MEMOIRS OF NAPOLEON BONAPARTE

COMPLETE

By

LOUIS ANTOINE
FAUVELET DE BOURRIENNE

WITH AN
INTRODUCTORY CHAPTER BY
RALPH WALDO EMERSON

First published in 1831

Read & Co.

This edition is published by Read & Co. History,
an imprint of Read & Co.

British Library Cataloguing-in-Publication Data
A catalogue record for this book is available
from the British Library.

Read & Co. is part of Read Books Ltd.
For more information visit
www.readandcobooks.co.uk

CONTENTS

VOLUME II

1800-1803

VOLUME III

1805-1814

VOLUME IV

1814-1821

THE DEATH OF NAPOLEON

By Isaac Mclellan

Wild was the night, yet a wilder night
  Hung round the soldier's pillow;
In his bosom there waged a fiercer fight
  Than the fight on the wrathful billow.

A few fond mourners were kneeling by,
  The few that his stern heart cherished;
They knew, by his glazed and unearthly eye,
  That life had nearly perished.

They knew by his awful and kingly look,
  By the order hastily spoken,
That he dreamed of days when the nations shook,
  And the nations' hosts were broken.

He dreamed that the Frenchman's sword still slew,
  And triumphed the Frenchman's eagle,
And the struggling Austrian fled anew,
  Like the hare before the beagle.

The bearded Russian he scourged again,
  The Prussian's camp was routed,
And again on the hills of haughty Spain
  His mighty armies shouted.

Over Egypt's sands, over Alpine snows,
  At the pyramids, at the mountain,
Where the wave of the lordly Danube flows,
  And by the Italian fountain,

On the snowy cliffs where mountain streams
  Dash by the Switzer's dwelling,
He led again, in his dying dreams,
  His hosts, the proud earth quelling.

Again Marengo's field was won,
  And Jena's bloody battle;
Again the world was overrun,
  Made pale at his cannon's rattle.

He died at the close of that darksome day,
  A day that shall live in story;
In the rocky land they placed his clay,
  And left him alone with his glory."

A poem from
Poems That Every Child Should Know, 1904

NAPOLEON — MAN OF THE WORLD

By Ralph Waldo Emerson

Among the eminent persons of the nineteenth century, Bonaparte is far the best known and the most powerful; and owes his predominance to the fidelity with which he expresses the tone of thought and belief, the aims of the masses of active and cultivated men. It is Swedenborg's theory that every organ is made up of homogeneous particles; or as it is sometimes expressed, every whole is made of similars; that is, the lungs are composed of infinitely small lungs; the liver, of infinitely small livers; the kidney, of little kidneys, etc. Following this analogy, if any man is found to carry with him the power and affections of vast numbers, if Napoleon is France, if Napoleon is Europe, it is because the people whom he sways are little Napoleons.

In our society there is a standing antagonism between the conservative and the democratic classes; between those who have made their fortunes, and the young and the poor who have fortunes to make; between the interests of dead labor,- that is, the labor of hands long ago still in the grave, which labor is now entombed in money stocks, or in land and buildings owned by idle capitalists,- and the interests of living labor, which seeks to possess itself of land and buildings and money stocks. The first class is timid, selfish, illiberal, hating innovation, and continually losing numbers by death. The second class is selfish also, encroaching, bold, self-relying, always outnumbering the other and recruiting its numbers every hour by births. It desires to keep open every avenue to the competition of all, and to multiply avenues: the class of business men in America, in England, in France and throughout Europe; the class of industry and skill. Napoleon is its representative. The instinct of active, brave, able men, throughout the middle class everywhere, has pointed out Napoleon as the incarnate Democrat. He had their virtues and their vices; above all, he had their spirit or aim. That tendency is material, pointing at a sensual success and employing the richest and most various means to that end; conversant with mechanical powers, highly intellectual, widely and accurately learned and skilful, but subordinating all intellectual and spiritual forces into means to a material success. To be the rich man, is the end. "God has granted," says the Koran, "to every people a prophet in its own tongue." Paris and London and New York, the spirit of commerce, of money and material power, were also to have their prophet; and Bonaparte was qualified and sent.

Every one of the million readers of anecdotes or memoirs or lives of Napoleon, delights in the page, because he studies in it his own history. Napoleon is thoroughly modern, and, at the highest point of his fortunes, has the very spirit of the newspapers. He is no saint,- to use his own word, "no capuchin," and he is no hero, in the high sense. The man in the street finds in him the qualities and powers of other men in the street. He finds him, like himself, by birth a citizen, who, by very intelligible merits, arrived at such a commanding position that he could indulge all those tastes which the common man possesses but is obliged to conceal and deny: good society, good books, fast travelling, dress, dinners, servants without number, personal weight, the execution of his ideas, the standing in the attitude of a benefactor to all persons about him, the refined enjoyments of pictures, statues, music, palaces and conventional honors,- precisely what is agreeable to the heart of every man in the nineteenth century, this powerful man possessed.

It is true that a man of Napoleon's truth of adaptation to the mind of the masses around him, becomes not merely representative but actually a monopolizer and usurper of other minds. Thus Mirabeau plagiarized every good thought, every good word that was spoken in France. Dumont relates that he sat in the gallery of the Convention and heard Mirabeau make a speech. It struck Dumont that he could fit it with a peroration, which he wrote in pencil immediately, and showed it to Lord Elgin, who sat by him. Lord Elgin approved it, and Dumont, in the evening, showed it to Mirabeau. Mirabeau read it, pronounced it admirable, and declared he would incorporate it into his harangue to-morrow, to the Assembly. "It is impossible," said Dumont, "as, unfortunately, I have shown it to Lord Elgin." "If you have shown it to Lord Elgin and to fifty persons beside, I shall still speak it to-morrow": and he did speak it, with much effect, at the next day's session. For Mirabeau, with his overpowering personality, felt that these things which his presence inspired were as much his own as if he had said them, and that his adoption of them gave them their weight. Much more absolute and centralizing was the successor to Mirabeau's popularity and to much more than his predominance in France. Indeed, a man of Napoleon's stamp almost ceases to have a private speech and opinion. He is so largely receptive, and is so placed, that he comes to be a bureau for all the intelligence, wit and power of the age and country. He gains the battle; he makes the code; he makes the system of weights and measures; he levels the Alps; he builds the road. All distinguished engineers, savans, statists, report to him: so likewise do all good heads in every kind: he adopts the best measures, sets his stamp on them, and not these alone, but on every happy and memorable expression. Every sentence spoken by Napoleon and every line of his writing, deserves reading, as it is the sense of France.

Bonaparte was the idol of common men because he had in transcendent degree the qualities and powers of common men. There is a certain satisfaction in coming down to the lowest ground of politics, for we get rid of cant and hypocrisy. Bonaparte wrought, in common with that great class he represented, for power and wealth,- but Bonaparte, specially, without any scruple as to the means. All the sentiments which embarrass men's pursuit of these objects, he set aside. The sentiments were for women and children. Fontanes, in 1804, expressed Napoleon's own sense, when in behalf of the Senate he addressed him,- "Sire, the desire of perfection is the worst disease that ever afflicted the human mind." The advocates of liberty and of progress are "ideologists";- a word of contempt often in his mouth;- "Necker is an ideologist": "Lafayette is an ideologist."

An Italian proverb, too well known, declares that "if you would succeed, you must not be too good." It is an advantage, within certain limits, to have renounced the dominion of the sentiments of piety, gratitude and generosity; since what was an impassable bar to us, and still is to others, becomes a convenient weapon for our purposes; just as the river which was a formidable barrier, winter transforms into the smoothest of roads.

Napoleon renounced, once for all, sentiments and affections, and would help himself with his hands and his head. With him is no miracle and no magic. He is a worker in brass, in iron, in wood, in earth, in roads, in buildings, in money and in troops, and a very consistent and wise master-workman. He is never weak and literary, but acts with the solidity and the precision of natural agents. He has not lost his native sense and sympathy with things. Men give way before such a man, as before natural events. To be sure there are men enough who are immersed in things, as farmers, smiths, sailors and mechanics generally; and we know how real and solid such men appear in the presence of scholars and grammarians: but these men ordinarily lack the power of arrangement, and are like hands without a head. But Bonaparte superadded to this mineral and animal force, insight and generalization, so that men saw in him combined the natural and the intellectual power, as if the sea and land had taken flesh and begun to cipher. Therefore the land and sea seem to presuppose him. He came unto his own and they received him. This ciphering operative knows what he is working with and what is the product. He knew the properties of gold and iron, of wheels and ships, of troops and diplomatists, and required that each should do after its kind.

The art of war was the game in which he exerted his arithmetic. It consisted, according to him, in having always more forces than the enemy, on the point where the enemy is attacked, or where he attacks: and his whole talent is strained by endless manoeuvre and evolution, to march always on the enemy at an angle, and destroy his forces in detail. It is obvious that a very small force, skilfully and rapidly manoeuvring so as always to bring two men against one at the point of engagement, will be an overmatch for a much larger body of men.

The times, his constitution and his early circumstances combined to develop this pattern democrat. He had the virtues of his class and the conditions for their activity. That common-sense which no sooner respects any end than it finds the means to effect it; the delight in the use of means; in the choice, simplification and combining of means; the directness and thoroughness of his work; the prudence with which all was seen and the energy with which all was done, make him the natural organ and head of what I may almost call, from its extent, the modern party.

Nature must have far the greatest share in every success, and so in his. Such a man was wanted, and such a man was born; a man of stone and iron, capable of sitting on horseback sixteen or seventeen hours, of going many days together without rest or food except by snatches, and with the speed and spring of a tiger in action; a man not embarrassed by any scruples; compact, instant, selfish, prudent, and of a perception which did not suffer itself to be baulked or misled by any pretences of others, or any superstition or any heat or haste of his own. "My hand of iron," he said, "was not at the extremity of my arm, it was immediately connected with my head." He respected the power of nature and fortune, and ascribed to it his superiority, instead of valuing himself, like inferior men, on his opinionativeness, and waging war with nature. His favorite rhetoric lay in allusion to his star; and he pleased himself, as well as the people, when he styled himself the "Child of Destiny." "They charge me," he said, "with the commission of great crimes: men of my stamp do not commit crimes. Nothing has been more simple than my elevation, 'tis in vain to ascribe it to intrigue or crime; it was owing to the peculiarity of the times and to my reputation of having fought well against the enemies of my country. I have always marched with the opinion of great masses and with events. Of what use then would crimes be to me?" Again he said, speaking of his son, "My son can not replace me; I could not replace myself. I am the creature of circumstances."

He had a directness of action never before combined with so much comprehension. He is a realist, terrific to all talkers and confused truth-obscuring persons. He sees where the matter hinges, throws himself on the precise point of resistance, and slights all other considerations. He is strong in the right manner, namely by insight. He never blundered into victory, but won his battles in his head before he won them on the field. His principal means are in himself. He asks counsel of no other. In 1796 he writes to the Directory: "I have conducted the campaign without consulting any one. I should have done no good if I had been under the necessity of conforming to the notions of another person. I have gained some advantages over superior forces and when totally destitute of every thing, because, in the persuasion that your confidence was reposed in me, my actions were as prompt as my thoughts."

History is full, down to this day, of the imbecility of kings and governors. They are a class of persons much to be pitied, for they know not what they should do. The weavers strike for bread, and the king and his ministers, knowing not what to do, meet them with bayonets. But Napoleon understood his business. Here was a man who in each moment and emergency knew what to do next. It is an immense comfort and refreshment to the spirits, not only of kings, but of citizens. Few men have any next; they live from hand to mouth, without plan, and are ever at the end of their line, and after each action wait for an impulse from abroad. Napoleon had been the first man of the world, if his ends had been purely public. As he is, he inspires confidence and vigor by the extraordinary unity of his action. He is firm, sure, self-denying, self-postponing, sacrificing every thing,- money, troops, generals, and his own safety also, to his aim; not misled, like common adventurers, by the splendor of his own means. "Incidents ought not to govern policy," he said, "but policy, incidents." "To be hurried away by every event is to have no political system at all." His victories were only so many doors, and he never for a moment lost sight of his way onward, in the dazzle and uproar of the present circumstance. He knew what to do, and he flew to his mark. He would shorten a straight line to come at his object. Horrible anecdotes may no doubt be collected from his history, of the price at which he bought his successes; but he must not therefore be set down as cruel, but only as one who knew no impediment to his will; not bloodthirsty, not cruel,- but woe to what thing or person stood in his way! Not bloodthirsty, but not sparing of blood,- and pitiless. He saw only the object: the obstacle must give way. "Sire, General Clarke can not combine with General Junot, for the dreadful fire of the Austrian battery."- "Let him carry the battery."- "Sire, every regiment that approaches the heavy artillery is sacrificed: Sire, what orders?"- "Forward, forward!" Seruzier, a colonel of artillery, gives, in his "Military Memoirs," the following sketch of a scene after the battle of Austerlitz.- "At the moment in which the Russian army was making its retreat, painfully, but in good order, on the ice of the lake, the Emperor Napoleon came riding at full speed toward the artillery. 'You are losing time,' he cried; 'fire upon those masses; they must be engulfed: fire upon the ice!' The order remained unexecuted for ten minutes. In vain several officers and myself were placed on the slope of a hill to produce the effect: their balls and mine rolled upon the ice without breaking it up. Seeing that, I tried a simple method of elevating light howitzers. The almost perpendicular fall of the heavy projectiles produced the desired effect. My method was immediately followed by the adjoining batteries, and in less than no time we buried" some "thousands of Russians and Austrians under the waters of the lake."

In the plenitude of his resources, every obstacle seemed to vanish. "There shall be no Alps," he said; and he built his perfect roads, climbing by graded galleries their steepest precipices, until Italy was as open to Paris as any town in France. He laid his bones to, and wrought for his crown. Having decided what was to be done, he did that with might and main. He put out all his strength. He risked every thing and spared nothing, neither ammunition, nor money, nor troops, nor generals, nor himself.

We like to see every thing do its office after its kind, whether it be a milch-cow or a rattlesnake; and if fighting be the best mode of adjusting national differences, (as large majorities of men seem to agree,) certainly Bonaparte was right in making it thorough. The grand principle of war, he said, was that an army ought always to be ready, by day and by night and at all hours, to make all the resistance it is capable of making. He never economized his ammunition, but, on a hostile position, rained a torrent of iron,- shells, balls, grape-shot,- to annihilate all defence. On any point of resistance he concentrated squadron on squadron in overwhelming numbers until it was swept out of existence. To a regiment of horse-chasseurs at Lobenstein, two days before the battle of Jena, Napoleon said, "My lads, you must not fear death; when soldiers brave death, they drive him into the enemy's ranks." In the fury of assault, he no more spared himself. He went to the edge of his possibility. It is plain that in Italy he did what he could, and all that he could. He came, several times, within an inch of ruin; and his own person was all but lost. He was flung into the marsh at Arcola. The Austrians were between him and his troops, in the melee, and he was brought off with desperate efforts. At Lonato, and at other places, he was on the point of being taken prisoner. He fought sixty battles. He had never enough. Each victory was a new weapon. "My power would fall, were I not to support it by new achievements. Conquest has made me what I am, and conquest must maintain me." He felt, with every wise man, that as much life is needed for conservation as for creation. We are always in peril, always in a bad plight, just on the edge of destruction and only to be saved by invention and courage.

This vigor was guarded and tempered by the coldest prudence and punctuality. A thunderbolt in the attack, he was found invulnerable in his intrenchments. His very attack was never the inspiration of courage, but the result of calculation. His idea of the best defence consists in being still the attacking party. "My ambition," he says, "was great, but was of a cold nature." In one of his conversations with Las Cases, he remarked, "As to moral courage, I have rarely met with the two-o'clock-in-the-morning kind: I mean unprepared courage; that which is necessary on an unexpected occasion, and which, in spite of the most unforeseen events, leaves full freedom of judgment and decision": and he did not hesitate to declare that he was himself eminently endowed with this two-o'clock-in-the-morning courage, and that he had met with few persons equal to himself in this respect.

Every thing depended on the nicety of his combinations, and the stars were not more punctual than his arithmetic. His personal attention descended to the smallest particulars. "At Montebello, I ordered Kellermann to attack with eight hundred horse, and with these he separated the six thousand Hungarian grenadiers, before the very eyes of the Austrian cavalry. This cavalry was half a league off and required a quarter of an hour to arrive on the field of action, and I have observed that it is always these quarters of an hour that decide the fate of a battle." "Before he fought a battle, Bonaparte thought little about what he should do in case of success, but a great deal about what he should do in case of a reverse of fortune." The same prudence and good sense mark all his behavior. His instructions to his secretary at the Tuileries are worth remembering. "During the night, enter my chamber as seldom as possible. Do not awake me when you have any good news to communicate; with that there is no hurry. But when you bring bad news, rouse me instantly, for then there is not a moment to be lost." It was a whimsical economy of the same kind which dictated his practice, when general in Italy, in regard to his burdensome correspondence. He directed Bourrienne to leave all letters unopened for three weeks, and then observed with satisfaction how large a part of the correspondence had thus disposed of itself and no longer required an answer. His achievement of business was immense, and enlarges the known powers of man. There have been many working kings, from Ulysses to William of Orange, but none who accomplished a tithe of this man's performance.

To these gifts of nature, Napoleon added the advantage of having been born to a private and humble fortune. In his later days he had the weakness of wishing to add to his crowns and badges the prescription of aristocracy; but he knew his debt to his austere education, and made no secret of his contempt for the born kings, and for "the hereditary asses," as he coarsely styled the Bourbons. He said that "in their exile they had learned nothing, and forgot nothing." Bonaparte had passed through all the degrees of military service, but also was citizen before he was emperor, and so has the key to citizenship. His remarks and estimates discover the information and justness of measurement of the middle class. Those who had to deal with him found that he was not to be imposed upon, but could cipher as well as another man. This appears in all parts of his Memoirs, dictated at St. Helena. When the expenses of the empress, of his household, of his palaces, had accumulated great debts, Napoleon examined the bills of the creditors himself, detected overcharges and errors, and reduced the claims by considerable sums.

His grand weapon, namely the millions whom he directed, he owed to the representative character which clothed him. He interests us as he stands for France and for Europe; and he exists as captain and king only as far as the Revolution, or the interest of the industrious masses, found an organ and a leader in him. In the social interests, he knew the meaning and value of labor, and threw himself naturally on that side. I like an incident mentioned by one of his biographers at St. Helena. "When walking with Mrs. Balcombe, some servants, carrying heavy boxes, passed by on the road, and Mrs. Balcombe desired them, in rather an angry tone, to keep back. Napoleon interfered, saying 'Respect the burden, Madam.'" In the time of the empire he directed attention to the improvement and embellishment of the markets of the capital. "The market-place," he said, "is the Louvre of the common people." The principal works that have survived him are his magnificent roads. He filled the troops with his spirit, and a sort of freedom and companionship grew up between him and them, which the forms of his court never permitted between the officers and himself. They performed, under his eye, that which no others could do. The best document of his relation to his troops is the order of the day on the morning of the battle of Austerlitz, in which Napoleon promises the troops that he will keep his person out of reach of fire. This declaration, which is the reverse of that ordinarily made by generals and sovereigns on the eve of a battle, sufficiently explains the devotion of the army to their leader.

But though there is in particulars this identity between Napoleon and the mass of the people, his real strength lay in their conviction that he was their representative in his genius and aims, not only when he courted, but when he controlled, and even when he decimated them by his conscriptions. He knew, as well as any Jacobin in France, how to philosophize on liberty and equality; and when allusion was made to the precious blood of centuries, which was spilled by the killing of the Duc d'Enghien, he suggested, "Neither is my blood ditchwater." The people felt that no longer the throne was occupied and the land sucked of its nourishment, by a small class of legitimates, secluded from all community with the children of the soil, and holding the ideas and superstitions of a long-forgotten state of society. Instead of that vampyre, a man of themselves held, in the Tuileries, knowledge and ideas like their own, opening of course to them and their children all places of power and trust. The day of sleepy, selfish policy, ever narrowing the means and opportunities of young men, was ended, and a day of expansion and demand was come. A market for all the powers and productions of man was opened; brilliant prizes glittered in the eyes of youth and talent. The old, iron-bound, feudal France was changed into a young Ohio or New York; and those who smarted under the immediate rigors of the new monarch, pardoned them as the necessary severities of the military system which had driven out the oppressor. And even when the majority of the people had begun to ask whether they had really gained any thing under the exhausting levies of men and money of the new master, the whole talent of the country, in every rank and kindred, took his part and defended him as its natural patron. In 1814, when advised to rely on the higher classes, Napoleon said to those around him, "Gentlemen, in the situation in which I stand, my only nobility is the rabble of the Faubourgs."

Napoleon met this natural expectation. The necessity of his position required a hospitality to every sort of talent, and its appointment to trusts; and his feeling went along with this policy. Like every superior person, he undoubtedly felt a desire for men and compeers, and a wish to measure his power with other masters, and an impatience of fools and underlings. In Italy, he sought for men and found none. "Good God!" he said, "how rare men are! There are eighteen millions in Italy, and I have with difficulty found two,- Dandolo and Melzi." In later years, with larger experience, his respect for mankind was not increased. In a moment of bitterness he said to one of his oldest friends, "Men deserve the contempt with which they inspire me. I have only to put some gold-lace on the coat of my virtuous republicans and they immediately become just what I wish them." This impatience at levity was, however, an oblique tribute of respect to those able persons who commanded his regard not only when he found them friends and coadjutors but also when they resisted his will. He could not confound Fox and Pitt, Carnot, Lafayette and Bernadotte, with the danglers of his court; and in spite of the detraction which his systematic egotism dictated toward the great captains who conquered with and for him, ample acknowledgments are made by him to Lannes, Duroc, Kleber, Dessaix, Massena, Murat, Ney and Augereau. If he felt himself their patron and the founder of their fortunes, as when he said, "I made my generals out of mud,"- he could not hide his satisfaction in receiving from them a seconding and support commensurate with the grandeur of his enterprise. In the Russian campaign he was so much impressed by the courage and resources of Marshal Ney, that he said, "I have two hundred millions in my coffers, and I would give them all for Ney." The characters which he has drawn of several of his marshals are discriminating, and though they did not content the insatiable vanity of French officers, are no doubt substantially just. And in fact every species of merit was sought and advanced under his government. "I know," he said, "the depth and draught of water of every one of my generals." Natural power was sure to be well received at his court. Seventeen men in his time were raised from common soldiers to the rank of king, marshal, duke, or general; and the crosses of his Legion of Honor were given to personal valor, and not to family connexion. "When soldiers have been baptized in the fire of a battlefield, they have all one rank in my eyes."

When a natural king becomes a titular king, every body is pleased and satisfied. The Revolution entitled the strong populace of the Faubourg St. Antoine, and every horse-boy and powder-monkey in the army, to look on Napoleon as flesh of his flesh and the creature of his party: but there is something in the success of grand talent which enlists an universal sympathy. For in the prevalence of sense and spirit over stupidity and malversation, all reasonable men have an interest; and as intellectual beings we feel the air purified by the electric shock, when material force is overthrown by intellectual energies. As soon as we are removed out of the reach of local and accidental partialities, Man feels that Napoleon fights for him; these are honest victories; this strong steam-engine does our work. Whatever appeals to the imagination, by transcending the ordinary limits of human ability, wonderfully encourages us and liberates us. This capacious head, revolving and disposing sovereignly trains of affairs, and animating such multitudes of agents; this eye, which looked through Europe; this prompt invention; this inexhaustible resource:- what events! what romantic pictures! what strange situations!- when spying the Alps, by a sunset in the Sicilian sea; drawing up his army for battle in sight of the Pyramids, and saying to his troops, "From the tops of those pyramids, forty centuries look down on you"; fording the Red Sea; wading in the gulf of the Isthmus of Suez. On the shore of Ptolemais, gigantic projects agitated him. "Had Acre fallen, I should have changed the face of the world." His army, on the night of the battle of Austerlitz, which was the anniversary of his inauguration as Emperor, presented him with a bouquet of forty standards taken in the fight. Perhaps it is a little puerile, the pleasure he took in making these contrasts glaring; as when he pleased himself with making kings wait in his antechambers, at Tilsit, at Paris and at Erfurt.

We can not, in the universal imbecility, indecision and indolence of men, sufficiently congratulate ourselves on this strong and ready actor, who took occasion by the beard, and showed us how much may be accomplished by the mere force of such virtues as all men possess in less degrees; namely, by punctuality, by personal attention, by courage and thoroughness. "The Austrians," he said, "do not know the value of time." I should cite him, in his earlier years, as a model of prudence. His power does not consist in any wild or extravagant force; in any enthusiasm like Mahomet's, or singular power of persuasion; but in the exercise of common-sense on each emergency, instead of abiding by rules and customs. The lesson he teaches is that which vigor always teaches;- that there is always room for it. To what heaps of cowardly doubts is not that man's life an answer. When he appeared it was the belief of all military men that there could be nothing new in war; as it is the belief of men to-day that nothing new can be undertaken in politics, or in church, or in letters, or in trade, or in farming, or in our social manners and customs; and as it is at all times the belief of society that the world is used up. But Bonaparte knew better than society; and moreover knew that he knew better. I think all men know better than they do; know that the institutions we so volubly commend are go-carts and baubles; but they dare not trust their presentiments. Bonaparte relied on his own sense, and did not care a bean for other people's. The world treated his novelties just as it treats everybody's novelties,- made infinite objection, mustered all the impediments; but he snapped his finger at their objections. "What creates great difficulty," he remarks, "in the profession of the land-commander, is the necessity of feeding so many men and animals. If he allows himself to be guided by the commissaries he will never stir, and all his expeditions will fail." An example of his common-sense is what he says of the passage of the Alps in winter, which all writers, one repeating after the other, had described as impracticable. "The winter," says Napoleon, "is not the most unfavorable season for the passage of lofty mountains. The snow is then firm, the weather settled, and there is nothing to fear from avalanches, the real and only danger to be apprehended in the Alps. On these high mountains there are often very fine days in December, of a dry cold, with extreme calmness in the air." Read his account, too, of the way in which battles are gained. "In all battles a moment occurs when the bravest troops, after having made the greatest efforts, feel inclined to run. That terror proceeds from a want of confidence in their own courage, and it only requires a slight opportunity, a pretence, to restore confidence to them. The art is, to give rise to the opportunity and to invent the pretence. At Arcola I won the battle with twenty-five horsemen. I seized that moment of lassitude, gave every man a trumpet, and gained the day with this handful. You see that two armies are two bodies which meet and endeavor to frighten each other; a moment of panic occurs, and that moment must be turned to advantage. When a man has been present in many actions, he distinguishes that moment without difficulty: it is as easy as casting up an addition."

This deputy of the nineteenth century added to his gifts a capacity for speculation on general topics. He delighted in running through the range of practical, of literary and of abstract questions. His opinion is always original and to the purpose. On the voyage to Egypt he liked, after dinner, to fix on three or four persons to support a proposition, and as many to oppose it. He gave a subject, and the discussions turned on questions of religion, the different kinds of government, and the art of war. One day he asked whether the planets were inhabited? On another, what was the age of the world? Then he proposed to consider the probability of the destruction of the globe, either by water or by fire: at another time, the truth or fallacy of presentiments, and the interpretation of dreams. He was very fond of talking of religion. In 1806 he conversed with Fournier, bishop of Montpellier, on matters of theology. There were two points on which they could not agree, viz. that of hell, and that of salvation out of the pale of the church. The Emperor told Josephine that he disputed like a devil on these two points, on which the bishop was inexorable. To the philosophers he readily yielded all that was proved against religion as the work of men and time, but he would not hear of materialism. One fine night, on deck, amid a clatter of materialism, Bonaparte pointed to the stars, and said, "You may talk as long as you please, gentlemen, but who made all that?" He delighted in the conversation of men of science, particularly of Monge and Berthollet; but the men of letters he slighted; they were "manufacturers of phrases." Of medicine too he was fond of talking, and with those of its practitioners whom he most esteemed,- with Corvisart at Paris, and with Antonomarchi at St. Helena. "Believe me," he said to the last, "we had better leave off all these remedies: life is a fortress which neither you nor I know any thing about. Why throw obstacles in the way of its defence? Its own means are superior to all the apparatus of your laboratories. Corvisart candidly agreed with me that all your filthy mixtures are good for nothing. Medicine is a collection of uncertain prescriptions, the results of which, taken collectively, are more fatal than useful to mankind. Water, air and cleanliness are the chief articles in my pharmacopoeia."

His memoirs, dictated to Count Montholon and General Gourgaud at St. Helena, have great value, after all the deduction that it seems is to be made from them on account of his known disingenuousness. He has the good-nature of strength and conscious superiority. I admire his simple, clear narrative of his battles;- good as Caesar's; his good-natured and sufficiently respectful account of Marshal Wurmser and his other antagonists; and his own equality as a writer to his varying subject. The most agreeable portion is the Campaign in Egypt.

He had hours of thought and wisdom. In intervals of leisure, either in the camp or the palace, Napoleon appears as a man of genius directing on abstract questions the native appetite for truth and the impatience of words he was wont to show in war. He could enjoy every play of invention, a romance, a bon mot, as well as a strategem in a campaign. He delighted to fascinate Josephine and her ladies, in a dim-lighted apartment, by the terrors of a fiction to which his voice and dramatic power lent every addition.

I call Napoleon the agent or attorney of the middle class of modern society; of the throng who fill the markets, shops, counting-houses, manufactories, ships, of the modern world, aiming to be rich. He was the agitator, the destroyer of prescription, the internal improver, the liberal, the radical, the inventor of means, the opener of doors and markets, the subverter of monopoly and abuse. Of course the rich and aristocratic did not like him. England, the centre of capital, and Rome and Austria, centres of tradition and genealogy, opposed him. The consternation of the dull and conservative classes, the terror of the foolish old men and old women of the Roman conclave, who in their despair took hold of any thing, and would cling to red-hot iron,- the vain attempts of statists to amuse and deceive him, of the emperor of Austria to bribe him; and the instinct of the young, ardent and active men every where, which pointed him out as the giant of the middle class, make his history bright and commanding. He had the virtues of the masses of his constituents: he had also their vices. I am sorry that the brilliant picture has its reverse. But that is the fatal quality which we discover in our pursuit of wealth, that it is treacherous, and is bought by the breaking or weakening of the sentiments; and it is inevitable that we should find the same fact in the history of this champion, who proposed to himself simply a brilliant career, without any stipulation or scruple concerning the means.

Bonaparte was singularly destitute of generous sentiments. The highest-placed individual in the most cultivated age and population of the world,- he has not the merit of common truth and honesty. He is unjust to his generals; egotistic and monopolizing; meanly stealing the credit of their great actions from Kellermann, from Bernadotte; intriguing to involve his faithful Junot in hopeless bankruptcy, in order to drive him to a distance from Paris, because the familiarity of his manners offends the new pride of his throne. He is a boundless liar. The official paper, his "Moniteur," and all his bulletins, are proverbs for saying what he wished to be believed; and worse,- he sat, in his premature old age, in his lonely island, coldly falsifying facts and dates and characters, and giving to history a theatrical eclat. Like all Frenchmen he has a passion for stage effect. Every action that breathes of generosity is poisoned by this calculation. His star, his love of glory, his doctrine of the immortality of the soul, are all French. "I must dazzle and astonish. If I were to give the liberty of the press, my power could not last three days." To make a great noise is his favorite design. "A great reputation is a great noise: the more there is made, the farther off it is heard. Laws, institutions, monuments, nations, all fall; but the noise continues, and resounds in after ages." His doctrine of immortality is simply fame. His theory of influence is not flattering. "There are two levers for moving men,- interest and fear. Love is a silly infatuation, depend upon it. Friendship is but a name. I love nobody. I do not even love my brothers: perhaps Joseph a little, from habit, and because he is my elder; and Duroc, I love him too; but why?- because his character pleases me: he is stern and resolute, and I believe the fellow never shed a tear. For my part I know very well that I have no true friends. As long as I continue to be what I am, I may have as many pretended friends as I please. Leave sensibility to women; but men should be firm in heart and purpose, or they should have nothing to do with war and government." He was thoroughly unscrupulous. He would steal, slander, assassinate, drown and poison, as his interest dictated. He had no generosity, but mere vulgar hatred; he was intensely selfish; he was perfidious; he cheated at cards; he was a prodigious gossip, and opened letters, and delighted in his infamous police, and rubbed his hands with joy when he had intercepted some morsel of intelligence concerning the men and women about him, boasting that "he knew every thing"; and interfered with the cutting the dresses of the women; and listened after the hurrahs and the compliments of the street, incognito. His manners were coarse. He treated women with low familiarity. He had the habit of pulling their ears and pinching their cheeks when he was in good humor, and of pulling the ears and whiskers of men, and of striking and horse-play with them, to his last days. It does not appear that he listened at key-holes, or at least that he was caught at it. In short, when you have penetrated through all the circles of power and splendor, you were not dealing with a gentleman, at last; but with an impostor and a rogue; and he fully deserves the epithet of Jupiter Scapin, or a sort of Scamp Jupiter.

In describing the two parties into which modern society divides itself,- the democrat and the conservative,- I said, Bonaparte represents the democrat, or the party of men of business, against the stationary or conservative party. I omitted then to say, what is material to the statement, namely that these two parties differ only as young and old. The democrat is a young conservative; the conservative is an old democrat. The aristocrat is the democrat ripe and gone to seed;- because both parties stand on the one ground of the supreme value of property, which one endeavors to get, and the other to keep. Bonaparte may be said to represent the whole history of this party, its youth and its age; yes, and with poetic justice its fate, in his own. The counter-revolution, the counter-party, still waits for its organ and representative, in a lover and a man of truly public and universal aims.

Here was an experiment, under the most favorable conditions, of the powers of intellect without conscience. Never was such a leader so endowed and so weaponed; never leader found such aids and followers. And what was the result of this vast talent and power, of these immense armies, burned cities, squandered treasures, immolated millions of men, of this demoralized Europe? It came to no result. All passed away like the smoke of his artillery, and left no trace. He left France smaller, poorer, feebler, than he found it; and the whole contest for freedom was to be begun again. The attempt was in principle suicidal. France served him with life and limb and estate, as long as it could identify its interest with him; but when men saw that after victory was another war; after the destruction of armies, new conscriptions; and they who had toiled so desperately were never nearer to the reward,- they could not spend what they had earned, nor repose on their down-beds, nor strut in their chateaux,- they deserted him. Men found that his absorbing egotism was deadly to all other men. It resembled the torpedo, which inflicts a succession of shocks on any one who takes hold of it, producing spasms which contract the muscles of the hand, so that the man can not open his fingers; and the animal inflicts new and more violent shocks, until he paralyzes and kills his victim. So this exorbitant egotist narrowed, impoverished and absorbed the power and existence of those who served him; and the universal cry of France and of Europe in 1814 was, "Enough of him"; "Assez de Bonaparte."

It was not Bonaparte's fault. He did all that in him lay to live and thrive without moral principle. It was the nature of things, the eternal law of man and of the world which baulked and ruined him; and the result, in a million experiments, will be the same. Every experiment, by multitudes or by individuals, that has a sensual and selfish aim, will fail. The pacific Fourier will be as inefficient as the pernicious Napoleon. As long as our civilization is essentially one of property, of fences, of exclusiveness, it will be mocked by delusions. Our riches will leave us sick; there will be bitterness in our laughter, and our wine will burn our mouth. Only that good profits which we can taste with all doors open, and which serves all men.

A CHAPTER FROM
Representative Men, 1850

PREFACE 1836 EDITION

In introducing the present edition of M. de Bourrienne's Memoirs to the public we are bound, as Editors, to say a few Words on the subject. Agreeing, however, with Horace Walpole that an editor should not dwell for any length of time on the merits of his author, we shall touch but lightly on this part of the matter. We are the more ready to abstain since the great success in England of the former editions of these Memoirs, and the high reputation they have acquired on the European Continent, and in every part of the civilised world where the fame of Bonaparte has ever reached, sufficiently establish the merits of M. de Bourrienne as a biographer. These merits seem to us to consist chiefly in an anxious desire to be impartial, to point out the defects as well as the merits of a most wonderful man; and in a peculiarly graphic power of relating facts and anecdotes. With this happy faculty Bourrienne would have made the life of almost any active individual interesting; but the subject of which the most favourable circumstances permitted him to treat was full of events and of the most extraordinary facts. The hero of his story was such a being as the world has produced only on the rarest occasions, and the complete counterpart to whom has, probably, never existed; for there are broad shades of difference between Napoleon and Alexander, Caesar, and Charlemagne; neither will modern history furnish more exact parallels, since Gustavus Adolphus, Frederick the Great, Cromwell, Washington, or Bolivar bear but a small resemblance to Bonaparte either in character, fortune, or extent of enterprise. For fourteen years, to say nothing of his projects in the East, the history of Bonaparte was the history of all Europe! With the copious materials he possessed, M. de Bourrienne has produced a work which, for deep interest, excitement, and amusement, can scarcely be paralleled by any of the numerous and excellent memoirs for which the literature of France is so justly celebrated.

M. de Bourrienne shows us the hero of Marengo and Austerlitz in his night-gown and slippers—with a 'trait de plume' he, in a hundred instances, places the real man before us, with all his personal habits and peculiarities of manner, temper, and conversation.

The friendship between Bonaparte and Bourrienne began in boyhood, at the school of Brienne, and their unreserved intimacy continued during the most brilliant part of Napoleon's career. We have said enough, the motives for his writing this work and his competency for the task will be best explained in M. de Bourrienne's own words, which the reader will find in the Introductory Chapter.

M. de Bourrienne says little of Napoleon after his first abdication and retirement to Elba in 1814: we have endeavoured to fill up the chasm thus left by following his hero through the remaining seven years of his life, to the "last scenes of all" that ended his "strange, eventful history,"—to his deathbed and alien grave at St. Helena. A completeness will thus be given to the work which it did not before possess, and which we hope will, with the other additions and improvements already alluded to, tend to give it a place in every well-selected library, as one of the most satisfactory of all the lives of Napoleon.

LONDON, 1836.

PREFACE 1885 EDITION

The Memoirs of the time of Napoleon may be divided into two classes—those by marshals and officers, of which Suchet's is a good example, chiefly devoted to military movements, and those by persons employed in the administration and in the Court, giving us not only materials for history, but also valuable details of the personal and inner life of the great Emperor and of his immediate surroundings. Of this latter class the Memoirs of Bourrienne are among the most important.

Long the intimate and personal friend of Napoleon both at school and from the end of the Italian campaigns in 1797 till 1802—working in the same room with him, using the same purse, the confidant of most of his schemes, and, as his secretary, having the largest part of all the official and private correspondence of the time passed through his hands, Bourrienne occupied an invaluable position for storing and recording materials for history. The Memoirs of his successor, Meneval, are more those of an esteemed private secretary; yet, valuable and interesting as they are, they want the peculiarity of position which marks those of Bourrienne, who was a compound of secretary, minister, and friend. The accounts of such men as Miot de Melito, Raederer, etc., are most valuable, but these writers were not in that close contact with Napoleon enjoyed by Bourrienne. Bourrienne's position was simply unique, and we can only regret that he did not occupy it till the end of the Empire. Thus it is natural that his Memoirs should have been largely used by historians, and to properly understand the history of the time, they must be read by all students. They are indeed full of interest for every one. But they also require to be read with great caution. When we meet with praise of Napoleon, we may generally believe it, for, as Thiers (Consulat., ii. 279) says, Bourrienne need be little suspected on this side, for although he owed everything to Napoleon, he has not seemed to remember it. But very often in passages in which blame is thrown on Napoleon, Bourrienne speaks, partly with much of the natural bitterness of a former and discarded friend, and partly with the curious mixed feeling which even the brothers of Napoleon display in their Memoirs, pride in the wonderful abilities evinced by the man with whom he was allied, and jealousy at the way in which he was outshone by the man he had in youth regarded as inferior to himself. Sometimes also we may even suspect the praise. Thus when Bourrienne defends Napoleon for giving, as he alleges, poison to the sick at Jaffa, a doubt arises whether his object was to really defend what to most Englishmen of this day, with remembrances of the deeds and resolutions of the Indian Mutiny, will seem an act to be pardoned, if not approved; or whether he was more anxious to fix the committal of the act on Napoleon at a time when public opinion loudly blamed it. The same may be said of his defence of the massacre of the prisoners of Jaffa.

Louis Antoine Fauvelet de Bourrienne was born in 1769, that is, in the same year as Napoleon Bonaparte, and he was the friend and companion of the future Emperor at the military school of Brienne-le-Chateau till 1784, when Napoleon, one of the sixty pupils maintained at the expense of the State, was passed on to the Military School of Paris. The friends again met in 1792 and in 1795, when Napoleon was hanging about Paris, and when

Bourrienne looked on the vague dreams of his old schoolmate as only so much folly. In 1796, as soon as Napoleon had assured his position at the head of the army of Italy, anxious as ever to surround himself with known faces, he sent for Bourrienne to be his secretary. Bourrienne had been appointed in 1792 as secretary of the Legation at Stuttgart, and had, probably wisely, disobeyed the orders given him to return, thus escaping the dangers of the Revolution. He only came back to Paris in 1795, having thus become an emigre. He joined Napoleon in 1797, after the Austrians had been beaten out of Italy, and at once assumed the office of secretary which he held for so long. He had sufficient tact to forbear treating the haughty young General with any assumption of familiarity in public, and he was indefatigable enough to please even the never-resting Napoleon. Talent Bourrienne had in abundance; indeed he is careful to hint that at school if any one had been asked to predict greatness for any pupil, it was Bourrienne, not Napoleon, who would have been fixed on as the future star. He went with his General to Egypt, and returned with him to France. While Napoleon was making his formal entry into the Tuileries, Bourrienne was preparing the cabinet he was still to share with the Consul. In this cabinet—our cabinet, as he is careful to call it—he worked with the First Consul till 1802.

During all this time the pair lead lived on terms of equality and friendship creditable to both. The secretary neither asked for nor received any salary: when he required money, he simply dipped into the cash-box of the First Consul. As the whole power of the State gradually passed into the hands of the Consul, the labours of the secretary became heavier. His successor broke down under a lighter load, and had to receive assistance; but, perhaps borne up by the absorbing interest of the work and the great influence given by his post, Bourrienne stuck to his place, and to all appearance might, except for himself, have come down to us as the companion of Napoleon during his whole life. He had enemies, and one of them[1]—has not shrunk from describing their gratification at the disgrace of the trusted secretary. Any one in favour, or indeed in office, under Napoleon was the sure mark of calumny for all aspirants to place; yet Bourrienne might have weathered any temporary storm raised by unfounded reports as successfully as Meneval, who followed him. But Bourrienne's hands were not clean in money matters, and that was an unpardonable sin in any one who desired to be in real intimacy with Napoleon. He became involved in the affairs of the House of Coulon, which failed, as will be seen in the notes, at the time of his disgrace; and in October 1802 he was called on to hand over his office to Meneval, who retained it till invalided after the Russian campaign.

As has been said, Bourrienne would naturally be the mark for many accusations, but the conclusive proof of his misconduct—at least for any one acquainted with Napoleon's objection and dislike to changes in office, whether from his strong belief in the effects of training, or his equally strong dislike of new faces round him—is that he was never again employed near his old comrade; indeed he really never saw the Emperor again at any private interview, except when granted the naval official reception in 1805, before leaving to take up his post at Hamburg, which he held till 1810. We know that his re-employment was urged by Josephine and several of his former companions. Savary himself says he tried his advocacy; but Napoleon was inexorable to those who, in his own phrase, had sacrificed to the golden calf.

Sent, as we have said, to Hamburg in 1805, as Minister Plenipotentiary to the Duke of

1 Boulay de la Meurthe.

Brunswick, the Duke of Mecklenburg-Schwerin, and to the Hanse towns, Bourrienne knew how to make his post an important one. He was at one of the great seats of the commerce which suffered so fearfully from the Continental system of the Emperor, and he was charged to watch over the German press. How well he fulfilled this duty we learn from Metternich, who writes in 1805: "I have sent an article to the newspaper editors in Berlin and to M. de Hofer at Hamburg. I do not know whether it has been accepted, for M. Bourrienne still exercises an authority so severe over these journals that they are always submitted to him before they appear, that he may erase or alter the articles which do not please him."

His position at Hamburg gave him great opportunities for both financial and political intrigues. In his Memoirs, as Meneval remarks, he or his editor is not ashamed to boast of being thanked by Louis XVIII. at St. Ouen for services rendered while he was the minister of Napoleon at Hamburg. He was recalled in 1810, when the Hanse towns were united, or, to use the phrase of the day, re-united to the Empire. He then hung about Paris, keeping on good terms with some of the ministers—Savary, not the most reputable of them, for example. In 1814 he was to be found at the office of Lavallette, the head of the posts, disguising, his enemies said, his delight at the bad news which was pouring in, by exaggerated expressions of devotion. He is accused of a close and suspicious connection with Talleyrand, and it is odd that when Talleyrand became head of the Provisional Government in 1814, Bourrienne of all persons should have been put at the head of the posts. Received in the most flattering manner by Louis XVIII, he was as astonished as poor Beugnot was in 1815, to find himself on 13th May suddenly ejected from office, having, however, had time to furnish post-horses to Manbreuil for the mysterious expedition, said to have been at least known to Talleyrand, and intended certainly for the robbery of the Queen of Westphalia, and probably for the murder of Napoleon.

In the extraordinary scurry before the Bourbons scuttled out of Paris in 1814, Bourrienne was made Prefet of the Police for a few days, his tenure of that post being signalised by the abortive attempt to arrest Fouché, the only effect of which was to drive that wily minister into the arms of the Bonapartists.

He fled with the King, and was exempted from the amnesty proclaimed by Napoleon. On the return from Ghent he was made a Minister of State without portfolio, and also became one of the Council. The ruin of his finances drove him out of France, but he eventually died in a madhouse at Caen.

When the Memoirs first appeared in 1829 they made a great sensation. Till then in most writings Napoleon had been treated as either a demon or as a demi-god. The real facts of the case were not suited to the tastes of either his enemies or his admirers. While the monarchs of Europe had been disputing among themselves about the division of the spoils to be obtained from France and from the unsettlement of the Continent, there had arisen an extraordinarily clever and unscrupulous man who, by alternately bribing and overthrowing the great monarchies, had soon made himself master of the mainland. His admirers were unwilling to admit the part played in his success by the jealousy of his foes of each other's share in the booty, and they delighted to invest him with every great quality which man could possess. His enemies were ready enough to allow his military talents, but they wished to attribute the first success of his not very deep policy to a marvellous duplicity, apparently considered by them the more wicked as possessed by a parvenu emperor, and far removed, in a moral point of view, from the statecraft so allowable in an ancient monarchy. But for Napoleon himself and his family and Court there was literally no limit to the really marvellous inventions of his enemies. He might enter every capital on the Continent, but there was some consolation in believing that he himself was a monster of wickedness, and his Court but the scene of one long protracted orgie.

There was enough against the Emperor in the Memoirs to make them comfortable reading for his opponents, though very many of the old calumnies were disposed of in them. They contained indeed the nearest approximation to the truth which had yet appeared. Metternich, who must have been a good judge, as no man was better acquainted with what he himself calls the "age of Napoleon," says of the Memoirs: "If you want something to read, both interesting and amusing, get the Memoires de Bourrienne. These are the only authentic Memoirs of Napoleon which have yet appeared. The style is not brilliant, but that only makes them the mere trustworthy." Indeed, Metternich himself in his own Memoirs often follows a good deal in the line of Bourrienne: among many formal attacks, every now and then he lapses into half involuntary and indirect praise of his great antagonist, especially where he compares the men he had to deal with in aftertimes with his former rapid and talented interlocutor. To some even among the Bonapartists, Bourrienne was not altogether distasteful. Lucien Bonaparte, remarking that the time in which Bourrienne treated with Napoleon as equal with equal did not last long enough for the secretary, says he has taken a little revenge in his Memoirs, just as a lover, after a break with his mistress, reveals all her defects. But Lucien considers that Bourrienne gives us a good enough idea of the young officer of the artillery, of the great General, and of the First Consul. Of the Emperor, says Lucien, he was too much in retirement to be able to judge equally well. But Lucien was not a fair representative of the Bonapartists; indeed he had never really thought well of his brother or of his actions since Lucien, the former "Brutus" Bonaparte, had ceased to be the adviser of the Consul. It was well for Lucien himself to amass a fortune from the presents of a corrupt court, and to be made a Prince and Duke by the Pope, but he was too sincere a republican not to disapprove of the imperial system. The real Bonapartists were naturally and inevitably furious with the Memoirs. They were not true, they were not the work of Bourrienne, Bourrienne himself was a traitor, a purloiner of manuscripts, his memory was as bad as his principles, he was not even entitled to the de before his name. If the Memoirs were at all to be pardoned, it was because his share was only really a few notes wrung from him by large pecuniary offers at a time when he was pursued by his creditors, and when his brain was already affected.

The Bonapartist attack on the Memoirs was delivered in full form, in two volumes, 'Bourrienne et ses Erreurs, Volontaires et Involontaires' (Paris, Heideloff, 1830), edited by the Comte d'Aure, the Ordonnateur en Chef of the Egyptian expedition, and containing communications from Joseph Bonaparte, Gourgaud, Stein, etc.[2]

Part of the system of attack was to call in question the authenticity of the Memoirs, and this was the more easy as Bourrienne, losing his fortune, died in 1834 in a state of imbecility. But this plan is not systematically followed, and the very reproaches addressed to the writer of the Memoirs often show that it was believed they were really written by Bourrienne. They undoubtedly contain plenty of faults. The editor (Villemarest, it is said) probably had a large share in the work, and Bourrienne must have forgotten or misplaced many dates and occurrences. In such a work, undertaken so many years after the events, it was inevitable that many errors should be made, and that many statements should be at least debatable. But

2 In the notes in this present edition these volumes are referred to in brief 'Erreurs'.

on close investigation the work stands the attack in a way that would be impossible unless it had really been written by a person in the peculiar position occupied by Bourrienne. He has assuredly not exaggerated that position: he really, says Lucien Bonaparte, treated as equal with equal with Napoleon during a part of his career, and he certainly was the nearest friend and confidant that Napoleon ever had in his life.

Where he fails, or where the Bonapartist fire is most telling, is in the account of the Egyptian expedition. It may seem odd that he should have forgotten, even in some thirty years, details such as the way in which the sick were removed; but such matters were not in his province; and it would be easy to match similar omissions in other works, such as the accounts of the Crimea, and still more of the Peninsula. It is with his personal relations with Napoleon that we are most concerned, and it is in them that his account receives most corroboration.

It may be interesting to see what has been said of the Memoirs by other writers. We have quoted Metternich, and Lucien Bonaparte; let us hear Meneval, his successor, who remained faithful to his master to the end: "Absolute confidence cannot be given to statements contained in Memoirs published under the name of a man who has not composed them. It is known that the editor of these Memoirs offered to M. de Bourrienne, who had then taken refuge in Holstein from his creditors, a sum said to be thirty thousand francs to obtain his signature to them, with some notes and addenda. M. de Bourrienne was already attacked by the disease from which he died a few years latter in a maison de sante at Caen. Many literary men co-operated in the preparation of his Memoirs. In 1825 I met M. de Bourrienne in Paris. He told me it had been suggested to him to write against the Emperor. 'Notwithstanding the harm he has done me,' said he, 'I would never do so. Sooner may my hand be withered.' If M. de Bourrienne had prepared his Memoirs himself, he would not have stated that while he was the Emperor's minister at Hamburg he worked with the agents of the Comte de Lille (Louis XVIII.) at the preparation of proclamations in favour of that Prince, and that in 1814 he accepted the thanks of the King, Louis XVIII., for doing so; he would not have said that Napoleon had confided to him in 1805 that he had never conceived the idea of an expedition into England, and that the plan of a landing, the preparations for which he gave such publicity to, was only a snare to amuse fools. The Emperor well knew that never was there a plan more seriously conceived or more positively settled. M. de Bourrienne would not have spoken of his private interviews with Napoleon, nor of the alleged confidences entrusted to him, while really Napoleon had no longer received him after the 20th October 1802. When the Emperor, in 1805, forgetting his faults, named him Minister Plenipotentiary at Hamburg, he granted him the customary audience, but to this favour he did not add the return of his former friendship. Both before and afterwards he constantly refused to receive him, and he did not correspond with him." (Meneval, ii. 378-79). And in another passage Meneval says: "Besides, it would be wrong to regard these Memoirs as the work of the man whose name they bear. The bitter resentment M. de Bourrienne had nourished for his disgrace, the enfeeblement of his faculties, and the poverty he was reduced to, rendered him accessible to the pecuniary offers made to him. He consented to give the authority of his name to Memoirs in whose composition he had only co-operated by incomplete, confused, and often inexact notes, materials which an editor was employed to put in order." And Meneval (iii. 29-30) goes on to quote what he himself had written in the Spectateur Militaire, in which he makes much the same assertions, and especially objects to the account of conversations with the Emperor after 1802, except always the one audience on taking leave for Hamburg.

Meneval also says that Napoleon, when he wished to obtain intelligence from Hamburg, did not correspond with Bourrienne, but deputed him, Meneval, to ask Bourrienne for what was wanted. But he corroborates Bourrienne on the subject of the efforts made, among others by Josephine, for his reappointment.

Such are the statements of the Bonapartists pure; and the reader, as has been said, can judge for himself how far the attack is good. Bourrienne, or his editor, may well have confused the date of his interviews, but he will not be found much astray on many points. His account of the conversation of Josephine after the death of the Duc d'Enghien may be compared with what we know from Madame de Rémusat, who, by the way, would have been horrified if she had known that he considered her to resemble the Empress Josephine in character.

We now come to the views of Savary, the Duc de Rovigo, who avowedly remained on good terms with Bourrienne after his disgrace, though the friendship of Savary was not exactly a thing that most men would have much prided themselves on. "Bourrienne had a prodigious memory; he spoke and wrote in several languages, and his pen ran as quickly as one could speak. Nor were these the only advantages he possessed. He knew the routine of public business and public law. His activity and devotion made him indispensable to the First Consul. I knew the qualities which won for him the unlimited confidence of his chief, but I cannot speak with the same assurance of the faults which made him lose it. Bourrienne had many enemies, both on account of his character and of his place" (Savary, i. 418-19).

Marmont ought to be an impartial critic of the Memoirs. He says, "Bourrienne . . . had a very great capacity, but he is a striking example of the great truth that our passions are always bad counsellors. By inspiring us with an immoderate ardour to reach a fixed end, they often make us miss it. Bourrienne had an immoderate love of money. With his talents and his position near Bonaparte at the first dawn of greatness, with the confidence and real good-will which Bonaparte felt for him, in a few years he would have gained everything in fortune and in social position. But his eager impatience mined his career at the moment when it might have developed and increased" (Marmont, i. 64). The criticism appears just. As to the Memoirs, Marmont says (ii. 224), "In general, these Memoirs are of great veracity and powerful interest so long as they treat of what the author has seen and heard; but when he speaks of others, his work is only an assemblage of gratuitous suppositions and of false facts put forward for special purposes."

The Comte Alexandre de Puymaigre, who arrived at Hamburgh soon after Bourrienne had left it in 1810, says (page 135) of the part of the Memoirs which relates to Hamburg, "I must acknowledge that generally his assertions are well founded. This former companion of Napoleon has only forgotten to speak of the opinion that they had of him in this town.

"The truth is, that he was believed to have made much money there."

Thus we may take Bourrienne as a clever, able man, who would have risen to the highest honours under the Empire had not his short-sighted grasping after lucre driven him from office, and prevented him from ever regaining it under Napoleon.

In the present edition the translation has been carefully compared with the original French text. Where in the original text information is given which has now become mere matter of history, and where Bourrienne merely quotes the documents well enough known at this day, his possession of which forms part of the charges of his opponents, advantage has been taken to lighten the mass of the Memoirs. This has been done especially where they deal with what the writer did not himself see or hear, the part of the Memoirs which are of least valve and of which Marmont's opinion has just been quoted. But in the personal and more valuable part of the Memoirs, where we have the actual knowledge of the secretary himself, the original text has been either fully retained, or some few passages previously omitted restored. Illustrative notes have been added from the Memoirs of the successor of Bourrienne, Meneval, Madame de Rémusat, the works of Colonel Iung on 'Bonaparte et Son Temps', and on 'Lucien Bonaparte', etc., and other books. Attention has also been paid to the attacks of the 'Erreurs', and wherever these criticisms are more than a mere expression of disagreement, their purport has been recorded with, where possible, some judgment of the evidence. Thus the reader will have before him the materials for deciding himself how far, Bourrienne's statements are in agreement with the facts and with the accounts of other writers.

At the present time too much attention has been paid to the Memoirs of Madame de Rémusat. She, as also Madame Junot, was the wife of a man on whom the full shower of imperial favours did not descend, and, womanlike, she saw and thought only of the Court life of the great man who was never less great than in his Court. She is equally astonished and indignant that the Emperor, coming straight from long hours of work with his ministers and with his secretary, could not find soft words for the ladies of the Court, and that, a horrible thing in the eyes of a Frenchwoman, when a mistress threw herself into his arms, he first thought of what political knowledge he could obtain from her. Bourrienne, on the other hand, shows us the other and the really important side of Napoleon's character. He tells us of the long hours in the Cabinet, of the never-resting activity of the Consul, of Napoleon's dreams, no ignoble dreams and often realised, of great labours of peace as well as of war. He is a witness, and the more valuable as a reluctant one, to the marvellous powers of the man who, if not the greatest, was at least the one most fully endowed with every great quality of mind and body the world has ever seen.

R. W. P.

AUTHOR'S INTRODUCTION

The trading upon an illustrious name can alone have given birth to the multitude of publications under the titles of historical memoirs, secret memoirs, and other rhapsodies which have appeared respecting Napoleon. On looking into them it is difficult to determine whether the impudence of the writers or the simplicity of certain readers is most astonishing. Yet these rude and ill digested compilations, filled with absurd anecdotes, fabricated speeches, fictitious crimes or virtues, and disfigured by numerous anachronisms, instead of being consigned to just contempt and speedy oblivion, have been pushed into notice by speculators, and have found zealous partisans and enthusiastic apologists.[3]

For a time I entertained the idea of noticing, one by one, the numerous errors which have been written respecting Napoleon; but I have renounced a task which would have been too laborious to myself, and very tedious to the reader. I shall therefore only correct those which come within the plan of my work, and which are connected with those facts, to a more accurate knowledge of which than any other person can possess I may lay claim. There are men who imagine that nothing done by Napoleon will ever be forgotten; but must not the slow but inevitable influence of time be expected to operate with respect to him? The effect of that influence is, that the most important event of an epoch soon sinks, almost imperceptibly and almost disregarded, into the immense mass of historical facts. Time, in its progress, diminishes the probability as well as the interest of such an event, as it gradually wears away the most durable monuments.

I attach only a relative importance to what I am about to lay before the public. I shall give authentic documents. If all persons who have approached Napoleon, at any time and in any place, would candidly record what they saw and heard, without passion, the future historian would be rich in materials. It is my wish that he who may undertake the difficult task of writing the history of Napoleon shall find in my notes information useful to the perfection of his work. There he will at least find truth. I have not the ambition to wish that what I state should be taken as absolute authority; but I hope that it will always be consulted.

I have never before published anything respecting Napoleon. That malevolence which fastens itself upon men who have the misfortune to be somewhat separated from the crowd has, because there is always more profit in saying ill than good, attributed to me several works on Bonaparte; among others, 'Les Memoires secrets d'un Homme qui ne l'a pas quitte', par M. B———-, and 'Memoires secrets sur Napoleon Bonaparte, par M. de B———, and 'Le Precis Historique sur Napoleon'. The initial of my name has served to propagate this error. The incredible ignorance which runs through those memoirs, the absurdities and inconceivable silliness with which they abound, do not permit a man of honour and common sense to allow such wretched rhapsodies to be imputed to him. I declared in 1816, and at later periods in the French and foreign journals, that I had no hand in those publications, and I

3 This Introduction has been reprinted as bearing upon the character of the work, but refers very often to events of the day at the time of its first appearance.

here formally repeat this declaration.

But it may be said to me, Why should we place more confidence in you than in those who have written before you?

My reply shall be plain. I enter the lists one of the last I have read all that my predecessors have published confident that all I state is true. I have no interest in deceiving, no disgrace to fear, no reward to expect. I neither wish to obscure nor embellish his glory. However great Napoleon may have been, was he not also liable to pay his tribute to the weakness of human nature? I speak of Napoleon such as I have seen him, known him, frequently admired and sometimes blamed him. I state what I saw, heard, wrote, and thought at the time, under each circumstance that occurred. I have not allowed myself to be carried away by the illusions of the imagination, nor to be influenced by friendship or hatred. I shall not insert a single reflection which did not occur to me at the very moment of the event which gave it birth. How many transactions and documents were there over which I could but lament!—how many measures, contrary to my views, to my principles, and to my character!—while the best intentions were incapable of overcoming difficulties which a most powerful and decided will rendered almost insurmountable.

I also wish the future historian to compare what I say with what others have related or may relate. But it will be necessary for him to attend to dates, circumstances, difference of situation, change of temperament, and age,—for age has much influence over men. We do not think and act at fifty as at twenty-five. By exercising this caution he will be able to discover the truth, and to establish an opinion for posterity.

The reader must not expect to find in these Memoirs an uninterrupted series of all the events which marked the great career of Napoleon; nor details of all those battles, with the recital of which so many eminent men have usefully and ably occupied themselves. I shall say little about whatever I did not see or hear, and which is not supported by official documents.

Perhaps I shall succeed in confirming truths which have been doubted, and in correcting errors which have been adopted. If I sometimes differ from the observations and statements of Napoleon at St. Helena, I am far from supposing that those who undertook to be the medium of communication between him and the public have misrepresented what he said. I am well convinced that none of the writers of St. Helena can be taxed with the slightest deception; disinterested zeal and nobleness of character are undoubted pledges of their veracity. It appears to me perfectly certain that Napoleon stated, dictated, or corrected all they have published. Their honour is unquestionable; no one can doubt it. That they wrote what he communicated must therefore be believed; but it cannot with equal confidence be credited that what he communicated was nothing but the truth. He seems often to have related as a fact what was really only an idea,—an idea, too, brought forth at St. Helena, the child of misfortune, and transported by his imagination to Europe in the time of his prosperity. His favourite phrase, which was every moment on his lips, must not be forgotten—"What will history say—what will posterity think?" This passion for leaving behind him a celebrated name is one which belongs to the constitution of the human mind; and with Napoleon its influence was excessive. In his first Italian campaign he wrote thus to General Clarke: "That ambition and the occupation of high offices were not sufficient for his satisfaction and happiness, which he had early placed in the opinion of Europe and the esteem of posterity." He often observed to me that with him the opinion of posterity was the real immortality of the soul.

It may easily be conceived that Napoleon wished to give to the documents which he knew historians would consult a favourable colour, and to direct, according to his own views, the judgment of posterity on his actions: But it is only by the impartial comparison of periods, positions, and age that a well founded decision will be given. About his fortieth year the physical constitution of Napoleon sustained considerable change; and it may be presumed that his moral qualities were affected by that change. It is particularly important not to lose sight of the premature decay of his health, which, perhaps, did not permit him always to, possess the vigour of memory otherwise consistent enough with his age. The state of our organisation often modifies our recollections, our feelings, our manner of viewing objects, and the impressions we receive. This will be taken into consideration by judicious and thinking men; and for them I write.

What M. de Las Casas states Napoleon to have said in May 1816 on the manner of writing his history corroborates the opinion I have expressed. It proves that all the facts and observations he communicated or dictated were meant to serve as materials. We learn from the Memorial that M. de Las Casas wrote daily, and that the manuscript was read over by Napoleon, who often made corrections with his own hand. The idea of a journal pleased him greatly. He fancied it would be a work of which the world could afford no other example. But there are passages in which the order of events is deranged; in others facts are misrepresented and erroneous assertions are made, I apprehend, not altogether involuntarily.

I have paid particular attention to all that has been published by the noble participators of the imperial captivity. Nothing, however, could induce me to change a word in these Memoirs, because nothing could take from me my conviction of the truth of what I personally heard and saw. It will be found that Napoleon in his private conversations often confirms what I state; but we sometimes differ, and the public must judge between us. However, I must here make one observation.

When Napoleon dictated or related to his friends in St. Helena the facts which they have reported he was out of the world,—he had played his part. Fortune, which, according to his notions, had conferred on him all his power and greatness, had recalled all her gifts before he sank into the tomb. His ruling passion would induce him to think that it was due to his glory to clear up certain facts which might prove an unfavourable escort if they accompanied him to posterity. This was his fixed idea. But is there not some ground for suspecting the fidelity of him who writes or dictates his own history? Why might he not impose on a few persons in St. Helena, when he was able to impose on France and Europe, respecting many acts which emanated from him during the long duration of his power? The life of Napoleon would be very unfaithfully written were the author to adopt as true all his bulletins and proclamations, and all the declarations he made at St. Helena. Such a history would frequently be in contradiction to facts; and such only is that which might be entitled, 'The History of Napoleon, written by Himself'.

I have said thus much because it is my wish that the principles which have guided me in the composition of these Memoirs may be understood. I am aware that they will not please every reader; that is a success to which I cannot pretend. Some merit, however, may be allowed me on account of the labour I have undergone. It has neither been of a slight nor an agreeable kind. I made it a rule to read everything that has been written respecting Napoleon, and I have had to decipher many of his autograph documents, though no longer so familiar with his scrawl as formerly. I say decipher, because a real cipher might often be much more readily understood than the handwriting of Napoleon. My own notes, too, which were often very hastily made, in the hand I wrote in my youth, have sometimes also much embarrassed me.

My long and intimate connection with Bonaparte from boyhood, my close relations with him when General, Consul, and Emperor, enabled me to see and appreciate all that was projected and all that was done during that considerable and momentous period of time. I not only had the opportunity of being present at the conception and the execution of the extraordinary deeds of one of the ablest men nature ever formed, but, notwithstanding an almost unceasing application to business, I found means to employ the few moments of leisure which Bonaparte left at my disposal in making notes, collecting documents, and in recording for history facts respecting which the truth could otherwise with difficulty be ascertained; and more particularly in collecting those ideas, often profound, brilliant, and striking, but always remarkable, to which Bonaparte gave expression in the overflowing frankness of confidential intimacy.

The knowledge that I possessed much important information has exposed me to many inquiries, and wherever I have resided since my retirement from public affairs much of my time has been spent in replying to questions. The wish to be acquainted with the most minute details of the life of a man formed on an unexampled model is very natural; and the observation on my replies by those who heard them always was, "You should publish your Memoirs!"

I had certainly always in view the publication of my Memoirs; but, at the same time, I was firmly resolved not to publish them until a period should arrive in which I might tell the truth, and the whole truth. While Napoleon was in the possession of power I felt it right to resist the urgent applications made to me on this subject by some persons of the highest distinction. Truth would then have sometimes appeared flattery, and sometimes, also, it might not have been without danger. Afterwards, when the progress of events removed Bonaparte to a far distant island in the midst of the ocean, silence was imposed on me by other considerations,-by considerations of propriety and feeling.

After the death of Bonaparte, at St. Helena, reasons of a different nature retarded the execution of my plan. The tranquillity of a secluded retreat was indispensable for preparing and putting in order the abundant materials in my possession. I found it also necessary to read a great number of works, in order to rectify important errors to which the want of authentic documents had induced the authors to give credit. This much-desired retreat was found. I had the good fortune to be introduced, through a friend, to the Duchesse de Brancas, and that lady invited me to pass some time on one of her estates in Hainault. Received with the most agreeable hospitality, I have there enjoyed that tranquillity which could alone have rendered the publication of these volumes practicable.

FAUVELET DE BOURRIENNE

NOTE

The Editor of the 1836 edition had added to the Memoirs several chapters taken from or founded on other works of the time, so as to make a more complete history of the period. These materials have been mostly retained, but with the corrections which later publications have made necessary. A chapter has now been added to give, a brief account of the part played by the chief historical personages during the Cent Jours, and another at the end to include the removal of the body of Napoleon from St. Helena to France.

Two special improvements have, it is hoped, been made in this edition. Great care has been taken to get names, dates, and figures rightly given,—points much neglected in most translations, though in some few cases, such as Davoust, the ordinary but not strictly correct spelling has been followed to suit the general reader. The number of references to other works which are given in the notes will, it is believed, be of use to any one wishing to continue the study of the history of Napoleon, and may preserve them from many of the errors too often committed. The present Editor has had the great advantage of having his work shared by Mr. Richard Bentley, who has brought his knowledge of the period to bear, and who has found, as only a busy man could do, the time to minutely enter into every fresh detail, with the ardour which soon seizes any one who long follows that enticing pursuit, the special study of an historical period.

R. W. P

January 1885.

MEMOIRS OF NAPOLEON BONAPARTE

VOLUME I

1769-1800

CHAPTER 1

1769-1783

NAPOLEON BONAPARTE was born at Ajaccio, in Corsica, on the 15th of August 1769;[4] the original orthography of his name was Buonaparte, but he suppressed the "u" during his first campaign in Italy. His motives for so doing were merely to render the spelling conformable with the pronunciation, and to abridge his signature. He signed Buonaparte even after the famous 13th Vendemiaire.

It has been affirmed that he was born in 1768, and that he represented himself to be a year younger than he really was. This is untrue. He always told me the 9th of August was his birthday, and, as I was born on the 9th of July 1769, our proximity of age served to strengthen our union and friendship when we were both at the Military College of Brienne.

The false and absurd charge of Bonaparte having misrepresented his age, is decidedly refuted by a note in the register of M. Berton, sub-principal of the College of Brienne, in which it is stated that M. Napoleon de Buonaparte, ecuyer, born in the city of Ajaccio, in Corsica, on the 15th of August 1769, left the Royal Military College of Brienne on the 17th October 1784.

The stories about his low extraction are alike devoid of foundation. His family was poor, and he was educated at the public expense, an advantage of which many honourable families availed themselves. A memorial addressed by his father, Charles Buonaparte, to the Minister of War states that his fortune had been reduced by the failure of some enterprise in which he had engaged, and by the injustice of the Jesuits, by whom he had been deprived of an inheritance. The object of this memorial was to solicit a sub-lieutenant's commission for

4 The following interesting trait of Napoleon's childhood is derived from the 'Memoirs of the Duchesse d'Arbranes':—"He was one day accused by one of his sisters of having eaten a basketful of grapes, figs, and citrons, which had come from the garden of his uncle the Canon. None but those who were acquainted with the Bonaparte family can form any idea of the enormity of this offence. To eat fruit belonging to the uncle the Canon was infinitely more criminal than to eat grapes and figs which might be claimed by anybody else. An inquiry took place. Napoleon denied the fact, and was whipped. He was told that if he would beg pardon he should be forgiven. He protested that he was innocent, but he was not believed. If I recollect rightly, his mother was at the time on a visit to M. de Marbeuf, or some other friend. The result of Napoleon's obstinacy was, that he was kept three whole days on bread and cheese, and that cheese was not 'broccio'. However, he would not cry: he was dull, but not sulky. At length, on the fourth day of his punishment a little friend of Marianne Bonaparte returned from the country, and on hearing of Napoleon's disgrace she confessed that she and Marianne had eaten the fruit. It was now Marianne's turn to be punished. When Napoleon was asked why he had not accused his sister, he replied that though he suspected that she was guilty, yet out of consideration to her little friend, who had no share in the falsehood, he had said nothing. He was then only seven years of age" (vol. i. p. 9, edit. 1883).

Napoleon, who was then fourteen years of age, and to get Lucien entered a pupil of the Military College. The Minister wrote on the back of the memorial, "Give the usual answer, if there be a vacancy;" and on the margin are these words—"This gentleman has been informed that his request is inadmissible as long as his second son remains at the school of Brienne. Two brothers cannot be placed at the same time in the military schools." When Napoleon was fifteen he was sent to Paris until he should attain the requisite age for entering the army. Lucien was not received into the College of Brienne, at least not until his brother had quitted the Military School of Paris.

Bonaparte was undoubtedly a man of good family. I have seen an authentic account of his genealogy, which he obtained from Tuscany. A great deal has been said about the civil dissensions which forced his family to quit Italy and take refuge in Corsica. On this subject I shall say nothing.

Many and various accounts have been given of Bonaparte's youth.

He has been described in terms of enthusiastic praise and exaggerated condemnation. It is ever thus with individuals who by talent or favourable circumstances are raised above their fellow-creatures. Bonaparte himself laughed at all the stories which were got up for the purpose of embellishing or blackening his character in early life. An anonymous publication, entitled the 'History of Napoleon Bonaparte', from his Birth to his last abdication, contains perhaps the greatest collection of false and ridiculous details about his boyhood. Among other things, it is stated that he fortified a garden to protect himself from the attacks of his comrades, who, a few lines lower down, are described as treating him with esteem and respect. I remember the circumstances which, probably, gave rise to the fabrication inserted in the work just mentioned; they were as follows.

During the winter of 1783-84, so memorable for heavy falls of snow, Napoleon was greatly at a loss for those retired walks and outdoor recreations in which he used to take much delight. He had no alternative but to mingle with his comrades, and, for exercise, to walk with them up and down a spacious hall. Napoleon, weary of this monotonous promenade, told his comrades that he thought they might amuse themselves much better with the snow, in the great courtyard, if they would get shovels and make hornworks, dig trenches, raise parapets, cavaliers, etc. "This being done," said he, "we may divide ourselves into sections, form a siege, and I will undertake to direct the attacks." The proposal, which was received with enthusiasm, was immediately put into execution. This little sham war was carried on for the space of a fortnight, and did not cease until a quantity of gravel and small stones having got mixed with the snow of which we made our bullets, many of the combatants, besiegers as well as besieged, were seriously wounded. I well remember that I was one of the worst sufferers from this sort of grapeshot fire.

It is almost unnecessary to contradict the story about the ascent in the balloon. It is now very well known that the hero of that headlong adventure was not young Bonaparte, as has been alleged, but one of his comrades, Dudont de Chambon, who was somewhat eccentric. Of this his subsequent conduct afforded sufficient proofs.

Bonaparte's mind was directed to objects of a totally different kind. He turned his attention to political science. During some of his vacations he enjoyed the society of the Abby Raynal, who used to converse with him on government, legislation, commercial relations, etc.

On festival days, when the inhabitants of Brienne were admitted to our amusements, posts were established for the maintenance of order. Nobody was permitted to enter the interior of the building without a card signed by the principal, or vice-principal. The rank of officers or sub-officers was conferred according to merit; and Bonaparte one day had the command of a post, when the following little adventure occurred, which affords an instance of his decision of character.

The wife of the porter of the school,[5] who was very well known, because she used to sell milk, fruit, etc., to the pupils, presented herself one Saint Louis day for admittance to the representation of the 'Death of Caesar, corrected', in which I was to perform the part of Brutus. As the woman had no ticket, and insisted on being admitted without one, some disturbance arose. The serjeant of the post reported the matter to the officer, Napoleon Bonaparte, who in an imperious tone of voice exclaimed: "Send away that woman, who comes here with her camp impudence." This was in 1782.

Bonaparte and I were eight years of, age when our friendship commenced. It speedily became very intimate, for there was a certain sympathy of heart between us. I enjoyed this friendship and intimacy until 1784, when he was transferred from the Military College of Brienne to that of Paris. I was one among those of his youthful comrades who could best accommodate themselves to his stern character. His natural reserve, his disposition to meditate on the conquest of Corsica, and the impressions he had received in childhood respecting the misfortunes of his country and his family, led him to seek retirement, and rendered his general demeanour, though in appearance only, somewhat unpleasing. Our equality of age brought us together in the classes of the mathematics and 'belles lettres'. His ardent wish to acquire knowledge was remarkable from the very commencement of his studies. When he first came to the college he spoke only the Corsican dialect, and the Sieur Dupuis,[6] who was vice-principal before Father Berton, gave him instructions in the French language. In this he made such rapid progress that in a short time he commenced the first rudiments of Latin. But to this study he evinced such a repugnance that at the age of fifteen he was not out of the fourth class. There I left him very speedily; but I could never get before him in the mathematical class, in which he was undoubtedly the cleverest lad at the college. I used sometimes to help him with his Latin themes and versions in return for the aid he afforded me in the solution of problems, at which he evinced a degree of readiness and facility which perfectly astonished me.

When at Brienne, Bonaparte was remarkable for the dark color of his complexion (which, subsequently, the climate of France somewhat changed), for his piercing and scrutinising glance, and for the style of his conversation both with his masters and comrades. His conversation almost always bore the appearance of ill-humour, and he was certainly not very amiable. This I attribute to the misfortunes his family had sustained and the impressions made on his mind by the conquest of his country.

The pupils were invited by turns to dine with Father Berton, the head of the school. One day, it being Bonaparte's turn to enjoy this indulgence, some of the professors who were at table designedly made some disrespectful remarks on Paoli, of whom they knew the young Corsican was an enthusiastic admirer. "Paoli," observed Bonaparte, "was a great man; he loved his country; and I will never forgive my father, who was his adjutant, for having concurred in the union of Corsica with France. He ought to have followed Paoli's fortune, and have

---

5 This woman, named Haute, was afterwards placed at Malmaison, with her husband. They both died as concierges of Malmaison. This shows that Napoleon had a memory.—Bourrienne.

6 He afterwards filled the post of librarian to Napoleon at Malmaison.

fallen with him."[7] Generally speaking, Bonaparte was not much liked by his comrades at Brienne. He was not social with them, and rarely took part in their amusements. His country's recent submission to France always caused in his mind a painful feeling, which estranged him from his schoolfellows. I, however, was almost his constant companion. During play-hours he used to withdraw to the library, where he-read with deep interest works of history, particularly Polybius and Plutarch. He was also fond of Arrianus, but did not care much for Quintus Gurtius. I often went off to play with my comrades, and left him by himself in the library.

The temper of the young Corsican was not improved by the teasing he frequently experienced from his comrades, who were fond of ridiculing him about his Christian name Napoleon and his country. He often said to me, "I will do these French all the mischief I can;" and when I tried to pacify him he would say, "But you do not ridicule me; you like me."

Father Patrauld, our mathematical professor, was much attached to Bonaparte. He was justly proud of him as a pupil. The other professors, in whose classes he was not distinguished, took little notice of him. He had no taste for the study of languages, polite literature, or the arts. As there were no indications of his ever becoming a scholar, the pedants of the establishment were inclined to think him stupid. His superior intelligence was, however, sufficiently perceptible, even through the reserve under which it was veiled. If the monks to whom the superintendence of the establishment was confided had understood the organisation of his mind, if they had engaged more able mathematical professors, or if we had had any incitement to the study of chemistry, natural philosophy, astronomy, etc., I am convinced that Bonaparte would have pursued these sciences with all the genius and spirit of investigation which he displayed in a career, more brilliant it is true, but less useful to mankind. Unfortunately, the monks did not perceive this, and were too poor to pay for good masters. However, after Bonaparte left the college they found it necessary to engage two professors from Paris, otherwise the college would have fallen to nothing. These two new professors, MM. Durfort and Desponts, finished my education; and I regretted that they did not come sooner. The often-repeated assertion of Bonaparte having received a careful education at Brienne is therefore untrue. The monks were incapable of giving it him; and, for my own part, I must confess that the extended information of the present day is to me a painful contrast with the limited course of education I received at the Military

7 The Duchesse d'Abrantes, speaking of the personal characteristics of Bonaparte in youth and manhood, says, "Saveria told me that Napoleon was never a pretty boy, as Joseph was, for example: his head always appeared too large for his body, a defect common to the Bonaparte family. When Napoleon grew up, the peculiar charm of his countenance lay in his eye, especially in the mild expression it assumed in his moments of kindness. His anger, to be sure, was frightful, and though I am no coward, I never could look at him in his fits of rage without shuddering. Though his smile was captivating, yet the expression of his mouth when disdainful or angry could scarcely be seen without terror. But that forehead which seemed formed to bear the crowns of a whole world; those hands, of which the most coquettish women might have been vain, and whose white skin covered muscles of iron; in short, of all that personal beauty which distinguished Napoleon as a young man, no traces were discernible in the boy. Saveria spoke truly when she said, that of all the children of Signora Laetitia, the Emperor was the one from whom future greatness was least to be prognosticated" (vol. i. p. 10, edit. 1883)

College. It is only surprising that the establishment should have produced a single able man.

Though Bonaparte had no reason to be satisfied with the treatment he received from his comrades, yet he was above complaining of it; and when he had the supervision of any duty which they infringed, he would rather go to prison than denounce the criminals.

I was one day his accomplice in omitting to enforce a duty which we were appointed to supervise. He prevailed on me to accompany him to prison, where we remained three days. We suffered this sort of punishment several times, but with less severity.

In 1783 the Duke of Orleans and Madame de Montesson visited Brienne; and, for upwards of a month, the magnificent chateau of the Comte de Brienne was a Versailles in miniature. The series of brilliant entertainments which were given to the august travellers made them almost forget the royal magnificence they had left behind them.

The Prince and Madame de Montesson expressed a wish to preside at the distribution of the prizes of our college. Bonaparte and I won the prizes in the class of mathematics, which, as I have already observed, was the branch of study to which he confined his attention, and in which he excelled. When I was called up for the seventh time Madame de Montesson said to my mother, who had come from Sens to be present at the distribution, "Pray, madame, crown your son this time; my hands are a-weary."

There was an inspector of the military schools, whose business it was to make an annual report on each pupil, whether educated at the public expense or paid for by his family. I copied from the report of 1784 a note which was probably obtained surreptitiously from the War Office. I wanted to purchase the manuscript, but Louis Bonaparte bought it. I did not make a copy of the note which related to myself, because I should naturally have felt diffident in making any use of it. It would, however, have served to show how time and circumstances frequently reversed the distinctions which arise at school or college. Judging from the reports of the inspector of military schools, young Bonaparte was not, of all the pupils at Brienne in 1784, the one most calculated to excite prognostics of future greatness and glory.

The note to which I have just alluded, and which was written by M. de Kerralio, then inspector of the military schools, describes Bonaparte in the following terms:

> INSPECTION OF MILITARY SCHOOLS, 1784.
> REPORT MADE FOR HIS MAJESTY BY M. DE KERALIO.
>
> M. de Buonaparte (Napoleon), born 15th August 1769, height 4 feet 10 inches 10 lines, is in the fourth class, has a good constitution, excellent health, character obedient, upright, grateful, conduct very regular; has been always distinguished by his application to mathematics. He knows history and geography very passably. He is not well up in ornamental studies or in Latin in which he is only in the fourth class. He will be an excellent sailor. He deserves to be passed on to the Military School of Paris.

Father Berton, however, opposed Bonaparte's removal to Paris, because he had not passed through the fourth Latin class, and the regulations required that he should be in the third.

I was informed by the vice-principal that a report relative to Napoleon was sent from the College of Brienne to that of Paris, in which he was described as being domineering, imperious, and obstinate.[8]

I knew Bonaparte well; and I think M. de Keralio's report of him was exceedingly just, except, perhaps, that he might have said he was very well as to his progress in history and geography, and very backward in Latin; but certainly nothing indicated the probability of his being an excellent seaman. He himself had no thought of the navy.[9]

What could have induced Sir Walter Scott to say that Bonaparte was the pride of the college, that our mathematical master was exceedingly fond of him, and that the other professors in the different sciences had equal reason to be satisfied with him? What I have above stated, together with the report of M. de Keralio, bear evidence of his backwardness in almost every branch of education except mathematics. Neither was it, as Sir Walter affirms, his precocious progress in mathematics that occasioned him to be removed to Paris. He had attained the proper age, and the report of him was favourable, therefore he was very naturally included among the number of the five who were chosen in 1784.

In a biographical account of Bonaparte I have read the following anecdote:—When he was fourteen years of age he happened to be at a party where some one pronounced a high eulogium on Turenne; and a lady in the company observed that he certainly was a great man, but that she should like him better if he had not burned the Palatinate. "What signifies

---

8 Napoleon remained upwards of five years at Brienne, from April 1779 till the latter end of 1784. In 1783 the Chevalier Keralio, sub-inspector of the military schools, selected him to pass the year following to the military school at Paris, to which three of the best scholars were annually sent from each of the twelve provincial military schools of France. It is curious as well as satisfactory to know the opinion at this time entertained of him by those who were the best qualified to judge. His old master, Le Guille, professor of history at Paris, boasted that, in a list of the different scholars, he had predicted his pupil's subsequent career. In fact, to the name of Bonaparte the following note is added: "a Corsican by birth and character—he will do something great, if circumstances favour him." Menge was his instructor in geometry, who also entertained a high opinion of him. M. Bauer, his German master, was the only one who saw nothing in him, and was surprised at being told he was undergoing his examination for the artillery. —Hazlitt.

9 In consequence of M. de Keralio's report, Bonaparte was transferred to the Military College of Paris, along with MM. Montarby de Dampierre, de Castres, de Comminges, and de Laugier de Bellecourt, who were all, like him, educated at the public expense, and all, at least, as favorably reported. Bourrienne is certainly wrong as to Bonaparte having no thought of the navy. In a letter of 1784 to the Minister of War his father says of Napoleon that, "following the advice of the Comte de Marbeuf, he has turned his studies towards the navy; and so well has he succeeded that he was intended by M. de Keralio for the school of Paris, and afterwards for the department of Toulon. The retirement of the former professor (Keralio) has changed the fate of my son." It was only on the failure of his intention to get into the navy that his father, on 15th July 1784 applied for permission for him to enter the artillery; Napoleon having a horror of the infantry, where he said they did nothing. It was on the success of this application that he was allowed to enter the school of Parts (Iung, tome i. pp. 91-103). Oddly enough, in later years, on 30th August 1792, having just succeeded in getting himself reinstated as captain after his absence, overstaying leave, he applied to pass into the Artillerie de la Marine. "The application was judged to be simply absurd, and was filed with this note, 'S. R.' ('sans reponse')" (Iung, tome ii. p. 201)

that," replied Bonaparte, "if it was necessary to the object he had in view?"

This is either an anachronism or a mere fabrication. Bonaparte was fourteen in the year 1783. He was then at Brienne, where certainly he did not go into company, and least of all the company of ladies.

CHAPTER II

1784-1794

Bonaparte was fifteen years and two months old when he went to the Military College of Paris.[10] I accompanied him in a carriole as far as Nogent Sur Seine, whence the coach was to start. We parted with regret, and we did not meet again till the year 1792. During these eight years we maintained an active correspondence; but so little did I anticipate the high destiny

10 Madame Junot relates some interesting particulars connected with Napoleon's first residence in Paris: "My mother's first care," says she, "on arriving in Paris was to inquire after Napoleon Bonaparte. He was at that time in the military school at Paris, having quitted Brienne in the September of the preceding year. My uncle Demetrius had met him just after he alighted from the coach which brought him to town; 'And truly.' said my uncle, 'he had the appearance of a fresh importation. I met him in the Palms Royal, where he was gaping and staring with wonder at everything he saw. He would have been an excellent subject for sharpers, if, indeed, he had had anything worth taking!' My uncle invited him to dine at his house; for though my uncle was a bachelor, he did not choose to dine at a 'traiteur' (the name 'restaurateur' was not then introduced). He told my mother that Napoleon was very morose. 'I fear,' added he, 'that that young man has more self-conceit than is suitable to his condition. When he dined with me he began to declaim violently against the luxury of the young men of the military school. After a little he turned the conversation on Mania, and the present education of the young Maniotes, drawing a comparison between it and the ancient Spartan system of education. His observations on this head he told me he intended to embody in a memorial to be presented to the Minister of War. All this, depend upon it, will bring him under the displeasure of his comrades; and it will be lucky if he escape being run through.' A few days afterwards my mother saw Napoleon, and then his irritability was at its height. He would scarcely bear any observations, even if made in his favour, and I am convinced that it is to this uncontrollable irritability that he owed the reputation of having been ill-tempered in his boyhood, and splenetic in his youth. My father, who was acquainted with almost all the heads of the military school, obtained leave for him sometimes to come out for recreation. On account of an accident (a sprain, if I recollect rightly) Napoleon once spent a whole week at our house. To this day, whenever I pass the Quai Conti, I cannot help looking up at a 'mansarde' at the left angle of the house on the third floor. That was Napoleon's chamber when he paid us a visit, and a neat little room it was. My brother used to occupy the one next to it. The two young men were nearly of the same age: my brother perhaps had the advantage of a year or fifteen months. My mother had recommended him to cultivate the friendship of young Bonaparte; but my brother complained how unpleasant it was to find only cold politeness where he expected affection. This repulsiveness on the part of Napoleon was almost offensive, and must have been sensibly felt by my brother, who was not only remarkable for the mildness of his temper and the amenity and grace of his manner, but whose society was courted in the most distinguished circles of Paris on account of his accomplishments. He perceived in Bonaparte a kind of acerbity and bitter irony, of which he long endeavoured to discover the cause. 'I believe,' said Albert one day to my mother, 'that the poor young man feels keenly his dependent situation.'" ('Memoirs of the Duchesse d'Abrantes, vol. i. p. 18, edit. 1883).

which, after his elevation, it was affirmed the wonderful qualities of his boyhood plainly denoted, that I did not preserve one of the letters he wrote to me at that period, but tore them up as soon as they were answered.[11]

On his arrival at the Military School of Paris, Bonaparte found the establishment on so brilliant and expensive a footing that he immediately addressed a memorial on the subject to the Vice-Principal Berton of Brienne.[12]

He showed that the plan of education was really pernicious, and far from being calculated to fulfil the object which every wise government must have in view. The result of the system, he said, was to inspire the pupils, who were all the sons of poor gentlemen, with a love of ostentation, or rather, with sentiments of vanity and self-sufficiency; so that, instead of returning happy to the bosom of their families, they were likely to be ashamed of their parents, and to despise their humble homes. Instead of the numerous attendants by whom they were surrounded, their dinners of two courses, and their horses and grooms, he suggested that they should perform little necessary services for themselves, such as brushing their clothes, and cleaning their boots and shoes; that they should eat the coarse bread made for soldiers, etc. Temperance and activity, he added, would render them robust, enable them to bear the severity of different seasons and climates, to brave the fatigues of war, and to inspire the respect and obedience of the soldiers under their command. Thus reasoned Napoleon at the age of sixteen, and time showed that he never deviated from these principles. The establishment of the military school at Fontainebleau is a decided proof of this.

As Napoleon was an active observer of everything passing around him, and pronounced his opinion openly and decidedly, he did not remain long at the Military School of Paris. His superiors, who were anxious to get rid of him, accelerated the period of his examination, and he obtained the first vacant sub-lieutenancy in a regiment of artillery.

I left Brienne in 1787; and as I could not enter the artillery, I proceeded in the following year to Vienna, with a letter of recommendation to M. de Montmorin, soliciting employment

---

11 I remember, however, that in a letter which I received from him about a year after his arrival in Paris he urged me to keep my promise of entering the army with him. Like him, I had passed through the studies necessary for the artillery service; and in 1787 I went for three months to Metz, in order to unite practice with theory. A strange Ordinance, which I believe was issued in 1778 by M. de Segur, required that a man should possess four quarterings of nobility before he could be qualified to serve his king and country as a military officer. My mother went to Paris, taking with her the letters patent of her husband, who died six weeks after my birth. She proved that in the year 1640 Louis XIII. had, by letters patent, restored the titles of one Fauvelet de Villemont, who in 1586 had kept several provinces of Burgundy subject to the king's authority at the peril of his life and the loss of his property; and that his family had occupied the first places in the magistracy since the fourteenth century. All was correct, but it was observed that the letters of nobility had not been registered by the Parliament, and to repair this little omission, the sum of twelve thousand francs was demanded. This my mother refused to pay, and there the matter rested.

12 A second memoir prepared by him to the same effect was intended for the Minister of War, but Father Berton wisely advised silence to the young cadet (Iung, tome i. p. 122). Although believing in the necessity of show and of magnificence in public life, Napoleon remained true to these principles. While lavishing wealth on his ministers and marshals, "In your private life," said be, "be economical and even parsimonious; in public be magnificent" (Meneval, tome i. p. 146).

in the French Embassy at the Court of Austria.

I remained two months at Vienna, where I had the honour of twice seeing the Emperor Joseph. The impression made upon me by his kind reception, his dignified and elegant manners, and graceful conversation, will never be obliterated from my recollection. After M. de Noailles had initiated me in the first steps of diplomacy, he advised me to go to one of the German universities to study the law of nations and foreign languages. I accordingly repaired to Leipsic, about the time when the French Revolution broke out.

I spent some time at Leipsic, where I applied myself to the study of the law of nations, and the German and English languages. I afterwards travelled through Prussia and Poland, and passed a part of the winter of 1791 and 1792 at Warsaw, where I was most graciously received by Princess Tyszicwiez, niece of Stanislaus Augustus, the last King of Poland, and the sister of Prince Poniatowski. The Princess was very well informed, and was a great admirer of French literature: At her invitation I passed several evenings in company with the King in a circle small enough to approach to something like intimacy. I remember that his Majesty frequently asked me to read the Moniteur; the speeches to which he listened with the greatest pleasure were those of the Girondists. The Princess Tyszicwiez wished to print at Warsaw, at her own expense, a translation I had executed of Kotzebue's 'Menschenhass and Reue, to which I gave the title of 'L'Inconnu'.[13]

I arrived at Vienna on the 26th of March 1792, when I was informed of the serious illness of the Emperor, Leopold II, who died on the following day. In private companies, and at public places, I heard vague suspicions expressed of his having been poisoned; but the public, who were admitted to the palace to see the body lie in state, were soon convinced of the falsehood of these reports. I went twice to see the mournful spectacle, and I never heard a word which was calculated to confirm the odious suspicion, though the spacious hall in which the remains of the Emperor were exposed was constantly thronged with people.

In the month of April 1792 I returned to Paris, where I again met Bonaparte,[14] and our college intimacy was fully renewed. I was not very well off, and adversity was hanging heavily on him; his resources frequently failed him. We passed our time like two young fellows of twenty-three who have little money and less occupation. Bonaparte was always poorer than I. Every day we conceived some new project or other. We were on the look-out for some profitable speculation. At one time he wanted me to join him in renting several houses, then building in the Rue Montholon, to underlet them afterwards. We found the demands of the landlords extravagant—everything failed.

At the same time he was soliciting employment at the War Office, and I at the office of

13 A play known on the English stage as *The Stranger.*

14 Bonaparte is said, on very doubtful authority, to have spent five or six weeks in London in 1791 or 1792, and to have "lodged in a house in George Street, Strand. His chief occupation appeared to be taking pedestrian exercise in the streets of London—hence his marvellous knowledge of the great metropolis which used to astonish any Englishmen of distinction who were not aware of this visit. He occasionally took his cup of chocolate at the 'Northumberland,' occupying himself in reading, and preserving a provoking taciturnity to the gentlemen in the room; though his manner was stern, his deportment was that of a gentleman." The story of his visit is probably as apocryphal as that of his offering his services to the English Government when the English forces wore blockading the coast of Corsica.

Foreign Affairs. I was for the moment the luckier of the two.

While we were spending our time in a somewhat vagabond way,[15] the 20th of June arrived. We met by appointment at a restaurateur's in the Rue St. Honore, near the Palais Royal, to take one of our daily rambles. On going out we saw approaching, in the direction of the market, a mob, which Bonaparte calculated at five or six thousand men. They were all in rags, ludicrously armed with weapons of every description, and were proceeding hastily towards the Tuilleries, vociferating all kinds of gross abuse. It was a collection of all that was most vile and abject in the purlieus of Paris. "Let us follow the mob," said Bonaparte. We got the start of them, and took up our station on the terrace of the banks of the river. It was there that he witnessed the scandalous scenes which took place; and it would be difficult to describe the surprise and indignation which they excited in him. When the King showed himself at the windows overlooking the garden, with the red cap, which one of the mob had put on his head, he could no longer repress his indignation. "Che coglione!" he loudly exclaimed. "Why have they let in all that rabble! They should sweep off four or five hundred of them with the cannon; the rest would then set off fast enough."

When we sat down to dinner, which I paid for, as I generally did, for I was the richer of the two, he spoke of nothing but the scene we had witnessed. He discussed with great good sense the causes and consequences of this unrepressed insurrection. He foresaw and developed with sagacity all that would ensue. He was not mistaken. The 10th of August soon arrived. I was then at Stuttgart, where I was appointed Secretary of Legation.

At St. Helena Bonaparte said, "On the news of the attack of the Tuilleries, on the 10th of August, I hurried to Fauvelet, Bourrienne's brother, who then kept a furniture warehouse at the Carrousel." This is partly correct. My brother was connected with what was termed an 'enterprise d'encan national', where persons intending to quit France received an advance of money, on depositing any effects which they wished to dispose of, and which were sold for them immediately. Bonaparte had some time previously pledged his watch in this way.

After the fatal 10th of August Bonaparte went to Corsica, and did not return till 1793. Sir Walter Scott says that after that time he never saw Corsica again. This is a mistake, as will be shown when I speak of his return from Egypt.[16]

Having been appointed Secretary of Legation to Stuttgart, I set off for that place on the 2d of August, and I did not again see my ardent young friend until 1795. He told me that my departure accelerated his for Corsica. We separated, as may be supposed, with but faint hopes of ever meeting again.

---

15 It was before the 20th of June that in our frequent excursions around Paris we went to St. Cyr to see his sister Marianne (Elisa). We returned to dine alone at Trianon.—Bourrienne.

16 Sir Walter appears to have collected his information for the Life of Napoleon only from those libels and vulgar stories which gratified the calumnious spirit and national hatred. His work is written with excessive negligence, which, added to its numerous errors, shows how much respect he must have entertained for his readers. It would appear that his object was to make it the inverse of his novels, where everything is borrowed from history. I have been assured that Marshal Macdonald having offered to introduce Scott to some generals who could have furnished him with the most accurate, information respecting military events, the glory of which they had shared, Sir Walter replied, "I thank you, but I shall collect my information from unprofessional reports."—Bourrienne.

By a decree of the 28th of March of 1793, all French agents abroad were ordered to return to France, within three months, under pain of being regarded as emigrants. What I had witnessed before my departure for Stuttgart, the excitement in which I had left the public mind, and the well-known consequences of events of this kind, made me fear that I should be compelled to be either an accomplice or a victim in the disastrous scenes which were passing at home. My disobedience of the law placed my name on the list of emigrants.

It has been said of me, in a biographical publication, that "it was as remarkable as it was fortunate for Bourrienne that, on his return, he got his name erased from the list of emigrants of the department of the Yonne, on which it had been inscribed during his first journey to Germany. This circumstance has been interpreted in several different ways, which are not all equally favourable to M. de Bourrienne."

I do not understand what favourable interpretations can be put upon a statement entirely false. General Bonaparte repeatedly applied for the erasure of my name, from the month of April 1797, when I rejoined him at Leoben, to the period of the signature of the treaty of Campo-Formio; but without success. He desired his brother Louis, Berthier, Bernadotte, and others, when he sent them to the Directory, to urge my erasure; but in vain. He complained of this inattention to his wishes to Bottot, when he came to Passeriano, after the 18th Fructidor. Bottot, who was secretary to Barras, was astonished that I was not erased, and he made fine promises of what he would do. On his return to France he wrote to Bonaparte: "Bourrienne is erased." But this was untrue. I was not erased until November 1797, upon the reiterated solicitations of General Bonaparte.

It was during my absence from France that Bonaparte, in the rank of 'chef de bataillon', performed his first campaign, and contributed so materially to the recapture of Toulon. Of this period of his life I have no personal knowledge, and therefore I shall not speak of it as an eye-witness. I shall merely relate some facts which fill up the interval between 1793 and 1795, and which I have collected from papers which he himself delivered to me. Among these papers is a little production, entitled 'Le Souper de Beaucaire', the copies of which he bought up at considerable expense, and destroyed upon his attaining the Consulate. This little pamphlet contains principles very opposite to those he wished to see established in 1800, a period when extravagant ideas of liberty were no longer the fashion, and when Bonaparte entered upon a system totally the reverse of those republican principles professed in 'Le Souper de Beaucaire.[17] It may be remarked, that in all that has come to us from St. Helena,

---

17 This is not, as Sir Walter says, a dialogue between Marat and a Federalist, but a conversation between a military officer, a native of Nismes, a native of Marseilles, and a manufacturer from Montpellier. The latter, though he takes a share in the conversation, does not say much. 'Le Souper de Beaucaire' is given at full length in the French edition of these Memoirs, tome i. pp. 319-347; and by Iung, tome ii. p. 354, with the following remarks: "The first edition of 'Le Souper de Beaucaire' was issued at the cost of the Public Treasury, in August 1798. Sabin Tournal, its editor, also then edited the 'Courrier d'Avignon'. The second edition only appeared twenty-eight years afterwards, in 1821, preceded by an introduction by Frederick Royou (Paris: Brasseur Aine, printer, Terrey, publisher, in octavo). This pamphlet did not make any sensation at the time it appeared. It was only when Napoleon became Commandant of the Army of Italy that M. Loubet, secretary and corrector of the press for M. Tournal, attached some value to the manuscript, and showed it to several persona. Louis Bonaparte, later, ordered several copies from M. Aurel. The pamphlet, dated 29th duly 1793, is in the form of a

not a word is said of this youthful production. Its character sufficiently explains this silence. In all Bonaparte's writings posterity will probably trace the profound politician rather than the enthusiastic revolutionist.

Some documents relative to Bonaparte's suspension and arrest, by order of the representatives Albitte and Salicetti, serve to place in their true light circumstances which have hitherto been misrepresented. I shall enter into some details of this event, because I have seen it stated that this circumstance of Bonaparte's life has been perverted and misrepresented by every person who has hitherto written about him; and the writer who makes this remark, himself describes the affair incorrectly and vaguely. Others have attributed Bonaparte's misfortune to a military discussion on war, and his connection with Robespierre the younger.[18]

It has, moreover, been said that Albitte and Salicetti explained to the Committee of Public Safety the impossibility of their resuming the military operations unaided by the talents of General Bonaparte. This is mere flattery. The facts are these:

On the 13th of July 1794 (25th Messidor, year II), the representatives of the people with the army of Italy ordered that General Bonaparte should proceed to Genoa, there, conjointly with the French 'charge d'affaires', to confer on certain subjects with the Genoese Government. This mission, together with a list of secret instructions, directing him to examine the fortresses of Genoa and the neighbouring country, show the confidence which Bonaparte, who was then only twenty-five, inspired in men who were deeply interested in making a prudent choice of their agents.

Bonaparte set off for Genoa, and fulfilled his mission. The 9th Thermidor arrived, and the deputies, called Terrorists, were superseded by Albitte and Salicetti. In the disorder which then prevailed they were either ignorant of the orders given to General Bonaparte, or persons envious of the rising glory of the young general of artillery inspired Albitte and

---

dialogue between an officer of the army, a citizen of Nismes, a manufacturer of Montpellier, and a citizen of Marseilles. Marseilles was then in a state of insurrection against the Convention. Its forces had seized Avignon, but had been driven out by the army of Cartesna, which was about to attack Marseilles itself." In the dialogue the officer gives most excellent military advice to the representative of Marseilles on the impossibility of their resisting the old soldiers of Carteaux. The Marseilles citizen argues but feebly, and is alarmed at the officer's representations; while his threat to call in the Spaniards turns the other speakers against him. Even Colonel Iung says, tome ii. p. 372, "In these concise judgments is felt the decision of the master and of the man of war .... These marvellous qualities consequently struck the members of the Convention, who made much of Bonaparte, authorised him to have it published at the public expense, and made him many promises." Lanfrey, vol. i. pp. 201, says of this pamphlets "Common enough ideas, expressed in a style only remarkable for its 'Italianisms,' but becoming singularly firm and precise every time the author expresses his military views. Under an apparent roughness, we find in it a rare circumspection, leaving no hold on the writer, even if events change."

18 It will presently be seen that all this is erroneous, and that Sir Walter commits another mistake when he says that Bonaparte's connection with Robespierre was attended with fatal consequences to him, and that his justification consisted in acknowledging that his friends were very different from what he had supposed them to be. —Bourrienne.

Salicetti with suspicions prejudicial to him. Be this as it may, the two representatives drew up a resolution, ordering that General Bonaparte should be arrested, suspended from his rank, and arraigned before the Committee of Public Safety; and, extraordinary as it may appear, this resolution was founded in that very journey to Genoa which Bonaparte executed by the direction of the representatives of the people.[19] Bonaparte said at St. Helena that he was a short time imprisoned by order of the representative Laporte; but the order for his arrest was signed by Albitte, Salicetti, and Laporte.[20]

Laporte was not probably the most influential of the three, for Bonaparte did not address his remonstrance to him. He was a fortnight under arrest.

Had the circumstance occurred three weeks earlier, and had Bonaparte been arraigned before the Committee of Public Safety previous to the 9th Thermidor, there is every probability that his career would have been at an end; and we should have seen perish on

---

19 Madame Junot throws some light on this Persecution of Bonaparte by Salicetti. "One motive (I do not mean to say the only one)," remarks this lady, "of the animosity shown by Salicetti to Bonaparte, in the affair of Loano, was that they were at one time suitors to the same lady. I am not sure whether it was in Corsica or in Paris, but I know for a fact that Bonaparte, in spite of his youth, or perhaps I should rather say on account of his youth, was the favoured lover. It was the opinion of my brother, who was secretary to Salicetti, that Bonaparte owed his life to a circumstance which is not very well known. The fact is, that Salicetti received a letter from Bonaparte, the contents of which appeared to make a deep impression on him. Bonaparte's papers had been delivered into Salicetti's hands, who, after an attentive perusal of them, laid them aside with evident dissatisfaction. He then took them up again, and read them a second time. Salicetti declined my brother's assistance is the examination of the papers, and after a second examination, which was probably as unsatisfactory as the first, he seated himself with a very abstracted air. It would appear that he had seen among the papers some document which concerned himself. Another curious fact is, that the man who had the care of the papers after they were sealed up was an inferior clerk entirely under the control of Salicetti; and my brother, whose business it was to have charge of the papers, was directed not to touch them. He has often spoken to me of this circumstance, and I mention it here as one of importance to the history of the time. Nothing that relates to a man like Napoleon can be considered useless or trivial. "What, after all, was the result of this strange business which might have cost Bonaparte his head?—for, had he been taken to Paris and tried by the Committee of Public Safety, there is little doubt that the friend of Robespierre the younger would have been condemned by Billaud-Varennes and Collot d'Herbois. The result was the acquittal of the accused. This result is the more extraordinary, since it would appear that at that time Salicetti stood in fear of the young general. A compliment is even paid to Bonaparte in the decree, by which he was provisionally restored to liberty. That liberation was said to be granted on the consideration that General Bonaparte might be useful to the Republic. This was foresight; but subsequently when measures were taken which rendered Bonaparte no longer an object of fear, his name was erased from the list of general officers, and it is a curious fact that Cambacérès, who was destined to be his colleague in the Consulate, was one of the persons who signed the act of erasure" (Memoirs of the Duchesse d'Abrantes, vol. i, p. 69, edit. 1843).

20 Albitte and Laporte were the representatives sent from the Convention to the army of the Alps, and Salicetti to the army of Italy.

the scaffold, at the age of twenty-five, the man who, during the twenty-five succeeding years, was destined to astonish the world by his vast conceptions, his gigantic projects, his great military genius, his extraordinary good fortune, his faults, reverses, and final misfortunes.

It is worth while to remark that in the post-Thermidorian resolution just alluded to no mention is made of Bonaparte's association with Robespierre the younger. The severity with which he was treated is the more astonishing, since his mission to Genoa was the alleged cause of it. Was there any other charge against him, or had calumny triumphed over the services he had rendered to his country? I have frequently conversed with him on the subject of this adventure, and he invariably assured me that he had nothing to reproach himself with, and that his defence, which I shall subjoin, contained the pure expression of his sentiments, and the exact truth.

In the following note, which he addressed to Albitte and Salicetti, he makes no mention of Laporte. The copy which I possess is in the handwriting of, Junot, with corrections in the General's hand. It exhibits all the characteristics of Napoleon's writing: his short sentences, his abrupt rather than concise style, sometimes his elevated ideas, and always his plain good sense.

TO THE REPRESENTATIVES ALBITTE AND SALICETTI:

You have suspended me from my duties, put me under arrest, and declared me to be suspected. Thus I am disgraced before being judged, or indeed judged before being heard. In a revolutionary state there are two classes, the suspected and the patriots. When the first are aroused, general measures are adopted towards them for the sake of security. The oppression of the second class is a blow to public liberty. The magistrate cannot condemn until after the fullest evidence and a succession of facts. This leaves nothing to arbitrary decision. To declare a patriot suspected is to deprive him of all that he most highly values—confidence and esteem. In what class am I placed? Since the commencement of the Revolution, have I not always been attached to its principles? Have I not always been contending either with domestic enemies or foreign foes? I sacrificed my home, abandoned my property, and lost everything for the Republic? I have since served with some distinction at Toulon, and earned a part of the laurels of the army of Italy at the taking of Saorgio, Oneille, and Tanaro. On the discovery of Robespierre's conspiracy, my conduct was that of a man accustomed to look only to principles. My claim to the title of patriot, therefore cannot be disputed. Why, then, am I declared suspected without being heard, and arrested eight days after I heard the news of the tyrant's death. I am declared suspected, and my papers are placed under seal. The reverse of this course ought to have been adopted. My papers should first have been sealed; then I should have been called on for my explanation; and, lastly, declared suspected, if there was reason for coming to, such a decision. It is wished that I should go to Paris with an order which declares me suspected. It will naturally be presumed that the representatives did not draw up this decree without accurate information, and I shall be judged with the bias which a man of that class merits. Though a patriot and an innocent and calumniated man, yet whatever measures may be adopted by the Committee I cannot complain. If three men declare

> that I have committed a crime, I cannot complain of the jury who condemns me. Salicetti, you know me; and I ask whether you have observed anything in my conduct for the last five years which can afford ground of suspicion? Albitte, you do not know me; but you have received proof of no fact against me; you have not heard me, and you know how artfully the tongue of calumny sometimes works. Must I then be confounded with the enemies of my country and ought the patriots inconsiderately to sacrifice a general who has not been useless to the Republic? Ought the representatives to reduce the Government to the necessity of being unjust and impolitic? Hear me; destroy the oppression that overwhelms me, and restore me to the esteem of the patriots. An hour after, if my enemies wish for my life, let them take it. I have often given proofs how little I value it. Nothing but the thought that I may yet be useful to my country makes me bear the burden of existence with courage.

It appears that this defence, which is remarkable for its energetic simplicity, produced an effect on Albitte and Salicetti. Inquiries more accurate, and probably more favourable to the General, were instituted; and on the 3d Fructidor (20th August 1794) the representatives of the people drew up a decree stating that, after a careful examination of General Bonaparte's papers, and of the orders he had received relative to his mission to Genoa, they saw nothing to justify any suspicion of his conduct; and that, moreover, taking into consideration the advantage that might accrue to the Republic from the military talents of the said General Bonaparte, it was resolved that he should be provisionally set at liberty.[21]

Salicetti afterwards became the friend and confidant of young Bonaparte; but their intimacy did not continue after his elevation.

What is to be thought of the motives for Bonaparte's arrest and provisional liberation, when his innocence and the error that had been committed were acknowledged? The importance of the General's military talents, though no mention is made about the impossibility of dispensing with them, is a pretence for restoring him to that liberty of which he had been unjustly deprived.

---

21 With reference to the arrest of Bonaparte (which lasted thirteen days) see 'Bourrienne et ses Erreurs', tome i. pp. 16-28, and Iung, tome ii. pp. 443-457. Both, in opposition to Bourrienne, attribute the arrest to his connection with the younger Robespierre. Apparently Albitte and Salicetti wets not acquainted with the secret plan of campaign prepared by the younger Robespierre and by Bonaparte, or with the real instructions given for the mission to Genoa. Jealousy between the representatives in the staff of the army of the Alps and those with the army of Italy, with which Napoleon was, also played a part in the affair. Iung looks on Salicetti as acting as the protector of the Bonapartes; but Napoleon does not seem to have regarded him in that light; see the letter given in Tunot, vol. i. p. 106, where in 1795 he takes credit for not returning the ill done to him; see also the same volume, p. 89. Salicetti eventually became Minister of Police to Joseph, when King of Naples, in 1806; but when he applied to return to France, Napoleon said to Mathieu Dumas, "Let him know that I am not powerful enough to protect the wretches who voted for the death of Louis XVI. from the contempt and indignation of the public" (Dumas, tome iii. p. 318). At the same time Napoleon described Salicetti as worse than the lazzaroni.

It was not at Toulon, as has been stated, that Bonaparte took Duroc into the artillery, and made him his 'aide de camp'.[22]

The acquaintance was formed at a subsequent period, in Italy. Duroc's cold character and unexcursive mind suited Napoleon, whose confidence he enjoyed until his death, and who entrusted him with missions perhaps above his abilities. At St. Helena Bonaparte often declared that he was much attached to Duroc. I believe this to be true; but I know that the attachment was not returned. The ingratitude of princes is proverbial. May it not happen that courtiers are also sometimes ungrateful?[23]

22 Michel Duroc (1773-1813) at first only aide de camp to Napoleon, was several times entrusted with special diplomatic missions (for example, to Berlin, etc.) On the formation of the Empire he became Grand Marechal du Palais, and Duc de Frioul. He always remained in close connection with Napoleon until he was killed in 1813. As he is often mentioned in contemporary memoirs under his abbreviated title of 'Marshal', he has sometimes been erroneously included in the number of the Marshals of the Empire—a military rank he never attained to.

23 It is only just to Duroc to add that this charge does not seem borne out by the impressions of those more capable than Bourrienne of judging in the matter.

CHAPTER III

1794-1795

General Bonaparte returned to Paris, where I also arrived from Germany shortly after him. Our intimacy was resumed, and he gave me an account of, all that had passed in the campaign of the south. He frequently alluded to the persecutions he had suffered, and he delivered to me the packet of papers noticed in the last chapter, desiring me to communicate their contents to my friends. He was very anxious, he said, to do away with the supposition that he was capable of betraying his country, and, under the pretence of a mission to Genoa, becoming a SPY on the interests of France. He loved to talk over his military achievements at Toulon and in Italy. He spoke of his first successes with that feeling of pleasure and gratification which they were naturally calculated to excite in him.

The Government wished to send him to La Vendée, with the rank of brigadier-general of infantry. Bonaparte rejected this proposition on two grounds. He thought the scene of action unworthy of his talents, and he regarded his projected removal from the artillery to the infantry as a sort of insult. This last was his most powerful objection, and was the only one he urged officially. In consequence of his refusal to accept the appointment offered him, the Committee of Public Safety decreed that he should be struck off the list of general officers.[24]

24 This statement as to the proposed transfer of Bonaparte to the infantry, his disobedience to the order, and his consequent dismissal, is fiercely attacked in the 'Erreurs', tome i. chap. iv. It is, however, correct in some points; but the real truths about Bonaparte's life at this time seem so little known that it may be well to explain the whole matter. On the 27th of March 1795 Bonaparte, already removed from his employment in the south, was ordered to proceed to the army of the west to command its artillery as brigadier-general. He went as far as Paris, and then lingered there, partly on medical certificate. While in Paris he applied, as Bourrienne says, to go to Turkey to organise its artillery. His application, instead of being neglected, as Bourrienne says, was favourably received, two members of the 'Comite de Saint Public' putting on its margin most favorable reports of him; one, Jean Debry, even saying that he was too distinguished an officer to be sent to a distance at such a time. Far from being looked on as the half-crazy fellow Bourrienne considered him at that time, Bonaparte was appointed, on the 21st of August 1795, one of four generals attached as military advisers to the Committee for the preparation of warlike operations, his own department being a most important one. He himself at the time tells Joseph that he is attached to the topographical bureau of the Comite de Saint Public, for the direction of the armies in the place of Carnot. It is apparently this significant appointment to which Madame Junot, wrongly dating it, alludes as "no great thing" (Junot, vol. i, p. 143). Another officer was therefore substituted for him as commander of Roches artillery, a fact made use of in the Erreurs (p. 31) to deny his having been dismissed—But a general re-classification of the generals was being made. The artillery generals were in excess of their establishment, and Bonaparte, as junior in age, was ordered on 13th June to join Hoche's army at Brest to command a brigade of infantry.

Deeply mortified at this unexpected stroke, Bonaparte retired into private life, and found himself doomed to an inactivity very uncongenial with his ardent character. He lodged in the Rue du Mail, in an hotel near the Place des Victoires, and we recommenced the sort of life we had led in 1792, before his departure for Corsica. It was not without a struggle that he determined to await patiently the removal of the prejudices which were cherished against him by men in power; and he hoped that, in the perpetual changes which were taking place, those men might be superseded by others more favourable to him. He frequently dined and spent the evening with me and my elder brother; and his pleasant conversation and manners made the hours pass away very agreeably. I called on him almost every morning, and I met at his lodgings several persons who were distinguished at the time; among others Salicetti, with whom he used to maintain very animated conversations, and who would often solicit a private interview with him. On one occasion Salicetti paid him three thousand francs, in assignats, as the price of his carriage, which his straitened circumstances obliged him to dispose of.[25]

All his efforts to get the order cancelled failed, and as he did not obey it he was struck off the list of employed general officers on the 15th of September 1795, the order of the 'Comite de Salut Public' being signed by Cambacérès, Berber, Merlin, and Boissy. His application to go to Turkey still, however, remained; and it is a curious thing that, on the very day he was struck off the list, the commission which had replaced the Minister of War recommended to the 'Comite de Saint Public' that he and his two aides de camp, Junot and Livrat, with other officers, under him, should be sent to Constantinople. So late as the 29th of September, twelve days later, this matter was being considered, the only question being as to any departmental objections to the other officers selected by him, a point which was just being settled. But on the 13th Vendemiaire (5th October 1795), or rather on the night before, only nineteen days after his removal, he was appointed second in command to Barras, a career in France was opened to him, and Turkey was no longer thought of. Thiers (vol. iv, p. 326) and most writers, contemporary and otherwise, say that Aubry gave the order for his removal from the list. Aubry, himself a brigadier-general of artillery, did not belong to the 'Comite de Salut Public' at the time Bonaparte was removed from the south; and he had left the Comite early is August, that is, before the order striking Bonaparte off was given. Aubry was, however, on the Comite in June 1795, and signed the order, which probably may have originated from him, for the transfer of Bonaparte to the infantry. It will be seen that, in the ordinary military sense of the term, Napoleon was only in Paris without employment from the 15th of September to the 4th or 6th of October 1796; all the rest of the time in Paris he had a command which he did not choose to take up. The distress under which Napoleon is said to have laboured in pecuniary matters was probably shared by most officers at that time; see 'Erreurs', tome i. p. 32. This period is fully described in Iung, tome ii. p. 476, and tome iii. pp. 1-93.

25 Of Napoleon's poverty at this time Madame Junot says, "On Bonaparte's return to Paris, after the misfortunes of which he accused Salicetti of being the cause, he was in very destitute circumstances. His family, who were banished from Corsica, found an asylum at Marseilles; and they could not now do for him what they would have done had they been in the country whence they derived their pecuniary resources. From time to time he received remittances of money, and I suspect they came from his excellent brother Joseph, who had then recently married 'Mademoiselle Clary; but with all his economy these supplies were insufficient.

I could, easily perceive that our young friend either was or wished to be initiated in some political intrigue; and I moreover suspected that Salicetti had bound him by an oath not to disclose the plans that were hatching.

He became pensive, melancholy, and anxious; and he always looked with impatience for Salicetti's daily visit.[26] Sometimes, withdrawing his mind from political affairs, he would envy the happiness of his brother Joseph, who had just then married Mademoiselle Clary, the daughter of a rich and respectable merchant of Marseilles. He would often say, "That Joseph is a lucky rogue."

Meanwhile time passed away, and none of his projects succeeded—none of his applications were listened to. He was vexed by the injustice with which he was treated, and tormented by the desire of entering upon some active pursuit. He could not endure the thought of remaining buried in the crowd. He determined to quit France; and the favourite idea, which he never afterwards relinquished, that the East is a fine field for glory, inspired him with the wish to proceed to Constantinople, and to enter the service of the Grand Seignior. What romantic plans, what stupendous projects he conceived! He asked me whether I would go with him? I replied in the negative. I looked upon him as a half-crazy young fellow, who was driven to extravagant enterprises and desperate resolutions by his restless activity of mind, joined to the irritating treatment he had experienced, and, perhaps, it may be added, his want of money. He did not blame me for my refusal to accompany him; and he told me that Junot, Marmont, and some other young officers whom he had known at Toulon, would be willing to follow his fortunes.

He drew up a note which commenced with the words 'Note for . . .' It was addressed to no one, and was merely a plan. Some days after he wrote out another, which, however, did not differ very materially from the first, and which he addressed to Aubert and Coni. I made him a fair copy of it, and it was regularly for forwarded. It was as follows:

Bonaparte was therefore in absolute distress. Junot often used to speak of the six months they passed together in Paris at this time. When they took an evening stroll on the Boulevard, which used to be the resort of young men, mounted on fine horses, and displaying all the luxury which they were permitted to show at that time, Bonaparte would declaim against fate, and express his contempt for the dandies with their whiskers and their 'orielles de chiene', who, as they rode Past, were eulogising in ecstasy the manner in which Madame Scio sang. And it is on such beings as these,' he would say, 'that Fortune confers her favours. Grand Dieu! how contemptible is human nature!'" (Memoirs of the Duchesse d'Abrantes, vol. i. p. 80, edit. 1883.)

26 Salicetti was implicated in the insurrection of the 20th May 1795, 1st Prairial, Year III., and was obliged to fly to Venice.

NOTE

Aubert	2500 artillerymen
Coni	

At a moment when the Empress of Russia has strengthened her union with the Emperor of Germany (Austria), it is the interest of France to do everything in her power to increase the military power of Turkey. That power possesses a numerous and brave militia but is very backward in the scientific part of the art of war. The organization and the service of the artillery, which, in our modern tactics, so powerfully facilitate the gaining of battles, and on which, almost exclusively, depend the attack and defence of fortresses, are especially the points in which France excels, and in which the Turks are most deficient. They have several times applied to us for artillery officers, and we have sent them some; but the officers thus sent have not been sufficiently powerful, either in numbers or talent, to produce any important result. General Bonaparte, who, from his youth, has served in the artillery, of which he was entrusted with the command at the siege of Toulon, and in the two campaigns of Italy, offers his services to proceed to Turkey, with a mission from the (French) Government. He proposes to take along with him six or seven officers, of different kinds, and who may be, altogether, perfect masters of the military art. He will have the satisfaction of being useful to his country in this new career, if he succeed in rendering the Turkish power more formidable, by completing the defence of their principal fortresses, and constructing new ones.

This note shows the error of the often-repeated assertion, that he proposed entering the service of the Turks against Austria. He makes no mention of such a thing; and the two countries were not at war.[27]

No answer was returned to this note. Turkey remained unaided, and Bonaparte unoccupied. I must confess that for the failure of this project, at least I was not sorry. I should have regretted to see a young man of great promise, and one for whom I cherished a sincere friendship, devote himself to so uncertain a fate. Napoleon has less than any man provoked the events which have favoured him; no one has more yielded to circumstances from which he was so skilful to derive advantages. If, however, a clerk of the War Office had but written on the note, "Granted," that little word would probably have changed the fate of Europe.

---

27 The Scottish biographer makes Bonaparte say that it would be strange if a little Corsican should become King of Jerusalem. I never heard anything drop from him which supports the probability of such a remark, and certainly there is nothing in his note to warrant the inference of his having made it.—Bourrienne.

Bonaparte remained in Paris, forming schemes for the gratification of his ambition, and his desire of making a figure in the world; but obstacles opposed all he attempted.

Women are better judges of character than men. Madame de Bourrienne, knowing the intimacy which subsisted between us, preserved some notes which she made upon Bonaparte, and the circumstances which struck her as most remarkable, during her early connection with him. My wife did not entertain so favourable an opinion of him as I did; the warm friendship I cherished for him probably blinded me to his faults. I subjoin Madame de Bourrienne's notes, word for word:

On the day after our second return from Germany, which was in May 1795, we met Bonaparte in the Palais Royal, near a shop kept by a man named Girardin. Bonaparte embraced Bourrienne as a friend whom he loved and was glad to see. We went that evening to the Theatre Francais. The performance consisted of a tragedy; and 'Le Sourd, ou l'Auberge pleine'. During the latter piece the audience was convulsed with laughter. The part of Dasnieres was represented by Batiste the younger, and it was never played better. The bursts of laughter were so loud and frequent that the actor was several times obliged to stop in the midst of his part. Bonaparte alone (and it struck me as being very extraordinary) was silent, and coldly insensible to the humour which was so irresistibly diverting to everyone else. I remarked at this period that his character was reserved, and frequently gloomy. His smile was hypocritical, and often misplaced; and I recollect that a few days after our return he gave us one of these specimens of savage hilarity which I greatly disliked, and which prepossessed me against him. He was telling us that, being before Toulon, where he commanded the artillery, one of his officers was visited by his wife, to whom he had been but a short time married, and whom he tenderly loved. A few days after, orders were given for another attack upon the town, in which this officer was to be engaged. His wife came to General Bonaparte, and with tears entreated him to dispense with her husband's services that day. The General was inexorable, as he himself told us, with a sort of savage exaltation. The moment for the attack arrived, and the officer, though a very brave man, as Bonaparte himself-assured us, felt a presentiment of his approaching death. He turned pale and trembled. He was stationed beside the General, and during an interval when the firing from the town was very heavy, Bonaparte called out to him, "Take care, there is a shell coming!" The officer, instead of moving to one side, stooped down, and was literally severed in two. Bonaparte laughed loudly while he described the event with horrible minuteness. At this time we saw him almost every day. He frequently came to dine with us. As there was a scarcity of bread, and sometimes only two ounces per head daily were distributed in the section, it was customary to request one's guests to bring their own bread, as it could not be procured for money. Bonaparte and his brother Louis (a mild, agreeable young man, who was the General's aide de army) used to bring with them their ration bread, which was black, and mixed with bran. I was sorry to observe that all this bad bread fell to the share of the poor aide de camp, for we provided the General with a finer kind, which was made clandestinely by a pastrycook, from flour which we contrived to smuggle from Sens, where my husband had some farms. Had we been denounced, the affair might have cost us our heads.

We spent six weeks in Paris, and we went frequently with Bonaparte to the theatres, and to the fine concerts given by Garat in the Rue St. Marc. These were the first brilliant entertainments that took place after the death of Robespierre. There was always something original in Bonaparte's behaviour, for he often slipped away from us without saying a word; and when we were supposing he had left the theatre, we would suddenly discover him in the second or third tier, sitting alone in a box, and looking rather sulky.

Before our departure for Sens, where my husband's family reside, and which was fixed upon for the place of my first accouchement, we looked out for more agreeable apartments than we had in the Rue Grenier St. Lazare, which we only had temporarily. Bonaparte used to assist us in our researches. At last we took the first floor of a handsome new house, No. 19 Rue des Marais. Bonaparte, who wished to stop in Paris, went to look at a house opposite to ours. He had thoughts of taking it for himself, his uncle Fesch (afterwards Cardinal Fesch), and a gentleman named Patrauld, formerly one of his masters at the Military School. One day he said, "With that house over there, my friends in it, and a cabriolet, I shall be the happiest fellow in the world."

We soon after left town for Sens. The house was not taken by him, for other and great affairs were preparing. During the interval between our departure and the fatal day of Vendemiaire several letters passed between him and his school companion. These letters were of the most amiable and affectionate description. They have been stolen. On our return, in November of the same year, everything was changed. The college friend was now a great personage. He had got the command of Paris in return for his share in the events of Vendemiaire. Instead of a small house in the Rue des Marais, he occupied a splendid hotel in the Rue des Capucines; the modest cabriolet was converted into a superb equipage, and the man himself was no longer the same. But the friends of his youth were still received when they made their morning calls. They were invited to grand dejeuners, which were sometimes attended by ladies; and, among others, by the beautiful Madame Tallien and her friend the amiable Madame de Beauharnais, to whom Bonaparte had begun to pay attention. He cared little for his friends, and ceased to address them in the style of familiar equality.

After the 13th of Vendemiaire M. de Bourrienne saw Bonaparte only at distant periods. In the month of February 1796 my husband was arrested, at seven in the morning, by a party of men, armed with muskets, on the charge of being a returned emigrant. He was torn from his wife and his child, only six months old, being barely allowed time to dress himself. I followed him. They conveyed him to the guard-house of the Section, and thence I know not whither; and, finally, in the evening, they placed him in the lockup-house of the prefecture of police, which, I believe, is now called the central bureau. There he passed two nights and a day, among men of the lowest description, some of whom were even malefactors. I and his friends ran about everywhere, trying to find somebody to rescue him, and, among the rest, Bonaparte was applied to. It was with great difficulty he could be seen. Accompanied by one of my husband's friends, I waited for the commandant of Paris until midnight, but he did not come home. Next morning I returned at an early hour, and found him. I stated what had happened to my husband, whose life was then at stake. He appeared to feel very little for the situation of his friend, but, however; determined to write to Merlin, the Minister of Justice. I carried the letter according to its address, and met the Minister as he was coming downstairs, on his way to the Directory. Being in grand costume, he wore a Henri IV. hat, surmounted with a multitude of plumes, a dress which formed a singular contrast with his person. He opened the letter; and whether it was that he cared as little for the General as for the cause of M. de Bourrienne's arrest, he replied that the matter was no longer in his hands, and that it was now under the cognisance of the public administrators of the laws. The Minister then stepped into his carriage, and the writer was conducted to several offices in his hotel. She passed through them with a broken heart, for she met with none but harsh men, who told her that the prisoner deserved death. From them she learned that on the following day he would be brought before the judge of the peace for his Section, who would decide whether there was ground for putting him on his trial. In fact, this proceeding took place next day. He was conveyed to the house of the judge of the peace for the Section of Bondy, Rue Grange-sue-Belles, whose name was Lemaire. His countenance was mild; and though his manner was cold, he had none of the harshness and ferocity common to the Government agents of that time. His examination of the charge was long, and he several times shook his head. The moment of decision had arrived, and everything seemed to indicate that the termination would be to place the prisoner under accusation. At seven o'clock be desired me to be called. I hastened to him, and beheld a most heart rending scene. Bourrienne was suffering under a hemorrhage, which had continued since two o'clock, and had interrupted the examination. The judge of the peace, who looked sad, sat with his head resting on his hand. I threw myself at his feet and implored his clemency. The wife and the two daughters of the judge visited this scene of sorrow, and assisted me in softening him. He was a worthy and feeling man, a good husband and parent, and it was evident that he struggled between compassion and duty. He kept referring to the laws on the subject, and, after long researches said to me, "To-morrow is Decadi, and no proceedings can take place on that day. Find, madams, two responsible persons, who will answer for the appearance of your husband, and I will permit him to go home with you, accompanied by the two guardians." Next day two friends were found, one of whom was M. Desmaisons, counsellor of the court, who became bail for M. de Bourrienne. He continued under these guardians six months, until a law compelled the persons who were inscribed on the fatal list to remove to the distance of ten leagues from Paris. One of the guardians was a man of straw; the other was a knight of St. Louis. The former was left in the antechamber; the latter made, every evening, one of our party at cards. The family of M. de Bourrienne have always felt the warmest gratitude to the judge of the peace and his family. That worthy man saved the life of M. de Bourrienne, who, when he returned from Egypt, and had it in his power to do him some service, hastened to his house; but the good judge was no more!

The letters mentioned in the narrative were at this time stolen from me by the police officers.

Everyone was now eager to pay court to a man who had risen from the crowd in consequence of the part he had acted at an extraordinary crisis, and who was spoken of as the future General of the Army of Italy. It was expected that he would be gratified, as he really was, by the restoration of some letters which contained the expression of his former very modest wishes, called to recollection his unpleasant situation, his limited ambition, his pretended aversion for public employment, and finally exhibited his intimate relations with those who were, without hesitation, characterised as emigrants, to be afterwards made the victims of confiscation and death.

The 13th of Vendemiaire (5th October 1795) was approaching. The National Convention had been painfully delivered of a new constitution, called, from the epoch of its birth, "the Constitution of Year III." It was adopted on the 22d of August 1795. The provident legislators did not forget themselves. They stipulated that two-thirds of their body should form part of the new legislature. The party opposed to the Convention hoped, on the contrary, that, by a general election, a majority would be obtained for its opinion. That opinion was against the continuation of power in the hands of men who had already so greatly abused it.

The same opinion was also entertained by a great part of the most influential Sections of Paris, both as to the possession of property and talent. These Sections declared that, in accepting the new constitution, they rejected the decree of the 30th of August, which required the re-election of two-thirds The Convention, therefore, found itself menaced in what it held most dear—its power;—and accordingly resorted to measures of defence. A declaration was put forth, stating that the Convention, if attacked, would remove to Chalons-sur-Marne; and the commanders of the armed force were called upon to defend that body.

The 5th of October, the day on which the Sections of Paris attacked the Convention, is certainly one which ought to be marked in the wonderful destiny of Bonaparte.

With the events of that day were linked, as cause and effect, many great political convulsions of Europe. The blood which flowed ripened the seeds of the youthful General's ambition. It must be admitted that the history of past ages presents few periods full of such extraordinary events as the years included between 1795 and 1815. The man whose name serves, in some measure, as a recapitulation of all these great events was entitled to believe himself immortal.

Living retired at Sens since the month of July, I only learned what had occasioned the insurrection of the Sections from public report and the journals. I cannot, therefore, say what part Bonaparte may have taken in the intrigues which preceded that day. He was officially characterised only as secondary actor in the scene. The account of the affair which was published announces that Barras was, on that very day, Commander-in-chief of the Army of the Interior, and Bonaparte second in command. Bonaparte drew up that account. The whole of the manuscript was in his handwriting, and it exhibits all the peculiarity of his style and orthography. He sent me a copy.

Those who read the bulletin of the 13th Vendemiaire, cannot fail to observe the care which Bonaparte took to cast the reproach of shedding the first blood on the men he calls rebels. He made a great point of representing his adversaries as the aggressors. It is certain he long regretted that day. He often told me that he would give years of his life to blot it out from the page of his history. He was convinced that the people of Paris were dreadfully irritated against him, and he would have been glad if Barras had never made that Speech in the Convention, with the part of which, complimentary to himself, he was at the time so well pleased. Barras said, "It is to his able and prompt dispositions that we are indebted for the defence of this assembly, around which he had posted the troops with so much skill." This is perfectly true, but it is not always agreeable that every truth should be told. Being out of Paris, and a total stranger to this affair, I know not how far he was indebted for his success to chance, or to his own exertions, in the part assigned to him by the miserable Government which then oppressed France. He represented himself only as secondary actor in this sanguinary scene in which Barras made him his associate. He sent to me, as already mentioned, an account of the transaction, written entirely in his own hand, and distinguished by all the peculiarities of his style and orthography.[28]

"On the 13th," says Bonaparte, "at five o'clock in the morning, the representative of the people, Barras, was appointed Commander-in-chief of the Army of the Interior, and General Bonaparte was nominated second in command.

"The artillery for service on the frontier was still at the camp of Sablons, guarded solely by 150 men; the remainder was at Marly with 200 men. The depot of Meudon was left unprotected. There were at the Feuillans only a few four-pounders without artillerymen,

28 Joseph Bonaparte, in a note on this peerage, insinuates that the account of the 13th Vendemiaire was never sent to Sens, but was abstracted by Bourrienne, with other documents, from Napoleon's Cabinet (Erreurs, tome i. p. 239).

and but 80,000 cartridges. The victualling depots were dispersed throughout Paris. In many Sections the drums beat to arms; the Section of the Theatre Francais had advanced posts even as far as the Pont Neuf, which it had barricaded.

"General Barras ordered the artillery to move immediately from the camp of Sablons to the Tuileries, and selected the artillerymen from the battalions of the 89th regiment, and from the gendarmerie, and placed them at the Palace; sent to Meudon 200 men of the police legion whom he brought from Versailles, 50 cavalry, and two companies of veterans; he ordered the property which was at Marly to be conveyed to Meudon; caused cartridges to be brought there, and established a workshop at that place for the manufacture of more. He secured means for the subsistence of the army and of the Convention for many days, independently of the depots which were in the Sections.

"General Verdier, who commanded at the Palais National, exhibited great coolness; he was required not to suffer a shot to be fired till the last extremity. In the meantime reports reached him from all quarters acquainting him that the Sections were assembled in arms, and had formed their columns. He accordingly arrayed his troops so as to defend the Convention, and his artillery was in readiness to repulse the rebels. His cannon was planted at the Feuillans to fire down the Rue Honore. Eight-pounders were pointed at every opening, and in the event of any mishap, General Verdier had cannon in reserve to fire in flank upon the column which should have forced a passage. He left in the Carrousel three howitzers (eight-pounders) to batter down the houses from which the Convention might be fired upon. At four o'clock the rebel columns marched out from every street to unite their forces. It was necessary to take advantage of this critical moment to attack the insurgents, even had they been regular troops. But the blood about to flow was French; it was therefore for these misguided people, already guilty of rebellion, to embrue their hands in the blood of their countrymen by striking the first blow.

"At a quarter before five o'clock the insurgents had formed. The attack was commenced by them on all sides. They were everywhere routed. French blood was spilled: the crime, as well as the disgrace, fell this day upon the Sections.

"Among the dead were everywhere to be recognized emigrants, landowners, and nobles; the prisoners consisted for the most part of the 'chouans' of Charette.

"Nevertheless the Sections did not consider themselves beaten: they took refuge in the church of St. Roch, in the theatre of the Republic, and in the Palais Egalite; and everywhere they were heard furiously exciting the inhabitants to arms. To spare the blood which would have been shed the next day it was necessary that no time should be given them to rally, but to follow them with vigour, though without incurring fresh hazards. The General ordered Montchoisy, who commanded a reserve at the Place de la Resolution, to form a column with two twelve-pounders, to march by the Boulevard in order to turn the Place Vendome, to form a junction with the picket stationed at headquarters, and to return in the same order of column.

"General Brune, with two howitzers, deployed in the streets of St. Nicaise and St. Honore. General Cartaux sent two hundred men and a four-pounder of his division by the Rue St. Thomas-du-Louvre to debouch in the square of the Palais Egalite. General Bonaparte, who had his horse killed under him, repaired to the Feuillans.

"The columns began to move, St. Roch and the theatre of the Republic were taken, by assault, when the rebels abandoned them, and retreated to the upper part of the Rue de la Loi, and barricaded themselves on all sides. Patrols were sent thither, and several cannon-shots were fired during the night, in order to prevent them from throwing up defences, which object was effectually accomplished.

"At daybreak, the General having learned that some students from the St. Genevieve side of the river were marching with two pieces of cannon to succour the rebels, sent a detachment of dragoons in pursuit of them, who seized the cannon and conducted them to the Tuileries. The enfeebled Sections, however, still showed a front. They had barricaded the Section of Grenelle, and placed their cannon in the principal streets. At nine o'clock General Beruyer hastened to form his division in battle array in the Place Vendome, marched with two eight-pounders to the Rue des Vieux-Augustins, and pointed them in the direction of the Section Le Pelletier. General Vachet, with a corps of 'tirailleurs', marched on his right, ready to advance to the Place Victoire. General Brune marched to the Perron, and planted two howitzers at the upper end of the Rue Vivienne. General Duvigier, with his column of six hundred men, and two twelve-pounders, advanced to the streets of St. Roch and Montmartre. The Sections lost courage with the apprehension of seeing their retreat cut off, and evacuated the post at the sight of our soldiers, forgetting the honour of the French name which they had to support. The Section of Brutus still caused some uneasiness. The wife of a representative had been arrested there. General Duvigier was ordered to proceed along the Boulevard as far as the Rue Poissonniere. General Beruyer took up a position at the Place Victoire, and General Bonaparte occupied the Pont-au-Change.

"The Section of Brutus was surrounded, and the troops advanced upon the Place de Greve, where the crowd poured in from the Isle St. Louis, from the Theatre Francais, and from the Palace. Everywhere the patriots had regained their courage, while the poniards of the emigrants, armed against us, had disappeared. The people universally admitted their error.

"The next day the two Sections of Les Pelletier and the Theatre Francais were disarmed."

The result of this petty civil war brought Bonaparte forward; but the party he defeated at that period never pardoned him for the past, and that which he supported dreaded him in the future. Five years after he will be found reviving the principles which he combated on the 5th of October 1795. On being appointed, on the motion of Barras, Lieutenant-General of the Army of the Interior, he established his headquarters in the Rue Neuve des Capucines. The statement in the 'Manuscrit de Sainte Helene', that after the 13th Brumaire he remained unemployed at Paris, is therefore obviously erroneous. So far from this, he was incessantly occupied with the policy of the nation, and with his own fortunes. Bonaparte was in constant, almost daily, communication with every one then in power, and knew how to profit by all he saw or heard.

To avoid returning to this 'Manuscrit de Sainte Helene', which at the period of its appearance attracted more attention than it deserved, and which was very generally attributed to Bonaparte, I shall here say a few words respecting it. I shall briefly repeat what I said in a note when my opinion was asked, under high authority, by a minister of Louis XVIII.

No reader intimately acquainted with public affairs can be deceived by the pretended authenticity of this pamphlet. What does it contain? Facts perverted and heaped together without method, and related in an obscure, affected, and ridiculously sententious style. Besides what appears in it, but which is badly placed there, it is impossible not to remark the omission of what should necessarily be there, were Napoleon the author. It is full of absurd and of insignificant gossip, of thoughts Napoleon never had, expressions unknown to him, and affectations far removed from his character. With some elevated ideas, more than one style and an equivocal spirit can be seen in it. Professed coincidences are put close to unpardonable anachronisms, and to the most absurd revelations. It contains neither his thoughts, his style, his actions, nor his life. Some truths are mimed up with an inconceivable mass of falsehoods. Some forms of expression used by Bonaparte are occasionally met with, but they are awkwardly introduced, and often with bad taste.

It has been reported that the pamphlet was written by M. Bertrand, formerly an officer of the army of the Vistula, and a relation of the Comte de Simeon, peer of France.[29]

---

29 'Manuscrit de Sainte Helene d'une maniere inconnue', London. Murray; Bruxelles, De Mat, 20 Avril 1817. This work merits a note. Metternich (vol, i. pp. 312-13) says, "At the time when it appeared the manuscript of St. Helena made a great impression upon Europe. This pamphlet was generally regarded as a precursor of the memoirs which Napoleon was thought to be writing in his place of exile. The report soon spread that the work was conceived and executed by Madame de Stael. Madame de Stael, for her part, attributed it to Benjamin Constant, from whom she was at this time separated by some disagreement." Afterwards it came to be known that the author was the Marquis Lullin de Chateauvieux, a man in society, whom no one had suspected of being able to hold a pen: Jomini (tome i. p. 8 note) says. "It will be remarked that in the course of this work [his life of Napoleon] the author has used some fifty pages of the pretended 'Manuscrit de Sainte Helene'. Far from wishing to commit a plagiarism, he considers he ought to render this homage to a clever and original work, several false points of view in which, however, he has combated. It would have been easy for him to rewrite these pages in other terms, but they appeared to him to be so well suited to the character of Napoleon that he has preferred to preserve them." In the will of Napoleon occurs (see end of this work): "I disavow the 'Manuscrit de Sainte Helene', and the other works under the title of Maxims, Sentences, etc., which they have been pleased to publish during the last six years. Such rules are not those which have guided my life: This manuscript must not be confused with the 'Memorial of Saint Helena'.

CHAPTER IV

1795-1797

After the 13th Vendemiaire I returned to Paris from Sens. During the short time I stopped there I saw Bonaparte less frequently than formerly. I had, however, no reason to attribute this to anything but the pressure of public business with which he was now occupied. When I did meet him it was most commonly at breakfast or dinner. One day he called my attention to a young lady who sat opposite to him, and asked what I thought of her. The way in which I answered his question appeared to give him much pleasure. He then talked a great deal to me about her, her family, and her amiable qualities; he told me that he should probably marry her, as he was convinced that the union would make him happy. I also gathered from his conversation that his marriage with the young widow would probably assist him in gaining the objects of his ambition. His constantly-increasing influence with her had already brought him into contact with the most influential persons of that epoch. He remained in Paris only ten days after his marriage, which took place on the 9th of March 1796. It was a union in which great harmony prevailed, notwithstanding occasional slight disagreements. Bonaparte never, to my knowledge, caused annoyance to his wife. Madame Bonaparte possessed personal graces and many good qualities.[30] I am convinced that all

30 "Eugène was not more than fourteen years of age when he ventured to introduce himself to General Bonaparte, for the purpose of soliciting his father's sword, of which he understood the General had become possessed. The countenance, air, and frank manner of Eugène pleased Bonaparte, and he immediately granted him the boon he sought. As soon as the sword was placed in the boy's hands he burst into tears, and kissed it. This feeling of affection for his father's memory, and the natural manner in which it was evinced, increased the interest of Bonaparte in his young visitor. Madame de Beauharnais, on learning the kind reception which the General had given her son, thought it her duty to call and thank him. Bonaparte was much pleased with Josephine on this first interview, and he returned her visit. The acquaintance thus commenced speedily led to their marriage."—Constant. Bonaparte himself, at St. Helena, says that he first met Josephine at Barras' (see Iung's Bonaparte, tome iii. p. 116). "Neither of his wives had ever anything to complain of from Napoleon's personal manners" (Metternich, vol. 1 p. 279). Madame de Rémusat, who, to paraphrase Thiers' saying on Bourrienne himself, is a trustworthy witness, for if she received benefits from Napoleon they did not weigh on her, says, "However, Napoleon had some affection for his first wife; and, in fact, if he has at any time been touched, no doubt it has been only for her and by her" (tome i. p. 113). "Bonaparte was young when he first knew Madame de Beauharnais. In the circle where he met her she had a great superiority by the name she bore and by the extreme elegance of her manners. . . . In marrying Madame de Beauharnais, Bonaparte believed he was allying himself to a very grand lady; thus this was one more conquest" (p. 114). But in speaking of Josephine's complaints to Napoleon of his love affairs, Madame de Rémusat says, "Her husband sometimes answered by violences, the excesses of which I do not dare to detail,

who were acquainted with her must have felt bound to speak well of her; to few, indeed, did she ever give cause for complaint. In the time of her power she did not lose any of her friends, because she forgot none of them. Benevolence was natural to her, but she was not always prudent in its exercise. Hence her protection was often extended to persons who did not deserve it. Her taste for splendour and expense was excessive. This proneness to luxury became a habit which seemed constantly indulged without any motive. What scenes have I not witnessed when the moment for paying the tradesmen's bills arrived! She always kept back one-half of their claims, and the discovery of this exposed her to new reproaches. How many tears did she shed which might have been easily spared!

When fortune placed a crown on her head she told me that the event, extraordinary as it was, had been predicted: It is certain that she put faith in fortune-tellers. I often expressed to her my astonishment that she should cherish such a belief, and she readily laughed at her own credulity; but notwithstanding never abandoned it: The event had given importance to the prophecy; but the foresight of the prophetess, said to be an old regress, was not the less a matter of doubt.

Not long before the 13th of Vendemiaire, that day which opened for Bonaparte his immense career, he addressed a letter to me at Sens, in which, after some of his usually friendly expressions, he said, "Look out a small piece of land in your beautiful valley of the Yonne. I will purchase it as soon as I can scrape together the money. I wish to retire there; but recollect that I will have nothing to do with national property."

Bonaparte left Paris on the 21st of March 1796, while I was still with my guardians. He no sooner joined the French army than General Colli, then in command of the Piedmontese army, transmitted to him the following letter, which, with its answer, I think sufficiently interesting to deserve preservation:

> GENERAL, I suppose that you are ignorant of the arrest of one of my officers, named Moulin, the bearer of a flag of truce, who has been detained for some days past at Murseco, contrary to the laws of war, and notwithstanding an immediate demand for his liberation being made by General Count Vital. His being a French emigrant cannot take from him the rights of a flag of truce, and I again claim him in that character.

---

until the moment when, his new fancy having suddenly passed, he felt his tenderness for his wife again renewed. Then he was touched by her sufferings, replaced his insults by caresses which were hardly more measured than his violences and, as she was gentle and untenacious, she fell back into her feeling of security" (p. 206). Miot de Melito, who was a follower of Joseph Bonaparte, says, "No woman has united so much kindness to so much natural grace, or has done more good with more pleasure than she did. She honoured me with her friendship, and the remembrance of the benevolence she has shown me, to the last moment of her too short existence, will never be effaced from my heart" (tome i. pp.101-2). Meneval, the successor of Bourrienne in his place of secretary to Napoleon, and who remained attached to the Emperor until the end, says of Josephine (tome i. p. 227), "Josephine was irresistibly attractive. Her beauty was not regular, but she had 'La grace, plus belle encore que la beaute', according to the good La Fontaine. She had the soft abandonment, the supple and elegant movements, and the graceful carelessness of the creoles.—(The reader must remember that the term 'Creole' does not imply any taint of black blood, but only that the person, of European family, has been born in the West Indies.)—Her temper was always the same. She was gentle and kind."

> The courtesy and generosity which I have always experienced from the generals of your nation induces me to hope that I shall not make this application in vain; and it is with regret that I mention that your chief of brigade, Barthelemy, who ordered the unjust arrest of my flag of truce, having yesterday by the chance of war fallen into my hands, that officer will be dealt with according to the treatment which M. Moulin may receive. I most sincerely wish that nothing may occur to change the noble and humane conduct which the two nations have hitherto been accustomed to observe towards each other. I have the honour, etc.,
>
> (*Signed*) COLLI.
> CEVA. *17th April 1796.*

Bonaparte replied as follows:

> GENERAL— An emigrant is a parricide whom no character can render sacred. The feelings of honour, and the respect due to the French people, were forgotten when M. Moulin was sent with a flag of truce. You know the laws of war, and I therefore do not give credit to the reprisals with which you threaten the chief of brigade, Barthelemy. If, contrary to the laws of war, you authorise such an act of barbarism, all the prisoners taken from you shall be immediately made responsible for it with the most deplorable vengeance, for I entertain for the officers of your nation that esteem which is due to brave soldiers.

The Executive Directory, to whom these letters were transmitted, approved of the arrest of M. Moulin; but ordered that he should be securely guarded, and not brought to trial, in consequence of the character with which he had been invested.

About the middle of the year 1796 the Directory proposed to appoint General Kellerman, who commanded the army of the Alps, second in command of the army of Italy.

On the 24th of May 1796 Bonaparte wrote to, Carnot respecting, this plan, which was far from being agreeable to him. He said, "Whether I shall be employed here or anywhere else is indifferent to me: to serve the country, and to merit from posterity a page in our history, is all my ambition. If you join Kellerman and me in command in Italy you will undo everything. General Kellerman has more experience than I, and knows how to make war better than I do; but both together, we shall make it badly. I will not willingly serve with a man who considers himself the first general in Europe."

Numbers of letters from Bonaparte to his wife have been published. I cannot deny their authenticity, nor is it my wish to do so. I will, however, subjoin one which appears to me to differ a little from the rest. It is less remarkable for exaggerated expressions of love, and a singularly ambitious and affected style, than most of the correspondence here alluded to. Bonaparte is announcing the victory of Arcola to Josephine.

VERONA, *the 29th, noon.*

At length, my adored Josephine, I live again. Death is no longer before me, and glory and honour are still in my breast. The enemy is beaten at Arcola. To-morrow we will repair the blunder of Vaubois, who abandoned Rivoli. In eight days Mantua will be ours, and then thy husband will fold thee in his arms, and give thee a thousand proofs of his ardent affection. I shall proceed to Milan as soon as I can: I am a little fatigued. I have received letters from Eugène and Hortense. I am delighted with the children. I will send you their letters as soon as I am joined by my household, which is now somewhat dispersed. We have made five thousand prisoners, and killed at least six thousand of the enemy. Adieu, my adorable Josephine. Think of me often. When you cease to love your Achilles, when your heart grows cool towards him, you wilt be very cruel, very unjust. But I am sure you will always continue my faithful mistress, as I shall ever remain your fond lover ('tendre amie'). Death alone can break the union which sympathy, love, and sentiment have formed. Let me have news of your health. A thousand and a thousand kisses.

It is impossible for me to avoid occasionally placing myself in the foreground in the course of these Memoirs. I owe it to myself to answer, though indirectly, to certain charges which, on various occasions, have been made against me. Some of the documents which I am about to insert belong, perhaps, less to the history of the General-in-Chief of the army of-Italy than to that of his secretary; but I must confess I wish to show that I was not an intruder, nor yet pursuing, as an obscure intriguer, the path of fortune. I was influenced much more by friendship than by ambition when I took a part on the scene where the rising-glory of the future Emperor already shed a lustre on all who were attached to his destiny. It will be seen by the following letters with what confidence I was then honoured; but these letters, dictated by friendship, and not written for history, speak also of our military achievements; and whatever brings to recollection the events of that heroic period must still be interesting to many.

HEADQUARTERS AT MILAN,
20th Prairial, year IV. (8th June 1796).

The General-in-Chief has ordered me, my dear Bourrienne, to make known to you the pleasure he experienced on hearing of you, and his ardent desire that you should join us. Take your departure, then, my dear Bourrienne, and arrive quickly. You may be certain of obtaining the testimonies of affection which are your due from all who know you; and we much regret that you were not with us to have a share in our success. The campaign which we have just concluded will be celebrated in the records of history. With less than 30,000 men, in a state of almost complete destitution, it is a fine thing to have, in the course of less than two months, beaten, eight different times, an army of from 65 to 70,000 men, obliged the King of Sardinia to make a humiliating peace, and driven the Austrians from Italy. The last victory, of which you have doubtless had an account, the passage of the Mincio, has closed our labours. There now remain for us the siege of Mantua and the castle of Milan; but these obstacles will not detain us long. Adieu, my dear Bourrienne: I repeat General Bonaparte's request that you should repair hither, and the testimony of his desire to see you. Receive, etc.,

(*Signed*) MARMONT.
Chief of Brigade (Artillery) and Aide de camp to the General-in-Chief.

I was obliged to remain at Sens, soliciting my erasure from the emigrant list, which I did not obtain, however, till 1797, and to put an end to a charge made against me of having fabricated a certificate of residence. Meanwhile I applied myself to study, and preferred repose to the agitation of camps. For these reasons I did not then accept his friendly invitation, notwithstanding that I was very desirous of seeing my young college friend in the midst of his astonishing triumphs. Ten months after, I received another letter from Marmont, in the following terms:—

HEADQUARTERS GORIZIA,
2d Germinal, year V. (22d March 1797).

The General-in-Chief, my dear Bourrienne, has ordered me to express to you his wish for your prompt arrival here. We have all along anxiously desired to see you, and look forward with great pleasure to the moment when we shall meet. I join with the General, my dear Bourrienne, in urging you to join the army without loss of time. You will increase a united family, happy to receive you into its bosom. I enclose an order written by the General, which will serve you as a passport. Take the post route and arrive as soon as you can. We are on the point of penetrating into Germany. The language is changing already, and in four days we shall hear no more Italian. Prince Charles has been well beaten, and we are pursuing him. If this campaign be fortunate, we may sign a peace, which is so necessary for Europe, in Vienna. Adieu, my dear Bourrienne: reckon for something the zeal of one who is much attached to you.

(*Signed*) MARMONT.

BONAPARTE, GENERAL-IN-CHIEF OF THE ARMY OF ITALY.

HEADQUARTERS, GORIZIA,
2d Germinal, year V.

The citizen Bourrienne is to come to me on receipt of the present order.

(Signed) BONAPARTE.

The odious manner in which I was then harassed, I know not why, on the part of the Government respecting my certificate of residence, rendered my stay in France not very agreeable. I was even threatened with being put on my trial for having produced a certificate of residence which was alleged to be signed by nine false witnesses. This time, therefore, I resolved without hesitation to set out for the army. General Bonaparte's order, which I registered at the municipality of Sens, answered for a passport, which otherwise would probably have been refused me. I have always felt a strong sense of gratitude for his conduct towards me on this occasion.

Notwithstanding the haste I made to leave Sens, the necessary formalities and precautions detained me some days, and at the moment I was about to depart I received the following letter:

HEADQUARTERS, JUDENBOURG,
19th Germinal, Year V. (8th April 1797).

The General-in-Chief again orders me, my dear Bourrienne, to urge you to come to him quickly. We are in the midst of success and triumphs. The German campaign begins even more brilliantly than did the Italian. You may judge, therefore, what a promise it holds out to us. Come, my dear Bourrienne, immediately—yield to our solicitations—share our pains and pleasures, and you will add to our enjoyments.

I have directed the courier to pass through Sens, that he may deliver this letter to you, and bring me back your answer.

(*Signed*) MARMONT.

To the above letter this order was subjoined:

The citizen Fauvelet de Bourrienne is ordered to leave Sens, and repair immediately by post to the headquarters of the army of Italy.

(*Signed*) BONAPARTE.

I arrived at the Venetian territory at the moment when the insurrection against the French was on the point of breaking out. Thousands of peasants were instigated to rise under the pretext of appeasing the troubles of Bergamo and Brescia. I passed through Verona on the 16th of April, the eve of the signature of the preliminaries of Leoben and of the revolt of Verona. Easter Sunday was the day which the ministers of Jesus Christ selected for preaching "that it was lawful, and even meritorious, to kill Jacobins." Death to Frenchmen!—Death to Jacobins! as they called all the French, were their rallying cries. At the time I had not the slightest idea of this state of things, for I had left Sens only on the 11th of April.

After stopping two hours at Verona, I proceeded on my journey without being aware of the massacre which threatened that city. When about a league from the town I was, however, stopped by a party of insurgents on their way thither, consisting, as I estimated, of about two thousand men. They only desired me to cry 'El viva Santo Marco', an order with which I speedily complied, and passed on. What would have become of me had I been in Verona on the Monday? On that day the bells were rung, while the French were butchered in the hospitals. Every one met in the streets was put to death. The priests headed the assassins, and more than four hundred Frenchmen were thus sacrificed. The forts held out against the Venetians, though they attacked them with fury; but repossession of the town was not obtained until after ten days. On the very day of the insurrection of Verona some Frenchmen were assassinated between that city and Vicenza, through which I passed on the day before without danger; and scarcely had I passed through Padua, when I learned that others had been massacred there. Thus the assassinations travelled as rapidly as the post.

I shall say a few words respecting the revolt of the Venetian States, which, in consequence of the difference of political opinions, has been viewed in very contradictory lights.

The last days of Venice were approaching, and a storm had been brewing for more than a year. About the beginning of April 1797 the threatening symptoms of a general insurrection appeared. The quarrel commenced when the Austrians entered Peschiera, and some pretext was also afforded by the reception given to Monsieur, afterwards Louis XVIII. It was certain that Venice had made military preparations during the siege of Mantua in 1796. The interests of the aristocracy outweighed the political considerations in our favour. On, the 7th of June 1796 General Bonaparte wrote thus to the Executive Directory:

> The Senate of Venice lately sent two judges of their Council here to ascertain definitively how things stand. I repeated my complaints. I spoke to them about the reception given to Monsieur. Should it be your plan to extract five or six millions from Venice, I have expressly prepared this sort of rupture for you. If your intentions be more decided, I think this ground of quarrel ought to be kept up. Let me know what you mean to do, and wait till the favourable moment, which I shall seize according to circumstances; for we must not have to do with all the world at once.

The Directory answered that the moment was not favourable; that it was first necessary to take Mantua, and give Wurmser a sound beating. However, towards the end of the year 1796 the Directory began to give more credit to the sincerity of the professions of neutrality made on the part of Venice. It was resolved, therefore, to be content with obtaining money and supplies for the army, and to refrain from violating the neutrality. The Directory had not then in reserve, like Bonaparte, the idea of making the dismemberment of Venice serve as a compensation for such of the Austrian possessions as the French Republic might retain.

In 1797 the expected favourable moment had arrived. The knell of Venice was rung; and Bonaparte thus wrote to the Directory on the 30th of April: "I am convinced that the only course to be now taken is to destroy this ferocious and sanguinary Government." On the 3d of May, writing from Palma Nuova, he says: "I see nothing that can be done but to obliterate the Venetian name from the face of the globe."

Towards the end of March 1797 the Government of Venice was in a desperate state. Ottolini, the Podesta of Bergamo, an instrument of tyranny in the hands of the State inquisitors, then harassed the people of Bergamo and Brescia, who, after the reduction of Mantua, wished to be separated from Venice. He drew up, to be sent to the Senate, a long report respecting the plans of separation, founded on information given him by a Roman advocate, named Marcelin Serpini; who pretended to have gleaned the facts he communicated in conversation with officers of the French army. The plan of the patriotic party was, to unite the Venetian territories on the mainland with Lombardy, and to form of the whole one republic. The conduct of Ottolini exasperated the party inimical to Venice, and augmented the prevailing discontent. Having disguised his valet as a peasant, he sent him off to Venice with the report he had drawn up on Serpini's communications, and other information; but this report never reached the inquisitors. The valet was arrested, his despatches taken, and Ottolini fled from Bergamo. This gave a beginning to the general rising of the Venetian States. In fact, the force of circumstances alone brought on the insurrection of those territories against their old insular government. General La Hoz, who commanded the Lombard Legion, was the active protector of the revolution, which certainly had its origin more in the progress of the prevailing principles of liberty than in the crooked policy of the Senate of Venice. Bonaparte, indeed, in his despatches to the Directory, stated that the Senate had instigated the insurrection; but that was not quite correct, and he could not wholly believe his own assertion.

Pending the vacillation of the Venetian Senate, Vienna was exciting the population of its States on the mainland to rise against the French. The Venetian Government had always exhibited an extreme aversion to the French Revolution, which had been violently condemned at Venice. Hatred of the French had been constantly excited and encouraged, and religious fanaticism had inflamed many persons of consequence in the country. From the end of 1796 the Venetian Senate secretly continued its armaments, and the whole conduct of that Government announced intentions which have been called perfidious, but the only object of which was to defeat intentions still more perfidious. The Senate was the irreconcilable enemy of the French Republic. Excitement was carried to such a point that in many places the people complained that they were not permitted to arm against the French. The Austrian generals industriously circulated the most sinister reports respecting the armies of the Sombre-et-Meuse and the Rhine, and the position of the French troops in the Tyrol. These impostures, printed in bulletins, were well calculated to instigate the Italians, and especially the Venetians, to rise in mass to exterminate the French, when the victorious army should penetrate into the Hereditary States.

The pursuit of the Archduke Charles into the heart of Austria encouraged the hopes which the Venetian Senate had conceived, that it would be easy to annihilate the feeble remnant of the French army, as the troops were scattered through the States of Venice on the mainland. Wherever the Senate had the ascendency, insurrection was secretly fomented; wherever the influence of the patriots prevailed, ardent efforts were made to unite the Venetian terra firma to the Lombard Republic.

Bonaparte skillfully took advantage of the disturbances, and the massacres consequent on them, to adopt towards the Senate the tone of an offended conqueror. He published a declaration that the Venetian Government was the most treacherous imaginable. The weakness and cruel hypocrisy of the Senate facilitated the plan he had conceived of making a peace for France at the expense of the Venetian Republic. On returning from Leoben, a conqueror and pacificator, he, without ceremony, took possession of Venice, changed the established government, and, master of all the Venetian territory, found himself, in the negotiations of Campo Formio, able to dispose of it as he pleased, as a compensation for the cessions which had been exacted from Austria. After the 19th of May he wrote to the Directory that one of the objects of his treaty with Venice was to avoid bringing upon us the odium of violating the preliminaries relative to the Venetian territory, and, at the same time, to afford pretexts and to facilitate their execution.

At Campo Formio the fate of this republic was decided. It disappeared from the number of States without effort or noise. The silence of its fall astonished imaginations warmed by historical recollections from the brilliant pages of its maritime glory. Its power, however, which had been silently undermined, existed no longer except in the prestige of those recollections. What resistance could it have opposed to the man destined to change the face of all Europe?

CHAPTER V

1797

I joined Bonaparte at Leoben on the 19th of April, the day after the signature of the preliminaries of peace. These preliminaries resembled in no respect the definitive treaty of Campo Formio. The still incomplete fall of the State of Venice did not at that time present an available prey for partition. All was arranged afterwards. Woe to the small States that come in immediate contact with two colossal empires waging war!

Here terminated my connection with Bonaparte as a comrade and equal, and those relations with him commenced in which I saw him suddenly great, powerful, and surrounded with homage and glory. I no longer addressed him as I had been accustomed to do. I appreciated too well his personal importance. His position placed too great a social distance between him and me not to make me feel the necessity of fashioning my demeanour accordingly. I made with pleasure, and without regret, the easy sacrifice of the style of familiar companionship and other little privileges. He said, in a loud voice, when I entered the salon where he was surrounded by the officers who formed his brilliant staff, "I am glad to see you, at last"—"Te voila donc, enfin;", but as soon as we were alone he made me understand that he was pleased with my reserve, and thanked me for it. I was immediately placed at the head of his Cabinet. I spoke to him the same evening respecting the insurrection of the Venetian territories, of the dangers which menaced the French, and of those which I had escaped, etc. "Care thou[31]' nothing about it," said he; "those rascals shall pay for it. Their republic has had its day, and is done." This republic was, however, still existing, wealthy and powerful. These words brought to my recollection what I had read in a work by one Gabriel Naude, who wrote during the reign of Louis XIII. for Cardinal de Bagin: "Do you see Constantinople, which flatters itself with being the seat of a double empire; and Venice, which glories in her stability of a thousand years? Their day will come."

In the first conversation which Bonaparte had with me, I thought I could perceive that he was not very well satisfied with the preliminaries. He would have liked to advance with his army to Vienna. He did not conceal this from me. Before he offered peace to Prince Charles, he wrote to the Directory that he intended to pursue his success, but that for this purpose he reckoned on the co-operation of the armies of the Sambre-et-Meuse and the Rhine. The Directory replied that he must not reckon on a diversion in Germany, and that the armies of the Sambre-et-Meuse and the Rhine were not to pass that river. A resolution so unexpected—a declaration so contrary to what he had constantly solicited, compelled him to terminate his triumphs, and renounce his favourite project of planting the standard of the republic on the ramparts of Vienna, or at least of levying contributions on the suburbs of that capital.

A law of the 23d of August 1794 forbade the use of any other names than those in the register of births. I wished to conform to this law, which very foolishly interfered with old

31 He used to 'tutoyer' me in this familiar manner until his return to Milan.

habits. My eldest brother was living, and I therefore designated myself Fauvelet the younger. This annoyed General Bonaparte. "Such change of name is absolute nonsense," said he. "I have known you for twenty years by the name of Bourrienne. Sign as you still are named, and see what the advocates with their laws will do."

On the 20th of April, as Bonaparte was returning to Italy, he was obliged to stop on an island of the Tagliamento, while a torrent passed by, which had been occasioned by a violent storm. A courier appeared on the right bank of the river. He reached the island. Bonaparte read in the despatches of the Directory that the armies of the Sambre-et-Meuse and the Rhine were in motion; that they were preparing to cross the Rhine, and had commenced hostilities on the very day of the signing of the preliminaries. This information arrived seven days after the Directory had written that "he must not reckon on the co-operation of the armies of Germany." It is impossible to describe the General's vexation on reading these despatches. He had signed the preliminaries only because the Government had represented the co-operation of the armies of the Rhine as impracticable at that moment, and shortly afterwards he was informed that the co-operation was about to take place! The agitation of his mind was so great that he for a moment conceived the idea of crossing to the left bank of the Tagliamento, and breaking off the negotiations under some pretext or other. He persisted for some time in this resolution, which, however, Berthier and some other generals successfully opposed. He exclaimed, "What a difference would there have been in the preliminaries, if, indeed, there had been any!"

His chagrin, I might almost say his despair, increased when, some days after his entry into the Venetian States, he received a letter from Moreau, dated the 23d of April, in which that general informed him that, having passed the Rhine on the 20th with brilliant success, and taken four thousand prisoners, it would not be long before he joined him. Who, in fact, can say what would have happened but for the vacillating and distrustful policy of the Directory, which always encouraged low intrigues, and participated in the jealousy excited by the renown of the young conqueror? Because the Directory dreaded his ambition they sacrificed the glory of our arms and the honour of the nation; for it cannot be doubted that, had the passage of the Rhine, so urgently demanded by Bonaparte, taken place some days sooner, he would have been able, without incurring any risk, to dictate imperiously the conditions of peace on the spot; or, if Austria were obstinate, to have gone on to Vienna and signed it there. Still occupied with this idea, he wrote to the Directory on the 8th of May: "Since I have received intelligence of the passage of the Rhine by Hoche and Moreau, I much regret that it did not take place fifteen days sooner; or, at least, that Moreau did not say that he was in a situation to effect it." (He had been informed to the contrary.) What, after this, becomes of the unjust reproach against Bonaparte of having, through jealousy of Moreau, deprived France of the advantages which a prolonged campaign would have procured her? Bonaparte was too devoted to the glory of France to sacrifice it to jealousy of the glory of any individual.

In traversing the Venetian States to return to Milan, he often spoke to me of Venice. He always assured me that he was originally entirely unconnected with the insurrections which had agitated that country; that common sense would show, as his project was to advance into the basin of the Danube, he had no interest in having his rear disturbed by revolts, and his communications interrupted or cut off: "Such an idea," said he, "would be absurd, and could never enter into the mind of a man to whom even his enemies cannot deny a certain degree of tact." He acknowledged that he was not vexed that matters had turned out as they had done, because he had already taken advantage of these circumstances in the preliminaries and hoped to profit still more from them in the definitive peace. "When I arrive at Milan," said he, "I will occupy myself with Venice." It is therefore quite evident to me that in reality the General-in-Chief had nothing to do with the Venetian insurrections; that subsequently he was not displeased with them; and that, later still, he derived great advantage from them.

We arrived at Milan on the 5th of May, by way of Lawbook, Thrust, Palma-Nova, Padua, Verona, and Mantua. Bonaparte soon took up his residence at Montebello, a very fine chateau, three leagues from Milan, with a view over the rich and magnificent plains of Lombard. At Montebello commenced the negotiations for the definitive peace which were terminated at Passeriano. The Marquis de Gallo, the Austrian plenipotentiary, resided half a league from Montebello.

During his residence at Montebello the General-in-Chief made an excursion to the Lake of Como and to the Ago Maguire. He visited the Borromean Islands in succession, and occupied himself on his return with the organization of the towns of Venice, Genoa, and Milan. He sought for men and found none. "Good God," said he, "how rare men are! There are eighteen millions in Italy, and I have with difficulty found two, Dandolo and Melzi."

He appreciated them properly. Dandolo was one of the men who, in those revolutionary times, reflected the greatest honour upon Italy. After being a member of the great council of the Cisalpine Republic, he exercised the functions of Proveditore-General in Dalmatia. It is only necessary to mention the name of Dandolo to the Dalmatians to learn from the grateful inhabitants how just and vigorous his administration was. The services of Melzi are known. He was Chancellor and Keeper of the Seals of the Italian monarchy, and was created Duke of Lodi.[32]

In those who have seen the world the truth of Napoleon's reproach excites little astonishment. In a country which, according to biographies and newspapers, abounds with extraordinary men, a woman of much talent—(Madame Roland.)—said, "What has most surprised me, since the elevation of my husband has afforded me the opportunity of knowing many persons, and particularly those employed in important affairs, is the universal mediocrity which exists. It surpasses all that the imagination can conceive, and it is observable in all ranks, from the clerk to the minister. Without this experience I never could have believed my species to be so contemptible."

Who does not remember Oxenstiern's remark to his son, who trembled at going so young to the congress of Munster: "Go, my son. You will see by what sort of men the world is governed."

32 Francesco, Comte de Melzi d'Eryl (1753-1816), vice President of the Italian Republic, 1802; Chancellor of the Kingdom of Italy, 1805; Duc de Loth, 1807.

CHAPTER VI

1797

During the time when the preliminaries of Leoben suspended military operations, Napoleon was not anxious to reply immediately to all letters. He took a fancy to do, not exactly as Cardinal Dubois did, when he threw into the fire the letters he had received, saying, "There! my correspondents are answered," but something of the same kind. To satisfy himself that people wrote too much, and lost, in trifling and useless answers, valuable time, he told me to open only the letters which came by extraordinary couriers, and to leave all the rest for three weeks in the basket. At the end of that time it was unnecessary to reply to four-fifths of these communications. Some were themselves answers; some were acknowledgments of letters received; others contained requests for favours already granted, but of which intelligence had not been received. Many were filled with complaints respecting provisions, pay, or clothing, and orders had been issued upon all these points before the letters were written. Some generals demanded reinforcements, money, promotion, etc. By not opening their letters Bonaparte was spared the unpleasing office of refusing. When the General-in-Chief compared the very small number of letters which it was necessary to answer with the large number which time alone had answered, he laughed heartily at his whimsical idea. Would not this mode of proceeding be preferable to that of causing letters to be opened by any one who may be employed, and replying to them by a circular to which it is only necessary to attach a date?

During the negotiations which followed the treaty of Leoben, the Directory ordered General Bonaparte to demand the liberty of MM. de La Fayette, Latour-Marbourg, and Bureau de Puzy, detained at Olmutz since 1792 as prisoners of state. The General-in-Chief executed this commission with as much pleasure as zeal, but he often met with difficulties which appeared to be insurmountable. It has been very incorrectly stated that these prisoners obtained their liberty by one of the articles of the preliminaries of Leoben. I wrote a great deal on this subject to the dictation of General Bonaparte, and I joined him only on the day after the signature of these preliminaries. It was not till the end of May of the year 1797 that the liberation of these captives was demanded, and they did not obtain their freedom till the end of August. There was no article in the treaty, public or secret, which had reference to them. Neither was it at his own suggestion that Bonaparte demanded the enlargement of the prisoners, but by order of the Directory. To explain why they did not go to France immediately after their liberation from Olmutz, it is necessary to recollect that the events of the 18th Fructidor occurred between the period when the first steps were taken to procure their liberty and the date of their deliverance. It required all Bonaparte's ascendency and vigour of character to enable him to succeed in his object at the end of three months.

We had arrived at the month of July, and the negotiations were tediously protracted. It was impossible to attribute the embarrassment which was constantly occurring to anything but the artful policy of Austria: Other affairs occupied Bonaparte. The news from Paris engrossed all his attention. He saw with extreme displeasure the manner in which the influential orators of the councils, and pamphlets written in the same spirit as they spoke, criticised him, his army, his victories, the affairs of Venice, and the national glory. He was quite indignant at the suspicions which it was sought to create respecting his conduct and ulterior views. The following excerpts, attributed to the pens of Dumouriez or Rivarol, are specimens of some of the comments of the time:

EXTRACTS OF LETTERS IN "LE SPECTATUER DU NORD" OF 1797

General Bonaparte is, without contradiction, the most brilliant warrior who has appeared at the head of the armies of the French Republic. His glory is incompatible with democratic equality, and the services he has rendered are too great to be recompensed except by hatred and ingratitude. He is very young, and consequently has to pursue a long career of accusations and of persecutions.

. . . Whatever may be the crowning event of his military career, Bonaparte is still a great man. All his glory is due to himself alone; because he alone has developed a character and a genius of which no one else has furnished an example.

EXTRACT OF LETTER OR 18TH APRIL 1797 IN "THE SPECTATEUR DU NORD"

Regard, for instance, this wretched war. Uncertain in Champagne, it becomes daring under Dumouriez, unbridled under the brigands who fought the Vendeeans, methodic under Pichegru, vulgar under Jourdan, skilled under Moreau, rash under Bonaparte. Each general has put the seal of his genius on his career, and has given life or death to his army. From the commencement of his career Bonaparte has developed an ardent character which is irritated by obstacles, and a quickness which forestalls every determination of the enemy. It is with heavier and heavier blows that, he strikes. He throws his army on the enemy like an unloosed torrent. He is all action, and he is so in everything. See him fight, negotiate, decree, punish, all is the matter of a moment. He compromises with Turin as with Rome. He invades Modena as he burns Binasco. He never hesitates; to cut the Gordian knot is always his method.

Bonaparte could not endure to have his conduct predicated; and enraged at seeing his campaigns depreciated, his glory and that of his army disparaged,[33] and intrigues formed against him in the Club of Clichy, he wrote the following letter to the Directory:—

33 The extraordinary folly of the opposition to the Directory in throwing Bonaparte on to the side of the Directory, will be seen by reading the speech of Dumolard, so often referred to by Bourrienne (Thiers, vol. v. pp. 110-111), and by the attempts of Mathieu Dumas to remove the impression that the opposition slighted the fortunate General. (See Dumas, tome iii. p. 80; see also Lanfrey, tome i. pp. 257-299).

To the President of the Executive Directory.

Citizens-Directors, I have just received, Citizens-Directors, a copy of the motion of Dumolard (23d June 1797). This motion, printed by order of the Assembly, it is evident, is directed against me. I was entitled, after, having five times concluded peace, and given a death-blow to the coalition, if not to civic triumphs, at least to live tranquilly under the protection of the first magistrates of the Republic. At present I find myself ill-treated, persecuted, and disparaged, by every shameful means, which their policy brings to the aid of persecution. I would have been indifferent to all except that species of opprobrium with which the first magistrates of the Republic endeavour to overwhelm me. After having deserved well of my country by my last act, I am not bound to hear myself accused in a manner as absurd as atrocious. I have not expected that a manifesto, signed by emigrants, paid by England, should obtain more credit with the Council of Five Hundred than the evidence of eighty thousand men—than mine! What! we were assassinated by traitors—upwards of four hundred men perished; and the first magistrates of the Republic make it a crime to have believed the statement for a moment. Upwards of four hundred Frenchmen were dragged through the streets. They were assassinated before the eyes of the governor of the fort. They were pierced wit a thousand blows of stilettos, such as I sent you and the representatives of the French people cause it to be printed, that if they believed this fact for an instant, they were excusable. I know well there are societies where it is said, "Is this blood, then, so pure?"

If only base men, who are dead to the feeling of patriotism and national glory, had spoken of me thus, I would not have complained. I would have disregarded it; but I have a right to complain of the degradation to which the first magistrates of the Republic reduce those who have aggrandised, and carried the French name to so high a pitch of glory. Citizens-Directors, I reiterate the demand I made for my dismissal; I wish to live in tranquillity, if the poniards of Clichy will allow me to live. You have employed me in negotiations. I am not very fit to conduct them.

About the same time he drew up the following note respecting the affairs of Venice, which was printed without the author's name, and circulated through the whole army:—

NOTE

Bonaparte, pausing before the gates of Turin, Parma, Rome, and Vienna, offering peace when he was sure of obtaining nothing but fresh triumphs—Bonaparte, whose every operation exhibits respect for religion, morality, and old age; who, instead of heaping, as he might have done, dishonour upon the Venetians, and humbling their republic to the earth, loaded her with acts of kindness, and took such great interest in her glory—is this the same Bonaparte who is accused of destroying the ancient Government of Venice, and democratising Genoa, and even of interfering in the affairs of the prudent and worthy people of the Swiss Cantons? Bonaparte had passed the Tagliamento, and entered Germany, when insurrections broke out in the Venetian States; these insurrections were, therefore, opposed to Bonaparte's project; surely, then, he could not favour them. When he was in the heart of Germany the Venetians massacred more than four hundred French troops, drove their quarters out of Verona, assassinated the unfortunate Laugier, and presented the spectacle of a fanatical party in arms. He returned to Italy; and on his arrival, as the winds cease their agitation at the presence of Neptune, the whole of Italy, which was in commotion, which was in arms, was restored to order. However, the deputies from Bonaparte drew up different articles conformable to the situation of the country, and in order to prevent, not a revolution in the Government, for the Government was defunct, and had died a natural death, but a crisis, and to save the city from convulsion, anarchy, and pillage. Bonaparte spared a division of his army to save Venice from pillage and massacre. All the battalions were in the streets of Venice, the disturbers were put down, and the pillage discontinued. Property and trade were preserved, when General Baragney d'Hilliers entered Venice with his division. Bonaparte, as usual, spared blood, and was the protector of Venice. Whilst the French troops remained they conducted themselves peaceably, and only interfered to support the provisional Government. Bonaparte could not say to the deputies of Venice, who came to ask his protection and assistance against the populace, who wished to plunder them, "I cannot meddle with your affairs." He could not say this, for Venice, and all its territories, had really formed the theatre of war; and, being in the rear of the army of Italy, the Republic of Venice was really under the jurisdiction of that army. The rights of war confer upon a general the powers of supreme police over the countries which are the seat of war. As the great Frederick said, "There are no neutrals where there is war." Ignorant advocates and babblers have asked, in the Club of Clichy, why we occupy the territory of Venice. These declaimers should learn war, and they would know that the Adige, the Brenta, and the Tagliamento, where we have been fighting for two years, are within the Venetian States. But, gentlemen of Clichy, we are at no loss to perceive your meaning. You reproach the army of Italy for having surmounted all difficulties—for subduing all Italy for having twice passed the Alps—for having marched on Vienna, and obliged Austria to acknowledge the Republic that, you, men of Clichy, would destroy. You accuse Bonaparte, I see clearly, for having brought about peace. But I know you, and I speak in the name of eighty thousand soldiers. The time is gone when base advocates and wretched declaimers could induce soldiers to revolt. If, however, you compel them, the soldiers of the army of Italy will soon appear at the Barrier of Clichy, with their General. But woe unto you if they do!

Bonaparte having arrived at Palma-Nova, issued a manifesto on the 2d of May 1797. Arrived at Mestre, where he posted his troops, the Government sent three deputies to him, with a decree of the Great Council, without Bonaparte having solicited it and without his having thought of making any change in the Government of that country: The governor of Venice was an old man, ninety-nine years-of age, confined by illness to his apartment. Everyone felt the necessity of renovating this Government of twelve hundred years' existence, and to simplify its machinery, in order to preserve its independence, honour, and glory. It was necessary to deliberate, first, on the manner of renovating the Government; secondly, on the means of atoning for the massacre of the French, the iniquity of which every one was sensible . . . Bonaparte, after having received the deputation at Mestre, told them that in order to obtain satisfaction, for the assassination of his brethren is arms, he wished the Great Council to arrest the inquisitors. He afterwards granted them an armistice, and appointed Milan as the place of conference. The deputies arrived at Milan on the . . . A negotiation commenced to re-establish harmony between the Governments. However, anarchy, with all its horrors, afflicted the city of Venice. Ten thousand Sclavonians threatened to pillage the shops. Bonaparte acquiesced in the proposition submitted by the deputies, who promised to verify the loss which had been sustained by pillage. Bonaparte also addressed a manifesto to the Doge, which appeared in all the public papers. It contained fifteen articles of complaint, and was followed by a decree ordering the French Minister to leave Venice, the Venetian agents to leave Lombard, and the Lion of St. Mark to be pulled down in all the Continental territories of Venice. The General-in-Chief now openly manifested his resolution of marching on Paris; and this disposition, which was well known in the army, was soon communicated to Vienna. At this period a letter from the Emperor Francis II. to his brother, the Grand Duke of Tuscany, was intercepted by Bonaparte. I translated the letter, which proved to him that Francis II. was acquainted with his project. He likewise saw with pleasure the assurances which the Emperor gave his brother of his love of peace, as well as the wavering of the imperial resolves, and the incertitude respecting the fate of the Italian princes, which the Emperor easily perceived to depend on Bonaparte. The Emperor's letter was as follows:—

> MY DEAR BROTHER—I punctually received your third letter, containing a description of your unhappy and delicate situation. You may be assured that I perceive it as clearly as you do yourself; and I pity you the more because, in truth, I do not know what advice to give you. You are, like me, the victim of the former inactivity of the princes of Italy, who ought, at once, to have acted with all their united forces, while I still possessed Mantua. If Bonaparte's project be, as I learn, to establish republics in Italy, this is likely to end in spreading republicanism over the whole country. I have already commenced negotiations for peace, and the preliminaries are ratified. If the French observe them as strictly as I do, and will do, then your situation will be improved; but already the French are beginning to disregard them. The principal problem which remains to be solved is, whether the French Directory approve of Bonaparte's proceedings, and whether the latter, as appears by some papers distributed through his army, is not disposed to revolt against his country, which also seems to be probable, from his severe conduct towards Switzerland, notwithstanding the assurances of the Directory, that he had been ordered to leave the country untouched. If this should be the case, new and innumerable difficulties may arise. Under these circumstances I can, at present, advise nothing; for, as to myself, it is only time and the circumstances of the moment which can point out how I am to act. There is nothing new here. We are all well; but the heat is extraordinary. Always retain your friendship and love for me. Make my compliments to your wife, and believe me ever
>
> Your best Friend and Brother,
>
> FRANCIS.
> HETZENDORF, *July 20, 1797.*

CHAPTER VII

1797

While Bonaparte was expressing his opinion on his campaigns and the injustice with which they had been criticised, it was generally believed that Carnot dictated to him from a closet in the Luxembourg all the plans of his operations, and that Berthier was at his right hand, without whom, notwithstanding Carnot's plans, which were often mere romances, he would have been greatly embarrassed. This twofold misrepresentation was very current for some time; and, notwithstanding it was contrary to the evidence of facts, it met with much credence, particularly abroad. There was, however, no foundation for the opinion: Let us render to Caesar that which is Caesar's due. Bonaparte was a creator in the art of war, and no imitator. That no man was superior to him in that art is incontestable. At the commencement of the glorious campaign in Italy the Directory certainly sent out instructions to him; but he always followed his own plans, and continually, wrote back that all would be lost if movements conceived at a distance from the scene of action were to be blindly executed. He also offered to resign. At length the Directory perceived the impossibility of prescribing operations of war according to the view of persons in Paris; and when I became the secretary of the General-in-Chief I saw a despatch of the Directory, dated May, 1796, committing the whole plan of the campaign to his judgment; and assuredly there was not a single operation or movement which did not originate with him. Carnot was obliged to yield to his firmness. When the Directory, towards the end of 1796, felt disposed to treat for peace, General Clarke, appointed to conclude the armistice, was authorised, in case Mantua should not be taken before the negotiation was brought to a close, to propose leaving the blockade in statu quo. Had such a condition been adopted it would doubtless had been stipulated that the Emperor of Austria should be allowed to provision the garrison and inhabitants of the city day by day. Bonaparte, convinced that an armistice without Mantua would by no means conduce to peace, earnestly opposed such a condition. He carried his point; Mantua capitulated, and the result is well known. Yet he was not blind to the hazards of war; while preparing, during the blockade, an assault on Mantua, he wrote thus to the Directory: "A bold stroke of this nature depends absolutely for success on a dog or a goose." This was about a question of surprise.

Bonaparte was exceedingly sensitive to the rumours which reached him respecting Carnot and Berthier. He one day said to me: "What gross stupidity, is this? It is very well to say to a general, 'Depart for Italy, gain battles, and sign a peace at Vienna;' but the execution that is not so easy. I never attached any value to the plans which the Directory sent me. Too many circumstances occur on the spot to modify them. The movement of a single corps of the enemy's army may confound a whole plan arranged by the fireside. Only fools can believe such stuff! As for Berthier, since you have been with me, you see what he is—he is a blockhead. Yet it is he who does it all; it is he who gathers a great part of the glory of the army of Italy." I told him that this erroneous opinion could not last long; that each person would be allowed his merit, and that at least posterity would judge rightly. This observation seemed to please him.

Berthier was a man full of honour, courage, and probity, and exceedingly regular in the performance of his duties. Bonaparte's attachment to him arose more from habit than liking. Berthier did not concede with affability, and refused with harshness. His abrupt, egotistic, and careless manners did not, however, create him many enemies, but, at the same time, did not make him many friends. In consequence of our frequent intercourse he had contracted the friendly practice of speaking to me in the second person singular; but he never wrote to me in that style. He was perfectly acquainted with the disposition of all the corps, and could name their commanders and their respective forces. Day or night he was always at hand and made out with clearness all the secondary orders which resulted from the dispositions of the General-in-Chief. In fact, he was, an excellent head of the staff of an army; but that is all the praise that can be given, and indeed he wished for no greater. He had such entire confidence in Bonaparte, and looked up to him with so much admiration, that he never would have presumed to oppose his plans or give any advise. Berthier's talent was very limited, and of a special nature; his character was one of extreme weakness. Bonaparte's friendship for him and the frequency of his name in the bulletins and official despatches have unduly elevated his reputation. Bonaparte, giving his opinion to the Directory respecting the generals employed in his army, said, "Berthier has talents, activity, courage, character—all in his favour." This was in 1796. He then made an eagle of him; at St. Helena he called him a goose. He should neither have, raised him so high nor sunk him so low.

Berthier neither merited the one nor the other. Bonaparte was a man of habit; he was much attached to all the people about him, and did not like new faces. Berthier loved him. He carried out his orders well, and that enabled him to pass off with his small portion of talent.

It was about this time that young Beauharnais came to Milan. He was seventeen years old. He had lived in Paris with his mother since the departure of Bonaparte. On his arrival he immediately entered the service as 'aide de camp' to the General-in-Chief, who felt for him an affection which was justified by his good qualities.

Comte Delaunay d'Entraigues, well known in the French Revolution, held a diplomatic post at Venice when that city was threatened by the French. Aware of his being considered the agent of all the machinations then existing against France, and especially against the army of Italy, he endeavoured to escape; but the city being, surrounded, he was seized, together with all his papers. The apparently frank manners of the Count pleased Bonaparte, who treated him with indulgence. His papers were restored, with the exception of three relating to political subjects. He afterwards fled to Switzerland, and ungratefully represented himself as having been oppressed by Bonaparte. His false statements have induced many writers to make of him an heroic victim. He was assassinated by his own servant in 1802.

I kept a copy of one of his most interesting papers. It has been much spoken of, and Fauche-Borel has, I believe, denied its authenticity and the truth of its contents. The manner in which it fell into the hands of the General-in-Chief, the importance attached to it by d'Entraigues, the differences I have observed between the manuscript I copied and versions which I have since read, and the knowledge of its authenticity, having myself transcribed it from the handwriting of the Count, who in my presence vouched for the truth of the facts it details—all these circumstances induce me to insert it here, and compel me to doubt that it was, as Fauche-Borel asserted, a fabrication.

This manuscript is entitled, 'My Conversation with Comte de Montgaillard, on the 4th of December 1796, from Six in the Afternoon till midnight, in the presence of the Abbe

Dumontel.' [On my copy are written the words, "Extracts from this conversation, made by me, from the original." I omitted what I thought unimportant, and transcribed only the most interesting passages. Montgaillard spoke of his escape, of his flight to England, of his return to France, of his second departure, and finally of his arrival at Bale in August 1795.]

The Prince de Condé soon afterwards, he said, called me to Mulheim, and knowing the connections I had had in France, proposed that I should sound General Pichegru, whose headquarters were at Altkirch, where he then was, surrounded by four representatives of the Convention.

I immediately went to Neufchatel, taking with me four or five hundred Louis. I cast my eyes on Fauche-Borel, the King's printer at Neufchatel, and also yours and mine, as the instrument by which to make the first overture, and I selected as his colleague M. Courant, a native of Neufchatel. I persuaded them to undertake the business: I supplied them with instructions and passports. They were foreigners: so I furnished them with all the necessary documents to enable them to travel in France as foreign merchants and purchasers of national property. I went to Bale to wait for news from them.

On the 13th of August Fauche and Courant set out for the headquarters at Altkirch. They remained there eight days without finding an opportunity to speak to Pichegru, who was surrounded by representatives and generals. Pichegru observed them, and seeing them continually wheresoever he went, he conjectured that they had something to say to him, and he called out in a loud voice, while passing them, "I am going to Huningen." Fauche contrived to throw himself in his way at the end of a corridor. Pichegru observed him, and fixed his eyes upon him, and although it rained in torrents, he said aloud, "I am going to dine at the chateau of Madame Salomon." This chateau was three leagues from Huningen, and Madame Salomon was Pichegru's mistress.

Fauche set off directly to the chateau, and begged to speak with General Pichegru. He told the general that, being in the possession of some of J. J. Rousseau's manuscripts, he wished to publish them and dedicate them to him. "Very good," said Pichegru; "but I should like to read them first; for Rousseau professed principles of liberty in which I do not concur, and with which I should not like to have my name connected."—"But," said Fauche, "I have something else to speak to you about."—"What is it, and on whose behalf?"— "On behalf of the Prince de Condé."—"Be silent, then, and follow me."

He conducted Fauche alone into a retired cabinet, and said to him, "Explain yourself; what does Monseigneur le Prince de Condé wish to communicate to me?" Fauche was embarrassed, and stammered out something unintelligible. "Compose yourself." said Pichegru; "my sentiments are the same, as the Prince de Condé's. What does he desire of me?" Fauche, encouraged by these words, replied, "The Prince wishes to join you. He counts on you, and wishes to connect himself with you."

"These are vague and unmeaning words," observed Pichegru. "All this amounts to nothing. Go back, and ask for written instructions, and return in three days to my headquarters at Altkirch. You will find me alone precisely at six o'clock in the evening."

Fauche immediately departed, arrived at Bale, and informed me of all that had passed. I spent the night in writing a letter to General Pichegru. (The Prince de Condé, who was invested with all the powers of Louis XVIII, except that of granting the 'cordon-bleu', had, by a note in his own handwriting, deputed to me all his powers, to enable me to maintain a negotiation with General Pichegru).

I therefore wrote to the general, stating, in the outset, everything that was calculated to awaken in him that noble sentiment of pride which is the instinct of great minds; and after pointing out to him the vast good it was in his power to effect, I spoke of the gratitude of the King, and the benefit he would confer on his country by restoring royalty. I told him that his Majesty would make him a marshal of France, and governor of Alsace, as no one could better govern the province than he who had so valiantly defended it. I added that he would have the 'cordon-rouge', the Chateau de Chambord, with its park, and twelve pieces of cannon taken from the Austrians, a million of ready money, 200,000 livres per annum, and an hotel in Paris; that the town of Arbors, Pichegru's native place, should bear his name, and be exempt from all taxation for twenty-five years; that a pension of 200,000 livres would be granted to him, with half reversion to his wife, and 50,000 livres to his heirs for ever, until the extinction of his family. Such were the offers, made in the name of the King, to General Pichegru. (Than followed the boons to be granted to the officers and soldiers, an amnesty to the people, etc). I added that the Prince de Coude desired that he would proclaim the King in the camps, surrender the city of Huningen to him, and join him for the purpose of marching on Paris.

Pichegru, having read my letter with great attention, said to Fauche, "This is all very well; but who is this M. de Montgaillard who talks of being thus authorised? I neither know him nor his signature. Is he the author?"—"Yes," replied Fauche. "But," said Pichegru, "I must, before making any negotiation on my part, be assured that the Prince de Condé, with whose handwriting I am well acquainted, approves of all that has been written is his name by M. de Montgaillard. Return directly to M. de Montgaillard, and tell him to communicate my answer to the Prince."

Fauche immediately departed, leaving M. Courant with Pichegru. He arrived at Bale at nine o'clock in the evening. I set off directly for Malheim, the Prince de Condé's headquarters, and arrived there at half-past twelve. The Prince was in bed, but I awoke him. He made me sit down by his bedside, and our conference then commenced.

After having informed the Prince of the state of affairs, all that remained was to prevail on him to write to General Pichegru to confirm the truth of what had been stated in his name. This matter, which appeared so simple, and so little liable to objection, occupied the whole night. The Prince, as brave a man as can possibly be, inherited nothing from the great Condé but his undaunted courage. In other respects he is the most insignificant of men; without resources of mind, or decision of character; surrounded by men of mediocrity, and even baseness; and though he knows them well, he suffers himself to be governed by them.

It required nine hours of hard exertion on my part to get him to write to General Pichegru a letter of eight lines. 1st. He did not wish it to be in his handwriting. 2d. He objected to dating it 3d. He was unwilling to call him General, lest he should recognise the republic by giving that title. 4th. He did not like to address it, or affix his seal to it.

At length he consented to all, and wrote to Pichegru that he might place full confidence in the letters of the Comte de Montgaillard. When all this was settled, after great difficulty, the Prince next hesitated about sending the letter; but at length he yielded. I set off for Bale, and despatched Fauche to Altkirch, to General Pichegru.

The general, after reading the letter of eight lines, and recognising the handwriting and signature, immediately returned it to Fauche, saying, "I have seen the signature: that is enough for me. The word of the Prince is a pledge with which every Frenchman ought to be satisfied. Take back his letter." He then inquired what was the Prince's wish. Fauche explained that he wished—1st. That Pichegru should proclaim the King to his troops, and hoist the White flag.

2d. That he should deliver up Huningen to the Prince. Pichegru objected to this. "I will never take part in such a plot," said he; "I have no wish to make the third volume of La Fayette and Dumouriez. I know my resources; they are as certain as they are vast. Their roots are not only in my army, but in Paris, in the Convention, in the departments, and in the armies of those generals, my colleagues, who think as I do. I wish to do nothing by halves. There must be a complete end of the present state of things. France cannot continue a Republic. She must have a king, and that king must be Louis XVIII. But we must not commence the counter-revolution until we are certain of effecting it. 'Surely and rightly' is my motto. The Prince's plan leads to nothing. He would be driven from Huningen in four days, and in fifteen I should be lost. My army is composed both of good men and bad. We must distinguish between them, and, by a bold stroke, assure the former of the impossibility of drawing back, and that their only safety lies in success. For this purpose I propose to pass the Rhine, at any place and any time that may be thought necessary. In the advance I will place those officers on whom I can depend, and who are of my way of thinking. I will separate the bad, and place them in situations where they can do no harm, and their position shall be such as to prevent them from uniting. That done, as soon as I shall be on the other side of the Rhine, I will proclaim the King, and hoist the white flag. Condé's corps and the Emperor's army will then join us. I will immediately repass the Rhine, and re-enter France. The fortresses will be surrendered, and will be held in the King's name by the Imperial troops. Having joined Condé's army, I immediately advance. All my means now develop themselves on every side. We march upon Paris, and in a fortnight will be there. But it is necessary that you should know that you must give the French soldier wine and a crown in his hand if you would have him cry 'Vive le Roi! Nothing must be wanting at the first moment. My army must be well paid as far as the fourth or fifth march in the French territory. There go and tell all this to the Prince, show my handwriting, and bring me back his answer."

During these conferences Pichegru was surrounded by four representatives of the people, at the head of whom was Merlin de Thionville, the most insolent and the most ferocious of inquisitors. These men, having the orders of the Committee, pressed Pichegru to pass the Rhine and go and besiege Manheim, where Merlin had an understanding with the inhabitants. Thus, if on the one hand the Committee by its orders made Pichegru wish to hasten the execution of his plan, on the other he had not a moment to lose; for to delay obeying the orders of the four representatives was to render himself suspected. Every consideration, therefore, called upon the Prince to decide, and decide promptly. Good sense required him also to do another thing, namely, to examine without prejudice what sort of man Pichegru was, to consider the nature of the sacrifice he made, and what were his propositions. Europe acknowledged his talents, and he had placed the Prince in a condition to judge of his good faith. Besides, his conduct and his plan afforded fresh proofs of his sincerity. By passing the Rhine and placing himself between the armies of Condé and Wurmser, he rendered desertion impossible; and, if success did not attend his attempt, his own acts forced him to become an emigrant. He left in the power of his fierce enemies his wife, his father, his children. Everything bore testimony to his honesty; the talents he had shown were a pledge for his genius, his genius for his resources; and the sacrifices he would have to make in case of failure proved that he was confident of success.

What stupid conceit was it for any one to suppose himself better able to command Pichegru's army than Pichegru himself!—to pretend to be better acquainted with the frontier provinces than Pichegru, who commanded them, and had placed his friends in them as commanders of the towns! This self-conceit, however, ruined the monarchy at this time, as well as at so many others. The Prince de Condé, after reading the plan, rejected it in toto. To render it successful it was necessary to make the Austrians parties to it. This Pichegru exacted, but the Prince of Condé would not hear a word of it, wishing to have confined to himself the glory of effecting the counter-revolution. He replied to Pichegru by a few observations, and concluded his answer by returning to his first plan—that Pichegru should proclaim the King without passing the Rhine, and should give up Huningen; that then the army of Condé by itself, and without the aid of the Austrians, would join him. In that case he could promise 100,000 crowns in louis, which he had at Bale, and 1,400,000 livres, which he had in good bills payable at sight.

No argument or entreaty had any effect on the Prince de Condo. The idea of communicating his plan to Wurmser and sharing his glory with him rendered him blind and deaf to every consideration. However, it was necessary to report to Pichegru the observations of the Prince de Condé, and Courant was commissioned to do so.

This document appeared so interesting to me that while Bonaparte was sleeping I was employed in copying it. Notwithstanding posterior and reiterated denials of its truth, I believe it to be perfectly correct.

Napoleon had ordered plans of his most famous battles to be engraved, and had paid in advance for them. The work was not done quickly enough for him. He got angry, and one day said to his geographer, Bacler d'Albe, whom he liked well enough, "Ah! do hurry yourself, and think all this is only the business of a moment. If you make further delay you will sell nothing; everything is soon forgotten!"

We were now in July, and the negotiations were carried on with a tardiness which showed that something was kept in reserve on both sides. Bonaparte at this time was anything but disposed to sign a peace, which he always hoped to be able to make at Vienna, after a campaign in Germany, seconded by the armies of the Rhine and the Sambre-et-Meuse. The minority of the Directory recommended peace on the basis of the preliminaries, but the majority wished for more honourable and advantageous terms; while Austria, relying on troubles breaking out in France, was in no haste to conclude a treaty. In these circumstances Bonaparte drew up a letter to be sent to the Emperor of Austria, in which he set forth the moderation of France; but stated that, in consequence of the many delays, nearly all hope of peace had vanished. He advised the Emperor not to rely on difficulties arising in France, and doubted, if war should continue and the Emperor be successful in the next campaign, that he would obtain a more advantageous peace than was now at his option. This letter was never sent to the Emperor, but was communicated as the draft of a proposed despatch to the Directory. The Emperor Francis, however, wrote an autograph letter to the General-in-Chief of the army of Italy, which will be noticed when I come to the period of its reception: It is certain that Bonaparte at this time wished for war. He was aware that the Cabinet of Vienna was playing with him, and that the Austrian Ministers expected some political convulsion in Paris, which they hoped would be favourable to the Bourbons. He therefore asked for reinforcements. His army consisted of 35,900 men, and he desired it to be raised to 60,000 infantry and 10,000 cavalry ready for the field.

General Desaix, profiting by the preliminaries of Leoben, came in the end of July to visit the scene of the army of Italy's triumphs. His conversations with Bonaparte respecting the army of the Rhine were far from giving him confidence in his military situation in Italy, or assurance of support from that army in the event of hostilities commencing beyond the mountains. It was at this period that their intimacy began. Bonaparte conceived for Desaix the greatest esteem and the sincerest friendship.[34]

When Desaix was named temporary commander of the force called the army of England, during the absence of General Bonaparte, the latter wrote to the Directory that they could not have chosen a more distinguished officer than Desaix; these sentiments he never belied. The early death of Desaix alone could break their union, which, I doubt not, would eventually have had great influence on the political and military career of General Bonaparte.

All the world knows the part which the General-in-Chief of the army of Italy took at the famous crisis of the 18th Fructidor; his proclamation, his addresses to the army, and his celebrated order of the day. Bonaparte went much into detail on this subject at St. Helena; and I shall now proceed to state what I knew at the time respecting that memorable event, which was in preparation in the month of June.

34 Desaix discontented with the conduct of affairs in Germany, seceded from the army of the Rhine, to which he belonged, to join that of Napoleon. He was sent to Italy to organise the part of the Egyptian expedition starting from Civita Vecchia. He took with him his two aides de camp, Rapp and Savary (later Duc de Rovigo), both of whom, on his death, were given the same post with Bonaparte.

CHAPTER VIII

1797

Bonaparte had long observed the struggle which was going on between the partisans of royalty and the Republic. He was told that royalism was everywhere on the increase. All the generals who returned from Paris to the army complained of the spirit of reaction they had noticed. Bonaparte was constantly urged by his private correspondents to take one side or the other, or to act for himself. He was irritated by the audacity of the enemies of the Republic, and he saw plainly that the majority of the councils had an evident ill-will towards him. The orators of the Club of Clichy missed no opportunity of wounding his self-love in speeches and pamphlets. They spared no insults, disparaged his success, and bitterly censured his conduct in Italy, particularly with respect to Venice. Thus his services were recompensed by hatred or ingratitude. About this time he received a pamphlet, which referred to the judgments pronounced upon him by the German journals, and more particularly by the Spectator of the North, which he always made me translate.

Bonaparte was touched to the quick by the comparison make between him and Moreau, and by the wish to represent him as foolhardy ("savants sous Moreau, fougueuse sous Buonaparte"). In the term of "brigands," applied to the generals who fought in La Vendée, he thought he recognized the hand of the party he was about to attack and overthrow. He was tired of the way in which Moreau's system of war was called "savants." But what grieved him still more was to see sitting in the councils of the nation Frenchmen who were detractors and enemies of the national glory.

He urged the Directory to arrest the emigrants, to destroy the influence of foreigners, to recall the armies, to suppress the journals sold to England, such as the 'Quotidienne', the 'Memorial', and the 'The', which he accused of being more sanguinary than Marat ever was. In case of there being no means of putting a stop to assassinations and the influence of Louis XVIII., he offered to resign.

His resolution of passing the Alps with 25,000 men and marching by Lyons and Paris was known in the capital, and discussions arose respecting the consequences of this passage of another Rubicon. On the 17th of August 1797 Carnot wrote to him: "People attribute to you a thousand absurd projects. They cannot believe that a man who has performed so many great exploits can be content to live as a private citizen." This observation applied to Bonaparte's reiterated request to be permitted to retire from the service on account of the state of his health, which, he said, disabled him from mounting his horse, and to the need which he constantly urged of having two years' rest.

The General-in-Chief was justly of opinion that the tardiness of the negotiations and the difficulties which incessantly arose were founded on the expectation of an event which would change the government of France, and render the chances of peace more favourable to Austria. He still urgently recommended the arrest of the emigrants, the stopping of the presses of the royalist journals, which he said were sold to England and Austria, the suppression of the Clichy Club. This club was held at the residence of Gerard Desodieres, in the Rue de Clichy. Aubry, was one of its warmest partisans, and he was the avowed enemy of the revolutionary cause which Bonaparte advocated at this period. Aubry's conduct at this time, together with the part he had taken in provoking Bonaparte's dismissal in 1795, inspired the General with an implacable hatred of him.

Bonaparte despised the Directory, which he accused of weakness, indecision, pusillanimity, wasteful expenditure, of many errors, and perseverance in a system degrading to the national glory.[35]

He knew that the Clichy party demanded his dismissal and arrest. He was given to understand that Dumolard was one of the most decided against him, and that, finally, the royalist party was on the point of triumphing.

Before deciding for one party or the other Bonaparte first thought of himself. He did not imagine that he had yet achieved enough to venture on possessing himself of that power which certainly he might easily have obtained. He therefore contented himself with joining the party which was, for the moment, supported by public opinion. I know he was determined to march upon Paris with 25,000 men had affairs taken a turn unfavourable to the Republic, which he preferred to royalty. He cautiously formed his plan. To defend the Directory was,

35 The Directory merited those accusations. The following sketches of two of their official sittings present a singular contrast: "At the time that the Directory were first installed in the Luxembourg (27th October 1795)." says M. Baileul, "there was hardly a single article of furniture in it. In a small room, round a little broken table, one of the legs of which had given way from age, on which table they had deposited a quire of letter-paper, and a writing desk 'a calamet', which luckily they had had the precaution to bring with them from the Committee of Public safety, seated on four rush-bottomed chairs, in front of some logs of wood ill-lighted, the whole borrowed from the porter Dupont; who would believe that it was in this deplorable condition that the member's of the new Government, after having examined all the difficulties, nay, let me add, all the horrors of their situation, resolved to confront all obstacles, and that they would either deliver France from the abyss in which she was plunged or perish in the attempt? They drew up on a sheet of letter-paper the act by which they declared themselves constituted, and immediately forwarded it to the Legislative Bodies." And the Comte de La Vallette, writing to M. Cuvillier Fleury, says: "I saw our five kings, dressed in the robes of Francis I., his hat, his pantaloons, and his lace: the face of La Reveilliere looked like a cork upon two pins, with the black and greasy hair of Clodion. M. de Talleyrand, in pantaloons of the colour of wine dregs, sat in a folding chair at the feet of the Director Barras, in the Court of the Petit Luxembourg, and gravely presented to his sovereigns as ambassador from the Grand Duke of Tuscany, while the French were eating his master's dinner, from the soup to the cheese. At the right hand there were fifty musicians and singers of the Opera, Laine, Lays, Regnault, and the actresses, not all dead of old age, roaring a patriotic cantata to the music of Mehul. Facing them, on another elevation, there were two hundred young and beautiful women, with their arms and bosoms bare, all in ecstasy at the majesty of our Pentarchy and the happiness of the Republic. They also wore tight flesh-coloured pantaloons, with rings on their toes. That was a sight that never will be seen again. A fortnight after this magnificent fete, thousands of families wept over their banished fathers, forty-eight departments were deprived of their representatives, and forty editors of newspapers were forced to go and drink the waters of the Elbe, the Synamary or the Ohio! It would be a curious disquisition to seek to discover what really were at that time the Republic and Liberty."

he conceived, to defend his own future fortune; that is to say, it was protecting a power which appeared to have no other object than to keep a place for him until his return.

The parties which rose up in Paris produced a reaction in the army. The employment of the word 'Monsieur' had occasioned quarrels, and even bloodshed. General Augereau, in whose division these contests had taken place, published an order of the day, setting forth that every individual in his division who should use the word 'Monsieur', either verbally or in writing, under any pretence whatever, should be deprived of his rank, and declared incapable of serving in the Republican armies. This order was read at the head of each company.

Bonaparte viewed the establishment of peace as the close of his military career. Repose and inactivity were to him unbearable. He sought to take part in the civil affairs of the Republic, and was desirous of becoming one of the five Directors, convinced that, if he obtained that object, he would speedily stand single and alone. The fulfilment of this wish would have prevented the Egyptian expedition, and placed the imperial crown much sooner upon his head. Intrigues were carried on in Paris in his name, with the view of securing to him a legal dispensation on the score of age. He hoped, though he was but eight-and-twenty, to supersede one of the two Directors who were to go out of office.[36]

His brothers and their friends made great exertions for the success of the project, which, however, was not officially proposed, because it was too adverse to the prevailing notions of the day, and seemed too early a violation of the constitution of the year III., which, nevertheless, was violated in another way a few months after.

The members of the Directory were by no means anxious to have Bonaparte for their colleague. They dissembled, and so did he. Both parties were lavish of their mutual assurances of friendship, while they cordially hated each other. The Directory, however, appealed for the support of Bonaparte, which he granted; but his subsequent conduct clearly proves that the maintenance of the constitution of the year III. was a mere pretext. He indeed defended it meanwhile, because, by aiding the triumph of the opposite party, he could not hope to preserve the influence which he exercised over the Directory. I know well that, in case of the Clichy party gaining the ascendency, he was determined to cross the Alps with his army, and to assemble all the friends of the Republic at Lyons, thence to march upon Paris.

In the Memorial of St. Helena it is stated, in reference to the 18th Fructidor, "that the triumph of the majority of the councils was his desire and hope, we are inclined to believe from the following fact, viz., that at the crisis of the contest between the two factions a secret resolution was drawn up by three of the members of the Directory, asking him for three millions to support the attack on the councils, and that Napoleon, under various pretences, did not send the money, though he might easily have done so."

This is not very comprehensible. There was no secret resolution of the members who applied for the three millions. It was Bonaparte who offered the money, which, however, he did not send; it was he who despatched Augereau; and he who wished for the triumph of the Directorial majority. His memory served him badly at St. Helena, as will be seen from some correspondence which I shall presently submit to the reader.

36 The Directors had to be forty years of ago before they could be appointed.

It is very certain that he did offer the money to the Directory; that is to say, to three of its members.[37]

Bonaparte had so decidedly formed his resolution that on the 17th of July, wishing to make Augereau his confidant, he sent to Vicenza for him by an extraordinary courier.

Bonaparte adds that when Bottot, the confidential agent of Barras, came to Passeriano, after the 18th Fructidor, he declared to him that as soon as La Vallette should make him acquainted with the real state of things the money should be transmitted. The inaccuracy of these statements will be seen in the correspondence relative to the event. In thus distorting the truth Napoleon's only object could have been to proclaim his inclination for the principles he adopted and energetically supported from the year 1800, but which, previously to that period, he had with no less energy opposed.

He decidedly resolved to support the majority of the Directory, and to oppose the royalist faction; the latter, which was beginning to be important, would have been listened to had it offered power to him. About the end of July he sent his 'aide de camp' La Vallette to Paris. La Vallette was a man of good sense and education, pleasing manners, pliant temper, and moderate opinions. He was decidedly devoted to Bonaparte. With his instructions he received a private cipher to enable him to correspond with the General-in-Chief.

Augereau went, after La Vallette, on the 27th of July. Bonaparte officially wrote to the Directory that Augereau "had solicited leave to go to Paris on his own private business."

But the truth is, Augereau was sent expressly to second the revolution which was preparing against the Clichy party and the minority of the Directory.

Bonaparte made choice of Augereau because he knew his staunch republican principles, his boldness, and his deficiency in political talent. He thought him well calculated to aid a commotion, which his own presence with the army of Italy prevented him from directing in person; and besides, Augereau was not an ambitious rival who might turn events to his own advantage. Napoleon said, at St. Helena, that he sent the addresses of the army of Italy by Augereau because he was a decided supporter of the opinions of the day. That was the true reason for choosing him.

Bernadotte was subsequently despatched on the same errand. Bonaparte's pretence for sending him was, that he wished to transmit to the Directory four flags, which, out of the twenty-one taken at the battle of Rivoli, had been left, by mistake, at Peschiera. Bernadotte, however, did not take any great part in the affair. He was always prudent.

The crisis of the 18th Fructidor, which retarded for three years the extinction of the pentarchy, presents one of the most remarkable events of its short existence. It will be seen how the Directors extricated themselves from this difficulty. I subjoin the correspondence relating to this remarkable episode of our Revolution, cancelling only such portions of it as are irrelevant to the subject. It exhibits several variations from the accounts given by Napoleon at St. Helena to his noble companions in misfortune.

Augereau thus expressed himself on the 18th Fructidor (4th September 1797):—

> At length, General, my mission is accomplished, and the promises of the army of Italy are fulfilled. The fear of being anticipated has caused measures to be hurried. At

---

37 Barras, La Revelliere-Lepaux, and Rewbell, the three Directors who carried out the 'coup d'etat' of the 18th Fructidor against their colleagues Carnot and Bartholemy. (See Thiers' "French Revolution", (vol. v. pp. 114,139, and 163.)

midnight I despatched orders to all the troops to march towards the points specified. Before day all the bridges and principal places were planted with cannon. At daybreak the halls of the councils were surrounded, the guards of the councils were amicably mingled with our troops, and the members, of whom I send you a list, were arrested and conveyed to the Temple. The greater number have escaped, and are being pursued. Carnot has disappeared.'[38] Paris is tranquil, and every one is astounded at an event which promised to be awful, but which has passed over like a fete. The stout patriots of the faubourgs proclaim the safety of the Republic, and the black collars are put down. It now remains for the wise energy of the Directory and the patriots of the two councils to do the rest. The place of sitting is changed, and the first operations promise well. This event is a great step towards peace; which it is your task finally to secure to us.

On the 24th Fructidor (10th September 1797) Augereau writes:

My 'aide de camp', de Verine, will acquaint you with the events of the 18th. He is also to deliver to you some despatches from the Directory, where much uneasiness is felt at not hearing from you. No less uneasiness is experienced on seeing in Paris one of your 'aides de camp',—(La Vallette)—whose conduct excites the dissatisfaction and distrust of the patriots, towards whom he has behaved very ill. The news of General Clarke's recall will have reached you by this time, and I suspect has surprised you. Amongst the thousand and one motives which have determined the Government to take this step may be reckoned his correspondence with Carnot, which has been communicated to me, and in which he treated the generals of the army of Italy as brigands. Moreau has sent the Directory a letter which throws a new light on Pichegru's treason. Such baseness is hardly to be conceived. The Government perseveres in maintaining the salutary measures which it has adopted. I hope it will be in vain for the remnant of the factions to renew their plots. The patriots will continue united. Fresh troops having been summoned to Paris, and my presence at their head being considered indispensable by the Government, I shall not have the satisfaction of seeing you so soon as I hoped. This has determined me to send for my horses and carriages, which I left at Milan.

Bernadotte wrote to Bonaparte on the 24th Fructidor as follows:—

The arrested deputies are removed to Rochefort, where they will be embarked for the island of Madagascar. Paris is tranquil. The people at first heard of the arrest of the deputies with indifference. A feeling of curiosity soon drew them into the streets; enthusiasm followed, and cries of 'Vive la Republique', which had not been heard for a long time, now resounded in every street. The neighbouring departments have expressed their discontent. That of Allier has, it is said, protested; but it will cut a

38 In 1824 Louis XVIII. sent letters of nobility to those members of the two councils who were, as it was termed, 'fructidorized'. —Bourrienne

> fine figure. Eight thousand men are marching to the environs of Paris. Part is already within the precincts; under the orders of General Lemoine. The Government has it at present in its power to elevate public spirit; but everybody feels that it is necessary the Directory should be surrounded by tried and energetic Republicans. Unfortunately a host of men, without talent and resources, already suppose that what has taken place has been done only in order to advance their interests. Time is necessary to set all to rights. The armies have regained consistency. The soldiers of the interior are esteemed, or at least feared. The emigrants fly, and the non-juring priests conceal themselves. Nothing could have happened more fortunately to consolidate the R*epublic.*

Bonaparte wrote as follows, to the Directory on the 26th Fructidor:

> Herewith you will receive a proclamation to the army, relative to the events of the 18th. I have despatched the 45th demi-brigade, commanded by General Bon, to Lyons, together with fifty cavalry; also General Lannes, with the 20th light infantry and the 9th regiment of the line, to Marseilles. I have issued the enclosed proclamation in the southern departments. I am about to prepare a proclamation for the inhabitants of Lyons, as soon as I obtain some information of what may have passed there. If I find there is the least disturbance, I will march there with the utmost rapidity. Believe that there are here a hundred thousand men, who are alone sufficient to make the measures you have taken to place liberty on a solid basis be respected. What avails it that we gain victories if we are not respected in our country. In speaking of Paris, one may parody what Cassius said of Rome: "Of what use to call her queen on the banks of the Seine, when she is the slave of Pitt's *gold?"*

After the 18th Fructidor Augereau wished to have his reward for his share in the victory, and for the service which he had rendered. He wished to be a Director. He got, however, only the length of being a candidate; honour enough for one who had merely been an instrument on that day.

CHAPTER IX

1797

Bonaparte was delighted when he heard of the happy issue of the 18th Fructidor. Its result was the dissolution of the Legislative Body and the fall of the Clichyan party, which for some months had disturbed his tranquillity. The Clichyans had objected to Joseph Bonaparte's right to sit as deputy for Liamone in the Council of Five Hundred.[39]

His brother's victory removed the difficulty; but the General-in-Chief soon perceived that the ascendant party abused its power, and again compromised the safety of the Republic, by recommencing the Revolutionary Government. The Directors were alarmed at his discontent and offended by his censure. They conceived the singular idea of opposing to Bonaparte, Augereau, of whose blind zeal they had received many proofs. The Directory appointed Augereau commander of the army of Germany. Augereau, whose extreme vanity was notorious, believed himself in a situation to compete with Bonaparte. What he built his arrogance on was, that, with a numerous troop, he had arrested some unarmed representatives, and torn the epaulettes from the shoulders of the commandant of the guard of the councils. The Directory and he filled the headquarters at Passeriano with spies and intriguers.

Bonaparte, who was informed of everything that was going on, laughed at the Directory, and tendered his resignation, in order that he might be supplicated to continue in command.

The following post-Thermidorian letters will prove that the General's judgment on this point was correct.

On the 2d Vendemiaire, year VI. (23d September 1797), he wrote to Augereau, after having announced the arrival of his 'aide de camp' as follows:

> The whole army applauds the wisdom and vigour which you have displayed upon this important occasion, and participates in the success of the country with the enthusiasm and energy which characterise our soldiers. It is only to be hoped, however, that the Government will not be playing at see saw, and thus throw itself into the opposite party. Wisdom and moderate views alone can establish the happiness of the country on a sure foundation. As for myself, this is the most ardent wish of my heart. I beg that you will sometimes let me know what you are doing in Paris.

On the 4th Vendemiaire Bonaparte wrote a letter to the Directory in the following terms:

> The day before yesterday an officer arrived at the army from Paris. He reported that he left Paris on the 25th, when anxiety prevailed there as to the feelings with which

39 He was ambassador to Rome, and not a deputy at this time. When he became a member of the council, after his return from Rome, he experienced no opposition (Bourrienne et ses Erreurs, tome i. p. 240).

> I viewed the events of the 18th He was the bearer of a sort of circular from General Augereau to all the generals of division; and he brought a letter of credit from the Minister of War to the commissary-general, authorising him to draw as much money as he might require for his journey. It is evident from these circumstances that the Government is acting towards me in somewhat the same way in which Pichegru was dealt with after Vendemiaire (year IV.). I beg of you to receive my resignation, and appoint another to my place. No power on earth shall make me continue in the service after this shocking mark of ingratitude on the part of the Government, which I was very far from expecting. My health, which is considerably impaired, imperiously demands repose and tranquillity. The state of my mind, likewise, requires me to mingle again in the mass of citizens. Great power has for a longtime been confided to my hands. I have employed it on all occasions for the advantage of my country; so much the worse for those who put no faith in virtue, and may have suspected mine. My recompense is in my own conscience, and in the opinion of posterity. Now that the country is tranquil and free from the dangers which have menaced it, I can, without inconvenience, quit the post in which I have been placed. Be sure that if there were a moment of danger, I would be found in the foremost rank of the defenders of liberty and of the constitution of the year III.

The Directory, judging from the account which Bottot gave of his mission that he had not succeeded in entirely removing the suspicions of Bonaparte, wrote the following letter on the 30th Vendemiaire:

> The Directory has itself been troubled about the impression made on you by the letter to the paymaster-general, of which an 'aide de camp' was the bearer. The composition of this letter has very much astonished the Government, which never appointed nor recognised such an agent: it is at least an error of office. But it should not alter the opinion you ought otherwise to entertain of the manner in which the Directory thinks of and esteems you. It appears that the 18th Fructidor was misrepresented in the letters which were sent to the army of Italy. You did well to intercept them, and it may be right to transmit the most remarkable to the Minister of Police. —(What an ignoble task to propose to the conqueror of Italy.) In your observations on the too strong tendency of opinion towards military government, the Directory recognises an equally enlightened and ardent friend of the Republic. Nothing is wiser than the maxim, 'cedant arma togae', for the maintenance of republics. To show so much anxiety on so important a point is not one of the least glorious features in the life of a general placed at the head of a triumphant army.

The Directory had sent General Clarke[40] to treat for peace, as second plenipotentiary. Bonaparte has often told me he had no doubt from the time of his arrival that General

40 H. J. G. Clarke, afterwards Minister of War under Napoleon, 1807-1814, acid under the Bourbons in 1816, when he wasmade a Marshal of France. He was created Duc de Feltre in 1819.

Clarke was charged with a secret mission to act as a spy upon him, and even to arrest him if an opportunity offered for so doing without danger. That he had a suspicion of this kind is certain; but I must own that I was never by any means able to discover its grounds; for in all my intercourse since with Clarke he never put a single question to me, nor did I ever hear a word drop from his mouth, which savoured of such a character. If the fact be that he was a spy, he certainly played his part well. In all the parts of his correspondence which were intercepted there never was found the least confirmation of this suspicion. Be this as it may, Bonaparte could not endure him; he did not make him acquainted with what was going on, and his influence rendered this mission a mere nullity. The General-in-Chief concentrated all the business of the negotiation in his own closet; and, as to what was going on, Clarke continued a mere cipher until the 18th Fructidor, when he was recalled. Bonaparte made but little count of Clarke's talents. It is but justice, however, to say that he bore him no grudge for the conduct of which he suspected he was guilty in Italy. "I pardon him because I alone have the right to be offended."

He even had the generosity to make interest for an official situation for him. These amiable traits were not uncommon with Bonaparte. Bonaparte had to encounter so many disagreeable contrarieties, both in the negotiators for peace and the events at Paris, that he often displayed a good deal of irritation and disgust. This state of mind was increased by the recollection of the vexation his sister's marriage had caused him, and which was unfortunately revived by a letter he received from her at this juncture. His excitement was such that he threw it down with an expression of anger. It has been erroneously reported in several publications that "Bacciocchi espoused Marie-Anne-Eliza Bonaparte on the 5th of May 1797. The brother of the bride was at the time negotiating the preliminaries of peace with Austria." In fact, the preliminaries were signed in the month of April, and it was for the definitive peace we were negotiating in May. But the reader will find by the subjoined letter that Christine applied to her brother to stand godfather to her third child. Three children in three months would be rather quick work.

AJACCIO,
14th, Thermidor, year V. (1st August 1797).

GENERAL—Suffer me to write to you and call you by the name of brother. My first child was born at a time when you were much incensed against us. I trust she may soon caress you, and so make you forget the pain my marriage has occasioned you. My second child was still-born. Obliged to quit Paris by your order,[41] I miscarried in Germany. In a month's time I hope to present you with a nephew. A favourable time, and other circumstances, incline me to hope my next will be a boy, and I promise you I will make a soldier of him; but I wish him to bear your name, and that you should be his godfather. I trust you will not refuse your sister's request. Will you send, for this purpose, your power of attorney to Baciocchi, or to whomsoever you think fit? I shall expect with impatience your assent. Because we are poor let not that cause you to despise us; for, after all, you are our brother, mine are the only children that call you

41 Napoleon had written in August 1796 to Carnot, to request that Lucien might be ordered to quit Paris; see Iung, tome iii. p. 223.

uncle, and we all love you more than we do the favours of fortune. Perhaps I may one day succeed in convincing you of the love I bear you.

Your affectionate sister,

CHRISTINE BONAPARTE.[42]

P.S.—Do not fail to remember me to your wife, whom I strongly desire to be acquainted with. They told me at Paris I was very like her. If you recollect my features you can judge. C. B.

This letter is in the handwriting of Lucien Bonaparte.[43]

General Bonaparte had been near a month at Passeriano when he received the following autograph letter from the Emperor of Austria:

TO MONSIEUR LE GENERAL BONAPARTE, GENERAL-IN-CHIEF OF THE ARMY OF ITALY.

MONSIEUR LE GENERAL BONAPARTE—When I thought I had given my plenipotentiaries full powers to terminate the important negotiation with which they were charged, I learn, with as much pain as surprise, that in consequence of swerving continually from the stipulations of the preliminaries, the restoration of tranquillity, with the tidings of which I desire to gladden the hearts of my subjects, and which the half of Europe devoutly prays for, becomes day after day more uncertain. Faithful to the performance of my engagements, I am ready to execute what was agreed to at Leoben, and require from you but the reciprocal performance of so sacred a duty. This is what has already been declared in my name, and what I do not now hesitate myself to declare. If, perhaps, the execution of some of the preliminary articles be now impossible, in consequence of the events which have since occurred, and in which I had no part, it may be necessary to substitute others in their stead equally adapted to the interests and equally conformable to the dignity of the two nations. To such alone will I put my hand. A frank and sincere explanation, dictated by the same feelings which govern me, is the only way to lead to so salutary a result. In order to accelerate this result as far as in me lies, and to put an end at once to the state of uncertainty we

42 Madame Bacciocchi went by the name of Marianne at St. Cyr, of Christine while on her travels, and of Eliza under the Consulate.— Bourrienne.

43 Joseph Bonaparte in his Notes says, "It is false that Madame Bonaparte ever called herself Christine; it is false that she ever wrote the letter of which M. de Bourrienne here gives a copy." It will be observed that Bourrienne says it was written by her brother Lucien. This is an error. The letter is obviously from Christine Boyer, the wife of Lucien Bonaparte, whose marriage had given such displeasure to Napoleon. (See Erreurs, tome i. p. 240, and Iung's Lucien, tome i p. 161).

remain in, and which has already lasted too long, I have determined to despatch to the place of the present negotiations Comte de Cobentzel, a man who possesses my most unlimited confidence, and who is instructed as to my intentions and furnished with my most ample powers. I have authorised him to receive and accept every proposition tending to the reconciliation of the two parties which may be in conformity with the principles of equity and reciprocal fitness, and to conclude accordingly. After this fresh assurance of the spirit of conciliation which animates me, I doubt not you will perceive that peace lies in your own hands, and that on your determination will depend the happiness or misery of many thousand men. If I mistake as to the means I think best adapted to terminate the calamities which for along time have desolated Europe, I shall at least have the consolation of reflecting that I have done all that depended on me. With the consequences which may result I can never be reproached.

I have been particularly determined to the course I now take by the opinion I entertain of your upright character, and by the personal esteem I have conceived towards you, of which I am very happy, M. le General Bonaparte, to give you here an assurance.

(Signed) FRANCIS.

In fact, it was only on the arrival of the Comte de Cobentzel that the negotiations were seriously set on foot. Bonaparte had all along clearly perceived that Gallo and Meerweldt were not furnished with adequate powers. He saw also clearly enough that if the month of September were, to be trifled away in unsatisfactory negotiations, as the month which preceded it had been, it would be difficult in October to strike a blow at the house of Austria on the side of Carinthia. The Austrian Cabinet perceived with satisfaction the approach of the bad weather, and insisted more strongly on its ultimatum, which was the Adige, with Venice.

Before the 18th Fructidor the Emperor of Austria hoped that the movement which was preparing in Paris would operate badly for France and favourably to the European cause. The Austrian plenipotentiaries, in consequence, raised their pretensions, and sent notes and an ultimatum which gave the proceedings more an air of trifling than of serious negotiation. Bonaparte's original ideas, which I have under his hand, were as follows:

1. The Emperor to have Italy as far as the Adda.
2. The King of Sardinia as far as the Adda.
3. The Genoese Republic to have the boundary of Tortona as far as the Po (Tortona to be demolished), as also the imperial fiefs. (Coni to be ceded to France, or to be demolished.)
4. The Grand Duke of Tuscany to be restored.
5. The Duke of Parma to be restored.

CHAPTER X

1797

After the 18th Fructidor Bonaparte was more powerful, Austria less haughty and confident. Venice was the only point of real difficulty. Austria wanted the line of the Adige, with Venice, in exchange for Mayence, and the boundary of the Rhine until that river enters Holland. The Directory wished to have the latter boundary, and to add Mantua to the Italian Republic, without giving up all the line of the Adige and Venice. The difficulties were felt to be so irreconcilable that within about a month of the conclusion of peace the Directory wrote to General Bonaparte that a resumption of hostilities was preferable to the state of uncertainty which was agitating and ruining France. The Directory, therefore, declared that both the armies of the Rhine should take the field. It appears from the Fructidorian correspondence, which has been already given, that the majority of the Directory then looked upon a peace such as Bonaparte afterwards made as infamous.

But Bonaparte, from the moment the Venetian insurrection broke out, perceived that Venice might be used for the pacification. Bonaparte, who was convinced that, in order to bring matters to an issue, Venice and the territory beyond the Adige must fall beneath the Hapsburg sceptre, wrote to the Directory that he could not commence operations, advantageously, before the end of March, 1798; but that if the objections to giving Venice to the Emperor of Austria were persisted in, hostilities would certainly be resumed in the month of October, for the Emperor would not renounce Venice. In that case it would be necessary to be ready on the Rhine for an advance in Germany, as the army of Italy, if it could make head against the Archduke Charles, was not sufficiently strong for any operations on a grand scale. At this period the conclusion of peace was certainly very doubtful; it was even seriously considered in what form the rupture should be notified.

Towards the end of September Bottot, Barras' secretary, arrived at Passeriano. He was despatched by the Directory. Bonaparte immediately suspected he was a new spy, come on a secret mission, to watch him. He was therefore received and treated with coolness; but Bonaparte never had, as Sir Walter Scott asserts, the idea of ordering him to be shot. That writer is also in error when he says that Bottot was sent to Passeriano to reproach Bonaparte for failing to fulfil his promise of sending money to the Directory.

Bonaparte soon gave Bottot an opportunity of judging of the kind of spirit which prevailed at headquarters. He suddenly tendered his resignation, which he had already several times called upon the Directory to accept. He accused the Government, at table, in Bottot's presence, of horrible ingratitude. He recounted all his subjects of complaint, in loud and impassioned language, without any restraint, and before twenty or thirty persons.

Indignant at finding that his reiterated demands for the erasure of my name from the list of emigrants had been slighted, and that, in spite of his representations, conveyed to Paris by General Bernadotte, Louis Bonaparte, and others, I was still included in that fatal list, he apostrophised M. Bottot at dinner one day, before forty individuals, among whom were the diplomatists Gallo, Cobentzel, and Meerweldt. The conversation turned upon the Directory.

"Yes, truly," cried Bonaparte, in a loud voice, "I have good reason to complain; and, to pass from great to little things, look, I pray you, at Bourrienne's case. He possesses my most unbounded confidence. He alone is entrusted, under my orders, with all the details of the negotiation. This you well know; and yet your Directory will not strike him off the list. In a word it is not only an inconceivable, but an extremely stupid piece of business; for he has all my secrets; he knows my ultimatum, and could by a single word realize a handsome fortune, and laugh at your obstinacy. Ask M. de Gallo if this be not true."

Bottot wished to offer some excuse; but the general murmur which followed this singular outburst reduced him to silence.

The Marquis de Gallo had conversed with me but three days before, in the park of Passeriano, on the subject of my position with regard to France, of the determination expressed by the Directory not to erase my name, and of the risk I thereby ran. "We have no desire," continued he, "to renew the war; we wish sincerely for peace; but it must be an honourable one. The Republic of Venice presents a large territory for partition, which would be sufficient for both parties. The cessions at present proposed are not, however, satisfactory. We want to know Bonaparte's ultimatum; and I am authorised to offer an estate in Bohemia, with a title and residence, and an annual revenue of 90,000 florins."

I quickly interrupted M. de Gallo, and assured him that both my conscience and my duty obliged me to reject his proposal; and so put at once an end to the conversation.

I took care to let the General-in-Chief know this story, and he was not surprised at my reply. His conviction, however, was strong, from all that M. de Gallo had said, and more particularly from the offer he had made, that Austria was resolved to avoid war, and was anxious for peace.

After I had retired to rest M. Bottot came to my bedroom and asked me, with a feigned surprise, if it was true that my name was still on the list of emigrants. On my replying in the affirmative, he requested me to draw up a note on the subject. This I declined doing, telling him that twenty notes of the kind he required already existed; that I would take no further steps; and that I would henceforth await the decision in a state of perfect inaction.

General Bonaparte thought it quite inexplicable that the Directory should express dissatisfaction at the view he took of the events of the 18th Fructidor, as, without his aid, they would doubtless have been overcome. He wrote a despatch, in which he repeated that his health and his spirits were affected—that he had need of some years' repose—that he could no longer endure the fatigue of riding; but that the prosperity and liberty of his country would always command his warmest interests. In all this there was not a single word of truth. The Directory thought as much, and declined to accept his resignation in the most flattering terms.

Bottot proposed to him, on the part of the Directory, to revolutionise Italy. The General inquired whether the whole of Italy would be included in the plan. The revolutionary commission had, however, been entrusted to Bottot in so indefinite a way that he could only hesitate, and give a vague reply. Bonaparte wished for more precise orders. In the interval peace was concluded, and the idea of that perilous and extravagant undertaking was no longer agitated. Bottot, soon after his return to Paris, wrote a letter to General Bonaparte, in which he complained that the last moments he had passed at Passeriano had deeply afflicted his heart. He said that cruel suspicions had followed him even to the gates of the Directory. These cruel suspicions had, however, been dissipated by the sentiments of admiration and affection which he had found the Directory entertained for the person of Bonaparte.

These assurances, which were precisely what Bonaparte had expected, did not avail to lessen the contempt he entertained for the heads of the Government, nor to change his conviction of their envy and mistrust of himself. To their alleged affection he made no return. Bottot assured the hero of Italy of "the Republican docility" of the Directory, and touched upon the reproaches Bonaparte had thrown out against them, and upon his demands which had not been granted. He said:

"The three armies, of the North, of the Rhine, and of the Sambre-et-Meuse, are to form only one, the army of Germany.—Augereau? But you yourself sent him. The fault committed by the Directory is owing to yourself! Bernadotte?—he is gone to join you. Cacault?—he is recalled. Twelve thousand men for your army?—they are on their march. The treaty with Sardinia?—it is ratified. Bourrienne?—he is erased. The revolution of Italy?—it is adjourned. Advise the Directory, then: I repeat it, they have need of information, and it is to you they look for it."

The assertion regarding me was false. For six months Bonaparte demanded my erasure without being able to obtain it. I was not struck off the list until the 11th of November 1797.

Just before the close of the negotiation Bonaparte, disgusted at the opposition and difficulties with which he was surrounded, reiterated again and again the offer of his resignation, and his wish to have a successor appointed. What augmented his uneasiness was an idea he entertained that the Directory had penetrated his secret, and attributed his powerful concurrence on the 18th Fructidor to the true cause—his personal views of ambition. In spite of the hypocritical assurances of gratitude made to him in writing, and though the Directory knew that his services were indispensable, spies were employed to watch his movements, and to endeavour by means of the persons about him to discover his views. Some of the General's friends wrote to him from Paris, and for my part I never ceased repeating to him that the peace, the power of making which he had in his own hands, would render him far more popular than the renewal of hostilities undertaken with all the chances of success and reverse. The signing of the peace, according to his own ideas, and in opposition to those of the Directory, the way in which he just halted at Rastadt, and avoided returning to the Congress, and, finally, his resolution to expatriate himself with an army in order to attempt new enterprises, sprung more than is generally believed from the ruling idea that he was distrusted, and that his ruin was meditated. He often recalled to mind what La Vallette had written to him about his conversation with Lacuee; and all he saw and heard confirmed the impression he had received on this subject.

The early appearance of bad weather precipitated his determination. On the 13th of October, at daybreak, on opening my window, I perceived the mountains covered with snow. The previous night had been superb, and the autumn till then promised to be fine and late. I proceeded, as I always did, at seven o'clock in the morning, to the General's chamber. I woke him, and told him what I had seen. He feigned at first to disbelieve me, then leaped from his bed, ran to the window, and, convinced of the sudden change, he calmly said, "What! before the middle of October! What a country is this! Well, we must make peace!" While he hastily put on his clothes I read the journals to him, as was my daily custom. He paid but little attention to them.

Shutting himself up with me in his closet, he reviewed with the greatest care all the returns from the different corps of his army. "Here are," said he, "nearly 80,000 effective men. I feed, I pay them: but I can bring but 60,000 into the field on the day of battle. I shall gain it, but afterwards my force will be reduced 20,000 men—by killed, wounded, and prisoners.

Then how oppose all the Austrian forces that will march to the protection of Vienna? It would be a month before the armies of the Rhine could support me, if they should be able; and in a fortnight all the roads and passages will be covered deep with snow. It is settled—I will make peace. Venice shall pay for the expense of the war and the boundary of the Rhine: let the Directory and the lawyers say what they like."

He wrote to the Directory in the following words: "The summits of the hills are covered with snow; I cannot, on account of the stipulations agreed to for the recommencement of hostilities, begin before five-and-twenty days, and by that time we shall be overwhelmed with snow."

Fourteen years after, another early winter, in a more severe climate, was destined to have a fatal influence on his fortunes. Had he but then exercised equal foresight!

It is well known that, by the treaty of Campo-Formio, the two belligerent powers made peace at the expense of the Republic of Venice, which had nothing to do with the quarrel in the first instance, and which only interfered at a late period, probably against her own inclination, and impelled by the force of inevitable circumstances. But what has been the result of this great political spoliation? A portion of the Venetian territory was adjudged to the Cisalpine Republic; it is now in the possession of Austria.

Another considerable portion, and the capital itself, fell to the lot of Austria in compensation for the Belgic provinces and Lombard, which she ceded to France. Austria has now retaken Lombard, and the additions then made to it, and Belgium is in the possession of the House of Orange. France obtained Corfu and some of the Ionian isles; these now belong to England.[44]

Romulus never thought he was founding Rome for Goths and priests. Alexander did not foresee that his Egyptian city would belong to the Turks; nor did Constantine strip Rome for the benefit of Mahomet II. Why then fight for a few paltry villages?

Thus have we been gloriously conquering for Austria and England. An ancient State is overturned without noise, and its provinces, after being divided among different bordering States, are now all under the dominion of Austria. We do not possess a foot of ground in all the fine countries we conquered, and which served as compensations for the immense acquisitions of the House of Hapsburgh in Italy. Thus that house was aggrandised by a war which was to itself most disastrous. But Austria has often found other means of extending her dominion than military triumphs, as is recorded in the celebrated distich of Mathias Corvinus:

> "Bella gerunt alli, to felix Austria nube;
> Nam quae Mars allis, dat tibi regna Venus."
>
> ["*Glad Austria wins by Hymen's silken chain*
> *What other States by doubtful battle gain,*
> *And while fierce Mars enriches meaner lands,*
> *Receives possession from fair Venus' hands.*"]

The Directory was far from being satisfied with the treaty of Campo-Formio, and with difficulty resisted the temptation of not ratifying it. A fortnight before the signature the

44 Afterwards to be ceded by her to Greece. Belgium is free.

Directors wrote to General Bonaparte that they would not consent to give to the Emperor Venice, Frioul, Padua, and the 'terra firma' with the boundary of the Adige. "That," said they, "would not be to make peace, but to adjourn the war. We shall be regarded as the beaten party, independently of the disgrace of abandoning Venice, which Bonaparte himself thought so worthy of freedom. France ought not, and never will wish, to see Italy delivered up to Austria. The Directory would prefer the chances of a war to changing a single word of its ultimatum, which is already too favourable to Austria."

All this was said in vain. Bonaparte made no scruple of disregarding his instructions. It has been said that the Emperor of Austria made an offer of a very considerable sum of money, and even of a principality, to obtain favourable terms. I was never able to find the slightest ground for this report, which refers to a time when the smallest circumstance could not escape my notice. The character of Bonaparte stood too high for him to sacrifice his glory as a conqueror and peacemaker for even the greatest private advantage. This was so thoroughly known, and he was so profoundly esteemed by the Austrian plenipotentiaries, that I will venture to say none of them would have been capable of making the slightest overture to him of so debasing a proposition. Besides, it would have induced him to put an end to all intercourse with the plenipotentiaries. Perhaps what I have just stated of M. de Gallo will throw some light upon this odious accusation. But let us dismiss this story with the rest, and among them that of the porcelain tray, which was said to have been smashed and thrown at the head of M. de Cobentzel. I certainly know nothing of any such scene; our manners at Passeriano were not quite so bad!

The presents customary on such occasions were given, and the Emperor of Austria also took that opportunity to present to General Bonaparte six magnificent white horses.

Bonaparte returned to Milan by way of Gratz, Laybach, Thrust, Mestre, Verona, and Mantua.

At this period Napoleon was still swayed by the impulse of the age. He thought of nothing but representative governments. Often has he said to me, "I should like the era of representative governments to be dated from my time." His conduct in Italy and his proclamations ought to give, and in fact do give, weight to this account of his opinion. But there is no doubt that this idea was more connected with lofty views of ambition than a sincere desire for the benefit of the human race; for, at a later period, he adopted this phrase: "I should like to be the head of the most ancient of the dynasties of Europe." What a difference between Bonaparte, the author of the 'Souper de Beaucaire', the subduer of royalism at Toulon; the author of the remonstrance to Albitte and Salicetti, the fortunate conqueror of the 13th Vendemiaire, the instigator and supporter of the revolution of Fructidor, and the founder of the Republics of Italy, the fruits of his immortal victories,—and Bonaparte, First Consul in 1800, Consul for life in 1802, and, above all, Napoleon, Emperor of the French in 1804, and King of Italy in 1805!

CHAPTER XI

1797

The day of the 18th Fructidor had, without any doubt, mainly contributed to the conclusion of peace at Campo Formio. On the one hand, the Directory, hitherto not very pacifically inclined, after having effected a 'coup d'etat', at length saw the necessity of appeasing the discontented by giving peace to France. On the other hand, the Cabinet of Vienna, observing the complete failure of all the royalist plots in the interior, thought it high time to conclude with the French Republic a treaty which, notwithstanding all the defeats Austria had sustained, still left her a preponderating influence over Italy.

Besides, the campaign of Italy, so fertile in glorious achievements of arms, had not been productive of glory alone. Something of greater importance followed these conquests. Public affairs had assumed a somewhat unusual aspect, and a grand moral influence, the effect of victories and of peace, had begun to extend all over France. Republicanism was no longer so sanguinary and fierce as it had been some years before. Bonaparte, negotiating with princes and their ministers on a footing of equality, but still with all that superiority to which victory and his genius entitled him, gradually taught foreign courts to be familiar with Republican France, and the Republic to cease regarding all States governed by Kings as of necessity enemies.

In these circumstances the General-in-Chief's departure and his expected visit to Paris excited general attention. The feeble Directory was prepared to submit to the presence of the conqueror of Italy in the capital.

It was for the purpose of acting as head of the French legation at the Congress of Rastadt that Bonaparte quitted Milan on the 17th of November. But before his departure he sent to the Directory one of those monuments, the inscriptions on which may generally be considered as fabulous, but which, in this case, were nothing but the truth. This monument was the "flag of the Army of Italy," and to General Joubert was assigned the honourable duty of presenting it to the members of the Executive Government.

On one side of the flag were the words "To the Army of Italy, the grateful country." The other contained an enumeration of the battles fought and places taken, and presented, in the following inscriptions, a simple but striking abridgment of the history of the Italian campaign.

> 150,000 PRISONERS; 170 STANDARDS; 550 PIECES OF SIEGE ARTILLERY; 600 PIECES OF FIELD ARTILLERY; FIVE PONTOON EQUIPAGES; NINE 64-GUN SHIPS; TWELVE 32-GUN FRIGATES; 12 CORVETTES; 18 GALLEYS; ARMISTICE WITH THE KING OF SARDINIA; CONVENTION WITH GENOA; ARMISTICE WITH THE DUKE OF PARMA; ARMISTICE WITH THE KING OF NAPLES; ARMISTICE WITH THE POPE; PRELIMINARIES OF LEOBEN; CONVENTION OF MONTEBELLO WITH THE REPUBLIC OF GENOA; TREATY OF PEACE WITH THE EMPEROR OF GERMANY AT CAMPO-FORMIO.

LIBERTY GIVEN TO THE PEOPLE OF BOLOGNA, FERRARA, MODENA, MASSA-CARRARA, LA ROMAGNA, LOMBARD, BRESCIA, BERGAMO, MANTUA, CREMONA. PART OF THE VERONESE, CHIAVENA, BORMIO, THE VALTELINE, THE GENOESE, THE IMPERIAL FIEFS, THE PEOPLE OF THE DEPARTMENTS OF CORCYRA, OF THE AEGEAN SEA, AND OF ITHACA.

SENT TO PARIS ALL THE MASTERPIECES OF MICHAEL ANGELO, OF GVERCINO, OF TITIAN, OF PAUL VERONESE, OF CORREGGIO, OF ALBANA, OF THE CARRACCI, OF RAPHAEL, AND OF LEONARDO DA VINCI.

Thus were recapitulated on a flag, destined to decorate the Hall of the Public Sittings of the Directory, the military deeds of the campaign in Italy, its political results, and the conquest of the monuments of art.

Most of the Italian cities looked upon their conqueror as a liberator—such was the magic of the word liberty, which resounded from the Alps to the Apennines. On his way to Mantua the General took up his residence in the palace of the ancient dukes. Bonaparte promised the authorities of Mantua that their department should be one of the most extensive; impressed on them the necessity of promptly organising a local militia, and of putting in execution the plans of Mari, the mathematician, for the navigation of the Mincio from Mantua to Peschiera.

He stopped two days at Mantua, and the morrow of his arrival was devoted to the celebration of a military funeral solemnity, in honour of General Hoche, who had just died. His next object was to hasten the execution of the monument which was erecting to the memory of Virgil. Thus, in one day, he paid honour to France and Italy, to modern and to ancient glory, to the laurels of war and to the laurels of poetry.

A person who saw Bonaparte on this occasion for the first time thus described him in a letter he wrote to Paris:—"With lively interest and extreme attention I have observed this extraordinary man, who has performed such great deeds, and about whom there is something which seems to indicate that his career is not yet terminated. I found him very like his portraits—little, thin, pale, with an air of fatigue, but not of ill-health, as has been reported of him. He appears to me to listen with more abstraction than interest, and that he was more occupied with what he was thinking of than with what was said to him. There is great intelligence in his countenance, along with which may be marked an air of habitual meditation, which reveals nothing of what is passing within. In that thinking head, in that bold mind, it is impossible not to believe that some daring designs are engendering which will have their influence an the destinies of Europe."

From the last phrase, in particular, of this letter, one might suspect that it was written after Bonaparte had made his name feared throughout Europe; but it really appeared in a journal in the month of December 1797, a little before his arrival in Paris.

There exists a sort of analogy between celebrated men and celebrated places; it was not, therefore, an uninteresting spectacle to see Bonaparte surveying the field of Morat, where, in 1476, Charles the Bold, Duke of Burgundy, daring like himself, fell with his powerful army under the effects of Helvetian valour. Bonaparte slept during the night at Maudon, where, as in every place through which he passed, the greatest honours were paid him. In the morning, his carriage having broken down, we continued our journey an foot, accompanied only by some officers and an escort of dragoons of the country. Bonaparte stopped near the Ossuary, and desired to be shown the spot where the battle of Morat was fought. A plain in front of the chapel was pointed out to him. An officer who had served in France was present, and explained to him how the Swiss, descending from the neighbouring mountains, were enabled, under cover of a wood, to turn the Burgundian army and put it to the rout. "What was the force of that army?" asked Bonaparte.—"Sixty thousand men."—"Sixty thousand men!" he exclaimed: "they ought to have completely covered these mountains!"—"The French fight better now," said Lannes, who was one of the officers of his suite. "At that time," observed Bonaparte, interrupting him, "the Burgundians were not Frenchmen."

Bonaparte's journey through Switzerland was not without utility; and his presence served to calm more than one inquietude. He proceeded on his journey to Rastadt by Aix in Savoy, Berne, and Bale. On arriving at Berne during night we passed through a double file of well-lighted equipages, filled with beautiful women, all of whom raised the cry of "Long live, Bonaparte!—long live the Pacificator!" To have a proper idea of this genuine enthusiasm it is necessary to have seen it.

The position in society to which his services had raised him rendered it unfit to address him in the second person singular and the familiar manner sometimes used by his old schoolfellows of Brienne. I thought, this very natural.

M. de Cominges, one of those who went with him to the military school at Paris, and who had emigrated, was at Bale. Having learned our arrival, he presented himself without ceremony, with great indecorum, and with a complete disregard of the respect due to a man who had rendered himself so illustrious. General Bonaparte, offended at this behaviour, refused to receive him again, and expressed himself to me with much warmth on the occasion of this visit. All my efforts to remove his displeasure were unavailing, this impression always continued, and he never did for M. de Cominges what his means and the old ties of boyhood might well have warranted.

On arriving at Rastadt[45] Bonaparte found a letter from the Directory summoning him to Paris. He eagerly obeyed this invitation, which drew him from a place where he could act only an insignificant part, and which he had determined to leave soon, never again to return. Some time after his arrival in Paris, on the ground that his presence was necessary for the execution of different orders, and the general despatch of business, he required that authority should be given to a part of his household, which he had left at Rastadt, to return.

How could it ever be said that the Directory "kept General Bonaparte away from the great interests which were under discussion at Rastadt"? Quite the contrary! The Directory would have been delighted to see him return there, as they would then have been relieved from his presence in Paris; but nothing was so disagreeable to Bonaparte as long and seemingly interminable negotiations. Such tedious work did not suit his character, and he had been sufficiently disgusted with similar proceedings at Campo-Formio.

On our arrival at Rastadt I soon found that General Bonaparte was determined to stay there only a short time. I therefore expressed to him my decided desire to remain in Germany. I was then ignorant that my erasure from the emigrant list had been ordered on the 11th of November, as the decree did not reach the commissary of the Executive Directory at Auxerre until the 17th of November, the day of our departure from Milan.

45 The conference for the formal peace with the Empire of Germany was held there. The peace of Leoben was only one made with Austria.

The silly pretext of difficulties by which my erasure, notwithstanding the reiterated solicitations of the victorious General, was so long delayed made me apprehensive of a renewal, under a weak and jealous pentarchy, of the horrible scenes of 1796. Bonaparte said to me, in atone of indignation, "Come, pass the Rhine; they will not dare to seize you while near me. I answer for your safety." On reaching Paris I found that my erasure had taken place. It was at this period only that General Bonaparte's applications in my favour were tardily crowned with success. Sotin, the Minister of General Police, notified the fact to Bonaparte; but his letter gave a reason for my erasure very different from that stated in the decree. The Minister said that the Government did not wish to leave among the names of traitors to their country the name of a citizen who was attached to the person of the conqueror of Italy; while the decree itself stated as the motive for removing my name from the list that I never had emigrated.

At St. Helena it seems Bonaparte said that he did not return from Italy with more than 300,000 francs; but I assert that he had at that time in his possession something more than 3,000,000.[46]

How could he with 300,000 francs have been able to provide for the extensive repairs, the embellishment, and the furnishing of his house in the Rue Chantereine? How could he have supported the establishment he did with only 15,000 francs of income and the emoluments of his rank? The excursion which he made along the coast, of which I have yet to speak, of itself cost near 12,000 francs in gold, which he transferred to me to defray the expense of the journey; and I do not think that this sum was ever repaid him. Besides, what did it signify, for any object he might have in disguising his fortune, whether he brought 3,000,000 or 300,000 francs with him from Italy? No one will accuse him of peculation. He was an inflexible administrator. He was always irritated at the discovery of fraud, and pursued those guilty of it with all the vigour of his character. He wished to be independent, which he well knew that no one could be without fortune. He has often said to me, "I am no Capuchin, not I." But after having been allowed only 300,000 francs on his arrival from the rich Italy, where fortune never abandoned him, it has been printed that he had 20,000,000 (some have even doubled the amount) on his return from Egypt, which is a very poor country, where money is scarce, and where reverses followed close upon his victories. All these reports are false. What he brought from Italy has just been stated, and it will be seen when we come to Egypt what treasure he carried away from the country of the Pharaohs.

Bonaparte's brothers, desirous of obtaining complete dominion over his mind, strenuously endeavoured to lessen the influence which Josephine possessed from the love of her husband. They tried to excite his jealousy, and took advantage of her stay at Milan after our departure, which had been authorised by Bonaparte himself. My intimacy with both the husband and the wife fortunately afforded me an opportunity of averting or lessening a good deal of mischief. If Josephine still lived she would allow me this merit. I never took part against her but once, and that unwillingly. It was on the subject of the marriage of her daughter Hortense. Josephine had never as yet spoken to me on the subject. Bonaparte wished to give his stepdaughter to Duroc, and his brothers were eager to promote the marriage, because they wished to separate Josephine from Hortense, for whom Bonaparte felt the tenderest affection. Josephine, on the other hand, wished Hortense to marry Louis Bonaparte. Her

46 Joseph says that Napoleon, when he exiled for Egypt, left with him all his fortune, and that it was much nearer 300,000 francs than 3,000,000. (See Erreurs, tome i. pp. 243, 259)

motives, as may easily be divined, were to, gain support in a family where she experienced nothing but enmity, and she carried her point.[47]

On his arrival from Rastadt the most magnificent preparations were made at the Luxembourg for the reception of Bonaparte. The grand court of the Palace was elegantly ornamented; and at its farther end, close to the Palace, a large amphitheatre was erected for the accommodation of official persons. Curiosity, as on all like occasions, attracted multitudes, and the court was filled. Opposite to the principal vestibule stood the altar of the country, surrounded by the statues of Liberty, Equality, and Peace. When Bonaparte entered every head was uncovered. The windows were full of young and beautiful females. But notwithstanding this great preparation an icy coldness characterized the ceremony. Every one seemed to be present only for the purpose of beholding a sight, and curiosity was the prevailing expression rather than joy or gratitude. It is but right to say, however, that an unfortunate event contributed to the general indifference. The right wing of the Palace was not occupied, but great preparations had been making there, and an officer had been directed to prevent anyone from ascending. One of the clerks of the Directory, however, contrived to get upon the scaffolding, but had scarcely placed his foot on the first plank when it tilted up, and the imprudent man fell the whole height into the court. This accident created a general stupor. Ladies fainted, and the windows were nearly deserted.

However, the Directory displayed all the Republican splendour of which they were so prodigal on similar occasions. Speeches were far from being scarce. Talleyrand, who was then Minister for Foreign Affairs, on introducing Bonaparte to the Directory, made a long oration, in the course of which he hinted that the personal greatness of the General ought not to excite uneasiness, even in a rising Republic. "Far from apprehending anything from his ambition, I believe that we shall one day be obliged to solicit him to tear himself from the pleasures of studious retirement. All France will be free, but perhaps he never will; such is his destiny."

Talleyrand was listened to with impatience, so anxious was every one to hear Bonaparte. The conqueror of Italy then rose, and pronounced with a modest air, but in a firm voice, a short address of congratulation on the improved position of the nation.

47 Previous to her marriage with Louis, Hortense cherished an attachment for Duroc, who was at that time a handsome man about thirty, and a great favourite of Bonaparte. However, the indifference with which Duroc regarded the marriage of Louis Bonaparte sufficiently proves that the regard with which he had inspired Hortense was not very ardently returned. It is certain that Duroc might have become the husband of Mademoiselle de Beauharnais had he been willing to accede to the conditions on which the First Consul offered him his step-daughter's hand. But Duroc looked forward to something better, and his ordinary prudence forsook him at a moment when he might easily have beheld a perspective calculated to gratify even a more towering ambition than his. He declined the proposed marriage; and the union of Hortense and Louis, which Madame Bonaparte, to conciliate the favour of her brothers-in-law, had endeavoured to bring about, was immediately determined on (Memoires de Constant). In allusion to the alleged unfriendly feeling of Napoleon's brothers towards Josephine, the following observation occurs in Joseph Bonaparte's Notes on Bourrienne: "None of Napoleon's brothers," he says, "were near him from the time of his departure for Italy except Louis who cannot be suspected of having intrigued against Josephine, whose daughter he married. These calumnies are without foundation" (Erreurs, tome i. p. 244)

Barras, at that time President of the Directory, replied to Bonaparte with so much prolixity as to weary everyone; and as soon as he had finished speaking he threw himself into the arms of the General, who was not much pleased with such affected displays, and gave him what was then called the fraternal embrace. The other members of the Directory, following the example of the President, surrounded Bonaparte and pressed him in their arms; each acted, to the best of his ability, his part in the sentimental comedy.

Chenier composed for this occasion a hymn, which Mehul set to music. A few days after an opera was produced, bearing the title of the 'Fall of Carthage', which was meant as an allusion to the anticipated exploits of the conqueror of Italy, recently appointed to the command of the "Army of England." The poets were all employed in praising him; and Lebrun, with but little of the Pindaric fire in his soul, composed the following distich, which certainly is not worth much:

"Heros, cher a la paix, aux arts, a la victoire—
Il conquit en deux ans mille siecles de gloire."

The two councils were not disposed to be behind the Directory in the manifestation of joy. A few days after they gave a banquet to the General in the gallery of the Louvre, which had recently been enriched by the masterpieces of painting conquered in Italy.

At this time Bonaparte displayed great modesty in all his transactions in Paris. The administrators of the department of the Seine having sent a deputation to him to inquire what hour and day he would allow them to wait on him, he carried himself his answer to the department, accompanied by General Berthier. It was also remarked that the judge of the peace of the arrondissement where the General lived having called on him on the 6th of December, the evening of his arrival, he returned the visit next morning. These attentions, trifling as they may appear, were not without their effect on the minds of the Parisians.

In consequence of General Bonaparte's victories, the peace he had effected, and the brilliant reception of which he had been the object, the business of Vendemiaire was in some measure forgotten. Every one was eager to get a sight of the young hero whose career had commenced with so much 'eclat'. He lived very retiredly, yet went often to the theatre. He desired me, one day, to go and request the representation of two of the best pieces of the time, in which Elleviou, Mesdames St. Aubin, Phillis, and other distinguished performers played. His message was, that he only wished these two pieces on the same night, if that were possible. The manager told me that nothing that the conqueror of Italy wished for was impossible, for he had long ago erased that word from the dictionary. Bonaparte laughed heartily at the manager's answer. When we went to the theatre he seated himself, as usual, in the back of the box, behind Madame Bonaparte, making me sit by her side. The pit and boxes, however, soon found out that he was in the house, and loudly called for him. Several times an earnest desire to see him was manifested, but all in vain, for he never showed himself.

Some days after, being at the Theatre des Arts, at the second representation of 'Horatius Cocles', although he was sitting at the back of a box in the second tier, the audience discovered that he was in the house. Immediately acclamations arose from all quarters; but he kept himself concealed as much as possible, and said to a person in the next box, "Had I known that the boxes were so exposed, I should not have come."

During Bonaparte's stay at Paris a woman sent a messenger to warn him that his life would be attempted, and that poison was to be employed for that purpose. Bonaparte had the bearer of this information arrested, who went, accompanied by the judge of the peace, to the woman's house, where she was found extended on the floor, and bathed in her blood. The men whose plot she had overheard, having discovered that she had revealed their secret, murdered her. The poor woman was dreadfully mangled: her throat was cut; and, not satisfied with that, the assassins had also hacked her body with sharp instruments.

On the night of the 10th of Nivôse the Rue Chantereine, in which Bonaparte had a small house (No. 6), received, in pursuance of a decree of the department, the name of Rue de la Victoire. The cries of "Vive Bonaparte!" and the incense prodigally offered up to him, did not however seduce him from his retired habits. Lately the conqueror and ruler of Italy, and now under men for whom he had no respect, and who saw in him a formidable rival, he said to me one day, "The people of Paris do not remember anything. Were I to remain here long, doing nothing, I should be lost. In this great Babylon one reputation displaces another. Let me be seen but three times at the theatre and I shall no longer excite attention; so I shall go there but seldom." When he went he occupied a box shaded with curtains. The manager of the opera wished to get up a special performance in his honour; but he declined the offer. When I observed that it must be agreeable to him to see his fellow-citizens so eagerly running after him, he replied, "Bah! the people would crowd as fast to see me if I were going to the scaffold."[48]

On the 28th of December Bonaparte was named a member of the Institute, in the class of the Sciences and arts.[49] He showed a deep sense of this honour, and wrote the following letter to Camus; the president of the class:

> CITIZEN PRESIDENT—The suffrage of the distinguished men who compose the institute confers a high honour on me. I feel well assured that, before I can be their equal, I must long be their scholar. If there were any way more expressive than another of making known my esteem for you, I should be glad to employ it. True conquests—the only ones which leave no regret behind them—are those which are made over ignorance. The most honourable, as well as the most useful, occupation for nations is the contributing to the extension of human knowledge. The true power of the French Republic should henceforth be made to consist in not allowing a single new idea to exist without making it part of its property.
>
> BONAPARTE.

The General now renewed, though unsuccessfully, the attempt he had made before the 18th Fructidor to obtain a dispensation of the age necessary for becoming a Director. Perceiving that the time was not yet favourable for such a purpose, he said to me, on the 29th of January 1798, "Bourrienne, I do not wish to remain here; there is nothing to do. They are

48 A similar remark made to William III. on his lending at Brixham elicited the comment, "Like the Jews, who cried one day 'Hosanna!' and the next 'Crucify Him! crucify Him!'"

49 Napoleon seems to have really considered this nomination as a great honour. He was fond of using the title in his proclamations; and to the last the allowance attached to the appointment figured in the Imperial accounts. He replaced Carnot, the exiled Director.

unwilling to listen to anything. I see that if I linger here, I shall soon lose myself. Everything wears out here; my glory has already disappeared. This little Europe does not supply enough of it for me. I must seek it in the East, the fountain of glory. However, I wish first to make a tour along the coast, to ascertain by my own observation what may be attempted. I will take you, Lannes, and Sulkowsky, with me. If the success of a descent on England appear doubtful, as I suspect it will, the army of England shall become the army of the East, and I will go to Egypt."

This and other conversations give a correct insight into his character. He always considered war and conquest as the most noble and inexhaustible source of that glory which was the constant object of his desire. He revolted at the idea of languishing in idleness at Paris, while fresh laurels were growing for him in distant climes. His imagination inscribed, in anticipation, his name on those gigantic monuments which alone, perhaps, of all the creations of man, have the character of eternity. Already proclaimed the most illustrious of living generals, he sought to efface the rival names of antiquity by his own. If Caesar fought fifty battles, he longed to fight a hundred—if Alexander left Macedon to penetrate to the Temple of Ammon, he wished to leave Paris to travel to the Cataracts of the Nile. While he was thus to run a race with fame, events would, in his opinion, so proceed in France as to render his return necessary and opportune. His place would be ready for him, and he should not come to claim it a forgotten or unknown man.

CHAPTER XII

1798

Bonaparte left Paris for the north on the 10th of February 1798—but he received no order, though I have seen it everywhere so stated, to go there—"for the purpose of preparing the operations connected with the intended invasion of England." He occupied himself with no such business, for which a few days certainly would not have been sufficient. His journey to the coast was nothing but a rapid excursion, and its sole object was to enable him to form an opinion on the main point of the question. Neither did he remain absent several weeks, for the journey occupied only one. There were four of us in his carriage—himself, Lannes, Sulkowsky, and I. Moustache was our courier. Bonaparte was not a little surprised on reading, in the 'Moniteur' of the 10th February, an article giving greater importance to his little excursion than it deserved.

> "General Bonaparte," said the 'Moniteur', "has departed for Dunkirk with some naval and engineer officers. They have gone to visit the coasts and prepare the preliminary operations for the descent (upon England). It may be stated that he will not return to Rastadt, and that the close of the session of the Congress there is approaching."

Now for the facts. Bonaparte visited Etaples, Ambleteuse, Boulogne, Calais, Dunkirk, Furnes, Niewport, Ostend, and the Isle of Walcheren. He collected at the different ports all the necessary information with that intelligence and tact for which he was so eminently distinguished. He questioned the sailors, smugglers, and fishermen, and listened attentively to the answers he received.

We returned to Paris by Antwerp, Brussels, Lille, and St. Quentin. The object of our journey was accomplished when we reached the first of these towns. "Well, General," said I, "what think you of our journey? Are you satisfied? For my part, I confess I entertain no great hopes from anything I have seen and heard." Bonaparte immediately answered, "It is too great a chance. I will not hazard it. I would not thus sport with the fate of my beloved France." On hearing this I already fancied myself in Cairo!

On his return to Paris Bonaparte lost no time in setting on foot the military and scientific preparations for the projected expedition to the banks of the Nile, respecting which such incorrect statements have appeared. It had long occupied his thoughts, as the following facts will prove.

In the month of August 1797 he wrote "that the time was not far distant when we should see that, to destroy the power of England effectually, it would be necessary to attack Egypt." In the same month he wrote to Talleyrand, who had just succeeded Charles de Lacroix as Minister of Foreign Affairs, "that it would be necessary to attack Egypt, which did not belong to the Grand Signior." Talleyrand replied, "that his ideas respecting Egypt were certainly grand, and that their utility could not fail to be fully appreciated." He concluded by saying he would write to him at length on the subject.

History will speak as favourably of M. de Talleyrand as his contemporaries have spoken ill of him. When a statesman, throughout a great, long, and difficult career, makes and preserves a number of faithful friends, and provokes but few enemies, it must be acknowledged that his character is honourable and his talent profound, and that his political conduct has been wise and moderate. It is impossible to know M. de Talleyrand without admiring him. All who have that advantage, no doubt, judge him as I do.

In the month of November of the same year Bonaparte sent Poussielgue, under the pretence of inspecting the ports of the Levant, to give the finishing stroke to the meditated expedition against Malta.

General Desaix, whom Bonaparte had made the confidant of all his plans at their interview in Italy after the preliminaries of Leoben, wrote to him from Affenbourg, on his return to Germany, that he regarded the fleet of Corfu with great interest. "If ever," said he, "it should be engaged in the grand enterprises of which I have heard you speak, do not, I beseech you, forget me." Bonaparte was far from forgetting him.

The Directory at first disapproved of the expedition against Malta, which Bonaparte had proposed long before the treaty of Campo-Formio was signed. The expedition was decided to be impossible, for Malta had observed strict neutrality, and had on several occasions even assisted our ships and seamen. Thus we had no pretext for going to war with her. It was said, too, that the legislative body would certainly not look with a favourable eye on such a measure. This opinion, which, however, did not last long, vexed Bonaparte. It was one of the disappointments which made him give a rough welcome to Bottot, Barras' agent, at the commencement of October 1797.

In the course of an animated conversation he said to Bottot, shrugging his shoulders, "Mon Dieu! Malta is for sale!" Sometime after he himself was told that "great importance was attached to the acquisition of Malta, and that he must not suffer it to escape." At the latter end of September 1797 Talleyrand, then Minister of Foreign Affairs, wrote to him that the Directory authorized him to give the necessary orders to Admiral Brueys for taking Malta. He sent Bonaparte some letters for the island, because Bonaparte had said it was necessary to prepare the public mind for the event.

Bonaparte exerted himself night and day in the execution of his projects. I never saw him so active. He made himself acquainted with the abilities of the respective generals, and the force of all the army corps. Orders and instructions succeeded each other with extraordinary rapidity. If he wanted an order of the Directory he ran to the Luxembourg to get it signed by one of the Directors. Merlin de Douai was generally the person who did him this service, for he was the most constant at his post. Lagarde, the Secretary-General, did not countersign any document relative to this expedition, Bonaparte not wishing him to be informed of the business. He transmitted to Toulon the money taken at Berne, which the Directory had placed at his disposal. It amounted to something above 3,000,000 francs. In those times of disorder and negligence the finances were very badly managed. The revenues were anticipated and squandered away, so that the treasury never possessed so large a sum as that just mentioned.

It was determined that Bonaparte should undertake an expedition of an unusual character to the East. I must confess that two things cheered me in this very painful interval; my friendship and admiration for the talents of the conqueror of Italy, and the pleasing hope of traversing those ancient regions, the historical and religious accounts of which had engaged the attention of my youth.

It was at Passeriano that, seeing the approaching termination of his labours in Europe, he first began to turn serious attention to the East. During his long strolls in the evening in the magnificent park there he delighted to converse about the celebrated events of that part of the world, and the many famous empires it once possessed. He used to say, "Europe is a mole-hill. There have never been great empires and revolutions except in the East, where there are 600,000,000 men." He considered that part of the world as the cradle of all religious, of all metaphysical extravagances. This subject was no less interesting than inexhaustible, and he daily introduced it when conversing with the generals with whom he was intimate, with Monge, and with me.

Monge entirely concurred in the General-in-Chief's opinions on this point; and his scientific ardour was increased by Bonaparte's enthusiasm. In short, all were unanimously of one opinion. The Directory had no share in renewing the project of this memorable expedition, the result of which did not correspond with the grand views in which it had been conceived. Neither had the Directory any positive control over Bonaparte's departure or return. It was merely the passive instrument of the General's wishes, which it converted into decrees, as the law required. He was no more ordered to undertake the conquest of Egypt than he was instructed as to the plan of its execution. Bonaparte organised the army of the East, raised money, and collected ships; and it was he who conceived the happy idea of joining to the expedition men distinguished in science and art, and whose labours have made known, in its present and past state, a country, the very name of which is never pronounced without exciting grand recollections.

Bonaparte's orders flew like lightning from Toulon to Civita Vecchia. With admirable precision he appointed some forces to assemble before Malta, and others before Alexandria. He dictated all these orders to me in his Cabinet.

In the position in which France stood with respect to Europe, after the treaty of Campo-Formio, the Directory, far from pressing or even facilitating this expedition, ought to have opposed it. A victory on the Adige would have been far better for France than one on the Nile. From all I saw, I am of opinion that the wish to get rid of an ambitious and rising man, whose popularity excited envy, triumphed over the evident danger of removing, for an indefinite period, an excellent army, and the possible loss of the French fleet. As to Bonaparte, he was well assured that nothing remained for him but to choose between that hazardous enterprise and his certain ruin. Egypt was, he thought, the right place to maintain his reputation, and to add fresh glory to his name.

On the 12th of April 1798 he was appointed General-in-Chief of the army of the East.

It was about this time that Marmont was married to Mademoiselle Perregaux; and Bonaparte's aide de camp, La Valletta, to Mademoiselle Beauharnais.[50]

Shortly before our departure I asked Bonaparte how long he intended to remain in Egypt. He replied, "A few months, or six years: all depends on circumstances. I will colonise the country. I will bring them artists and artisans of every description; women, actors, etc. We are but nine-and-twenty now, and we shall then be five-and-thirty. That is not an old age. Those six years will enable me, if all goes well, to get to India. Give out that you are going to Brest. Say so even to your family." I obeyed, to prove my discretion and real attachment to him.

50 Sir Walter Scott informs us that Josephine, when she became Empress, brought about the marriage between her niece and La Vallette. This is another fictitious incident of his historical romance.—Bourrienne.

Bonaparte wished to form a camp library of cabinet editions, and he gave me a list of the books which I was to purchase. This list is in his own writing, and is as follows:

CAMP LIBRARY

1. ARTS AND SCIENCE.—Fontenelle's Worlds, 1 vol. Letters to a German Princess, 2 vols. Courses of the Normal School, 6 vols. The Artillery Assistant, 1 vol. Treatise on Fortifications, 3 vols. Treatise on Fireworks, 1 vol.
2. GEOGRAPHY AND TRAVELS.—Barclay's Geography, 12 vols. Cook's Voyages, 3 vols. La Harpe's Travels, 24 vols.
3. HISTORY.—Plutarch, 12 vols. Turenne, 2 vols. Condé, 4 vols. Villars, 4 vols. Luxembourg, 2 vols. Duguesclin, 2 vols. Saxe, 3 vols. Memoirs of the Marshals of France, 20 vols. President Hainault, 4 vols. Chronology, 2 vols. Marlborough, 4 vols. Prince Eugène, 6 vols. Philosophical History of India, 12 vols. Germany, 2 vols. Charles XII., 1 vol. Essay on the Manners of Nations, 6 vols. Peter the Great, 1 vol. Polybius, 6 vols. Justin, 2 vols. Arrian, 3 vols. Tacitus, 2 vols. Titus Livy, Thucydides, 2 vols. Vertot, 4 vols. Denina, 8 vols. Frederick II, 8 vols.
4. POETRY.—Osaian, 1 vol. Tasso, 6 vols. Ariosto, 6 vols. Homer, 6 vols. Virgil, 4 vols. The Henriade, 1 vol. Telemachus, 2 vols. Les Jardin, 1 vol. The Chefs-d'Oeuvre of the French Theatre, 20 vols. Select Light Poetry, 10 vols. La Fontaine.
5. ROMANCE.—Voltaire, 4 vols. Heloise, 4 vols. Werther, 1 vol. Marmontel, 4 vols. English Novels, 40 vols. Le Sage, 10 vols. Prevost, 10 vols.
6. POLITICS AND MORALS.—The Old Testament. The New Testament. The Koran. The Vedan. Mythology. Montesquieu. The Esprit des Lois.

It will be observed that he classed the books of the religious creeds of nations under the head of "politics." The autograph copy of the above list contains some of those orthographical blunders which Bonaparte so frequently committed. Whether these blunders are attributable to the limited course of instruction he received at Brienne, to his hasty writing, the rapid flow of his ideas, or the little importance he attached to that indispensable condition of polite education, I know not. Knowing so well as he did the authors and generals whose names appear in the above list, it is curious that he should have written Ducecling for Duguesclin, and Ocean for Ossian. The latter mistake would have puzzled me not a little had I not known his predilection for the Caledonian bard.

Before his departure Bonaparte laid in a considerable stock of Burgundy. It was supplied by a man named James, of Dijon. I may observe that on this occasion we had an opportunity of ascertaining that good Burgundy, well racked off, and in casks hermetically sealed, does not lose its quality on a sea voyage. Several cases of this Burgundy twice crossed the desert of the Isthmus of Suez on camels' backs. We brought some of it back with us to Fréjus, and it was as good as when we departed. James went with us to Egypt.

During the remainder of our stay in Paris nothing occurred worthy of mention, with the exception of a conversation between Bonaparte and me some days before our departure for Toulon. He went with me to the Luxembourg to get signatures to the official papers connected with his expedition. He was very silent. As we passed through the Rue Sainte

Anne I asked him, with no other object than merely to break a long pause, whether he was still determined to quit France. He replied, "Yes: I have tried everything. They do not want me (probably alluding to the office of Director). I ought to overthrow them, and make myself King; but it will not do yet. The nobles will never consent to it. I have tried my ground. The time is not yet come. I should be alone. But I will dazzle them again." I replied, "Well, we will go to Egypt;" and changed the conversation.[51] The squabble with Bernadotte at Vienna delayed our departure for a fortnight, and might have had the most disastrous influence on the fate of the squadron, as Nelson would most assuredly have waited between Malta and Sicily if he had arrived there before us.[52]

It is untrue that he ever entertained the idea of abandoning the expedition in consequence of Bernadotte's affair. The following letter to Brueys, dated the 28th of April 1798, proves the contrary:

> Some disturbances which have arisen at Vienna render my presence in Paris necessary for a few days. This will not change any of the arrangements for the expedition. I have sent orders by this courier for the troops at Marseilles to embark and proceed to Toulon. On the evening of the 30th I will send you a courier with orders for you to embark and proceed with the squadron and convoy to Genoa, where I will join you.
>
> The delay which this fresh event has occasioned will, I imagine, have enabled you to complete every preparation.

We left Paris on the 3d of May 1798. Ten days before Bonaparte's departure for Egypt a prisoner (Sir Sidney Smith) escaped from the Temple who was destined to contribute materially to his reverses. An escape so unimportant in itself afterwards caused the failure of the most gigantic projects and daring conceptions. This escape was pregnant with future events; a false order of the Minister of Police prevented the revolution of the East!

---

51 Lucien and the Bonapartists of course deny that Napoleon wished to become Director, or to seize on power at this time; see Lucien, tome 1. p. 154. Thiers (vol. v. p. 257) takes the same view. Lanfrey (tome i. p. 363) believes Napoleon was at last compelled by the Directory to start and he credits the story told by Desaix to Mathieu Dumas, or rather to the wife of that officer, that there was a plot to upset the Directory, but that when all was ready Napoleon judged that the time was not ripe. Lanfrey, however, rather enlarges what Dumas says; see Dumas, tome iii. p. 167. See also the very remarkable conversation of Napoleon with Miot de Melito just before leaving Italy for Rastadt: "I cannot obey any longer. I have tasted the pleasures of command, and I cannot renounce it. My decision is taken. If I cannot be master, I shall quit France." (Miot, tome i. p. 184).

52 Sir Walter Scott, without any authority, states that, at the moment of his departure, Bonaparte seemed disposed to abandon the command of an expedition so doubtful and hazardous, and that for this purpose he endeavoured to take advantage of what had occurred at Vienna. This must be ranked in the class of inventions, together with Barras mysterious visit to communicate the change of destination, and also the ostracism and honourable exile which the Directory wished to impose on Bonaparte.—Bourrienne.

We were at Toulon on the 8th. Bonaparte knew by the movements of the English that not a moment was to be lost; but adverse winds detained us ten days, which he occupied in attending to the most minute details connected with the fleet.

Bonaparte, whose attention was constantly occupied with his army, made a speech to the soldiers, which I wrote to his dictation, and which appeared in the public papers at the time. This address was followed by cries of "The Immortal Republic for ever!" and the singing of national hymns.

Those who knew Madame Bonaparte are aware that few women were more amiable and fascinating. Bonaparte was passionately fond of her, and to enjoy the pleasure of her society as long as possible he brought her with him to Toulon. Nothing could be more affecting than their parting. On leaving Toulon Josephine went to the waters of Plombieres. I recollect that during her stay at Plombieres she incurred great danger from a serious accident. Whilst she was one day sitting at the balcony of the hotel, with her suite, the balcony suddenly gave way, and all the persons in it fell into the street. Madame Bonaparte was much hurt, but no serious consequences ensued.

Bonaparte had scarcely arrived at Toulon when he heard that the law for the death of emigrants was enforced with frightful rigour; and that but recently an old man, upwards of eighty, had been shot. Indignant at this barbarity, he dictated to me, in a tone of anger, the following letter:

HEADQUARTERS TOULON,
27th Floréal, year VI. (16th May 1798).

BONAPARTE, MEMBER OF THE NATIONAL INSTITUTE, TO THE MILITARY COMMISSIONERS OF THE NINTH DIVISION, ESTABLISHED BY THE LAW OF THE 19TH FRUCTIDOR.

I have learned, citizens, with deep regret, that an old man, between seventy and eighty years of age, and some unfortunate women, in a state of pregnancy, or surrounded with children of tender age, have been shot on the charge of emigration. Have the soldiers of liberty become executioners? Can the mercy which they have exercised even in the fury of battle be extinct in their hearts? The law of the 19th Fructidor was a measure of public safety. Its object was to reach conspirators, not women and aged men.

I therefore exhort you, citizens, whenever the law brings to your tribunals women or old men, to declare that in the field of battle you have respected the women and old men of your enemies. The officer who signs a sentence against a person incapable of bearing arms is a coward.

(Signed) BONAPARTE.

This letter saved the life of an unfortunate man who came under the description of persons to whom Bonaparte referred. The tone of this note shows what an idea he already entertained of his power. He took upon him, doubtless from the noblest motives, to step out of his way to interpret and interdict the execution of a law, atrocious, it is true, but which even in those times of weakness, disorder, and anarchy was still a law. In this instance, at least, the power of his name was nobly employed. The letter gave great satisfaction to the army destined for the expedition.

A man named Simon, who had followed his master in emigration, and dreaded the application of the law, heard that I wanted a servant. He came to me and acknowledged his situation. He suited me, and I hired him. He then told me he feared he should be arrested whilst going to the port to embark. Bonaparte, to whom I mentioned the circumstance, and who had just given a striking proof of his aversion to these acts of barbarity, said to me in a tone of kindness, "Give him my portfolio to carry, and let him remain with you." The words "Bonaparte, General-in-Chief of the Army of the East," were inscribed in large gold letters on the green morocco. Whether it was the portfolio or his connection with us that prevented Simon from being arrested I know not; but he passed on without interruption. I reprimanded him for having smiled derisively at the ill humour of the persons appointed to arrest him. He served me faithfully, and was even sometimes useful to Bonaparte.

CHAPTER XIII

1798

The squadron sailed on the 19th of May. The Orient, which, owing to her heavy lading, drew too much water, touched the ground; but she was got off without much difficulty.

We arrived off Malta on the 10th of June. We had lost two days in waiting for some convoys which joined us at Malta.

The intrigues throughout Europe had not succeeded in causing the ports of that island to be opened to us immediately on our arrival. Bonaparte expressed much displeasure against the persons sent from Europe to arrange measures for that purpose. One of them, however, M. Dolomieu, had cause to repent his mission, which occasioned him to be badly treated by the Sicilians. M. Poussielgue had done all he could in the way of seduction, but he had not completely succeeded. There was some misunderstanding, and, in consequence, some shots were interchanged. Bonaparte was very much pleased with General Baraguay d'Hilliers' services in Italy. He could not but praise his military and political conduct at Venice when, scarcely a year before, he had taken possession of that city by his orders. General Baraguay d'Hilliers joined us with his division,—which had embarked in the convoy that sailed from Genoa. The General-in-Chief ordered him to land and attack the western part of the island. He executed this order with equal prudence and ability, and highly to the satisfaction of the General-in-Chief. As every person in the secret knew that all this was a mere form, these hostile demonstrations produced no unpleasant consequences. We wished to save the honour of the knights—that was all; for no one who has seen Malta can imagine that an island surrounded with such formidable and perfect fortifications would have surrendered in two days to a fleet which was pursued by an enemy. The impregnable fortress of Malta is so secure against a 'coup de main' that General Caffarelli, after examining its fortifications, said to the General-in-Chief, in my presence, "Upon my word, General, it is luck: there is some one in the town to open the gates for us."

By comparing the observation of General Caffarelli with what has been previously stated respecting the project of the expedition to Egypt and Malta, an idea may be formed of the value of Bonaparte's assertion at St. Helena:

"The capture of Malta was not owing to private intrigues, but to the sagacity of the Commander-in-chief. I took Malta when I was in Mantua!"

It is not the less true, however, that I wrote, by his dictation, a mass of instructions for private intrigues. Napoleon also said to another noble companion of his exile at St Helena, "Malta certainly possessed vast physical means of resistance; but no moral means. The knights did nothing dishonourable, nobody is obliged to do impossibilities. No; but they were sold; the capture of Malta was assured before we left Toulon."

The General-in-Chief proceeded to that part of the port where the Turks made prisoners by the knights were kept.

The disgusting galleys were emptied of their occupants: The same principles which, a few days after, formed the basis of Bonaparte's proclamation to the Egyptians, guided him in this act of reason and humanity.

He walked several times in the gardens of the grandmaster. They were in beautiful order, and filled with magnificent orange-trees. We regaled ourselves with their fruit, which the great heat rendered most delicious.

On the 19th of June, after having settled the government and defence of the island, the General left Malta, which he little dreamed he had taken for the English, who have very badly requited the obligation. Many of the knights followed Bonaparte and took civil and military appointments.

During the night of the 22d of June the English squadron was almost close upon us. It passed at about six leagues from the French fleet. Nelson, who learned the capture of Malta at Messina on the day we left the island, sailed direct for Alexandria, without proceeding into the north. He considered that city to be the place of our destination. By taking the shortest course, with every sail set, and unembarrassed by any convoy, he arrived before Alexandria on the 28th of June, three days before the French fleet, which, nevertheless, had sailed before him from the shores of Malta. The French squadron took the direction of Candia, which we perceived on the 25th of June, and afterwards stood to the south, favoured by the Etesian winds, which regularly prevail at that season. The French fleet did not reach Alexandria till the 30th of June.

When on board the 'Orient' he took pleasure in conversing frequently with Monge and Berthollet. The subjects on which they usually talked were chemistry, mathematics, and religion. General Caffarelli, whose conversation, supplied by knowledge, was at once energetic, witty, and lively, was one of those with whom he most willingly discoursed. Whatever friendship he might entertain for Berthollet, it was easy to perceive that he preferred Monge, and that he was led to that preference because Monge, endowed with an ardent imagination, without exactly possessing religious principles, had a kind of predisposition for religious ideas which harmonised with the notions of Bonaparte. On this subject Berthollet sometimes rallied his inseparable friend Monge. Besides, Berthollet was, with his cold imagination, constantly devoted to analysis and abstractions, inclined towards materialism, an opinion with which the General was always much dissatisfied.

Bonaparte sometimes conversed with Admiral Brueys. His object was always to gain information respecting the different manoeuvres, and nothing astonished the Admiral more than the sagacity of his questions. I recollect that one day, Bonaparte having asked Brueys in what manner the hammocks were disposed of when clearing for action, he declared, after he had received an answer, that if the case should occur he would order every one to throw his baggage overboard.

He passed a great part of his time in his cabin, lying on a bed, which, swinging on a kind of castors, alleviated the severity of the sea-sickness from which he frequently suffered much when the ship rolled.

I was almost always with him in his cabin, where I read to him some of the favourite works which he had selected for his camp library. He also frequently conversed, for hours together, with the captains of the vessels which he hailed. He never failed to ask whence they came? what was their destination? what ships they had met? what course they had sailed? His curiosity being thus satisfied, he allowed them to continue their voyage, after making them promise to say nothing of having seen the French squadron.

Whilst we were at sea he seldom rose before ten o'clock in the morning. The 'Orient' had the appearance of a populous town, from which women had been excluded; and this floating city was inhabited by 2000 individuals, amongst whom were a great number of distinguished men. Bonaparte every day invited several persons to dine with him, besides Brueys, Berthier, the colonels, and his ordinary household, who were always present at the table of the General-in-Chief. When the weather was fine he went up to the quarter-deck, which, from its extent, formed a grand promenade.

I recollect once that when walking the quarter-deck with him whilst we were in Sicilian waters I thought I could see the summits of the Alps beautifully lighted by the rays of the setting sun. Bonaparte laughed much, and joked me about it. He called Admiral Brueys, who took his telescope and soon confirmed my conjecture. The Alps!

At the mention of that word by the Admiral I think I can see Bonaparte still. He stood for a long time motionless; then, suddenly bursting from his trance, exclaimed, "No! I cannot behold the land of Italy without emotion! There is the East: and there I go; a perilous enterprise invites me. Those mountains command the plains where I so often had the good fortune to lead the French to victory. With them we will conquer again."

One of Bonaparte's greatest pleasures during the voyage was, after dinner, to fix upon three or four persons to support a proposition and as many to oppose it. He had an object in view by this. These discussions afforded him an opportunity of studying the minds of those whom he had an interest in knowing well, in order that he might afterwards confide to each the functions for which he possessed the greatest aptitude: It will not appear singular to those who have been intimate with Bonaparte, that in these intellectual contests he gave the preference to those who had supported an absurd proposition with ability over those who had maintained the cause of reason; and it was not superiority of mind which determined his judgment, for he really preferred the man who argued well in favour of an absurdity to the man who argued equally well in support of a reasonable proposition. He always gave out the subjects which were to be discussed; and they most frequently turned upon questions of religion, the different kinds of government, and the art of war. One day he asked whether the planets were inhabited; on another, what was the age of the world; then he proposed to consider the probability of the destruction of our globe, either by water or fire; at another time, the truth or fallacy of presentiments, and the interpretation of dreams. I remember the circumstance which gave rise to the last proposition was an allusion to Joseph, of whom he happened to speak, as he did of almost everything connected with the country to which we were bound, and which that able administrator had governed. No country came under Bonaparte's observation without recalling historical recollections to his mind. On passing the island of Candia his imagination was excited, and he spoke with enthusiasm of ancient Crete and the Colossus, whose fabulous renown has surpassed all human glories. He spoke much of the fall of the empire of the East, which bore so little resemblance to what history has preserved of those fine countries, so often moistened with the blood of man. The ingenious fables of mythology likewise occurred to his mind, and imparted to his language something of a poetical, and, I may say, of an inspired character. The sight of the kingdom of Minos led him to reason on the laws best calculated for the government of nations; and the birthplace of Jupiter suggested to him the necessity of a religion for the mass of mankind. This animated conversation lasted until the favourable north winds, which drove the clouds into the valley of the Nile, caused us to lose sight of the island of Candia.

The musicians on board the Orient sometimes played serenades; but only between decks, for Bonaparte was not yet sufficiently fond of music to wish to hear it in his cabin. It may be said that his taste for this art increased in the direct ratio of his power; and so it was with his taste for hunting, of which he gave no indication until after his elevation to the empire; as though he had wished to prove that he possessed within himself not only the genius of sovereignty for commanding men, but also the instinct for those aristocratical pleasures, the enjoyment of which is considered by mankind to be amongst the attributes of kings.

It is scarcely possible that some accidents should not occur during a long voyage in a crowded vessel—that some persons should not fall overboard. Accidents of this kind frequently happened on board the 'Orient'. On those occasions nothing was more remarkable than the great humanity of the man who has since been so prodigal of the blood of his fellow-creatures on the field of battle, and who was about to shed rivers of it even in Egypt, whither we were bound. When a man fell into the sea the General-in-Chief was in a state of agitation till he was saved. He instantly had the ship hove-to, and exhibited the greatest uneasiness until the unfortunate individual was recovered. He ordered me to reward those who ventured their lives in this service. Amongst these was a sailor who had incurred punishment for some fault. He not only exempted him from the punishment, but also gave him some money. I recollect that one dark night we heard a noise like that occasioned by a man falling into the sea. Bonaparte instantly caused the ship to be hove-to until the supposed victim was rescued from certain death. The men hastened from all sides, and at length they picked up-what?—the quarter of a bullock, which had fallen from the hook to which it was hung. What was Bonaparte's conduct? He ordered me to reward the sailors who had exerted themselves in this occasion even more generously than usual, saying, "It might have been a sailor, and these brave fellows have shown as much activity and courage as if it had."

After the lapse of thirty years all these things are as fresh in my recollection as if they were passing at the present moment. In this manner Bonaparte employed his time on board the Orient during the voyage, and it was also at this time that he dictated to me the following proclamation:

HEADQUARTERS ON BOARD THE "ORIENT,"
The 4th Messidor, Year VI.

BONAPARTE, MEMBER OF THE NATIONAL INSTITUTE, GENERAL-IN-CHIEF.

SOLDIERS—You are about to undertake a conquest the effects of which on civilisation and commerce are incalculable. The blow you are about to give to England will be the best aimed, and the most sensibly felt, she can receive until the time arrive when you can give her her deathblow. We must make some fatiguing marches; we must fight several battles; we shall succeed in all we undertake. The destinies are with us. The Mameluke Beys who favour exclusively English commerce, whose extortions oppress our merchants, and who tyrannise over the unfortunate inhabitants of the Nile, a few days after our arrival will no longer exist. The people amongst whom we are going to live are Mahometans. The first article of their faith is this: "There is no God but God, and Mahomet is his prophet." Do not contradict them. Behave to them as you have behaved to the Jews—to the Italians. Pay respect to their muftis, and their Imaums, as you did to the rabbis and the bishops. Extend to the ceremonies prescribed by the Koran and to the mosques the same toleration which you showed to the synagogues, to the religion of Moses and of Jesus Christ. The Roman legions protected all religions. You will find here customs different from those of Europe. You must accommodate yourselves to them. The people amongst whom we are to mix differ from us in the treatment of women; but in all countries he who violates is a monster. Pillage enriches only a small number of men; it dishonours us; it destroys our resources; it converts into enemies the people whom it is our interest to have for friends. The first town we shall come to was built by Alexander. At every step we shall meet with grand recollections, worthy of exciting the emulation of Frenchmen.

BONAPARTE.

During the voyage, and particularly between Malta and Alexandria, I often conversed with the brave and unfortunate Admiral Brueys. The intelligence we heard from time to time augmented his uneasiness. I had the good fortune to obtain the confidence of this worthy man. He complained bitterly of the imperfect manner in which the fleet had been prepared for sea; of the encumbered state of the ships of the line and frigates, and especially of the 'Orient'; of the great number of transports; of the bad Outfit of all the ships and the weakness of their crews. He assured me that it required no little courage to undertake the command of a fleet so badly equipped; and he often declared, that in the event of our falling in with the enemy, he could not answer for the consequences. The encumbered state of the vessels, the immense quantity of civic and military baggage which each person had brought, and would wish to save, would render proper manoeuvres impracticable. In case of an attack, added Brueys, even by an inferior squadron, the confusion and disorder amongst so great a number of persons would produce an inevitable catastrophe. Finally, if the English had appeared with ten vessels only, the Admiral could not have guaranteed a fortunate result. He considered victory to be a thing that was impossible, and even with a victory, what would have become of the expedition? "God send," he said, with a sigh, "that we may pass the English without meeting them!" He appeared to foresee what did afterwards happen to him, not in the open sea, but in a situation which he considered much more favourable to his defence.

On the morning of the 1st of July the expedition arrived off the coast of Africa, and the column of Septimus-Severus pointed out to us the city of Alexandria. Our situation and frame of mind hardly permitted us to reflect that in the distant point we beheld the city of the Ptolemies and Caesars, with its double port, its pharos, and the gigantic monuments of its ancient grandeur. Our imaginations did not rise to this pitch.

Admiral Brueys had sent on before the frigate Juno to fetch M. Magallon, the French Consul. It was near four o'clock when he arrived, and the sea was very rough. He informed the General-in-Chief that Nelson had been off Alexandria on the 28th—that he immediately dispatched a brig to obtain intelligence from the English agent. On the return of the brig Nelson instantly stood away with his squadron towards the north-east. But for a delay which our convoy from Civita Vecchia occasioned, we should have been on this coast at the same time as Nelson.

It appeared that Nelson supposed us to be already at Alexandria when he arrived there. He had reason to suppose so, seeing that we left Malta on the 19th of June, whilst he did not sail from Messina till the 21st. Not finding us where he expected, and being persuaded we ought to have arrived there had Alexandria been the place of our destination; he sailed for Alexandretta in Syria, whither he imagined we had gone to effect a landing. This error saved the expedition a second time.

Bonaparte, on hearing the details which the French Consul communicated, resolved to disembark immediately. Admiral Brueys represented the difficulties and dangers of a disembarkation—the violence of the surge, the distance from the coast,—a coast, too, lined with reefs of rocks, the approaching night, and our perfect ignorance of the points suitable for landing. The Admiral, therefore, urged the necessity of waiting till next morning; that is to say, to delay the landing twelve hours. He observed that Nelson could not return from Syria for several days. Bonaparte listened to these representations with impatience and ill-humour. He replied peremptorily, "Admiral, we have no time to lose. Fortune gives me but three days; if I do not profit by them we are lost." He relied much on fortune; this chimerical idea constantly influenced his resolutions.

Bonaparte having the command of the naval as well as the military force, the Admiral was obliged to yield to his wishes.

I attest these facts, which passed in my presence, and no part of which could escape my observation. It is quite false that it was owing to the appearance of a sail which, it is pretended, was descried, but of which, for my part, I saw nothing, that Bonaparte exclaimed, "Fortune, have you abandoned me? I ask only five days!" No such thing occurred.

It was one o'clock in the morning of the 2d of July when we landed on the soil of Egypt, at Marabou, three leagues to the west of Alexandria. We had to regret the loss of some lives; but we had every reason to expect that our losses would have been greater.

At three o'clock the same morning the General-in-Chief marched on Alexandria with the divisions of Kléber, Bon, and Menou. The Bedouin Arabs, who kept hovering about our right flank and our rear, picked up the stragglers.

Having arrived within gunshot of Alexandria, we scaled the ramparts, and French valour soon triumphed over all obstacles.

The first blood I saw shed in war was General Kléber's. He was struck in the head by a ball, not in storming the walls, but whilst heading the attack. He came to Pompey's Pillar, where many members of the staff were assembled, and where the General-in-Chief was watching the attack. I then spoke to Kléber for the first time, and from that day our friendship commenced. I had the good fortune to contribute somewhat towards the assistance of which he stood in need, and which, as we were situated, could not be procured very easily.

It has been endeavoured to represent the capture of Alexandria, which surrendered after a few hours, as a brilliant exploit. The General-in-Chief himself wrote that the city had been taken after a few discharges of cannon; the walls, badly fortified, were soon scaled. Alexandria was not delivered up to pillage, as has been asserted, and often repeated. This would have been a most impolitic mode of commencing the conquest of Egypt, which had no strong places requiring to be intimidated by a great example.

Bonaparte, with some others, entered the city by a narrow street which scarcely allowed two persons to walk abreast; I was with him. We were stopped by some musket-shots fired from a low window by a man and a woman. They repeated their fire several times. The guides who preceded their General kept up a heavy fire on the window. The man and woman fell dead, and we passed on in safety, for the place had surrendered.

Bonaparte employed the six days during which he remained in Alexandria in establishing order in the city and province, with that activity and superior talent which I could never sufficiently admire, and in directing the march of the army across the province of Bohahire'h. He sent Desaix with 4500 infantry and 60 cavalry to Beda, on the road to Damanhour. This general was the first to experience the privations and sufferings which the whole army had soon to endure. His great mind, his attachment to Bonaparte, seemed for a moment about to yield to the obstacles which presented themselves. On the 15th of July he wrote from Bohahire'h as follows: "I beseech you do not let us stop longer in this position. My men are discouraged and murmur. Make us advance or fall back without delay. The villages consist merely of huts, absolutely without resources."

In these immense plains, scorched by the vertical rays of a burning sun, water, everywhere else so common, becomes an object of contest. The wells and springs, those secret treasures of the desert, are carefully concealed from the travellers; and frequently, after our most oppressive marches, nothing could be found to allay the urgent cravings of thirst but a little brackish water of the most disgusting description.[53]

---

53 Some idea of the misery endured by the French troops on this occasion may be gathered from the following description is Napoleon's Memoirs, dictated at St. Helena: "As the Hebrews wandering in the wilderness complained, and angrily asked Moses for the onions and flesh-pots of Egypt, the French soldiers constantly regretted the luxuries of Italy. In vain were they assured that the country was the most fertile in the world, that it was even superior to Lombard; how were they to be persuaded of this when they could get neither bread nor wine? We encamped on immense quantities of wheat, but there was neither mill nor oven in the country. The biscuit brought from Alexandria had long been exhausted; the soldiers were even reduced to bruise the wheat between two stones and to make cake which they baked under the ashes. Many parched the wheat in a pan, after which they boiled it. This was the best way to use the grain; but, after all, it was not bread. The apprehensions of the soldiers increased daily, and rose to such a pitch that a great number of them said there was no great city of calm; and that the place bring that name was, like Damanhour, a vast assemblage of mere huts, destitute of everything that could render life comfortable or agreeable. To such a melancholy state of mind had they brought themselves that two dragoons threw themselves, completely clothed, into the Nile, where they were drowned. It is nevertheless true that, though there was neither bread nor wine, the resources which were procured with wheat, lentils, meat, and sometimes pigeons, furnished the army with food of some kind. But the evil was, in the ferment of the mind. The officers complained more loudly than the soldiers, because the comparison was proportionately more disadvantageous to them. In Egypt they found neither the quarters, the good table, nor the luxury of Italy. The General-in-Chief, wishing to set an example, tried to bivouac in the midst of the army, and in the least commodious spots. No one had either tent or provisions; the dinner of Napoleon and his staff consisted of a dish of lentils. The soldiers passed the evenings in political conversations, arguments, and complaints. 'For what purpose are we come here?' said some of them, 'the Directory has transported us.' 'Caffarelli,' said others, 'is the agent that has been made use of to deceive the General-in-Chief.' Many of them, having observed that wherever there were vestiges of antiquity they were carefully searched, vented their spite in invective against the savants, or scientific men, who, they said, had started the idea of she expedition to order to make these searches. Jests were showered upon them, even in their presence. The men called an ass a savant; and said of Caffarelli Dufalga, alluding to his wooden leg, 'He laughs at all these troubles; he has one foot to France.'"

CHAPTER XIV

1798

On the 7th of July General Bonaparte left Alexandria for Damanhour. In the vast plains of Bohahire'h the mirage every moment presented to the eye wide sheets of water, while, as we advanced, we found nothing but barren ground full of deep cracks. Villages, which at a distance appear to be surrounded with water, are, on a nearer approach, discovered to be situated on heights, mostly artificial, by which they are raised above the inundations of the Nile. This illusion continually recurs; and it is the more treacherous, inasmuch as it presents to the eye the perfect representation of water, at the time when the want of that article is most felt. This mirage is so considerable in the plain of Pelusium that shortly after sunrise no object is recognisable. The same phenomenon has been observed in other countries. Quintus Curtius says that in the deserts of Sogdiana, a fog rising from the earth obscures the light, and the surrounding country seems like a vast sea. The cause of this singular illusion is now fully explained; and, from the observations of the learned Monge, it appears that the mirage will be found in almost every country situated between the tropics where the local circumstances are similar.

The Arabs harassed the army without intermission. The few wells met with in the desert were either filled up or the water was rendered unfit for use. The intolerable thirst with which the troops were tormented, even on this first march, was but ill allayed by brackish and unwholesome water. The army crossed the desert with the rapidity of lightning, scarcely tasting a drop of water. The sufferings of the troops were frequently expressed by discouraging murmurs.

On the first night a mistake occurred which might have proved fatal. We were advancing in the dark, under feeble escort, almost sleeping on our horses, when suddenly we were assailed by two successive discharges of musketry. We aroused ourselves and reconnoitred, and to our great satisfaction discovered that the only mischief was a alight wound received by one of our guides. Our assailants were the division of General Desaix, who, forming the advanced guard of the army, mistook us for a party of the enemy, and fired upon us. It was speedily ascertained that the little advanced guard of the headquarters had not heard the "Qui vive?" of Desaix's advanced posts.

On reaching Damanhour our headquarters were established at the residence of a sheik. The house had been new whitened, and looked well enough outside, but the interior was inconceivably wretched. Every domestic utensil was broken, and the only seats were a few dirty tattered mats. Bonaparte knew that the sheik was rich, and having somewhat won his confidence, he asked him, through the medium of the interpreter, why, being in easy circumstances, he thus deprived himself of all comfort. "Some years ago," replied the sheik, "I repaired and furnished my house. When this became known at Cairo a demand was made upon me for money, because it was said my expenses proved me to be rich. I refused to pay the money, and in consequence I was ill-treated, and at length forced to pay it. From that time I have allowed myself only the bare necessaries of life, and I shall buy no furniture for my house." The old man was lame in consequence of the treatment he had suffered. Woe to him who in this country is suspected of having a competency—a hundred spies are always ready to denounce him. The appearance of poverty is the only security against the rapine of power and the cupidity of barbarism.

A little troop of Arabs on horseback assailed our headquarters. Bonaparte, who was at the window of the sheik's house, indignant at this insolence, turned to one of his aides de camp, who happened to be on duty, and said, "Croisier, take a few guides and drive those fellows away!" In an instant Croisier was in the plain with fifteen guides. A little skirmish ensued, and we looked on from the window. In the movement and in the attack of Croisier and his party there was a sort of hesitation which the General-in-Chief could not comprehend. "Forward, I say! Charge!" he exclaimed from the window, as if he could have been heard. Our horsemen seemed to fall back as the Arabs returned to the attack; and after a little contest, maintained with tolerable spirit, the Arabs retired without loss, and without being molested in their retreat. Bonaparte could no longer repress his rage; and when Croisier returned he experienced such a harsh reception that the poor fellow withdrew deeply mortified and distressed. Bonaparte desired me to follow him and say something to console him: but all was in vain. "I cannot survive this," he said. "I will sacrifice my life on the first occasion that offers itself. I will not live dishonoured." The word coward had escaped the General's lips. Poor Croisier died at Saint Jean d'Acre.

On the 10th of July our headquarters were established at Rahmahanie'h, where they remained during the 11th and 12th. At this place commences the canal which was cut by Alexander to convey water to his new city; and to facilitate commercial intercourse between Europe and the East.

The flotilla, commanded by the brave chief of division Perree, had just arrived from Rosette. Perree was on board the xebec 'Cerf'.[54] Bonaparte placed on board the Cerf and the other vessels of the flotilla those individuals who, not being military, could not be serviceable in engagements, and whose horses served to mount a few of the troops.

On the night of the 14th of July the General-in-Chief directed his march towards the south, along the left bank of the Nile. The flotilla sailed up the river parallel with the left wing of the army. But the force of the wind, which at this season blows regularly from the Mediterranean into the valley of the file, carried the flotilla far in advance of the army, and frustrated the plan of their mutually defending and supporting each other. The flotilla thus unprotected fell in with seven Turkish gunboats coming from Cairo, and was exposed simultaneously to their fire and to that of the Mamelukes, fellahs, and Arabs who lined both banks of the river. They had small guns mounted on camels.

Perree cast anchor, and an engagement commenced at nine o'clock on the 14th of July, and continued till half past twelve.

At the same time the General-in-Chief met and attacked a corps of about 4000 Mamelukes. His object, as he afterwards said, was to turn the corps by the left of the village of Chebreisse, and to drive it upon the Nile.

About eleven in the morning Perree told me that the Turks were doing us more harm than we were doing them; that our ammunition would soon be exhausted; that the army was far inland, and that if it did not make a move to the left there would be no hope for us.

---

54 Bonaparte had great confidence in him. He had commanded, under the General's orders, the naval forces in the Adriatic in 1797.— Bourrienne

Several vessels had already been boarded and taken by the Turks, who massacred the crews before our eyes, and with barbarous ferocity showed us the heads of the slaughtered men.

Perree, at considerable risk, despatched several persons to inform the General-in-Chief of the desperate situation of the flotilla. The cannonade which Bonaparte had heard since the morning, and the explosion of a Turkish gunboat, which was blown up by the artillery of the xebec, led him to fear that our situation was really perilous. He therefore made a movement to the left, in the direction of the Nile and Chebreisse, beat the Mamelukes, and forced them to retire on Cairo. At sight of the French troops the commander of the Turkish flotilla weighed anchor and sailed up the Nile. The two banks of the river were evacuated, and the flotilla escaped the destruction which a short time before had appeared inevitable. Some writers have alleged that the Turkish flotilla was destroyed in this engagement. The truth is, the Turks did us considerable injury, while on their part they suffered but little. We had twenty men killed and several wounded. Upwards of 1500 cannon-shots were fired during the action.

General Berthier, in his narrative of the Egyptian expedition, enumerates the individuals who, though not in the military service, assisted Perree in this unequal and dangerous engagement. He mentions Monge, Berthollet, Andreossy, the paymaster, Junot, and Bourrienne, secretary to the General-in-Chief. It has also been stated that Sucy, the commissary-general, was seriously wounded while bravely defending a gunboat laden with provisions; but this is incorrect.

We had no communication with the army until the 23d of July. On the 22d we came in sight of the Pyramids, and were informed that we were only about, ten leagues from Gizeh, where they are situated. The cannonade which we heard, and which augmented in proportion as the north wind diminished, announced a serious engagement; and that same day we saw the banks of the Nile strewed with heaps of bodies, which the waves were every moment washing into the sea. This horrible spectacle, the silence of the surrounding villages, which had hitherto been armed against us, and the cessation of the firing from the banks of the river, led us to infer, with tolerable certainty, that a battle fatal to the Mamelukes had been fought. The misery we suffered on our passage from Rahmahanie'h to Gizeh is indescribable. We lived for eleven days on melons and water, besides being momentarily exposed to the musketry of the Arabs and the fellahs. We luckily escaped with but a few killed and wounded. The rising of the Nile was only beginning. The shallowness of the river near Cairo obliged us to leave the xebec and get on board a djerm. We reached Gizeh at three in the afternoon of the 23d of July.

When I saluted the General, whom I had not seen for twelve days, he thus addressed me: "So you are here, are you? Do you know that you have all of you been the cause of my not following up the battle of Chebreisse? It was to save you, Monge, Berthollet, and the others on board the flotilla that I hurried the movement of my left upon the Nile before my right had turned Chebreisse. But for that, not a single Mameluke would have escaped."

"I thank you for my own part," replied I; "but in conscience could you have abandoned us, after taking away our horses, and making us go on board the xebec, whether we would or not?" He laughed, and then told me how sorry he was for the wound of Sucy, and the death of many useful men, whose places could not possibly be filled up.

He made me write a letter to his brother Louis, informing him that he had gained a complete victory over the Mamelukes at Embabeh, opposite Boulac, and that the enemy's loss was 2000 men killed and wounded, 40 guns, and a great number of horses.

The occupation of Cairo was the immediate consequence of the victory of Embabeh. Bonaparte established his head-quarters in the home of Elfy Bey, in the great square of Ezbekye'h.

The march of the French army to Cairo was attended by an uninterrupted succession of combats and victories. We had won the battles of Rahmahanie'h, Chebreisse, and the Pyramids. The Mamelukes were defeated, and their chief, Mourad Bey, was obliged to fly into Upper Egypt. Bonaparte found no obstacle to oppose his entrance into the capital of Egypt, after a campaign of only twenty days.

No conqueror, perhaps, ever enjoyed a victory so much as Bonaparte, and yet no one was ever less inclined to abuse his triumphs.

We entered Cairo on the 24th of July, and the General-in-Chief immediately directed his attention to the civil and military organization of the country. Only those who saw him in the vigour of his youth can form an idea of his extraordinary intelligence and activity. Nothing escaped his observation. Egypt had long been the object of his study; and in a few weeks he was as well acquainted with the country as if he had lived in it ten years. He issued orders for observing the strictest discipline, and these orders were punctually obeyed.

The mosques, the civil and religious institutions, the harems, the women, the customs of the country—all were scrupulously respected. A few days after they entered Cairo the French were freely admitted into the shops, and were seen sociably smoking their pipes with the inhabitants, assisting them in their occupations, and playing with their children.

The day after his arrival in Cairo Bonaparte addressed to his brother Joseph the following letter, which was intercepted and printed. Its authenticity has been doubted, but I saw Napoleon write it, and he read it to me before he sent it off.

CAIRO,
7th. Thermidor (25th July 1798)

> You will see in the public papers the bulletins of the battles and conquest of Egypt, which were sufficiently contested to add another wreath to the laurels of this army. Egypt is richer than any country in the world in coin, rice, vegetables, and cattle. But the people are in a state of utter barbarism. We cannot procure money, even to pay the troops. I maybe in France in two months. Engage a country-house, to be ready for me on my arrival, either near Paris or in Burgundy, where I mean to pass the winter.[55]
>
> *(Signed)* BONAPARTE

55 Bonaparte's autograph note, after enumerating the troops and warlike stores he wished to be sent, concluded with the following list: 1st, a company of actors; 2d, a company of dancers; 3d, some dealers in marionettes, at least three or four; 9th, a hundred French women; 5th, the wives of all the men employed in the corps; 6th, twenty surgeons, thirty apothecaries, and ten Physicians; 7th, some founders; 8th, some distillers and dealers in liquor; 9th fifty gardeners with their families, and the seeds of every kind of vegetable; 10th, each party to bring with them: 200,000 pints of brandy; 11th, 30,000 ells of blue and scarlet cloth; 12th, a supply of soap and oil.—Bourrienne.

This announcement of his departure to his brother is corroborated by a note which he despatched some days after, enumerating the supplies and individuals which he wished to have sent to Egypt. His note proves, more convincingly than any arguments, that Bonaparte earnestly wished to preserve his conquest, and to make it a French colony. It must be borne in mind that the note here alluded to, as well as the letter above quoted, was written long before the destruction of the fleet.

CHAPTER XV

1798

From the details I have already given respecting Bonaparte's plans for colonising Egypt, it will be seen that his energy of mind urged him to adopt anticipatory measures for the accomplishment of objects which were never realised. During the short interval in which he sheathed his sword he planned provisional governments for the towns and provinces occupied by the French troops, and he adroitly contrived to serve the interests of his army without appearing to violate those of the country.

After he had been four days at Cairo, during which time he employed himself in examining everything, and consulting every individual from whom he could obtain useful information, he published the following order:

HEADQUARTERS, CAIRO,
9th Thermidor, year VI.

BONAPARTE, MEMBER OF THE NATIONAL INSTITUTE, AND GENERAL-IN-CHIEF, ORDERS:

ART. 1. There shall be in each province of Egypt a divan, composed of seven individuals, whose duty will be to superintend the interests of the province; to communicate to me any complaints that may be made; to prevent warfare among the different villages; to apprehend and punish criminals (for which purpose they may demand assistance from the French commandant); and to take every opportunity of enlightening the people.

ART. 2. There shall be in each province an aga of the Janizaries, maintaining constant communication with the French commandant. He shall have with him a company of sixty armed natives, whom he may take wherever he pleases, for the maintenance of good order, subordination, and tranquillity.

ART. 3. There shall be in each province an intendant, whose business will be to levy the miri, the feddam, and the other contributions which formerly belonged to the Mamelukes, but which now belong to the French Republic. The intendants shall have as many agents as may be necessary.

ART. 4. The said intendant shall have a French agent to correspond with the Finance Department, and to execute all the orders he may receive.

(*Signed*) BONAPARTE.

While Bonaparte was thus actively taking measures for the organization of the country,[56] General Desaix had marched into Upper Egypt in pursuit of Mourad Bey. We learned that Ibrahim, who, next to Mourad, was the most influential of the beys, had proceeded towards Syria, by the way of Belbeis and Salehye'h. The General-in-Chief immediately determined to march in person against that formidable enemy, and he left Cairo about fifteen days after he had entered it. It is unnecessary to describe the well-known engagement in which Bonaparte drove Ibrahim back upon El-Arish; besides, I do not enter minutely into the details of battles, my chief object being to record events which I personally witnessed.

At the battle of Salehye'h Bonaparte thought he had lost one of his 'aides de camp', Sulkowsky, to whom he was much attached, and who had been with us during the whole of the campaign of Italy. On the field of battle one object of regret cannot long engross the mind; yet, on his return to Cairo, Bonaparte frequently spoke to me of Sulkowsky in terms of unfeigned sorrow.

"I cannot," said he one day, "sufficiently admire the noble spirit and determined courage of poor Sulkowsky." He often said that Sulkowsky would have been a valuable aid to whoever might undertake the resuscitation of Poland. Fortunately that brave officer was not killed on that occasion, though seriously wounded. He was, however, killed shortly after.

The destruction of the French squadron in the roads of Aboukir occurred during the absence of the General-in-Chief. This event happened on the 1st of August. The details are generally known; but there is one circumstance to which I cannot refrain from alluding, and which excited deep interest at the time. This was the heroic courage of the son of Casablanca, the captain of the 'Orient'. Casablanca was among the wounded, and when the vessel was blown up his son, a lad of ten years of age, preferred perishing with him rather than saving himself, when one of the seamen had secured him the means of escape. I told the 'aide de camp', sent by General Kléber, who had the command of Alexandria, that the General-in-Chief was near Salehye'h. He proceeded thither immediately, and Bonaparte hastened back to Cairo, a distance of about thirty-three leagues.

In spite of any assertions that may have been made to the contrary, the fact is, that as soon as the French troops set foot in Egypt, they were filled with dissatisfaction, and ardently longed to return home.[57]

56 Far more thoroughly and actively than those taken by the English Government in 1882-3-4

57 'Erreurs' objects to this description of the complaints of the army, but Savary (tome i. pp. 66, 67, and tome i. p. 89) fully confirms it, giving the reason that the army was not a homogeneous body, but a mixed force taken from Rome, Florence, Milan, Venice, Genoa, and Marseilles; see also Thiers, tome v. p. 283. But the fact is not singular. For a striking instance, in the days of the Empire, of the soldiers in 1809, in Spain, actually threatening Napoleon in his own hearing, see De Gonneville (tome i. pp. 190-193): "The soldiers of Lapisse's division gave loud expression to the most sinister designs against the Emperor's person, stirring up each other to fire a shot at him, and bandying accusations of cowardice for not doing it." He heard it all

The illusion of the expedition had disappeared, and only its reality remained. What bitter murmuring have I not heard from Murat, Lannes, Berthier, Bessières, and others! Their complaints were, indeed, often so unmeasured as almost to amount to sedition. This greatly vexed Bonaparte, and drew from him severe reproaches and violent language.[58] When the news arrived of the loss of the fleet, discontent increased. All who had acquired fortunes under Napoleon now began to fear that they would never enjoy them. All turned their thoughts to Paris, and its amusements, and were utterly disheartened at the idea of being separated from their homes and their friends for a period, the termination of which it was impossible to foresee.

The catastrophe of Aboukir came like a thunderbolt upon the General-in-Chief. In spite of all his energy and fortitude, he was deeply distressed by the disasters which now assailed him. To the painful feelings excited by the complaints and dejection of his companions in arms was now added the irreparable misfortune of the burning of our fleet. He measured the fatal consequences of this event at a single glance. We were now cut off from all communication with France, and all hope of returning thither, except by a degrading capitulation with an implacable and hated enemy. Bonaparte had lost all chance of preserving his conquest, and to him this was indeed a bitter reflection. And at what a time did this disaster befall him? At the very moment when he was about to apply for the aid of the mother-country.

From what General Bonaparte communicated to me previously to the 1st of August, his object was, having once secured the possession of Egypt; to return to Toulon with the fleet; then to send troops and provisions of every kind to Egypt; and next to combine with the fleet all the forces that could be supplied, not only by France, but by her allies, for the purpose of attacking England. It is certain that previously to his departure for Egypt he had laid before the Directory a note relative to his plans. He always regarded a descent upon England as possible, though in its result fatal, so long as we should be inferior in naval strength; but he hoped by various manoeuvres to secure a superiority on one point.

His intention was to return to France. Availing himself of the departure of the English fleet for the Mediterranean, the alarm excited by his Egyptian expedition, the panic that would be inspired by his sudden appearance at Boulogne, and his preparations against England, he hoped to oblige that power to withdraw her naval force from the Mediterranean, and to prevent her sending out troops to Egypt. This project was often in his head. He would have thought it sublime to date an order of the day from the ruins of Memphis, and three months later, one from London. The loss of the fleet converted all these bold conceptions into mere romantic visions.

When alone with me he gave free vent to his emotion. I observed to him that the disaster

---

as plainly as we did, and seemed as if he did not care a bit for it, but "sent the division into good quarters, when the men were as enthusiastic as they were formerly mutinous." In 1796 d'Entraigues, the Bourbon spy, reports, "As a general rule, the French soldier grumbles and is discontented. He accuses Bonaparte of being a thief and a rascal. But to-morrow the very same soldier will obey him blindly" (Iung's Bonaparte, tome iii. p. 152).

58 Napoleon related at St. Helena that in a fit of irritation he rushed among a group of dissatisfied generals, and said to one of them, who was remarkable for his stature, "you have held seditious language; but take care I do not perform my duty. Though you are five feet ten inches high, that shall not save you from being shot."—Bourrienne.

was doubtless great, but that it would have been infinitely more irreparable had Nelson fallen in with us at Malta, or had he waited for us four-and-twenty hours before Alexandria, or in the open sea. "Any one of these events," said I, "which were not only possible but probable, would have deprived us of every resource. We are blockaded here, but we have provisions and money. Let us then wait patiently to see what the Directory will do for us."—"The Directory!" exclaimed he angrily, "the Directory is composed of a set of scoundrels! they envy and hate me, and would gladly let me perish here. Besides, you see how dissatisfied the whole army is: not a man is willing to stay."

The pleasing illusions which were cherished at the outset of the expedition vanished long before our arrival in Cairo. Egypt was no longer the empire of the Ptolemies, covered with populous and wealthy cities; it now presented one unvaried scene of devastation and misery. Instead of being aided by the inhabitants, whom we had ruined, for the sake of delivering them from the yoke of the beys, we found all against us: Mamelukes, Arabs, and fellahs. No Frenchman was secure of his life who happened to stray half a mile from any inhabited place, or the corps to which he belonged. The hostility which prevailed against us and the discontent of the army were clearly developed in the numerous letters which were written to France at the time, and intercepted.

The gloomy reflections which at first assailed Bonaparte, were speedily banished; and he soon recovered the fortitude and presence of mind which had been for a moment shaken by the overwhelming news from Aboukir. He, however, sometimes repeated, in a tone which it would be difficult to describe, "Unfortunate Brueys, what have you done!"

I have remarked that in some chance observations which escaped Napoleon at St. Helena he endeavoured to throw all the blame of the affair on Admiral Brueys. Persons who are determined to make Bonaparte an exception to human nature have unjustly reproached the Admiral for the loss of the fleet.

CHAPTER XVI

1798

The loss of the fleet convinced General Bonaparte of the necessity of speedily and effectively organising Egypt, where everything denoted that we should stay for a considerable time, excepting the event of a forced evacuation, which the General was far from foreseeing or fearing. The distance of Ibrahim Bey and Mourad Bey now left him a little at rest. War, fortifications, taxation, government, the organization of the divans, trade, art, and science, all occupied his attention. Orders and instructions were immediately despatched, if not to repair the defeat, at least to avert the first danger that might ensue from it. On the 21st of August Bonaparte established at Cairo an institute of the arts and sciences, of which he subsequently appointed me a member in the room of M. de Sucy, who was obliged to return to France, in consequence of the wound he received on board the flotilla in the Nile.[59]

In founding this Institute, Bonaparte wished to afford an example of his ideas of civilisation. The minutes of the sittings of that learned body, which have been printed, bear evidence of its utility, and of Napoleon's extended views. The objects of the Institute were the advancement and propagation of information in Egypt, and the study and publication of all facts relating to the natural history, trade, and antiquities of that ancient country.

On the 18th Bonaparte was present at the ceremony of opening the dyke of the canal of Cairo, which receives the water of the Nile when it reaches the height fired by the Mequyas.

Two days after came the anniversary festival of the birth of Mahomet. At this Napoleon was also present, in company with the sheik El Bekri, who at his request gave him two young Mamelukes, Ibrahim, and Roustan.[60] It has been alleged that Bonaparte, when in Egypt, took

59 The Institute of Egypt was composed of members of the French Institute, and of the men of science and artists of the commission who did not belong to that body. They assembled and added to their number several officers of the artillery and staff, and others who had cultivated the sciences and literature. The Institute was established in one of the palaces of the bey's. A great number of machines, and physical, chemical, and astronomical instruments had been brought from France. They were distributed in the different rooms, which were also successively filled with all the curiosities of the country, whether of the animal, vegetable, or mineral kingdom. The garden of the palace became a botanical garden. A chemical laboratory was formed at headquarters; Berthollet performed experiments there several times every week, which Napoleon and a great number of officers attended ('Memoirs of Napoleon')

60 The General-in-Chief went to celebrate the feast of the Prophet at the house of the sheik El Bekri. The ceremony was begun by the recital of a kind of litany, containing the life of Mahomet from his birth to his death. About a hundred sheiks, sitting in a circle, on carpets, with their legs crossed, recited all the verses, swinging their bodies violently backwards and forwards, and altogether. A grand dinner was afterwards served up, at which the guests sat on carpets, with their legs across. There were twenty tables, and five or six people at each

part in the religious ceremonies and worship of the Mussulmans; but it cannot be said that he celebrated the festivals of the overflowing of the Nile and the anniversary of the Prophet. The Turks invited him to these merely as a spectator; and the presence of their new master was gratifying to the people. But he never committed the folly of ordering any solemnity. He neither learned nor repeated any prayer of the Koran, as many persons have asserted; neither did he advocate fatalism, polygamy, or any other doctrine of the Koran. Bonaparte employed himself better than in discussing with the Imaums the theology of the children of Ismael. The ceremonies, at which policy induced him to be present, were to him, and to all who accompanied him, mere matters of curiosity. He never set foot in a mosque; and only on one occasion, which I shall hereafter mention, dressed himself in the Mahometan costume. He attended the festivals to which the green turbans invited him. His religious tolerance was the natural consequence of his philosophic spirit.[61] Doubtless Bonaparte did, as he was bound to do, show respect for the religion of the country; and he found it necessary to act more like a Mussulman than a Catholic. A wise conqueror supports his triumphs by protecting and even elevating the religion of the conquered people. Bonaparte's principle was, as he himself has often told me, to look upon religions as the work of men, but to respect them everywhere

table. That of the General-in-Chief and the sheik El Bekri was in the middle; a little slab of a precious kind of wood ornamented with mosaic work was placed eighteen inches above the floor and covered with a great number of dishes in succession. They were pillaws of rice, a particular kind of roast, entrees, and pastry, all very highly spiced. The sheiks picked everything with their fingers. Accordingly water was brought to wash the hands three times during dinner. Gooseberry-water, lemonade, and other sorts of sherbets were served to drink, and abundance of preserves and confectionery with the dessert. On the whole, the dinner was not disagreeable; it was only the manner of eating it that seemed strange to us. In the evening the whole city was illuminated. After dinner the party went into the square of El Bekri, the illumination of which, in coloured lamps, was very beautiful. An immense concourse of people attended. They were all placed in order, in ranks of from twenty to a hundred persons, who, standing close together, recited the prayers and litanies of the Prophet with movements which kept increasing, until at length they seemed to be convulsive, and some of the most zealous fainted away ('Memoirs of Napoleon').]— —[Roustan or Rustan, a Mameluke, was always with Napoleon from the time of the return from Egypt till 1814, when he abandoned his master. He slept at or near the door of Napoleon. See Rémusat, tome i, p. 209, for an amusing description of the alarm of Josephine, and the precipitate flight of Madame de Rémusat, at the idea of being met and killed by this man in one of Josephine's nocturnal attacks on the privacy of her husband when closeted with his mistress.

61 From this Sir Walter Scott infers that he did not scruple to join the Musselmans in the external ceremonies of their religion. He embellishes his romance with the ridiculous farce of the sepulchral chamber of the grand pyramid, and the speeches which were addressed to the General as well as to the muftis and Imaums; and he adds that Bonaparte was on the point of embracing Islamism. All that Sir Walter says on this subject is the height of absurdity, and does not even deserve to be seriously refuted. Bonaparte never entered a mosque except from motives of curiosity,(see contradiction in previous paragraph. D.W.) and he never for one moment afforded any ground for supposing that he believed in the mission of Mahomet.—Bourrienne.

as a powerful engine of government. However, I will not go so far as to say that he would not have changed his religion had the conquest of the East been the price of that change. All that he said about Mahomet, Islamism, and the Koran to the great men of the country he laughed at himself. He enjoyed the gratification of having all his fine sayings on the subject of religion translated into Arabic poetry, and repeated from mouth to mouth. This of course tended to conciliate the people.

I confess that Bonaparte frequently conversed with the chiefs of the Mussulman religion on the subject of his conversion; but only for the sake of amusement. The priests of the Koran, who would probably have been delighted to convert us, offered us the most ample concessions. But these conversations were merely started by way of entertainment, and never could have warranted a supposition of their leading to any serious result. If Bonaparte spoke as a Mussulman, it was merely in his character of a military and political chief in a Mussulman country. To do so was essential to his success, to the safety of his army, and, consequently, to his glory. In every country he would have drawn up proclamations and delivered addresses on the same principle. In India he would have been for Ali, at Thibet for the Dalai-lama, and in China for Confucius.[62]

The General-in-Chief had a Turkish dress made, which he once put on, merely in joke. One day he desired me to go to breakfast without waiting for him, and that he would follow me. In about a quarter of an hour he made his appearance in his new costume. As soon as

62 On the subject of his alleged conversion to Mahometanism Bonaparte expressed himself at St. Helena as follows: "I never followed any of the tenets of that religion. I never prayed in the mosques. I never abstained from wine, or was circumcised, neither did I ever profess it. I said merely that we were the friends of the Mussulmans, and that I respected Mahomet their prophet, which was true; I respect him now. I wanted to make the Imaums cause prayers to be offered up in the mosques for me, in order to make the people respect me still more than they actually did, and obey me more readily. The Imaums replied that there was a great obstacle, because their Prophet in the Koran had inculcated to them that they were not to obey, respect, or hold faith with infidels, and that I came under that denomination. I then desired them to hold a consultation, and see what was necessary to be done in order to become a Mussulman, as some of their tenets could not be practised by us. That, as to circumcision, God had made us unfit for that. That, with respect to drinking wine, we were poor cold people, inhabitants of the north, who could not exist without it. They consulted together accordingly, and in about three weeks issued a fetham, declaring that circumcision might be omitted, because it was merely a profession; that as to drinking wine, it might be drunk by Mussulmans, but that those who drank it would not go to paradise, but to hell. I replied that this would not do; that we had no occasion to make ourselves Mussulmans in order to go to hell, that there were many ways of getting there without coming to Egypt, and desired them to hold another consultation. After deliberating and battling together for I believe three months, they finally decided that a man might become a Mussulman, and neither circumcise nor abstain from wine; but that, in proportion to the wine drunk, some good works must be done. I then told them that we were all Mussulmans and friends of the Prophet, which they really believed, as the French soldiers never went to church, and had no priests with them. For you must know that during the Revolution there was no religion whatever in the French army. Menou," continued Napoleon, "really turned Mahometan, which was the reason I left him behind." — (Voices from St. Helena.)

he was recognised he was received with a loud burst of laughter. He sat down very coolly; but he found himself so encumbered and ill at ease in his turban and Oriental robe that he speedily threw them off, and was never tempted to a second performance of the masquerade.

About the end of August Bonaparte wished to open negotiations with the Pasha of Acre, nicknamed the Butcher. He offered Djezzar his friendship, sought his in return, and gave him the most consolatory assurances of the safety of his dominions. He promised to support him against the Grand Seignior, at the very moment when he was assuring the Egyptians that he would support the Grand Seignior against the beys. But Djezzar, confiding in his own strength and in the protection of the English, who had anticipated Bonaparte, was deaf to every overture, and would not even receive Beauvoisin, who was sent to him on the 22d of August. A second envoy was beheaded at Acre. The occupations of Bonaparte and the necessity of obtaining a more solid footing in Egypt retarded for the moment the invasion of that pashalic, which provoked vengeance by its barbarities, besides being a dangerous neighbour.

From the time he received the accounts of the disaster of Aboukir until the revolt of Cairo on the 22d of October, Bonaparte sometimes found the time hang heavily on his hands. Though he devoted attention to everything, yet there was not sufficient occupation for his singularly active mind. When the heat was not too great he rode on horseback; and on his return, if he found no despatches to read (which often happened), no orders to send off; or no letters to answer, he was immediately absorbed in reverie, and would sometimes converse very strangely. One day, after a long pause, he said to me:

"Do you know what I am thinking of?"—"Upon my word, that would be very difficult; you think of such extraordinary things."—"I don't know," continued he, "that I shall ever see France again; but if I do, my only ambition is to make a glorious campaign in Germany—in the plains of Bavaria; there to gain a great battle, and to avenge France for the defeat of Hochstadt. After that I would retire into the country, and live quietly."

He then entered upon a long dissertation on the preference he would give to Germany as the theatre of war; the fine character of the people, and the prosperity and wealth of the country, and its power of supporting an army. His conversations were sometimes very long; but always replete with interest.[63] In these intervals of leisure Bonaparte was accustomed to retire to bed early. I used to read to him every evening. When I read poetry he would fall asleep; but when he asked for the Life of Cromwell I counted on sitting up pretty late. In the course of the day he used to read and make notes. He often expressed regret at not receiving news from France; for correspondence was rendered impracticable by the numerous English and Turkish cruisers. Many letters were intercepted and scandalously published. Not even family secrets and communications of the most confidential nature were respected.

About the middle of September in this year (1798), Bonaparte ordered to be brought to the house of Elfy Bey half a dozen Asiatic women whose beauty he had heard highly extolled.

---

63 So early as 1794 Napoleon had suggested that Austria should always be attacked in Germany, not in Italy. "It is Germany that should be overwhelmed; that done, Italy and Spain fall of themselves. Germany should be attacked, not Spain or Italy. If we obtain great success, advantage should never be taken of it to penetrate into Italy while Germany, unweakened, offers a formidable front" (Iung's Bonaparte, tome ii. p. 936), He was always opposed to the wild plans which had ruined so many French armies in Italy, and which the Directory tried to force on him, of marching on Rome and Naples after every success in the north.

But their ungraceful obesity displeased him, and they were immediately dismissed. A few days after he fell violently in love with Madame Foures, the wife of a lieutenant of infantry. She was very pretty, and her charms were enhanced by the rarity of seeing a woman in Egypt who was calculated to please the eye of a European. Bonaparte engaged for her a house adjoining the palace of Elfy Bey, which we occupied. He frequently ordered dinner to be prepared there, and I used to go there with him at seven o'clock, and leave him at nine.

This connection soon became the general subject of gossip at head-quarters. Through a feeling of delicacy to M. Foures, the General-in-Chief gave him a mission to the Directory. He embarked at Alexandria, and the ship was captured by the English, who, being informed of the cause of his mission, were malicious enough to send him back to Egypt, instead of keeping him prisoner. Bonaparte wished to have a child by Madame Foures, but this wish was not realised.

A celebrated soothsayer was recommended to Bonaparte by the inhabitants of Cairo, who confidentially vouched for the accuracy with which he could foretell future events. He was sent for, and when he arrived, I, Venture, and a sheik were with the General. The prophet wished first to exercise his skill upon Bonaparte, who, however, proposed that I should have my fortune told first, to which I acceded without hesitation. To afford an idea of his prophetic skill I must mention that since my arrival in Cairo I had been in a very weak state. The passage of the Nile and the bad food we had had for twelve days had greatly reduced me, so that I was miserably pale and thin.

After examining my hands, feeling my pulse, my forehead, and the nape of my neck, the fortune-teller shrugged his shoulders, and, in a melancholy tone, told Venture that he did not think it right to inform me of my fate. I gave him to understand that he might say what he pleased, as it was a matter of indifference to me. After considerable hesitation on his part and pressing on mine, he announced to me that the earth of Egypt would receive me in two months.

I thanked him, and he was dismissed. When we were alone the General said to me, "Well, what do you think of that?" I observed that the fortune-teller did not run any great risk in foretelling my death, which was a very probable circumstance in the state in which I was; "but," added I, "if I procure the wines which I have ordered from France, you will soon see me get round again."

The art of imposing on mankind has at all times been an important part of the art of governing; and it was not that portion of the science of government which Bonaparte was the least acquainted with. He neglected no opportunity of showing off to the Egyptians the superiority of France in arts and sciences; but it happened, oftener than once, that the simple instinct of the Egyptians thwarted his endeavours in this way. Some days after the visit of the pretended fortune-teller he wished, if I may so express myself, to oppose conjurer to conjurer. For this purpose he invited the principal sheiks to be present at some chemical experiments performed by M. Berthollet. The General expected to be much amused at their astonishment; but the miracles of the transformation of liquids, electrical commotions and galvanism, did not elicit from them any symptom of surprise. They witnessed the operations of our able chemist with the most imperturbable indifference. When they were ended, the sheik El Bekri desired the interpreter to tell M. Berthollet that it was all very fine; "but," said he, "ask him whether he can make me be in Morocco and here at one and the same moment?" M. Berthollet replied in the negative, with a shrug of his shoulders. "Oh! then," said the sheik, "he is not half a sorcerer."

Our music produced no greater effect upon them. They listened with insensibility to all the airs that were played to them, with the exception of "Marlbrook." When that was played they became animated, and were all in motion, as if ready to dance.

An order which had been issued on our arrival in Cairo for watching the criers of the mosques had for some weeks been neglected. At certain hours of the night these criers address prayers to the Prophet. As it was merely a repetition of the same ceremony over and over again, in a short time no notice was taken of it. The Turks, perceiving this negligence, substituted for their prayers and hymns cries of revolt, and by this sort of verbal telegraph, insurrectionary excitement was transmitted to the northern and southern extremities of Egypt. By this means, and by the aid of secret emissaries, who eluded our feeble police, and circulated real or forged firmans of the Sultan disavowing the concord between France and the Porte, and provoking war, the plan of a revolution was organised throughout the country.

The signal for the execution of this plan was given from the minarets on the night of the 20th of October, and on the morning of the 21st it was announced at headquarters that the city of Cairo was in open insurrection. The General-in-Chief was not, as has been stated, in the isle of Raeuddah: he did not hear the firing of the alarm-guns. He rose when the news arrived; it was then five o'clock. He was informed that all the shops were closed, and that the French were attacked. A moment after he heard of the death of General Dupuis, commandant of the garrison, who was killed by a lance in the street. Bonaparte immediately mounted his horse, and, accompanied by only thirty guides, visited all the threatened points, restored confidence, and, with great presence of mind, adopted measures of defence.

He left me at headquarters with only one sentinel; but he had been accurately informed of the situation of the insurgents; and such was my confidence in his activity and foresight that I had no apprehension, and awaited his return with perfect composure. This composure was not disturbed even when I saw a party of insurgents attack the house of M. Estève, our paymaster-general, which was situated on the opposite side of Ezbekye'h Place. M. Estève was, fortunately, able to resist the attack until troops from Boulac came up to his assistance.

After visiting all the posts, and adopting every precautionary measure, Bonaparte returned to headquarters. Finding me still alone with the sentinel, he asked me, smiling, "whether I had not been frightened?"—"Not at all, General, I assure you," replied I.

—It was about half-past eight in the morning when Bonaparte returned to headquarters, and while at breakfast he was informed that some Bedouin Arabs, on horseback, were trying to force their entrance into Cairo. He ordered his aide de camp, Sulkowsky, to mount his horse, to take with him fifteen guides, and proceed to the point where the assailants were most numerous. This was the Bab-el-Nasser, or the gate of victory. Croisier observed to the General-in-Chief that Sulkowsky had scarcely recovered from the wounds at Salehye'h, and he offered to take his place. He had his motives for this. Bonaparte consented; but Sulkowsky had already set out. Within an hour after, one of the fifteen guides returned, covered with blood, to announce that Sulkowsky and the remainder of his party had been cut to pieces. This was speedy work, for we were still at table when the sad news arrived.

Mortars were planted on Mount Mokatam, which commands Cairo. The populace, expelled from all the principal streets by the troops, assembled in the square of the Great Mosque, and in the little streets running into it, which they barricaded. The firing of the artillery on the heights was kept up with vigour for two days.

About twelve of the principal chiefs of Cairo were arrested and confined in an apartment at headquarters. They awaited with the calmest resignation the death they knew they merited;

but Bonaparte merely detained them as hostages. The aga in the service of Bonaparte was astonished that sentence of death was not pronounced upon them; and he said, shrugging his shoulders, and with a gesture apparently intended to provoke severity, "You see they expect it."

On the third the insurrection was at an end, and tranquillity restored. Numerous prisoners were conducted to the citadel. In obedience to an order which I wrote every evening, twelve were put to death nightly. The bodies were then put into sacks and thrown into the Nile. There were many women included in these nocturnal executions.

I am not aware that the number of victims amounted to thirty per day, as Bonaparte assured General Reynier in a letter which he wrote to him six days after the restoration of tranquillity. "Every night," said he, "we cut off thirty heads. This, I hope, will be an effectual example." I am of opinion that in this instance he exaggerated the extent of his just revenge.

Some time after the revolt of Cairo the necessity of ensuring our own safety forced the commission of a terrible act of cruelty. A tribe of Arabs in the neighbourhood of Cairo had surprised and massacred a party of French. The General-in-Chief ordered his aide de camp Croisier to proceed to the spot, surround the tribe, destroy the huts, kill all the men, and conduct the rest of the population to Cairo. The order was to decapitate the victims, and bring their heads in sacks to Cairo to be exhibited to the people. Eugène Beauharnais accompanied Croisier, who joyfully set out on this horrible expedition, in hope of obliterating all recollection of the affair of Damanhour.

On the following day the party returned. Many of the poor Arab women had been delivered on the road, and the children had perished of hunger, heat, and fatigue. About four o'clock a troop of asses arrived in Ezbekye'h Place, laden with sacks. The sacks were opened and the heads rolled out before the assembled populace. I cannot describe the horror I experienced; but I must nevertheless acknowledge that this butchery ensured for a considerable time the tranquillity and even the existence of the little caravans which were obliged to travel in all directions for the service of the army.

Shortly before the loss of the fleet the General-in Chief had formed the design of visiting Suez, to examine the traces of the ancient canal which united the Nile to the Gulf of Arabia, and also to cross the latter. The revolt at Cairo caused this project to be adjourned until the month of December.

Before his departure for Suez, Bonaparte granted the commissary Sucy leave to return to France. He had received a wound in the right hand, when on board the xebec 'Cerf'. I was conversing with him on deck when he received this wound. At first it had no appearance of being serious; but some time after he could not use his hand. General Bonaparte despatched a vessel with sick and wounded, who were supposed to be incurable, to the number of about eighty. All envied their fate, and were anxious to depart with them, but the privilege was conceded to very few. However, those who were, disappointed had, no cause for regret. We never know what we wish for. Captain Marengo, who landed at Augusta in Sicily, supposing it to be a friendly land, was required to observe quarantine for twenty-two days, and information was given of the arrival of the vessel to the court, which was at Palermo. On the 25th of January 1799 all on board the French vessel were massacred, with the exception of twenty-one who were saved by a Neapolitan frigate, and conducted to Messing, where they were detained.

Before he conceived the resolution of attacking the Turkish advanced guard in the valleys of Syria, Bonaparte had formed a plan of invading British India from Persia. He had ascertained, through the medium of agents, that the Shah of Persia would, for a sum of money paid in advance, consent to the establishment of military magazines on certain points of his territory. Bonaparte frequently told me that if, after the subjugation of Egypt, he could have left 15,000 men in that country, and have had 30,000 disposable troops, he would have marched on the Euphrates. He was frequently speaking about the deserts which were to be crossed to reach Persia.

How many times have I seen him extended on the ground, examining the beautiful maps which he had brought with him, and he would sometimes make me lie down in the same position to trace to me his projected march. This reminded him of the triumphs of his favourite hero, Alexander, with whom he so much desired to associate his name; but, at the same time, he felt that these projects were incompatible with our resources, the weakness of the Government; and the dissatisfaction which the army already evinced. Privation and misery are inseparable from all these remote operations.

This favourite idea still occupied his mind a fortnight before his departure for Syria was determined on, and on the 25th of January 1799 he wrote to Tippoo Saib as follows:—

> You are of course already informed of my arrival on the banks of the Red Sea, with a numerous and invincible army. Eager to deliver you from the iron yoke of England, I hasten to request that you will send me, by the way of Mascate or Mocha, an account of the political situation in which you are. I also wish that you could send to Suez, or Grand Cairo, some able man, in your confidence, with whom I may confer.[64]

64 It is not true, as has often been stated, that Tippoo Saib wrote to General Bonaparte. He could not reply to a letter written on the 23th of January, owing to the great difficulty of communication, the considerable distance, and the short interval which elapsed between the 25th of January and the fall of the Empire of Mysore, which happened on the 20th of April following. The letter to Tippo Saib commenced "Citizen-Sultan!"—Bourrienne

CHAPTER XVII

1798-1799

On the 24th of December we set out for Suez, where we arrived on the 26th. On the 25th we encamped in the desert some leagues before Ad-Geroth. The heat had been very great during the day; but about eleven at night the cold became so severe as to be precisely in an inverse ratio to the temperature of the day. This desert, which is the route of the caravans from Suez, from Tor and the countries situated on the north of Arabia, is strewed with the bones of the men and animals who, for ages past, have perished in crossing it. As there was no wood to be got, we collected a quantity of these bones for fuel. Monge himself was induced to sacrifice some of the curious skulls of animals which he had picked up on the way and deposited in the Berlin of the General-in-Chief. But no sooner had we kindled our fires than an intolerable effluvium obliged us to raise our camp and advance farther on, for we could procure no water to extinguish the fires.

On the 27th Bonaparte employed himself in inspecting the town and port of Suez, and in giving orders for some naval and military works. He feared—what indeed really occurred after his departure from Egypt—the arrival of some English troops from the East Indies, which he had intended to invade. These regiments contributed to the loss of his conquest.[65]

On the morning of the 28th we crossed the Red Sea dry-shod, to go to the Wells of Moses, which are nearly a myriametre from the eastern coast, and a little southeast of Suez. The Gulf of Arabia terminates at about 5,000 metres north of that city. Near the port the Red Sea is not above 1,500 metres wide, and is always fordable at low water. The caravans from Tor and Mount Sinai always pass at that part,[66] either in going to or returning from Egypt. This shortens their journey nearly a myriametre. At high tide the water rises five or six feet at Suez, and when the wind blows fresh it often rises to nine or ten feet.

We spent a few hours seated by the largest of the springs called the Wells of Moses,

65 Sir David Baird, with a force of about 7000 men sent from India, landed at Cosseir in July 1801.

66 I shall say nothing of the Cenobites of Mount Sinai, as I had not the honour of seeing them. Neither did I see the register containing the names of Ali, Salah-Eddin, Ibrahim or Abraham, on which Bonaparte is said to have inscribed his name. I perceived at a distance some high hills which were said to be Mount Sinai. I conversed, through the medium of an interpreter, with some Arabian chiefs of Tor and its neighbourhood. They had been informed of our excursion to the Wells, and that they might there thank the French General for the protection granted to their caravans and their trade with Egypt. On the 19th of December, before his departure from Suez, Bonaparte signed a sort of safeguard, or exemption from duties, for the convent of Mount Sinai. This had been granted out of respect to Moses and the Jewish nation, and also because the convent of Mount Sinai is a seat of learning and civilisation amidst the barbarism of the deserts.—Bourrienne.

situated on the eastern shore of the Gulf of Arabia. We made coffee with the water from these springs, which, however, gave it such a brackish taste that it was scarcely drinkable.

Though the water of the eight little springs which form the Wells of Moses is not so salt as that of many wells dug in other parts of the deserts, it is, nevertheless, exceedingly brackish, and does not allay thirst so well as fresh water.

Bonaparte returned to Suez that same night. It was very dark when we reached the sea-shore. The tide was coming up, and the water was pretty high. We deviated a little from the way we had taken in the morning; we crossed a little too low down; we were thrown into disorder, but we did not lose ourselves in the marshes as has been stated. There were none. I have read somewhere, though I did not see the fact, nor did I hear it mentioned at the time, that the tide, which was coming up, would have been the grave of the General-in-Chief had not one of the guides saved him by carrying him on his shoulders. If any such danger had existed, all who had not a similar means of escape must have perished.

This is a fabrication. General Caffarelli was the only person who was really in danger, for his wooden leg prevented his sitting firmly on his horse in the water; but some persons came to his assistance and supported him.[67]

On his return to Cairo the General-in-Chief wished to discover the site of the canal which in ancient times formed a junction between the Red Sea and the Nile by Belbeis. M. Lepère, who was a member of the Egyptian Institute, and is now inspector-general of bridges and highways, executed on the spot a beautiful plan, which may confidently be consulted by those who wish to form an accurate idea of that ancient communication, and the level of the two seas.[68]

On his arrival at the capital Bonaparte again devoted all his thoughts to the affairs of the army, which he had not attended to during his short absence. The revenues of Egypt were far from being sufficient to meet the military expenditure. To defray his own expenses Bonaparte raised several considerable loans in Genoa through the medium of M. James. The connection of James with the Bonaparte family takes its date from this period.[69]

Since the month of August the attention of General Bonaparte had been constantly fixed on Syria. The period of the possible landing of an enemy in Egypt had now passed away, and could not return until the month of July in the following year. Bonaparte was fully convinced that that landing would take place, and he was not deceived. The Ottoman Porte had, indeed, been persuaded that the conquest of Egypt was not in her interest. She preferred enduring a rebel whom she hoped one day to subdue to supporting a power which, under the specious pretext of reducing her insurgent beys to obedience, deprived her of one of her finest provinces, and threatened the rest of the empire.

---

67 Bonaparte extricated himself as the others did from the real danger he and his escort had run. At St. Helena he said, "Profiting by the low tide, I crossed the Red Sea dry-shod. On my return I was overtaken by the night and went astray in the middle of the rising tide. I ran the greatest danger. I nearly perished in the same manner as Pharaoh did. This would certainly have furnished all the Christian preachers with a magnificent test against me." —Bourrienne.

68 Since accurately ascertained during the progress of the works for the Suez Canal.

69 Joseph Bonaparte says that the fathers of Napoleon and of M. James had long known one another, and that Napoleon had met James at Autun. ('Erreurs', tome i, p. 296).

On his return to Cairo the General-in-Chief had no longer any doubt as to the course which the Porte intended to adopt. The numerous class of persons who believed that the Ottoman Porte had consented to our occupation of Egypt were suddenly undeceived. It was then asked how we could, without that consent, have attempted such an enterprise? Nothing, it was said, could justify the temerity of such an expedition, if it should produce a rupture between France, the Ottoman empire, and its allies. However, for the remainder of the year Bonaparte dreaded nothing except an expedition from Gaza and El-Arish, of which the troops of Djezzar had already taken possession. This occupation was justly regarded as a decided act of hostility; war was thus practically declared. "We must adopt anticipatory measures," thought Napoleon; "we must destroy this advanced guard of the Ottoman empire, overthrow the ramparts of Jaffa and Acre, ravage the country, destroy all her resources, so as to render the passage of an army across the desert impracticable." Thus was planned the expedition against Syria.

General Berthier, after repeated entreaties, had obtained permission to return to France. The 'Courageuse' frigate, which was to convey him home, was fitting out at Alexandria; he had received his instructions, and was to leave Cairo on the 29th of January, ten days before Bonaparte's departure for Syria. Bonaparte was sorry to part with him; but he could not endure to see an old friend, and one who had served him well in all his campaigns, dying before his eyes, the victim of nostalgia and romantic love. Besides, Berthier had been for some time past, anything but active in the discharge of his duties. His passion, which amounted almost to madness, impaired the feeble faculties with which nature had endowed him. Some writers have ranked him in the class of sentimental lovers: be this as it may, the homage which Berthier rendered to the portrait of the object of his adoration more frequently excited our merriment than our sensibility.

One day I went with an order from Bonaparte to the chief of his staff, whom I found on his knees before the portrait of Madame Visconti, which was hanging opposite the door. I touched him, to let him know I was there. He grumbled a little, but did not get angry.

The moment was approaching when the two friends were to part, perhaps forever. Bonaparte was sincerely distressed at this separation, and the chief of his staff was informed of the fact. At a moment when it was supposed Berthier was on his way to Alexandria, he presented himself to the General-in-Chief. "You are, then, decidedly going to Asia?" said he.—"You know," replied the General, "that all is ready, and I shall set out in a few days."—"Well, I will not leave you. I voluntarily renounce all idea of returning to France. I could not endure to forsake you at a moment when you are going to encounter new dangers. Here are my instructions and my passport." Bonaparte, highly pleased with this resolution, embraced Berthier; and the coolness which had been excited by his request to return home was succeeded by a sincere reconciliation.

Louis Bonaparte, who was suffering from the effects of the voyage, was still at Alexandria. The General-in-Chief, yielding to the pacific views of his younger brother, who was also beginning to evince some symptoms of nostalgia, consented to his return home. He could not, however, depart until the 11th of March 1799. I felt the absence of Louis very much.

On his return to France Louis passed through Sens, where he dined with Madame de Bourrienne, to whom he presented a beautiful shawl, which General Berthier had given me. This, I believe, was the first Cashmere that had ever been seen in France. Louis was much surprised when Madame de Bourrienne showed him the Egyptian correspondence, which had been seized by the English and printed in London. He found in the collection some letters addressed to himself, and there were others, he said, which were likely to disturb the peace of more than one family on the return of the army.

On the 11th of February 1799 we began our march for Syria, with about 12,000 men. It has been erroneously stated that the army amounted to only 6000: nearly that number was lost in the course of the campaign. However, at the very moment we were on our way to Syria, with 12,000 men, scarcely as many being left in Egypt, the Directory published that, "according to the information which had been received," we had 60,000 infantry and 10,000 cavalry; that the army had doubled its numbers by battles; and that since our arrival in Egypt, we had lost only 300 men. Is history to be written from such documents?

We arrived, about four o'clock in the afternoon, at Messoudiah, or, "the Fortunate Spot." Here we witnessed a kind of phenomenon, which was not a little agreeable to us. Messoudiah is a place situated on the coast of the Mediterranean, surrounded with little dunes of very fine sand, which the copious rains of winter readily penetrate. The rain remains in the sand, so that on making with the fingers holes of four or five inches in depth at the bottom of these little hills, the water immediately flows out. This water was, indeed, rather thick, but its flavour was agreeable; and it would have become clear if we could have spared time to allow it to rest and deposit the particles of sand it contained.

It was a curious spectacle to behold us all lying prostrate, digging wells in miniature; and displaying a laughable selfishness in our endeavours to obtain the most abundant source. This was a very important discovery to us. We found these sand-wells at the extremity of the desert, and it contributed, in no small degree, to revive the courage of our soldiers; besides, when men are, as was the case with us, subject to privations of every kind, the least benefit which accrues inspires the hope of a new advantage. We were approaching the confines of Syria, and we enjoyed by anticipation, the pleasure we were about to experience, on treading a soil which, by its variety of verdure and vegetation, would remind us of our native land. At Messoudiah we likewise possessed the advantage of bathing in the sea, which was not more than fifty paces from our unexpected water-supply.

Whilst near the wells of Messoudiah, on the way to El-Arish, I one day saw Bonaparte walking alone with Junot, as he was often in the habit of doing. I stood at a little distance, and my eyes, I know not why, were fixed on him during their conversation. The General's countenance, which was always pale, had, without my being able to divine the cause, become paler than usual. There was something convulsive in his features—a wildness in his look, and he several times struck his head with his hand. After conversing with Junot about a quarter of an hour he quitted him and came towards me. I never saw him exhibit such an air of dissatisfaction, or appear so much under the influence of some prepossession. I advanced towards him, and as soon as we met, he exclaimed in an abrupt and angry tone, "So! I find I cannot depend upon you.—These women!—Josephine! —if you had loved me, you would before now have told me all I have heard from Junot—he is a real friend—Josephine!—and I 600 leagues from her—you ought to have told me.—That she should thus have deceived me!—'Woe to them!—I will exterminate the whole race of fops and puppies!—As to her—divorce!—yes, divorce! a public and open divorce!—I must write!—I know all!—It is your fault—you ought to have told me!"

These energetic and broken exclamations, his disturbed countenance and altered voice informed me but too well of the subject of his conversation with Junot. I saw that Junot had been drawn into a culpable indiscretion; and that, if Josephine had committed any faults, he had cruelly exaggerated them. My situation was one of extreme delicacy. However, I had the good fortune to retain my self-possession, and as soon as some degree of calmness succeeded to this first burst, I replied that I knew nothing of the reports which Junot might have communicated to him; that even if such reports, often the offspring of calumny, had reached my ear, and if I had considered it my duty to inform him of them, I certainly would not have selected for that purpose the moment when he was 600 leagues from France. I also did not conceal how blamable Junot's conduct appeared to me, and how ungenerous I considered it thus rashly to accuse a woman who was not present to justify or defend herself; that it was no great proof of attachment to add domestic uneasiness to the anxiety, already sufficiently great, which the situation of his brothers in arms, at the commencement of a hazardous enterprise, occasioned him.

Notwithstanding these observations, which, however, he listened to with some calmness, the word "divorce" still escaped his lips; and it is necessary to be aware of the degree of irritation to which he was liable when anything seriously vexed him, to be able to form an idea of what Bonaparte was during this painful scene. However, I kept my ground. I repeated what I had said. I begged of him to consider with what facility tales were fabricated and circulated, and that gossip such as that which had been repeated to him was only the amusement of idle persons; and deserved the contempt of strong minds. I spoke of his glory. "My glory!" cried he. "I know not what I would not give if that which Junot has told me should be untrue; so much do I love Josephine! If she be really guilty a divorce must separate us for ever. I will not submit to be a laughing-stock for all the imbeciles in Paris. I will write to Joseph; he will get the divorce declared."

Although his agitation continued long, intervals occurred in which he was less excited. I seized one of these moments of comparative calm to combat this idea of divorce which seemed to possess his mind. I represented to him especially that it would be imprudent to write to his brother with reference to a communication which was probably false. "The letter might be intercepted; it would betray the feelings of irritation which dictated it. As to a divorce, it would be time to think of that hereafter, but advisedly."

These last words produced an effect on him which I could not have ventured to hope for so speedily. He became tranquil, listened to me as if he had suddenly felt the justice of my observations, dropped the subject, and never returned to it; except that about a fortnight after, when we were before St. Jean d'Acre, he expressed himself greatly dissatisfied with Junot, and complained of the injury he had done him by his indiscreet disclosures, which he began to regard as the inventions of malignity. I perceived afterwards that he never pardoned Junot for this indiscretion; and I can state, almost with certainty, that this was one of the reasons why Junot was not created a marshal of France, like many of his comrades whom Bonaparte had loved less. It may be supposed that Josephine, who was afterwards informed by Bonaparte of Junot's conversation, did not feel particularly interested in his favour. He died insane on the 27th of July 1813.[70]

70 However indiscreet Junot might on this occasion have shown himself in interfering in so delicate a matter, it is pretty certain that his suspicions were breathed to no other ear than that of Bonaparte himself. Madame Junot, in speaking of the ill-suppressed enmity between her husband and Madame Bonaparte, says that he never uttered a word even to her of the subject of his conversation with the General-in-Chief to Egypt. That Junot's testimony, however, notwithstanding the countenance it obtained from Bonaparte's relations, ought to be cautiously received, the following passage from the Memoirs of the Duchesse d'Abrantes,

Our little army continued its march on El-Arish, where we arrived on the 17th of February. The fatigues experienced in the desert and the scarcity of water excited violent murmurs amongst the soldiers during their march across the isthmus. When any person on horseback passed them they studiously expressed their discontent. The advantage possessed by the horsemen provoked their sarcasms. I never heard the verses which they are said to have repeated, but they indulged in the most violent language against the Republic, the men of science, and those whom they regarded as the authors of the expedition. Nevertheless these brave fellows, from whom it was not astonishing that such great privations should extort complaints, often compensated by their pleasantries for the bitterness of their reproaches.

Many times during the crossing of the isthmus I have seen soldiers, parched with thirst, and unable to wait till the hour for distribution of water, pierce the leathern bottles which contained it; and this conduct, so injurious to all, occasioned numerous quarrels.

El-Arish surrendered on the 17th of February. It has been erroneously stated that the garrison of this insignificant place, which was set at liberty on condition of not again serving against us, was afterwards found amongst the besieged at Jaffa. It has also been stated that it was because the men composing the El-Arish garrison did not proceed to Bagdad, according to the capitulation, that we shot them at Jaffa. We shall presently see the falsehood of these assertions.

On the 28th of February we obtained the first glimpse of the green and fertile plains of Syria, which, in many respects, reminded us of the climate and soil of Europe. We now had rain, and sometimes rather too much. The feelings which the sight of the valleys and

vol. i. p. 250, demonstrative of the feelings of irritation between the parties, will show: "Junot escorted Madame Bonaparte when she went to join the General-in-Chief in Italy. I am surprised that M. de Bourrienne has omitted mentioning this circumstance in his Memoirs. He must have known it, since he was well acquainted with everything relating to Josephine, and knew many facts of high interest in her life at this period and subsequently. How happens it too that he makes no mention of Mademoiselle Louise, who might be called her 'demoiselle de compagnie' rather than her 'femme de chambre'? At the outset of the journey to Italy she was such a favourite with Josephine that she dressed like her mistress, ate at table with her, and was in all respects her friend and confidante. "The journey was long, much too long for Junot, though he was very much in love with Mademoiselle Louise. But he was anxious to join the army, for to him his General was always the dearest of mistresses. Junot has often spoken to me, and to me alone, of the vexations he experienced on this journey. He might have added to his circumstantial details relative to Josephine the conversation he is reported to have had with Bonaparte to Egypt; but he never breathed a word on the subject, for his character was always noble and generous. The journey to Italy did not produce the effect which usually arises from such incidents in common life; namely, a closer friendship and intimacy between the parties. On the contrary, Madame Bonaparte from that moment evinced some degree of ill-humour towards Junot, and complained with singular warmth of the want of respect which he had shown her, in making love to her 'femme de chambre' before her face." According to 'Erreurs (tome i. pp. 4, 50) Junot was not then in Syria. On 10th February Napoleon was at Messoudiah. Junot only arrived from Egypt at Gaza on the 25th February. Madame d'Abrantes (ii. 32) treats this conversation as apocryphal. "This (an anecdote of her own) is not an imaginary episode like that, for example, of making a person speak at Messoudiah who never was there."

mountains called forth made us, in some degree, forget the hardships and vexations of an expedition of which few persons could foresee the object or end. There are situations in life when the slightest agreeable sensation alleviates all our ills.

On the 1st of March we slept at Ramleh, in a small convent occupied by two monks, who paid us the greatest attention. They gave us the church for a hospital. These good fathers did not fail to tell us that it was through this place the family of Jesus Christ passed into Egypt, and showed us the wells at which they quenched their thirst.[71] The pure and cool water of these wells delighted us.

We were not more than about six leagues from Jerusalem.

I asked the General whether he did not intend to direct his march by the way of that city, so celebrated in many respects. He replied, "Oh no! Jerusalem is not in my line of operations. I do not wish to be annoyed by mountaineers in difficult roads. And, besides, on the other side of the mountain I should be assailed by swarms of cavalry. I am not ambitious of the fate of Cassius."

We therefore did not enter Jerusalem, which was not disturbed by the war. All we did was to send a written declaration to the persons in power at Jerusalem, assuring them that we had no design against that country, and only wished them to remain at peace. To this communication no answer was returned, and nothing more passed on the subject.[72]

We found at Ramleh between two and three hundred Christians in a pitiable state of servitude, misery, and dejection. On conversing with them I could not help admiring how much the hope of future rewards may console men under present ills. But I learned from many of them that they did not live in harmony together. The feelings of hatred and jealousy are not less common amongst these people than amongst the better-instructed inhabitants of rich and populous cities.

---

71 Ramleh, the ancient Arimathea, is situated at the base of a chain of mountains, the eastern extremity of which is washed by the Persian Gulf, and the western by the Mediterranean. Bourrienne.

72 Sir Walter Scott says, speaking of Bonaparte, that he believes that little officer of artillery dreamed of being King of Jerusalem. What I have just stated proves that he never thought of such a thing. The "little officer of artillery" had a far more splendid dream in his head.—Bourrienne.

CHAPTER XVIII

1799

On arriving before Jaffa, where there were already some troops, the first person I met was Adjutant-General Gresieux, with whom I was well acquainted. I wished him good-day, and offered him my hand. "Good God! what are you about?" said he, repulsing me with a very abrupt gesture; "you may have the plague. People do not touch each other here!" I mentioned the circumstance to Bonaparte, who said, "If he be afraid of the plague, he will die of it." Shortly after, at St. Jean d'Acre, he was attacked by that malady, and soon sank under it.

On the 4th of March we commenced the siege of Jaffa. That paltry place, which, to round a sentence, was pompously styled the ancient Joppa, held out only to the 6th of March, when it was taken by storm, and given up to pillage. The massacre was horrible. General Bonaparte sent his aides de camp Beauharnais and Croisier to appease the fury of the soldiers as much as possible, and to report to him what was passing. They learned that a considerable part of the garrison had retired into some vast buildings, a sort of caravanserai, which formed a large enclosed court. Beauharnais and Croisier, who were distinguished by wearing the 'aide de camp' scarf on their arms, proceeded to that place. The Arnauts and Albanians, of whom these refugees were almost entirely composed, cried from the windows that they were willing to surrender upon an assurance that they would be exempted from the massacre to which the town was doomed; if not, they threatened to fire on the 'aides de camp', and to defend themselves to the last extremity. The two officers thought that they ought to accede to the proposition, notwithstanding the decree of death which had been pronounced against the whole garrison, in consequence of the town being taken by storm. They brought them to our camp in two divisions, one consisting of about 2500 men, the other of about 1600.

I was walking with General Bonaparte, in front of his tent, when he beheld this mass of men approaching, and before he even saw his 'aides de camp' he said to me, in a tone of profound sorrow, "What do they wish me to do with these men? Have I food for them?—ships to convey them to Egypt or France? Why, in the devil's name, have they served me thus?" After their arrival, and the explanations which the General-in-Chief demanded and listened to with anger, Eugène and Croisier received the most severe reprimand for their conduct. But the deed was done. Four thousand men were there. It was necessary to decide upon their fate. The two aides de camp observed that they had found themselves alone in the midst of numerous enemies, and that he had directed them to restrain the carnage. "Yes, doubtless," replied the General-in-Chief, with great warmth, "as to women, children, and old men—all the peaceable inhabitants; but not with respect to armed soldiers. It was your duty to die rather than bring these unfortunate creatures to me. What do you want me to do with them?" These words were pronounced in the most angry tone.

The prisoners were then ordered to sit down, and were placed, without any order, in front of the tents, their hands tied behind their backs. A sombre determination was depicted on their countenances. We gave them a little biscuit and bread, squeezed out of the already scanty supply for the army.

On the first day of their arrival a council of war was held in the tent of the General-in-Chief, to determine what course should be pursued with respect to them. The council deliberated a long time without coming to any decision.

On the evening of the following day the daily reports of the generals of division came in. They spoke of nothing but the insufficiency of the rations, the complaints of the soldiers—of their murmurs and discontent at seeing their bread given to enemies who had been withdrawn from their vengeance, inasmuch as a decree of death, in conformity with the laws of war, had been passed on Jaffa. All these reports were alarming, and especially that of General Bon, in which no reserve was made. He spoke of nothing less than the fear of a revolt, which would be justified by the serious nature of the case.

The council assembled again. All the generals of division were summoned to attend, and for several hours together they discussed, under separate questions, what measures might be adopted, with the most sincere desire to discover and execute one which would save the lives of these unfortunate prisoners.

(1.) Should they be sent into Egypt? Could it be done?

To do so, it would be necessary to send with them a numerous escort, which would too much weaken our little army in the enemy's country. How, besides, could they and the escort be supported till they reached Cairo, having no provisions to give them on setting out, and their route being through a hostile territory, which we had exhausted, which presented no fresh resources, and through which we, perhaps, might have to return.

(2.) Should they be embarked?

Where were the ships?—Where could they be found? All our telescopes, directed over the sea, could not descry a single friendly sail. Bonaparte, I affirm, would have regarded such an event as a real favour of fortune. It was, and—I am glad to have to say it, this sole idea, this sole hope, which made him brave, for three days, the murmurs of his army. But in vain was help looked for seaward. It did not come.

(3.) Should the prisoners be set at liberty?

They would then instantly proceed to St. Jean d'Acre to reinforce the pasha, or else, throwing themselves into the mountains of Nablous, would greatly annoy our rear and right-flank, and deal out death to us, as a recompense for the life we had given them. There could be no doubt of this. What is a Christian dog to a Turk? It would even have been a religious and meritorious act in the eye of the Prophet.

(4.) Could they be incorporated, disarmed, with our soldiers in the ranks?

Here again the question of food presented itself in all its force. Next came to be considered the danger of having such comrades while marching through an enemy's country. What might happen in the event of a battle before St. Jean d'Acre? Could we even tell what might occur during the march? And, finally, what must be done with them when under the ramparts of that town, if we should be able to take them there? The same embarrassments with respect to the questions of provisions and security would then recur with increased force.

The third day arrived without its being possible, anxiously as it was desired, to come to any conclusion favourable to the preservation of these unfortunate men. The murmurs in the camp grew louder—the evil went on increasing—remedy appeared impossible—the danger was real and imminent. The order for shooting the prisoners was given and executed on the 10th of March. We did not, as has been stated, separate the Egyptians from the other prisoners. There were no Egyptians.

Many of the unfortunate creatures composing the smaller division, which was fired on close to the seacoast, at some distance from the other column, succeeded in swimming to some reefs of rocks out of the reach of musket-shot. The soldiers rested their muskets on the sand, and, to induce the prisoners to return, employed the Egyptian signs of reconciliation in use in the country. They came back; but as they advanced they were killed, and disappeared among the waves.

I confine myself to these details of this act of dreadful necessity, of which I was an eye-witness. Others, who, like myself, saw it, have fortunately spared me the recital of the sanguinary result. This atrocious scene, when I think of it, still makes me shudder, as it did on the day I beheld it; and I would wish it were possible for me to forget it, rather than be compelled to describe it. All the horrors imagination can conceive, relative to that day of blood, would fall short of the reality.

I have related the truth, the whole truth. I was present at all the discussions, all the conferences, all the deliberations. I had not, as may be supposed, a deliberative voice; but I am bound to declare that the situation of the army, the scarcity of food, our small numerical strength, in the midst of a country where every individual was an enemy, would have induced me to vote in the affirmative of the proposition which was carried into effect, if I had a vote to give. It was necessary to be on the spot in order to understand the horrible necessity which existed.

War, unfortunately, presents too many occasions on which a law, immutable in all ages, and common to all nations, requires that private interests should be sacrificed to a great general interest, and that even humanity should be forgotten. It is for posterity to judge whether this terrible situation was that in which Bonaparte was placed. For my own part, I have a perfect conviction that he could not do otherwise than yield to the dire necessity of the case. It was the advice of the council, whose opinion was unanimous in favour of the execution, that governed him. Indeed I ought in truth to say, that he yielded only in the last extremity, and was one of those, perhaps, who beheld the massacre with the deepest pain.

After the siege of Jaffa the plague began to exhibit itself with a little more virulence. We lost between seven and eight hundred, men by the contagion during the campaign of Syria.[73] During our march on St. Jean d'Acre, which was commenced on the 14th of March, the army neither obtained the brilliant triumphs nor encountered the numerous obstacles spoken of in certain works. Nothing of importance occurred but a rash skirmish of General Lannes who, in spite of contrary orders from Bonaparte, obstinately pursued a troop of mountaineers into the passes of Nablous. On returning, he found the mountaineers placed in ambush in great numbers amongst rocks, the windings of which they were well acquainted with, whence they fired close upon our troops, whose situation rendered them unable to defend themselves. During the time of this foolish and useless enterprise, especially while the firing was brisk, Bonaparte exhibited much impatience, and it must be confessed, his anger was but natural. The Nablousians halted at the openings of the mountain defiles. Bonaparte reproached Lannes bitterly for having uselessly exposed himself, and "sacrificed, without any object, a number of brave men." Lannes excused himself by saying that the mountaineers had defied him, and he wished to chastise the rabble. "We are not in a condition to play the swaggerer," replied Napoleon.

In four days we arrived before St. Jean d'Acre, where we learned that Djezzar had cut

73 Sir Walter Scott says, that Heaven sent this pestilence amongst us to avenge the massacre of Jaffa

off the head of our envoy, Mailly-de-Chateau-Renaud, and thrown his body into the sea in a sack. This cruel pasha was guilty of a great number of similar executions. The waves frequently drove dead bodies towards the coast, and we came upon them whilst bathing.

The details of the siege of Acre are well known. Although surrounded by a wall, flanked with strong towers, and having, besides, a broad and deep ditch defended by works this little fortress did not appear likely to hold out against French valour and the skill of our corps of engineers and artillery; but the ease and rapidity with which Jaffa had been taken occasioned us to overlook in some degree the comparative strength of the two places, and the difference of their respective situations. At Jaffa we had sufficient artillery: at St. Jean d'Acre we had not. At Jaffa we had to deal only with a garrison left to itself: at St. Jean d'Acre we were opposed by a garrison strengthened by reinforcements of men and supplies of provisions, supported by the English fleet, and assisted by European Science. Sir Sidney Smith was, beyond doubt, the man who did us the greatest injury.[74] Much has been said respecting his communications with the General-in-Chief. The reproaches which the latter cast upon him for endeavouring to seduce the soldiers and officers of the army by tempting offers were the more singular, even if they were well founded, inasmuch as these means are frequently employed by leaders in war.[75] As to the embarking of French prisoners on board a vessel in which the plague existed, the improbability of the circumstance alone, but especially the notorious facts of the case, repel this odious accusation. I observed the conduct of Sir Sidney Smith closely at the time, and I remarked in him a chivalric spirit, which sometimes hurried him into trifling eccentricities; but I affirm that his behaviour towards the French was that of a gallant enemy. I have seen many letters, in which the writers informed him that they "were very sensible of the good treatment which the French experienced when they fell into his hands." Let any one examine Sir Sidney's conduct before the capitulation of El-Arish, and after its rupture, and then they can judge of his character.[76] All our manoeuvres, our works,

---

74 Sir Sidney Smith was the only Englishman besides the Duke of Wellington who defeated Napoleon in military operations. The third Englishman opposed to him, Sir John Moore, was compelled to make a precipitate retreat through the weakness of his force

75 At one time the French General was so disturbed by them as to endeavour to put a stop to them; which object he effected by interdicting all communication with the English, and signifying, in an order of the day, that their Commodore was a madman. This, being believed in the army, so enraged Sir Sidney Smith, that in his wrath he sent a challenge to Napoleon. The latter replied, that he had too many weighty affairs on his hands to trouble himself in so trifling a matter. Had it, indeed, been the great Marlborough, it might have been worthy his attention. Still, if the English sailor was absolutely bent upon fighting, he would send him a bravo from the army, and show them a small portion of neutral ground, where the mad Commodore might land, and satisfy his humour to the full.— (Editor of 1836 edition.)

76 Napoleon, when at St. Helena, in speaking of the siege of Acre, said,—Sidney Smith is a brave officer. He displayed considerable ability in the treaty for the evacuation of Egypt by the French. He took advantage of the discontent which he found to prevail amongst the French troops at being so long away from France, and other circumstances. He manifested great honour in sending immediately to Kléber the refusal of Lord Keith to ratify the treaty, which saved the French army; if he had kept it a secret seven or eight days longer, Cairo would

and attacks were made with that levity and carelessness which over-confidence inspires. Kléber, whilst walking with me one day in the lines of our camp, frequently expressed his surprise and discontent. "The trenches," said, he, "do not come up to my knees." Besieging artillery was, of necessity, required: we commenced with field artillery. This encouraged the besieged, who perceived the weakness of our resources. The besieging artillery, consisting only of three twenty-four pounders and six eighteen pounders, was not brought up until the end of April, and before that period three assaults had taken place with very serious loss. On the 4th of May our powder began to fail us. This cruel event obliged us to slacken our fire. We also wanted shot; and an order of the day fixed a price to be given for all balls, according to their calibre, which might be picked up after being fired from the fortress or the two ships of the line, the 'Tiger' and 'Theseus', which were stationed on each side of the harbour. These two vessels embarrassed the communication between the camp and the trenches; but though they made much noise, they did little harm. A ball from one of them killed an officer on the evening the siege was raised.

The enemy had within the walls some excellent riflemen, chiefly Albanians. They placed stones, one over the other, on the walls, put their firearms through the interstices, and thus, completely sheltered, fired with destructive precision.

On the 9th of April General Caffarelli, so well known for his courage and talents, was passing through the trench, his hand resting as he stooped on his hip, to preserve the equilibrium which his wooden leg impaired; his elbow only was raised above the trench. He was warned that the enemy's shot, fired close upon us, did not miss the smallest object.

---

have been given up to the Turks, and the French army necessarily obliged to surrender to the English. He also showed great humanity and honour in all his proceedings towards the French who felt into his hands. He landed at Havre, for some 'sottise' of a bet he had made, according to some, to go to the theatre; others said it was for espionage; however that may be, he was arrested and confined in the Temple as a spy; and at one time it was intended to try and execute him. Shortly after I returned from Italy he wrote to me from his prison, to request that I would intercede for him; but, under the circumstances in which he was taken, I could do nothing for him. He is active, intelligent, intriguing, and indefatigable; but I believe that he is 'mezzo pazo'. "The chief cause of the failure at Acre was, that he took all my battering train, which was on board of several small vessels. Had it not been for that, I would have taken Acre in spite of him. He behaved very bravely, and was well seconded by Phillipeaux, a Frenchman of talent, who had studied with me as an engineer. There was a Major Douglas also, who behaved very gallantly. The acquisition of five or six hundred seamen as gunners was a great advantage to the Turks, whose spirits they revived, and whom they showed how to defend the fortress. But he committed a great fault in making sorties, which cost the lives of two or three hundred brave fellows without the possibility of success. For it was impossible he could succeed against the number of the French who were before Acre. I would lay a wage that he lost half of his crew in them. He dispersed Proclamations amongst my troops, which certainly shook some of them, and I in consequence published an order, stating that he was mad, and forbidding all communication with him. Some days after he sent, by means of a flag of truce, a lieutenant or a midshipman with a letter containing a challenge to me to meet him at some place he pointed out in order to fight a duel. I laughed at this, and sent him back an intimation that when he brought Marlborough to fight me I would meet him. Notwithstanding this, I like the character of the man." (Voices from St. Helena, vol. 4, p. 208).

He paid no attention to any observation of this kind, and in a few instants his elbow joint was fractured. Amputation of the arm was judged indispensable. The General survived the operation eighteen days. Bonaparte went regularly twice a day to his tent. By his order, added to my friendship for Caffarelli, I scarcely ever quitted him. Shortly before he expired he said to me, "My dear Bourrienne, be so good as to read to me Voltaire's preface to 'Esprit des Lois'." When I returned to the tent of the General-in-Chief he asked, "How is Caffarelli?" I replied, "He is near his end; but he asked me to read him Voltaire's preface to the 'Esprit de Lois', he has just fallen asleep." Bonaparte said, "Bah! to wish to hear that preface? how singular!" He went to see Caffarelli, but he was still asleep. I returned to him that evening and received his last breath. He died with the utmost composure. His death was equally regretted by the soldiers and the men of science, who accompanied us. It was a just regret due to that distinguished man, in whom very extensive information was united with great courage and amiable disposition.

On the 10th of May, when an assault took place, Bonaparte proceeded at an early hour to the trenches.[77]

Croisier, who was mentioned on our arrival at Damanhour and on the capture of Jaffa, had in vain courted death since the commencement of the siege. Life had become insupportable to him since the unfortunate affair at Jaffa. He as usual accompanied his General to the trenches. Believing that the termination of the siege, which was supposed to be near, would postpone indefinitely the death which he sought, he mounted a battery. In this situation his tall figure uselessly provoked all the enemy's shots. "Croisier, come down, I command you; you have no business there," cried Bonaparte, in a loud and imperative tone. Croisier remained without making any reply. A moment after a ball passed through his right leg. Amputation was not considered indispensable. On the day of our departure he was placed on a litter, which was borne by sixteen men alternately, eight at a time. I received his farewell between Gaza and El-Arish, where he died of tetanus. His modest tomb will not be often visited.

The siege of St. Jean d'Acre lasted sixty days. During that time eight assaults and twelve sorties took place. In the assault of the 8th of May more than 200 men penetrated into the town. Victory was already shouted; but the breach having been taken in reverse by the Turks, it was not approached without some degree of hesitation, and the men who had entered were not supported. The streets were barricaded. The cries, the howlings of the women, who ran through the streets throwing, according to the custom of the country, dust in the air, excited the male inhabitants to a desperate resistance, which rendered unavailing this short occupation of the town, by a handful of men, who, finding themselves left without assistance, retreated towards the breach. Many who could not reach it perished in the town.

During this assault Duroc, who was in the trench, was wounded in the right thigh by the splinter from a shell fired against the fortifications. Fortunately this accident only carried away the flesh from the bone, which remained untouched. He had a tent in common with several other 'aides de camp'; but for his better accommodation I gave him mine, and I scarcely ever quitted him. Entering his tent one day about noon, I found him in a profound sleep. The excessive heat had compelled him to throw off all covering, and part of his wound was exposed. I perceived a scorpion which had crawled up the leg of the camp-bed and

77 Sir Sidney Smith, in his official report of the assault of the 8th of May, says that Napoleon was distinctly seen directing the operation.

approached very near to the wound. I was just in time to hurl it to the ground. The sudden motion of my hand awoke Duroc.

We often bathed in the sea. Sometimes the English, perhaps after taking a double allowance of grog, would fire at our heads, which appeared above water. I am not aware that any accident was occasioned by their cannonade; but as we were beyond reach of their guns, we paid scarcely any attention to the firing. It was seen a subject of amusement to us.

Had our attack on St. Jean d'Acre been less precipitate, and had the siege been undertaken according to the rules of war, the place would not have held out three days; one assault, like that of the 8th of May, would have been sufficient. If, in the situation in which we were on the day when we first came in sight of the ramparts of Acre; we had made a less inconsiderate estimate of the strength of the place; if we had likewise taken into consideration the active co-operation of the English and the Ottoman Porte, our absolute want of artillery of sufficient calibre, our scarcity of gunpowder and the difficulty of procuring food, we certainly should not have undertaken the siege; and that would have been by far the wisest course.

Towards the end of the siege the General-in-Chief received intelligence of some trifling insurrections in northern Egypt. An angel had excited them, and the heavenly messenger, who had condescended to assume a name, was called the Mahdi, or El Mohdy. This religious extravagance, however, did not last long, and tranquillity was soon restored. All that the fanatic Mahdi, who shrouded himself in mystery, succeeded in doing was to attack our rear by some vagabonds, whose illusions were dissipated by a few musket shots.

CHAPTER XIX

1799

The siege of St. Jean d'Acre was raised on the 20th of May. It cost us a loss of nearly 3000 men, in killed, deaths by the plague, or wounds. A great number were wounded mortally. In those veracious documents, the bulletins, the French loss was made 500 killed, and 1000 wounded, and the enemy's more than 15,000.

Our bulletins may form curious materials for history; but their value certainly will not depend on the credit due to their details. Bonaparte attached the greatest importance to those documents; generally drawing them up himself, or correcting them, when written by another hand, if the composition did not please him.

It must be confessed that at that time nothing so much flattered self-love as being mentioned in a bulletin. Bonaparte was well aware of this; he knew that to insert a name in a bulletin was conferring a great honour, and that its exclusion was a severe disappointment. General Berthier, to whom I had expressed a strong desire to examine the works of the siege, took me over them; but, notwithstanding his promise of secrecy, he mentioned the circumstance to the General-in-Chief, who had desired me not to approach the works. "What did you go there for?" said Bonaparte to me, with some severity; "that is not your place." I replied that Berthier told me that no assault would take place that day; and he believed there would be no sortie, as the garrison had made one the preceding evening. "What matters that? There might have been another. Those who have nothing to do in such places are always the first victims. Let every man mind his own business. Wounded or killed, I would not even have noticed you in the bulletin. You could have been laughed at, and that justly."

Bonaparte, not having at this time experienced reverses, having continually proceeded from triumph to triumph, confidently anticipated the taking of St. Jean d'Acre. In his letters to the generals in Egypt he fixed the 25th of April for the accomplishment of that event. He reckoned that the grand assault against the tower could not be made before that day; it took place, however, twenty-four hours sooner. He wrote to Desaix on the 19th of April, "I count on being master of Acre in six days." On the 2d of May he told Junot, "Our 18 and 24 pounders have arrived. We hope to enter Acre in a few days. The fire of their artillery is completely extinguished." Letters have been printed, dated 30th Floréal (19th May), in which he announces to Dugua and to Poussielque that they can rely on his being in Acre on 6th Floréal (25th April). Some mistake has evidently been made. "The slightest circumstances produce the greatest events," said Napoleon, according to the Memorial of St. Helena; "had St. Jean d'Acre fallen, I should have changed the face of the world." And again, "The fate of the East lay in that small town." This idea is not one which he first began to entertain at St. Helena; he often repeated the very same words at St. Jean d'Acre. On the shore of Ptolemes gigantic projects agitated him, as, doubtless, regret for not having carried them into execution tormented him at St. Helena.

Almost every evening Bonaparte and myself used to walk together, at a little distance from the sea-shore. The day after the unfortunate assault of the 8th of May Bonaparte, afflicted at seeing the blood of so many brave men uselessly shed, said to me, "Bourrienne, I see that this wretched place has cost me a number of men, and wasted much time. But things are too far advanced not to attempt a last effort. If I succeed, as I expect, I shall find in the town the pasha's treasures, and arms for 300,000 men. I will stir up and arm the people of Syria, who are disgusted at the ferocity of Djezzar, and who, as you know, pray for his destruction at every assault. I shall then march upon Damascus and Aleppo. On advancing into the country, the discontented will flock round my standard, and swell my army. I will announce to the people the abolition of servitude and of the tyrannical governments of the pashas. I shall arrive at Constantinople with large masses of soldiers. I shall overturn the Turkish empire, and found in the East a new and grand empire, which will fix my place in the records of posterity. Perhaps I shall return to Paris by Adrianople, or by Vienna, after having annihilated the house of Austria." After I had made some observations which these grand projects naturally suggested, he replied, "What! do you not see that the Druses only wait for the fall of Acre to rise in rebellion? Have not the keys of Damascus already been offered me? I only stay till these walls fall because until then I can derive no advantage from this large town. By the operation which I meditate I cut off all kind of succour from the beys, and secure the conquest of Egypt. I will have Desaix nominated commander-in-chief; but if I do not succeed in the last assault I am about to attempt, I set off directly. Time presses,—I shall not be at Cairo before the middle of June; the winds will then lie favourable for ships bound to Egypt, from the north. Constantinople will send troops to Alexandria and Rosetta. I must be there. As for the army, which will arrive afterwards by land, I do not fear it this year. I will cause everything to be destroyed, all the way to the entrance of the desert. I will render the passage of an army impossible for two years. Troops cannot exist amoung ruins."

As soon as I returned to my tent I committed to paper this conversation, which was then quite fresh in my memory, and, I may venture to say that every word I put down is correct. I may add, that during the siege our camp was constantly filled with the inhabitants, who invoked Heaven to favour our arms, and prayed fervently at every assault for our success, many of them on their knees, with their faces to the city. The people of Damascus, too, had offered the keys to Bonaparte. Thus everything contributed to make him confident in his favourite plan.

The troops left St. Jean d'Acre on the 20th of May, taking advantage of the night to avoid a sortie from the besieged, and to conceal the retreat of the army, which had to march three leagues along the shore, exposed to the fire of the English vessels lying in the roads of Mount Carmel. The removal of the wounded and sick commenced on the 18th and 19th of May.

Bonaparte then made a proclamation, which from one end to the other offends against truth. It has been published in many works. The season of the year for hostile landing is there very dexterously placed in the foreground; all the rest is a deceitful exaggeration. It must be observed that the proclamations which Bonaparte regarded as calculated to dazzle an ever too credulous public were amplifications often ridiculous and incomprehensible upon the spot, and which only excited the laughter of men of common sense. In all Bonaparte's correspondence there is an endeavour to disguise his reverses, and impose on the public, and even on his own generals. For example, he wrote to General Dugua, commandant of Cairo, on the 15th of February, "I will bring you plenty of prisoners and flags!" One would almost be inclined to say that he had resolved, during his stay in the East, thus to pay a tribute to the country of fables.[78] Thus terminated this disastrous expedition. I have read somewhere that during this immortal campaign the two heroes Murat and Mourad had often been in face of one another. There is only a little difficulty; Mourad Bey never put his foot in Syria.

We proceeded along the coast, and passed Mount Carmel. Some of the wounded were carried on litters, the remainder on horses, mules, and camels. At a short distance from Mount Carmel we were informed that three soldiers, ill of the plague, who were left in a convent (which served for a hospital), and abandoned too confidently to the generosity of the Turks, had been barbarously put to death.

A most intolerable thirst, the total want of water, an excessive heat, and a fatiguing march over burning sand-hills, quite disheartened the men, and made every generous sentiment give way to feelings of the grossest selfishness and most shocking indifference. I saw officers, with their limbs amputated, thrown off the litters, whose removal in that way had been ordered, and who had themselves given money to recompense the bearers. I saw the amputated, the wounded, the infected, or those only suspected of infection, deserted and left to themselves. The march was illumined by torches, lighted for the purpose of setting fire to the little towns, villages, and hamlets which lay in the route, and the rich crops with which the land was then covered. The whole country was in a blaze. Those who were ordered to preside at this work of destruction seemed eager to spread desolation on every side, as if they could thereby avenge themselves for their reverses, and find in such dreadful havoc an alleviation of their sufferings. We were constantly surrounded by plunderers, incendiaries, and the dying, who, stretched on the sides of the road, implored assistance in a feeble voice, saying, "I am not infected—I am only wounded;" and to convince those whom they addressed, they reopened their old wounds, or inflicted on themselves fresh ones. Still nobody attended to them. "It is all over with him," was the observation applied to the unfortunate beings in succession, while every one pressed onward. The sun, which shone in an unclouded sky in all its brightness, was often darkened by our conflagrations. On our right lay the sea; on our left, and behind us, the desert made by ourselves; before were the privations and sufferings which awaited us. Such was our true situation.

We reached Tentoura on the 20th of May, when a most oppressive heat prevailed, and produced general dejection. We had nothing to sleep on but the parched and burning sand; on our right lay a hostile sea; our losses in wounded and sick were already considerable since leaving Acre; and there was nothing consolatory in the future. The truly afflicting condition in which the remains of an army called triumphant were plunged, produced, as might well be expected, a corresponding impression on the mind of the General-in-Chief. Scarcely had he arrived at Tentoura when he ordered his tent to be pitched. He then called me, and with a mind occupied by the calamities of our situation, dictated an order that every one should march on foot; and that all the horses, mules, and camels should be given up to the wounded, the sick, and infected who had been removed, and who still showed signs of life. "Carry that to Berthier," said he; and the order was instantly despatched. Scarcely had I returned to the tent when the elder Vigogne, the General-in-Chief's groom, entered, and raising his hand to

78 The prisoners and flags were sent. The Turkish flags were entrusted by Berthier to the Adjutant-Commandant Boyer, who conducted a convoy of sick and wounded to Egypt. Sidney Smith acknowledges the loss of some flags by the Turks. The Turkish prisoners were used as carriers of the litters for the wounded, and were, for the most part, brought into Egypt. (Erreurs, tome i. pp. 47 and 160)

his cap, said, "General, what horse do you reserve for yourself?" In the state of excitement in which Bonaparte was this question irritated him so violently that, raising his whip, he gave the man a severe blow on the head, saying in a terrible voice, "Every-one must go on foot, you rascal—I the first—Do you not know the order? Be off!"

Every one in parting with his horse was now anxious to avoid giving it to any unfortunate individual supposed to be suffering from plague. Much pains were taken to ascertain the nature of the diseases of the sick; and no difficulty was made in accommodating the wounded of amputated. For my part I had an excellent horse; a mule, and two camels, all which I gave up with the greatest pleasure; but I confess that I directed my servant to do all he could to prevent an infected person from getting my horse. It was returned to me in a very short time. The same thing happened to many others. The cause may be easily conjectured.

The remains of our heavy artillery were lost in the moving sands of Tentoura, from the want of horses, the small number that remained being employed in more indispensable services. The soldiers seemed to forget their own sufferings, plunged in grief at the loss of their bronze guns, often the instruments of their triumphs, and which had made Europe tremble.

We halted at Caesarea on the 22d of May, and we marched all the following night. Towards daybreak a man, concealed in a bush upon the left of the road (the sea was two paces from us on the right), fired a musket almost close to the head of the General-in-Chief, who was sleeping on his horse. I was beside him. The wood being searched, the Nablousian was taken without difficulty, and ordered to be shot on the spot. Four guides pushed him towards the sea by thrusting their carbines against his back; when close to the water's edge they drew the triggers, but all the four muskets hung fire: a circumstance which was accounted for by the great humidity of the night. The Nablousian threw himself into the water, and, swimming with great agility and rapidity, gained a ridge of rocks so far off that not a shot from the whole troop, which fired as it passed, reached him. Bonaparte, who continued his march, desired me to wait for Kléber, whose division formed the rear-guard, and to tell him not to forget the Nablousian. He was, I believe, shot at last.

We returned to Jaffa on the 24th of May, and stopped there during the 25th, 26th, 27th, and 28th. This town had lately been the scene of a horrible transaction, dictated by necessity, and it was again destined to witness the exercise of the same dire law. Here I have a painful duty to perform—I will perform it. I will state what I know, what I saw.

I have seen the following passage in a certain, work:—"Bonaparte, having arrived at Jaffa, ordered three removals of the infected: one by sea to Damietta, and also by land; the second to Gaza; and the third to El-Arish!" So, many words, so many errors!

Some tents were pitched on an eminence near the gardens east of Jaffa. Orders were given directly to undermine the fortifications and blow them up; and on the 27th of May, upon the signaling given, the town was in a moment laid bare. An hour afterwards the General-in-Chief left his tent and repaired to the town, accompanied by Berthier, some physicians and surgeons, and his usual staff. I was also one of the party. A long and sad deliberation took place on the question which now arose relative to the men who were incurably ill of the plague, or who were at the point of death. After a discussion of the most serious and conscientious kind it was decided to accelerate a few moments, by a potion, a death which was inevitable, and which would otherwise be painful and cruel.

Bonaparte took a rapid view of the destroyed ramparts of the town and returned to the hospital, where there were men whose limbs had been amputated, many wounded, many afflicted with ophthalmia, whose lamentations were distressing, and some infected with the plague. The beds of the last description of patients were to the right on entering the first ward. I walked by the General's side, and I assert that I never saw him touch any one of the infected. And why should he have done so? They were in the last stage of the disease. Not one of them spoke a word to him, and Bonaparte well knew that he possessed no protection against the plague. Is Fortune to be again brought forward here? She had, in truth, little favoured him during the last few months, when he had trusted to her favours. I ask, why should he have exposed himself to certain death, and have left his army in the midst of a desert created by our ravages, in a desolate town, without succour, and without the hope of ever receiving any? Would he have acted rightly in doing so—he who was evidently so necessary, so indispensable to his army; he on whom depended at that moment the lives of all who had survived the last disaster, and who had proved their attachment to him by their sufferings, their privations, and their unshaken courage, and who had done all that he could have required of men, and whose only trust was in him?

Bonaparte walked quickly through the rooms, tapping the yellow top of his boot with a whip he held in his hand. As he passed along with hasty steps he repeated these words: "The fortifications are destroyed. Fortune was against me at St. Jean d'Acre. I must return to Egypt to preserve it from the enemy, who will soon be there: In a few hours the Turks will be here. Let all those who have strength enough rise and come along with us. They shall be carried on litters and horses." There were scarcely sixty cases of plague in the hospital; and all accounts stating a greater number are exaggerated. The perfect silence, complete dejection, and general stupor of the patients announced their approaching end. To carry them away in the state in which they were would evidently have been doing nothing else than inoculating the rest of the army with the plague. I have, it is true, learned, since my return to Europe, that some persons touched the infected with impunity; nay; that others went so far as to inoculate themselves with the plague in order to learn how to cure those whom it might attack. It certainly was a special protection from Heaven to be preserved from it; but to cover in some degree the absurdity of such a story, it is added that they knew how to elude the danger, and that any one else who braved it without using precautions met with death for their temerity. This is, in fact, the whole point of the question. Either those privileged persons took indispensable precautions; and in that case their boasted heroism is a mere juggler's trick; or they touched the infected without using precautions, and inoculated themselves with the plague, thus voluntarily encountering death, and then the story is really a good one.

The infected were confided, it has been stated, to the head apothecary of the army, Royer, who, dying in Egypt three years after, carried the secret with him to the grave. But on a moment's reflection it will be evident that the leaving of Royer alone in Jaffa would have been to devote to certain death; and that a prompt and cruel one, a man who was extremely useful to the army, and who was at the time in perfect health. It must be remembered that no guard could be left with him, and that the Turks were close at our heels. Bonaparte truly said, while walking through the rooms of the hospital, that the Turks would be at Jaffa in a few hours. With this conviction, would he have left the head apothecary in that town?

Recourse has been had to suppositions to support the contrary belief to what I state. For example, it is said that the infected patients were embarked in ships of war. There were no such ships. Where had they disembarked, who had received them; what had been done with them? No one speaks of them. Others, not doubting that the infected men died at Jaffa, say, that the rearguard under Kléber, by order of Bonaparte, delayed its departure for three days, and only began its march when death had put an end to the sufferings of these unfortunate beings, unshortened by any sacrifice. All this is incorrect. No rear-guard was left—it could not be done. Pretence is made of forgetting that the ramparts were destroyed, that the town was as open and as defenceless as any village, so this small rear-guard would have been left for certain destruction. The dates themselves tell against these suppositions. It is certain, as can be seen by the official account, that we arrived at Jaffa on 24th May, and stayed there the 25th, 26th, and 27th. We left it on the 28th. Thus the rear-guard, which, according to these writers, left-on the 29th, did not remain, even according to their own hypothesis, three days after the army to see the sick die. In reality it left on the 29th of May, the day after we did. Here are the very words of the Major-General (Berthier) in his official account, written under the eye and under the dictation of the Commander-in-Chief:—

> The army arrived at Jaffa, 5th Prairial (24th May), and remained there the 6th, 7th, and 8th (25th-27th May). This time was employed in punishing the village, which had behaved badly. The fortifications of Jaffa were blown up. All the iron guns of the place were thrown into the sea. The wounded were removed by sea and by land. There were only a few ships, and to give time to complete the evacuation by land, the departure of the army had to be deferred until the 9th (28th May). Kléber's division formed the rear-guard, and only left Jaffa on the 10th (29th *May).*

The official report of what passed at Jaffa was drawn up by Berthier, under the eye of Bonaparte. It has been published; but it may be remarked that not a word about the infected, not a word of the visit to the hospital, or the touching of the plague-patients with impunity, is there mentioned. In no official report is anything said about the matter. Why this silence? Bonaparte was not the man to conceal a fact which would have afforded him so excellent and so allowable a text for talking about his fortune. If the infected were removed, why not mention it? Why be silent on so important an event? But it would have been necessary to confess that being obliged to have recourse to so painful a measure was the unavoidable consequence of this unfortunate expedition. Very disagreeable details must have been entered into; and it was thought more advisable to be silent on the subject.

But what did Napoleon himself say on the subject at St. Helena? His statement there was to the following effect:—"I ordered a consultation as to what was best to be done. The report which was made stated that there were seven or eight men (the question is not about the number) so dangerously ill that they could not live beyond twenty-four hours, and would besides infect the rest of the army with the plague. It was thought it would be an act of charity to anticipate their death a few hours."

Then comes the fable of the 500 men of the rear guard, who, it is pretended, saw them die! I make no doubt that the story of the poisoning was the invention of Den——. He was a babbler, who understood a story badly, and repeated it worse. I do not think it would have been a crime to have given opium to the infected. On the contrary, it would have been obedience to the dictates of reason. Where is the man who would not, in such a situation, have preferred a prompt death, to being exposed to the lingering tortures inflicted by barbarians? If my child, and I believe I love him as much as any father does his, had been in such a state, my advice would have been the same; if I had been among the infected myself, I should have demanded to be so treated.

Such was the reasoning at St. Helena, and such was the view which he and every one else took of the case twenty years ago at Jaffa.

Our little army arrived at Cairo on the 14th of June, after a painful and harassing march of twenty-five days. The heats during the passage of the desert between El-Arish and Belbeis exceeded thirty-three degrees. On placing the bulb of the thermometer in the sand the mercury rose to forty-five degrees. The deceitful mirage was even more vexatious than in the plains of Bohahire'h. In spite of our experience an excessive thirst, added to a perfect illusion, made us goad on our wearied horses towards lakes which vanished at our approach, and left behind nothing but salt and arid sand. In two days my cloak was completely covered with salt, left on it after the evaporation of the moisture which held it in solution. Our horses, who ran eagerly to the brackish springs of the desert, perished in numbers, after travelling about a quarter of a league from the spot where they drank the deleterious fluid.

Bonaparte preceded his entry into the capital of Egypt by one of those lying bulletins which only imposed on fools. "I will bring with me," said he, "many prisoners and flags. I have razed the palace of the Djezzar and the ramparts of Acre—not a stone remains upon another. All the inhabitants have left the city, by sea. Djezzar is severely wounded."

I confess that I experienced a painful sensation in writing, by his dictation, these official words, everyone of which was an imposition. Excited by all I had just witnessed, it was difficult for me to refrain from making the observation; but his constant reply was, "My dear fellow, you are a simpleton: you do not understand this business." And he observed, when signing the bulletin, that he would yet fill the world with admiration, and inspire historians and poets.

Our return to Cairo has been attributed to the insurrections which broke out during the unfortunate expedition into Syria. Nothing is more incorrect. The term insurrection cannot be properly applied to the foolish enterprises of the angel El-Mahdi in the Bohahire'h, or to the less important disturbances in the Charkyeh. The reverses experienced before St. Jean d'Acre, the fear, or rather the prudent anticipation of a hostile landing, were sufficient motives, and the only ones, for our return to Egypt. What more could we do in Syria but lose men and time, neither of which the General had to spare?

Frenchmen one of the most brilliant achievements of their arms.[79]

After the battle, which took place on the 25th of July, Bonaparte sent a flag of truce on board the English Admiral's ship. Our intercourse was full of politeness, such as might be expected in the communications of the people of two civilised nations. The English Admiral gave the flag of truce some presents in exchange for some we sent, and likewise a copy of the French Gazette of Frankfort, dated 10th of June 1799. For ten months we had received no news from France. Bonaparte glanced over this journal with an eagerness which may easily be conceived.[80]

"Heavens!" said he to me, "my presentiment is verified: the fools have lost Italy. All the

---

79 As M. de Bourrienne gives no details of the battle, the following extract from the Duc de Rovigo's Memoirs, tome i, p. 167, will supply the deficiency: "General Bonaparte left Cairo in the utmost haste to place himself at the head of the troops which he had ordered to quit their cantonments and march down to the coast. "Whilst the General was making these arrangements and coming in person from Cairo, the troops on board the Turkish fleet had effected a landing and taken possession of the fort of Aboukir, and of a redoubt placed behind the village of that name which ought to have been put into a state of defence six months before, but had been completely neglected. "The Turks had nearly destroyed the weak garrisons that occupied those two military points when General Marmont (who commanded at Alexandria) came to their relief. This general, seeing the two posts in the power of the Turks, returned to shut himself up in Alexandria, where he would probably have been blockaded by the Turkish army had it not been for the arrival of General Bonaparte with his forces, who was very angry when he saw that the fort and redoubt had been taken; but he did not blame Marmont for retreating to Alexandria with the forces at his disposal. "General Bonaparte arrived at midnight with his guides and the remaining part of his army, and ordered the Turks to be attacked the next morning. In this battle, as in the preceding ones, the attack, the encounter, and the rout were occurrences of a moment, and the result of a single movement on the part of our troops. The whole Turkish army plunged into the sea to regain its ships, leaving behind them everything they had brought on shore. "Whilst this event was occurring on the seashore a pasha had left the field of battle with a corps of about 3000 men in order to throw himself into the fort of Aboukir. They soon felt the extremities of thirst, which compelled them, after the lapse of a few days, to surrender unconditionally to General Menou, who was left to close the operations connected with the recently defeated Turkish army."

80 The French, on their return from St. Jean d'Acre were totally ignorant of all that had taken place in Europe for several months. Napoleon, eager to obtain intelligence, sent a flag of truce on board the Turkish admiral's ship, under the pretence of treating for the ransom of the prisoners taken at Aboukir, not doubting but the envoy would be stopped by Sir Sidney Smith, who carefully prevented all direct communication between the French and the Turks. Accordingly the French flag of truce received directions from Sir Sidney to go on board his ship. He experienced the handsomest treatment; and the English commander having, among other things, ascertained that the disasters of Italy were quite unknown to Napoleon, indulged in the malicious pleasure of sending him a file of newspapers. Napoleon spent the whole night in his tent perusing the papers; and he came to the determination of immediately proceeding to Europe to repair the disasters of France; and if possible, to save her from destruction (Memorial de Sainte Helene)

fruits of our victories are gone! I must leave Egypt!"

He sent for Berthier, to whom he communicated the news, adding that things were going on very badly in France—that he wished to return home—that he (Berthier) should go along with him, and that, for the present, only he, Gantheaume, and I were in the secret. He recommended Berthier to be prudent, not to betray any symptoms of joy, nor to purchase or sell anything, and concluded by assuring him that he depended on him. "I can answer," said he, "for myself and for Bourrienne." Berthier promised to be secret, and he kept his word. He had had enough of Egypt, and he so ardently longed to return to France, that there was little reason to fear he would disappoint himself by any indiscretion.

Gantheaume arrived, and Bonaparte gave him orders to fit out the two frigates, the 'Muiron' and the 'Carrère', and the two small vessels, the 'Revanche' and the 'Fortune', with a two months' supply of provisions for from four to five hundred men. He enjoined his secrecy as to the object of these preparations, and desired him to act with such circumspection that the English cruisers might have no knowledge of what was going on. He afterwards arranged with Gantheaume the course he wished to take. No details escaped his attention.

Bonaparte concealed his preparations with much care, but still some vague rumours crept abroad. General Dugua, the commandant of Cairo, whom he had just left for the purpose of embarking, wrote to him on the 18th of August to the following effect:

> I have this moment heard that it is reported at the Institute you are about to return to France, taking with you Monge, Berthollet, Berthier, Lannes, and Murat. This news has spread like lightning through the city, and I should not be at all surprised if it produce an unfavourable effect, which, however, I hope you will obviate.

Bonaparte embarked five days after the receipt of Dugua's letter, and, as may be supposed, without replying to it.

On the 18th of August he wrote to the divan of Cairo as follows:

> I set out to-morrow for Menouf, whence I intend to make various excursions in the Delta, in order that I may myself witness the acts of oppression which are committed there, and acquire some knowledge of the people.

He told the army but half the truth:

> The news from Europe (said he) has determined me to proceed to France. I leave the command of the army to General Kléber. The army shall hear from me forthwith. At present I can say no more. It costs me much pain to quit troops to whom I am so strongly attached. But my absence will be but temporary, and the general I leave in command has the confidence of the Government as well as mine.

I have now shown the true cause of General Bonaparte's departure for Europe. This circumstance, in itself perfectly natural, has been the subject of the most ridiculous conjectures to those who always wish to assign extraordinary causes for simple events. There is no truth whatever in the assertion of his having planned his departure before the battle of Aboukir. Such an idea never crossed his mind. He had no thought whatever of his departure for France when he made the journey to the Pyramids, nor even when he received the news of the landing of the Anglo-Turkish force.

At the end of December 1798 Bonaparte thus wrote to the Directory: "We are without any news from France. No courier has arrived since the month of June."

Some writers have stated that we received news by the way of Tunis, Algiers, or Morocco; but there is no contradicting a positive fact. At that period I had been with Bonaparte more than two years, and during that time not a single despatch on any occasion arrived of the contents of which I was ignorant. How then should the news alluded to have escaped me?[81]

Almost all those who endeavour to avert from Bonaparte the reproach of desertion quote a letter from the Directory, dated the 26th of May 1799. This letter may certainly have been written, but it never reached its destination. Why then should it be put upon record?

The circumstance I have stated above determined the resolution of Bonaparte, and made him look upon Egypt as an exhausted field of glory, which it was high time he had quitted, to play another part in France. On his departure from Europe Bonaparte felt that his reputation was tottering. He wished to do something to raise up his glory, and to fix upon him the attention of the world. This object he had in great part accomplished; for, in spite of serious disasters, the French flag waved over the cataracts of the Nile and the ruins of Memphis, and the battles of the Pyramids, and Aboukir were calculated in no small degree to dazzle the imagination. Cairo and Alexandria too were ours. Finding that the glory of his arms no longer supported the feeble power of the Directory, he was anxious to see whether he could not share it, or appropriate it to himself.

A great deal has been said about letters and secret communications from the Directory, but Bonaparte needed no such thing. He could do what he pleased: there was no power to

81 Details on the question of the correspondence of Napoleon with France while he was to Egypt will be found in Colonel Iung's work, Lucien Bonaparte (Paris. Charpentier, 1882), tome i. pp. 251-274. It seems most probable that Napoleon was in occasional communication with his family and with some of the Directors by way of Tunis and Tripoli. It would not be his interest to let his army or perhaps even Bourrienne know of the disasters in Italy till he found that they were sure to hear of them through the English. This would explain his affected ignorance till such a late date. On the 11th of April Barras received a despatch by which Napoleon stated his intention of returning to France if the news brought by Hamelin was confirmed. On the 26th of May 1799 three of the Directors, Barras, Rewbell, and La Révellière-Lepeaux, wrote to Napoleon that Admiral Bruix had been ordered to attempt every means of bringing back his army. On the 15th of July Napoleon seems to have received this and other letters. On the 20th of July he warns Admiral Gantheaume to be ready to start. On the 11th of September the Directors formally approved the recall of the army from Egypt. Thus at the time Napoleon landed in France (on the 8th October), his intended return had been long known to and approved by the majority of the Directors, and had at last been formally ordered by the Directory. At the most he anticipated the order. He cannot be said to have deserted his post. Lantrey (tome i. p. 411) remarks that the existence and receipt of the letter from Joseph denied by Bourrienne is proved by Miot (the commissary, the brother of Miot de Melito) and by Joseph himself. Talleyrand thanks the French Consul at Tripoli for sending news from Egypt, and for letting Bonaparte know what passed in Europe. See also Ragusa (Marmont), tome i. p. 441, writing on 24th December 1798: "I have found an Arab of whom I am sure, and who shall start to-morrow for Derne. . . . This means can be used to send a letter to Tripoli, for boats often go there."

check him; such had been the nature of his arrangements on leaving France. He followed only the dictates of his own will, and probably, had not the fleet been destroyed, he would have departed from Egypt much sooner. To will and to do were with him one and the same thing. The latitude he enjoyed was the result of his verbal agreement with the Directory, whose instructions and plans he did not wish should impede his operations.

Bonaparte left Alexandria on the 5th of August, and on the 10th arrived at Cairo. He at first circulated the report of a journey to Upper Egypt. This seemed so much the more reasonable, as he had really entertained that design before he went to the Pyramids, and the fact was known to the army and the inhabitants of Cairo. Up to this time our secret had been studiously kept. However, General Lanusse, the commandant at Menouf, where we arrived on the 20th of August, suspected it. "You are going to France," said he to me. My negative reply confirmed his suspicion. This almost induced me to believe the General-in-Chief had been the first to make the disclosure. General Lanusse, though he envied our good fortune, made no complaints. He expressed his sincere wishes for our prosperous voyage, but never opened his mouth on the subject to any one.

On the 21st of August we reached the wells of Birkett. The Arabs had rendered the water unfit for use, but the General-in-Chief was resolved to quench his thirst, and for this purpose squeezed the juice of several lemons into a glass of the water; but he could not swallow it without holding his nose and exhibiting strong feelings of disgust.

The next day we reached Alexandria, where the General informed all those, who had accompanied him from Cairo that France was their destination. At this announcement joy was pictured in every countenance.

General Kléber, to whose command Bonaparte had resigned the army, was invited to come from Damietta to Rosetta to confer with the General-in-Chief on affairs of extreme importance. Bonaparte, in making an appointment which he never intended to keep, hoped to escape the unwelcome freedom of Kléber's reproaches. He afterwards wrote to him all he had to say; and the cause he assigned for not keeping his appointment was, that his fear of being observed by the English cruisers had forced him to depart three days earlier than he intended. But when he wrote Bonaparte well knew that he would be at sea before Kléber could receive his letter. Kléber, in his letter to the Directory, complained bitterly of this deception. The singular fate that befell this letter will be seen by and by.

CHAPTER XXI

1799

We were now to return to our country—again to cross the sea, to us so pregnant with danger—Caesar and his fortune were once more to embark. But Caesar was not now advancing to the East to add Egypt to the conquests of the Republic. He was revolving in his mind vast schemes, unawed by the idea of venturing everything to chance in his own favour the Government for which he had fought. The hope of conquering the most celebrated country of the East no longer excited the imagination, as on our departure from France. Our last visionary dream had vanished before the walls of St. Jean d'Acre, and we were leaving on the burning sands of Egypt most of our companions in arms. An inconceivable destiny seemed to urge us on, and we were obliged to obey its decrees.

On the 23d of August we embarked on board two frigates, the 'Muiron'[82] and 'Carrère'. Our number was between four and five hundred. Such was our squadron, and such the formidable army with which Bonaparte had resolved, as he wrote to the divan of Cairo, "to annihilate all his enemies." This boasting might impose on those who did not see the real state of things; but what were we to think of it? What Bonaparte himself thought the day after.

The night was dark when we embarked in the frigates which lay at a considerable distance from the port of Alexandria; but by the faint light of the stars we perceived a corvette, which appeared to be observing our silent nocturnal embarkation.[83]

Next morning, just as we were on the point of setting sail, we saw, coming from the port of Alexandria a boat, on board of which was M. Parseval Grandmaison. This excellent man, who was beloved by all of us, was not included among the persons whose return to France had been determined by the General-in-Chief. In his anxiety to get off Bonaparte would not hear of taking him on board. It will readily be conceived how urgent were the entreaties of Parseval; but he would have sued in vain had not Gantheaume, Monge, Berthollet, and

82 Named after Bonaparte's aide de camp killed in the Italian campaign

83 The horses of the escort had been left to run loose on the beach, and all was perfect stillness in Alexandria, when the advanced posts of the town were alarmed by the wild galloping of horses, which from a natural instinct, were returning to Alexandria through the desert. The picket ran to arms on seeing horses ready saddled and bridled, which were soon discovered to belong to the regiment of guides. They at first thought that a misfortune had happened to some detachment in its pursuit of the Arabs. With these horses came also those of the generals who had embarked with General Bonaparte; so that Alexandria was for a time in considerable alarm. The cavalry was ordered to proceed in all haste in the direction whence the horses came, and every one was giving himself up to the most gloomy conjectures, when the cavalry returned to the city with the Turkish groom, who was bringing back General Bonaparte's horse to Alexandria (Memoirs of the Duc de Rovigo, tome i. p. 182).

I interceded for him. With some difficulty we overcame Bonaparte's resistance, and our colleague of the Egyptian Institute got on board after the wind had filled our sails.

It has been erroneously said that Admiral Gantheaume had full control of the frigates, as if any one could command when Bonaparte was present. On the contrary, Bonaparte declared to the admiral, in my hearing, that he would not take the ordinary course and get into the open sea. "Keep close along the coast of the Mediterranean," said he, "on the African side, until you get south of Sardinia. I have here a handful of brave fellows and a few pieces of artillery; if the English should appear I will run ashore, and with my party, make my way by land to Oran, Tunis, or some other port, whence we may find an opportunity of getting home." This was his irrevocable determination.

For twenty-one days adverse winds, blowing from west or north-west, drove us continually on the coast of Syria, or in the direction of Alexandria. At one time it was even proposed that we should again put into the port; but Bonaparte declared he would rather brave every danger than do so. During the day we tacked to a certain distance northward, and in the evening we stood towards Africa, until we came within sight of the coast. Finally after no less than twenty-one days of impatience and disappointment, a favourable east wind carried us past that point of Africa on which Carthage formerly stood, and we soon doubled Sardinia. We kept very near the western coast of that island, where Bonaparte had determined to land in case of our falling in with the English squadron. From thence his plan was to reach Corsica, and there to await a favourable opportunity of returning to France.

Everything had contributed to render our voyage dull and monotonous; and, besides, we were not entirely without uneasiness as to the steps which might be taken by the Directory, for it was certain that the publication of the intercepted correspondence must have occasioned many unpleasant disclosures. Bonaparte used often to walk on deck to superintend the execution of his orders. The smallest sail that appeared in view excited his alarm.

The fear of falling into the hands of the English never forsook him. That was what he dreaded most of all, and yet, at a subsequent period, he trusted to the generosity of his enemies.

However, in spite of our well-founded alarm, there were some moments in which we sought to amuse ourselves, or, to use a common expression, to kill time. Cards afforded us a source of recreation, and even this frivolous amusement served to develop the character of Bonaparte. In general he was not fond of cards; but if he did play, vingt-et-un was his favourite game, because it is more rapid than many others, and because, in short, it afforded him an opportunity of cheating. For example, he would ask for a card; if it proved a bad one he would say nothing, but lay it down on the table and wait till the dealer had drawn his. If the dealer produced a good card, then Bonaparte would throw aside his hand, without showing it, and give up his stake. If, on the contrary, the dealer's card made him exceed twenty-one, Bonaparte also threw his cards aside without showing them, and asked for the payment of his stake. He was much diverted by these little tricks, especially when they were played off undetected; and I confess that even then we were courtiers enough to humour him, and wink at his cheating. I must, however, mention that he never appropriated to himself the fruit of these little dishonesties, for at the end of the game he gave up all his winnings, and they were equally divided. Gain, as may readily be supposed, was not his object; but he always expected that fortune would grant him an ace or a ten at the right moment with the same confidence with which he looked for fine weather on the day of battle. If he were disappointed he wished nobody to know it.

Bonaparte also played at chess, but very seldom, because he was only a third-rate player, and he did not like to be beaten at that game, which, I know not why, is said to bear a resemblance to the grand game of war. At this latter game Bonaparte certainly feared no adversary. This reminds me that when we were leaving Passeriano he announced his intention of passing through Mantua. He was told that the commandant of that town, I believe General Beauvoir, was a great chess-player, and he expressed a wish to play a game with him. General Beauvoir asked him to point out any particular pawn with which he would be checkmated; adding, that if the pawn were taken, he, Bonaparte, should be declared the winner. Bonaparte pointed out the last pawn on the left of his adversary. A mark was put upon it, and it turned out that he actually was checkmated with that very pawn. Bonaparte was not very well pleased at this. He liked to play with me because, though rather a better player than himself, I was not always able to beat him. As soon as a game was decided in his favour he declined playing any longer, preferring to rest on his laurels.

The favourable wind which had constantly prevailed after the first twenty days of our voyage still continued while we kept along the coast of Sardinia; but after we had passed that island the wind again blew violently from the west, and on the 1st of October we were forced to enter the Gulf of Ajaccio. We sailed again next day but we found it impossible to work our way out of the gulf. We were therefore obliged to put into the port and land at Ajaccio. Adverse winds obliged us to remain there until the 7th of October. It may readily be imagined how much this delay annoyed Bonaparte. He sometimes expressed his impatience, as if he could enforce the obedience of the elements as well as of men. He was losing time, and time was everything to him.

There was one circumstance which seemed to annoy him as much as any of his more serious vexations. "What will become of me," said he, "if the English, who are cruising hereabout, should learn that I have landed in Corsica? I shall be forced to stay here. That I could never endure. I have a torrent of relations pouring upon me." His great reputation had certainly prodigiously augmented the number of his family. He was overwhelmed with visits, congratulations, and requests. The whole town was in a commotion. Every one of its inhabitants wished to claim him as their cousin; and from the prodigious number of his pretended godsons and goddaughters, it might have been supposed that he had held one-fourth of the children of Ajaccio at the baptismal font.

Bonaparte frequently walked with us in the neighbourhood of Ajaccio; and when in all the plenitude of his power he did not count his crowns with greater pleasure than he evinced in pointing out to us the little domains of his ancestors.

While we were at Ajaccio M. Fesch gave Bonaparte French money in exchange for a number of Turkish sequins, amounting in value to 17,000 francs. This sum was all that the General brought with him from Egypt. I mention this fact because he was unjustly calumniated in letters written after his departure, and which were intercepted and published by the English. I ought also to add, that as he would never for his own private use resort to the money-chest of the army, the contents of which were, indeed, never half sufficient to defray the necessary expenses, he several times drew on Genoa, through M. James, and on the funds he possessed in the house of Clary, 16,000, 25,000, and up to 33,000 francs. I can bear witness that in Egypt I never saw him touch any money beyond his pay; and that he left the country poorer than he had entered it is a fact that cannot be denied. In his notes on Egypt it appears that in one year 12,600,000 francs were received. In this sum were included at least 2,000,000 of contributions, which were levied at the expense of many decapitations. Bonaparte was fourteen months in Egypt, and he is said to have brought away with him 20,000,000. Calumny may be very gratifying to certain persons, but they should at least give it a colouring of probability. The fact is, that Bonaparte had scarcely enough to maintain himself at Ajaccio and to defray our posting expenses to Paris.

On our arrival at Ajaccio we learnt the death of Joubert, and the loss of the battle of Novi, which was fought on the 15th of August. Bonaparte was tormented by anxiety; he was in a state of utter uncertainty as to the future. From the time we left Alexandria till our arrival in Corsica he had frequently talked of what he should do during the quarantine, which he supposed he would be required to observe on reaching Toulon, the port at which he had determined to land.

Even then he cherished some illusions respecting the state of affairs; and he often said to me, "But for that confounded quarantine, I would hasten ashore, and place myself at the head of the army of Italy. All is not over; and I am sure that there is not a general who would refuse me the command. The news of a victory gained by me would reach Paris as soon as the battle of Aboukir; that, indeed, would be excellent."

In Corsica his language was very different. When he was informed of our reverses, and saw the full extent of the evil, he was for a moment overwhelmed. His grand projects then gave way to the consideration of matters of minor import, and he thought about his detention in the Lazaretto of Toulon. He spoke of the Directory, of intrigues, and of what would be said of him. He accounted his enemies those who envied him, and those who could not be reconciled to his glory and the influence of his name. Amidst all these anxieties Bonaparte was outwardly calm, though he was moody and reflective.

Providing against every chance of danger, he had purchased at Ajaccio a large launch which was intended to be towed by the 'Muiron', and it was manned by twelve of the best sailors the island could furnish. His resolution was, in case of inevitable danger, to jump into this boat and get ashore. This precaution had well-nigh proved useful.[84]

After leaving the Gulf of Ajaccio the voyage was prosperous and undisturbed for one day; but on the second day, just at sunset, an English squadron of fourteen sail hove in sight. The English, having advantage of the lights which we had in our faces, saw us better than we could see them. They recognised our two frigates as Venetian built; but luckily for us, night came on, for we were not far apart. We saw the signals of the English for a long time, and heard the report of the guns more and more to our left, and we thought it was the intention of the cruisers to intercept us on the south-east. Under these circumstances Bonaparte had reason to thank fortune; for it is very evident that had the English suspected our two frigates of coming from the East and going to France, they would have shut us out from land by running between us and it, which to them was very easy. Probably they took us for a convoy of provisions going from Toulon to Genoa; and it was to this error and the darkness that we were indebted for escaping with no worse consequence than a

---

84 Sir Walter Scott, at the commencement of his Life of Napoleon, says that Bonaparte did not see his native City after 1793. Probably to avoid contradicting himself, the Scottish historian observes that Bonaparte was near Ajaccio on his return from Egypt. He spent eight days there.—Bourrienne.

fright.[85] During the remainder of the night the utmost agitation prevailed on board the Muiron. Gantheaume especially was in a state of anxiety which it is impossible to describe, and which it was painful to witness: he was quite beside himself, for a disaster appeared inevitable. He proposed to return to Corsica. "No, no!" replied Bonaparte imperiously. "No! Spread all sail! Every man at his post! To the north-west! To the north-west!" This order saved us; and I am enabled to affirm that in the midst of almost general alarm Bonaparte was solely occupied in giving orders. The rapidity of his judgment seemed to grow in the face of danger. The remembrance of that night will never be effaced from my mind. The hours lingered on; and none of us could guess upon what new dangers the morrow's sun would shine.

However, Bonaparte's resolution was taken: his orders were given, his arrangements made. During the evening he had resolved upon throwing himself into the long boat; he had already fixed on the persons who were to share his fate, and had already named to me the papers which he thought it most important to save. Happily our terrors were vain and our arrangements useless. By the first rays of the sun we discovered the English fleet sailing to the north-east, and we stood for the wished-for coast of France.

The 8th of October, at eight in the morning, we entered the roads of Fréjus. The sailors not having recognised the coast during the night, we did not know where we were. There was, at first, some hesitation whether we should advance. We were by no means expected, and did not know how to answer the signals, which has been changed during our absence. Some guns were even fired upon us by the batteries on the coast; but our bold entry into the roads, the crowd upon the decks of the two frigates, and our signs of joy, speedily banished all doubt of our being friends. We were in the port, and approaching the landing-place, when the rumour spread that Bonaparte was on board one of the frigates. In an instant the sea was covered with boats. In vain we begged them to keep at a distance; we were carried ashore, and when we told the crowd, both of men and women who were pressing about us, the risk they ran, they all exclaimed, "We prefer the plague to the Austrians!"

What were our feelings when we again set foot on the soil of France I will not attempt to describe. Our escape from the dangers that threatened us seemed almost miraculous. We had lost twenty days at the beginning of our voyage, and at its close had been almost taken by an English squadron. Under these circumstances, how rapturously we inhaled the balmy air of Provence! Such was our joy, that we were scarcely sensible of the disheartening news which arrived from all quarters. At the first moment of our arrival, by a spontaneous impulse, we all repeated, with tears in our eyes, the beautiful lines which Voltaire has put into the mouth of the exile of Sicily.

Bonaparte has been reproached with having violated the sanitary laws; but, after what I have already stated respecting his intentions, I presume there can remain no doubt of the

85 Here Bourrienne says in a note "Where did Sir Walter Scott learn that we were neither seen nor recognised? We were not recognised, but certainly seen," This is corroborated by the testimony of the Duc de Rovigo, who, in his Memoirs, says, "I have met officers of the English navy who assured me that the two frigates had been seen but were considered by the Admiral to belong to his squadron, as they steered their course towards him; and as he knew we had only one frigate in the Mediterranean, and one in Toulon harbour, he was far from supposing that the frigates which he had descried could have General Bonaparte on board." (Savary, tome i. p. 226).

falsehood of this accusation. All the blame must rest with the inhabitants of Fréjus, who on this occasion found the law of necessity more imperious than the sanitary laws. Yet when it is considered that four or five hundred persons, and a quantity of effects, were landed from Alexandria, where the plague had been raging during the summer, it is almost a miracle that France, and indeed Europe escaped the scourge.

CHAPTER XXII

1799

The effect produced in France and throughout Europe by the mere intelligence of Bonaparte's return is well known. I shall not yet speak of the vast train of consequences which that event entailed. I must, however, notice some accusations which were brought against him from the time of our landing to the 9th of November. He was reproached for having left Egypt, and it was alleged that his departure was the result of long premeditation. But I, who was constantly with him, am enabled positively to affirm that his return to France was merely the effect of a sudden resolution. Of this the following fact is in itself sufficient evidence.

While we were at Cairo, a few days before we heard of the landing of the Anglo-Turkish fleet, and at the moment when we were on the point of setting off to encamp at the Pyramids, Bonaparte despatched a courier to France. I took advantage of this opportunity to write to my wife. I almost bade her an eternal adieu. My letter breathed expressions of grief such as I had not before evinced. I said, among other things, that we knew not when or how it would be possible for us to return to France. If Bonaparte had then entertained any thought of a speedy return I must have known it, and in that case I should not certainly have distressed my family by a desponding letter, when I had not had an opportunity of writing for seven months before.

Two days after the receipt of my letter my wife was awoke very early in the morning to be informed of our arrival in France. The courier who brought this intelligence was the bearer of a second letter from me, which I had written on board ship, and dated from Fréjus. In this letter I mentioned that Bonaparte would pass through Sens and dine with my mother.

In fulfilment of my directions Madame de Bourrienne set off for Paris at five in the morning. Having passed the first post-house she met a Berlin containing four travellers, among whom she recognised Louis Bonaparte going to meet the General on the Lyons road. On seeing Madame de Bourrienne Louis desired the postillion to stop, and asked her whether she had heard from me. She informed him that we should pass through Sens, where the General wished to dine with my mother, who had made every preparation for receiving him. Louis then continued his journey. About nine o'clock my wife met another Berlin, in which were Madame Bonaparte and her daughter. As they were asleep, and both carriages were driving at a very rapid rate, Madame de Bourrienne did not stop them. Josephine followed the route taken by Louis. Both missed the General, who changed his mind at Lyons, and proceeded by way of Bourbonnais. He arrived fifteen hours after my wife; and those who had taken the Burgundy road proceeded to Lyons uselessly.

Determined to repair in all haste to Paris, Bonaparte had left Fréjus on the afternoon of the day of our landing. He himself had despatched the courier to Sens to inform my mother of his intended visit to her; and it was not until he got to Lyons that he determined to take the Bourbonnais road. His reason for doing so will presently be seen. All along the road, at Aix, at Lyons, in every town and village, he was received, as at Fréjus, with the most rapturous demonstrations of joy.[86] Only those who witnessed his triumphal journey can form any notion of it; and it required no great discernment to foresee something like the 18th Brumaire.

The provinces, a prey to anarchy and civil war, were continually threatened with foreign invasion. Almost all the south presented the melancholy spectacle of one vast arena of conflicting factions. The nation groaned beneath the yoke of tyrannical laws; despotism was systematically established; the law of hostages struck a blow at personal liberty, and forced loans menaced every man's property. The generality of the citizens had declared themselves against a pentarchy devoid of power, justice, and morality, and which had become the sport of faction and intrigue. Disorder was general; but in the provinces abuses were felt more sensibly than elsewhere. In great cities it was found more easy to elude the hand of despotism and oppression.

A change so earnestly wished for could not fail to be realised, and to be received with transport. The majority of the French people longed to be relieved from the situation in which they then stood. There were two dangers bar to cope with—anarchy and the Bourbons. Every one felt the urgent and indispensable necessity of concentrating the power of the Government in a single hand; at the same time maintaining the institutions which the spirit of the age demanded, and which France, after having so dearly purchased, was now about to lose. The country looked for a man who was capable of restoring her to tranquillity; but as yet no such man had appeared. A soldier of fortune presented himself, covered with glory; he had planted the standard of France on the Capitol and on the Pyramids. The whole world acknowledged his superior talent; his character, his courage, and his victories had raised him to the very highest rank. His great works, his gallant actions, his speeches, and his proclamations ever since he had risen to eminence left no doubt of his wish to secure happiness and freedom to France, his adopted country. At that critical moment the necessity of a temporary dictatorship, which sometimes secures the safety of a state, banished all reflections on the consequences of such a power, and nobody seemed to think glory incompatible with personal liberty. All eyes were therefore directed on the General, whose past conduct guaranteed his capability of defending the Republic abroad, and liberty at home,—on the General whom his flatterers, and indeed some of his sincere friends, styled, "the hero of liberal ideas," the title to which he aspired.

Under every point of view, therefore, he was naturally chosen as the chief of a generous nation, confiding to him her destiny, in preference to a troop of mean and fanatical hypocrites, who, under the names of republicanism and liberty, had reduced France to the most abject slavery.

Among the schemes which Bonaparte was incessantly revolving in his mind may undoubtedly be ranked the project of attaining the head of the French Government; but it would be a mistake to suppose that on his return from Egypt he had formed any fixed plan. There was something vague in his ambitious aspirations; and he was, if I may so express myself, fond of building those imaginary edifices called castles in the air. The current of

86 From Fréjus to Aix a crowd of men kindly escorted us, carrying torches alongside the carriage of the General, not so much to show their enthusiasm as to ensure our safety (Bourrienne) These brigands became so bad in France that at one time soldiers were placed in the imperials of all the diligences, receiving from the wits the curiously anticipative name of "imperial armies"

events was in accordance with his wishes; and it may truly be said that the whole French nation smoothed for Bonaparte the road which led to power. Certainly the unanimous plaudits and universal joy which accompanied him along a journey of more than 200 leagues must have induced him to regard as a national mission that step which was at first prompted merely by his wish of meddling with the affairs of the Republic.

This spontaneous burst of popular feeling, unordered and unpaid for, loudly proclaimed the grievances of the people, and their hope that the man of victory would become their deliverer. The general enthusiasm excited by the return of the conqueror of Egypt delighted him to a degree which I cannot express, and was, as he has often assured me, a powerful stimulus in urging him to the object to which the wishes of France seemed to direct him.

Among people of all classes and opinions an 18th Brumaire was desired and expected. Many royalists even believed that a change would prove favourable to the King. So ready are we to persuade ourselves of the reality of what we wish.

As soon as it was suspected that Bonaparte would accept the power offered him, an outcry was raised about a conspiracy against the Republic, and measures were sought for preserving it. But necessity, and indeed, it must be confessed, the general feeling of the people, consigned the execution of those measures to him who was to subvert the Republic. On his return to Paris Bonaparte spoke and acted like a man who felt his own power; he cared neither for flattery, dinners, nor balls,—his mind took a higher flight.

We arrived in Paris on the 24th Vendemiaire (the 16th of October). As yet he knew nothing of what was going on; for he had seen neither his wife nor his brothers, who were looking for him on the Burgundy road. The news of our landing at Fréjus had reached Paris by a telegraphic despatch. Madame Bonaparte, who was dining with M. Gohier when that despatch was communicated to him, as president of the Directory, immediately set off to meet her husband, well knowing how important it was that her first interview with him should not be anticipated by his brothers.

The imprudent communications of Junot at the fountains of Messoudiah will be remembered, but, after the first ebullition of jealous rage, all traces of that feeling had apparently disappeared. Bonaparte however, was still harassed by secret suspicion, and the painful impressions produced by Junot were either not entirely effaced or were revived after our arrival in Paris. We reached the capital before Josephine returned. The recollection of the past, the ill-natured reports of his brothers,[87] and the exaggeration of facts had irritated Napoleon to the very highest pitch, and he received Josephine with studied coldness, and with an air of the most cruel indifference. He had no communication with her for three days, during which time he frequently spoke to me of suspicions which his imagination converted into certainty; and threats of divorce escaped his lips with no less vehemence than when we were on the confines of Syria. I took upon me the office of conciliator, which I had before discharged with success. I represented to him the dangers to be apprehended from the publicity and scandal of such an affair; and that the moment when his grand views might possibly be realized was not the fit time to entertain France and Europe with the details of a charge of adultery. I spoke to him of Hortense and Eugène, to whom he was much attached. Reflection, seconded by his ardent affection for Josephine, brought about a complete reconciliation. After these three days of conjugal misunderstanding their

87 Joseph Bonaparte remarks on this that Napoleon met Josephine at Paris before his brothers arrived there, (Compare d'Abrantès, vol. 1, pp. 260-262 and Rémusat, tome i. pp. 147-148.)

happiness was never afterwards disturbed by a similar cause.[88]

88 In speaking of the unexpected arrival of Bonaparte and of the meeting between him and Josephine, Madame Junot says: "On the 10th October Josephine set off to meet her husband, but without knowing exactly what road he would take. She thought it likely he would come by way of Burgundy, and therefore Louis and she set off for Lyons. "Madame Bonaparte was a prey to great and well-founded aspersions. Whether she was guilty or only imprudent, she was strongly accused by the Bonaparte family, who were desirous that Napoleon should obtain a divorce. The elder M. de Caulaincourt stated to us his apprehensions on this point; but whenever the subject was introduced my mother changed the conversation, because, knowing as she did the sentiments of the Bonaparte family, she could not reply without either committing them or having recourse to falsehood. She knew, moreover, the truth of many circumstances which M. de Caulaincourt seemed to doubt, and which her situation with respect to Bonaparte prevented her from communicating to him. "Madame Bonaparte committed a great fault in neglecting at this juncture to conciliate her mother-in-law, who might have protected her against those who sought her ruin and effected it nine years later; for the divorce in 1809 was brought about by the joint efforts of all the members of the Bonaparte family, aided by some of Napoleon's most confidential servants, whom Josephine, either as Madame Bonaparte or as Empress, had done nothing to make her friends. "Bonaparte, on his arrival in Paris, found his house deserted: but his mother, sisters, and sisters-in-law, and, in short, every member of his family, except Louis, who had attended Madame Bonaparte to Lyons, came to him immediately. The impression made upon him by the solitude of his home and its desertion by its mistress was profound and terrible, and nine years afterwards, when the ties between him and Josephine were severed for ever, he showed that it was not effaced. From not finding her with his family he inferred that she felt herself unworthy of their presence, and feared to meet the man she had wronged. He considered her journey to Lyons as a mere pretence. "M. de Bourrienne says that for some days after Josephine's return Bonaparte treated her with extreme coldness. As he was an eyewitness, why does he not state the whole truth, and say that on her return Bonaparte refused to see her and did not see her? It was to the earnest entreaties of her children that she owed the recovery, not of her husband's love, for that had long ceased, but of that tenderness acquired by habit, and that intimate intercourse which made her still retain the rank of consort to the greatest man of his age. Bonaparte was at this period much attached to Eugène Beauharnais, who, to do him justice, was a charming youth. He knew less of Hortense; but her youth and sweetness of temper, and the protection of which, as his adopted daughter, she besought him not to deprive her, proved powerful advocates, and overcame his resistance. "In this delicate negotiation it was good policy not to bring any other person into play, whatever might be their influence with Bonaparte, and Madame Bonaparte did not, therefore, have recourse either to Barras, Bourrienne, or Berthier. It was expedient that they who interceded for her should be able to say something without the possibility of a reply. Now Bonaparte could not with any degree of propriety explain to such children as Eugène or Hortense the particulars of their mother's conduct. He was therefore constrained to silence, and had no argument to combat the tears of two innocent creatures at his feet exclaiming, 'Do not abandon our mother; she will break her heart! and ought injustice to take from us, poor orphans, whose natural protector the scaffold has already deprived us of, the support of one whom Providence has sent to replace him!' "The scene, as Bonaparte has since stated, was long and painful, and the two children at length introduced their mother,

On the day after his arrival Bonaparte visited the Directors.[89] The interview was cold. On the 24th of October he said to me, "I dined yesterday at Gohier's; Sieyès was present, and I pretended not to see him. I observed how much he was enraged at this mark of disrespect."—"But are you sure he is against you?" inquired I. "I know nothing yet; but he is a scheming man, and I don't like him." Even at that time Bonaparte had thoughts of getting himself elected a member of the Directory in the room of Sieyès.

---

and placed her in his arms. The unhappy woman had awaited his decision at the door of a small back staircase, extended at almost full length upon the stairs, suffering the acutest pangs of mental torture. "Whatever might be his wife's errors, Bonaparte appeared entirely to forget them, and the reconciliation was complete. Of all the members of the family Madame Leclerc was most vexed at the pardon which Napoleon had granted to his wife. Bonaparte's mother was also very ill pleased; but she said nothing. Madame Joseph Bonaparte, who was always very amiable, took no part in these family quarrels; therefore she could easily determine what part to take when fortune smiled on Josephine. As to Madame Bacciocchi, she gave free vent to her ill-humour and disdain; the consequence was that her sister-in-law could never endure her. Christine who was a beautiful creature, followed the example of Madame Joseph, and Caroline was so young that her opinion could have no weight in such an affair. As to Bonaparte's brothers, they were at open war with Josephine."

89 The Directors at this time were Barras, Sieyès, Moulins, Gohier, and Roger Ducos.

CHAPTER XXIII

1799

To throw a clear light on the course of the great events which will presently be developed it is necessary to state briefly what intrigues had been hatched and what ambitious hopes had risen up while we were in Egypt. When in Egypt Bonaparte was entirely deprived of any means of knowing what was going on in France; and in our rapid journey from Fréjus to Paris we had no opportunity of collecting much information. Yet it was very important that we should know the real state of affairs, and the sentiments of those whom Bonaparte had counted among his rivals in glory, and whom he might now meet among his rivals in ambition.

Moreau's military reputation stood very high, and Bernadotte's firmness appeared inflexible. Generally speaking, Bonaparte might have reckoned among his devoted partisans the companions of his glory in Italy, and also those whom he subsequently denominated "his Egyptians." But brave men had distinguished themselves in the army of the Rhine; and if they did not withhold their admiration from the conqueror of Italy, they felt at least more personally interested in the admiration which they lavished on him who had repaired the disaster of Scherer. Besides, it must be borne in mind that a republican spirit prevailed, almost without exception, in the army, and that the Directory appeared to be a Government invented expressly to afford patronage to intriguers. All this planted difficulties in our way, and rendered it indispensably necessary that we should know our ground. We had, it is true, been greeted by the fullest measure of popular enthusiasm on our arrival; but this was not enough. We wanted suffrages of a more solid kind.

During the campaign of Egypt, Bernadotte, who was a zealous republican, had been War Minister,[90] but he had resigned the portfolio to Dubois-Crancé three weeks before Bonaparte's return to France. Some partisans of the old Minister were endeavouring to get him recalled, and it was very important to Bonaparte's interests that he should prevent the success of this design. I recollect that on the second day of our arrival Bonaparte said to me, "I have learned many things; but we shall see what will happen. Bernadotte is a singular man. When he was War Minister Augereau, Salicetti, and some others informed him that the Constitution was in danger, and that it was necessary to get rid of Sieyès, Barras, and Fouché, who were at the head of a plot. What did Bernadotte do? Nothing. He asked for proofs. None could be produced. He asked for powers. Who could grant them? Nobody. He should have taken them; but he would not venture on that. He wavered. He said he could not enter into the schemes which were proposed to him. He only promised to be silent on condition that they were renounced. Bernadotte is not a help; he is an obstacle. I have heard from good authority that a great number of influential persons wished to invest him with extensive power for the public good; but he was obstinate, and would listen to nothing."

---

90 Bernadotte was Minister of War from 2d July 1799 to 14th September 1799, when, as he himself wrote to the Directory, they "accepted" the resignation he had not offered.

After a brief interval of silence, during which Bonaparte rubbed his forehead with his right hand, he then resumed:

"I believe I shall have Bernadotte and Moreau against me. But I do not fear Moreau. He is devoid of energy. I know he would prefer military to political power. The promise of the command of an army would gain him over. But Bernadotte has Moorish blood in his veins. He is bold and enterprising. He is allied to my brothers.[91]

"He does not like me, and I am almost certain that he will oppose me. If he should become ambitious he will venture anything. And yet, you recollect in what a lukewarm way he acted on the 18th Fructidor, when I sent him to second Augereau. This devil of a fellow is not to be seduced. He is disinterested and clever. But, after all, we have but just arrived, and know not what may happen."

Bernadotte, it was reported, had advised that Bonaparte should be brought to a court-martial, on the two-fold charge of having abandoned his army and violated the quarantine laws. This report came to the ear of Bonaparte; but he refused to believe it and he was right. Bernadotte thought himself bound to the Constitution which he had sworn to defend. Hence the opposition he manifested to the measures of the 18th Brumaire. But he cherished no personal animosity against Bonaparte as long as he was ignorant of his ambitious designs. The extraordinary and complicated nature of subsequent events rendered his possession of the crown of Sweden in no way incompatible with his fidelity to the Constitution of the year III.

On our first arrival in Paris, though I was almost constantly with the General, yet, as our routine of occupation was not yet settled, I was enabled now and then to snatch an hour or two from business. This leisure time I spent in the society of my family and a few friends, and in collecting information as to what had happened during our absence, for which purpose I consulted old newspapers and pamphlets. I was not surprised to learn that Bonaparte's brothers—that is to say, Joseph and Lucien—had been engaged in many intrigues. I was told that Sieyès had for a moment thought of calling the Duke of Brunswick to the head of the Government; that Barras would not have been very averse to favouring the return of the Bourbons; and that Moulins, Roger Ducos, and Gohier alone believed or affected to believe, in the possibility of preserving the existing form of government. From what I heard at the time I have good reasons for believing that Joseph and Lucien made all sorts of endeavours to inveigle Bernadotte into their brother's party, and in the hope of accomplishing that object they had assisted in getting him appointed War Minister. However, I cannot vouch for the truth of this. I was told that Bernadotte had at first submitted to the influence of Bonaparte's two brothers; but that their urgent interference in their client's behalf induced him to shake them off, to proceed freely in the exercise of his duties, and to open the eyes of the Directory on what the Republic might have to apprehend from the enterprising character of Bonaparte.

91 Joseph Bonaparte and Bernadotte had married sisters. Marie-Julie and Eugénie Bernardine-Desirée Clary. The feeling of Bourrienne for Bernadotte makes this passage doubtful. It is to be noticed that in the same conversation he makes Napoleon describe Bernadotte as not venturing to act without powers and as enterprising. The stern republican becoming Prince de Monte Carlo and King of Sweden, in a way compatible with his fidelity to the Constitution of the year III., is good. Lanfrey attributes Bernadotte's refusal to join more to rivalry than to principle (Lanfrey, tome i. p. 440). But in any case Napoleon did not dread Bernadotte, and was soon threatening to shoot him; see Lucien, tome ii. p. 107.

It is certain that what I have to relate respecting the conduct of Bernadotte to Bonaparte is calculated to give credit to these assertions.

All the generals who were in Paris, with the exception of Bernadotte, had visited Bonaparte during the first three days which succeeded his arrival. Bernadotte's absence was the more remarkable because he had served under Bonaparte in Italy. It was not until a fortnight had elapsed, and then only on the reiterated entreaties of Joseph and Madame Joseph Bonaparte (his sister-in-law), that he determined to go and see his old General-in-Chief. I was not present at their interview, being at that moment occupied in the little cabinet of the Rue Chantereine. But I soon discovered that their conversation had been long and warm; for as soon as it was ended Bonaparte entered the cabinet exceedingly agitated, and said to me, "Bourrienne, how do you think Bernadotte has behaved? You have traversed France with me—you witnessed the enthusiasm which my return excited—you yourself told me that you saw in that enthusiasm the desire of the French people to be relieved from the disastrous position in which our reverses have placed them. Well! would you believe it? Bernadotte boasts, with ridiculous exaggeration, of the brilliant and victorious situation of France! He talks about the defeat of the Russians, the occupation of Genoa, the innumerable armies that are rising up everywhere. In short, I know not what nonsense he has got in his head."—"What can all this mean?" said I. "Did he speak about Egypt?"—"Oh, yes! Now you remind me. He actually reproached me for not having brought the army back with me! 'But,' observed I, 'have you not just told me that you are absolutely overrun with troops; that all your frontiers are secure, that immense levies are going on, and that you will have 200,000 infantry?—If this be true, what do you want with a few thousand men who may ensure the preservation of Egypt?' He could make no answer to this. But he is quite elated by the honour of having been War Minister, and he told me boldly that he looked upon the army of Egypt as lost nay, more. He made insinuations. He spoke of enemies abroad and enemies at home; and as he uttered these last words he looked significantly at me. I too gave him a glance! But stay a little. The pear will soon be ripe! You know Josephine's grace and address. She was present. The scrutinising glance of Bernadotte did not escape her, and she adroitly turned the conversation. Bernadotte saw from my countenance that I had had enough of it, and he took his leave. But don't let me interrupt you farther. I am going back to speak to Josephine."

I must confess that this strange story made me very impatient to find myself alone with Madame Bonaparte, for I wished to hear her account of the scene. An opportunity occurred that very evening. I repeated to her what I had heard from the General, and all that she told me tended to confirm its accuracy. She added that Bernadotte seemed to take the utmost pains to exhibit to the General a flattering picture of the prosperity of France; and she reported to me, as follows, that part of the conversation which was peculiarly calculated to irritate Bonaparte:—"'I do not despair of the safety of the Republic, which I am certain can restrain her enemies both abroad and at home.' As Bernadotte uttered these last words,'" continued Josephine, "his glance made me shudder. One word more and Bonaparte could have commanded himself no longer! It is true," added she, "that it was in some degree his own fault, for it was he who turned the conversation on politics; and Bernadotte, in describing the flourishing condition of France, was only replying to the General, who had drawn a very opposite picture of the state of things. You know, my dear Bourrienne, that Bonaparte is not always very prudent. I fear he has said too much to Bernadotte about the necessity of changes in the Government." Josephine had not yet recovered from the agitation into which this violent scene had thrown her. After I took leave of her I made notes of what she had told me.

A few days after, when Bonaparte, Josephine, Hortense, Eugène, and I were together in the drawing-room, Bernadotte unexpectedly entered. His appearance, after what had passed, was calculated to surprise us. He was accompanied by a person whom he requested permission to introduce to Bonaparte. I have forgotten his name, but he was, I think, secretary-general while Bernadotte was in office. Bonaparte betrayed no appearance of astonishment. He received Bernadotte with perfect ease, and they soon entered into conversation. Bonaparte, who seemed to acquire confidence from the presence of those who were about him, said a great deal about the agitation which prevailed among the republicans, and expressed himself in very decided terms against the 'Manège Club.'[92] I seconded him by observing that M. Moreau de Worms of my department, who was a member of that club, had himself complained to me of the violence that prevailed in it. "But, General," said Bernadotte, "your brothers were its most active originators. Yet," added he in a tone of firmness, "you accuse me of having favoured that club, and I repel the charge. It cannot be otherwise than false. When I came into office I found everything in the greatest disorder. I had no leisure to think about any club to which my duties did not call me. You know well that your friend Salicetti, and that your brother, who is in your confidence, are both leading men in the Manège Club. To the instructions of I know not whom is to be attributed the violence of which you complain." At these words, and especially the tone in which Bernadotte uttered 'I know not whom,' Bonaparte could no longer restrain himself. "Well, General," exclaimed he furiously, "I tell you plainly, I would rather live wild in the woods than in a state of society which affords no security." Bernadotte then said, with great dignity of manner, "Good God! General, what security would you have?" From the warmth evinced by Bonaparte I saw plainly that the conversation would soon be converted into a dispute, and in a whisper I requested Madame Bonaparte to change the conversation, which she immediately did by addressing a question to some one present. Bernadotte, observing Madame Bonaparte's design, checked his warmth. The subject of conversation was changed, and it became general. Bernadotte soon took up his hat and departed.

One morning, when I entered Bonaparte's chamber—it was, I believe, three or four days after the second visit of Bernadotte—he said:

"Well, Bourrienne, I wager you will not guess with whom I am going to breakfast this morning?"—"Really, General, I —"—"With Bernadotte; and the best of the joke is, that I have invited myself. You would have seen how it was all brought about if you had been with us at the Théâtre Français, yesterday evening. You know we are going to visit Joseph today at Mortfontaine. Well, as we were coming out of the theatre last night, finding myself side by side with Bernadotte and not knowing what to talk about, I asked him whether he was to be of our party to-day? He replied in the affirmative; and as we were passing his house in the Rue Cisalpine.[93]

---

92 The Manège Club, the last resort of the Jacobins, formed in 1799, and closed seven or eight months afterwards. Joseph Bonaparte (Erreurs, time i. p. 251) denies that he or Lucien—for whom the allusion is meant—were members of this club, and he disputes this conversation ever having taken place. Lucien (tome i. p. 219) treats this club as opposed to his party.

93 Joseph Bonaparte lays great stress on the fact that Napoleon would not have passed this house, which was far from the theatre (Erreurs, tome i, p. 251).

"I told him, without any ceremony, that I should be happy to come and take a cup of coffee with him in the morning. He seemed pleased. What do you think of that, Bourrienne?"—"Why, General, I hope you may have reason on your part to be pleased with him."—"Never fear, never fear. I know what I am about. This will compromise him with Gohier. Remember, you must always meet your enemies with a bold face, otherwise they think they are feared, and that gives them confidence."

Bonaparte stepped into the carriage with Josephine, who was always ready when she had to go out with him, for he did not like to wait. They proceeded first to Bernadotte's to breakfast, and from thence to Mortfontaine. On his return Bonaparte told me very little about what had passed during the day, and I could see that he was not in the best of humours. I afterwards learned that Bonaparte had conversed a good deal with Bernadotte, and that he had made every effort to render himself agreeable, which he very well knew how to do when he chose! but that, in spite of all his conversational talent; and supported as he was by the presence of his three brothers, and Regnault de St. Jean d'Angély, he could not withstand the republican firmness of Bernadotte. However, the number of his partisans daily augmented; for all had not the uncompromising spirit of Bernadotte; and it will soon be seen that Moreau himself undertook charge of the Directors who were made prisoners on the 18th Brumaire.

Bernadotte's shrewd penetration made him one of the first to see clearly into Bonaparte's designs. He was well convinced of his determination to overthrow the constitution and possess himself of power. He saw the Directory divided into two parties; the one duped by the promises and assurances of Bonaparte, and the other conniving with him for the accomplishment of his plans. In these circumstances Bernadotte offered his services to all persons connected with the Government who, like himself, were averse to the change which he saw good reason to apprehend. But Bonaparte was not the man to be outdone in cunning or activity; and every moment swelled the ranks of his adherents.

On the 16th Brumaire I dined in the Rue de la Victoire. Bernadotte was present, and I believe General Jourdan also. While the grand conspiracy was hastening to its accomplishment Madame Bonaparte and I had contrived a little plot of a more innocent kind. We let no one into our secret, and our 16th Brumaire was crowned with complete success. We had agreed to be on the alert to prevent any fresh exchange of angry words. All succeeded to the utmost of our wishes. The conversation languished during dinner; but it was not dulness that we were afraid of. It turned on the subject of war, and in that vast field Bonaparte's superiority over his interlocutors was undeniable.

When we retired to the drawing-rooms a great number of evening visitors poured in, and the conversation then became animated, and even gay. Bonaparte was in high spirits. He said to some one, smiling, and pointing to Bernadotte, "You are not aware that the General yonder is a Chouan."—"A Chouan?" repeated Bernadotte, also in a tone of pleasantry. "Ah! General you contradict yourself. Only the other day you taxed me with favouring the violence of the friends of the Republic, and now you accuse me of protecting the Chouans.[94]

"You should at least be consistent." A few moments after, availing himself of the confusion occasioned by the throng of visitors, Bernadotte slipped off.

As a mark of respect to Bonaparte the Council of the Five Hundred appointed Lucien

94 The "Chouans," so called from their use of the cry of the screech-owl (chathouan) as a signal, were the revolted peasants of Brittany and of Maine.

its president. The event proved how important this nomination was to Napoleon. Up to the 19th Brumaire, and especially on that day, Lucien evinced a degree of activity, intelligence, courage, and presence of mind which are rarely found united in one individual. I have no hesitation in stating that to Lucien's nomination and exertions must be attributed the success of the 19th Brumaire.

The General had laid down a plan of conduct from which he never deviated during the twenty-three days which intervened between his arrival in Paris and the 18th Brumaire. He refused almost all private invitations, in order to avoid indiscreet questions, unacceptable offers, and answers which might compromise him.

It was not without some degree of hesitation that he yielded to a project started by Lucien, who, by all sorts of manoeuvring, had succeeded in prevailing on a great number of his colleagues to be present at a grand subscription dinner to be given to Bonaparte by the Council of the Ancients.

The disorder which unavoidably prevailed in a party amounting to upwards of 250 persons, animated by a diversity of opinions and sentiments; the anxiety and distrust arising in the minds of those who were not in the grand plot, rendered this meeting one of the most disagreeable I ever witnessed. It was all restraint and dulness. Bonaparte's countenance sufficiently betrayed his dissatisfaction; besides, the success of his schemes demanded his presence elsewhere. Almost as soon as he had finished his dinner he rose, saying to Berthier and me, "I am tired: let us be gone." He went round to the different tables, addressing to the company compliments and trifling remarks, and departed, leaving at table the persons by whom he had been invited.

This short political crisis was marked by nothing more grand, dignified, or noble than the previous revolutionary commotions. All these plots were so contemptible, and were accompanied by so much trickery, falsehood, and treachery, that, for the honour of human nature, it is desirable to cover them with a veil.

General Bonaparte's thoughts were first occupied with the idea he had conceived even when in Italy, namely, to be chosen a Director. Nobody dared yet to accuse him of being a deserter from the army of the East. The only difficulty was to obtain a dispensation on the score of age. And was this not to be obtained? No sooner was he installed in his humble abode in the Rue de la Victoire than he was assured that, on the retirement of Rewbell, the majority of suffrages would have devolved on him had he been in France, and had not the fundamental law required the age of forty; but that not even his warmest partisans were disposed to violate the yet infant Constitution of the year III.

Bonaparte soon perceived that no efforts would succeed in overcoming this difficulty, and he easily resolved to possess himself wholly of an office of which he would nominally have had only a fifth part had he been a member of the Directory.

As soon as his intentions became manifest he found himself surrounded by all those who recognised in him the man they had long looked for. These persons, who were able and influential in their own circles, endeavoured to convert into friendship the animosity which existed between Sieyès and Bonaparte. This angry feeling had been increased by a remark made by Sieyès, and reported to Bonaparte. He had said, after the dinner at which Bonaparte treated him so disrespectfully, "Do you see how that little insolent fellow behaves to a member of a Government which would do well to order him to be SHOT?"

But all was changed when able mediators pointed out to Bonaparte the advantage of uniting with Sieyès for the purpose of overthrowing a Constitution which he did not like.

He was assured how vain it would be to think of superseding him, and that it would be better to flatter him with the hope of helping to subvert the constitution and raising up a new one. One day some one said to Bonaparte in my hearing, "Seek for support among the party who call the friends of the Republic Jacobins, and be assured that Sieyès is at the head of that party."

On the 25th Vendémiaire (17th of October) the Directory summoned General Bonaparte to a private sitting. "They offered me the choice of any army I would command," said he to me the next morning. "I would not refuse, but I asked to be allowed a little time for the recovery of my health; and, to avoid any other embarrassing offers, I withdrew. I shall go to no more of their sittings." (He attended only one after this.) "I am determined to join Sieyès' party. It includes a greater diversity of opinions than that of the profligate Barras. He proclaims everywhere that he is the author of my fortune. He will never be content to play an inferior part, and I will never bend to such a man. He cherishes the mad ambition of being the support of the Republic. What would he do with me? Sieyès, on the contrary, has no political ambition."

No sooner did Sieyès begin to grow friendly with Bonaparte than the latter learned from him that Barras had said, "The 'little corporal' has made his fortune in Italy and does not want to go back again." Bonaparte repaired to the Directory for the sole purpose of contradicting this allegation. He complained to the Directors of its falsehood, boldly affirmed that the fortune he was supposed to possess had no existence, and that even if he had made his fortune it was not, at all events, at the expense of the Republic "You know," said he to me, "that the mines of Hydria have furnished the greater part of what I possess."—"Is it possible," said I, "that Barras could have said so, when you know so well of all the peculations of which he has been guilty since your return?"

Bonaparte had confided the secret of his plans to very few persons—to those only whose assistance he wanted. The rest mechanically followed their leaders and the impulse which was given to them; they passively awaited the realisation of the promises they had received, and on the faith of which they had pledged themselves.

CHAPTER XXIV

The parts of the great drama which was shortly to be enacted were well distributed. During the three days preceding the 18th Brumaire every one was at his post. Lucien, with equal activity and intelligence, forwarded the conspiracy in the two Councils; Sieyès had the management of the Directory; Réal,[95] under the instructions of Fouché,[96] negotiated with the departments, and dexterously managed, without compromising Fouché, to ruin those from whom that Minister had received his power. There was no time to lose; and Fouché said to me on the 14th Brumaire, "Tell your General to be speedy; if he delays, he is lost."

On the 17th, Regnault de St. Jean d'Angély told Bonaparte that the overtures made to Cambacérès and Lebrun had not been received in a very decided way. "I will have no tergiversation," replied Bonaparte with warmth. "Let them not flatter themselves that I stand in need of them. They must decide to-day; to-morrow will be too late. I feel myself strong enough now to stand alone."

Cambacérès[97] and Lebrun[98] were almost utter strangers to the intrigues which preceded the 18th Brumaire. Bonaparte had cast his eyes on the Minister of Justice to be one of his colleagues when he should be at liberty to name them, because his previous conduct had pledged him as a partisan of the Revolution. To him Bonaparte added Lebrun, to counterbalance the first choice. Lebrun was distinguished for honourable conduct and moderate principles. By selecting these two men Bonaparte hoped to please every one; besides, neither of them were able to contend against his fixed determination and ambitious views.

---

95 Pierre Francois Réal (1757-1834); public accuser before the revolutionary criminal tribunal; became, under Napoleon, Conseiller d'Etat and Comte, and was charged with the affairs of the "haute police."

96 Joseph Fouché (1754-1820); Conventionalist; member of extreme Jacobin party; Minister of Police under the Directory, August 1799; retained by Napoleon in that Ministry till 1802, and again from 1804 to 1810; became Duc d'Otrante in 1809; disgraced in 1810, and sent in 1813 as governor of the Illyrian Provinces; Minister of Police during the 'Cent Jours'; President of the Provisional Government, 1815; and for a short time Minister of Police under second restoration.

97 Cambacérès (J. J. Régis de) (1763-1824) Conventionalist; Minister of Justice under Directory, 1799; second Consul, 25th December 1799; Arch-Chancellor of the Empire, 1804; Duc de Parma, 1806; Minister of Justice during the 'Cent Jours': took great part in all the legal and administrative projects of the Consulate and Empire.

98 Charles Francois Lebrun (1757-1824). Deputy to the National Assembly, and member of the Council of the Five Hundred; Third Consul, 25th December 1799; Arch-Treasurer of the Empire, 1804; Duc de Plaisance, 1806; Governor-General of Holland, 1806; Lieutenant-Governor of Holland, 1810 to 1813; chiefly engaged in financial measures

What petty intrigues marked the 17th Brumaire! On that day I dined with Bonaparte; and after dinner he said, "I have promised to dine to-morrow with Gohier; but, as you may readily suppose, I do not intend going. However, I am very sorry for his obstinacy. By way of restoring his confidence Josephine is going to invite him to breakfast with us to-morrow. It will be impossible for him to suspect anything. I saw Barras this morning, and left him much disturbed. He asked me to return and visit him to-night. I promised to do so, but I shall not go. To-morrow all will be over. There is but little time; he expects me at eleven o'clock to-night. You shall therefore take my carriage, go there, send in my name, and then enter yourself. Tell him that a severe headache confines me to my bed, but that I will be with him without fail tomorrow. Bid him not be alarmed, for all will soon be right again. Elude his questions as much as possible; do not stay long, and come to me on your return."

At precisely eleven o'clock I reached the residence of Barras, in General Bonaparte's carriage. Solitude and silence prevailed in all the apartments through which I passed to Barras' cabinet. Bonaparte was announced, and when Barras saw me enter instead of him, he manifested the greatest astonishment and appeared much cast down. It was easy to perceive that he looked on himself as a lost man. I executed my commission, and stayed only a short time. I rose to take my leave, and he said, while showing me out, "I see that Bonaparte is deceiving me: he will not come again. He has settled everything; yet to me he owes all." I repeated that he would certainly come tomorrow, but he shook his head in a way which plainly denoted that he did not believe me. When I gave Bonaparte an account of my visit he appeared much pleased. He told me that Joseph was going to call that evening on Bernadotte, and to ask him to come tomorrow. I replied that, from all I knew, he would be of no use to him. "I believe so too," said he; "but he can no longer injure me, and that is enough. Well, good-night; be here at seven in the morning." It was then one o'clock.

I was with him a little before seven o'clock on the morning of the 18th Brumaire, and on my arrival I found a great number of generals and officers assembled. I entered Bonaparte's chamber, and found him already up—a thing rather unusual with him. At this moment he was as calm as on the approach of a battle. In a few moments Joseph and Bernadotte arrived. Joseph had not found him at home on the preceding evening, and had called for him that morning. I was surprised to see Bernadotte in plain clothes, and I stepped up to him and said in a low voice, "General, every one here, except you and I, is in uniform."—"Why should I be in uniform?" said he. As he uttered these words Bonaparte, struck with the same surprise as myself, stopped short while speaking to several persons around him, and turning quickly towards Bernadotte said, "How is this? you are not in uniform!"—"I never am on a morning when I am not on duty," replied Bernadotte.—"You will be on duty presently."—"I have not heard a word of it: I should have received my orders sooner."

Bonaparte then led Bernadotte into an adjoining room. Their conversation was not long, for there was no time to spare.

On the other hand, by the influence of the principal conspirators the removal of the legislative body to St. Cloud was determined on the morning of the 18th Brumaire, and the command of the army was given to Bonaparte.

All this time Barras was no doubt waiting for Bonaparte, and Madame Bonaparte was expecting Gohier to breakfast. At Bonaparte's were assembled all the generals who were devoted to him. I never saw so great a number before in the Rue de la Victoire. They were all, except Bernadotte, in full uniform; and there were, besides, half a dozen persons there initiated in the secrets of the day. The little hotel of the conqueror of Italy was much too small for such an assemblage, and several persons were standing in the court-yard. Bonaparte was acquainted with the decree of the Council of the Ancients, and only waited for its being brought to him before he should mount his horse. That decree was adopted in the Council of the Ancients by what may be called a false majority, for the members of the Council were summoned at different hours, and it was so contrived that sixty or eighty of them, whom Lucien and his friends had not been able to gain over, should not receive their notices in time.

As soon as the message from the Council of the Ancients arrived Bonaparte requested all the officers at his house to follow him. At that announcement a few who were in ignorance of what was going on did not follow—at least I saw two groups separately leave the hotel. Bernadotte said to me, "I shall stay with you." I perceived there was a good deal of suspicion in his manner. Bonaparte, before going down the stairs which led from the small round dining-room into the courtyard, returned quickly to bid Bernadotte follow him. He would not, and Bonaparte then said to me, while hurrying off, "Gohier is not come—so much the worse for him," and leaped on his horse. Scarcely was he off when Bernadotte left me. Josephine and I being now left alone, she acquainted me with her anxiety. I assured her that everything had been so well prepared that success was certain. She felt much interest about Gohier on account of her friendship for his wife. She asked me whether I was well acquainted with Gohier. "You know, Madame," replied I, "that we have been only twenty days in Paris, and that during that time I have only gone out to sleep in the Rue Martel. I have seen M. Gohier several times, when he came to visit the General, and have talked to him about the situation of our affairs in Switzerland, Holland, France, and other political matters, but I never exchanged a word with him as to what is now going on. This is the whole extent of my acquaintance with him."

"I am sorry for it," resumed Josephine, "because I should have asked you to write to him, and beg him to make no stir, but imitate Sieyès and Roger, who will voluntarily retire, and not to join Barras, who is probably at this very moment forced to do so. Bonaparte has told me that if Gohier voluntarily resigns, he will do everything for him." I believe Josephine communicated directly with the President of the Directory through a friend of Madame Gohier's.

Gohier and Moulins, no longer depending on Sieyès and Roger Ducos, waited for their colleague, Barras, in the hall of the Directory, to adopt some measure on the decree for removing the Councils to St. Cloud. But they were disappointed; for Barras, whose eyes had been opened by my visit on the preceding night, did not join them. He had been invisible to his colleagues from the moment that Bruix and M. de Talleyrand had informed him of the reality of what he already suspected, and insisted on his retirement.

On the 18th Brumaire a great number of military, amounting to about 10,000 men, were assembled in the gardens of the Tuileries, and were reviewed by Bonaparte, accompanied by Generals Beurnonville, Moreau, and Macdonald. Bonaparte read to them the decree just issued by the commission of inspectors of the Council of the Ancients, by which the legislative body was removed to St. Cloud; and by which he himself was entrusted with the execution of that decree, and appointed to the command of all the military force in Paris, and afterwards delivered an address to the troops.

Whilst Bonaparte was haranguing the soldiers, the Council of the Ancients published an address to the French people, in which it was declared that the seat of the legislative body was changed, in order to put down the factions, whose object was to control the national representation.

While all this was passing abroad I was at the General's house in the Rue de la Victoire; which I never left during the whole day. Madame Bonaparte and I were not without anxiety in Bonaparte's absence. I learned from Josephine that Joseph's wife had received a visit from Adjutant-General Rapatel, who had been sent by Bonaparte and Moreau to bring her husband to the Tuileries. Joseph was from home at the time, and so the message was useless. This circumstance, however, awakened hopes which we had scarcely dared to entertain. Moreau was then in accordance with Bonaparte, for Rapatel was sent in the name of both Generals. This alliance, so long despaired of, appeared to augur favourably. It was one of Bonaparte's happy strokes. Moreau, who was a slave to military discipline, regarded his successful rival only as a chief nominated by the Council of the Ancients. He received his orders and obeyed them. Bonaparte appointed him commander of the guard of the Luxembourg, where the Directors were under confinement. He accepted the command, and no circumstance could have contributed more effectually to the accomplishment of Bonaparte's views and to the triumph of his ambition.

At length Bonaparte, whom we had impatiently expected, returned. Almost everything had gone well with him, for he had had only to do with soldiers. In the evening he said to me, "I am sure that the committee of inspectors of the hall are at this very moment engaged in settling what is to be done at St. Cloud to-morrow. It is better to let them decide the matter, for by that means their vanity is flattered. I will obey orders which I have myself concerted." What Bonaparte was speaking of had been arranged nearly two or three days previously. The committee of inspectors was under the influence of the principal conspirators.

In the evening of this anxious day, which was destined to be succeeded by a stormy morrow, Bonaparte, pleased with having gained over Moreau, spoke to me of Bernadotte's visit in the morning.—"I saw," said he, "that you were as much astonished as I at Bernadotte's behaviour. A general out of uniform! He might as well have come in slippers. Do you know what passed when I took him aside? I told him all; I thought that the best way. I assured him that his Directory was hated, and his Constitution worn out; that it was necessary to turn them all off, and give another impulse to the government. 'Go and put on your uniform said I: I cannot wait for you long. You will find me at the Tuileries, with the rest of our comrades. Do not depend on Moreau, Beurnonville, or the generals of your party. When you know them better you will find that they promise much but perform little. Do not trust them.' Bernadotte then said that he would not take part in what he called a rebellion. A rebellion! Bourrienne, only think of that! A set of imbeciles, who from morning to night do nothing but debate in their kennels! But all was in vain. I could not move Bernadotte. He is a bar of iron. I asked him to give me his word that he would do nothing against me; what do you think was his answer?"—"Something unpleasant, no doubt."—"Unpleasant! that is too mild a word. He said, 'I will remain quiet as a citizen; but if the Directory order me to act, I will march against all disturbers.' But I can laugh at all that now. My measures are taken, and he will have no command. However, I set him at ease as to what would take place. I flattered him with a picture of private life, the pleasures of the country, and the charms of Malmaison; and I left him with his head full of pastoral dreams. In a word, I am very well satisfied with my day's work. Good-night, Bourrienne; we shall see what will turn up to-morrow."

On the 19th I went to St. Cloud with my friend La Vallette. As we passed the Place Louis XV., now Louis XVI., he asked me what Napoleon was doing, and what my opinion was as to the coming events? Without entering into any detail I replied, "My friend, either we shall sleep tomorrow at the Luxembourg, or there will be an end of us." Who could tell which of the two things would happen! Success legalised a bold enterprise, which the slightest accident might have changed into a crime.

The sitting of the Ancients, under the presidency of Lemercier, commenced at one o'clock. A warm discussion took place upon the situation of affairs, the resignation of the members of the Directory, and the immediate election of others. Great heat and agitation prevailed during the debate. Intelligence was every minute carried to Bonaparte of what was going forward, and he determined to enter the hall and take part in the discussion. He entered in a hasty and angry way, which did not give me a favourable foreboding of what he was about to say. We passed through a narrow passage to the centre of the hall; our backs were turned to the door. Bonaparte had the President to his right. He could not see him full in the face. I was close to the General on his right. Berthier was at his left.

All the speeches which have been subsequently passed off as having been delivered by Bonaparte on this occasion differ from each other; as well they may, for he delivered none to the Ancients, unless his confused conversation with the President, which was alike devoid of dignity and sense, is to be called a speech. He talked of his "brothers in arms" and the "frankness of a soldier." The questions of the President followed each other rapidly: they were clear; but it is impossible to conceive anything more confused or worse delivered than the ambiguous and perplexed replies of Bonaparte. He talked without end of "volcanoes; secret agitations, victories, a violated constitution!" He blamed the proceedings of the 18th Fructidor, of which he was the first promoter and the most powerful supporter. He pretended to be ignorant of everything until the Council of Ancients had called him to the aid of his country. Then came "Caesar—Cromwell—tyrant!" and he several times repeated, "I have nothing more to say to you!" though, in fact, he had said nothing. He alleged that he had been called to assume the supreme authority, on his return from Italy, by the desire of the nation, and afterwards by his comrades in arms. Next followed the words "liberty—equality!" though it was evident he had not come to St. Cloud for the sake of either. No sooner did he utter these words, than a member of the Ancients, named, I think, Linglet, interrupting him, exclaimed, "You forget the Constitution!" His countenance immediately lighted up; yet nothing could be distinguished but, "The 18th Fructidor—the 30th Prairial—hypocrites—intriguers—I will disclose all!—I will resign my power, when the danger which threatens the Republic shall have passed away!"

Bonaparte, believing all his assertions to be admitted as proved, assumed a little confidence, and accused the two directors Barras and Moulins of having proposed to put him at the head of a party whose object was to oppose all men professing liberal ideas.

At these words, the falsehood of which was odious, a great tumult arose in the hall. A general committee was loudly called for to hear the disclosures. "No, no!" exclaimed others, "no general committee! conspirators have been denounced: it is right that France should know all!"

Bonaparte was then required to enter into the particulars of his accusation against Barras and Moulins, and of the proposals which had been made to him: "You must no longer conceal anything."

Embarrassed by these interruptions and interrogatories Bonaparte believed that he was completely lost. Instead of giving an explanation of what he had said, he began to make fresh accusations; and against whom? The Council of the Five Hundred, who, he said, wished for "scaffolds, revolutionary committees, and a complete overthrow of everything."

Violent murmurs arose, and his language became more and more incoherent and inconsequent. He addressed himself at one moment to the representatives of the people, who were quite overcome by astonishment; at another to the military in the courtyard, who could not hear him. Then, by an unaccountable transition, he spoke of "the thunderbolts of war!" and added, that he was "attended by the God of war and the God of fortune."

The President, with great calmness, told him that he saw nothing, absolutely nothing, upon which the Council could deliberate; that there was vagueness in all he had said. "Explain yourself; reveal the plot which you say you were urged to join."

Bonaparte repeated again the same things. But only those who were present can form any idea of his manner. There was not the slightest connection in what he stammered out. Bonaparte was then no orator. It may well be supposed that he was more accustomed to the din of war than to the discussions of the tribunes. He was more at home before a battery than before a President's chair.

Perceiving the bad effect which this unconnected babbling produced on the assembly, as well as the embarrassment of Bonaparte, I said, in a low voice, pulling him gently by the skirt of his coat, "withdraw, General; you know not what you are saying." I made signs to Berthier, who was on his left, to second me in persuading him to leave the hall; and all at once, after having stammered out a few more words, he turned round exclaiming, "Let those who love me follow me!" The sentinels at the door offered no opposition to his passing. The person who went before him quietly drew aside the tapestry which concealed the door, and General Bonaparte leaped upon his horse, which stood in the court-yard. It is hard to say what would have happened if, on seeing the General retire, the President had said, "Grenadiers, let no one pass!" Instead of sleeping next day at the Luxembourg he would, I am convinced, have ended his career on the Place de la Revolution.

CHAPTER XXV

1799

The scene which occurred at the sitting of the Council of the Ancients was very different from that which passed outside. Bonaparte had scarcely reached the courtyard and mounted his horse when cries of "Vive Bonaparte!" resounded on all sides. But this was only a sunbeam between two storms. He had yet to brave the Council of the Five Hundred, which was far more excited than the Council of the Ancients. Everything tended to create a dreadful uncertainty; but it was too late to draw back. We had already staked too heavily. The game was desperate, and everything was to be ventured. In a few hours all would be determined.

Our apprehensions were not without foundation. In the Council of the Five Hundred agitation was at its height. The most serious alarm marked its deliberations. It had been determined to announce to the Directory the installation of the Councils, and to inquire of the Council of the Ancients their reasons for resolving upon an extraordinary convocation. But the Directory no longer existed. Sieyès and Roger Ducos had joined Bonaparte's party. Gohier and Moulins were prisoners in the Luxembourg, and in the custody of General Moreau; and at the very moment when the Council of the Five Hundred had drawn up a message to the Directory, the Council of the Ancients transmitted to them the following letter, received from Barras. This letter; which was addressed to the Council of the Ancients, was immediately read by Lucien Bonaparte, who was President of the Council of the Five Hundred.

> CITIZEN PRESIDENT—Having entered into public affairs solely from my love of liberty, I consented to share the first magistracy of the State only that I might be able to defend it in danger; to protect against their enemies the patriots compromised in its cause; and to ensure to the defenders of their country that attention to their interests which no one was more calculated to feel than a citizen, long the witness of their heroic virtues, and always sensible to their wants. The glory which accompanies the return of the illustrious warrior to whom I had the honour of opening the path of glory, the striking marks of confidence given him by the legislative body, and the decree of the National Convention, convince me that, to whatever post he may henceforth be called, the dangers to liberty will be averted, and the interests of the army ensured. I cheerfully return to the rank of a private citizen: happy, after so many storms, to resign, unimpaired, and even more glorious than ever, the destiny of the Republic, which has been, in part, committed to my care.
>
> (*Signed*) BARRAS.

This letter occasioned a great sensation in the Council of the Five Hundred. A second reading was called for, and a question was started, whether the retirement was legal, or was the result of collusion, and of the influence of Bonaparte's agents; whether to believe Barras, who declared the dangers of liberty averted, or the decree for the removal of the legislative corps, which was passed and executed under the pretext of the existence of imminent peril? At that moment Bonaparte appeared, followed by a party of grenadiers, who remained at the entrance of the hall.

I did not accompany him to the Council of the Five Hundred. He had directed me to send off an express to ease the apprehensions of Josephine, and to assure her that everything would go well. It was some time before I joined him again.

However, without speaking as positively as if I had myself been an eye-witness of the scene, I do not hesitate to declare that all that has been said about assaults and poniards is pure invention. I rely on what was told me, on the very night, by persons well worthy of credit, and who were witnessess of all that passed.

As to what passed at the sitting, the accounts, given both at the time and since, have varied according to opinions. Some have alleged that unanimous cries of indignation were excited by the appearance of the military. From all parts of the hall resounded, "The sanctuary of the laws is violated. Down with the tyrant!—down with Cromwell!—down with the Dictator!" Bonaparte stammered out a few words, as he had done before the Council of the Ancients, but his voice was immediately drowned by cries of "Vive la Republique!" "Vive la Constitution!" "Outlaw the Dictator!" The grenadiers are then said to have rushed forward, exclaiming, "Let us save our General!" at which indignation reached its height, and cries, even more violent than ever, were raised; that Bonaparte, falling insensible into the arms of the grenadiers, said, "They mean to assassinate me!" All that regards the exclamations and threats I believe to be correct; but I rank with the story of the poniards the assertion of the members of the Five Hundred being provided with firearms, and the grenadiers rushing into the hall; because Bonaparte never mentioned a word of anything of the sort to me, either on the way home, or when I was with him in his chamber. Neither did he say anything on the subject to his wife, who had been extremely agitated by the different reports which reached her.

After Bonaparte left the Council of the Five Hundred the deliberations were continued with great violence. The excitement caused by the appearance of Bonaparte was nothing like subsided when propositions of the most furious nature were made. The President, Lucien, did all in his power to restore tranquillity. As soon as he could make himself heard he said, "The scene which has just taken place in the Council proves what are the sentiments of all; sentiments which I declare are also mine. It was, however, natural to believe that the General had no other object than to render an account of the situation of affairs, and of something interesting to the public. But I think none of you can suppose him capable of projects hostile to liberty."

Each sentence of Lucien's address was interrupted by cries of "Bonaparte has tarnished his glory! He is a disgrace to the Republic!"

Lucien[99] made fresh efforts to be heard, and wished to be allowed to address the assembly

---

99 The next younger brother of Napoleon, President of the Council of the Five Hundred in 1799; Minister of the Interior, 1st December 1799 to 1841; Ambassador in Spain, 1801 to December 1801; left France in disgrace in 1804; retired to Papal States; Prisoner in Malta and England, 1810 to 1814; created by Pope in 1814 Prince de Canino and Duc de Musignano; married firstly, 1794, Christine Boyer, who died 1800; married secondly, 1802 or 1803, a Madame Jonberthon. Of his part in the 18th Brumaire Napoleon said

as a member of the Council, and for that purpose resigned the Presidentship to Chasal. He begged that the General might be introduced again and heard with calmness. But this proposition was furiously opposed. Exclamations of "Outlaw Bonaparte! outlaw him!" rang through the assembly, and were the only reply given to the President. Lucien, who had reassumed the President's chair, left it a second time, that he might not be constrained to put the question of outlawry demanded against his brother. Braving the displeasure of the assembly, he mounted the tribune, resigned the Presidentship, renounced his seat as a deputy, and threw aside his robes.

Just as Lucien left the Council I entered. Bonaparte, who was well informed of all that was passing,[100] had sent in soldiers to the assistance of his brother; they carried him off from the midst of the Council, and Bonaparte thought it a matter of no little importance to have with him the President of an assembly which he treated as rebellious. Lucien was reinstalled in office; but he was now to discharge his duties, not in the President's chair, but on horseback, and at the head of a party of troops ready to undertake anything. Roused by the danger to which both his brother and himself were exposed he delivered on horseback the following words, which can never be too often remembered, as showing what a man then dared to say, who never was anything except from the reflection of his brother's glory:—

> CITIZENS! SOLDIERS!—The President of the Council of the Five Hundred declares to you that the majority of that Council is at this moment held in terror by a few representatives of the people, who are armed with stilettoes, and who surround the tribune, threatening their colleagues with death, and maintaining most atrocious discussions. I declare to you that these brigands, who are doubtless in the pay of England, have risen in rebellion against the Council of the Ancients, and have dared to talk of outlawing the General, who is charged with the execution of its decree, as if the word "outlaw" was still to be regarded as the death-warrant of persons most beloved by their country. I declare to you that these madmen have outlawed themselves by their attempts upon the liberty of the Council.
>
> In the name of that people, which for so many years have been the sport of terrorism, I consign to you the charge of rescuing the majority of their representatives; so that, delivered from stilettoes by bayonets, they may deliberate on the fate of the Republic. General, and you, soldiers, and you, citizens, you will not acknowledge, as legislators of France, any but those who rally round me. As for those who remain in the orangery, let force expel them.

---

to him in 1807, "I well know that you were useful to me on the 18th Brumaire, but it is not so clear to me that you saved me then" (Iung's Lucien, tome iii. p.89).

100 Lucien distinctly states that he himself, acting within his right as President, had demanded an escort of the grenadiers of the Councils as soon as he saw his withdrawal might be opposed. Then the first entry of the soldiers with Napoleon would be illegal. The second, to withdraw Lucien, was nominally legal (see Iung's Lucien, tome i, pp, 318-322)

They are not the representatives of the people, but the representatives of the poniard. Let that be their title, and let it follow them everywhere; and whenever they dare show themselves to the people, let every finger point at them, and every tongue designate them by the well-merited title of representatives of the poniard!

VIVE LA REPUBLIQUE!

Notwithstanding the cries of "Vive Bonaparte!" which followed this harangue, the troops still hesitated. It was evident that they were not fully prepared to turn their swords against the national representatives. Lucien then drew his sword, exclaiming, "I swear that I will stab my own brother to the heart if he ever attempt anything against the liberty of Frenchmen." This dramatic action was perfectly successful; hesitation vanished; and at a signal given by Bonaparte, Murat, at the head of his grenadiers, rushed into the hall, and drove out the representatives. Everyone yielded to the reasoning of bayonets, and thus terminated the employment of the armed force on that memorable day.

At ten o'clock at night the palace of St. Cloud, where so many tumultuous scenes had occurred, was perfectly tranquil. All the deputies were still there, pacing the hall, the corridors, and the courts. Most of them had an air of consternation; others affected to have foreseen the event, and to appear satisfied with it; but all wished to return to Paris, which they could not do until a new order revoked the order for the removal of the Councils to St. Cloud.

At eleven o'clock Bonaparte, who had eaten nothing all day, but who was almost insensible to physical wants in moments of great agitation, said to me, "We must go and write, Bourrienne; I intend this very night to address a proclamation to the inhabitants of Paris. To-morrow morning I shall be all the conversation of the capital." He then dictated to me the following proclamation, which proves, no less than some of his reports from Egypt, how much Bonaparte excelled in the art of twisting the truth to own advantage:

TO THE PEOPLE.

19th Brumaire, 11 o'clock, p.m.

FRENCHMEN!—On my return to France I found division reigning amongst all the authorities. They agreed only on this single point, that the Constitution was half destroyed, and was unable to protect liberty! Each party in turn came to me, confided to me their designs, imparted their secrets, and requested my support. I refused to be the man of a party.

The Council of the Ancients appealed to me. I answered their appeal. A plan of general restoration had been concerted by men whom the nation has been accustomed to regard as the defenders of liberty, equality, and property. This plan required calm and free deliberation, exempt from all influence and all fear. The Ancients, therefore, resolved upon the removal of the legislative bodies to St. Cloud. They placed at my disposal the force necessary to secure their independence. I was bound, in duty to my fellow-citizens, to the soldiers perishing in our armies, and to the national glory, acquired at the cost of so much blood, to accept the command. The Councils assembled at St. Cloud. Republican troops guaranteed their safety from without, but assassins created terror within. Many members of the Council of the Five Hundred, armed with stilettoes and pistols, spread menaces of death around them.

The plans which ought to have been developed were withheld. The majority of the Council was rendered inefficient; the boldest orators were disconcerted, and the inutility of submitting any salutary proposition was quite evident.

I proceeded, filled with indignation and grief, to the Council of the Ancients. I besought them to carry their noble designs into execution. I directed their attention to the evils of the nation, which were their motives for conceiving those designs. They concurred in giving me new proofs of their uniform goodwill, I presented myself before the Council of the Five Hundred, alone, unarmed, my head uncovered, just as the Ancients had received and applauded me. My object was to restore to the majority the expression of its will, and to secure to it its power.

The stilettoes which had menaced the deputies were instantly raised against their deliverer. Twenty assassins rushed upon me and aimed at my breast. The grenadiers of the legislative body, whom I had left at the door of the hall, ran forward, and placed themselves between me and the assassins. One of these brave grenadiers (Thome) had his clothes pierced by a stiletto. They bore me off.[101]

At the same moment cries of "Outlaw him!" were raised against the defender of the law. It was the horrid cry of assassins against the power destined to repress them.

They crowded round the President, uttering threats. With arms in their hands they commanded him to declare "the outlawry." I was informed of this. I ordered him to be rescued from their fury, and six grenadiers of the legislative body brought him out. Immediately afterwards some grenadiers of the legislative body charged into the hall and cleared it.

The factions, intimidated, dispersed and fled. The majority, freed from their assaults, returned freely and peaceably into the hall; listened to the propositions made for the public safety, deliberated, and drew up the salutary resolution which will become the new and provisional law of the Republic.

Frenchmen, you doubtless recognise in this conduct the zeal of a soldier of liberty, of a citizen devoted to the Republic. Conservative, tutelary, and liberal ideas resumed their

101 Thome merely had a small part of his coat torn by a deputy, who took him by the collar. This constituted the whole of the attempted assassinations of the 19th Brumaire.—Bourrienne

> authority upon the dispersion of the factions, who domineered in the Councils, and who, in rendering themselves the most odious of men, did not cease to be the most contemptible.
>
> (*Signed*) BONAPARTE,
> *General, etc.*

The day had been passed in destroying a Government; it was necessary to devote the night to framing a new one. Talleyrand, Raederer, and Sieyès were at St. Cloud. The Council of the Ancients assembled, and Lucien set himself about finding some members of the Five Hundred on whom he could reckon. He succeeded in getting together only thirty, who, with their President, represented the numerous assembly of which they formed part. This ghost of representation was essential, for Bonaparte, notwithstanding his violation of all law on the preceding day, wished to make it appear that he was acting legally. The Council of the Ancients had, however, already decided that a provisional executive commission should be appointed, composed of three members, and was about to name the members of the commission—a measure which should have originated with the Five Hundred—when Lucien came to acquaint Bonaparte that his chamber 'introuvable' was assembled.

This chamber, which called itself the Council of the Five Hundred, though that Council was now nothing but a Council of Thirty, hastily passed a decree, the first article of which was as follows:

> The Directory exists no longer; and the individuals hereafter named are no longer members of the national representation, on account of the excesses and illegal acts which they have constantly committed, and more particularly the greatest part of them, in the sitting of this morning.

Then follow the names of sixty-one members expelled.

By other articles of the same decree the Council instituted a provisional commission, similar to that which the Ancients had proposed to appoint, resolved that the said commission should consist of three members, who should assume the title of Consuls; and nominated as Consuls Sieyès, Roger Ducos, and Bonaparte. The other provisions of the nocturnal decree of St. Cloud had for their object merely the carrying into effect those already described. This nocturnal sitting was very calm, and indeed it would have been strange had it been otherwise, for no opposition could be feared from the members of the Five Hundred, who were prepared to concur with Lucien. All knew beforehand what they would have to do. Everything was concluded by three o'clock in the morning; and the palace of St. Cloud, which had been so agitated since the previous evening, resumed in the morning its wonted stillness, and presented the appearance of a vast solitude.

All the hurrying about, the brief notes which I had to write to many friends, and the conversations in which I was compelled to take part, prevented me from dining before one o'clock in the morning. It was not till then that Bonaparte, having gone to take the oath as Consul before the Five Hundred, afforded me an opportunity of taking some refreshment with Admiral Bruix and some other officers.

At three o'clock in the morning I accompanied Bonaparte, in his carriage to Paris. He was extremely fatigued after so many trials and fatigues. A new future was opened before him. He was completely absorbed in thought, and did not utter a single word during the journey. But when he arrived at his house in the Rue de la Victoire, he had no sooner entered his chamber and wished good morning to Josephine, who was in bed, and in a state of the greatest anxiety on account of his absence, than he said before her, "Bourrienne, I said many ridiculous things?"—"Not so very bad, General"—"I like better to speak to soldiers than to lawyers. Those fellows disconcerted me. I have not been used to public assemblies; but that will come in time."

We then began, all three, to converse. Madame Bonaparte became calm, and Bonaparte resumed his wonted confidence. The events of the day naturally formed the subject of our conversation. Josephine, who was much attached to the Gohier family, mentioned the name of that Director in a tone of kindness. "What would you have, my dear?" said Bonaparte to her. "It is not my fault. He is a respectable man, but a simpleton. He does not understand me!—I ought, perhaps, to have him transported. He wrote against me to the Council of the Ancients; but I have his letter, and they know nothing about it. Poor man! he expected me to dinner yesterday. And this man thinks himself a statesman!—Speak no more of him."

During our discourse the name of Bernadotte was also mentioned. "Have you seen him, Bourrienne?" said Bonaparte to me.—"No, General"—"Neither have I. I have not heard him spoken of. Would you imagine it? I had intelligence to-day of many intrigues in which he is concerned. Would you believe it? he wished nothing less than to be appointed my colleague in authority. He talked of mounting his horse and marching with the troops that might be placed under his command. He wished, he said, to maintain the Constitution: nay, more; I am assured that he had the audacity to add that, if it were necessary to outlaw me, the Government might come to him and he would find soldiers capable of carrying the decree into execution."—"All this, General, should give you an idea how inflexible his principles are."—"Yes, I am well aware of it; there is something in that: he is honest. But for his obstinacy, my brothers would have brought him over. They are related to him. His wife, who is Joseph's sister-in-law, has ascendency over him. As for me, have I not, I ask you, made sufficient advances to him? You have witnessed them. Moreau, who has a higher military reputation than he, came over to me at once. However, I repent of having cajoled Bernadotte. I am thinking of separating him from all his coteries without any one being able to find fault with the proceeding. I cannot revenge myself in any other manner. Joseph likes him. I should have everybody against me. These family considerations are follies! Goodnight, Bourrienne.—By the way, we will sleep in the Luxembourg to-morrow."

I then left the General, whom, henceforth, I will call the First Consul, after having remained with him constantly during nearly twenty-four hours, with the exception of the time when he was at the Council of the Five Hundred. I retired to my lodging, in the Rue Martel, at five o'clock in the morning.

It is certain that if Gohier had come to breakfast on the morning of the 18th Brumaire, according to Madame Bonaparte's invitation, he would have been one of the members of the Government. But Gohier acted the part of the stern republican. He placed himself, according to the common phrase of the time, astride of the Constitution of the year III.; and as his steed made a sad stumble, he fell with it.

It was a singular circumstance which prevented the two Directors Gohier and Moulins from defending their beloved Constitution. It was from their respect for the Constitution that they allowed it to perish, because they would have been obliged to violate the article which did not allow less than three Directors to deliberate together. Thus a king of Castile was burned to death, because there did not happen to be in his apartment men of such rank as etiquette would permit to touch the person of the monarch.

CHAPTER XXVI

1799

It cannot be denied that France hailed, almost with unanimous voice, Bonaparte's accession to the Consulship as a blessing of Providence. I do not speak now of the ulterior consequences of that event; I speak only of the fact itself, and its first results, such as the repeal of the law of hostages, and the compulsory loan of a hundred millions. Doubtless the legality of the acts of the 18th Brumaire may be disputed; but who will venture to say that the immediate result of that day ought not to be regarded as a great blessing to France? Whoever denies this can have no idea of the wretched state of every branch of the administration at that deplorable epoch. A few persons blamed the 18th Brumaire; but no one regretted the Directory, with the exception, perhaps, of the five Directors themselves. But we will say no more of the Directorial Government. What an administration! In what a state were the finances of France! Would it be believed? on the second day of the Consulate, when Bonaparte wished to send a courier to General Championet, commander-in-chief of the army of Italy, the treasury had not 1200 francs disposable to give to the courier!

It may be supposed that in the first moments of a new Government money would be wanted. M. Collot, who had served under Bonaparte in Italy, and whose conduct and administration deserved nothing but praise, was one of the first who came to the Consul's assistance. In this instance M. Collot was as zealous as disinterested. He gave the Consul 500,000 francs in gold, for which service he was badly rewarded. Bonaparte afterwards behaved to M. Collot as though he was anxious to punish him for being rich. This sum, which at the time made so fine an appearance in the Consular treasury, was not repaid for a long time after, and then without interest. This was not, indeed, the only instance in which M. Collot had cause to complain of Bonaparte, who was never inclined to acknowledge his important services, nor even to render justice to his conduct.

On the morning of the 20th Brumaire Bonaparte sent his brother Louis to inform the Director Gohier that he was free. This haste in relieving Gohier was not without a reason, for Bonaparte was anxious to install himself in the Luxembourg, and we went there that same evening.

Everything was to be created. Bonaparte had with him almost the whole of the army, and on the soldiers he could rely. But the military force was no longer sufficient for him. Wishing to possess a great civil power established by legal forms, he immediately set about the composition of a Senate and Tribunate; a Council of State and a new legislative body, and, finally, a new Constitution.[102]

102 The Constitution of the year VIII. was presented on the 18th of December 1799 (22d Frimaire, year VIII.), and accepted by the people on the 7th of February 1800 (18th Pluviôse, year VIII.). It established a Consular Government, composed of Bonaparte, First Consul, appointed for ten years; Cambacérès, Second Consul, also for ten years; and Lebrun, Third Consul appointed for five years. It established a conservative Senate, a legislative body of

As Bonaparte had not time to make himself acquainted with the persons by whom he was about to be surrounded, he requested from the most distinguished men of the period, well acquainted with France and the Revolution, notes respecting the individuals worthy and capable of entering the Senate, the Tribunate, and the Council of State. From the manner in which all these notes were drawn up it was evident that the writers of them studied to make their recommendation correspond with what they conceived to be Bonaparte's views, and that they imagined he participated in the opinions which were at that time popular. Accordingly they stated, as grounds for preferring particular candidates, their patriotism, their republicanism, and their having had seats in preceding assemblies.

Of all qualities, that which most influenced the choice of the First Consul was inflexible integrity; and it is but just to say that in this particular he was rarely deceived. He sought earnestly for talent; and although he did not like the men of the Revolution, he was convinced that he could not do without them. He had conceived an extreme aversion for mediocrity, and generally rejected a man of that character when recommended to him; but if he had known such a man long, he yielded to the influence of habit, dreading nothing so much as change, or, as he was accustomed to say himself, new faces.[103]

Bonaparte then proceeded to organise a complaisant Senate, a mute legislative body, and a Tribunate which was to have the semblance of being independent, by the aid of some fine speeches and high-sounding phrases. He easily appointed the Senators, but it was different with the Tribunate. He hesitated long before he fixed upon the candidates for that body, which inspired him with an anticipatory fear. However, on arriving at power he dared not oppose himself to the exigencies of the moment, and he consented for a time to delude the ambitious dupes who kept up a buzz of fine sentiments of liberty around him. He saw that circumstances were not yet favourable for refusing a share in the Constitution to this third portion of power, destined apparently to advocate the interests of the people before the legislative body. But in yielding to necessity, the mere idea of the Tribunate filled him with the utmost uneasiness; and, in a word, Bonaparte could not endure the public discussions on his projects[104].

Bonaparte composed the first Consular Ministry as follows: Berthier was Minister of

---

800 members, and a Tribunate composed of 100 members. The establishment of the Council of State took place on the 29th of December 1799. The installation of the new legislative body and the Tribunate was fixed for the 1st of January 1800.—Bourrienne. Lanfrey (tome i. p. 329) sees this Constitution foreshadowed in that proposed by Napoleon in 1797 for the Cisalpine Republic.

103 Napoleon loved only men with strong passions and great weakness; he judged the most opposite qualities in men by these defects (Metternich, tome iii. p.589)

104 The Tribunate under this Constitution of the year VIII. was the only body allowed to debate in public on proposed laws, the legislative body simply hearing in silence the orators sent by the Council of State and by the Tribunals to state reasons for or against propositions, and then voting in silence. Its orators were constantly giving umbrage to Napoleon. It was at first purified, early in 1802, by the Senate naming the members to go out in rotation then reduced to from 100 to 50 members later in 1802, and suppressed in 1807; its disappearance being regarded by Napoleon as his last break with the Revolution.

War; Gaudin, formerly employed in the administration of the Post Office, was appointed Minister of Finance; Cambacérès remained Minister of Justice; Forfait was Minister of Marine; La Place of the Interior; Fouché of Police; and Reinhard of Foreign Affairs.

Reinhard and La Place were soon replaced, the former by the able M. Talleyrand, the latter by Lucien Bonaparte.[105] It may be said that Lucien merely passed through the Ministry on his way to a lucrative embassy in Spain. As to La Place, Bonaparte always entertained a high opinion of his talents. His appointment to the Ministry of the Interior was a compliment paid to science; but it was not long before the First Consul repented of his choice. La Place, so happily calculated for science, displayed the most inconceivable mediocrity in administration. He was incompetent to the most trifling matters; as if his mind, formed to embrace the system of the world, and to interpret the laws of Newton and Kepler, could not descend to the level of subjects of detail, or apply itself to the duties of the department with which he was entrusted for a short, but yet, with regard to him, too long a time.

On the 26th Brumaire (17th November 1799) the Consuls issued a decree, in which they stated that, conformably with Article III. of the law of the 19th of the same month, which especially charged them with the reestablishment of public tranquillity, they decreed that thirty-eight individuals, who were named, should quit the continental territory of the Republic, and for that purpose should proceed to Rochefort, to be afterwards conducted to, and detained in, the department of French Guiana. They likewise decreed that twenty-three other individuals, who were named, should proceed to the commune of Rochelle, in the department of the lower Charente, in order to be afterwards filed and detained in such part of that department as should be pointed out by the Minister of General Police. I was fortunate enough to keep my friend M. Moreau de Worms, deputy from the Youne, out of the fiat of exiles. This produced a mischievous effect. It bore a character of wanton severity quite inconsistent with the assurances of mildness and moderation given at St. Cloud on the 19th Brumaire. Cambacérès afterwards made a report, in which he represented that it was unnecessary for the maintenance of tranquillity to subject the proscribed to banishment, considering it sufficient to place them under the supervision of the superior police. Upon receiving the report the Consuls issued a decree, in which they directed all the individuals included in the proscription to retire respectively into the different communes which should be fixed upon by the Minister of Justice, and to remain there until further orders.

At the period of the issuing of these decrees Sieyès was still one of the Consuls, conjointly with Bonaparte and Roger Ducos; and although Bonaparte had, from the first moment, possessed the whole power of the government, a sort of apparent equality was, nevertheless, observed amongst them. It was not until the 25th of December that Bonaparte assumed the title of First Consul, Cambacérès and Lebrun being then joined in the office with him. He had fixed his eyes on them previously to the 18th Brumaire, and he had no cause to reproach them with giving him much embarrassment in his rapid progress towards the imperial throne.

I have stated that I was so fortunate as to rescue M. Moreau de Worms from the list of proscription. Some days after Sieyès entered Bonaparte's cabinet and said to him, "Well, this

105 When I quitted the service of the First Consul Talleyrand was still at the head of the Foreign Department. I have frequently been present at this great statesman's conferences with Napoleon, and I can declare that I never saw him flatter his dreams of ambition; but, on the contrary, he always endeavoured to make him sensible of his true interests.—Bourrienne.

M. Moreau de Worms, whom M. Bourrienne induced you to save from banishment, is acting very finely! I told you how it would be! I have received from Sens, his native place, a letter which informs me that Moreau is in that town, where he has assembled the people in the market-place, and indulged in the most violent declamations against the 18th Brumaire,"—"Can you rely upon your agent" asked Bonaparte.—"Perfectly. I can answer for the truth of his communication." Bonaparte showed me the bulletin of Sieyès' agent, and reproached me bitterly. "What would you say, General," I observed, "if I should present this same M. Moreau de Worms, who is declaiming at Sens against the 18th Brumaire, to you within an hour?"—"I defy you to do it."—"I have made myself responsible for him, and I know what I am about. He is violent in his politics; but he is a man of honour, incapable of failing in his word."—"Well, we shall see. Go and find him." I was very sure of doing what I had promised, for within an hour before I had seen M. Moreau de Worms. He had been concealed since the 19th Brumaire, and had not quitted Paris. Nothing was easier than to find him, and in three-quarters of an hour he was at the Luxembourg. I presented him to Bonaparte, who conversed with him a long time concerning the 18th Brumaire. When M. Moreau departed Bonaparte said to me, "You are right. That fool Sieyès is as inventive as a Cassandra. This proves that one should not be too ready to believe the reports of the wretches whom we are obliged to employ in the police." Afterwards he added, "Bourrienne, Moreau is a nice fellow: I am satisfied with him; I will do something for him." It was not long before M. Moreau experienced the effect of the Consul's good opinion. Some days after, whilst framing the council of prizes, he, at my mere suggestion, appointed M. Moreau one of the members, with a salary of 10,000 francs. On what extraordinary circumstances the fortunes of men frequently depend! As to Sieyès, in the intercourse, not very frequent certainly, which I had with him, he appeared to be far beneath the reputation which he then enjoyed.[106] He reposed a blind confidence in a multitude of agents, whom he sent into all parts of France. When it happened, on other occasions, that I proved to him, by evidence as sufficient as that in the case of M. Moreau, the falseness of the reports he had received, he replied, with a confidence truly ridiculous, "I can rely on my men." Sieyès had written in his countenance, "Give me money!" I recollect that I one day alluded to this expression in the anxious face of Sieyès to the First Consul. "You are right," observed he to me, smiling; "when money is in question, Sieyès is quite a matter-of-fact man. He sends his ideology to the right about and thus becomes easily manageable. He readily abandons his constitutional dreams for a good round sum, and that is very convenient."[107]

Bonaparte occupied, at the Little Luxembourg, the apartments on the ground floor which

106 M. de Talleyrand, who is so capable of estimating men, and whose admirable sayings well deserve to occupy a place in history, had long entertained a similar opinion of Sieyès. One day, when he was conversing with the Second Consul concerning Sieyès, Cambacérès said to him. "Sieyès, however, is a very profound man."—"Profound?" said Talleyrand. "Yes, he is, a cavity, a perfect cavity, as you would say."—Bourrienne.

107 Everybody knows, in fact, that Sieyès refused to resign his consular dignities unless he received in exchange a beautiful farm situated in the park of Versailles, and worth about 15,000 livres a year. The good abbé consoled himself for no longer forming a third of the republican sovereignty by making himself at home in the ancient domain of the kings of France.—Bourrienne.

lie to the right on entering from the Rue de Vaugirard. His cabinet was close to a private staircase, which conducted me to the first floor, where Josephine dwelt. My apartment was above.

After breakfast, which was served at ten o'clock, Bonaparte would converse for a few moments with his usual guests, that is to say, his 'aides de camp', the persons he invited, and myself, who never left him. He was also visited very often by Deferment, Regnault (of the town of St. Jean d'Angély), Boulay (de la Meurthe), Monge, and Berber, who were, with his brothers, Joseph and Lucien, those whom he most delighted to see; he conversed familiarly with them. Cambacérès generally came at mid-day, and stayed some time with him, often a whole hour. Lebrun visited but seldom. Notwithstanding his elevation, his character remained unaltered; and Bonaparte considered him too moderate, because he always opposed his ambitious views and his plans to usurp power. When Bonaparte left the breakfast-table it was seldom that he did not add, after bidding Josephine and her daughter Hortense good-day, "Come, Bourrienne, come, let us to work."

After the morning audiences I stayed with Bonaparte all the day, either reading to him, or writing to his dictation. Three or four times in the week he would go to the Council. On his way to the hall of deliberation he was obliged to cross the courtyard of the Little Luxembourg and ascend the grand staircase. This always vexed him, and the more so as the weather was very bad at the time. This annoyance continued until the 25th of December, and it was with much satisfaction that he saw himself quit of it. After leaving the Council he used to enter his cabinet singing, and God knows how wretchedly he sung! He examined whatever work he had ordered to be done, signed documents, stretched himself in his arm-chair, and read the letters of the preceding day and the publications of the morning. When there was no Council he remained in his cabinet, conversed with me, always sang, and cut, according to custom, the arm of his chair, giving himself sometimes quite the air of a great boy. Then, all at once starting up, he would describe a plan for the erection of a monument, or dictate some of those extraordinary productions which astonished and dismayed the world. He often became again the same man, who, under the walls of St. Jean d'Acre, had dreamed of an empire worthy his ambition.

At five o'clock dinner was served up. When that was over the First Consul went upstairs to Josephine's apartments, where he commonly received the visits of the Ministers. He was always pleased to see among the number the Minister of Foreign Affairs, especially since the portfolio of that department had been entrusted to the hands of M. de Talleyrand. At midnight, and often sooner, he gave the signal for retiring by saying in a hasty manner, "Allons nous coucher."

It was at the Luxembourg, in the salons of which the adorable Josephine so well performed the honours, that the word 'Madame' came again into use. This first return towards the old French politeness was startling to some susceptible Republicans; but things were soon carried farther at the Tuileries by the introduction of 'Votre Altesse' on occasions of state ceremony, and Monseigneur in the family circle.

If, on the one hand, Bonaparte did not like the men of the Revolution, on the other he dreaded still more the partisans of the Bourbons. On the mere mention of the name of those princes he experienced a kind of inward alarm; and he often spoke of the necessity of raising a wall of brass between France and them. To this feeling, no doubt, must be attributed certain nominations, and the spirit of some recommendations contained in the notes with which he was supplied on the characters of candidates, and which for ready reference were arranged alphabetically. Some of the notes just mentioned were in the handwriting of Regnault de St. Jean d'Angély, and some in Lucien Bonaparte's.[108]

At the commencement of the First Consul's administration, though he always consulted the notes he had collected, he yet received with attention the recommendations of persons with whom he was well acquainted; but it was not safe for them to recommend a rogue or a fool. The men whom he most disliked were those whom he called babblers, who are continually prating of everything and on everything. He often said,—"I want more head and less tongue." What he thought of the regicides will be seen farther on, but at first the more a man had given a gage to the Revolution, the more he considered him as offering a guarantee against the return of the former order of things. Besides, Bonaparte was not the man to attend to any consideration when once his policy was concerned.

As I have said a few pages back, on taking the government into his own hands Bonaparte knew so little of the Revolution and of the men engaged in civil employments that it was indispensably necessary for him to collect information from every quarter respecting men and things. But when the conflicting passions of the moment became more calm and the spirit of party more prudent, and when order had been, by his severe investigations, introduced where hitherto unbridled confusion had reigned, he became gradually more scrupulous in granting places, whether arising from newly-created offices, or from those changes which the different departments often experienced. He then said to me, "Bourrienne, I give up your department to you. Name whom you please for the appointments; but remember you must be responsible to me."

What a list would have been which should contain the names of all the prefects, sub-prefects, receivers-general, and other civil officers to whom I gave places! I have kept no memoranda of their names; and indeed, what advantage would there have been in doing so? It was impossible for me to have a personal knowledge of all the fortunate candidates; but I relied on recommendations in which I had confidence.

I have little to complain of in those I obliged; though it is true that, since my separation from Bonaparte, I have seen many of them take the opposite side of the street in which I was walking, and by that delicate attention save me the trouble of raising my hat.

---

108 Among them was the following, under the title of "General Observations": "In choosing among the men who were members of the Constituent Assembly it is necessary to be on guard against the Orleans' party, which is not altogether a chimera, and may one day or other prove dangerous. "There is no doubt that the partisans of that family are intriguing secretly; and among many other proofs of this fact the following is a striking one: the journal called the 'Aristargue', which undisguisedly supports royalism, is conducted by a man of the name of Voidel, one of the hottest patriots of the Revolution. He was for several months president of the committee of inquiry which caused the Marquis de Favras to be arrested and hanged, and gave so much uneasiness to the Court. There was no one in the Constituent Assembly more hateful to the Court than Voidel, so much on account of his violence as for his connection with the Duke of Orleans, whose advocate and counsel he was. When the Duke of Orleans was arrested, Voidel, braving the fury of the revolutionary tribunals, had the courage to defend him, and placarded all the walls of Paris with an apology for the Duke and his two sons. This man, writing now in favour of royalism, can have no other object than to advance a member of the Orleans family to the throne."—Bourrienne.

CHAPTER XXVII

1799-1800

When a new Government rises on the ruins of one that has been overthrown, its best chance of conciliating the favour of the nation, if that nation be at war, is to hold out the prospect of peace; for peace is always dear to a people. Bonaparte was well aware of this; and if in his heart he wished otherwise, he knew how important it was to seem to desire peace. Accordingly, immediately after his installation at the Luxembourg he notified to all the foreign powers his accession to the Consulate, and, for the same purpose, addressed letters to all the diplomatic agents of the French Government abroad.

The day after he got rid of his first two colleagues, Sieyès and Roger Ducos, he prepared to open negotiations with the Cabinet of London. At that time we were at war with almost the whole of Europe. We had also lost Italy. The Emperor of Germany was ruled by his Ministers, who in their turn were governed by England. It was no easy matter to manage equally the organization of the Consular Government and the no less important affairs abroad; and it was very important to the interests of the First Consul to intimate to foreign powers, while at the same time he assured himself against the return of the Bourbons, that the system which he proposed to adopt was a system of order and regeneration, unlike either the demagogic violence of the Convention or the imbecile artifice of the Directory. In fulfilment of this object Bonaparte directed M. de Talleyrand, the new Minister for Foreign Affairs, to make the first friendly overtures to the English Cabinet: A correspondence ensued, which was published at the time, and which showed at once the conciliatory policy of Bonaparte and the arrogant policy of England.

The exchange of notes which took place was attended by no immediate result. However, the First Consul had partly attained his object: if the British Government would not enter into negotiations for peace, there was at least reason to presume that subsequent overtures of the Consular Government might be listened to. The correspondence had at all events afforded Bonaparte the opportunity of declaring his principles, and above all, it had enabled him to ascertain that the return of the Bourbons to France (mentioned in the official reply of Lord Grenville) would not be a sine qua non condition for the restoration of peace between the two powers.

Since M. de Talleyrand had been Minister for Foreign Affairs the business of that department had proceeded with great activity. It was an important advantage to Bonaparte to find a nobleman of the old regime among the republicans. The choice of M. de Talleyrand was in some sort an act of courtesy to the foreign Courts. It was a delicate attention to the diplomacy of Europe to introduce to its members, for the purpose of treating with them, a man whose rank was at least equal to their own, and who was universally distinguished for a polished elegance of manner combined with solid good qualities and real talents.

It was not only with England that Bonaparte and his Minister endeavoured to open negotiations; the Consular Cabinet also offered peace to the House of Austria; but not at the same time. The object of this offer was to sow discord between the two powers. Speaking to me one day of his earnest wish to obtain peace Bonaparte said, "You see, Bourrienne, I have two great enemies to cope with. I will conclude peace with the one I find most easy to deal with. That will enable me immediately to assail the other. I frankly confess that I should like best to be at peace with England. Nothing would then be more easy than to crush Austria. She has no money except what she gets through England."

For a long time all negotiations proved abortive. None of the European powers would acknowledge the new Government, of which Bonaparte was the head; and the battle of Marengo was required before the peace of Amiens could be obtained.

Though the affairs of the new Government afforded abundant occupation to Bonaparte, he yet found leisure to direct attention to the East—to that land of despotism whence, judging from his subsequent conduct, it might be presumed he derived his first principles of government. On becoming the head of the State he wished to turn Egypt, which he had conquered as a general, to the advantage of his policy as Consul. If Bonaparte triumphed over a feeling of dislike in consigning the command of the army to Kléber, it was because he knew Kléber to be more capable than any other of executing the plans he had formed; and Bonaparte was not the man to sacrifice the interests of policy to personal resentment. It is certainly true that he then put into practice that charming phrase of Molière's—"I pardon you, but you shall pay me for this!"

With respect to all whom he had left in Egypt Bonaparte stood in a very singular situation. On becoming Chief of the Government he was not only the depositary of all communications made to the Directory; but letters sent to one address were delivered to another, and the First Consul received the complaints made against the General who had so abruptly quitted Egypt. In almost all the letters that were delivered to us he was the object of serious accusation. According to some he had not avowed his departure until the very day of his embarkation; and he had deceived everybody by means of false and dissembling proclamations. Others canvassed his conduct while in Egypt: the army which had triumphed under his command he had abandoned when reduced to two-thirds of its original force and a prey to all the horrors of sickness and want. It must be confessed that these complaints and accusations were but too well founded, and one can never cease wondering at the chain of fortunate circumstances which so rapidly raised Bonaparte to the Consular seat. In the natural order of things, and in fulfilment of the design which he himself had formed, he should have disembarked at Toulon, where the quarantine laws would no doubt have been observed; instead of which, the fear of the English and the uncertainty of the pilots caused him to go to Fréjus, where the quarantine laws were violated by the very persons most interested in respecting them. Let us suppose that Bonaparte had been forced to perform quarantine at Toulon. What would have ensued? The charges against him would have fallen into the hands of the Directory, and he would probably have been suspended, and put upon his trial.

Among the letters which fell into Bonaparte's hands, by reason of the abrupt change of government, was an official despatch (of the 4th Vendemiaire, year VIII.) from General Kléber at Cairo to the Executive Directory, in which that general spoke in very stringent terms of the sudden departure of Bonaparte and of the state in which the army in Egypt had been left. General Kléber further accused him of having evaded, by his flight, the difficulties which he thus transferred to his successor's shoulders, and also of leaving the army "without a sou in the chest," with pay in arrear, and very little supply of munitions or clothing.

The other letters from Egypt were not less accusatory than Kléber's; and it cannot be doubted that charges of so precise a nature, brought by the general who had now become commander-in-chief against his predecessor, would have had great weight, especially backed as they were by similar complaints from other quarters. A trial would have been inevitable; and then, no 18th Brumaire, no Consulate, no Empire, no conquest of Europe—but also, it may be added, no St. Helena. None of these events would have ensued had not the English squadron, when it appeared off Corsica, obliged the Muiron to scud about at hazard, and to touch at the first land she could reach.

The Egyptian expedition filled too important a place in the life of Bonaparte for him to neglect frequently reviving in the public mind the recollection of his conquests in the East. It was not to be forgotten that the head of the Republic was the first of her generals. While Moreau received the command of the armies of the Rhine, while Massena, as a reward for the victory of Zurich, was made Commander-in-Chief in Italy, and while Brune was at the head of the army of Batavia, Bonaparte, whose soul was in the camps, consoled himself for his temporary inactivity by a retrospective glance on his past triumphs. He was unwilling that Fame should for a moment cease to blazon his name. Accordingly, as soon as he was established at the head of the Government, he caused accounts of his Egyptian expedition to be from time to time published in the Moniteur. He frequently expressed his satisfaction that the accusatory correspondence, and, above all, Kléber's letter, had fallen into his own hands. Such was Bonaparte's perfect self-command that immediately after perusing that letter he dictated to me the following proclamation, addressed to the army of the East:

> SOLDIERS!—The Consuls of the French Republic frequently direct their attention to the army of the East. France acknowledges all the influence of your conquests on the restoration of her trade and the civilisation of the world.
>
> The eyes of all Europe are upon you, and in thought I am often with you. In whatever situation the chances of war may place you, prove yourselves still the soldiers of Rivoli and Aboukir—you will be invincible. Place in Kléber the boundless confidence which you reposed in me. He deserves it. Soldiers, think of the day when you will return victorious to the sacred territory of France. That will be a glorious day for the whole nation.

Nothing can more forcibly show the character of Bonaparte than the above allusion to Kléber, after he had seen the way in which Kléber spoke of him to the Directory. Could it ever have been imagined that the correspondence of the army, to whom he addressed this proclamation, teemed with accusations against him? Though the majority of these accusations were strictly just, yet it is but fair to state that the letters from Egypt contained some calumnies. In answer to the well-founded portion of the charges Bonaparte said little; but he seemed to feel deeply the falsehoods that were stated against him, one of which was, that he had carried away millions from Egypt. I cannot conceive what could have given rise to this false and impudent assertion. So far from having touched the army chest, Bonaparte had not even received all his own pay. Before he constituted himself the Government the Government was his debtor.

Though he knew well all that was to be expected from the Egyptian expedition, yet those who lauded that affair were regarded with a favourable eye by Bonaparte. The correspondence which had fallen into his hands was to him of the highest importance in enabling him to ascertain the opinions which particular individuals entertained of him.

It was the source of favours and disgraces which those who were not in the secret could not account for. It serves to explain why many men of mediocrity were elevated to the highest dignities and honours, while other men of real merit fell into disgrace or were utterly neglected.

CHAPTER XXVIII

1800

In perusing the history of the distinguished characters of past ages, how often do we regret that the historian should have portrayed the hero rather than the man! We wish to know even the most trivial habits of those whom great talents and vast reputation have elevated above their fellow-creatures. Is this the effect of mere curiosity, or rather is it not an involuntary feeling of vanity which prompts us to console ourselves for the superiority of great men by reflecting on their faults, their weaknesses, their absurdities; in short, all the points of resemblance between them and common men? For the satisfaction of those who are curious in details of this sort, I will here endeavour to paint Bonaparte, as I saw him, in person and in mind, to describe what were his tastes and habits, and even his whims and caprices.

Bonaparte was now in the prime of life, and about thirty. The person of Bonaparte has served as a model for the most skilful painters and sculptors; many able French artists have successfully delineated his features, and yet it may be said that no perfectly faithful portrait of him exists. His finely-shaped head, his superb forehead, his pale countenance, and his usual meditative look, have been transferred to the canvas; but the versatility of his expression was beyond the reach of imitation. All the various workings of his mind were instantaneously depicted in his countenance; and his glance changed from mild to severe, and from angry to good-humoured, almost with the rapidity of lightning. It may truly be said that he had a particular look for every thought that arose in his mind.

Bonaparte had beautiful hands, and he was very proud of them; while conversing he would often look at them with an air of self-complacency. He also fancied he had fine teeth, but his pretension to that advantage was not so well founded as his vanity on the score of his hands.

When walking, either alone or in company with any one, in his apartments or in his gardens, he had the habit of stooping a little, and crossing his hands behind his back. He frequently gave an involuntary shrug of his right shoulder, which was accompanied by a movement of his mouth from left to right. This habit was always most remarkable when his mind was absorbed in the consideration of any profound subject. It was often while walking that he dictated to me his most important notes. He could endure great fatigue, not only on horseback but on foot; he would sometimes walk for five or six hours in succession without being aware of it.

When walking with any person whom he treated with familiarity he would link his arm into that of his companion, and lean on it.

He used often to say to me, "You see, Bourrienne, how temperate, and how thin I am; but, in spite of that, I cannot help thinking that at forty I shall become a great eater, and get very fat. I foresee that my constitution will undergo a change. I take a great deal of exercise; but yet I feel assured that my presentiment will be fulfilled." This idea gave him great uneasiness, and as I observed nothing which seemed to warrant his apprehensions, I omitted no opportunity of assuring him that they were groundless. But he would not listen to me, and all the time I was about him, he was haunted by this presentiment, which, in the end, was but too well verified.

His partiality for the bath he mistook for a necessity. He would usually remain in the bath two hours, during which time I used to read to him extracts from the journals and pamphlets of the day, for he was anxious to hear and know all that was going on. While in the bath he was continually turning on the warm water to raise the temperature, so that I was sometimes enveloped in such a dense vapour that I could not see to read, and was obliged to open the door.

Bonaparte was exceedingly temperate, and averse to all excess. He knew the absurd stories that were circulated about him, and he was sometimes vexed at them. It has been repeated, over and over again, that he was subject to attacks of epilepsy; but during the eleven years that I was almost constantly with him I never observed any symptom which in the least degree denoted that malady. His health was good and his constitution sound. If his enemies, by way of reproach, have attributed to him a serious periodical disease, his flatterers, probably under the idea that sleep is incompatible with greatness, have evinced an equal disregard of truth in speaking of his night-watching. Bonaparte made others watch, but he himself slept, and slept well. His orders were that I should call him every morning at seven. I was therefore the first to enter his chamber; but very frequently when I awoke him he would turn himself, and say, "Ah, Bourrienne! let me lie a little longer." When there was no very pressing business I did not disturb him again till eight o'clock. He in general slept seven hours out of the twenty-four, besides taking a short nap in the afternoon.

Among the private instructions which Bonaparte gave me, one was very curious. "During the night," said he, "enter my chamber as seldom as possible. Do not awake me when you have any good news to communicate: with that there is no hurry. But when you bring bad news, rouse me instantly; for then there is not a moment to be lost."

This was a wise regulation, and Bonaparte found his advantage in it.

As soon as he rose his 'valet de chambre' shaved him and dressed his hair. While he was being shaved I read to him the newspapers, beginning always with the 'Moniteur.' He paid little attention to any but the German and English papers. "Pass over all that," he would say, while I was perusing the French papers; "I know it already. They say only what they think will please me." I was often surprised that his valet did not cut him while I was reading; for whenever he heard anything interesting he turned quickly round towards me.

When Bonaparte had finished his toilet, which he did with great attention, for he was scrupulously neat in his person, we went down to his cabinet. There he signed the orders on important petitions which had been analysed by me on the preceding evening. On reception and parade days he was particularly exact in signing these orders, because I used to remind him that he would be likely to see most of the petitioners, and that they would ask him for answers. To spare him this annoyance I used often to acquaint them beforehand of what had been granted or refused, and what had been the decision of the First Consul. He next perused the letters which I had opened and laid on his table, ranging them according to their importance. He directed me to answer them in his name; he occasionally wrote the answers himself, but not often.

At ten o'clock the 'maître d'hôtel' entered, and announced breakfast, saying, "The General is served." We went to breakfast, and the repast was exceedingly simple. He ate almost every morning some chicken, dressed with oil and onions. This dish was then, I believe, called 'poulet à la Provençale'; but our restaurateurs have since conferred upon it the more ambitious name of 'poulet à la Marengo.'

Bonaparte drank little wine, always either claret or Burgundy, and the latter by preference. After breakfast, as well as after dinner, he took a cup of strong coffee.[109] I never saw him take any between his meals, and I cannot imagine what could have given rise to the assertion of his being particularly fond of coffee. When he worked late at night he never ordered coffee, but chocolate, of which he made me take a cup with him. But this only happened when our business was prolonged till two or three in the morning.

All that has been said about Bonaparte's immoderate use of snuff has no more foundation in truth than his pretended partiality for coffee. It is true that at an early period of his life he began to take snuff, but it was very sparingly, and always out of a box; and if he bore any resemblance to Frederick the Great, it was not by filling his waistcoat-pockets with snuff, for I must again observe he carried his notions of personal neatness to a fastidious degree.

Bonaparte had two ruling passions, glory and war. He was never more gay than in the camp, and never more morose than in the inactivity of peace. Plans for the construction of public monuments also pleased his imagination, and filled up the void caused by the want of active occupation. He was aware that monuments form part of the history of nations, of whose civilisation they bear evidence for ages after those who created them have disappeared from the earth, and that they likewise often bear false-witness to remote posterity of the reality of merely fabulous conquests. Bonaparte was, however, mistaken as to the mode of accomplishing the object he had in view. His ciphers, his trophies, and subsequently his eagles, splendidly adorned the monuments of his reign. But why did he wish to stamp false initials on things with which neither he nor his reign had any connection; as, for example the old Louvre? Did he imagine that the letter, "N" which everywhere obtruded itself on the eye, had in it a charm to controvert the records of history, or alter the course of time?[110]

Be this as it may, Bonaparte well knew that the fine arts entail lasting glory on great actions, and consecrate the memory of princes who protect and encourage them. He oftener than once said to me, "A great reputation is a great noise; the more there is made, the farther off it is heard. Laws, institutions, monuments, nations, all fall; but the noise continues and resounds in after ages." This was one of his favourite ideas. "My power," he would say at other times, "depends on my glory, and my glory on my victories. My power would fall were I not to support it by new glory and new victories. Conquest has made me what I am, and conquest alone can maintain me." This was then, and probably always continued to be, his predominant idea, and that which prompted him continually to scatter the seeds of war through Europe. He thought that if he remained stationary he would fall, and he was tormented with the desire of continually advancing. Not to do something great and decided was, in his opinion, to do nothing. "A newly-born Government," said he to me, "must dazzle and astonish. When it ceases to do that it falls." It was vain to look for rest from a man who was restlessness itself.

---

109 M. Brillat de Savarin, whose memory is dear to all gourmands, had established, as a gastronomic principle, that "he who does not take coffee after each meal is assuredly not a man of taste."— Bourrienne.

110 When Louis XVIII. returned to the Tuileries in 1814 he found that Bonaparte had been an excellent tenant, and that he had left everything in very good condition.

His sentiments towards France now differed widely from what I had known them to be in his youth. He long indignantly cherished the recollection of the conquest of Corsica, which he was once content to regard as his country. But that recollection was effaced, and it might be said that he now ardently loved France. His imagination was fired by the very thought of seeing her great, happy, and powerful, and, as the first nation in the world, dictating laws to the rest. He fancied his name inseparably connected with France, and resounding in the ears of posterity. In all his actions he lost sight of the present moment, and thought only of futurity; so, in all places where he led the way to glory, the opinion of France was ever present in his thoughts. As Alexander at Arbela pleased himself less in having conquered Darius than in having gained the suffrage of the Athenians, so Bonaparte at Marengo was haunted by the idea of what would be said in France. Before he fought a battle Bonaparte thought little about what he should do in case of success, but a great deal about what he should do in case of a reverse of fortune. I mention this as a fact of which I have often been a witness, and leave to his brothers in arms to decide whether his calculations were always correct. He had it in his power to do much, for he risked everything and spared nothing. His inordinate ambition goaded him on to the attainment of power; and power when possessed served only to augment his ambition. Bonaparte was thoroughly convinced of the truth that trifles often decide the greatest events; therefore he watched rather than provoked opportunity, and when the right moment approached, he suddenly took advantage of it. It is curious that, amidst all the anxieties of war and government, the fear of the Bourbons incessantly pursued him, and the Faubourg St. Germain was to him always a threatening phantom.

He did not esteem mankind, whom, indeed, he despised more and more in proportion as he became acquainted with them. In him this unfavourable opinion of human nature was justified by many glaring examples of baseness, and he used frequently to repeat, "There are two levers for moving men,—interest and fear." What respect, indeed, could Bonaparte entertain for the applicants to the treasury of the opera? Into this treasury the gaming-houses paid a considerable sum, part of which went to cover the expenses of that magnificent theatre. The rest was distributed in secret gratuities, which were paid on orders signed by Duroc. Individuals of very different characters were often seen catching the little door in the Rue Rameau. The lady who was for a while the favourite of the General-in-Chief in Egypt, and whose husband was maliciously sent back by the English, was a frequent visitor to the treasury. On an occasion would be seen assembled there a distinguished scholar and an actor, a celebrated orator and a musician; on another, the treasurer would have payments to make to a priest, a courtesan, and a cardinal.

One of Bonaparte's greatest misfortunes was, that he neither believed in friendship not felt the necessity of loving. How often have I heard him say, "Friendship is but a name; I love nobody. I do not even love my brothers. Perhaps Joseph, a little, from habit and because he is my elder; and Duroc, I love him too. But why? Because his character pleases me. He is stern and resolute; and I really believe the fellow never shed a tear. For my part, I know very well that I have no true friends. As long as I continue what I am, I may have as many pretended friends as I please. Leave sensibility to women; it is their business. But men should be firm in heart and in purpose, or they should have nothing to do with war or government."

In his social relations Bonaparte's temper was bad; but his fits of ill-humour passed away like a cloud, and spent themselves in words. His violent language and bitter imprecations were frequently premeditated. When he was going to reprimand any one he liked to have a witness present. He would then say the harshest things, and level blows against which few could bear up. But he never gave way to those violent ebullitions of rage until he acquired undoubted proofs of the misconduct of those against whom they were directed. In scenes of this sort I have frequently observed that the presence of a third person seemed to give him confidence. Consequently, in a 'tête-à-tête' interview, any one who knew his character, and who could maintain sufficient coolness and firmness, was sure to get the better of him. He told his friends at St. Helena that he admitted a third person on such occasions only that the blow might resound the farther. That was not his real motive, or the better way would have been to perform the scene in public. He had other reasons. I observed that he did not like a 'tête-à-tête'; and when he expected any one, he would say to me beforehand, "Bourrienne, you may remain;" and when any one was announced whom he did not expect, as a minister or a general, if I rose to retire he would say in a half-whisper, "Stay where you are." Certainly this was not done with the design of getting what he said reported abroad; for it belonged neither to my character nor my duty to gossip about what I had heard. Besides, it may be presumed, that the few who were admitted as witnesses to the conferences of Napoleon were aware of the consequences attending indiscreet disclosures under a Government which was made acquainted with all that was said and done.

Bonaparte entertained a profound dislike of the sanguinary men of the Revolution, and especially of the regicides. He felt, as a painful burden, the obligation of dissembling towards them. He spoke to me in terms of horror of those whole he called the assassins of Louis XVI, and he was annoyed at the necessity of employing them and treating them with apparent respect. How many times has he not said to Cambacérès, pinching him by the ear, to soften, by that habitual familiarity, the bitterness of the remark, "My dear fellow, your case is clear; if ever the Bourbons come back you will be hanged!" A forced smile would then relax the livid countenance of Cambacérès, and was usually the only reply of the Second Consul, who, however, on one occasion said in my hearing, "Come, come, have done with this joking."

One thing which gave Bonaparte great pleasure when in the country was to see a tall, slender woman, dressed in white, walking beneath an alley of shaded trees. He detested coloured dresses, and especially dark ones. To fat women he had an invincible antipathy, and he could not endure the sight of a pregnant woman; it therefore rarely happened that a female in that situation was invited to his parties. He possessed every requisite for being what is called in society an agreeable man, except the will to be so. His manner was imposing rather than pleasing, and those who did not know him well experienced in his presence an involuntary feeling of awe. In the drawing-room, where Josephine did the honours with so much grace and affability, all was gaiety and ease, and no one felt the presence of a superior; but on Bonaparte's entrance all was changed, and every eye was directed towards him, to read his humour in his countenance, whether he intended to be silent or talkative, dull or cheerful.

He often talked a great deal, and sometimes a little too much; but no one could tell a story in a more agreeable and interesting way. His conversation rarely turned on gay or humorous subjects, and never on trivial matters. He was so fond of argument that in the warmth of discussion it was easy to draw from him secrets which he was most anxious to conceal. Sometimes, in a small circle, he would amuse himself by relating stories of presentiments and apparitions. For this he always chose the twilight of evening, and he would prepare his hearers for what was coming by some solemn remark. On one occasion of this kind he said, in a very grave tone of voice, "When death strikes a person whom we love, and who is distant from us, a foreboding almost always denotes the event, and the dying person appears to us at the moment of his dissolution." He then immediately related the following anecdote: "A gentleman of the Court of Louis XIV. was in the gallery of Versailles at the time that the King was reading to his courtiers the bulletin of the battle of Friedlingen gained by Villars. Suddenly the gentleman saw, at the farther end of the gallery, the ghost of his son, who served under Villars. He exclaimed, 'My son is no more!' and next moment the King named him among the dead."

When travelling Bonaparte was particularly talkative. In the warmth of his conversation, which was always characterised by original and interesting ideas, he sometimes dropped hints of his future views, or, at least, he said things which were calculated to disclose what he wished to conceal. I took the liberty of mentioning to him this indiscretion, and far from being offended, he acknowledged his mistake, adding that he was not aware he had gone so far. He frankly avowed this want of caution when at St. Helena.

When in good humour his usual tokens of kindness consisted in a little rap on the head or a slight pinch of the ear. In his most friendly conversations with those whom he admitted into his intimacy he would say, "You are a fool"—"a simpleton"—"a ninny"—"a blockhead." These, and a few other words of like import, enabled him to vary his catalogue of compliments; but he never employed them angrily, and the tone in which they were uttered sufficiently indicated that they were meant in kindness.

Bonaparte had many singular habits and tastes. Whenever he experienced any vexation, or when any unpleasant thought occupied his mind, he would hum something which was far from resembling a tune, for his voice was very unmusical. He would, at the same time, seat himself before the writing-table, and swing back in his chair so far that I have often been fearful of his falling.

He would then vent his ill-humour on the right arm of his chair, mutilating it with his penknife, which he seemed to keep for no other purpose. I always took care to keep good pens ready for him; for, as it was my business to decipher his writing, I had a strong interest in doing what I could to make it legible.

The sound of bells always produced in Bonaparte pleasurable sensations, which I could never account for. When we were at Malmaison, and walking in the alley leading to the plain of Ruel, how many times has the bell of the village church interrupted our most serious conversations!

He would stop, lest the noise of our footsteps should drown any portion of the delightful sound. He was almost angry with me because I did not experience the impressions he did. So powerful was the effect produced upon him by the sound of these bells that his voice would falter as he said, "Ah! that reminds me of the first years I spent at Brienne! I was then happy!" When the bells ceased he would resume the course of his speculations, carry himself into futurity, place a crown on his head, and dethrone kings.

Nowhere, except on the field of battle, did I ever see Bonaparte more happy than in the gardens of Malmaison. At the commencement of the Consulate we used to go there every Saturday evening, and stay the whole of Sunday, and sometimes Monday. Bonaparte used to spend a considerable part of his time in walking and superintending the improvements which he had ordered. At first he used to make excursions about the neighbourhood, but the reports of the police disturbed his natural confidence, and gave him reason to fear the attempts of concealed royalist partisans.

During the first four or five days that Bonaparte spent at Malmaison he amused himself after breakfast with calculating the revenue of that domain. According to his estimates it amounted to 8000 francs. "That is not bad!" said he; "but to live here would require an income of 30,000 livres!" I could not help smiling to see him seriously engaged in such a calculation.

Bonaparte had no faith in medicine. He spoke of it as an art entirely conjectural, and his opinion on this subject was fired and incontrovertible. His vigorous mind rejected all but demonstrative proofs.

He had little memory for proper names, words, or dates, but he had a wonderful recollection of facts and places. I recollect that, on going from Paris to Toulon, he pointed out to me ten places calculated for great battles, and he never forgot them. They were memoranda of his first youthful journeys.

Bonaparte was insensible to the charms of poetic harmony. He had not even sufficient ear to feel the rhythm of poetry, and he never could recite a verse without violating the metre; yet the grand ideas of poetry charmed him. He absolutely worshipped Corneille; and, one day, after having witnessed a performance of 'Cinna', he said to me, "If a man like Corneille were living in my time I would make him my Prime Minister. It is not his poetry that I most admire; it is his powerful understanding, his vast knowledge of the human heart, and his profound policy!" At St. Helena he said that he would have made Corneille a prince; but at the time he spoke to me of Corneille he had no thought of making either princes or kings.

Gallantry to women was by no means a trait in Bonaparte's character. He seldom said anything agreeable to females, and he frequently addressed to them the rudest and most extraordinary remarks. To one he would say, "Heavens, how red your elbows are!" To another, "What an ugly headdress you have got!" At another time he would say, "Your dress is none of the cleanest . . . . Do you ever change your gown? I have seen you in that twenty times!" He showed no mercy to any who displeased him on these points. He often gave Josephine directions about her toilet, and the exquisite taste for which she was distinguished might have helped to make him fastidious about the costume of other ladies. At first he looked to elegance above all things: at a later period he admired luxury and splendour, but he always required modesty. He frequently expressed his disapproval of the low-necked dresses which were so much in fashion at the beginning of the Consulate.

Bonaparte did not love cards, and this was very fortunate for those who were invited to his parties; for when he was seated at a card-table, as he sometimes thought himself obliged to be, nothing could exceed the dulness of the drawing-room either at the Luxembourg or the Tuileries. When, on the contrary, he walked about among the company, all were pleased, for he usually spoke to everybody, though he preferred the conversation of men of science, especially those who had been with him in in Egypt; as for example, Monge and Berthollet. He also liked to talk with Chaptal and Lacépède, and with Lemercier, the author of 'Agamemnon'.

Bonaparte was seen to less advantage in a drawing-room than at the head of his troops. His military uniform became him much better than the handsomest dress of any other kind. His first trials of dress-coats were unfortunate. I have been informed that the first time he wore one he kept on his black cravat. This incongruity was remarked to him, and he replied, "So much the better; it leaves me something of a military air, and there is no harm in that." For my own part, I neither saw the black cravat nor heard this reply.

The First Consul paid his own private bills very punctually; but he was always tardy in settling the accounts of the contractors who bargained with Ministers for supplies for the public service. He put off these payments by all sorts of excuses and shufflings. Hence arose immense arrears in the expenditure, and the necessity of appointing a committee of liquidation. In his opinion the terms contractor and rogue were synonymous. All that he avoided paying them he regarded as a just restitution to himself; and all the sums which were struck off from their accounts he regarded as so much deducted from a theft. The less a Minister paid out of his budget the more Bonaparte was pleased with him; and this ruinous system of economy can alone explain the credit which Decrès so long enjoyed at the expense of the French navy.

On the subject of religion Bonaparte's ideas were very vague. "My reason," said he, "makes me incredulous respecting many things; but the impressions of my childhood and early youth throw me into uncertainty." He was very fond of talking of religion. In Italy, in Egypt, and on board the 'Orient' and the 'Muiron', I have known him to take part in very animated conversations on this subject.

He readily yielded up all that was proved against religion as the work of men and time: but he would not hear of materialism. I recollect that one fine night, when he was on deck with some persons who were arguing in favour of materialism, Bonaparte raised his hand to heaven and, pointing to the stars, said, "You may talk as long as you please, gentlemen, but who made all that?" The perpetuity of a name in the memory of man was to him the immortality of the soul. He was perfectly tolerant towards every variety of religious faith.

Among Bonaparte's singular habits was that of seating himself on any table which happened to be of a suitable height for him. He would often sit on mine, resting his left arm on my right shoulder, and swinging his left leg, which did not reach the ground; and while he dictated to me he would jolt the table so that I could scarcely write.

Bonaparte had a great dislike to reconsider any decision, even when it was acknowledged to be unjust. In little as well as in great things he evinced his repugnance to retrograde. An instance of this occurred in the affair of General Latour-Foissac. The First Consul felt how much he had wronged that general; but he wished some time to elapse before he repaired his error. His heart and his conduct were at variance; but his feelings were overcome by what he conceived to be political necessity. Bonaparte was never known to say, "I have done wrong:" his usual observation was, "I begin to think there is something wrong."

In spite of this sort of feeling, which was more worthy of an ill-humoured philosopher than the head of a government, Bonaparte was neither malignant nor vindictive. I cannot certainly defend him against all the reproaches which he incurred through the imperious law of war and cruel necessity; but I may say that he has often been unjustly accused. None but those who are blinded by fury will call him a Nero or a Caligula. I think I have avowed his faults with sufficient candour to entitle me to credit when I speak in his commendation; and I declare that, out of the field of battle, Bonaparte had a kind and feeling heart. He was very fond of children, a trait which seldom distinguishes a bad man. In the relations of private life to call him amiable would not be using too strong a word, and he was very indulgent to the weakness of human nature. The contrary opinion is too firmly fixed in some minds for me to hope to root it out. I shall, I fear, have contradictors, but I address myself to those who look for truth. To judge impartially we must take into account the influence which time and circumstances exercise on men; and distinguish between the different characters of the Collegian, the General, the Consul, and the Emperor.

CHAPTER XXIX

1800

It is not my purpose to say much about the laws, decrees, and 'Senatus-Consultes', which the First Consul either passed, or caused to be passed, after his accession to power, what were they all, with the exception of the Civil Code? The legislative reveries of the different men who have from time to time ruled France form an immense labyrinth, in which chicanery bewilders reason and common sense; and they would long since have been buried in oblivion had they not occasionally served to authorise injustice. I cannot, however, pass over unnoticed the happy effect produced in Paris, and throughout the whole of France, by some of the first decisions of the Consuls. Perhaps none but those who witnessed the state of society during the reign of Terror can fully appreciate the satisfaction which the first steps towards the restoration of social order produced in the breasts of all honest men. The Directory, more base and not less perverse than the Convention, had retained the horrible 21st of January among the festivals of the Republic. One of Bonaparte's first ideas on attaining the possession of power was to abolish this; but such was the ascendency of the abettors of the fearful event that he could not venture on a straightforward course. He and his two colleagues, who were Sieyès and Roger Ducos, signed, on the 5th Nivôse, a decree, setting forth that in future the only festivals to be celebrated by the Republic were the 1st Vendemiaire and the 14th of July, intending by this means to consecrate provisionally the recollection of the foundation of the Republic and of liberty.

All was calculation with Bonaparte. To produce effect was his highest gratification. Thus he let slip no opportunity of saying or doing things which were calculated to dazzle the multitude. While at the Luxembourg, he went sometimes accompanied by his 'aides de camp' and sometimes by a Minister, to pay certain official visits. I did not accompany him on these occasions; but almost always either on his return, after dinner, or in the evening, he related to me what he had done and said. He congratulated himself on having paid a visit to Daubenton, at the Jardin des Plantes, and talked with great self-complacency of the distinguished way in which he had treated the contemporary of Buffon.

On the 24th Brumaire he visited the prisons. He liked to make these visits unexpectedly, and to take the governors of the different public establishments by surprise; so that, having no time to make their preparations, he might see things as they really were. I was in his cabinet when he returned, for I had a great deal of business to go through in his absence. As he entered he exclaimed, "What brutes these Directors are! To what a state they have brought our public establishments! But, stay a little! I will put all in order. The prisons are in a shockingly unwholesome state, and the prisoners miserably fed. I questioned them, and I questioned the jailers, for nothing is to be learned from the superiors. They, of course, always speak well of their own work! When I was in the Temple I could not help thinking of the unfortunate Louis XVI. He was an excellent man, but too amiable, too gentle for the times. He knew not how to deal with mankind! And Sir Sidney Smith! I made them show me his apartment. If the fools had not let him escape I should have taken St. Jean d'Acre! There are too many painful recollections connected with that prison! I will certainly have it pulled down some day or other! What do you think I did at the Temple? I ordered the jailers' books to be brought to me, and finding that some hostages were still in confinement I liberated them. 'An unjust law,' said I, 'has deprived you of liberty; my first duty is to restore it to you.' 'Was not this well done, Bourrienne?' As I was, no less than Bonaparte himself, an enemy to the revolutionary laws, I congratulated him sincerely; and he was very sensible to my approbation, for I was not accustomed to greet him with 'Good; very good,' on all occasions. It is true, knowing his character as I did, I avoided saying anything that was calculated to offend him; but when I said nothing, he knew very well how to construe my silence. Had I flattered him I should have continued longer in favour."

Bonaparte always spoke angrily of the Directors he had turned off. Their incapacity disgusted and astonished him. "What simpletons! what a government!" he would frequently exclaim when he looked into the measures of the Directory. "Bourrienne," said he, "can you imagine anything more pitiable than their system of finance? Can it for a moment be doubted that the principal agents of authority daily committed the most fraudulent peculations? What venality! what disorder! what wastefulness! everything put up for sale: places, provisions, clothing, and military, all were disposed of. Have they not actually consumed 75,000,000 in advance? And then, think of all the scandalous fortunes accumulated, all the malversations! But are there no means of making them refund? We shall see."

In these first moments of poverty it was found necessary to raise a loan, for the funds of M. Collot did not last long, and 12,000,000 were advanced by the different bankers of Paris, who, I believe, were paid by bills of the receivers-general, the discount of which then amounted to about 33 per cent. The salaries of the first offices were not very considerable, and did not amount to anything like the exorbitant stipends of the Empire.

Bonaparte's salary was fixed at 500,000 francs. What a contrast to the 300,000,000 in gold which were reported to have been concealed in 1811 in the cellars of the Tuileries!

In mentioning Bonaparte's nomination to the Institute, and his affectation in putting at the head of his proclamation his title of member of that learned body before that of General-in-Chief, I omitted to state what value he really attached to that title. The truth is that, when young and ambitious, he was pleased with the proffered title, which he thought would raise him in public estimation. How often have we laughed together when he weighed the value of his scientific titles! Bonaparte, to be sure, knew something of mathematics, a good deal of history, and, I need not add, possessed extraordinary military talent; but he was nevertheless a useless member of the Institute.

On his return from Egypt he began to grow weary of a title which gave him so many colleagues. "Do you not think," said he one day to me, "that there is something mean and humiliating in the words, 'I have the honour to be, my dear Colleague'! I am tired of it!" Generally speaking, all phrases which indicated equality displeased him. It will be recollected how gratified he was that I did not address him in the second person singular on our meeting at Leoben, and also what befell M. de Cominges at Bâle because he did not observe the same precaution.

The figure of the Republic seated and holding a spear in her hand, which at the commencement of the Consulate was stamped on official letters, was speedily abolished. Happy would it have been if Liberty herself had not suffered the same treatment as her emblem! The title of First Consul made him despise that of Member of the Institute. He no longer entertained the least predilection for that learned body, and subsequently he regarded it with much suspicion. It was a body, an authorised assembly; these were reasons sufficient for him to take umbrage at it, and he never concealed his dislike of all bodies possessing the privilege of meeting and deliberating.

While we were at the Luxembourg Bonaparte despatched Duroc on a special mission to the King of Prussia. This happened, I think, at the very beginning of the year 1800. He selected Duroc because he was a man of good education and agreeable manners, and one who could express himself with elegance and reserve, qualities not often met with at that period. Duroc had been with us in Italy, in Egypt, and on board the 'Muiron', and the Consul easily guessed that the King of Prussia would be delighted to hear from an eye-witness the events of Bonaparte's campaigns, especially the siege of St. Jean d'Acre, and the scenes which took place during the months of March and May at Jaffa. Besides, the First Consul considered it indispensable that such circumstantial details should be given in a way to leave no doubt of their correctness. His intentions were fully realised; for Duroc told me, on his return, that nearly the whole of the conversation he had with the King turned upon St. Jean d'Acre and Jaffa. He stayed nearly two whole hours with his Majesty, who, the day after, gave him an invitation to dinner. When this intelligence arrived at the Luxembourg I could perceive that the Chief of the Republic was flattered that one of his aides de camp should have sat at table with a King, who some years after was doomed to wait for him in his antechamber at Tilsit.

Duroc never spoke on politics to the King of Prussia, which was very fortunate, for, considering his age and the exclusively military life he had led, he could scarcely have been expected to avoid blunders. Some time later, after the death of Paul I., he was sent to congratulate Alexander on his accession to the throne. Bonaparte's design in thus making choice of Duroc was to introduce to the Courts of Europe, by confidential missions, a young man to whom he was much attached, and also to bring him forward in France. Duroc went on his third mission to Berlin after the war broke out with Austria. He often wrote to me, and his letters convinced me how much he had improved himself within a short time.

Another circumstance which happened at the commencement of the Consulate affords an example of Bonaparte's inflexibility when he had once formed a determination. In the spring of 1799, when we were in Egypt, the Directory gave to General Latour-Foissac, a highly distinguished officer, the command of Mantua, the taking of which had so powerfully contributed to the glory of the conqueror of Italy. Shortly after Latour's appointment to this important post the Austrians besieged Mantua. It was well known that the garrison was supplied with provisions and ammunition for a long resistance; yet, in the month of July it surrendered to the Austrians. The act of capitulation contained a curious article, viz. "General Latour-Foissac and his staff shall be conducted as prisoners to Austria; the garrison shall be allowed to return to France." This distinction between the general and the troops entrusted to his command, and at the same time the prompt surrender of Mantua, were circumstances which, it must be confessed, were calculated to excite suspicions of Latour-Foissac. The consequence was, when Bernadotte was made War Minister he ordered an inquiry into the general's conduct by a court-martial. Latour-Foissac had no sooner returned to France than he published a justificatory memorial, in which he showed the impossibility of his having made a longer defence when he was in want of many objects of the first necessity.

Such was the state of the affair on Bonaparte's elevation to the Consular power. The loss of Mantua, the possession of which had cost him so many sacrifices, roused his indignation to so high a pitch that whenever the subject was mentioned he could find no words to express his rage. He stopped the investigation of the court-martial, and issued a violent decree against Latour-Foissac even before his culpability had been proved. This proceeding occasioned much discussion, and was very dissatisfactory to many general officers, who, by this arbitrary decision, found themselves in danger of forfeiting the privilege of being tried by their natural judges whenever they happened to displease the First Consul. For my own part, I must say that this decree against Latour-Foissac was one which I saw issued with considerable regret. I was alarmed for the consequences. After the lapse of a few days I ventured to point out to him the undue severity of the step he had taken; I reminded him of all that had been said in Latour-Foissac's favour, and tried to convince him how much more just it would be to allow the trial to come to a conclusion. "In a country," said I, "like France, where the point of honour stands above every thing, it is impossible Foissac can escape condemnation if he be culpable."—"Perhaps you are right, Bourrienne," rejoined he; "but the blow is struck; the decree is issued. I have given the same explanation to every one; but I cannot so suddenly retrace my steps. To retro-grade is to be lost. I cannot acknowledge myself in the wrong. By and by we shall see what can be done. Time will bring lenity and pardon. At present it would be premature." Such, word for word, was Bonaparte's reply. If with this be compared what he said on the subject at St. Helena it will be found that his ideas continued nearly unchanged; the only difference is that, instead of the impetuosity of 1800, he expressed himself with the calmness which time and adversity naturally produce.[111]

Bonaparte, as I have before observed, loved contrasts; and I remember at the very time he was acting so violently against Latour-Foissac he condescended to busy himself about a company of players which he wished to send to Egypt, or rather that he pretended to wish to send there, because the announcement of such a project conveyed an impression of the prosperous condition of our Oriental colony. The Consuls gravely appointed the Minister of the Interior to execute this business, and the Minister in his turn delegated his powers to Florence, the actor. In their instructions to the Minister the Consuls observed that it would be advisable to include some female dancers in the company; a suggestion which corresponds with Bonaparte's note, in which were specified all that he considered necessary for the Egyptian expedition.

The First Consul entertained singular notions respecting literary property. On his hearing that a piece, entitled 'Misanthropie et Repentir', had been brought out at the Odeon, he said to me, "Bourrienne, you have been robbed."—"I, General? how?"—"You have been robbed, I tell you, and they are now acting your piece." I have already mentioned that during my stay at Warsaw I amused myself with translating a celebrated play of Kotzebue. While we were in Italy I lent Bonaparte my translation to read, and he expressed himself much pleased with it. He greatly admired the piece, and often went to see it acted at the Odeon. On his return he invariably gave me fresh reasons for my claiming what he was pleased to call my property. I represented to him that the translation of a foreign work belonged to any one who chose to execute it. He would not, however, give up his point, and I was obliged to assure him that my occupations in his service left me no time to engage in a literary lawsuit. He then exacted

111 "It was," says the 'Memorial of St. Helena', "an illegal and tyrannical act, but still it was a necessary evil. It was the fault of the law. He was a hundred, nay, a thousand fold guilty, and yet it was doubtful whether he would be condemned. We therefore assailed him with the shafts of honour and public opinion. Yet I repeat it was a tyrannical act, and one of those violent measures which are at times necessary in great nations and in extraordinary circumstances."

a promise from me to translate Goethe's 'Werther'. I told him it was already done, though indifferently, and that I could not possibly devote to the subject the time it merited. I read over to him one of the letters I had translated into French, and which he seemed to approve.

That interval of the Consular Government during which Bonaparte remained at the Luxembourg may be called the preparatory Consulate. Then were sown the seeds of the great events which he meditated, and of those institutions with which he wished to mark his possession of power. He was then, if I may use the expression, two individuals in one: the Republican general, who was obliged to appear the advocate of liberty and the principles of the Revolution; and the votary of ambition, secretly plotting the downfall of that liberty and those principles.

I often wondered at the consummate address with which he contrived to deceive those who were likely to see through his designs. This hypocrisy, which some, perhaps, may call profound policy, was indispensable to the accomplishment of his projects; and sometimes, as if to keep himself in practice, he would do it in matters of secondary importance. For example, his opinion of the insatiable avarice of Sieyès is well known; yet when he proposed, in his message to the Council of Ancients, to give his colleague, under the title of national recompense, the price of his obedient secession, it was, in the words of the message, a recompense worthily bestowed on his disinterested virtues.

While at the Luxembourg Bonaparte showed, by a Consular act, his hatred of the liberty of the press above all liberties, for he loved none. On the 27th Nivôse the Consuls, or rather the First Consul, published a decree, the real object of which was evidently contrary to its implied object.

This decree stated that:

The Consuls of the Republic, considering that some of the journals printed at Paris are instruments in the hands of the enemies of the Republic, over the safety of which the Government is specially entrusted by the people of France to watch, decree—

That the Minister of Police shall, during the continuation of the war, allow only the following journals to be printed and published, viz. (list of 20 publications) . . . and those papers which are exclusively devoted to science, art, literature, commerce, and advertisements.

Surely this decree may well be considered as preparatory; and the fragment I have quoted may serve as a standard for measuring the greater part of those acts by which Bonaparte sought to gain, for the consolidation of his power, what he seemed to be seeking solely for the interest of the friends of the Republic. The limitation to the period of the continuance of the war had also a certain provisional air which afforded hope for the future. But everything provisional is, in its nature, very elastic; and Bonaparte knew how to draw it out ad infinitum. The decree, moreover, enacted that if any of the uncondemned journals should insert articles against the sovereignty of the people they would be immediately suppressed. In truth, great indulgence was shown on this point, even after the Emperor's coronation.

The presentation of swords and muskets of honour also originated at the Luxembourg; and this practice was, without doubt, a preparatory step to the foundation of the Legion of Honour.[112] A grenadier sergeant, named Léon Aune, who had been included in the first

112 "Armes d'honneur," decreed 25th December 1799. Muskets for infantry, carbines for cavalry, grenades for artillery, swords for the officers. Gouvion St. Cyr received the first sword (Thiers, tome i. p. 126).

distribution, easily obtained permission to write to the First Consul to thank him. Bonaparte, wishing to answer him in his own name, dictated to me the following letter for Aune:—

> I have received your letter, my brave comrade. You needed not to have told me of your exploits, for you are the bravest grenadier in the whole army since the death of Benezete. You received one of the hundred sabres I distributed to the army, and all agreed you most deserved it.
>
> I wish very much again to see you. The War Minister sends you an order to come to Paris.

This wheedling wonderfully favoured Bonaparte's designs. His letter to Aune could not fail to be circulated through the army. A sergeant called my brave comrade by the First Consul—the First General of France! Who but a thorough Republican, the stanch friend of equality, would have done this? This was enough to wind up the enthusiasm of the army. At the same time it must be confessed that Bonaparte began to find the Luxembourg too little for him, and preparations were set on foot at the Tuileries.

Still this great step towards the re-establishment of the monarchy was to be cautiously prepared. It was important to do away with the idea that none but a king could occupy the palace of our ancient kings. What was to be done? A very fine bust of Brutus had been brought from Italy. Brutus was the destroyer of tyrants! This was the very thing; and David was commissioned to place it in a gallery of the Tuileries. Could there be a greater proof of the Consul's horror of tyranny?

To sleep at the Tuileries, in the bedchamber of the kings of France, was all that Bonaparte wanted; the rest would follow in due course. He was willing to be satisfied with establishing a principle the consequences of which were to be afterwards deduced. Hence the affectation of never inserting in official acts the name of the Tuileries, but designating that place as the Palace of the Government. The first preparations were modest, for it did not become a good Republican to be fond of pomp. Accordingly Lecomte, who was at that time architect of the Tuileries, merely received orders to clean the Palace, an expression which might bear more than one meaning, after the meetings which had been there. For this purpose the sum of 500,000 francs was sufficient. Bonaparte's drift was to conceal, as far as possible, the importance he attached to the change of his Consular domicile. But little expense was requisite for fitting up apartments for the First Consul. Simple ornaments, such as marbles and statues, were to decorate the Palace of the Government.

Nothing escaped Bonaparte's consideration. Thus it was not merely at hazard that he selected the statues of great men to adorn the gallery of the Tuileries. Among the Greeks he made choice of Demosthenes and Alexander, thus rendering homage at once to the genius of eloquence and the genius of victory. The statue of Hannibal was intended to recall the memory of Rome's most formidable enemy; and Rome herself was represented in the Consular Palace by the statues of Scipio, Cicero, Cato, Brutus and Caesar—the victor and the immolator being placed side by side. Among the great men of modern times he gave the first place to Gustavus Adolphus, and the next to Turenne and the great Condé, to Turenne in honour of his military talent, and to Condé to prove that there was nothing fearful in the recollection of a Bourbon. The remembrance of the glorious days of the French navy was revived by the statue of Duguai Trouin. Marlborough and Prince Eugène had also their places in the gallery, as if to attest the disasters which marked the close of the great reign; and Marshal Sage, to show that Louis XV.'s reign was not without its glory. The statues of Frederick and Washington were emblematic of false philosophy on a throne and true wisdom founding a free state. Finally, the names of Dugommier, Dampierre, and Joubert were intended to bear evidence of the high esteem which Bonaparte cherished for his old comrades,—those illustrious victims to a cause which had now ceased to be his.

The reader has already been informed of the attempts made by Bonaparte to induce England and Austria to negotiate with the Consular Government, which the King of Prussia was the first of the sovereigns of Europe to recognise. These attempts having proved unavailing, it became necessary to carry on the war with renewed vigour, and also to explain why the peace, which had been promised at the beginning of the Consulate, was still nothing but a promise. In fulfilment of these two objects Bonaparte addressed an energetic proclamation to the armies, which was remarkable for not being followed by the usual sacred words, "Vive la République!"

At the same time Bonaparte completed the formation of the Council of State, and divided it into five sections:—(1) The Interior; (2) Finance; (3) Marine; (4) The War Department; (5) Legislation. He fixed the salaries of the Councillors of the State at 25,000 francs, and that of the Precedents of Sections at 30,000. He settled the costume of the Consuls, the Ministers, and the different bodies of the State. This led to the re-introduction of velvet, which had been banished with the old regime, and the encouragement of the manufactures of Lyons was the reason alleged for employing this un-republican article in the different dresses, such as those of the Consuls and Ministers. It was Bonaparte's constant aim to efface the Republic, even in the utmost trifles, and to prepare matters so well that the customs and habits of monarchy being restored, there should only then remain a word to be changed.

I never remember to have seen Bonaparte in the Consular dress, which he detested, and which he wore only because duty required him to do so at public ceremonies. The only dress he was fond of, and in which he felt at ease, was that in which he subjugated the ancient Eridanus and the Nile, namely, the uniform of the Guides, to which corps Bonaparte was always sincerely attached.

The masquerade of official dresses was not the only one which Bonaparte summoned to the aid of his policy. At that period of the year VIII. which corresponded with the carnival of 1800, masques began to be resumed at Paris. Disguises were all the fashion, and Bonaparte favoured the revival of old amusements; first, because they were old, and next, because they were the means of diverting the attention of the people: for, as he had established the principle that on the field of battle it is necessary to divide the enemy in order to beat him, he conceived it no less advisable to divert the people in order to enslave them. Bonaparte did not say 'panem et circenses', for I believe his knowledge of Latin did not extend even to that well-known phrase of Juvenal, but he put the maxim in practice. He accordingly authorised the revival of balls at the opera, which they who lived during that period of the Consulate know was an important event in Paris. Some gladly viewed it as a little conquest in favour of the old regime; and others, who for that very reason disapproved it, were too shallow to understand the influence of little over great things. The women and the young men did not bestow a thought on the subject, but yielded willingly to the attractions of pleasure. Bonaparte, who was delighted at having provided a diversion for the gossiping of the Parisian salons, said to me one day, "While they are chatting about all this, they do not babble upon politics, and that is what I want. Let them dance and amuse themselves as long as they do not thrust their noses into the Councils of the Government; besides, Bourrienne," added he, "I have other reasons for encouraging this, I see other advantages in it. Trade is languishing; Fouché tells me that there are great complaints. This will set a little money in circulation; besides, I am on my guard about the Jacobins. Everything is not bad, because it is not new. I prefer the opera-balls to the saturnalia of the Goddess of Reason. I was never so enthusiastically applauded as at the last parade."

A Consular decision of a different and more important nature had, shortly before, namely, at the commencement of Nivôse, brought happiness to many families. Bonaparte, as every one knows, had prepared the events of the 18th Fructidor that he might have some plausible reasons for overthrowing the Directors. The Directory being overthrown, he was now anxious, at least in part, to undo what he had done on the 18th Fructidor. He therefore ordered a report on the persons exiled to be presented to him by the Minister of Police. In consequence of this report he authorised forty of them to return to France, placing them under the observation of the Police Minister, and assigning them their place of residence. However, they did not long remain under these restrictions, and many of them were soon called to fill high places in the Government. It was indeed natural that Bonaparte, still wishing, at least in appearance, to found his government on those principles of moderate republicanism which had caused their exile, should invite them to second his views.

Barrère wrote a justificatory letter to the First Consul, who, however, took no notice of it, for he could not get so far as to favour Barrère. Thus did Bonaparte receive into the Councils of the Consulate the men who had been exiled by the Directory, just as he afterwards appointed the emigrants and those exiles of the Revolution to high offices under the Empire. The time and the men alone differed; the intention in both cases was the same.

CHAPTER XXX

1800

The first communications between Bonaparte and Paul I. commenced a short time after his accession to the Consulate. Affairs then began to look a little less unfavourable for France; already vague reports from Switzerland and the banks of the Rhine indicated a coldness existing between the Russians and the Austrians; and at the same time, symptoms of a misunderstanding between the Courts of London and St. Petersburg began to be perceptible. The First Consul, having in the meantime discovered the chivalrous and somewhat eccentric character of Paul I., thought the moment a propitious one to attempt breaking the bonds which united Russia and England. He was not the man to allow so fine an opportunity to pass, and he took advantage of it with his usual sagacity. The English had some time before refused to include in a cartel for the exchange of prisoners 7000 Russians taken in Holland. Bonaparte ordered them all to be armed, and clothed in new uniforms appropriate to the corps to which they had belonged, and sent them back to Russia, without ransom, without exchange, or any condition whatever. This judicious munificence was not thrown away. Paul I. showed himself deeply sensible of it, and closely allied as he had lately been with England, he now, all at once, declared himself her enemy. This triumph of policy delighted the First Consul.

Thenceforth the Consul and the Czar became the best friends possible. They strove to outdo each other in professions of friendship; and it may be believed that Bonaparte did not fail to turn this contest of politeness to his own advantage. He so well worked upon the mind of Paul that he succeeded in obtaining a direct influence over the Cabinet of St. Petersburg.

Lord Whitworth, at that time the English ambassador in Russia, was ordered to quit the capital without delay, and to retire to Riga, which then became the focus of the intrigues of the north which ended in the death of Paul. The English ships were seized in all the ports, and, at the pressing instance of the Czar, a Prussian army menaced Hanover. Bonaparte lost no time, and, profiting by the friendship manifested towards him by the inheritor of Catherine's power, determined to make that friendship subservient to the execution of the vast plan which he had long conceived: he meant to undertake an expedition by land against the English colonies in the East Indies.

The arrival of Baron Sprengporten at Paris caused great satisfaction among the partisans of the Consular Government, that is to say, almost every one in Paris. M. Sprengporten was a native of Swedish Finland. He had been appointed by Catherine chamberlain and lieutenant-general of her forces, and he was not less in favour with Paul, who treated him in the most distinguished manner. He came on an extraordinary mission, being ostensibly clothed with the title of plenipotentiary, and at the same time appointed confidential Minister to the Consul. Bonaparte was extremely satisfied with the ambassador whom Paul had selected, and with the manner in which he described the Emperor's gratitude for the generous conduct of the First Consul. M. Sprengporten did not conceal the extent of Paul's dissatisfaction with his allies. The bad issue, he said, of the war with France had already disposed the Czar to connect himself with that power, when the return of his troops at once determined him.

We could easily perceive that Paul placed great confidence in M. Sprengporten. As he had satisfactorily discharged the mission with which he had been entrusted, Paul expressed pleasure at his conduct in several friendly and flattering letters, which Sprengporten always allowed us to read. No one could be fonder of France than he was, and he ardently desired that his first negotiations might lead to a long alliance between the Russian and French Governments. The autograph and very frequent correspondence between Bonaparte and Paul passed through his hands. I read all Paul's letters, which were remarkable for the frankness with which his affection for Bonaparte was expressed. His admiration of the First Consul was so great that no courtier could have written in a more flattering manner.

This admiration was not feigned on the part of the Emperor of Russia: it was no less sincere than ardent, and of this he soon gave proofs. The violent hatred he had conceived towards the English Government induced him to defy to single combat every monarch who would not declare war against England and shut his ports against English ships. He inserted a challenge to the King of Denmark in the St. Petersburg Court Gazette; but not choosing to apply officially to the Senate of Hamburg to order its insertion in the 'Correspondant', conducted by M. Stoves, he sent the article, through Count Pahlen, to M. Schramm, a Hamburg merchant. The Count told M. Schramm that the Emperor would be much pleased to see the article of the St. Petersburg Court Gazette copied into the Correspondant; and that if it should be inserted, he wished to have a dozen copies of the paper printed on vellum, and sent to him by an extraordinary courier. It was Paul's intention to send a copy to every sovereign in Europe; but this piece of folly, after the manner of Charles XII., led to no further results.

Bonaparte never felt greater satisfaction in the whole course of his life than he experienced from Paul's enthusiasm for him. The friendship of a sovereign seemed to him a step by which he was to become a sovereign himself. At the same time the affairs of La Vendée began to assume a better aspect, and he hoped soon to effect that pacification in the interior which he so ardently desired.

It was during the First Consul's residence at the Luxembourg that the first report on the civil code was made to the legislative body. It was then, also, that the regulations for the management of the Bank of France were adopted, and that establishment so necessary to France was founded.

There was at this time in Paris a man who has acquired an unfortunate celebrity, the most unlucky of modern generals—in a word, General Mack. I should not notice that person here were it not for the prophetic judgment which Bonaparte then pronounced on him. Mack had been obliged to surrender himself at Championnet some time before our landing at Fréjus. He was received as a prisoner of war, and the town of Dijon had been appointed his place of residence, and there he remained until after the 18th Brumaire. Bonaparte, now Consul, permitted him to come to Paris, and to reside there on his parole. He applied for leave to go to Vienna, pledging himself to return again a prisoner to France if the Emperor Francis would not consent to exchange him for Generals Pérignon and Grouchy, then prisoners in Austria. His request was not granted, but his proposition was forwarded to Vienna. The Court of Vienna refused to accede to it, not placing perhaps so much importance on the deliverance of Mack as he had flattered himself it would.

Bonaparte speaking to me of him one day said, "Mack is a man of the lowest mediocrity

I ever saw in my life; he is full of self-sufficiency and conceit, and believes himself equal to anything. He has no talent. I should like to see him opposed some day to one of our good generals; we should then see fine work. He is a boaster, and that is all. He is really one of the most silly men existing; and, besides all that, he is unlucky." Was not this opinion of Bonaparte, formed on the past, fully verified by the future?

It was at Malmaison that Bonaparte thus spoke of General Mack. That place was then far from resembling what it afterwards became, and the road to it was neither pleasant nor sure. There was not a house on the road; and in the evening, during the season when we were there, it was not frequented all the way from St. Germain. Those numerous vehicles, which the demands of luxury and an increasing population have created, did not then, as now, pass along the roads in the environs of Paris. Everywhere the road was solitary and dangerous; and I learned with certainty that many schemes were laid for carrying off the First Consul during one of his evening journeys. They were unsuccessful, and orders were given to enclose the quarries, which were too near to the road. On Saturday evening Bonaparte left the Luxembourg, and afterwards the Tuileries, to go to Malmaison, and I cannot better express the joy he then appeared to experience than by comparing it to the delight of a school-boy on getting a holiday.

Before removing from the Luxembourg to the Tuileries Bonaparte determined to dazzle the eyes of the Parisians by a splendid ceremony. He had appointed it to take place on the 'decadi', Pluviôse 20 (9th February 1800), that is to say, ten days before his final departure from the old Directorial palace. These kinds of fetes did not resemble what they afterwards became; their attraction consisted in the splendour of military dress: and Bonaparte was always sure that whenever he mounted his horse, surrounded by a brilliant staff from which he was to be distinguished by the simplicity of his costume, his path would be crowded and himself greeted with acclamations by the people of Paris. The object of this fete was at first only to present to the 'Hôtel des Invalides', then called the Temple of Mars, seventy-two flags taken from the Turks in the battle of Aboukir and brought from Egypt to Paris; but intelligence of Washington's death, who expired on the 14th of December 1799, having reached Bonaparte, he eagerly took advantage of that event to produce more effect, and mixed the mourning cypress with the laurels he had collected in Egypt.

Bonaparte did not feel much concerned at the death of Washington, that noble founder of rational freedom in the new world; but it afforded him an opportunity to mask his ambitious projects under the appearance of a love of liberty. In thus rendering honour to the memory of Washington everybody would suppose that Bonaparte intended to imitate his example, and that their two names would pass in conjunction from mouth to mouth. A clever orator might be employed, who, while pronouncing a eulogium on the dead, would contrive to bestow some praise on the living; and when the people were applauding his love of liberty he would find himself one step nearer the throne, on which his eyes were constantly fixed. When the proper time arrived, he would not fail to seize the crown; and would still cry, if necessary, "Vive la Liberté!" while placing it on his imperial head.

The skilful orator was found. M. de Fontanes[113] was commissioned to pronounce the funeral eulogium on Washington, and the flowers of eloquence which he scattered about did not all fall on the hero of America.

---

113 L. de Fontanes (1767-1821) became president of the Corps Legislatif, Senator, and Grand Master of the University. He was the centre of the literary group of the Empire.

Lannes was entrusted by Bonaparte with the presentation of the flags; and on the 20th Pluviôse he proceeded, accompanied by strong detachments of the cavalry then in Paris, to the council-hall of the Invalides, where he was met by the Minister of War, who received the colours. All the Ministers, the councillors of State, and generals were summoned to the presentation. Lannes pronounced a discourse, to which Berthier replied, and M. de Fontanes added his well-managed eloquence to the plain military oratory of the two generals. In the interior of this military temple a statue of Mars sleeping had been placed, and from the pillars and roof were suspended the trophies of Denain, Fontenoy, and the campaign of Italy, which would still have decorated that edifice had not the demon of conquest possessed Bonaparte. Two Invalides, each said to be a hundred years old, stood beside the Minister of War; and the bust of the emancipator of America was placed under the trophy composed of the flags of Aboukir. In a word, recourse was had to every sort of charlatanism usual on such occasions. In the evening there was a numerous assembly at the Luxembourg, and Bonaparte took much credit to himself for the effect produced on this remarkable day. He had only to wait ten days for his removal to the Tuileries, and precisely on that day the national mourning for Washington was to cease, for which a general mourning for freedom might well have been substituted.

I have said very little about Murat in the course of these Memoirs except mentioning the brilliant part he performed in several battles. Having now arrived at the period of his marriage with one of Napoleon's sisters I take the opportunity of returning to the interesting events which preceded that alliance.

His fine and well-proportioned form, his great physical strength and somewhat refined elegance of manner,—the fire of his eye, and his fierce courage in battle, gave to Murat rather the character of one of those 'preux chevaliers' so well described by Ariosto and Taro, than that a Republican soldier. The nobleness of his look soon made the lowness of his birth be forgotten. He was affable, polished, gallant; and in the field of battle twenty men headed by Murat were worth a whole regiment. Once only he showed himself under the influence of fear, and the reader shall see in what circumstance it was that he ceased to be himself.[114]

When Bonaparte in his first Italian campaign had forced Wurmser to retreat into Mantua with 28,000 men, he directed Miollis, with only 4000 men, to oppose any sortie that might be attempted by the Austrian general. In one of these sorties Murat, who was at the head of a very weak detachment, was ordered to charge Wurmser. He was afraid, neglected to execute the order, and in a moment of confusion said that he was wounded. Murat immediately fell into disgrace with the General-in-Chief, whose 'aide de camp' he was.

Murat had been previously sent to Paris to present to the Directory the first colours taken by the French army of Italy in the actions of Dego and Mondovi, and it was on this occasion that he got acquainted with Madame Tallien and the wife of his General. But he already knew the beautiful Caroline Bonaparte, whom he had seen at Rome in the residence of her brother Joseph, who was then discharging the functions of ambassador of the Republic. It appears that Caroline was not even indifferent to him, and that he was the successful rival of

114 Marshal Lannes, so brave and brilliant in war and so well able to appreciate courage, one day sharply rebuked a colonel for having punished a young officer just arrived from school at Fontainebleau because he gave evidence of fear in his first engagement. "Know, colonel," said he, "none but a poltroon (the term was even more strong) will boast that he never was afraid."—Bourrienne.

the Princess Santa Croce's son, who eagerly sought the honour of her hand. Madame Tallien and Madame Bonaparte received with great kindness the first 'aide de camp', and as they possessed much influence with the Directory, they solicited, and easily obtained for him, the rank of brigadier-general. It was somewhat remarkable at that time Murat, notwithstanding his newly-acquired rank, to remain Bonaparte's 'aide de camp', the regulations not allowing a general-in-chief an 'aide de camp' of higher rank than chief of brigade, which was equal to that of colonel. This insignificant act was, therefore, rather a hasty anticipation of the prerogatives everywhere reserved to princes and kings.

It was after having discharged this commission that Murat, on his return to Italy, fell into disfavour with the General-in Chief. He indeed looked upon him with a sort of hostile feeling, and placed him in Reille's division, and afterwards Baraguey d'Hilliers'; consequently, when we went to Paris, after the treaty of Campo-Formio, Murat was not of the party. But as the ladies, with whom he was a great favourite, were not devoid of influence with the Minister of War, Murat was, by their interest, attached to the engineer corps in the expedition to Egypt. On board the Orient he remained in the most complete disgrace. Bonaparte did not address a word to him during the passage; and in Egypt the General-in-Chief always treated him with coldness, and often sent him from the headquarters on disagreeable services. However, the General-in-Chief having opposed him to Mourad Bey, Murat performed such prodigies of valour in every perilous encounter that he effaced the transitory stain which a momentary hesitation under the walls of Mantua had left on his character. Finally, Murat so powerfully contributed to the success of the day at Aboukir that Bonaparte, glad to be able to carry another laurel plucked in Egypt to France, forgot the fault which had made so unfavourable an impression, and was inclined to efface from his memory other things that he had heard to the disadvantage of Murat; for I have good reasons for believing, though Bonaparte never told me so, that Murat's name, as well as that of Charles, escaped from the lips of Junot when he made his indiscreet communication to Bonaparte at the walls of Messoudiah. The charge of grenadiers, commanded by Murat on the 19th Brumaire in the hall of the Five Hundred, dissipated all the remaining traces of dislike; and in those moments when Bonaparte's political views subdued every other sentiment of his mind, the rival of the Prince Santa Croce received the command of the Consular Guard.[115]

It may reasonably be supposed that Madame Bonaparte, in endeavouring to win the friendship of Murat by aiding his promotion, had in view to gain one partisan more to oppose to the family and brothers of Bonaparte; and of this kind of support she had much need. Their jealous hatred was displayed on every occasion; and the amiable Josephine, whose only fault was being too much of the woman, was continually tormented by sad presentiments. Carried away by the easiness of her character, she did not perceive that the coquetry which enlisted for her so many defenders also supplied her implacable enemies with weapons to use against her.

In this state of things Josephine, who was well convinced that she had attached Murat to herself by the bonds of friendship and gratitude, and ardently desired to see him united to Bonaparte by a family connection, favoured with all her influence his marriage with Caroline.

---

115 Joachim Murat (1771-1616), the son of an innkeeper, aide de camp to Napoleon in Italy, etc.; Marshal, 1804; Prince in 1806; Grand Admiral; Grand Duc de Berg et de Clesves, 1808; King of Naples, 1808. Shot by Bourbons 13th October 1815. Married Caroline Bonaparte (third sister of Napoleon) 20th January 1800.

She was not ignorant that a close intimacy had already sprung up at Milan between Caroline and Murat, and she was the first to propose a marriage. Murat hesitated, and went to consult M. Collot, who was a good adviser in all things, and whose intimacy with Bonaparte had initiated him into all the secrets of the family. M. Collot advised Murat to lose no time, but to go to the First Consul and formally demand the hand of his sister. Murat followed his advice. Did he do well? It was to this step that he owed the throne of Naples. If he had abstained he would not have been shot at Pizzo. 'Sed ipsi Dei fata rumpere non possunt!'

However that might be, Bonaparte received, more in the manner of a sovereign than of a brother in arms, the proposal of Murat. He heard him with unmoved gravity, said that he would consider the matter, but gave no positive answer.

This affair was, as may be supposed, the subject of conversation in the evening in the salon of the Luxembourg. Madame Bonaparte employed all her powers of persuasion to obtain the First Consul's consent, and her efforts were seconded by Hortense, Eugène, and myself, "Murat," said he, among other things, "Murat is an innkeeper's son. In the elevated rank where glory and fortune have placed me, I never can mix his blood with mine! Besides, there is no hurry: I shall see by and by." We forcibly described to him the reciprocal affection of the two young people, and did not fail to bring to his observation Murat's devoted attachment to his person, his splendid courage and noble conduct in Egypt. "Yes," said he, with warmth, "I agree with you; Murat was superb at Aboukir." We did not allow so favourable a moment to pass by. We redoubled our entreaties, and at last he consented. When we were together in his cabinet in the evening, "Well, Bourrienne," said he to me, "you ought to be satisfied, and so am I, too, everything considered. Murat is suited to my sister, and then no one can say that I am proud, or seek grand alliances. If I had given my sister to a noble, all your Jacobins would have raised a cry of counter-revolution. Besides, I am very glad that my wife is interested in this marriage, and you may easily suppose the cause. Since it is determined on, I will hasten it forward; we have no time to lose. If I go to Italy I will take Murat with me. I must strike a decisive blow there. Adieu."

When I entered the First Consul's chamber at seven o'clock the next day he appeared even more satisfied than on the preceding evening with the resolution he had taken. I easily perceived that in spite of all his cunning, he had failed to discover the real motive which had induced Josephine to take so lively an interest respecting Murat's marriage with Caroline. Still Bonaparte's satisfaction plainly showed that his wife's eagerness for the marriage had removed all doubt in his mind of the falsity of the calumnious reports which had prevailed respecting her intimacy with Murat.

The marriage of Murat and Caroline was celebrated at the Luxembourg, but with great modesty. The First Consul did not yet think that his family affairs were affairs of state. But previously to the celebration a little comedy was enacted in which I was obliged to take a part, and I will relate how.

At the time of the marriage of Murat Bonaparte had not much money, and therefore only gave his sister a dowry of 30,000 francs. Still, thinking it necessary to make her a marriage present, and not possessing the means to purchase a suitable one, he took a diamond necklace which belonged to his wife and gave it to the bride. Josephine was not at all pleased with this robbery, and taxed her wits to discover some means of replacing her necklace.

Josephine was aware that the celebrated jeweler Foncier possessed a magnificent collection of fine pearls which had belonged, as he said, to the late Queen, Marie Antoinette. Having ordered them to be brought to her to examine them, she thought there were sufficient to make a very fine necklace. But to make the purchase 250,000 francs were required, and how to get them was the difficulty. Madame Bonaparte had recourse to Berthier, who was then Minister of War. Berthier, after biting his nails according to his usual habit, set about the liquidation of the debts due for the hospital service in Italy with as much speed as possible; and as in those days the contractors whose claims were admitted overflowed with gratitude towards their patrons, through whom they obtained payment, the pearls soon passed from Foncier's shop to the casket of Madame Bonaparte.

The pearls being thus obtained, there was still another difficulty, which Madame Bonaparte did not at first think of. How was she to wear a necklace purchased without her husband's knowledge? Indeed it was the more difficult for her to do so as the First Consul knew very well that his wife had no money, and being, if I may be allowed the expression, something of the busybody, he knew, or believed he knew, all Josephine's jewels. The pearls were therefore condemned to remain more than a fortnight in Madame Bonaparte's casket without her daring to use them. What a punishment for a woman! At length her vanity overcame her prudence, and being unable to conceal the jewels any longer, she one day said to me, "Bourrienne, there is to be a large party here to-morrow, and I absolutely must wear my pearls. But you know he will grumble if he notices them. I beg, Bourrienne, that you will keep near me. If he asks me where I got my pearls I must tell him, without hesitation, that I have had them a long time."

Everything happened as Josephine feared and hoped.

Bonaparte, on seeing the pearls, did not fail to say to Madame, "What is it you have got there? How fine you are to-day! Where did you get these pearls? I think I never saw them before."—"Oh! 'mon Dieu'! you have seen them a dozen times! It is the necklace which the Cisalpine Republic gave me, and which I now wear in my hair."—"But I think—"—"Stay: ask Bourrienne, he will tell you."—"Well, Bourrienne, what do you say to it? Do you recollect the necklace?"—"Yes, General, I recollect very well seeing it before." This was not untrue, for Madame Bonaparte had previously shown me the pearls. Besides, she had received a pearl necklace from the Cisalpine Republic, but of incomparably less value than that purchased from Foncier. Josephine performed her part with charming dexterity, and I did not act amiss the character of accomplice assigned me in this little comedy. Bonaparte had no suspicions. When I saw the easy confidence with which Madame Bonaparte got through this scene, I could not help recollecting Suzanne's reflection on the readiness with which well-bred ladies can tell falsehoods without seeming to do so.

CHAPTER XXXI

1800

Before taking up his quarters in the Tuileries the First Consul organised his secret police, which was intended, at the same time, to be the rival or check upon Fouché's police. Duroc and Moncey were at first the Director of this police; afterwards Davoust and Junot. Madame Bonaparte called this business a vile system of espionage. My remarks on the inutility of the measure were made in vain. Bonaparte had the weakness at once to fear Fouché and to think him necessary. Fouché, whose talents at this trade are too well known to need my approbation, soon discovered this secret institution, and the names of all the subaltern agents employed by the chief agents. It is difficult to form an idea of the nonsense, absurdity, and falsehood contained in the bulletins drawn up by the noble and ignoble agents of the police. I do not mean to enter into details on this nauseating subject; and I shall only trespass on the reader's patience by relating, though it be in anticipation, one fact which concerns myself, and which will prove that spies and their wretched reports cannot be too much distrusted.

During the second year of the Consulate we were established at Malmaison. Junot had a very large sum at his disposal for the secret police of the capital. He gave 3000 francs of it to a wretched manufacturer of bulletins; the remainder was expended on the police of his stable and his table. In reading one of these daily bulletins I saw the following lines:

> "M. de Bourrienne went last night to Paris. He entered an hotel of the Faubourg St. Germain, Rue de Varenne, and there, in the course of a very animated discussion, he gave it to be understood that the First Consul wished to make himself King."

As it happens, I never had opened my mouth, either respecting what Bonaparte had said to me before we went to Egypt or respecting his other frequent conversations with me of the same nature, during this period of his Consulship. I may here observe, too, that I never quitted, nor ever could quit Malmaison for a moment. At any time, by night or day, I was subject to be called for by the First Consul, and, as very often was the case, it so happened that on the night in question he had dictated to me notes and instructions until three o'clock in the morning.

Junot came every day to Malmaison at eleven o'clock in the morning. I called him that day into my cabinet, when I happened to be alone. "Have you not read your bulletin?" said I, "Yes, I have."—"Nay, that is impossible."—"Why?"—"Because, if you had, you would have suppressed an absurd story which relates to me."—"Ah!" he replied, "I am sorry on your account, but I can depend on my agent, and I will not alter a word of his report." I then told him all that had taken place on that night; but he was obstinate, and went away unconvinced.

Every morning I placed all the papers which the First Consul had to read on his table, and among the first was Junot's report. The First Consul entered and read it; on coming to the passage concerning me he began to smile.

"Have you read this bulletin?"—"Yes, General."—"What an ass that Junot is! It is a long time since I have known that."—"How he allows himself to be entrapped! Is he still here?"—"I believe so. I have just seen him, and made observations to him, all in good part, but he would hear nothing."—"Tell him to come here." When Junot appeared Bonaparte began—"Imbecile that you are! how could you send me such reports as these? Do you not read them? How shall I be sure that you will not compromise other persons equally unjustly? I want positive facts, not inventions. It is some time since your agent displeased me; dismiss him directly." Junot wanted to justify himself, but Bonaparte cut him short—"Enough!—It is settled!"

I related what had passed to Fouché, who told me that, wishing to amuse himself at Junot's expense, whose police agents only picked up what they heard related in coffeehouses, gaming-houses, and the Bourse, he had given currency to this absurd story, which Junot had credited and reported, as he did many other foolish tales. Fouché often caught the police of the Palace in the snares he laid for them, and thus increased his own credit.

This circumstance, and others of the same nature, induced the First Consul to attach less importance than at first he had to his secret police, which seldom reported anything but false and silly stories. That wretched police! During the time I was with him it embittered his life, and often exasperated him against his wife, his relations, and friends.[116] Rapp, who was as frank as he was brave, tells us in his Memoirs (p. 233) that when Napoleon, during his retreat from Moscow, while before Smolenski, heard of the attempt of Mallet, he could not get over the adventure of the Police Minister, Savary, and the Prefect of Police, Pasquier. "Napoleon," says Rapp, "was not surprised that these wretches (he means the agents of the police) who crowd the salons and the taverns, who insinuate themselves everywhere and obstruct everything, should not have found out the plot, but he could not understand the weakness of the Duc de Rovigo. The very police which professed to divine everything had let themselves be taken by surprise." The police possessed no foresight or faculty of prevention. Every silly thing that transpired was reported either from malice or stupidity. What was heard was misunderstood or distorted in the recital, so that the only result of the plan was mischief and confusion.

The police as a political engine is a dangerous thing. It foments and encourages more false conspiracies than it discovers or defeats real ones. Napoleon has related "that M. de la Rochefoucauld formed at Paris a conspiracy in favour of the King, then at Mittau, the first act of which was to be the death of the Chief of the Government. The plot being discovered, a trusty person belonging to the police was ordered to join it and become one of the most active agents. He brought letters of recommendation from an old gentleman in Lorraine who had held a distinguished rank in the army of Condé." After this, what more can be wanted? A hundred examples could not better show the vileness of such a system. Napoleon, when fallen, himself thus disclosed the scandalous means employed by his Government.

Napoleon on one occasion, in the Isle of Elba, said to an officer who was conversing with him about France, "You believe, then, that the police agents foresee everything and know everything? They invent more than they discover. Mine, I believe, was better than that they have got now, and yet it was often only by mere chance, the imprudence of the parties implicated, or the treachery of some of them, that something was discovered after a week or fortnight's exertion." Napoleon, in directing this officer to transmit letters to him under the cover of a commercial correspondence, to quiet his apprehensions that the

116 Bourrienne, it must be remembered, was a sufferer from the vigilance of this police.

correspondence might be discovered, said, "Do you think, then, that all letters are opened at the post office? They would never be able to do so. I have often endeavoured to discover what the correspondence was that passed under mercantile forms, but I never succeeded. The post office, like the police, catches only fools."

Since I am on the subject of political police, that leprosy of modern society, perhaps I may be allowed to overstep the order of time, and advert to its state even in the present day.

The Minister of Police, to give his prince a favourable idea of his activity, contrives great conspiracies, which he is pretty sure to discover in time, because he is their originator. The inferior agents, to find favour in the eyes of the Minister, contrive small plots. It would be difficult to mention a conspiracy which has been discovered, except when the police agents took part in it, or were its promoters. It is difficult to conceive how those agents can feed a little intrigue, the result at first, perhaps, of some petty ill-humour and discontent which, thanks to their skill, soon becomes a great affair. How many conspiracies have escaped the boasted activity and vigilance of the police when none of its agents were parties. I may instance Babeuf's conspiracy, the attempt at the camp at Grenelle, the 18th Brumaire, the infernal machine, Mallet, the 20th of March, the affair of Grenoble, and many others.

The political police, the result of the troubles of the Revolution, has survived them. The civil police for the security of property, health, and order, is only made a secondary object, and has been, therefore, neglected. There are times in which it is thought of more consequence to discover whether a citizen goes to mass or confession than to defeat the designs of a band of robbers. Such a state of things is unfortunate for a country; and the money expended on a system of superintendence over persons alleged to be suspected, in domestic inquisitions, in the corruption of the friends, relations, and servants of the man marked out for destruction might be much better employed. The espionage of opinion, created, as I have said, by the revolutionary troubles, is suspicious, restless, officious, inquisitorial, vexatious, and tyrannical. Indifferent to crimes and real offences, it is totally absorbed in the inquisition of thoughts. Who has not heard it said in company, to some one speaking warmly, "Be moderate, M——— is supposed to belong to the police." This police enthralled Bonaparte himself in its snares, and held him a long time under the influence of its power.

I have taken the liberty thus to speak of a scourge of society of which I have been a victim. What I here state may be relied on. I shall not speak of the week during which I had to discharge the functions of Prefect of Police, namely, from the 13th to the 20th of March, 1815. It may well be supposed that though I had not held in abhorrence the infamous system which I have described, the important nature of the circumstances and the short period of my administration must have prevented me from making complete use of the means placed at my disposal. The dictates of discretion, which I consider myself bound to obey, forbid me giving proofs of what I advance. What it was necessary to do I accomplished without employing violent or vexatious means; and I can take on myself to assert that no one has cause to complain of me. Were I to publish the list of the persons I had orders to arrest, those of them who are yet living would be astonished that the only knowledge they had of my being the Prefect of Police was from the Moniteur. I obtained by mild measures, by persuasion, and reasoning what I could never have got by violence. I am not divulging any secrets of office, but I believe I am rendering a service to the public in pointing out what I have often observed while an unwilling confidant in the shameful manoeuvres of that political institution.

The word ideologue was often in Bonaparte's mouth; and in using it he endeavoured to throw ridicule on those men whom he fancied to have a tendency towards the doctrine of indefinite perfectibility. He esteemed them for their morality, yet he looked on them as dreamers seeking for the type of a universal constitution, and considering the character of man in the abstract only. The ideologues, according to him, looked for power in institutions; and that he called metaphysics. He had no idea of power except in direct force. All benevolent men who speculate on the amelioration of human society were regarded by Bonaparte as dangerous, because their maxims and principles were diametrically opposed to the harsh and arbitrary system he had adopted. He said that their hearts were better than their heads, and, far from wandering with them in abstractions, he always said that men were only to be governed by fear and interest. The free expression of opinion through the press has been always regarded by those who are not led away by interest or power as useful to society. But Bonaparte held the liberty of the press in the greatest horror; and so violent was his passion when anything was urged in its favour that he seemed to labour under a nervous attack. Great man as he was, he was sorely afraid of little paragraphs.[117]

117 Joseph Bonaparte fairly enough remarks on this that such writings had done great harm in those extraordinary times (Erreurs, tome i, p. 259). Metternich, writing in 1827 with distrust of the proceedings of Louis XVIII., quotes, with approval, Napoleon's sentiments on this point. "Napoleon, who could not have been wanting in the feeling of power, said to me, 'You see me master of France; well, I would not undertake to govern her for three months with liberty of the press. Louis XVIII., apparently thinking himself stronger than Napoleon, is not content with allowing the press its freedom, but has embodied its liberty in the charter" (Metternich, tome iv, p. 391.)

CHAPTER XXXII

1800

Of the three brothers to whom the 18th Brumaire gave birth Bonaparte speedily declared himself the eldest, and hastened to assume all the rights of primogeniture. He soon arrogated to himself the whole power. The project he had formed, when he favoured the revolution of the 18th Fructidor, was now about to be realized. It was then an indispensable part of his plan that the Directory should violate the constitution in order to justify a subsequent subversion of the Directory. The expressions which escaped him from time to time plainly showed that his ambition was not yet satisfied, and that the Consulship was only a state of probation preliminary to the complete establishment of monarchy. The Luxembourg was then discovered to be too small for the Chief of the Government, and it was resolved that Bonaparte should inhabit the Tuileries. Still great prudence was necessary to avoid the quicksands which surrounded him! He therefore employed great precaution in dealing with the susceptibilities of the Republicans, taking care to inure them gradually to the temperature of absolute power. But this mode of treatment was not sufficient; for such was Bonaparte's situation between the Jacobins and the Royalists that he could not strike a blow at one party without strengthening the other. He, however, contrived to solve this difficult problem, and weakened both parties by alternately frightening each. "You see, Royalists," he seemed to say, "if you do not attach yourselves to my government the Jacobins will again rise and bring back the reign of terror and its scaffold." To the men of the Revolution he, on the other hand, said, "See, the counter-Revolution appears, threatening reprisals and vengeance. It is ready to overwhelm you; my buckler can alone protect you from its attacks." Thus both parties were induced, from their mutual fear of each other, to attach themselves to Bonaparte; and while they fancied they were only placing themselves under the protection of the Chief of the Government, they were making themselves dependent on an ambitious man, who, gradually bending them to his will, guided them as he chose in his political career. He advanced with a firm step; but he never neglected any artifice to conceal, as long as possible, his designs.

I saw Bonaparte put in motion all his concealed springs; and I could not help admiring his wonderful address.

But what most astonished me was the control he possessed over himself, in repressing any premature manifestation of his intentions which might prejudice his projects. Thus, for instance, he never spoke of the Tuileries but under the name of "the Palace of the Government," and he determined not to inhabit, at first, the ancient palace of the kings of France alone. He contented himself with selecting the royal apartments, and proposed that the Third Consul should also reside in the Tuileries, and in consequence he occupied the Pavilion of Flora. This skilful arrangement was perfectly in accordance with the designation of "Palace of the Government" given to the Tuileries, and was calculated to deceive, for a time, the most clear-sighted.

The moment for leaving the Luxembourg having arrived, Bonaparte still used many deceptive precautions. The day filed for the translation of the seat of government was the

30th Pluviôse, the previous day having been selected for publishing the account of the votes taken for the acceptance of the new Constitution. He had, besides, caused the insertion in the 'Moniteur' of the eulogy on Washington, pronounced, by M. de Fontanes, the decadi preceding, to be delayed for ten days. He thought that the day when he was about to take so large a step towards monarchy would be well chosen for entertaining the people of Paris with grand ideas of liberty, and for coupling his own name with that of the founder of the free government of the United States.

At seven o'clock on the morning of the 30th Pluviôse I entered, as usual, the chamber of the First Consul. He was in a profound sleep, and this was one of the days on which I had been desired to allow him to sleep a little longer than usual. I have often observed that General Bonaparte appeared much less moved when on the point of executing any great design than during the time of projecting it, so accustomed was he to think that what he had resolved on in his mind, was already done.

When I returned to Bonaparte he said to me, with a marked air of satisfaction, "Well, Bourrienne, to-night, at last, we shall sleep in the Tuileries. You are better off than I: you are not obliged to make a spectacle of yourself, but may go your own road there. I must, however, go in procession: that disgusts me; but it is necessary to speak to the eyes. That has a good effect on the people. The Directory was too simple, and therefore never enjoyed any consideration. In the army simplicity is in its proper place; but in a great city, in a palace, the Chief of the Government must attract attention in every possible way, yet still with prudence. Josephine is going to look out from Lebrun's apartments; go with her, if you like; but go to the cabinet as soon as you see me alight from my horse."

I did not go to the review, but proceeded to the Tuileries, to arrange in our new cabinet the papers which it was my duty to take care of, and to prepare everything for the First Consul's arrival. It was not until the evening that I learned, from the conversation in the salon, where there was a numerous party, what had taken place in the course of the day.

At one o'clock precisely Bonaparte left the Luxembourg. The procession was, doubtless, far from approaching the magnificent parade of the Empire: but as much pomp was introduced as the state of things in France permitted. The only real splendour of that period consisted in fine troops. Three thousand picked men, among whom was the superb regiment of the Guides, had been ordered out for the occasion: all marched in the greatest order; with music at the head of each corps. The generals and their staffs were on horseback, the Ministers in carriages, which were somewhat remarkable, as they were almost the only private carriages then in Paris, for hackney-coaches had been hired to convey the Council of State, and no trouble had been taken to alter them, except by pasting over the number a piece of paper of the same colour as the body of the vehicle. The Consul's carriage was drawn by six white horses. With the sight of those horses was associated the recollection of days of glory and of peace, for they had been presented to the General-in-Chief of the army of Italy by the Emperor of Germany after the treaty of Campo-Formio. Bonaparte also wore the magnificent sabre given him by the Emperor Francis. With Cambacérès on his left, and Lebrun in the front of the carriage, the First Consul traversed a part of Paris, taking the Rue de Thionville, and the Quai Voltaire to the Pont Royal. Everywhere he was greeted by acclamations of joy, which at that time were voluntary, and needed not to be commanded by the police.

From the wicket of the Carrousel to the gate of the Tuileries the troops of the Consular Guard were formed in two lines, through which the procession passed—a royal custom, which made a singular contrast with an inscription in front of which Bonaparte passed on entering the courtyard. Two guard-houses had been built, one on the right and another on the left of the centre gate. On the one to the right were written these words:

> "THE TENTH OF AUGUST 1792.—ROYALTY IN FRANCE IS ABOLISHED; AND SHALL NEVER BE RE-ESTABLISHED!"

It was already re-established!

In the meantime the troops had been drawn up in line in the courtyard. As soon as the Consul's carriage stopped Bonaparte immediately alighted, and mounted, or, to speak more properly, leaped on his horse, and reviewed his troops, while the other two Consuls proceeded to the state apartments of the Tuileries, where the Council of State and the Ministers awaited them. A great many ladies, elegantly dressed in Greek costume, which was then the fashion, were seated with Madame Bonaparte at the windows of the Third Consul's apartments in the Pavilion of Flora. It is impossible to give an idea of the immense crowds which flowed in from all quarters. The windows looking to the Carrousel were let for very large sums; and everywhere arose, as if from one voice, shouts of "Long live the First Consul!" Who could help being intoxicated by so much enthusiasm?

Bonaparte prolonged the review for some time, passed down all the ranks, and addressed the commanders of corps in terms of approbation and praise. He then took his station at the gate of the Tuileries, with Murat on his right, and Lannes on his left, and behind him a numerous staff of young warriors, whose complexions had been browned by the sun of Egypt and Italy, and who had been engaged in more battles than they numbered years. When the colours of the 96th, 43d, and 34th demi-brigades, or rather their flagstaffs surmounted by some shreds, riddled by balls and blackened by powder, passed before him, he raised his hat and inclined his head in token of respect. Every homage thus paid by a great captain to standards which had been mutilated on the field of battle was saluted by a thousand acclamations. When the troops had finished defiling before him, the First Consul, with a firm step, ascended the stairs of the Tuileries.

The General's part being finished for the day, that of the Chief of the State began; and indeed it might already be said that the First Consul was the whole Consulate. At the risk of interrupting my narrative of what occurred on our arrival at the Tuileries, by a digression, which may be thought out of place, I will relate a fact which had no little weight in hastening Bonaparte's determination to assume a superiority over his colleagues. It may be remembered that when Roger Ducos and Sieyès bore the title of Consuls the three members of the Consular commission were equal, if not in fact at least in right. But when Cambacérès and Lebrun took their places, Talleyrand, who had at the same time been appointed to succeed M. Reinhart as Minister of Foreign Affairs, obtained a private audience of the First Consul in his cabinet, to which I was admitted. The observations of Talleyrand on this occasion were highly agreeable to Bonaparte, and they made too deep an impression on my mind to allow me to forget them.

"Citizen Consul," said he to him, "you have confided to me the office of Minister for Foreign Affairs, and I will justify your confidence; but I must declare to you that from this moment, I will not transact business with any but yourself. This determination does not proceed from any vain pride on my part, but is induced by a desire to serve France. In order that France may be well governed, in order that there may be a unity of action in the government, you must be First Consul, and the First Consul must have the control over all that relates directly to politics; that is to say, over the Ministry of the Interior, and the Ministry of Police, for Internal Affairs, and over my department, for Foreign Affairs; and, lastly, over the two great means of execution, the military and naval forces. It will therefore be most convenient that the Ministers of those five departments should transact business with you. The Administration of Justice and the ordering of the Finances are objects certainly connected with State politics by numerous links, which, however, are not of so intimate a nature as those of the other departments. If you will allow me, General, I should advise that the control over the Administration of Justice be given to the Second Consul, who is well versed in jurisprudence; and to the Third Consul, who is equally well acquainted with Finance, the control over that department. That will occupy and amuse them, and you, General, having at your disposal all the vital parts of the government, will be able to reach the end you aim at, the regeneration of France."

Bonaparte did not hear these remarkable words with indifference. They were too much in accordance with his own secret wishes to be listened to without pleasure; and he said to me as soon as Talleyrand had taken leave, "Do you know, Bourrienne, I think Talleyrand gives good advice. He is a man of great understanding."—"Such is the opinion," I replied, "of all who know him."—"He is perfectly right." Afterwards he added, smiling, "Tallyrand is evidently a shrewd man. He has penetrated my designs. What he advises you know I am anxious to do. But again I say, he is right; one gets on quicker by oneself. Lebrun is a worthy man, but he has no policy in his head; he is a book-maker. Cambacérès carries with him too many traditions of the Revolution. My government must be an entirely new one."

Talleyrand's advice had been so punctually followed that even on the occasion of the installation of the Consular Government, while Bonaparte was receiving all the great civil and military officers of the State in the hall of presentation, Cambacérès and Lebrun stood by more like spectators of the scene than two colleagues of the First Consul. The Minister of the Interior presented the civil authorities of Paris; the Minister of War, the staff of the 17th military division; the Minister of Marine, several naval officers; and the staff of the Consular Guard was presented by Murat. As our Consular republicans were not exactly Spartans, the ceremony of the presentations was followed by grand dinner-parties. The First Consul entertained at his table, the two other Consuls, the Ministers, and the Presidents of the great bodies of the State. Murat treated the heads of the army; and the members of the Council of State, being again seated in their hackney-coaches with covered numbers, drove off to dine with Lucien.

Before taking possession of the Tuileries we had frequently gone there to see that the repairs, or rather the whitewashing, which Bonaparte had directed to be done, was executed. On our first visit, seeing a number of red caps of liberty painted on the walls, he said to M. Lecomte, at that time the architect in charge, "Get rid of all these things; I do not like to see such rubbish."

The First Consul gave directions himself for what little alterations he wanted in his own apartments. A state bed—not that of Louis XVI.—was placed in the chamber next his cabinet, on the south side, towards the grand staircase of the Pavilion of Flora. I may as well mention here that he very seldom occupied that bed, for Bonaparte was very simple in his manner of living in private, and was not fond of state, except as a means of imposing on mankind. At the Luxembourg, at Malmaison, and during the first period that he occupied the Tuileries, Bonaparte, if I may speak in the language of common life, always slept with his wife. He went every evening down to Josephine by a small staircase leading from a wardrobe attached to his cabinet, and which had formerly been the chapel of Maria de Medici. I never went to Bonaparte's bedchamber but by this staircase; and when he came to our cabinet it was always by the wardrobe which I have mentioned. The door opened opposite the only window of our room, and it commanded a view of the garden.

As for our cabinet, where so many great, and also small events were prepared, and where I passed so many hours of my life, I can, even now, give the most minute description of it to those who like such details.

There were two tables. The best, which was the First Consul's, stood in the middle of the room, and his armchair was turned with its back to the fireplace, having the window on the right. To the right of this again was a little closet where Duroc sat, through which we could communicate with the clerk of the office and the grand apartments of the Court. When the First Consul was seated at his table in his chair (the arms of which he so frequently mutilated with his penknife) he had a large bookcase opposite to him. A little to the right, on one side of the bookcase, was another door, opening into the cabinet which led directly to the state bedchamber which I have mentioned. Thence we passed into the grand Presentation Saloon, on the ceiling of which Lebrun had painted a likeness of Louis XIV. A tri-coloured cockade placed on the forehead of the great King still bore witness of the imbecile turpitude of the Convention. Lastly came the hall of the Guards, in front of the grand staircase of the Pavilion of Flora.

My writing-table, which was extremely plain, stood near the window, and in summer I had a view of the thick foliage of the chestnut-trees; but in order to see the promenaders in the garden I was obliged to raise myself from my seat. My back was turned to the General's side, so that it required only a slight movement of the head to speak to each other. Duroc was seldom in his little cabinet, and that was the place where I gave some audiences. The Consular cabinet, which afterwards became the Imperial, has left many impressions on my mind; and I hope the reader, in going through these volumes, will not think that they have been of too slight a description.

CHAPTER XXXIII

1800

The morning after that ardently wished-for day on which we took possession of the Palace of the Kings of France I observed to Bonaparte on entering his chamber, "Well, General, you have got here without much difficulty, and with the applause of the people! Do you remember what you said to me in the Rue St. Anne nearly two years ago?"—"Ay, true enough, I recollect. You see what it is to have the mind set on a thing. Only two years have gone by! Don't you think we have not worked badly since that time? Upon the whole I am very well content. Yesterday passed off well. Do you imagine that all those who came to flatter me were sincere? No, certainly not: but the joy of the people was real. They know what is right. Besides, consult the grand thermometer of opinion, the price of the funds: on the 17th Brumaire at 11 francs, on the 20th at 16 and to-day at 21. In such a state of things I may let the Jacobins prate as they like. But let them not talk too loudly either!"

As soon as he was dressed we went to look through the Gallery of Diana and examine the statues which had been placed there by his orders. We ended our morning's work by taking complete possession of our new residence. I recollect Bonaparte saying to me, among other things, "To be at the Tuileries, Bourrienne, is not all. We must stay here. Who, in Heaven's name, has not already inhabited this palace? Ruffians, conventionalists! But hold! there is your brother's house! Was it not from those windows I saw the Tuileries besieged, and the good Louis XVI. carried off? But be assured they will not come here again!"

The Ambassadors and other foreign Ministers then in Paris were presented to the First Consul at a solemn audience. On this occasion all the ancient ceremonials belonging to the French Court were raked up, and in place of chamberlains and a grand master of ceremonies a Counsellor of State, M. Benezech, who was once Minister for Foreign Affairs, officiated.

When the Ambassadors had all arrived M. Benezech conducted them into the cabinet, in which were the three Consuls, the Ministers, and the Council of State. The Ambassadors presented their credentials to the First Consul, who handed them to the Minister for Foreign Affairs. These presentations were followed by others; for example, the Tribunal of Cassation, over which the old advocate, Target, who refused to defend Louis XVI., then presided. All this passed in view of the three Consuls; but the circumstance which distinguished the First Consul from his colleagues was, that the official personages, on leaving the audience-chamber, were conducted to Madame Bonaparte's apartments, in imitation of the old practice of waiting on the Queen after presentation to the King.

Thus old customs of royalty crept by degrees into the former abodes of royalty. Amongst the rights attached to the Crown, and which the Constitution of the year VIII. did not give to the First Consul, was one which he much desired to possess, and which, by the most happy of all usurpations, he arrogated to himself. This was the right of granting pardon. Bonaparte felt a real pleasure in saving men under the sentence of the law; and whenever the imperious necessity of his policy, to which, in truth, he sacrificed everything, permitted it, he rejoiced in the exercise of mercy. It would seem as if he were thankful to the persons to whom he rendered such service merely because he had given them occasion to be thankful to him. Such was the First Consul: I do not speak of the Emperor. Bonaparte, the First Consul, was accessible to the solicitations of friendship in favour of persons placed under proscription. The following circumstance, which interested me much, affords an incontestable proof of what I state:—

Whilst we were still at the Luxembourg, M. Defeu, a French emigrant, was taken in the Tyrol with arms in his hand by the troops of the Republic. He was carried to Grenoble, and thrown into the military prison of that town. In the course of January General Ferino, then commanding at Grenoble, received orders to put the young emigrant on his trial. The laws against emigrants taken in arms were terrible, and the judges dared not be indulgent. To be tried in the morning, condemned in the course of the day, and shot in the evening, was the usual course of those implacable proceedings. One of my cousins, the daughter of M. Poitrincourt, came from Sens to Paris to inform me of the dreadful situation of M. Defeu. She told me that he was related to the most respectable families of the town of Sens, and that everybody felt the greatest interest in his fate.

I had escaped for a few moments to keep the appointment I made with Mademoiselle Poitrincourt. On my return I perceived the First Consul surprised at finding himself alone in the cabinet, which I was not in the habit of quitting without his knowledge. "Where have you been?" said he. "I have been to see one of my relations, who solicits a favour of you."—"What is it?" I then informed him of the unfortunate situation of M. Defeu. His first answer was dreadful. "No pity! no pity for emigrants! Whoever fights against his country is a child who tries to kill his mother!" This first burst of anger being over, I returned to the charge. I urged the youth of M. Defeu, and the good effect which clemency would produce. "Well," said he, "write—

"The First Consul orders the judgment on M. Defeu to be suspended."

He signed this laconic order, which I instantly despatched to General Ferino. I acquainted my cousin with what had passed, and remained at ease as to the result of the affair.

Scarcely had I entered the chamber of the First Consul the next morning when he said to me, "Well, Bourrienne, you say nothing about your M. Defeu. Are you satisfied?"—"General, I cannot find terms to express my gratitude."—"Ah, bah! But I do not like to do things by halves. Write to Ferino that I wish M. Defeu to be instantly set at liberty. Perhaps I am serving one who will prove ungrateful. Well, so much the worse for him. As to these matters, Bourrienne, always ask them from me. When I refuse, it is because I cannot help it."

I despatched at my own expense an extraordinary courier, who arrived in time to save M. Defeu's life. His mother, whose only son he was, and M. Blanchet, his uncle, came purposely from Sens to Paris to express their gratitude to me. I saw tears of joy fall from the eyes of a mother who had appeared to be destined to shed bitter drops, and I said to her as I felt, "that I was amply recompensed by the success which had attended my efforts."

Emboldened by this success, and by the benevolent language of the First Consul, I ventured to request the pardon of M. de Frotte, who was strongly recommended to me by most honourable persons. Comte Louis de Frotte had at first opposed all negotiation for the pacification of La Vendée. At length, by a series of unfortunate combats, he was, towards the end of January, reduced to the necessity of making himself the advances which he had rejected when made by others. At this period he addressed a letter to General Guidal, in which he offered pacificatory proposals. A protection to enable him to repair to Alençon was transmitted to him. Unfortunately for M. de Frotte, he did not confine himself to writing to General Guidal, for whilst the safe-conduct which he had asked was on the way to him, he wrote to his lieutenants, advising them not to submit or consent to be disarmed. This letter was intercepted. It gave all the appearance of a fraudulent stratagem to his proposal to treat for peace. Besides, this opinion appeared to be confirmed by a manifesto of M. de Frotte, anterior, it is true, to the offers of pacification, but in which he announced to all his partisans the approaching end of Bonaparte's "criminal enterprise."

I had more trouble than in M. Defeu's case to induce the First Consul to exercise his clemency. However, I pressed him so much, I laboured so hard to convince him of the happy effect of such indulgence, that at length I obtained an order to suspend the judgment. What a lesson I then experienced of the evil which may result from the loss of time! Not supposing that matters were so far advanced as they were, I did not immediately send off the courier with the order for the suspension of the judgment. Besides, the Minister-of-Police had marked his victim, and he never lost time when evil was to be done. Having, therefore, I know not for what motive, resolved on the destruction of M. de Frotte, he sent an order to hasten his trial.

Comte Louis de Frotte was brought to trial on the 28th Pluviôse, condemned the same day, and executed the next morning, the day before we entered the Tuileries. The cruel precipitation of the Minister rendered the result of my solicitations abortive. I had reason to think that after the day on which the First Consul granted me the order for delay he had received some new accusation against M. de Frotte, for when he heard of his death he appeared to me very indifferent about the tardy arrival of the order for suspending judgment. He merely said to me, with unusual insensibility, "You should take your measures better. You see it is not my fault."

Though Bonaparte put no faith in the virtue of men, he had confidence in their honour. I had proof of this in a matter which deserves to be recorded in history. When, during the first period of our abode at the Tuileries, he had summoned the principal chiefs of La Vendée to endeavour to bring about the pacification of that unhappy country, he received Georges Cadoudal in a private audience. The disposition in which I beheld him the evening before the day appointed for this audience inspired me with the most flattering hopes. Rapp introduced Georges into the grand salon looking into the garden. Rapp left him alone with the First Consul, but on returning to the cabinet where I was he did not close either of the two doors of the state bedchamber which separated the cabinet from the salon. We saw the First Consul and Georges walk from the window to the bottom of the salon—then return—then go back again. This lasted for a long time. The conversation appeared very animated, and we heard several things, but without any connection. There was occasionally a good deal of ill-humour displayed in their tone and gestures. The interview ended in nothing. The First Consul, perceiving that Georges entertained some apprehensions for his personal safety, gave him assurances of security in the most noble manner, saying, "You take a wrong view of things, and are wrong in not coming to some understanding; but if you persist in wishing to return to your country you shall depart as freely as you came to Paris." When Bonaparte returned to his cabinet he said to Rapp, "Tell me, Rapp, why you left these doors open, and stopped with Bourrienne?" Rapp replied, "If you had closed the doors I would have opened them again. Do you think I would have left you alone with a man like that? There would have been danger in it."—"No, Rapp," said Bonaparte, "you cannot think so." When we were alone the First Consul appeared pleased with Rapp's attachment, but very vexed at Georges' refusal. He said, "He does not take a correct view of things; but the extravagance of his principles has its source in noble sentiments, which must give him great influence over his countrymen. It is necessary, however, to bring this business soon to an end."

Of all the actions of Louis XIV. that which Bonaparte most admired was his having made the Doge of Genoa send ambassadors to Paris to apologise to him. The slightest insult offered in a foreign country to the rights and dignity of France put Napoleon beside himself. This anxiety to have the French Government respected exhibited itself in an affair which made much noise at the period, but which was amicably arranged by the soothing influence of gold.

Two Irishmen, Napper Tandy and Blackwell, who had been educated in France, and whose names and rank as officers appeared in the French army list, had retired to Hamburg. The British Government claimed them as traitors to their country, and they were given up; but, as the French Government held them to be subjects of France, the transaction gave rise to bitter complaints against the Senate of Hamburg.

Blackwell had been one of the leaders of the united Irishmen. He had procured his naturalisation in France, and had attained the rank of chef d'escadron. Being sent on a secret mission to Norway, the ship in which he was embarked was wrecked on the coast of that kingdom. He then repaired to Hamburg, where the Senate placed him under arrest on the demand of Mr. Crawford, the English Minister. After being detained in prison a whole year he was conveyed to England to be tried. The French Government interfered, and preserved, if not his liberty, at least his life.

Napper Tandy was also an Irishman. To escape the search made after him, on account of the sentiments of independence which had induced him to engage in the contest for the liberty of his country, he got on board a French brig, intending to land at Hamburg and pass into Sweden. Being exempted from the amnesty by the Irish Parliament, he was claimed by the British Government, and the Senators of Hamburg forgot honour and humanity in their alarm at the danger which at that moment menaced their little republic both from England and France. The Senate delivered up Napper Tandy; he was carried to Ireland, and condemned to death, but owed the suspension of his execution to the interference of France. He remained two years in prison, when M. Otto, who negotiated with Lord Hawkesbury the preliminaries of peace, obtained the release of Napper Tandy, who was sent back to France.

The First Consul spoke at first of signal vengeance; but the Senate of Hamburg sent him a memorial, justificatory of its conduct, and backed the apology with a sum of four millions and a half, which mollified him considerably. This was in some sort a recollection of Egypt—one of those little contributions with which the General had familiarised the pashas; with this difference, that on the present occasion not a single sous went into the national treasury. The sum was paid to the First Consul through the hands of M. Chapeau Rouge.[118] I kept the four millions and a half in Dutch bonds in a secretaire for a week. Bonaparte then determined to distribute them; after paying Josephine's debts, and the whole of the great expenses incurred at Malmaison, he dictated to me a list of persons to whom he wished to make presents. My name did not escape his lips, and consequently I had not the trouble to transcribe it; but

118 A solemn deputation from the Senate arrived at the Tuileries to make public apologies to Napoleon. He again testified his indignation: and when the envoys urged their weakness he said to them. "Well and had you not the resource of weak states? was it not in your power to let them escape?" (Napoleon's Memoirs).

some time after he said to me, with the most engaging kindness, "Bourrienne, I have given you none of the money which came from Hamburg, but I will make you amends for it." He took from his drawer a large and broad sheet of printed paper, with blanks filled up in his own handwriting, and said to me, "Here is a bill for 300,000 Italian livres on the Cisalpine Republic, for the price of cannon furnished. It is endorsed Halter and Collot—I give it you." To make this understood, I ought to state that cannon had been sold to the Cisalpine Republic, for the value of which the Administrator-general of the Italian finances drew on the Republic, and the bills were paid over to M. Collot, a provision contractor, and other persons. M. Collot had given one of these bills for 300,000 livres to Bonaparte in quittance of a debt, but the latter had allowed the bill to run out without troubling himself about it. The Cisalpine Republic kept the cannons and the money, and the First Consul kept his bill. When I had examined it I said, "General, it has been due for a long time; why have you not got it paid? The endorsers are no longer liable."—"France is bound to discharge debts of this kind;" said he; "send the paper to de Fermont: he will discount it for three per cent. You will not have in ready money more than about 9000 francs of rentes, because the Italian livre is not equal to the franc." I thanked him, and sent the bill to M. de Fermont. He replied that the claim was bad, and that the bill would not be liquidated because it did not come within the classifications made by the laws passed in the months the names of which terminated in 'aire, ose, al, and or'.

I showed M. de Fermont's answer to the First Consul, who said, "Ah, bah! He understands nothing about it—he is wrong: write." He then dictated a letter, which promised very favourably for the discounting of the bill; but the answer was a fresh refusal. I said, "General, M. de Fermont does not attend to you any more than to myself." Bonaparte took the letter, read it, and said, in the tone of a man who knew beforehand what he was about to be informed of, "Well, what the devil would you have me do, since the laws are opposed to it? Persevere; follow the usual modes of liquidation, and something will come of it!" What finally happened was, that by a regular decree this bill was cancelled, torn, and deposited in the archives. These 300,000 livres formed part of the money which Bonaparte brought from Italy. If the bill was useless to me it was also useless to him. This scrap of paper merely proves that he brought more than 25,000 francs from Italy.

I never had, from the General-in-Chief of the army of Italy, nor from the General in-Chief of the army of Egypt, nor from the First Consul, for ten years, nor from the Consul for life, any fixed salary: I took from his drawer what was necessary for my expenses as well as his own. He never asked me for any account. After the transaction of the bill on the insolvent Cisalpine Republic he said to me, at the beginning of the winter of 1800, "Bourrienne, the weather is becoming very bad; I will go but seldom to Malmaison. Whilst I am at council get my papers and little articles from Malmaison; here is the key of my secretaire, take out everything that is there." I got into the carriage at two o'clock and returned at six. When he had dined I placed upon the table of his cabinet the various articles which I had found in his secretaire including 15,000 francs (somewhere about L 600 of English money) in banknotes which were in the corner of a little drawer. When he looked at them he said, "Here is money—what is the meaning of this?" I replied, "I know nothing about it, except that it was in your secretaire."— "Oh yes; I had forgotten it. It was for my trifling expenses. Here, take it." I remembered well that one summer morning he had given me his key to bring him two notes of 1000 francs for some incidental expense, but I had no idea that he had not drawn further on his little treasure.

I have stated the appropriation of the four millions and a half, the result of the extortion inflicted on the Senate of Hamburg, in the affair of Napper Tandy and Blackwell.

The whole, however, was not disposed of in presents. A considerable portion was reserved for paying Josephine's debts, and this business appears to me to deserve some remarks.

The estate of Malmaison had cost 160,000 francs. Josephine had purchased it of M. Lecouteulx while we were in Egypt. Many embellishments, and some new buildings, had been made there; and a park had been added, which had now become beautiful. All this could not be done for nothing, and besides, it was very necessary that what was due for the original purchase should be entirely discharged; and this considerable item was not the only debt of Josephine. The creditors murmured, which had a bad effect in Paris; and I confess I was so well convinced that the First Consul would be extremely displeased that I constantly delayed the moment of speaking to him on the subject. It was therefore with extreme satisfaction I learned that M. de Talleyrand had anticipated me. No person was more capable than himself of gilding the pill, as one may say, to Bonaparte. Endowed with as much independence of character as of mind, he did him the service, at the risk of offending him, to tell him that a great number of creditors expressed their discontent in bitter complaints respecting the debts contracted by Madame Bonaparte during his expedition to the East. Bonaparte felt that his situation required him promptly to remove the cause of such complaints. It was one night about half-past eleven o'clock that M. Talleyrand introduced this delicate subject. As soon he was gone I entered the little cabinet; Bonaparte said to me, "Bourrienne, Talleyrand has been speaking to me about the debts of my wife. I have the money from Hamburg—ask her the exact amount of her debts: let her confess all. I wish to finish, and not begin again. But do not pay without showing me the bills of those rascals: they are a gang of robbers."

Hitherto the apprehension of an unpleasant scene, the very idea of which made Josephine tremble, had always prevented me from broaching this subject to the First Consul; but, well pleased that Talleyrand had first touched upon it, I resolved to do all in my power to put an end to the disagreeable affair.

The next morning I saw Josephine. She was at first delighted with her husband's intentions; but this feeling did not last long. When I asked her for an exact account of what she owed she entreated me not to press it, but content myself with what she should confess. I said to her, "Madame, I cannot deceive you respecting the disposition of the First Consul. He believes that you owe a considerable sum, and is willing to discharge it. You will, I doubt not, have to endure some bitter reproaches, and a violent scene; but the scene will be just the same for the whole as for a part. If you conceal a large proportion of your debts at the end of some time murmurs will recommence, they will reach the ears of the First Consul, and his anger will display itself still more strikingly. Trust to me—state all; the result will be the same; you will hear but once the disagreeable things he will say to you; by reservations you will renew them incessantly." Josephine said, "I can never tell all; it is impossible. Do me the service to keep secret what I say to you. I owe, I believe, about 1,200,000 francs, but I wish to confess only 600,000; I will contract no more debts, and will pay the rest little by little out of my savings."—"Here, Madame, my first observations recur. As I do not believe he estimates your debts at so high a sum as 600,000 francs, I can warrant that you will not experience more displeasure for acknowledging to 1,200,000 than to 600,000; and by going so far you will get rid of them for ever."—"I can never do it, Bourrienne; I know him; I can never support his violence." After a quarter of an hour's further discussion on the subject

I was obliged to yield to her earnest solicitation, and promise to mention only the 600,000 francs to the First Consul.

The anger and ill-humour of Bonaparte may be imagined. He strongly suspected that his wife was dissembling in some respect; but he said, "Well, take 600,000 francs, but liquidate the debts for that sum, and let me hear nothing more on the subject. I authorise you to threaten these tradesmen with paying nothing if they do not reduce their enormous charges. They ought to be taught not to be so ready in giving credit." Madame Bonaparte gave me all her bills. The extent to which the articles had been overcharged, owing to the fear of not being paid for a long period, and of deductions being made from the amount, was inconceivable. It appeared to me, also, that there must be some exaggeration in the number of articles supplied. I observed in the milliner's bill thirty-eight new hats, of great price, in one month. There was likewise a charge of 1800 francs for heron plumes, and 800 francs for perfumes. I asked Josephine whether she wore out two hats in one day? She objected to this charge for the hats, which she merely called a mistake. The impositions which the saddler attempted, both in the extravagance of his prices and in charging for articles which he had not furnished, were astonishing. I need say nothing of the other tradesmen, it was the same system of plunder throughout.

I availed myself fully of the First Consul's permission, and spared neither reproaches nor menaces. I am ashamed to say that the greater part of the tradesmen were contented with the half of what they demanded. One of them received 35,000 francs for a bill of 80,000; and he had the impudence to tell me that he made a good profit nevertheless. Finally, I was fortunate enough, after the most vehement disputes, to settle everything for 600,000 francs. Madame Bonaparte, however, soon fell again into the same excesses, but fortunately money became more plentiful. This inconceivable mania of spending money was almost the sole cause of her unhappiness. Her thoughtless profusion occasioned permanent disorder in her household until the period of Bonaparte's second marriage, when, I am informed, she became regular in her expenditure. I could not say so of her when she was Empress in 1804.[119] The amiable Josephine had not less ambition in little things than her husband had in great. She felt pleasure in acquiring and not in possessing. Who would suppose it? She grew tired of the beauty of the park of Malmaison, and was always asking me to take her out on the high road, either in the direction of Nanterre, or on that of Marly, in the midst of the dust occasioned by the passing of carriages. The noise of the high road appeared to her preferable

119 Notwithstanding her husband's wish, she could never bring her establishment into any order or rule. He wished that no tradesmen should ever reach her, but he was forced to yield on this point. The small inner rooms were filled with them, as with artists of all sorts. She had a mania for having herself painted, and gave her portraits to whoever wished for one, relations, 'femmes de chambre', even to tradesmen. They never ceased bringing her diamonds, jewels, shawls, materials for dresses, and trinkets of all kinds; she bought everything without ever asking the price; and generally forgot what she had purchased. . . All the morning she had on a shawl which she draped on her shoulders with a grace I have seen in no one else. Bonaparte, who thought her shawls covered her too much, tore them off, and sometimes threw them into the fire; then she sent for another (Rémusat, tome ii. pp. 343-345). After the divorce her income, large as it was, was insufficient, but the Emperor was more compassionate then, and when sending the Comte Mollien to settle her affairs gave him strict orders "not to make her weep" (Meneval, tome iii. p.237)

to the calm silence of the beautiful avenues of the park, and in this respect Hortense had the same taste as her mother. This whimsical fancy astonished Bonaparte, and he was sometimes vexed at it. My intercourse with Josephine was delightful; for I never saw a woman who so constantly entered society with such an equable disposition, or with so much of the spirit of kindness, which is the first principle of amiability. She was so obligingly attentive as to cause a pretty suite of apartments to be prepared at Malmaison for me and my family.

She pressed me earnestly, and with all her known grace, to accept it; but almost as much a captive at Paris as a prisoner of state, I wished to have to myself in the country the moments of liberty I was permitted to enjoy. Yet what was this liberty? I had bought a little house at Ruel, which I kept during two years and a half. When I saw my friends there, it had to be at midnight, or at five o'clock in the morning; and the First Consul would often send for me in the night when couriers arrived. It was for this sort of liberty I refused Josephine's kind offer. Bonaparte came once to see me in my retreat at Ruel, but Josephine and Hortense came often. It was a favourite walk with these ladies.

At Paris I was less frequently absent from Bonaparte than at Malmaison. We sometimes in the evening walked together in the garden of the Tuileries after the gates were closed. In these evening walks he always wore a gray greatcoat, and a round hat. I was directed to answer, "The First Consul," to the sentinel's challenge of, "Who goes there?" These promenades, which were of much benefit to Bonaparte, and me also, as a relaxation from our labours, resembled those which we had at Malmaison. As to our promenades in the city, they were often very amusing.

At the period of our first inhabiting the Tuileries, when I saw Bonaparte enter the cabinet at eight o'clock in the evening in his gray coat, I knew he would say, "Bourrienne, come and take a turn." Sometimes, then, instead of going out by the garden arcade, we would take the little gate which leads from the court to the apartments of the Duc d'Angoulême. He would take my arm, and we would go to buy articles of trifling value in the shops of the Rue St. Honoré; but we did not extend our excursions farther than Rue de l'Arbre Sec. Whilst I made the shopkeeper exhibit before us the articles which I appeared anxious to buy he played his part in asking questions.

Nothing was more amusing than to see him endeavouring to imitate the careless and jocular tone of the young men of fashion. How awkward was he in the attempt to put on dandy airs when pulling up the corners of his cravat he would say, "Well, Madame, is there anything new to-day? Citizen, what say they of Bonaparte? Your shop appears to be well supplied. You surely have a great deal of custom. What do people say of that buffoon, Bonaparte?" He was made quite happy one day when we were obliged to retire hastily from a shop to avoid the attacks drawn upon us by the irreverent tone in which Bonaparte spoke of the First Consul.

CHAPTER XXXIV

1800

The destruction of men and the construction of monuments were two things perfectly in unison in the mind of Bonaparte. It may be said that his passion for monuments almost equalled his passion for war;[120] but as in all things he disliked what was little and mean, so he liked vast constructions and great battles. The sight of the colossal ruins of the monuments of Egypt had not a little contributed to augment his natural taste for great structures. It was not so much the monuments themselves that he admired, but the historical recollections they perpetuate, the great names they consecrate, the important events they attest. What should he have cared for the column which we beheld on our arrival in Alexandria had it not been Pompey's pillar? It is for artists to admire or censure its proportions and ornaments, for men of learning to explain its inscriptions; but the name of Pompey renders it an object of interest to all.

When endeavouring to sketch the character of Bonaparte, I ought to have noticed his taste for monuments, for without this characteristic trait something essential is wanting to the completion of the portrait. This taste, or, as it may more properly be called, this passion for monuments, exercised no small influence on his thoughts and projects of glory; yet it did not deter him from directing attention to public improvements of a less ostentatious kind. He wished for great monuments to perpetuate the recollection of his glory; but at the same time he knew how to appreciate all that was truly useful. He could very rarely be reproached for rejecting any plan without examination; and this examination was a speedy affair, for his natural tact enabled him immediately to see things in their proper light.

Though most of the monuments and embellishments of Paris are executed from the plans of men of talent, yet some owe their origin to circumstances merely accidental. Of this I can mention an example.

I was standing at the window of Bonaparte's' cabinet, which looked into the garden of the Tuileries. He had gone out, and I took advantage of his absence to arise from my chair, for I was tired of sitting. He had scarcely been gone a minute when he unexpectedly returned to ask me for a paper. "What are you doing there, Bourrienne? I'll wager anything you are admiring the ladies walking on the terrace."—"Why, I must confess I do sometimes amuse myself in that way," replied I; "but I assure you, General, I was now thinking of something else. I was looking at that villainous left bank of the Seine, which always annoys me with the gaps in its dirty quay, and the floodings which almost every winter prevent communication

120 Take pleasure, if you can, in reading your returns. The good condition of my armies is owing to my devoting to them one or two hours in every day. When the monthly returns of my armies and of my fleets, which form twenty thick volumes, are sent to me, I give up every other occupation in order to read them in detail and to observe the difference between one monthly return and another. No young girl enjoys her novel so much as I do these returns! (Napoleon to Joseph, 20th August 1806—Du Casse, tome iii. p. 145).

with the Faubourg St. Germain; and I was thinking I would speak to you on the subject." He approached the window, and, looking out, said, "You are right, it is very ugly; and very offensive to see dirty linen washed before our windows. Here, write immediately: 'The quay of the École de Natation is to be finished during next campaign.' Send that order to the Minister of the Interior." The quay was finished the year following.

An instance of the enormous difference which frequently appears between the original estimates of architects and their subsequent accounts I may mention what occurred in relation to the Palace of St. Cloud. But I must first say a word about the manner in which Bonaparte originally refused and afterwards took possession of the Queen's pleasure-house. Malmaison was a suitable country residence for Bonaparte as long as he remained content with his town apartments in the little Luxembourg; but that Consular 'bagatelle' was too confined in comparison with the spacious apartments in the Tuileries. The inhabitants of St. Cloud, well-advised, addressed a petition to the Legislative Body, praying that their deserted chateau might be made the summer residence of the First Consul. The petition was referred to the Government; but Bonaparte, who was not yet Consul for life, proudly declared that so long as he was at the head of affairs, and, indeed, for a year afterwards, he would accept no national recompense. Sometime after we went to visit the palace of the 18th Brumaire. Bonaparte liked it exceedingly, but all was in a state of complete dilapidation. It bore evident marks of the Revolution. The First Consul did not wish, as yet, to burden the budget of the State with his personal expenses, and he was alarmed at the enormous sum required to render St. Cloud habitable. Flattery had not yet arrived at the degree of proficiency which it subsequently attained; but even then his flatterers boldly assured him he might take possession of St. Cloud for 25,000 francs. I told the First Consul that considering the ruinous state of the place, I could to say that the expense would amount to more than 1,200,000 francs. Bonaparte determined to have a regular estimate of the expense, and it amounted to nearly 3,000,000. He thought it a great sum; but as he had resolved to make St. Cloud his residence he gave orders for commencing the repairs, the expense of which, independently of the furniture, amounted to 6,000,000. So much for the 3,000,000 of the architect and the 25,000 francs of the flatterers.

When the First Consul contemplated the building of the Pont des Arts we had a long conversation on the subject. I observed that it would be much better to build the bridge of stone. "The first object of monuments of this kind," said I, "is public utility. They require solidity of appearance, and their principal merit is duration. I cannot conceive, General, why, in a country where there is abundance of fine stone of every quality, the use of iron should be preferred."—"Write," said Bonaparte, "to Fontaine and Percier, the architects, and ask what they think of it." I wrote and they stated in their answer that "bridges were intended for public utility and the embellishment of cities. The projected bridge between the Louvre and the Quatre-Nations would unquestionably fulfil the first of these objects, as was proved by the great number of persons who daily crossed the Seine at that point in boats; that the site fixed upon between the Pont Neuf and the Tuileries appeared to be the best that could be chosen for the purpose; and that on the score of ornament Paris would gain little by the construction of an iron bridge, which would be very narrow, and which, from its light form, would not correspond with the grandeur of the two bridges between which it would be placed."

When we had received the answer of MM. Percier and Fontaine, we again had a conversation on the subject of the bridge. I told the First Consul that I perfectly concurred in the opinion of MM. Fontaine and Percier; however, he would have his own way, and thus was authorised the construction of the toy which formed a communication between the Louvre and the Institute. But no sooner was the Pont des Arts finished than Bonaparte pronounced it to be mean and out of keeping with the other bridges above and below it. One day when visiting the Louvre he stopped at one of the windows looking towards the Pont des Arts and said, "There is no solidity, no grandeur about that bridge. In England, where stone is scarce, it is very natural that iron should be used for arches of large dimensions. But the case is different in France, where the requisite material is abundant."

The infernal machine of the 3d Nivôse, of which I shall presently speak more at length, was the signal for vast changes in the quarter of the Tuileries. That horrible attempt was at least so far attended by happy results that it contributed to the embellishment of Paris. It was thought more advisable for the Government to buy and pull down the houses which had been injured by the machine than to let them be put under repair. As an example of Bonaparte's grand schemes in building I may mention that, being one day at the Louvre, he pointed towards St. Germain l'Auxerrois and said to me, "That is where I will build an imperial street. It shall run from here to the Barrière du Trône. It shall be a hundred feet broad, and have arcades and plantations. This street shall be the finest in the world."

The palace of the King of Rome, which was to face the Pont de Jena and the Champ de Mars, would have been in some measure isolated from Paris, with which, however, it was to be connected by a line of palaces. These were to extend along the quay, and were destined as splendid residences for the Ambassadors of foreign sovereigns, at least as long as there should be any sovereigns in Europe except Napoleon. The Temple of Glory, too, which was to occupy the site of the Church of la Madeleine, was never finished. If the plan of this monument proved the necessity, which Bonaparte felt of constantly holding out stimulants to his soldiers, its relinquishment was at least a proof of his wisdom. He who had reestablished religious worship in France, and had restored to its destination the church of the Invalides, which was for a time metamorphosed into the Temple of Mars, foresaw that a Temple of Glory would give birth to a sort of paganism incompatible with the ideas of the age.

The recollection of the magnificent Necropolis of Cairo frequently recurred to Bonaparte's mind. He had admired that city of the dead, which he had partly contributed to people; and his design was to make, at the four cardinal points of Paris, four vast cemeteries on the plan of that at Cairo.

Bonaparte determined that all the new streets of Paris should be 40 feet wide, and be provided with foot-pavements; in short, he thought nothing too grand for the embellishment of the capital of a country which he wished to make the first in the world. Next to war, he regarded the embellishment of Paris as the source of his glory; and he never considered a victory fully achieved until he had raised a monument to transmit its memory to posterity. He, wanted glory, uninterrupted glory, for France as well as for himself. How often, when talking over his schemes, has he not said, "Bourrienne, it is for France I am doing all this! All I wish, all I desire, the end of all my labours is, that my name should be indissolubly connected with that of France!"

Paris is not the only city, nor is France the only kingdom, which bears traces of Napoleon's passion for great and useful monuments. In Belgium, in Holland, in Piedmont, in all Italy, he executed great improvements. At Turin a splendid bridge was built over the Po, in lieu of an old bridge which was falling in ruins.

How many things were undertaken and executed in Napoleon's short and eventful reign!

To obviate the difficulty of communication between Metz and Mayence a magnificent road was made, as if by magic, across impracticable marshes and vast forests. Mountains were cut through and ravines filled up. He would not allow nature more than man to resist him. One day when he was proceeding to Belgium by the way of Givet, he was detained for a short time at Little Givet, on the right bank of the Meuse, in consequence of an accident which happened to the ferry-boat. He was within a gunshot of the fortress of Charlemont, on the left bank, and in the vexation which the delay occasioned he dictated the following decree: "A bridge shall be built over the Meuse to join Little Givet to Great Givet. It shall be terminated during the ensuing campaign." It was completed within the prescribed time. In the great work of bridges and highways Bonaparte's chief object was to remove the obstacles and barriers which nature had raised up as the limits of old France so as to form a junction with the provinces which he successively annexed to the Empire. Thus in Savoy a road, smooth as a garden-walk, superseded the dangerous ascents and descents of the wood of Bramant; thus was the passage of Mont Cenis a pleasant promenade at almost every season of the year; thus did the Simplon bow his head, and Bonaparte might have said, "There are now my Alps," with more reason than Louis XIV. said, "There are now no Pyrenees."[121]

Such was the implicit confidence which Bonaparte reposed in me that I was often alarmed at the responsibility it obliged me to incur.[122]

121 Metternich (tome iv. p. 187) says on this subject, 'If you look closely at the course of human affairs you will make strange discoveries. For instance, that the Simplon Pass has contributed as surely to Napoleon's immortality as the numerous works done in the reign of the Emperor Francis will fail to add to his.

122 Of this confidence the following instructions for me, which he dictated to Duroc, afford sufficient proof:— "1st. Citizen Bourrienne shall open all the letters addressed to the First Consul, Vol, and present them to him three times a day, or oftener in case of urgent business. The letters shall be deposited in the cabinet when they are opened. Bourrienne is to analyse all those which are of secondary interest, and write the First Consul's decision on each letter. The hours for presenting the letters shall be, first, when the Consul rises; second, a quarter of an hour before dinner; and third, at eleven at night. "2d. He is to have the superintendence of the Topographical office, and of an office of Translation, in which there shall be a German and an English clerk. Every day he shall present to the First Consul, at the hours above mentioned the German and English journals, together with a translation. With respect to the Italian journals, it will only be necessary to mark what the First Consul is to read. "3d. He shall keep a register of appointments to offices under Government; a second, for appointments to judicial posts; a third for appointments to places abroad; and a fourth, for the situations of receivers and great financial posts, where he is to inscribe the names of all the individuals whom the First Consul may refer to him. These registers must be written by his own hand, and must be kept entirely private. "4th. Secret correspondence, and the different reports of surveillance, are to be addressed directly to Bourrienne, and transmitted by him to the hand of the First Consul, by whom they will be returned without the intervention of any third party. "6th. There shall be a register for all that relates to secret extraordinary expenditure. Bourrienne shall write the whole with his own hand, in order that the business may be kept from the knowledge of any one. "7th. He shall despatch all the business which may be referred to him, either from Citizen Duroc, or from the cabinet of the First Consul, taking care to arrange everything so

Official business was not the only labour that devolved upon me. I had to write to the dictation of the First Consul during a great part of the day, or to decipher his writing, which was always the most laborious part of my duty. I was so closely employed that I scarcely ever went out; and when by chance I dined in town, I could not arrive until the very moment of dinner, and I was obliged to run away immediately after it. Once a month, at most, I went without Bonaparte to the Comédie Française, but I was obliged to return at nine o'clock, that being the hour at which we resumed business. Corvisart, with whom I was intimately acquainted, constantly expressed his apprehensions about my health; but my zeal carried me through every difficulty, and during our stay at the Tuileries I cannot express how happy I was in enjoying the unreserved confidence of the man on whom the eyes of all Europe were filed. So perfect was this confidence that Bonaparte, neither as General, Consul, nor Emperor, ever gave me any fixed salary. In money matters we were still comrades: I took from his funds what was necessary to defray my expenses, and of this Bonaparte never once asked me for any account.

He often mentioned his wish to regenerate public education, which he thought was ill managed. The central schools did not please him; but he could not withhold his admiration from the Polytechnic School, the finest establishment of education that was ever founded, but which he afterwards spoiled by giving it a military organisation. In only one college of Paris the old system of study was preserved: this was the Louis-le-Grand, which had received the name of Pritanée. The First Consul directed the Minister of the Interior to draw up a report on that establishment; and he himself went to pay an unexpected visit to the Pritanée, accompanied by M. Lebrun and Duroc. He remained there upwards of an hour, and in the evening he spoke to me with much interest on the subject of his visit. "Do you know, Bourrienne," said he, "that I have been performing the duties of professor?"—"You, General!"—"Yes! and I did not acquit myself badly. I examined the pupils in the mathematical class; and I recollected enough of my Bezout to make some demonstrations before them. I went everywhere, into the bedrooms and the dining-room. I tasted the soup, which is better than we used to have at Brienne. I must devote serious attention to public education and the management of the colleges. The pupils must have a uniform. I observed some well and others ill dressed. That will not do. At college, above all places, there should be equality. But I was much pleased with the pupils of the Pritanée. I wish to know the names of those I examined, and I have desired Duroc to report them to me. I will give them rewards; that stimulates young people. I will provide for some of them."

On this subject Bonaparte did not confine himself to an empty scheme. After consulting with the headmaster of the Pritanée, he granted pensions of 200 francs to seven or eight of the most distinguished pupils of the establishment, and he placed three of them in the department of Foreign Affairs, under the title of diplomatic pupils.[123]

What I have just said respecting the First Consul's visit to the Pritanée reminds me of a very extraordinary circumstance which arose out of it. Among the pupils at the Pritanée there was a son of General Miackzinski, who died fighting under the banners of the Republic. Young Miackzinski was then sixteen or seventeen years of age. He soon quitted the college,

---

as to secure secrecy. "(*Signed*) "BONAPARTE, *First Consul. "Paris, 13th Germinal, year VIII.* "(3d. April 1800.)"

123 This institution of diplomatic pupils was originally suggested by M. de Talleyrand.

entered the army as a volunteer, and was one of a corps reviewed by Bonaparte, in the plain of Sablons. He was pointed out to the First Consul, who said to him, "I knew your father. Follow his example, and in six months you shall be an officer." Six months elapsed, and Miackzinski wrote to the First Consul, reminding him of his promise. No answer was returned, and the young man then wrote a second letter as follows:

> You desired me to prove myself worthy of my father; I have done so.
> You promised that I should be an officer in six months; seven have elapsed since that promise was made. When you receive this letter I shall be no more. I cannot live under a Government the head of which breaks his word.

Poor Miackzinski kept his word but too faithfully. After writing the above letter to the First Consul he retired to his chamber and blew out his brains with a pistol. A few days after this tragical event Miackzinski's commission was transmitted to his corps, for Bonaparte had not forgotten him. A delay in the War Office had caused the death of this promising young man. Bonaparte was much affected at the circumstance, and he said to me, "These Poles have such refined notions of honour . . . Poor Sulkowski, I am sure, would have done the same."

At the commencement of the Consulate it was gratifying to see how actively Bonaparte was seconded in the execution of plans for the social regeneration of France; all seemed animated with new life, and every one strove to do good as if it were a matter of competition.

Every circumstance concurred to favour the good intentions of the First Consul. Vaccination, which, perhaps, has saved as many lives as war has sacrificed, was introduced into France by M. d'Liancourt; and Bonaparte, immediately appreciating the value of such a discovery, gave it his decided approbation. At the same time a council of Prizes was established, and the old members of the Constituent Assembly were invited to return to France. It was for their sake and that of the Royalists that the First Consul recalled them, but it was to please the Jacobins, whom he was endeavouring to conciliate, that their return was subject to restrictions. At first the invitation to return to France extended only to those who could prove that they had voted in favour of the abolition of nobility. The lists of emigrants were closed, and committees were appointed to investigate their claims to the privilege of returning.

From the commencement of the month of Germinal the reorganisation of the army of Italy had proceeded with renewed activity. The presence in Paris of the fine corps of the Consular Guard, added to the desire of showing themselves off in gay uniforms, had stimulated the military ardour of many respectable young men of the capital. Taking advantage of this circumstance the First Consul created a corps of volunteers destined for the army of reserve, which was to remain at Dijon. He saw the advantage of connecting a great number of families with his cause, and imbuing them with the spirit of the army. This volunteer corps wore a yellow uniform which, in some of the salons of Paris where it was still the custom to ridicule everything, obtained for them the nickname of "canaries." Bonaparte, who did not always relish a joke, took this in very ill part, and often expressed to me his vexation at it. However, he was gratified to observe in the composition of this corps a first specimen of privileged soldiers; an idea which he acted upon when he created the orderly gendarmes in the campaign of Jena, and when he organised the guards of honour after the disasters of Moscow.

In every action of his life Bonaparte had some particular object in view. I recollect his saying to me one day, "Bourrienne, I cannot yet venture to do anything against the regicides; but I will let them see what I think of them. To-morrow I shall have some business with Abrial respecting the organisation of the court of Cassation. Target, who is the president of that court, would not defend Louis XVI. Well, whom do you think I mean to appoint in his place? . . . Tronchet, who did defend the king. They may say what they please; I care not."[124]

Tronchet was appointed.

Nearly about the same time the First Consul, being informed of the escape of General Mack, said to me, "Mack may go where he pleases; I am not afraid of him. But I will tell you what I have been thinking. There are some other Austrian officers who were prisoners with Mack; among the number is a Count Dietrichstein, who belongs to a great family in Vienna. I will liberate them all. At the moment of opening a campaign this will have a good effect. They will see that I fear nothing; and who knows but this may procure me some admirers in Austria." The order for liberating the Austrian prisoners was immediately despatched. Thus Bonaparte's acts of generosity, as well as his acts of severity and his choice of individuals, were all the result of deep calculation.

This unvarying attention to the affairs of the Government was manifest in all he did. I have already mentioned the almost simultaneous suppression of the horrible commemoration of the month of January, and the permission for the revival of the opera balls. A measure something similar to this was the authorisation of the festivals of Longchamps, which had been forgotten since the Revolution. He at the same time gave permission for sacred music to be performed at the opera. Thus, while in public acts he maintained the observance of the Republican calendar, he was gradually reviving the old calendar by seasons of festivity. Shrove-Tuesday was marked by a ball, and Passion-week by promenades and concerts.

124 On this, as on many other occasions, the cynicism of Bonaparte's language does not admit of a literal translation.

CHAPTER XXXV

1800

It sometimes happens that an event which passes away unnoticed at the time of its occurrence acquires importance from events which subsequently ensue. This reflection naturally occurs to my mind now that I am about to notice the correspondence which passed between Louis XVIII. and the First Consul. This is certainly not one of the least interesting passages in the life of Bonaparte.

But I must first beg leave to make an observation on the 'Memorial of St. Helena.' That publication relates what Bonaparte said respecting the negotiations between Louis XVIII. and himself; and I find it necessary to quote a few lines on the subject, in order to show how far the statements contained in the Memorial differ from the autograph letters in my possession.

At St. Helena Napoleon said that he never thought of the princes of the House of Bourbon. This is true to a certain point. He did not think of the princes of the House of Bourbon with the view of restoring them to their throne; but it has been shown, in several parts of these Memoirs, that he thought of them very often, and on more than one occasion their very names alarmed him.[125]

The substance of the two letters given in the 'Memorial of St. Helena' is correct. The ideas are nearly the same as those of the original letters. But it is not surprising that, after the lapse of so long an interval, Napoleon's memory should somewhat have failed him. However, it will not, I presume, be deemed unimportant if I present to the reader literal copies of this correspondence; together with the explanation of some curious circumstances connected with it.

The following is Louis XVIII's letter:—

125 The Memorial states that "A letter was delivered to the First Consul by Lebrun who received it from the Abbé de Montesquieu, the secret agent of the Bourbons in Paris." This letter which was very cautiously written, said:— "You are long delaying the restoration of my throne. It is to be feared you are suffering favourable moments to escape. You cannot secure the happiness of France without me, and I can do nothing for France without you. Hasten, then, to name the offices which you would choose for your friends." The answer, Napoleon said, was as follows:— "I have received your royal highness' letter. I have always taken a lively interest in your misfortunes, and those of your family. You must not think of appearing in France; you could only return here by trampling over a hundred thousand dead bodies. I shall always be happy to do anything that can alleviate your fate and help to banish the recollection of your misfortunes."—Bourrienne.

February 20,1800.

> SIR—Whatever may be their apparent conduct, men like you never inspire alarm. You have accepted an eminent station, and I thank you for having done so. You know better than any one how much strength and power are requisite to secure the happiness of a great nation. Save France from her own violence, and you will fulfil the first wish of my heart. Restore her King to her, and future generations will bless your memory. You will always be too necessary to the State for me ever to be able to discharge, by important appointments, the debt of my family and myself.
>
> (*Signed*) LOUIS.

The First Consul was much agitated on the reception of this letter. Though he every day declared his determination to have nothing to do with the Princes, yet he hesitated whether or no he should reply to this overture. The numerous affairs which then occupied his mind favoured this hesitation. Josephine and Hortense conjured him to hold out hope to the King, as by so doing he would in no way pledge himself, and would gain time to ascertain whether he could not ultimately play a far greater part than that of Monk. Their entreaties became so urgent that he said to me, "These devils of women are mad! The Faubourg St. Germain has turned their heads! They make the Faubourg the guardian angel of the royalists; but I care not; I will have nothing to do with them."

Madame Bonaparte said she was anxious he should adopt the step she proposed in order to banish from his mind all thought of making himself King. This idea always gave rise to a painful foreboding which she could never overcome. In the First Consul's numerous conversations with me he discussed with admirable sagacity Louis XVIII.'s proposition and its consequences. "The partisans of the Bourbons," said he, "are deceived if they suppose I am the man to play Monk's part." Here the matter rested, and the King's letter remained on the table. In the interim Louis XVIII. wrote a second letter, without any date. It was as follows:

> You must have long since been convinced, General, that you possess my esteem. If you doubt my gratitude, fix your reward and mark out the fortune of your friends. As to my principles, I am a Frenchman, merciful by character, and also by the dictates of reason. No, the victor of Lodi, Castiglione, and Arcola, the conqueror of Italy and Egypt, cannot prefer vain celebrity to real glory. But you are losing precious time. We may ensure the glory of France. I say we, because I require the aid of Bonaparte, and he can do nothing without me. General, Europe observes you. Glory awaits you, and I am impatient to restore peace to my people.
>
> (*Signed*) LOUIS.

This dignified letter the First Consul suffered to remain unanswered for several weeks; at length he proposed to dictate an answer to me. I observed, that as the King's letters were autographs, it would be more proper that he should write himself. He then wrote with his own hand the following:

> SIR—I have received your letter, and I thank you for the compliments you address to me. You must not seek to return to France. To do so you must trample over a hundred thousand dead bodies. Sacrifice your interest to the repose and happiness of France, and history will render you justice. I am not insensible to the misfortunes of your family. I shall learn with pleasure, and shall willingly contribute to ensure, the tranquillity of your retirement.
>
> (*Signed*) BONAPARTE.

He showed me this letter, saying, "What do you think of it? is it not good?" He was never offended when I pointed out to him an error of grammar or style, and I therefore replied, "As to the substance, if such be your resolution, I have nothing to say against it; but," added I, "I must make one observation on the style. You cannot say that you shall learn with pleasure to ensure, etc." On reading the passage over again he thought he had pledged himself too far in saying that he would willingly contribute, etc. He therefore scored out the last sentence, and interlined, "I shall contribute with pleasure to the happiness and tranquillity of your retirement."

The answer thus scored and interlined could not be sent off, and it lay on the table with Bonaparte's signature affixed to it.

Some time after he wrote another answer, the three first paragraphs of which were exactly alike that first quoted; but for the last paragraph he substituted the following:

> "I am not insensible to the misfortunes of your family; and I shall learn with pleasure that you are surrounded with all that can contribute to the tranquillity of your retirement."

By this means he did not pledge himself in any way, not even in words, for he himself made no offer of contributing to the tranquillity of the retirement. Every day which augmented his power and consolidated his position diminished, he thought, the chances of the Bourbons; and seven months were suffered to intervene between the date of the King's first letter and the answer of the First Consul, which was written on the 2d Vendemiaire, year IX. (24th September 1800) just when the Congress of Luneville was on the point of opening.

Some days after the receipt of Louis XVIII.'s letter we were walking in the gardens of Malmaison; he was in good humour, for everything was going on to his mind. "Has my wife been saying anything more to you about the Bourbons?" said he.—"No, General."—"But when you converse with her you concur a little in her opinions. Tell me why you wish the Bourbons back? You have no interest in their return, nothing to expect from them. Your family rank is not high enough to enable you to obtain any great post. You would be nothing under them. Through the patronage of M. de Chambonas you got the appointment of Secretary of Legation at Stuttgart; but had it not been for the change you would have remained all your life in that or some inferior post. Did you ever know men rise by their own merit under kings? Everything depends on birth, connection, fortune, and intrigue. Judge things more accurately; reflect more maturely on the future."—"General," replied I, "I am quite of your opinion on one point. I never received gift, place, or favour from the Bourbons; and I have not the vanity to believe that I should ever have attained any important Appointment. But you must not forget that my nomination as Secretary of Legation at Stuttgart preceded the overthrow of the throne only by a few days; and I cannot infer, from what took place under circumstances unfortunately too certain, what might have happened in the reverse case. Besides, I am not actuated by personal feelings; I consider not my own interests, but those of France. I wish you to hold the reins of government as long as you live; but you have no children, and it is tolerably certain that you will have none by Josephine. What will become of us when you are gone? You talk of the future; but what will be the future fate of France? I have often heard you say that your brothers are not—"—"You are right," said he, abruptly interrupting me. "If I do not live thirty years to complete my work you will have a long series of civil wars after my death. My brothers will not suit France; you know what they are. A violent conflict will therefore arise among the most distinguished generals, each of whom will think himself entitled to succeed me."—"Well, General, why not take means to obviate the mischief you foresee?"—"Do you imagine I do not think of it? But look at the difficulties that stand in my way. How are so many acquired rights and material results to be secured against the efforts of a family restored to power, and returning with 80,000 emigrants and the influence of fanaticism? What would become of those who voted for the death of the King—the men who acted a conspicuous part in the Revolution—the national domains, and a multitude of things that have been done during twelve years? Can you see how far reaction would extend?"—"General, need I remind you that Louis, in his letter, guarantees the contrary of all you apprehend? I know what will be your answer; but are you not able to impose whatever conditions you may think fit? Grant what is asked of you only at that price. Take three or four years; in that time you may ensure the happiness of France by institutions conformable to her wants. Custom and habit would give them a power which it would not be easy to destroy; and even supposing such a design were entertained, it could not be accomplished. I have heard you say it is wished you should act the part of Monk; but you well know the difference between a general opposing the usurper of a crown, and one whom victory and peace have raised above the ruins of a subverted throne, and who restores it voluntarily to those who have long occupied it. You are well aware what you call ideology will not again be revived; and—"—"I know what you are going to say; but it all amounts to nothing. Depend upon it, the Bourbons will think they have reconquered their inheritance, and will dispose of it as they please. The most sacred pledges, the most positive promises, will be violated. None but fools will trust them. My resolution is formed; therefore let us say no more on the subject. But I know how these women torment you. Let them mind their knitting, and leave me to do what I think right."

Every one knows the adage, 'Si vis pacem para bellum'. Had Bonaparte been a Latin scholar he would probably have reversed it and said, 'Si vis bellum para pacem'. While seeking to establish pacific relations with the powers of Europe the First Consul was preparing to strike a great blow in Italy. As long as Genoa held out, and Massena continued there, Bonaparte did not despair of meeting the Austrians in those fields which not four years before had been the scenes of his success. He resolved to assemble an army of reserve at Dijon. Where there was previously nothing he created everything. At that period of his life the fertility of his imagination and the vigour of his genius must have commanded the admiration of even his bitterest enemies. I was astonished at the details into which he entered. While every moment was engrossed by the most important occupations he sent 24,000 francs to the hospital of Mont St. Bernard. When he saw that his army of reserve was forming, and everything was going on to his liking, he said to me, "I hope to fall on the rear of Melas before he is aware I am in Italy . . . that is to say, provided Genoa holds out. But MASSENA is defending it."

On the 17th of March, in a moment of gaiety and good humour, he desired me to unroll Chauchard's great map of Italy. He lay down upon it, and desired me to do likewise. He then stuck into it pins, the heads of which were tipped with wax, some red and some black. I silently observed him; and awaited with no little curiosity the result of this plan of campaign. When he had stationed the enemy's corps, and drawn up the pins with red heads on the points where he hoped to bring his own troops, he said to me, "Where do you think I shall beat Melas?"—"How the devil should I know?"—"Why, look here, you fool! Melas is at Alessandria with his headquarters. There he will remain until Genoa surrenders. He has in Alessandria his magazines, his hospitals, his artillery, and his reserves. Crossing the Alps here (pointing to the Great Mont St. Bernard) I shall fall upon Melas, cut off his communications with Austria, and meet him here in the plains of Scrivia" (placing a red pin at San Giuliano). Finding that I looked on this manoeuvre of pins as mere pastime, he addressed to me some of his usual compliments, such as fool, ninny, etc., and then proceeded to demonstrate his plans more clearly on the map. At the expiration of a quarter of an hour we rose; I folded up the map, and thought no more of the matter.

Four months after this, when I was at San Giuliano with Bonaparte's portfolio and despatches, which I had saved from the rout which had taken place during the day, and when that very evening I was writing at Torre di Galifolo the bulletin of the battle to Napoleon's dictation, I frankly avowed my admiration of his military plans. He himself smiled at the accuracy of his own foresight.

The First Consul was not satisfied with General Berthier as War Minister, and he superseded him by Carnot,[126] who had given great proofs of firmness and integrity, but who, nevertheless, was no favourite of Bonaparte, on account of his decided republican principles. Berthier was too slow in carrying out the measures ordered, [duplicated line removed here D.W.] and too lenient in the payment of past charges and in new contracts. Carnot's appointment took place on the 2d of April 1800; and to console Berthier, who, he knew, was more at home in the camp than in the office, he dictated to me the following letter for him:—

PARIS, *2d April 1800.*

> CITIZEN-GENERAL,—The military talents of which you have given so many proofs, and the confidence of the Government, call you to the command of an army. During the winter you have *reorganised* the War Department, and you have provided, as far as circumstances would permit, for the wants of our armies. During the spring and summer it must be your task to lead our troops to victory, which is the effectual means of obtaining peace and consolidating the Republic.

126 There were special reasons for the appointment of Carnot, Berthier was required with his master in Italy, while Carnot, who had so long ruled the armies of the Republic, was better fitted to influence Moreau, at this time advancing into Germany. Carnot probably fulfilled the main object of his appointment when he was sent to Moreau, and succeeded in getting that general, with natural reluctance, to damage his own campaign by detaching a large body of troops into Italy. Berthier was reappointed to the Ministry on the 8th of October 1800,—a very speedy return if he had really been disgraced.

Bonaparte laughed heartily while he dictated this epistle, especially when he uttered the word which I have marked in italics. Berthier set out for Dijon, where he commenced the formation of the army of reserve.

The Consular Constitution did not empower the First Consul to command an army out of the territory of France. Bonaparte therefore wished to keep secret his long-projected plan of placing himself at the head of the army of Italy, which he then for the first time called the grand army. I observed that by his choice of Berthier nobody could be deceived, because it must be evident that he would have made another selection had he not intended to command in person. He laughed at my observation.

Our departure from Paris was fixed for the 6th of May, or, according to the republican calendar, the 16th Floréal. Bonaparte had made all his arrangements and issued all his orders; but still he did not wish it to be known that he was going to take the command of the army. On the eve of our departure, being in conference with the two other Consuls and the Ministers, he said to Lucien, "Prepare, to-morrow morning, a circular to the prefects, and you, Fouché, will publish it in the journals. Say I am gone to Dijon to inspect the army of reserve. You may add that I shall perhaps go as far as Geneva; but you must affirm positively that I shall not be absent longer than a fortnight. You, Cambacérès, will preside to-morrow at the Council of State. In my absence you are the Head of the Government. State that my absence will be but of short duration, but specify nothing. Express my approbation of the Council of State; it has already rendered great services, and I shall be happy to see it continue in the course it has hitherto pursued. Oh! I had nearly forgotten—you will at the same time announce that I have appointed Joseph a Councillor of State. Should anything happen I shall be back again like a thunderbolt. I recommend to you all the great interests of France, and I trust that I shall shortly be talked of in Vienna and in London."

We set out at two in the morning, taking the Burgundy road, which we had already so often travelled under very different circumstances.

On the journey Bonaparte conversed about the warriors of antiquity, especially Alexander, Caesar, Scipio, and Hannibal. I asked him which he preferred, Alexander or Caesar. "I place Alexander in the first rank," said he, "yet I admire Caesar's fine campaign in Africa. But the ground of my preference for the King of Macedonia is the plan, and above all the execution, of his campaign in Asia. Only those who are utterly ignorant of war can blame Alexander for having spent seven months at the siege of Tyre. For my part, I would have stayed there seven years had it been necessary. This is a great subject of dispute; but I look upon the siege of Tyre, the conquest of Egypt, and the journey to the Oasis of Ammon as a decided proof of the genius of that great captain. His object was to give the King of Persia (of whose force he had only beaten a feeble advance-guard at the Granicus and Issus) time to reassemble his troops, so that he might overthrow at a blow the colossus which he had as yet only shaken. By pursuing Darius into his states Alexander would have separated himself from his reinforcements, and would have met only scattered parties of troops who would have drawn him into deserts where his army would have been sacrificed. By persevering in the taking of Tyre he secured his communications with Greece, the country he loved as dearly as I love France, and in whose glory he placed his own. By taking possession of the rich province of Egypt he forced Darius to come to defend or deliver it, and in so doing to march half-way to meet him. By representing himself as the son of Jupiter he worked upon the ardent feelings of the Orientals in a way that powerfully seconded his designs. Though he died at thirty-three what a name he has left behind him!"

Though an utter stranger to the noble profession of arms, yet I could admire Bonaparte's clever military plans and his shrewd remarks on the great captains of ancient and modern times. I could not refrain from saying, "General, you often reproach me for being no flatterer, but now I tell you plainly I admire you." And certainly, I really spoke the true sentiments of my mind.

VOLUME II

1800-1803

CHAPTER I

1800

It cannot be denied that if, from the 18th Brumaire to the epoch when Bonaparte began the campaign, innumerable improvements had been made in the internal affairs of France, foreign affairs could not be seen with the same satisfaction. Italy had been lost, and from the frontiers of Provence the Austrian camp fires were seen. Bonaparte was not ignorant of the difficulties of his position, and it was even on account of these very difficulties that, whatever might be the result of his hardy enterprise, he wished to escape from it as quickly as possible. He cherished no illusions, and often said all must be staked to gain all.

The army which the First Consul was preparing to attack was numerous, well disciplined, and victorious.

His, with the exception of a very small number of troops, was composed of conscripts; but these conscripts were commanded by officers whose ardour was unparalleled. Bonaparte's fortune was now to depend on the winning or losing of a battle. A battle lost would have dispelled all the dreams of his imagination, and with them would have vanished all his immense schemes for the future of France. He saw the danger, but was not intimidated by it; and trusting to his accustomed good fortune, and to the courage and fidelity of his troops, he said, "I have, it is true, many conscripts in my army, but they are Frenchmen. Four years ago did I not with a feeble army drive before me hordes of Sardinians and Austrians, and scour the face of Italy? We shall do so again. The sun which now shines on us is the same that shone at Arcola and Lodi. I rely on Massena. I hope he will hold out in Genoa. But should famine oblige him to surrender, I will retake Genoa in the plains of the Scrivia. With what pleasure shall I then return to my dear France! Ma belle France."

At this moment, when a possible, nay, a probable chance, might for ever have blasted his ambitious hopes, he for the first time spoke of France as his. Considering the circumstances in which we then stood, this use of the possessive pronoun "my" describes more forcibly than anything that can be said the flashes of divination which crossed Bonaparte's brain when he was wrapped up in his chimerical ideas of glory and fortune.

In this favourable disposition of mind the First Consul arrived at Martigny on the 20th of May. Martigny is a convent of Bernardins, situated in a valley where the rays of the sun scarcely ever penetrate. The army was in full march to the Great St. Bernard. In this gloomy solitude did Bonaparte wait three days, expecting the fort of Bard, situated beyond the mountain and covering the road to Yvree, to surrender. The town was carried on the 21st of May, and on the third day he learned that the fort still held out, and that there were no indications of its surrender. He launched into complaints against the commander of the siege, and said, "I am weary of staying in this convent; those fools will never take Bard; I must go myself and see what can be done. They cannot even settle so contemptible an affair without me!" He immediately gave orders for our departure.

The grand idea of the invasion of Italy by crossing Mont St. Bernard emanated exclusively from the First Consul. This miraculous achievement justly excited the admiration of the world. The incredible difficulties it presented did not daunt the courage of Bonaparte's troops. His generals, accustomed as they had been to brave fatigue and danger, regarded without concern the gigantic enterprise of the modern Hannibal.

A convent or hospice, which had been established on the mountain for the purpose of affording assistance to solitary travellers, sufficiently bespeaks the dangers of these stormy regions. But the St. Bernard was now to be crossed, not by solitary travellers, but by an army. Cavalry, baggage, limbers, and artillery were now to wend their way along those narrow paths where the goat-herd cautiously picks his footsteps. On the one hand masses of snow, suspended above our heads, every moment threatened to break in avalanches, and sweep us away in their descent. On the other, a false step was death. We all passed, men and horse, one by one, along the goat paths. The artillery was dismounted, and the guns, put into excavated trunks of trees, were drawn by ropes.

I have already mentioned that the First Consul had transmitted funds to the hospice of the Great St. Bernard. The good fathers had procured from the two valleys a considerable supply of cheese, bread, and wine. Tables were laid out in front of the hospice, and each soldier as he defiled past took a glass of wine and a piece of bread and cheese, and then resigned his place to the next. The fathers served, and renewed the portions with admirable order and activity.

The First Consul ascended the St. Bernard with that calm self-possession and that air of indifference for which he was always remarkable when he felt the necessity of setting an example and exposing himself to danger. He asked his guide many questions about the two valleys, inquired what were the resources of the inhabitants, and whether accidents were as frequent as they were said to be. The guide informed him that the experience of ages enabled the inhabitants to foresee good or bad weather, and that they were seldom deceived.

Bonaparte, who wore his gray greatcoat, and had his whip in his hand, appeared somewhat disappointed at not seeing any one come from the valley of Aorta to inform him of the taking of the fort of Bard. I never left him for a moment during the ascent. We encountered no personal danger, and escaped with no other inconvenience than excessive fatigue.

On his arrival at the convent the First Consul visited the chapel and the three little libraries. He had time to read a few pages of an old book, of which I have forgotten the title.

Our breakfast-dinner was very frugal. The little garden was still covered with snow, and I said to one of the fathers, "You can have but few vegetables here."—"We get our vegetables from the valleys," he replied; "but in the month of August, in warm seasons, we have a few lettuces of our own growing."

When we reached the summit of the mountain we seated ourselves on the snow and slid down. Those who went first smoothed the way for those who came behind them. This rapid descent greatly amused us, and we were only stopped by the mud which succeeded the snow at the distance of five or six hundred toises down the declivity.

We crossed, or rather climbed up, Mont Albaredo to avoid passing under the fort of Bard, which closes the valley of Aorta. As it was impossible to get the artillery up this mountain it was resolved to convey it through the town of Bard, which was not fortified. For this operation we made choice of night, and the wheels of the cannon and caissons, and even the horses' feet, being wrapped in straw, the whole passed quietly through the little town. They were, indeed, under the fire of the fort; however, it did not so completely command the street but that the houses would have protected them against any very fatal consequences. A great part of the army had passed before the surrender of the fort, which so completely commands the narrow valley leading to Aorta that it is difficult to comprehend the negligence of the Austrians in not throwing up more efficient works; by very simple precautions they might have rendered the passage of St. Bernard unavailing.

On the 23d we came within sight of the fort of Bard, which commands the road bounded by the Doria Baltea on the right and Mont Albaredo on the left. The Doria Baltea is a small torrent which separates the town of Bard from the fort. Bonaparte, whose retinue was not very numerous, crossed the torrent. On arriving within gunshot of the fort he ordered us to quicken our pace to gain a little bridle-path on the left, leading to the summit of Mont Albaredo, and turning the town and fort of Bard.

We ascended this path on foot with some difficulty. On reaching the summit of the mountain, which commands the fort, Bonaparte levelled his telescope on the grass, and stationing himself behind some bushes, which served at once to shelter and conceal him, he attentively reconnoitered the fort. After addressing several questions to the persons who had come to give him information, he mentioned, in a tone of dissatisfaction, the faults that had been committed, and ordered the erection of a new battery to attack a point which he marked out, and from whence, he guaranteed, the firing of a few shots would oblige the fort to surrender. Having given these orders he descended the mountain and went to sleep that night at Yvree. On the 3d of June he learned that the fort had surrendered the day before.

The passage of Mont St. Bernard must occupy a great place in the annals of successful temerity. The boldness of the First Consul seemed, as it were, to have fascinated the enemy, and his enterprise was so unexpected that not a single Austrian corps defended the approaches of the fort of Bard. The country was entirely exposed, and we only encountered here and there a few feeble parties, who were incapable of checking our march upon Milan. Bonaparte's advance astonished and confounded the enemy, who thought of nothing but marching back the way he came, and renouncing the invasion of France. The bold genius which actuated Bonaparte did not inspire General Melas, the commander-in-chief of the Austrian forces. If Melas had had the firmness which ought to belong to the leader of an army—if he had compared the respective positions of the two parties—if he had considered that there was no longer time to regain his line of operations and recover his communication with the Hereditary States, that he was master of all the strong places in Italy, that he had nothing to fear from Massena, that Suchet could not resist him:—if, then, following Bonaparte's example, he had marched upon Lyons, what would have become of the First Consul? Melas would have found few obstacles, and almost everywhere open towns, while the French army would have been exhausted without having an enemy to fight. This is, doubtless, what Bonaparte would have done had he been Melas; but, fortunately for us, Melas was not Bonaparte.

We arrived at Milan on the 2d of June, the day on which the First Consul heard that the fort of Bard was taken. But little resistance was opposed to our entrance to the capital of Lombardy, and the term "engagements" can scarcely be applied to a few affairs of advance posts, in which success could not be for a moment doubtful; the fort of Milan was immediately blockaded. Murat was sent to Piacenza, of which he took possession without difficulty, and Lannes beat General Ott at Montebello. He was far from imagining that by that exploit he conquered for himself a future duchy!

The First Consul passed six days at Milan. On the day after our arrival there a spy who had served us very well in the first campaign in Italy was announced. The First Consul recollected him, and ordered him to be shown into his cabinet.—"What, are you here?" he exclaimed; "so you are not shot yet!"—"General," replied the spy, "when the war recommenced I determined to serve the Austrians because you were far from Europe. I always follow the fortunate; but the truth is, I am tired of the trade. I wish to have done with it, and to get enough to enable me to retire. I have been sent to your lines by General Melas, and I can render you an important service. I will give an exact account of the force and the position of all the enemy's corps, and the names of their commanders. I can tell you the situation in which Alessandria now is. You know me, I will not deceive you; but, I must carry back some report to my general. You need not care for giving me some true particulars which I can communicate to him."—"Oh! as to that," resumed the First Consul, "the enemy is welcome to know my forces and my positions, provided I know his, and he be ignorant of my plans. You shall be satisfied; but do not deceive me: you ask for 1000 Louis, you shall have them if you serve me well." I then wrote down from the dictation of the spy, the names of the corps, their amount, their positions, names of the generals commanding them. The Consul stuck pins in the map to mark his plans on places respecting which he received information from the spy. We also learned that Alexandria was without provisions, that Melas was far from expecting a siege, that many of his troops were sick, and that he wanted medicines. Berthier was ordered to draw up for the spy a nearly accurate statement of our positions.

The information given by this man proved so accurate and useful that on his return from Marengo Bonaparte ordered me to pay him the 1000 Louis. The spy afterwards informed him that Melas was delighted with the way in which he had served him in this affair, and had rewarded him handsomely. He assured us that he had bidden farewell to his odious profession. The First Consul regarded this little event as one of the favours of fortune.

In passing through Geneva the First Consul had an interview with M. Necker.[127]

I know not how it happened, but at the time he did not speak to me of this interview. However, I was curious to know what he thought of a man who had acquired much celebrity in France. One evening, when we were talking of one thing and another, I managed to turn the conversation on that subject. "M. Necker," said he, "appears to me very far below his reputation. He did not equal the idea I had formed of him. I tried all I could to get him to talk; but he said nothing remarkable. He is an ideologist[128]— a banker. It is impossible that such a man can have any but narrow views; and, besides, most celebrated people lose on a close view."— "Not always, General," observed I—"Ah!" said he, smiling, "that is not bad, Bourrienne. You are improving. I see I shall make something of you in time!"

The day was approaching when all was to be lost or won. The First Consul made all his arrangements, and sent off the different corps to occupy the points he had marked out. I have already mentioned that Murat's task was the occupation of Piacenza. As soon as he was in possession of that town he intercepted a courier of General Melas. The despatch, which was addressed to the Aulic Council of Vienna, was delivered to us on the night of the 8th

127 Madame de Stael briefly mention this interview in her'Considerations sur la Revolution Francaise' "M. Necker," she says,"had an interview with Bonaparte, when he was on his way to Italy bythe passage of Mont. St. Bernard, a few days before the battle of Marengo. During this conversation, which lasted two hours, the First Consul made a very favourable impression on my father by theconfident way he spoke of his future projects."—Bourrienne.

128 This was a constant term of reproach with Bonaparte. He set allthe metaphysicians of the Continent against him by exclaiming, "Jene veux point d'ideologues."

of June. It announced the capitulation of Genoa, which took place on the 4th, after the long and memorable defence which reflected so much honour on Massena. Melas in his despatch spoke of what he called our pretended army of reserve with inconceivable contempt, and alluded to the presence of Bonaparte in Italy as a mere fabrication. He declared he was still in Paris. It was past three in the morning when Murat's courier arrived. I immediately translated the despatch, which was in German. About four o'clock I entered the chamber of the First Consul, whom I was obliged to shake by the arm in order to wake him. He had desired me; as I have already mentioned, never to respect his repose an the arrival of bad news; but on the receipt of good news to let him sleep. I read to him the despatch, and so much was he confounded by this unexpected event that his first exclamation was, "Bah! you do not understand German." But hardly had he uttered these words when he arose, and by eight o'clock in the morning orders were despatched for repairing the possible consequences of this disaster, and countermanding the march of the troops on the Scrivia. He himself proceeded the same day to Stradella.

I have seen it mentioned in some accounts that the First Consul in person gained the battle of Montebello. This is a mistake. He did not leave Milan until the 9th of June, and that very day Lannes was engaged with the enemy. The conflict was so terrible that Lannes, a few days after, describing it in my presence to M. Collot, used these remarkable words, which I well remember: "Bones were cracking in my division like a shower of hail falling on a skylight."

By a singular chance Desaix, who was to contribute to the victory and stop the rout of Marengo, arrived from Egypt at Toulon, on the very day on which we departed from Paris. He was enabled to leave Egypt in consequence of the capitulation of El-Arish, which happened on the 4th of January 1800. He wrote me a letter, dated 16th Floréal, year VIII. (6th of May 1800), announcing his arrival. This letter I did not receive until we reached Martigny. I showed it to the First Consul. "Ah!" exclaimed he, "Desaix in Paris!" and he immediately despatched an order for him to repair to the headquarters of the army of Italy wherever they might be. Desaix arrived at Stradella on the morning of the 11th of June. The First Consul received him with the warmest cordiality, as a man for whom he had a high esteem, and whose talents and character afforded the fairest promise of what might one day be expected of him. Bonaparte was jealous of some generals, the rivalry of whose ambition he feared; but on this subject Desaix gave him no uneasiness; equally remarkable for his unassuming disposition, his talent, and information, he proved by his conduct that he loved glory for her own sake, and that every wish for the possession of political power was foreign to his mind. Bonaparte's friendship for him was enthusiastic. At this interview at Stradella, Desaix was closeted with the First Consul for upwards of three hours. On the day after his arrival an order of the day communicated to the army that Desaix was appointed to the command of Boudet's division.[129] I expressed to Bonaparte my surprise at his long interview with Desaix. "Yes," replied he, "he has been a long time with me; but you know what a favourite he is. As soon as I return to Paris I will make him War Minister. I would make him a prince if I could.

129 Boudet was on terms of great intimacy with Bonaparte, who, nodoubt, was much affected at his death. However, the only remark hemade on receiving the intelligence, was "Who the devil shall I getto supply Boudet's place?"—Bourrienne. The command given to Desaix was a corps especially formed of the twodivisions of Boudet and Monnier (Savary, tome i. p. 262). Boudetwas not killed at Marengo, still less before (see Erreurs, tome i.p. 14).

He is quite an antique character." Desaix died two days after he had completed his thirty-third year, and in less than a week after the above observations.

About this time M. Collot came to Italy and saw Bonaparte at Milan. The latter received him coldly, though he had not yet gained the battle of Marengo. M. Collot had been on the most intimate footing with Bonaparte, and had rendered him many valuable services. These circumstances sufficiently accounted for Bonaparte's coolness, for he would never acknowledge himself under obligations to any one, and he did not like those who were initiated into certain family secrets which he had resolved to conceal.[130]

---

130 The day after the interview I had a long conversation with M. Collot while Bonaparte was gone to review some corps stationed at Milan. M. Collot perfectly understood the cause of the unkindtreatment he had experienced, and of which he gave me the followingexplanation: Some days before the Consulate—that is to say, two or three daysafter our return from Egypt,—Bonaparte, during his jealous fit,spoke to M. Collot about his wife, her levities, and theirpublicity. "Henceforth," said Bonaparte, "I will have nothing to dowith her."—"What, would you part from her?"—"Does not her conductjustify me in so doing?"—"I do not know; but is this the time tothink of such a thing, when the eyes of all France are fixed uponyou? These domestic squabbles will degrade you in the eyes of thepeople, who expect you to be wholly devoted to their interests; andyou will be laughed at, like one of Molière's husbands, if you aredispleased with your wife's conduct you can call her to account whenyou have nothing better to do. Begin by raising up the state. After that you may find a thousand reasons for your resentment whennow you would not find one. You know the French people well enoughto see how important it is that you should not commence with thisabsurdity." By these and other similar remarks M. Collot thought he had producedsome impression, when Bonaparte suddenly exclaimed: "No, mydetermination is fixed; she shall never again enter my house. Icare not what people say. They will gossip about the affair for twodays, and on the third it will be forgotten. She shall go to Malmaison, and I will live here. The public know enough, not to bemistaken as to the reasons of her removal." M. Collot vainly endeavoured to calm his irritation. Bonapartevented a torrent of reproaches upon Josephine. "All this violence,"observed M. Collot, "proves that you still love her. Do but seeher, she will explain the business to your satisfaction and you willforgive her."—"I forgive her! Never! Collot, you know me. If Iwere not sure of my own resolution, I would tear out this heart, andcast it into the fire." Here anger almost choked his utterance, andhe made a motion with his hand as if tearing his breast. When this violent paroxysm had somewhat subsided M. Collot withdrew;but before he went away Bonaparte invited him to breakfast on thefollowing morning. At ten o'clock M. Collot was there, and as he was passing throughthe courtyard he was informed that Madame Bonaparte, who, as I havealready mentioned, had gone to Lyons without meeting the General,had returned during the night. On M. Collot's entrance Bonaparteappeared considerably embarrassed. He led him into a side room, notwishing to bring him into the room where I was writing. "Well,"said Bonaparte to M. Collot, "she is here."—"I rejoice to hear it. You have done well for yourself as well as for us."—"But do notimagine I have forgiven her. As long as I live I shall suspect. The fact is, that on her arrival I desired her to be gone; but thatfool Joseph was there. What could I do, Collot? I saw her descendthe staircase followed by Eugine and Hortense. They were allweeping; and I have not a heart to resist tears. Eugène was with mein Egypt. I have been accustomed to look upon him as my adoptedson. He is a fine brave lad. Hortense is just about to beintroduced into society, and she is admired by all

On the 13th the First Consul slept at Torre di Galifolo. During the evening he ordered a staff-officer to ascertain whether the Austrians had a bridge across the Bormida. A report arrived very late that there was none. This information set Bonaparte's mind at rest, and he went to bed very well satisfied; but early next morning, when a firing was heard, and he learned that the Austrians had debouched on the plain, where the troops were engaged, he flew into a furious passion, called the staff-officer a coward, and said he had not advanced far enough. He even spoke of bringing the matter to an investigation.

From motives of delicacy I refrain from mentioning the name of the officer here alluded to.

Bonaparte mounted his horse and proceeded immediately to the scene of action. I did not see him again until six in the evening. In obedience to his instructions; I repaired to San Giuliano, which is not above two leagues from the place where the engagement commenced. In the course of the afternoon I saw a great many wounded passing through the village, and shortly afterwards a multitude of fugitives. At San Giuliano nothing was talked of but a retreat, which, it was said, Bonaparte alone firmly opposed. I was then advised to leave San Giuliano, where I had just received a courier for the General-in-Chief. On the morning of the 14th General Desaix was sent towards Novi to observe the road to Genoa, which city had fallen several days before, in spite of the efforts of its illustrious defender, Massena. I returned with this division to San Giuliano. I was struck with the numerical weakness of the corps which was marching to aid an army already much reduced and dispersed. The battle was looked upon as lost, and so indeed it was. The First Consul having asked Desaix what he thought of it, that brave General bluntly replied, "The battle is completely lost; but it is only two o'clock, we have time to gain another to-day." I heard this from Bonaparte himself the same evening. Who could have imagined that Desaix's little corps, together with the few heavy cavalry commanded by General Kellerman, would, about five o'clock, have changed the fortune of the day? It cannot be denied that it was the instantaneous inspiration of Kellerman that converted a defeat into a victory, and decided the battle of Marengo.

That memorable battle, of which the results were incalculable, has been described in various ways. Bonaparte had an account of it commenced no less than three times; and I must confess that none of the narratives are more correct than that contained in the 'Memoirs of the Duke of Rovigo'. The Emperor Napoleon became dissatisfied with what had been said by the First Consul Bonaparte. For my part, not having had the honour to bear a sword, I cannot say that I saw any particular movement executed this or that way; but I may mention here what I heard on the evening of the battle of Marengo respecting the probable chances of that event. As to the part which the First Consul took in it, the reader, perhaps, is sufficiently acquainted with his character to account for it. He did not choose that a result so decisive should be attributed to any other cause than the combinations of his genius,

---

who know her. I confess, Collot, I was deeply moved; I could not endure thedistress of the two poor children. 'Should they,' thought I,'suffer for their mother's faults?' I called back Eugène and Hortense, and their mother followed them. What could I say, whatcould I do? I should not be a man without some weakness."—"Be assured they will reward you for this."—"They ought, Collotthey ought; for it has cost me a hard struggle." After thisdialogue Bonaparte and M. Collot entered the breakfast-parlour,where I was then sitting. Eugène breakfasted with us, but neither Josephine nor Hortense. I have already related how I acted the partof mediator in this affair. Next day nothing was wanting tocomplete the reconciliation between the Conqueror of Egypt and thecharming woman who conquered Bonaparte.—Bourrienne.

and if I had not known his insatiable thirst for glory I should have been surprised at the sort of half satisfaction evinced at the cause of the success amidst the joy manifested for the success itself. It must be confessed that in this he was very unlike Jourdan, Hoche, Kléber, and Moreau, who were ever ready to acknowledge the services of those who had fought under their orders.

Within two hours of the time when the divisions commanded by Desaix left San Giuliano I was joyfully surprised by the triumphant return of the army, whose fate, since the morning, had caused me so much anxiety. Never did fortune within so short a time show herself under two such various faces. At two o'clock all denoted the desolation of a defeat, with all its fatal consequences; at five victory was again faithful to the flag of Arcola. Italy was reconquered by a single blow, and the crown of France appeared in the perspective.

At seven in the evening, when I returned with the First Consul to headquarters, he expressed to me his sincere regret for the loss of Desaix, and then he added, "Little Kellerman made a lucky charge. He did it at just the right moment. We are much indebted to him. You see what trifling circumstances decide these affairs."

These few words show that Bonaparte sufficiently appreciated the services of Kellerman. However, when that officer approached the table at which were seated the First Consul and a number of his generals, Bonaparte merely said, "You made a pretty good charge." By way of counter-balancing this cool compliment he turned towards Bessières, who commanded the horse grenadiers of the Guard, and said, "Bessières, the Guard has covered itself with glory." Yet the fact is, that the Guard took no part in the charge of Kellerman, who could assemble only 500 heavy cavalry; and with this handful of brave men he cut in two the Austrian column, which had overwhelmed Desaix's division, and had made 6000 prisoners. The Guard did not charge at Marengo until nightfall.

Next day it was reported that Kellerman, in his first feeling of dissatisfaction at the dry congratulation he had received, said to the First Consul, "I have just placed the crown on your head!" I did not hear this, and I cannot vouch for the truth of its having been said. I could only have ascertained that fact through Bonaparte, and of course I could not, with propriety, remind him of a thing which must have been very offensive to him. However, whether true or not, the observation was circulated about, verbally and in writing, and Bonaparte knew it. Hence the small degree of favour shown to Kellerman, who was not made a general of division on the field of battle as a reward for his charge at Marengo.[131]

---

131 If Savary's story be correct, and he was then aide de camp to Desaix, and Bourrienne acknowledges his account to be the best, theinspiration of the charge did not come from the young Kellerman. Savary says that Desaix sent him to tell Napoleon that he could notdelay his attack, and that he must be supported by some cavalry. Savary was then sent by Napoleon to a spot where he was told hewould find Kellerman, to order him to charge in support of Desaix. Desaix and Kellerman were so placed as to be out of sight of eachother (Savary, tome i. pp. 279-279). Thiers (tome i, p. 445)follows Savary. It may here be mentioned that Savary, in his account of the battle,expressly states that he carried the order from Bonaparte to Kellerman to make this charge. He also makes the followingobservations on the subject:— After the fall of the Imperial Government some pretended friends of General Kellerman have presumed to claim for him the merit oforiginating the charge of cavalry. That general, whose share ofglory is sufficiently brilliant to gratify his most sanguine wishes,can have no knowledge of so presumptuous a pretension. I the morereadily acquit him from the circumstance that, as

M. Delaforet, the Postmaster-general, sometimes transacted business with the First Consul. The nature of this secret business may easily be guessed at.[132] On the occasion of one of their interviews the First Consul saw a letter from Kellerman to Lasalle, which contained the following passage: "Would you believe, my friend, that Bonaparte has not made me a general of division though I have just placed the crown on his head?" The letter was sealed again and sent to its address; but Bonaparte never forgot its contents.

Whether Kellerman did or did not give the crown of France to the First Consul, it is very certain that on the evening of the battle of Marengo he gave him a supper, of which his famishing staff and the rest of us partook. This was no inconsiderable service in the destitute condition in which we were. We thought ourselves exceeding fortunate in profiting by the precaution of Kellerman, who had procured provisions from one of those pious retreats which are always well supplied, and which soldiers are very glad to fall in with when campaigning. It was the convent del Bosco which on this occasion was laid under contribution; and in return for the abundance of good provisions and wine with which they supplied the commander of the heavy cavalry the holy fathers were allowed a guard to protect them against pillage and the other disastrous concomitants of war.

After supper was over the First Consul dictated to me the bulletin of the battle. When

---

we were conversingone day respecting that battle, I called to his mind my havingbrought, to him the First Consul's orders, and he appeared not tohave forgotten that fact. I am far from suspecting his friends ofthe design of lessening the glory of either General Bonaparte or General Desaix; they know as well as myself that theirs are names sorespected that they can never be affected by such detractions, andthat it would be as vain to dispute the praise due to the Chief whoplanned the battle was to attempt to depreciate the brilliant sharewhich General Kellerman had in its successful result. I will add tothe above a few observations."From the position which he occupied General Desaix could not see General Kellerman; he had even desired me to request the First Consul to afford him the support of some cavalry. Neither could General Kellerman, from the point where he was stationed, perceive General Desaix's division; it is even probable that he was not awareof the arrival of that General, who had only joined the army twodays before. Both were ignorant of each other's position, which the First Consul was alone acquainted with; he alone could introduceharmony into their movements; he alone could make their effortsrespectively conduce to the same object."The fate of the battle was decided by Kellerman's bold charge; hadit, however, been made previously to General Desaix's attack, in allprobability it would have had a quite different result. Kellermanappears to have been convinced of it, since he allowed the Austriancolumn to cross our field of battle and extend its front beyond thatof the troops we had still in line without making the least attemptto impede its progress. The reason of Kellerman's not charging itsooner was that it was too serious a movement, and the consequencesof failure would have been irretrievable: that charge, therefore,could only enter into a general combination of plans, to which hewas necessarily a stranger" (Memoirs of the Duke of Rovigo, tome i.pp. 218-280).

132 When M. Delaforet was replaced soon after this by Lavalette, Napoleon ordered the discontinuance of the practice followed untilthen of allowing letters to be opened by subordinate officials. This right was restricted, as in England, to the Minister. Howeverbad this practice, it was limited, not extended, in his reign. See Mineval, tome iii. pp. 60-62, and Lavalette, tome ii. p. 10.

we were alone I said to him, "General, here is a fine victory! You recollect what you said the other day about the pleasure with which you would return to France after striking a grand blow in Italy; surely you must be satisfied now?"—"Yes, Bourrienne, I am satisfied.—But Desaix! . . . Ah, what a triumph would this have been if I could have embraced him to-night on the field of battle!" As he uttered these words I saw that Bonaparte was on the point of shedding tears, so sincere and profound was his grief for the death of Desaix. He certainly never loved, esteemed, or regretted any man so much.

The death of Desaix has been variously related, and I need not now state that the words attributed to him in the bulletin were imaginary. Neither did he die in the arms of his aide de camp, Lebrun, as I wrote from the dictation of the First Consul. The following facts are more correct, or at all events more probable:—the death of Desaix was not perceived at the moment it took place. He fell without saying a word, at a little distance from Lefebre-Desnouettes. A sergeant of battalion of the 9th brigade light infantry, commanded by Barrois, seeing him extended on the ground, asked permission to pick up his cloak. It was found to be perforated behind; and this circumstance leaves it doubtful whether Desaix was killed by some unlucky inadvertency, while advancing at the head of his troops, or by the enemy when turning towards his men to encourage them. However, the event was so instantaneous, the disorder so complete, and the change of fortune so sudden, that it is not surprising there should be no positive account of the circumstances which attended his death.

Early next morning the Prince of Liechtenstein came from General Melas with negotiations to the First Consul. The propositions of the General did not suit Bonaparte, and he declared to the Prince that the army shut up in Alessandria should evacuate freely, and with the honours of war; but on those conditions, which are well known, and by which Italy was to be fully restored to the French domination. That day were repaired the faults of Scherer, whose inertness and imbecility had paralysed everything, and who had fled, and been constantly beaten, from the Adriatic to Mont Cenis. The Prince of Liechtenstein begged to return to render an account of his mission to General Melas. He came back in the evening, and made many observations on the hard nature of the conditions. "Sir," replied the First Consul, in a tone of marked impatience, "carry my final determination to your General, and return quickly. It is irrevocable! Know that I am as well acquainted with your position as you are yourselves. I did not begin to learn the art of war yesterday. You are blocked up in Alessandria; you have many sick and wounded; you are in want of provisions and medicines. I occupy the whole of your rear. Your finest troops are among the killed and wounded. I might insist on harder conditions; my position would warrant me in so doing; but I moderate my demands in consideration of the gray hairs of your General, whom I respect."

This reply was delivered with considerable dignity and energy. I showed the Prince out, and he said to me, "These conditions are very hard, especially that of giving up Genoa, which surrendered to us only a fortnight ago, after so long a siege." It is a curious fact that the Emperor of Austria received intelligence of the capitulation and restitution of Genoa at the same time.

When the First Consul returned to Milan he made Savary and Rapp his aides de camp. They had previously served in the same rank under Desaix. The First Consul was at first not much disposed to take them, alleging that he had aides de camp enough. But his respect for the choice of Desaix, added to a little solicitation on my part, soon removed every obstacle. These two officers served him to the last hour of his political career with unfailing zeal and fidelity.

I have seen nothing in the Memoirs of the Duc de Rovigo (Savary) about my having had anything to do with his admission to the honour. I can probably tell the reason why one of the two aides de camp has risen higher than the other. Rapp had an Alsatian frankness which always injured him.

CHAPTER II

1800

What little time, and how few events sometimes suffice to change the destiny of nations! We left Milan on the 13th of June, Marengo on the 14th, and on the 15th Italy was ours! A suspension of hostilities between the French and Austrian armies was the immediate result of a single battle; and by virtue of a convention, concluded between Berthier and Melas, we resumed possession of all the fortified places of any importance, with the exception of Mantua. As soon as this convention was signed Bonaparte dictated to me at Torre di Galifolo the following letter to his colleagues:

> The day after the battle of Marengo, CITIZENS CONSULS, General Melastransmitted a message to our advance posts requesting permission tosend General Skal to me. During the day the convention, of which Isend you a copy, was drawn up, and at night it was signed by Generals Berthier and Melas. I hope the French people will besatisfied with the conduct, of their army.
>
> (*Signed*) BONAPARTE

The only thing worthy of remark in this letter would be the concluding sentence, in which the First Consul still affected to acknowledge the sovereignty of the people, were it not that the words "Citizens Consuls" were evidently foisted in with a particular design. The battle was gained; and even in a trifling matter like this it was necessary that the two, other Consuls should feel that they were not so much the colleagues as the subordinates of the First Consul.

We returned to Milan, and our second occupation of that city was marked by continued acclamations wherever the First Consul showed himself. At Milan the First Consul now saw Massena for the first time since our departure for Egypt. Bonaparte lavished upon him the highest praises, but not higher than he deserved, for his admirable defence of Genoa. He named him his successor in the command of the army of Italy. Moreau was on the Rhine, and therefore none but the conqueror of Zurich could properly have succeeded the First Consul in that command. The great blow was struck; but there might still occur an emergency requiring the presence of a skillful experienced general, well acquainted with the country. And besides, we could not be perfectly at ease, until it was ascertained what conditions would be adhered to by the Cabinet of Vienna, which was then entirely under the influence of the Cabinet of London. After our return from the battle the popular joy was general and heartfelt not only among the higher and middle ranks of society, but in all classes; and the affection evinced from all quarters to the First Consul was unfeigned. In what a tone of sincerity did he say to me one day, when returning from the parade, "Bourrienne, do you hear the acclamations still resounding? That noise is as sweet to me as the sound of Josephine's voice. How happy and proud I am to be loved by such a people!"

During our stay at Milan Bonaparte had arranged a new government for Piedmont; he had ever since cherished the wish to unite that rich and fertile country to the French territory because some Piedmontese provinces had been possessed by Louis XIV. That monarch was the only king whom the First Consul really admired. "If," said he one day, "Louis XIV. had not been born a king, he would have been a great man. But he did not know mankind; he could not know them, for he never knew misfortune." He admired the resolution of the old King, who would rather bury himself under the ruins of the monarchy than submit to degrading conditions, after having commanded the sovereigns of Europe. I recollect that Bonaparte was extremely pleased to see in the reports which he ordered to be made that in Casal, and in the valleys of Pignerol, Latour, and Luzerne, there still existed many traces of the period when those countries belonged to France; and that the French language was yet preserved there. He already began to identify himself with the past; and abusing the old kings of France was not the way to conciliate his favour.

The First Consul appointed for the government of Piedmont a Council which, as may naturally be imagined; he composed of those Piedmontese who were the declared partisans of France. He stated as the grounds of this arrangement that it was to give to Piedmont a new proof of the affection and attachment of the French people. He afterwards appointed General Dupont President of the Council, with the title of Minister-Extraordinary of the French government. I will here mention a secret step taken by Bonaparte towards the overthrowing of the Republic. In making the first draught of General Dupont's appointment I had mechanically written, "Minister-Extraordinary of the French Republic."—"No! no!" said Bonaparte, "not of the Republic; say of the Government."

On his return to Paris the First Consul gave almost incredible proofs of his activity. The day after his arrival he promulgated a great number of decrees, and afterwards allotted the rewards to his soldiers. He appointed Kellerman General of division which, on every principle of justice, he ought to have done on the field of battle. He distributed sabres of honour, with the following inscription, highly complimentary to himself:—

> "Battle of Maringo[133], commanded in person by the First Consul. —Given by the Government of the Republic to General Lannes."

Similar sabres where presented to Generals Victor, Watrin, Gardanne, and Murat; and sabres of less value to other officers: and also muskets and drumsticks of honour to the soldiers and drummers who had distinguished themselves at Marengo, or in the army of the Rhine; for Bonaparte took care that the officers and men who had fought under Moreau should be included among those to whom the national rewards were presented. He even had a medal struck to perpetuate the memory of the entry of the French army into Munich. It is worthy of remark that while official fabrications and exaggerated details of facts were published respecting Marengo and the short campaign of Italy, by a feigned modesty the victorious army of Marengo received the unambitious title of 'Army of Reserve'. By this artifice the honour of the Constitution was saved. The First Consul had not violated it. If he had marched to the field, and staked everything on a chance it was merely accidentally, for he commanded only an "Army of Reserve," which nevertheless he had greeted with the title of Grand Army before he entered upon the campaign. It is scarcely conceivable that

133 spelt for some time, I do not know why, as, Maringo—Bourrienne

Bonaparte, possessing as he did an extraordinary mind, should have descended to such pitiful artifices.[134] Even foreigners and prisoners were objects of Bonaparte's designing intentions. I recollect one evening his saying to me; "Bourrienne, write to the Minister of War, and tell him to select a fine brace of pistols, of the Versailles manufacture, and send them, in my name, to General Zach. He dined with me to-day, and highly praised our manufacture of arms. I should like to give him a token of remembrance; besides—the matter will be talked of at Vienna, and may perhaps do good!"

As soon as the news of the battle of Marengo reached Paris Lucien Bonaparte, Minister of the Interior, ordered preparations for the festival, fixed for the 14th of July, in commemoration of the first Federation. This festival and that of the 1st Vendemiaire were the only ones preserved by the Consular Government. Indeed, in those memorable days, when the Revolution appeared in its fairest point of view, France had never known such joy as that to which the battle of Marengo gave rise. Still, amidst all this popular transport there was a feeling of regret. The fame of Desaix, his heroic character, his death, the words attributed to him and believed to be true, caused mourning to be mingled with joy. It was agreed to open a subscription for erecting a national monument to his memory. A reflection naturally arises here upon the difference between the period referred to and the present time. France has endowed with nearly a million the children of one of her greatest orators and most eloquent defenders of public liberty, yet, for the monument to the memory of Desaix scarcely 20,000 francs were subscribed. Does not this form a singular contrast with the patriotic munificence displayed at the death of General Foy? The pitiful monument to Desaix, on the Place Dauphins, sufficiently attests the want of spirit on the part of the subscribers. Bonaparte, who was much dissatisfied with it, gave the name of Desaix to a new quay, the first stone of which was laid with great solemnity on the 14th of July.

On that day the crowd was immense in the Champ-de-Mars and in the Temple of Mars, the name which at that the Church of the Invalides still preserved. Lucien delivered a speech on the encouraging prospects of France, and Lannes made an appropriate address on presenting to the Government the flags taken at Marengo. Two more followed; one from an aide de camp of Massena, and the other from an aide de camp of Lecourbe; and after the distribution of some medals the First Consul then delivered the following address:—

> CITIZENS! SOLDIERS!—The flags presented to the Government, in thepresence of the people of this immense capital, attest at once thegenius of the Commanders-in-Chief Moreau, Massena, and Berthier; themilitary talents of the generals, their lieutenants; and bravery ofthe French soldiers. On your return to the camp tell your comrades that for the 1st Vendemiaire, when we shall celebrate the anniversary of the Republic, the French people expect either peace or, if the enemyobstinately refuse it, other flags, the fruit of fresh victories.

After this harangue of the First Consul, in which he addressed to the military in the

134 Thiers (tome. vi., p. 70) says the title Grande Armee was firstgiven by Napoleon to the force prepared in 1805 for the campaignagainst Austria. The Constitution forbad the First Consul tocommand the armies in person. Hence the title, "Army of Reserve,"gives to the force which fought Marengo.

name of the people, and ascribed to Berthier the glory of Marengo, a hymn was chanted, the words of which were written by M. de Fontanes and the music composed by Mehul. But what was most remarkable in this fete was neither the poetry, music, nor even the panegyrical eloquence of Lucien,—it was the arrival at the Champ-de-Mars, after the ceremony at the Invalides, of the Consular Guard returning from Marengo. I was at a window of the Ecole-Militaire, and I can never forget the commotion, almost electrical, which made the air resound with cries of enthusiasm at their appearance. These soldiers did not defile before the First Consul in fine uniforms as at a review. Leaving the field of battle when the firing ceased, they had crossed Lombardy, Piedmont, Mont Cenis, Savoy, and France in the space of twenty-nine days. They appeared worn by the fatigue of a long journey, with faces browned by the summer sun of Italy, and with their arms and clothing showing the effects of desperate struggles. Do you wish to have an idea of their appearance? You will find a perfect type in the first grenadier put by Gerard at one side of his picture of the battle of Austerlitz.

At the time of this fete, that is to say, in the middle of the month of July, the First Consul could not have imagined that the moderate conditions he had proposed after the victory would not be accepted by Austria. In the hope, therefore, of a peace which could not but be considered probable, he, for the first time since the establishment of the Consular Government, convoked the deputies of the departments, and appointed their time of assembling in Paris for the 1st Vendemiaire, a day which formed the close of one remarkable century and marked the commencement of another.

The remains of Marshal Turenne; to which Louis XIV. had awarded the honours of annihilation by giving them a place among the royal tombs in the vaults of St. Denis, had been torn from their grave at the time of the sacrilegious violation of the tombs. His bones, mingled indiscriminately with others, had long lain in obscurity in a garret of the College of Medicine when M. Lenoir collected and restored them to the ancient tomb of Turenne in the Mussee des Petits Augustins. Bonaparte resolved to enshrine these relics in that sculptured marble with which the glory of Turenne could so well dispense. This was however, intended as a connecting link between the past days of France and the future to which he looked forward. He thought that the sentiments inspired by the solemn honours rendered to the memory of Turenne would dispose the deputies of the departments to receive with greater enthusiasm the pacific communications he hoped to be able to make.

However, the negotiations did not take the favourable turn which the First Consul had expected; and, notwithstanding all the address of Lucien, the communication was not heard without much uneasiness. But Lucien had prepared a speech quite to the taste of the First Consul. After dilating for some time on the efforts of the Government to obtain peace he deplored the tergiversations of Austria, accused the fatal influence of England, and added in a more elevated and solemn tone, "At the very moment when, the Consuls were leaving the Palace of the Government a courier arrived bearing despatches which the First Consul has directed me to communicate to you." He then read a note declaring that the Austrian Government consented to surrender to France the three fortresses of Ulm, Philipsburg, and Ingolstadt. This was considered as a security for the preliminaries of peace being speedily signed. The news was received with enthusiasm, and that anxious day closed in a way highly gratifying to the First Consul.

Whilst victory confirmed in Italy the destinies of the First Consul, his brothers were more concerned about their own interests than the affairs of France. They loved money as much as Bonaparte loved glory. A letter from Lucien to his brother Joseph, which I shall subjoin, shows how ready they always were to turn to their own advantage the glory and fortune of him to whom they were indebted for all their importance. I found this letter among my papers, but I cannot tell why and how I preserved it. It is interesting, inasmuch as it shows, the opinion that family of future kings entertained of their own situation, and of what their fate would have been had Bonaparte, like Desaix, fallen on the field of Marengo. It is, besides, curious to observe the philosopher Lucien causing Te Deum, to be chanted with the view of influencing the public funds. At all events I copy Lucien's letter as he wrote it, giving the words marked in italics and the numerous notes of exclamation which distinguish the original.

> MY BROTHER—I send you a courier; I particularly wish that the First Consul would give me notice of his arrival twenty-four hours beforehand, and that he would inform *me alone* of the barrier by which he will enter. The city wishes to prepare triumphal arches for him, and it deserves not to be disappointed.
>
> *At my request* a Te Deum was chanted yesterday. There were 60,000 persons present.
>
> The intrigues of Auteuil continue.[135]—It has been found difficult to decide between C—— and La F——. The latter has proposed his daughter in marriage to me. Intrigue has been carried to the last extreme. I do not know yet whether the High Priest has decided for one party or the other. I believe that he would cheat them both for an Orleans, and your friend of Auteuil was at the bottom of all. The news of the battle of Marengo petrified them, and yet next day the High Priest certainly spent three hours with your friend of Auteuil. As to us, had the victory of Marengo closed the First Consul's career we should now have been Proscribed.
>
> Your letters say nothing of what I expected to hear. I hope at least to be informed of the answer from Vienna before any one. I am sorry you have not paid me back for the battle of Marengo.

---

135 This intrigue, so called from Talleyrand one of its heads, livingin the suburb of Auteuil, arose from the wish of many of the mostinfluential men to be prepared in case of the death of Napoleon inany action in Italy: It was simply a continuation of the samecombinations which had been attempted or planned in 1799, till the arrival of Bonaparte from Egypt made the party choose him as the instrument for the overthrow of the Directors. There was littlesecrecy about their plans; see Miot de Melito (tome i p. 276),where Joseph Bonaparte tells his friends all that was being proposedin case his brother fell. Carnot seems to have been the mostprobable choice as leader and replacer of Bonaparte. In the aboveletter "C——," stands for Carrot, "La F——" for La Fayette, the"High Priest" is Sieyès, and the "friend of Auteuil" is Talleyrand;see Iung's Lucien, tome i. p. 411. The postscript seems to refer toa wretched scandal about Caroline, and Lucien; see Iung's Lucien,tome i. pp. 411, 432-433. The reader should remark the retentionof this and other documents by Bourrienne, which forms one of thecharges brought against him farther on.

The festival of the 14th of July will be very gratifying. We expect peace as a certainty, and the triumphant return of the First Consul. The family is all well. Your wife and all her family are at Mortfontaine. Ney is at Paris. Why do you return with the First Consul?

Peace! and Italy! Think of our last interview. I embrace you.

(Signed) LUCIEN.

On the margin is written—

P.S.—Read the letter addressed to the Consul, and give it to him *after you have carefully closed it.* Forward the enclosed. Madame Murat never lodged in my house. Her husband is a fool, whom his wife ought to punish by not writing to him for a month.

(Signed) LUCIEN BONAPARTE

Bonaparte, confirmed in his power by the victory of Marengo, remained some days longer at Milan to settle the affairs of Italy. He directed one to furnish Madame Grassini with money to pay her expenses to Paris. We departed amidst the acclamations of the inhabitants, and took the road to Turin. The First Consul stopped at Turin for some hours, and inspected the citadel, which had been surrendered to us in pursuance of the capitulation of Alessandria. In passing over Mont Cenis we observed the carriage of Madame Kellerman, who was going to meet her husband. Bonaparte on recognizing the lady stopped his carriage and congratulated her on the gallant conduct of her husband at the battle of Marengo.

On our arrival at Lyons we alighted at the Hotel des Celestins, and the loud acclamations of a numerous multitude assembled round the hotel obliged Bonaparte to show himself on the balcony. Next day he proceeded to the Square of Bellecour, where, amidst the plaudits of the people, he laid the first stone of some new buildings destined to efface one of the disasters of the Revolution.

We left Lyons that evening and continued our journey by way of Dijon. On our arrival in that town the joy of the inhabitants was very great. I never saw a more graceful and captivating sight than that which was presented by a group of beautiful young females, crowned with flowers, who accompanied Bonaparte's carriage, and which at that period, when the Revolution had renewed all the republican recollections of Greece and Rome, looked like the chorus of females dancing around the victor at the Olympic games.

But all our journey was not so agreeable. Some accidents awaited us. The First Consul's carriage broke down between Villeneuve-le-Roi and Sens. He sent a courier to inform my mother that he would stop at her house till his carriage was repaired. He dined there, and we started again at seven in the evening.

But we had other disasters to encounter. One of our off-wheels came off, and as we were driving at a very rapid pace the carriage was overturned on the bridge at a short distance from Montreau-Faut-Yonne. The First Consul, who sat on my left, fell upon me, and sustained no injury. My head was slightly hurt by striking against some things which were in the pocket of the carriage; but this accident was not worth stopping for, and we arrived at Paris on the same night, the 2d of July. Duroc, who was the third in the carriage, was not hurt.

I have already mentioned that Bonaparte was rather talkative when travelling; and as we were passing through Burgundy, on our return to Paris from Marengo, he said exultingly, "Well, a few more events like this campaign, and I may go down to posterity."—"I think," replied I, "that you have already done enough to secure great and lasting fame."—"Yes," resumed he, "I have done enough, it is true. In less than two years I have won Cairo, Paris, and Milan; but for all that, my dear fellow, were I to die to-morrow I should not at the end of ten centuries occupy half a page of general history!"

On the very day when Desaix fell on the field of Marengo Kléber was assassinated by a fanatical Mussulman, named Soleiman Haleby, who stabbed him with a dagger, and by that blow decided the fate of Egypt.[136]

Thus was France, on the same day, and almost at the same hour, deprived of two of her most distinguished generals. Menou, as senior in command, succeeded Kléber, and the First Consul confirmed the appointment. From that moment the loss of Egypt was inevitable.

I have a few details to give respecting the tragical death of Kléber. The house of Elfy Bey, which Bonaparte occupied at Cairo, and in which Kléber lived after his departure; had a terrace leading from a salon to an old ruined cistern, from which, down a few steps, there was an entrance into the garden. The terrace commanded a view of the grand square of El Beguyeh, which was to the right on coming out of the salon, while the garden was on the left. This terrace was Bonaparte's favourite promenade, especially in the evenings, when he used to walk up and down and converse with the persons about him, I often advised him to fill up the reservoir, and to make it level with the terrace. I even showed him, by concealing myself in it, and coming suddenly behind him, how easy it would be for any person to attempt his life and then escape, either by jumping into the square, or passing through the garden. He told me I was a coward, and was always in fear of death; and he determined not to make the alteration I suggested, which, however, he acknowledged to be advisable. Kléber's assassin availed himself of the facility which I so often apprehended might be fatal to Bonaparte.

I shall not atop to refute all the infamous rumours which were circulated respecting Kléber's death. When the First Consul received the unexpected intelligence he could scarcely believe it. He was deeply affected; and on reading the particulars of the assassination he instantly called to mind how often he had been in the same situation as that in which Kléber was killed, and all I had said respecting the danger of the reservoir—a danger from which it is inconceivable he should have escaped, especially after his Syrian expedition had excited the fury of the natives. Bonaparte's knowledge of Kléber's talents—the fact of his having

136 "This fellah was, at most, eighteen or twenty years of age: hewas a native of Damascus, and declared that he had quitted hisnative city by command of the grand vizier, who had entrusted himwith the commission of repairing to Egypt and killing the grandsultan of the French [Bonaparte being probably intended]. That forthis purpose alone he had left his family, and performed the wholejourney on foot and had received from the grand vizier no othermoney than what was absolutely requisite for the exigencies of thejourney. On arriving at Cairo he had gone forthwith to perform hisdevotions in the great mosque, and it was only on the eve ofexecuting his project that he confided it to one of the scherifs ofthe mosque" (Duc de Rovigo's Memoirs, tome 1. p. 367)

confided to him the command of the army, and the aid which he constantly endeavoured to transmit to him, repelled at once the horrible suspicion of his having had the least participation in the crime, and the thought that he was gratified to hear of it.

It is very certain that Bonaparte's dislike of Kléber was as decided as the friendship he cherished for Desaix. Kléber's fame annoyed him, for he was weak enough to be annoyed at it. He knew the manner in which Kléber spoke of him, which was certainly not the most respectful. During the long and sanguinary siege of St. Jean d'Acre Kléber said to me, "That little scoundrel Bonaparte, who is no higher than my boot, will enslave France. See what a villainous expedition he has succeeded in involving us in." Kléber often made the same remark to others as well as to me. I am not certain that it was ever reported to Bonaparte; but there is reason to believe that those who found it their interest to accuse others did not spare Kléber.

Kléber, who was a sincere republican, saw and dreaded for his country's sake the secret views and inordinate ambition of Bonaparte. He was a grumbler by nature; yet he never evinced discontent in the discharge of his duties as a soldier. He swore and stormed, but marched bravely to the cannon's mouth: he was indeed courage personified. One day when he was in the trench at St. Jean d'Acre, standing up, and by his tall stature exposed to every shot, Bonaparte called to him, "Stoop down, Kléber, stoop down!"—"Why;" replied he, "your confounded trench does not reach to my knees." He never regarded the Egyptian expedition with a favourable eye. He thought it too expensive, and utterly useless to France. He was convinced that in the situation in which we stood, without a navy or a powerful Government, it would have been better to have confined our attention to Europe than to have wasted French blood and money on the banks of the Nile, and among the ruined cities of Syria. Kléber, who was a cool, reflecting man, judged Bonaparte without enthusiasm, a thing somewhat rare at that time, and he was not blind to any of his faults.

Bonaparte alleged that Kléber said to him, "General, you are as great as the world!" Such a remark is in direct opposition to Kléber's character. He was too sincere to say anything against his conviction. Bonaparte, always anxious to keep Egypt, of which the preservation alone could justify the conquest, allowed Kléber to speak because he acted at the same time. He knew that Kléber's sense of military duty would always triumph over any opposition he might cherish to his views and plans. Thus the death of his lieutenant, far from causing Bonaparte any feeling of satisfaction, afflicted him the more, because it almost totally deprived him if the hope of preserving a conquest which had cost France so dear, and which was his work.

The news of the death of Kléber arrived shortly after our return to Paris. Bonaparte was anxiously expecting accounts from Egypt, none having been received for a considerable time. The arrival of the courier who brought the fatal intelligence gave rise to a scene which I may relate here. It was two o'clock in the morning when the courier arrived at the Tuileries. In his hurry the First Consul could not wait to rouse any one to call me up. I had informed him some days before that if he should want me during the night he should send for me to the corridor, as I had changed my bedchamber on account of my wife's accouchement. He came up himself and instead of knocking at my door knocked at that of my secretary. The latter immediately rose, and opening the door to his surprise saw the First Consul with a candle in his hand, a Madras handkerchief on his head, and having on his gray greatcoat. Bonaparte, not knowing of the little step down into the room, slipped and nearly fell, "Where is Bourrienne?" asked he. The surprise of my secretary at the apparition of the First Consul can be imagined. "What; General, is it you?"—"Where is Bourrienne?" Then my secretary, in his shirt, showed the First Consul my door. After having told him that he was sorry at having called him up, Napoleon came to me. I dressed in a hurry, and we went downstairs to my usual room. We rang several times before they opened the door for us. The guards were not asleep, but having heard so much running to and fro feared we were thieves. At last they opened the door, and the First Consul threw on the table the immense packet of despatches which he had just received. They had been fumigated and steeped in vinegar. When he read the announcement of the death of Kléber the expression of his countenance sufficiently denoted the painful feelings which arose in his mind. I read in his face; EGYPT IS LOST!

CHAPTER III

The happy events of the campaign of Italy had been crowned by the armistice, concluded on the 6th of July. This armistice was broken on the 1st of September, and renewed after the battle of Hohenlinden. On his return from Marengo Bonaparte was received with more enthusiasm than ever. The rapidity with which, in a campaign of less than two months, he had restored the triumph of the French standard, excited universal astonishment. He then actively endeavoured to open negotiations with England and Austria; but difficulties opposed him in every direction. He frequently visited the theatre, where his presence attracted prodigious throngs of persons, all eager to see and applaud him.

The immense number of letters which were at this time addressed to the First Consul is scarcely conceivable. They contained requests for places, protestations of fidelity, and, in short, they were those petitionary circulars that are addressed to all persons in power. These letters were often exceedingly curious, and I have preserved many of them; among the rest was one from Durosel Beaumanoir, an emigrant who had fled to Jersey. This letter contains some interesting particulars relative to Bonaparte's family. It is dated Jersey, 12th July 1800, and the following are the most remarkable passages it contains:

> I trust; General, that I may, without indiscretion, intrude upon your notice, to remind you of what, I flatter myself, you have not totally forgotten, after having lived eighteen or nineteen years at Ajaccio. But you will, perhaps, be surprised that so trifling an item should be the subject of the letter which I have the honour to address to you. You cannot have forgotten, General, that when your late father was obliged to take your brothers from the college of Autun, from whence he went to see you at Brienne, he was unprovided with money, and he asked me for twenty-five louis, which I lent him with pleasure. After his return he had no opportunity of paying me, and when I left Ajaccio your mother offered to dispose of some plate in order to pay the debt. To this I objected, and told her that I would wait until she could pay me at her convenience, and previous to the breaking out of the revolution I believe it was not in her power to fulfil her wish of discharging the debt. I am sorry, General, to be obliged to trouble you about such a trifle. But such is my unfortunate situation that even this trifle is of some importance to me. Driven from my country, and obliged to take refuge in this island, where everything is exceedingly expensive, the little sum I have mentioned, which was formerly a matter of indifference, would now be of great service to me. You will understand, General, that at the age of eighty-six, after serving served my country well for sixty years, without the least interruption, not counting the time of emigration, chased from every place, I have been obliged to take refuge here, to subsist on the scanty succour given by the English Government to the French emigrant. I say emigrant because I have been forced to be one. I had no intention of being one, but a

horde of brigands, who came from Caen to my house to assassinate me, considered I had committed the great crime in being the senior general of the canton and in having the Grand Cross of St. Louis: this was too much for them; if it had not been for the cries of my neighbours, my door would have been broken open, and I should have been assassinated; and I had but time to fly by a door at the back, only carrying away what I had on me. At first I retired to Paris, but there they told me that I could do nothing but go into a foreign country, so great was the hate entertained for me by my fellow-citizens, although I lived in retirement, never having any discussion with any one. Thus, General; I have abandoned all I possessed, money and goods, leaving them at the mercy of what they call the nation, which has profited a good deal by this, as I have nothing left in the world, not even a spot to put my foot on. If even a horse had been reserved for me, General, I could ask for what depends on you, for I have heard it said that some emigrants have been allowed to return home. I do not even ask this favour, not having a place to rest my foot. And, besides, I have with me here an exiled brother, older than I am, very ill and in perfect second childhood, whom I could not abandon. I am resigned to my own unhappy fate, but my sole and great grief is that not only I myself have been ill-treated, but that my fate has, contrary to the law, injured relations whom I love and respect. I have a mother-in-law, eighty years old, who has been refused the dower I had given her from my property, and this will make me die a bankrupt if nothing is changed, which makes me miserable. I acknowledge, General, that I know little of the new style, but, according to the old form, I am your humble servant,

DUROSEL BEAUMANOIR.

I read this letter to the First Consul, who immediately said, "Bourrienne, this is sacred! Do not lose a minute. Send the old man ten times the sum. Write to General Durosel that he shall be immediately erased from the list of emigrants. What mischief those brigands of the Convention have done! I can never repair it all." Bonaparte uttered these words with a degree of emotion which I rarely saw him evince. In the evening he asked me whether I had executed his orders, which I had done without losing a moment. The death of M. Froth had given me a lesson as to the value of time!

Availing myself of the privilege I have already frequently taken of making abrupt transitions from one subject to another, according as the recollection of past circumstances occurs to my mind, I shall here note down a few details, which may not improperly be called domestic, and afterwards describe a conspiracy which was protected by the very man against whom it was hatched.

At the Tuileries, where the First Consul always resided during the winter and sometimes a part of the summer, the grand salon was situated between his cabinet and the Room in which he received the persons with whom he had appointed audiences. When in this audience-chamber, if he wanted anything or had occasion to speak to anybody, he pulled a bell which was answered by a confidential servant named Landoire, who was the messenger of the First Consul's cabinet. When Bonaparte's bell rung it was usually for the purpose of making some inquiry of me respecting a paper, a name, a date, or some matter of that sort; and then Landoire had to pass through the cabinet and salon to answer the bell and afterwards to return and to tell me I was wanted. Impatient at the delay occasioned by this running about, Bonaparte, without saying anything to me, ordered the bell to be altered so that it should ring within the cabinet; and exactly above my table. Next morning when I entered the cabinet I saw a man mounted-upon a ladder. "What are you doing here?" said I. "I am hanging a bell, sir." I called Landoire and asked him who had given the order. "The First Consul," he replied. I immediately ordered the man to come down and remove the ladder, which he accordingly did. When I went, according to custom, to awaken the First Consul and read the newspapers to him I said, "General, I found a man this morning hanging a bell in your cabinet. I was told it was by your orders; but being convinced there must be some mistake I sent him away. Surely the bell was not intended for you, and I cannot imagine it was intended for me: who then could it be for?—" "What a stupid fellow that Landoire is!" said Bonaparte. "Yesterday, when Cambacérès was with me, I wanted you. Landoire did not come when I touched the bell. I thought it was broken, and ordered him to get it repaired. I suppose the bell-hanger was doing it when you saw him, for you know the wire passes through the cabinet." I was satisfied with this explanation, though I was not deceived, by it. For the sake of appearance he reproved Landoire, who, however, had done nothing more than execute the order he had received. How could he imagine I would submit to such treatment, considering that we had been friends since our boyhood, and that I was now living on full terms of confidence and familiarity with him?

Before I speak of the conspiracy of Ceracchi, Arena, Topino-Lebrun, and others, I must notice a remark made by Napoleon at St. Helena. He said, or is alleged to have said, "The two attempts which placed me in the greatest danger were those of the sculptor Ceracchi and of the fanatic of Schoenbrun." I was not at Schoenbrun at the time; but I am convinced that Bonaparte was in the most imminent danger. I have been informed on unquestionable authority that Staps set out from Erfurth with the intention of assassinating the Emperor; but he wanted the necessary courage for executing the design. He was armed with a large dagger, and was twice sufficiently near Napoleon to have struck him. I heard this from Rapp, who seized Stags, and felt the hilt of the dagger under his coat. On that occasion Bonaparte owed his life only to the irresolution of the young 'illuminato' who wished to sacrifice him to his fanatical fury. It is equally certain that on another occasion, respecting which the author of the St. Helena narrative observes complete silence, another fanatic—more dangerous than Steps attempted the life of Napoleon.[137]

The following is a correct statement of the facts relative to Ceracchi's conspiracy. The plot itself was a mere shadow; but it was deemed advisable to give it substance, to exaggerate, at least in appearance, the danger to which the First Consul had been exposed:—

There was at that time in Paris an idle fellow called Harrel; he had been a 'chef de battalion', but he had been dismissed the service, and was consequently dissatisfied. He became connected with Cerracchi, Arena, Topino-Lebrun, and Demerville. From different motives all these individuals were violently hostile to the First Consul, who on his part, was no friend to Cerracchi and Arena, but scarcely knew the two others. These four individuals formed, in conjunction with Harrel, the design of assassinating the First Consul, and the

137 At the time of this attempt I was not with Napoleon; but he directed me to see the madmen who had formed the design of assassinating him. It will be seen in the course of these Memoirs what were his plans, and what was the result of them—Bourrienne

time fixed for the perpetration of the deed was one evening when Bonaparte intended to visit the opera.

On the 20th of September 1804 Harrel came to me at the Tuileries. He revealed to me the plot in which he was engaged, and promised that his accomplices should be apprehended in the very act if I would supply him with money to bring the plot to maturity. I knew not how to act upon this disclosure, which I, however, could not reject without incurring too great a responsibility. I immediately communicated the business to the First Consul, who ordered me to supply Harrel with money; but not to mention the affair to Fouché, to whom he wished to prove that he knew better how to manage the police than he did.

Harrel came nearly every evening at eleven o'clock to inform me of the progress of the conspiracy, which I immediately communicated to the First Consul, who was not sorry to find Arena and Ceracchi deeply committed. But the time passed on, and nothing was done. The First Consul began to grow impatient. At length Harrel came to say that they had no money to purchase arms. Money was given him. He, however, returned next day to say that the gunsmith refused to sell them arms without authority. It was now found necessary to communicate the business to Fouché in order that he might grant the necessary permission to the gunsmith, which I was not empowered to do.

On the 10th of October the Consuls, after the breaking up of the Council, assembled in the cabinet of their colleague. Bonaparte asked them in my presence whether they thought he ought to go to the opera. They observed that as every precaution was taken no danger could be apprehended, and that it was desirable to show the futility of attempts against the First Consul's life. After dinner Bonaparte put on a greatcoat over his green uniform and got into his carriage accompanied by me and Duroc. He seated himself in front of his box, which at that time was on the left of the theatre between the two columns which separated the front and side boxes. When we had been in the theatre about half an hour the First Consul directed me to go and see what was doing in the corridor. Scarcely had I left the box than I heard a great uproar, and soon discovered that a number of persons, whose names I could not learn, had been arrested. I informed the First Consul of what I had heard, and we immediately returned to the Tuileries.

It is certain that the object of the conspiracy was to take the First Consul's life, and that the conspirators neglected nothing which could further the accomplishment of their atrocious design. The plot, however, was known through the disclosures of Harrel; and it would have been easy to avert instead of conjuring up the storm. Such was, and such still is, my opinion. Harrel's name was again restored to the army list, and he was appointed commandant of Vincennes. This post he held at the time of the Duc d'Enghien's assassination. I was afterwards told that his wife was foster-sister to the unfortunate prince, and that she recognised him when he entered the prison which in a few short hours was to prove his grave.

Carbonneau, one of the individuals condemned, candidly confessed the part he had taken in the plot, which he said was brought to maturity solely by the agents of the police, who were always eager to prove their zeal to their employers by some new discovery.

Although three months intervened between the machinations of Ceracchi and Arena and the horrible attempt of the 3d Nivôse, I shall relate these two events in immediate succession; for if they had no other points of resemblance they were at least alike in their object. The conspirators in the first affair were of the revolutionary faction. They sought Bonaparte's life as if with the view of rendering his resemblance to Caesar so complete that not even a Brutus should be wanting. The latter, it must with regret be confessed, were of the Royalist party, and in their wish to destroy the First Consul they were not deterred by the fear of sacrificing a great number of citizens.

The police knew nothing of the plot of the 3d Nivôse for two reasons; first, because they were no parties to it, and secondly, because two conspirators do not betray and sell each other when they are resolute in their purpose. In such cases the giving of information can arise only from two causes, the one excusable, the other infamous, viz. the dread of punishment, and the hope of reward. But neither of these causes influenced the conspirators of the 3d Nivôse, the inventors and constructors of that machine which has so justly been denominated infernal!

On the 3d Nivôse (24th December 1800) the first performance of Haydn's magnificent oratorio of the "Creation" took place at the opera, and the First Consul had expressed his intention of being present. I did not dine with him that day, but as he left me he said, "Bourrienne, you know I am going to the opera to-night, and you may go too; but I cannot take you in the carriage, as Lannes, Berthier, and Lauriston are going with me." I was very glad of this, for I much wished to hear one of the masterpieces of the German school of composition. I got to the opera before Bonaparte, who on his entrance seated himself, according to custom, in front of the box. The eyes of all present were fixed upon him, and he appeared to be perfectly calm and self-possessed. Lauriston, as soon as he saw me, came to my box, and told me that the First Consul, on his way to the opera, had narrowly escaped being assassinated in the Rue St. Nicaise by the explosion of a barrel of gunpowder, the concussion of which had shattered the windows of his carriage. "Within ten seconds after our escape," added Lauriston, "the coachman having turned the corner of the Rue St Honore, stopped to take the First Consul's orders; and he coolly said, 'To the opera.'"[138] On hearing

138 The following particulars respecting the affair of the infernal machine are related by Rapp, who attended Madame Bonaparte to the opera. He differs from Bourrienne as to the total ignorance of the police: "The affair of the infernal machine has never been properly understood by the public. The police had intimated to Napoleon that an attempt would be made against his life and cautioned him not to go out. Madame Bonaparte, Mademoiselle Beauharnais, Madame Murat, Lannes, Bessières, the aide de camp on duty, Lieutenant Lebrun, now duke of Placenza were all assembled in the salon, while the First Consul was writing in his cabinet. Haydn's oratorio was to be performed that evening; the ladies were anxious to hear the music, and we also expressed a wish to that effect. The escort piquet was ordered out; and Lannes requested that Napoleon would join the party. He consented; his carriage was ready, and he took along with him Bessières and the aide de camp on duty. I was directed to attend the ladies. Josephine had received a magnificent shawl from Constantinople and she that evening wore it for the first time. 'Permit me to observe,' said I, 'that your shawl is not thrown on with your usual elegance.' She good-humouredly begged that I would fold it after the fashion of the Egyptian ladies. While I was engaged in this operation we heard Napoleon depart. 'Come sister,' said Madame Murat, who was impatient to get to the theatre: 'Bonaparte is going.' We stopped into the carriage: the First Consul's equipage had already reached the middle of the Place du Carrousel. We drove after it, but we had scarcely entered the place when the machine exploded. Napoleon escaped by a singular chance, St. Regent, or his servant Francois, had stationed himself in the middle of the Rue Nicaise. A grenadier of the escort, supposing he was really what he appeared to be, a water-carrier, gave him a few blows with the flat of his sabre and drove him off. The cart was turned round, and the machine

this I left the theatre and returned to the Palace, under the expectation that I should speedily be wanted. Bonaparte soon returned home; and as intelligence of the affair had spread through Paris the grand salon on the ground-floor was filled with a crowd of functionaries, eager to read in the eye of their master what they were to think and say on the occasion. He did not keep them long in suspense. "This," exclaimed he vehemently, "is the work of the Jacobins: they have attempted my life ...... There are neither nobles, priests, nor Chouans in this affair! .... I know what I am about, and they need not think to impose on me. These are the Septembrizers who have been in open revolt and conspiracy, and arrayed against every succeeding Government. It is scarce three months since my life was attempted by Uracchi, Arena; Topino-Lebrun, and Demerville. They all belong to one gang! The cutthroats of September, the assassins of Versailles, the brigands of the 81st of May, the conspirators of Prairial are the authors of all the crimes committed against established Governments! If they cannot be checked they must be crashed! France must be purged of these ruffians!" It is impossible to form any idea of the bitterness with which Bonaparte, pronounced these words. In vain did some of the Councillors of State, and Fouché in particular, endeavour to point out to him that there was no evidence against any one, and that before he pronounced people to be guilty it would be right to ascertain the fact. Bonaparte repeated with increased violence what he had before said of the Jacobins; thus adding; not without some ground of suspicion, one crime more to, the long catalogue for which they had already to answer.

Fouché had many enemies, and I was not, therefore, surprised to find some of the Ministers endeavouring to take advantage of the difference between his opinion and that of the First Consul; and it must be owned that the utter ignorance of the police respecting this event was a circumstance not very favourable to Fouché. He, however, was like the reed in the fable—he bent with the wind, but was soon erect again. The most skilful actor could scarcely imitate the inflexible calmness he maintained during Bonaparte's paroxysm of rage, and the patience with which he allowed himself to be accused.

Fouché, when afterwards conversing with me, gave me clearly to understand that he did not think the Jacobins guilty. I mentioned this to the First Consul, but nothing could make him retract his opinion. "Fouché," said he, "has good reason for his silence. He is serving his own party. It is very natural that he should seek to screen a set of men who are polluted with blood and crimes! He was one of their leaders. Do not I know what he did at Lyons and the Loire? That explains Fouché's conduct now!"

This is the exact truth; and now let me contradict one of the thousand fictions about this event. It has been said and printed that "the dignitaries and the Ministers were assembled at

---

exploded between the carriages of Napoleon and Josephine. The ladies shrieked on hearing the report; the carriage windows were broken, and Mademoiselle Beauharnais received a slight hurt on her hand. I alighted and crossed the Rue Nicaise which was strewed with the bodies of those who had been thrown down, and the fragments of the walls that had been shattered with the explosion. Neither the consul nor any individual of his suite sustained any serious injury. When I entered the theatre Napoleon was seated in his box; calm and composed, and looking at the audience through his opera-glass. Fouché was beside him. 'Josephine' said he as soon as he observed me. She entered at that instant and he did not finish his question 'The rascals' said he very cooly, 'wanted to blow me up: Bring me a book of the oratorio'" (Memoirs of General Count Rape. P. 19)

the Tuileries. 'Well,' said the First Consul, advancing angrily towards Fouché, 'will you still say that this is the Royalist party?' Fouché, better informed than was believed, answered coolly, 'Yes, certainly, I shall say so; and, what is more, I shall prove it.' This speech caused general astonishment, but was afterwards fully borne out." This is pure invention. The First Consul only said to Fouché; "I do not trust to your police; I guard myself, and I watch till two in the morning." This however, was very rarely the case.

On the day after the explosion of the infernal machine a considerable concourse assembled at the Tuileries. There was absolutely a torrent of congratulations. The prefect of the Seine convoked the twelve mayors of Paris and came at their head to wait on the First Consul. In his reply to their address Bonaparte said, "As long as this gang of assassins confined their attacks to me personally I left the law to take its course; but since, by an unparalleled crime, they have endangered the lives of a portion of the population of Paris, their punishment must be as prompt as exemplary. A hundred of these wretches who have libeled liberty by perpetrating crimes in her name must be effectually prevented from renewing their atrocities." He then conversed with the Ministers, the Councillors of State, etc., on the event of the preceding day; and as all knew the First Consul's opinion of the authors of the crime each was eager to confirm it. The Council was several times assembled when the Senate was consulted, and the adroit Fouché, whose conscience yielded to the delicacy of his situation, addressed to the First Consul a report worthy of a Mazarin. At the same time the journals were filled with recollections of the Revolution, raked up for the purpose of connecting with past crimes the individuals on whom it was now wished to cast odium. It was decreed that a hundred persons should be banished; and the senate established its character for complaisance by passing a 'Senatus-consulte' conformable to the wishes of the First Consul.

A list was drawn up of the persons styled Jacobins, who were condemned to transportation. I was fortunate enough to obtain the erasure of the names of several whose opinions had perhaps been violent, but whose education and private character presented claims to recommendation. Some of my readers may probably recollect them without my naming them, and I shall only mention M. Tissot, for the purpose of recording, not the service I rendered him, but an instance of grateful acknowledgment.

When in 1815 Napoleon was on the point of entering Paris M. Tissot came to the prefecture of police, where I then was, and offered me his house as a safe asylum; assuring me I should there run no risk of being discovered. Though I did not accept the offer yet I gladly seize on this opportunity of making it known. It is gratifying to find that difference of political opinion does not always exclude sentiments of generosity and honour! I shall never forget the way in which the author of the essays on Virgil uttered the words 'Domus mea'.

But to return to the fatal list. Even while I write this I shudder to think of the way in which men utterly innocent were accused of a revolting crime without even the shadow of a proof. The name of an individual, his opinions, perhaps only assumed, were sufficient grounds for his banishment. A decree of the Consuls, dated 4th of January 1801, confirmed by a 'Senates-consulte' on the next day, banished from the territory of the Republic, and placed under special inspectors, 130 individuals, nine of whom were merely designated in the report as Septembrizers.

The exiles, who in the reports and in the public acts were so unjustly accused of being the authors of the infernal machine, were received at Nantes, with so much indignation that the military were compelled to interfere to save them from being massacred.

In the discussions which preceded the decree of the Consuls few persons had the courage to express a doubt respecting the guilt of the accused. Truguet was the first to mount the breach. He observed that without denying the Government the extraordinary means for getting rid of its enemies he could not but acknowledge that the emigrants threatened the purchasers of national domains, that the public mind was corrupted by pamphlets, and that—Here the First Consul, interrupting him, exclaimed, "To what pamphlets do you allude?"—"To pamphlets which are publicly circulated."—"Name them!"—"You know them as well as I do."[139]

After a long and angry ebullition the First Consul abruptly dismissed the Council. He observed that he would not be duped; that the villains were known; that they were Septembrizers, the hatchers of every mischief. He had said at a sitting three days before, "If proof should fail, we must take advantage of the public excitement. The event is to me merely the opportunity. They shall be banished for the 2d September, for the 31st May, for Baboeuf's conspiracy—or anything else."

On leaving one of the sittings of the Council, at which the question of a special tribunal had been discussed, he told me that he had been a little ruffled; that he had said a violent blow must be struck; that blood must be spilt; and that as many of the guilty should be shot as there had been victims of the explosion (from fifteen to twenty); that 200 should be banished, and the Republic purged of these scoundrels.

The arbitrariness and illegality of the proceeding were so evident that the 'Senatus-consulte' contained no mention of the transactions of the 3d Nivôse, which was very remarkable. It was, however, declared that the measure of the previous day had been adopted with a view to the preservation of the Constitution. This was promising.

The First Consul manifested the most violent hatred of the Jacobins; for this he could not have been blamed if under the title of Jacobins he had not comprised every devoted advocate of public liberty. Their opposition annoyed him and he could never pardon them for having presumed to condemn his tyrannical acts, and to resist the destruction of the freedom which he had himself sworn to defend, but which he was incessantly labouring to overturn. These were the true motives of his conduct; and, conscious of his own faults, he regarded with dislike those who saw and disapproved of them. For this reason he was more afraid of those whom he called Jacobins than of the Royalists.

I am here recording the faults of Bonaparte, but I excuse him; situated as he was, any other person would have acted in the same way. Truth now reached him with difficulty, and when it was not agreeable he had no disposition to hear it. He was surrounded by flatterers; and, the greater number of those who approached him, far from telling him what they really thought; only repeated what he had himself been thinking. Hence he admired the wisdom of his Counsellors. Thus Fouché, to maintain himself in favour, was obliged to deliver up to his master 130 names chosen from among his own most intimate friends as objects of proscription.

Meanwhile Fouché, still believing that he was not deceived as to the real authors of the attempt of the 3d Nivôse, set in motion with his usual dexterity all the springs of the police. His efforts, however, were for sometime unsuccessful; but at length on Saturday, the 31st January 1801, about two hours after our arrival at Malmaison, Fouché presented himself and produced authentic proofs of the accuracy of his conjectures. There was no longer any doubt

139 The Parallel between Caesar, Cromwell, and Bonaparte, of which I shall speak a little farther on, is here alluded to.—Bourrienne.

on the subject; and Bonaparte saw clearly that the attempt of the 3d Nivôse was the result of a plot hatched by the partisans of royalty. But as the act of proscription against those who were jumbled together under the title of the Jacobins had been executed, it was not to be revoked.

Thus the consequence of the 3d Nivôse was that both the innocent and guilty were punished; with this difference, however, that the guilty at least had the benefit of a trial.

When the Jacobins, as they were called, were accused with such precipitation, Fouché had no positive proofs of their innocence; and therefore their illegal condemnation ought not to be attributed to him. Sufficient odium is attached to his memory without his being charged with a crime he never committed. Still, I must say that had he boldly opposed the opinion of Bonaparte in the first burst of his fury he might have averted the blow. Every time he came to the Tuileries, even before he had acquired any traces of the truth, Fouché always declared to me his conviction of the innocence of the persons first accused. But he was afraid to make the same observation to Bonaparte. I often mentioned to him the opinion of the Minister of Police; but as proof was wanting he replied to me with a triumphant air, "Bah! bah! This is always the way with Fouché. Besides, it is of little consequence. At any rate we shall get rid of them. Should the guilty be discovered among the Royalists they also shall be punished."

The real criminals being at length discovered through the researches of Fouché, St. Regent and Carbon expiated their crimes by the forfeit of their heads. Thus the First Consul gained his point, and justice gained hers.[140] I have often had occasion to notice the multifarious means employed by Bonaparte to arrive at the possession of supreme power, and to prepare men's minds for so great change. Those who have observed his life must have so remarked how entirely he was convinced of the truth that public opinion wastes itself on the rumour of a project and possesses no energy at the moment of its execution. In order, therefore, to direct public attention to the question of hereditary power a pamphlet was circulated about Paris, and the following is the history of it:—

In the month of December 1800, while Fouché was searching after the real authors of the attempt of the 3d Nivôse, a small pamphlet, entitled "Parallel between Caesar, Cromwell, and Bonaparte," was sent to the First Consul. He was absent when it came. I read it, and perceived that it openly advocated hereditary monarchy. I then knew nothing about the origin of this pamphlet, but I soon learned that it issued from the office of the Minister of the Interior [Lucien Bonaparte], and that it had been largely circulated. After reading it I laid it on the table. In a few minutes Bonaparte entered, and taking up the pamphlet pretended to look through it: "Have you read this?" said he.—"Yes, General."— "Well! what is your opinion of it?"—"I think it is calculated to produce an unfavourable effect on the public mind: it is ill-timed, for it prematurely reveals your views." The First Consul took the pamphlet and threw it on the ground, as he did all the stupid publications of the day after having slightly glanced over them. I was not singular in my opinion of the pamphlet, for next day the prefects in the immediate neighbourhood of Paris sent a copy of it to the First Consul, complaining of its mischievous effect; and I recollect that in one of their letters it was stated that such a

140 It was St. Regent, or St. Rejeant, who fired the infernal machine. The violence of the shock flung him against a post and part of his breast bone was driven in. He was obliged to resort to a surgeon, and it would seem that this man denounced him. (Memoirs of Miot de Melito, tome i. p. 264). The discussions which took place in the Council of State on this affair are remarkable, both for the violence of Napoleon and for the resistance made in the Council, to a great extent successfully, to his views as to the plot being one of the Jacobin party.

work was calculated to direct against him the poniards of new assassins. After reading this correspondence he said to me, "Bourrienne, send for Fouché; he must come directly, and give an account of this matter." In half an hour Fouché was in the First Consul's cabinet. No sooner had he entered than the following dialogue took place, in which the impetuous warmth of the one party was strangely contrasted with the phlegmatic and rather sardonic composure of the other.

"What pamphlet is this? What is said about it in Paris?"—"General, there is but one opinion of its dangerous tendency."—"Well, then, why did you allow it to appear?"—"General, I was obliged to show some consideration for the author!"—"Consideration for the author! What do you mean? You should have sent him to the temple."—"But, General, your brother Lucien patronises this pamphlet. It has been printed and published by his order. In short, it comes from the office of the Minister of the Interior."—"No matter for that! Your duty as Minister of Police was to have arrested Lucien, and sent him to the Temple. The fool does nothing but contrive how he can commit me!"

With these words the First Consul left the cabinet, shutting the door violently behind him. Being now alone with Fouché, I was eager to get an explanation of the suppressed smile which had more than once curled his lips during Bonaparte's angry expostulation. I easily perceived that there was something in reserve. "Send the author to the Temple!" said Fouché; "that would be no easy matter! Alarmed at the effect which this parallel between Caesar, Cromwell, and Bonaparte was likely to produce, I went to Lucien to point out to him his imprudence. He made me no answer, but went and got a manuscript, which he showed me, and which contained corrections and annotations in the First Consul's handwriting."

When Lucien heard how Bonaparte had expressed his displeasure at the pamphlet, he also came to the Tuileries to reproach his brother with having thrust him forward and then abandoned him. "'Tis your own fault," said the First Consul. "You have allowed yourself to be caught! So much the worse for you! Fouché is too cunning for you! You are a mere fool compared with him!" Lucien tendered his resignation, which was accepted, and he departed for Spain. This diplomatic mission turned to his advantage. It was necessary that one should veil the Machiavellian invention of the 'Parallel.'[141] Lucien, among other instructions, was directed to use all his endeavours to induce Spain to declare against Portugal in order to compel that power to separate herself from England.

The First Consul had always regarded Portugal as an English colony, and he conceived that to attack it was to assail England. He wished that Portugal should no longer favour

141 The 'Parallel' has been attributed to different writers; some phrases seemed the work of Lucien, but, says Thiers (tome ii p. 210), its rare elegance of language and its classical knowledge of history should attribute it to its real anchor, Fontanel, Joseph Bonaparte (Erreurs tome i. p. 270) says that Fontanel wrote it, and Lucien Bonaparte corrected it. See Meneval, tome iii. p. 105. Whoever wrote it Napoleon certainly planned its issue. "It was," said he to Roederer, "a work of which he himself had given the idea, but the last pages were by a fool" (Miot, tome i, p. 318). See also Lanfrey, tome ii. p. 208; and compare the story in Iung's Lucien, tome ii. p. 490. Miot, then in the confidence of Joseph, says, that Lucien's removal from, office was the result of an angry quarrel between him and Fouché in the presence of Napoleon, when Fouché attacked Lucien, not only for the pamphlet, but also for the disorder of his public and his private life; but Miot (tome i, p, 319) places the date of this as the 3d November, while Bourrienne dates the disapproval of the pamphlet in December.

England in her commercial relations, but that, like Spain, she should become dependent on him. Lucien was therefore sent as ambassador to Madrid, to second the Ministers of Charles IV. in prevailing on the King to invade Portugal. The King declared war, but it was not of long duration, and terminated almost without a blow being struck, by the taking of Olivenza. On the 6th of June 1801 Portugal signed the treaty of Badajoz, by which she promised to cede Olivenza, Almeida, and some other fortresses to Spain, and to close her ports against England. The First Consul, who was dissatisfied with the treaty, at first refused to ratify it. He still kept his army in Spain, and this proceeding determined Portugal to accede to some slight alterations in the first treaty. This business proved very advantageous to Lucien and Godoy.

The cabinet of the Tuileries was not the only place in which the question of hereditary succession was discussed. It was the constant subject of conversation in the salons of Paris, where a new dynasty was already spoken of. This was by no means displeasing to the First Consul; but he saw clearly that he had committed a mistake in agitating the question prematurely; for this reason he waged war against the Parallel, as he would not be suspected of having had any share in a design that had failed. One day he said to me, "I believe I have been a little too precipitate. The pear is not quite ripe!" The Consulate for life was accordingly postponed till 1802, and the hereditary empire till 1804.

After the failure of the artful publication of the pamphlet Fouché invited me to dine with him. As the First Consul wished me to dine out as seldom as possible, I informed him of the invitation I had received. He was, however, aware of it before, and he very readily gave me leave to go. At dinner Joseph was placed on the right of Fouché, and I next to Joseph, who talked of nothing but his brother, his designs, the pamphlet, and the bad effect produced by it. In all that fell from him there was a tone of blame and disapproval. I told him my opinion, but with greater reserve than I had used towards his brother. He seemed to approve of what I said; his confidence encouraged me, and I saw with pleasure that he entertained sentiments entirely similar to my own. His unreserved manner so imposed upon me that, notwithstanding the experience I had acquired, I was far from suspecting myself to be in the company of a spy. Next day the First Consul said to me very coldly, "Leave my letters in the basket, I will open them myself." This unexpected direction surprised me exceedingly, and I determined to play him a trick in revenge for his unfounded distrust. For three mornings I laid at the bottom of the basket all the letters which I knew came from the Ministers, and all the reports which were addressed to me for the First Consul. I then covered them over with those which; judging from their envelopes and seals, appeared to be of that trifling kind with which the First Consul was daily overwhelmed: these usually consisted of requests that he would name the number of a lottery ticket, so, that the writer might have the benefit of his good luck—solicitations that he would stand godfather to a child—petitions for places—announcements of marriages and births—absurd eulogies, etc. Unaccustomed to open the letters, he became impatient at their number, and he opened very few. Often on the same day, but always on the morrow, came a fresh letter from a Minister, who asked for an answer to his former one, and who complained of not having received one. The First Consul unsealed some twenty letters and left the rest.

The opening of all these letters, which he was not at other times in the habit of looking at, annoyed him extremely; but as I neither wished to carry the joke too far, nor to remain in the disagreeable position in which Joseph's treachery had placed me, I determined to bring the matter to a conclusion. After the third day, when the business of the night, which had been interrupted by little fits of ill-humour, was concluded, Bonaparte retired to bed. Half an hour after I went to his chamber, to which I was admitted at all hours. I had a candle in my hand, and, taking a chair, I sat down on the right side of the bed, and placed the candle on the table. Both he and Josephine awoke. "What is the matter?" he asked with surprise. "General, I have come to tell you that I can no longer remain here, since I have lost your confidence. You know how sincerely I am devoted to you; if you have, then, anything to reproach me with, let me at least know it, for my situation during the last three days has been very painful."—"What has Bourrienne done?" inquired Josephine earnestly.—"That does not concern you," he replied. Then turning to me he said, "'Tis true, I have cause to complain of you. I have been informed that you have spoken of important affairs in a very indiscreet manner."—"I can assure you that I spoke to none but your brother. It was he who led me into the conversation, and he was too well versed in the business for me to tell him any secret. He may have reported to you what he pleased, but could not I do the same by him? I could accuse and betray him as he has accused and betrayed me. When I spoke in confidence to your brother, could I regard him as an inquisitor?"—"I must confess," replied Bonaparte, "that after what I heard from Joseph I thought it right to put my confidence in quarantine."—"The quarantine has lasted three days, General; surely that is long enough."—"Well, Bourrienne, let us say no more about it. Open my letters as usual; you will find the answers a good deal in arrear, which has much vexed me; and besides, I was always stumbling on some stupid nonsense or other!"

I fancy I still see and hear the amiable Josephine sitting up in bed and saying, in her gentle way, "What! Bonaparte, is it possible you could suspect Bourrienne, who is so attached to you, and who is your only friend? How could you suffer such a snare to be laid for him? What! a dinner got up on purpose! How I hate these odious police manoeuvres!"—"Go to sleep," said Bonaparte; "let women mind their gewgaws, and not interfere with politics." It was near two in the morning before I retired.

When, after a few hours' sleep, I again saw the First Consul, he was more kind to me than ever, and I perceived that for the present every cloud had dispersed.' [142]

142 Joseph Bonaparte (Erreurs, tome i. p. 273) says what he reported to his brother was Bourrienne's conversation to him in the First Consul's cabinet during Napoleon's absence. It is curious that at the only time when Napoleon became dissatisfied with Meneval (Bourrienne's successor), and ordered him not to open the letters, he used the same expression when returning to the usual order of business, which in this case was to a few hours. "My dear Meneval," said he, "there are circumstances in which I am forced to put my confidence in quarantine." (Meneval, tome i. p. 123). For any one who has had to manage an office it is pleasant to find that even Napoleon was much dependent on a good secretary. In an illness of his secretary he said, showing the encumbrance of his desk, "with Meneval I should soon clear off all that." (Meneval, tome i. p. 151.)

CHAPTER IV

1800-1801

The armistice concluded after the battle of Marengo, which had been first broken and then resumed, continued to be observed for some time between the armies of the Rhine and Italy and the Imperial armies. But Austria, bribed by a subsidy of 2,000,000 sterling, would not treat for peace without the participation of England. She did not despair of recommencing the war successfully.

M. de St. Julien had signed preliminaries at Paris; but the Court of Vienna disavowed them, and Duroc, whom Bonaparte sent to convey the preliminaries to Vienna for the Imperial ratification, was not permitted to pass the Austrian advance posts. This unexpected proceeding, the result of the all-powerful influence of England, justly incensed the First Consul, who had given decided proofs of moderation and a wish for peace. "I want peace," said he to me, "to enable me to organise the interior; the people also want it. You see the conditions I offer. Austria, though beaten, obtains all she got at Campo-Formio. What can she want more? I could make further exactions; but, without fearing the reverses of 1799, I must think of the future. Besides, I want tranquillity, to enable me to settle the affairs of the interior, and to send aid to Malta and Egypt. But I will not be trifled with. I will force an immediate decision!"

In his irritation the First Consul despatched orders to Moreau, directing him to break the armistice and resume hostilities unless he regained possession of the bridges of the Rhine and the Danube by the surrender of Philipsburg, Ulm, and Ingolstadt. The Austrians then offered to treat with France on new bases. England wished to take part in the Congress, but to this the First Consul would not consent until she should sign a separate armistice and cease to make common cause with Austria.

The First Consul received intelligence of the occupation of the three garrisons on the 23d of September, the day he had fixed in his ultimatum to England for the renewal of hostilities. But for the meanwhile he was satisfied with the concessions of Austria: that power, in the expectation of being supported by England, asked her on what terms she was to treat.

During these communications with Austria M. Otto was in London negotiating for the exchange of prisoners. England would not hear of an armistice by sea like that which France had concluded with Austria by land. She alleged that, in case of a rupture, France would derive from that armistice greater advantage than Austria would gain by that already concluded. The difficulty and delay attending the necessary communications rendered these reasons plausible. The First Consul consented to accept other propositions from England, and to allow her to take part in the discussions of Luneville, but on condition that she should sign a treaty with him without the intervention of Austria. This England refused to do. Weary of this uncertainty, and the tergiversation of Austria, which was still under the influence of England, and feeling that the prolongation of such a state of things could only turn to his disadvantage, Bonaparte broke the armistice. He had already consented to sacrifices which his successes in Italy did not justify. The hope of an immediate peace had alone made him lose sight of the immense advantages which victory had given him.

Far from appearing sensible to the many proofs of moderation which the First Consul evinced, the combined insolence of England and Austria seemed only to increase. Orders were immediately given for resuming the offensive in Germany and Italy, and hostilities then recommenced.

The chances of fortune were long doubtful. After a reverse Austria made promises, and after an advantage she evaded them; but finally, fortune proved favourable to France. The French armies in Italy and Germany crossed the Mincio and the Danube, and the celebrated battle of Hohenlinden brought the French advanced posts within ten leagues of Vienna. This victory secured peace; for, profiting by past experience, the First Consul would not hear of any suspension of arms until Austria should consent to a separate treaty. Driven into her last intrenchments, Austria was obliged to yield. She abandoned England; and the English Cabinet, in spite of the subsidy of 2,000,000 sterling, consented to the separation. Great Britain was forced to come to this arrangement in consequence of the situation to which the successes of the army of Moreau had reduced Austria, which it was certain would be ruined by longer resistance.

England wished to enter into negotiations at Luneville. To this the First Consul acceded; but, as he saw that England was seeking to deceive him, he required that she should suspend hostilities with France, as Austria had done. Bonaparte very reasonably alleged that an indefinite armistice on the Continent would be more to the disadvantage of France than a long armistice by sea would be unfavourable to England. All this adjourned the preliminaries to 1801 and the peace to 1802.

The impatience and indignation of the First Consul had been highly excited by the evasions of Austria and the plots of England, for he knew all the intrigues that were carrying on for the restoration of the Bourbons. His joy may be therefore conceived when the battle of Hohenlinden balanced the scale of fortune in his favour. On the 3d of December 1800 Moreau gained that memorable victory which at length put an end to the hesitations of the Cabinet of Vienna.[143] On the 6th of December the First Consul received intelligence of the battle of Hohenlinden. It was on a Saturday, and he had just returned from the theatre when I delivered the despatches to him. He literally danced for joy. I must say that he did not expect so important a result from the movements of the army of the Rhine. This victory gave a new face to his negotiations for peace, and determined the opening of the Congress of Luneville, which took place on the 1st of January following.

On receiving information of the battle of Hohenlinden, Madame Moreau came to the Tuileries to call on the First Consul and Madame Bonaparte. She did not see them, and repeated her calls several times with no better success. The last time she came she was accompanied by her mother, Madame Hulot. She waited for a considerable time in vain, and when she was going away her mother, who could no longer restrain her feelings, said aloud, before me and several persons of the household, that "it ill became the wife of the conqueror of Hohenlinden to dance attendance in this way." This remark reached the ears of those to

143 On the eve of the battle of Hohenlinden Moreau was at supper with his aides de camp and several general officers, when a despatch was delivered to him. After he had read it be said to his guests, though he was far from being in the habit of boasting, "I am here made acquainted with Baron Kray's movements. They are all I could wish. To-morrow we will take from him 10,000 prisoners." Moreau took 40,000, besides a great many flags.—Bourrienne.

whom it was directed. Madame Moreau shortly after rejoined her husband in Germany; and some time after her departure Madame Hulot came to Malmaison to solicit promotion for her eldest son, who was in the navy. Josephine received Madame Hulot very kindly, and requested her to stay to dinner. She accepted the invitation. The First Consul, who did not see her until the hour of dinner, treated her very coolly: he said little to her, and retired as soon as dinner was over. His rudeness was so marked and offensive that Josephine, who was always kind and amiable, thought it necessary to apologise, by observing that his mind was disturbed by the non-arrival of a courier whom he expected.

Bonaparte entertained no dislike of Moreau, because he did not fear him; and after the battle of Hohenlinden he spoke of him in the highest terms, and frankly acknowledged the services he had rendered on that important occasion; but he could not endure his wife's family, who, he said, were a set of intriguers.[144]

Luneville having been fixed upon for the Congress, the First Consul sent his brother Joseph to treat with Count Louis de Cobentzel. On his way Joseph met M. de Cobentzel, who had passed Luneville, and was coming to Paris to sound the sentiments of the French Government. Joseph returned to Paris with him. After some conversation with the First Consul they set out next day for Luneville, of which place Bonaparte appointed General Clarke governor. This appeared to satisfy Clarke, who was very anxious to be something, and had long been importuning Bonaparte for an appointment.

A day or two after the news of the battle of Hohenlinden M. Maret came to present for Bonaparte's signature some, decrees made in Council. While affixing the signatures, and without looking up, the First Consul said to M. Maret, who was a favourite with him, and who was standing at his right hand, "Are you rich, Maret?"—"No, General."—"So much the worse: a man should be independent."—"General, I will never be dependent on any one but you." The First Consul then raised his eyes to Maret and said, "Hem! that is not bad!" and when the secretary-general was gone he said to me, "Maret is not deficient in cleverness: he made me a very good answer."

On the 9th of February 1801, six weeks after the opening of the Congress of Luneville, peace was signed between Austria and France. This peace—the fruit of Marengo and Hohenlinden—restored France to that honourable position which had been put in jeopardy by the feeble and incapable government of the pentarchy and the reverses of 1799. This peace, which in the treaty, according to custom, was called perpetual, lasted four years.

Joseph Bonaparte, while treating for France at Luneville, was speculating on the rise of the funds which he thought the peace would produce. Persons more wise, who were like him in the secret, sold out their stock at the moment when the certainty of the peace became known. But Joseph purchased to a great extent, in the hope of selling to advantage on the signature of peace. However, the news had been discounted, and a fall took place. Joseph's loss was considerable, and he could not satisfy the engagements in which his greedy and silly speculations had involved him. He applied to his brother, who neither wished nor was

144 Napoleon had good reason for his opinion. "Moreau had a mother- in-law and a wife lively and given to intrigue. Bonaparte could not bear intriguing women. Besides, on one occasion Madame Moreau's mother, when at Malmaison, had indulged in sharp remarks on a suspected scandalous intimacy between Bonaparte and his young sister Caroline, then just married. The Consul had not forgiven such conversation" (Rémusat tome i. P. 192). see also Meneval, tome iii. p. 57, as to the mischief done by Madame Hulot.

able to advance him the necessary sum. Bonaparte was, however, exceedingly sorry to see his elder brother in this embarrassment. He asked me what was to be done. I told him I did not know; but I advised him to consult M. de Talleyrand, from whom he had often received good advice. He did so, and M. de Talleyrand replied, with that air of coolness which is so peculiar to him, "What! is that all? Oh! that is nothing. It is easily settled. You have only to raise the price of the funds."—"But the money?"— "Oh, the money may be easily obtained. Make some deposits in the Mont-de-Piste, or the sinking fund. That will give you the necessary money to raise the funds; and then Joseph may sell out, and recover his losses." M. de Talleyrand's advice was adopted, and all succeeded as he had foretold. None but those who have heard M. de Talleyrand converse can form an accurate idea of his easy manner of expressing himself, his imperturbable coolness, the fixed unvarying expression of his countenance, and his vast fund of wit.[145] During the sitting of the Congress the First Consul learnt that the Government couriers conveyed to favoured individuals in Paris various things, but especially the delicacies of the table, and he ordered that this practice should be discontinued. On the very evening on which this order was issued Cambacérès entered the salon, where I was alone with the First Consul, who had already been laughing at the mortification which he knew this regulation would occasion to his colleague: "Well, Cambacérès, what brings you here at this time of night?"—"I come to solicit an exception to the order which you have just given to the Director of the Posts. How do you think a man can make friends unless he keeps a good table? You know very well how much good dinners assist the business of Government." The First Consul laughed, called him a gourmand, and, patting him on the shoulder, said, "Do not distress yourself, my dear Cambacérès; the couriers shall continue to bring you your 'dindes aux truffes', your Strasburg 'pates', your Mayence hams, and your other titbits."

Those who recollect the magnificent dinners given by Cambacérès and others, which were a general topic of conversation at the time, and who knew the ingenious calculation which was observed in the invitation of the guests, must be convinced of the vast influence of a good dinner in political affairs. As to Cambacérès, he did not believe that a good government could exist without good dinners; and his glory (for every man has his own particular glory) was to know that the luxuries of his table were the subject of eulogy throughout Paris, and even Europe. A banquet which commanded general suffrage was to him a Marengo or a Friedland.[146] At the commencement of 1801 Fulton presented to Bonaparte his memorial on

145 Talleyrand had a large experience in all sorts of speculation. When old he gave this counsel to one of his proteges: "Do not speculate. I have always speculated on assured information, and that has cost me so many millions;" and he named his losses. We may believe that in this reckoning he rather forgot the amount of his gains (Sainte-Beuve, Talleyrand, 93).

146 Bourrienne does not exaggerate this excellent quality of the worthy Cambacérès. When Beugnot was sent to administer the Grand Duchy of Berg, Cambacérès said to him, "My dear Beugnot, the Emperor arranges crowns as he chooses; here is the Grand Duke of Berg (Murat) going to Naples; he is welcome, I have no objection, but every year the Grand Duke sent me a couple of dozen hams from his Grand Duchy, and I warn you I do not intend to lose them, so you must make your preparations.". . . . I never once omitted to acquit myself of the obligation, and if there were any delay, . . . his Highness never failed to cause one of his secretaries to write a good scolding to my house steward; but when the hams arrived exactly, his highness

steamboats. I urged a serious examination of the subject. "Bah!" said he, "these projectors are all either intriguers or visionaries. Don't trouble me about the business." I observed that the man whom he called an intriguer was only reviving an invention already known, and that it was wrong to reject the scheme without examination. He would not listen to me; and thus was adjourned, for some time, the practical application of a discovery which has given such an important impulse to trade and navigation.

Paul I. fell by the hands of assassins on the night of the 24th of March 1801. The First Consul was much shocked on receiving the intelligence. In the excitement caused by this unexpected event, which had so important an influence on his policy, he directed me to send the following note to the Moniteur:—

> Paul I. died on the night of the 24th of March, and the English squadron passed the Sound on the 30th. History will reveal the connection which probably exists between these two events.

Thus were announced the crime of the 24th of March and the not ill-founded suspicions of its authors.[147] The amicable relations of Paul and Bonaparte had been daily strengthened. "In concert with the Czar," said Bonaparte, "I was sure of striking a mortal blow at the English power in India. A palace revolution has overthrown all my projects." This resolution, and the admiration of the Autocrat of Russia for the head of the French Republic, may certainly be numbered among the causes of Paul's death. The individuals generally accused at the time were those who were violently and perseveringly threatened, and who had the strongest

never failed to write to my wife himself to thank her. This was not all; the hams were to come carriage free. This petty jobbery occasioned discontent, . . . and it would not have cost me more to pay the carriage. The Prince would not allow it. There was an agreement between him and Lavalette (the head of the Posts), . . . And my Lord appeared to lay as much stress on the performance of this treaty as on the procuring of the ham, (Beugnot, tome i. p. 262). Cambacérès never suffered the cares of Government to distract his attention from the great object of life. On one occasion, for example, being detained in consultation with Napoleon beyond the appointed hour of dinner—it is said that the fate of the Duc d'Enghien was the topic under discussion—he was observed, when the hour became very late, to show great symptoms of impatience and restlessness. He at last wrote a note which he called a gentleman usher in waiting to carry. Napoleon, suspecting the contents, nodded to an aide de camp to intercept the despatch. As he took it into his hands Cambacérès begged earnestly that he would not read a trifling note upon domestic matters. Napoleon persisted, and found it to be a note to the cook containing only the following words, "Gardez les entremetes—les rotis sont perdue." When Napoleon was in good humor at the result of a diplomatic conference he was accustomed to take leave of the plenipotentiaries with, "Go and dine Cambacérès." His table was in fact an important state engine, as appears from the anecdote of the trout sent to him by the municipality of Geneva, and charged 300 francs in their accounts. The Imperial 'Cour des Comptes' having disallowed the item, was interdicted from meddling with similar municipal affairs in future (Hayward's Art of Dining, p. 20).

147 We do not attempt to rescue the fair name of our country. This is one among many instances in which Bourrienne was misled.—Editor of 1886 edition.

interest in the succession of a new Emperor. I have seen a letter from a northern sovereign which in my mind leaves no doubt on this subject, and which specified the reward of the crime, and the part to be performed by each actor. But it must also be confessed that the conduct and character of Paul I., his tyrannical acts, his violent caprices, and his frequent excesses of despotism, had rendered him the object of accumulated hatred, for patience has its limit. These circumstances did not probably create the conspiracy, but they considerably facilitated the execution of the plot which deprived the Czar of his throne and his life.

As soon as Alexander ascended the throne the ideas of the First Consul respecting the dismemberment of Poland were revived, and almost wholly engrossed his mind. During his first campaign in Italy, and several times when in Egypt, he told Sulkowsky that it was his ardent wish to reestablish Poland, to avenge the iniquity of her dismemberment, and by that grand repertory act to restore the former equilibrium of Europe. He often dictated to me for the 'Moniteur' articles tending to prove, by various arguments, that Europe would never enjoy repose until those great spoilations were avenged and repaired; but he frequently destroyed these articles instead of sending them to press. His system of policy towards Russia changed shortly after the death of Paul. The thought of a war against that empire unceasingly occupied his mind, and gave birth to the idea of that fatal campaign which took place eleven years afterwards, and which had other causes than the re-establishment of Poland. That object was merely set forward as a pretext.

Duroc was sent to St. Petersburg to congratulate the Emperor Alexander on his accession to the throne. He arrived in the Russian capital on the 24th of May. Duroc, who was at this time very young, was a great favourite of the First Consul. He never importuned Bonaparte by his solicitations, and was never troublesome in recommending any one or busying himself as an agent for favour; yet he warmly advocated the cause of those whom he thought injured, and honestly repelled accusations which he knew to be false. These moral qualities; joined to an agreeable person and elegant manners, rendered him a very superior man.

The year 1801 was, moreover, marked by the fatal creation of special tribunals, which were in no way justified by the urgency of circumstances. This year also saw the re-establishment of the African Company, the treaty of Luneville (which augmented the advantages France had obtained by the treaty of Campo-Formio), and the peace concluded between Spain and Portugal by means of Lucien. On the subject of this peace I may mention that Portugal, to obtain the cession of Olivenza, secretly offered Bonaparte, through me, 8,000,000 of francs if he would contribute his influence towards the acquisition of that town by Portugal. He, rejected this offer indignantly, declaring that he would never sell honour for money. He has been accused of having listened to a similar proposition at Passeriano, though in fact no such proposition was ever made to him. Those who bring forward such accusations little know the inflexibility of his principles on this point.

One evening in April 1801 an English paper—the London Gazette—arrived at Malmaison. It announced the landing in Egypt of the army commanded by Abercromby, the battle given by the English, and the death of their General. I immediately translated the article, and presented it to the First Consul, with the conviction that the news would be very painful to him. He doubted its truth, or at least pretended to do so. Several officers and aides de camp who were in the salon coincided in his opinion, especially Lannes, Bessières, and Duroc. They thought by so doing to please the First Consul, who then said to me, in a jeering tone, "Bah! you do not understand English. This is the way with you: you are always inclined to believe bad news rather than good!" These words, and the approving smiles of the gentlemen present, ruffled me, and I said with some warmth, "How, General, can you believe that the English Government would publish officially so important an event if it were not true? Do you think that a Government that has any self-respect would, in the face of Europe, state a falsehood respecting an affair the truth of which cannot long remain unknown? Did you ever know an instance of so important an announcement proving untrue after it had been published in the London Gazette? I believe it to be true, and the smiles of these gentlemen will not alter my opinion." On these observations the First Consul rose and said, "Come, Bourrienne, I want you in the library." After we had left the salon he added, "This is always the way with you. Why are you vexed at such trifles? I assure you I believe the news but too confidently, and I feared it before it came. But they think they please me by thus appearing to doubt it. Never mind them."—"I ask your pardon," said I, "but I conceive the best way of proving my attachment to you is to tell you what I believe to be true. You desire me not to delay a moment in announcing bad news to you. It would be far worse to disguise than to conceal it."

CHAPTER V

1801-1802

Before he placed two crowns on his own head Bonaparte thought it would promote the interests of his policy to place one on the head of a prince, and even a prince of the House of Bourbon. He wished to accustom the French to the sight of a king. It will hereafter be seen that he gave sceptres, like his confidence, conditionally, and that he was always ready to undo his own work when it became an obstacle to his ambitious designs.

In May 1801 the Infanta of Spain, Maria Louisa, third daughter of Charles IV., visited Paris. The Infante Louis de Bourbon, eldest son of the Duke of Parma, had gone to Madrid in 1798 to contract a marriage with Maria Amelia, the sister of Maria Louisa; but he fell in love with the latter. Godoy favoured the attachment, and employed all his influence to bring about the marriage. The son who, six years later, was born of this union, was named Charles Louis, after the King of Spain. France occupied the Duchy of Parma, which, in fulfilment of the conventions signed by Lucien Bonaparte, was to belong to her after the death of the reigning Duke. On the other hand, France was to cede the Grand Duchy of Tuscany to the son of the Duke of Parma; and Spain paid to France, according to stipulation, a considerable sum of money. Soon after the treaty was communicated to Don Louis and his wife they left Madrid and travelled through France. The prince took the title of Count of Leghorn. All accounts are unanimous as to the attentions which the Prince and Princess received on their journey. Among the fetes in honour of the illustrious couple that given by M. de Talleyrand at Neuilly was remarkable for magnificence.

When the Count of Leghorn was coming to pay his first visit to Malmaison Bonaparte went into the drawing-room to see that everything was suitably prepared for his reception. In a few minutes he returned to his cabinet and said to me, somewhat out of humour, "Bourrienne, only think of their stupidity; they had not taken down the picture representing me on the summit of the Alps pointing to Lombardy and commanding the conquest of it. I have ordered its removal. How mortifying it would have been if the Prince had seen it!"

Another picture in the drawing-room at Malmaison represented the First Consul sleeping on the snow on the summit of the Alps before the battle of Marengo.

The Count of Leghorn's visit to Paris imparted brilliancy to the first years of the reign of Bonaparte, of whom it was at that time said, "He made kings, but would not be one!"

At the representation of Oedipus, the following expression of Philactetes was received with transport:—

> "J'ai fait des Souverains, et n'ai pas voulu l'etre."
> *["Monarchs I've made, but one I would not be."]*

The First Consul, on leaving the theatre, did not conceal his satisfaction. He judged, from the applause with which that verse had been received, that his pamphlet was forgotten. The manner, moreover, in which a king, crowned by his hands, had been received by the public, was no indifferent matter to him, as he expected that the people would thus again become familiar with what had been so long proscribed.

This King, who, though well received and well entertained, was in all respects a very ordinary man, departed for Italy. I say very ordinary, not that I had an opportunity of judging of his character myself, but the First Consul told me that his capabilities were extremely limited; that he even felt repugnance to take a pen in his hand; that he never cast a thought on anything but his pleasures: in a word, that he was a fool.

One day, after the First Consul had spent several hours in company with him and his consort, he said to me, "I am quite tired. He is a mere automaton. I put a number of questions to him, but he can answer none. He is obliged to consult his wife, who makes him understand as well as she is able what he ought to say." The First Consul added, "The poor Prince will set off to-morrow, without knowing what he is going to do." I observed that it was a pity to see the happiness of the people of Tuscany entrusted to such a prince. Bonaparte replied, "Policy requires it. Besides, the young man is not worse than the usual run of kings." The Prince fully justified in Tuscany the opinion which the First Consul formed of him.[148]

In order to show still further attention to the King of Etruria, after his three weeks' visit to Paris, the First Consul directed him to be escorted to Italy by a French guard, and selected his brother-in-law Murat for that purpose.

The new King of a new kingdom entered Florence on the 12th of April 1801; but the reception given him by the Tuscans was not at all similar to what he had experienced at Paris. The people received the royal pair as sovereigns imposed on them by France. The ephemeral kingdom of Etruria lasted scarcely six years. The King died in 1803, in the flower of his age, and in 1807 the Queen was expelled from her throne by him who had constructed it for her.

At this period a powerful party urged Bonaparte to break with the Pope, and to establish a Gallican Church, the head of which should reside in France. They thought to flatter his ambition by indicating to him a new source of power which might establish a point

148 This unfortunate Prince was very ill-calculated to recommend, by his personal character, the institutions to which the nobility clung with so much fondness. Nature had endowed him with an excellent heart, but with very limited talents; and his mind had imbibed the false impress consequent upon his monastic education. He resided at Malmaison nearly the whole time of his visit to Paris. Madame Bonaparte used to lead the Queen to her own apartments; and as the First Consul never left his closet except to sit down to meals, the aides de camp were under the necessity of keeping the King company, and of endeavoring to entertain him, so wholly was he devoid of intellectual resources. It required, indeed, a great share of patience to listen to the frivolities which engrossed his attention. His turn of mind being thus laid open to view, care was taken to supply him with the playthings usually placed in the hands of children; he was, therefore, never at a loss for occupation. His nonentity was a source of regret to us: we lamented to see a tall handsome youth, destined to rule over his fellow-men, trembling at the neigh of a horse, and wasting his time in the game of hide-and-seek, or at leap-frog and whose whole information consisted in knowing his prayers, and in saying grace before and after meals. Such, nevertheless, was the man to whom the destinies of a nation were about to be committed! When he left France to repair to his kingdom, "Rome need not be uneasy," said the First Consul to us after the farewell audience, "there is no danger of his crossing the Rubicon" (Memoirs of the Duke of Rovigo, vol. i. p. 363).

of comparison between him and the first Roman emperors. But his ideas did not coincide with theirs on this subject. "I am convinced," said he, "that a part of France would become Protestant, especially if I were to favour that disposition. I am also certain that the much greater portion would remain Catholic, and would oppose, with the greatest zeal and fervour, the schism of a part of their fellow-citizens. I dread the religious quarrels, the family dissensions, and the public distractions, which such a state of things would inevitably occasion. In, reviving a religion which has always prevailed in the country, and which still prevails in the hearts of the people, and in giving the liberty of exercising their worship to the minority, I shall satisfy every one."

The First Consul, taking a superior view of the state of France, considered that the re-establishment of religious worship would prove a powerful support to his Government: and he had been occupied ever since the commencement of 1801 in preparing a Concordat with the Pope. It was signed in the month of July in the same year. It required some time to enable the parties to come to an understanding on the subject.

Cardinal Consalvi arrived, in the month of June 1801, at Paris, to arrange matters on the part of the Pope. Cardinal Caprara and M. de Spina also formed part of the embassy sent by the Holy Father. There were, besides, several able theologians, among whom Doctor C—— was distinguished.[149] He was a member of the Pope's chancery; his knowledge gave him so much influence over his colleagues that affairs advanced only as much as he pleased. However, he was gained over by honours conferred on him, and promises of money. Business then went on a little quicker. The Concordat was signed on the 15th of July 1801, and made a law of the State in the following April. The plenipotentiaries on the part of Bonaparte were Joseph Bonaparte, Cretet, and the Abby Bernier, afterwards Bishop of Versailles.[150]

A solemn Te Deum was chanted at the cathedral of Notre Dame on Sunday, the 11th of April. The crowd was immense, and the greater part of those present stood during the ceremony, which was splendid in the extreme; but who would presume to say that the general feeling was in harmony with all this pomp? Was, then, the time for this innovation not yet arrived? Was it too abrupt a transition from the habits of the twelve preceding years? It is unquestionably true that a great number of the persons present at the ceremony expressed, in their countenances and gestures, rather a feeling of impatience and displeasure than of satisfaction or of reverence for the place in which they were. Here and there murmurs arose expressive of discontent. The whispering, which I might more properly call open

149 The "Doctor C——" was Caselti, later Archbishop of Parma. Bonier was green the Bishopric of Orleans, not Versailles; see Erreurs, tome i, p. 276. The details of the surprise attempted at the last moment by putting before Cardinal Consalvi for his signature an altered copy of the Concordat should be read in his Memoirs (tome i. p. 355), or in Lanfrey (tome ii. p. 267). As for Napoleon's belief that part of the nation might become Protestant, Narbonne probably put the matter truly when he said there was not religion enough in France to stand a division. It should be noted that the Concordat did not so much restore the Catholic Church as destroy the old Gallican Church, with all its liberties, which might annoy either Pope or Emperor. But on this point see The Gallican Church and the Revolution, by Jervis: London, Began Paul, Trench and Co., 1882. The clergy may, it is true, have shown wisdom in acceding to any terms of restoration.

150 Orleans not Versailles. — D.W.

conversation, often interrupted the divine service, and sometimes observations were made which were far from being moderate. Some would turn their heads aside on purpose to take a bit of chocolate-cake, and biscuits were openly eaten by many who seemed to pay no attention to what was passing.

The Consular Court was in general extremely irreligious; nor could it be expected to be otherwise, being composed chiefly of those who had assisted in the annihilation of all religious worship in France, and of men who, having passed their lives in camps, had oftener entered a church in Italy to carry off a painting than to hear the Mass. Those who, without being imbued with any religious ideas, possessed that good sense which induces men to pay respect to the belief of others, though it be one in which they do not participate, did not blame the First Consul for his conduct, and conducted themselves with some regard to decency. But on the road from the Tuileries to Notre Dame, Lannes and Augereau wanted to alight from the carriage as soon as they saw that they were being driven to Mass, and it required an order from the First Consul to prevent their doing so. They went therefore to Notre Dame, and the next day Bonaparte asked Augereau what he thought of the ceremony. "Oh! it was all very fine," replied the General; "there was nothing wanting, except the million of men who have perished in the pulling down of what you are setting up." Bonaparte was much displeased at this remark.[151]

During the negotiations with the Holy Father Bonaparte one day said to me, "In every country religion is useful to the Government, and those who govern ought to avail themselves of it to influence mankind. I was a Mahometan in Egypt; I am a Catholic in France. With relation to the police of the religion of a state, it should be entirely in the hands of the sovereign. Many persons have urged me to found a Gallican Church, and make myself its head; but they do not know France. If they did, they would know that the majority of the people would not like a rupture with Rome. Before I can resolve on such a measure the Pope must push matters to an extremity; but I believe he will not do so."—"You are right, General, and you recall to my memory what Cardinal Consalvi said: 'The Pope will do all the First Consul desires.'"—"That is the best course for him. Let him not suppose that he has to do with an idiot. What do you think is the point his negotiations put most forward? The salvation of my soul! But with me immortality is the recollection one leaves in the memory of man. That idea prompts to great actions. It would be better for a man never to have lived than to leave behind him no traces of his existence."

Many endeavours were made to persuade the First Consul to perform in public the duties imposed by the Catholic religion. An influential example, it was urged, was required. He told me once that he had put an end to that request by the following declaration: "Enough of this. Ask me no more. You will not obtain your object. You shall never make a hypocrite of me. Let us remain where we are."

I have read in a work remarkable on many accounts that it was on the occasion of the Concordat of the 15th July 1801 that the First Consul abolished the republican calendar and

151 This remark has been attributed elsewhere to General Delmas. According to a gentleman who played a part in this empty pageantry, Lannes at one moment did get out of the carriage, and Augereau kept swearing in no low whisper during the whole of the chanted Mass. Most of the military chiefs who sprang out of the Revolution had no religion at all, but there were some who were Protestants, and who were irritated by the restoration of Catholicism as the national faith.—Editor of 1896 edition.

reestablished the Gregorian. This is an error. He did not make the calendar a religious affair. The 'Senatus-consulte', which restored the use of the Gregorian calendar, to commence in the French Empire from the 11th Nivôse, year XIV. (1st January 1806), was adopted on the 22d Fructidor, year XIII. (9th September 1805), more than four years after the Concordat. The re-establishment of the ancient calendar had no other object than to bring us into harmony with the rest of Europe on a point so closely connected with daily transactions, which were much embarrassed by the decadary calendar.

Bonaparte at length, however, consented to hear Mass, and St. Cloud was the place where this ancient usage was first re-established. He directed the ceremony to commence sooner than the hour announced in order that those who would only make a scoff at it might not arrive until the service was ended.

Whenever the First Consul determined to hear Mass publicly on Sundays in the chapel of the Palace a small altar was prepared in a room near his cabinet of business. This room had been Anne of Austria's oratory. A small portable altar, placed on a platform one step high, restored it to its original destination. During the rest of the week this chapel was used as a bathing-room. On Sunday the door of communication was opened, and we heard Mass sitting in our cabinet of business. The number of persons there never exceeded three or four, and the First Consul seldom failed to transact some business during the ceremony, which never lasted longer than twelve minutes. Next day all the papers had the news that the First Consul had heard Mass in his apartments. In the same way Louis XVIII. has often heard it in his!

On the 19th of July 1801 a papal bull absolved Talleyrand from his vows. He immediately married Madame Grandt, and the affair obtained little notice at the time. This statement sufficiently proves how report has perverted the fact. It has been said that Bonaparte on becoming Emperor wished to restore that decorum which the Revolution had destroyed, and therefore resolved to put an end to the improper intimacy which subsisted between Talleyrand and Madame Grandt. It is alleged that the Minister at first refused to marry the lady, but that he at last found it necessary to obey the peremptory order of his master. This pretended resurrection of morality by Bonaparte is excessively ridiculous. The bull was not registered in the Council of State until the 19th of August 1802.[152]

I will end this chapter by a story somewhat foreign to the preceding transactions, but which personally concerns myself. On the 20th of July 1801 the First Consul, 'ex proprio motu', named me a Councillor of State extraordinary. Madame Bonaparte kindly condescended to have an elegant but somewhat ideal costume made for me. It pleased the First Consul, however, and he had a similar one made for himself. He wore it a short time and then left it off. Never had Bonaparte since his elevation shown himself so amiable as on this occasion.

---

152 The First Consul had on several occasions urged M. de Talleyrand to return to holy orders. He pointed out to him that that course would be most becoming his age and high birth, and promised that he should be made a cardinal, thus raising him to a par with Richelieu, and giving additional lustre to his administration (Memoirs of the Duke of Rovigo, vol. i. p. 426). But M. de Talleyrand vindicated his choice, saying, "A clever wife often compromises her husband; a stupid one only compromises herself" (Historical Characters, p.122, Bulwer, Lord Dulling).

CHAPTER VI

1802

For the last time in these Memoirs I shall return to the affairs of Egypt—to that episode which embraces so short a space of time and holds so high a place in the life of Bonaparte. Of all his conquests he set the highest value on Egypt, because it spread the glory of his name throughout the East. Accordingly he left nothing unattempted for the preservation of that colony. In a letter to General Kléber he said, "You are as able as I am to understand how important is the possession of Egypt to France. The Turkish Empire, in which the symptoms of decay are everywhere discernible, is at present falling to pieces, and the evil of the evacuation of Egypt by France would now be the greater, as we should soon see that fine province pass into the possession of some other European power." The selection of Gantheaume, however, to carry assistance to Kléber was not judicious. Gantheaume had brought the First Consul back from Egypt, and though the success of the passage could only be attributed to Bonaparte's own plan, his determined character, and superior judgment, yet he preserved towards Gantheaume that favourable disposition which is naturally felt for one who has shared a great danger with us, and upon whom the responsibility may be said to have been imposed.

This confidence in mediocrity, dictated by an honourable feeling, did not obtain a suitable return. Gantheaume, by his indecision and creeping about in the Mediterranean, had already failed to execute a commission entrusted to him. The First Consul, upon finding he did not leave Brest after he had been ordered to the Mediterranean, repeatedly said to me, "What the devil is Gantheaume about?" With one of the daily reports sent to the First Consul he received the following quatrain, which made him laugh heartily:

> "Vaisseaux lestes, tete sans lest,
> Ainsi part l'Amiral Gantheaume;
> Il s'en va de Brest a Bertheaume,
> Et revient de Bertheaume a Brest!"
>
> ["*With ballast on board, but none in his brain,*
> *Away went our gallant Gantheaume,*
> *On a voyage from Brest to Bertheaume,*
> *And then from Bertheaume—to Brest back again!*"]

Gantheaume's hesitation, his frequent tergiversations, his arrival at Toulon, his tardy departure, and his return to that port on the 19th of February 1801, only ten days prior to Admiral Keith's appearance with Sir Ralph Abercromby off Alexandria, completely foiled all the plans which Bonaparte had conceived of conveying succour and reinforcements to a colony on the brink of destruction.

Bonaparte was then dreaming that many French families would carry back civilisation, science, and art to that country which was their cradle. But it could not be concealed that his departure from Egypt in 1799 had prepared the way for the loss of that country, which was hastened by Kléber's death and the choice of Menou as his successor.

A sure way of paying court to the First Consul and gaining his favour was to eulogise his views about Egypt, and to appear zealous for maintaining the possession of that country. By these means it was that Menou gained his confidence. In the first year of the occupation of that country he laid before him his dreams respecting Africa. He spoke of the negroes of Senegal, Mozambique, Mehedie, Marabout, and other barbarous countries which were all at once to assume a new aspect, and become civilised, in consequence of the French possession of Egypt. To Menou's adulation is to be attributed the favourable reception given him by the First Consul, even after his return from Egypt, of which his foolish conduct had allowed the English to get possession. The First Consul appointed him Governor of Piedmont, and at my request gave my elder brother the situation of Commissary-General of Police in that country; but I am in candour obliged to confess that the First Consul was obliged to retract this mark of his favour in consequence of my brother's making an abuse of it.

It was also by flattering the First Consul on the question of the East that Davoust, on his return from Egypt in 1800 in consequence of the Convention of El-Ariah, insinuated himself into Bonaparte's good graces and, if he did not deserve, obtained his favour. At that time Davoust certainly had no title whatever to the good fortune which he suddenly experienced. He obtained, without first serving in a subordinate rank, the command-in-chief of the grenadiers of the Consular Guard; and from that time commenced the deadly hatred which Davoust bore towards me. Astonished at the great length of time that Bonaparte had been one day conversing with him I said, as soon as he was gone, "How could you talk so long with a man whom you have always called a stupid fellow?"—"Ah! but I did not know him well enough before. He is a better man, I assure you, than he is thought; and you will come over to my opinion."—"I hope so." The First Consul, who was often extremely indiscreet, told Davoust my opinion of him, and his hostility against me ceased but with his life.

The First Consul could not forget his cherished conquest in the East. It was constantly the object of his thoughts. He endeavoured to send reinforcements to his army from Brest and Toulon, but without success. He soon had cause to repent having entrusted to the hands of Menou the command-in-chief, to which he became entitled only by seniority, after the assassination of Kléber by Soleiman Heleby. But Bonaparte's indignation was excited when he became acquainted with Menou's neglect and mismanagement, when he saw him giving reins to his passion for reform, altering and destroying everything, creating nothing good in its stead, and dreaming about forming a land communication with the Hottentots and Congo instead of studying how to preserve the country. His pitiful plans of defence, which were useless from their want of combination, appeared to the First Consul the height of ignorance. Forgetful of all the principles of strategy, of which Bonaparte's conduct afforded so many examples, he opposed to the landing of Abercromby a few isolated corps, which were unable to withstand the enemy's attack, while the English army might have been entirely annihilated had all the disposable troops been sent against it.

The great admiration which Menou expressed at the expedition to Egypt; his excessive fondness for that country, the religion of which he had ridiculously enough embraced under the name of Abdallah; the efforts he made, in his sphere, to preserve the colony; his enthusiasm and blind attachment to Bonaparte; the flattering and encouraging accounts he gave of the situation of the army, at first had the effect of entirely covering Menou's incapacity.[153] This alone can account for the First Consul's preference of him. But I am far from concurring in what has been asserted by many persons, that France lost Egypt at the very moment when it seemed most easy of preservation. Egypt was conquered by a genius of vast intelligence, great capacity, and profound military science. Fatuity, stupidity, and incapacity lost it. What was the result of that memorable expedition? The destruction of one of our finest armies; the loss of some of our best generals; the annihilation of our navy; the surrender of Malta; and the sovereignty of England in the Mediterranean. What is the result at present? A scientific work. The gossiping stories and mystifications of Herodotus, and the reveries of the good Rollin, are worth as much, and have not cost so dear.

The First Consul had long been apprehensive that the evacuation of Egypt was unavoidable. The last news he had received from that country was not very encouraging, and created a presentiment of the approach of the dreaded catastrophe. He, however, published the contrary; but it was then of great importance that, an account of the evacuation should not reach England until the preliminaries of peace were signed, for which purpose M. Otto was exerting all his industry and talent. We made a great merit of abandoning our conquests in Egypt; but the sacrifice would not have been considered great if the events which took place at the end of August had been known in London before the signing of the preliminaries on the 1st of October. The First Consul himself answered M. Otto's last despatch, containing a copy of the preliminaries ready to be adopted by the English Ministry. Neither this despatch nor the answer was communicated to M. de Talleyrand, then Minister for Foreign Affairs. The First Consul, who highly appreciated the great talents and knowledge of that Minister, never closed any diplomatic arrangement without first consulting him; and he was right in so doing. On this occasion, however, I told him that as M. de Talleyrand was, for his health, taking the waters of Bourbon-l'Archambault, four days must elapse before his reply could be received, and that the delay might cause the face of affairs to change. I reminded him that Egypt was on the point of yielding. He took my advice, and it was well for him that he did, for the news of the compulsory evacuation of Egypt arrived in London the day after the signing of the preliminaries. M. Otto informed the First Consul by letter that Lord Hawkesbury, ill communicating to him the news of the evacuation, told him he was very glad everything was settled, for it would have been impossible for him to have treated on the same basis after the arrival of such news. In reality we consented at Paris to the voluntary evacuation of Egypt, and that was something for England, while Egypt was at that very time evacuated by a convention made on the spot. The definitive evacuation of Egypt took place on the 30th of August 1801; and thus the conquest of that country, which had cost so dear, was rendered useless, or rather injurious.

---

153 For a ludicrous description of Menou see the Memoirs of Marmont:— "Clever and gay, he was an agreeable talker, but a great liar. He was not destitute of some education. His character, one of the oddest in the world, came very near to lunacy: Constantly writing, always in motion in his room, riding for exercise every day, he was never able to start on any necessary of useful journey. . . . When, later, Bonaparte, then First Consul, gave him by special favour the administration of Piedmont, he put off his departure from day to day for six months; and then he only did start because his friend Maret himself put him into his carriage, with post-horses already harnessed to it. . . . When he left this post they found in his cabinet 900 letters which he had not opened. He was an eccentric lunatic, amusing enough sometimes, but a curse to everything which depended on him." (Memoirs of the Duc de Raguse, tome i. p. 410).

CHAPTER VII

1802

The epoch of the peace of Amiens must be considered as the most glorious in the history of France, not excepting the splendid period of Louis XIV.'s victories and the more brilliant era of the Empire. The Consular glory was then pure, and the opening prospect was full of flattering hope; whereas those who were but little accustomed to look closely into things could discern mighty disasters lurking under the laurels of the Empire.

The proposals which the First Consul made in order to obtain peace sufficiently prove his sincere desire for it. He felt that if in the commencement of his administration he could couple his name with so hoped for an act he should ever experience the affection and gratitude of the French. I want no other proof of his sentiments than the offer he made to give up Egypt to the Grand Seignior, and to restore all the ports of the Gulf of Venice and of the Mediterranean to the States to which they had previously belonged; to surrender Malta to the order of the Knights of St. John, and even to raze its fortifications if England should think such a measure necessary for her interests. In the Indies, Ceylon was to be left to him,[154] and he required the surrender of the Cape of Good Hope and all the places taken by the English in the West Indies.

England had firmly resolved to keep Malta, the Gibraltar of the Mediterranean, and the Cape of Good Hope, the caravanserai of the Indies. She was therefore unwilling to close with the proposition respecting Malta; and she said that an arrangement might be made by which it would be rendered independent both of Great Britain and France. We clearly saw that this was only a lure, and that, whatever arrangements might be entered into, England would keep Malta, because it was not to be expected that the maritime power would willingly surrender an island which commands the Mediterranean. I do not notice the discussions respecting the American islands, for they were, in my opinion, of little consequence to us.[155] They cost

154 Ceylon belonged to Holland, but was retained by England under the treaty of Amiens.

155 It is strange that Bourrienne does not allude to one of the first arbitrary acts of Napoleon, the discussions on which formed part of those conversations between Napoleon and his brother Lucien of which Bourrienne complained to Josephine he knew nothing. In 1763 France had ceded to England the part of Louisiana on the east of the Mississippi, and the part on the west of that river, with New Orleans, to Spain. By the treaty negotiated with Spain by Lucien Bonaparte in 1800 her share was given back to France. On the 80th April 1803 Napoleon sold the whole to the United States for 80,000,000 francs (L 3,260,000), to the intense anger of his brothers Joseph and Lucien. Lucien was especially proud of having obtained the cession for which Napoleon was, at that time, very anxious; but both brothers were horrified when Napoleon disclosed how little he cared for constitutional forms by telling them that if the Legislature, as his brothers threatened, would not ratify the treaty, he would do without the ratification; see Iung's Letter, tome ii. p. 128. Napoleon's most obvious motives were want of

more than they produce; and they will escape from us, some time or other, as all colonies ultimately do from the parent country. Our whole colonial system is absurd; it forces us to pay for colonial produce at a rate nearly double that for which it may be purchased from our neighbours.

When Lord Hawkesbury consented to evacuate Malta, on condition that it should be independent of France and Great Britain, he must have been aware that such a condition would never be fulfilled. He cared little for the order of St. John, and he should have put, by way of postscript, at the bottom of his note, "We will keep Malta in spite of you." I always told the First Consul that if he were in the situation of the English he would act the same part; and it did not require much sagacity to foretell that Malta would be the principal cause of the rupture of peace. He was of my opinion; but at that moment he thought everything depended on concluding the negotiations, and I entirely agreed with him. It happened, as was foreseen, that Malta caused the renewal of war. The English, on being called upon to surrender the island, eluded the demand, shifted about, and at last ended by demanding that Malta should be placed under the protection of the King of Naples,—that is to say, under the protection of a power entirely at their command, and to which they might dictate what they pleased. This was really too cool a piece of irony!

I will here notice the quarrel between the First Consul and the English newspapers, and give a new proof of his views concerning the freedom of the press. However, liberty of the press did once contribute to give him infinite gratification, namely, when all the London journals mentioned the transports of joy manifested in London on the arrival of General Lauriston, the bearer of the ratification of the preliminaries of peace.

The First Consul was at all times the declared enemy of the liberty of the press, and therefore he ruled the journals with a hand of iron.[156] I have often heard him say, "Were I

---

money and the certainty of the seizure of the province by England, as the rupture with her was now certain. But there was perhaps another cause. The States had already been on the point of seizing the province from Spain, which had interfered with their trade (Hinton's United States, p. 435, and Thiers tome iv, p. 320). Of the sum to be paid, 20,000,000 were to go to the States, to cover the illegal seizures of American ships by the French navy, a matter which was not settled for many years later. The remaining 80,000,000 were employed in the preparations for the invasion of England; see Thiers, tome iv. pp. 320 and 326, and Lanfrey, tome iii. p. 48. The transaction is a remarkable one, as forming the final withdrawal of France from North America (with the exception of some islands on the Newfoundland coast), where she had once held such a proud position. It also eventually made an addition to the number of slave States.

156 An incident, illustrative of the great irritation which Bonaparte felt at the plain speaking of the English press, also shows the important character of Coleridge's writings in the 'Morning Post'. In the course of a debate in the House of Commons Fox asserted that the rupture of the Peace of Amiens had its origin in certain essays which had appeared in the Morning POST, and which were known to have proceeded from the pen of Coleridge. But Fox added an ungenerous and malicious hint that the writer was at Rome, within the reach of Bonaparte. The information reached the ears for which it was uttered, and an order was sent from Paris to compass the arrest of Coleridge. It was in the year 1806, when the poet was making a tour in Italy. The news reached him at Naples, through a brother of the illustrious Humboldt, as Mr.

to slacken the reins, I should not continue three months in power." He unfortunately held the same opinion respecting every other prerogative of public freedom. The silence he had imposed in France he wished, if he could, to impose in England. He was irritated by the calumnies and libels so liberally cast upon him by the English journals, and especially by one written in French, called 'L'Ambigu', conducted by Peltier, who had been the editor of the 'Actes des Apotres' in Paris. The 'Ambigu' was constantly teeming with the most violent attacks on the First Consul and the French nation. Bonaparte could never, like the English, bring himself to despise newspaper libels, and he revenged himself by violent articles which he caused to be inserted in the 'Moniteur'. He directed M. Otto to remonstrate, in an official note, against a system of calumny which he believed to be authorised by the English Government. Besides this official proceeding he applied personally to Mr. Addington, the Chancellor of the Exchequer, requesting him to procure the adoption of legislative measures against the licentious writings complained of; and, to take the earliest opportunity of satisfying his hatred against the liberty of the press, the First Consul seized the moment of signing the preliminaries to make this request.

Mr. Addington wrote a long answer to the First Consul, which I translated for him. The English Minister refuted, with great force, all the arguments which Bonaparte had employed against the press. He also informed the First Consul that, though a foreigner, it was competent in him to institute a complaint in the courts of law; but that in such case he must be content to see all the scandalous statements of which he complained republished in the report of the trial. He advised him to treat the libels with profound contempt, and do as he and others did, who attached not the slightest importance to them. I congratulate myself on having in some degree prevented a trial taking place at that time.

Things remained in this state for the moment; but after the peace of Amiens the First Consul prosecuted Pettier, whose journal was always full of violence and bitterness against him. Pettier was defended by the celebrated Mackintosh, who, according to the accounts of the time, displayed great eloquence on this occasion, yet, in spite of the ability of his counsel, he was convicted. The verdict, which public opinion considered in the light of a triumph for the defendant, was not followed up by any judgment, in consequence of the rupture of the peace occurring soon after. It is melancholy to reflect that this nervous susceptibility to the libels of the English papers contributed certainly as much as, and perhaps more than, the consideration of great political interests to the renewal of hostilities. The public would be astonished at a great many things if they could only look under the cards.

I have anticipated the rupture of the treaty of Amiens that I might not interrupt what I had to mention respecting Bonaparte's hatred of the liberty of the press. I now return to the end of the year 1801, the period of the expedition against St. Domingo.

The First Consul, after dictating to me during nearly: the whole of one night instructions

---

Gillman says—or in a friendly warning from Prince Jerome Bonaparte, as we have it on the authority of Mr. Cottle—and the Pope appears to have been reluctant to have a hand in the business, and, in fact, to have furnished him with a passport, if not with a carriage for flight, Coleridge eventually got to Leghorn, where he got a passage by an American ship bound for England; but his escape coming to the ears of Bonaparte, a look-out was kept for the ship, and she was chased by a French cruiser, which threw the captain into such a state of terror that he made Coleridge throw all his journals and papers overboard (Andrews' History of Journalism, vol. ii. p. 28).

for that expedition, sent for General Leclerc, and said to him in my presence, "Here, take your instructions; you have a fine opportunity for filling your purse. Go, and no longer tease me with your eternal requests for money." The friendship which Bonaparte felt for his sister Pauline had a good deal of influence in inducing him to take this liberal way of enriching her husband.

The expedition left the ports of France on the 14th of December 1801, and arrived off Cape St. Domingo on the 1st of February 1802. The fatal result of the enterprise is well known, but we are never to be cured of the folly of such absurd expeditions. In the instructions given to Leclerc everything was foreseen; but it was painful to know that the choice of one of the youngest and least capable of all the generals of the army left no hope of a successful result. The expedition to St. Domingo was one of Bonaparte's great errors. Almost every person whom he consulted endeavoured to dissuade him from it. He attempted a justification through the medium of his historians of St. Helena; but does he succeed when he says, "that he was obliged to yield to the advice of his Council of State?" He, truly, was a likely man to submit a question of war to the discussion of the Council of State, or to be guided in such an affair by any Council! We must believe that no other motive influenced the First Consul but the wish, by giving him the means of enriching himself, to get rid of a brother-in-law who had the gift of specially annoying him. The First Consul, who did not really much like this expedition, should have perhaps reflected longer on the difficulties of attempting to subdue the colony by force. He was shaken by this argument, which I often repeated to him, and he agreed with it, but the inconceivable influence which the members of his family exercised on him always overcame him.

Bonaparte dictated to me a letter for Toussaint, full of sounding words and fine promises, informing him that his two children, who had been educated in Paris, were sent back to him, offering him the title of vice-governor, and stating that he ought readily to assist in an arrangement which would contribute to reconnect the colony with the mother-country. Toussaint, who had at first shown a disposition to close with the bargain, yet feeling afraid of being deceived by the French, and probably induced by ambitious motives, resolved on war. He displayed a great deal of talent; but, being attacked before the climate had thinned the French ranks, he was unable to oppose a fresh army, numerous and inured to war. He capitulated, and retired to a plantation, which he was not to leave without Leclerc's permission. A feigned conspiracy on the part of the blacks formed a pretence for accusing Toussaint, and he was seized and sent to France.

Toussaint was brought to Paris in the beginning of August. He was sent, in the first instance, to the Temple, whence he was removed to the Chateau de Joux. His imprisonment was rigorous; few comforts were allowed him. This treatment, his recollection of the past, his separation from the world, and the effects of a strange climate, accelerated his death, which took place a few months after his arrival in France. The reports which spread concerning his death, the assertion that it was not a natural one, and that it had been caused by poison, obtained no credit. I should add that Toussaint wrote a letter to Bonaparte; but I never saw in it the expression attributed to him, "The first man of the blacks to the first man of the whites" Bonaparte acknowledged that the black leader possessed energy, courage, and great skill. I am sure that he would have rejoiced if the result of his relations with St. Domingo had been something else than the kidnaping and transportation of Toussaint.

Leclerc, after fruitless efforts to conquer the colony, was himself carried off by the yellow fever. Rochambeau succeeded him by right of seniority, and was as unsuccessful as Menou had been in Egypt. The submission of the blacks, which could only have been obtained by conciliation, he endeavoured to compel by violence. At last, in December 1803, he surrendered to an English squadron, and abandoned the island to Dessalines.

Bonaparte often experienced severe bodily pain, and I have now little doubt, from the nature of his sufferings, that they were occasioned by the commencement of that malady which terminated his life at St. Helena. These pains, of which he frequently complained, affected him most acutely on the night when he dictated to me the instructions for General Leclerc. It was very late when I conducted him to his apartment. We had just been taking a cup of chocolate, a beverage of which we always partook when our business lasted longer than one o'clock in the morning. He never took a light with him when he went up to his bedroom. I gave him my arm, and we had scarcely got beyond the little staircase which leads to the corridor, when he was rudely run against by a man who was endeavouring to escape as quickly as possible by the staircase. The First Consul did not fall because I supported him. We soon gained his chamber, where we, found Josephine, who, having heard the noise, awoke greatly alarmed. From the investigations which were immediately made it appeared that the uproar was occasioned by a fellow who had been keeping an assignation and had exceeded the usual hour for his departure.

On the 7th of January 1802 Mademoiselle Hortense was married to Louis Bonaparte. As the custom was not yet resumed of adding the religious ceremony to the civil contract, the nuptial benediction was on this occasion privately given by a priest at the house Rue de la Victoire. Bonaparte also caused the marriage of his sister Caroline, (The wife of Murat, and the cleverest of Bonaparte's sisters.) which had taken place two years earlier before a mayor, to be consecrated in the same manner; but he and his wife did not follow the example. Had he already, then, an idea of separating from Josephine, and therefore an unwillingness to render a divorce more difficult by giving his marriage a religious sanction? I am rather inclined to think, from what he said to me, that his neglecting to take a part in the religious ceremony arose from indifference.

Bonaparte said at St. Helena, speaking of Louis and Hortense, that "they loved each other when they married: they desired to be united. The marriage was also the result of Josephine's intrigues, who found her account in it." I will state the real facts. Louis and Hortense did not love one another at all. That is certain. The First Consul knew it, just as he well knew that Hortense had a great inclination for Duroc, who did not fully return it. The First Consul agreed to their union, but Josephine was troubled by such a marriage, and did all she could to prevent it. She often spoke to me about it, but rather late in the day. She told me that her brothers-in law were her declared enemies, that I well knew their intrigues, and that I well knew there was no end to the annoyances they made her undergo. In fact, I did know all this perfectly. She kept on repeating to me that with this projected marriage she would not have any support; that Duroc was nothing except by the favour of Bonaparte; that he had neither fortune, fame, nor reputation, and that he could be no help to her against the well-known ill-will of the brothers of Bonaparte. She wanted some assurance for the future. She added that her husband was very fond of Louis, and that if she had the good fortune to unite him to her daughter this would be a counterpoise to the calumnies and persecutions of her other brothers-in-law. I answered her that she had concealed her intentions too long from me, and that I had promised my services to the young people, and the more willingly as I knew the favourable opinion of the First Consul, who had often said to me, "My wife has done well; they suit one another, they shall marry one another. I like Duroc; he is of good family. I have rightly given Caroline to Murat, and Pauline to Leclerc, and I can well give Hortense to Duroc, who is a fine fellow. He is worth more than the others. He is now general of a division there is nothing against this marriage. Besides, I have other plans for Louis." In speaking to Madame Bonaparte I added that her daughter burst into tears when spoken to about her marriage with Louis.

The First Consul had sent a brevet of general of division to Duroc by a special courier, who went to Holland, through which the newly-made general had to pass on his return from St. Petersburg, where, as I have already said, he had been sent to compliment the Emperor Alexander on his accession to the throne. The First Consul probably paid this compliment to Duroc in the belief that the marriage would take place.

During Duroc's absence the correspondence of the lovers passed, by their consent, through my hands. Every night I used to make one in a party at billiards, at which Hortense played very well. When I told her, in a whisper, that I had got a letter for her, she would immediately leave off playing and run to her chamber, where I followed and gave her Duroc's epistle. When she opened it her eyes would fill with tears, and it was some time before she could return to the salon. All was useless for her. Josephine required a support in the family against the family. Seeing her firm resolution, I promised to no longer oppose her wishes, which I could not disapprove, but I told her I could only maintain silence and neutrality in these little debates, and she seemed satisfied.

When we were at Malmaison those intrigues continued. At the Tuileries the same conduct was pursued, but then the probability of success was on Duroc's side; I even congratulated him on his prospects, but he received my compliments in a very cold manner. In a few days after Josephine succeeded in changing the whole face of affairs. Her heart was entirely set on the marriage of Louis with her daughter; and prayers, entreaties, caresses, and all those little arts which she so well knew how to use, were employed to win the First Consul to her purpose.

On the 4th of January the First Consul, after dinner, entered our cabinet, where I was employed. "Where is Duroc?" he inquired.—"He has gone to the opera, I believe."—"Tell him, as soon as he returns, that I have promised Hortense to him, and he shall have her. But I wish the marriage to take place in two days at the latest. I will give him 500,000 francs, and name him commandant of the eighth military division; but he must set out the day after his marriage with his wife for Toulon. We must live apart; I want no son-in-law at home. As I wish to come to some conclusion, let me know to-night whether this plan will satisfy him."—"I think it will not."—"Very well! then she shall marry Louis."—"Will she like that?"—"She must like it." Bonaparte gave me these directions in a very abrupt manner, which made me think that some little domestic warfare had been raging, and that to put an end to it he had come to propose his ultimatum. At half-past ten in the evening Duroc returned; I reported to him, word for word, the proposition of the First Consul. "Since it has come to that, my good friend," said he, "tell him he may keep his daughter for me. I am going to see the ——," and, with an indifference for which I cannot account, he took his hat and went off.[157]

157 Duroc eventually married a Mademoiselle Hervae d'Almenara, the daughter of a Spanish banker, who was later Minister of Joseph, and was created Marquis of Abruenara. The lady was neither handsome nor amiable, but she possessed a vast fortune, and Bonaparte himself solicited her hand for his aide de camp. After the death of Duroc his widow married a M. Fabvier, and Napoleon gave his Duchy of Frioul to his daughter.

The First Consul, before going to bed, was informed of Duroc's reply, and Josephine received from him the promise that Louis and Hortense should be married. The marriage took place a few days after, to the great regret of Hortense, and probably to the satisfaction of Duroc. Louis submitted to have forced on him as a wife a woman who had hitherto avoided him as much as possible. She always manifested as much indifference for him as he displayed repugnance for her, and those sentiments have not been effaced.[158] Napoleon said at St. Helena that he wished to unite Louis with a niece of Talleyrand. I can only say that I never heard a word of this niece, either from himself, his wife, or his daughter; and I rather think that at that time the First Consul was looking after a royal alliance for Louis. He often expressed regret at the precipitate marriages of his sisters. It should be recollected that we were now in the year which saw the Consulship for life established, and which, consequently, gave presage of the Empire. Napoleon said truly to the companions of his exile that "Louis' marriage was the result of Josephine's intrigues," but I cannot understand how he never mentioned the intention he once had of uniting Hortense to Duroc. It has been erroneously stated that the First Consul believed that he reconciled the happiness of his daughter with his policy. Hortense did not love Louis, and dreaded this marriage. There was no hope of happiness for her, and the event has proved this. As for the policy of the First Consul, it is not easy to see how it was concerned with the marriage of Louis to Hortense, and in any case the grand policy which professed so loudly to be free from all feminine influences would have been powerless against the intrigues of Josephine, for at this time at the Tuileries the boudoir was often stronger than the cabinet. Here I am happy to have it in my power to contradict most formally and most positively certain infamous insinuations which have prevailed respecting Bonaparte and Hortense. Those who have asserted that Bonaparte ever entertained towards Hortense any other sentiments than those of a father-in-law for a daughter-in-law have, as the ancient knights used to say, "lied in their throats." We shall see farther on what he said to me on this subject, but it is never too soon to destroy such a base calumny. Authors unworthy of belief have stated, without any proof, that not only was there this criminal liaison, but they have gone so far as to say that Bonaparte was the father of the eldest son of Hortense. It is a lie, a vile lie. And yet the rumour has spread through all France and all Europe. Alas! has calumny such powerful charms that, once they are submitted to, their yoke cannot be broken?[159]

---

158 The marriage of Louis Bonaparte took place on the 7th January. The bride and bridegroom were exceedingly dull, and Mademoiselle Hortense wept during the whole of the ceremony. Josephine, knowing that this union, which commenced so inauspiciously, was her own work, anxiously endeavoured to establish a more cordial feeling between her daughter and son-in-law. But all her efforts were vain, and the marriage proved a very unhappy one (Memoirs de Constant). Napoleon III. was the son of the Queen of Holland (Hortense Beauharnais).

159 Bourrienne's account of this marriage, and his denial of the vile calumny about Napoleon, is corroborated by Madame Rémusat. After saying that Hortense had refused to marry the son of Rewbell and also the Comte de Nun, she goes on: "A short time afterwards Duroc, then aide de camp to the Consul, and already noted by him, fell in love with Hortense. She returned the feeling, and believed she had found that other half of herself which she sought. Bonaparte looked favourably on their union, but Madame Bonaparte in her turn was inflexible. 'My daughter,' said she, 'must marry a gentleman or a Bonaparte.' Louis was then thought of. He

had no fancy for Hortense; defeated the Beauharnais family, and had a supreme contempt for his sister-in-law. But as he was silent, he was believed to be gentle; and as he was severe by character, he was believed to be upright. Madame Louis told me afterwards that at the news of this arrangement she experienced violent grief. Not only was she forbidden to think of the man she loved, but she was about to be given to another of whom she had a secret distrust" (Rémusat, tome i. p. 156). For the cruel treatment of Hortense by Louis see the succeeding pages of Rémusat. As for the vile scandal about Hortense and Napoleon, there is little doubt that it was spread by the Bonapartist family for interested motives. Madame Louis became enceinte soon after her marriage. The Bonapartists, and especially Madame Murat (Caroline); had disliked this marriage because Joseph having only daughters, it was forseen that the first son of Louis and the grandson of Madame Bonaparte would be the object of great interest. They therefore spread the revolting story that this was the result of a connection of the First Consul with his daughter-in-law, encouraged by the mother herself. "The public willingly believed this suspicion.' Madame Murat told Louis," etc. (Rémusat, tome i, p. 169). This last sentence is corroborated by Miot de Melito (tome ii. p. 170), who, speaking of the later proposal of Napoleon to adopt this child, says that Louis "remembered the damaging stories which ill-will had tried to spread among the public concerning Hortense Beauharnais before he married her, and although a comparison of the date of his marriage with that of the birth of his son must have shown him that these tales were unfounded, he felt that they would be revived by the adoption of this child by the First Consul." Thus this wretched story did harm in every way. The conduct of Josephine must be judged with leniency, engaged as she was in a desperate struggle to maintain her own marriage,—a struggle she kept up with great skill; see Metternich, tome ii. p. 296. "she baffled all the calculations, all the manoeuvres of her adversaries." But she was foolish enough to talk in her anger as if she believed some of the disgraceful rumours of Napoleon. "Had he not seduced his sisters, one after the other?" (Rémusat, tome i. p. 204). As to how far this scandal was really believed by the brothers of Napoleon, see Iung's Lucien (tome ii. pp. 268-269), where Lucien describes Louis as coming three times to him for advice as to his marriage with Hortense, both brothers referring to this rumour. The third time Louis announces he is in love with Hortense. "You are in love? Why the devil, then, do you come to me for advice? If so, forget what has been rumoured, and what I have advised you. Marry, and may God bless you." Thiers (tome iii. p. 308) follows Bourrienne's account. Josephine, alluding to Louis Bonaparte, said, "His family have maliciously informed him of the disgraceful stories which have been spread on the conduct of my daughter and on the birth of her son. Hate assigns this child to Napoleon." (Rémusat, tome i, p. 206). The child in question was Napoleon Charles (1802-1807).]—

CHAPTER VIII

1802-1803

Bonaparte was anxious to place the Cisalpine Republic on a footing of harmony with the Government of France. It was necessary to select a President who should perfectly agree with Bonaparte's views; and in this respect no one could be so suitable as Bonaparte himself. The two Presidencies united would serve as a transition to the throne. Not wishing to be long absent from Paris, and anxious to avoid the trouble of the journey to Milan, he arranged to meet the deputation half-way at Lyons. Before our departure I said to him, "Is it possible that you do not wish to revisit Italy, the first scene of your glory, and the beautiful capital of Lombardy, where you were the object of so much homage?"—"I certainly should," replied the First Consul, "but the journey to Milan would occupy too much precious time. I prefer that the meeting should take place in France. My influence over the deputies will be more prompt and certain at Lyons than at Milan; and then I should be glad to see the noble wreck of the army of Egypt, which is collected at Lyons."

On the 8th of January 1802 we set out. Bonaparte who was now ready to ascend the throne of France, wished to prepare the Italians for one day crowning him King of Italy, in imitation of Charlemagne, of whom in anticipation he considered himself the successor. He saw that the title of President of the Cisalpine Republic was a great advance towards the sovereignty of Lombardy, as he afterwards found that the Consulate for life was a decisive step towards the throne of France. He obtained the title of President without much difficulty on the 36th of January 1802. The journey to Lyons and the conferences were only matters of form; but high sounding words and solemn proceedings were required for the public mind.

The attempts which had been made on the life of the First Consul gave rise to a report that he took extraordinary precautions for his safety during this journey to Lyons. I never saw those precautions, and Bonaparte was at all times averse to adopt any. He often repeated "That whoever would risk his own life might take his." It is not true that guards preceded his carriage and watched the roads. The Consul travelled like a private person, and very rarely had arms in his carriage.[160]

160 Bonaparte may have been careless of his own safety, but that he took great pains in regard to his brother's may be inferred from the following letter, written a few years later: "Take care that your valets de chambre, your cooks, the guards that sleep in your apartments, and those who come during the night to awaken you with despatches, are all Frenchmen. No one should enter your room during the night except your aides de camp, who should sleep in the chamber that precedes your bedroom. Your door should be fastened inside, and you ought not to open it, even to your aide de camp, until you have recognised his voice; he himself should not knock at your door until he has locked that of the room which he is in, to make sure of being alone, and of being followed by no one. These precautions are important; they give no trouble, and they inspire confidence—besides, they may really save your life. You should establish these habits immediately and permanently; You ought not to be obliged to have resource to them

At this time, when the ambition of Bonaparte every day took a farther flight, General Clarke took it into his head to go into the box of the First Consul at the "Francais," and to place himself in the front seat. By chance the First Consul came to the theatre, but Clarke, hardly rising, did not give up his place. The First Consul only stayed a short time, and when he came back he showed great discontent at this affectation of pride and of vanity. Wishing to get rid of a man whom he looked on as a blundering flatterer and a clumsy critic, he sent him away as charge d'affaires to the young extemporized King of Etruria, where Clarke expiated his folly in a sort of exile. This is all the "great disfavour" which has been so much spoken about, In the end General Clarke returned to favour. Berlin knows and regrets it.

On the 25th of March of the same year England signed, at Amiens, a suspension of arms for fourteen months, which was called a treaty of peace. The clauses of this treaty were not calculated to inspire the hope of a very long peace. It was evident, as I have already said, that England would not evacuate Malta; and that island ultimately proved the chief cause of the rupture of the treaty of Amiens. But England, heretofore so haughty in her bearing to the First Consul, had at length treated with him as the Head of the French Government. This, as Bonaparte was aware, boded well for the consolidation of his power.

At that time, when he saw his glory and power augmenting, he said to me in one of our walks at Malmaison, in a moment of hilarity, and clapping me on the shoulder, "Well, Bourrienne, you also will be immortal!"— "Why, General?"—"Are you not my secretary?"— "Tell me the name of Alexander's," said I.[161] Bonaparte then turned to me and laughing, said, "Hem! that is not bad." There was, to be sure, a little flattery conveyed in my question, but that never displeased him, and I certainly did not in that instance deserve the censure he often bestowed on me for not being enough of a courtier and flatterer.

Madame Murat gave a grand fete in honour of Bonaparte at her residence at Neuilly. At dinner Bonaparte sat opposite Madame Murat at the principal table, which was appropriated to the ladies. He ate fast, and talked but little. However, when the dessert was served, he put a question to each lady. This question was to inquire their respective ages. When Madame Bourrienne's turn came he said to her, "Oh! I know yours." This was a great deal for his gallantry, and the other ladies were far from being pleased at it.

Next day, while walking with me in his favourite alley at Malmaison, he received one of those stupid reports of the police which were so frequently addressed to him. It mentioned the observations which had been made in Paris about a green livery he had lately adopted. Some said that green had been chosen because it was the colour of the House of Artois. On reading that a slight sneer was observable in his countenance, and he said, "What are these idiots dreaming of? They must be joking, surely. Am I no better than M. d'Artois? They shall soon see the difference."

---

on some emergency, which would hurt the feelings of those around you. Do not trust only to your own experience. The Neapolitan character has been violent in every age, and you have to do with a woman [Queen of Naples] who is the impersonation of crime" (Napoleon to Joseph, May 31, 1806.—Du Casse, tome ii. p. 260).

161 Bonaparte did not know the name of Alexander's secretary, and I forgot at the moment to tell him it was Clallisthenes. He wrote Alexander's Memoirs, as I am writing Bonaparte's; but, notwithstanding this coincidence, I neither expect nor desire the immortality of my name.—Bourrienne.

Until the middle of the year 1801 the erasures from the emigrant list had always been proposed by the Minister of Police. The First Consul having been informed that intrigue and even bribery had been employed to obtain them, determined that in future erasures should be part of the business of his cabinet. But other affairs took up his attention, and a dozen or fifteen erasures a week were the most that were made. After Te Deum had been chanted at Malmaison for the Concordat and the peace, I took advantage of that moment of general joy to propose to Bonaparte the return of the whole body of emigrants. "You have," said I in a half-joking way, "reconciled Frenchmen to God—now reconcile them to each other. There have never been any real emigrants, only absentees; and the proof of this is, that erasures from the list have always been, and will always be, made daily." He immediately seized the idea. "We shall see," said he; "but I must except a thousand persons belonging to high families, especially those who are or have been connected with royalty or the Court."

I said in the Chamber of Deputies, and I feel pleasure in repeating here, that the plan of the 'Senatus-consults', which Bonaparte dictated to me, excepted from restitution only such mansions as were used for public establishments. These he would neither surrender nor pay rent for. With those exceptions he was willing to restore almost all that was possessed by the State and had not been sold.

The First Consul, as soon as he had finished this plan of a decree, convoked a Grand Council to submit it to their consideration. I was in an adjoining room to that in which they met, and as the deliberations were carried on with great warmth, the members talking very loudly, sometimes even vociferating, I heard all that passed. The revolutionary party rejected all propositions of restitution. They were willing to call back their victims, but they would not part with the spoil.

When the First Consul returned to his cabinet, dissatisfied with the ill success of his project, I took the liberty of saying to him, "you cannot but perceive, General, that your object has been defeated, and your project unsuccessful. The refusal to restore to the emigrants all that the State possesses takes from the recall all its generosity and dignity of character. I wonder how you could yield to such an unreasonable and selfish opposition."—"The revolutionary party," replied he, "had the majority in the Council. What could I do? Am I strong enough to overcome all those obstacles?"—"General, you can revive the question again, and oppose the party you speak of."—"That would be difficult," he said; "they still have a high hand in these matters. Time is required. However, nothing is definitively arranged. We shall see what can be done." The 'Senatus-consulte', published on the 6th Floréal, year X. (26th of April 1802), a fortnight after the above conversation took place, is well known. Bonaparte was then obliged to yield to the revolutionary party, or he would have adhered to his first proposition.[162] Napoleon referred to this matter at St. Helena. He himself says that he "would have been able" (he should have said that he wished) to grant everything, that for a moment he thought of doing so, and that it was a mistake not to do so. "This limitation on my part," he adds, "destroyed all the good effect of the return of the emigrants. The mistake was the greater since I thought of doing it, but I was alone, surrounded by oppositions and by spies: all were against your party, you cannot easily picture the matter to yourself, but

162 The Senatus-consulte retained the woods and forests of the emigrants, and made their recall an "amnesty." In the end this retention of the forests was used by Napoleon with great dexterity as a means of placing them under personal obligation to him for restoring this species of property. See Thiers tome iii, p. 458, livre xiv.

important affairs hurried me, time pressed, and I was obliged to act differently." Afterwards he speaks of a syndicate he wished to form, but I have never heard a word of that. I have said how things really happened, and what has been just read confirms this.[163]

The Royalists, dissatisfied with the state of political affairs, were not better pleased with the illiberal conditions of the recall of the emigrants. The friends of public liberty, on the other hand, were far from being satisfied with the other acts of the First Consul, or with the conduct of the different public authorities, who were always ready to make concessions to him. Thus all parties were dissatisfied.

Bonaparte was much pleased with General Sebastiani's conduct when he was sent to Constantinople, after the peace of Amiens, to induce the Grand Seignior to renew amicable relations with France.

At the period here alluded to, namely, before the news of the evacuation of Egypt, that country greatly occupied Bonaparte's attention. He thought that to send a man like Sebastiani travelling through Northern Africa, Egypt, and Syria might inspire the sovereigns of those countries with a more favourable idea of France than they now entertained, and might remove the ill impressions which England was endeavouring to produce. On this mission Sebastiani was accordingly despatched. He visited all the Barbary States, Egypt, Palestine, and the Ionian Isles. Everywhere he drew a highly-coloured picture of the power of Bonaparte, and depreciated the glory of England.[164] He strengthened old connections, and contracted new ones with the chiefs of each country. He declared to the authorities of the Ionian Isles that they might rely on the powerful protection of France. Bonaparte, in my opinion, expected too much from the labours of a single individual furnished with but vague instructions. Still Sebastiani did all that could be done. The interesting details of his proceedings were published in the 'Moniteur'. The secret information respecting the means of successfully attacking the English establishments in India was very curious, though not affording the hope of speedy success.

The published abstract of General Sebastiani's report was full of expressions hostile to England. Among other things it was stated that Egypt might be conquered with 6000 men, and that the Ionian Isles where disposed to throw off the yoke. There can be little doubt that this publication hastened the rupture of the treaty of Amiens.

England suspended all discussions respecting Malta, and declared that she would not resume them till the King of Great Britain should receive satisfaction for what was called an act of hostility. This was always put forward as a justification, good or bad, for breaking the treaty of Amiens, which England had never shown herself very ready to execute.

Bonaparte, waiving the usual forma of etiquette, expressed his wish to have a private conference with Lord Whitworth, the ambassador from London to Paris, and who had been the English ambassador at St. Petersburg previous to the rupture which preceded the death of Paul I. Bonaparte counted much on the effect he might produce by that captivating manner which he so well knew how to assume in conversation; but all was in vain. In signing

163 This was by no means the only time that Napoleon's wishes were opposed successfully in his Council of State. On such occasions he used to describe himself as "repulsed with losses." See the interesting work of St. Hilaire, Napoleon au Conseil d'Etat.

164 This General, or Count Sebastian, was afterwards ambassador for Louis Philippe at our Court.

the treaty of Amiens the British Minister was well aware that he would be the first to break it.

About the commencement of the year 1802 Napoleon began to feel acute pains in his right side. I have often seen him at Malmaison, when sitting up at night, lean against the right arm of his chair, and unbuttoning his coat and waistcoat exclaim,—"What pain I feel!" I would then accompany him to his bedchamber, and have often been obliged to support him on the little staircase which led from his cabinet to the corridor. He frequently used to say at this time, "I fear that when I am forty I shall become a great eater: I have a foreboding that I shall grow very corpulent." This fear of obesity, though it annoyed him very much, did not appear to have the least foundation, judging from his habitual temperance and spare habit of body. He asked me who was my physician. I told him M. Corvisart, whom his brother Louis had recommended to me. A few days after he called in Corvisart, who three years later was appointed first physician to the Emperor. He appeared to derive much benefit from the prescriptions of Corvisart, whose open and good-humoured countenance at once made a favourable impression on him.

The pain which the First Consul felt at this time increased his irritability. Perhaps many of the sets of this epoch of his life should be attributed to this illness. At the time in question his ideas were not the same in the evening as they had been in the morning; and often in the morning he would tear up, even without the least remark, notes he had dictated to me at night and which he had considered excellent. At other times I took on myself not to send to the Moniteur, as he wished me to do, notes which, dictated by annoyance and irascibility, might have produced a bad effect in Europe. When the next day he did not see the article, I attributed this to the note being too late, or to the late arrival of the courier. But I told him it was no loss, for it would be inserted the next day. He did not answer at once, but a quarter of an hour afterwards he said to me, "Do not send my note to the 'Moniteur' without showing it to me." He took it and reread it. Sometimes he was astonished at what he had dictated to me, and amused himself by saying that I had not understood him properly. "That is not much good, is it? "—"'Pon my word, I don't quite know."—"Oh no, it is worthless; what say you?" Then he bowed his head a little, and tore up the paper. Once when we were at the Tuileries he sent me at two o'clock in the morning a small note in his own writing, in which was, "To Bourrienne. Write to Maret to make him erase from the note which Fleurieu has read to the Tribunate the phrase (spelt frase) concerning Costaz, and to soften as much as possible what concerns the reporter of the Tribunate."

This change, after time for reflection, arose, as often happened with him, from observations I had made to him, and which he had at first angrily repulsed.

After the peace of Amiens the First Consul, wishing to send an ambassador to England, cast his eyes—for what reason I know not—on General Andreossi. I took the liberty of making some observation on a choice which did not appear to me to correspond with the importance of the mission. Bonaparte replied, "I have not determined on it; I will talk to Talleyrand on the subject." When we were at Malmaison in the evening M. de Talleyrand came to transact business with the First Consul. The proposed appointment of an ambassador to England was mentioned. After several persons had been named the First Consul said, "I believe I must send Andreossi." M. de Talleyrand, who was not much pleased with the choice, observed in a dry sarcastic tone, "You must send Andre 'aussi', I Pray, who is this Andre?"—"I did not mention any Andre; I said Andreossi. You know Andreossi, the general of artillery?"—"Ah! true; Andreossi: I did not think of him: I was thinking only of the diplomatic men, and did not recollect any of that name. Yes, yes; Andreossi is in the artillery!" The general was appointed ambassador, and went to London after the treaty of Amiens; but he returned again in a few months. He had nothing of consequence to do, which was very lucky for him.

In 1802 Jerome was at Brest in the rank of 'enseigne de vaisseau.' [165] He launched into expenses far beyond what his fortune or his pay could maintain. He often drew upon me for sums of money which the First Consul paid with much unwillingness. One of his letters in particular excited Napoleon's anger. The epistle was filled with accounts of the entertainments Jerome was giving and receiving, and ended by stating that he should draw on me for 17,000 francs. To this Bonaparte wrote the following reply:—

> I have read your letter, Monsieur l'Enseigne de Vaisseau; and I am waiting to hear that you are studying on board your corvette a profession which you ought to consider as your road to glory. Die young, and I shall have some consolatory reflection; but if you live to sixty without having served your country, and without leaving behind you any honourable recollections, you had better not have lived at all.

Jerome never fulfilled the wishes of his brother, who always called him a little profligate. From his earliest years his conduct was often a source of vexation to his brother and his family. Westphalia will not soon forget that he was her King; and his subjects did not without reason surname him "Heliogabalus in miniature."

The First Consul was harassed by the continual demands for money made on him by his brothers. To get rid of Joseph, who expended large sums at Mortfontaine, as Lucien did at Neuilly, he gave M. Collot the contract for victualling the navy, on the condition of his paying Joseph 1,600,000 francs a year out of his profits. I believe this arrangement answered Joseph's purpose very well; but it was anything but advantageous to M. Collot. I think a whole year elapsed without his pocketing a single farthing. He obtained an audience of the First Consul, to whom he stated his grievances. His outlays he showed were enormous, and he could get no payment from the navy office. Upon which the Consul angrily interrupted him, saying, "Do you think I am a mere capuchin? Decres must have 100,000 crowns, Duroc 100,000, Bourrienne 100,000; you must make the payments, and don't come here troubling me with your long stories. It is the business of my Ministers to give me accounts of such matters; I will hear Decres, and that's enough. Let me be teased no longer with these complaints; I cannot attend to them." Bonaparte then very unceremoniously dismissed M. Collot. I learned afterwards that he did not get a settlement of the business until after a great deal of trouble. M. Collot once said to me, "If he had asked me for as much money as would have built a frigate he should have had it. All I want now is to be paid, and to get rid of the business." M. Collot had reason and honour on his side; but there was nothing but shuffling on the other.

---

165 A rank in the navy equivalent to that of our lieutenant.

CHAPTER IX

1802

The historian of these times ought to put no faith in the bulletins, despatches, notes, and proclamations which have emanated from Bonaparte, or passed through his hands. For my part, I believe that the proverb, "As great a liar as a bulletin," has as much truth in it as the axiom, two and two make four.

The bulletins always announced what Bonaparte wished to be believed true; but to form a proper judgment on any fact, counter-bulletins must be sought for and consulted. It is well known, too, that Bonaparte attached great importance to the place whence he dated his bulletins; thus, he dated his decrees respecting the theatres and Hamburg beef at Moscow.

The official documents were almost always incorrect. There was falsity in the exaggerated descriptions of his victories, and falsity again in the suppression or palliation of his reverses and losses. A writer, if he took his materials from the bulletins and the official correspondence of the time, would compose a romance rather than a true history. Of this many proofs have been given in the present work.

Another thing which always appeared to me very remarkable was, that Bonaparte, notwithstanding his incontestable superiority, studied to depreciate the reputations of his military commanders, and to throw on their shoulders faults which he had committed himself. It is notorious that complaints and remonstrances, as energetic as they were well founded, were frequently addressed to General Bonaparte on the subject of his unjust and partial bulletins, which often attributed the success of a day to some one who had very little to do with it, and made no mention of the officer who actually had the command. The complaints made by the officers and soldiers stationed at Damietta compelled General Lanusse, the commander, to remonstrate against the alteration of a bulletin, by which an engagement with a body of Arabs was represented as an insignificant affair, and the loss trifling, though the General had stated the action to be one of importance, and the loss considerable. The misstatement, in consequence of his spirited and energetic remonstrances, was corrected.

Bonaparte took Malta, as is well known, in forty-eight hours. The empire of the Mediterranean, secured to the English by the battle of Aboukir, and their numerous cruising vessels, gave them the means of starving the garrison, and of thus forcing General Vaubois, the commandant of Malta, who was cut off from all communication with France, to capitulate. Accordingly on the 4th of September 1800 he yielded up the Gibraltar of the Mediterranean, after a noble defence of two years. These facts require to be stated in order the better to understand what follows.

On 22d February 1802 a person of the name of Doublet, who was the commissary of the French Government at Malta when we possessed that island, called upon me at the Tuileries. He complained bitterly that the letter which he had written from Malta to the First Consul on the 2d Ventose, year VIII. (9th February 1800), had been altered in the 'Moniteur'. "I congratulated him," said M. Doublet, "on the 18th Brumaire, and informed him of the state of Malta, which was very alarming. Quite the contrary was printed in the 'Moniteur', and that is what I complain of. It placed me in a very disagreeable situation at Malta, where I was accused of having concealed the real situation of the island, in which I was discharging a public function that gave weight to my words." I observed to him that as I was not the editor of the 'Moniteur' it was of no use to apply to me; but I told him to give me a copy of the letter, and I would mention the subject to the First Consul, and communicate the answer to him. Doublet searched his pocket for the letter, but could not find it. He said he would send a copy, and begged me to discover how the error originated. On the same day he sent me the copy of the letter, in which, after congratulating Bonaparte on his return, the following passage occurs:—"Hasten to save Malta with men and provisions: no time is to be lost." For this passage these words were substituted in the 'Moniteur': "His name inspires the brave defenders of Malta with fresh courage; we have men and provisions."

Ignorant of the motives of so strange a perversion, I showed this letter to the First Consul. He shrugged up his shoulders and said, laughing, "Take no notice of him, he is a fool; give yourself no further trouble about it."

It was clear there was nothing more to be done. It was, however, in despite of me that M. Doublet was played this ill turn. I represented to the First Consul the inconveniences which M. Doublet might experience from this affair. But I very rarely saw letters or reports published as they were received. I can easily understand how particular motives might be alleged in order to justify such falsifications; for, when the path of candour and good faith is departed from, any pretext is put forward to excuse bad conduct. What sort of a history would he write who should consult only the pages of the 'Moniteur'?

After the vote for adding a second ten years to the duration of Bonaparte's Consulship he created, on the 19th of May, the order of the Legion of Honour. This institution was soon followed by that of the new nobility. Thus, in a short space of time, the Concordat to tranquillize consciences and re-establish harmony in the Church; the decree to recall the emigrants; the continuance of the Consular power for ten years, by way of preparation for the Consulship for life, and the possession of the Empire; and the creation, in a country which had abolished all distinctions, of an order which was to engender prodigies, followed closely on the heels of each other. The Bourbons, in reviving the abolished orders, were wise enough to preserve along with them the Legion of Honour.

It has already been seen how, in certain circumstances, the First Consul always escaped from the consequences of his own precipitation, and got rid of his blunders by throwing the blame on others—as, for example, in the affair of the parallel between Caesar, Cromwell, and Bonaparte. He was indeed so precipitate that one might say, had he been a gardener, he would have wished to see the fruits ripen before the blossoms had fallen off. This inconsiderate haste nearly proved fatal to the creation of the Legion of Honour, a project which ripened in his mind as soon as he beheld the orders glittering at the button-holes of the Foreign Ministers. He would frequently exclaim, "This is well! These are the things for the people!"

I was, I must confess, a decided partisan of the foundation in France of a new chivalric order, because I think, in every well-conducted State, the chief of the Government ought to do all in his power to stimulate the honour of the citizens, and to render them more sensible to honorary distinctions than to pecuniary advantages. I tried, however, at the same time to warn the First Consul of his precipitancy. He heard me not; but I must with equal frankness confess that on this occasion I was soon freed from all apprehension with respect to the consequences of the difficulties he had to encounter in the Council and in the other constituted orders of the State.

On the 4th of May 1801 he brought forward, for the first time officially, in the Council of State the question of the establishment of the Legion of Honour, which on the 19th May 1802 was proclaimed a law of the State. The opposition to this measure was very great, and all the power of the First Consul, the force of his arguments, and the immense influence of his position, could procure him no more than 14 votes out of 24. The same feeling was displayed at the Tribunate; where the measure only passed by a vote of 56 to 38. The balance was about the same in the Legislative Body, where the votes were 166 to 110. It follows, then, that out of the 394 voters in those three separate bodies a majority only of 78 was obtained. Surprised at so feeble a majority, the First Consul said in the evening, "Ah! I see very clearly the prejudices are still too strong. You were right; I should have waited. It was not a thing of such urgency. But then, it must be owned, the speakers for the measure defended it badly. The strong minority has not judged me fairly."— "Be calm," rejoined I: "without doubt it would have been better to wait; but the thing is done, and you will soon find that the taste for these distinctions is not near gone by. It is a taste which belongs to the nature of man. You may expect some extraordinary circumstances from this creation—you will soon see them."

In April 1802 the First Consul left no stone unturned to get himself declared Consul for life. It is perhaps at this epoch of his career that he most brought into play those principles of duplicity and dissimulation which are commonly called Machiavellian. Never were trickery, falsehood, cunning, and affected moderation put into play with more talent or success.

In the month of March hereditary succession and a dynasty were in everybody's mouths. Lucien was the most violent propagator of these ideas, and he pursued his vocation of apostle with constancy and address. It has already been mentioned that, by his brother's confession; he published in 1800 a pamphlet enforcing the same ideas; which work Bonaparte afterwards condemned as a premature development of his projects. M. de Talleyrand, whose ideas could not be otherwise than favourable to the monarchical form of government, was ready to enter into explanations with the Cabinets of Europe on the subject. The words which now constantly resounded in every ear were "stability and order," under cloak of which the downfall of the people's right was to be concealed. At the same time Bonaparte, with the view of disparaging the real friends of constitutional liberty, always called them ideologues,[166] or terrorists. Madame Bonaparte opposed with fortitude the influence of counsels which she believed fatal to her husband. He indeed spoke rarely, and seldom confidentially, with her on politics or public affairs. "Mind your distaff or your needle," was with him a common phrase.

166 I have classed all these people under the denomination of Ideologues, which, besides, is what specially and literally fits them,—searchers after ideas (ideas generally empty). They have been made more ridiculous than even I expected by this application, a correct one, of the term ideologue to them. The phrase has been successful, I believe, because it was mine (Napoleon in Iung's Lucien, tome ii. p, 293). Napoleon welcomed every attack on this description of sage. Much pleased with a discourse by Royer Collard, he said to Talleyrand, "Do you know, Monsieur is Grand Electeur, that a new and serious philosophy is rising in my university, which may do us great honour and disembarrass us completely of the ideologues, slaying them on the spot by reasoning?" It is with something of the same satisfaction that Renan, writing of 1898, says that the finer dreams had been disastrous when brought into the domain of facts, and that human concerns only began to improve when the ideologues ceased to meddle with them (Souvenirs, p. 122).

The individuals who applied themselves with most perseverance in support of the hereditary question were Lucien, Roederer, Regnault de St. Jean d'Angély, and Fontanel. Their efforts were aided by the conclusion of peace with England, which, by re-establishing general tranquillity for a time, afforded the First Consul an opportunity of forwarding any plan.

While the First Consul aspired to the throne of France, his brothers, especially Lucien, affected a ridiculous pride and pretension. Take an almost incredible example of which I was witness. On Sunday, the 9th of May, Lucien came to see Madame Bonaparte, who said to him, "Why did you not come to dinner last Monday?"—"Because there was no place marked for me: the brothers of Napoleon ought to have the first place after him."— "What am I to understand by that?" answered Madame Bonaparte. "If you are the brother of Bonaparte, recollect what you were. At my house all places are the same. Eugène world never have committed such a folly."[167] At this period, when the Consulate for life was only in embryo, flattering counsels poured in from all quarters, and tended to encourage the First Consul in his design of grasping at absolute power.

Liberty rejected an unlimited power, and set bounds to the means he wished and had to employ in order to gratify his excessive love of war and conquest. "The present state of things, this Consulate of ten years," said he to me, does not satisfy me; "I consider it calculated to excite unceasing troubles." On the 7th of July 1801, he observed, "The question whether France will be a Republic is still doubtful: it will be decided in five or six years." It was clear that he thought this too long a term. Whether he regarded France as his property, or considered himself as the people's delegate and the defender of their rights, I am convinced the First Consul wished the welfare of France; but then that welfare was in his mind inseparable from absolute power. It was with pain I saw him following this course. The friends of liberty, those who sincerely wished to maintain a Government constitutionally free, allowed themselves to be prevailed upon to consent to an extension of ten years of power beyond the ten years originally granted by the constitution. They made this sacrifice to glory and to that power which was its consequence; and they were far from thinking they were lending their support to shameless intrigues. They were firm, but for the moment only, and the nomination for life was rejected by the Senate, who voted only ten years more power to Bonaparte, who saw the vision of his ambition again adjourned.

The First Consul dissembled his displeasure with that profound art which, when he

167 On such points there was constant trouble with the Bonapartist family, as will be seen in Madame de Rémusat's Memoirs. For an instance, in 1812, where Joseph insisted on his mother taking precedence of Josephine at a dinner in his house, when Napoleon settled the matter by seizing Josephine's arm and leading her in first, to the consternation of the party. But Napoleon, right in this case, had his own ideas on such points, The place of the Princess Elisa, the eldest of his sisters, had been put below that of Caroline, Queen of Naples. Elisa was then only princess of Lucca. The Emperor suddenly rose, and by a shift to the right placed the Princess Elisa above the Queen. 'Now,' said he, 'do not forget that in the imperial family I am the only King.' (Iung's Lucien, tome ii. p. 251), This rule he seems to have adhered to, for when he and his brothers went in the same carriage to the Champ de Mai in 1815, Jerome, titular King of Westphalia, had to take the front seat, while his elder brother, Lucien, only bearing the Roman title of Prince de Canino, sat on one of the seats of honour alongside Napoleon. Jerome was disgusted, and grumbled at a King having to give way to a mere Roman Prince, See Iung's Lucien, tome ii. p, 190.

could not do otherwise, he exercised to an extreme degree. To a message of the Senate on the subject of that nomination he returned a calm but evasive and equivocating answer, in which, nourishing his favourite hope of obtaining more from the people than from the Senate, he declared with hypocritical humility, "That he would submit to this new sacrifice if the wish of the people demanded what the Senate authorised." Such was the homage he paid to the sovereignty of the people, which was soon to be trampled under his feet!

An extraordinary convocation of the Council of State took place on Monday, the 10th of May. A communication was made to them, not merely of the Senate's consultation, but also of the First Consul's adroit and insidious reply. The Council regarded the first merely as a notification, and proceeded to consider on what question the people should be consulted. Not satisfied with granting to the First Consul ten years of prerogative, the Council thought it best to strike the iron while it was hot, and not to stop short in the middle of so pleasing a work. In fine, they decided that the following question should be put to the people: "Shall the First Consul be appointed for life, and shall he have the power of nominating his successor?" The reports of the police had besides much influence on the result of this discussion, for they one and all declared that the whole of Paris demanded a Consul for life, with the right of naming a successor. The decisions on these two questions were carried as it were by storm. The appointment for life passed unanimously, and the right of naming the successor by a majority. The First Consul, however, formally declared that he condemned this second measure, which had not originated with himself. On receiving the decision of the Council of State the First Consul, to mask his plan for attaining absolute power, thought it advisable to appear to reject a part of what was offered him. He therefore cancelled that clause which proposed to give him the power of appointing a successor, and which had been carried by a small majority.

CHAPTER X

1802

Having arrived at nearly the middle of the career which I have undertaken to trace, before I advance farther I must go back for a few moments, as I have already frequently done, in order to introduce some circumstances which escaped my recollection, or which I purposely reserved, that I might place them amongst facts analogous to them: Thus, for instance, I have only referred in passing to a man who, since become a monarch, has not ceased to honour me with his friendship, as will be seen in the course of my Memoirs, since the part we have seen him play in the events of the 18th Brumaire. This man, whom the inexplicable combination of events has raised to a throne for the happiness of the people he is called to govern, is Bernadotte.

It was evident that Bernadotte must necessarily fall into a kind of disgrace for not having supported Bonaparte's projects at the period of the overthrow of the Directory. The First Consul, however, did not dare to avenge himself openly; but he watched for every opportunity to remove Bernadotte from his presence, to place him in difficult situations, and to entrust him with missions for which no precise instructions were given, in the hope that Bernadotte would commit faults for which the First Consul might make him wholly responsible.

At the commencement of the Consulate the deplorable war in La Vendée raged in all its intensity. The organization of the Chouans was complete, and this civil war caused Bonaparte much more uneasiness than that which he was obliged to conduct on the Rhine and in Italy, because, from the success of the Vendeans might arise a question respecting internal government, the solution of which was likely to be contrary to Bonaparte's views. The slightest success of the Vendeans spread alarm amongst the holders of national property; and, besides, there was no hope of reconciliation between France and England, her eternal and implacable enemy, as long as the flame of insurrection remained unextinguished.

The task of terminating this unhappy struggle was obviously a difficult one. Bonaparte therefore resolved to impose it on Bernadotte; but this general's conciliatory disposition, his chivalrous manners, his tendency to indulgence, and a happy mixture of prudence and firmness, made him succeed where others would have failed. He finally established good order and submission to the laws.

Some time after the pacification of La Vendée a rebellious disposition manifested itself at Tours amongst the soldiers of a regiment stationed there. The men refused to march until they received their arrears of pay. Bernadotte, as commander-in-chief of the army of the west, without being alarmed at the disturbance, ordered the fifty-second demi-brigade—the one in question—to be drawn up in the square of Tours, where, at the very head of the corps, the leaders of the mutiny were by his orders arrested without any resistance being offered. Carnot who was then Minister of War, made a report to the First Consul on this affair, which, but for the firmness of Bernadotte, might have been attended with disagreeable results. Carnet's report contained a plain statement of the facts, and of General Bernadotte's conduct. Bonaparte was, however, desirous to find in it some pretext for blaming him, and made me write these words on the margin of the report: "General Bernadotte did not act discreetly in adopting such severe measures against the fifty-second demi-brigade, he not having the means, if he had been unsuccessful, of re-establishing order in a town the garrison of which was not strong enough to subdue the mutineers."

A few days after, the First Consul having learned that the result of this affair was quite different from that which he affected to dread, and being convinced that by Bernadotte's firmness alone order had been restored, he found himself in some measure constrained to write to the General, and he dictated the following letter to me:

PARIS,
11th Vendemiaire. Year XI.

CITIZEN-GENERAL—I have read with interest the account of what you did to re-establish order in the fifty-second demi-brigade, and also the report of General Liebert, dated the 5th Vendemiaire. Tell that officer that the Government is satisfied with his conduct. His promotion from the rank of Colonel to that of General of brigade is confirmed. I wish that brave officer to come to Paris. He has afforded an example of firmness and energy which does honour to a soldier.

(Signed) BONAPARTE.

Thus in the same affair Bonaparte, in a few days, from the spontaneous expression of blame dictated by hate, was reduced to the necessity of declaring his approbation, which he did, as may be seen, with studied coldness, and even taking pains to make his praises apply to Colonel Liebert, and not to the general-in-chief.

Time only served to augment Bonaparte's dislike of Bernadotte. It might be said that the farther he advanced in his rapid march towards absolute power the more animosity he cherished against the individual who had refused to aid his first steps in his adventurous career. At the same time the persons about Bonaparte who practised the art of flattering failed not to multiply reports and insinuations against Bernadotte. I recollect one day, when there was to be a grand public levee, seeing Bonaparte so much out of temper that I asked him the cause of it. "I can bear it no longer," he replied impetuously. "I have resolved to have a scene with Bernadotte to-day. He will probably be here. I will open the fire, let what will come of it. He may do what he pleases. We shall see! It is time there should be an end of this."

I had never before observed the First Consul so violently irritated. He was in a terrible passion, and I dreaded the moment when the levee was to open. When he left me to go down to the salon I availed myself of the opportunity to get there before him, which I could easily do, as the salon was not twenty steps from the cabinet. By good luck Bernadotte was the first person I saw. He was standing in the recess of a window which looked on the square of the Carrousel. To cross the salon and reach the General was the work of a moment. "General!" said I, "trust me and retire!—I have good reasons for advising it!" Bernadotte, seeing my extreme anxiety, and aware of the sincere sentiments of esteem end friendship which I entertained for him, consented to retire, and I regarded this as a triumph; for, knowing Bernadotte's frankness of character and his nice sense of honour, I was quite certain that he would not submit to the harsh observations which Bonaparte intended to address to him.

My stratagem had all the success I could desire. The First Consul suspected nothing, and remarked only one thing, which was that his victim was absent. When the levee was over he said to me, "What do you think of it, Bourrienne?—-Bernadotte did not come."—"So much the better for him, General," was my reply. Nothing further happened. The First Consul on returning from Josephine found me in the cabinet, and consequently could suspect nothing, and my communication with Bernadotte did not occupy five minutes. Bernadotte always expressed himself much gratified with the proof of friendship I gave him at this delicate conjuncture. The fact is, that from a disposition of my mind, which I could not myself account for, the more Bonaparte'a unjust hatred of Bernadotte increased the more sympathy and admiration I felt for the noble character of the latter.

The event in question occurred in the spring of 1802. It was at this period that Bonaparte first occupied St. Cloud, which he was much pleased with, because he found himself more at liberty there than at the Tuileries; which palace is really only a prison for royalty, as there a sovereign cannot even take the air at a window without immediately being the object of the curiosity of the public, who collect in large crowds. At St. Cloud, on the contrary, Bonaparte could walk out from his cabinet and prolong his promenade without being annoyed by petitioners. One of his first steps was to repair the cross road leading from St. Cloud to Malmaison, between which places Bonaparte rode in a quarter of an hour. This proximity to the country, which he liked, made staying at St. Cloud yet pleasanter to him. It was at St. Cloud that the First Consul made, if I may so express it, his first rehearsals of the grand drama of the Empire. It was there he began to introduce, in external forms, the habits and etiquette which brought to mind the ceremonies of sovereignty. He soon perceived the influence which pomp of ceremony, brilliancy of appearance, and richness of costume, exercise over the mass of mankind. "Men," he remarked to me a this period, "well deserve the contempt I feel for them. I have only to put some gold lace on the coats of my virtuous republicans and they immediately become just what I wish them."

I remember one day, after one of his frequent sallies of contempt for human kind, I observed to him that although baubles might excite vulgar admiration, there were some distinguished men who did not permit themselves to be fascinated by their allurements; and I mentioned the celebrated Fox by way of example, who, previous to the conclusion of the peace of Amiens, visited Paris, where he was remarked for his extreme simplicity. The First Consul said, "Ah! you are right with respect to him. Mr. Fox is a truly great man, and pleases me much."

In fact, Bonaparte always received Mr. Fox's visits with the greatest satisfaction; and after every conversation they had together he never failed to express to me the pleasure which he experienced in discoursing with a man every way worthy of the great celebrity he had attained. He considered him a very superior man, and wished he might have to treat with him in his future negotiations with England. It may be supposed that Mr. Fox, on his part, never forgot the terms of intimacy, I may say of confidence, on which he had been with the First Consul. In fact, he on several occasions informed him in time of war of the plots formed against his life. Less could not be expected from a man of so noble a character. I can likewise affirm, having more than once been in possession of proofs of the fact, that the English Government constantly rejected with indignation all such projects. I do not mean those which had for their object the overthrow of the Consular or Imperial Government, but all plans of assassination and secret attacks on the person of Bonaparte, whether First Consul or Emperor. I will here request the indulgence of the reader whilst I relate a circumstance which occurred a year before Mr. Fox's journey to Paris; but as it refers to Moreau, I believe that the transposition will be pardoned more easily than the omission.

During the summer 1801 the First Consul took a fancy to give a grand military dinner at a restaurateur's. The restaurateur he favoured with his company was Veri, whose establishment was situated on the terrace of the Feuillans with an entrance into the garden of the Tuileries. Bonaparte did not send an invitation to Moreau, whom I met by chance that day in the following manner:—The ceremony of the dinner at Veri's leaving me at liberty to dispose of my time, I availed myself of it to go and dine at a restaurateur's named Rose, who then enjoyed great celebrity amongst the distinguished gastronomes. I dined in company with M. Carbonnet, a friend of Moreau's family, and two or three other persons. Whilst we were at table in the rotunda we were informed by the waiter who attended on us that General Moreau and his wife, with Lacuee and two other military men, were in an adjoining apartment. Suchet, who had dined at Veri's, where he said everything was prodigiously dull, on rising from the table joined Moreau's party. These details we learned from M. Carbonnet, who left us for a few moments to see the General and Madame Moreau.

Bonaparte's affectation in not inviting Moreau at the moment when the latter had returned a conqueror from the army of the Rhine, and at the same time the affectation of Moreau in going publicly the same day to dine at another restaurateur's, afforded ground for the supposition that the coolness which existed between them would soon be converted into enmity. The people of Paris naturally thought that the conqueror of Marengo might, without any degradation, have given the conqueror of Hohenlinden a seat at his table.

By the commencement of the year 1802 the Republic had ceased to be anything else than a fiction, or an historical recollection. All that remained of it was a deceptive inscription on the gates of the Palace. Even at the time of his installation at the Tuileries, Bonaparte had caused the two trees of liberty which were planted in the court to be cut down; thus removing the outward emblems before he destroyed the reality. But the moment the Senatorial decisions of the 2d and 4th of August were published it was evident to the dullest perceptions that the power of the First Consul wanted nothing but a name.

After these 'Consultes' Bonaparte readily accustomed himself to regard the principal authorities of the State merely as necessary instruments for the exercise of his power. Interested advisers then crowded round him. It was seriously proposed that he should restore the ancient titles, as being more in harmony with the new power which the people had confided to him than the republican forms. He was still of opinion, however, according to his phrase, that "the pear was not yet ripe," and would not hear this project spoken of for a moment. "All this," he said to me one day, "will come in good time; but you must see, Bourrienne, that it is necessary I should, in the first place, assume a title, from which the others that I will give to everybody will naturally take their origin.

The greatest difficulty is surmounted. There is no longer any person to deceive. Everybody sees as clear as day that it is only one step which separates the throne from the Consulate for life. However, we must be cautious. There are some troublesome fellows in the Tribunate, but I will take care of them."

Whilst these serious questions agitated men's minds the greater part of the residents at Malmaison took a trip to Plombieres. Josephine, Bonaparte's mother, Madame Beauharnais-Lavallette, Hortense, and General Rapp, were of this party.

It pleased the fancy of the jocund company to address to me a bulletin of the pleasant and unpleasant occurrences of the journey. I insert this letter merely as a proof of the intimacy which existed between the writers and myself. It follows, precisely as I have preserved it, with the exception of the blots, for which it will be seen they apologised.

AN ACCOUNT OF THE JOURNEY TO PLOMBIERES.

TO THE INHABITANTS OF MALMAISON.

The whole party left Malmaison in tears, which brought on such dreadful headaches that all the amiable persons were quite overcome by the idea of the journey. Madame Bonaparte, mere, supported the fatigues of this memorable day with the greatest courage; but Madame Bonaparte, Consulesse, did not show any. The two young ladies who sat in the dormouse, Mademoiselle Hortense and Madame Lavallette, were rival candidates for a bottle of Eau de Cologne; and every now and then the amiable M. Rapp made the carriage stop for the comfort of his poor little sick heart, which overflowed with bile: in fine, he was obliged to take to bed on arriving at Epernay, while the rest of the amiable party tried to drown their sorrows in champagne. The second day was more fortunate on the score of health and spirits, but provisions were wanting, and great were the sufferings of the stomach. The travellers lived on the hope of a good supper at Toul; but despair was at its height when, on arriving there, they found only a wretched inn, and nothing in it. We saw some odd-looking folks there, which indemnified us a little for spinach dressed in lamp-oil, and red asparagus fried with curdled milk. Who would not have been amused to see the Malmaison gourmands seated at a table so shockingly served! In no record of history is there to be found a day passed in distress so dreadful as that on which we arrived at Plombieres. On departing from Toul we intended to breakfast at Nancy, for every stomach had been empty for two days; but the civil and military authorities came out to meet us, and prevented us from executing our plan. We continued our route, wasting away, so that you might, see us growing thinner every moment. To complete our misfortune, the dormouse, which seemed to have taken a fancy to embark on the Moselle for Metz, barely escaped an overturn. But at Plombieres we have been well compensated for this unlucky journey, for on our arrival we were received with all kinds of rejoicings. The town was illuminated, the cannon fired, and the faces of handsome women at all the windows give us reason to hope that we shall bear our absence from Malmaison with the less regret. With the exception of some anecdotes, which we reserve for chit-chat on our return, you have here a correct account of our journey, which we, the undersigned, hereby certify.

JOSEPHINE BONAPARTE. BEAUHARNAIS-LAPALLETTE. HORTENSE BEAUHARNAIS. RAPP. BONAPARTE, mere.

The company ask pardon for the blots.
21st Messidor.

It is requested that the person who receives this journal will show it to all who take an interest in the fair travellers.

This journey to Plombieres was preceded by a scene which I should abstain from describing if I had not undertaken to relate the truth respecting the family of the First Consul. Two or three days before her departure Madame Bonaparte sent for me. I obeyed the summons, and found her in tears. "What a man-what a man is that Lucien!" she exclaimed in accents of grief. "If you knew, my friend, the shameful proposals he has dared to make to me! 'You are going to the waters,' said he; 'you must get a child by some other person since you cannot have one by him.' Imagine the indignation with which I received such advice. 'Well,' he continued, 'if you do not wish it, or cannot help it, Bonaparte must get a child by another woman, and you must adopt it, for it is necessary to secure an hereditary successor. It is for your interest; you must know that.'— 'What, sir!' I replied, 'do you imagine the nation will suffer a bastard to govern it? Lucien! Lucien! you would ruin your brother! This is dreadful! Wretched should I be, were any one to suppose me capable of listening, without horror, to your infamous proposal! Your ideas are poisonous; your language horrible!'—'Well, Madame,' retorted he, 'all I can say to that is, that I am really sorry for you!'"

The amiable Josephine was sobbing whilst she described this scene to me, and I was not insensible to the indignation which she felt. The truth is, that at that period Lucien, though constantly affecting to despise power for himself, was incessantly labouring to concentrate it in the hands of his brother; and he considered three things necessary to the success of his views, namely, hereditary succession, divorce, and the Imperial Government.

Lucien had a delightful house near Neuilly. Some days before the deplorable scene which I have related he invited Bonaparte and all the inmates at Malmaison to witness a theatrical representation. 'Alzire' was the piece performed. Elise played Alzire, and Lucien, Zamore. The warmth of their declarations, the energetic expression of their gestures, the too faithful nudity of costume, disgusted most of the spectators, and Bonaparte more than any other. When the play was over he was quite indignant. "It is a scandal," he said to me in an angry tone; "I ought not to suffer such indecencies—I will give Lucien to understand that I will have no more of it." When his brother had resumed his own dress, and came into the salon, he addressed him publicly, and gave him to understand that he must for the future desist from such representations. When we returned to Malmaison; he again spoke of what had passed with dissatisfaction. "What!" said he, "when I am endeavouring to restore purity of manners, my brother and sister must needs exhibit themselves upon the boards almost in a state of nudity! It is an insult!"

Lucien had a strong predilection for theatrical exhibitions, to which he attached great importance. The fact is, he declaimed in a superior style, and might have competed with the best professional actors. It was said that the turban of Orosmane, the costume of America, the Roman toga, or the robe of the high priest of Jerusalem, all became him equally well; and I believe that this was the exact truth. Theatrical representations were not confined to Neuilly. We had our theatre and our company of actors at Malmaison; but there everything was conducted with the greatest decorum; and now that I have got behind the scenes, I will not quit them until I have let the reader into the secrets of our drama.

By the direction of the First Consul a very pretty little theatre was built at Malmaison. Our usual actors were Eugène BEAUHARNAIS, Hortense, Madame Murat, Lauriston, M. Didelot, one of the prefects of the Palace, some other individuals belonging to the First Consul's household, and myself. Freed from the cares of government, which we confined as much as possible to the Tuileries, we were a very happy colony at Malmaison; and, besides, we were young, and what is there to which youth does not add charms? The pieces which the First Consul most liked to see us perform were, 'Le Barbier de Seville' and 'Defiance et Malice'. In Le Barbier Lauriston played the part of Count Almaviva; Hortense, Rosins; Eugène, Basil; Didelot, Figaro; I, Bartholo; and Isabey, l'Aveille. Our other stock pieces were, Projets de Mariage, La Gageltre, the Dapit Anloureux, in which I played the part of the valet; and L'Impromptu de Campagne, in which I enacted the Baron, having for my Baroness the young and handsome Caroline Murat.

Hortense's acting was perfection, Caroline was middling, Eugène played very well, Lauriston was rather heavy, Didelot passable, and I may venture to assert, without vanity, that I was not quite the worst of the company. If we were not good actors it was not for want of good instruction and good advice. Talma and Michot came to direct us, and made us rehearse before them, sometimes altogether and sometimes separately. How many lessons have I received from Michot whilst walking in the beautiful park of Malmaison! And may I be excused for saying, that I now experience pleasure in looking back upon these trifles, which are matters of importance when one is young, and which contrasted so singularly with the great theatre on which we did not represent fictitious characters? We had, to adopt theatrical language, a good supply of property. Bonaparte presented each of us with a collection of dramas very well bound; and, as the patron of the company, he provided us with rich and elegant dresses.[168]

Bonaparte took great pleasure in our performances. He liked to see plays acted by persons with whom he was familiar. Sometimes he complimented us on our exertions. Although I was as much amused with the thing as others, I was more than once obliged to remind him that my occupations left me but little time to learn my parts. Then he would assume his coaxing manner and say, "Come, do not vex me! You have such a memory! You know that it amuses me. You see that these performances render Malmaison gay and animated; Josephine takes much pleasure in them. Rise earlier in the morning.—In fact, I sleep too much; is not that the cafe—Come, Bourrienne, do oblige me. You make me laugh so

168 While Bourrienne, belonging to the Malmaison company, considered that the acting at Neuilly was indecent, Lucien, who refused to act at Malmaison, naturally thought the Malmaison troupe was dull. "Hortense and Caroline filled the principal parts. They were very commonplace. In this they followed the unfortunate Marie Antoinette and her companions. Louis XVI., not naturally polite, when seeing them act, had said that it was royally badly acted" (see Madame Campan's Life of Marie Antoinette, tome i. p. 299). "The First Consul said of his troupe that it was sovereignly badly acted . . . Murat, Lannes, and even Caroline ranted. Elisa, who, having been educated at Saint Cyr, spoke purely and without accent, refused to act. Janot acted well the drunken parts, and even the others he undertook. The rest were decidedly bad. Worse than bad—ridiculous" (Iung's Lucien's, tome ii. p. 256). Rival actors are not fair critics. Let us hear Madame Junot (tome ii. p. 103). "The cleverest of our company was M. de Bourrienne. He played the more dignified characters in real perfection, and his talent was the more pleasing as it was not the result of study, but of a perfect comprehension of his part." And she goes on to say that even the best professional actors might have learnt from him in some parts. The audience was not a pleasant one to face. It was the First Consul's habit to invite forty persons to dinner, and a hundred and fifty for the evening, and consequently to hear, criticise, and banter us without mercy" (Memoirs of Duchesse d'Abrantes, tome ii. p. 108).

heartily! Do not deprive me of this pleasure. I have not over much amusement, as you well know."—"All, truly! I would not deprive you of any pleasure. I am delighted to be able to contribute to your amusement." After a conversation of this sort I could not do less than set about studying my part.

At this period, during summer, I had half the Sunday to myself. I was, however, obliged to devote a portion of this precious leisure to pleasing Bonaparte by studying a new part as a surprise for him. Occasionally, however, I passed the time at Ruel. I recollect that one day, when I had hurried there from Malmaison, I lost a beautiful watch made by Breguet. It was four o'clock in the afternoon, and the road was that day thronged with people. I made my loss publicly known by means of the crier of Ruel. An hour after, as I was sitting down to table, a young lad belonging to the village brought me my watch. He had found it on the high road in a wheel rut. I was pleased with the probity of this young man, and rewarded both him and his father, who accompanied him. I reiterated the circumstance the same evening to the First Consul, who was so struck with this instance of honesty that he directed me to procure information respecting the young man and his family. I learned that they were honest peasants. Bonaparte gave employment to three brothers of this family; and, what was most difficult to persuade him to, he exempted the young man who brought me the watch from the conscription.

When a fact of this nature reached Bonaparte's ear it was seldom that he did not give the principal actor in it some proof of his satisfaction. Two qualities predominated in his character—kindness and impatience. Impatience, when he was under its influence, got the better of him; it was then impossible for him to control himself. I had a remarkable proof of it about this very period.

Canova having arrived in Paris came to St. Cloud to model the figure of the First Consul, of whom he was about to make a colossal statue. This great artist came often, in the hope of getting his model to stand in the proper attitude; but Bonaparte was so tired, disgusted, and fretted by the process, that he very seldom put himself in the required attitude, and then only for a short time. Bonaparte notwithstanding had the highest regard for Canova. Whenever he was announced the First Consul sent me to keep him company until he was at leisure to give him a sitting; but he would shrug up his shoulders and say, "More modeling! Good Heavens, how vexatious!" Canova expressed great displeasure at not being able to study his model as he wished to do, and the little anxiety of Bonaparte on the subject damped the ardour of his imagination. Everybody agrees in saying that he has not succeeded in the work, and I have explained the reason. The Duke of Wellington afterwards possessed this colossal statue, which was about twice his own height.

CHAPTER XI

1802

It is a principle particularly applicable to absolute governments that a prince should change his ministers as seldom as possible, and never except upon serious grounds. Bonaparte acted on this principle when First Consul, and also when he became Emperor. He often allowed unjust causes to influence him, but he never dismissed a Minister without cause; indeed, he more than once, without any reason, retained Ministers longer than he ought to have done in the situations in which he had placed them. Bonaparte's tenacity in this respect, in some instances, produced very opposite results. For instance, it afforded M. Gaudin' time to establish a degree of order in the administration of Finance which before his time had never existed; and on the other hand, it enabled M. Decres to reduce the Ministry of Marine to an unparalleled state of confusion.

Bonaparte saw nothing in men but helps and obstacles. On the 18th Brumaire Fouché was a help. The First Consul feared that he would become an obstacle; it was necessary, therefore, to think of dismissing him. Bonaparte's most sincere friends had from the beginning been opposed to Fouché's having any share in the Government. But their disinterested advice produced no other result than their own disgrace, so influential a person had Fouché become. How could it be otherwise? Fouché was identified with the Republic by the death of the King, for which he had voted; with the Reign of Terror by his sanguinary missions to Lyons and Nevers; with the Consulate by his real though perhaps exaggerated services; with Bonaparte by the charm with which he might be said to have fascinated him; with Josephine by the enmity of the First Consul's brothers. Who would believe it? Fouché ranked the enemies of the Revolution amongst his warmest partisans. They overwhelmed him with eulogy, to the disparagement even of the Head of the State, because the cunning Minister, practising an interested indulgence, set himself up as the protector of individuals belonging to classes which, when he was proconsul, he had attacked in the mass. Director of public opinion, and having in his hands the means at his pleasure of inspiring fear or of entangling by inducements, it was all in his favour that he had already directed this opinion. The machinery he set in motion was so calculated that the police was rather the police of Fouché than that of the Minister of the General Police. Throughout Paris, and indeed throughout all France, Fouché obtained credit for extraordinary ability; and the popular opinion was correct in this respect, namely, that no man ever displayed such ability in making it be supposed that he really possessed talent. Fouché's secret in this particular is the whole secret of the greater part of those persons who are called statesmen.

Be this as it may, the First Consul did not behold with pleasure the factitious influence of which Fouché had possessed himself. For some time past, to the repugnance which at bottom he had felt towards Fouché, were added other causes of discontent. In consequence of having been deceived by secret reports and correspondence Bonaparte began to shrug up his shoulders with an expression of regret when he received them, and said, "Would you believe, Bourrienne, that I have been imposed on by these things? All such denunciations are useless—scandalous. All the reports from prefects and the police, all the intercepted letters, are a tissue of absurdities and lies. I desire to have no more of them." He said so, but he still received them. However, Fouché's dismissal was resolved upon. But though Bonaparte wished to get rid of him, still, under the influence of the charm, he dared not proceed against him without the greatest caution. He first resolved upon the suppression of the office of Minister of Police in order to disguise the motive for the removal of the Minister. The First Consul told Fouché that this suppression, which he spoke of as being yet remote, was calculated more than anything else to give strength to the Government, since it would afford a proof of the security and internal tranquillity of France. Overpowered by the arguments with which Bonaparte supported his proposition, Fouché could urge no good reasons in opposition to it, but contented himself with recommending that the execution of the design, which was good in intention, should, however, be postponed for two years. Bonaparte appeared to listen favourably to Fouché's recommendation, who, as avaricious for money as Bonaparte of glory, consoled himself by thinking that for these two years the administration of the gaming tables would still be for him a Pactolus flowing with gold. For Fouché, already the possessor of an immense fortune, always dreamed of increasing it, though he himself did not know how to enjoy it. With him the ambition of enlarging the bounds of his estate of Pont-Carre was not less felt than with the First Consul the ambition of extending the frontier of France.

Not only did the First Consul not like Fouché, but it is perfectly true that at this time the police wearied and annoyed him. Several times he told me he looked on it as dangerous, especially for the possessor of power. In a Government without the liberty of the press he was quite right. The very services which the police had rendered to the First Consul were of a nature to alarm him, for whoever had conspired against the Directory in favour of the Consulate might also conspire against the Consulate in favour of any other Government. It is needless to say that I only allude to the political police, and not to the municipal police, which is indispensable for large towns, and which has the honourable mission of watching over the health and safety of the citizens.

Fouché, as has been stated, had been Minister of Police since the 18th Brumaire. Everybody who was acquainted with, the First Consul's character was unable to explain the ascendency which he had suffered Fouché to acquire over him, and of which Bonaparte himself was really impatient. He saw in Fouché a centre around which all the interests of the Revolution concentrated themselves, and at this he felt indignant; but, subject to a species of magnetism, he could not break the charm which enthralled him. When he spoke of Fouché in his absence his language was warm, bitter, and hostile. When Fouché was present, Bonaparte's tone was softened, unless some public scene was to be acted like that which occurred after the attempt of the 3d Nivôse.

The suppression of the Ministry of Police being determined on, Bonaparte did not choose to delay the execution of his design, as he had pretended to think necessary. On the evening of the 12th of September we went to Mortfontaine. We passed the next day, which was Monday, at that place, and it was there, far removed from Fouché, and urged by the combined persuasions of Joseph and Lucien, that the First Consul signed the decree of suppression. The next morning we returned to Paris. Fouché came to Malmaison, where we were, in the regular execution of his duties. The First Consul transacted business with him as usual without daring to tell him of his dismissal, and afterwards sent Cambacérès to inform him of it. After this act, respecting which he had hesitated so long, Bonaparte still endeavoured to modify his rigour. Having appointed Fouché a Senator, he said in the letter which he wrote to the Senate to notify the appointment:

> "Fouché, as Minister of Police, in times of difficulty, has by his talent, his activity, and his attachment to the Government done all that circumstances required of him. Placed in the bosom of the Senate, if events should again call for a Minister of Police the Government cannot find one more worthy of its confidence."

From this moment the departments of Justice and Police united were confided to the hands of Regnier.' Bonaparte's aversion for Fouché strangely blinded him with respect to the capabilities of his successor. Besides, how could the administration of justice, which rests on fixed, rigid, and unchangeable bases, proceed hand in hand with another administration placed on the quicksand of instantaneous decisions, and surrounded by stratagems and deceptions? Justice should never have anything to do with secret police, unless it be to condemn it.[169]

What could be expected from Regnier, charged as he was with incompatible functions? What, under such circumstances, could have been expected even from a man gifted with great talents? Such was the exact history of Fouché's disgrace. No person was more afflicted at it than Madame Bonaparte, who only learned the news when it was announced to the public. Josephine, on all occasions, defended Fouché against her husband's sallies. She believed that he was the only one of his Ministers who told him the truth. She had such a high opinion of the way in which Fouché managed the police that the first time I was alone with her after our return from Mortfontaine she said to me, "My dear Bourrienne; speak openly to me; will Napoleon know all about the plots from the police of Moncey, Duroc, Junot, and of Davoust? You know better than I do that these are only wretched spies. Has not Savary also eventually got his police? How all this alarms me. They take away all my supports, and surround me only with enemies."—"To justify your regrets we should be sure that Fouché has never been in agreement with Lucien in favour of the divorce."—"Oh, I do not believe that. Bonaparte does not like him, and he would have been certain to tell me of it when I spoke favourably to him of Fouché. You will see that his brothers will end by bringing him into their plan."

I have already spoken of Josephine's troubles, and of the bad conduct of Joseph, but more particularly of Lucien, towards her; I will therefore describe here, as connected with the disgrace of Fouché, whom Madame Bonaparte regretted as a support, some scenes which occurred about this period at Malmaison. Having been the confidant of both parties, and an involuntary actor in those scenes, now that twenty-seven years have passed since they occurred what motive can induce me to disguise the truth in any respect?

Madame Louis Bonaparte was enceinte. Josephine, although she tenderly loved her children, did not seem to behold the approaching event which the situation of her daughter indicated with the interest natural to the heart of a mother. She had long been aware of the calumnious reports circulated respecting the supposed connection between Hortense

---

169 M. Abrial, Minister of Justice, was called to the Senate at the same time as Fouché. Understanding that the assimilation of the two men was more a disgrace to Abrial than the mere loss of the Ministry, the First Consul said to M. Abrial: "In uniting the Ministry of Police to that of Justice I could not retain you in the Ministry, you are too upright a man to manage the police." Not a flattering speech for Regnier.—Bourrienne.

and the First Consul, and that base accusation cost her many tears. Poor Josephine paid dearly for the splendour of her station! As I knew how devoid of foundation these atrocious reports were, I endeavoured to console her by telling her what was true, that I was exerting all my efforts to demonstrate their infamy and falsehood. Bonaparte, however, dazzled by the affection which was manifested towards him from all quarters, aggravated the sorrow of his wife by a silly vanity. He endeavoured to persuade her that these reports had their origin only in the wish of the public that he should have a child, so that these seeming consolations offered by self-love to Josephine's grief gave force to existing conjugal alarms, and the fear of divorce returned with all its horrors. Under the foolish illusion of his vanity Bonaparte imagined that France was desirous of being governed even by a bastard if supposed to be a child of his,—a singular mode truly of founding a new legitimacy!

Josephine, whose susceptibility appears to me even now excusable, well knew my sentiments on the subject of Bonaparte's founding a dynasty, and she had not forgotten my conduct when two years before the question had been agitated on the occasion of Louis XVIII.'s letters to the First Consul. I remember that one day, after the publication of the parallel of Caesar, Cromwell, and Bonaparte, Josephine having entered our cabinet without being announced, which she sometimes did when from the good humour exhibited at breakfast she reckoned upon its continuance, approached Bonaparte softly, seated herself on his knee, passed her hand gently through his hair and over his face, and thinking the moment favourable, said to him in a burst of tenderness, "I entreat of you, Bonaparte, do not make yourself a King! It is that wretch Lucien who urges you to it. Do not listen to him!" Bonaparte replied, without anger, and even smiling as he pronounced the last words, "You are mad, my poor Josephine. It is your old dowagers of the Faubourg St. Germain, your Rochefoucaulds, who tell you all these fables! . . . . Come now, you interrupt me—leave me alone."

What Bonaparte said that day good-naturedly to his wife I have often heard him declare seriously. I have been present at five or six altercations on the subject. That there existed, too, an enmity connected with this question between the family of BEAUHARNAIS and the family of Bonaparte cannot be denied.

Fouché, as I have stated, was in the interest of Josephine, and Lucien was the most bitter of her enemies. One day Raederer inveighed with so much violence against Fouché in the presence of Madame Bonaparte that she replied with extreme warmth, "The real enemies of Bonaparte are those who feed him with notions of hereditary descent, of a dynasty, of divorce, and of marriage!" Josephine could not check this exclamation, as she knew that Roederer encouraged those ideas, which he spread abroad by Lucien's direction. I recollect one day when she had been to see us at our little house at Ruel: as I walked with her along the high road to her carriage, which she had sent forward, I acknowledged too unreservedly my fears on account of the ambition of Bonaparte, and of the perfidious advice of his brothers. "Madame," said I, "if we cannot succeed in dissuading the General from making himself a King, I dread the future for his sake. If ever he re-establishes royalty he will in all probability labour for the Bourbons, and enable them one day to re-ascend the throne which he shall erect. No one, doubtless, without passing for a fool, can pretend to say with certainty what series of chances and events such a proceeding will produce; but common sense alone is sufficient to convince any one that unfavourable chances must long be dreaded. The ancient system being re-established, the occupation of the throne will then be only a family question, and not a question of government between liberty and despotic power. Why should not

France, if it ceases to be free, prefer the race of her ancient kings? You surely know it. You had not been married two years when, on returning from Italy, your husband told me that he aspired to royalty. Now he is Consul for life. Would he but resolve to stop there! He already possesses everything but an empty title. No sovereign in Europe has so much power as he has. I am sorry for it, Madame, but I really believe that, in spite of yourself, you will be made Queen or Empress."

Madame Bonaparte had allowed me to speak without interruption, but when I pronounced the words Queen and Empress she exclaimed, "My God! Bourrienne, such ambition is far from my thoughts. That I may always continue the wife of the First Consul is all I desire. Say to him all that you have said to me. Try and prevent him from making himself King."—"Madame," I replied, "times are greatly altered. The wisest men, the strongest minds, have resolutely and courageously opposed his tendency to the hereditary system. But advice is now useless. He would not listen to me. In all discussions on the subject he adheres inflexibly to the view he has taken. If he be seriously opposed his anger knows no bounds; his language is harsh and abrupt, his tone imperious, and his authority bears down all before him."—"Yet, Bourrienne, he has so much confidence in you that of you should try once more!"—"Madame, I assure you he will not listen to me. Besides, what could I add to the remarks I made upon his receiving the letters of Louis XVIII., when I fearlessly represented to him that being without children he would have no one to whom to bequeath the throne—that, doubtless, from the opinion which he entertained of his brothers, he could not desire to erect it for them?" Here Josephine again interrupted me by exclaiming, "My kind friend, when you spoke of children did he say anything to you? Did he talk of a divorce?"—"Not a word, Madame, I assure you."—"If they do not urge him to it, I do not believe he will resolve to do such a thing. You know how he likes Eugène, and Eugène behaves so well to him. How different is Lucien. It is that wretch Lucien, to whom Bonaparte listens too much, and of whom, however, he always speaks ill to me."—"I do not know, Madame, what Lucien says to his brother except when he chooses to tell me, because Lucien always avoids having a witness of his interviews with your husband, but I can assure you that for two years I have not heard the word 'divorce' from the General's mouth."—"I always reckon on you, my dear Bourrienne; to turn him away from it; as you did at that time."—"I do not believe he is thinking of it, but if it recurs to him, consider, Madame, that it will be now from very different motives: He is now entirely given up to the interests of his policy and his ambition, which dominate every other feeling in him. There will not now be any question of scandal, or of a trial before a court, but of an act of authority which complaisant laws will justify and which the Church perhaps will sanction."—"That's true. You are right. Good God! how unhappy I am."[170]

Such was the nature of one of the conversations I had with Madame Bonaparte on a subject to which she often recurred. It may not perhaps be uninteresting to endeavour to

170 When Bourrienne complains of not knowing what passed between Lucien and Napoleon, we can turn to Lucien's account of Bourrienne, apparently about this very time. "After a stormy interview with Napoleon," says Lucien, "I at once went into the cabinet where Bourrienne was working, and found that unbearable busybody of a secretary, whose star had already paled more than once, which made him more prying than ever, quite upset by the time the First Consul had taken to come out of his bath. He must, or at least might, have heard some noise, for enough had been made. Seeing that he wanted to know the cause from me, I took up a newspaper to avoid being bored by his conversation" (Iung's Lucien, tome ii. p.156)

compare with this what Napoleon said at St. Helena, speaking of his first wife. According to the Memorial Napoleon there stated that when Josephine was at last constrained to renounce all hope of having a child, she often let fall allusions to a great political fraud, and at length openly proposed it to him. I make no doubt Bonaparte made use of words to this effect, but I do not believe the assertion. I recollect one day that Bonaparte, on entering our cabinet, where I was already seated, exclaimed in a transport of joy impossible for me to describe, "Well, Bourrienne, my wife is at last enceinte!" I sincerely congratulated him, more, I own, out of courtesy than from any hope of seeing him made a father by Josephine, for I well remembered that Corvisart, who had given medicines to Madame Bonaparte, had nevertheless assured me that he expected no result from them. Medicine was really the only political fraud to which Josephine had recourse; and in her situation what other woman would not have done as much? Here, then, the husband and the wife are in contradiction, which is nothing uncommon. But on which side is truth? I have no hesitation in referring it to Josephine. There is indeed an immense difference between the statements of a women—trusting her fears and her hopes to the sole confidant of her family secrets, and the tardy declaration of a man who, after seeing the vast edifice of his ambition leveled with the dust, is only anxious, in his compulsory retreat, to preserve intact and spotless the other great edifice of his glory. Bonaparte should have recollected that Caesar did not like the idea of his wife being even suspected.

CHAPTER XII

1802

Citizen Fesch, who, when we were forced to stop at Ajaccio on our return from Egypt, discounted at rather a high rate the General-in-Chief's Egyptian sequins, became again the Abbe Fesch, as soon as Bonaparte by his Consular authority re-erected the altars which the Revolution had overthrown. On the 15th of August 1802 he was consecrated Bishop, and the following year received the Cardinal's hat. Thus Bonaparte took advantage of one of the members of his family being in orders to elevate him to the highest dignities of the Church. He afterwards gave Cardinal Fesch the Archbishopric of Lyons, of which place he was long the titular.[171] The First Consul prided himself a good deal on his triumph, at least in appearance, over the scruples which the persons who surrounded him had manifested against the re-establishment of worship. He read with much self-satisfaction the reports made to him, in which it was stated that the churches were well frequented: Indeed, throughout the year 1802, all his attention was directed to the reformation of manners, which had become more dissolute under the Directory than even during the Reign of Terror.

In his march of usurpation the First Consul let slip no opportunity of endeavouring to obtain at the same time the admiration of the multitude and the approbation of judicious men. He was very fond of the arts, and was sensible that the promotion of industry ought to be the peculiar care of the head of the Government. It must, however, at the same time be owned that he rendered the influence of his protection null and void by the continual violations he committed on that liberty which is the animating principle of all improvement.

During the supplementary days of the year X., that is to say, about the beginning of the autumn of 1802, there was held at the Louvre an exhibition of the products of industry. The First Consul visited the exhibition, and as even at that period he had begun to attribute every good result to himself, he seemed proud of the high degree of perfection the manufacturing

171 Like Cambacérès the Cardinal was a bit of a gourmet, and on one occasion had invited a large party of clerical magnates to dinner. By a coincidence two turbots of singular beauty arrived as presents to his Eminence on the very morning of the feast. To serve both would have appeared ridiculous, but the Cardinal was most anxious to have the credit of both. He imparted his embarrassment to his chef: "'Be of good faith, your Eminence,' was the reply, 'both shall appear and enjoy the reception so justly their due.' The dinner was served: one of the turbots relieved the soup. Delight was on every face—it was the moment of the 'eprouvette positive'. The 'maitre a'hotel' advances; two attendants raise the turbot and carry him off to cut him up; but one of them loses his equilibrium: the attendants and the turbot roll together on the floor. At this sad sight the assembled Cardinals became as pale as death, and a solemn silence reigned in the 'conclave'—it was the moment of the 'eprouvette negative'; but the 'maitre a'hotel' suddenly turns to one of the attendants, Bring another turbot,' said he, with the most perfect coolness. The second appeared, and the eprouvette positive was gloriously renewed." (Hayward's Art of Dining, P. 65.)

arts had attained in France. He was, above all, delighted with the admiration this exhibition excited among the numerous foreigners who resorted to Paris during the peace.

In fact, throughout the year 1802 the capital presented an interesting and animating-spectacle. The appetite for luxury and pleasure had insinuated itself into manners—which were no longer republican, and the vast number of Russians and English who drove about everywhere with brilliant equipages contributed not a little to this metamorphosis. All Paris flocked to the Carrousel on review days, and regarded with eyes of delight the unusual sight of rich foreign liveries and emblazoned carriages. The parties at the Tuileries were brilliant and numerous, and nothing was wanting but the name of levees. Count Markoff, who succeeded M. de Kalitscheff as Russian ambassador; the Marquis de Lucchesini, the Prussian ambassador; and Lord Whitworth, the Minister from England, made numerous presentations of their countrymen to the First Consul, who was well pleased that the Court he was forming should have examples set by foreign courtiers. Never since the meeting of the States-General had the theatres been so frequented, or fetes so magnificent; and never since that period had Paris presented so cheering an aspect. The First Consul, on his part, spared no exertion to render the capital more and more worthy the admiration of foreigners. The statue of the Venus de Medicis, which had been robbed from the gallery of the Grand Duke of Tuscany, now decorated the gallery of the Louvre, and near it was placed that of the Velletrian Pallas, a more legitimate acquisition, since it was the result of the researches of some French engineers at Velletri. Everywhere an air of prosperity was perceptible, and Bonaparte proudly put in his claim to be regarded as the author of it all. With what heartfelt satisfaction did he likewise cast his eye upon what he called the grand thermometer of opinion, the price of the funds! For if he saw them doubled in value in consequence of the revolution of the 18th Brumaire, rising as they did at that period from seven to sixteen francs, this value was even more than tripled after the vote of Consulship for life and the 'Senates-consulte' of the 4th of August,—when they rose to fifty-two francs.

While Paris presented so satisfactory an aspect the departments were in a state of perfect tranquillity; and foreign affairs had every appearance of security. The Court of the Vatican, which since the Concordat may be said to have become devoted to the First Consul, gave, under all circumstances, examples of submission to the wishes of France. The Vatican was the first Court which recognised the erection of Tuscany into the Kingdom of Etruria, and the formation of the Helvetic, Cisalpine, and Batavian Republics. Prussia soon followed the example of the Pope, which was successively imitated by the other powers of Europe.

The whole of these new states, realms, or republics were under the immediate influence of France. The Isle of Elba, which Napoleon's first abdication afterwards rendered so famous, and Piedmont, divided into six departments, were also united to France, still called it Republic. Everything now seemed to concur in securing his accession to absolute power. We were now at peace with all the world, and every circumstance tended to place in the hands of the First Consul that absolute power which indeed was the only kind of government he was capable of forming any conception of. Indeed, one of the characteristic signs of Napoleon's government, even under the Consular system, left no doubt as to his real intentions. Had he wished to found a free Government it is evident that he world have made the Ministers responsible to the country, whereas he took care that there should be no responsibility but to himself. He viewed them, in fact, in the light of instruments which he might break as he pleased. I found this single index sufficient to disclose all his future designs. In order to make the irresponsibility of his Ministers to the public perfectly clear, he had all the acts of his Government signed merely by M. Maret, Secretary of State. Thus the Consulship for life was nothing but an Empire in disguise, the usufruct of which could not long satisfy the First Consul's ambition. His brothers influenced him, and it was resolved to found a new dynasty.

It was not in the interior of France that difficulties were likely first to arise on Bonaparte's carrying his designs into effect, but there was some reason to apprehend that foreign powers, after recognising and treating with the Consular Government, might display a different feeling, and entertain scruples with regard to a Government which had resumed its monarchical form. The question regarding the Bourbons was in some measure kept in the background as long as France remained a Republic, but the re-establishment of the throne naturally called to recollection the family which had occupied it for so many ages. Bonaparte fully felt the delicacy of his position, but he knew how to face obstacles, and had been accustomed to overcome them: he, however, always proceeded cautiously, as when obstacles induced him to defer the period of the Consulship for life.

Bonaparte laboured to establish in France not only an absolute government, but, what is still worse, a military one. He considered a decree signed by his hand possessed of a magic virtue capable of transforming his generals into able diplomatists, and so he sent them on embassies, as if to show the Sovereigns to whom they were accredited that he soon meant to take their thrones by assault. The appointment of Lannes to the Court of Lisbon originated from causes which probably will be read with some interest, since they serve to place Bonaparte's character in, its true light, and to point out, at the same time, the means he disdained not to resort to, if he wished to banish his most faithful friends when their presence was no longer agreeable to him.

Bonaparte had ceased to address Lannes in the second person singular; but that general continued the familiarity of thee and thou in speaking to Napoleon. It is hardly possible to conceive how much this annoyed the First Consul. Aware of the unceremonious candour of his old comrade, whose daring spirit he knew would prompt him to go as great lengths in civil affairs as on the field of battle, Bonaparte, on the great occasion of the 18th Brumaire, fearing his reproaches, had given him the command of Paris in order to ensure his absence from St. Cloud.

After that time, notwithstanding the continually growing greatness of the First Consul, which, as it increased, daily exacted more and more deference, Lannes still preserved his freedom of speech, and was the only one who dared to treat Bonaparte as a comrade, and tell him the truth without ceremony. This was enough to determine Napoleon to rid himself of the presence of Lannes. But under what pretext was the absence of the conqueror of Montebello to be procured? It was necessary to conjure up an excuse; and in the truly diabolical machination resorted to for that purpose, Bonaparte brought into play that crafty disposition for which he was so remarkable.

Lannes, who never looked forward to the morrow, was as careless of his money as of his blood. Poor officers and soldiers partook largely of his liberality. Thus he had no fortune, but plenty of debts when he wanted money, and this was not seldom, he used to come, as if it were a mere matter of course, to ask it of the First Consul, who, I must confess, never refused him. Bonaparte, though he well knew the general's circumstances, said to him one day, "My friend, you should attend a little more to appearances. You must have your establishment suitable to your rank. There is the Hotel de Noailles—why don't you take it, and furnish it in proper style?" Lannes, whose own candour prevented him from suspecting the artful designs of others, followed the advice of the First Consul. The Hotel de Noailles was taken and superbly fitted up. Odiot supplied a service of plate valued at 200,000 francs.

General Lannes having thus conformed to the wishes of Bonaparte came to him and requested 400,000 francs, the amount of the expense incurred, as it were, by his order. "But," said the First Consul, "I have no money."—"You have no money! What the devil am I to do, then?"

"But is there none in the Guard's chest? Take what you require, and we will settle it, hereafter."

Mistrusting nothing, Lannes went to the treasurer of the Guards, who made some objections at first to the advance required, but who soon yielded on learning that the demand was made with the consent of the First Consul.

Within twenty-four hours after Lannes had obtained the 400,000 francs the treasurer received from the head commissary an order to balance his accounts. The receipt for the 400,000 francs advanced to Lannes, was not acknowledged as a voucher. In vain the treasurer alleged the authority of the First Consul for the transaction. Napoleon's memory had suddenly failed him; he had entirely forgotten all about it. In a word, it was incumbent on Lannes to refund the 400,000 francs to the Guards' chest; and, as I have already said, he had no property on earth, but debts in abundance. He repaired to General Lefebre, who loved him as his son, and to him he related all that had passed. "Simpleton," said Lefebvre, "why did you not come to me? Why did you go and get into debt with that ——-? Well, here are the 400,000 francs; take them to him, and let him go to the devil!"

Lannes hastened to the First Consul. "What!"—he exclaimed, "is it possible you can be guilty of such baseness as this? To treat me in such a manner! To lay such a foul snare for me after all that I have done for you; after all the blood I have shed to promote your ambition! Is this the recompense you had in store for me? You forget the 13th Vendemiaire, to the success of which I contributed more than you! You forget Millesimo: I was colonel before you! For whom did I fight at Bassano? You were witness of what I did at Lodi and at Governolo, where I was wounded; and yet you play me such a trick as this! But for me, Paris would have revolted on the 18th Brumaire. But for me, you would have lost the battle of Marengo. I alone, yes, I alone, passed the Po, at Montebello, with my whole division. You gave the credit of that to Berthier, who was not there; and this is my reward—humiliation. This cannot, this shall not be. I will——" Bonaparte, pale with anger, listened without stirring, and Lannes was on the point of challenging him when Junot, who heard the uproar, hastily entered. The unexpected presence of this general somewhat reassured the First Consul, and at the same time calmed, in some degree, the fury of Lannes. "Well," said Bonaparte, "go to Lisbon. You will get money there; and when you return you will not want any one to pay your debts for you." Thus was Bonaparte's object gained. Lannes set out for Lisbon, and never afterwards annoyed the First Consul by his familiarities, for on his return he ceased to address him with thee and thou.

Having described Bonaparte's ill-treatment of Lannes I may here subjoin a statement of the circumstances which led to a rupture between the First Consul and me. So many false stories have been circulated on the subject that I am anxious to relate the facts as they really were.

Nine months had now passed since I had tendered my resignation to the First Consul. The business of my office had become too great for me, and my health was so much endangered by over-application that my physician, M. Corvisart, who had for a long time impressed upon me the necessity of relaxation, now formally warned me that I should not long hold out under the fatigue I underwent. Corvisart had no doubt spoken to the same effect to the First Consul, for the latter said to me one day, in a tone which betrayed but little feeling, "Why, Corvisart says you have not a year to live." This was certainly no very welcome compliment in the mouth of an old college friend, yet I must confess that the doctor risked little by the prediction.

I had resolved, in fact, to follow the advice of Corvisart; my family were urgent in their entreaties that I would do so, but I always put off the decisive step. I was loath to give up a friendship which had subsisted so long, and which had been only once disturbed: on that occasion when Joseph thought proper to play the spy upon me at the table of Fouché. I remembered also the reception I had met with from the conqueror of Italy; and I experienced, moreover, no slight pain at the thought of quitting one from whom I had received so many proofs of confidence, and to whom I had been attached from early boyhood. These considerations constantly triumphed over the disgust to which I was subjected by a number of circumstances, and by the increasing vexations occasioned by the conflict between my private sentiments and the nature of the duties I had to perform.

I was thus kept in a state of perplexity, from which some unforeseen circumstance alone could extricate me. Such a circumstance at length occurred, and the following is the history of my first rupture with Napoleon:

On the 27th of February 1802, at ten at night, Bonaparte dictated to me a despatch of considerable importance and urgency, for M. de Talleyrand, requesting the Minister for Foreign Affairs to come to the Tuileries next morning at an appointed hour. According to custom, I put the letter into the hands of the office messenger that it might be forwarded to its destination.

This was Saturday. The following day, Sunday, M. de Talleyrand came as if for an audience about mid-day. The First Consul immediately began to confer with him on the subject of the letter sent the previous evening, and was astonished to learn that the Minister had not received it until the morning. He immediately rang for the messenger, and ordered me to be sent for. Being in a very bad humour, he pulled the bell with so much fury that he struck his hand violently against the angle of the chimney-piece. I hurried to his presence. "Why," he said, addressing me hastily, "why was not my letter delivered yesterday evening?"—"I do not know: I put it at once into the hands of the person whose duty it was to see that it was sent."—"Go and find the cause of the delay, and come back quickly." Having rapidly made my inquiries, I returned to the cabinet. "Well?" said the First Consul, whose irritation seemed to have increased. "Well, General, it is not the fault of anybody, M. de Talleyrand was not to be found, either at the office or at his own residence, or at the houses of any of his friends where he was thought likely to be." Not knowing with whom to be angry, restrained by the coolness of M. de Talleyrand, yet at the same time ready to burst with rage, Bonaparte rose from his seat, and proceeding to the hall, called the messenger and questioned him sharply. The man, disconcerted by the anger of the First Consul, hesitated in his replies, and gave confused answers. Bonaparte returned to his cabinet still more irritated than he had left it.

I had followed him to the hall, and on my way back to the cabinet I attempted to soothe him, and I begged him not to be thus discomposed by a circumstance which, after all, was of no great moment. I do not know whether his anger was increased by the sight of the blood which flowed from his hand, and which he was every moment looking at; but however that might be, a transport of furious passion, such as I had never before witnessed, seized him; and as I was about to enter the cabinet after him he threw back the door with so much violence that, had I been two or three inches nearer him, it must infallibly have struck me in the face. He accompanied this action, which was almost convulsive, with an appellation, not to be borne; he exclaimed before M. de Talleyrand, "Leave me alone; you are a fool." At an insult so atrocious I confess that the anger which had already mastered the First Consul suddenly seized on me. I thrust the door forward with as much impetuosity as he had used in throwing it back, and, scarcely knowing what I said, exclaimed, "You are a hundredfold a greater fool than I am!" I then banged the door and went upstairs to my apartment, which was situated over the cabinet.

I was as far from expecting as from wishing such an occasion of separating from the First Consul. But what was done could not be undone; and therefore, without taking time for reflection, and still under the influence of the anger that had got the better of me, I penned the following positive resignation:

> GENERAL—The state of my health no longer permits me to continue in your service. I therefore beg you to accept my resignation.
>
> BOURRIENNE.

Some moments after this note was written I saw Bonaparte's saddle-horses brought up to the entrance of the Palace. It was Sunday morning, and, contrary to his usual custom on that day, he was going to ride out.

Duroc accompanied him. He was no sooner done than I, went down into his cabinet, and placed my letter on his table. On returning at four o'clock with Duroc Bonaparte read my letter. "Ah! ah!" said he, before opening it, "a letter from Bourrienne." And he almost immediately added, for the note was speedily perused, "He is in the sulks.—Accepted." I had left the Tuileries at the moment he returned, but Duroc sent to me where I was dining the following billet:

> The First Consul desires me, my dear Bourrienne, to inform you that he accepts your resignation, and to request that you will give me the necessary information respecting your papers.—Yours,
>
> DUROC.
>
> P.S.:—I will call on you presently.

Duroc came to me at eight o'clock the same evening. The First Consul was in his cabinet when we entered it. I immediately commenced giving my intended successor the necessary explanations to enable him to enter upon his new duties. Piqued at finding that I did not speak to him, and at the coolness with which I instructed Duroc, Bonaparte said to me in a harsh tone, "Come, I have had enough of this! Leave me." I stepped down from the ladder on which I had mounted for the purpose of pointing out to Duroc the places in which the various papers were deposited and hastily withdrew. I too had quite enough of it!

I remained two more days at the Tuileries until I had suited myself with lodgings. On Monday I went down into the cabinet of the First Consul to take my leave of him. We conversed together for a long time, and very amicably. He told me he was very sorry I was going to leave him, and that he would do all he could for me. I pointed out several places to him; at last I mentioned the Tribunate. "That will not do for you," he said; "the members are a set of babblers and phrasemongers, whom I mean to get rid of. All the troubles of States proceed from such debatings. I am tired of them." He continued to talk in a strain which left me in no doubt as to his uneasiness about the Tribunate, which, in fact, reckoned among its members many men of great talent and excellent character.[172]

The following day, Tuesday, the First Consul asked me to breakfast with him. After breakfast, while he was conversing with some other person, Madame Bonaparte and Hortense pressed me to make advances towards obtaining a re-instalment in my office, appealing to me on the score of the friendship and kindness they had always shown me. They told me that I had been in the wrong, and that I had forgotten myself. I answered that I considered the evil beyond remedy; and that, besides, I had really need of repose. The First Consul then called me to him, and conversed a considerable time with me, renewing his protestations of goodwill towards me.

At five o'clock I was going downstairs to quit the Tuileries for good when I was met by the office messenger, who told me that the First Consul wished to see me. Duroc; who was in the room leading to the cabinet, stopped me as I passed, and said, "He wishes you to remain. I beg of you not to refuse; do me this favour. I have assured him that I am incapable of filling your office. It does not suit my habits; and besides, to tell you the truth, the business is too irksome for me." I proceeded to the cabinet without replying to Duroc. The First Consul came up to me smiling, and pulling me by the ear, as he did when he was in the best of humours, said to me, "Are you still in the sulks?" and leading me to my usual seat he added, "Come, sit down."

Only those who knew Bonaparte can judge of my situation at that moment. He had at times, and when he chose, a charm in his manners which it was quite impossible to resist. I could offer no opposition, and I resumed my usual office and my accustomed labours. Five minutes afterwards it was announced that dinner was on table. "You will dine with me?" he said. "I cannot; I am expected at the place where I was going when Duroc called me back. It is an engagement that I cannot break."—"Well, I have nothing to say, then. But give me your word that you will be here at eight o'clock."—"I promise you." Thus I became again the private secretary of the First Consul, and I believed in the sincerity of our reconciliation.

---

172 In 1802 the First Consul made a reduction of fifty members of the Tribunate, and subsequently the whole body was suppressed.—Bourrienne.

CHAPTER XIII

1802-1803

It may truly be said that history affords no example of an empire founded like that of France, created in all its parts under the cloak of a republic. Without any shock, and in the short space of four years, there arose above the ruins of the short-lived Republic a Government more absolute than ever was Louis XIV.'s. This extraordinary change is to be assigned to many causes; and I had the opportunity of observing the influence which the determined will of one man exercised over his fellow-men.

The great object which Bonaparte had at heart was to legitimate his usurpations by institutions. The Concordat had reconciled him with the Court of Rome; the numerous erasures from the emigrant list gathered round him a large body of the old nobility; and the Legion of Honour, though at first but badly received, soon became a general object of ambition. Peace, too, had lent her aid in consolidating the First Consul's power by affording him leisure to engage in measures of internal prosperity.

The Council of State, of which Bonaparte had made me a member, but which my other occupations did not allow me to attend, was the soul of the Consular Government. Bonaparte felt much interest in the discussions of that body, because it was composed of the most eminent men in the different branches of administration; and though the majority evinced a ready compliance with his wishes, yet that disposition was often far from being unanimous. In the Council of State the projects of the Government were discussed from the first with freedom and sincerity, and when once adopted they were transmitted to the Tribunate, and to the Legislative Body. This latter body might be considered as a supreme Legislative Tribunal, before which the Tribunes pleaded as the advocates of the people, and the Councillors of State, whose business it was to support the law projects, as the advocates of the Government. This will at once explain the cause of the First Consul's animosity towards the Tribunate, and will show to what the Constitution was reduced when that body was dissolved by a sudden and arbitrary decision.

During the Consulate the Council of State was not only a body politic collectively, but each individual member might be invested with special power; as, for example, when the First Consul sent Councillors of State on missions to each of the military divisions where there was a Court of Appeal, the instructions given them by the First Consul were extensive, and might be said to be unlimited. They were directed to examine all the branches of the administration, so that their reports collected and compared together presented a perfect description of the state of France. But this measure, though excellent in itself, proved fatal to the State. The reports never conveyed the truth to the First Consul, or at least if they did, it was in such a disguised form as to be scarcely recognisable; for the Councillors well knew that the best way to pay their court to Bonaparte was not to describe public feeling as it really was, but as he wished it to be. Thus the reports of the councillors of State only furnished fresh arguments in favour of his ambition.

I must, however, observe that in the discussions of the Council of State Bonaparte was not at all averse to the free expression of opinion. He, indeed, often encouraged it; for although fully resolved to do only what he pleased, he wished to gain information; indeed, it is scarcely conceivable how, in the short space of two years, Bonaparte adapted his mind so completely to civil and legislative affairs. But he could not endure in the Tribunate the liberty of opinion which he tolerated in the Council; and for this reason—that the sittings of the Tribunate were public, while those of the Council of State were secret, and publicity was what he dreaded above all things. He was very well pleased when he had to transmit to the Legislative Body or to the Tribunate any proposed law of trifling importance, and he used then to say that he had thrown them a bone to gnaw.

Among the subjects submitted to the consideration of the Council and the Tribunate was one which gave rise to a singular discussion, the ground of which was a particular word, inserted in the third article of the treaty of Russia with France. This word seemed to convey a prophetic allusion to the future condition of the French people, or rather an anticipated designation of what they afterwards became. The treaty spoke of "the subjects of the two Governments." This term applied to those who still considered themselves citizens, and was highly offensive to the Tribunate. Chenier most loudly remonstrated against the introduction of this word into the dictionary of the new Government. He said that the armies of France had shed their blood that the French people might be citizens and not subjects. Chenier's arguments, however, had no effect on the decision of the Tribunate, and only served to irritate the First Consul. The treaty was adopted almost unanimously, there being only fourteen dissentient voices, and the proportion of black balls in the Legislative Body was even less.

Though this discussion passed off almost unnoticed, yet it greatly displeased the First Consul, who expressed his dissatisfaction in the evening. "What is it," said he, "these babblers want? They wish to be citizens—why did they not know how to continue so? My government must treat on an equal footing with Russia. I should appear a mere puppet in the eyes of foreign Courts were I to yield to the stupid demands of the Tribunate . . . Those fellows tease me so that I have a great mind to end matters at once with them." I endeavoured to soothe his anger, and observed, that one precipitate act might injure him. "You are right," he continued; "but stay a little, they shall lose nothing by waiting."

The Tribunate pleased Bonaparte better in the great question of the Consulate for life, because he had taken the precaution of removing such members as were most opposed to the encroachments of his ambition. The Tribunate resolved that a marked proof of the national gratitude should be offered to the First Consul, and the resolution was transmitted to the Senate. Not a single voice was raised against this proposition, which emanated from Chabot de l'Allier, the President of the Tribunate. When the First Consul came back to his cabinet after receiving the deputation of the Tribunate he was very cheerful, and said to me, "Bourrienne, it is a blank cheque that the Tribunate has just offered me; I shall know how to fill it up. That is my business."

The Tribunate having adopted the indefinite proposition of offering to the First Consul a marked proof of the national gratitude, it now only remained to determine what that proof should be. Bonaparte knew well what he wanted, but he did not like to name it in any positive way. Though in his fits of impatience, caused by the lingering proceedings of the Legislative Body and the indecision of some of its members, he often talked of mounting on horseback and drawing his sword, yet he so far controlled himself as to confine violence to his conversations with his intimate friends. He wished it to be thought that he himself was yielding to compulsion; that he was far from wishing to usurp permanent power contrary to the Constitution; and that if he deprived France of liberty it was all for her good, and out of mere love for her. Such deep-laid duplicity could never have been conceived and maintained in any common mind; but Bonaparte's was not a mind of the ordinary cast. It must have required extraordinary self-command to have restrained so long as he did that daring spirit which was so natural to him, and which was rather the result of his temperament than his character. For my part, I confess that I always admired him more for what he had the fortitude not to do than for the boldest exploits he ever performed.

In conformity with the usual form, the proposition of the Tribunate was transmitted to the Senate. From that time the Senators on whom Bonaparte most relied were frequent in their visits to the Tuileries. In the preparatory conferences which preceded the regular discussions in the Senate it has been ascertained that the majority was not willing that the marked proof of gratitude should be the Consulate for life; it was therefore agreed that the reporter should limit his demand to a temporary prolongation of the dignity of First Consul in favour of Bonaparte. The reporter, M. de Lacepede, acted accordingly, and limited the prolongation to ten years, commencing from the expiration of the ten years granted by the Constitution. I forget which of the Senators first proposed the Consulate for life; but I well recollect that Cambacérès used all his endeavours to induce those members of the Senate whom he thought he could influence to agree to that proposition. Whether from flattery or conviction I know not, but the Second Consul held out to his colleague, or rather his master, the hope of complete success. Bonaparte on hearing him shook his head with an air of doubt, but afterwards said to me, "They will perhaps make some wry faces, but they must come to it at last!"

It was proposed in the Senate that the proposition of the Consulate for life should take the priority of that of the decennial prolongation; but this was not agreed to; and the latter proposition being adopted, the other, of course, could not be discussed.

There was something very curious in the 'Senatus-consulte' published on the occasion. It spoke in the name of the French people, and stated that, "in testimony of their gratitude to the Consuls of the Republic," the Consular reign was prolonged for ten years; but that the prolongation was limited to the First Consul only.

Bonaparte, though much dissatisfied with the decision of the Senate, disguised his displeasure in ambiguous language. When Tronchet, then President of the Senate, read to him, in a solemn audience, at the head of the deputation, the 'Senatus-consulte' determining the prorogation, he said in reply that he could not be certain of the confidence of the people unless his continuance in the Consulship were sanctioned by their suffrages. "The interests of my glory and happiness," added he, "would seem to have marked the close of my public life at the moment when the peace of the world is proclaimed. But the glory and the happiness of the citizen must yield to the interests of the State and wishes of the public. You, Senators, conceive that I owe to the people another sacrifice. I will make it if the voice of the people commands what your suffrage authorises."

The true meaning of these words was not understood by everybody, and was only manifest to those who were initiated in the secret of Bonaparte's designs. He did not accept the offer of the Senate, because he wished for something more. The question was to be renewed and to be decided by the people only; and since the people had the right to refuse what the Senate offered, they possessed, for the same reason, the right to give what the Senate did not offer.

The moment now arrived for consulting the Council of State as to the mode to be adopted for invoking and collecting the suffrages of the people. For this purpose an extraordinary meeting of the Council of State was summoned on the 10th of May. Bonaparte wished to keep himself aloof from all ostensible influence; but his two colleagues laboured for him more zealously than he could have worked for himself, and they were warmly supported by several members of the Council. A strong majority were of opinion that Bonaparte should not only be invested with the Consulship for life, but that he should be empowered to nominate his successor. But he, still faithful to his plan, affected to venerate the sovereignty of the people, which he held in horror, and he promulgated the following decree, which was the first explanation of his reply to the Senate.

> The Consuls of the Republic, considering that the resolution of the First Consul is an homage rendered to the sovereignty of the People, and that the People, when consulted on their dearest interests, will not go beyond the limits of those interests, decree as follows:— First, that the French people shall be consulted on the question whether Napoleon Bonaparte is to be made Consul for life, etc.

The other articles merely regulated the mode of collecting the votes.

This decree shows the policy of the First Consul in a new point of view, and displays his art in its fullest extent. He had just refused the less for the sake of getting the greater; and now he had contrived to get the offer of the greater to show off his moderation by accepting only the less. The Council of State sanctioned the proposition for conferring on the First Consul the right of nominating his successor, and, of his own accord, the First Consul declined this. Accordingly the Second Consul, when he, the next day, presented the decree to the Council of State, did not fail to eulogise this extreme moderation, which banished even the shadow of suspicion of any ambitious after-thought. Thus the Senate found itself out-manoeuvred, and the decree of the Consuls was transmitted at once to the Legislative Body and to the Tribunate.

In the Legislative Body, M. de Vaublanc was distinguished among all the deputies who applauded the conduct of the Government; and it was he who delivered the apologetic harangue of the deputation of the Legislative Body to the First Consul. After having addressed the Government collectively he ended by addressing the First Consul individually—a sort of compliment which had not hitherto been put in practice, and which was far from displeasing him who was its object. As M. de Vaublanc's speech had been communicated beforehand to the First Consul, the latter prepared a reply to it which sufficiently showed how much it had gratified him. Besides the flattering distinction which separated him from the Government, the plenitude of praise was not tempered by anything like advice or comment. It was not so with the address of the Tribunate. After the compliments which the occasion demanded, a series of hopes were expressed for the future, which formed a curious contrast with the events which actually ensued. The Tribunate, said the address, required no guarantee, because Bonaparte's elevated and generous sentiments would never permit him to depart from those principles which brought about the Revolution and founded the Republic;—he loved real glory too well ever to stain that which he had acquired by the abuse of power;—the nation which he was called to govern was free and generous he would respect and consolidate her liberty; he would distinguish his real friends, who spoke truth to him, from flatterers who might seek to deceive him. In short, Bonaparte would surround himself with the men who, having made the Revolution, were interested in supporting it.

To these and many other fine things the Consul replied, "This testimony of the affection of the Tribunate is gratifying to the Government. The union of all bodies of the State is a guarantee of the stability and happiness of the nation. The efforts of the Government will be constantly directed to the interests of the people, from whom all power is derived, and whose welfare all good men have at heart."

So much for the artifice of governments and the credulity of subjects! It is certain that, from the moment Bonaparte gained his point in submitting the question of the Consulate for life to the decision of the people, there was no longer a doubt of the result being in his favour. This was evident, not only on account of the influential means which a government always has at its command, and of which its agents extend the ramifications from the centre to the extremities, but because the proposition was in accordance with the wishes of the majority. The Republicans were rather shy in avowing principles with which people were now disenchanted;—the partisans of a monarchy without distinction of family saw their hopes almost realised in the Consulate for life; the recollection of the Bourbons still lived in some hearts faithful to misfortune but the great mass were for the First Consul, and his external acts in the new step he had taken towards the throne had been so cautiously disguised as to induce a belief in his sincerity. If I and a few others were witness to his accomplished artifice and secret ambition, France beheld only his glory, and gratefully enjoyed the blessings of peace which he had obtained for her. The suffrages of the people speedily realised the hopes of the First Consul, and thus was founded the CONSULATE FOR LIFE.

CHAPTER XIV

1802-1803

When nothing was wanting to secure the Consulate for life but the votes of the people, which there was no doubt of obtaining, the First Consul set off to spend a few days at Malmaison.

On the day of our arrival, as soon as dinner was ended, Bonaparte said to me, "Bourrienne, let us go and take a walk." It was the middle of May, so that the evenings were long. We went into the park: he was very grave, and we walked for several minutes without his uttering a syllable. Wishing to break silence in a way that would be agreeable to him, I alluded to the facility with which he had nullified the last 'Senatus-consulte'. He scarcely seemed to hear me, so completely was his mind absorbed in the subject on which he was meditating. At length, suddenly recovering from his abstraction, he said, "Bourrienne, do you think that the pretender to the crown of France would renounce his claims if I were to offer him a good indemnity, or even a province in Italy?" Surprised at this abrupt question on a subject which I was far from thinking of, I replied that I did not think the pretender would relinquish his claims; that it was very unlikely the Bourbons would return to France as long as he, Bonaparte, should continue at the head of the Government, though they would look forward to their ultimate return as probable. "How so?" inquired he. "For a very simple reason, General. Do you not see every day that your agents conceal the truth from you, and flatter you in your wishes, for the purpose of ingratiating themselves in your favour? are you not angry when at length the truth reaches your ear?"—"And what then?"—"why, General, it must be just the same with the agents of Louis XVIII. in France. It is in the course of things, in the nature of man, that they should feed the Bourbons with hopes of a possible return, were it only to induce a belief in their own talent and utility."—"That is very true! You are quite right; but I am not afraid. However, something might perhaps be done—we shall see." Here the subject dropped, and our conversation turned on the Consulate for life, and Bonaparte spoke in unusually mild terms of the persons who had opposed the proposition. I was a little surprised at this, and could not help reminding him of the different way in which he had spoken of those who opposed his accession to the Consulate. "There is nothing extraordinary in that," said he. "Worthy men may be attached to the Republic as I have made it. It is a mere question of form. I have nothing to say against that; but at the time of my accession to the Consulate it was very different. Then, none but Jacobins, terrorists, and rogues resisted my endeavours to rescue France from the infamy into which the Directory had plunged her. But now I cherish no ill-will against those who have opposed me."

During the intervals between the acts of the different bodies of the State, and the collection of the votes, Lucien renewed his intrigues, or rather prosecuted them with renewed activity, for the purpose of getting the question of hereditary succession included in the votes. Many prefects transmitted to M. Chaptal anonymous circulars which had been sent to them: all stated the ill effect produced by these circulars, which had been addressed to the principal individuals of their departments. Lucien was the originator of all this, though I cannot positively say whether his brother connived with him, as in the case of the pamphlet to which I have already alluded. I believe, however, that Bonaparte was not entirely a stranger to the business; for the circulars were written by Raederer at the instigation of Lucien, and Raederer was at that time in favour at the Tuileries. I recollect Bonaparte speaking to me one day very angrily about a pamphlet which had just, been published by Camille Jordan on the subject of the national vote on the Consulate for life. Camille Jordan did not withhold his vote, but gave it in favour of the First Consul; and instead of requiring preliminary conditions, he contented himself, like the Tribunate, with enumerating all the guarantees which he expected the honour of the First Consul would grant. Among these guarantees were the cessation of arbitrary imprisonments, the responsibility of the agents of Government, and the independence of the judges. But all these demands were mere peccadilloes in comparison with Camille Jordan's great crime of demanding the liberty of the press.

The First Consul had looked through the fatal pamphlet, and lavished invectives upon its author. "How!" exclaimed he, "am I never to have done with these fire brands?—These babblers, who think that politics may be shown on a printed page like the world on a map? Truly, I know not what things will come to if I let this go on. Camille Jordan, whom I received so well at Lyons, to think that he should—ask for the liberty of the press! Were I to accede to this I might as well pack up at once and go and live on a farm a hundred leagues from Paris." Bonaparte's first act in favour of the liberty of the press was to order the seizure of the pamphlet in which Camille Jordan had extolled the advantages of that measure. Publicity, either by words or writing, was Bonaparte's horror. Hence his aversion to public speakers and writers.

Camille Jordan was not the only person who made unavailing efforts to arrest Bonaparte in the first steps of his ambition. There were yet in France many men who, though they had hailed with enthusiasm the dawn of the French Revolution, had subsequently been disgusted by its crimes, and who still dreamed of the possibility of founding a truly Constitutional Government in France. Even in the Senate there were some men indignant at the usual compliance of that body, and who spoke of the necessity of subjecting the Constitution to a revisal, in order to render it conformable to the Consulate for life.

The project of revising the Constitution was by no means unsatisfactory to Bonaparte. It afforded him an opportunity of holding out fresh glimmerings of liberty to those who were too shortsighted to see into the future. He was pretty certain that there could be no change but to his advantage. Had any one talked to him of the wishes of the nation he would have replied, "3,577,259 citizens have voted. Of these how many were for me? 3,368,185. Compare the difference! There is but one vote in forty-five against me. I must obey the will of the people!" To this he would not have failed to add, "Whose are the votes opposed to me? Those of ideologists, Jacobins, and peculators under the Directory." To such arguments what could have been answered? It must not be supposed that I am putting these words into Bonaparte's mouth. They fell from him oftener than once.

As soon as the state of the votes was ascertained the Senate conceived itself under the necessity of repairing the only fault it had committed in the eyes of the First Consul, and solemnly presented him with a new 'Senatus-consulte', and a decree couched in the following terms:

ARTICLE I. The French people nominate and the Senate proclaim Napoleon Bonaparte Consul for life.

ARTICLE II. A statue representing Peace, holding in one hand the laurel of victory, and in the other the decree of the senate, shall commemorate to posterity the gratitude of the Nation.

ARTICLE III. The Senate will convey to the First Consul the expression of the confidence, the love, and the admiration of the French people.

Bonaparte replied to the deputation from the Senate, in the presence of the Diplomatic Body, whose audience had been appointed for that day in order that the ambassadors might be enabled to make known to their respective Courts that Europe reckoned one King more. In his reply he did not fail to introduce the high-sounding words "liberty and equality." He commenced thus: "A citizen's life belongs to his country. The French people wish that mine should be entirely devoted to their service. I obey."

On the day this ceremony took place, besides the audience of the Diplomatic Body there was an extraordinary assemblage of general officers and public functionaries. The principal apartments of the Tuileries's presented the appearance of a fete. This gaiety formed a striking contrast with the melancholy of Josephine, who felt that every step of the First Consul towards the throne removed him farther from her.

She had to receive a party that evening, and though greatly depressed in spirits she did the honours with her usual grace.

Let a Government be what it may, it can never satisfy everyone. At the establishment of the Consulate for life, those who were averse to that change formed but a feeble minority. But still they met, debated, corresponded, and dreamed of the possibility of overthrowing the Consular Government.

During the first six months of the year 1802 there were meetings of the discontented, which Fouché, who was then Minister of the Police, knew and would not condescend to notice; but, on the contrary, all the inferior agents of the police contended for a prey which was easily seized, and, with the view of magnifying their services, represented these secret meetings as the effect of a vast plot against the Government. Bonaparte, whenever he spoke to me on the subject, expressed himself weary of the efforts which were made to give importance to trifles; and yet he received the reports of the police agents as if he thought them of consequence. This was because he thought Fouché badly informed, and he was glad to find him at fault; but when he sent for the Minister of Police the latter told him that all the reports he had received were not worth a moment's attention. He told the First Consul all, and even a great deal more than had been revealed to him, mentioning at the same time how and from whom Bonaparte had received his information.

But these petty police details did not divert the First Consul's attention from the great object he had in view. Since March 1802 he had attended the sittings of the Council of State with remarkable regularity. Even while we were at the Luxembourg he busied himself in drawing up a new code of laws to supersede the incomplete collection of revolutionary laws, and to substitute order for the sort of anarchy which prevailed in the legislation. The man who were most distinguished for legal knowledge had cooperated in this laborious task, the result of which was the code first distinguished by the name of the Civil Code, and afterwards called the Code Napoleon. The labours of this important undertaking being completed, a committee was appointed for the presentation of the code. This committee, of which Cambacérès was the president, was composed of MM. Portalis, Merlin de Douai, and Tronchet. During all the time the discussions were pending, instead of assembling as usual three times a week, the Council of State assembled every day, and the sittings, which on ordinary occasions only lasted two or three hours, were often prolonged to five or six. The First Consul took such interest in these discussions that, to have an opportunity of conversing upon them in the evening, he frequently invited several members of the Council to dine with him. It was during these conversations that I most admired the inconceivable versatility of Bonaparte's genius, or rather, that superior instinct which enabled him to comprehend at a glance, and in their proper point of view, legislative questions to which he might have been supposed a stranger. Possessing as he did, in a supreme degree, the knowledge of mankind, ideas important to the science of government flashed upon his mind like sudden inspirations.

Some time after his nomination to the Consulate for life, anxious to perform a sovereign act, he went for the first time to preside at the Senate. Availing myself that day of a few leisure moments I went out to see the Consular procession. It was truly royal. The First Consul had given orders that the military should-be ranged in the streets through which he had to pass. On his first arrival at the Tuileries, Napoleon had the soldiers of the Guard ranged in a single line in the interior of the court, but he now ordered that the line should be doubled, and should extend from the gate of the Tuileries to that of the Luxembourg. Assuming a privilege which old etiquette had confined exclusively to the Kings of France, Bonaparte now for the first time rode in a carriage drawn by eight horses. A considerable number of carriages followed that of the First Consul, which was surrounded by generals and aides de camp on horseback. Louis XIV. going to hold a bed of justice at the Parliament of Paris never displayed greater pomp than did Bonaparte in this visit to the Senate. He appeared in all the parade of royalty; and ten Senators came to meet him at the foot of the staircase of the Luxembourg.

The object of the First Consul's visit to the Senate was the presentation of five plans of 'Senatus-consultes'. The other two Consuls were present at the ceremony, which took place about the middle of August.

Bonaparte returned in the same style in which he went, accompanied by M. Lebrun, Cambacérès remaining at the Senate, of which he was President. The five 'Senatus-consultes' were adopted, but a restriction was made in that which concerned the forms of the Senate. It was proposed that when the Consuls visited the Senate they should be received by a deputation of ten members at the foot of the staircase, as the First Consul had that day been received; but Bonaparte's brothers Joseph and Lucien opposed this, and prevented the proposition from being adopted, observing that the Second and Third Consuls being members of the Senate could not be received with such honours by their colleagues. This little scene of political courtesy, which was got up beforehand, was very well acted.

Bonaparte's visit to the Senate gave rise to a change of rank in the hierarchy of the different authorities composing the Government. Hitherto the Council of State had ranked higher in public opinion; but the Senate, on the occasion of its late deputation to the Tuileries, had for the first time, received the honour of precedency. This had greatly displeased some of the Councillors of State, but Bonaparte did not care for that. He instinctively saw that the Senate would do what he wished more readily than the other constituted bodies, and he determined to augment its rights and prerogatives even at the expense of the rights of the Legislative Body. These encroachments of one power upon another, authorised by the First

Consul, gave rise to reports of changes in ministerial arrangements. It was rumoured in Paris that the number of the ministers was to be reduced to three, and that Lucien, Joseph, and M. de Talleyrand were to divide among them the different portfolios. Lucien helped to circulate these reports, and this increased the First Consul's dissatisfaction at his conduct. The letters from Madrid, which were filled with complaints against him, together with some scandalous adventures, known in Paris, such as his running away with the wife of a 'limonadier', exceedingly annoyed Bonaparte, who found his own family more difficult to govern than France.

France, indeed, yielded with admirable facility to the yoke which, the First Consul wished to impose on her. How artfully did he undo all that the Revolution had done, never neglecting any means of attaining his object! He loved to compare the opinions of those whom he called the Jacobins with the opinions of the men of 1789; and even them he found too liberal. He felt the ridicule which was attached to the mute character of the Legislative Body, which he called his deaf and dumb assembly. But as that ridicule was favourable to him he took care to preserve the assembly as it was, and to turn it into ridicule whenever he spoke of it. In general, Bonaparte's judgment must not be confounded with his actions. His accurate mind enabled him to appreciate all that was good; but the necessity of his situation enabled him to judge with equal shrewdness what was useful to himself.

What I have just said of the Senate affords me an opportunity of correcting an error which has frequently been circulated in the chit-chat of Paris. It has erroneously been said of some persons that they refused to become members of the Senate, and among the number have been mentioned M. Ducis, M. de La Fayette, and the Marechal de Rochambeau. The truth is, that no such refusals were ever made. The following fact, however, may have contributed to raise these reports and give them credibility. Bonaparte used frequently to say to persons in his salon and in his cabinet; "You should be a Senator—a man like you should be a Senator." But these complimentary words did not amount to a nomination. To enter the Senate certain legal forms were to be observed. It was necessary to be presented by the Senate, and after that presentation no one ever refused to become a member of the body, to which Bonaparte gave additional importance by the creation of "Senatoreries."[173] This creation took place in the beginning of 1803.

173 Districts presided over by a Senator.

CHAPTER XV

1802

Perhaps one of the happiest ideas that ever were expressed was that of the Athenian who said, "I appeal from Philip drunk to Philip sober." The drunkenness here alluded to is not of that kind which degrades a man to the level of a brute, but that intoxication which is occasioned by success, and which produces in the heads of the ambitious a sort of cerebral congestion. Ordinary men are not subject to this excitement, and can scarcely form an idea of it. But it is nevertheless true that the fumes of glory and ambition occasionally derange the strongest heads; and Bonaparte, in all the vigour of his genius, was often subject to aberrations of judgment; for though his imagination never failed him, his judgment was frequently at fault.

This fact may serve to explain, and perhaps even to excuse the faults with which the First Consul has been most seriously reproached. The activity of his mind seldom admitted of an interval between the conception and the execution of a design; but when he reflected coolly on the first impulses of his imperious will, his judgment discarded what was erroneous. Thus the blind obedience, which, like an epidemic disease, infected almost all who surrounded Bonaparte, was productive of the most fatal effects. The best way to serve the First Consul was never to listen to the suggestions of his first ideas, except on the field of battle, where his conceptions were as happy as they were rapid. Thus, for example, MM. Maret, de Champagny, and Savary evinced a ready obedience to Bonaparte's wishes, which often proved very unfortunate, though doubtless dictated by the best intentions on their part. To this fatal zeal may be attributed a great portion of the mischief which Bonaparte committed. When the mischief was done, and past remedy, Bonaparte deeply regretted it. How often have I heard him say that Maret was animated by an unlucky zeal! This was the expression he made use of.

M. de Talleyrand was almost the only one among the ministers who did not flatter Bonaparte, and who really served both the First Consul and the Emperor. When Bonaparte said to M. de Talleyrand, "Write so and so, and send it off by a special courier," that minister was never in a hurry to obey the order, because he knew the character of the First Consul well enough to distinguish between what his passion dictated and what his reason would approve: in short, he appealed from Philip drunk to Philip sober. When it happened that M. de Talleyrand suspended the execution of an order, Bonaparte never evinced the least displeasure. When, the day after he had received any hasty and angry order, M. de Talleyrand presented himself to the First Consul, the latter would say, "Well, did you send off the courier?"—"No," the minister would reply, "I took care not to do so before I showed you my letter." Then the First Consul would usually add, "Upon second thoughts I think it would be best not to send it." This was the way to deal with Bonaparte. When M. de Talleyrand postponed sending off despatches, or when I myself have delayed the execution of an order which I knew had been dictated by anger, and had emanated neither from his heart nor his understanding, I have heard him say a hundred times, "It was right, quite right. You understand me: Talleyrand understands me also. This is the way to serve me: the others do not leave me time for reflection: they are too precipitate." Fouché also was one of those who did not on all occasions blindly obey Bonaparte's commands. His other ministers, on the other hand, when told to send off a courier the next morning, would have more probably sent him off the same evening. This was from zeal, but was not the First Consul right in saying that such zeal was unfortunate?

Of Talleyrand and Fouché, in their connections with the First Consul, it might be said that the one represented the Constituent Assembly, with a slight perfume of the old regime, and the other the Convention in all its brutality. Bonaparte regarded Fouché as a complete personification of the Revolution. With him, therefore, Fouché's influence was merely the influence of the Revolution. That great event was one of those which had made the most forcible impression on Bonaparte's ardent mind, and he imagined he still beheld it in a visible form as long as Fouché continued at the head of his police. I am now of opinion that Bonaparte was in some degree misled as to the value of Fouché's services as a minister. No doubt the circumstance of Fouché being in office conciliated those of the Revolutionary party who were his friends. But Fouché cherished an undue partiality for them, because he knew that it was through them he held his place. He was like one of the old Condottieri, who were made friends of lest they should become enemies, and who owed all their power to the soldiers enrolled under their banners.

Such was Fouché, and Bonaparte perfectly understood his situation. He kept the chief in his service until he could find an opportunity of disbanding his undisciplined followers. But there was one circumstance which confirmed his reliance on Fouché. He who had voted the death of the King of France, and had influenced the minds of those who had voted with him, offered Bonaparte the best guarantee against the attempts of the Royalists for raising up in favour of the Bourbons the throne which the First Consul himself had determined to ascend. Thus, for different reasons, Bonaparte and Fouché had common interests against the House of Bourbon, and the master's ambition derived encouragement from the supposed terror of the servant.

The First Consul was aware of the existence in Paris of a Royalist committee, formed for the purpose of corresponding with Louis XVIII. This committee consisted of men who must not be confounded with those wretched intriguers who were of no service to their employers, and were not unfrequently in the pay of both Bonaparte and the Bourbons. The Royalist committee, properly so called, was a very different thing. It consisted of men professing rational principles of liberty, such as the Marquis de Clermont Gallerande, the Abbe de Montesqieu, M. Becquet, and M. Royer Collard. This committee had been of long standing; the respectable individuals whose names I have just quoted acted upon a system hostile to the despotism of Bonaparte, and favourable to what they conceived to be the interests of France. Knowing the superior wisdom of Louis XVIII., and the opinions which he had avowed and maintained in the Assembly of the Notables, they wished to separate that Prince from the emigrants, and to point him out to the nation as a suitable head of a reasonable Constitutional Government. Bonaparte, whom I have often heard speak on the subject, dreaded nothing so much as these ideas of liberty, in conjunction with a monarchy. He regarded them as reveries, called the members of the committee idle dreamers, but nevertheless feared the triumph of their ideas. He confessed to me that it was to counteract the possible influence of the Royalist committee that he showed himself so indulgent to those of the emigrants whose monarchical prejudices he knew were incompatible with liberal opinions. By the presence of emigrants who acknowledged nothing short of absolute power, he thought he might paralyse the influence of the Royalists of the interior; he therefore granted all such emigrants permission to return.

About this time I recollect having read a document, which had been signed, purporting to be a declaration of the principles of Louis XVIII. It was signed by M. d'Andre, who bore evidence to its authenticity. The principles contained in the declaration were in almost all points conformable to the principles which formed the basis of the charter. Even so early as 1792, and consequently previous to the fatal 21st of January, Louis XVI., who knew the opinions of M. de Clermont Gallerande, sent him on a mission to Coblentz to inform the Princes from him, and the Queen, that they would be ruined by their emigration. I am accurately informed, and I state this fact with the utmost confidence. I can also add with equal certainty that the circumstance was mentioned by M. de Clermont Gallerande in his Memoirs, and that the passage relative to his mission to Coblentz was cancelled before the manuscript was sent to press.

During the Consular Government the object of the Royalist committee was to seduce rather than to conspire. It was round Madame Bonaparte in particular that their batteries were raised, and they did not prove ineffectual. The female friends of Josephine filled her mind with ideas of the splendour and distinction she would enjoy if the powerful hand which had chained the Revolution should raise up the subverted throne. I must confess that I was myself, unconsciously, an accomplice of the friends of the throne; for what they wished for the interest of the Bourbons I then ardently wished for the interest of Bonaparte.

While endeavours were thus made to gain over Madame Bonaparte to the interest of the royal family, brilliant offers were held out for the purpose of dazzling the First Consul. It was wished to retemper for him the sword of the constable Duguesclin; and it was hoped that a statue erected to his honour would at once attest to posterity his spotless glory and the gratitude of the Bourbons. But when these offers reached the ears of Bonaparte he treated them with indifference, and placed no faith in their sincerity. Conversing on the subject one day with M. de La Fayette he said, "They offer me a statue, but I must look to the pedestal. They may make it my prison." I did not hear Bonaparte utter these words; but they were reported to me from a source, the authenticity of which may be relied on.

About this time, when so much was said in the Royalist circles and in the Faubourg St. Germain, of which the Hotel de Luynes was the headquarters, about the possible return of the Bourbons, the publication of a popular book contributed not a little to direct the attention of the public to the most brilliant period of the reign of Louis XIV. The book was the historical romance of Madame de la Valloire, by Madame de Genlis, who had recently returned to France. Bonaparte read it, and I have since understood that he was very well pleased with it, but he said nothing to me about it. It was not until some time after that he complained of the effect which was produced in Paris by this publication, and especially by engravings representing scenes in the life of Louis XIV., and which were exhibited in the shop-windows. The police received orders to suppress these prints; and the order was implicitly obeyed; but it was not Fouché's police. Fouché saw the absurdity of interfering with trifles. I recollect that immediately after the creation of the Legion of Honour, it being summer, the young men of Paris indulged in the whim of wearing a carnation in a button-hole, which at a distance had rather a deceptive effect. Bonaparte took this very seriously. He sent for Fouché, and desired him to arrest those who presumed thus to turn the new order into ridicule. Fouché merely replied that he would wait till the autumn; and the First Consul understood that trifles were often rendered matters of importance by being honoured with too much attention.

But though Bonaparte was piqued at the interest excited by the engravings of Madame de Genlis' romance he manifested no displeasure against that celebrated woman, who had been recommended to him by MM. de Fontanes and Fievee and who addressed several letters to him. As this sort of correspondence did not come within the routine of my business I did not see the letters; but I heard from Madame Bonaparte that they contained a prodigious number of proper names, and I have reason to believe that they contributed not a little to magnify, in the eyes of the First Consul, the importance of the Faubourg St. Germain, which, in spite of all his courage, was a scarecrow to him.

Bonaparte regarded the Faubourg St. Germain as representing the whole mass of Royalist opinion; and he saw clearly that the numerous erasures from the emigrant list had necessarily increased dissatisfaction among the Royalists, since the property of the emigrants had not been restored to its old possessors, even in those cases in which it had not been sold. It was the fashion in a certain class to ridicule the unpolished manners of the great men of the Republic compared with the manners of the nobility of the old Court. The wives of certain generals had several times committed themselves by their awkwardness. In many circles there was an affectation of treating with contempt what are called the parvenus; those people who, to use M. de Talleyrand's expression, do not know how to walk upon a carpet. All this gave rise to complaints against the Faubourg St. Germain; while, on the other hand, Bonaparte's brothers spared no endeavours to irritate him against everything that was calculated to revive the recollection of the Bourbons.

Such were Bonaparte's feelings, and such was the state of society during the year 1802. The fear of the Bourbons must indeed have had a powerful influence on the First Consul before he could have been induced to take a step which may justly be regarded as the most inconsiderate of his whole life. After suffering seven months to elapse without answering the first letter of Louis XVIII., after at length answering his second letter in the tone of a King addressing a subject, he went so far as to write to Louis, proposing that he should renounce the throne of his ancestors in his, Bonaparte's, favour, and offering him as a reward for this renunciation a principality in Italy, or a considerable revenue for himself and his family.[174]

174 Napoleon seems to have always known, as with Cromwell and the Stuarts, that if his dynasty failed the Bourbons must succeed him. "I remember," says Metternich, "Napoleon said to me, 'Do you know why Louis XVIII. is not now sitting opposite to you? It is only because it is I who am sitting here. No other person could maintain his position; and if ever I disappear in consequence of a catastrophe no one but a Bourbon could sit here.'" (Metternich, tome i. p. 248). Farther, he said to Metternich, "The King overthrown, the Republic was master of the soil of France. It is that which I have replaced. The old throne of France is buried under its rubbish. I had to found a new one. The Bourbons could not reign over this creation. My strength lies in my fortune. I am new, like the Empire; there is, therefore, a perfect homogeneity between the Empire and myself."—"However," says Metternich, "I have often thought that Napoleon, by talking in this way, merely sought to study the opinion of others, or to confuse it, and the direct advance which he made to Louis XVIII., in 1804 seemed to confirm this suspicion. Speaking to me one day of this advance he said, 'Monsieur's reply was grand; it was full of fine traditions. There is something in legitimate rights which appeals to more than the mere mind. If Monsieur had consulted his mind only he would have arranged

The reader will recollect the curious question which the First Consul put to me on the subject of the Bourbons when we were walking in the park of Malmaison. To the reply which I made to him on that occasion I attribute the secrecy he observed towards me respecting the letter just alluded to. I am indeed inclined to regard that letter as the result of one of his private conferences with Lucien; but I know nothing positive on the subject, and merely mention this as a conjecture. However, I had an opportunity of ascertaining the curious circumstances which took place at Mittau, when Bonaparte's letter was delivered to Louis XVIII.

That Prince was already much irritated against Bonaparte by his delay in answering his first letter, and also by the tenor of his tardy reply; but on reading the First Consul's second letter the dethroned King immediately sat down and traced a few lines forcibly expressing his indignation at such a proposition. The note, hastily written by Louis XVIII. in the first impulse of irritation, bore little resemblance to the dignified and elegant letter which Bonaparte received, and which I shall presently lay before the reader. This latter epistle closed very happily with the beautiful device of Francis I., "All is lost but honour." But the first letter was stamped with a more chivalrous tone of indignation. The indignant sovereign wrote it with his hand supported on the hilt of his sword; but the Abbe Andre, in whom Louis XVIII. reposed great confidence, saw the note, and succeeded, not without some difficulty, in soothing the anger of the King, and prevailing on him to write the following letter:

---

with me, and I should have made for him a magnificent future'" (Metternich, tome i, p. 276). According to Iung's Lucien (tome ii. p. 421), the letter written and signed by Napoleon, but never sent, another draft being substituted, is still in the French archives. Metternich speaks of Napoleon making a direct advance to Louis XVIII. in 1804. According to Colonel Iung (Lucien Bonaparte, tome ii. pp. 4211-426) the attempt was made through the King of Prussia in 1802, the final answer of Louis being made on the 28th February 1803, as given in the text, but with a postscript of his nephew in addition, "With the permission of the King, my uncle, I adhere with heart and soul to the contents of this note. "(*signed*) LOUIS ANTOINE, *Duc d'Angouleme.*" The reader will remark that there is no great interval between this letter and the final break with the Bourbons by the death of the Duc d'Enghien. At this time, according to Savory (tome iii. p. 241), some of the Bourbons were receiving French pensions. The Prince de Conti, the Duchesse de Bourbon, and the Duchesse d'Orleans, when sent out of France by the Directory, were given pensions of from 20,000 to 26,000 francs each. They lived in Catalonia. When the French troops entered Spain in 1808 General Canclaux, a friend of the Prince de Conti, brought to the notice of Napoleon that the tiresome formalities insisted on by the pestilent clerks of all nations were observed towards these regal personages. Gaudin, the Minister of Finance, apparently on his own initiative, drew up a decree increasing the pensions to 80,000 francs, and doing away with the formalities. "The Emperor signed at once, thanking the Minister of Finance." The reader, remembering the position of the French Princes then, should compare this action of Napoleon with the failure of the Bourbons in 1814 to pay the sums promised to Napoleon, notwithstanding the strong remonstrances made at Vienna to Talleyrand by Alexander and Lord Castlereagh. See Talleyrand's Correspondence with Louis XVIII., tome ii. pp. 27, 28; or French edition, pp. 285, 288.

I do not confound M. Bonaparte with those who have preceded him. I esteem his courage and his military talents. I am grateful for some acts of his government; for the benefits which are conferred on my people will always be prized by me. But he errs in supposing that he can induce me to renounce my rights; so far from that, he would confirm them, if they could possibly be doubtful, by the step he has now taken. I am ignorant of the designs of Heaven respecting me and my subjects; but I know the obligations which God has imposed upon me. As a Christian, I will fulfil my duties to my last breath—as the son of St. Louis, I would, like him, respect myself even in chains— as the successor of Francis I., I say with him—'Tout est perdu 'hors l'honneur'.

MITTAU, 1802.

LOUIS.

Louis XVIII.'s letter having reached Paris, the Royalist committee assembled, and were not a little embarrassed as to what should be done. The meeting took place at Neuilly. After a long deliberation it was suggested that the delivery of the letter should be entrusted to the Third Consul, with whom the Abby de Montesqieu had kept up acquaintance since the time of the Constituent Assembly. This suggestion was adopted. The recollections of the commencement of his career, under Chancellor Maupeou, had always caused M. Lebrun to be ranked in a distinct class by the Royalists. For my part, I always looked upon him as a very honest man, a warm advocate of equality, and anxious that it should be protected even by despotism, which suited the views of the First Consul very well. The Abbe de Montesquiou accordingly waited upon M. Lebrun, who undertook to deliver the letter. Bonaparte received it with an air of indifference; but whether that indifference were real or affected, I am to this day unable to determine. He said very little to me about the ill success of the negotiation with Louis XVIII. On this subject he dreaded, above all, the interference of his brothers, who created around him a sort of commotion which he knew was not without its influence, and which on several occasions had excited his anger.

The letter of Louis XVIII. is certainly conceived in a tone of dignity which cannot be too highly admired; and it may be said that Bonaparte on this occasion rendered a real service to Louis by affording him the opportunity of presenting to the world one of the finest pages in the history of a dethroned King. This letter, the contents of which were known in some circles of Paris, was the object of general approbation to those who preserved the recollection of the Bourbons, and above all, to the Royalist committee. The members of that committee, proud of the noble spirit evinced by the unfortunate monarch, whose return they were generously labouring to effect, replied to him by a sort of manifesto, to which time has imparted interest, since subsequent events have fulfilled the predictions it contained.

CHAPTER XVI

1802

I shall now return to the circumstances which followed my first disgrace, of which I have already spoken. The day after that on which I had resumed my functions I went as usual to awaken the First Consul at seven in the morning. He treated me just the same as if nothing had happened between us; and on my part I behaved to him just as usual, though I really regretted being obliged to resume labours which I found too oppressive for me. When Bonaparte came down into his cabinet he spoke to me of his plans with his usual confidence, and I saw, from the number of letters lying in the basket, that during the few days my functions had been suspended Bonaparte had not overcome his disinclination to peruse this kind of correspondence. At the period of this first rupture and reconciliation the question of the Consulate for life was yet unsettled. It was not decided until the 2d of August, and the circumstances to which I am about to refer happened at the end of February.

I was now restored to my former footing of intimacy with the First Consul, at least for a time; but I soon perceived that, after the scene which M. de Talleyrand had witnessed, my duties in the Tuileries were merely provisional, and might be shortened or prolonged according to circumstances. I saw at the very first moment that Bonaparte had sacrificed his wounded pride to the necessity (for such I may, without any vanity, call it) of employing my services. The forced preference he granted to me arose from the fact of his being unable to find any one able to supply my place; for Duroc, as I have already said, showed a disinclination to the business. I did not remain long in the dark respecting the new situation in which I stood. I was evidently still under quarantine; but the period of my quitting the port was undetermined.

A short time after our reconciliation the First Consul said to me, in a cajoling tone of which I was not the dupe, "My dear Bourrienne, you cannot do everything. Business increases, and will continue to increase. You know what Corvisart says. You have a family; therefore it is right you should take care of your health. You must not kill yourself with work; therefore some one must be got to assist you. Joseph tells me that he can recommend a secretary, one of whom he speaks very highly. He shall be under your direction; he can make out your copies, and do all that can consistently be required of him. This, I think, will be a great relief to you."—"I ask for nothing better," replied I, "than to have the assistance of some one who, after becoming acquainted with the business, may, some time or other, succeed me." Joseph sent M. de Meneval, a young man who, to a good education, added the recommendations of industry and prudence. I had every reason to be satisfied with him.

It was now that Napoleon employed all those devices and caresses which always succeeded so well with him, and which yet again gained the day, to put an end to the inconvenience caused to him by my retirement, and to retain me. Here I call every one who knew me as witnesses that nothing could equal my grief and despair to find myself obliged to again begin my troublesome work. My health had suffered much from it. Corvisart was a clever counsellor, but it was only during the night that I could carry out his advice. To resume my duties was to renounce all hope of rest, and even of health.[175]

I soon perceived the First Consul's anxiety to make M. de Meneval acquainted with the routine of business, and accustomed to his manner. Bonaparte had never pardoned me for having presumed to quit him after he had attained so high a degree of power; he was only waiting for an opportunity to punish me, and he seized upon an unfortunate circumstance as an excuse for that separation which I had previously wished to bring about.

I will explain this circumstance, which ought to have obtained for me the consolation and assistance of the First Consul rather than the forfeiture of his favour. My rupture with him has been the subject of various misstatements, all of which I shall not take the trouble to correct; I will merely notice what I have read in the Memoirs of the Duc de Rovigo, in which it is stated that I was accused of peculation. M. de Rovigo thus expresses himself:

> Ever since the First Consul was invested with the supreme power his life had been a continued scene of personal exertion. He had for his private secretary M. de Bourrienne, a friend and companion of his youth, whom he now made the sharer of all his labours. He frequently sent for him in the dead of the night, and particularly insisted upon his attending him every morning at seven. Bourrienne was punctual in his attendance with the public papers, which he had previously glanced over. The First Consul almost invariably read their contents himself; he then despatched some business, and sat down to table just as the clock struck nine. His breakfast, which lasted six minutes, was no sooner over than he returned to his cabinet, only left it for dinner, and resumed his close occupation immediately after, until ten at night, which was his usual hour for retiring to rest.
>
> Bourrienne was gifted with a most wonderful memory; he could speak and write many languages, and would make his pen follow as fast as words were uttered. He possessed many other advantages; he was well acquainted with the administrative departments, was versed in the law of nations, and possessed a zeal and activity which rendered his services quite indispensable to the First Consul. I have known the several grounds upon which the unlimited confidence placed in him by his chief rested, but am unable to speak with equal assurance of the errors which occasioned his losing that confidence. Bourrienne had many enemies; some were owing to his personal character, a greater number to the situation which he held. Others were jealous of the credit he enjoyed with the Head of the Government; others, again, discontented at his not making that credit subservient to their personal advantage. Some even imputed to him the want of success that had attended their claims. It was impossible to bring any charge against him on the score of deficiency of talent or of indiscreet conduct; his personal habits were watched—it was ascertained that he engaged in financial speculations. An imputation could easily be founded on this circumstance. Peculation

175 There is considerable truth in this statement about the effect on his health. His successor, Meneval, without the same amount of work, broke down and had to receive assistance (Meneval, tome i. p. 149).

was accordingly laid to his charge. This was touching the most tender ground, for the First Consul held nothing in greater abhorrence than unlawful gains. A solitary voice, however, would have failed in an attempt to defame the character of a man for whom he had so long felt esteem and affection; other voices, therefore, were brought to bear against him. Whether the accusations were well founded or otherwise, it is beyond a doubt that all means were resorted to for bringing them to the knowledge of the First Consul.

The most effectual course that suggested itself was the opening a correspondence either with the accused party direct, or with those with whom it was felt indispensable to bring him into contact; this correspondence was carried on in a mysterious manner, and related to the financial operations that had formed the grounds of a charge against him.—Thus it is that, on more than one occasion, the very channels intended for conveying truth to the knowledge of a sovereign have been made available to the purpose of communicating false intelligence to him. To give an instance.

Under the reign of Louis XV., and even under the Regency, the Post Office was organized into a system of minute inspection, which did not indeed extend to every letter, but was exercised over all such as afforded grounds for suspicion. They were opened, and, when it was not deemed safe to suppress them, copies were taken, and they were returned to their proper channel without the least delay. Any individual denouncing another may, by the help of such an establishment, give great weight to his denunciation. It is sufficient for his purpose that he should throw into the Post Office any letter so worded as to confirm the impression which it is his object to convey. The worthiest man may thus be committed by a letter which he has never read, or the purport of which is wholly unintelligible to him.

I am speaking from personal experience. It once happened that a letter addressed to myself, relating to an alleged fact which had never occurred, was opened. A copy of the letter so opened was also forwarded to me, as it concerned the duties which I had to perform at that time; but I was already in possession of the original, transmitted through the ordinary channel. Summoned to reply to the questions to which such productions had given rise, I took that opportunity of pointing out the danger that would accrue from placing a blind reliance upon intelligence derived from so hazardous a source. Accordingly, little importance was afterwards attached to this means of information; but the system was in operation at the period when M. de Bourrienne was disgraced; his enemies took care to avail themselves of it; they blackened his character with M. de Barbe Marbois, who added to their accusations all the weight of his unblemished character. The opinion entertained by this rigid public functionary, and many other circumstances, induced the First Consul to part with his secretary (tome i. p. 418).

Peculation is the crime of those who make a fraudulent use of the public money. But as it was not in my power to meddle with the public money, no part of which passed through my hands, I am at loss to conceive how I can be charged with peculation! The Duc de Rovigo is not the author, but merely the echo, of this calumny; but the accusation to which his Memoirs gave currency afforded M. de Barbe Marbois an opportunity of adding one more to the many proofs he has given of his love of justice.

I had seen nothing of the Memoirs of the Duc de Rovigo except their announcement in the journals, when a letter from M. de Barbe Marbois was transmitted to me from my family. It was as follows:

> SIR—My attention has been called to the enclosed article in a recent publication. The assertion it contains is not true, and I conceive it to be a duty both to you and myself to declare that I then was, and still am, ignorant of the causes of the separation in question:—I am, etc.
>
> *(Signed)* MARBOIS

I need say no more in my justification. This unsolicited testimony of M. de Marbois is a sufficient contradiction to the charge of peculation which has been raised against me in the absence of correct information respecting the real causes of my rupture with the First Consul.

M. le Duc de Rovigo also observes that my enemies were numerous. My concealed adversaries were indeed all those who were interested that the sovereign should not have about him, as his confidential companion, a man devoted to his glory and not to his vanity. In expressing his dissatisfaction with one of his ministers Bonaparte had said, in the presence of several individuals, among whom was M. Maret, "If I could find a second Bourrienne I would get rid of you all." This was sufficient to raise against me the hatred of all who envied the confidence of which I was in possession.

The failure of a firm in Paris in which I had invested a considerable sum of money afforded an opportunity for envy and malignity to irritate the First Consul against me. Bonaparte, who had not yet forgiven me for wishing to leave him, at length determined to sacrifice my services to a new fit of ill-humour.

A mercantile house, then one of the most respectable in Patna, had among its speculations undertaken some army contracts. With the knowledge of Berthier, with whom, indeed, the house had treated, I had invested some money in this business. Unfortunately the principals were, unknown to me, engaged in dangerous speculations in the Funds, which in a short time so involved them as to occasion their failure for a heavy amount. This caused a rumour that a slight fall of the Funds, which took place at that period, was occasioned by the bankruptcy; and the First Consul, who never could understand the nature of the Funds, gave credit to the report. He was made to believe that the business of the Stock Exchange was ruined. It was insinuated that I was accused of taking advantage of my situation to produce variations in the Funds, though I was so unfortunate as to lose not only my investment in the bankrupt house, but also a sum of money for which I had become bound, by way of surety, to assist the house in increasing its business. I incurred the violent displeasure of the First Consul, who declared to me that he no longer required my services. I might, perhaps have cooled his irritation by reminding him that he could not blame me for purchasing an interest in a contract, since he himself had stipulated for a gratuity of 1,500,000 francs for his brother Joseph out of the contract for victualling the navy. But I saw that for some time past M. de Meneval had begun to supersede me, and the First Consul only wanted such an opportunity as this for coming to a rupture with me.

Such is a true statement of the circumstances which led to my separation from Bonaparte. I defy any one to adduce a single fact in support of the charge of peculation, or any transaction of the kind; I fear no investigation of my conduct. When in the service of Bonaparte I caused many appointments to be made, and many names to be erased from the emigrant list before the 'Senatus-consulte' of the 6th Floréal, year X.; but I never counted upon gratitude, experience having taught me that it was an empty word.

The Duc de Rovigo attributed my disgrace to certain intercepted letters which injured me in the eyes of the First Consul. I did not know this at the time, and though I was pretty well aware of the machinations of Bonaparte's adulators, almost all of whom were my enemies, yet I did not contemplate such an act of baseness. But a spontaneous letter from M. de Barbe Marbois at length opened my eyes, and left little doubt on the subject. The following is the postscript to that noble peer's letter:

> I recollect that one Wednesday the First Consul, while presiding at a Council of Ministers at St. Cloud, opened a note, and, without informing us what it contained, hastily left the Board, apparently much agitated. In a few minutes he returned and told us that your functions had ceased.

Whether the sudden displeasure of the First Consul was excited by a false representation of my concern in the transaction which proved so unfortunate to me, or whether Bonaparte merely made that a pretence for carrying into execution a resolution which I am convinced had been previously adopted, I shall not stop to determine; but the Duc de Rovigo having mentioned the violation of the secrecy of letters in my case, I shall take the opportunity of stating some particulars on that subject.

Before I wrote these Memoirs the existence in the Post Office of the cabinet, which had obtained the epithet of black, had been denounced in the chamber of deputies, and the answer was, that it no longer existed, which of course amounted to an admission that it had existed. I may therefore, without indiscretion, state what I know respecting it.

The "black cabinet" was established in the reign of Louis XV., merely for the purpose of prying into the scandalous gossip of the Court and the capital. The existence of this cabinet soon became generally known to every one. The numerous postmasters who succeeded each other, especially in latter times, the still more numerous Post Office clerks, and that portion of the public who are ever on the watch for what is held up as scandalous, soon banished all the secrecy of the affair, and none but fools were taken in by it. All who did not wish to be committed by their correspondence chose better channels of communication than the Post; but those who wanted to ruin an enemy or benefit a friend long continued to avail themselves of the black cabinet, which, at first intended merely to amuse a monarch's idle hours, soon became a medium of intrigue, dangerous from the abuse that might be made of it.

Every morning, for three years, I used to peruse the portfolio containing the bulletins of the black cabinet, and I frankly confess that I never could discover any real cause for the public indignation against it, except inasmuch as it proved the channel of vile intrigue. Out of 30,000 letters, which daily left Paris to be distributed through France and all parts of the world, ten or twelve, at most, were copied, and often only a few lines of them.

Bonaparte at first proposed to send complete copies of intercepted letters to the ministers whom their contents might concern; but a few observations from me induced him to direct that only the important passages should be extracted and sent. I made these extracts, and transmitted them to their destinations, accompanied by the following words: "The First Consul directs me to inform you that he has just received the following information," etc. Whence the information came was left to be guessed at.

The First Consul daily received through this channel about a dozen pretended letters, the writers of which described their enemies as opponents of the Government, or their friends as models of obedience and fidelity to the constituted authorities. But the secret purpose of this vile correspondence was soon discovered, and Bonaparte gave orders that no more of it should be copied. I, however, suffered from it at the time of my disgrace, and was well-nigh falling a victim to it at a subsequent period.

The letter mentioned by M. de Marbois, and which was the occasion of this digression on the violation of private correspondence, derived importance from the circumstance that Wednesday, the 20th of October, when Bonaparte received it, was the day on which I left the Consular palace.

I retired to a house which Bonaparte had advised me to purchase at St. Cloud, and for the fitting up and furnishing of which he had promised to pay. We shall see how he kept this promise! I immediately sent to direct Landoire, the messenger of Bonaparte's cabinet, to place all letters sent to me in the First Consul's portfolio, because many intended for him came under cover for me. In consequence of this message I received the following letter from M. de Meneval:

> MY DEAR BOURRIENNE—I cannot believe that the First Consul would wish that your letters should be presented to him. I presume you allude only to those which may concern him, and which come addressed under cover to you. The First Consul has written to citizens Lavallette and Mollien directing them to address their packets to him. I cannot allow Landoire to obey the order you sent. The First Consul yesterday evening evinced great regret. He repeatedly said, "How miserable I am! I have known that man since he was seven years old." I cannot but believe that he will reconsider his unfortunate decision. I have intimated to him that the burden of the business is too much for me, and that he must be extremely at a loss for the services of one to whom he was so much accustomed, and whose situation, I am confident, nobody else can satisfactorily fill. He went to bed very low-spirited. I am, etc.
>
> *(Signed)* MENEVAL.
>
> 19 *Vendemiaire, an X.* (*21st October 1802.)*

Next day I received another letter from M. Meneval as follows:—

> I send you your letters. The First Consul prefers that you should break them open, and send here those which are intended for him. I enclose some German papers, which he begs you to translate. Madame Bonaparte is much interested in your behalf;

> and I can assure you that no one more heartily desires than the First Consul himself to see you again at your old post, for which it would be difficult to find a successor equal to you, either as regards fidelity or fitness. I do not relinquish the hope of seeing you here again.

A whole week passed away in conflicts between the First Consul's friendship and pride. The least desire he manifested to recall me was opposed by his flatterers. On the fifth day of our separation he directed me to come to him. He received me with the greatest kindness, and after having good-humouredly told me that I often expressed myself with too much freedom—a fault I was never solicitous to correct—he added: "I regret your absence much. You were very useful to me. You are neither too noble nor too plebeian, neither too aristocratic nor too Jacobinical. You are discreet and laborious. You understand me better than any one else; and, between ourselves be it said, we ought to consider this a sort of Court. Look at Duroc, Bessières, Maret. However, I am very much inclined to take you back; but by so doing I should confirm the report that I cannot do without you."

Madame Bonaparte informed me that she had heard persons to whom Bonaparte expressed a desire to recall me observe, "What would you do? People will say you cannot do without him. You have got rid of him now; therefore think no more about him: and as for the English newspapers, he gave them more importance than they really deserved: you will no longer be troubled with them." This will bring to mind a scene—which occurred at Malmaison on the receipt of some intelligence in the 'London Gazette'.

I am convinced that if Bonaparte had been left to himself he would have recalled me, and this conviction is warranted by the interval which elapsed between his determination to part with me and the formal announcement of my dismissal. Our rupture took place on the 20th of October, and on the 8th of November following the First Consul sent me the following letter:

> CITIZEN BOURRIENNE, MINISTER OF STATE—I am satisfied with the services which you have rendered me during the time you have been with me; but henceforth they are no longer necessary. I wish you to relinquish, from this time, the functions and title of my private secretary. I shall seize an early opportunity of providing for you in a way suited to your activity and talents, and conducive to the public service.
>
> (*Signed*) BONAPARTE.

If any proof of the First Consul's malignity were wanting it would be furnished by the following fact:—A few days after the receipt of the letter which announced my dismissal I received a note from Duroc; but, to afford an idea of the petty revenge of him who caused it to be written, it will be necessary first to relate a few preceding circumstances.

When, with the view of preserving a little freedom, I declined the offer of apartments which Madame Bonaparte had prepared at Malmaison for myself and my family, I purchased a small house at Ruel: the First Consul had given orders for the furnishing of this house, as well as one which I possessed in Paris. From the manner in which the orders were given I had not the slightest doubt but that Bonaparte intended to make me a present of the furniture. However, when I left his service he applied to have it returned.

As at first I paid no attention to his demand, as far as it concerned the furniture at Ruel, he directed Duroc to write the following letter to me:

> The First Consul, my dear Bourrienne, has just ordered me to send him this evening the keys of your residence in Paris, from which the furniture is not to be removed. He also directs me to put into a warehouse whatever furniture you may have at Ruel or elsewhere which you have obtained from Government. I beg of you to send me an answer, so as to assist me in the execution of these orders. You promised me to have everything settled before the First Consul's return. I must excuse myself in the best way I can.
>
> (*Signed*) DUROC.
>
> *24 Brumaire, an X. (15th November 1802.)*

Believing myself to be master of my own actions, I had formed the design of visiting England, whither I was called by some private business. However, I was fully aware of the peculiarity of my situation, and I was resolved to take no step that should in any way justify a reproach.

On the 11th of January I therefore wrote to Duroc:

> My affairs require my presence in England for some time. I beg of you, my dear Duroc, to mention my intended journey to the First Consul, as I do not wish to do anything inconsistent with his views. I would rather sacrifice my own interest than displease him. I rely on your friendship for an early answer to this, for uncertainty would be fatal to me in many respects.

The answer, which speedily arrived, was as follows:—

> MY DEAR BOURRIENNE—I have presented to the First Consul the letter I just received from you. He read it, and said, "No!" That is the only answer I can give you.
>
> (*Signed*) DUROC.

This monosyllable was expressive. It proved to me that Bonaparte was conscious how ill he had treated me; and, suspecting that I was actuated by the desire of vengeance, he was afraid of my going to England, lest I should there take advantage of that liberty of the press which he had so effectually put down in France. He probably imagined that my object was to publish statements which would more effectually have enlightened the public respecting his government and designs than all the scandalous anecdotes, atrocious calumnies, and ridiculous fabrications of Pelletier, the editor of the 'Ambigu'. But Bonaparte was much deceived in this supposition; and if there can remain any doubt on that subject, it will be removed on referring to the date of these Memoirs, and observing the time at which I consented to publish them.

I was not deceived as to the reasons of Bonaparte's unceremonious refusal of my application;

and as I well knew his inquisitorial character, I thought it prudent to conceal my notes. I acted differently from Camoens. He contended with the sea to preserve his manuscripts; I made the earth the depository of mine. I carefully enclosed my most valuable notes and papers in a tin box, which I buried under ground. A yellow tinge, the commencement of decay, has in some places almost obliterated the writing.

It will be seen in the sequel that my precaution was not useless, and that I was right in anticipating the persecution of Bonaparte, provoked by the malice of my enemies. On the 20th of April Duroc sent me the following note:

> I beg, my dear Bourrienne, that you will come to St. Cloud this morning. I have something to tell you on the part of the First Consul.
>
> (*Signed*) DUROC.

This note caused me much anxiety. I could not doubt but that my enemies had invented some new calumny; but I must say that I did not expect such baseness as I experienced.

As soon as Duroc had made me acquainted with the business which the First Consul had directed him to communicate, I wrote on the spot the subjoined letter to Bonaparte:

> At General Duroc's desire I have this moment waited upon him, and he informs me that you have received notice that a deficit of 100,000 francs has been discovered in the Treasury of the Navy, which you require me to refund this day at noon. Citizen First Consul, I know not what this means! I am utterly ignorant of the matter. I solemnly declare to you that this charge is a most infamous calumny. It is one more to be added to the number of those malicious charges which have been invented for the purpose of destroying any influence I might possess with you. I am in General Duroc's apartment, where I await your orders.

Duroc carried my note to the First Consul as soon as it was written. He speedily returned. "All's right!" said he. "He has directed me to say it was entirely a mistake!—that he is now convinced he was deceived! that he is sorry for the business, and hopes no more will be said about it."

The base flatterers who surrounded Bonaparte wished him to renew his Egyptian extortions upon me; but they should have recollected that the fusillade employed in Egypt for the purpose of raising money was no longer the fashion in France, and that the days were gone by when it was the custom to 'grease the wheels of the revolutionary car.'

CHAPTER XVII

1803

The First Consul never anticipated a long peace with England. He wished for peace merely because, knowing it to be ardently desired by the people, after ten years of war he thought it would increase his popularity and afford him the opportunity of laying the foundation of his government. Peace was as necessary to enable him to conquer the throne of France as war was essential to secure it, and to enlarge its base at the expense of the other thrones of Europe. This was the secret of the peace of Amiens, and of the rupture which so suddenly followed, though that rupture certainly took place sooner than the First Consul wished. On the great questions of peace and war Bonaparte entertained elevated ideas; but in discussions on the subject he always declared himself in favour of war. When told of the necessities of the people, of the advantages of peace, its influence on trade, the arts, national industry, and every branch of public prosperity, he did not attempt to deny the argument; indeed, he concurred in it; but he remarked, that all those advantages were only conditional, so long as England was able to throw the weight of her navy into the scale of the world, and to exercise the influence of her gold in all the Cabinets of Europe. Peace must be broken; since it was evident that England was determined to break it. Why not anticipate her? Why allow her to have all the advantages of the first step? We must astonish Europe! We must thwart the policy of the Continent! We must strike a great and unexpected blow. Thus reasoned the First Consul, and every one may judge whether his actions agreed with his sentiments.

The conduct of England too well justified the foresight of Bonaparte's policy; or rather England, by neglecting to execute her treaties, played into Bonaparte's hand, favoured his love for war, and justified the prompt declaration of hostilities in the eyes of the French nation, whom he wished to persuade that if peace were broken it would be against his wishes. England was already at work with the powerful machinery of her subsidies, and the veil beneath which she attempted to conceal her negotiations was still sufficiently transparent for the lynx eye of the First Consul. It was in the midst of peace that all those plots were hatched, while millions who had no knowledge of their existence were securely looking forward to uninterrupted repose.

Since the Revolution Paris had never presented such a spectacle as during the winter of 1802-3. At that time the concourse of foreigners in the French capital was immense. Everything wore the appearance of satisfaction, and the external signs of public prosperity. The visible regeneration in French society exceedingly annoyed the British Ministry. The English who flocked to the Continent discovered France to be very different from what she was described to be by the English papers. This caused serious alarm on the other side of the Channel, and the English Government endeavoured by unjust complaints to divert attention from just dissatisfaction, which its own secret intrigues excited. The King of England sent a message to Parliament, in which he spoke of armaments preparing in the ports of France, and of the necessity of adopting precautions against meditated aggressions. This instance of bad faith highly irritated the First Consul, who one day, in a fit of displeasure, thus addressed

Lord Whitworth in the salon, where all the foreign Ambassadors were assembled:

"What is the meaning of this? Are you then tired of peace? Must Europe again be deluged with blood? Preparations for war indeed! Do you think to overawe us by this? You shall see that France may be conquered, perhaps destroyed, but never intimidated—never!"

The English Ambassador was astounded at this unexpected sally, to which he made no reply. He contented himself with writing to his Government an account of an interview in which the First Consul had so far forgotten himself,-whether purposely or not I do not pretend to say.

That England wished for war there could be no doubt. She occupied Malta, it is true, but she had promised to give it up, though she never had any intention of doing so. She was to have evacuated Egypt, yet there she still remained; the Cape of Good Hope was to have been surrendered, but she still retained possession of it. England had signed, at Amiens, a peace which she had no intention of maintaining. She knew the hatred of the Cabinets of Europe towards France, and she was sure, by her intrigues and subsidies, of arming them on her side whenever her plans reached maturity. She saw France powerful and influential in Europe, and she knew the ambitious views of the First Consul, who, indeed, had taken little pains to conceal them.

The First Consul, who had reckoned on a longer duration of the peace of Amiens, found himself at the rupture of the treaty in an embarrassing situation. The numerous grants of furloughs, the deplorable condition of the cavalry, and the temporary absence of artillery, in consequence of a project for refounding all the field-pieces, caused much anxiety to Bonaparte. He had recourse to the conscription to fill up the deficiencies of the army; and the project of refounding the artillery was abandoned. Supplies of money were obtained from the large towns, and Hanover, which was soon after occupied, furnished abundance of good horses for mounting the cavalry.

War had now become inevitable; and as soon as it was declared the First Consul set out to visit Belgium and the seaboard departments to ascertain the best means of resisting the anticipated attacks of the English. In passing through Compiegne he received a visit from Father Berton, formerly principal of the military school of Brienne. He was then rector of the school of arts at Compiegne, a situation in which he had been placed by Bonaparte. I learned the particulars of this visit through Josephine. Father Berton, whose primitive simplicity of manner was unchanged since the time when he held us under the authority of his ferule, came to invite Bonaparte and Josephine to breakfast with him, which invitation was accepted. Father Berton had at that time living with him one of our old comrades of Brienne, named Bouquet; but he expressly forbade him to show himself to Bonaparte or any one of his suite, because Bouquet, who had been a commissary at headquarters in Italy, was in disgrace with the First Consul. Bouquet promised to observe Father Berton's injunctions, but was far from keeping his promise. As soon as he saw Bonaparte's carriage drive up, he ran to the door and gallantly handed out Josephine. Josephine, as she took his hand, said, "Bouquet,—you have ruined yourself!" Bonaparte, indignant at what he considered an unwarrantable familiarity, gave way to one of his uncontrollable fits of passion, and as soon as he entered the room where the breakfast was laid, he seated himself, and then said to his wife in an imperious tone, "Josephine, sit there!" He then commenced breakfast, without telling Father Becton to sit down, although a third plate had been laid for him. Father Becton stood behind his old pupil's chair apparently confounded at his violence. The scene produced such an effect on the old man that he became incapable of discharging his duties at Compiegne. He retired to Rheims, and his intellect soon after became deranged. I do not pretend to say whether this alienation of mind was caused by the occurrence I have just related, and the account of which I received from Josephine. She was deeply afflicted at what had passed. Father Berton died insane. What I heard from Josephine was afterwards confirmed by the brother of Father Becton. The fact is, that in proportion as Bonaparte acquired power he was the more annoyed at the familiarity of old companions; and, indeed, I must confess that their familiarity often appeared very ridiculous.

The First Consul's visit to the northern coast took place towards the end of the year 1803, at which time the English attacked the Dutch settlements of Surinam, Demerara, and Essequibo, and a convention of neutrality was concluded between France, Spain, and Portugal. Rapp accompanied the First Consul, who attentively inspected the preparations making for a descent on England, which it was never his intention to effect, as will be shortly shown.

On the First Consul's return I learned from Rapp that I had been spoken of during the journey, and in the following way:—Bonaparte, being at Boulogne, wanted some information which no one there could give, him. Vexed at receiving no satisfactory answer to his inquiries he called Rapp, and said, "Do you know, Rapp, where Bourrienne is?"—"General, he is in Paris."—"Write to him to come here immediately, and send off one of my couriers with the letter." The rumour of the First Consul's sudden recollection of me spread like lightning, and the time required to write the letter and despatch the courier was more than sufficient for the efforts of those whom my return was calculated to alarm. Artful representations soon checked these spontaneous symptoms of a return to former feelings and habits. When Rapp carried to the First Consul the letter he had been directed to write the order was countermanded. However, Rapp advised me not to leave Paris, or if I did, to mention the place where I might be found, so that Duroc might have it in his power to seize on any favourable circumstance without delay. I was well aware of the friendship of both Rapp and Duroc, and they could as confidently rely on mine.

CHAPTER XVIII

1803

At the time of the rupture with England Bonaparte was, as I have mentioned, quite unprepared in most branches of the service; yet everything was created as if by magic, and he seemed to impart to others a share of his own incredible activity. It is inconceivable how many things had been undertaken and executed since the rupture of the peace. The north coast of France presented the appearance of one vast arsenal; for Bonaparte on this occasion employed his troops like Roman soldiers, and made the tools of the artisan succeed to the arms of the warrior.

On his frequent journeys to the coast Bonaparte usually set off at night, and on the following morning arrived at the post office of Chantilly, where he breakfasted. Rapp, whom I often saw when he was in Paris, talked incessantly of these journeys, for he almost always accompanied the First Consul, and it would have been well had he always been surrounded by such men. In the evening the First Consul supped at Abbeville, and arrived early next day at the bridge of Brique. "It would require constitutions of iron to go through what we do," said Rapp. "We no sooner alight from the carriage than we mount on horseback, and sometimes remain in our saddles for ten or twelve hours successively. The First Consul inspects and examines everything, often talks with the soldiers. How he is beloved by them! When shall we pay a visit to London with those brave fellows?"

Notwithstanding these continual journeys the First Consul never neglected any of the business of government, and was frequently present at the deliberations of the Council. I was still with him when the question as to the manner in which the treaties of peace should be concluded came under the consideration of the Council. Some members, among whom Truguet was conspicuous, were of opinion that, conformably with an article of the Constitution, the treaties should be proposed by the Head of the Government, submitted to the Legislative Body, and after being agreed to promulgated as part of the laws. Bonaparte thought differently. I was entirely of his opinion, and he said to me, "It is for the mere pleasure of opposition that they appeal to the Constitution, for if the Constitution says so it is absurd. There are some things which cannot become the subject of discussion in a public assembly; for instance, if I treat with Austria, and my Ambassador agrees to certain conditions, can those conditions be rejected by the Legislative Body? It is a monstrous absurdity! Things would be brought to a fine pass in this way! Lucchesini and Markow would give dinners every day like Cambacérès; scatter their money about, buy men who are to be sold, and thus cause our propositions to be rejected. This would be a fine way to manage matters!"

When Bonaparte, according to his custom, talked to me in the evening of what had passed in the Council, his language was always composed of a singular mixture of quotations from antiquity, historical references, and his own ideas. He talked about the Romans, and I remember when Mr. Fox was at Paris that he tried to distinguish himself before that Foreign Minister, whom he greatly esteemed. In his enlarged way of viewing the world Bonaparte divided it into two large states, the East and the West: "What matters," he would often say, "that two countries are separated by rivers or mountains, that they speak different languages? With very slight shades of variety France, Spain, England, Italy, and Germany, have the same manners and customs, the same religion, and the same dress. In them a man can only marry one wife; slavery is not allowed; and these are the great distinctions which divide the civilised inhabitants of the globe. With the exception of Turkey, Europe is merely a province of the world, and our warfare is but civil strife. There is also another way of dividing nations, namely, by land and water." Then he would touch on all the European interests, speak of Russia, whose alliance he wished for, and of England, the mistress of the seas. He usually ended by alluding to what was then his favourite scheme—an expedition to India.

When from these general topics Bonaparte descended to the particular interests of France, he still spoke like a sovereign; and I may truly say that he showed himself more jealous than any sovereign ever was of the dignity of France, of which he already considered himself the sole representative. Having learned that a captain of the English navy had visited the dockyard of Brest passing himself off as a merchant, whose passport he had borrowed, he flew into a rage because no one had ventured to arrest him[176]. Nothing was lost on Bonaparte, and he made use of this fact to prove to the Council of State the necessity of increasing the number of commissary-generals of police. At a meeting of the Council he said, "If there had been a commissary of police at Brest he would have arrested the English captain and sent him at once to Paris. As he was acting the part of a spy I would have had him shot as such. No Englishman, not even a nobleman, or the English Ambassador, should be admitted into our dockyards. I will soon regulate all this." He afterwards said to me, "There are plenty of wretches who are selling me every day to the English without my being subjected to English spying."[177]

He had on one occasion said before an assemblage of generals, senators, and high officers of State, who were at an audience of the Diplomatic Body, "The English think that I am afraid of war, but I am not." And here the truth escaped him, in spite of himself. "My power will lose nothing by war. In a very short time I can have 2,000,000 of men at my disposal. What has been the result of the first war? The union of Belgium and Piedmont to France. This is greatly to our advantage; it will consolidate our system. France shall not be restrained by foreign fetters. England has manifestly violated the treaties! It would be better to render homage to the King of England, and crown him King of France at Paris, than to submit to the insolent caprices of the English Government. If, for the sake of preserving peace, at most for only two months longer, I should yield on a single point, the English would become the more treacherous and insolent, and would enact the more in proportion as we yield. But they little know me! Were we to yield to England now, she would next prohibit our navigation in certain parts of the world. She would insist on the surrender of our ships. I know not what she would not demand; but I am not the man to brook such indignities. Since England wishes for war she shall have it, and that speedily!"

---

176 See James' Naval History for an account of Sir Sidney Smith's daring exploit.

177 During the short and hollow peace of Amiens Bonaparte sent over to England as consuls and vice-consuls, a number of engineers and military men, who were instructed to make plans of all the harbours and coasts of the United Kingdom. They worked in secrecy, yet not so secretly but that they were soon suspected: the facts were proved, and they were sent out of the country without ceremony.— Editor of 1836 edition.

On the same day Bonaparte said a great deal more about the treachery of England. The gross calumnies to which he was exposed in the London newspapers powerfully contributed to increase his natural hatred of the liberty of the press; and he was much astonished that such attacks could be made upon him by English subjects when he was at peace with the English Government.

I had one day a singular proof of the importance which Bonaparte attached to the opinion of the English people respecting any misconduct that was attributed to him. What I am about to state will afford another example of Bonaparte's disposition to employ petty and roundabout means to gain his ends. He gave a ball at Malmaison when Hortense was in the seventh month of her pregnancy.[178] I have already mentioned that he disliked to see women in that situation, and above all could not endure to see them dance. Yet, in spite of this antipathy, he himself asked Hortense to dance at the ball at Malmaison. She at first declined, but Bonaparte was exceedingly importunate, and said to her in a tone of good-humoured persuasion, "Do, I beg of you; I particularly wish to see you dance. Come, stand up, to oblige me." Hortense at last consented. The motive for this extraordinary request I will now explain.

On the day after the ball one of the newspapers contained some verses on Hortense's dancing. She was exceedingly annoyed at this, and when the paper arrived at Malmaison she expressed, displeasure at it. Even allowing for all the facility of our newspaper wits, she was nevertheless at a loss to understand how the lines could have been written and printed respecting a circumstance which only occurred the night before. Bonaparte smiled, and gave her no distinct answer. When Hortense knew that I was alone in the cabinet she came in and asked me to explain the matter; and seeing no reason to conceal the truth, I told her that the lines had been written by Bonaparte's direction before the ball took place. I added, what indeed was the fact, that the ball had been prepared for the verses, and that it was only for the appropriateness of their application that the First Consul had pressed her to dance. He adopted this strange contrivance for contradicting an article which appeared in an English journal announcing that Hortense was delivered. Bonaparte was highly indignant at that premature announcement, which he clearly saw was made for the sole purpose of giving credit to the scandalous rumours of his imputed connection with Hortense. Such were the petty machinations which not unfrequently found their place in a mind in which the grandest schemes were revolving.

178 This refers to the first son of Louis and of Hortense, Napoleon Charles, the intended successor of Napoleon, who was born 1802, died 1807, elder brother of Napoleon III.

CHAPTER XIX

1803

One of the circumstances which foretold the brief duration of the peace of Amiens was, that Mr. Pitt was out of office at the time of its conclusion. I mentioned this to Bonaparte, and I immediately perceived by his hasty "What do you say?" that my observation had been heard—but not liked. It did not, however, require any extraordinary shrewdness to see the true motive of Mr. Pitt's retirement. That distinguished statesman conceived that a truce under the name of a peace was indispensable for England; but, intending to resume the war with France more fiercely than ever, he for a while retired from office, and left to others the task of arranging the peace; but his intention was to mark his return to the ministry by the renewal of the implacable hatred he had vowed against France. Still, I have always thought that the conclusion of peace, however necessary to England, was an error of the Cabinet of London. England alone had never before acknowledged any of the governments which had risen up in France since the Revolution; and as the past could not be blotted out, a future war, however successful to England, could not take from Bonaparte's Government the immense weight it had acquired by an interval of peace. Besides, by the mere fact of the conclusion of the treaty England proved to all Europe that the restoration of the Bourbons was merely a pretext, and she defaced that page of her history which might have shown that she was actuated by nobler and more generous sentiments than mere hatred of France. It is very certain that the condescension of England in treating with the First Consul had the effect of rallying round him a great many partisans of the Bourbons, whose hopes entirely depended on the continuance of war between Great Britain and France. This opened the eyes of the greater number, namely, those who could not see below the surface, and were not previously aware that the demonstrations of friendship so liberally made to the Bourbons by the European Cabinets, and especially by England, were merely false pretences, assumed for the purpose of disguising, beneath the semblance of honourable motives, their wish to injure France, and to oppose her rapidly increasing power.

When the misunderstanding took place, France and England might have mutually reproached each other, but justice was apparently on the side of France. It was evident that England, by refusing to evacuate Malta, was guilty of a palpable infraction of the treaty of Amiens, while England could only institute against France what in the French law language is called a suit or process of tendency. But it must be confessed that this tendency on the part of France to augment her territory was very evident, for the Consular decrees made conquests more promptly than the sword. The union of Piedmont with France had changed the state of Europe. This union, it is true, was effected previously to the treaty of Amiens; but it was not so with the states of Parma and Piacenza, Bonaparte having by his sole authority constituted himself the heir of the Grand Duke, recently deceased. It may therefore be easily imagined how great was England's uneasiness at the internal prosperity of France and the insatiable ambition of her ruler; but it is no less certain that, with respect to Malta, England acted with decidedly bad faith; and this bad faith appeared in its worst light from the following circumstance:—It had been stipulated that England should withdraw her troops from Malta three months after the signing of the treaty, yet more than a year had elapsed, and the troops were still there. The order of Malta was to be restored as it formerly was; that is to say, it was to be a sovereign and independent order, under the protection of the Holy See. The three Cabinets of Vienna, Berlin, and St. Petersburg were to guarantee the execution of the treaty of Amiens. The English Ambassador, to excuse the evasions of his Government, pretended that the Russian Cabinet concurred with England in the delayed fulfilment of the conditions of the treaty; but at the very moment he was making that excuse a courier arrived from the Cabinet of St. Petersburg bearing despatches completely, at variance with the assertion of Lord Whitworth. His lordship left Paris on the night of the 12th May 1803, and the English Government, unsolicited, sent passports to the French embassy in London. The news of this sudden rupture made the English console fall four per cent., but did not immediately produce such a retrograde effect on the French funds, which were then quoted at fifty-five francs;—a very high point, when it is recollected that they were at seven or eight francs on the eve of the 18th Brumaire.

In this state of things France proposed to the English Government to admit of the mediation of Russia; but as England had declared war in order to repair the error she committed in concluding peace, the proposition was of course rejected. Thus the public gave the First Consul credit for great moderation and a sincere wish for peace. Thus arose between England and France a contest resembling those furious wars which marked the reigns of King John and Charles VII. Our beaux esprits drew splendid comparisons between the existing state of things and the ancient rivalry of Carthage and Rome, and sapiently concluded that, as Carthage fell, England must do so likewise.

Bonaparte was at St. Cloud when Lord Whitworth left Paris. A fortnight was spent in useless attempts to renew negotiations. War, therefore, was the only alternative. Before he made his final preparations the First Consul addressed a message to the Senate, the Legislative Body, and the Tribunate. In this message he mentioned the recall of the English Ambassador, the breaking out of hostilities, the unexpected message of the King of England to his Parliament, and the armaments which immediately ensued in the British ports. "In vain," he said, "had France tried every means to induce England to abide by the treaty. She had repelled every overture, and increased the insolence of her demands. France," he added, "will not submit to menaces, but will combat for the faith of treaties, and the honour of the French name, confidently trusting that the result of the contest will be such as she has a right to expect from the justice of her cause and the courage of her people."

This message was dignified, and free from that vein of boasting in which Bonaparte so frequently indulged. The reply of the Senate was accompanied by a vote of a ship of the line, to be paid for out of the Senatorial salaries. With his usual address Bonaparte, in acting for himself, spoke in the name of the people, just as he did in the question of the Consulate for life. But what he then did for his own interests turned to the future interests of the Bourbons. The very treaty which had just been broken off gave rise to a curious observation. Bonaparte, though not yet a sovereign, peremptorily required the King of England to renounce the empty title of King of France, which was kept up as if to imply that old pretensions were not yet renounced. The proposition was acceded to, and to this circumstance was owing the disappearance of the title of King of France from among the titles of the King of England, when the treaty of Paris was concluded on the return of the Bourbons.

The first grievance complained of by England was the prohibition of English merchandise, which had been more rigid since the peace than during the war. The avowal of Great Britain on this point might well have enabled her to dispense with any other subject of complaint; for the truth is, she was alarmed at the aspect of our internal prosperity, and at the impulse given to our manufactures. The English Government had hoped to obtain from the First Consul such a commercial treaty as would have proved a death-blow to our rising trade; but Bonaparte opposed this, and from the very circumstance of his refusal he might easily have foreseen the rupture at which he affected to be surprised. What I state I felt at the time, when I read with great interest all the documents relative to this great dispute between the two rival nations, which eleven years afterwards was decided before the walls of Paris.

It was evidently disappointment in regard to a commercial treaty which created the animosity of the English Government, as that circumstance was alluded to, by way of reproach, in the King of England's declaration. In that document it was complained that France had sent a number of persona into the ports of Great Britain and Ireland in the character of commercial agents, which character, and the privileges belonging to it, they could only have acquired by a commercial treaty. Such was, in my opinion, the real cause of the complaints of England; but as it would have seemed too absurd to make it the ground of a declaration of war, she enumerated other grievances, viz., the union of Piedmont and of the states of Parma and Piacenza with France, and the continuance of the French troops in Holland. A great deal was said about the views and projects of France with respect to Turkey, and this complaint originated in General Sebastiani's mission to Egypt. On that point I can take upon me to say that the English Government was not misinformed. Bonaparte too frequently spoke to me of his ideas respecting the East, and his project of attacking the English power in India, to leave any doubt of his ever having renounced them. The result of all the reproaches which the two Governments addressed to each other was, that neither acted with good faith.

The First Consul, in a communication to the Legislative Body on the state of France and on her foreign relations; had said, "England, single-handed, cannot cope with France." This sufficed to irritate the susceptibility of English pride, and the British Cabinet affected to regard it as a threat. However, it was no such thing. When Bonaparte threatened, his words were infinitely more energetic. The passage above cited was merely an assurance to France; and if we only look at the past efforts and sacrifices made by England to stir up enemies to France on the Continent, we may be justified in supposing that her anger at Bonaparte's declaration arose from a conviction of its truth. Singly opposed to France, England could doubtless have done her much harm, especially by assailing the scattered remnants of her navy; but she could have done nothing against France on the Continent. The two powers, unaided by allies, might have continued long at war without any considerable acts of hostility.

The first effect of the declaration of war by England was the invasion of Hanover by the French troops under General Mortier. The telegraphic despatch by which this news was communicated to Paris was as laconic as correct, and contained, in a few words, the complete history of the expedition. It ran as follows: "The French are masters of the Electorate of Hanover, and the enemy's army are made prisoners of war." A day or two after the shop windows of the print-sellers were filled with caricatures on the English, and particularly on the Duke of Cambridge. I recollect seeing one in which the Duke was represented reviewing his troops mounted on a crab. I mention these trifles because, as I was then living entirely at leisure, in the Rue Hauteville, I used frequently to take a stroll on the Boulevards, where I was sometimes much amused with these prints; and I could not help remarking, that in large cities such trifles have more influence on the public mind than is usually supposed.

The First Consul thought the taking of the prisoners in Hanover a good opportunity to exchange them for those taken from us by the English navy. A proposition to this effect was accordingly made; but the English Cabinet was of opinion that, though the King of England was also Elector of Hanover, yet there was no identity between the two Governments, of both which George III. was the head. In consequence of this subtle distinction the proposition for the exchange of prisoners fell to the ground. At this period nothing could exceed the animosity of the two Governments towards each other, and Bonaparte, on the declaration of war, marked his indignation by an act which no consideration can justify; I allude to the order for the arrest of all the English in France—a truly barbarious measure; for; can anything be more cruel and unjust than to visit individuals with the vengeance due to the Government whose subjects they may happen to be? But Bonaparte, when under the influence of anger, was never troubled by scruples.

I must here notice the fulfilment of a remark Bonaparte often made, use of to me during the Consulate. "You shall see, Bourrienne," he would say, "what use I will make of the priests."

War being declared, the First Consul, in imitation of the most Christian kings of olden times, recommended the success of his arms to the prayers of the faithful through the medium of the clergy. To this end he addressed a circular letter, written in royal style, to the Cardinals, Archbishops, and Bishops of France.

It was as follows:

> MONSIEUR—The motives of the present war are known throughout Europe. The bad faith of the King of England, who has violated his treaties by refusing to restore Malta to the order of St. John of Jerusalem, and attacked our merchant vessels without a previous declaration of war, together with the necessity of a just defence, forced us to have recourse to arms. I therefore wish you to order prayers to be offered up, in order to obtain the benediction of Heaven on our enterprises. The proofs I have received of your zeal for the public service give me an assurance of your readiness to conform with my wishes.
>
> Given at *St. Cloud, 18 Prairial, an XI. (7th June 1803).*
>
> *(Signed)* BONAPARTE.

This letter was remarkable in more than one respect. It astonished most of his old brothers-in-arms, who turned it into ridicule; observing that Bonaparte needed no praying to enable him to conquer Italy twice over. The First Consul, however, let them laugh on, and steadily followed the line he had traced out. His letter was admirably calculated to please the Court of Rome, which he wished should consider him in the light of another elder son of the Church. The letter was, moreover, remarkable for the use of the word "Monsieur," which the First Consul now employed for the first time in an act destined for publicity. This circumstance would seem to indicate that he considered Republican designations incompatible with the forms due to the clergy: the clergy were especially interested in the restoration of monarchy. It may, perhaps, be thought that I dwell too much on trifles; but I lived long enough in Bonaparte's confidence to know the importance he attached to trifles. The First Consul restored the old names of the days of the week, while he allowed the names of the months, as set down in the Republican calendar, to remain. He commenced by ordering the Moniteur to be dated "Saturday," such a day of "Messidor." "See," said he one day, "was there ever such an inconsistency? We shall be laughed at! But I will do away with the Messidor. I will efface all the inventions of the Jacobins."

The clergy did not disappoint the expectations of the First Consul. They owed him much already, and hoped for still more from him. The letter to the Bishops, etc., was the signal for a number of circulars full of eulogies on Bonaparte.

These compliments were far from displeasing to the First Consul, who had no objection to flattery though he despised those who meanly made themselves the medium of conveying it to him. Duroc once told me that they had all great difficulty in preserving their gravity when the cure of a parish in Abbeville addressed Bonaparte one day while he was on his journey to the coast. "Religion," said the worthy cure, with pompous solemnity, "owes to you all that it is, we owe to you all that we are; and I, too, owe to you all that I am."[179]

179 Not so fulsome as some of the terms used a year later when Napoleon was made Emperor. "I am what I am," was placed over a seat prepared for the Emperor. One phrase, "God made Napoleon and then rested," drew from Narbonne the sneer that it would have been better if the Deity had rested sooner. "Bonaparte," says Joseph de Maistre, "has had himself described in his papers as the 'Messenger of God.' Nothing more true. Bonaparte comes straight from heaven, like a thunderbolt." (Saints-Benve, Caureries, tome iv. p. 203.)

CHAPTER XX

1803

In the month of April 1803 Prince Borghese, who was destined one day to become Bonaparte's brother-in-law by marrying the widow of Leclerc, was introduced to the First Consul by Cardinal Caprara.

About the end of June Bonaparte proceeded, with Josephine, on his journey to Belgium and the seaboard departments. Many curious circumstances were connected with this journey, of which I was informed by Duroc after the First Consul's return. Bonaparte left Paris on the 24th of June, and although it was not for upwards of a year afterwards that his brow was encircled with the imperial-diadem, everything connected with the journey had an imperial air. It was formerly the custom, when the Kings of France entered the ancient capital of Picardy, for the town of Amiens to offer them in homage some beautiful swans. Care was taken to revive this custom, which pleased Bonaparte greatly, because it was treating him like a King. The swans were accepted, and sent to Paris to be placed in the basin of the Tuileries, in order to show the Parisians the royal homage which the First Consul received when absent from the capital.

It was also during this journey that Bonaparte began to date his decrees from the places through which he passed. He had hitherto left a great number of signatures in Paris, in order that he might be present, as it were, even during his absence, by the acts of his Government. Hitherto public acts had been signed in the name of the Consuls of the Republic. Instead of this formula, he substituted the name of the Government of the Republic. By means of this variation, unimportant as it might appear, the Government was always in the place where the First Consul happened to be. The two other Consuls were now mere nullities, even in appearance. The decrees of the Government, which Cambacérès signed during the campaign of Marengo, were now issued from all the towns of France and Belgium which the First Consul visited during his six weeks' journey. Having thus centred the sole authority of the Republic in himself, the performers of the theatre of the Republic became, by a natural consequence, his; and it was quite natural that they should travel in his suite, to entertain the inhabitants of the towns in which he stopped by their performances. But this was not all. He encouraged the renewal of a host of ancient customs. He sanctioned the revival of the festival of Joan of Arc at Orleans, and he divided the Institute into four classes, with the intention of recalling the recollection of the old academies, the names of which, however, he rejected, in spite of the wishes and intrigues of Suard and the Abby Morellet, who had gained over Lucien upon this point.

However, the First Consul did not give to the classes of the Institute the rank which they formerly possessed as academies. He placed the class of sciences in the first rank, and the old French Academy in the second rank. It must be acknowledged that, considering the state of literature and science at that period, the First Consul did not make a wrong estimate of their importance.

Although the literature of France could boast of many men of great talent, such as La Harpe, who died during the Consulate, Ducis, Bernardin de Saint-Pierre, Chenier, and Lemercier, yet they could not be compared with Lagrange, Laplace, Monge, Fourcroy, Berthollet, and Cuvier, whose labours have so prodigiously extended the limits of human knowledge. No one, therefore, could murmur at seeing the class of sciences in the Institute take precedence of its elder sister. Besides, the First Consul was not sorry to show, by this arrangement, the slight estimation in which he held literary men. When he spoke to me respecting them he called them mere manufacturers of phrases. He could not pardon them for excelling him in a pursuit in which he had no claim to distinction. I never knew a man more insensible than Bonaparte to the beauties of poetry or prose. A certain degree of vagueness, which was combined with his energy of mind, led him to admire the dreams of Ossian, and his decided character found itself, as it were, represented in the elevated thoughts of Corneille. Hence his almost exclusive predilection for these two authors. With this exception, the finest works in our literature were in his opinion merely arrangements of sonorous words, void of sense, and calculated only for the ear.

Bonaparte's contempt, or, more properly speaking, his dislike of literature, displayed itself particularly in the feeling he cherished towards some men of distinguished literary talent. He hated Chenier, and Ducis still more. He could not forgive Chenier for the Republican principles which pervaded his tragedies; and Ducis excited in him; as if instinctively, an involuntary hatred. Ducis, on his part, was not backward in returning the Consul's animosity, and I remember his writing some verses which were inexcusably violent, and overstepped all the bounds of truth. Bonaparte was so singular a composition of good and bad that to describe him as he was under one or other of these aspects would serve for panegyric or satire without any departure from truth. Bonaparte was very fond of Bernardin Saint-Pierre's romance of 'Paul and Virginia', which he had read in his boyhood. I remember that he one day tried to read 'Les etudes de la Nature', but at the expiration of a quarter of an hour he threw down the book, exclaiming, "How can any one read such silly stuff. It is insipid and vapid; there is nothing in it. These are the dreams of a visionary! What is nature? The thing is vague and unmeaning. Men and passions are the subjects to write about—there is something there for study. These fellows are good for nothing under any government. I will, however, give them pensions, because I ought to do so, as Head of the State. They occupy and amuse the idle. I will make Lagrange a Senator—he has a head."

Although Bonaparte spoke so disdainfully of literary men it must not be taken for granted that he treated them ill. On the contrary, all those who visited at Malmaison were the objects of his attention, and even flattery. M. Lemercier was one of those who came most frequently, and whom Bonaparte received with the greatest pleasure. Bonaparte treated M. Lemercier with great kindness; but he did not like him. His character as a literary man and poet, joined to a polished frankness, and a mild but inflexible spirit of republicanism, amply sufficed to explain Bonaparte's dislike. He feared M. Lemercier and his pen; and, as happened more than once, he played the part of a parasite by flattering the writer. M. Lemercier was the only man I knew who refused the cross of the Legion of Honour.

Bonaparte's general dislike of literary men was less the result of prejudice than circumstances. In order to appreciate or even to read literary works time is requisite, and time was so precious to him that he would have wished, as one may say, to shorten a straight line. He liked only those writers who directed their attention to positive and precise things, which excluded all thoughts of government and censures on administration. He looked with a jealous eye on political economists and lawyers; in short, as all persons who in any way whatever meddled with legislation and moral improvements. His hatred of discussions on those subjects was strongly displayed on the occasion of the classification of the Institute. Whilst he permitted the reassembling of a literary class, to the number of forty, as formerly, he suppressed the class of moral and political science. Such was his predilection for things of immediate and certain utility that even in the sciences he favoured only such as applied to terrestrial objects. He never treated Lalande with so much distinction as Monge and Lagrange. Astronomical discoveries could not add directly to his own greatness; and, besides, he could never forgive Lalande for having wished to include him in a dictionary of atheists precisely at the moment when he was opening negotiations with the court of Rome.

Bonaparte wished to be the sole centre of a world which he believed he was called to govern. With this view he never relaxed in his constant endeavour to concentrate the whole powers of the State in the hands of its Chief. His conduct upon the subject of the revival of public instruction affords evidence of this fact. He wished to establish 6000 bursaries, to be paid by Government, and to be exclusively at his disposal, so that thus possessing the monopoly of education, he could have parcelled it out only to the children of those who were blindly devoted to him. This was what the First Consul called the revival of public instruction. During the period of my closest intimacy with him he often spoke to me on this subject, and listened patiently to my observations. I remember that one of his chief arguments was this: "What is it that distinguishes men? Education—is it not? Well, if the children of nobles be admitted into the academies, they will be as well educated as the children of the revolution, who compose the strength of my government. Ultimately they will enter into my regiments as officers, and will naturally come in competition with those whom they regard as the plunderers of their families. I do not wish that!"

My recollections have caused me to wander from the journey of the First Consul and Madame Bonaparte to the seabord departments and Belgium. I have, however, little to add to what I have already stated on the subject. I merely remember that Bonaparte's military suite, and Lauriston and Rapp in particular, when speaking to me about the journey, could not conceal some marks of discontent on account of the great respect which Bonaparte had shown the clergy, and particularly to M. de Roquelaure, the Archbishop of Malines (or Mechlin). That prelate, who was a shrewd man, and had the reputation of having been in his youth more addicted to the habits of the world than to those of the cloister, had become an ecclesiastical courtier. He went to Antwerp to pay his homage to the First Consul, upon whom he heaped the most extravagant praises. Afterwards, addressing Madame Bonaparte, he told her that she was united to the First Consul by the sacred bonds of a holy alliance. In this harangue, in which unction was singularly blended with gallantry, surely it was a departure from ecclesiastical propriety to speak of sacred bonds and holy alliance when every one knew that those bonds and that alliance existed only by a civil contract. Perhaps M. de Roquelaure merely had recourse to what casuists call a pious fraud in order to engage the married couple to do that which he congratulated them on having already done. Be this as it may, it is certain that this honeyed language gained M. de Roquelaure the Consul's favour, and in a short time after he was appointed to the second class of the Institute.

CHAPTER XXI

1804

The time was passed when Bonaparte, just raised to the Consulate, only proceeded to the Temple to release the victims of the "Loi des suspects" by his sole and immediate authority. This state prison was now to be filled by the orders of his police. All the intrigues of Europe were in motion. Emissaries came daily from England, who, if they could not penetrate into the interior of France, remained in the towns near the frontiers, where they established correspondence, and published pamphlets, which they sent to Paris by post, in the form of letters.

The First Consul, on the other hand, gave way, without reserve, to the natural irritation which that power had excited by her declaration of war. He knew that the most effective war he could carry on against England would be a war against her trade.

As a prelude to that piece of madness, known by the name of the Continental system, the First Consul adopted every possible preventive measure against the introduction of English merchandise. Bonaparte's irritation against the English was not without a cause. The intelligence which reached Paris from the north of France was not very consolatory. The English fleets not only blockaded the French ports, but were acting on the offensive, and had bombarded Granville. The mayor of the town did his duty, but his colleagues, more prudent, acted differently. In the height of his displeasure Bonaparte issued a decree, by which he bestowed a scarf of honour on Letourneur, the mayor, and dismissed his colleagues from office as cowards unworthy of trust. The terms of this decree were rather severe, but they were certainly justified by the conduct of those who had abandoned their posts at a critical moment.

I come now to the subject of the invasion of England, and what the First Consul said to me respecting it. I have stated that Bonaparte never had any idea of realising the pretended project of a descent on England. The truth of this assertion will appear from a conversation which I had with him after he returned from his journey to the north. In this conversation he repeated what he had often before mentioned to me in reference to the projects and possible steps to which fortune might compel him to resort.

The peace of Amiens had been broken about seven months when, on the 15th of December 1803, the First Consul sent for me to the Tuileries. His incomprehensible behaviour to me was fresh in my mind; and as it was upwards of a year since I had seen him, I confess I did not feel quite at ease when I received the summons. He was perfectly aware that I possessed documents and data for writing his history which would describe facts correctly, and destroy the illusions with which his flatterers constantly, entertained the public. I have already stated that at that period I had no intention of the kind; but those who laboured constantly to incense him against me might have suggested apprehensions on the subject. At all events the fact is, that when he sent for me I took the precaution of providing myself with a night-cap, conceiving it to be very likely that I should be sent to sleep at Vincennes. On the day appointed for the interview Rapp was on duty. I did not conceal from him my opinion as to the possible result of my visit. "You need not be afraid," said Rapp; "the First Consul merely wishes to talk with you." He then announced me.

Bonaparte came into the grand salon where I awaited him, and addressing me in the most good-humoured way said, "What do the gossips say of my preparations for the invasion of England?"—"There is a great difference of opinion on the subject, General," I replied. "Everyone speaks according to his own views. Suchet, for instance, who comes to see me very often, has no doubt that it will take place, and hopes to give you on the occasion fresh proofs of his gratitude and fidelity."—"But Suchet tells me that you do not believe it will be attempted."—"That is true, I certainly do not."—"Why?"—"Because you told me at Antwerp, five years ago, that you would not risk France on the cast of a die—that the adventure was too hazardous—and circumstances have not altered since that time."—"You are right. Those who look forward to the invasion of England are blockheads. They do not see the affair in its true light. I can, doubtless, land in England with 100,000 men. A great battle will be fought, which I shall gain; but I must reckon upon 30,000 men killed, wounded, and prisoners. If I march on London, a second battle must be fought. I will suppose myself again victorious; but what should I do in London with an army diminished three-fourths and without the hope of reinforcements? It would be madness. Until our navy acquires superiority it is useless to think of such a project. The great assemblage of troops in the north has another object. My Government must be the first in the world, or it must fall." Bonaparte then evidently wished it to be supposed that he entertained the design of invading England in order to divert the attention of Europe to that direction.

From Dunkirk the First Consul proceeded to Antwerp, where also he had assembled experienced men to ascertain their opinions respecting the surest way of attempting a landing, the project of which was merely a pretence. The employment of large ships of war, after many discussions, abandoned in favour of a flotilla.[180]

After visiting Belgium, and giving directions there, the First Consul returned from Brussels to Paris by way of Maestricht, Liege, and Soissons.

Before my visit to the Tuileries, and even before the rupture of the peace of Amiens, certain intriguing speculators, whose extravagant zeal was not less fatal to the cause of the Bourbons than was the blind subserviency of his unprincipled adherents to the First Consul, had taken part in some underhand manoeuvres which could have no favourable result. Amongst these great contrivers of petty machinations the well-known Fauche Borel, the bookseller of Neufchatel, had long been conspicuous. Fauche Borel, whose object was to create a stir, and who wished nothing better than to be noticed and paid, failed not to come to France as soon as the peace of Amiens afforded him the opportunity. I was at that time still with Bonaparte, who was aware of all these little plots, but who felt no personal anxiety on the subject, leaving to his police the care of watching their authors.

The object of Fauche Borel's mission was to bring about a reconciliation between

180 At this period a caricature (by Gillray) appeared in London. which was sent to Paris, and strictly sought after by the police. One of the copies was shown to the First Consul, who was highly indignant at it. The French fleet was represented by a number of nut-shells. An English sailor, seated on a rock, was quietly smoking his pipe, the whiffs of which were throwing the whole squadron into disorder.—Bourrienne. Gillray's caricatures should be at the reader's side during the perusal of this work, also English Caricature and Satire on Napoleon I., by J. Ashton Chatto: and Windus, 1884.

Moreau and Pichegru. The latter general, who was banished on the 18th Fructidor 4th (September 1797), had not obtained the First Consul's permission to return to France. He lived in England, where he awaited a favourable opportunity for putting his old projects into execution. Moreau was in Paris, but no longer appeared at the levees or parties of the First Consul, and the enmity of both generals against Bonaparte, openly avowed on the part of Pichegru; and still disguised by Moreau, was a secret to nobody. But as everything was prosperous with Bonaparte he evinced contempt rather than fear of the two generals. His apprehensions were, indeed, tolerably allayed by the absence of the one and the character of the other. Moreau's name had greater weight with the army than that of Pichegru; and those who were plotting the overthrow of the Consular Government knew that that measure could not be attempted with any chance of success without the assistance of Moreau. The moment was inopportune; but, being initiated in some secrets of the British Cabinet, they knew that the peace was but a truce, and they determined to profit by that truce to effect a reconciliation which might afterwards secure a community of interests. Moreau and Pichegru had not been friends since Moreau sent to the Directory the papers seized in M. de Klinglin's carriage, which placed Pichegru's treason in so clear a light. Since that period Pichegru's name possessed no influence over the minds of the soldiers, amongst whom he had very few partisans, whilst the name of Moreau was dear to all who had conquered under his command.

Fauche Borel's design was to compromise Moreau without bringing him to any decisive step. Moreau's natural indolence, and perhaps it may be said his good sense, induced him to adopt the maxim that it was necessary to let men and things take their course; for temporizing policy is often as useful in politics as in war. Besides, Moreau was a sincere Republican; and if his habit of indecision had permitted him to adopt any resolution, it is quite certain that he would not then have assisted in the reestablishment of the Bourbons, as Pichegru wished.

What I have stated is an indispensable introduction to the knowledge of plots of more importance which preceded the great event that marked the close of the Consulship: I allude to the conspiracy of Georges, Cadoudal, Moreau, and Pichegru, and that indelible stain on the character of Napoleon,—the death of the Duc d'Enghien. Different opinions have been expressed concerning Georges' conspiracy. I shall not contradict any of them. I will relate what I learned and what I saw, in order to throw some light on that horrible affair. I am far from believing what I have read in many works, that it was planned by the police in order to pave the First Consul's way to the throne. I think that it was contrived by those who were really interested in it, and encouraged by Fouché in order to prepare his return to office.

To corroborate my opinion respecting Fouché's conduct and his manoeuvres I must remind the reader that about the close of 1803 some persons conceived the project of reconciling Moreau and Pichegru. Fouché, who was then out of the Ministry, caused Moreau to be visited by men of his own party, and who were induced, perhaps unconsciously, by Fouché's art, to influence and irritate the general's mind. It was at first intended that the Abbe David, the mutual friend of Moreau and Pichegru, should undertake to effect their reconciliation; but he, being arrested and confined in the Temple, was succeeded by a man named Lajolais, whom every circumstance proves to have been employed by Fouché. He proceeded to London, and, having prevailed on Pichegru and his friends to return to France, he set off to announce their arrival and arrange everything for their reception and destruction. Moreau's discontent was the sole foundation of this intrigue. I remember that one day, about the end of January 1804, I called on Fouché, who informed me that he had been at St. Cloud, where he had had a long conversation with the First Consul on the situation of affairs. Bonaparte told him that he was satisfied with the existing police, and hinted that it was only to make himself of consequence that he had given a false colouring to the picture. Fouché asked him what he would say if he told him that Georges and Pichegru had been for some time in Paris carrying on the conspiracy of which he had received information. The First Consul, apparently delighted at what he conceived to be Fouché's mistake, said, with an air of contempt, "You are well informed, truly! Regnier has just received a letter from London stating that Pichegru dined three days ago at Kingston with one of the King of England's ministers."

As Fouché, however, persisted in his assertion, the First Consul sent to Paris for the Grand Judge, Regnier, who showed Fouché the letter he had received. The First Consul triumphed at first to see Fouché at fault; but the latter so clearly proved that Georges and Pichegru were actually in Paris that Regnier began to fear he had been misled by his agents, whom his rival paid better than he did. The First Consul, convinced that his old minister knew more than his new one, dismissed Regnier, and remained a long time in consultation with Fouché, who on that occasion said nothing about his reinstatement for fear of exciting suspicion. He only requested that the management of the business might be entrusted to Real, with orders to obey whatever instructions he might receive from him. I will return hereafter to the arrest of Moreau and the other persons accused, and will now subjoin the account of a long interview which I had with Bonaparte in the midst of these important events.

On the 8th of March 1804, some time after the arrest but before the trial of General Moreau, I had an audience of the First Consul, which was unsought on my part. Bonaparte, after putting several unimportant questions to me as to what I was doing, what I expected he should do for me, and assuring me that he would bear me in mind, gave a sudden turn to the conversation, and said, "By the by, the report of my connection with Hortense is still kept up: the most abominable rumours have been spread as to her first child. I thought at the time that these reports had only been admitted by the public in consequence of the great desire that I should not be childless. Since you and I separated have you heard them repeated?"—"Yes, General, oftentimes; and I confess I could not have believed that this calumny would have existed so long."—"It is truly frightful to think of! You know the truth—you have seen all—heard all—nothing could have passed without your knowledge; you were in her full confidence during the time of her attachment to Duroc. I therefore expect, if you should ever write anything about me, that you will clear me from this infamous imputation. I would not have it accompany my name to posterity. I trust in you. You have never given credit to the horrid accusation?"—"No, General, never." Napoleon then entered into a number of details on the previous life of Hortense; on the way in which she conducted herself, and on the turn which her marriage had taken. "It has not turned out," he said, "as I wished: the union has not been a happy one. I am sorry for it, not only because both are dear to me, but because the circumstance countenances the infamous reports that are current among the idle as to my intimacy with her." He concluded the conversation with these words:—"Bourrienne, I sometimes think of recalling you; but as there is no good pretext for so doing, the world would say that I have need of you, and I wish it to be known that I stand in need of nobody." He again said a few words about Hortense. I answered that it would fully coincide with my conviction of the truth to do what he desired, and that I would do it; but that suppressing the false reports did not depend on me.

Hortense, in fact, while she was Mademoiselle BEAUHARNAIS, regarded Napoleon with respectful awe. She trembled when she spoke to him, and never dared to ask him a favour. When she had anything to solicit she applied to me; and if I experienced any difficulty in obtaining for her what she sought, I mentioned her as the person for whom I pleaded. "The little simpleton!" Napoleon would say, "why does she not ask me herself: is the girl afraid of me?" Napoleon never cherished for her any feeling but paternal tenderness. He loved her after his marriage with her mother as he would have loved his own child. During three years I was a witness to all their most private actions, and I declare that I never saw or heard anything that could furnish the least ground for suspicion, or that afforded the slightest trace of the existence of a culpable intimacy. This calumny must be classed among those with which malice delights to blacken the characters of men more brilliant than their fellows, and which are so readily adopted by the light-minded and unreflecting. I freely declare that did I entertain the smallest doubt with regard to this odious charge, of the existence of which I was well aware before Napoleon spoke to me on the subject, I would candidly avow it. He is no more: and let his memory be accompanied only by that, be it good or bad, which really belongs to it. Let not this reproach be one of those charged against him by the impartial historian. I must say, in concluding this delicate subject, that the principles of Napoleon on points of this kind were rigid in the utmost degree, and that a connection of the nature of that charged against him was neither in accordance with his morals nor his tastes.

I cannot tell whether what followed was a portion of his premeditated conversation with me, or whether it was the result of the satisfaction he had derived from ascertaining my perfect conviction of the purity of his conduct with regard to Hortense, and being assured that I would express that conviction. Be this as it may, as I was going out at the door he called me back, saying, "Oh! I have forgotten something." I returned. "Bourrienne," said he, "do you still keep up your acquaintance with the Fauchers?"—"Yes, General; I see them frequently."—"You are wrong."— "Why should I not? They are clever, well-educated men, and exceedingly pleasant company, especially Caesar. I derive great pleasure from their society; and then they are almost the only persons whose friendship has continued faithful to me since I left you. You know people do not care for those who can render them no service."—"Maret will not see the Fauchers."—"That may be, General; but it is nothing to me; and you must recollect that as it was through him I was introduced to them at the Tuileries, I think he ought to inform me of his reasons for dropping their acquaintance."—"I tell you again he has closed his door against them. Do you the same; I advise you." As I did not seem disposed to follow this advice without some plausible reason, the First Consul added, "You must know, then, that I learn from Caesar all that passes in your house. You do not speak very ill of me yourself, nor does any one venture to do so in your presence. You play your rubber and go to bed. But no sooner are you gone than your wife, who never liked me, and most of those who visit at your house, indulge in the most violent attacks upon me. I receive a bulletin from Caesar Faucher every day when he visits at your house; this is the way in which he requites you for your kindness, and for the asylum you afforded his brother.[181] But enough; you see I know all—farewell;" and he left me.

181 Constantine Rancher had been condemned in contumacy for the forgery of a public document.—Bourrienne.

The grave having closed over these two brothers[182], I shall merely state that they wrote me a letter the evening preceding their execution, in which they begged me to forgive their conduct towards me. The following is an extract from this letter:

In our dungeon we hear our sentence of death being cried in the streets. To-morrow we shall walk to the scaffold; but we will meet death with such calmness and courage as shall make our executioners blush. We are sixty years old, therefore our lives will only be shortened by a brief space. During our lives we have shared in common, illness, grief, pleasure, danger, and good fortune. We both entered the world on the same day, and on the same day we shall both depart from it. As to you, sir . . . . . .

I suppress what relates to myself.

The hour of the grand levee arrived just as the singular interview which I have described terminated. I remained a short time to look at this phantasmagoria. Duroc was there. As soon as he saw me he came up, and taking me into the recess of a window told me that Moreau's guilt was evident, and that he was about to be put on his trial. I made some observations on the subject, and in particular asked whether there were sufficient proofs of his guilt to justify his condemnation? "They should be cautious," said I; "it is no joke to accuse the conqueror of Hohenlinden." Duroc's answer satisfied me that he at least had no doubt on the subject. "Besides," added he, "when such a general as Moreau has been between two gendarmes he is lost, and is good for nothing more. He will only inspire pity." In vain I tried to refute this assertion so entirely contrary to facts, and to convince Duroc that Moreau would never be damaged by calling him "brigand," as was the phrase then, without proofs. Duroc persisted in his opinion. As if a political crime ever sullied the honour of any one! The result has proved that I judged rightly.

No person possessing the least degree of intelligence will be convinced that the conspiracy of Moreau, Georges, Pichegru, and the other persons accused would ever have occurred but for the secret connivance of Fouché's police.

Moreau never for a moment desired the restoration of the Bourbons. I was too well acquainted with M. Carbonnet, his most intimate friend, to be ignorant of his private sentiments. It was therefore quite impossible that he could entertain the same views as Georges, the Polignacs, Riviera, and others; and they had no intention of committing any overt acts. These latter persons had come to the Continent solely to investigate the actual state of affairs, in order to inform the Princes of the House of Bourbon with certainty how far they might depend on the foolish hopes constantly held out to them by paltry agents, who were always ready to advance their own interests at the expense of truth. These agents did indeed conspire, but it was against the Treasury of London, to which they looked for pay.

Without entering into all the details of that great trial I will relate some facts which may assist in eliciting the truth from a chaos of intrigue and falsehood.

Most of the conspirators had been lodged either in the Temple or La Force, and one of them, Bouvet de Lozier, who was confined in the Temple, attempted to hang himself. He made use of his cravat to effect his purpose, and had nearly succeeded, when a turnkey by chance entered and found him at the point of death. When he was recovered he acknowledged that though he had the courage to meet death, he was unable to endure the interrogatories

182 The Fauchers were twin brothers, distinguished in the war of the Revolution, and made brigadier-generals at the same time on the field of battle. After the Cent Jours they refused to recognise the Bourbons, and were shot by sentence of court-martial at Bordeaux. (Bouillet)

of his trial, and that he had determined to kill himself, lest he might be induced to make a confession. He did in fact confess, and it was on the day after this occurred that Moreau was arrested, while on his way from his country-seat of Grosbois to Paris.

Fouché, through the medium of his agents, had given Pichegru, Georges, and some other partisans of royalty, to understand that they might depend on Moreau, who, it was said, was quite prepared. It is certain that Moreau informed Pichegru that he (Pichegru) had been deceived, and that he had never been spoken to on the subject. Russillon declared on the trial that on the 14th of March the Polignacs said to some one, "Everything is going wrong—they do not understand each other. Moreau does not keep his word. We have been deceived." M. de Riviera declared that he soon became convinced they had been deceived, and was about to return to England when he was arrested. It is certain that the principal conspirators obtained positive information which confirmed their suspicions. They learned Moreau's declaration from Pichegru. Many of the accused declared that they soon discovered they had been deceived; and the greater part of them were about to quit Paris, when they were all arrested, almost at one and the same moment. Georges was going into La Vendée when he was betrayed by the man who, with the connivance of the police, had escorted him ever since his departure from London, and who had protected him from any interruption on the part of the police so long as it was only necessary to know where he was, or what he was about. Georges had been in Paris seven months before it was considered that the proper moment had arrived for arresting him.

The almost simultaneous arrest of the conspirators proves clearly that the police knew perfectly well where they could lay their hands upon them.

When Pichegru was required to sign his examination he refused. He said it was unnecessary; that, knowing all the secret machinery of the police, he suspected that by some chemical process they would erase all the writing except the signature, and afterwards fill up the paper with statements which he had never made. His refusal to sign the interrogatory, he added, would not prevent him from repeating before a court of justice the truth which he had stated in answer to the questions proposed to him. Fear was entertained of the disclosures he might make respecting his connection with Moreau, whose destruction was sought for, and also with respect to the means employed by the agents of Fouché to urge the conspirators to effect a change which they desired.

On the evening of the 15th of February I heard of Moreau's arrest, and early next morning I proceeded straight to the Rue St. Pierre, where M. Carbonnet resided with his nephew. I was anxious to hear from him the particulars of the general's arrest. What was my surprise! I had hardly time to address myself to the porter before he informed me that M. Carbonnet and his nephew were both arrested. "I advise you, sir," added the man, "to retire without more ado, for I can assure you that the persons who visit M. Carbonnet are watched."—"Is he still at home?" said I. "Yes, Sir; they are examining his papers."—"Then," said I, "I will go up." M. Carbonnet, of whose friendship I had reason to be proud, and whose memory will ever be dear to me, was more distressed by the arrest of his nephew and Moreau than by his own. His nephew was, however, liberated after a few hours. M. Carbonnet's papers were sealed up, and he was placed in solitary confinement at St. Pelagic.

Thus the police, who previously knew nothing, were suddenly informed of all. In spite of the numerous police agents scattered over France, it was only discovered by the declarations of Bouvet de Lozier that three successive landings had been effected, and that a fourth was expected, which, however, did not take place, because General Savary was despatched by the

First Consul with orders to seize the persons whose arrival was looked for. There cannot be a more convincing proof of the fidelity of the agents of the police to their old chief, and their combined determination of trifling with their new one.

CHAPTER XXII

1804

In order to form a just idea of the events which succeeded each other so rapidly at the commencement of 1804 it is necessary to consider them both separately and connectedly. It must be borne in mind that all Bonaparte's machinations tended to one object, the foundation of the French Empire in his favour; and it is also essential to consider how the situation of the emigrants, in reference to the First Consul, had changed since the declaration of war. As long as Bonaparte continued at peace the cause of the Bourbons had no support in foreign Cabinets, and the emigrants had no alternative but to yield to circumstances; but on the breaking out of a new war all was changed. The cause of the Bourbons became that of the powers at war with France; and as many causes concurred to unite the emigrants abroad with those who had returned but half satisfied, there was reason to fear something from their revolt, in combination with the powers arrayed against Bonaparte.

Such was the state of things with regard to the emigrants when the leaders and accomplices of Georges' conspiracy were arrested at the very beginning of 1804. The assassination of the Duc d'Enghien[183] took place on the 21st of March; on the 30th of April appeared the proposition of the Tribunate to found a Government in France under the authority of one individual; on the 18th of May came the 'Senatus-consulte', naming Napoleon Bonaparte EMPEROR, and lastly, on the 10th. of June, the sentence of condemnation on Georges and his accomplices. Thus the shedding of the blood of a Bourbon, and the placing of the crown of France on the head of a soldier of fortune were two acts interpolated in the sanguinary drama of Georges' conspiracy. It must be remembered, too, that during the period of these events we were at war with England, and on the point of seeing Austria and the Colossus of the north form a coalition against the new Emperor.

I will now state all I know relative to the death of the Duc d'Enghien. That unfortunate Prince, who was at Ettenheim, in consequence of a love affair, had no communication whatever with those who were concocting a plot in the interior. Machiavelli says that when the author of a crime cannot be discovered we should seek for those to whose advantage it turns. In the present case Machiavelli's advice will find an easy application, since the Duke's death could be advantageous only to Bonaparte, who considered it indispensable to his accession to the crown of France. The motives may be explained, but can they be justified? How could it ever be said that the Duc d'Enghien perished as a presumed accomplice in the

183 Louis Antoine Henri de Bourbon, Duc d'Enghien (1772-1804), son of the Duc de Bourbon, and grandson of the Prince de Condé, served against France in the army of Condé. When this force was disbanded he stayed at Ettenheim on account of a love affair with the Princesse Charlotte de Rohan-Rochefort. Arrested in the territory of Baden, he was taken to Vincennes, and after trial by court-martial shot in the moat, 21st May 1804. With him practically ended the house of Bourbon-Condé as his grandfather died in 1818, leaving only the Duc de Bourbon, and the Princesee Louise Adelaide, Abbesse de Remiremont, who died in 1824.

conspiracy of Georges?

Moreau was arrested on the 15th of February 1804, at which time the existence of the conspiracy was known. Pichegru and Georges were also arrested in February, and the Duc d'Enghien not till the 15th of March. Now if the Prince had really been concerned in the plot, if even he had a knowledge of it, would he have remained at Ettenheim for nearly a month after the arrest of his presumed accomplices, intelligence of which he might have obtained in the space of three days? Certainly not. So ignorant was he of that conspiracy that when informed at Ettenheim of the affair he doubted it, declaring that if it were true his father and grandfather would have made him acquainted with it. Would so long an interval have been suffered to elapse before he was arrested? Alas! cruel experience has shown that that step would have been taken in a few hours.

The sentence of death against Georges and his accomplices was not pronounced till the 10th of June 1804, and the Duc d'Enghien was shot on the 21st of March, before the trials were even commenced. How is this precipitation to be explained? If, as Napoleon has declared, the young Bourbon was an accomplice in the crime, why was he not arrested at the time the others were? Why was he not tried along with them, on the ground of his being an actual accomplice; or of being compromised, by communications with them; or, in short, because his answers might have thrown light on that mysterious affair? How was it that the name of the illustrious accused was not once mentioned in the course of that awful trial?

It can scarcely be conceived that Napoleon could say at St. Helena, "Either they contrived to implicate the unfortunate Prince in their project, and so pronounced his doom, or, by omitting to inform him of what was going on, allowed him imprudently to slumber on the brink of a precipice; for he was only a stone's cast from the frontier when they were about to strike the great blow in the name and for the interest of his family."

This reasoning is not merely absurd, it is atrocious. If the Duke was implicated by the confession of his accomplices, he should have been arrested and tried along with them. Justice required this. If he was not so implicated, where is the proof of his guilt? Because some individuals, without his knowledge, plotted to commit a crime in the name of his family he was to be shot! Because he was 130 leagues from the scene of the plot, and had no connection with it, he was to die! Such arguments cannot fail to inspire horror. It is absolutely impossible any reasonable person can regard the Duc d'Enghien as an accomplice of Cadoudal; and Napoleon basely imposed on his contemporaries and posterity by inventing such falsehoods, and investing them with the authority of his name.

Had I been then in the First Consul's intimacy I may aver, with as much confidence as pride, that the blood of the Duc d'Enghien would not have imprinted an indelible stain on the glory of Bonaparte. In this terrible matter I could have done what no one but me could even attempt, and this on account of my position, which no one else has since held with Bonaparte. I quite admit that he would have preferred others to me, and that he would have had more friendship for them than for me, supposing friendship to be compatible with the character of Bonaparte, but I knew him better than any one else. Besides, among those who surrounded him I alone could have permitted myself some return to our former familiarity on account of our intimacy of childhood. Certainly, in a matter which permanently touched the glory of Bonaparte, I should not have been restrained by the fear of some transitory fit of anger, and the reader has seen that I did not dread disgrace. Why should I have dreaded it? I had neither portfolio, nor office, nor salary, for, as I have said, I was only with Bonaparte as a friend, and we had, as it were, a common purse. I feel a conviction that it would have been very possible for me to have dissuaded Bonaparte from his fatal design, inasmuch as I positively know that his object, after the termination of the peace, was merely to frighten the emigrants, in order to drive them from Ettenheim, where great numbers, like the Duc d'Enghien, had sought refuge. His anger was particularly directed against a Baroness de Reith and a Baroness d'Ettengein, who had loudly vituperated him, and distributed numerous libels on the left bank of the Rhine. At that period Bonaparte had as little design against the Duc d'Enghien's life as against that of any other emigrant. He was more inclined to frighten than to harm him, and certainly his first intention was not to arrest the Prince, but, as I have said, to frighten the 'emigres', and to drive them to a distance. I must, however, admit that when Bonaparte spoke to Rapp and Duroc of the emigrants on the other side of the Rhine he expressed himself with much irritability: so much so, indeed, that M. de Talleyrand, dreading its effects for the Duc d'Enghien, warned that Prince, through the medium of a lady to whom he was attached, of his danger, and advised him to proceed to a greater distance from the frontier. On receiving this notice the Prince resolved to rejoin his grandfather, which he could not do but by passing through the Austrian territory. Should any doubt exist as to these facts it may be added that Sir Charles Stuart wrote to M. de Cobentzel to solicit a passport for the Duc d'Enghien; and it was solely owing to the delay of the Austrian Cabinet that time was afforded for the First Consul to order the arrest of the unfortunate Prince as soon as he had formed the horrible resolution of shedding the blood of a Bourbon. This resolution could have originated only with himself, for who would have dared to suggest it to him? The fact is, Bonaparte knew not what he did. His fever of ambition amounted to delirium; and he knew not how he was losing himself in public opinion because he did not know that opinion, to gain which he would have made every sacrifice.

When Cambacérès (who, with a slight reservation, had voted the death of Louis XVI.) warmly opposed in the Council the Duc d'Enghien's arrest, the First Consul observed to him, "Methinks, Sir, you have grown very chary of Bourbon blood!"

Meanwhile the Duc d'Enghien was at Ettenheim, indulging in hope rather than plotting conspiracies. It is well known that an individual made an offer to the Prince de Condé to assassinate the First Consul, but the Prince indignantly rejected the proposition, and nobly refused to recover the rights of the Bourbons at the price of such a crime. The individual above-mentioned was afterwards discovered to be an agent of the Paris police, who had been commissioned to draw the Princes into a plot which would have ruined them, for public feeling revolts at assassination under any circumstances.

It has been alleged that Louis XVIII.'s refusal to treat with Bonaparte led to the fatal catastrophe of the Duc d'Enghien's death. The first correspondence between Louis XVIII. and the First Consul, which has been given in these Memoirs, clearly proves the contrary. It is certainly probable that Louis XVIII.'s refusal to renounce his rights should have irritated Bonaparte. But it was rather late to take his revenge two years after, and that too on a Prince totally ignorant of those overtures. It is needless to comment on such absurdities. It is equally unnecessary to speak of the mysterious being who often appeared at meetings in the Faubourg St. Germain, and who was afterwards discovered to be Pichegru.

A further light is thrown on this melancholy catastrophe by a conversation Napoleon had, a few days after his elevation to the imperial throne, with M. Masaias, the French Minister at the Court of the Grand Duke of Baden. This conversation took place at Aix-la-Chapelle. After some remarks on the intrigues of the emigrants Bonaparte observed, "You ought at least to have prevented the plots which the Duc d'Enghien was hatching at Ettenheim."—"Sire, I am too old to learn to tell a falsehood. Believe me, on this subject your Majesty's ear has been abused."—"Do you not think, then, that had the conspiracy of Georges and Pichegru proved successful, the Prince would have passed the Rhine, and have come post to Paris?"

M. Massias, from whom I had these particulars, added, "At this last question of the Emperor I hung down my head and was silent, for I saw he did not wish to hear the truth."

Now let us consider, with that attention which the importance of the subject demands, what has been said by the historians of St. Helena.

Napoleon said to his companions in exile that "the Duc d'Enghien's death must be attributed either to an excess of zeal for him (Napoleon), to private views, or to mysterious intrigues. He had been blindly urged on; he was, if he might say so, taken by surprise. The measure was precipitated, and the result predetermined."

This he might have said; but if he did so express himself, how are we to reconcile such a declaration with the statement of O'Meara? How give credit to assertions so very opposite?

Napoleon said to M. de Las Casas:

> "One day when alone, I recollect it well, I was taking my coffee, half seated on the table at which I had just dined, when suddenly information was brought to me that a new conspiracy had been discovered. I was warmly urged to put an end to these enormities; they represented to me that it was time at last to give a lesson to those who had been day after day conspiring against my life; that this end could only be attained by shedding the blood of one of them; and that the Duc d'Enghien, who might now be convicted of forming part of this new conspiracy, and taken in the very act, should be that one. It was added that he had been seen at Strasburg; that it was even believed that he had been in Paris; and that the plan was that he should enter France by the east at the moment of the explosion, whilst the Duc de Berri was disembarking in the west. I should tell you," observed the Emperor, "that I did not even know precisely who the Duc d'Enghien was (the Revolution having taken place when I was yet a very young man, and I having never been at Court), and that I was quite in the dark as to where he was at that moment. Having been informed on those points I exclaimed that if such were the case the Duke ought to be arrested, and that orders should be given to that effect. Everything had been foreseen and prepared; the different orders were already drawn up, nothing remained to be done but to sign them, and the fate of the young Prince was thus decided."

Napoleon next asserts that in the Duke's arrest and condemnation all the usual forms were strictly observed. But he has also declared that the death of that unfortunate Prince will be an eternal reproach to those who, carried away by a criminal zeal, waited not for their Sovereign's orders to execute the sentence of the court-martial. He would, perhaps, have allowed the Prince to live; but yet he said, "It is true I wished to make an example which should deter."

It has been said that the Duc d'Enghien addressed a letter to Napoleon, which was not delivered till after the execution. This is false and absurd! How could that Prince write to Bonaparte to offer him his services and to solicit the command of an army? His interrogatory makes no mention of this letter, and is in direct opposition to the sentiments which that letter would attribute to him. The truth is, no such letter ever existed. The individual who was with the Prince declared he never wrote it. It will never be believed that any one would have presumed to withhold from Bonaparte a letter on which depended the fate of so august a victim.

In his declarations to his companions in exile Napoleon endeavoured either to free himself of this crime or to justify it. His fear or his susceptibility was such, that in discoursing with strangers he merely said, that had he known of the Prince's letter, which was not delivered to him.—God knows why!—until after he had breathed his last, he would have pardoned him. But at a subsequent date he traced, with his own hand, his last thoughts, which he supposed would be consecrated in the minds of his contemporaries, and of posterity. Napoleon, touching on the subject which he felt would be one of the most important attached to his memory, said that if the thing were to do again he would act as he then did. How does this declaration tally with his avowal, that if he had received the Prince's letter he should have lived? This is irreconcilable. But if we compare all that Napoleon said at St. Helena, and which has been transmitted to us by his faithful followers; if we consider his contradictions when speaking of the Duc d'Enghien's death to strangers, to his friends, to the public, or to posterity, the question ceases to be doubtful. Bonaparte wished to strike a blow which would terrify his enemies. Fancying that the Duc de Berri was ready to land in France, he despatched his aide de camp Savary, in disguise, attended by gendarmes, to watch the Duke's landing at Biville, near Dieppe. This turned out a fruitless mission. The Duke was warned in time not to attempt the useless and dangerous enterprise, and Bonaparte, enraged to see one prey escape him, pounced upon another. It is well known that Bonaparte often, and in the presence even of persons whom he conceived to have maintained relations with the partisans of the Bourbons at Paris, expressed himself thus: "I will put an end to these conspiracies. If any of the emigrants conspire they shall be shot. I have been told that Cobentzel harbours some of them. I do not believe this; but if it be true, Cobentzel shall be arrested and shot along with them. I will let the Bourbons know I am not to be trifled with." The above statement of facts accounts for the suppositions respecting the probable influence of the Jacobins in this affair. It has been said, not without some appearance of reason, that to get the Jacobins to help him to ascend the throne Bonaparte consented to sacrifice a victim of the blood royal, as the only pledge capable of ensuring them against the return of the proscribed family. Be this as it may, there are no possible means of relieving Bonaparte from his share of guilt in the death of the Duc d'Enghien.

To the above facts, which came within my own knowledge, I may add the following curious story, which was related to me by an individual who himself heard it from the secretary of General Davoust.

Davoust was commanding a division in the camp of Boulogne, and his secretary when proceeding thither to join him met in the diligence a man who seemed to be absorbed in affliction. This man during the whole journey never once broke silence but by some deep sighs, which he had not power to repress. General Davoust's secretary observed him with curiosity and interest, but did not venture to intrude upon his grief by any conversation. The concourse of travellers from Paris to the camp was, however, at that time very great, and the inn at which the diligence stopped in the evening was so crowded that it was impossible to assign a chamber to each traveller. Two, therefore, were put into one room, and it so happened that the secretary was lodged with his mysterious travelling companion.

When they were alone he addressed him in a torso of interest which banished all appearance of intrusion. He inquired whether the cause of his grief was of a nature to admit of any alleviation, and offered to render him any assistance in his power. "Sir," replied the stranger, "I am much obliged for the sympathy you express for me—I want nothing. There is no possible consolation for me. My affliction can end only with my life. You shall judge for yourself, for the interest you seem to take in my misfortune fully justifies my confidence. I was quartermaster in the select gendarmerie, and formed part of a detachment which was ordered to Vincennes. I passed the night there under arms, and at daybreak was ordered down to the moat with six men. An execution was to take place. The prisoner was brought out, and I gave the word to fire. The man fell, and after the execution I learned that we had shot the Duc d'Enghien. Judge of my horror! . . . I knew the prisoner only by the name of the brigand of La Vendée! . . . I could no longer remain in the service—I obtained my discharge, and am about to retire to my family. Would that I had done so sooner!" The above has been related to me and other persons by Davoust's secretary, whom I shall not name.

CHAPTER XXIII

1804

I will now narrate more fully the sanguinary scene which took place at Vincennes. General Ordener, commanding the mounted grenadiers of the Guard, received orders from the War Minister to proceed to the Rhine, to give instructions to the chiefs of the gendarmerie of New Brissac, which was placed at his disposal. General Ordener sent a detachment of gendarmerie to Ettenheim, where the Duc d'Enghien was arrested on the 15th of March. He was immediately conducted to the citadel of Strasburg, where he remained till the 18th, to give time for the arrival of orders from Paris. These orders were given rapidly, and executed promptly, for the carriage which conveyed the unfortunate Prince arrived at the barrier at eleven o'clock on the morning of the 20th, where it remained for five hours, and afterwards proceeded by the exterior boulevards on the road to Vincennes, where it arrived at night. Every scene of this horrible drama was acted under the veil of night: the sun did not even shine upon its tragical close. The soldiers received orders to proceed to Vincennes at night. It was at night that the fatal gates of the fortress were closed upon the Prince. At night the Council assembled and tried him, or rather condemned him without trial. When the clock struck six in the morning the orders were given to fire, and the Prince ceased to exist.

Here a reflection occurs to me. Supposing one were inclined to admit that the Council held on the 10th of March had some connection with the Duc d'Enghien's arrest, yet as no Council was held from the time of the Duke's arrival at the barrier to the moment of his execution, it could only be Bonaparte himself who issued the orders which were too punctually obeyed. When the dreadful intelligence of the Duc d'Enghien's death was spread in Paris it excited a feeling of consternation which recalled the recollection of the Reign of Terror. Could Bonaparte have seen the gloom which pervaded Paris, and compared it with the joy which prevailed on the day when he returned victorious from the field of Marengo, he would have felt that he had tarnished his glory by a stain which could never be effaced.

About half-past twelve on the 22d of March I was informed that some one wished to speak with me. It was Harrel.[184] I will relate word for word what he communicated to me. Harrel probably thought that he was bound in gratitude to acquaint me with these details; but he owed me no gratitude, for it was much against my will that he had encouraged the conspiracy of Ceracchi, and received the reward of his treachery in that crime. The following is Harrel's statement:—

"On the evening of the day before yesterday, when the Prince arrived, I was asked whether I had a room to lodge a prisoner in; I replied, No—that there were only my apartments and the Council-chamber. I was told to prepare instantly a room in which a prisoner could sleep

184 Harrel, who had been unemployed till the plot of Arena and Ceracchi on the 18th Vendemiairean IX (10th October 1800) which he had feigned to join, and had then revealed to the police (see ante), had been made Governor of Vincennes.

who was to arrive that evening. I was also desired to dig a pit in the courtyard.[185]

"I replied that that could not be easily done, as the courtyard was paved. The moat was then fixed upon, and there the pit was dug. The Prince arrived at seven o'clock in the evening; he was perishing with cold and hunger. He did not appear dispirited. He said he wanted something to eat, and to go to bed afterwards. His apartment not being yet sufficiently aired, I took him into my own, and sent into the village for some refreshment. The Prince sat down to table, and invited me to eat with him. He then asked me a number of questions respecting Vincennes—what was going on there, and other particulars. He told me that he had been brought up in the neighbourhood of the castle, and spoke to me with great freedom and kindness. 'What do they want with me?' he said. 'What do they mean to do with me?' But these questions betrayed no uneasiness or anxiety. My wife, who was ill, was lying in the same room in an alcove, closed by a railing. She heard, without being perceived, all our conversation, and she was exceedingly agitated, for she recognised the Prince, whose foster-sister she was, and whose family had given her a pension before the Revolution.

"The Prince hastened to bed, but before he could have fallen asleep the judges sent to request his presence in the Council-chamber. I was not present at his examination; but when it was concluded he returned to his chamber, and when they came to read his sentence to him he was in a profound sleep. In a few moments after he was led out for execution. He had so little suspicion of the fate that awaited him that on descending the staircase leading to the moat he asked where they were taking him. He received no answer. I went before the Prince with a lantern. Feeling the cold air which came up the staircase he pressed my arm and said, 'Are they going to put me into a dungeon?'"

The rest is known. I can yet see Harrel shuddering while thinking of this action of the Prince's.

Much has been said about a lantern which it is pretended was attached to one of the Duc d'Enghien's button-holes. This is a pure invention. Captain Dautancourt, whose sight was not very good, took the lantern out of Harrel's hand to read the sentence to the victim, who had been condemned with as little regard to judicial forms as to justice. This circumstance probably gave rise to the story about the lantern to which I have just alluded. The fatal event took place at six o'clock on the morning of the 21st of March, and it was then daylight.

General Savary did not dare to delay the execution of the sentence, although the Prince urgently demanded to have an interview with the First Consul. Had Bonaparte seen the prince there can be little doubt but that he would have saved his life. Savary, however, thought himself bound to sacrifice his own opinions to the powerful faction which then controlled the First Consul; and whilst he thought he was serving his master, he was in fact only serving the faction to which, I must say, he did not belong. The truth is, that General Savary can only be reproached for not having taken upon himself to suspend the execution, which very probably would not have taken place had it been suspended. He was merely an instrument, and regret on his part would, perhaps, have told more in his favour than his vain efforts to justify Bonaparte. I have just said that if there had been any suspension there would have

185 This fact must be noted. Harrel is told to dig a trench before the sentence. Thus it was known that they had come to kill the Duc d'Enghien. How can this be answered? Can it possibly be supposed that anyone, whoever it was, would have dared to give each an order in anticipation if the order had not been the carrying out of a formal command of Bonaparte? That is incredible.—Bourrienne.

been no execution; and I think this is almost proved by the uncertainty which must have existed in the mind of the First Consul. If he had made up his mind all the measures would have been taken in advance, and if they had been, the carriage of the Duke would certainly not have been kept for five hours at the barriers. Besides, it is certain that the first intention was to take the Prince to the prison of the Temple.

From all that I have stated, and particularly from the non-suspension of the execution, it appears to me as clear as day that General Savary had received a formal order from Bonaparte for the Duc d'Enghien's death, and also a formal order that it should be so managed as to make it impossible to speak to Bonaparte again on the subject until all should be over. Can there be a more evident, a more direct proof of this than the digging of the grave beforehand? I have repeated Harrel's story just as he related it to me. He told it me without solicitation, and he could not invent a circumstance of this nature.

General Savary was not in the moat during the execution, but on the bank, from whence he could easily see all that passed. Another circumstance connected with the Duc d'Enghien's death has been mentioned, which is true. The Prince had a little dog; this faithful animal returned incessantly to the fatal spot in the moat. There are few who have not seen that spot. Who has not made a pilgrimage to Vincennes and dropped a tear where the victim fell? The fidelity of the poor dog excited so much interest that the police prevented any one from visiting the fatal spot, and the dog was no longer heard to howl over his master's grave.

I promised to state the truth respecting the death of the Duc d'Enghien, and I have done so, though it has cost me some pain. Harrel's narrative, and the shocking circumstance of the grave being dug beforehand, left me no opportunity of cherishing any doubts I might have wished to entertain; and everything which followed confirmed the view I then took of the subject. When Harrel left me on the 22d I determined to go to Malmaison to see Madame Bonaparte, knowing, from her sentiments towards the House of Bourbon, that she would be in the greatest affliction. I had previously sent to know whether it would be convenient for her to see me, a precaution I had never before observed, but which I conceived to be proper upon that occasion. On my arrival I was immediately introduced to her boudoir, where she was alone with Hortense and Madame de Rémusat. They were all deeply afflicted. "Bourrienne," exclaimed Josephine, as soon as she perceived me, "what a dreadful event! Did you but know the state of mind Bonaparte is in! He avoids, he dreads the presence of every one! Who could have suggested to him such an act as this?" I then acquainted Josephine with the particulars which I had received from Harrel. "What barbarity!" she resumed. "But no reproach can rest upon me, for I did everything to dissuade him from this dreadful project. He did not confide the secret to me, but I guessed it, and he acknowledged all. How harshly he repelled my entreaties! I clung to him! I threw myself at his feet! 'Meddle with what concerns you!' he exclaimed angrily. 'This is not women's business! Leave me!' And he repulsed me with a violence which he had never displayed since our first interview after your return from Egypt. Heavens! what will become of us?"

I could say nothing to calm affliction and alarm in which I participated, for to my grief for the death of the Duc d'Enghien was added my regret that Bonaparte should be capable of such a crime. "What," said Josephine, "can be thought of this in Paris? He must be the object of universal, imprecation, for even here his flatterers appear astounded when they are out of his presence. How wretched we have been since yesterday; and he! . . . . . . You know what he is when he is dissatisfied with himself. No one dare speak to him, and all is mournful around us. What a commission he gave to Savary! You know I do not like the general, because he is one of those whose flatteries will contribute to ruin Bonaparte. Well! I pitied Savary when he came yesterday to fulfil a commission which the Duc d'Enghien had entrusted to him. Here," added Josephine, "is his portrait and a lock of his hair, which he has requested me to transmit to one who was dear to him. Savary almost shed tears when he described to me the last moments of the Duke; then, endeavouring to resume his self-possession, he said: 'It is in vain to try to be indifferent, Madame! It is impossible to witness the death of such a man unmoved!'"

Josephine afterwards informed me of the only act of courage which occurred at this period—namely, the resignation which M. de Chateaubriand had sent to Bonaparte. She admired his conduct greatly, and said: "What a pity he is not surrounded by men of this description! It would be the means of preventing all the errors into which he is led by the constant approbation of those about him." Josephine thanked me for my attention in coming to see her at such an unhappy juncture; and I confess that it required all the regard I cherished for her to induce me to do so, for at that moment I should not have wished to see the First Consul, since the evil was irreparable. On the evening of that day nothing was spoken of but the transaction of the 21st of March, and the noble conduct of M. de Chateaubriand. As the name of that celebrated man is for ever written in characters of honour in the history of that period, I think I may with propriety relate here what I know respecting his previous connection with Bonaparte.

I do not recollect the precise date of M. de Chateaubriand's return to France; I only know that it was about the year 1800, for we were, I think, still at the Luxembourg: However, I recollect perfectly that Bonaparte began to conceive prejudices against him; and when I one day expressed my surprise to the First Consul that M. de Chateaubriand's name did not appear on any of the lists which he had ordered to be presented to him for filling up vacant places, he said: "He has been mentioned to me, but I replied in a way to check all hopes of his obtaining any appointment. He has notions of liberty and independence which will not suit my system. I would rather have him my enemy than my forced friend. At all events, he must wait awhile; I may, perhaps, try him first in a secondary place, and, if he does well, I may advance him."

The above is, word for word, what Bonaparte said the first time I conversed with him about M. de Chateaubriand. The publication of 'Atala' and the 'Genie du Christianisme' suddenly gave Chateaubriand celebrity, and attracted the attention of the First Consul. Bonaparte who then meditated the restoration of religious worship: in France, found himself wonderfully supported by the publication of a book which excited the highest interest, and whose superior merit led the public mind to the consideration of religious topics. I remember Madame Bacciocchi coming one day to visit her brother with a little volume in her hand; it was 'Atala'. She presented it to the First Consul, and begged he would read it. "What, more romances!" exclaimed he. "Do you think I have time to read all your fooleries?" He, however, took the book from his sister and laid it down on my desk. Madame Bacciocchi then solicited the erasure of M. de Chateaubriand's name from the list of emigrants. "Oh! oh!" said Bonaparte, "it is Chateaubriand's book, is it? I will read it, then. Bourrienne, write to Fouché to erase his name from the list."

Bonaparte, at that time paid so little attention to what was doing in the literary world that he was not aware of Chateaubriand being the author of 'Atala'. It was on the recommendation of M. de Fontanel that Madame Bacciocchi tried this experiment, which was attended by complete success. The First Consul read 'Atala', and was much pleased with it. On the publication of the 'Genie du Christianisme' some time after, his first prejudices were wholly removed. Among the persons about him there were many who dreaded to see a man of de Chateaubriand's talent approach the First Consul, who knew how to appreciate superior merit when it did not exite his envy.

Our relations with the Court of the Vatican being renewed, and Cardinal Fesch appointed Ambassador to the Holy See, Bonaparte conceived the idea of making M. de Chateaubriand first secretary to the Embassy, thinking that the author of the 'Genie du Christianisme' was peculiarly fitted to make up for his uncle's deficiency of talent in the capital of the Christian world, which was destined to become the second city of the Empire.

It was not a little extraordinary to let a man, previously, a stranger to diplomatic business; stepping over all the intermediate degrees; and being at once invested with the functions of first secretary to an important Embassy. I oftener than once heard the First Consul congratulate himself on having made the appointment. I knew, though Bonaparte was not aware of the circumstance at the time, that Chateaubriand at first refused the situation, and that he was only induced to accept it by the entreaties of the head of the clergy, particularly of the Abby Emery, a man of great influence. They represented to the author of the 'Genie du Christianisme' that it was necessary he should accompany the uncle of the First Consul to Rome; and M. de Chateaubriand accordingly resolved to do so.

However, clouds, gathered; I do not know from what cause, between the ambassador and his secretary. All I know is, that on Bonaparte being informed of the circumstance he took the part of the Cardinal, and the friends of M. de Chateaubriand expected to see him soon deprived of his appointment, when, to the great astonishment of every one, the secretary to the Roman Embassy, far from being disgraced, was raised by the First Consul to the rank of Minister Plenipotentiary to the Valais, with leave to travel in Switzerland and Italy, together with the promise of the first vacant Embassy.

This favour excited a considerable sensation at the Tuileries; but as it was known to be the will and pleasure of the First Consul all expression of opinion on the subject was confined to a few quiet murmurs that Bonaparte had done for the name of Chateaubriand what, in fact, he had done only on account of his talent. It was during the continuance of this favour that the second edition of the 'Genie du Christianisme' was dedicated to the First Consul.

M. de Chateaubriand returned to France previously to entering on the fulfilment of his new mission. He remained for some months in Paris, and on the day appointed for his departure he went to take leave of the First Consul. By a singular chance it happened to be the fatal morning of the 21st of March, and consequently only a few hours after the Duc d'Enghien had been shot. It is unnecessary to observe that M. de Chateaubriand was ignorant of the fatal event. However, on his return home he said to his friends that he had remarked a singular change in the appearance of the First Consul, and that there was a sort of sinister expression in his countenance. Bonaparte saw his new minister amidst the crowd who attended the audience, and several times seemed inclined to step forward to speak to him, but as often turned away, and did not approach him the whole morning. A few hours after, when M. de Chateaubriand mentioned his observations to some of his friends; he was made acquainted with the cause of that agitation which, in spite of all his strength of mind and self-command, Bonaparte could not disguise.

M. de Chateaubriand instantly resigned his appointment of Minister Plenipotentiary to the Valais. For several days his friends were much alarmed for his safety, and they called every morning early to ascertain whether he had not been carried off during the night.

Their fears were not without foundation. I must confess that I, who knew Bonaparte well, was somewhat surprised that no serious consequence attended the anger he manifested on receiving the resignation of the man who had dedicated his work to him. In fact, there was good reason for apprehension, and it was not without considerable difficulty that Elisa succeeded in averting the threatened storm. From this time began a state of hostility between Bonaparte and Chateaubriand which only terminated at the Restoration.

I am persuaded, from my knowledge of Bonaparte's character, that though he retained implacable resentment against a returned emigrant who had dared to censure his conduct in so positive a manner, yet, his first burst of anger being soothed, that which was the cause of hatred was at the same time the ground of esteem. Bonaparte's animosity was, I confess, very natural, for he could not disguise from himself the real meaning of a resignation made under such circumstances. It said plainly, "You have committed a crime, and I will not serve your Government, which is stained with the blood of a Bourbon!" I can therefore very well imagine that Bonaparte could never pardon the only man who dared to give him such a lesson in the midst of the plenitude of his power. But, as I have often had occasion to remark, there was no unison between Bonaparte's feelings and his judgment.

I find a fresh proof of this in the following passage, which he dictated to M. de Montholon at St. Helena (Memoires, tome iv. p 248). "If," said he, "the royal confidence had not been placed in men whose minds were unstrung by too important circumstances, or who, renegade to their country, saw no safety or glory for their master's throne except under the yoke of the Holy Alliance; if the Duc de Richelieu, whose ambition was to deliver his country from the presence of foreign bayonets; if Chateaubriand, who had just rendered valuable services at Ghent; if they had had the direction of affairs, France would have emerged from these two great national crises powerful and redoubtable. Chateaubriand had received from Nature the sacred fire-his works show it! His style is not that of Racine but of a prophet. Only he could have said with impunity in the chamber of peers, 'that the redingote and cocked hat of Napoleon, put on a stick on the coast of Brest, would make all Europe run to arms.'"

The immediate consequences of the Duc d'Enghien's death were not confined to the general consternation which that unjustifiable stroke of state policy produced in the capital. The news spread rapidly through the provinces and foreign countries, and was everywhere accompanied by astonishment and sorrow. There is in the departments a separate class of society, possessing great influence, and constituted entirely of persons usually called the "Gentry of the Chateaux," who may be said to form the provincial Faubourg St. Germain, and who were overwhelmed by the news. The opinion of the Gentry of the Chateaux was not hitherto unfavourable to the First Consul, for the law of hostages which he repealed had been felt very severely by them. With the exception of some families accustomed to consider themselves, in relation to the whole world, what they were only within the circle of a couple of leagues; that is to say, illustrious personages, all the inhabitants of the provinces, though they might retain some attachment to the ancient order of things, had viewed with satisfaction the substitution of the Consular for the Directorial government, and entertained no personal dislike to the First Consul. Among the Chateaux, more than anywhere else, it had always been the custom to cherish Utopian ideas respecting the management of public affairs, and to criticise the acts of the Government. It is well known that at this time there was not in all France a single old mansion surmounted by its two weathercocks which had not a systems of policy peculiar to itself, and in which the question whether the First Consul would play the part of Cromwell or Monk was not frequently canvassed. In those innocent controversies the little news which the Paris papers were allowed to publish was freely discussed, and a confidential letter from Paris sometimes furnished food for the conversation of a whole week.

While I was with Bonaparte he often talked to me about the life in the Chateaux, which he considered as the happiest for men with sufficient income and exempt from ambition. He knew and could appreciate this sort of life, for he often told me the period of his life which he remembered. with the greatest pleasure was that which he had passed in a Chateau of the family of Boulat du Colombier near Valence. Bonaparte set great value on the opinion of the Chateaux, because while living in the country he had observed the moral influence which their inhabitants exercise over their neighbourhood. He had succeeded to a great degree in conciliating them, but the news of the death of the Duc d'Enghien alienated from him minds which were still wavering, and even those which had already declared in his favour. That act of tyranny dissolved the charm which had created hope from his government and awakened affections which had as yet only slumbered. Those to whom this event was almost indifferent also joined in condemning it; for there are certain aristocratic ideas which are always fashionable in a certain class of society. Thus for different causes this atrocity gave a retrograde direction to public opinion, which had previously been favourably disposed to Bonaparte throughout the whole of France.

The consequences were not less important, and might have been disastrous with respect to foreign Courts. I learned, through a channel which does not permit me to entertain any doubt of the correctness of my information, that as soon as the Emperor Alexander received the news it became clear that England might conceive a well-founded hope of forming a new coalition against France. Alexander openly expressed his indignation. I also learned with equal certainty that when Mr. Pitt was informed of the death of the French Prince he said, "Bonaparte has now done himself more mischief than we have done him since the last declaration of war."[186]

Pitt was not the man to feel much concern for the death of any one; but he understood and seized all the advantages afforded to him by this great error of policy committed by the most formidable enemy of England. In all the Treasury journals published in London Bonaparte was never spoken of under any other name than that of the "assassin of the Duc d'Enghien." The inert policy of the Cabinet of Vienna prevented the manifestation of its displeasure by remonstrances, or by any outward act. At Berlin, in consequence of the neighbourhood of the French troops in Hanover, the commiseration for the death of the Duc d'Enghien was also confined to the King's cabinet, and more particularly to the salons of the Queen of Prussia; but it is certain that that transaction almost everywhere changed the disposition of sovereigns towards the First Consul, and that if it did not cause, it at least hastened the success of the negotiations which England was secretly carrying on with Austria and Prussia. Every Prince of Germany was offended by the violation of the Grand Duke of Baden's territory, and the death of a Prince could not fail everywhere to irritate that kind of sympathy of blood and of race which had hitherto always influenced the crowned heads and sovereign families of Europe; for it was felt as an injury to all of them.

When Louis XVIII. learned the death of the Duc d'Enghien he wrote to the King of Spain, returning him the insignia of the Order of the Golden Fleece (which had also been conferred

186 The remark made on this murder by the astute cold-blooded Fouché is well known. He said, "It was worse than a crime—it was a blunder!"—Editor of 1836 Edition..

on Bonaparte), with the accompanying letter:

> SIRE, MONSIEUR, AND DEAR COUSIN—It is with regret that I send back to you the insignia of the Order of the Golden Fleece which his Majesty, your father, of glorious memory conferred upon me. There can be nothing in common between me and the great criminal whom audacity and fortune have placed on my throne, since he has had the barbarity to stain himself with the blood of a Bourbon, the Duc d'Enghien. Religion might make me pardon an assassin, but the tyrant of my people must always be my enemy. In the present age it is more glorious to merit a sceptre than to possess one. Providence, for incomprehensible reasons, may condemn me to end my days in exile, but neither my contemporaries nor posterity shall ever have to say, that in the period of adversity I showed my self unworthy of occupying the throne of my ancestors.
>
> LOUIS

The death of the Duc d'Enghien was a horrible episode in the proceedings of the great trial which was then preparing, and which was speedily followed by the accession of Bonaparte to the Imperial dignity. It was not one of the least remarkable anomalies of the epoch to see the judgment by which criminal enterprises against the Republic were condemned pronounced in the name of the Emperor who had so evidently destroyed that Republic. This anomaly certainly was not removed by the subtlety, by the aid of which he at first declared himself Emperor of the Republic, as a preliminary to his proclaiming himself Emperor of the French. Setting aside the means, it must be acknowledged that it is impossible not to admire the genius of Bonaparte, his tenacity in advancing towards his object, and that adroit employment of suppleness and audacity which made him sometimes dare fortune, sometimes avoid difficulties which he found insurmountable, to arrive, not merely at the throne of Louis XVI., but at the reconstructed throne of Charlemagne.

CHAPTER XXIV

1804

I shall now proceed to relate what I knew at the time and what I have since learnt of the different phases of the trial of Georges, Pichegru, Moreau and the other persons accused of conspiracy,—a trial to all the proceedings of which I closely attended. From those proceedings I was convinced that Moreau was no conspirator, but at the same time I must confess that it is very probable the First Consul might believe that he had been engaged in the plot, and I am also of opinion that the real conspirators believed Moreau to be their accomplice and their chief; for the object of the machinations of the police agents was to create a foundation for such a belief, it being important to the success of their scheme.

It has been stated that Moreau was arrested on the day after the confessions made by Bouvet de Lozier; Pichegru was taken by means of the most infamous treachery that a man can be guilty of. The official police had at last ascertained that he was in Paris, but they could not learn the place of his concealment. The police agents had in vain exerted all their efforts to discover him, when an old friend, who had given him his last asylum, offered to deliver him up for 100,000 crowns. This infamous fellow gave an exact description of the chamber which Pichegru occupied in the Rue de Chabanais, and in consequence of his information Comminges, commissary of police, proceeded thither, accompanied by some determined men. Precautions were necessary, because it was known that Pichegru was a man of prodigious bodily strength, and that besides, as he possessed the means of defence, he would not allow himself to be taken without making a desperate resistance. The police entered his chamber by using false keys, which the man who had sold him had the baseness to get made for them. A light was burning on his night table. The party of police, directed by Comminges, overturned the table, extinguished the light, and threw themselves on the general, who struggled with all his strength, and cried out loudly. They were obliged to bind him, and in this state the conqueror of Holland was removed to the Temple, out of which he was destined never to come alive.

It must be owned that Pichegru was far from exciting the same interest as Moreau. The public, and more especially the army, never pardoned him for his negotiations with the Prince de Condé prior to the 18th Fructidor. However, I became acquainted with a trait respecting him while he was in Paris which I think does him much honour. A son of M. Lagrenee, formerly director of the French Academy at Rome, had been one of Pichegru's aides de camp. This young man, though he had obtained the rank of captain, resigned on the banishment of his general, and resumed the pencil, which he had lad aside for the sword. Pichegru, while he was concealed in Paris; visited his former aide de camp, who insisted upon giving him an asylum; but Pichegru positively refused to accept M. Lagrenee's offer, being determined not to commit a man who had already given him so strong a proof of friendship. I learned this fact by a singular coincidence. At this period Madame de Bourrienne wished to have a portrait of one of our children; she was recommended to M. Lagrenee, and he related the circumstance to her.

It was on the night of the 22d of February that Pichegru was arrested in the manner I have described. The deceitful friend who gave him up was named Le Blanc, and he went to settle at Hamburg with the reward of his treachery, I had entirely lost sight of Pichegru since we left Brienne, for Pichegru was also a pupil of that establishment; but, being older than either Bonaparte or I, he was already a tutor when we were only scholars, and I very well recollect that it was he who examined Bonaparte in the four first rules of arithmetic.

Pichegru belonged to an agricultural family of Franche-Comte. He had a relation, a minim,' in that country. The minim, who had the charge of educating the pupils of the Military School of Brienne, being very poor, and their poverty not enabling them to hold out much inducement to other persons to assist them, they applied to the minims of Franche-Comte. In consequence of this application Pichegru's relation, and some other minims, repaired to Brienne. An aunt of Pichegru, who was a sister of the order of charity, accompanied them, and the care of the infirmary was entrusted to her. This good woman took her nephew to Brienne with her, and he was educated at the school gratuitously. As soon as his age permitted, Pichegru was made a tutor; but all, his ambition was to become a minim. He was, however, dissuaded from that pursuit by his relation, and he adopted the military profession. There is this further remarkable circumstance in the youth of Pichegru, that, though he was older by several years than Bonaparte, they were both made lieutenants of artillery at the same time. What a difference in their destiny! While the one was preparing to ascend a throne the other was a solitary prisoner in the dungeon of the Temple.

I had no motive to induce me to visit either the Temple or La Force, but I received at the time circumstantial details of what was passing in those prisons, particularly in the former; I went, however, frequently to St. Pelagie, where M. Carbonnet was confined. As soon as I knew that he was lodged in that prison I set about getting an admission from Real, who smoothed all difficulties. M. Carbonnet was detained two months in solitary confinement. He was several times examined, but the interrogatories produced no result, and, notwithstanding the desire to implicate him in consequence of the known intimacy between him and Moreau, it was at last found impossible to put him on trial with the other parties accused.

The Temple had more terrors than St. Pelagie, but not for the prisoners who were committed to it, for none of those illustrious victims of police machination displayed any weakness, with the exception of Bouvet de Lozier, who, being sensible of his weakness, wished to prevent its consequences by death. The public, however, kept their attention riveted on the prison in which Moreau was confined. I have already mentioned that Pichegru was conveyed thither on the night of the 22d of February; a fortnight later Georges was arrested, and committed to the same prison.

Either Real or Desmarets, and sometimes both together, repaired to the Temple to examine the prisoners. In vain the police endeavoured to direct public odium against the prisoners by placarding lists of their names through the whole of Paris, even before they were arrested. In those lists they were styled "brigands," and at the head of "the brigands," the name of General Moreau shone conspicuously. An absurdity without a parallel. The effect produced was totally opposite to that calculated on; for, as no person could connect the idea of a brigand with that of a general who was the object of public esteem, it was naturally concluded that those whose names were placarded along with his were no more brigands than he.

Public opinion was decidedly in favour of Moreau, and every one was indignant at seeing him described as a brigand. Far from believing him guilty, he was regarded as a victim fastened on because his reputation embarrassed Bonaparte; for Moreau had always been looked up to as capable of opposing the accomplishment of the First Consul's ambitious views. The whole crime of Moreau was his having numerous partisans among those who still clung to the phantom of the Republic, and that crime was unpardonable in the eyes of the First Consul, who for two years had ruled the destinies of France as sovereign master. What means were not employed to mislead the opinion of the public respecting Moreau? The police published pamphlets of all sorts, and the Comte de Montgaillard was brought from Lyons to draw up a libel implicating him with Pichegru and the exiled Princes. But nothing that was done produced the effect proposed.

The weak character of Moreau is known. In fact, he allowed himself to be circumvented by a few intriguers, who endeavoured to derive advantage from the influence of his name. But he was so decidedly opposed to the reestablishment of the ancient system that he replied to one of the agents who addressed' him, "I cannot put myself at the head of any movement for the Bourbons, and such an attempt would not succeed. If Pichegru act on another principle—and even in that case I have told him that the Consuls and the Governor of Paris must disappear—I believe that I have a party strong enough in the Senate to obtain possession of authority, and I will immediately make use of it to protect his friends; public opinion will then dictate what may be fit to be done, but I will promise nothing in writing." Admitting these words attributed to Moreau to be true, they prove that he was dissatisfied with the Consular Government, and that he wished a change; but there is a great difference between a conditional wish and a conspiracy.

The commander of the principal guard of the Temple was General Savory, and he had reinforced that guard by his select gendarmerie. The prisoners did not dare to communicate one with another for fear of mutual injury, but all evinced a courage which created no little alarm as to the consequences of the trial. Neither offers nor threats produced any confessions in the course of the interrogatories. Pichegru, in particular, displayed an extraordinary firmness, and Real one day, on leaving the chamber where he had been examining him, said aloud in the presence of several persons, "What a man that Pichegru is!"

Forty days elapsed after the arrest of General Pichegru when, on the morning of the 6th of April, he was found dead in the chamber he occupied in the Temple. Pichegru had undergone ten examinations; but he had made no confessions, and no person was committed by his replies.

All his declarations, however, gave reason to believe that he would speak out, and that too in a lofty and energetic manner during the progress of the trial. "When I am before my judges," said he, "my language shall be conformable to truth and the interests of my country." What would that language have been? Without doubt there was no wish that it should be heard. Pichegru would have kept his promise, for he was distinguished for his firmness of character above everything, even above his qualities as a soldier; differing in this respect from Moreau, who allowed himself to be guided by his wife and mother-in-law, both of whom displayed ridiculous pretensions in their visits to Madame Bonaparte.

The day on which Real spoke before several persons of Pichegru in the way I have related was the day of his last examination. I afterwards learned, from a source on which I can rely, that during his examination Pichegru, though careful to say nothing which could affect the other prisoners, showed no disposition to be tender of him who had sought and resolved his death, but evinced a firm resolution to unveil before the public the odious machinery of the plot into which the police had drawn him. He also declared that he and his companions had no longer any object but to consider of the means of leaving Paris, with the view of escaping from the snares laid for them when their arrest took place. He declared that they had all of them given up the idea of overturning the power of Bonaparte, a scheme into which they had been enticed by shameful intrigues. I am convinced the dread excited by his manifestation of a resolution to speak out with the most rigid candour hastened the death of Pichegru. M. Real, who is still living, knows better than any one else what were Pichegru's declarations, as he interrogated him. I know not whether that gentleman will think fit, either at the present or some future period, to raise the veil of mystery which hangs over these events, but of this I am sure, he will be unable to deny anything I advance. There is evidence almost amounting to demonstration that Pichegru was strangled in prison, and consequently all idea of suicide must be rejected as inadmissible. Have I positive and substantive proof of what I assert? I have not; but the concurrence of facts and the weight of probabilities do not leave me in possession of the doubts I should wish to entertain on that tragic event. Besides, there exists a certain popular instinct, which is rarely at fault, and it must be in the recollection of many, not only that the general opinion favoured the notion of Pichegru's assassination, but that the pains taken to give that opinion another direction, by the affected exhibition of the body, only served to strengthen it. He who spontaneously says, I have not committed such or such a crime, at least admits there is room for suspecting his guilt.

The truth is, the tide of opinion never set in with such force against Bonaparte as during the trial of Moreau; nor was the popular sentiment in error on the subject of the death of Pichegru, who was clearly strangled in the Temple by secret agents. The authors, the actors, and the witnesses of the horrible prison scenes of the period are the only persons capable of removing the doubts which still hang over the death of Pichegru; but I must nevertheless contend that the preceding circumstances, the general belief at the time, and even probability, are in contradiction with any idea of suicide on the part of Pichegru. His death was considered necessary, and this necessity was its real cause.

CHAPTER XXV

1804

Georges was arrested about seven o'clock, on the evening of the 9th of March, with another conspirator, whose name, I think, was Leridan. Georges was stopped in a cabriolet on the Place de l'Odeon, whither he had no doubt been directed by the police agent, who was constantly about him. In not seizing him at his lodgings, the object, probably, was to give more publicity to his arrest, and to produce an effect upon the minds of the multitude. This calculation cost the life of one man, and had well-nigh sacrificed the lives of two, for Georges, who constantly carried arms about him, first shot dead the police officer who seized the horse's reins, and wounded another who advanced to arrest him is the cabriolet. Besides his pistols there was found upon him a poniard of English manufacture.

Georges lodged with a woman named Lemoine, who kept a fruiterer's shop in the Rue de la Montagne St. Genevieve, and on the evening of the 9th of March he had just left his lodging to go, it was said, to a perfumer's named Caron. It is difficult to suppose that the circumstance of the police being on the spot was the mere effect of chance. The fruiterer's daughter was putting into the cabriolet a parcel belonging to Georges at the moment of his arrest. Georges, seeing the officers advance to seize him, desired the girl to get out of the way, fearing lest he should shoot her when he fired on the officers. She ran into a neighbouring house, taking the parcel along with her. The police, it may readily be supposed, were soon after her. The master of the house in which she had taken refuge, curious to know what the parcel contained, had opened it, and discovered, among other things, a bag containing 1000 Dutch sovereigns, from which he acknowledged he had abstracted a considerable sum. He and his wife, as well as the fruiterer's daughter, were all arrested; as to Georges, he was taken that same evening to the Temple, where he remained until his removal to the Conciergerie when the trial commenced.

During the whole of the legal proceedings Georges and the other important prisoners were kept in solitary confinement. Immediately on Pichegru's death the prisoners were informed of the circumstance. As they were all acquainted with the general, and none believed the fact of his reported suicide, it may easily be conceived what consternation and horror the tragical event excited among them. I learned, and I was sorry to hear of it, that Louis Bonaparte, who was an excellent man, and, beyond all comparison, the best of the family, had the cruel curiosity to see Georges in his prison a few days after the death of Pichegru, and when the sensation of horror excited by that event in the interior of the Temple was at its height, Louis repaired to the prison, accompanied by a brilliant escort of staff-officers, and General Savary introduced him to the prisoners. When Louis arrived, Georges was lying on his bed with his hands strongly bound by manacles. Lauriston, who accompanied Louis, related to me some of the particulars of this visit, which, in spite of his sincere devotedness to the first Consul, he assured me had been very painful to him.

After the arrest of Georges there were still some individuals marked out as accomplices in the conspiracy who had found means to elude the search of the police. The persons last arrested were, I think, Villeneuve, one of the principal confidants of Georges, Burban Malabre, who went by the name of Barco, and Charles d'Hozier. They were not taken till five days after the arrest of the Duc d'Enghien. The famous Commissioner Comminges, accompanied by an inspector and a detachment of gendarmes d'Elite, found Villeneuve and Burban Malabre in the house of a man named Dubuisson, in the Rue Jean Robert.

This Dubuisson and his wife had sheltered some of the principal persons proscribed by the police. The Messieurs de Polignac and M. de Riviere had lodged with them. When the police came to arrest Villeneuve and Burban Malabre the people with whom they lodged declared that they had gone away in the morning. The officers, however, searched the house, and discovered a secret door within a closet. They called, and receiving no answer, the gendarmerie had recourse to one of those expedients which were, unfortunately, too familiar to them. They fired a pistol through the door. Villeneuve, who went by the name of Joyau, was wounded in the arm, which obliged him and his companion to come from the place of their concealment, and they were then made prisoners.

Moreau was not treated with the degree of rigour observed towards the other prisoners. Indeed, it would not have been safe so to treat him, for even in his prison he received the homage and respect of all the military, not excepting even those who were his guards. Many of these soldiers had served under him, and it could not be forgotten how much he was beloved by the troops he had commanded. He did not possess that irresistible charm which in Bonaparte excited attachment, but his mildness of temper and excellent character inspired love and respect. It was the general opinion in Paris that a single word from Moreau to the soldiers in whose custody he was placed would in a moment have converted the gaoler-guard into a guard of honour, ready to execute all that might be required for the safety of the conqueror of Hohenlinden. Perhaps the respect with which he was treated and the indulgence of daily seeing his wife and child were but artful calculations for keeping him within the limits of his usual character. Besides, Moreau was so confident of the injustice of the charge brought against him that he was calm and resigned, and showed no disposition to rouse the anger of an enemy who would have been happy to have some real accusation against him. To these causes combined I always attributed the resignation; and I may say the indifference, of Moreau while he was in prison and on his trial.

When the legal preparations for the trial were ended the prisoners of the Temple were permitted to communicate with each other, and, viewing their fate with that indifference which youth, misfortune, and courage inspired, they amused themselves with some of those games which usually serve for boyish recreation. While they were thus engaged the order arrived for their removal to the Conciergerie. The firmness of all remained unshaken, and they made their preparations for departure as if they were going about any ordinary business. This fortitude was particularly remarkable in Georges, in whose manner a change had taken place which was remarked by all his companions in misfortune.

For some time past the agents of Government throughout France had been instructed to solicit the First Consul to grant for the people what the people did not want, but what Bonaparte wished to take while he appeared to yield to the general will, namely, unlimited sovereign authority, free from any subterfuge of denomination. The opportunity of the great conspiracy just discovered, and in which Bonaparte had not incurred a moment's danger, as he did at the time of the infernal machine, was not suffered to escape; that opportunity was, on the contrary, eagerly seized by the authorities of every rank, civil, ecclesiastical, and military, and a torrent of addresses, congratulations, and thanksgivings inundated the Tuileries. Most of the authors of these addressee did not confine themselves to mere congratulations; they entreated Bonaparte to consolidate his work, the true meaning of which was that it was time he should make himself Emperor and establish hereditary succession. Those who on other occasions had shown an officious readiness to execute Bonaparte's commands did not now fear to risk his displeasure by opposing the opinion he had expressed in the Council of State on the discussion of the question of the Consulate for life. Bonaparte then said, "Hereditary succession is absurd. It is irreconcilable with the principle of the sovereignty of the people, and impossible in France."

In this scene of the grand drama Bonaparte played his part with his accustomed talent, keeping himself in the background and leaving to others the task of preparing the catastrophe. The Senate, who took the lead in the way of insinuation, did not fail, while congratulating the First Consul on his escape from the plots of foreigners, or, as they were officially styled, the daggers of England, to conjure him not to delay the completion of his work. Six days after the death of the Duc d'Enghien the Senate first expressed this wish. Either because Bonaparte began to repent of a useless crime, and felt the ill effect it must produce on the public mind, or because he found the language of the Senate somewhat vague, he left the address nearly a month unanswered, and then only replied by the request that the intention of the address might be more completely expressed. These negotiations between the Senate and the Head of the Government were not immediately published. Bonaparte did not like publicity except for what had arrived at a result; but to attain the result which was the object of his ambition it was necessary that the project which he was maturing should be introduced in the Tribunate, and the tribune Curee had the honour to be the first to propose officially, on the 30th of April 1804, the conversion of the Consular Republic into an Empire, and the elevation of Bonaparte to the title of Emperor; with the rights of hereditary succession.

If any doubts could exist respecting the complaisant part which Curee acted on this occasion one circumstance would suffice to remove them; that is, that ten days before the development of his proposition Bonaparte had caused the question of founding the Empire and establishing hereditary succession in his family to be secretly discussed in the Council of State. I learned from one of the Councillors of State all that passed on that occasion, and I may remark that Cambacérès showed himself particularly eager in the Council of State, as well as afterwards in the Senate, to become the exalted subject of him who had been his first colleague in the Consulate.

About the middle of April, the Council of State being assembled as for an ordinary sitting, the First Consul, who was frequently present at the sittings, did not appear. Cambacérès arrived and took the Presidency in his quality of Second Consul, and it was remarked that his air was more solemn than usual, though he at all times affected gravity.

The partisans of hereditary succession were the majority, and resolved to present an address to the First Consul. Those of the Councillors who opposed this determined on their part to send a counter-address; and to avoid this clashing of opinions Bonaparte signified his wish that each member of the Council should send him his opinion individually, with his signature affixed. By a singular accident it happened to be Berlier's task to present to the First Consul the separate opinions of the Council. Out of the twenty-seven Councillors present only seven opposed the question. Bonaparte received them all most graciously, and told them, among other things, that he wished for hereditary power only for the benefit of France; that the citizens would never be his subjects, and that the French people would never be his people. Such were the preliminaries to the official proposition of Curee to the Tribunate, and upon reflection it was decided that, as all opposition would be useless and perhaps dangerous to the opposing party, the minority should join the majority. This was accordingly done.

The Tribunate having adopted the proposition of Curee, there was no longer any motive for concealing the overtures of the Senate. Its address to the First Consul was therefore published forty days after its date: the pear was then ripe. This period is so important that I must not omit putting together the most remarkable facts which either came within my own observation, or which I have learned since respecting the foundation of the Empire.

Bonaparte had a long time before spoken to me of the title of Emperor as being the most appropriate for the new sovereignty which he wished to found in France. This, he observed, was not restoring the old system entirely, and he dwelt much on its being the title which Caesar had borne. He often said, "One may be the Emperor of a republic, but not the King of a republic, those two terms are incongruous."

In its first address the Senate had taken as a test the documents it had received from the Government in relation to the intrigues of Drake, who had been sent from England to Munich. That text afforded the opportunity for a vague expression of what the Senate termed the necessities of France. To give greater solemnity to the affair the Senate proceeded in a body to the Tuileries, and one thing which gave a peculiar character to the preconcerted advances of the Senate was that Cambacérès, the Second Consul, fulfilled his functions of President on this occasion, and delivered the address to the First Consul.

However, the First Consul thought the address of the Senate, which, I have been informed, was drawn up by Francois de Neufchateau, was not expressed with sufficient clearness; he therefore, after suffering a little interval to elapse, sent a message to the Senate signed by himself, in which he said, "Your address has been the object of my earnest consideration." And though the address contained no mention of hereditary succession, he added, "You consider the hereditary succession of the supreme magistracy necessary to defend the French people against the plots of our enemies and the agitation arising from rival ambition. At the same time several of our institutions appear to you to require improvement so as to ensure the triumph of equality and public liberty, and to offer to the nation and the Government the double guarantee they require." From the subsequent passages of the message it will be sufficient to extract the following: "We have been constantly guided by this great truth: that the sovereignty dwells with the French people, and that it is for their interest, happiness, and glory that the Supreme Magistracy, the Senate, the Council of State, the Legislative Body, the Electoral Colleges, and the different branches of the Government, are and must be instituted." The omission of the Tribunate in this enumeration is somewhat remarkable. It announced a promise which was speedily realised.

The will of Bonaparte being thus expressed in his message to the—Senate, that body, which was created to preserve the institutions consecrated by the Constitution of the year VIII., had no alternative but to submit to the intentions manifested by the First Consul. The reply to the message was, therefore, merely a counterpart of the message itself. It positively declared that hereditary government was essential to the happiness, the glory, and the prosperity of France, and that that government could be confided only to Bonaparte and his family. While the Senate so complaisantly played its part in this well-get-up piece, yet, the better to impose on the credulity of the multitude, its reply, like Bonaparte's message, resounded with the words liberty and equality. Indeed, it was impudently asserted in that reply that Bonaparte's accession to hereditary power would be a certain guarantee for the liberty of the press, a liberty which Bonaparte held in the greatest horror, and without which all other liberty is but a vain illusion.

By this reply of the Senate the most important step was performed. There now remained merely ceremonies to regulate and formulas to fill up. These various arrangements occasioned a delay of a fortnight. On the 18th of May the First Consul was greeted for the first time by the appellation of Sire by his former colleague, Cambacérès, who at the head of the Senate went to present to Bonaparte the organic 'Senatus-consulte' containing the foundation of the Empire. Napoleon was at St. Cloud, whither the Senate proceeded in state. After the speech of Cambacérès, in which the old designation of Majesty was for the first time revived, the EMPEROR replied:—

> All that can contribute to the welfare of the country is essentially connected with my happiness. I accept the title which you believe to be conducive to the glory of the nation. I submit to the sanction of the people the law of hereditary succession. I hope that France will never repent the honours she may confer on my family. At all events, my spirit will not be with my posterity when they cease to merit the confidence and love of the great nation.

Cambacérès next went to congratulate the Empress, and then was realised to Josephine the prediction which I had made to her three years before at Malmaison.[187]

Bonaparte's first act as Emperor, on the very day of his elevation to the Imperial throne, was the nomination of Joseph to the dignity of Grand Elector, with the title of Imperial Highness. Louis was raised to the dignity of Constable, with the same title, and Cambacérès and Lebrun were created Arch-Chancellor and Arch-Treasurer of the Empire. On the same day Bonaparte wrote the following letter to Cambacérès, the first which he signed as

---

187 In the original motion as prepared by Curee, the Imperial dignity was to be declared hereditary in the family of Napoleon. Previous to being formerly read before the Tribunate, the First Consul sent for the document, and when it was returned it was found that the word family was altered to descendants. Fabre, the President of the Tribunate, who received the altered document from Maret, seeing the effect the alteration would have on the brothers of Napoleon, and finding that Maret affected to crest the change as immaterial, took on himself to restore the original form, and in that shape it was read by the unconscious Curee to the Tribunals. On this curious, passage see Miot de Melito, tome ii, p. 179. As finally settled the descent of the crown in default of Napoleon's children was limited to Joseph and Louis and their descendants, but the power of adoption was given to Napoleon. The draft of the 'Senates-consulte' was heard by the Council of State in silence, and Napoleon tried in vain to get even the most talkative of the members now to speak. The Senate were not unanimous in rendering the 'Senatus-consulte'. The three votes given against it were said to have been Gregoire, the former constitutional Bishop of Blois, Carat, who as Minister of Justice had read to Louis XVI. the sentence of death, and Lanjuinais, one of the very few survivors of the Girondists, Thiers says there was only one dissentient voice. For the fury of the brothers of Napoleon, who saw the destruction of all their ambitions hopes in any measure for the descent of the crown except in the family, see Miot, tome ii. p . . . 172, where Joseph is described as cursing the ambition of his brother, and desiring his death as a benefit for France and his family.

Emperor, and merely with the name of Napoleon:—

> CITIZEN CONSUL CAMBACERES—Your title has changed; but your functions and my confidence remain the same. In the high dignity with which you are now invested you will continue to manifest, as you have hitherto done in that of Consul, that wisdom and that distinguished talent which entitle you to so important a share in all the good which I may have effected. I have, therefore, only to desire the continuance of the sentiments you cherish towards the State and me.
>
> Given at the *Palace of St. Cloud, 28th Floréal, an XII.* (*18th May 1804*).
>
> (*Signed*) NAPOLEON.
> *By the Emperor.* H. B. MARET.

I have quoted this first letter of the Emperor because it is characteristic of Bonaparte's art in managing transitions. It was to the Citizen Consul that the Emperor addressed himself, and it was dated according to the Republican calendar. That calendar, together with the delusive inscription on the coin, were all that now remained of the Republic. Next day the Emperor came to Paris to hold a grand levee at the Tuileries, for he was not the man to postpone the gratification that vanity derived from his new dignity and title. The assembly was more numerous and brilliant than on any former occasion. Bessières having addressed the Emperor on the part of the Guards, the Emperor replied in the following terms: "I know the sentiments the Guards cherish towards me. I repose perfect confidence in their courage and fidelity. I constantly see, with renewed pleasure, companions in arms who have escaped so many dangers, and are covered with so many honourable wounds. I experience a sentiment of satisfaction when I look at the Guards, and think that there has not, for the last fifteen years, in any of the four quarters of the world, been a battle in which some of them have not taken part."

On the same day all the generals and colonels in Paris were presented to the Emperor by Louis Bonaparte, who had already begun to exercise his functions of Constable. In a few days everything assumed a new aspect; but in spite of the admiration which was openly expressed the Parisians secretly ridiculed the new courtiers. This greatly displeased Bonaparte, who was very charitably informed of it in order to check his prepossession in favour of the men of the old Court, such as the Comte de Segur, and at a later period Comte Louis de Narbonne.

To give all possible solemnity to his accession Napoleon ordered that the Senate itself should proclaim in Paris the organic 'Senates-consulte', which entirely changed the Constitution of the State. By one of those anomalies which I have frequently had occasion to remark, the Emperor fixed for this ceremony Sunday, the 30th Floral. That day was a festival in all Paris, while the unfortunate prisoners were languishing in the dungeons of the Temple.

On the day after Bonaparte's accession the old formulae were restored. The Emperor determined that the French Princes and Princesses should receive the title of Imperial Highness; that his sisters should take the same title; that the grand dignitaries of the Empire should be called Serene Highnesses; that the Princes and titularies of the grand dignitaries should be addressed by the title of Monseigneur; that M. Maret, the Secretary of State, should have the rank of Minister; that the ministers should retain the title of Excellency, to which should be added that of Monseigneur in the petitions addressed to them; and that the title of Excellency should be given to the President of the Senate.

At the same time Napoleon appointed the first Marshals of the Empire, and determined that they should be called Monsieur le Marechal when addressed verbally, and Monseigneur in writing. The following are the names of these sons of the Republic transformed into props of the Empire: Berthier, Murat, Moncey, Jourdan, Massena, Augereau, Bernadotte, Soult, Brune, Lannes, Mortier, Ney, Davoust, and Besaieres. The title of Marshal of the Empire was also granted to the generals Kellerman, Lefebvre, Perignon, and Serrurier, as having served as commander-in-chief.

The reader cannot have failed to observe that the name of Lucien has not been mentioned among the individuals of Bonaparte's family on whom dignities were conferred. The fact is, the two brothers were no longer on good terms with each other. Not, as it has been alleged, because Lucien wished to play the part of a Republican, but because he would not submit to the imperious will of Napoleon in a circumstance in which the latter counted on his brother's docility to serve the interests of his policy. In the conferences which preceded the great change in the form of government it was not Lucien but Joseph who, probably for the sake of sounding opinion, affected an opposition, which was by some mistaken for Republicanism. With regard to Lucien, as he had really rendered great services to Napoleon on the 19th Brumaire at St. Cloud, and as he himself exaggerated the value of those services, he saw no reward worthy of his ambition but a throne independent of his brother. It is certain that when at Madrid he had aspired to win the good graces of a Spanish Infanta, and on that subject reports were circulated with which I have nothing to do, because I never had any opportunity of ascertaining their truth. All I know is that, Lucien's first wife being dead, Bonaparte, wished him to marry a German Princess, by way of forming the first great alliance in the family. Lucien, however, refused to comply with Napoleon's wishes, and he secretly married the wife of an agent, named, I believe, Joubertou, who for the sake of convenience was sent to the West Indies, where he: died shortly after. When Bonaparte heard of this marriage from the priest by whom it had been clandestinely performed, he fell into a furious passion, and resolved not to confer on Lucien the title of French Prince, on account of what he termed his unequal match. Lucien, therefore, obtained no other dignity than that of Senator.[188] Jerome, who pursued an opposite line of conduct, was afterwards

188 According to Lucien himself, Napoleon wished him to marry the Queen of Etruria Maria-Louise, daughter of Charles IV. of Spain, who had married, 1795 Louie de Bourbon, Prince of Parma, son of the Duke of Parma, to whom Napoleon had given Tuscany in 1801 as the Kingdom of, Etruria. Her husband had died in May 1808, and she governed in the name of her son. Lucien, whose first wife, Anne Christine Boyer, had died in 1801, had married his second wife, Alexandrine Laurence de Bleschamps, who had married, but who had divorced, a M. Jonberthon. When Lucien had been ambassador in Spain in 1801, charged among other things with obtaining Elba, the Queen, he says, wished Napoleon should marry an Infanta,—Donna Isabella, her youngest daughter, afterwards Queen of Naples, an overture to which Napoleon seems not to have made any answer. As for Lucien, he objected to his brother that the Queen was ugly, and laughed at Napoleon's representations as to her being "propre": but at last he acknowledged his marriage with Madame Jouberthon. This made a complete break between the brothers, and on hearing of the execution of the Duc d'Enghien, Lucien said to

made a King. As to Lucien's Republicanism, it did not survive the 18th Brumaire, and he was always a warm partisan of hereditary succession.

But I pass on to relate what I know respecting the almost incredible influence which, on the foundation of the Empire, Bonaparte exercised over the powers which did not yet dare to declare war against him. I studied Bonaparte's policy closely, and I came to this conclusion on the subject, that he was governed by ambition, by the passion of dominion, and that no relations, on a footing of equality, between himself and any other power, could be of long duration. The other States of Europe had only to choose one of two things—submission or war. As to secondary States, they might thenceforth be considered as fiefs of the French Government; and as they could not resist, Bonaparte easily accustomed them to bend to his yoke. Can there be a stronger proof of this arbitrary influence than what occurred at Carlsruhe, after the violation of the territory of Baden, by the arrest of the Duc d'Enghien? Far from venturing to make any observation on that violation, so contrary to the rights of nations, the Grand Duke of Baden was obliged to publish, in his own State, a decree evidently dictated by Bonaparte. The decree stated, that many individuals formerly belonging to the army of Condé having come to the neighbourhood of Carlsruhe, his Electoral Highness had felt it his duty to direct that no individual coming from Condé's army, nor indeed any French emigrant, should, unless he had permission previously to the place, make a longer sojourn than was allowed to foreign travellers. Such was already the influence which Bonaparte exercised over Germany, whose Princes, to use an expression which he employed in a later decree, were crushed by the grand measures of the Empire.

But to be just, without however justifying Bonaparte, I must acknowledge that the intrigues which England fomented in all parts of the Continent were calculated to excite his natural irritability to the utmost degree. The agents of England were spread over the whole of Europe, and they varied the rumours which they were commissioned to circulate, according to the chances of credit which the different places afforded. Their reports were generally false; but credulity gave ear to them, and speculators endeavoured, each according to his interest, to give them support. The headquarters of all this plotting was Munich, where Drake, who was sent from England, had the supreme direction. His correspondence, which was seized by the French Government, was at first placed amongst the documents to be produced on the trial of Georges, Moreau, and the other prisoners; but in the course of the preliminary proceedings the Grand Judge received directions to detach them, and make them the subject of a special report to the First Consul, in order that their publication beforehand might influence public opinion, and render it unfavourable to those who were doomed to be sacrificed. The instructions given by Drake to his agents render it impossible to doubt that England wished to overthrow the Government of Bonaparte. Drake wrote as follows to a man who was appointed to travel through France:—

---

his wife, "Alexandrine, let us go; he has tasted blood." He went to Italy, and in 1810 tried to go to the United States. Taken prisoner by the English, he was detained first at Malta, and then in England, at Ludlow Castle and at Thorngrove, till 1814, when he went to Rome. The Pope, who ever showed a kindly feeling towards the Bonapartes, made the ex-"Brutus" Bonaparte Prince de Canino and Duc de Musignano. In 1815 he joined Napoleon and on the final fall of the Empire he was interned at Rome till the death of his brother.

> The principal object of your journey being the overthrow of the existing Government, one of the means of effecting it is to acquire a knowledge of the enemy's plans. For this purpose it is of the highest importance to begin, in the first place, by establishing communications with persons who may be depended upon in the different Government offices in order to obtain exact information of all plans with respect to foreign or internal affairs. The knowledge of these plans will supply the best means of defeating them; and failure is the way to bring the Government into complete discredit—the first and most important step towards the end proposed. Try to gain over trustworthy agents in the different Government departments. Endeavour, also, to learn what passes in the secret committee, which is supposed to be established at St Cloud, and composed of the friends of the First Consul. Be careful to furnish information of the various projects which Bonaparte may entertain relative to Turkey and Ireland. Likewise send intelligence respecting the movements of troops, respecting vessels and ship-building, and all military preparations.

Drake, in his instructions, also recommended that the subversion of Bonaparte's Government should, for the time, be the only object in view, and that nothing should be said about the King's intentions until certain information could be obtained respecting his views; but most of his letters and instructions were anterior to 1804. The whole bearing of the seized documents proved what Bonaparte could not be ignorant of, namely, that England was his constant enemy; but after examining them, I was of opinion that they contained nothing which could justify the belief that the Government of Great Britain authorised any attempt at assassination.

When the First Consul received the report of the Grand Judge relative to Drake's plots' against his Government he transmitted a copy of it to the Senate, and it was in reply to this communication that the Senate made those first overtures which Bonaparte thought vague, but which, nevertheless, led to the formation of the Empire. Notwithstanding this important circumstance, I have not hitherto mentioned Drake, because his intrigues for Bonaparte's overthrow appeared to me to be more immediately connected with the preliminaries of the trial of Georges and Moreau, which I shall notice in my next chapter.[189]

At the same time that Bonaparte communicated to the Senate the report of the Grand Judge, the Minister for Foreign Affairs addressed the following circular letter to the members of the Diplomatic Body:

---

189 These were not plots for assassination. Bonaparte, in the same way, had his secret agents in every country of Europe, without excepting England. Alison (chap. xxxvii. par. 89) says on this matter of Drake that, though the English agents were certainly attempting a counter-revolution, they had no idea of encouraging the assassination of Napoleon, while "England was no match for the French police agents in a transaction of this description, for the publication of Regular revealed the mortifying fact that the whole correspondence both of Drake and Spencer Smith had been regularly transmitted, as fast as it took place, to the police of Paris, and that their principal corresponded in that city, M. Mehu de la Tonche, was himself an agent of the police, employed to tempt the British envoys into this perilous enterprise."

> The First Consul has commanded me to forward to your Excellency a copy of a report which has been presented to him, respecting a conspiracy formed in France by Mr. Drake, his Britannic Majesty's Minister at the Court of Munich, which, by its object as well as its date, is evidently connected with the infamous plot now in the course of investigation. The printed copy of Mr. Drake's letters and authentic documents is annexed to the report. The originals will be immediately sent, by order of the First Consul, to the Elector of Bavaria. Such a prostitution of the most honourable function which can be intrusted to a man is unexampled in the history of civilised nations. It will astonish and afflict Europe as an unheard of crime, which hitherto the most perverse Governments have not dared to meditate. The First Consul is too well acquainted with sentiments of the Diplomatic Body accredited to him not to be fully convinced that every one of its members will behold, with profound regret, the profanation of the sacred character of Ambassador, basely transformed into a minister of plots, snares, and corruption.

All the ambassadors, ministers, plenipotentiaries, envoys, ordinary or extraordinary, whatever might be their denomination, addressed answers to the Minister for Foreign Affairs, in which they expressed horror and indignation at the conduct of England and Drake's machinations. These answers were returned only five days after the Duc d'Enghien's death; and here one cannot help admiring the adroitness of Bonaparte, who thus compelled all the representatives of the European Governments to give official testimonies of regard for his person and Government.

CHAPTER XXVI

1804

On the 28th of May, about ten days after Napoleon had been declared Emperor, the trials of Moreau and others commenced. No similar event that has since occurred can convey an idea of the fermentation which then prevailed in Paris. The indignation excited by Moreau's arrest was openly manifested, and braved the observation of the police. Endeavours had been successfully made to mislead public opinion with respect to Georges and some others among the accused, who were looked upon as assassins in the pay of England, at least by that numerous portion of the public who lent implicit faith to declarations presented to them as official. But the case was different with regard to those individuals who were particularly the objects of public interest,—viz. MM. de Polignac, de Riviere, Charles d'Hozier, and, above all, Moreau. The name of Moreau towered above all the rest, and with respect to him the Government found itself not a little perplexed. It was necessary on the one hand to surround him with a guard sufficiently imposing, to repress the eagerness of the people and of his friends, and yet on the other hand care was required that this guard should not be so strong as to admit of the possibility of making it a rallying-point, should the voice of a chief so honoured by the army appeal to it for defence. A rising of the populace in favour of Moreau was considered as a very possible event,—some hoped for it, others dreaded it. When I reflect on the state of feeling which then prevailed, I am certain that a movement in his favour would infallibly have taken place had judges more complying than even those who presided at the trial condemned Moreau to capital punishment.

It is impossible to form an idea of the crowd that choked up the avenues of the Palace of Justice on the day the trials commenced. This crowd continued during the twelve days the proceedings lasted, and was exceedingly great on the day the sentence was pronounced. Persons of the highest class were anxious to be present.

I was one of the first in the Hall, being determined to watch the course of these solemn proceedings. The Court being assembled, the President ordered the prisoners to be brought in. They entered in a file, and ranged themselves on the benches each between two gendarmes. They appeared composed and collected, and resignation was depicted on the countenances of all except Bouvet de Lozier, who did not dare to raise his eyes to his companions in misfortune, whom his weakness, rather than his will, had betrayed. I did not recognise him until the President proceeded to call over the prisoners, and to put the usual questions respecting their names, professions, and places of abode. Of the forty-nine prisoners, among whom were several females, only two were personally known to me; namely, Moreau, whose presence on the prisoner's bench seemed to wring every heart, and Georges, whom I had seen at the Tuileries in the First Consul's cabinet.

The first sitting of the Court was occupied with the reading of the act of accusation or indictment, and the voices of the ushers, commanding silence, could scarce suppress the buzz which pervaded the Court at the mention of Moreau's name. All eyes were turned towards the conqueror of Hohenlinden, and while the Procureur Imperial read over the long indictment and invoked the vengeance of the law on an attempt against the head of the Republic, it was easy to perceive how he tortured his ingenuity to fasten apparent guilt on the laurels of Moreau. The good sense of the public discerned proofs of his innocence in the very circumstances brought forward against him. I shall never forget the effect produced—so contrary to what was anticipated by the prosecutors—by the reading of a letter addressed by Moreau from his prison in the Temple to the First Consul, when the judges appointed to interrogate him sought to make his past conduct the subject of accusation, on account of M. de Klinglin's papers having fallen into his hands. He was reproached with having too long delayed transmitting these documents to the Directory; and it was curious to see the Emperor Napoleon become the avenger of pretended offences committed against the Directory which he had overthrown.

In the letter here alluded to Moreau said to Bonaparte, then First Consul—

> "In the short campaign of the year V. (from the 20th to the 23d of March 1797) we took the papers belonging to the staff of the enemy's army, and a number of documents were brought to me which General Desaix, then wounded, amused himself by perusing. It appeared from this correspondence that General Pichegru had maintained communications with the French Princes. This discovery was very painful, and particularly to me, and we agreed to say nothing of the matter. Pichegru, as a member of the Legislative Body, could do but little to injure the public cause, since peace was established. I nevertheless took every precaution for protecting the army against the ill effects of a system of espionage. . . . The events of the 18th Fructidor occasioned so much anxiety that two officers, who knew of the existence of the correspondence, prevailed on me to communicate it to the Government. . . . I felt that, as a public functionary, I could no longer remain silent. . . . During the two last campaigns in Germany, and since the peace, distant overtures have been made to me, with the view of drawing me into connection with the French Princes. This appeared so absurd that I took no notice of these overtures. As to the present conspiracy, I can assure you I have been far from taking any share in it. I repeat to you, General, that whatever proposition to that effect was made me, I rejected it, and regarded it as the height of madness. When it was represented to me that the invasion of England would offer a favourable opportunity for effecting a change in the French Government, I invariably answered that the Senate was the authority to which the whole of France would naturally cling in the time of trouble, and that I would be the first to place myself under its orders. To such overtures made to a private individual, who wished to preserve no connection either with the army, of whom nine-tenths have served under me, or any constituted authority, the only possible answer was a refusal. Betrayal of confidence I disdained. Such a step, which is always base, becomes doubly odious when the treachery is committed against those to whom we owe gratitude, or have been bound by old friendship. "This, General, is all I have to tell you respecting my relations with Pichegru, and it must convince you that very false and hasty inferences have been drawn from conduct which, though perhaps imprudent, was far from being criminal."

Moreau fulfilled his duty as a public functionary by communicating to the Directory the papers which unfolded a plot against the Government, and which the chances of war had thrown into his hands. He fulfilled his duty as a man of honour by not voluntarily incurring the infamy which can never be wiped from the character of an informer. Bonaparte in Moreau's situation would have acted the same part, for I never knew a man express stronger indignation than himself against informers, until he began to consider everything a virtue which served his ambition, and everything a crime which opposed it.

The two facts which most forcibly obtruded themselves on my attention during the trial were the inveterate violence of the President of the Court towards the prisoners and the innocence of Moreau.[190]

But, in spite of the most insidious examinations which can be conceived, Moreau never once fell into the least contradiction. If my memory fail me not, it was on the fourth day that he was examined by Thuriot, one of the judges. The result, clear as day to all present, was, that Moreau was a total stranger to all the plots, all the intrigues which had been set on foot in London. In fact, during the whole course of the trial, to which I listened with as much attention as interest, I did not discover the shadow of a circumstance which could in the least commit him, or which had the least reference to him. Scarcely one of the hundred and thirty-nine witnesses who were heard for the prosecution knew him, and he himself declared on the fourth sitting, which took place on the 31st of May, that there was not an individual among the accused whom he knew,—not one whom he had ever seen. In the course of the long proceedings, notwithstanding the manifest efforts of Thuriot to extort false admissions and force contradictions, no fact of any consequence was elicited to the prejudice of Moreau. His appearance was as calm as his conscience; and as he sat on the bench he had the appearance of one led by curiosity to be present at this interesting trial, rather than of an accused person, to whom the proceedings might end in condemnation and death. But for the fall of Moreau in the ranks of the enemy,—but for the foreign cockade which disgraced the cap of the conqueror of Hohenlinden, his complete innocence would long since have been put beyond doubt, and it would have been acknowledged that the most infamous machinations were employed for his destruction. It is evident that Lajolais, who had passed from London to Paris, and from Paris to London, had been acting the part of an intriguer rather than of a conspirator; and that the object of his missions was not so much to reconcile Moreau and Pichegru as to make Pichegru the instrument of implicating Moreau. Those who supposed Lajolais to be in the pay of the British Government were egregiously imposed on. Lajolais was only in the pay of the secret police; he was condemned to death, as was expected, but he received his pardon, as was agreed upon. Here was one of the disclosures which Pichegru might have made; hence the necessity of getting him out of the way before the trial. As to the evidence of the man named Rolland, it was clear to everybody that Moreau was right when he said to the President, "In my opinion, Rolland is either a creature of the police, or he has given his evidence under the influence of fear." Rolland made two declarations the first contained nothing at all; the second was in answer to the following observations: "You see you stand in a terrible situation; you must either be held to be an accomplice in the conspiracy, or you must be taken as evidence. If you say nothing, you will be considered in the light of an accomplice; if you confess, you will be saved." This single circumstance may

190 It is strange that Bourrienne does not acknowledge that he was charged by Napoleon with the duty of attending this trial of Moreau, and of sending in a daily report of the proceedings.

serve to give an idea of the way the trials were conducted so as to criminate Moreau. On his part the general repelled the attacks, of which he was the object, with calm composure and modest confidence, though flashes of just indignation would occasionally burst from him. I recollect the effect he produced upon the Court and the auditors at one of the sittings, when the President had accused him of the design of making himself Dictator. He exclaimed, "I Dictator! What, make myself Dictator at the head of the partisans of the Bourbons! Point out my partisans! My partisans would naturally be the soldiers of France, of whom I have commanded nine-tenths, and saved more than fifty thousand. These are the partisans I should look to! All my aides de camp, all the officers of my acquaintance, have been arrested; not the shadow of a suspicion could be found against any of them, and they have been set at liberty. Why, then, attribute to me the madness of aiming to get myself made Dictator by the aid of the adherents of the old French Princes, of persons who have fought in their cause since 1792? You allege that these men, in the space of four-and-twenty hours, formed the project of raising me to the Dictatorship! It is madness to think of it! My fortune and my pay have been alluded to; I began the world with nothing; I might have had by this time fifty millions; I have merely a house and a bit of ground; as to my pay, it is forty thousand francs. Surely that sum will not be compared with my services."

During the trial Moreau delivered a defence, which I knew had been written by his friend Garat, whose eloquence I well remember was always disliked by Bonaparte. Of this I had a proof on the occasion of a grand ceremony which took place in the Place des Victoires, on laying the first stone of a monument which was to have been erected to the memory of Desaix, but which was never executed. The First Consul returned home in very ill-humour, and said to me, "Bourrienne, what a brute that Garat is! What a stringer of words! I have been obliged to listen to him for three-quarters of an hour. There are people who never know when to hold their tongues!"

Whatever might be the character of Garat's eloquence or Bonaparte's opinion of it, his conduct was noble on the occasion of Moreau's trial; for he might be sure Bonaparte would bear him a grudge for lending the aid of his pen to the only man whose military glory, though not equal to that of the First Consul, might entitle him to be looked upon as his rival in fame. At one of the sittings a circumstance occurred which produced an almost electrical effect. I think I still see General Lecourbe, the worthy friend of Moreau, entering unexpectedly into the Court, leading a little boy. Raising the child in his arms, he exclaimed aloud, and with considerable emotion, "Soldiers, behold the son of your general!"[191]

At this unexpected movement all the military present spontaneously rose and presented arms; while a murmur of approbation from the spectators applauded the act. It is certain that had Moreau at that moment said but one word, such was the enthusiasm in his favour, the tribunal would have been broken up and the prisoners liberated. Moreau, however, was

191 This action of Lecourbe, together with the part played in this trial by his brother, one of the judges, was most unfortunate, not only for Lecourbe but for France, which consequently lost the services of its best general of mountain warfare. His campaigns of Switzerland in 1799 on the St. Gothard against Suwarrow are well known. Naturally disgraced for the part he took with Moreau, he was not again employed till the Cent Jours, when he did good service, although he had disapproved of the defection of Ney from the Royalist cause. He died in 1816; his brother, the judge, had a most furious reception from Napoleon, who called him a prevaricating judge, and dismissed him from his office (Rémusat, tome ii. p. 8).

silent, and indeed appeared the only unconcerned person in Court. Throughout the whole course of the trial Moreau inspired so much respect that when he was asked a question and rose to reply the gendarmes appointed to guard him rose at the same time and stood uncovered while he spoke.

Georges was far from exciting the interest inspired by Moreau. He was an object of curiosity rather than of interest. The difference of their previous conduct was in itself sufficient to occasion a great contrast in their situation before the Court. Moreau was full of confidence and Georges full of resignation. The latter regarded his fate with a fierce kind of resolution. He occasionally resumed the caustic tone which he seemed to have renounced when he harangued his associates before their departure from the Temple. With the most sarcastic bitterness he alluded to the name and vote of Thuriot, one of the most violent of the judges, often terming him 'Tue-roi';[192] and after pronouncing his name, or being forced to reply to his interrogatories, he would ask for a glass of brandy to wash his mouth.

Georges had the manners and bearing of a rude soldier; but under his coarse exterior he concealed the soul of a hero. When the witnesses of his arrest had answered the questions of the President Hemart, this judge turned towards the accused, and inquired whether he had anything to say in reply.—"No."—"Do you admit the facts?"—"Yes." Here Georges busied himself in looking over the papers which lay before him, when Hemart warned him to desist, and attend to the questions. The following dialogue then commenced. "Do you confess having been arrested in the place designated by the witness?"—"I do not know the name of the place."—"Do you confess having been arrested?"—"Yes."—"Did you twice fire a pistol?"—"Yes."—"Did you kill a man?"—"Indeed I do not know."— "Had you a poniard?"—"Yes."—"And two pistols?"—"Yes."—"Who was in company with you?"—"I do not know the person."—"Where did you lodge in Paris?"—"Nowhere."—"At the time of your arrest did you not reside in the house of a fruiterer in the Rue de la Montagne St. Genevieve?"— "At the time of my arrest I was in a cabriolet. I lodged nowhere."— "Where did you sleep on the evening of your arrest?"—"Nowhere."—"What were you doing in Paris?"—"I was walking about."—"Whom have you seen in Paris?"—"I shall name no one; I know no one."

From this short specimen of the manner in which Georges replied to the questions of the President we may judge of his unshaken firmness during the proceedings. In all that concerned himself he was perfectly open; but in regard to whatever tended to endanger his associates he maintained the most obstinate silence, notwithstanding every attempt to overcome his firmness.

That I was not the only one who justly appreciated the noble character of Georges is rendered evident by the following circumstance. Having accompanied M. Carbonnet to the police, where he went to demand his papers, on the day of his removal to St. Pelagic, we were obliged to await the return of M. Real, who was absent. M. Desmarets and several other persons were also in attendance. M. Real had been at the Conciergerie, where he had seen Georges Cadoudal, and on his entrance observed to M. Desmarets and the others, sufficiently loud to be distinctly heard by M. Carbonnet and myself, "I have had an interview with Georges who is an extraordinary man. I told him that I was disposed to offer him a pardon if he would promise to renounce the conspiracy and accept of employment under Government. But to my arguments and persuasions he only replied, 'My comrades followed

192 Thuriot and the President Hemart both voted for the death of the King. Merlin, the imperial Procureur-General, was one of the regicides.—Bourrienne.

me to France, and I shall follow them, to death.'" In this he kept his word.

Were we to judge these memorable proceedings from the official documents published in the Moniteur and other journals of that period, we should form a very erroneous opinion. Those falsities were even the object of a very serious complaint on the part of Cosier St. Victor, one of the accused.

After the speech of M. Gauthier, the advocate of Coster St. Victor, the President inquired of the accused whether he had anything further to say in his defence, to which he replied, "I have only to add that the witnesses necessary to my exculpation have not yet appeared. I must besides express my surprise at the means which have been employed to lead astray public opinion, and to load with infamy not only the accused but also their intrepid defenders. I have read with pain in the journals of to-day that the proceedings—" Here the President interrupting, observed that "these were circumstances foreign to the case."—"Not in the least," replied Cosier St. Victor; "on the contrary, they bear very materially on the cause, since mangling and misrepresenting our defence is a practice assuredly calculated to ruin us in the estimation of the public. In the journals of to-day the speech of M. Gauthier is shamefully garbled, and I should be deficient in gratitude were I not here to bear testimony to the zeal and courage which he has displayed in my defence. I protest against the puerilities and absurdities which have been put into his mouth, and I entreat him not to relax in his generous efforts. It is not on his account that I make this observation; he does not require it at my hands; it is for 'myself, it is for the accused, whom such arts tend to injure in the estimation of the public."

Coster St. Victor had something chivalrous in his language and manners which spoke greatly in his favour; he conveyed no bad idea of one of the Fiesco conspirators, or of those leaders of the Fronds who intermingled gallantry with their politics.

An anecdote to this effect was current about the period of the trial. Coster St. Victor, it is related, being unable any longer to find a secure asylum in Paris, sought refuge for a single night in the house of a beautiful actress, formerly in the good graces of the First Consul; and it is added that Bonaparte, on the same night, having secretly arrived on a visit to the lady, found himself unexpectedly in the presence of Coster St. Victor, who might have taken his life; but that only an interchange of courtesy took place betwixt the rival gallants.

This ridiculous story was doubtless intended to throw additional odium on the First Consul, if Cosier St. Victor should be condemned and not obtain a pardon, in which case malignity would not fail to attribute his execution to the vengeance of a jealous lover.

I should blush to relate such stories, equally destitute of probability and truth, had they not obtained some credit at the time. Whilst I was with Bonaparte he never went abroad during the night; and it was not surely at a moment when the saying of Fouché, "The air is full of poniards," was fully explained that he would have risked such nocturnal adventures.

Wright was heard in the sixth sitting, on the 2d of June, as the hundred and thirty-fourth witness in support of the prosecution. He, however, refused to answer any interrogatories put to him, declaring that, as a prisoner of war, he considered himself only amenable to his own Government.

The Procureur-General requested the President to order the examinations of Captain Wright on the 21st of May' and at a later period to be read over to him; which being done, the witness replied, that it was omitted to be stated that on these occasions the questions had been accompanied with the threat of transferring him to a military tribunal, in order to be shot, if he did not betray the secrets of his country.

In the course of the trial the most lively interest was felt for MM. de Polignac[193]— Charles d'Hozier, and de Riviere. So short a period had elapsed since the proscription of the nobility that, independently of every feeling of humanity, it was certainly impolitic to exhibit before the public the heirs of an illustrious name, endowed with that devoted heroism which could not fail to extort admiration even from those who condemned their opinions and principles.

The prisoners were all young, and their situation create universal sympathy. The greatest number of them disdained to have recourse to a denial, and seemed less anxious for the preservation of their own lives than for the honour of the cause in which they had embarked, not with the view of assassination, as had been demonstrated, but for the purpose of ascertaining the true state of the public feeling, which had been represented by some factious intriguers as favourable to the Bourbons. Even when the sword of the law was suspended over their heads the faithful adherents of the Bourbons displayed on every occasion their attachment and fidelity to the royal cause. I recollect that the Court was dissolved in tears when the President adduced as a proof of the guilt of M. de Riviere his having worn a medal of the Comte d'Artois, which the prisoner requested to examine; and, on its being handed to him by an officer, M. de Riviere pressed it to his lips and his heart, then returning it, he said that he only wished to render homage to the Prince whom he loved.

The Court was still more deeply affected on witnessing the generous fraternal struggle which took place during the last sitting between the two De Polignacs. The emotion was general when the eldest of the brothers, after having observed that his always going out alone and during the day did not look like a conspirator anxious for concealment, added these remarkable words which will remain indelibly engraven on my memory: "I have now only one wish, which is that, as the sword is suspended over our heads, and threatens to cut short the existence of several of the accused, you would, in consideration of his youth if not of his innocence, spare my brother, and shower down upon me the whole weight of your vengeance." It was during the last sitting but one, on Friday the 8th of June, that M. Armand de Polignac made the above affecting appeal in favour of his brother. The following day, before the fatal sentence was pronounced, M. Jules de Polignac addressed the judges, saying, "I was so deeply affected yesterday, while my brother was speaking, as not fully to have attended to what I read in my own defence: but being now perfectly tranquil, I entreat, gentlemen, that you will not regard what he urged in my behalf. I repeat, on the contrary,

193 The eldest of the Polignacs, Armand (1771-1847), condemned to death, had that penalty remitted, but was imprisoned in Ham till permitted to escape m 1813. He became Duc de Richelieu in 1817. His younger brother, Jules (1780-1847) was also imprisoned and escaped. In 1814 he was one of the first to display the white flag in Paris. In 1829 he became Minister of Charles X. and was responsible for the ordinances which cost his master his throne in 1830. Imprisoned, nominally for life, he was released in 1836, and after passing some time in England returned to France. The remission of the sentence of death on Prince Armand was obtained by the Empress Josephine. Time after time, urged on by Madame de Rémusat, she implored mercy from Napoleon, who at last consented to see the wife of the Prince. Unlike the Bourbon Louis XVIII., who could see Madame de Lavalette only to refuse the wretched woman's prayer for her husband, for Napoleon to grant the interview was to concede the pardon. The Prince escaped death, and his wife who had obtained the interview by applying to Madame de Rémusat, when she met her benefactress in the times of the Restoration, displayed a really grand forgetfulness of what had passed (see Rémusat, tome ii. chap. i.).

and with most justice, if one of us must fall a sacrifice, if there be yet time, save him, restore him to the tears of his wife; I have no tie like him, I can meet death unappalled;—too young to have tasted the pleasures of the world, I cannot regret their loss."—"No, no," exclaimed his brother, "you are still in the outset of your career; it is I who ought to fall."

At eight in the morning the members of the Tribunal withdrew to the council-chamber. Since the commencement of the proceedings the crowd, far from diminishing, seemed each day to increase; this morning it was immense, and, though the sentence was not expected to be pronounced till a late hour, no one quitted the Court for fear of not being able to find a place when the Tribunal should resume its sitting.

Sentence of death was passed upon Georges Caudoudal, Bouvet de Lozier, Rusillon, Rochelle, Armand de Polignac, Charles d'Hozier, De Riviere, Louis Ducorps, Picot, Lajolais, Roger, Coster St. Victor, Deville, Gaillard, Joyaub, Burban; Lemercier, Jean Cadudol, Lelan, and Merille; while Lies de Polignac, Leridant, General Moreau,[194] Rolland, and Hisay were only condemned to two years' imprisonment.

This decree was heard with consternation by the assembly, and soon spread throughout Paris. I may well affirm it to have been a day of public mourning; even though it was Sunday every place of amusement was nearly deserted. To the horror inspired by a sentence of death passed so wantonly, and of which the greater number of the victims belonged to the most distinguished class of society, was joined the ridicule inspired by the condemnation of Moreau; of the absurdity of which no one seemed more sensible than Bonaparte himself, and respecting which he expressed himself in the most pointed terms. I am persuaded that every one who narrowly watched the proceedings of this celebrated trial must have been convinced that all means were resorted to in order that Moreau, once accused, should not appear entirely free from guilt.

Bonaparte is reported to have said, "Gentlemen, I have no control over your proceedings; it is your duty strictly to examine the evidence before presenting a report to me. But when it has once the sanction of your signatures, woe to you if an innocent man be condemned." This remark is in strict conformity with his usual language, and bears a striking similarity to the conversation I held with him on the following Thursday; but though this language might be appropriate from the lips of a sovereign whose ministers are responsible, it appears but a lame excuse in the mouth of Bonaparte, the possessor of absolute power.

The condemned busied themselves in endeavouring to procure a repeal of their sentence, the greatest number of them yielded in this respect to the entreaties of their friends, who lost no time in taking the steps requisite to obtain the pardon of those in whom they were most interested. Moreau at first also determined to appeal; but he relinquished his purpose before the Court of Cessation commenced its sittings.

As soon as the decree of the special Tribunal was delivered, Murat, Governor of Paris, and brother-in-law to the Emperor, sought his presence and conjured him in the most urgent manner to pardon all the criminals, observing that such an act of clemency would redound greatly to his honour in the opinion of France and all Europe, that it would be said the Emperor pardoned the attempt against the life of the First Consul, that this act of mercy would shed more glory over the commencement of his reign than any security which could accrue from the execution of the prisoners. Such was the conduct of Murat; but he did not solicit, as has been reported, the pardon of any one in particular.

194 General Moreau's sentence was remitted, and he was allowed to go to America.

Those who obtained the imperial pardon were Bouvet de Lozier, who expected it from the disclosures he had made; Rusillon, de Riviere, Rochelle, Armand de Polignac, d'Hozier, Lajolais, who had beforehand received a promise to that effect, and Armand Gaillard.

The other ill-fated victims of a sanguinary police underwent their sentence on the 25th of June, two days after the promulgation of the pardon of their associates.

Their courage and resignation never forsook them even for a moment, and Georges, knowing that it was rumoured he had obtained a pardon, entreated that he might die the first, in order that his companions in their last moments might be assured he had not survived them.

CHAPTER XXVII

1804

The judges composing the Tribunal which condemned Moreau were not all like Thuriot and Hemart. History has recorded an honourable contrast to the general meanness of the period in the reply given by M. Clavier, when urged by Hemart to vote for the condemnation of Moreau. "Ah, Monsieur, if we condemn him, how shall we be able to acquit ourselves?" I have, besides, the best reason for asserting that the judges were tampered with, from, a circumstance which occurred to myself. Bonaparte knew that I was intimately connected with M. Desmaisons, one of the members of the Tribunal, and brother in-law to Corvisart; he also knew that Desmaisons was inclined to believe in Moreau's innocence, and favourable to his acquittal. During the progress of the trial Corvisart arrived at my house one morning at a very early hour, in a state of such evident embarrassment that, before he had time to utter a word, I said to him, "What is the matter? Have you heard any bad news?"

"No," replied Corvisart, "but I came by the Emperor's order. He wishes you to see my brother-in-law. 'He is,' said he to me, 'the senior judge, and a man of considerable eminence; his opinion will carry with it great weight, and I know that he is favourable to Moreau; he is in the wrong. Visit Bourrienne, said the Emperor, and concert with him respecting the best method of convincing Desmaisons of his error, for I repeat he is wrong, he is deceived.' This is the mission with which I am entrusted."

"How," said I, with thorough astonishment, "how came you to be employed in this affair? Could you believe for one moment that I would tamper with a magistrate in order to induce him to exercise an unjust rigour?"

"No, rest assured," replied Corvisart, "I merely visited you this morning in obedience to the order of the Emperor; but I knew beforehand in what manner you would regard the proposition with which I was charged. I knew your opinions and your character too well to entertain the smallest doubt in this respect, and I was convinced that I ran no risk in becoming the bearer of a commission which would be attended with no effect. Besides, had I refused to obey the Emperor, it would have proved prejudicial to your interest, and confirmed him in the opinion that you were favourable to the acquittal of Moreau. For myself," added Corvisart, "it is needless to affirm that I have no intention of attempting to influence the opinion of my brother-in-law; and if I had, you know him sufficiently well to be convinced in what light he would regard such a proceeding."

Such were the object and result of Corvisart's visit, and I am thence led to believe that similar attempts must have been made to influence other members of the Tribunal.[195]

195 "The judges had been pressed and acted on in a thousand ways by the hangers on of the Palace and especially by Real, the natural intermediary between justice and the Government. Ambition, servility, fear, every motive capable of influencing them, had been used: even their humane scruples were employed" (Lanfrey tome iii. p. 193, who goes on to say that the judges were urged to sentence Moreau to death in order that the Emperor might fully pardon him).

But however this may be, prudence led me to discontinue visiting M. Desmaisons, with whom I was in habits of the strictest friendship.

About this period I paid a visit which occupies an important place in my recollections. On the 14th of June 1804, four days after the condemnation of Georges and his accomplices, I received a summons to attend the Emperor at St. Cloud. It was Thursday, and as I thought on the great events and tragic scenes about to be acted, I was rather uneasy respecting his intentions.

But I was fortunate enough to find my friend Rapp in waiting, who said to me as I entered, "Be not alarmed; he is in the best of humours at present, and wishes to have some conversation with you."

Rapp then announced me to the Emperor, and I was immediately admitted to his presence. After pinching my ear and asking his usual questions, such as, "What does the world say? How are your children? What are you about? etc.," he said to me, "By the by, have you attended the proceedings against Moreau?"—"Yes, Sire, I have not been absent during one of the sittings."—"Well, Bourrienne, are you of the opinion that Moreau is innocent?"—"Yes, Sire; at least I am certain that nothing has come out in the course of the trial tending to criminate him; I am even surprised how he came to be implicated in this conspiracy, since nothing has appeared against him which has the most remote connexion with the affair."—"I know your opinion on this subject; Duroc related to me the conversation you held with him at the Tuileries; experience has shown that you were correct; but how could I act otherwise? You know that Bouvet de Lozier hanged himself in prison, and was only saved by accident. Real hurried to the Temple in order to interrogate him, and in his first confessions he criminated Moreau, affirming that he had held repeated conferences with Pichegru. Real immediately reported to me this fact, and proposed that Moreau should be arrested, since the rumours against him seemed to be well founded; he had previously made the same proposition. I at first refused my sanction to this measure; but after the charge made against him by Bouvet de Lozier, how could I act otherwise than I did? Could I suffer such open conspiracies against the Government? Could I doubt the truth of Bouvet de Lozier's declaration, under the circumstances in which it was made? Could I foresee that he would deny his first declaration when brought before the Court? There was a chain of circumstances which human sagacity could not penetrate, and I consented to the arrest of Moreau when it was proved that he was in league with Pichegru. Has not England sent assassins?"—"Sire," said I, "permit me to call to your recollection the conversation you had in my presence with Mr. Fox, after which you said to me, 'Bourrienne, I am very happy at having heard from the mouth of a man of honour that the British Government is incapable of seeking my life; I always wish to esteem my enemies."—"Bah! you are a fool! Parbleu! I did not say that the English Minister sent over an assassin, and that he said to him, 'Here is gold and a poniard; go and kill the First Consul.' No, I did not believe that; but it cannot be denied that all those foreign conspirators against my Government were serving England, and receiving pay from that power. Have I agents in London to disturb the Government of Great Britain? I have waged with it honourable warfare; I have not attempted to awaken a remembrance of the Stuarts amongst their old partisans. Is not Wright, who landed Georges and his accomplices at Dieppe, a captain in the British navy? But rest assured that, with the exception of a few babblers, whom I can easily silence, the hearts of the French people are with me; everywhere public opinion has been declared in my favour, so that I have nothing to apprehend from giving the greatest publicity to these plots, and bringing the accused to a solemn trial. The greater number of those gentlemen wished me to bring the prisoners before a military commission, that summary judgment might be obtained; but I refused my consent to this measure. It might have been said that I dreaded public opinion; and I fear it not. People may talk as much as they please, well and good, I am not obliged to hear them; but I do not like those who are attached to my person to blame what I have done."

As I could not wholly conceal an involuntary emotion, in which the Emperor saw something more than mere surprise, he paused, took me by the ear, and, smiling in the most affectionate manner, said, "I had no reference to you in what I said, but I have to complain of Lacuee. Could you believe that during the trial he went about clamouring in behalf of Moreau? He, my aide de camp—a man who owes everything to me! As for you, I have said that you acted very well in this affair."—"I know not, Sire, what has either been done or said by Lacuee,—whom I have not seen for a long time; what I said to Duroc is what history teaches in every page."—"By the by," resumed the Emperor, after a short silence, "do you know that it was I myself who discovered that Pichegru was in Paris. Everyone said to me, Pichegru is in Paris; Fouché, Real, harped on the same string, but could give me no proof of their assertion. 'What a fool you are,' said I to Real, when in an instant you may ascertain the fact. Pichegru has a brother, an aged ecclesiastic, who resides in Paris; let his dwelling be searched, and should he be absent, it will warrant a suspicion that Pichegru is here; if, on the contrary, his brother should be at home, let him be arrested: he is a simple-minded man, and in the first moments of agitation will betray the truth. Everything happened as I had foreseen, for no sooner was he arrested than, without waiting to be questioned, he inquired if it was a crime to have received his brother into his house. Thus every doubt was removed, and a miscreant in the house in which Pichegru lodged betrayed him to the police. What horrid degradation to betray a friend for the sake of gold."

Then reverting to Moreau, the Emperor talked a great deal respecting that general. "Moreau," he said, "possesses many good qualities; his bravery is undoubted; but he has more courage than energy; he is indolent and effeminate. When with the army he lived like a pasha; he smoked, was almost constantly in bed, and gave himself up to the pleasures of the table. His dispositions are naturally good; but he is too indolent for study; he does not read, and since he has been tied to his wife's apronstrings is fit for nothing. He sees only with the eyes of his wife and her mother, who have had a hand in all these late plots; and then, Bourrienne, is it not very strange that it was by my advice that he entered into this union? I was told that Mademoiselle Hulot was a creole, and I believed that he would find in her a second Josephine; how greatly was I mistaken! It is these women who have estranged us from each other, and I regret that he should have acted so unworthily. You must remember my observing to you more than two years ago that Moreau would one day run his head against the gate of the Tuileries; that he has done so was no fault of mine, for you know how much I did to secure his attachment. You cannot have forgotten the reception I gave him at Malmaison. On the 18th Brumaire I conferred on him the charge of the Luxembourg, and in that situation he fully justified my choice. But since that period he has behaved towards me with the utmost ingratitude—entered into all the silly cabala against me, blamed all my measures, and turned into ridicule the Legion of Honour. Have not some of the intriguers put it into his head that I regard him with jealousy? You must be aware of that. You must also know as well as I how anxious the members of the Directory were to exalt the reputation of Moreau. Alarmed at my success in Italy, they wished to have in the armies a general to serve as a counterpoise to my renown. I have ascended the throne and he is the inmate of a prison! You are aware of the incessant clamouring raised against me by the whole family, at which I confess I was very much displeased; coming from those whom I had treated so well! Had he attached himself to me, I would doubtless have conferred on him the title of First Marshal of the Empire; but what could I do? He constantly depreciated my campaigns and my government. From discontent to revolt there is frequently only one step, especially when a man of a weak character becomes the tool of popular clubs; and therefore when I was first informed that Moreau was implicated in the conspiracy of Georges I believed him to be guilty, but hesitated to issue an order for his arrest till I had taken the opinion of my Council. The members having assembled, I ordered the different documents to be laid before them, with an injunction to examine them with the utmost care, since they related to an affair of importance, and I urged them candidly to inform me whether, in their opinion, any of the charges against Moreau were sufficiently strong to endanger his life. The fools! their reply was in the affirmative; I believe they were even unanimous! Then I had no alternative but to suffer the proceedings to take their course. It is unnecessary to affirm to you, Bourrienne, that Moreau never should have perished on a scaffold! Most assuredly I would have pardoned him; but with the sentence of death hanging over his head he could no longer have proved dangerous; and his name would have ceased to be a rallying-point for disaffected Republicans or imbecile Royalists. Had the Council expressed any doubts respecting his guilt I would have intimated to him that the suspicions against him were so strong as to render any further connection between us impossible; and that the best course he could pursue would be to leave France for three years, under the pretext of visiting some of the places rendered celebrated during the late wars; but that if he preferred a diplomatic mission I would make a suitable provision for his expenses; and the great innovator, Time, might effect great changes during the period of his absence. But my foolish Council affirmed to me that his guilt, as a principal, being evident, it was absolutely necessary to bring him to trial; and now his sentence is only that of a pickpocket. What think you I ought to do? Detain him? He might still prove a rallying-point. No. Let him sell his property and quit? Can I confine him in the Temple? It is full enough without him. Still, if this had been the only great error they had led me to commit—"

"Sire, how greatly you have been deceived."

"Oh yes, I have been so; but I cannot see everything with my own eyes."

At this part of our conversation, of which I have suppressed my own share as much as possible, I conceived that the last words of Bonaparte alluded to the death of the Duc d'Enghien; and I fancied he was about to mention that event but he again spoke of Moreau.

"He is very much mistaken," resumed the Emperor, "if he conceives I bore any ill-will towards him. After his arrest I sent Lauriston to the Temple, whom I chose because he was of an amiable and conciliating disposition; I charged him to tell Moreau to confess he had only seen Pichegru, and I would cause the proceedings against him to be suspended. Instead of receiving this act of generosity as he ought to have done, he replied to it with great haughtiness, so much was he elated that Pichegru had not been arrested; he afterwards, however, lowered his tone. He wrote to me a letter of excuse respecting his anterior conduct, which I caused to be produced on the trial. He was the author of his own ruin; besides, it would have required men of a different stamp from Moreau to conspire against me. Amoung, the conspirators, for example, was an individual whose fate I regret; this Georges in my hands might have achieved great things. I can duly appreciate the firmness of character he displayed, and to which I could have given a proper direction. I caused Real to intimate to him that, if he would attach himself to me, not only should he be pardoned, but that I would give him the command of a regiment. Perhaps I might even have made him my aide de camp. Complaints would have been made, but, parbleu, I should not have cared. Georges refused all my offers; he was as inflexible as iron. What could I do? he underwent his fate, for he was a dangerous man; circumstances rendered his death a matter of necessity. Examples of severity were called for, when England was pouring into France the whole offscouring of the emigration; but patience, patience! I have a long arm, and shall be able to reach them, when necessary. Moreau regarded Georges merely as a ruffian—I viewed him in a different light. You may remember the conversation I had with him at the Tuileries—you and Rapp were in an adjoining cabinet. I tried in vain to influence him—some of his associates were affected at the mention of country and of glory; he alone stood cold and unmoved. I addressed myself to his feelings, but in vain; he was insensible to everything I said. At that period Georges appeared to me little ambitious of power; his whole wishes seemed to centre in commanding the Vendeans. It was not till I had exhausted every means of conciliation that I assumed the tone and language of the first magistrate. I dismissed him with a strong injunction to live retired—to be peaceable and obedient—not to misinterpret the motives of my conduct towards himself—nor attribute to weakness what was merely the result of moderation and strength. 'Rest assured,' I added, 'and repeat to your associates, that while I hold the reins of authority there will be neither chance nor salvation for those who dare to conspire against me: How he conformed to this injunction the event has shown. Real told me that when Moreau and Georges found themselves in the presence of Pichegru they could not come to any understanding, because Georges would not act against the Bourbons. Well, he had a plan, but Moreau had none; he merely wished for my overthrow, without having formed any ulterior views whatever. This showed that he was destitute of even common sense. Apropos, Bourrienne, have you seen Corvisart?"—"Yes, Sire."—"Well!" "He delivered to me the message with which you entrusted him."—"And Desmaisons!—I wager that you have not spoken to him in conformity to my wishes."—"Sire, the estimation in which I hold Desmaisons deterred me from a course so injurious to him; for in what other light could he have considered what I should have said to him? I have never visited at his house since the commencement of the trial."—"Well! well! Be prudent and discreet, I shall not forget you." He then waved a very gracious salute with his hand, and withdrew into his cabinet.

The Emperor had detained me more than an hour. On leaving the audience-chamber I passed through the outer salon, where a number of individuals were waiting; and I perceived that an observance of etiquette was fast gaining ground, though the Emperor had not yet adopted the admirable institution of Court Chamberlains.

I cannot deny that I was much gratified with my reception; besides I was beginning to be weary of an inactive life, and was anxious to obtain a place, of which I stood in great need, from the losses I had sustained and the unjust resumption which Bonaparte had made of his gifts. Being desirous to speak of Napoleon with the strictest impartiality, I prefer drawing my conclusions from those actions in which I had no personal concern. I shall therefore only relate here, even before giving an account of my visit to the Empress on leaving the audience-chamber, the former conduct of Napoleon towards myself and Madame de Bourrienne, which will justify the momentary alarm with which I was seized when summoned to the Tuileries, and the satisfaction I felt at my reception. I had a proof of what Rapp said of the Emperor being in good-humour, and was flattered by the confidential manner in which he spoke to me concerning some of the great political secrets of his Government. On seeing me come out Rapp observed, "You have had a long audience."—"Yes, not amiss;" and this circumstance procured for me a courtly salutation from all persons waiting in the antechamber.'

I shall now relate how I spent the two preceding years. The month after I tendered my resignation to the First Consul, and which he refused to accept, the house at St. Cloud belonging to Madame Deville was offered to me; it was that in which the Duc d'Angouleme and the Duc de Berri were inoculated. I visited this mansion, thinking it might be suitable for my family; but, notwithstanding the beauty of its situation, it seemed far too splendid either for my taste or my fortune. Except the outer walls, it was in a very dilapidated state, and would require numerous and expensive repairs. Josephine, being informed that Madame de Bourrienne had set her face against the purchase, expressed a wish to see the mansion, and accompanied us for that purpose. She was so much delighted with it that she blamed my wife for starting any objections to my becoming, its possessor. "With regard to the expense," Josephine replied to her, "ah, we shall arrange that." On our return to Malmaison she spoke of it in such high terms that Bonaparte said to me, "Why don't you purchase it, Bourrienne, since the price is so reasonable?"

The house was accordingly purchased. An outlay of 20,000 francs was immediately required to render it habitable. Furniture was also necessary for this large mansion, and orders for it were accordingly given. But no sooner were repairs begun than everything crumbled to pieces, which rendered many additional expenses necessary.

About this period Bonaparte hurried forward the works at St. Cloud, to which place he immediately removed. My services being constantly required, I found it so fatiguing to go twice or thrice a day from Ruel to St. Cloud that I took possession of my new mansion, though it was still filled with workmen. Scarcely eight days had elapsed from this period when Bonaparte intimated that he no longer had occasion for my services. When my wife went to take leave Napoleon spoke to her in a flattering manner of my good qualities, my merit, and the utility of my labours, saying that he was himself the most unfortunate of the three, and that my loss could never be replaced. He then added, "I shall be absent for a month, but Bourrienne may be quite easy; let him remain in retirement, and on my return I shall reward his services, should I even create a place on purpose for him."

Madame de Bourrienne then requested leave to retain the apartments appropriated to her in the Tuileries till after her accouchement, which was not far distant, to which he replied, "You may keep them as long as you please; for it will be some time before I again reside in Paris."

Bonaparte set out on his journey, and shortly afterwards I went with my family to visit Madame de Coubertin, my cousin-german, who received us with her usual kindness. We passed the time of the First Consul's absence at her country seat, and only returned to St. Cloud on the day Bonaparte was expected.

Scarcely a quarter of an hour had elapsed after his arrival when I received an intimation to give up, in twenty-four hours, the apartments in the Tuileries, which he had promised my wife should retain till after her confinement. He reclaimed at the same time the furniture of Ruel, which he presented to me two years before, when I purchased that small house on purpose to be near him.

I addressed several memorials to him on this subject, stating that I had replaced the worn-out furniture with new and superior articles; but this he wholly disregarded, compelling me to give up everything, even to the greatest trifle. It may be right to say that on his return the Emperor found his table covered with information respecting my conduct in Paris, though

I had not held the smallest communication with any one in the capital, nor once entered it during his absence.

After my departure for Hamburg, Bonaparte took possession of my stables and coach-house, which he filled with horses. Even the very avenues and walks were converted into stabling. A handsome house at the entrance to the park was also appropriated to similar purposes; in fact, he spared nothing. Everything was done in the true military style; I neither had previous intimation of the proceedings nor received any remuneration for my loss. The Emperor seemed to regard the property as his own; but though he all but ordered me to make the purchase, he did not furnish the money that was paid for it. In this way it was occupied for more than four years.

The recollection of those arbitrary and vexatious proceedings on the part of Bonaparte has led me farther than I intended. I shall therefore return to the imperial residence of St. Cloud. On leaving the audience-chamber, as already stated, I repaired to the apartments of the Empress, who, knowing that I was in the Palace, had intimated her wishes for my attendance. No command could have been more agreeable to me, for every one was certain of a gracious reception from Josephine. I do not recollect which of the ladies in waiting was in attendance when my name was announced; but she immediately retired, and left me alone with Josephine. Her recent elevation had not changed the usual amenity of her disposition. After some conversation respecting the change in her situation, I gave her an account of what had passed between the Emperor and myself.

I faithfully related all that he had said of Moreau, observing that at one moment I imagined he was about to speak of the Duc d'Enghien, when he suddenly reverted to what he had been saying, and never made the slightest allusion to the subject.

Madame Bonaparte replied to me, "Napoleon has spoken the truth respecting Moreau. He was grossly deceived by those who believed they could best pay their court to him by calumniating that general. His silence on the subject of the Duc d'Enghien does not surprise me; he says as little respecting it as possible, and always in a vague manner, and with manifest repugnance. When you see Bonaparte again be silent on the subject, and should chance bring it forward, avoid every expression in the smallest degree indicative of reproach; he would not suffer it; you would ruin yourself for ever in his estimation, and the evil is, alas! without remedy. When you came to Malmaison I told you that I had vainly endeavoured to turn him from his fatal purpose, and how he had treated me. Since then he has experienced but little internal satisfaction; it is only in the presence of his courtiers that he affects a calm and tranquil deportment; but I perceive his sufferings are the greater from thus endeavouring to conceal them. By the by, I forgot to mention that he knew of the visit you paid me on the day after the catastrophe. I dreaded that your enemies, the greater number of whom are also mine, might have misrepresented that interview; but, fortunately, he paid little attention to it. He merely said, 'So you have seen Bourrienne? Does he sulk at me? Nevertheless I must do something for him.' He has again spoken in the same strain, and repeated nearly the same expressions three days ago; and since he has commanded your presence to-day, I have not a doubt but he has something in view for your advantage."—"May I presume to inquire what it is?"—"I do not yet know; but I would recommend to you, in the meantime, to be more strictly on your guard than ever; he is so suspicious, and so well informed of all that is done or said respecting himself. I have suffered so much since I last saw you; never can I forget the unkind manner in which he rejected my entreaties! For several days I laboured under a depression of spirits which greatly irritated him, because he clearly saw whence it proceeded. I am not dazzled by the title of Empress; I dread some evil will result from this step to him, to my children, and to myself. The miscreants ought to be satisfied; see to what they have driven us! This death embitters every moment of my life. I need not say to you, Bourrienne, that I speak this in confidence."—"You cannot doubt my prudence."—"No, certainly not, Bourrienne. I do not doubt it. My confidence in you is unbounded. Rest assured that I shall never forget what you have done for me, under various circumstances, and the devotedness you evinced to me on your return from Egypt.—Adieu, my friend. Let me see you soon again."

It was on the 14th of June 1804 that I had this audience of the Emperor, and afterwards attended the Empress.

On my return home I spent three hours in making notes of all that was said to me by these two personages; and the substance of these notes I have now given to the reader.

CHAPTER XXVIII

1804

Louis XVIII., being at Warsaw when he was informed of the elevation of Napoleon to the Imperial dignity, addressed to the sovereigns of Europe a protest against that usurpation of his throne. Fouché, being the first who heard of this protest, immediately communicated the circumstance to the Emperor, observing that doubtless the copies would be multiplied and distributed amongst the enemies of his Government, in the Faubourg St. Germain, which might produce the worst effects, and that he therefore deemed it his duty to inform him that orders might be given to Regnier and Real to keep a strict watch over those engaged in distributing this document.

"You may judge of my surprise," added Fouché, "you who know so well that formerly the very mention of the Bourbons rendered Bonaparte furious, when, after perusing the protest, he returned it to me, saying, 'Ah, ah, so the Comte de Lille makes his protest! Well, well, all in good time. I hold my right by the voice of the French nation, and while I wear a sword I will maintain it! The Bourbons ought to know that I do not fear them; let them, therefore, leave me in tranquillity. Did you say that the fools of the Faubourg St. Germain would multiply the copies of this protest of Comte de Lille? well, they shall read it at their ease. Send it to the Moniteur, Fouché; and let it be inserted to-morrow morning.'" This passed on the 30th of June, and the next day the protest of Louis XVIII. did actually appear in that paper.

Fouché was wholly indifferent respecting the circulation of this protest; he merely wished to show the Emperor that he was better informed of passing events than Regnier, and to afford Napoleon another proof of the inexperience and inability of the Grand Judge in police; and Fouché was not long in receiving the reward which he expected from this step. In fact, ten days after the publication of the protest, the Emperor announced to Regnier the re-establishment of the Ministry of General Police.

The formula, I Pray God to have you in His holy keeping, with which the letter to Regnier closed, was another step of Napoleon in the knowledge of ancient usages, with which he was not sufficiently familiar when he wrote Cambacérès on the day succeeding his elevation to the Imperial throne; at the same time it must be confessed that this formula assorted awkwardly with the month of "Messidor," and the "twelfth year of the Republic!"

The errors which Regnier had committed in the affair of Georges were the cause which determined Bonaparte to re-establish the Ministry of Police, and to bestow it on a man who had created a belief in the necessity of that measure, by a monstrous accumulation of plots and intrigues. I am also certain that the Emperor was swayed by the probability of a war breaking out, which would force him to leave France; and that he considered Fouché as the most proper person to maintain the public tranquillity during his absence, and detect any cabala that might be formed in favour of the Bourbons.

At this period, when Bonaparte had given the finishing blow to the Republic, which had only been a shadow since the 19th Brumaire, it was not difficult to foresee that the Bourbons would one day remount the throne of their ancestors; and this presentiment was not, perhaps, without its influence in rendering the majority greater in favour of the foundation of the Empire than for the establishment of a Consulate for life. The reestablishment of the throne was a most important step in favour of the Bourbons, for that was the thing most difficult to be done. But Bonaparte undertook the task; and, as if by the aid of a magic rod, the ancient order of things was restored in the twinkling of an eye. The distinctions of rank—orders—titles, the noblesse—decorations—all the baubles of vanity—in short, all the burlesque tattooing which the vulgar regard as an indispensable attribute of royalty, reappeared in an instant. The question no longer regarded the form of government, but the individual who should be placed at its head. By restoring the ancient order of things, the Republicans had themselves decided the question, and it could no longer be doubted that when an occasion presented itself the majority of the nation would prefer the ancient royal family, to whom France owed her civilisation, her greatness, and her power, and who had exalted her to such a high degree of glory and prosperity.

It was not one of the least singular traits in Napoleon's character that during the first year of his reign he retained the fete of the 14th of July. It was not indeed strictly a Republican fate, but it recalled the recollection of two great popular triumphs,—the taking of the Bastille and the first Federation. This year the 14th of July fell on a Saturday, and the Emperor ordered its celebration to be delayed till the following day, because it was Sunday; which was in conformity with the sentiments he delivered respecting the Concordat. "What renders me," he said, "most hostile to the re-establishment of the Catholic worship is the number of festivals formerly observed. A saint's day is a day of indolence, and I wish not for that; the people must labour in order to live. I consent to four holidays in the year, but no more; if the gentlemen from Rome are not satisfied with this, they may take their departure."

The loss of time seemed to him so great a calamity that he seldom failed to order an indispensable solemnity to be held on the succeeding holiday. Thus he postponed the Corpus Christi to the following Sunday.

On Sunday, the 15th of July 1804, the Emperor appeared for the first time before the Parisians surrounded by all the pomp of royalty. The members of the Legion of Honour, then in Paris, took the oath prescribed by the new Constitution, and on this occasion the Emperor and Empress appeared attended for the first time by a separate and numerous retinue.

The carriages in the train of the Empress crossed the garden of the Tuileries, hitherto exclusively appropriated to the public; then followed the cavalcade of the Emperor, who appeared on horseback, surrounded by his principal generals, whom he had created Marshals of the Empire. M. de Segur, who held the office of Grand Master of Ceremonies, had the direction of the ceremonial to be observed on this occasion, and with, the Governor received the Emperor on the threshold of the Hotel des Invalides. They conducted the Empress to a tribune prepared for her reception, opposite the Imperial throne which Napoleon alone occupied, to the right of the altar. I was present at this ceremony, notwithstanding the repugnance I have to such brilliant exhibitions; but as Duroc had two days before presented me with tickets, I deemed it prudent to attend on the occasion, lest the keen eye of Bonaparte should have remarked my absence if Duroc had acted by his order.

I spent about an hour contemplating the proud and sometimes almost ludicrous demeanour of the new grandees of the Empire; I marked the manoeuvring of the clergy, who, with Cardinal Belloy at their head, proceeded to receive the Emperor on his entrance into the church. What a singular train of ideas was called up to my mind when I beheld my former comrade at the school of Brienne seated upon an elevated throne, surrounded by his brilliant staff, the great dignitaries of his Empire—his Ministers and Marshals! I involuntarily recurred to the 19th Brumaire, and all this splendid scene vanished; when I thought of Bonaparte stammering to such a degree that I was obliged to pull the skirt of his coat to induce him to withdraw.

It was neither a feeling of animosity nor of jealousy which called up such reflections; at no period of our career would I have exchanged my situation for his; but whoever can reflect, whoever has witnessed the unexpected elevation of a former equal, may perhaps be able to conceive the strange thoughts that assailed my mind, for the first time, on this occasion.

When the religious part of the ceremony terminated, the church assumed, in some measure, the appearance of a profane temple. The congregation displayed more devotion to the Emperor than towards the God of the Christians,—more enthusiasm than fervour. The mass had been heard with little attention; but when M. de Lacepede, Grand Chancellor of the Legion of Honour, after pronouncing a flattering discourse, finished the call of the Grand Officers of the Legion, Bonaparte covered, as did the ancient kings of France when they held a bed of justice. A profound silence, a sort of religious awe, then reigned throughout the assembly, and Napoleon, who did not now stammer as in the Council of the Five Hundred, said in a firm voice:

"Commanders, officers, legionaries, citizens, soldiers; swear upon your honour to devote yourselves to the service of the Empire—to the preservation of the integrity of the French territory—to the defence of the Emperor, of the laws of the Republic, and of the property which they have made sacred—to combat by all the means which justice, reason, and the laws authorise every attempt to reestablish the feudal system; in short, swear to concur with all your might in maintaining liberty and equality, which are the bases of all our institutions. Do you swear?"

Each member of the Legion of Honour exclaimed, "I swear;" adding, "Vive l'Empereur!" with an enthusiasm it is impossible to describe, and in which all present joined.

What, after all, was this new oath? It only differed from that taken by the Legion of Honour, under the Consulate, in putting the defence of the Emperor before that of the laws of the Republic; and this was not merely a form. It was, besides, sufficiently laughable and somewhat audacious, to make them swear to support equality at the moment so many titles and monarchical distinctions had been re-established.

On the 18th of July, three days after this ceremony, the Emperor left Paris to visit the camp at Boulogne. He was not accompanied by the Empress on this journey, which was merely to examine the progress of the military operations. Availing myself of the invitation Josephine had given me, I presented myself at St. Cloud a few days after the departure of Napoleon; as she did not expect my visit, I found her surrounded by four or five of the ladies in waiting, occupied in examining some of the elegant productions of the famous Leroi and Madame Despeaux; for amidst the host of painful feelings experienced by Josephine she was too much of a woman not to devote some attention to the toilet.

On my introduction they were discussing the serious question of the costume to be worn by the Empress on her journey to Belgium to meet Napoleon at the Palace of Lacken, near Brussels. Notwithstanding those discussions respecting the form of hats, the colour and shape of dresses, etc., Josephine received me in her usual gracious manner. But not being able to converse with me, she said, without giving it an appearance of invitation but in a manner sufficiently evident to be understood, that she intended to pass the following morning at Malmaison.

I shortened my visit, and at noon next day repaired to that delightful abode, which always created in my mind deep emotion. Not an alley, not a grove but teemed with interesting recollections; all recalled to me the period when I was the confidant of Bonaparte. But the time was past when he minutely calculated how much a residence at Malmaison would cost, and concluded by saying that an income of 30,000 livres would be necessary.

When I arrived Madame Bonaparte was in the garden with Madame de Rémusat, who was her favourite from the similarity of disposition which existed between them.

Madame de Rémusat was the daughter of the Minister Vergennes, and sister to Madame de Nansouty, whom I had sometimes seen with Josephine, but not so frequently as her elder sister. I found the ladies in the avenue which leads to Ruel, and saluted Josephine by inquiring respecting the health of Her Majesty. Never can I forget the tone in which she replied: "Ah! Bourrienne, I entreat that you will suffer me, at least here, to forget that I am an Empress." As she had not a thought concealed from Madame de Rémusat except some domestic vexations, of which probably I was the only confidant, we conversed with the same freedom as if alone, and it is easy to define that the subject of our discourse regarded Bonaparte.

After having spoken of her intended journey to Belgium, Josephine said to me, "What a pity, Bourrienne, that the past cannot be recalled! He departed in the happiest disposition: he has bestowed some pardons and I am satisfied that but for those accursed politics he would have pardoned a far greater number. I would have said much more, but I endeavoured to conceal my chagrin because the slightest contradiction only renders him the more obstinate. Now, when in the midst of his army, he will forget everything. How much have I been afflicted that I was not able to obtain a favourable answer to all the petitions which were addressed to me. That good Madame de Monteason came from Romainville to St. Cloud to solicit the pardon of MM. de Riviere and de Polignac; we succeeded in gaining an audience for Madame de Polignac; . . . how beautiful she is! Bonaparte was greatly affected on beholding her; he said to her, 'Madame, since it was only my life your husband menaced, I may pardon him.' You know Napoleon, Bourrienne; you know that he is not naturally cruel; it is his counsellors and flatterers who have induced him to commit so many villainous actions. Rapp has behaved extremely well; he went to the Emperor, and would not leave him till he had obtained the pardon of another of the condemned, whose name I do not recollect. How much these Polignacs have interested me! There will be then at least some families who will owe him gratitude! Strive, if it be possible, to throw a veil over the past; I am sufficiently miserable in my anticipations of the future. Rest assured, my dear Bourrienne, that I shall not fail to exert myself during our stay in Belgium in your behalf, and inform you of the result. Adieu!"

During the festival in celebration of the 14th of July, which I have already alluded to, the Emperor before leaving the Hotel des Invalides had announced that he would go in person to distribute the decorations of the Legion of Honour to the army assembled in the camp of Boulogne. He was not long before he fulfilled his promise. He left St. Cloud on the 18th and travelled with such rapidity that the next morning, whilst every one was busy with preparations for his reception, he was already at that port, in the midst of the labourers, examining the works. He seemed to multiply himself by his inconceivable activity, and one might say that he was present everywhere.

At the Emperor's departure it was generally believed at Paris that the distribution of the crosses at the camp of Boulogne was only a pretext, and that Bonaparte had at length gone to carry into execution the project of an invasion of England, which every body supposed he contemplated. It was, indeed, a pretext. The Emperor wished to excite more and more the enthusiasm of the army—to show himself to the military invested in his new dignity, to be present at some grand manoeuvres, and dispose the army to obey the first signal he might give. How indeed, on beholding such great preparations, so many transports created, as it were, by enchantment, could any one have supposed that he did not really intend to attempt a descent on England? People almost fancied him already in London; it was known that all the army corps echelloned on the coast from Maples to Ostend were ready to embark. Napoleon's arrival in the midst of his troops inspired them, if possible, with a new impulse. The French ports on the Channel had for a long period been converted into dockyards and arsenals, where works were carried on with that inconceivable activity which Napoleon knew so well how to inspire. An almost incredible degree of emulation prevailed amongst the commanders of the different camps, and it descended from rank to rank to the common soldiers and even to the labourers.

As every one was eager to take advantage of the slightest effects of chance, and exercised his ingenuity in converting them into prognostics of good fortune for the Emperor, those who had access to him did not fail to call his attention to some remains of a Roman camp which had been discovered at the Tour d'Ordre, where the Emperor's tent was pitched. This was considered an evident proof that the French Caesar occupied the camp which the Roman Caesar had formerly constructed to menace Great Britain. To give additional force to this allusion, the Tour d'Ordre resumed the name of Caesar's Tower. Some medals of William the Conqueror, found in another spot, where, perhaps, they had been buried for the purpose of being dug up, could not fail to satisfy the most incredulous that Napoleon must conquer England.

It was not far from Caesar's Tower that 80,000 men of the camps of Boulogne and Montreuil, under the command of Marshal Soult, were assembled in a vast plain to witness the distribution of the crosses of the Legion of Honour impressed with the Imperial effigy. This plain, which I saw with Bonaparte in our first journey to the coast, before our departure to Egypt, was circular and hollow; and in the centre was a little hill. This hill formed the Imperial throne of Bonaparte in the midst of his soldiers. There he stationed himself with his staff and around this centre of glory the regiments were drawn up in lines and looked like so many diverging rays. From this throne, which had been erected by the hand of nature, Bonaparte delivered in a loud voice the same form of oath which he had pronounced at the Hotel des Invalides a few days before. It was the signal for a general burst of enthusiasm, and Rapp, alluding to this ceremony, told me that he never saw the Emperor appear more pleased. How could he be otherwise? Fortune then seemed obedient to his wishes. A storm came on during this brilliant day, and it was apprehended that part of the flotilla would have suffered.

Bonaparte quitted the hill from which he had distributed the crosses and proceeded to the port to direct what measures should be taken, when upon his arrival the storm[196]—

196 The following description of the incident when Napoleon nearly occasioned the destruction of the Boulogne flotilla was forwarded to the 'Revue Politique et Litteraire' from a private memoir. The writer, who was an eye-witness, says— One morning, when the Emperor was mounting his horse, he announced that he intended to hold a review of his naval forces, and gave the order that the vessels which lay in the harbour should alter their positions, as the review was to be held on the open sea. He started on his usual ride, giving orders that

everything should be arranged on his return, the time of which he indicated. His wish was communicated to Admiral Bruix, who responded with imperturbable coolness that he was very sorry, but that the review could not take place that day. Consequently not a vessel was moved. On his return back from his ride the Emperor asked whether all was ready. He was told what the Admiral had said. Twice the answer had to be repeated to him before he could realise its nature, and then, violently stamping his foot on the ground, he sent for the Admiral. The Emperor met him halfway. With eyes burning with rage, he exclaimed in an excited voice, "Why have my orders not been executed?" With respectful firmness Admiral Bruix replied, "Sire, a terrible storm is brewing. Your Majesty may convince yourself of it; would you without need expose the lives of so many men?" The heaviness of the atmosphere and the sound of thunder in the distance more than justified the fears of the Admiral. "Sir, said the Emperor, getting more and more irritated, "I have given the orders once more; why have they not been executed? The consequences concern me alone. Obey!" 'Sire, I will not obey,' replied the Admiral. "You are insolent!" And the Emperor, who still held his riding-whip in his hand, advanced towards the admiral with a threatening gesture. Admiral Bruix stepped back and put his hand on the sheath of his sword and said, growing very pale, "sire, take care!" The whole suite stood paralysed with fear. The Emperor remained motionless for some time, his hand lifted up, his eyes fixed on the Admiral, who still retained his menacing attitude. At last the Emperor threw his whip on the floor. M. Bruix took his hand off his sword, and with uncovered head awaited in silence the result of the painful scene. Rear-Admiral Magon was then ordered to see that the Emperor's orders were instantly executed. "As for you, sir," said the Emperor, fixing his eyes on Admiral Bruix, you leave Boulogne within twenty-four hours and depart for Holland. Go!" M. Magon ordered the fatal movement of the fleet on which the Emperor had insisted. The first arrangements had scarcely been made when the sea became very high. The black sky was pierced by lightning, the thunder rolled and every moment the line of vessels was broken by the wind, and shortly after, that which the Admiral had foreseen came to pass, and the most frightful storm dispersed the vessels in each a way that it seamed impossible to save them. With bent head, arms crossed, and a sorrowful look in his face, the Emperor walked up and down on the beach, when suddenly the most terrible cries were heard. More than twenty gunboats filled with soldiers and sailors were being driven towards the shore, and the unfortunate men were vainly fighting against the furious waves, calling for help which nobody could give them. Deeply touched by the spectacle and the heart-rending cries and lamentations of the multitude which had assembled on the beach, the Emperor, seeing his generals and officers tremble with horror, attempted to set an example of devotion, and, in spite of all efforts to keep him back, he threw himself into a boat, saying, "Let me go! let me go! they must be brought out of this." In a moment the boat was filled with water. The waves poured over it again and again, and the Emperor was drenched. One wave larger than the others almost threw him overboard and his hat was carried sway. Inspired by so much courage, officers, soldiers, seamen, and citizens tried to succour the drowning, some in boats, some swimming. But, alas! only a small number could be saved of the unfortunate men.
The following day more than 200 bodies were thrown ashore, and with them the hat of the conqueror of Marengo. That sad day was one of desolation for Boulogne and for the camp. The Emperor groaned under the burden of an accident which he had to attribute solely to his own obstinacy. Agents were despatched to all parts of the town to subdue with gold the murmurs which were ready to break out into a tumult.

ceased as if by enchantment. The flotilla entered the port safe and sound and he went back to the camp, where the sports and amusements prepared for the soldiers commenced, and in the evening the brilliant fireworks which were let off rose in a luminous column, which was distinctly seen from the English coast[197].

When he reviewed the troops he asked the officers, and often the soldiers, in what battles they had been engaged, and to those who had received serious wounds he gave the cross. Here, I think, I may appropriately mention a singular piece of charlatanism to which the Emperor had recourse, and which powerfully contributed to augment the enthusiasm of his troops. He would say to one of his aides de camp, "Ascertain from the colonel of such a regiment whether he has in his corps a man who has served in the campaigns of Italy or the campaigns of Egypt. Ascertain his name, where he was born, the particulars of his family, and what he has done. Learn his number in the ranks, and to what company he belongs, and furnish me with the information."

On the day of the review Bonaparte, at a single glance, could perceive the man who had been described to him. He would go up to him as if he recognised him, address him by his name, and say, "Oh! so you are here! You are a brave fellow—I saw you at Aboukir—how is your old father? What! have you not got the Cross? Stay, I will give it you." Then the delighted soldiers would say to each other, "You see the Emperor knows us all; he knows our families; he knows where we have served." What a stimulus was this to soldiers, whom he succeeded in persuading that they would all some time or other become Marshals of the Empire!

Lauriston told me, amongst other anecdotes relating to Napoleon's sojourn at the camp at Boulogne, a remarkable instance of intrepidity on the part of two English sailors. These men had been prisoners at Verdun, which was the most considerable depot of English prisoners in France at the rupture of the peace of Amiens. They effected their escape from Verdun, and arrived at Boulogne without having been discovered on the road, notwithstanding the vigilance with which all the English were watched. They remained at Boulogne for some time, destitute of money, and without being able to effect their escape. They had no hope of getting aboard a boat, on account of the strict watch that was kept upon vessels of every kind. These two sailors made a boat of little pieces of wood, which they put together as well as they could, having no other tools than their knives. They covered it with a piece of sail-cloth. It was only three or four feet wide, and not much longer, and was so light that a man could easily carry it on his shoulders,—so powerful a passion is the love of home and liberty! Sure of being shot if they were discovered, almost equally sure of being drowned if they effected their escape, they, nevertheless, resolved to attempt crossing the Channel in their fragile skiff. Perceiving an English frigate within sight of the coast, they pushed off and endeavoured to reach her. They had not gone a hundred toises from the shore when they were perceived by the custom-house officers, who set out in pursuit of them, and brought them back again. The news of this adventure spread through the camp, where the extraordinary courage of the two sailors was the subject of general remark. The circumstance reached the Emperor's ears. He wished to see the men, and they were conducted to his presence, along with their little boat. Napoleon, whose imagination was struck by everything extraordinary, could not conceal his surprise at so bold a project, undertaken with such feeble means of execution. "Is it really true," said the Emperor to them, "that you thought of crossing the

197 It appears that Napoleon was so well able to cover up this fiasco that not even Bourrienne ever heard the true story. —D.W.

sea in this?"—"Sire," said they, "if you doubt it, give us leave to go, and you shall see us depart."—"I will. You are bold and enterprising men—I admire courage wherever I meet it. But you shall not hazard your lives. You are at liberty; and more than that, I will cause you to be put on board an English ship. When you return to London tell how I esteem brave men, even when they are my enemies." Rapp, who with Lauriaton, Duroc, and many others were present at this scene, were not a little astonished at the Emperor's generosity. If the men had not been brought before him, they would have been shot as spies, instead of which they obtained their liberty, and Napoleon gave several pieces of gold to each. This circumstance was one of those which made the strongest impression on Napoleon, and he recollected it when at St. Helena, in one of his conversations with M. de Las Casas.

No man was ever so fond of contrasts as Bonaparte. He liked, above everything, to direct the affairs of war whilst seated in his easy chair, in the cabinet of St. Cloud, and to dictate in the camp his decrees relative to civil administration. Thus, at the camp of Boulogne, he founded the decennial premiums, the first distribution of which he intended should take place five years afterwards, on the anniversary of the 18th Brumaire, which was an innocent compliment to the date of the foundation of the Consular Republic. This measure also seemed to promise to the Republican calendar a longevity which it did not attain. All these little circumstances passed unobserved; but Bonaparte had so often developed to me his theory of the art of deceiving mankind that I knew their true value. It was likewise at the camp of Boulogne that, by a decree emanating from his individual will, he destroyed the noblest institution of the Republic, the Polytechnic School, by converting it into a purely military academy. He knew that in that sanctuary of high study a Republican spirit was fostered; and whilst I was with him he had often told me it was necessary that all schools, colleges, and establishments for public instruction should be subject to military discipline. I frequently endeavoured to controvert this idea, but without success.

It was arranged that Josephine and the Emperor should meet in Belgium. He proceeded thither from the camp of Boulogne, to the astonishment of those who believed that the moment for the invasion of England had at length arrived. He joined the Empress at the Palace of Lacken, which the Emperor had ordered to be repaired and newly furnished with great magnificence.

The Emperor continued his journey by the towns bordering on the Rhine. He stopped first in the town of Charlemagne, passed through the three bishoprics,[198] —on his way Cologne

198 There are two or three little circumstances in connection with this journey that seem worth inserting here: Mademoiselle Avrillion was the 'femme de chambre' of Josephine, and was constantly about her person from the time of the first Consulship to the death of the Empress in 1814. In all such matters as we shall quote from them, her memoirs seem worthy of credit. According to Mademoiselle, the Empress during her stay at Aix-la- Chapelle, drank the waters with much eagerness and some hope. As the theatre there was only supplied with some German singers who were not to Josephine's taste, she had part of a French operatic company sent to her from Paris. The amiable creole had always a most royal disregard of expense. When Bonaparte joined her, he renewed his old custom of visiting his wife now and then at her toilet, and according to Mademoiselle Avrillion, he took great interest in the subject of her dressing. She says, "It was a most extraordinary thing for us to see the man whose head was filled with such vast affairs enter into the most minute details of the female toilet and of what dresses, what robes, and what jewels the Empress should wear on such and such an

and Coblentz, which the emigration had rendered so famous, and arrived at Mayence, where his sojourn was distinguished by the first attempt at negotiation with the Holy See, in order to induce the Pope to come to France to crown the new Emperor, and consolidate his power by supporting it with the sanction of the Church. This journey of Napoleon occupied three months, and he did not return to St. Cloud till October. Amongst the flattering addresses which the Emperor received in the course of his journey I cannot pass over unnoticed the speech of M. de la Chaise, Prefect of Arras, who said, "God made Bonaparte, and then rested." This occasioned Comte Louis de Narbonne, who was not yet attached to the Imperial system, to remark "That it would have been well had God rested a little sooner."

During the Emperor's absence a partial change took place in the Ministry. M. de Champagny succeeded M. Chaptal as Minister of the Interior. At the camp of Boulogne the pacific Joseph found himself, by his brother's wish, transformed into a warrior, and placed in command of a regiment of dragoons, which was a subject of laughter with a great number of generals. I recollect that one day Lannes, speaking to me of the circumstance in his usual downright and energetic way, said, "He had better not place him under my orders, for upon the first fault I will put the scamp under arrest."

---

occasion. One day he daubed her dress with ink because he did not like it, and wanted her to put on another. Whenever he looked into her wardrobe he was sure to throw everything topsy-turvy." This characteristic anecdote perfectly agrees with what we have heard from other persons. When the Neapolitan Princess di——- was at the Tuileries as 'dame d'honneur' to Bonaparte's sister Caroline Murat, then Queen of Naples, on the grand occasion of the marriage with Maria Louisa, the, Princess, to her astonishment, saw the Emperor go up to a lady of the Court and address her thus: "This is the same gown you wore the day before yesterday! What's the meaning of this, madame? This is not right, madame!" Josephine never gave him a similar cause of complaint, but even when he was Emperor she often made him murmur at the profusion of her expenditure under this head. The next anecdote will give some idea of the quantity of dresses which she wore for a day or so, and then gave away to her attendants, who appear to have carried on a very active trade in them. "While we were at Mayence the Palace was literally besieged by Jews, who continually brought manufactured and other goods to show to the followers of the Court; and we had the greatest difficulty to avoid buying them. At last they proposed that we should barter with them; and when Her Majesty had given us dresses that were far too rich for us to wear ourselves, we exchanged them with the Jews for piecegoods. The robes we thus bartered did not long remain in the hands of the Jews, and there must have been a great demand for them among the belles of Mayence, for I remember a ball there at which the Empress might have seen all the ladies of a quadrille party dressed in her cast-off clothes.—I even saw German Princesses wearing them" (Memoires de Mademoiselle Avrillion).

CHAPTER XXIX

1804

England was never so much deceived by Bonaparte as during the period of the encampment at Boulogne. The English really believed that an invasion was intended, and the Government exhausted itself in efforts for raising men and money to guard against the danger of being taken by surprise. Such, indeed, is the advantage always possessed by the assailant. He can choose the point on which he thinks it most convenient to act, while the party which stands on the defence, and is afraid of being attacked, is compelled to be prepared in every point. However, Napoleon, who was then in the full vigour of his genius and activity, had always his eyes fixed on objects remote from those which surrounded him, and which seemed to absorb his whole attention. Thus, during the journey of which I have spoken, the ostensible object of which was the organisation of the departments on the Rhine, he despatched two squadrons from Rochefort and Boulogne, one commanded by Missiessy, the other by Villeneuve—I shall not enter into any details about those squadrons; I shall merely mention with respect to them that, while the Emperor was still in Belgium, Lauriston paid me a sudden and unexpected visit. He was on his way to Toulon to take command of the troops which were to be embarked on Villeneuve's squadron, and he was not much pleased with the service to which he had been appointed.

Lauriston's visit was a piece of good fortune for me. We were always on friendly terms, and I received much information from him, particularly with respect to the manner in which the Emperor spent his time. "You can have no idea," said he, "how much the Emperor does, and the sort of enthusiasm which his presence excites in the army. But his anger at the contractors is greater than ever, and he has been very severe with some of them." These words of Lauriaton did not at all surprise me, for I well knew Napoleon's dislike to contractors, and all men who had mercantile transactions with the army. I have often heard him say that they were a curse and a leprosy to nations; that whatever power he might attain, he never would grant honours to any of them, and that of all aristocracies, theirs was to him the most insupportable. After his accession to the Empire the contractors were no longer the important persons they had been under the Directory, or even during the two first years of the Consulate. Bonaparte sometimes acted with them as he had before done with the Beya of Egypt, when he drew from them forced contributions.[199]

I recollect another somewhat curious circumstance respecting the visit of Lauriston, who

199 Lauriston, one of Napoleon's aides de camp, who was with him at the Military School of Paris, and who had been commissioned in the artillery at the same time as Napoleon, considered that he should have had the post of Grand Ecuyer which Caulaincourt had obtained. He had complained angrily to the Emperor, and after a stormy interview was ordered to join the fleet of Villeneuve—In consequence he was at Trafalgar. On his return after Austerlitz his temporary disgrace was forgotten, and he was sent as governor to Venice. He became marshal under the Restoration.

had left the Emperor and Empress at Aix-la-Chapelle. Lauriston was the best educated of the aides de camp, and Napoleon often conversed with him on such literary works as he chose to notice. "He sent for me one day," said Lauriston, "when I was on duty at the Palace of Lacken, and spoke to me of the decennial prizes, and the tragedy of 'Carion de Nisas', and a novel by Madame de Stael, which he had just read, but which I had not seen, and was therefore rather embarrassed in replying to him. Respecting Madame de Stael and her Delphine, he said some remarkable things. 'I do not like women,' he observed, 'who make men of themselves, any more than I like effeminate men. There is a proper part for every one to play in the world. What does all this flight of imagination mean? What is the result of it? Nothing. It is all sentimental metaphysics and disorder of the mind. I cannot endure that woman; for one reason, that I cannot bear women who make a set at me, and God knows how often she has tried to cajole me!'"

The words of Lauriston brought to my recollection the conversations I had often had with Bonaparte respecting Madame de Stael, of whose advances made to the First Consul, and even to the General of the Army of Italy, I had frequently been witness. Bonaparte knew nothing at first of Madame de Stael but that she was the daughter of M. Necker, a man for whom, as I have already shown, he had very little esteem. Madame de Stael had not been introduced to him, and knew nothing more of him than what fame had published respecting the young conqueror of Italy, when she addressed to him letters full of enthusiasm. Bonaparte read some passages of them to me, and, laughing, said, "What do you think, Bourrienne, of these extravagances. This woman is mad." I recollect that in one of her letters Madame de Stael, among other things, told him that they certainly were created for each other—that it was in consequence of an error in human institutions that the quiet and gentle Josephine was united to his fate—that nature seemed to have destined for the adoration of a hero such as he, a soul of fire like her own. These extravagances disgusted Bonaparte to a degree which I cannot describe. When he had finished reading these fine epistles he used to throw them into the fire, or tear them with marked ill-humour, and would say, "Well, here is a woman who pretends to genius—a maker of sentiments, and she presumes to compare herself to Josephine! Bourrienne, I shall not reply to such letters."

I had, however, the opportunity of seeing what the perseverance of a woman of talent can effect. Notwithstanding Bonaparte's prejudices against Madame de Stael, which he never abandoned, she succeeded in getting herself introduced to him; and if anything could have disgusted him with flattery it would have been the admiration, or, to speak more properly, the worship, which she paid him; for she used to compare him to a god descended on earth,—a kind of comparison which the clergy, I thought, had reserved for their own use. But, unfortunately, to please Madame de Stael it would have been necessary that her god had been Plutua; for behind her eulogies lay a claim for two millions, which M. Necker considered still due to him on account of his good and worthy services. However, Bonaparte said on this occasion that whatever value he might set on the suffrage of Madame de Stael, he did not think fit to pay so dear for it with the money of the State. The conversion of Madame de Stael's enthusiasm into hatred is well known, as are also the petty vexations, unworthy of himself, with which the Emperor harassed her in her retreat at Coppet.

Lauriston had arrived at Paris, where he made but a short stay, some days before Caffarelli, who was sent on a mission to Rome to sound the Papal Court, and to induce the Holy Father to come to Paris to consecrate Bonaparte at his coronation. I have already described the nature of Bonaparte's ideas on religion. His notions on the subject seemed to amount to a sort of vague feeling rather than to any belief founded on reflection. Nevertheless, he had a high opinion of the power of the Church; but not because he considered it dangerous to Governments, particularly to his own. Napoleon never could have conceived how it was possible that a sovereign wearing a crown and a sword could have the meanness to kneel to a Pope, or to humble his sceptre before the keys of St. Peter. His spirit was too great to admit of such a thought. On the contrary, he regarded the alliance between the Church and his power as a happy means of influencing the opinions of the people, and as an additional tie which was to attach them to a Government rendered legitimate by the solemn sanction of the Papal authority. Bonaparte was not deceived. In this, as well as in many other things, the perspicacity of his genius enabled him to comprehend all the importance of a consecration bestowed on him by the Pope; more especially as Louis XVIII., without subjects, without territory, and wearing only an illusory crown, had not received that sacred unction by which the descendants of Hugh Capet become the eldest sons of the Church.

As soon as the Emperor was informed of the success of Caffarelli's mission, and that the Pope, in compliance with his desire, was about to repair to Paris to confirm in his hands the sceptre of Charlemagne, nothing was thought of but preparations for that great event, which had been preceded by the recognition of Napoleon as Emperor of the French on the part of all the States of Europe, with the exception of England.

On the conclusion of the Concordat Bonaparte said to me, "I shall let the Republican generals exclaim as much as they like against the Mass. I know what I am about; I am working for posterity." He was now gathering the fruits of his Concordat. He ordered that the Pope should be everywhere treated in his journey through the French territory with the highest distinction, and he proceeded to Fontainebleau to receive his Holiness. This afforded an opportunity for Bonaparte to re-establish the example of those journeys of the old Court, during which changes of ministers used formerly to be made. The Palace of Fontainebleau, now become Imperial, like all the old royal chateaux, had been newly furnished with a luxury and taste corresponding to the progress of modern art. The Emperor was proceeding on the road to Nemours when courtiers informed him of the approach of Pius VII. Bonaparte's object was to avoid the ceremony which had been previously settled. He had therefore made the pretext of going on a hunting-party, and was in the way as it were by chance when the Pope's carriage was arriving. He alighted from horseback, and the Pope came out of his carriage. Rapp was with the Emperor, and I think I yet hear him describing, in his original manner and with his German accent, this grand interview, upon which, however, he for his part looked with very little respect. Rapp, in fact, was among the number of those who, notwithstanding his attachment to the Emperor, preserved independence of character, and he knew he had no reason to dissemble with me. "Fancy to yourself," said he, "the amusing comedy that was played." After the Emperor and the Pope had well embraced they went into the same carriage; and, in order that they might be upon a footing of equality, they were to enter at the same time by opposite doors. All that was settled; but at breakfast the Emperor had calculated how he should manage, without appearing to assume anything, to get on the righthand side of the Pope, and everything turned out as he wished. "As to the Pope," said Rapp, "I must own that I never saw a man with a finer countenance or more respectable appearance than Pius VII."

After the conference between the Pope and the Emperor at Fontainebleau, Pius VII. set off for Paris first. On the road the same honours were paid to him as to the Emperor. Apartments were prepared for him in the Pavilion de Flore in the Tuileries, and his bedchamber was arranged and furnished in the same manner as his chamber in the Palace of Monte-Cavallo, his usual residence in Rome. The Pope's presence in Paris was so extraordinary a circumstance that it was scarcely believed, though it had some time before been talked of. What, indeed, could be more singular than to see the Head of the Church in a capital where four years previously the altars had been overturned, and the few faithful who remained had been obliged to exercise their worship in secret!

The Pope became the object of public respect and general curiosity. I was exceedingly anxious to see him, and my wish was gratified on the day when he went to visit the Imperial printing office, then situated where the Bank of France now is.

A pamphlet, dedicated to the Pope, containing the "Pater Noster," in one hundred and fifty different languages, was struck off in the presence of his Holiness. During this visit to the printing office an ill-bred young man kept his hat on in the Pope's presence. Several persons, indignant at this indecorum, advanced to take off the young man's hat. A little confusion arose, and the Pope, observing the cause of it, stepped up to the young man and said to him, in a tone of kindness truly patriarchal, "Young man, uncover, that I may give thee my blessing. An old man's blessing never yet harmed any one." This little incident deeply affected all who witnessed it. The countenance and figure of Pope Pius VII. commanded respect. David's admirable portrait is a living likeness of him.

The Pope's arrival at Paris produced a great sensation in London, greater indeed there than anywhere else, notwithstanding the separation of the English Church from the Church of Rome. The English Ministry now spared no endeavours to influence public opinion by the circulation of libels against Bonaparte. The Cabinet of London found a twofold advantage in encouraging this system, which not merely excited irritation against the powerful enemy of England, but diverted from the British Government the clamour which some of its measures were calculated to create. Bonaparte's indignation against England was roused to the utmost extreme, and in truth this indignation was in some degree a national feeling in France.

Napoleon had heard of the success of Caffarelli's negotiations previous to his return to Paris, after his journey to the Rhine. On arriving at St. Cloud he lost no time in ordering the preparations for his coronation. Everything aided the fulfilment of his wishes. On 28th November the Pope arrived at Paris, and two days after, viz. on the 1st of December, the Senate presented to the Emperor the votes of the people for the establishment of hereditary succession in his family: for as it was pretended that the assumption of the title of Emperor was no way prejudicial to the Republic, the question of hereditary succession only had been proposed for public sanction. Sixty thousand registers had been opened in different parts of France,—at the offices of the ministers, the prefects, the mayors of the communes, notaries, solicitors, etc. France at that time contained 108 departments, and there were 3,574,898 voters. Of these only 2569 voted against hereditary succession. Bonaparte ordered a list of the persons who had voted against the question to be sent to him, and he often consulted it. They proved to be not Royalist, but for the most part staunch Republicans. To my knowledge many Royalists abstained from voting at all, not wishing to commit themselves uselessly, and still less to give their suffrages to the author of the Duc d'Enghien's death. For my part, I gave my vote in favour of hereditary succession in Bonaparte's family; my situation, as may well be imagined, did not allow me to do otherwise.

Since the month of October the Legislative Body had been convoked to attend the Emperor's coronation. Many deputies arrived, and with them a swarm of those presidents of cantons who occupied a conspicuous place in the annals of ridicule at the close of the year 1804. They became the objects of all sorts of witticisms and jests. The obligation of wearing swords made their appearance very grotesque. As many droll, stories were told of them as were ten years afterwards related of those who were styled the voltigeurs of Louis XIV. One of these anecdotes was so exceedingly ludicrous that, though it was probably a mere invention, yet I cannot refrain from relating it. A certain number of these presidents were one day selected to be presented to the Pope; and as most of them were very poor they found it necessary to combine economy with the etiquette necessary to be observed under the new order of things. To save the expense of hiring carriages they therefore proceeded to the Pavilion de Flore on foot, taking the precaution of putting on gaiters to preserve their white silk stockings from the mud which covered the streets, for it was then the month of December. On arriving at the Tuileries one of the party put his gaiters into his pocket. It happened that the Pope delivered such an affecting address that all present were moved to tears, and the unfortunate president who had disposed of his gaiters in the way just mentioned drew them out instead of his handkerchief and smeared his face over with mud. The Pope is said to have been much amused at this mistake. If this anecdote should be thought too puerile to be repeated here, I may observe that it afforded no small merriment to Bonaparte, who made Michot the actor relate it to the Empress at Paris one evening after a Court performance.

Napoleon had now attained the avowed object of his ambition; but his ambition receded before him like a boundless horizon. On the 1st of December; the day on which the Senate presented to the Emperor the result of the votes for hereditary succession, Francois de Neufchateau delivered an address to him, in which there was no want of adulatory expressions. As President of the Senate he had had some practice in that style of speechmaking; and he only substituted the eulogy of the Monarchical Government for that of the Republican Government 'a sempre bene', as the Italians say.

If I wished to make comparisons I could here indulge in some curious ones. Is it not extraordinary that Fontainebleau should have witnessed, at the interval of nearly ten years, Napoleon's first interview with the Pope, and his last farewell to his army, and that the Senate, who had previously given such ready support to Bonaparte, should in 1814 have pronounced his abdication at Fontainebleau.

The preparations for the Coronation proved very advantageous to the trading classes of Paris. Great numbers of foreigners and people from the provinces visited the capital, and the return of luxury and the revival of old customs gave occupation to a variety of tradespeople who could get no employment under the Directory or Consulate, such as saddlers, carriage-makers, lacemen, embroiderers, and others. By these positive interests were created more partisans of the Empire than by opinion and reflection; and it is but just to say that trade had not been so active for a dozen years before. The Imperial crown jewels were exhibited to the public at Biennais the jeweller's. The crown was of a light form, and, with its leaves of gold, it less resembled the crown of France than the antique crown of the Caesars. These things were afterwards placed in the public treasury, together with the imperial insignia of Charlemagne, which Bonaparte had ordered to be brought from Aix-la-Chapelle. But while Bonaparte was thus priding himself in his crown and his imagined resemblance to Charlemagne, Mr. Pitt, lately recalled to the Ministry, was concluding at Stockholm a treaty with Sweden, and agreeing to pay a subsidy to that power to enable it to maintain hostilities against France.

This treaty was concluded on the 3d of December, the day after the Coronation.[200]

It cannot be expected that I should enter into a detail of the ceremony which took place on the 2d of December. The glitter of gold, the waving plumes, and richly-caparisoned horses of the Imperial procession; the mule which preceded the Pope's cortege, and occasioned so much merriment to the Parisians, have already been described over and over again. I may, however, relate an anecdote connected with the Coronation, told me by Josephine, and which is exceedingly characteristic of Napoleon.

When Bonaparte was paying his addresses to Madame de BEAUHARNAIS, neither the one nor the other kept a carriage; and therefore Bonaparte frequently accompanied her when she walked out. One day they went together to the notary Raguideau, one of the shortest men I think I ever saw in my life, Madame de Beauharnais placed great confidence, in him, and went there on purpose to acquaint him of her intention to marry the young general of artillery,—the protege of Barras. Josephine went alone into, the notary's cabinet, while Bonaparte waited for her in an adjoining room. The door of Raguideau's cabinet did not shut close, and Bonaparte plainly heard him dissuading Madame de Beauharnais from her projected marriage. "You are going to take a very wrong step," said he, "and you will be sorry for it, Can you be so mad as to marry a young man who has nothing but his cloak and his sword?" Bonaparte, Josephine told me, had never mentioned this to her, and she never supposed that he had heard what fell from Raguideau. "Only think, Bourrienne," continued

200 The details of the preparation for the Coronation caused many stormy scenes between Napoleon and his family. The Princesses, his sisters and sisters-in-law, were especially shocked at having to carry the train of the Imperial mantle of Josephine, and even when Josephine was actually moving from the altar to the throne the Princesses evinced their reluctance so plainly that Josephine could not advance and an altercation took place which had to be stopped by Napoleon himself. Joseph was quite willing himself give up appearing in a mantle with a train, but he wished to prevent his wife bearing the mantle of the Empress; and he opposed his brother on so many points that Napoleon ended by calling on him to either give up his position and retire from all politics, or else to fully accept the imperial regime. How the economical Cambercerers used up the ermine he could not wear will be seen in Junot tome iii. p. 196. Josephine herself was in the greatest anxiety as to whether the wish of the Bonaparte family that she should be divorced would carry the day with her husband. When she had gained her cause for the time and after the Pope had engaged to crown her, she seems to have most cleverly managed to get the Pope informed that she was only united to Napoleon by a civil marriage. The Pope insisted on a religious marriage. Napoleon was angry, but could not recede, and the religions rite was performed by Cardinal Fesch the day, or two days, before the Coronation. The certificate of the marriage was carefully guarded from Napoleon by Josephine, and even placed beyond his reach at the time of the divorce. Such at least seems to be the most probable account of this mysterious and doubtful matter. The fact that Cardinal Fesch maintained that the religious rite had been duly performed, thirteen of the Cardinals (not, however including Fesch) were so convinced of the legality of the marriage that they refused to appear at the ceremony of marriage with Marie Louise, thus drawing down the wrath of the Emperor, and becoming the "Cardinals Noirs," from being forbidden; to wear their own robes, seems to leave no doubt that the religious rite had been performed. The marriage was only pronounced to be invalid in 1809 by the local canonical bodies, not by the authority of the pope.

she, "what was my astonishment when, dressed in the Imperial robes on the Coronation day, he desired that Raguideau might be sent for, saying that he wished to see him immediately; and when Raguideau appeared; he said to him, 'Well, sir! have I nothing but my cloak and my sword now?'"

Though Bonaparte had related to me almost all the circumstances of his life, as they occurred to his memory, he never once mentioned this affair of Raguideau, which he only seemed to have suddenly recollected on his Coronation day.

The day after the Coronation all the troops in Paris were assembled in the Champ de Mars the Imperial eagles might be distributed to each regiment, in lieu of the national flags. I had stayed away from the Coronation in the church of Notre Dame, but I wished to see the military fete in the Champ de Mars because I took real pleasure in seeing Bonaparte amongst his soldiers. A throne was erected in front of the Military School, which, though now transformed into a barrack, must have recalled, to Bonaparte's mind some singular recollections of his boyhood. At a given signal all the columns closed and approached the throne. Then Bonaparte, rising, gave orders for the distribution of the eagles, and delivered the following address to the deputations of the different corps of the army:

> "Soldiers, Soldiers! behold your colours. These eagles will always be your rallying-point! They will always be where your Emperor may think them necessary for the defence of his throne and of his people. Swear to sacrifice your lives to defend them, and by your courage to keep them constantly in the path of victory.—Swear!"

It would be impossible to describe the acclamations which followed this address; there is something so seductive in popular enthusiasm that even indifferent persons cannot help yielding to its influence. And yet the least reflection would have shown how shamefully Napoleon forswore the declaration he made to the Senate, when the organic 'Senatus-consulte' for the foundation of the Empire was presented to him at St: Cloud: On that occasion he said; "The French people shall never be MY people!" And yet the day after his Coronation his eagles were to be carried wherever they might be necessary for the defence of his people.

By a singular coincidence, while on the 2d of December 1804 Bonaparte was receiving from the head of the Church the Imperial crown of France, Louis XVIII., who was then at Colmar, prompted as it were by an inexplicable presentiment, drew up and signed a declaration to the French people, in which he declared that he then, swore never to break the sacred bond which united his destiny to theirs, never to renounce the inheritance of his ancestors, or to relinquish his rights.

CHAPTER XXX

1805

I must now mention an event which concerns myself personally, namely, my appointment as Minister Plenipotentiary, to the Dukes of Brunswick and Mecklenburg-Schwerin, and to the Hanse towns.

This appointment took place on the 22d of March 1806. Josephine, who had kindly promised to apprise me of what the Emperor intended to do for me, as soon as she herself should know his intentions, sent a messenger to acquaint me with my appointment, and to tell me that the Emperor wished to see me. I had not visited Josephine since her departure for Belgium. The pomp and ceremonies of the Coronation had, I may say, dazzled me, and deterred me from presenting myself at the Imperial Palace, where I should have been annoyed by the etiquette which had been observed since the Coronation. I cannot describe what a disagreeable impression this parade always produced on me. I could not all at once forget the time when I used without ceremony to go into Bonaparte's chamber and wake him at the appointed hour. As to Bonaparte I had not seen him since he sent for me after the condemnation of Georges, when I saw that my candour relative to Moreau was not displeasing to him. Moreau had since quitted France without Napoleon's subjecting him to the application of the odious law which has only been repealed since the return of the Bourbons, and by virtue of which he was condemned to the confiscation of his property. Moreau sold his estate of Gros Bois to Berthier, and proceeded to Cadiz, whence he embarked for America. I shall not again have occasion to speak of him until the period of the intrigues into which he was drawn by the same influence which ruined him in France.

On the evening of the day when I received the kind message from Josephine I had an official invitation to proceed the next day to Malmaison, where the Emperor then was. I was much pleased at the idea of seeing him there rather than at the Tuileries, or even at St. Cloud. Our former intimacy at Malmaison made me feel more at my ease respecting an interview of which my knowledge of Bonaparte's character led me to entertain some apprehension. Was I to be received by my old comrade of Brienne, or by His Imperial Majesty? I was received by my old college companion.

On my arrival at Malmaison I was ushered into the tentroom leading to the library. How I was astonished at the good-natured familiarity with which he received me! This extraordinary man displayed, if I may employ the term, a coquetry towards me which surprised me, notwithstanding my past knowledge of his character. He came up to me with a smile on his lips, took my hand (which he had never done since he was Consul), pressed it affectionately, and it was impossible that I could look upon him as the Emperor of France and the future King of Italy. Yet I was too well aware of his fits of pride to allow his familiarity to lead me beyond the bounds of affectionate respect. "My dear Bourrienne," said he, "can you suppose that the elevated rank I have attained has altered my feelings towards you? No. I do not attach importance to the glitter of Imperial pomp; all that is meant for the people; but I must still be valued according to my deserts. I have been very well satisfied with your services, and I have appointed you to a situation where I shall have occasion for them. I know that I can rely upon you." He then asked with great warmth of friendship what I was about, and inquired after my family, etc. In short, I never saw him display less reserve or more familiarity and unaffected simplicity; which he did the more readily, perhaps, because his greatness was now incontestable.

"You know," added Napoleon, "that I set out in a week for Italy. I shall make myself King; but that is only a stepping-stone. I have greater designs respecting Italy.

"It must be a kingdom comprising all the Transalpine States, from Venice to the Maritime Alps. The union of Italy with France can only be temporary; but it is necessary, in order to accustom the nations of Italy to live under common laws. The Genoese, the Piedmontese, the Venetians, the Milanese, the inhabitants of Tuscany, the Romans, and the Neapolitans, hate each other. None of them will acknowledge the superiority of the other, and yet Rome is, from the recollections connected with it, the natural capital of Italy. To make it so, however, it is necessary that the power of the Pope should be confined within limits purely spiritual. I cannot now think of this; but I will reflect upon it hereafter. At present I have only vague ideas on the subject, but they will be matured in time, and then all depends on circumstances. What was it told me, when we were walking like two idle fellows, as we were, in the streets of Paris, that I should one day be master of France—my wish—merely a vague wish. Circumstances have done the rest. It is therefore wise to look into the future, and that I do. With respect to Italy, as it will be impossible with one effort to unite her so as to form a single power, subject to uniform laws, I will begin by making her French. All these little States will insensibly become accustomed to the same laws, and when manners shall be assimilated and enmities extinguished, then there will be an Italy, and I will give her independence. But for that I must have twenty years, and who can count on the future? Bourrienne, I feel pleasure in telling you all this. It was locked up in my mind. With you I think aloud."

I do not believe that I have altered two words of what Bonaparte said to me respecting Italy, so perfect, I may now say without vanity, was my memory then, and so confirmed was my habit of fixing in it all that he said to me. After having informed me of his vague projects Bonaparte, with one of those transitions so common to him, said, "By the by, Bourrienne, I have something to tell you. Madame de Brienne has begged that I will pass through Brienne, and I promised that I will. I will not conceal from you that I shall feel great pleasure in again beholding the spot which for six years was the scene of our boyish sports and studies." Taking advantage of the Emperor's good humour I ventured to tell him what happiness it would give me if it were possible that I could share with him the revival of all recollections which were mutually dear to us. But Napoleon, after a moment's pause, said with extreme kindness, "Hark ye, Bourrienne, in your situation and mine this cannot be. It is more than two years since we parted. What would be said of so sudden a reconciliation? I tell you frankly that I have regretted you, and the circumstances in which I have frequently been placed have often made me wish to recall you. At Boulogne I was quite resolved upon it. Rapp, perhaps, has informed you of it. He liked you, and he assured me that he would be delighted at your return. But if upon reflection I changed my mind it was because, as I have often told you, I will not have it said that I stand in need of any one. No. Go to Hamburg. I have formed some projects respecting Germany in which you can be useful to me. It is there I will give a mortal blow to England. I will deprive her of the Continent,—besides, I have some ideas not yet matured which extend much farther. There is not sufficient unanimity amongst the nations of Europe. European society must be regenerated—a superior power must control the other powers, and compel them to live in peace with each other; and France is well situated for that purpose. For details you will receive instructions from Talleyrand; but I recommend you, above all things, to keep a strict watch on the emigrants. Woe to them if they become too dangerous! I know that there are still agitators,—among them all the 'Marquis de Versailles', the courtiers of the old school. But they are moths who will burn themselves in the candle. You have been an emigrant yourself, Bourrienne; you feel a partiality for them, and you know that I have allowed upwards of two hundred of them to return upon your recommendation. But the case is altered. Those who are abroad are hardened. They do not wish to return home. Watch them closely. That is the only particular direction I give you. You are to be Minister from France to Hamburg; but your place will be an independent one; besides your correspondence with the Minister for Foreign Affairs, I authorise you to write to me personally, whenever you have anything particular to communicate. You will likewise correspond with Fouché."

Here the Emperor remained silent for a moment, and I was preparing to retire, but he detained me, saying in the kindest manner, "What, are you going already, Bourrienne? Are you in a hurry? Let us chat a little longer. God knows, when we may see each other again!" Then after two or three moments' silence he said, "The more I reflect on our situation, on our former intimacy, and our subsequent separation, the more I see the necessity of your going to Hamburg. Go, then, my dear fellow, I advise you. Trust me. When do you think of setting out?" "In May."—"In May? . . . Ah, I shall be in Milan then, for I wish to stop at Turin. I like the Piedmontese; they are the best soldiers in Italy."—"Sire, the King of Italy will be the junior of the Emperor of France!"[201] —"Ah! so you recollect what I said one day at the Tuileries; but, my dear fellow, I have yet a devilish long way to go before I gain my point."—"At the rate, Sire, at which you are going you will not be long in reaching it."—"Longer than you imagine. I see all the obstacles in my way; but they do not alarm me. England is everywhere, and the struggle is between her and me. I see how it will be. The whole of Europe will be our instruments; sometimes serving one, sometimes the other, but at bottom the dispute is wholly between England and France.

"A propos," said the Emperor, changing the subject, for all who knew him are aware that this 'a propos' was his favourite, and, indeed, his only mode of transition; a propos, Bourrienne, you surely must have heard of the departure of Jaubert,[202] and his mission. What is said on the subject?"—"Sire, I have only heard it slightly alluded to. His father, however, to whom he said nothing respecting the object of his journey, knowing I was intimate with Jaubert, came to me to ascertain whether I could allay his anxiety respecting a journey of

201 I alluded to a conversation which I had with Napoleon when we first went to the Tuileries. He spoke to me about his projects of royalty, and I stated the difficulties which I thought he would experience in getting himself acknowledged by the old reigning families of Europe. "If it comes to that," he replied. "I will dethrone them all, and then I shall be the oldest sovereign among them."—Bourrienne.

202 Amedee Jaubart had been with Napoleon in Egypt, and was appointed to the cabinet of the Consul as secretary interpreter of Oriental languages. He was sent on several missions to the East, and brought back, is 1818, goats from Thibet, naturalising in France the manufacture of cashmeres. He became a peer of France under the Monarchy of July.

the duration of which he could form no idea. The precipitate departure of his son had filled him with apprehension I told him the truth, viz., that Jaubert had said no more to me on the subject than to him."—"Then you do not know where he is gone?"—"I beg your pardon, Sire; I know very well."—"How, the devil!" said Bonaparte, suddenly turning on me a look of astonishment. "No one, I, declare, has ever told me; but I guessed it. Having received a letter from Jaubert dated Leipsic, I recollected what your Majesty had often told me of your views respecting Persia and India. I have not forgotten our conversation in Egypt, nor the great projects which you enfolded to me to relieve the solitude and sometimes the weariness of the cabinet of Cairo. Besides, I long since knew your opinion of Amedee, of his fidelity, his ability, and his courage. I felt convinced, therefore, that he had a mission to the Shah of Persia."—"You guessed right; but I beg of you, Bourrienne, say nothing of this to any person whatever. Secrecy on this point is of great importance. The English would do him an ill turn, for they are well aware that my views are directed against their possessions and their influence in the East."—"I think, Sire, that my answer to Amedee's worthy father is a sufficient guarantee for my discretion. Besides, it was a mere supposition on my part, and I could have stated nothing with certainty before your Majesty had the kindness to inform me of the fact. Instead of going to Hamburg, if your Majesty pleases, I will join Jaubert, accompany him to Persia, and undertake half his mission."— "How! would you go with him?"—"Yes, Sire; I am much attached to him. He is an excellent man, and I am sure that he would not be sorry to have me with him."—"But . . . Stop, Bourrienne, . . . this, perhaps, would not be a bad idea. You know a little of the East. You are accustomed to the climate. You could assist Jaubert. . . . But. . . . No! Daubert must be already far off—I, fear you could not overtake him. And besides you have a numerous family. You will be more useful to me in Germany. All things considered, go to Hamburg—you know the country, and, what is better you speak the language."

I could see that Bonaparte still had something to say to me. As we were walking up and down the room he stopped; and looking at me with an expression of sadness, he said, "Bourrienne, you must, before I proceed to Italy, do me a service. You sometimes visit my wife, and it is right; it is fit you should. You have been too long one of the family not to continue your friendship with her. Go to her.[203]

"Endeavour once more to make her sensible of her mad extravagance. Every day I discover new instances of it, and it distresses me. When I speak to her—on the subject I am vexed; I get angry—she weeps. I forgive her, I pay her bills—she makes fair promises; but the same

203 This employment of Bourrienne to remonstrate with Josephine is a complete answer to the charge sometimes made that Napoleon, while scolding, really encouraged the foolish expenses of his wife, as keeping her under his control. Josephine was incorrigible. "On the very day of her death," says Madame de Rémusat "she wished to put on a very pretty dressing-gown because she thought the Emperor of Russia would perhaps come to see her. She died all covered with ribbons and rose-colored satin." "One would not, sure, be frightful when one's dead!" As for Josephine's great fault—her failure to give Napoleon an heir—he did not always wish for one. In 1802, on his brother Jerome jokingly advising Josephine to give the Consul a little Caesar. Napoleon broke out, "Yea, that he may end in the same manner as that of Alexander? Believe me, Messieurs, that at the present time it is better not to have children: I mean when one is condemned to rule nations." The fate of the King of Rome shows that the exclamation was only too true!

thing occurs over and over again. If she had only borne me a child! It is the torment of my life not to have a child. I plainly perceive that my power will never be firmly established until I have one. If I die without an heir, not one of my brothers is capable of supplying my place. All is begun, but nothing is ended. God knows what will happen! Go and see Josephine, and do not forget my injunctions . . . "

Then he resumed the gaiety which he had exhibited at intervals during our conversation, far clouds driven by the wind do not traverse the horizon with such rapidity as different ideas and sensations succeeded each other in Napoleon's mind. He dismissed me with his usual nod of the head, and seeing him in such good humour I said on departing, "well, Sire, you are going to hear the old bell of Brienne. I have no doubt it will please you better than the bells of Ruel." He replied, "That's true—you are right. Adieu!"

Such are my recollections of this conversation, which lasted for more than an hour and a half. We walked about all the time, for Bonaparte was indefatigable in audiences of this sort, and would, I believe, have walked and talked for a whole day without being aware of it. I left him, and, according to his desire, went to see Madame Bonaparte, which indeed I had intended to do before he requested it.

I found Josephine with Madame de la Rochefoucauld, who had long been in her suite, and who a short time before had obtained the title of lady of honour to the Empress. Madame de la Rochefoucauld was a very amiable woman, of mild disposition, and was a favourite with Josephine. When I told the Empress that I had just left the Emperor, she, thinking that I would not speak freely before a third person, made a sign to Madame de la Rochefoucauld to retire. I had no trouble in introducing the conversation on the subject concerning which Napoleon had directed me to speak to Josephine, for; after the interchange of a few indifferent remarks, she herself told me of a violent scene, which had occurred between her and the Emperor two days before. "When I wrote to you yesterday," said she, "to announce your appointment, and to tell you that Bonaparte would recall you, I hoped that you would come to see me on quitting him, but I did not think that he would have sent for you so soon. Ah! how I wish that you were still with him, Bourrienne; you could make him hear reason. I know not who takes pleasure in bearing tales to him; but really I think there are persons busy everywhere in finding out my debts, and telling him of them."

These complaints, so gently uttered by Josephine rendered less difficult the preparatory mission with which I commenced the exercise of my diplomatic functions. I acquainted Madame Bonaparte with all that the Emperor had said to me. I reminded her of the affair of the 1,200,000 francs which we had settled with half that sum. I even dropped some allusions to the promises she had made.

"How can I help it?" Said she. "Is it my fault?" Josephine uttered these words in a tone of sincerity which was at once affecting and ludicrous. "All sorts of beautiful things are brought to me," she continued; "they are praised up; I buy them—I am not asked for the money, and all of a sudden, when I have got none, they come upon me with demands for payment. This reaches Napoleon's ears, and he gets angry. When I have money, Bourrienne you know how I employ it. I give it principally to the unfortunate who solicit my assistance, and to poor emigrants. But I will try to be more economical in future. Tell him so if you see him again, But is it not my duty to bestow as much in charity as I can?"—"Yes, Madame; but permit me to say that nothing requires greater discernment than the distribution of charity. If you had always sat upon a throne you might have always supposed that your bounty always fall into the hands of the deserving; but you cannot be ignorant that it oftener falls to the lot of intrigue than to the meritorious needy. I cannot disguise from you that the Emperor was very earnest when he spoke on this subject; and he desired me to tell you so."—"Did he reproach me with nothing else?"—"No Madame. You know the influence you have over him with respect to everything but what relates to politics. Allow a faithful and sincere friend to prevail upon you seriously not to vex him on this point."—"Bourrienne, I give you my word. Adieu! my friend."

In communicating to Josephine what the Emperor had said to me I took care not to touch a chord which would have awakened feelings far more painful to her than even the Emperor's harsh reproof on account of her extravagance. Poor Josephine! how I should have afflicted her had I uttered a word of Bonaparte's regret at not having a child. She always had a presentiment of the fate that one day awaited her. Besides, Josephine told the truth in assuring me that it was not her fault that, she spent as she did; at least all the time I was with both of them, order and economy were no more compatible with her than moderation and—patience with Napoleon. The sight of the least waste put him beside himself, and that was a sensation his wife hardly ever spared him. He saw with irritation the eagerness of his family to gain riches; the more he gave, the more insatiable they appeared, with the exception of Louis, whose inclinations were always upright, and his tastes moderate. As for the other members of his family, they annoyed him so much by their importunity that one day he said, "Really to listen to them it would be thought that I had wasted the heritage of our father."

CHAPTER XXXI

1805

Voltaire says that it is very well to kiss the feet of Popes provided their hands are tied. Notwithstanding the slight estimation in which Bonaparte held Voltaire, he probably, without being aware of this irreverent satire, put it into practice. The Court of Rome gave him the opportunity of doing so shortly after his Coronation. The Pope, or rather the Cardinals, his advisers' conceiving that so great an instance of complaisance as the journey of His Holiness to Paris ought not to go for nothing; demanded a compensation, which, had they been better acquainted with Bonaparte's character and policy, they would never have dreamed of soliciting. The Holy see demanded the restitution of Avignon, Bologna, and some parts of the Italian territory which had formerly been subject to the Pope's dominion. It may be imagined how such demands were received by Napoleon, particularly after he had obtained all he wanted from the Pope. It was, it must be confessed, a great mistake of the Court of Rome, whose policy is usually so artful and adroit, not to make this demand till after the Coronation. Had it been made the condition of the Pope's journey to France perhaps Bonaparte would have consented to give up, not Avignon, certainly, but the Italian territories, with the intention of taking them back again. Be this as it may, these tardy claims, which were peremptorily rejected, created an extreme coolness between Napoleon and Pius VII. The public did not immediately perceive it, but there is in the public an instinct of reason which the most able politicians never can impose upon; and all eyes were opened when it was known that the Pope, after having crowned Napoleon as Emperor of France, refused to crown him as sovereign of the regenerated kingdom of Italy.

Napoleon left Paris on the 1st of April to take possession of the Iron Crown at Milan. The Pope remained some time longer in the French capital. The prolonged presence of His Holiness was not without its influence on the religious feelings of the people, so great was the respect inspired by the benign countenance and mild manners of the Pope. When the period of his persecutions arrived it would have been well for Bonaparte had Pius VII. never been seen in Paris, for it was impossible to view in any other light than as a victim the man whose truly evangelic meekness had been duly appreciated.

Bonaparte did not evince great impatience to seize the Crown of Italy, which he well knew could not escape him. He stayed a considerable time at Turin, where he resided in the Stupinis Palace, which may be called the St. Cloud of the Kings of Sardinia. The Emperor cajoled the Piedmontese. General Menou, who was made Governor of Piedmont, remained there till Napoleon founded the general government of the Transalpine departments in favour of his brother-in-law, the Prince Borghese, of whom he would have, found it difficult to make anything else than a Roman Prince. Napoleon was still at Turin when the Pope passed through that city on his return to Rome. Napoleon had a final interview with His Holiness to whom he now affected to show the greatest personal deference. From Turin Bonaparte proceeded to Alessandria, where he commenced those immense works on which such vast sums were expended. He had many times spoken to me of his projects respecting

Alessandria, as I have already observed, all his great measures as Emperor were merely the execution of projects conceived at a time when his future elevation could have been only a dream of the imagination. He one day said to Berthier, in my presence, during our sojurn at Milan after the battle of Marengo, "With Alessandria in my possession I should always be master of Italy. It might be made the strongest fortress in the world; it is capable of containing a garrison of 40,000 men, with provisions for six months. Should insurrection take place, should Austria send a formidable force here, the French troops might retire to Alessandria, and stand a six months' siege. Six months would be more than sufficient, wherever I might be, to enable me to fall upon Italy, rout the Austrians, and raise the siege of Alessandria!"

As he was so near the field of Marengo the Emperor did not fail to visit it, and to add to this solemnity he reviewed on the field all the corps of French troops which were in Italy. Rapp told me afterwards that the Emperor had taken with him from Paris the dress and the hat which he wore on the day of that memorable battle, with the intention of wearing them on the field where it was fought. He afterwards proceeded by the way of Casal to Milan.

There the most brilliant reception he had yet experienced awaited him. His sojourn at Milan was not distinguished by outward demonstrations of enthusiasm alone. M. Durszzo, the last Doge of Genoa, added another gem to the Crown of Italy by supplicating the Emperor in the name of the Republic, of which he was the representative, to permit Genoa to exchange her independence for the honour of becoming a department of France. This offer, as may be guessed, was merely a plan contrived beforehand. It was accepted with an air of protecting kindness, and at the same moment that the country of Andrea Doria was effaced from the list of nations its last Doge was included among the number of French Senators. Genoa, which formerly prided herself in her surname, the Superb, became the chief station of the twenty-seventh military division. The Emperor went to take possession of the city in person, and slept in the Doria Palace, in the bed where Charles V. had lain. He left M. le Brun at Genoa as Governor-General.

At Milan the Emperor occupied the Palace of Monza. The old Iron Crown of the Kings of Lombardy was brought from the dust in which it had been buried, and the new Coronation took place in the cathedral at Milan, the largest in Italy, with the exception of St. Peter's at Rome. Napoleon received the crown from the hands of the Archbishop of Milan, and placed it on his head, exclaiming, "Dieu me l'a donnee, gare a qui la touche." This became the motto of the Order of the Iron Crown, which the Emperor founded in commemoration of his being crowned King of Italy.

Napoleon was crowned in the month of May 1805: and here I cannot avoid correcting some gross and inconceivable errors into which Napoleon must have voluntarily fallen at St. Helena. The Memorial states "that the celebrated singer Madame Grasaini attracted his attention at the time of the Coronation." Napoleon alleges that Madame Grassini on that occasion said to him, "When I was in the prime of my beauty and talent all I wished was that you would bestow a single look upon me. That wish was not fulfilled, and now you notice me when I am no longer worthy your attention."

I confess I am at a loss to conceive what could induce Napoleon to invent such a story. He might have recollected his acquaintance with Madame Grassini at Milan before the battle of Marengo. It was in 1800, and not in 1805, that I was first introduced to her, and I know that I several times took tea with her and Bonaparte in the General's apartments I remember also another circumstance, which is, that on the night when I awoke Bonaparte to announce to him the capitulation of Genoa, Madame Grassini also awoke. Napoleon was charmed with

Madame Grasaini's delicious voice, and if his imperious duties had permitted it he would have listened with ecstasy to her singing for hours together. Whilst Napoleon was at Milan, priding himself on his double sovereignty, some schemes were set on foot at Vienna and St. Petersburg which I shall hereafter have occasion to notice. The Emperor, indeed, gave cause for just complaint by the fact of annexing Genoa to the Empire within four months after his solemn declaration to the Legislative Body, in which he pledged himself in the face of France and Europe not to seek any aggrandisement of territory. The pretext of a voluntary offer on the part of Genoa was too absurd to deceive any one. The rapid progress of Napoleon's ambition could not escape the observation of the Cabinet of Vienna, which began to allow increased symptoms of hostility. The change which was effected in the form of the Government of the Cisalpine Republic was likewise an act calculated to excite remonstrance on the part of all the powers who were not entirely subject to the yoke of France. He disguised the taking of Genoa under the name of a gift, and the possession of Italy under the appearance of a mere change of denomination. Notwithstanding these flagrant outrages the exclusive apologists of Napoleon have always asserted that he did not wish for war, and he himself maintained that assertion at St. Helena. It is said that he was always attacked, and hence a conclusion is drawn in favour of his love of peace. I acknowledge Bonaparte would never have fired a single musket-shot if all the powers of Europe had submitted to be pillaged by him one after the other without opposition. It was in fact declaring war against them to place them under the necessity of breaking a peace, during the continuance of which he was augmenting his power, and gratifying his ambition, as if in defiance of Europe. In this way Napoleon commenced all the wars in which he was engaged, with the exception of that which followed the peace of Marengo, and which terminated in Moreau's triumph at Hohenlinden. As there was no liberty of the press in France he found it easy to deceive the nation. He was in fact attacked, and thus he enjoyed the pleasure of undertaking his great military expeditions without being responsible in the event of failure.

During the Emperor's stay in the capital of the new kingdom of Italy he received the first intelligence of the dissatisfaction of Austria and Russia. That dissatisfaction was not of recent date. When I entered on my functions at Hamburg I learned some curious details (which I will relate in their proper place) respecting the secret negotiations which had been carried on for a considerable time previously to the commencement of hostilities. Even Prussia was no stranger to the dissatisfaction of Austria and Russia; I do not mean the King, but the Cabinet of Berlin, which was then under the control of Chancellor Hardenberg; for the King of Prussia had always personally declared himself in favour of the exact observance of treaties, even when their conditions were not honourable. Be that as it may, the Cabinet of Berlin, although dissatisfied in 1806 with the rapid progress of Napoleon's ambition, was nevertheless constrained to conceal its discontent, owing to the presence of the French troops in Hanover.

On returning from Milan the Emperor ordered the erection, of a monument on the Great St. Bernard in commemoration of the victory of Marengo. M. Denon who accompanied Napoleon, told me that he made a useless search to discover the body of Desaix, which Bonaparte wished to be buried beneath the monument and that it was at length found by General Savary. It is therefore certain that the ashes of the brave Desaix repose on the summit of the Alps.

The Emperor arrived in Paris about the end of June and instantly set off for the camp at Boulogne. It was now once more believed that the project of invading England would be accomplished. This idea obtained the greater credit because Bonaparte caused some experiments for embarkation to be made, in his presence. These experiments, however, led to no result. About this period a fatal event but too effectually contributed to strengthen the opinion of the inferiority of our navy. A French squadron consisting of fifteen ships, fell in with the English fleet commanded by Admiral Calder, who had only nine vessels under his command, and in an engagement, which there was every reason to expect would terminate in our favour, we had the misfortune to lose two ships. The invasion of England was as little the object of this as of the previous journey to Boulogne; all Napoleon had in view was to stimulate the enthusiasm of the troops, and to hold out those threats against England when conceived necessary for diverting attention from the real motive of his hostile preparations, which was to invade Germany and repulse the Russian troops, who had begun their march towards Austria. Such was the true object of Napoleons last journey to Boulogne.

I had been some time at Hamburg when these events took place, and it was curious to observe the effect they produced. But I must not forget one circumstance in which I am personally concerned, and which brings me back to the time when I was in Paris. My new title of Minister Plenipotentiary obliged me to see a little more of society than during the period when prudence required me to live as it were in retirement. I had received sincere congratulations from Duroc, Rape, and Lauriston, the three friends who had shown the greatest readiness to serve my interests with the Emperor; and I had frequent occasion to see M. Talleyrand, as my functions belonged to his department. The Emperor, on my farewell audience, having informed me that I was to correspond directly with the Minister of the General Police, I called on Fouché, who invited me to spend some days at his estate of Pont-Carre. I accepted the invitation because I wanted to confer with him, and I spent Sunday and Monday, the 28th and 29th of April, at Pont-Carre.

Fouché, like the Emperor, frequently revealed what he intended to conceal; but he had such a reputation for cunning that this sort of indiscretion was attended by no inconvenience to him. He was supposed to be such a constant dissembler that those who did not know him well looked upon the truth when he spoke it merely as an artful snare laid to entrap them. I, however, knew that celebrated person too well to confound his cunning with his indiscretion. The best way to get out of him more than he was aware of was to let him talk on without interruption. There were very few visitors at Pont-Carre, and during the two days I spent there I had several conversations with Fouché. He told me a great deal about the events of 1804, and he congratulated himself on having advised Napoleon to declare himself Emperor—"I have no preference," says Fouché, "for one form of government more than another. Forms signify nothing. The first object of the Revolution was not the overthrow of the Bourbons, but merely the reform of abuses and the destruction of prejudices. However, when it was discovered that Louis XVI. had neither firmness to refuse what he did not wish to grant, nor good faith to grant what his weakness had led him to promise, it was evident that the Bourbons could no longer reign over France and things were carried to such a length that we were under the necessity of condemning Louis XVI. and resorting to energetic measures. You know all that passed up to the 18th Brumaire, and after. We all perceived that a Republic could not exist in France; the question, therefore, was to ensure the perpetual removal of the Bourbons; and I believed the only means for so doing was to transfer the inheritance of their throne to another family. Some time before the 18th Brumaire I had a conversation with Sieyès and Barras, in which it was proposed, in case of the Directory being threatened, to recall the Duke of Orleans; and I could see very well that Barras favoured that suggestion, although he alluded to it merely as a report that was circulated about, and recommended me to pay attention to it. Sieyès said nothing, and I settled the question by observing, that if any such thing had been agitated I must have been informed of it through the reports of my agents. I added, that the restoration of the throne to a collateral branch of the Bourbons would be an impolitic act, and would but temporarily change the position of those who had brought about the Revolution. I rendered an account of this interview with Barras to General Bonaparte the first time I had an opportunity of conversing with him after your return from Egypt. I sounded him; and I was perfectly convinced that in the state of decrepitude into which the Directory had fallen he was just the man we wanted. I therefore adopted such measures with the police as tended to promote his elevation to the First Magistracy. He soon showed himself ungrateful, and instead of giving me all his confidence he tried to outwit me. He put into the hands of a number of persons various matters of police which were worse than useless. Most of their agents, who were my creatures, obeyed my instructions in their reports; and it often happened that the First Consul thought he had discovered, through the medium of others, information that came from me, and of the falsehood of which I easily convinced him. I confess I was at fault on the 3d Nivoise; but are there any human means of preventing two men, who have no accomplices, from bringing a plot to execution? You saw the First Consul on his return from the opera; you heard all his declamations. I felt assured that the infernal machine was the work of the Royalists. I told the Emperor this, and he was, I am sure, convinced of it; but he, nevertheless, proscribes a number of men on the mere pretence of their old opinions. Do you suppose I am ignorant of what he said of me and of my vote at the National Convention? Most assuredly it ill becomes him to reproach the Conventionists. It was that vote which placed the crown upon his head. But for the situation in which we were placed by that event, which circumstances had rendered inevitable, what should we have cared for the chance of seeing the Bourbons return? You must have remarked that the Republicans, who were not Conventionists, were in general more averse than we to the proceedings of the 18th Brumaire, as, for example, Bernadotte and Moreau. I know positively that Moreau was averse to the Consulate; and that it was only from irresolution that he accepted the custody of the Directory. I know also that he excused himself to his prisoners for the duty which had devolved upon him. They themselves told me this."

Fouché entered further into many details respecting his conduct, and the motives which had urged him to do what he did in favour of the First Consul. My memory does not enable me to report all he told me, but I distinctly recollect that the impression made on my mind by what fell from him was, that he had acted merely with a view to his own interests. He did not conceal his satisfaction at having outwitted Regnier, and obliged Bonaparte to recall him, that he set in motion every spring calculated to unite the conspirators, or rather to convert the discontented into conspirators, is evident from the following remarks which fell from him: "With the information I possessed, had I remained in office it is probable that I might have prevented the conspiracy, but Bonaparte would still have had to fear the rivalry of Moreau. He would not have been Emperor; and we should still have had to dread the return of the Bourbons, of which, thank God, there is now no fear."

During my stay at Pont-Carry I said but little to Fouché about my long audience with the Emperor. However, I thought I might inform him that I was authorised to correspond directly with his Majesty. I thought it useless to conceal this fact, since he would soon learn it through his agents. I also said a few words about Bonaparte's regret at not having children.

My object was to learn Fouché's opinion on this subject, and it was not without a feeling of indignation that I heard him say, "It is to be hoped the Empress will soon die. Her death will remove many difficulties. Sooner or later he must take a wife who will bear him a child; for as long as he has no direct heir there is every chance that his death will be the signal for a Revolution. His brothers are perfectly incapable of filling his place, and a new party would rise up in favour of the Bourbons; which must be prevented above all things. At present they are not dangerous, though they still have active and devoted agents. Altona is full of them, and you will be surrounded by them. I beg of you to keep a watchful eye upon them, and render me a strict account of all their movements, and even of their most trivial actions. As they have recourse to all sorts of disguises, you cannot be too vigilant; therefore it will be advisable, in the first place, to establish a good system of espionage; but have a care of the spies who serve both sides, for they swarm in Germany."

This is all I recollect of my conversations with Fouché at Pont-Carre. I returned to Paris to make preparations for my journey to Hamburg.

CHAPTER XXXII

1805

I left Paris on the 20th of May 1805. On the 5th of June following I delivered my credentials to the Senate of Hamburg, which was represented by the Syndic Doormann and the Senator Schutte. M. Reinhart, my predecessor, left Hamburg on the 12th of June.

The reigning Dukes of Mecklenburg-Schwerin and Brunswick, to whom I had announced my arrival as accredited Minister to them, wrote me letters recognising me in that character. General Walmoden had just signed the capitulation of Sublingen with Marshal Mortier, who had the command in Hanover. The English Government refused to ratify this, because it stipulated that the troops should be prisoners of war. Bonaparte had two motives for relaxing this hard condition. He wished to keep Hanover as a compensation for Malta, and to assure the means of embarrassing and attacking Prussia, which he now began to distrust. By advancing upon Prussia he would secure his left, so that when convenient he might march northward. Mortier, therefore, received orders to reduce the conditions of the capitulation to the surrender of the arms, baggage, artillery, and horses. England, which was making great efforts to resist the invasion with which she thought herself threatened, expended considerable sums for the transport of the troops from Hanover to England. Her precipitation was indescribable, and she paid the most exorbitant charges for the hire of ships. Several houses in Hamburg made fortunes on this occasion. Experience has long since proved that it is not at their source that secret transactions are most readily known. The intelligence of an event frequently resounds at a distance, while the event itself is almost entirely unknown in the place of its occurrence. The direct influence of political events on commercial speculations renders merchants exceedingly attentive to what is going on. All who are engaged in commercial pursuits form a corporation united by the strongest of all bonds, common interest; and commercial correspondence frequently presents a fertile field for observation, and affords much valuable information, which often escapes the inquiries of Government agents.

I resolved to form a connection with some of the mercantile houses which maintained extensive and frequent communications with the Northern States. I knew that by obtaining their confidence I might gain a knowledge of all that was going on in Russia, Sweden, England, and Austria. Among the subjects upon which it was desirable to obtain information I included negotations, treaties, military measures—such as recruiting troops beyond the amount settled for the peace establishment, movements of troops, the formation of camps and magazines, financial operations, the fitting-out of ships, and many other things, which, though not important in themselves, frequently lead to the knowledge of what is important.

I was not inclined to place reliance on all public reports and gossiping stories circulated on the Exchange without close investigation; for I wished to avoid transmitting home as truths what might frequently be mere stock-jobbing inventions. I was instructed to keep watch on the emigrants, who were exceedingly numerous in Hamburg and its neighbourhood, Mecklenburg, Hanover, Brunswick, and Holstein; but I must observe that my inspection was to extend only to those who were known to be actually engaged in intrigues and plots.

I was also to keep watch on the state of the public mind, and on the journals which frequently give it a wrong direction, and to point out those articles in the journals which I thought censurable. At first I merely made verbal representations and complaints, but I could not always confine myself to this course. I received such distinct and positive orders that, in spite of myself, inspection was speedily converted into oppression. Complaints against the journals filled one-fourth of my despatches.

As the Emperor wished to be made acquainted with all that was printed against him, I sent to Paris, in May 1805, and consequently a very few days after my arrival in Hamburg, a pamphlet by the celebrated Kotzebue, entitled 'Recollections of my Journey to Naples and Rome'. This publication, which was printed at Berlin, was full of indecorous attacks and odious allusions on the Emperor.

I was informed at that time, through a certain channel, that the Emperor Alexander had solicited General Moreau to enter his service, and take the command of the Russian infantry. He offered him 12,000 roubles to defray his travelling expenses. At a subsequent period Moreau unfortunately accepted these offers, and died in the enemy's ranks.

On the 27th of June M. Bouligny arrived at Hamburg. He was appointed to supersede M. d'Ocariz at Stockholm. The latter minister had left Hamburg on the 11th of June for Constantinople, where he did not expect to stay three months. I had several long conversations with him before his departure, and he did not appear to be satisfied with his destination. We frequently spoke of the King of Sweden, whose conduct M. d'Ocariz blamed. He was, he said, a young madman, who, without reflecting on the change of time and circumstances, wished to play the part of Gustavus Adolphus, to whom he bore no resemblance but in name. M. d'Ocariz spoke of the King of Sweden's camp in a tone of derision. That Prince had returned to the King of Prussia the cordon of the Black Eagle because the order had been given to the First Consul. I understood that Frederick William was very much offended at this proceeding, which was as indecorous and absurd as the return of the Golden Fleece by Louis XVII. to the King of Spain was dignified and proper. Gustavus Adolphus was brave, enterprising, and chivalrous, but inconsiderate and irascible. He called Bonaparte Monsieur Napoleon. His follies and reverses in Hanover were without doubt the cause of his abdication. On the 31st of October 1805 he published a declaration of war against France in language highly insulting to the Emperor.

Fouché overwhelmed me with letters. If I had attended to all his instructions I should have left nobody unmolested. He asked me for information respecting a man named Lazoret, of the department of Gard, a girl, named Rosine Zimbenni, having informed the police that he had been killed in a duel at Hamburg. I replied that I knew but of four Frenchmen who had been killed in that way; one, named Clement, was killed by Tarasson; a second, named Duparc, killed by Lezardi; a third, named Sadremont, killed by Revel; and a fourth, whose name I did not know, killed by Lafond. This latter had just arrived at Hamburg when he was killed, but he was not the man sought for.

Lafond was a native of Brabant, and had served in the British army. He insulted the Frenchman because he wore the national cockade—A duel was the consequence, and the offended party fell. M. Reinhart, my predecessor wished to punish Lafond, but the Austrian Minister having claimed him as the subject of his sovereign, he was not molested. Lafond took refuge in Antwerp, where he became a player.

During the first months which succeeded my arrival in Hamburg I received orders for the arrest of many persons, almost all of whom were designated as dangerous and ill disposed men. When I was convinced that the accusation was groundless I postponed the arrest. The matter was then forgotten, and nobody complained.

A title, or a rank in foreign service, was a safeguard against the Paris inquisition. Of this the following is an instance. Count Gimel, of whom I shall hereafter have occasion to speak more at length, set out about this time for Carlsbad. Count Grote the Prussian Minister, frequently spoke to me of him. On my expressing apprehension that M. de Gimel might be arrested, as there was a strong prejudice against him, M. Grote replied, "Oh! there is no fear of that. He will return to Hamburg with the rauk of an English colonel."

On the 17th of July there appeared in the Correspondent an article exceedingly insulting to France. It had been inserted by order of Baron Novozilzow, who was at Berlin, and who had become very hostile to France, though it was said he had been sent from St. Petersburg on a specific mission to Napoleon. The article in question was transmitted from Berlin by an extraordinary courier, and Novozilzow in his note to the Senate said it might be stated that the article was inserted at the request of His Britannic Majesty. The Russian Minister at Berlin, M. Alopaeus, despatched also an 'estafette' to the Russian charge d'affaires at Hamburg, with orders to apply for the insertion of the article, which accordingly appeared. In obedience to the Emperor's instructions, I complained of it, and the Senate replied that it never opposed the insertion of an official note sent by any Government; that insults would redound against those from whom they came; that the reply of the French Government would be published; and that the Senate had never deviated from this mode of proceeding.

I observed to the Senate that I did not understand why the Correspondent should make itself the trumpet of M. Novozilzow; to which the Syndic replied, that two great powers, which might do them much harm, had required the insertion of the article, and that it could not be refused.

The hatred felt by the foreign Princes, which the death of the Duc d'Enghien had considerably increased; gave encouragement to the publication of everything hostile to Napoleon. This was candidly avowed to me by the Ministers and foreigners of rank whom I saw in Hamburg. The King of Sweden was most violent in manifesting the indignation which was generally excited by the death of the Duc d'Enghien. M. Wetterstadt, who had succeeded M. La Gerbielske in the Cabinet of Stockholm, sent to the Swedish Minister at Hamburg a long letter exceedingly insulting to Napoleon. It was in reply to an article inserted in the 'Moniteur' respecting the return of the Black Eagle to the King of Prussia. M. Peyron, the Swedish Minister at Hamburg, who was very far from approving all that his master did, transmitted to Stockholm some very energetic remarks on the ill effect which would be produced by the insertion of the article in the 'Correspondent'. The article was then a little modified, and M. Peyron received formal orders to get it inserted. However; on my representations the Senate agreed to suppress it, and it did not appear.

Marshal Bernadotte, who had the command of the French troops in Hanover, kept up a friendly correspondence with me unconnected with the duties of our respective functions.

On the occupation of Hanover Mr. Taylor, the English Minister at Cassel, was obliged to leave that place; but he soon returned in spite of the opposition of France. On this subject the marshal furnished me with the following particulars:

I have just received, my dear Bourrienne, information which leaves no doubt of what has taken place at Cassel with respect to Mr. Taylor. That Minister has been received in spite of the representations of M. Bignon, which, however, had previously been merely verbal. I know that the Elector wrote to London to request that Mr. Taylor should not return. In answer to this the English Government sent him back. Our Minister has done everything he could to obtain his dismissal; but the pecuniary interests of the Elector have triumphed over every other consideration. He would not risk quarrelling with the Court from which he expects to receive more than 12,000,000 francs. The British Government has been written to a second time, but without effect. The Elector himself, in a private letter, has requested the King of England to recall Mr. Taylor, but it is very probable that the Cabinet of London will evade this request. Under these circumstances our troops have approached nearer to Cassel. Hitherto the whole district of Gottingen had been exempt from quartering troops. New arrangements, tendered necessary by the scarcity of forage, have obliged me to send a squadron of 'chasseurs de cheval' to Munden, a little town four leagues from Cassel. This movement excited some alarm in the Elector, who expressed a wish to see things restored to the same footing as before. He has requested M. Bignon to write to me, and to assure me again that he will be delighted to become acquainted with me at the waters of Nemidorff, where he intends to spend some time. But on this subject I shall not alter the determination I have already mentioned to you. —Yours, etc.,

(Signed) BERNADOTTE.

STADE,
10th Thermidor (29th July, 1805).

CHAPTER XXXIII

1805

At the beginning of August 1805 a treaty of alliance between Russia and England was spoken of. Some persons of consequence, who had the means of knowing all that was going on in the political world, had read this treaty, the principal points of which were communicated to me.

Article 1st stated that the object of the alliance was to restore the balance of Europe. By art. 2d the Emperor of Russia was to place 36,000 men at the disposal of England. Art. 3d stipulated that neither of the two powers would consent to treat with France, nor to lay down arms until the King of Sardinia should either be restored to his dominions or receive an equivalent indemnity in the northeast of Italy. By art. 4th Malta was to be evacuated by the English, and occupied by the Russians. By art. 5th the two powers were to guarantee the independence of the Republic of the Ionian Isles, and England was to pledge herself to assist Russia in her war against Persia. If this plan of a treaty, of the existence of which I was informed on unquestionable authority, had been brought to any result it is impossible to calculate what might have been its consequences.

At that time an immediate Continental war was confidently expected by every person in the north of Europe; and it is very certain that, had not Napoleon taken the hint in time and renounced his absurd schemes at Boulogne, France would have stood in a dangerous situation.

M. Forshmann, the Russian charge d'affaires, was intriguing to excite the north of Europe against France. He repeatedly received orders to obtain the insertion of irritating articles in the 'Correspondent'. He was an active, intriguing, and spiteful little man, and a declared enemy of France; but fortunately his stupidity and vanity rendered him less dangerous than he wished to be. He was universally detested, and he would have lost all credit but that the extensive trade carried on between Russia and Hamburg forced the inhabitants and magistrates of that city to bear with a man who might have done them, individually, considerable injury.

The recollection of Duroc's successful mission to Berlin during the Consulate induced Napoleon to believe that that general might appease the King of Prussia, who complained seriously of the violation of the territory of Anspach, which Bernadotte, in consequence of the orders he received, had not been able to respect. Duroc remained about six weeks in Berlin.

The following letter from Duroc will show that the facility of passing through Hesse seemed to excuse the second violation of the Prussian territory; but there was a great difference between a petty Prince of Hesse and the King of Prussia.

> I send you, my dear Bourrienne, two despatches, which I have received for you. M. de Talleyrand, who sends them, desires me to request that you will transmit General Victor's by a sure conveyance. I do not yet know whether I shall stay long in Berlin.

> By the last accounts I received the Emperor is still in Paris, and numerous forces are assembling on the Rhine. The hopes of peace are vanishing every day, and Austria does everything to promote war. I have received accounts from Marshal Bernadotte. He has effected his passage through Hesse. Marshal Bernadotte was much pleased with the courtesy he experienced from the Elector.

The junction of the corps commanded by Bernadotte with the army of the Emperor was very important, and Napoleon therefore directed the Marshal to come up with him as speedily as possible, and by the shortest road. It was necessary he should arrive in time for the battle of Austerlitz. Gustavus, King of Sweden, who was always engaged in some enterprise, wished to raise an army composed of Swedes, Prussians, and English; and certainly a vigorous attack in the north would have prevented Bernadotte from quitting the banks of the Elbe and the Weser, and reinforcing the Grand Army which was marching on Vienna. But the King of Sweden's coalition produced no other result than the siege of the little fortress of Hameln.

Prussia would not come to a rupture with France, the King of Sweden was abandoned, and Bonaparte's resentment against him increased. This abortive project of Gustavus contributed not a little to alienate the affections of his subjects, who feared that they might be the victims of the revenge excited by the extravagant plans of their King, and the insults he had heaped upon Napoleon, particularly since the death of the Duc d'Enghien.

On the 13th of September 1805 I received a letter from the Minister of Police soliciting information about Swedish Pomerania.

Astonished at not obtaining from the commercial Consuls at Lübeck and Stettin any accounts of the movements of the Russians, I had sent to those ports, four days before the receipt of the Police Minister's letter, a confidential agent, to observe the Baltic: though we were only 64 leagues from Stralsund the most uncertain and contradictory accounts came to hand. It was, however, certain that a landing of the Russians was expected at Stralsund, or at Travemtinde, the port of Lübeck, at the mouth of the little river Trave. I was positively informed that Russia had freighted a considerable number of vessels for those ports.

The hatred of the French continued to increase in the north of Europe. About the end of September there appeared at Kiel, in Denmark, a libellous pamphlet, which was bought and read with inconceivable avidity. This pamphlet, which was very ably written, was the production of some fanatic who openly preached a crusade against France. The author regarded the blood of millions of men as a trifling sacrifice for the great object of humiliating France and bringing her back to the limits of the old monarchy. This pamphlet was circulated extensively in the German departments united to France, in Holland, and in Switzerland. The number of incendiary publications which everywhere abounded indicated but too plainly that if the nations of the north should be driven back towards the Arctic regions they would in their turn repulse their conquerors towards the south; and no man of common sense could doubt that if the French eagles were planted in foreign capitals, foreign standards would one day wave over Paris.

On the 30th of September 1805 I received, by an 'estafette', intelligence of the landing at Stralsund of 6000 Swedes, who had arrived from Stockholm in two ships of war.

About the end of September the Hamburg exchange on Paris fell alarmingly. The loss was twenty per cent. The fall stopped at seventeen below par.

The speculation for this fall of the exchange had been made with equal imprudence and animosity by the house of Osy and Company.

The head of that house, a Dutch emigrant, who had been settled at Hamburg about six years, seized every opportunity of manifesting his hatred of France. An agent of that rich house at Rotterdam was also very hostile to us, a circumstance which shows that if many persons sacrifice their political opinions to their interests there are others who endanger their interests for the triumph of their opinions.

On the 23d of October 1805 I received official intelligence of the total destruction of the first Austrian army: General Barbou, who was in Hanover, also informed me of that event in the following terms: "The first Austrian army has ceased to exist." He alluded to the brilliant affair of Ulm. I immediately despatched twelve estafettes to different parts; among other places to Stralsund and Husum. I thought that these prodigies, which must have been almost incredible to those who were unacquainted with Napoleon's military genius, might arrest the progress of the Russian troops, and produces some change in the movements of the enemy's forces. A second edition of the 'Correspondent' was published with this intelligence, and 6000 copies were sold at four times the usual price.

I need not detain the reader with the details of the capitulation of Ulm, which have already been published, but I may relate the following anecdote, which is not generally known. A French general passing before the ranks of his men said to them, "Well, comrades, we have prisoners enough here."—"yes indeed," replied one of the soldiers, "we never saw so many . . . collected together before." It was stated at the time, and I believe it, that the Emperor was much displeased when he heard of this, and remarked that it was "atrocious to insult brave men to whom the fate of arms had proved unfavourable."

In reading the history of this period we find that in whatever place Napoleon happened to be, there was the central point of action. The affairs of Europe were arranged at his headquarters in the same manner as if he had been in Paris. Everything depended on his good or bad fortune. Espionage, seduction, false promises, exactions,—all were put in force to promote the success of his projects; but his despotism, which excited dissatisfaction in France, and his continual aggressions, which threatened the independence of foreign States, rendered him more and more unpopular everywhere.

The battle of Trafalgar took place while Napoleon was marching on Vienna, and on the day after the capitulation of Ulm. The southern coast of Spain then witnessed an engagement between thirty-one French and about an equal number of English ships, and in spite of this equality of force the French fleet was destroyed.[204] This great battle afforded another proof of our naval inferiority. Admires Calder first gave us the lesson which Nelson completed, but which cost the latter his life. According to the reports which Duroc transmitted to me, courage gave momentary hope to the French; but they were at length forced to yield to the superior naval tactics of the enemy. The battle of Trafalgar paralysed our naval force, and banished all hope of any attempt against England.

The favour which the King, of Prussia had shown to Duroc was withdrawn when his Majesty received intelligence of the march of Bernadotte's troops through the Margravate of Anspach. All accounts concurred respecting the just umbrage which that violation of territory occasioned to the King of Prussia. The agents whom I had in that quarter overwhelmed me with reports of the excesses committed by the French in passing through the Margravate. A

204 The actual forces present were 27 English ships of the line and 38 Franco-Spanish ships of the line; see James' Naval History, vol. iii. p. 459.

letter I received from Duroc contains the following remarks on this subject:

> The corps of Marshal Bernadotte has passed through Anapach and by some misunderstanding this has been regarded at Berlin as an insult to the King, a violence committed upon his neutrality. How can it be supposed, especially under present circumstances, that the Emperor could have any intention of insulting or committing violence upon his friend? Besides, the reports have been exaggerated, and have been made by persons who wish to favour our enemies rather than us. However, I am perfectly aware that Marshal Bernadotte's 70,000 men are not 70,000 virgins. Be this as it may, the business might have been fatal, and will, at all events, be very injurious to us. Laforeat and I are treated very harshly, though we do not deserve it. All the idle stories that have been got up here must have reached you. Probably Prussia will not forget that France was, and still may be, the only power interested in her glory and aggrandisement.

At the end of October the King of Prussia, far from thinking of war, but in case of its occurrence wishing to check its disasters as far as possible, proposed to establish a line of neutrality. This was the first idea of the Confederation of the North. Duroc, fearing lest the Russians should enter Hamburg, advised me, as a friend, to adopt precautions. But I was on the spot; I knew all the movement the little detached corps, and I was under no apprehension.

The editor of the Hamburg 'Correspondent' sent me every evening a proof of the number which was to appear next day,—a favour which was granted only to the French Minister. On the 20th of November I received the proof as usual, and saw nothing objectionable in it. How great, therefore, was my astonishment when next morning I read in the same journal an article personally insulting to the Emperor, and in which the legitimate sovereigns of Europe were called upon to undertake a crusade against the usurper etc. I immediately sent for M. Doormann, first Syndic of the Senate of Hamburg. When he appeared his mortified look sufficiently informed me that he knew what I had to say to him. I reproached him sharply, and asked him how, after all I had told him of the Emperor's susceptibility, he could permit the insertion of such an article. I observed to him that this indecorous diatribe had no official character, since it had no signature; and that, therefore, he had acted in direct opposition to a decree of the Senate, which prohibited the insertion in the journals of any articles which were not signed. I told him plainly that his imprudence might be attended with serious consequences. M. Doormann did not attempt to justify himaelt but merely explained to me how the thing had happened.

On the 20th of November, in the evening, M. Forshmann, the Russian charge d'affaires who had in the course of the day arrived from the Russian headquarters presented to the editor of the Correspondent the article in question. The editor, after reading the article, which he thought exceedingly indecorous, observed to M. Forshmann that his paper was already made up, which was the fact, for I had seen a proof. M. Forshmann, however, insisted on the insertion of the article. The editor then told him that he could not admit it without the approbation of the Syndic Censor. M. Forshmann immediately waited upon M. Doormann, and when the latter begged that he would not insist on the insertion of the article, M. Forshmann produced a letter written in French, which, among other things, contained the following: "You will get the enclosed article inserted in the Correspondent without suffering a single word to be altered. Should the censor refuse, you must apply to the directing Burgomaster, and, in case of his refusal, to General Tolstoy, who will devise some means of rendering the Senate more complying, and forcing it to observe an impartial deference."

M. Doorman, thinking he could not take upon himself to allow the insertion of the article, went, accompanied by M. Forshmann, to wait upon M. Von Graffen, the directing Burgomaster. MM. Doorman and Von Graffen earnestly pointed out the impropriety of inserting the article; but M. Forshmann referred to his order, and added that the compliance of the Senate on this point was the only means of avoiding great mischief. The Burgomaster and the Syndic, finding themselves thus forced to admit the article, entreated that the following passage at least might be suppressed: "I know a certain chief, who, in defiance of all laws divine and human,—in contempt of the hatred he inspires in Europe, as well as among those whom he has reduced to be his subjects, keeps possession of a usurped throne by violence and crime. His insatiable ambition would subject all Europe to his rule. But the time is come for avenging the rights of nations . . . ." M. Forshmann again referred to his orders, and with some degree of violence insisted on the insertion of the article in its complete form. The Burgomaster then authorised the editor of the Correspondent to print the article that night, and M. Forshmann, having obtained that authority, carried the article to the office at half-past eleven o'clock.

Such was the account given me by M. Doormann. I observed that I did not understand how the imaginary apprehension of any violence on the part of Russia should have induced him to admit so insolent an attack upon the most powerful sovereign in Europe, whose arms would soon dictate laws to Germany. The Syndic did not dissemble his fear of the Emperor's resentment, while at the same time he expressed a hope that the Emperor would take into consideration the extreme difficulty of a small power maintaining neutrality in the extraordinary circumstances in which Hamburg was placed, and that the articles might be said to have been presented almost at the point of the Cossacks' spears. M. Doormann added that a refusal, which world have brought Russian troops to Hamburg, might have been attended by very unpleasant consequences to me, and might have committed the Senate in a very different way. I begged of him, once for all, to set aside in these affairs all consideration of my personal danger: and the Syndic, after a conversation of more than two hours, departed more uneasy in his mind than when he arrived, and conjuring me to give a faithful report of the facts as they had happened.

M. Doormann was a very worthy man, and I gave a favourable representation of his excuses and of the readiness which he had always evinced to keep out of the Correspondent articles hostile to France; as, for example, the commencement of a proclamation of the Emperor of Germany to his subjects, and a complete proclamation of the King of Sweden. As it happened, the good Syndic escaped with nothing worse than a fright; I was myself astonished at the success of my intercession. I learned from the Minister for Foreign Affairs that the Emperor was furiously indignant on reading the article, in which the French army was outraged as well as he. Indeed, he paid but little attention to insults directed against himself personally. Their eternal repetition had inured him to them; but at the idea of his army being insulted he was violently enraged, and uttered the most terrible threats.

It is worthy of remark that the Swedish and English Ministers, as soon as they read the article, waited upon the editor of the Correspondent, and expressed their astonishment that such a libel should have been published. "Victorious armies," said they, "should be answered by cannonballs and not by insults as gross as they are ridiculous." This opinion was shared by all the foreigners at that time in Hamburg.

CHAPTER XXXIV

1805

The brief detail I have given in the two or three preceding chapters of the events which occurred previously to and during the campaign of Austerlitz, with the letters of Duroc and Bernadotte, may afford the reader some idea of my situation during the early part of my residence in Hamburg. Events succeeded each other with such incredible rapidity as to render my labour excessive. My occupations were different, but not less laborious, than those which I formerly performed when near the Emperor; and, besides, I was now loaded with a responsibility which did not attach to me as the private secretary of General Bonaparte and the First Consul. I had, in fact, to maintain a constant watch over the emigrants in Altona, which was no easy matter—to correspond daily with the Minister for Foreign Affairs and the Minister of Police—to confer with the foreign Ministers accredited at Hamburg—to maintain active relations with the commanders of the French army—to interrogate my secret agents, and keep a strict surveillance over their proceedings; it was, besides, necessary to be unceasingly on the watch for scurrilous articles against Napoleon in the Hamburg 'Corespondent'. I shall frequently have occasion to speak of all these things, and especially of the most marked emigrants, in a manner less irregular, because what I have hitherto said may, in some sort, be considered merely as a summary of all the facts relating to the occurrences which daily passed before my eyes.

In the midst of these multifarious and weighty occupations I received a packet with the Strasburg postmark at the time the Empress was in that city. This packet had not the usual form of a diplomatic despatch, and the superscription announced that it came from the residence of Josephine. My readers, I venture to presume, will not experience less gratification than I did on a perusal of its contents, which will be found at the end of this chapter; but before satisfying the curiosity to which I have perhaps given birth, I may here relate that one of the peculiarities of Bonaparte was a fondness of extempore narration; and it appears he had not discontinued the practice even after he became Emperor.

In fact, Bonaparte, during the first year after his elevation to the Imperial throne, usually passed those evenings in the apartments of the Empress which he could steal from public business. Throwing himself on a sofa, he would remain absorbed in gloomy silence, which no one dared to interrupt. Sometimes, however, on the contrary, he would give the reins to his vivid imagination and his love of the marvelous, or, to speak more correctly, his desire to produce effect, which was perhaps one of his strongest passions, and would relate little romances, which were always of a fearful description and in unison with the natural turn of his ideas. During those recitals the ladies-in-waiting were always present, to one of whom I am indebted for the following story, which she had written nearly in the words of Napoleon. "Never," said this lady in her letter to me, "did the Emperor appear more extraordinary. Led away by the subject, he paced the salon with hasty strides; the intonations of his voice varied according to the characters of the personages he brought on the scene; he seemed to multiply himself in order to play the different parts, and no person needed to feign the terror which he really inspired, and which he loved to see depicted in the countenances of those who surrounded him." In this tale I have made no alterations, as can be attested by those who, to my knowledge, have a copy of it. It is curious to compare the impassioned portions of it with the style of Napoleon in some of the letters addressed to Josephine.

VOLUME III

1805-1814

CHAPTER I

1805

I had been three months at Hamburg when I learned that the Emperor had at last resolved to abolish the only remaining memorial of the Republic, namely, the revolutionary calendar. That calendar was indeed an absurd innovation, for the new denominations of the months were not applicable in all places, even in France; the corn of Provence did not wait to be opened by the sun of the month of Messidor. On the 9th of September a 'Senates-consulte' decreed that on the 1st of January following the months and days should resume their own names. I read with much interest Laplace's report to the Senate, and must confess I was very glad to see the Gregorian calendar again acknowledged by law, as it had already been acknowledged in fact. Frenchmen in foreign countries experienced particular inconvenience from the adoption of a system different from all the rest of the world.

A few days after the revival of the old calendar the Emperor departed for the army. When at Hamburg it may well be supposed that I was anxious to obtain news, and I received plenty from the interior of Germany and from some friends in Paris. This correspondence enables me to present to my readers a comprehensive and accurate picture of the state of public affairs up to the time when Napoleon took the field. I have already mentioned how artfully he always made it appear that he was anxious for peace, and that he was always the party attacked; his, conduct previous to the first conquest of Vienna affords a striking example of this artifice. It was pretty evident that the transformation of the Cisalpine Republic into the kingdom of Italy, and the union of Genoa to France were infractions of treaties; yet the Emperor, nevertheless, pretended that all the infractions were committed by Austria. The truth is, that Austria was raising levies as secretly as possible, and collecting her troops on the frontiers of Bavaria. An Austrian corps even penetrated into some provinces of the Electorate; all this afforded Napoleon a pretext for going to the aid of his allies.

In the memorable sitting preceding his departure the Emperor presented a project of a 'Senatus-consulte' relative to the re-organisation of the National Guard. The Minister for Foreign Affairs read an explanation of the reciprocal conduct of France and Austria since the peace of Luneville, in which the offences of France were concealed with wonderful skill. Before the sitting broke up the Emperor addressed the members, stating that he was about to leave the capital to place himself at the head of the army to afford prompt succour to his allies, and defend the dearest interests of his people. He boasted of his wish to preserve peace, which Austria and Russia, as he alleged, had, through the influence of England, been induced to disturb.

This address produced a very powerful impression in Hamburg. For my part, I recognised in it Napoleon's usual boasting strain; but on this occasion events seemed bent on justifying it. The Emperor may certainly have performed more scientific campaigns than that of Austerlitz, but never any more glorious in results. Everything seemed to partake of the marvellous, and I have often thought of the secret joy which Bonaparte must have felt on seeing himself at last an the point of commencing a great war in Germany, for which he had so often expressed an ardent desire. He proceeded first to Strasburg, whither Josephine accompanied him.

All the reports that I received agreed with the statements of my private correspondence in describing the incredible enthusiasm which prevailed in the army on learning that it was to march into Germany. For the first time Napoleon had recourse to an expeditious mode of transport, and 20,000 carriages conveyed his army, as if by enchantment, from the shores of the Channel to the banks of the Rhine. The idea of an active campaign fired the ambition of the junior part of the army. All dreamed of glory, and of speedy promotion, and all hoped to distinguish themselves before the eyes of a chief who was idolised by his troops. Thus during his short stay at Strasburg the Emperor might with reason prophesy the success which crowned his efforts under the walls of Vienna.

Rapp, who accompanied him, informed me that on leaving Strasburg he observed, in the presence of several persons, "It will be said that I made Mack's plan of campaign for him. The Caudine Forks are at Ulm."[205]

Experience proved that Bonaparte was not deceived; but I ought on this occasion to contradict a calumnious report circulated at that time, and since maliciously repeated. It has been said that there existed an understanding between Mack and Bonaparte, and that the general was bought over to deliver up the gates of Ulm. I have received positive proof that this assertion is a scandalous falsehood; and the only thing that could give it weight was Napoleon's intercession after the campaign that Mack might not be put on his trial. In this intercession Napoleon was actuated only by humanity.

On taking the field Napoleon placed himself at the head of the Bavarians, with whom be opposed the enemy's army before the arrival of his own troops. As soon as they were assembled he published the following proclamation, which still further excited the ardour of the troops.

> SOLDIERS—The war of the third coalition is commenced. The Austrian army has passed the Inn, violated treaties, attacked and driven our ally from his capital. You yourselves have been obliged to hasten, by forced marches, to the defence of our frontiers. But you have now passed the Rhine; and we will not stop till we have secured the independence of the Germanic body, succoured our allies, and humbled the pride of our unjust assailants. We will not again make peace without a sufficient guarantee! Our generosity shall not again wrong our policy. Soldiers, your Emperor is among you! You are but the advanced guard of the great people. If it be necessary they will all rise at my call to confound and dissolve this new league, which has been created by the malice and the gold of England. But, soldiers, we shall have forced marches to make, fatigues and privations of every kind to endure. Still, whatever obstacles may be opposed to us, we will conquer them; and we will never rest until we have planted our eagles on the territory of our enemies!

In the confidential notes of his diplomatic agents, in his speeches, and in his proclamations, Napoleon always described himself as the attacked party, and perhaps his very earnestness

205 This allusion to the Caudine Forks was always in Napoleon's mouth when he saw an enemy's army concentrated on a point, and foresaw its defeat—Bourrienne.

in so doing sufficed to reveal the truth to all those who had learned to read his thoughts differently from what his words expressed them.

At the commencement of the campaign of Austerlitz a circumstance occurred from which is to be dated the fortune of a very meritorious man. While the Emperor was at Strasburg he asked General Marescot, the commander-in-chief of the engineers, whether he could recommend from his corps a brave, prudent, and intelligent young officer, capable of being entrusted with an important reconnoitering mission. The officer selected by General Marescot was a captain in the engineers, named Bernard, who had been educated in the Polytechnic School. He set off on his mission, advanced almost to Vienna, and returned to the headquarters of the Emperor at the capitulation of Ulm.

Bonaparte interrogated him himself, and was well satisfied with his replies; but, not content with answering verbally the questions put by Napoleon, Captain Bernard had drawn up a report of what he observed, and the different routes which might be taken. Among other things he observed that it would be a great advantage to direct the whole army upon Vienna, without regard to the fortified places; for that, once master of the capital of Austria, the Emperor might dictate laws to all the Austrian monarchy. "I was present," said Rapp to me, "at this young officer's interview with the Emperor. After reading the report, would you believe that the Emperor flew into a furious passion? 'How!' cried he, 'you are very bold, very presumptuous! A young officer to take the liberty of tracing out a plan of campaign for me! Begone, and await my orders.'"

This, and some other circumstances which I shall have to add respecting Captain Bernard, completely reveal Napoleon's character. Rapp told me that as soon as the young officer had left the Emperor all at once changed his tone. "That," said he, "is a clever young man; he has taken a proper view of things. I shall not expose him to the chance of being shot. Perhaps I shall sometime want his services. Tell Berthier to despatch an order for his departure for Elyria."

This order was despatched, and Captain Bernard, who, like his comrades, was ardently looking forward to the approaching campaign, regarded as a punishment what was, on the Emperor's part, a precaution to preserve a young man whose merit he appreciated. At the close of the campaign, when the Emperor promoted those officers who had distinguished themselves, Bernard, who was thought to be in disgrace, was not included in Berthier's list among the captains of engineers whom he recommended to the rank of chef de bataillon; but Napoleon himself inscribed Bernard's name before all the rest. However, the Emperor forgot him for some time; and it was only an accidental circumstance that brought him to his recollection. I never had any personal acquaintance with Bernard, but I learned from Rapp, how he afterwards became his colleague as aide de camp to the Emperor; a circumstance which I shall now relate, though it refers to a later period.

Before the Emperor left Paris for the campaign of 1812 he wished to gain precise information respecting Ragusa and Elyria. He sent for Marmont, but was not satisfied with his answers. He then interrogated several other generals, but the result of his inquiries always was, "This is all very well; but it is not what I want. I do not know Ragusa." He then sent for General Dejean, who had succeeded M. de Marescot as first inspector of the Engineers.

"Have you any one among your officers," he asked, "who is well acquainted with Ragusa?" Dejean, after a little reflection, replied, "Sire, there is a chef de bataillon who has been a long time forgotten, but who knows Elyria perfectly."—"What's his name?"—"Bernard."—"Ah! stop . . . Bernard! I remember that name. Where is he?"—"At Antwerp, Sire, employed on the fortifications."—"Let a telegraphic despatch be immediately, transmitted[206], desiring him to mount his horse and come with all speed to Paris."

The promptitude with which the Emperor's orders were always executed is well known. A few days after Captain Bernard was in the Emperor's cabinet in Paris. Napoleon received him very graciously. The first thing he said was, "Talk to me about Ragusa." This was a favourite mode of interrogation with him in similar cases, and I have heard him say that it was a sure way of drawing out all that a man had observed in any country that he had visited. Be that as it may, he was perfectly satisfied with M. Bernard's information respecting Elyria; and when the chef de bataillon had finished speaking Napoleon said, "Colonel Bernard, I am now acquainted with Ragusa." The Emperor afterwards conversed familiarly with him, entered into details respecting the system of fortification adopted at Antwerp, referred to the plan of the works, criticised it, and showed how he would, if he besieged the town, render the means of defence unavailing. The new Colonel explained so well how he would defend the town against the Emperor's attack that Bonaparte was delighted, and immediately bestowed upon, the young officer a mark of distinction which, as far as I know, he never granted but upon that single occasion. The Emperor was going to preside at the Council of State, and desired Colonel Bernard to accompany him, and many times during the sittings be asked him for his opinion upon the points which were under discussion. On leaving the Council Napoleon said, "Bernard, you are in future my aide de camp." After the campaign he was made General of Brigade, soon after General of Division, and now he is acknowledged to be one of the ablest engineer officers in existence. Clarke's silly conduct deprived France of this distinguished man, who refused the brilliant offers of several sovereigns of Europe for the sake of retiring to the United States of America, where he commands the Engineers, and has constructed fortifications on the coast of the Floridas which are considered by engineers to be masterpieces of military art.

206 By semaphore arms.

CHAPTER II

1805

To convey an idea of the brilliant campaign of 1805 from an abstract of the reports and letters I received at Hamburg I should, like the almanac-makers, be obliged to note down a victory for every day. Was not the rapidity of the Emperor's first operations a thing hitherto unprecedented? He departed from Paris on the 24th of September, and hostilities commenced on the 2d of October. On the 6th and 7th the French passed the Danube, and turned the enemy's army. On the 8th Murat, at the battle of Wertingen, on the Danube, took 2000 Austrian prisoners, amongst whom, besides other general officers, was Count Auffemberg. Next day the Austrians fell back upon Gunsburg, retreating before our victorious legions, who, pursuing their triumphal course, entered Augsburg on the 10th, and Munich on the 12th. When I received my despatches I could have fancied I was reading a fabulous narrative. Two days after the French entered Munich—that is to say, on the 14th—an Austrian corps of 6000 men surrendered to Marshal Soult at Memingen, whilst Ney conquered, sword in hand, his future Duchy of Elchingen. Finally, on the 17th of October, came the famous capitulation of General Mack at Ulm,' and on the same day hostilities commenced in Italy between the French and Austrians, the former commanded by Massena and the latter by Prince Charles.[207]

207 Prince Maurice Liechtenstein was sent by General Mack as a flag of truce to the Imperial headquarters before Ulm. He was, according to custom, led blindfold on horseback. Rapp, who was present, together with several of Napoleon's aides de camp, afterwards spoke to me of the Prince's interview with the Emperor. I think he told me that Berthier was present likewise. "Picture to yourself," said Rapp, "the astonishment, or rather confusion, of the poor Prince when the bandage was removed from his eyes. He knew nothing of what had been going on, and did not even suspect that the Emperor had yet joined the army. When he understood that he was in the presence of Napoleon he could not suppress an exclamation of surprise, which did not escape the Emperor, and he ingenuously acknowledged that General Mack had no idea he was before the walls of Ulm." Prince Liechtenstein proposed to capitulate on condition that the garrison of Ulm should be allowed to return into Austria. This proposal, in the situation in which the garrison stood, Rapp said, made the Emperor smile. "How can you expect," said Napoleon, "that I can accede to such a proposition? What shall I gain by it? Eight days. In eight days you will be in my power without any condition. Do you suppose I am not acquainted with everything? . . You expect the Russians? . . . At the nearest they are in Bohemia. Were I to allow you to march out, what security can I have that you will not join them, and afterwards fight against me? Your generals have deceived me often enough, and I will no longer be duped. At Marengo I was weak enough to allow the troops of Melas to march out of Alessandria. He promised to treat for peace. What happened? Two months after Moreau had to fight with the garrison of Alessandria. Besides, this war is not an ordinary war. After the conduct of your Government I am not bound to keep any terms with it. I

Napoleon, who was so violently irritated by any obstacle which opposed him, and who treated with so much hauteur everybody who ventured to resist his inflexible will, was no longer the same man when, as a conqueror, he received the vanquished generals at Ulm. He condoled with them on their misfortune; and this, I can affirm, was not the result of a feeling of pride concealed beneath a feigned generosity. Although he profited by their defeat he pitied them sincerely. How frequently has he observed to me, "How much to be pitied is a general on the day after a lost battle." He had himself experienced this misfortune when he was obliged to raise the siege of St. Jean d'Acre. At that moment he would, I believe, have strangled Djezzar; but if Djezzar had surrendered, he would have treated him with the same attention which he showed to Mack and the other generals of the garrison of Ulm. These generals were seventeen in number, and among them was Prince Liechtenstein. There were also General Klenau (Baron de Giulay), who had acquired considerable military reputation in the preceding wars, and General Fresnel, who stood in a more critical situation than his companions in misfortune, for he was a Frenchman, and an emigrant.

Rapp told me that it was really painful to see these generals. They bowed respectfully to the Emperor, having Mack at their head. They preserved a mournful silence, and Napoleon was the first to speak, which he did in the following terms: "Gentlemen, I feel sorry that such brave men as you are should be the victims of the follies of a Cabinet which cherishes insane projects, and which does not hesitate to commit the dignity of the Austrian nation by trafficking with the services of its generals. Your names are known to me—they are honourably known wherever you have fought. Examine the conduct of those who have

---

have no faith in its promises. You have attacked me. If I should agree to what you ask, Mack would pledge his word, I know. But, even relying on his good faith, would be he able to keep his promise? As far as regards himself—yes; but as regards his army—no. If the Archduke Ferdinand were still with you I could rely upon his word, because he would be responsible for the conditions, and he would not disgrace himself; but I know he has quitted Ulm and passed the Danube. I know how to reach him, however." Rapp said it was impossible to imagine the embarrassment of Prince Liechtenstein whilst the Emperor was speaking. He, however, somewhat regained his self-possession, and observed that, unless the conditions which he proposed were granted the army would not capitulate. "If that be the case," said Napoleon. "you may as well go back to Mack, for I will never grant such conditions. Are you jesting with me? Stay; here is the capitulation of Memingen—show it to your General—let him surrender on the same conditions—I will consent to no others. Your officers may return to Austria, but the soldiers must be prisoners. Tell him to be speedy, for I have no time to lose. The more he delays the worse he will render his own condition and yours. To-morrow I shall have here the corps to which Memingen capitulated, and then we shall see what is to be done. Make Mack clearly understand that he has no alternative but to conform to my will." The imperious tones which Napoleon employed towards his enemies almost always succeeded, and it produced the accustomed effect upon Mack. On the same day that Prince Liechtenstein had been at our headquarters Mack wrote to the Emperor, stating that he would not have treated with any other on such terms; but that he yielded to the ascendency of Napoleon's fortune; and on the following day Berthier was sent into Ulm, from whence he returned with the capitulation signed. Thus Napoleon was not mistaken respecting the Caudine Forks of the Austrian army. The garrison of Ulm marched out with what are called the honours of war, and were led prisoners into France.—Bourrienne.

committed you. What could be more iniquitous than to attack me without a declaration of war? Is it not criminal to bring foreign invasion upon a country? Is it not betraying Europe to introduce Asiatic barbarities into her disputes? If good policy had been followed the Aulic Council, instead of attacking me, would have sought my alliance in order to drive back the Russians to the north. The alliance which your Cabinet has formed will appear monstrous in history. It is the alliance of dogs, shepherds, and wolves against sheep—such a scheme could never have been planned in the mind of a statesman. It is fortunate for you that I have not been defeated in the unjust struggle to which I have been provoked; if I had, the Cabinet of Vienna would have soon perceived its error, for which, perhaps, it will yet one day pay dearly."

What a change fifteen days of success, crowned by the capture of Ulm, had made in affairs! At Hamburg I knew through my agents to what a degree of folly the hopes of Napoleon's enemies had risen before he began the campaign. The security of the Cabinet of Vienna was really inexplicable; not only did they not dream of the series of victories which made Napoleon master of all the Austrian monarchy, but the assistants of Drake and all the intriguers of that sort treated France already as a conquered country, and disposed of some of our provinces. In the excess of their folly, to only give one instance, they promised the town of Lyons to the King of Sardinia, to recompense him for the temporary occupation of Piedmont.[208] While Napoleon flattered his prisoners at the expense of their Government he wished to express satisfaction at the conduct of his own army, and with this view he published a remarkable proclamation, which in some measure presented an abstract of all that had taken place since the opening of the campaign.

This proclamation was as follows:—

> SOLDIERS OF THE GRAND ARMY—In a fortnight we have finished an entire campaign. What we proposed to do has been done. We have driven the Austrian troops from Bavaria, and restored our ally to the sovereignty of his dominions. That army, which, with equal presumption and imprudence, marched upon our frontiers, is annihilated. But what does this signify to England? She has gained her object. We are no longer at Boulogne, and her subsidy will be neither more nor less. Of a hundred thousand men who composed that army, sixty thousand are prisoners. They will replace our conscripts in the labours of agriculture. Two hundred pieces of cannon, the whole park of artillery, ninety flags, and all their generals are in our power. Fifteen thousand men only have escaped. Soldiers! I announced to you the result of a great battle; but, thanks to the ill-devised schemes of the enemy, I was enabled to secure the wished-for result without incurring any danger, and, what is unexampled in the history of nations, that result has been gained at the sacrifice of scarcely fifteen hundred men killed and wounded. Soldiers! this success is due to your unlimited confidence in your Emperor, to your patience in enduring fatigues and privations of every kind, and to your singular courage and intrepidity. But we will not stop here. You are impatient to commence another campaign! The Russian army, which English gold has brought from the extremities of the universe, shall experience the same fate

208 In the treaties and declarations (see Martens and Thiers, tome v. p. 355) there is rather a tendency to sell the skin of the bear before killing him.

> as that which we have just defeated. In the conflict in which we are about to engage the honour of the French infantry is especially concerned. We shall now see another decision of the question which has already been determined in Switzerland and Holland; namely, whether the French infantry is the first or the second in Europe. Among the Russians there are no generals in contending against whom I can acquire any glory. All I wish is to obtain the victory with the least possible bloodshed. My soldiers are, my children.

This proclamation always appeared to me a masterpiece of military eloquence. While he lavished praises on his troops, he excited their emulation by hinting that the Russians were capable of disputing with them the first rank among the infantry of Europe, and he concluded his address by calling them his children.

The second campaign, to which Napoleon alleged they so eagerly looked forward, speedily ensued, and hostilities were carried on with a degree of vigour which fired the enthusiasm of the army. Heaven knows what accounts were circulated of the Russians, who, as Bonaparte solemnly stated in his proclamation, had come from the extremity of the world. They were represented as half-naked savages, pillaging, destroying and burning wherever they went. It was even asserted that they were cannibals, and had been seen to eat children. In short, at that period was introduced the denomination of northern barbarians which has since been so generally applied to the Russians. Two days after the capitulation of Ulm Murat obtained the capitulation of Trochtelfingen from General Yarneck, and made 10,000 prisoners, so that, without counting killed and wounded, the Austrian army had sustained a diminution of 50,000 men after a campaign of twenty days. On the 27th of October the French army crossed the Inn, and thus penetrated into the Austrian territory. Salzburg and Brannan were immediately taken. The army of Italy, under the command of Massena, was also obtaining great advantages. On the 30th of October, that is to say, the very day on which the Grand Army took the above-mentioned fortresses, the army of Italy, having crossed the Adige, fought a sanguinary battle at Caldiero, and took 5000 Austrian prisoners.

In the extraordinary campaign, which has been distinguished by the name of "the Campaign of Austerlitz," the exploits of our troops succeeded each other with the rapidity of thought. I confess I was equally astonished and delighted when I received a note from Duroc, sent by an extraordinary courier, and commencing laconically with the words, "We are in Vienna; the Emperor is well."

Duroc's letter was dated the 13th November, and the words, "We are in Vienna," seemed to me the result of a dream. The capital of Austria, which from time immemorial had not been occupied by foreigners—the city which Sobieski had saved from Ottoman violence, had become the prey of the Imperial eagle of France, which, after a lapse of three centuries, avenged the humiliations formerly imposed upon Francis I. by the 'Aquila Grifagna' of Charles V. Duroc had left the Emperor before the camp of Boulogne was raised; his mission to Berlin being terminated, he rejoined the Emperor at Lintz.[209]

Before I noticed the singular mission of M. Haugwitz to the Emperor Napoleon, and the

209 As soon as Bonaparte became Emperor he constituted himself the avenger of all the insults given to the sovereigns, whom he styled his predecessors. All that related to the honour of France was sacred to him. Thus he removed the column of Rosbach from the Prussian territory.—Bourrienne.

result of that mission, which circumstances rendered diametrically the reverse of its object, I will relate what came to my knowledge respecting some other negotiations on the part of Austria, the evident intent of which was to retard Napoleon's progress, and thereby to dupe him. M. de Giulay, one of the generals included in the capitulation of Ulm, had returned home to acquaint his sovereign with the disastrous event. He did not conceal, either from the Emperor Francis or the Cabinet of Vienna, the destruction of the Austrian army, and the impossibility of arresting the rapid advance of the French. M. de Giulay was sent with a flag of truce to the headquarters of Napoleon, to assure him of the pacific intentions of the Emperor of Austria, and to solicit an armistice. The snare was too clumsy not to be immediately discovered by so crafty a man as Napoleon.[210] He had always pretended a love for peace, though he was overjoyed at the idea of continuing a war so successfully commenced, and he directed General Giulay to assure the Emperor of Austria that he was not less anxious for peace than he, and that he was ready to treat for it, but without suspending the course of his operations. Bonaparte, indeed, could not, without a degree of imprudence of which he was incapable, consent to an armistice; for M. de Giulay, though entrusted with powers from Austria, had received none from Russia. Russia, therefore, might disavow the armistice and arrive in time to defend Vienna, the occupation of which was so important to the French army. The Russians, indeed, were advancing to oppose us, and the corps of our army, commanded by Mortier on the left bank of the Danube, experienced in the first engagement a check at Dirnstein, which not a little vexed the Emperor. This was the first reverse of fortune we had sustained throughout the campaign. It was trivial, to be sure, but the capture by the Russians of three French eagles, the first that had fallen into the hands of the enemy, was very mortifying to Napoleon, and caused him to prolong for some days his staff at St. Folten, where he then was.

The rapid occupation of Vienna was due to the successful temerity of Lannes and Murat, two men alike distinguished for courage and daring spirit. A bold artifice of these generals prevented the destruction of the Thabor bridge at Vienna, without which our army would have experienced considerable difficulty in penetrating into the Austrian capital. This act of courage and presence of mind, which had so great an influence on the events of the campaign, was described to me by Lannes, who told the story with an air of gaiety, unaccompanied by any self-complacency, and seemed rather pleased with the trick played upon the Austrians than proud of the brilliant action which had been performed. Bold enterprises were so natural to Lannes that he was frequently the only person who saw nothing extraordinary in his own exploits. Alas! what men were sacrificed to Napoleon's ambition!

The following is the story of the Bridge of Thabor as I heard it from Lannes[211]:— Such,

210 Metternich (tome ii. p. 346, compare French edition, tome ii. p. 287) says, "Let us hold always the sword in one hand and the olive branch in the other; always ready to negotiate, but only negotiating while advancing." Here is Napoleons system.

211 I was one day walking with Murat, on the right bank of the Danube, and we observed on the left bank, which was occupied by the Austrians, some works going on, the evident object of which was to blow up the bridge on the approach of our troops. The fools had the impudence to make these preparations under our very noses; but we gave them a good lesson. Having arranged our plan, we returned to give orders, and I entrusted the command of my column of grenadiers to an officer on whose courage and intelligence I could rely. I then returned to the

as well as I can recollect, was the account given by Lannes, who laughed immoderately in describing the consternation of the Austrian officers when they discovered the trick that had been played upon them. When Lannes performed this exploit he had little idea of the important consequences which would attend, it. He had not only secured to the remainder of the French army a sure and easy entrance to Vienna, but, without being aware of it, he created an insurmountable impediment to the junction of the Russian army with the Austrian corps, commanded by Prince Charles, who, being pressed by Massena, hastily advanced into the heart of the Hereditary States, where he fully expected a great battle would take place.

As soon as the corps of Murat and Lannes had taken possession of Vienna the Emperor ordered all the divisions of the army to march upon that capital.[212]

Napoleon established his headquarters at Schoenbrunn, where he planned his operations for compelling the corps of Prince Charles to retire to Hungary, and also for advancing his own forces to meet the Russians. Murat and Lannes always commanded the advanced guard during the forced marches ordered by Napoleon, which were executed in a way truly miraculous.

To keep up the appearance of wishing to conclude peace as soon as reasonable propositions should be made to him, Napoleon sent for his Minister for foreign Affairs, who speedily arrived at Vienna, and General Savary was sent on a mission to the Emperor Alexander. The details of this mission I have learned only from the account of it given by the Duc de Rovigo in his apologetic Memoirs. In spite of the Duke's eagerness to induce a belief in Napoleon's pacific disposition, the very facts on which he supports his argument lead to the contrary conclusion. Napoleon wished to dictate his conditions before the issue of a battle the success of which might appear doubtful to the young Emperor of Russia, and these conditions were such as he might impose when victory should be declared in favour of our eagles. It must

---

bridge, accompanied by Murat and two or three other officers. We advanced, unconcernedly, and entered into conversation with the commander of a post in the middle of the bridge. We spoke to him about an armistice which was to be speedily concluded: While conversing with the Austrian officers we contrived to make them turn their eyes towards the left bank, and then, agreeably to the orders we had given, my column of grenadiers advanced on the bridge. The Austrian cannoneers, on the left bank, seeing their officers in the midst of us, did not dare to fire, and my column advanced at a quick step. Murat and I, at the head of it, gained the left bank. All the combustibles prepared for blowing up the bridge were thrown into the river, and my men took possession of the batteries erected for the defence of the bridge head. The poor devils of Austrian officers were perfectly astounded when I told them they were my prisoners.

212 The story to told in much the same way in Theirs (tome vi, p. 260), Rupp (p. 57), and Savory (tome ii. p. 162), but as Erreurs (tome i. p. 814) points out, Bourrienne makes an odd mistake in believing the Thabor Bridge gave the French access to Vienna. The capital is on the right bank, and was already in their power. The possession of the bridge enabled them to pass over to the left bank, and to advance towards Austerlitz before the Archduke Charles, coming from Italy, could make his junction with the allied army. See plan 48 of Thiers' Atlas, or 58 of Alison's. The immediate result of the success of this rather doubtful artifice would have been the destruction of the corps of Kutusoff; but Murat in his turn was deceived by Bagration into belief in an armistice. In fact, both sides at this time fell into curious errors.

be clear to every reflecting person that by always proposing what he knew could not be honourably acceded to, he kept up the appearance of being a pacificator, while at the same time he ensured to himself the pleasure of carrying on the war.

CHAPTER III

1805

I must now relate how, in conformity with my instructions, I was employed in Hamburg in aiding the success of the French army. I had sent an agent to observe the Russian troops, which were advancing by forced marches to the banks of the Elbe. This agent transmitted to me from Gadbusch an account of the routes taken by the different columns. It was then supposed that they would march upon Holland by the way of Bremen and Oldenburg. On the receipt of thus intelligence the Electorate of Hanover was evacuated by the French, and General Barbou, who had commanded there concentrated his forces in Hamelin.

On the 2d of November 1805 the King of Sweden arrived at Stralsund. I immediately intimated to our Government that this circumstance would probably give a new turn to the operations of the combined army, for hitherto the uncertainty of its movements and the successive counter- orders afforded no possibility of ascertaining any determined plan. The intention seemed to be, that all the Swedo-Russian troops should cross the Elbe at the same point; viz., Lauenburg, six miles from Hamburg.

There was not on the 5th of November a single Russian on the southern bank of the Elbe.

The first column of the grand Russian army passed through Warsaw on the 1st of November, and on the 2d the Grand-Duke Constantine was expected with the Guards. This column, which amounted to 6000 men, was the first that passed through Prussian Poland.

At this time we momentarily expected to see the Hanoverian army landed on the banks of the Weser or the Elbe, augmented by some thousands of English. Their design apparently was either to attack Holland, or to attempt some operation on the rear of our Grand Army.

The French Government was very anxious to receive accurate accounts of the march of the Swedo-Russian troops through Hanover, and of the Russian army through Poland. My agents at Warsaw and Stralsund, who were exceedingly active and intelligent, enabled me to send off a bulletin describing the state of Hanover, the movements of the Russians and Swedes, together with information of the arrival of English troops in the Elbe, and a statement of the force of the combined army in Hanover, which consisted of 15,000 Russians, 8000 Swedes, and 12,000 English; making in all 35,000 men.

It was probably on account of this bulletin that Napoleon expressed to Duroc his satisfaction with my services. The Emperor on recalling Duroc from Berlin did not manifest the least apprehension respecting Prussia. Duroc wrote to me the following letter on the occasion of his recall:

> My Dear Bourrienne—The Emperor having thought my services necessary to the army has recalled me. I yesterday had a farewell audience of the King and Queen, who treated me very graciously. His Majesty presented me with his portrait set in diamonds.

The Emperor Alexander will probably depart to morrow, and the Archduke Anthony vary speedily. We cannot but hope that their presence here will facilitate a good understanding.

(*Signed*) DUROC.

Whenever foreign armies were opposing France the hopes of the emigrants revived. They falsely imagined that the powers coalesced against Napoleon were labouring in their cause; and many of them entered the Russian and Austrian armies. Of this number was General Dumouriez. I received information that he had landed at Stade on the 21st of November; but whither he intended to proceed was not known. A man named St. Martin, whose wife lived with Dumouriez, and who had accompanied the general from England to Stade, came to Hamburg, where he observed great precautions for concealment, and bought two carriages, which were immediately forwarded to Stade. St, Martin himself immediately proceeded to the latter place. I was blamed for not having arrested this man; but he had a commission attesting that he was in the English service, and, as I have before mentioned; a foreign commission was a safeguard; and the only one which could not be violated in Hamburg.

In December 1805 the English recruiting in Hanover was kept up without interruption, and attended with extraordinary success. Sometimes a hundred men were raised in a day. The misery prevailing in Germany, which had been ravaged by the war, the hatred against the French, and the high bounty that was offered enabled the English to procure as many men as they wished.

The King of Sweden, meditating on the stir he should make in Hanover, took with him a camp printing-press to publish the bulletins of the grand Swedish army.—The first of these bulletins announced to Europe that his Swedish Majesty was about to leave Stralsund; and that his army would take up its position partly between Nelsen and Haarburg, and partly between Domitz and the frontiers of Hamburg.

Among the anecdotes of Napoleon connected with this campaign I find in my notes the following, which was related to me by Rapp. Some days before his entrance into Vienna Napoleon, who was riding on horseback along the road, dressed in his usual uniform of the chasseurs of the Guard, met an open carriage, in which were seated a lady and a priest. The lady was in tears, and Napoleon could not refrain from stopping to ask her what was the cause of her distress. "Sir," she replied, for she did not know the Emperor, "I have been pillaged at my estate, two leagues from hence, by a party of soldiers, who have murdered my gardener. I am going to seek your Emperor, who knows my family, to whom he was once under great obligations."—"What is your name?" inquired Napoleon.—"De Bunny," replied the lady. "I am the daughter of M de Marbeuf, formerly Governor of Corsica."—"Madame," exclaimed Napoleon, "I am the Emperor. I am delighted to have the opportunity of serving you."—"You cannot conceive," continued Rapp, "the attention which the Emperor showed Madame de Bunny. He consoled her, pitied her, almost apologised for the misfortune she had sustained. 'Will you have the goodness, Madame,' said he, 'to go and wait for me at my head-quarters? I will join you speedily; every member of M. de Marbeuf's family has a claim on my respect.' The Emperor immediately gave her a picquet of chasseurs of his guard to escort her. He saw her again during the day, when he loaded her with attentions, and liberally indemnified her for the losses she had sustained."

For some time previous to the battle of Austerlitz the different corps of the army intersected every part of Germany and Italy, all tending towards Vienna as a central point. At the beginning of November the corps commanded by Marshal Bernadotte arrived at Saltzburg at the moment when the Emperor had advanced his headquarters to Braunau, where there were numerous magazines of artillery and a vast quantity of provisions of every kind. The junction of the corps commanded by Bernadotte in Hanover with the Grand Army was a point of such high importance that Bonaparte had directed the Marshal to come up with him as speedily as possible, and to take the shortest road. This order obliged Bernadotte to pass through the territory of the two Margravates.

At that time we were at peace with Naples. In September the Emperor had concluded with Ferdinand IV. a treaty of neutrality. This treaty enabled Carra St. Cyr, who occupied Naples, to evacuate that city and to join Massena in Upper Italy; both reached the Grand Army on the 28th of November. But no sooner had the troops commanded by Carra St. Cyr quitted the Neapolitan territory than the King of Naples, influenced by his Ministers, and above all by Queen Caroline, broke the treaty of neutrality, ordered hostile preparations against France, opened his ports to the enemies of the Emperor, and received into his States 12,000 Russians and 8000 English. It was on the receipt of this news that Bonaparte, in one of his most violent bulletins, styled the Queen of Naples a second Fredegonda. The victory of Austerlitz having given powerful support to his threats, the fall of Naples was decided, and shortly after his brother Joseph was seated on the Neapolitan throne.

At length came the grand day when, to use Napoleon's expression, the Sun of Austerlitz rose. All our forces were concentrated on one point, at about 40 leagues beyond Vienna. There remained nothing but the wreck of the Austrian army, the corps of Prince Charles being by scientific manoeuvres kept at a distance from the line of operations; but the Russians alone were superior to us in numbers, and their army was almost entirely composed of fresh troops. The most extraordinary illusion prevailed in the enemy's camp. The north of Europe has its Gascons as well as the south of France, and the junior portion of the Russian army at this period assumed an absurd braggadocio tone. On the very eve of the battle the Emperor Alexander sent one of his aides de camp, Prince Dolgorouki, as a flag of truce to Napoleon. The Prince could not repress his self-sufficiency even in the presence of the Emperor, and Rapp informed me that on dismissing him the Emperor said, "If you were on 'the heights of Montmartre,' I would answer such impertinence only by cannon-balls." This observation was very remarkable, inasmuch as subsequent events rendered it a prophecy.

As to the battle itself, I can describe it almost as well as if I had witnessed it, for some time after I had the pleasure of seeing my friend Rapp, who was sent an a mission to Prussia. He gave me the following account:

> "When we arrived at Austerlitz the Russians were not aware of the scientific plans which the Emperor had laid for drawing them upon the ground he had marked out; and seeing our advanced guards fall back before theirs they already considered themselves conquerors. They supposed that their Guard alone would secure an easy triumph. But the action commenced, and they experienced an energetic resistance on all points. At one o'clock the victory was yet uncertain, for they fought admirably. They wished to make a last effort by directing close masses against our centre. Their Imperial Guard deployed; their artillery, cavalry, and infantry marched upon a bridge which they attacked, and this movement, which was concealed by the rising and

falling of the ground, was not observed by Napoleon. I was at that moment near the Emperor, awaiting his orders. We heard a well-maintained firing of musketry. The Russians were repulsing one of our brigades. The Emperor ordered me to take some of the Mamelukes, two squadrons of chasseurs, and one of grenadiers of the Guard, and to go and reconnoitre the state of things. I set off at full gallop, and soon discovered the disaster. The Russian cavalry had penetrated our squares, and was sabring our men. I perceived in the distance some masses of cavalry and infantry; which formed the reserve of the Russians. At that moment the enemy advanced to meet us, bringing with him four pieces of artillery, and ranged himself in order of battle. I had the brave Morland on my left, and General D'Allemagne on my right. 'Forward, my lads!' exclaimed I to my troop. 'See how your brothers and friends are being cut to pieces. Avenge them! avenge our flag! Forward!' These few words roused my men. We advanced as swiftly as our horses could carry us upon the artillery, which was taken. The enemy's cavalry, which awaited us firmly, was repulsed by the same shock, and fled in disorder, galloping as we did over the wrecks of our squares. The Russians rallied but a squadron of horse grenadiers came up to reinforce me, and thus enabled me to hold ground against the reserves of the Russian Guard. We charged again, and this charge was terrible. The brave Morland was killed by my side. It was downright butchery. We were opposed man to man, and were so mingled together that the infantry of neither one nor the other side could venture to fire for fear of killing its own men. At length the intrepidity of our troops overcame every obstacle, and the Russians fled in disorder, in sight of the two Emperors of Russia and Austria, who had stationed themselves on a height in order to witness the battle. They saw a desperate one," said Rapp, "and I trust they were satisfied. For my part, my dear friend, I never spent so glorious a day. What a reception the Emperor gave me when I returned to inform him that we had won the battle! My sword was broken, and a wound which I received on my head was bleeding copiously, so that I was covered with blood! He made me a General of Division. The Russians did not return to the charge; we had taken all their cannon and baggage, and Prince Repnin was among the prisoners."

Thus it was that Rapp related to me this famous battle of which he was the hero, as Kellerman had been the hero of Marengo. What now remains of Austerlitz? The recollection, the glory, and the magnificent picture of Gerard, the idea of which was suggested to the Emperor by the sight of Rapp with the blood streaming from his wound.

I cannot forbear relating here a few particulars which I learned from Rapp respecting his mission after the cure of his wound; and the marriage of Prince Eugène to the Princess Augusta of Bavaria. The friendship which Rapp cherished for me was of the most sincere kind. During my disgrace he did not even conceal it from Napoleon; and whoever knows anything of the Emperor's Court will acknowledge that that was a greater mark of courage than the carrying of a redoubt or making the most brilliant charge of cavalry. Rapp possessed courage of every kind, an excellent heart, and a downright frankness, which for a time brought him into disgrace with Napoleon.

The only thing for which Rapp could be reproached was his extreme prejudice against the nobility, which I am convinced was the sole reason why he was not created a Duke. The

Emperor made him a Count because he wished that all his aides de camp should have titles.

> "He had been a fortnight at Schoenbrunn," said Rapp to me, "and I had not yet resumed my duties, when the Emperor sent for me. He asked me whether I was able to travel, and on my replying in the affirmative, he said, 'Go then, and give an account of the battle of Austerlitz to Marmont, and vex him for not having been at it.' I set off, and in conformity with the instructions I had received from the Emperor I proceeded to Gratz, where I found Marmont, who was indeed deeply mortified at not having had a share in the great battle. I told him, as the Emperor had directed me, that the negotiations were commenced, but that nothing was yet concluded, and that therefore, at all events, he must hold himself in readiness. I ascertained the situation of his army in Styria, and the amount of the enemy's force before him: The Emperor wished him to send a number of spies into Hungary, and to transmit to him a detailed report from their communications. I next proceeded to Laybach, where I found Massena at the head of the eighth corps, and I informed him that the Emperor wished him to march in all haste upon Vienna, in case he should hear of the rupture of the negotiations. I continued the itinerary marked out for me until I reached Venice, and thence till I met the troops of Carra St. Cyr, who had received orders to march back upon Naples as soon as the Emperor heard of the treachery of the King of Naples and the landing of the English and Russians. Having fulfilled these different missions I proceeded to Klagenfurth, where I saw Marshal Ney, and I afterwards rejoined the Emperor at Munich. There I had the pleasure of finding our friends assembled, and among them Josephine, still as affable and amiable as ever. How delighted I was when, an my arrival, I learned that the Emperor had adopted Eugène. I was present at his marriage with the Princess Augusta of Bavaria. As to me, you know I am not very fond of fetes, and the Emperor might have dispensed with my performing the duties of Chamberlain; Eugène had no idea of what was going on when the Emperor sent to desire his presence at Munich with all possible speed. He, too, remains unchanged; he is still our old comrade. At first he was not much pleased with the idea of a political marriage; but when he saw his bride he was quite enchanted; and no wonder, for I assure you she is a very charming woman."

CHAPTER IV

1805

At the moment when the Emperor had reason to hope that the news of his extraordinary success would animate public spirit he was informed that considerable disquietude prevailed, and that the Bank of France was assailed by demands for the payment of its paper, which had fallen, more than 5 per cent. I was not ignorant of the cause of this decline. I had been made acquainted, through the commercial correspondence between Hamburg and Paris, with a great financial operation, planned by M. Ouvrard, in consequence of which he was to obtain piastres from Spanish America at a price much below the real value; and I had learned that he was obliged to support this enterprise by the funds which he and his partners previously employed in victualling the forces. A fresh investment of capital was therefore necessary for this service, which, when on a large scale, requires extensive advances, and the tardy payment of the Treasury at that period was well known.

I was well acquainted with M. Ouvrard, and in what I am about to say I do not think there will be found anything offensive or disagreeable to him. I observed the greater number of the facts to which I shall refer in their origin, and the rest I learned from M. Ouvrard himself, who, when he visited Hamburg in 1808, communicated to me a variety of details respecting his immense transaction with the King of Spain. Among other things I recollect he told me that before the 18th Brumaire he was possessed of 60,000,000, without owing a franc to any person.

This celebrated financier has been the object of great public attention. The prodigious variations of fortune which he has experienced, the activity of his life, the immense commercial operations in which he has been engaged; the extent and the boldness of his enterprises, render it necessary, in forming a judgment of M. Ouvrard, to examine his conduct with due care and deliberation. The son of a stationer, who was able merely through his own resources to play so remarkable a part, could be no ordinary man. It may be said of M. Ouvrard what Beaumarchais said of himself, that his life was really a combat. I have known him long, and I saw much of him in his relations with Josephine. He always appeared to me to possess great knowledge of the world, accompanied by honourable principles, and a high degree of generosity, which added greatly to the value of his prudence and discretion. No human power, no consideration, not even the ingratitude of those whom he had obliged, could induce him to disclose any sacrifice which he had made at the time when, under the Directory, the public revenue may be said to have been always at the disposal of the highest bidder, and when no business could be brought to a conclusion except by him who set about it with his hands full of money. To this security, with which M. Ouvrard impressed all official persons who rendered him services, I attribute the facility with which he obtained the direction of the numerous enterprises in which he engaged, and which produced so many changes in his fortune. The discretion of M. Ouvrard was not quite agreeable to the First Consul, who found it impossible to extract from him the information he wanted. He tried every method to obtain from him the names of persons to whom he had given those kind of subsidies which in vulgar language are called sops in the pan, and by ladies pin money. Often have I seen Bonaparte resort to every possible contrivance to gain his object. He would sometimes endeavour to alarm M. Ouvrard by menaces, and at other times to flatter him by promises, but he was in no instance successful.

While we were at the Luxembourg, on, as I recollect, the 25th of January 1800, Bonaparte said to me during breakfast, "Bourrienne, my resolution is taken. I shall have Ouvrard arrested."—"General, have you proofs against him?"—"Proofs, indeed! He is a money-dealer, a monopoliser; we must make him disgorge. All the contractors, the provision agents, are rogues. How have they made their fortunes? At the expense of the country, to be sure. I will not suffer such doings. They possess millions, they roll in an insolent luxury, while my soldiers have neither bread nor shoes! I will have no more of that! I intend to speak on the business to-day in the Council, and we shall see what can be done."

I waited with impatience for his return from the Council to know what had passed. "Well, General?" said I "The order is given." On hearing this I became anxious about the fate of M. Ouvrard, who was thus to be treated more like a subject of the Grand Turk than a citizen of the Republic; but I soon learned that the order had not been executed because he could not be found.

Next day I learned that a person, whom I shall not name, who was present at the Council, and who probably was under obligations to Ouvrard, wrote him a note in pencil to inform him of the vote for his arrest carried by the First Consul. This individual stepped out for a moment and despatched his servant with the note to Ouvrard. Having thus escaped the writ of arrest, Ouvrard, after a few days had passed over, reappeared, and surrendered himself prisoner. Bonaparte was at first furious on learning that he had got out of the way; but on hearing that Ouvrard had surrendered himself he said to me, "The fool! he does not know what is awaiting him! He wishes to make the public believe that he has nothing to fear; that his hands are clean. But he is playing a bad game; he will gain nothing in that way with me. All talking is nonsense. You may be sure, Bourrienne, that when a man has so much money he cannot have got it honestly, and then all those fellows are dangerous with their fortunes. In times of revolution no man ought to have more than 3,000,000 francs, and that is a great deal too much."

Before going to prison Ouvrard took care to secure against all the searches of the police any of his papers which might have committed persons with whom he had dealings; and I believe that there were individuals connected with the police itself who had good reason for not regretting the opportunity which M. Ouvrard had taken for exercising this precaution. Seals, however, were put upon his papers; but on examining them none of the information Bonaparte so much desired to obtain was found. Nevertheless on one point his curiosity was satisfied, for on looking over the documents he found from some of them that Madame Bonaparte had been borrowing money from Ouvrard.

As Ouvrard had a great number of friends they bestirred themselves to get some person of influence to speak to the First Consul in his favour. But this was a commission no one was willing to undertake; because, prejudiced as Bonaparte was, the least hint of the kind would have appeared to him to be dictated by private interest. Berthier was very earnestly urged to interfere, but he replied, "That is impossible. He would say that it was underhand work to get money for Madame Visconti."

I do not recollect to what circumstance Ouvrard was indebted for his liberty, but it is certain that his captivity did not last long. Sometime after he had left his prison Bonaparte asked him for 12,000,000, which M. Ouvrard refused.

On his accession to the Consulate Bonaparte found M. Ouvrard contractor for supplying the Spanish fleet under the command of Admiral Massaredo. This business introduced him to a correspondence with the famous Godoy, Prince of the Peace. The contract lasted three years, and M. Ouvrard gained by it a net profit of 15,000,000. The money was payable in piastres, at the rate of 3 francs and some centimes each, though the piastre was really worth 5 francs 40 centimes. But to recover it at this value it was necessary for M. Ouvrard to go and get the money in Mexico. This he was much inclined to do, but he apprehended some obstacle on the part of the First Consul, and, notwithstanding his habitual shrewdness, he became the victim of his over-precaution. On his application M. de Talleyrand undertook to ask the First Consul for authority to give him a passport. I was in the cabinet at the time, and I think I still hear the dry and decided "No," which was all the answer M. de Talleyrand obtained. When we were alone the First Consul said to me, "Do you not see, Bourrienne, this Ouvrard must have made a good thing of his business with the Prince of the Peace? But the fool! Why did he get Talleyrand to ask me for a passport? That is the very thing that raised my suspicion. Why did he not apply for a passport as every one else does? Have I the giving of them? He is an ass; so much the worse for him."

I was sorry for Ouvrard's disappointment, and I own none the less so because he had intimated his willingness to give me a share in the business he was to transact its Spain; and which was likely to be very profitable. His brother went to Mexico in his stead.

In 1802 a dreadful scarcity afflicted France. M. Ouvrard took upon himself, in concert with Wanlerberghe, the task of importing foreign grain to prevent the troubles which might otherwise have been expected. In payment of the grain the foreign houses who sent it drew upon Ouvrard and Wanlerberghe for 26,000,000 francs in Treasury bills, which, according to the agreement with the Government, were to be paid. But when the bills of the foreign houses became due there was no money in the Treasury, and payment was refused. After six months had elapsed payment was offered, but on condition that the Government should retain half the profit of the commission! This Ouvrard and Wanlerberghe refused, upon which the Treasury thought it most economical to pay nothing, and the debt remained unsettled. Notwithstanding this transaction Ouvrard and Wanlerberghe engaged to victual the navy, which they supplied for six years and three months. After the completion of these different services the debt due to them amounted to 68,000,000.

In consequence of the long delay of, payment by the Treasury the disbursements for supplies of grain amounted at least to more than 40,000,000; and the difficulties which arose had a serious effect on the credit of the principal dealers with those persons who supplied them. The discredit spread and gradually reached the Treasury, the embarrassments of which augmented with the general alarm. Ouvrard, Wanlerberghe, and Seguin were the persons whose capital and credit rendered them most capable of relieving the Treasury, and they agreed to advance for that purpose 102,000,000, in return for which they were allowed bonds of the Receivers-General to the amount of 150,000,000. M. Desprez undertook to be the medium through which the 102,000,000 were to be paid into the Treasury, and the three partners transferred the bands to him.

Spain had concluded a treaty with France, by which she was bound to pay a subsidy of 72,000,000 francs, and 32,000,000 had become due without any payment being made: It was thought advisable that Ouvrard should be sent to Madrid to obtain a settlement, but he was afraid that his business in Paris would suffer during his absence, and especially the transaction in which he was engaged with Desprez. The Treasury satisfied him on this point by agreeing to sanction the bargain with Desprez, and Ouvrard proceeded to Madrid. It was on this occasion he entered into the immense speculation for trading with Spanish America.

Spain wished to pay the 32,000,000 which were due to France as soon as possible, but her coffers were empty, and goodwill does not ensure ability; besides, in addition to the distress of the Government, there was a dreadful famine in Spain. In this state of things Ouvrard proposed to the Spanish Government to pay the debt due to France, to import a supply of corn, and to advance funds for the relief of the Spanish Treasury. For this he required two conditions. (1.) The exclusive right of trading with America. (2.) The right of bringing from America on his own account all the specie belonging to the Crown, with the power of making loans guaranteed and payable by the Spanish Treasuries.

About the end of July 1805 the embarrassment which sometime before had begun to be felt in the finances of Europe was alarmingly augmented. Under these circumstances it was obviously the interest of Ouvrard to procure payment as soon as possible of the 32,000,000 which he had advanced for Spain to the French Treasury. He therefore redoubled his efforts to bring his negotiation to a favourable issue, and at last succeeded in getting a deed of partnership between himself and Charles IV. which contained the following stipulation:— "Ouvrard and Company are authorised to introduce into the ports of the New World every kind of merchandise and production necessary for the consumption of those countries, and to export from the Spanish Colonies, during the continuance of the war with England; all the productions and all specie derivable from them." This treaty was only to be in force during the war with England, and it was stipulated that the profits arising from the transactions of the Company should be equally divided between Charles IV. and the rest of the Company; that is to say, one-half to the King and the other half to his partners.

The consequences of this extraordinary partnership between a King and a private individual remain to be stated. On the signing of the deed Ouvrard received drafts from the Treasury of Madrid to the extent of 52,500,000 piastres; making 262,500,000 francs; but the piastres were to be brought from America, while the terms of the treaty required that the urgent wants of the Spanish Government should be immediately supplied, and, above all, the progress of the famine checked. To accomplish this object fresh advances to an enormous amount were necessary, for M. Ouvrard had to begin by furnishing 2,000,000 of quintals of grain at the rate of 26 francs the quintal. Besides all this, before he could realise a profit and be reimbursed for the advances he had made to the Treasury of Paris, he had to get the piastres conveyed from America to Europe. After some difficulty the English Government consented to facilitate the execution of the transaction by furnishing four frigates for the conveyance of the piastres.

Ouvrard had scarcely completed the outline of his extraordinary enterprise when the Emperor suddenly broke up his camp at Boulogne to march to Germany. It will readily be conceived that Ouvrard's interests then imperatively required his presence at Madrid; but he was recalled to Paris by the Minister of the Treasury, who wished to adjust his accounts. The Emperor wanted money for the war on which he was entering, and to procure it for the Treasury Ouvrard was sent to Amsterdam to negotiate with the House of Hope. He succeeded, and Mr. David Parish became the Company's agent.

Having concluded this business Ouvrard returned in all haste to Madrid; but in the midst of the most flattering hopes and most gigantic enterprises he suddenly found himself threatened with a dreadful crisis. M. Desprez, as has been stated, had, with the concurrence of the Treasury, been allowed to take upon himself all the risk of executing the treaty, by which 150,000,000 were to be advanced for the year 1804, and 400,000,000 for the year 1805. Under the circumstances which had arisen the Minister of the Treasury considered himself entitled to call upon Ouvrard to place at his disposal 10,000,000 of the piastres which he had received from Spain. The Minister at the same time informed him that he had made arrangements on the faith of this advance, which he thought could not be refused at so urgent a moment.

The embarrassment of the Treasury, and the well-known integrity of the Minister, M. de Barbe Marbois, induced Ouvrard to remit the 10,000,000 piastres. But a few days after he had forwarded the money a Commissioner of the Treasury arrived at Madrid with a ministerial despatch, in which Ouvrard was requested to deliver to the Commissioner all the assets he could command, and to return immediately to Paris.

The Treasury was then in the greatest difficulty, and a general alarm prevailed. This serious financial distress was occasioned by the following circumstances. The Treasury had, by a circular, notified to the Receivers-General that Desprez was the holder of their bonds. They were also authorised to transmit to him all their disposable funds, to be placed to their credit in an account current. Perhaps the giving of this authority was a great error; but, be that as it may, Desprez, encouraged by the complaisance of the Treasury, desired the Receivers-General to transmit to him all the sums they could procure for payment of interest under 8 per cent., promising to allow them a higher rate of interest. As the credit of the house of Desprez stood high, it may be easily conceived that on such conditions the Receivers-General, who were besides secured by the authority of the Treasury, would enter eagerly into the proposed plan. In short, the Receivers-General soon transmitted very considerable sums. Chests of money arrived daily from every point of France. Intoxicated by this success, Desprez engaged in speculations which in his situation were extremely imprudent. He lent more than 50,000,000 to the merchants of Paris, which left him no command of specie. Being obliged to raise money, he deposited with the Bank the bonds of the Receivers-General which had been consigned to him, but which were already discharged by the sums transmitted to their credit in the account current. The Bank, wishing to be reimbursed for the money advanced to Desprez, applied to the Receivers-General whose bonds were held an security. This proceeding had become necessary on the part of the Bank, as Desprez, instead of making his payments in specie, sent in his acceptances. The Directors of the Bank, who conducted that establishment with great integrity and discretion, began to be alarmed, and required Desprez to explain the state of his affairs. The suspicions of the Directors became daily stronger, and were soon shared by the public. At last the Bank was obliged to stop payment, and its notes were soon at a discount of 12 per cent.

The Minister of the Treasury, dismayed, as well may be supposed, at such a state of things during the Emperor's absence, convoked a Council, at which Joseph Bonaparte presided, and to which Desprez and Wanlerberghe were summoned. Ouvrard being informed of this financial convulsion made all possible haste from Madrid, and on his arrival at Paris sought assistance from Amsterdam. Hope's house offered to take 15,000,000 piastres at the rate of 3 francs 75 centimes each. Ouvrard having engaged to pay the Spanish Government only 3 francs, would very willingly have parted with them at that rate, but his hasty departure from Madrid, and the financial events at Paris, affected his relations with the Spanish Treasury, and rendered it impossible for him to afford any support to the Treasury of France; thus the alarm continued, until the news of the battle of Austerlitz and the consequent hope of peace tranquillised the public mind. The bankruptcy of Desprez was dreadful; it was followed by the failure of many houses, the credit of which was previously undoubted.

To temper the exultation which victory was calculated to excite, the news of the desperate situation of the Treasury and the Bank reached the Emperor on the day after the battle of Austerlitz. The alarming accounts which he received hastened his return to France; and on the very evening on which he arrived in Paris he pronounced, while ascending the stairs of the Tuileries, the dismissal of M. de Barbs Marbois. This Minister had made numerous enemies by the strict discharge of his duty, and yet, notwithstanding his rigid probity, he sunk under the accusation of having endangered the safety of the State by weakness of character. At this period even Madame de Stael said, in a party where the firmness of M. Barbs Marbois was the topic of conversation—"What, he inflexible? He is only a reed bronzed!" But whatever may be the opinion entertained of the character of this Minister, it is certain that Napoleon's rage against him was unbounded. Such was the financial catastrophe which occurred during the campaign of Vienna; but all was not over with Ouvrard, and in so great a confusion of affairs it was not to be expected that the Imperial hand, which was not always the hand of justice, should not make itself somewhere felt.

In the course of the month of February 1806 the Emperor issued two decrees, in which he declared Ouvrard, Wanlerberghe, and Michel, contractors for the service of 1804, and Desprez their agent, debtors to the amount of 87,000,000, which they had misapplied in private speculations, and in transactions with Spain "for their personal interests." Who would not suppose from this phrase that Napoleon had taken no part whatever in the great financial operation between Spain and South America? He was, however, intimately acquainted with it, and was himself really and personally interested. But whenever any enterprise was unsuccessful he always wished to deny all connection with it. Possessed of title-deeds made up by himself—that is to say, his own decrees—the Emperor seized all the piastres and other property belonging to the Company, and derived from the transaction great pecuniary advantage,—though such advantage never could be regarded by a sovereign as any compensation for the dreadful state into which the public credit had been brought.

CHAPTER V

1805-1806

I have been somewhat diffuse respecting the vast enterprises of M. Ouvrard, and on the disastrous state of the finances during the campaign of Vienna. Now, if I may so express myself, I shall return to the Minister Plenipotentiary's cabinet, where several curious transactions occurred. The facts will not always be given in a connected series, because there was no more relation between the reports which I received on a great variety of subjects than there is in the pleading of the barristers who succeed each other in a court of justice.

On the 2d of January 1806 I learned that many houses in Hamburg had received by post packets, each containing four copies of a declaration of Louis XVIII. Dumouriez had his carriage filled with copies of this declaration when he passed through Brunswick; and in that small town alone more than 3000 were distributed. The size of this declaration rendered its transmission by post very easy, even in France.

All my letters from the Minister recommended that I should keep a strict watch over the motions of Dumouriez; but his name was now as seldom mentioned as if he had ceased to exist. The part he acted seemed to be limited to disseminating pamphlets more or less insignificant.

It is difficult to conceive the great courage and presence of mind sometimes found in men so degraded as are the wretches who fill the office of spies. I had an agent amongst the Swedo-Russians, named Chefneux, whom I had always found extremely clever and correct. Having for a long time received no intelligence from him I became very anxious,—an anxiety which was not without foundation. He had, in fact, been arrested at Lauenburg, and conducted, bound, tied hand and foot, by some Cossacks to Luneburg. There was found on him a bulletin which he was about to transmit to me, and he only escaped certain death by having in his possession a letter of recommendation from a Hamburg merchant well known to M. Alopaeus, the Russian Minister in that city. This precaution, which I had taken before he set out, saved his life. M. Alopaeus replied to the merchant that, in consequence of his recommendation the spy should be sent back safe and sound, but that another time neither the recommended nor the recommender should escape so easily. Notwithstanding this, Chefneux would certainly have paid with his head for the dangerous business in which he was embarked but for the inconceivable coolness he displayed under the most trying circumstances. Though the bulletin which was found upon him was addressed to M. Schramm, merchant, they strongly suspected that it was intended for me. They demanded of the prisoner whether he knew me; to which he boldly replied that he had never seen me. They endeavoured, by every possible means, to extort a confession from him, but without success. His repeated denials, joined to the name of M. Schramm, created doubts in the minds of his interrogators; they hesitated lest they should condemn an innocent man. They, however, resolved to make a last effort to discover the truth, and Chefneux, condemned to be shot, was conducted to the plain of Luneburg. His eyes were bandaged, and he heard the command of preparation given to the platoon, which was to fire upon him; at that moment a man approaching him whispered in his ear, in a tone of friendship and compassion, "They are going to fire; but I am your friend; only acknowledge that you know M. de Bourrienne and you are safe."—"No," replied Chefneux in a firm tone; "if I said so I should tell a falsehood." Immediately the bandage was removed from his eyes, and he was set at liberty. It would be difficult to cite a more extraordinary instance of presence of mind.

Much as I execrate the system of espionage I am nevertheless compelled to admit that the Emperor was under the necessity of maintaining the most unremitting vigilance amidst the intrigues which were going forward in the neighbourhood of Hamburg, especially when the English, Swedes, and Russians were in arms, and there were the strongest grounds for suspecting the sincerity of Prussia.

On the 5th of January 1806 the King of Sweden arrived before the gates of Hamburg. The Senate of that city, surrounded on all sides by English, Swedish, and Russian troops, determined to send a deputation to congratulate the Swedish monarch, who, however, hesitated so long about receiving this homage that fears were entertained lest his refusal should be followed by some act of aggression. At length, however, the deputies were admitted, and they returned sufficiently well satisfied with their reception.

The King of Sweden then officially declared, "That all the arrangements entered into with relation to Hanover had no reference to hint, as the Swedish army was under the immediate command of its august sovereign."

The King, with his 6000 men, seemed inclined to play the part of the restorer of Germany, and to make himself the Don Quixote of the treaty of Westphalia. He threatened the Senate of Hamburg with the whole weight of his anger, because on my application the colours which used to be suspended over the door of the house for receiving Austrian recruits had been removed. The poor Senate of Hamburg was kept in constant alarm by so dangerous a neighbour.

The King of Sweden had his headquarters at Boetzenburg, on the northern bank of the Elbe. In order to amuse himself he sent for Dr. Gall, who was at Hamburg, where he delivered lectures on his system of phrenology, which was rejected in the beginning by false science and prejudice, and afterwards adopted in consequence of arguments, in my opinion, unanswerable. I had the pleasure of living some time with Dr. Gall, and I owe to the intimacy which subsisted between us the honour he conferred on me by the dedication of one of his works. I said to him, when he departed for the headquarters of the King of Sweden, "My dear doctor, you will certainly discover the bump of vanity." The truth is, that had the doctor at that period been permitted to examine the heads of the sovereigns of Europe they would have afforded very curious craniological studies.

It was not the King of Sweden alone who gave uneasiness to Hamburg; the King of Prussia threatened to seize upon that city, and his Minister publicly declared that it would very soon belong to his master. The Hamburgers were deeply afflicted at this threat; in fact, next to the loss of their independence, their greatest misfortune would have been to fall under the dominion of Prussia, as the niggardly fiscal system of the Prussian Government at that time would have proved extremely detrimental to a commercial city. Hanover, being evacuated by the French troops, had become a kind of recruiting mart for the British army, where every man who presented himself was enrolled, to complete the Hanoverian legion which was then about to be embodied. The English scattered gold by handfuls. One hundred and fifty carriages, each with six horses, were employed in this service, which confirmed me in the belief I had previously entertained, that the English were to join with the Russians in an expedition against Holland. The aim of the Anglo-Russians was to make a diversion which might disconcert the movements of the French armies in Germany, the allies being at that time unacquainted with the peace concluded at Presburg. Not a moment was therefore to be lost in uniting the whole of our disposable force for the defence of Holland; but it is not of this expedition that I mean to speak at present. I only mention it to afford some idea of our situation at Hamburg, surrounded, as we then were, by Swedish, English, and Russian troops. At this period the Russian Minister at Hamburg, M. Forshmann, became completely insane; his conduct had been more injurious than advantageous to his Government. He was replaced by M. Alopcous, the Russian Minister at Berlin; and they could not have exchanged a fool for a more judicious and able diplomatist.

I often received from the Minister of Marine letters said packets to transmit to the Isle of France,(Mauritius) of which the Emperor was extremely anxious to retain possession; and I had much trouble in finding any vessels prepared for that colony by which I could forward the Minister's communications. The death of Pitt and the appointment of Fox as his successor had created a hope of peace. It was universally known that Mr. Fox, in succeeding to his office, did not inherit the furious hatred of the deceased Minister against France and her Emperor. There moreover existed between Napoleon and Mr. Fox a reciprocal esteem, and the latter had shown himself really disposed to treat. The possibility of concluding a peace had always been maintained by that statesman when he was in opposition to Mr. Pitt; and Bonaparte himself might have been induced, from the high esteem he felt for Mr. Fox, to make concessions from which he would before have recoiled. But there were two obstacles, I may say almost insurmountable ones. The first was the conviction on the part of England that any peace which might be made would only be a truce, and that Bonaparte would never seriously relinquish his desire of universal dominion. On the other side, it was believed that Napoleon had formed the design of invading England. Had he been able to do so it would have been less with the view of striking a blow at her commerce and destroying her maritime power, than of annihilating the liberty of the press, which he had extinguished in his own dominions. The spectacle of a free people, separated only by six leagues of sea, was, according to him, a seductive example to the French, especially to those among them who bent unwillingly under his yoke.

At an early period of Mr. Fox's ministry a Frenchman made the proposition to him of assassinating the Emperor, of which information was immediately transmitted to M. de Talleyrand. In this despatch the Minister said that, though the laws of England did not authorise the permanent detention of any individual not convicted of a crime, he had on this occasion taken it on himself to secure the miscreant till such time as the French Government could be put on its guard against his attempts. Mr. Fox said in his letter that he had at first done this individual "the honour to take him for a spy," a phrase which sufficiently indicated the disgust with which the British Minister viewed him.

This information was the key which opened the door to new negotiations. M. de Talleyrand was ordered to express, in reply to the communication of Mr. Fox, that the Emperor was sensibly affected at the index it afforded of the principles by which the British Cabinet was actuated. Napoleon did not limit himself to this diplomatic courtesy; he deemed it a favourable occasion to create a belief that he was actuated by a sincere love of peace. He summoned to Paris Lord Yarmouth, one of the most distinguished amongst the English who had been so unjustly detained prisoners at Verdun on the rupture of the peace of Amiens. He gave his lordship instructions to propose to the British Government a new form of negotiations, offering to guarantee to England the Cape of Good Hope and Malta. Some have been inclined from this concession to praise the moderation of Bonaparte; others to blame him for offering to resign these two places, as if the Cape and Malta could be put in competition with the title of Emperor, the foundation of the Kingdom of Italy, the acquisition of Genoa and of all the Venetian States, the dethronement of the King of Naples and the gift of his kingdom to Joseph, and finally, the new partition of Germany. These transactions, of which Bonaparte said not a word, and from which he certainly had no intention of departing, were all long after the treaty of Amiens.

Every day brought with it fresh proofs of insatiable ambition. In fact, Napoleon longed to obtain possession of the Hanse Towns. I was, however, in the first place, merely charged to make overtures to the Senates of each of these towns, and to point out the advantages they would derive from the protection of Napoleon in exchange for the small sacrifice of 6,000,000 francs in his favour. I had on this subject numerous conferences with the magistrates: they thought the sum too great, representing, to me that the city was not so rich as formerly, because their commerce had been much curtailed by the war; in short, the Senate declared that, with the utmost goodwill, their circumstances would not permit them to accept the "generous proposal" of the Emperor.

I was myself, indeed, at a loss to conceive how the absurdity of employing me to make such a proposition was overlooked, for I had, really no advantage to offer in return to the Hanse Towns. Against whom did Bonaparte propose to protect them? The truth is, Napoleon then wished to seize these towns by direct aggression, which, however, he was not able to accomplish until four years afterwards.

During five years I witnessed the commercial importance of these cities, and especially of Hamburg. Its geographical situation, on a great river navigable by large vessels to the city, thirty leagues from the mouth of the Elbe; the complete independence it enjoyed; its municipal regulations and paternal government, were a few amongst the many causes which had raised Hamburg to its enviable height of prosperity. What, in fact, was the population of these remnants of the grand Hanseatic League of the Middle Ages? The population of Hamburg when I was there amounted to 90,000, and that of its small surrounding territory to 25,000. Bremen had 36,000 inhabitants, and 9000 in its territory; the city of Lübeck, which is smaller and its territory a little more extensive than that of Bremen, contained a population of 24,000 souls within and 16,000 without the walls. Thus the total population of the Hanse Towns amounted to only 200,000 individuals; and yet this handful of men carried on an extensive commerce, and their ships ploughed every sea, from the shores of India to the frozen regions of Greenland.

The Emperor arrived at Paris towards the end of January 1806. Having created kings in Germany he deemed the moment favourable for surrounding his throne with new princes. It was at this period that he created Murat, Grand Duke of Cleves and Berg; Bernadotte, Prince of Ponte-Corvo; M. de Talleyrand, Duke of Benevento; and his two former colleagues, Cambacérès and Lebrun, Dukes of Parma and Piacenza. He also gave to his sister Pauline, a short time after her second marriage with the Prince Borghese, the title of Duchess of Guastalla. Strange events! who could then have foreseen that the duchy of Cambacérès would become the refuge of a Princess of Austria, the widowed wife of Napoleon Bonaparte? In the midst of the prosperity of the Imperial family, when the eldest of the Emperor's brothers had ascended the throne of Naples, when Holland was on the eve of being offered to Louis, and Jerome had exchanged his legitimate wife for the illegitimate throne of Westphalia, the

Imperial pillow was still far from being free from anxiety. Hostilities did not actually exist with the Continental powers; but this momentary state of repose lacked the tranquillity of peace. France was at war with Russia and England, and the aspect of the Continent presented great uncertainty, while the treaty of Vienna had only been executed in part. In the meantime Napoleon turned his eyes towards the East. General Sebastiani was sent to Constantinople. The measures be pursued and his judicious conduct justified the choice of the Emperor. He was adroit and conciliating, and peace with Turkey was the result of his mission. The negotiations with England did not terminate so happily, although, after the first overtures made to Lord Yarmouth, the Earl of Lauderdale had been sent to Paris by Mr. Fox. In fact, these negotiations wholly failed. The Emperor had drawn enormous sums from Austria, without counting the vases, statues, and pictures. With which he decorated the Louvre, and the bronze with which he clothed the column of the Place Vendome,—in my opinion the finest monument of his reign and the most beautiful one in Paris. As Austria was exhausted all the contributions imposed on her could not be paid in cash, and they gave the Emperor bills in payment. I received one for about 7,000,000 on Hamburg on account of the stipulations of the treaty of Presburg.

The affairs of the Bourbon Princes became more and more unfavourable, and their finances, as well as their chances of success, were so much diminished that about this period it was notified to the emigrants in Brunswick that the pretender (Louis XVIII.) had no longer the means of continuing their pensions. This produced great consternation amongst those emigrants, many of whom had no other means of existence; and notwithstanding their devotion to the cause of royalty they found a pension very useful in strengthening their zeal[213].

Amongst those emigrants was one whose name will occupy a certain place in history; I mean Dumouriez, of whom I have already spoken, and who had for some time employed himself in distributing pamphlets. He was then at Stralsund; and it was believed that the King of Sweden would give him a command. The vagrant life of this general, who ran everywhere hegging employment from the enemies of his country without being able to obtain it, subjected him to general ridicule; in fact, he was everywhere despised.

To determine the difficulties which had arisen with regard to Holland, which Dumouriez dreamed of conquering with an imaginary army, and being discontented besides with the Dutch for not rigorously excluding English vessels from their ports, the Emperor constituted the Batavian territory a kingdom under his brother Louis. When I notified to the States of the circle of Lower Saxony the accession of Louis Bonaparte to the throne of Holland, and the nomination of Cardinal Fesch as coadjutor and successor of the Arch-chancellor of the Germanic Empire, along with their official communications, the Duke of Mecklenburg-Schwerin was the only member of the circle who forebore to reply, and I understood he had applied to the Court of Russia to know "whether" and "how" he should reply. At the same time he made known to the Emperor the marriage of his daughter, the Princess Charlotte

213 When Louis XVIII. returned to France, and Fouché was his Minister of Police, the King asked Fouché whether during his (the King's) exile, had not set spies over him, and who they were. Fouché hesitated to reply, but the King insisting he said: "If your Majesty presses for an answer, it was the Duc de Blacas to whom this matter was confided."—"And how much did you pay him?" said the King. "Deux cents mille livres de rents, Sire."—"Ah, so!" said the King, "then he has played fair; we went halves."—Henry Greville's Diary, p. 430.

Frederica, with Prince Christian Frederick of Denmark.

At this period it would have been difficult to foresee the way in which this union would terminate. The Prince was young and handsome, and of an amiable disposition, which seemed to indicate that he would prove a good husband. As for the Princess, she was as beautiful as love; but she was heedless and giddy; in fact, she was a spoiled child. She adored her husband, and during several years their union proved happy. I had the honour of knowing them at the period when the Duke of Mecklenburg, with his family, sought refuge at Altona. Before leaving that town the Duchess of Mecklenburg, a Princess of Saxony, paid a visit to Madame de Bourrienne and loaded her with civilities. This Princess was perfectly amiable, and was therefore generally regretted when, two years afterwards, death snatched her from her family. Before leaving Altona the Duke of Mecklenburg gave some parties by way of bidding adieu to Holstein, where he had been so kindly received; and I can never forget the distinguished reception and many kindnesses Madame de Bourrienne and myself received from that illustrious family.

It consisted of the hereditary Prince, so distinguished by his talents and acquirements (he was at that time the widower of a Grand Duchess of Russia, a sister of the Emperor Alexander), of Prince Gustavus, so amiable and graceful, and of Princess Charlotte and her husband, the Prince Royal of Denmark.

This happy couple were far from foreseeing that in two years they would be separated for ever. The Princess was at this period in all the splendour of her beauty; several fetes were given on her account on the banks of the Elbe, at which the Prince always opened the ball with Madame de Bourrienne. Notwithstanding her amiability the Princess Charlotte was no favourite at the Danish Court. Intrigues were formed against her. I know not whether any foundation existed for the calumnies spread to her disadvantage, but the Court dames accused her of great levity of conduct, which, true or false, obliged her husband to separate from her; and at the commencement of 1809 he sent her to Altona, attended by a chamberlain and a maid of honour. On her arrival she was in despair; hers was not a silent grief, for she related her story to every one. This unfortunate woman really attracted pity, as she shed tears for her son, three years of age, whom she was doomed never again to behold. But her natural levity returned; she did not always maintain the reserve suitable to her rank, and some months afterwards was sent into Jutland, where I believe she still lives.

The enemies of the French Government did not confine themselves to writing and publishing invectives against it. More than one wretch was ready to employ daggers against the Emperor. Among this number was a man named Louis Loizeau, recently arrived from London. He repaired to Altona, there to enjoy the singular privilege which that city afforded of sheltering all the ruffians, thieves, and bankrupts who fled from the justice of their own Governments. On the 17th of July Loizeau presented himself to Comte de Gimel, who resided at Altona, as the agent of the Comte de Lille. He offered to repair to Paris and assassinate the Emperor. Comte de Gimel rejected the proposal with indignation; and replied, that if he had no other means of serving the Bourbons than cowardly assassination he might go elsewhere and find confederates. This fact, which was communicated to me by a friend of M. de Gimel, determined me to arrest Loizeau. Not being warranted, however, to take this step at Altona, I employed a trusty agent to keep watch, and draw him into a quarrel the moment he should appear on the Hamburg side of a public walk which divides that city from Altona, and deliver him up to the nearest Hamburg guard-house. Loizeau fell into the snare; but finding that he was about to be conducted from the guardhouse to the prison of Hamburg, and that it was at my request he had been arrested, he hastily unloosed his cravat, and tore with his teeth the papers it contained, part of which he swallowed. He also endeavoured to tear some other papers which were concealed under his arm, but was prevented by the guard. Furious at this disappointment, he violently resisted the five soldiers who had him in custody, and was not secured until he had been slightly wounded. His first exclamation on entering prison was, "I am undone!" Loizeau was removed to Paris, and, though I am ignorant of the ultimate fate of this wretch, I am pretty certain that Fouché would take effectual means to prevent him from doing any further mischief.

CHAPTER VI

1806

The moment now approached when war was about to be renewed in Germany, and in proportion as the hopes of peace diminished Prussia redoubled her threats, which were inspired by the recollection of the deeds of the great Frederick. The idea of peace was hateful to Prussia. Her measures, which till now had been sufficiently moderate, suddenly assumed a menacing aspect on learning that the Minister of the King of England had declared in Parliament that France had consented to the restitution of Hanover. The French Ministry intimated to the Prussian Government that this was a preliminary step towards a general peace, and that a large indemnity would be granted in return. But the King of Prussia, who was well informed, and convinced that the House of Hanover clung to this ancient domain, which gave to England a certain preponderance in Germany, considered himself trifled with, and determined on war.

Under these circumstances Lord Lauderdale was recalled from Paris by his Government. War continued with England, and was about to commence with Prussia. The Cabinet of Berlin sent an ultimatum which could scarcely be regarded in any other light than a defiance, and from the well-known character of Napoleon we may judge of his irritation at this ultimatum[214].

The Emperor, after his stay of eight months in Paris passed in abortive negotiations for peace, set out on the 25th of September for the Rhine.

Hostilities commenced on the 10th of October 1806 between France and Prussia, and I demanded of the Senate that a stop should be put to the Prussians recruiting. The news of a great victory gained by the Emperor over the Prussians on the 14th of October reached Hamburg on the 19th, brought by some fugitives, who gave such exaggerated accounts of the loss of the French army that it was not until the arrival of the official despatches on the 28th of October that we knew whether to mourn or to rejoice at the victory of Jena.

The Duke of Brunswick, who was dangerously wounded at the battle of Auerstadt, arrived on the 29th of October at Altona.[215] His entrance into that city afforded a striking example of the vicissitudes of fortune. That Prince entered Altona on a wretched litter, borne by ten men, without officers, without domestics, followed by a troop of vagabonds and children, who were drawn together by curiosity. He was lodged in a wretched inn, and so much worn out by fatigue and the pain of his eyes that on the day after his arrival a report of his death very generally prevailed. Doctor Unzer was immediately sent for to attend the unfortunate Duke, who, during the few days that he survived his wounds, saw no one else except his wife,

214 The severity with which Bonaparte treated the press may be inferred from the case of Palm the publisher. In 1808 Johann Phillip Palm, of Nuremberg, was shot by Napoleon's order for issuing a pamphlet against the rule of the French in Germany.

215 This Prince was in the seventy-second year of his age, and extremely infirm.

who arrived on the 1st of November. He expired on the 10th of the same month[216].

At this juncture Bernadotte returned to Hamburg. I asked him how I was to account for his conduct while he was with Davoust, who had left Nuremberg to attack the Prussian army; and whether it was true that he had refused to march with that general, and afterwards to aid him when he attacked the Prussians on the Weimar road. "The letters I received," observed I, "state that you took no part in the battle of Auerstadt; that I did not believe, but I suppose you saw the bulletin which I received a little after the battle, and which stated that Bonaparte said at Nuremberg, in the presence of several officers, 'Were I to bring him before a court-martial he would be shot. I shall say nothing to him about it, but I will take care he shall know what I think of his behaviour. He has too keen a sense of honour not to be aware that he acted disgracefully.'—"I think him very likely," rejoined Bernadotte, "to have made these observations. He hates me because he knows I do not like him; but let him speak to me and he shall have his answer. If I am a Gascon, he is a greater one. I might have felt piqued at receiving something like orders from Davoust, but I did my duty."[217]

In the beginning of November the Swedes entered Lübeck; but on the 8th of that month the town was taken by assault, and the Swedes, as well as the rest of the corps which had escaped from Jena, were made prisoners.

A troop of Prussians had advanced within four leagues of Hamburg, and that town had already prepared for a vigorous resistance, in case they should attempt an entrance, when Major Amiel attacked them at Zollenspieker and made some prisoners. Hamburg was, however, threatened with another danger, for Major Amiel expressed his intention of entering with all his prisoners, notwithstanding the acknowledged neutrality of the town. Amiel was a partisan leader in the true sense of the word; he fought rather on his own account than with the intention of contributing to the success of the operations of the army. His troop did not consist of more than forty men, but that was more than sufficient to spread terror and devastation in the surrounding villages. He was a bold fellow, and when, with his handful of men, he threw himself upon Hamburg, the worthy inhabitants thought he had

216 For the mistimed but rather pathetic belief of the old dying Duke in the courtesy with which he and his States would be treated by the French, see Beugnot, tome 1. p. 80: "I feel sure that there is a courier of the Emperor's on the road to know how I am."

217 The complaints of Bernadotte's conduct on the 14th of October 1806. when he gave no assistance to Davoust in repulsing the main body of the Prussians at Aneratadt, are well known. Jomini says that Davoust proposed to Bernadotte to march with him, and even offered him the command of the two corps. Bernadotte refused, and marched away to Dornburg, where he was of no use, "his obstinacy, difficult to explain, nearly compromised both Davoust and the success of the battle;" See also Thiers (tome vii. p. 172), who attributes Bernadotte's conduct to a profound aversion for Davoust conceived on the most frivolous grounds. Bernadotte had frequently given cause of complaint to Napoleon in the two campaigns of 1806 and 1806. In the movement on Vienna Napoleon considered he showed want of activity and of zeal. These complaints seem to have been made in good faith, for in a letter to Bernadotte's brother-in-law, Joseph, Napoleon suggests that health may have been the causes (Du Cases, tome i. p. 322). Bernadotte was equally unfortunate in putting in his appearance too late at Eylan (see Duc de Rovigo's Memoirs, tome ii. p. 48), and also incurred the displeasure of Napoleon at Wagram (see later on).

20,000 troops with him. He had pillaged every place through which he passed, and brought with him 300 prisoners, and a great many horses he had taken on his road. It was night when he presented himself at the gates of the city, which he entered alone, having left his men and booty at the last village. He proceeded to the French Embassy. I was not there at the time, but I was sent for, and about seven o'clock in the evening I had my first interview with the Major. He was the very, beau ideal of a bandit, and would have been an admirable model for a painter. I was not at all surprised to hear that on his arrival his wild appearance and huge mustachios had excited some degree of terror among those who were in the salon. He described his exploits on the march, and did not disguise his intention of bringing his troops into Hamburg next day. He talked of the Bank and of pillage. I tried for some time to divert him from this idea, but without effect, and at length said to him, "Sir, you know that this is not the way the Emperor wishes to be served. During the seven years that I have been about him, I have invariably heard him express his indignation against those who aggravate the misery which war naturally brings in her train. It is the express wish of the Emperor that no damage, no violence whatever, shall be committed on the city or territory of Hamburg." These few words produced a stronger effect than any entreaties I could have used, for the mere name of the Emperor made even the boldest tremble, and Major Amiel next thought of selling his booty. The Senate were so frightened at the prospect of having Amiel quartered upon them that to get rid of him they determined to purchase his booty at once, and even furnished him with guards for his prisoners. I did not learn till some time afterwards that among the horses Major Amiel had seized upon the road were those of the Countess Walmoden. Had I known this fact at the time I should certainly have taken care to have had them restored to her. Madame Walmoden was then a refugee at Hamburg, and between her and my family a close intimacy existed. On the very day, I believe, of the Major's departure the Senate wrote me a letter of thanks for the protection I afforded the town.

Before the commencement of the Prussian campaign, while anxiety was entertained respecting the designs of the Cabinet of Berlin, my task was not an easy one. I exerted all my efforts to acquaint the French Government with what was passing on the Spree. I announced the first intelligence of an unexpected movement which had taken place among the Prussian troops cantoned in the neighbourhood of Hamburg. They suddenly evacuated Lauenburg, Platzburg, Haarburg, Stade, Twisenfelth, and Cuxhaven. This extraordinary movement gave rise to a multitude of surmises. I was not wrong when I informed the French Government that, according to every probability, Prussia was about to declare hostilities against France, and to enter into an alliance with England.

I much regretted that my situation did not allow me more frequent opportunities of meeting Mr. Thornton, the English Minister to the circle of Lower Saxony. However; I saw him sometimes, and had on two different occasions the opportunity of rendering him some service. Mr. Thornton had requested me to execute a little private business for him, the success of which depended on the Emperor. I made the necessary communication to the Minister for Foreign Affairs, adding in my letter that Mr. Thornton's conduct towards the French who had come in any way in contact with him had ever been just and liberal, and that I should receive great pleasure in being able to announce to him the success of his application. His request was granted.

On another occasion Mr. Thornton applied to me for my services, and I had once more the pleasure of rendering them. He wished to procure some information respecting an Englishman named Baker, who had gone to Terracina, in the Campagna di Roma, for the benefit of sea-bathing. He was there arrested, without any cause assigned, by order of the commandant of the French troops in Terracina. The family of Mr. Baker, not having heard from him for some months, became very uneasy respecting him, for they had not the least idea of his arrest. His relations applied to Mr. Thornton, and that gentleman, notwithstanding the circumstances which, as I have stated, prevented our frequent intercourse, hesitated not a moment in requesting me to furnish him with some information respecting his countryman. I lost no time in writing to M. Alquier, our Ambassador at Rome, and soon enabled Mr. Thornton to ease the apprehension of Mr. Baker's friends.

I had every opportunity of knowing what was passing in Italy, for I had just been invested with a new dignity. As the new King of Naples, Joseph, had no Minister in Lower Saxony, he wished that I should discharge the function of Minister Plenipotentiary for Naples. His Ministers accordingly received orders to correspond with me upon all business connected with his government and his subjects. The relations between Hamburg and Naples were nearly nil, and my new office made no great addition to my labours.

I experienced, however, a little more difficulty in combining all the post-offices of Hamburg in the office of the Grand Duchy of Berg, thus detaching them from the offices of Latour and Taxis, so named after the German family who for a length of time had had the possession of them, and who were devoted to Austria.

After some days of negotiation I obtained the suppression of these offices, and their union with the postoffice of the Grand Duc de Berg (Murat), who thus received letters from Italy, Hungary, Germany, Poland, part of Russia, and the letters from England for these countries.

The affair of the post-offices gained for me the approbation of Napoleon. He expressed his satisfaction through the medium of a letter I received from Duroc, who at the same time recommended me to continue informing the Emperor of all that was doing in Germany with relation to the plans of the Confederation of the North. I therefore despatched to the Minister for Foreign Affairs a detailed letter, announcing that Baron Grote, the Prussian Minister at Hamburg, had set off on a visit to Bremen and Lübeck. Among those who accompanied him on this excursion was a person wholly devoted to me; and I knew that Baron Grote's object was to offer to these towns verbal propositions for their union with the Confederation of the North, which the King of Prussia wished to form as a counterpoise to the Confederation of the Rhine, just created by Napoleon. Baron Grote observed the strictest secrecy in all his movements. He showed, in confidence, to those to whom he addressed himself, a letter from M. Haugwitz, the Minister of the King of Prussia[218], who endeavoured to point out to the Hanse Towns how much the Confederation of the North would turn to their advantage, it being the only means of preserving their liberty, by establishing a formidable power. However, to the first communication only an evasive answer was returned. M. Van Sienen, the Syndic of Hamburg, was commissioned by the Senate to inform the Prussian Minister

218 In July 1806, after Austerlitz, Napoleon had formed the "Confederation du Rhin." to include the smaller States of Germany, who threw off all connection with the German Empire, and formed a Confederation furnishing a considerable army. The Emperor of Germany, Francis IL, had already in 1804, on Napoleon taking the title of Emperor, declared himself Hereditary Emperor of Austria. After the formation of the Rhenish Confederation and Napoleon's refusal to acknowledge the German Empire any longer, he released the States of the Holy Roman Empire from their allegiance, declared the Empire dissolved, and contented himself with the title of Emperor of Austria, as Francis I.

that the affair required the concurrence of the burghers, and that before he could submit it to them it would be necessary to know its basis and conditions. Meanwhile the Syndic Doormann proceeded to Lübeck, where there was also a deputy from Bremen. The project of the Confederation, however, never came to anything.

I scrupulously discharged the duties of my functions, but I confess I often found it difficult to execute the orders I received, and more than once I took it upon myself to modify their severity. I loved the frank and generous character of the Hamburgers, and I could not help pity the fate of the Hanse Towns, heretofore so happy, and from which Bonaparte had exacted such immense sacrifices.

On the principal gate of the Hanse Towns is inscribed the following motto, well expressing the pacific spirit of the people: 'Da nobis pacem, Domine, in diebus nostris'. The paternal and elected government, which did everything to secure the happiness of these towns, was led to believe that the sacrifices imposed on them would be recompensed by the preservation of their neutrality. No distrust was entertained, and hope was kept alive by the assurances given by Napoleon. He published in the Moniteur that the Hanse Towns could not be included in any particular Confederation. He thus strangled in its birth the Confederation of the North, to which those feeble States would otherwise have been obliged to consent. When in 1806 Napoleon marched against Prussia, he detached Marshal Mortier from the Grand Army when it had passed the Rhine, and directed him to invade the Electorate of Hesse, and march on Hamburg. On the 19th of November the latter town was occupied by the French army in the name of the Emperor, amidst the utmost order and tranquillity.

I must acknowledge that I was under much apprehension as to this event. At the intelligence of the approach of the French army consternation was great and universal in Hamburg, which was anxious to maintain its neutrality unimpaired. At the urgent request of the magistrates of the city I assumed functions more than diplomatic, and became, in some respects, the first magistrate of the town. I went to meet Marshal Mortier to endeavour to dissuade him from entering. I thought I should by this means better serve the interests of France than by favouring the occupation of a neutral town by our troops. But all my remonstrances were useless. Marshal Mortier had received formal orders from the Emperor.

No preparations having been made at Hamburg for the reception of Marshal Mortier, he quartered himself and his whole staff upon me. The few troops he had with him were disposed of in my courtyard, so that the residence of a Minister of peace was all at once converted into headquarters. This state of things continued until a house was got ready for the Marshal.

Marshal Mortier had to make very rigorous exactions, but my representations suspended for a while Napoleon's orders for taking possession of the Bank of Hamburg. I am here bound to bear testimony to the Marshal's honourable principles and integrity of character. The representations which I had sent to Marshal Mortier were transmitted by the latter to the Emperor at Berlin; and Mortier stated that he had suspended the execution of the orders until he should receive others. The Emperor approved of this. It was, indeed, a happy event for France and for Europe, even more so than for Hamburg. Those who suggested to the Emperor the idea of pillaging that fine establishment must have been profoundly ignorant of its importance. They thought only of the 90,000,000 of marks banco deposited in its cellars.

By the famous decree of Berlin, dated 21st November 1806, Mortier was compelled to order the seizure of all English merchandise in the Hanse Towns, but he enforced the decree only so far as to preserve the appearance of having obeyed his orders.

Mortier, on leaving Hamburg for Mecklenburg, was succeeded by General Michaud, who in his turn was succeeded by Marshal Brune in the beginning of 1807. I am very glad to take the present opportunity of correcting the misconceptions which arose through the execution of certain acts of Imperial tyranny. The truth is, Marshal Brune, during his government, constantly endeavoured to moderate, as far as he could, the severity of the orders he received. Bernadotte became Governor of Hamburg when the battle of Jena rendered Napoleon master of Prussia and the north of Germany.

The Prince of Ponte-Corvo lightened, as far as possible, the unjust burdens and vexations to which that unfortunate town was subject. He never refused his assistance to any measures which I adopted to oppose a system of ruin and persecution. He often protected Hamburg against exorbitant exactions, The Hanse Towns revived a little under his government, which continued longer than that of Mortier, Michaud, and Brune. The memory of Bernadotte will always be dear to the Hamburgers; and his name will never be pronounced without gratitude. His attention was especially directed to moderate the rigour of the custom-houses; and perhaps the effect which his conduct produced on public opinion may be considered as having, in some measure, led to the decision which, four years after, made him Hereditary Prince of Sweden.

CHAPTER VII

1806

In September 1806 it became very manifest that, as soon as war should break out between France and Prussia, Russia would not be slow in forming an alliance with the latter power. Peace had, however, been reestablished between Napoleon and Alexander by virtue of a treaty just signed at Paris. By that treaty Russia was to evacuate the Bouches du Cattaro,[219] a condition with which she was in no hurry to comply. I received a number of the Court Gazette of St. Petersburg, containing a ukase of the Emperor of Russia, in which Alexander pointed out the danger which again menaced Europe, showed the necessity of adopting precautions for general tranquillity and the security of his own Empire, and declared his determination of not only completing but augmenting his army. He therefore ordered a levy of four men out of every 500 inhabitants.

Before the commencement of hostilities Duroc was sent to the King of Prussia with the view of discovering whether there was any possibility of renewing negotiations; but affairs were already too much embarrassed. All Duroc's endeavours were in vain, and perhaps it was no longer in the power of the King of Prussia to avoid war with France. Besides, he had just grounds of offence against the Emperor. Although the latter had given him Hanover in exchange for the two Margravates, he had, nevertheless, offered to England the restoration of that province as one of the terms of the negotiations commenced with Mr. Fox. This underhand work was not unknown to the Berlin Cabinet, and Napoleon's duplicity rendered Duroc's mission useless. At this time the King of Prussia was at Weimar.

Victory everywhere favoured the French arms. Prince Hohenlohe, who commanded a corps of the Prussian army, was forced to capitulate at Prentzlau. After this capitulation General Blücher took the command of the remains of the corps, to which he joined the troops whose absence from Prentzlau exempted them from the capitulation. These corps, added to those which Blücher had at Auerstadt, were then almost the only ramparts of the Prussian monarchy. Soult and Bernadotte received orders from Murat to pursue Blücher, who was using all his efforts to draw from Berlin the forces of those two generals. Blücher marched in the direction of Lübeck.

General Murat pursued the wreck of the Prussian army which had escaped from Saxony by Magdeburg. Blücher was driven upon Lübeck. It was very important to the army at Berlin that this numerous corps should be destroyed, commanded as it was by a skillful and brave general, who drew from the centre of the military operations numerous troops, with which he might throw himself into Hanover, or Hesse, or even Holland, and by joining the English troops harass the rear of the Grand Army. The Grand Duke of Berg explained to me his plans and expectations, and soon after announced their fulfilment in several letters which contained, among other things, the particulars of the taking of Lübeck.

---

219 The Bouches do Cattaro, on the eastern coast of the Adriatic, had formed part of the Dalmatian possessions of Venice.

In two of these letters Murat, who was probably deceived by his agents, or by some intriguer, informed me that General Moreau had passed through Paris on the 12th of October, and had arrived in Hamburg on the 28th of October. The proof which Murat possessed of this circumstance was a letter of Fauche-Borel, which he had intercepted. I recollect a curious circumstance which serves to show the necessity of mistrusting the vague intelligence furnished to persons in authority. A fortnight before I received Murat's first letter a person informed me that General Moreau was in Hamburg. I gave no credit to this intelligence, yet I endeavoured to ascertain whether it had any foundation, but without effect. Two days later I was assured that an individual had met General Moreau, that he had spoken to him, that he knew him well from having served under him—together with various other circumstances, the truth of which there appeared no reason to doubt. I immediately sent for the individual in question, who told me that he knew Moreau, that he had met him, that the General had inquired of him the way to the Jungfersteige (a promenade at Hamburg), that he had pointed it out to him, and then said, "Have I not the honour to speak to General Moreau?" upon which the General answered, "Yes, but say nothing about having seen me; I am here incognito." All this appeared to me so absurd that, pretending not to know Moreau, I asked the person to describe him to me. He described a person bearing little resemblance to Moreau, and added that he wore a braided French coat and the national cockade in his hat. I instantly perceived the whole was a mere scheme for getting a little money. I sent the fellow about his business. In a quarter of an hour after I had got rid of him M. la Chevardiere called on me, and introduced M. Billaud, the French Consul at Stettin. This gentleman wore a braided coat and the national cockade in his hat. He was the hero of the story I had heard from the informer. A slight personal resemblance between the Consul and the General had caused several persons to mistake them for each other.

During the Prussian campaign nothing was talked of throughout Germany but Napoleon's generous conduct with respect to Prince Hatzfeld. I was fortunate enough to obtain a copy of a letter which the Emperor wrote to Josephine on the subject, and which I shall presently lay before the reader. In conformity with the inquisitorial system which too frequently characterised the Emperor's government, and which he extended to every country of which he had military possession, the first thing done on entering a town was to take possession of the post-office, and then, Heaven knows how little respect was shown to the privacy of correspondence. Among the letters thus seized at Berlin and delivered to Napoleon was one addressed to the King of Prussia by Prince Hatzfeld, who had imprudently remained in the Prussian capital. In this letter the Prince gave his Sovereign an account of all that had occurred in Berlin since he had been compelled to quit at; and at the same time he informed him of the force and situation of the corps of the French army. The Emperor, after reading this letter, ordered that the Prince should be arrested, and tried by a court-martial on the charge of being a spy.

The Court was summoned, and little doubt could be entertained as to its decision when Madame Hatzfeld repaired to Duroc, who on such occasions was always happy when he could facilitate communication with the Emperor. On that day Napoleon had been at a review. Duroc knew Madame Hatzfeld, whom he had several times seen on his visits to Berlin. When Napoleon returned from the review he was astonished to see Duroc at the palace at that hour, and inquired whether he had brought any news. Duroc answered in the affirmative, and followed the Emperor into his Cabinet, where he soon introduced Madame Hatzfeld. The remainder of the scene is described in Napoleon's letter. It may easily be perceived that this letter is an answer to one from Josephine reproaching him for the manner in which he spoke of women, and very probably of the beautiful and unfortunate Queen of Prussia, respecting whom he had expressed himself with too little respect in one of his bulletins. The following is Napoleon's letter:—

> I have received your letter, in which you seem to reproach me for speaking ill of women. It is true that I dislike female intriguers above all things. I am used to kind, gentle, and conciliatory women. I love them, and if they have spoiled me it is not my fault, but yours. However, you will see that I have done an act of kindness to one deserving woman. I allude to Madame de Hatzfeld. When I showed her her husband's letter she stood weeping, and in a tone of mingled grief and ingenuousness said, "It is indeed his writing!" This went to my heart, and I said, "Well, madame, throw the letter into the fire, and then I shall have no proof against your husband." She burned the letter, and was restored to happiness. Her husband now is safe: two hours later, and he would have been lost. You see, therefore, that I like women who are simple, gentle, and amiable; because they alone resemble you.
>
> *November 6, 1806, 9 o'clock P.M.*

When Marshal Bernadotte had driven Blücher into Lübeck and made him prisoner, he sent to inform me of the circumstance; but I was far from, expecting that the prisoner would be confided to my charge. Such, however, was the case. After his capitulation he was sent to Hamburg, where he had the whole city for his prison.

I was curious to become acquainted with this celebrated man, and I saw him very frequently. I found that he was an enthusiastic Prussian patriot—a brave man, enterprising even to rashness, of limited education, and almost to an incredible degree devoted to pleasure, of which he took an ample share while he remained in Hamburg. He sat an enormous time at table, and, notwithstanding his exclusive patriotism, he rendered full justice to the wines of France. His passion for women was unbounded, and one of his most favourite sources of amusement was the gaming-table, at which he spent a considerable portion of his time. Blücher was of an extremely gay disposition; and considered merely as a companion he was very agreeable. The original style of his conversation pleased me much. His confidence in the deliverance of Germany remained unshaken in spite of the disasters of the Prussian army. He often said to me, "I place great reliance on the public spirit of Germany—on the enthusiasm which prevails in our universities. The events of war are daily changing, and even defeats con tribute to nourish in a people sentiments of honour and national glory. You may depend upon it that when a whole nation is determined to shake off a humiliating yoke it will succeed. There is no doubt but we shall end by having a landwehr very different from any militia to which the subdued spirit of the French people could give birth. England will always lend us the support of her navy and her subsidies, and we will renew alliances with Russia and Austria. I can pledge myself to the truth of a fact of which I have certain knowledge, and you may rely upon it; namely, that none of the allied powers engaged in the present war entertain views of territorial aggrandisement. All they unanimously desire is to put an end to the system of aggrandisement which your Emperor has established and acts upon with such alarming rapidity. In our first war against France, at the commencement of your Revolution, we fought for questions respecting the rights of sovereigns, for which, I assure you, I care very little; but now the case is altered, the whole population of Prussia makes common cause with its Government. The people fight in defence of their homes, and reverses destroy our armies without changing the spirit of the nation. I rely confidently on the future because I foresee that fortune will not always favour your Emperor. It is impossible; but the time will come when all Europe, humbled by his exactions, and impatient of his depredations, will rise up against him. The more he enslaves nations, the more terrible will be the reaction when they break their chains. It cannot be denied that he is tormented with an insatiable desire of acquiring new territories. To the war of 1805 against Austria and Russia the present war has almost immediately succeeded. We have fallen. Prussia is occupied; but Russia still remains undefeated. I cannot foresee what will be the termination of the war; but, admitting that the issue should be favourable to you, it will end only to break out again speedily. If we continue firm, France, exhausted by her conquests, must in the end fall. You may be certain of it. You wish for peace. Recommend it! By so doing You will give strong proofs of love for your country."

In this strain Blücher constantly spoke to me; and as I never thought it right to play the part of the public functionary in the drawing-room I replied to him with the reserve necessary in my situation. I could not tell him how much my anticipations frequently coincided with his; but I never hesitated to express to him how much I wished to see a reasonable peace concluded.

Blücher's arrival at Hamburg was preceded by that of Prince Paul of Wutrtemberg, the second son of one of the two kings created by Napoleon, whose crowns were not yet a year old. This young Prince, who was imbued with the ideas of liberty and independence which then prevailed in Germany, had taken a headlong step. He had quitted Stuttgart to serve in the Prussian campaign without having asked his father's permission, which inconsiderate proceeding might have drawn Napoleon's anger upon the King of Wurtemberg. The King of Prussia advanced Prince Paul to the rank of general, but he was taken prisoner at the very commencement of hostilities. Prince Paul was not, as has been erroneously stated, conducted to Stuttgart by a captain of gendarmerie. He came to Hamburg, where I received many visits from him. He did not yet possess very definite ideas as to what he wished; for after he was made prisoner he expressed to me his strong desire to enter the French service, and often asked me to solicit for him an interview with the Emperor. He obtained this interview, and remained for a long time in Paris, where I know he has frequently resided since the Restoration.

The individuals whom I had to observe in Hamburg gave me much less trouble than our neighbours at Altona. The number of the latter had considerably augmented, since the events of the war had compelled a great number of emigrants who had taken refuge at Munster to leave that town. They all proceeded to Altona. Conquered countries became as dangerous to them as the land which they had forsaken. The most distinguished amongst the individuals assembled at Altona were Vicomte de Sesmaisons, the Bailly d'Hautefeuille, the Duchess of Luxembourg, the Marquis de Bonnard, the Duc d'Aumont (then Duc de Villequier), the wife of Marshal de Brogue and her daughter, Cardinal de Montmorency, Madame de Cosse, her two daughters and her son (and a priest), and the Bishop of Boulogne.

Bonaparte stayed long enough at Berlin to permit of the arrival of a deputation from the French Senate to congratulate him on his first triumphs. I learned that in this instance the Senatorial deputation, departing from its accustomed complaisance, ventured not to confine itself to compliments and felicitations, but went so far as to interfere with the Emperor's plan of the campaign, to speak of the danger that might be incurred and finally to express a desire to in passing the Oder, see peace concluded. Napoleon received this communication with a very bad grace. He thought the Senators very bold to meddle with his affairs, treated the conscript fathers of France as if they had been inconsiderate youths, protested, according to custom, his sincere love of peace, and told the deputation that it was Prussia, backed by Russia, and not he, who wished for war!

All the German Princes who had taken part against Napoleon fled to Altona after the battle of Jena with as much precipitation as the emigrants themselves. The Hereditary Prince of Weimar, the Duchess of Holstein, Prince Belmonte-Pignatelli, and a multitude of other persons distinguished for rank and fortune, arrived there almost simultaneously. Among the persons who took refuge in Altona were some intriguers, of whom Fauche-Borel was one. I remember receiving a report respecting a violent altercation which Fauche had the audacity to enter into with Comte de Gimel because he could not extort money from the Count in payment of his intrigues. Comte de Gimel had only funds for the payment of pensions, and, besides, he had too much sense to suppose there was any utility in the stupid pamphlets of Fauche-Borel, and therefore he dismissed him with a refusal. Fauche was insolent, which compelled Comte de Gimel to send him about his business as he deserved. This circumstance, which was first communicated to me in a report, has since been confirmed by a person who witnessed the scene. Fauche-Borel merely passed through Hamburg, and embarked for London on board the same ship which took Lord Morpeth back to England[220].

220 Louis Fauche-Borel (1762-1829), a Swiss who devoted himself to the cause of the Royalists. As Louis stepped on the shore of France in 1814, Fauche-Borel was ready to assist him from the boat, and was met with the gracious remark that he was always at hand when a service was required. His services were however left unrewarded.

CHAPTER VIII

1806

At this critical moment Hamburg was menaced on all sides; the French even occupied a portion of its territory. The French troops, fortunately for the country, were attached to the corps commanded by the Prince de Ponte-Corvo. This military occupation alarmed the town of Hamburg, to which, indeed, it proved very injurious. I wrote to Marshal Bernadotte on the subject. The grounds on which the Senate appealed for the evacuation of their territory were such that Bernadotte could not but acknowledge their justice. The prolonged stay of the French troops in the bailiwick of Bergdorf, which had all the appearance of an occupation, might have led to the confiscation of all Hamburg property in England, to the laying an embargo on the vessels of the Republic, and consequently to the ruin of a great part of the trade of France and Holland, which was carried on under the flag of Hamburg. There was no longer any motive for occupying the bailiwick of Bergdorf when there were no Prussians in that quarter. It would have been an absurd misfortune that eighty men stationed in that bailiwick should, for the sake of a few louis and a few ells of English cloth, have occasioned the confiscation of Hamburg, French, and Dutch property to the amount of 80,000,000 francs.

Marshal Bernadotte replied to me on the 16th of November, and said, "I hasten to inform you that I have given orders for the evacuation of the bailiwick of Bergdorf and all the Hamburg territory. If you could obtain from the Senate of Hamburg, by the 19th of this month, two or three thousand pairs of shoes, you would oblige me greatly. They shall be paid for in goods or in money."

I obtained what Bernadotte required from the Senate, who knew his integrity, while they were aware that that quality was not the characteristic of all who commanded the French armies! What extortions took place during the occupation of Prussia! I will mention one of the means which, amongst others, was employed at Berlin to procure money. Bills of exchange were drawn, on which endorsements were forged, and these bills were presented to the bankers on whom they were purported to be drawn. One day some of these forged bills to a large amount were presented to Messrs. Mathiesen and Silleine of Hamburg, who, knowing the endorsement to be forged, refused to cash them. The persons who presented the bills carried their impudence so far as to send for the gendarmes, but the bankers persisted in their refusal. I was informed of this almost incredible scene, which had drawn together a great number of people. Indignant at such audacious robbery, I instantly proceeded to the spot and sent away the gendarmes, telling them it was not their duty to protect robbers, and that it was my business to listen to any just claims which might be advanced. Under Clarke's government at Berlin the inhabitants were subjected to all kinds of oppression and exaction. Amidst these exactions and infamous proceedings, which are not the indispensable consequences of war, the Dutch generals distinguished themselves by a degree of rapacity which brought to mind the period of the French Republican peculations in Italy. It certainly was not their new King who set the example of this conduct. His moderation was well known, and it was as much the result of his disposition as of his honest principles. Louis Bonaparte, who was a King in spite of himself, afforded an example of all that a good man could suffer upon a usurped throne.

When the King of Prussia found himself defeated at every point he bitterly repented having undertaken a war which had delivered his States into Napoleon's power in less time than that in which Austria had fallen the preceding year. He wrote to the Emperor, soliciting a suspension of hostilities. Rapp was present when Napoleon received the King of Prussia's letter. "It is too late," said he; "but, no matter, I wish to stop the effusion of blood; I am ready to agree to anything which is not prejudicial to the honour or interests of the nation." Then calling Duroc, he gave him orders to visit the wounded, and see that they wanted for nothing. He added, "Visit every man on my behalf; give them all the consolation of which they stand in need; afterwards find the King of Prussia, and if he offers reasonable proposals let me know them."

Negotiations were commenced, but Napoleon's conditions were of a nature which was considered inadmissible. Prussia still hoped for assistance from the Russian forces. Besides, the Emperor's demands extended to England, who at that moment had no reason to accede to the pretensions of France. The Emperor wished England to restore to France the colonies which she had captured since the commencement of the war, that Russia should restore to the Porte Moldavia and Wallachia, which she then occupied; in short, he acted upon the advice which some tragedy-king gives to his ambassador: "Demand everything, that you may obtain nothing." The Emperor's demands were, in fact, so extravagant that it was scarcely possible he himself could entertain the hope of their being accepted. Negotiations, alternately resumed and abandoned, were carried on with coldness on both sides until the moment when England prevailed on Russia to join Prussia against France; they then altogether ceased: and it was for the sake of appearing to wish for their renewal, on bases still more favourable to France, that Napoleon sent Duroc to the King of Prussia. Duroc found the King at Osterode, on the other side of the Vistula. The only answer he received from His Majesty was, "The time is passed;" which was very much like Napoleon's observation; "It is too late."

Whilst Duroc was on his mission to the King of Prussia I was myself negotiating at Hamburg. Bonaparte was very anxious to detach Sweden from the coalition, and to terminate the war with her by a separate treaty. Sweden, indeed, was likely to be very useful to him if Prussia, Russia, and England should collect a considerable mass of troops in the north. Denmark was already with us, and by gaining over Sweden also the union of those two powers might create a diversion, and give serious alarm to the coalition, which would be obliged to concentrate its principal force to oppose the attack of the grand army in Poland. The opinions of M. Peyron, the Swedish Minister at Hamburg, were decidedly opposed to the war in which his sovereign was engaged with France. I was sorry that this gentleman left Hamburg upon leave of absence for a year just at the moment I received my instructions from the Emperor upon this subject. M. Peyron was succeeded by M. Netzel, and I soon had the pleasure of perceiving that his opinions corresponded in every respect with those of his predecessor.

As soon as he arrived M. Netzel sought an interview to speak to me on the subject of the Swedes, who had been taken prisoners on the Drave. He entreated me to allow the officers to return to Sweden on their parole. I was anxious to get Netzel's demand acceded to, and availed myself of that opportunity to lead him gradually to the subject of my instructions.

I had good reason to be satisfied with the manner in which he received my first overtures. I said nothing to him of the justice of which he was not previously convinced. I saw he understood that his sovereign would have everything to gain by a reconciliation with France, and he told me that all Sweden demanded peace. Thus encouraged, I told him frankly that I was instructed to treat with him. M. Netzel assured me that M. de Wetterstedt, the King of Sweden's private secretary, with whom he was intimate, and from whom he showed me several letters, was of the same opinion on the subject as himself. He added, that he had permission to correspond with the King, and that he would; write the same evening to his sovereign and M . . . de Wetterstedt to acquaint them with our conversation.

It will be perceived, from what I have stated, that no negotiation was ever commenced under more favourable auspices; but who could foresee what turn the King of Sweden would take? That unlucky Prince took M. Netzel's letter in very ill part, and M. de Wetterstedt himself received peremptory orders to acquaint M. Netzel with his sovereign's displeasure at his having presumed to visit a French Minster, and, above all, to enter into a political conversation with him, although it was nothing more than conversation. The King did not confine himself to reproaches; M. Netzel came in great distress to inform me he had received orders to quit Hamburg immediately, without even awaiting the arrival of his successor. He regarded his disgrace as complete. I had the pleasure of seeing M. Netzel again in 1809 at Hamburg, where he was on a mission from King Charles XIII.

CHAPTER IX

1806

I have a few remarks to make on the famous Continental system, which was a subject of such engrossing interest. I had, perhaps, better opportunities than any other person of observing the fraud and estimating the fatal consequences of this system. It took its rise during the war in 1806, and was brought into existence by a decree; dated from Berlin. The project was conceived by weak counsellors, who; perceiving the Emperor's just indignation at the duplicity of England, her repugnance to enter, into negotiations with him, and her constant endeavours to raise enemies against France, prevailed upon him to issue the decree, which I could only regard as an act of madness and tyranny. It was not a decree, but fleets, that were wanting. Without a navy it was ridiculous to declare the British Isles in a state of blockade, whilst the English fleets were in fact blockading all the French ports. This declaration was, however, made in the Berlin Decree. This is what was called the Continental system! which, in plain terms, was nothing but a system of fraud and pillage.

One can now scarcely conceive how Europe could for a single day endure that fiscal tyranny which extorted exorbitant prices for articles which the habits of three centuries had rendered indispensable to the poor as well as to the rich. So little of truth is there in the pretence that this system had for its sole and exclusive object to prevent the sale of English goods, that licences for their disposal were procured at a high price by whoever was rich enough to pay for them. The number and quality of the articles exported from France were extravagantly exaggerated. It was, indeed, necessary to take out some of the articles is compliance with the Emperor's wishes, but they were only thrown into the sea. And yet no one had the honesty to tell the Emperor that England sold on the continent but bought scarcely anything. The speculation in licences was carried to a scandalous extent only to enrich a few, and to satisfy the short-sighted views of the contrivers of the system.

This system proves what is written in the annals of the human heart and mind, that the cupidity of the one is insatiable, and the errors of the other incorrigible. Of this I will cite an example, though it refers to a period posterior to the origin of the Continental system. In Hamburg, in 1811, under Davoust's government, a poor man had well-nigh been shot for having introduced into the department of the Elbe a small loaf of sugar for the use of his family, while at the same moment Napoleon was perhaps signing a licence for the importation of a million of sugar-loaves.[221] Smuggling on a small scale was punished with

221 In this same year (1811) Murat, as King of Naples, not only winked at the infringement of the Continental system, but almost openly broke the law himself. His troops in Calabria and all round his immense line sea coast, carried on an active trade with Sicilian and English smugglers. This was so much the case that an officer never set out from Naples to join, without, being, requested by his wife, his relations or friends, to bring them some English muslins, some sugar and coffee, together with a few needles, pen-knives, and razors. Some of the Neapolitan officers embarked in really large commercial operations, going shares with

death, whilst the Government themselves carried it on extensively. The same cause filled the Treasury with money, and the prisons with victims:

The custom-house laws of this period, which waged open war against rhubarb, and armed the coasts of the Continent against the introduction of senna, did not save the Continental system from destruction. Ridicule attended the installation of the odious prevotal courts. The president of the Prevotal Court at Hamburg, who was a Frenchman, delivered an address, in which he endeavoured to prove that in the time of the Ptolemies there had existed extraordinary fiscal tribunals, and that it was to those Egypt owed her prosperity. Terror was thus introduced by the most absurd folly. The ordinary customhouse officers, formerly so much abhorred in Hamburg, declared with reason that they would soon be regretted, and than the difference between them and the prevotal courts would soon be felt. Bonaparte's counsellors led him to commit the folly of requiring that a ship which had obtained a licence should export merchandise equivalent to that of the colonial produce to be imported under the authority of the licence. What was the consequence? The speculators bought at a low price old stores of silk-which change of fashion had made completely unsaleable, and as those articles were prohibited in England they were thrown into the sea without their loss being felt. The profits of the speculation made ample amends for the sacrifice. The Continental system was worthy only of the ages of ignorance and barbarism, and had it been admissible in theory, was impracticable in application[222]. It cannot be sufficiently stigmatised. They were not the friends of the Emperor who recommended a system calculated to rouse the indignation of Europe, and which could not fail to create reaction. To tyrannize over the human species, and to exact uniform admiration and submission, is to require an impossibility. It would seem that fate, which had still some splendid triumphs in store for Bonaparte, intended to prepare beforehand the causes which were to deprive him of all his triumphs at once, and plunge him into reverses even greater than the good fortune which had favoured his elevation.

The prohibition of trade, the habitual severity in the execution of this odious system, made it operate like a Continental impost. I will give a proof of this, and I state nothing but what came under my own observation. The fiscal regulations were very rigidly enforced at Hamburg, and along the two lines of Cuxhaven and Travemunde. M. Eudel, the director of that department, performed his duty with zeal and disinterestedness. I feel gratified in rendering him this tribute. Enormous quantities of English merchandise and colonial produce were accumulated at Holstein, where they almost all arrived by way of Kiel and Hudsum, and were smuggled over the line at the expense of a premium of 33 and 40 per cent.

---

the custom house people who were there to enforce the law, and making their soldiers load and unload the contraband vessels. The Comte de ——-, a French officer on Murat's staff, was very noble, but very poor, and excessively extravagant. After making several vain efforts to set him up in the world, the King told him one day he would give him the command of the troops round the Gulf of Salerno; adding that the devil was in it if he could not make a fortune in such a capital smuggling district, in a couple of years.—The Count took the hint, and did make a fortune.—Editor 1836 edition.

222 Sydney Smith was struck with the, ridiculous side of the war of tariffs: "We are told that the Continent is to be reconquered by the want of rhubarb and plums." (Essays of Sydney Smith, p. 533, edition of 1861).

Convinced of this fact by a thousand proofs, and weary of the vexations of the preventive system, I took upon myself to lay my opinions on the subject before the Emperor. He had given me permission to write to him personally, without any intermediate agency, upon everything that I might consider essential to his service. I sent an extraordinary courier to Fontainebleau, where he then was, and in my despatch I informed him that, notwithstanding his preventive guard, every prohibited article was smuggled in because the profits on the sale in Germany, Poland, Italy, and even France, into which the contrabrand goods found their way, were too considerable not to induce persons to incur all risks to obtain them. I advised him, at the very time he was about to unite the Hanse Towns to the French Empire, to permit merchandise to be imported subject to a duty of 33 per cent., which was about equal to the amount of the premium for insurance. The Emperor adopted my advice without hesitation, and in 1811 the regulation produced a revenue of upwards of 60,000,000 francs in Hamburg alone.

This system, however, embroiled us with Sweden and Russia, who could not endure that Napoleon should enact a strict blockade from them, whilst he was himself distributing licences in abundance. Bernadotte, on his way to Sweden, passed through Hamburg in October 1810. He stayed with me three days, during which time he scarcely saw any person but myself. He asked my opinion as to what he should do in regard to the Continental system. I did not hesitate to declare to him, not as a French Minister, but as a private individual to his friend, that in his place, at the head of a poor nation, which could only subsist by the exchange of its territorial productions with England, I would open my ports, and give the Swedes gratuitously that general licence which Bonaparte sold in detail to intrigue and cupidity.

The Berlin decree could not fail to cause a reaction against the Emperor's fortune by raising up whole nations against him. The hurling of twenty kings from their thrones would have excited less hatred than this contempt for the wants of nations. This profound ignorance of the maxims of political economy caused general privation and misery, which in their turn occasioned general hostility. The system could only succeed in the impossible event of all the powers of Europe honestly endeavouring to carry it into effect. A single free port would have destroyed it. In order to ensure its complete success it was necessary to conquer and occupy all countries, and never to evacuate them. As a means of ruining England it was contemptible. It was necessary that all Europe should be compelled by force of arms to join this absurd coalition, and that the same force should be constantly employed to maintain it. Was this possible? The captain "rapporteur" of a court-martial allowed a poor peasant to escape the punishment due to the offence of having bought a loaf of sugar beyond the custom-house barrier. This officer was some time afterwards at a dinner given by Marshal Davoust; the latter said to him, "You have a very scrupulous conscience, sir; go to headquarters and you will find an order there for you." This order sent him eighty leagues from Hamburg. It is necessary to have witnessed, as I have, the numberless vexations and miseries occasioned by the unfortunate Continental system to understand the mischief its authors did in Europe, and how much that mischief contributed to Napoleon's fall.[223]

223 The so-called Continental system was framed by Napoleon in revenge for the English very extended system of blockades, after Trafalgar had put it out of his power to attempt to keep the seas. By these decrees all ports occupied by the French were closed to the English, and all English goods were to be destroyed wherever found in any country occupied by the French. All States under French influence had to adopt this system. It must be remembered that

Napoleon eventually held or enforced his system on all the coastlines of Europe, except that of Spain and Turkey; but as Bourrienne shows the plan of giving licences to break his own system was too lucrative to be resisted by him, or, still more, by his officers. For the working of the system in the occupied lands, Laffite the banker told Savary it was a grand idea, but impracticable (Savary, tome v. p. 110). The Emperor Alexander is reported to have said, after visiting England in 1814, that he believed the system would have reduced England if it had lasted another year. The English, who claimed the right of blockading any coast with but little regard to the effectiveness of the blockade, retaliated by orders in Council, the chief of which are dated 7th January 1807, and 11th November 1807, by which no ships of any power were allowed to trade between any French ports, or the ports of any country closed to England. Whatever the real merits of the system, and although it was the cause of war between the United States and England, its execution did most to damage France and Napoleon, and to band all Europe against it. It is curious that even in 1831 a treaty had to be made to settle the claims of the United States on France for unjust seizures under these decrees.

CHAPTER X

1806-1807

Bonaparte was not only beyond all comparison the greatest captain of modern times, but he may be said to have wrought a complete change in the art of war. Before his time the most able generals regulated the fighting season by the almanac. It was customary in Europe to brave the cannon's mouth only from the first fine days of spring to the last fine days of autumn; and the months of rain, snow, and frost were passed in what were called winter quarters. Pichegru, in Holland, had set the example of indifference to temperature. At Austerlitz, too, Bonaparte had braved the severity of winter; this answered his purpose well, and he adopted the same course in 1806. His military genius and activity seemed to increase, and, proud of his troops, he determined to commence a winter campaign in a climate more rigorous than any in which he had yet fought. The men, chained to his destiny, were now required to brave the northern blast, as they had formerly braved the vertical sun of Egypt. Napoleon, who, above all generals, was remarkable for the choice of his fields of battle, did not wish to wait tranquilly until the Russian army, which was advancing towards Germany, should come to measure its strength with him in the plains of conquered Prussia; he resolved to march to meet it, and to reach it before it should arose the Vistula; but before he left Berlin to explore and conqueror, Poland and the confines of Russia; he addressed a proclamation to his troops, in which he stated all that had hitherto been achieved by the French army, and at the same time announced his future intentions. It was especially advisable that he should march forward, for, had he waited until the Russians had passed the Vistula, there could probably have been no winter campaign, and he would have been obliged either to take up miserable winter quarters between the Vistula and the Oder, or to recross the Oder to combat the enemy in Prussia. Napoleon's military genius and indefatigable activity served him admirably on this occasion, and the proclamation just alluded to, which was dated from Berlin before his departure from Charlottenburg; proves that he did not act fortuitously, as he frequently did, but that his calculations were well-made.[224]

A rapid and immense impulse given to great masses of men by the will of a single individual may produce transient lustre and dazzle the eyes of the multitude; but when, at a distance from the theatre of glory, we flee only the melancholy results which have been produced. The genius of conquest can only be regarded as the genius of destruction. What a sad picture was often presented to my eyes! I was continually doomed to hear complaints of the general distress, and to execute orders which augmented the immense sacrifices already made by the city of Hamburg. Thus, for example, the Emperor desired me to furnish him with 50,000 cloaks which I immediately did. I felt the importance of such an order

224 Before leaving the capital of Prussia Bonaparte stole from the monument, of Frederick the Great his sword and military orders. He also plundered the galleries of Berlin and Potsdam of their best pictures and statues, thus continuing the system he had began is Italy. All those things he sent to Paris as trophies of victory and glory.—Editor of as 1836 edition.

with the approach of winter, and in a climate—the rigour of which our troops had not yet encountered. I also received orders to seize at Lübeck (Which town, as I have already stated, had been alternately taken and retaken try Blücher and Bernadotte) 400,000 lasts of corn,—(A last weighs 2000 kilogrammes)—and to send them to Magdeburg. This corn belonged to Russia. Marshal Mortier, too, had seized some timber for building, which also belonged to Russia; and which was estimated at 1,400,000 francs.

Meanwhile our troops continued to advance with such rapidity that before the end of November Murat arrived at Warsaw, at the head of the advanced guard of the Grand Army, of which, he had the command. The Emperor's headquarters, were then at Posen, and, he received deputations from all parts soliciting the re-establishment and independence of the Kingdom of Poland.

Rapp informed me that after receiving the deputation from Warsaw the Emperor said to him, "I love the Poles; their enthusiastic character pleases me; I should like to make them independent, but that is a difficult matter. Austria, Russia, and Prussia have all had a slice of the cake; when the match is once kindled who knows where, the conflagration may stop? My first duty, is towards France, which I must not sacrifice to Poland; we must refer this matter to the sovereign of all things—Time, he will presently show us what we must do." Had Sulkowsky lived Napoleon might have recollected what he had said to him in Egypt, and, in all probability he would have raised up a power, the dismemberment of which; towards the close of the last century, began to overturn the political equilibrium which had subsisted in Europe since the peace of Westphalia in 1648.

It was at the headquarters at Posen that Duroc rejoined the Emperor after his mission to the King of Prussia. His carriage overturned on the way, and he had the misfortune to break his collar-bone. All the letters I received were nothing but a succession of complaints on the bad state of the roads. Our troops were absolutely fighting in mud, and it was with extreme difficulty that the artillery and caissons of the army could be moved along. M. de Talleyrand had been summoned to headquarters by the Emperor, in the expectation of treating for peace, and I was informed that his carriage stuck in the mud and he was detained on his journey for twelve hours. A soldier having asked one of the persons in M. de Talleyrand's suite who the traveller was, was informed that he was the Minister for Foreign Affairs. "Ah! bah!" said the soldier, "why does he come with his diplomacy to such a devil of a country as this?"

The Emperor entered Warsaw on the 1st of January 1807. Most of the reports which he had received previous to his entrance had concurred in describing the dissatisfaction of the troops, who for some time had had to contend with bad roads, bad weather, and all aorta of privations.' Bonaparte said to the generals who informed him that the enthusiasm of his troops had been succeeded by dejection and discontent, "Does their spirit fail them when they come in sight of the enemy?"—"No, Sire."— "I knew it; my troops are always the same." Then turning to Rapp he said, "I must rouse them;" and he dictated the following proclamation:

> SOLDIERS—It is a year this very hour since you were on the field of Austerlitz, where the Russian battalions fled in disorder, or surrendered up their arms to their conquerors. Next day proposals, of peace were talked of; but they were deceptive. No sooner had the Russians escaped, by perhaps, blamable generosity from the disasters of the third coalition than they contrived a fourth. But the ally on whose tactics they

> founded their principal hope was no more. His capital, his fortresses; his magazines; his arsenals, 280 flags, and 700 field-pieces have fallen into our power. The Oder, the Wartha, the deserts of Poland, and the inclemency of the season have not for a moment retarded your progress. You have braved all; surmounted all; every obstacle has fled at your approach. The Russians have in vain endeavoured to defend the capital of ancient and illustrious Poland. The French eagle hovers over the Vistula. The brave and unfortunate Poles, on beholding you, fancied they saw the legions of Sobieski, returning from their memorable expedition. Soldiers, we will not lay down our arms until a general peace has secured the power of our allies and restored to us our colonies and our freedom of trade. We have gained on the Elbe and the Oder, Pondicherry, our Indian establishments, the Cape of Good Hope, and the Spanish colonies. Why should the Russians have the right of opposing destiny and thwarting our just designs? They and we are still the soldiers who fought at Austerlitz.

Rapp thus describes the entrance of the French into Warsaw, and adds a few anecdotes connected with that event:

> "At length we entered the Polish capital. The King of Naples had preceded us, and had driven the Russians from the city. Napoleon was received with enthusiasm. The Poles thought that the moment of their regeneration had arrived, and that their wishes were fulfilled. It would be difficult to describe the joy thus evinced, and the respect with which they treated us. The French troops, however, were not quite so well pleased; they manifested the greatest repugnance to crossing the Vistula. The idea of want and bad weather had inspired them with the greatest aversion to Poland, and they were inexhaustible, in their jokes on the country."

When Bonaparte dictated his proclamations—and how many have I not written from his dictation!—he was for the moment inspired, and he evinced all the excitement which distinguishes the Italian improvisatori. To follow him it was necessary to write with inconceivable rapidity. When I have read over to him what he has dictated I have often known him to smile triumphantly at the effect which he expected any particular phrase would produce. In general his proclamations turned on three distinct points—(1) Praising his soldiers for what they had done; (2) pointing out to them what they had yet to do; and (3) abusing his enemies. The proclamation to which I have just now alluded was circulated profusely through Germany, and it is impossible to conceive the effect it produced. on the whole army. The corps stationed in the rear burned too pass, by forced marches, the space which still separated them from headquarters; and those who were nearer the Emperor forgot their fatigues and privations and were only anxious to encounter the enemy. They frequently could not understand what Napoleon said in these proclamations; but no matter for that, they would have followed him cheerfully barefooted and without provisions. Such was the enthusiasm, or rather the fanaticism, which Napoleon could inspire among his troops when he thought proper to rouse them, as he termed it.

When, on a former occasion, I spoke of the Duke of, Mecklenburg-Schwerin and his family, I forgot a circumstance respecting my intercourse with him which now occurs to my memory. When, on his expulsion from his States, after the battle of Jena, he took refuge in

Altona, he requested, through the medium of his Minister at Hamburg, Count von Plessen, that I would give him permission occasionally to visit that city. This permission I granted without hesitation; but the Duke observed no precaution in his visits, and I made some friendly observations to him on the subject. I knew the object of his visits. It was a secret connection in Hamburg; but in consequence of my observations he removed the lady to Altona, and assured me that he adopted that determination to avoid committing me. He afterwards came very seldom to Hamburg; but as we were on the best understanding with Denmark I frequently saw his daughter, and son-in-law, who used to visit me at a house I had in Holstein, near Altona.

There I likewise saw, almost every day, the Duke of Weimar, an excellent old man. I had the advantage of being on such terms of intimacy with him that my house was in some measure his. He also had lost his States. I was so happy as to contribute to their restitution, for my situation enabled me to exercise some influence on the political indulgences or severities of the Government. I entertained a sincere regard for the Duke of Weimar, and I greatly regretted his departure. No sooner had he arrived in Berlin than he wrote me a letter of, thanks, to which he added the present of a diamond, in token of his grateful remembrance of me. The Duke of Mecklenburg was not so fortunate as the Duke of Weimar, in spite of his alliance with the reigning family of Denmark. He was obliged to remain at Altona until the July following, for his States were restored only by the Treaty of Tilsit. As soon as it was known that the Emperor had returns to Paris the Duke's son, the Hereditary Prince, visited me in Hamburg, and asked me whether I thought he could present himself to the Emperor, for the purpose of expressing his own and his father's gratitude. He was a very well-educated young man. He set out, accompanied by M. Oertzen and Baron von Brandstaten. Some time afterwards I saw his name in the Moniteur, in one of the lists of presentations to Napoleon, the collection of which, during the Empire, might be regarded as a general register of the nobility of Europe. It is commonly said that we may accustom ourselves to anything, but to me this remark is subject to an exception; for, in spite of the necessity to which I was reduced of employing spies, I never could surmount the disgust I felt at them, especially when I saw men destined to fill a respectable rank in society degrade themselves to that infamous profession. It is impossible to conceive the artifices to which these men resort to gain the confidence of those whom they wish to betray. Of this the following example just now occurs to my mind. One of those wretches who are employed in certain circumstances, and by all parties, came to offer his services to me. His name was Butler, and he had been sent from England to the Continent as a spy upon the French Government. He immediately came to me, complaining of pretended enemies and unjust treatment. He told me he had the greatest wish to serve the Emperor, and that he would make any sacrifice to prove his fidelity. The real motive of his change of party was, as it is with all such men, merely the hope of a higher reward. Most extraordinary were the schemes he adopted to prevent his old employers from suspecting that he was serving new ones. To me he continually repeated how happy he was to be revenged on his enemies in London. He asked me to allow him to go to Paris to be examined by the Minister of Police. The better to keep up the deception he requested that on his arrival in Paris he might be confined in the Temple, and that there might be inserted in the French journals an announcement in the following terms:

> "John Butler, commonly called Count Butler, has just been arrested and sent to Paris under a good escort by the French Minister at Hamburg."

At the expiration of a few weeks Butler, having received his instruction's, set out for London, but by way of precaution he said it would be well to publish in the journals another announcement; which was as follows:

> "John Butler, who has been arrested in Hamburg as an English agent, and conveyed to Paris, is ordered to quit France and the territories occupied by the French armies and their allies, and not to appear there again until the general peace."

In England Butler enjoyed the honours of French prosecution. He was regarded as a victim who deserved all the confidence of the enemies of France. He furnished Fouché with a considerable amount of information, and he was fortunate enough to escape being hanged.

Notwithstanding the pretended necessity of employing secret agents, Bonaparte was unwilling that, even under that pretext, too many communications should be established between France and England: Fouché, nevertheless, actively directed the evolutions of his secret army. Ever ready to seize on anything that could give importance to the police and encourage the suspicions of the Emperor, Fouché wrote to me that the government had received certain—information that many Frenchmen traveling for commercial houses in France were at Manchester purchasing articles of English manufacture. This was true; but how was it to be prevented? These traveling clerks passed through Holland, where they easily procured a passage to England.

Louis Bonaparte, conceiving that the King of Holland ought to sacrifice the interests of his new subjects to the wishes of his brother, was at first very lenient as to the disastrous Continental system. But at this Napoleon soon manifested his displeasure, and about the end of the year 1806 Louis was reduced to the necessity of ordering the strict observance of the blockade. The facility with which the travelers of French commercial houses passed from Holland to England gave rise to other alarms on the part of the French Government. It was said that since Frenchmen could so easily pass from the Continent to Great Britain, the agents of the English Cabinet might, by the same means, find their way to the Continent. Accordingly the consuls were directed to keep a watchful eye, not only upon individuals who evidently came from England, but upon those who might by any possibility come from that country. This plan was all very well, but how was it to be put into execution? . . . The Continent was, nevertheless, inundated with articles of English manufacture, for this simple reason, that, however powerful may be the will of a sovereign, it is still less powerful and less lasting than the wants of a people. The Continental system reminded me of the law created by an ancient legislator, who, for a crime which he conceived could not possibly be committed, condemned the person who should be guilty of it to throw a bull over Mount Taurus.

It is not my present design to trace a picture of the state of Europe at the close of 1806. I will merely throw together a few facts which came to my knowledge at the time, and which I find in my correspondence. I have already mentioned that the Emperor arrived at Warsaw on the 1st of January. During his stay at Posen he had, by virtue of a treaty concluded with the Elector of Saxony, founded a new kingdom, and consequently extended his power in Germany, by the annexation of the new Kingdom of Saxony to the Confederation of the Rhine. By the terms of this treaty Saxony, so justly famed for her cavalry, was to furnish the Emperor with a contingent of 20,000 men and horses.

It was quite a new spectacle to the Princes of Germany, all accustomed to old habits of etiquette, to see an upstart sovereign treat them as subjects, and even oblige them to consider themselves as such. Those famous Saxons, who had made Charlemagne tremble, threw themselves on the protection of the Emperor; and the alliance of the head of the House of Saxony was not a matter of indifference to Napoleon, for the new King was, on account of his age, his tastes, and his character, more revered than any other German Prince.

From the moment of Napoleon's arrival at Warsaw until the commencement of hostilities against the Russians he was continually solicited to reestablish the throne of Poland, and to restore its chivalrous independence to the ancient empire of the Jagellons. A person who was at that time in Warsaw told me that the Emperor was in the greatest uncertainty as to what he should do respecting Poland. He was entreated to reestablish that ancient and heroic kingdom; but he came to no decision, preferring, according to custom, to submit to events, that he might appear to command them. At Warsaw, indeed, the Emperor passed a great part of his time in fetes and reviews, which, however, did not prevent him from watching, with his eagle eye, every department of the public service, both interior and exterior. He himself was in the capital of Poland, but his vast influence was present everywhere. I heard Duroc say, when we were conversing together about the campaign of Tilsit, that Napoleon's activity and intelligence were never more conspicuously developed.

One very remarkable feature of the imperial wars was, that, with the exception of the interior police, of which Fouché was the soul, the whole government of France was at the headquarters of the Emperor. At Warsaw Napoleon's attention was not only occupied with the affairs of his army, but he directed the whole machinery of the French Government just the same as if he had been in Paris. Daily estafettes, and frequently the useless auditors of the Council of State, brought him reports more or less correct, and curious disclosures which were frequently the invention of the police. The portfolios of the Ministers arrived every week, with the exception of those of the Minister for Foreign Affairs and the Minister of the War Department; the former had first stopped at Mayence with the Empress, but had been called on to Warsaw; and the latter, Clarke, was, for the misfortune of Berlin, governor of that city. This state of things lasted during the ten months of the Emperor's absence from Paris. Louis XIV. said, "I am myself the State." Napoleon did not say this; but, in fact, under his reign the Government of France was always at his headquarters. This circumstance had well-nigh proved fatal to him, on the occasion of the extraordinary conspiracy of Malet, with some points of which I alone, perhaps, am thoroughly acquainted. The Emperor employed the month of January in military preparations for the approaching attack of the Russians, but at the same time he did not neglect the business of the cabinet: with him nothing was suffered to linger in arrear.

While Napoleon was at Warsaw a battle was not the only thing to be thought about; affairs were much more complicated than during the campaign of Vienna. It was necessary, on the one hand, to observe Prussia, which was occupied; and on the other to anticipate the Russians, whose movements indicated that they were inclined to strike the first blow. In the preceding campaign Austria, before the taking of Vienna, was engaged alone. The case was different now: Austria had had only soldiers; and Prussia, as Blücher declared to me, was beginning to have citizens. There was no difficulty in returning from Vienna, but a great deal in returning from Warsaw, in case of failure, notwithstanding the creation of the Kingdom of Saxony, and the provisional government given to Prussia, and to the other States of Germany which we had conquered. None of these considerations escaped the penetration of Napoleon: nothing was omitted in the notes, letters, and official correspondence which came to me from all quarters. Receiving, as I did, accurate information from my own correspondents of all that was passing in Germany, it often happened that I transmitted to the Government the same news which it transmitted to me, not supposing that I previously knew it. Thus, for example, I thought I was apprising the Government of the arming of Austria, of which I received information from headquarters a few days after.

During the Prussian campaign Austria played precisely the same waiting game which Prussia had played clueing the campaign of Austria. As Prussia had, before the battle of Austerlitz, awaited the success or defeat of the French to decide whether she should remain neutral or declare herself against France, so Austria, doubtless supposing that Russia would be more fortunate as the ally of Prussia than she had been as her ally, assembled a corps of 40,000 men in Bohemia. That corps was called an army of observation; but the nature of these armies of observation is well known; they belong to the class of armed neutralities, like the ingenious invention of sanitary cordons. The fact is, that the 40,000 men assembled in Bohemia were destined to aid and assist the Russians in case they should be successful (and who can blame the Austrian Government for wishing to wash away the shame of the Treaty of Presburg?). Napoleon had not a moment to lose, but this activity required no spur; he had hastened the battle of Austerlitz to anticipate Prussia, and he now found it necessary to anticipate Russia in order to keep Austria in a state of indecision.

The Emperor, therefore, left Warsaw about the end of January, and immediately gave orders for engaging the Russian army in the beginning of February; but, in spite of his desire of commencing the attack, he was anticipated. On the 8th of February, at seven in the morning, he was attacked by the Russians, who advanced during a terrible storm of snow, which fell in large flakes. They approached Preussich-Eylau, where the Emperor was, and the Imperial Guard stopped the Russian column. Nearly the whole French army was engaged in that battle-one of the most sanguinary ever fought in Europe. The corps commanded by Bernadotte was not engaged, in the contest; it had been stationed on the left at Mohrungen, whence it menaced Dantzic. The issue of the battle would have been very different had the four, divisions of infantry and the two of cavalry composing Bernadotte's corps arrived in time; but unfortunately the officer instructed to convey orders to Bernadotte to march without delay on Preussich-Eylau was taken by a body of Cossacks; Bernadotte, therefore, did not arrive. Bonaparte, who always liked to throw blame on some one if things did not turn out exactly as he wished, attributed the doubtful success of the day to the absence of Bernadotte; in this he was right; but to make his absence a reproach to that Marshal was a gross injustice. Bernadotte was accused of not having been willing to march on Preussich-Eylau, though, as it was alleged, General d'Hautpoult had informed him of the necessity of his presence. But how can that fact be ascertained, since General d'Hautpoult was killed on that same day? Who can assure us that that General had been able to communicate with the Marshal?

Those who knew Bonaparte, his cunning, and the artful advantage he would sometimes take of words which he attributed to the dead, will easily solve the enigma. The battle of Eylau was terrible. Night came on—Bernadotte's corps was instantly, but in vain, expected; and after a great loss the French army had the melancholy honour of passing the night on the field of battle. Bernadotte at length arrived, but too late. He met the enemy, who were retreating without the fear of being molested towards Konigsberg, the only capital remaining to Prussia. The King of Prussia was then at Memel, a small port on the Baltic, thirty leagues from Konigsberg.

After the battle of Eylau both sides remained stationary, and several days elapsed without anything remarkable taking place. The offers of peace made by the Emperor, with very little earnestness it is true, were disdainfully rejected, as if a victory disputed with Napoleon was to be regarded as a triumph. The battle of Eylau seemed to turn the heads of the Russians, who chanted Te Deum on the occasion. But while the Emperor was making preparations to advance, his diplomacy was taking effect in a distant quarter, and raising up against Russia an old and formidable enemy. Turkey declared war against her. This was a powerful diversion, and obliged Russia to strip her western frontiers to secure a line of defence on the south.

Some time after General Gardanne set out on the famous embassy to Persia; for which the way had been paved by the success of the mission of my friend, Amedee Jaubert. This embassy was not merely one of those pompous legations such as Charlemagne, Louis XIV., and Louis XVI. received from the Empress Irene, the King of Siam, and Tippoo Saib. It was connected with ideas which Bonaparte had conceived at the very dawn of his power. It was, indeed, the light from the East which fast enabled him to see his greatness in perspective; and that light never ceased to fix his attention and dazzle his imagination. I know well that Gardanne's embassy was at first conceived on a much grander scale than that on which it was executed. Napoleon had resolved to send to the Shah of Persia 4000 infantry, commanded by chosen and experienced officers, 10,000 muskets, and 50 pieces, of cannon; and I also know that orders were given for the execution of this design. The avowed object of the Emperor was to enable the Shah of Persia to make an important diversion, with 80,000 men, in, the eastern provinces of Russia. But there was likewise another, an old and constant object, which was always, uppermost in Napoleon's mind, namely the wish to strike at England in the very heart of her Asiatic possessions. Such was the principal motive of Gardanne's mission, but circumstances did not permit the Emperor, to, give, it, all the importance he desired. He contented himself with sending a few officers of engineers and artillery, to Persia, who, on their arrival, were astonished at the number of English they found there.

CHAPTER XI

1807

Meanwhile the internal affairs of the towns over which my diplomatic jurisdiction extended soon gave me more employment than ever. The greatest misfortune of the Empire was, perhaps, the abuse of the right arrogated by the wearers of epaulettes. My situation gave me an opportunity of observing all the odious character of a military government. Another in my place could not have done all that I did. I say this confidently, for my situation was a distinct and independent one, as Bonaparte had told me: Being authorised to correspond directly with the Emperor; the military chiefs feared, if they did not yield to my just representations, that I would made private reports; this apprehension was wonderfully useful in enabling me to maintain the rights of the towns, which had adopted me as their first citizen.

A circumstance occurred in which I had to defend the rights of the diplomatic and commercial agents against the pretensions of military power. Marshal Brune during his government at Hamburg, went to Bremman. to watch the strict execution of the illusive blockade against England. The Marshal acting no doubt, in conformity with the instructions of Clarke, then Minister of War and Governor of Berlin, wished to arrogate the right of deciding on the captures made by our cruisers.

He attempted to prevent the Consul Lagau from selling the confiscated ships in order to sell them himself. Of this M. Lagau complained to me. The more I observed a disposition to encroach on the part of the military authorities, the more I conceived it necessary to maintain the rights of the consuls, and to favour their influence, without which they would have lost their consideration. To the complaints of M. Lagau I replied, "That to him alone belonged the right of deciding, in the first instance, on the fate of the ships; that he could not be deprived of that right without changing the law; that he was free to sell the confiscated Prussian ships; that Marshall Brune was at Bremen only for the execution of the decree respecting the blockade of England, and that he ought not to interfere in business unconnected with that decree." Lagau showed this letter to Brune, who then allowed him to do as he wished; but it was an affair of profit, and the Marshal for a long time owed me a grudge.

Bernadotte was exceedingly disinterested, but he loved to be talked about. The more the Emperor endeavoured to throw accusations upon him, the more he was anxious to give publicity to all his actions. He sent to me an account of the brilliant affair of Braunsburg, in which a division of the first corps had been particularly distinguished. Along with this narrative he sent me a note in the following terms:—"I send you, my dear. Minister, an account of the affair of Braunsburg. You will, perhaps, think proper to publish it. In that case I shall be obliged by your getting it inserted in the Hamburg journals," I did so. The injustice of the Emperor, and the bad way in which he spoke of Bernadotte, obliged the latter,—for the sake of his own credit, to make the truth known to the world.

I have already mentioned that I received an order from the Emperor to supply 50,000 cloaks for the army. With this order, which was not the only one I received of the same kind, some circumstances were connected which I may take the present opportunity of explaining.

The Emperor gave me so many orders for army clothing that all that could be supplied by the cities of Hamburg, Bremen, and Lübeck would have been insufficient for executing the commissions. I entered into a treaty with a house in Hamburg, which I authorised, in spite of the Berlin decree, to bring cloth and leather from England. Thus I procured these articles in a sure and cheap way. Our troops might have perished of cold had the Continental system and the absurd mass of inexecutable decrees relative to English merchandise been observed.

The Director of the Customs at Hamburg got angry, but I held firm: my cloths and my leather arrived; cloaks, coats; boots, all were promptly made, and our soldiers thus were sheltered from the severity of the season. To preserve peace with the Imperial Custom-house I wrote to M. Collie, then Director-General, that M. Eudel having wished to put in execution the law of the 10th Brumaire and complaints had been made on every side. Marshal Brune asked for my opinion on this matter, and I gave it to him. I declared to M. Collie that the full execution of the decree of 31st October 1796 was impracticable, injurious to France, and to the Hanseatic Towns, without doing harm to England. Indeed, what said article 5 of this law? "All goods imported from foreign countries, whatever may be their origin, are to be considered as coming from English manufacturers." According to this article France was a foreign country for the Hanseatic Towns, and none of the objects enumerated in this article ought to enter Hamburg! But the town received from England a large quantity of fine cloths, buttons; ironmongery, toys, china; and from France only clocks, bronzes, jewellery, ribbons, bonnets, gauzes and gloves. "Let," said I to M. Eudel, "the Paris Duane be asked what that town alone exports in matters of this sort and it will be seen how important it is not to stop a trade all the more profitable to France, as the workmanship forms the greatest part of the price of the goods which make up this trade. What would happen if the importation of these goods were absolutely prohibited in Hamburg? The consignments would cease, and one of the most productive sources of trade for France, and especially for Paris would be cut off."

At this time neither Hamburg nor its territory had any manufacture of cloth. All woollen stuffs were prohibited, according to M. Eudel, and still my duty was to furnish, and I had furnished, 50,000 cloaks for the Grand Army. In compliance with a recent Imperial decree I had to have made without delay 16,000 coats, 37,000 waistcoats, and the Emperor required of me 200,000 pairs of boots, besides the 40,000 pairs I had sent in. Yet M. Eudel said that tanned and worked leather ought not to enter Hamburg! If such a ridiculous application of the law of 1796 had been made it would have turned the decree of 21st November 1796 against France, without fulfilling its object.

These reflections, to which I added other details, made the Government conclude that I was right, and I traded with England to the great advantage of the armies, which were well clothed and shod. What in the world can be more ridiculous than commercial laws carried out to one's own detriment?

At the beginning of 1807 my occupations at Hamburg were divided between the furnishing of supplies for the army and the inspection of the emigrants, whom Fouché pretended to dread in order to give greater importance to his office.

I never let slip an opportunity of mitigating the rigour of Fouché's orders, which, indeed, were sometimes so absurd that I did not attempt to execute them. Of this an instance occurs to my recollection. A printer at Hamburg had been arrested on the charge of having printed a libel in the German language. The man was detained in prison because, very much to his honour, he would not disclose the name of the writer of the pamphlet. I sent for him and questioned him. He told me, with every appearance of sincerity, that he had never but once seen the man who had brought him the manuscript. I was convinced of the truth of what he said, and I gave an order for his liberation. To avoid irritating the susceptibility of the Minister of Police I wrote to him the following few lines:—"The libel is the most miserable rhapsody imaginable. The author, probably with the view of selling his pamphlet in Holstein, predicts that Denmark will conquer every other nation and become the greatest kingdom in the world. This alone will suffice to prove to you how little clanger there is in rubbish written in the style of the Apocalypse."

After the battle of Eylau I received a despatch from M. de Talleyrand, to which was added an account in French of that memorable battle, which was more fatal to the conqueror than to the other party,—I cannot say the conquered in speaking of the Russians, the more especially when I recollect the precautions which were then taken throughout Germany to make known the French before the Russian version. The Emperor was exceedingly anxious that every one should view that event as he himself viewed it. Other accounts than his might have produced an unfavourable impression in the north. I therefore had orders to publish that account. I caused 2000 copies of it to be issued, which were more than sufficient for circulation in the Hanse Towns and their territories.

The reader will perhaps complain that I have been almost silent with respect to the grand manoeuvres of the French army from the battle of Eylau to that of Friedland, where, at all events, our success was indisputable. There was no necessity for printing favourable versions of that event, and, besides, its immense results were soon felt throughout Europe. The interview at Tilsit is one of the culminating points of modern history, and the waters of the Niemen reflected the image of Napoleon at the height of his glory. The interview between the two Emperors at Tilsit, and the melancholy situation of the King of Prussia, are generally known. I was made acquainted with but few secret details relative to those events, for Rapp had gone to Dantzic, and it was he who most readily communicated to me all that the Emperor said and did, and all that was passing around him.[225] I, however, learned one

225 Savory gives the following account of the interview between Napoleon and Alexander at Tilsit. "The Emperor Napoleon, whose courtesy was manifest in all his actions, ordered a large raft to be floated in the middle of the river, upon which was constructed a room well covered in and elegantly decorated having two doors on opposite aides, each of which opened into an antechamber. The work could not have been better executed in Paris. The roof was surmounted by two weathercocks: one displaying the eagle of Russia, and the other the eagle of France. The two outer doors were also surmounted by the eagles of the two countries. "The raft was precisely in the middle of the river, with the two doors of the salon facing the two opposite banks. "The two sovereigns appeared on the banks of the river, and embarked at the same moment But the Emperor Napoleon having a good boat, manned by marines of the Guard, arrived first on the raft, entered the room, and went to the opposite door, which he opened, and then stationed himself on the edge of the raft to receive the Emperor Alexander, who had not yet arrived, not having each good rowers as the Emperor Napoleon. "The two Emperors met in the most amicable way, et least to all appearance. They remained together for a considerable time, and then took leave of each other with as friendly an air as that with which they had met. "Next day the Emperor of Russia established himself at Tilsit with a battalion of his Guard. Orders were given for evacuating that part of the town where he and his battalion were to be quartered; and, though we were very much pressed for room, no

circumstance peculiarly worthy of remark which occurred in the Emperor's apartments at Tilsit the first time he received a visit from the King of Prussia. That unfortunate monarch, who was accompanied by Queen Louisa, had taken refuge in a mill beyond the town. This was his sole habitation, whilst the Emperors occupied the two portions of the town, which is divided by the Niemen. The fact I am about to relate reached me indirectly through the medium of an offices of the Imperial Guard, who was on duty in Napoleon's apartments and was an eye-witness of it. When the Emperor Alexander visited Napoleon they continued for a long time in conversation on a balcony below, where as immense crowd hailed their meeting with enthusiastic shouts. Napoleon commenced the conversation, as he did the year preceding with the Emperor of Austria, by speaking of the uncertain fate of war. Whilst they were conversing the King of Prussia was announced. The King's emotion was visible, and may easily be imagined; for as hostilities were suspended, and his territory in possession of the French, his only hope was in the generosity of the conqueror. Napoleon himself, it is said, appeared moved by his situation, and invited him, together with the Queen, to dinner. On sitting down to table Napoleon with great gallantry told the beautiful Queen that he would restore to her Silesia, a province which she earnestly wished should be retained in the new arrangements which were necessarily about to take place.[226]

---

encroachment on the space allotted to the Russians was thought of. "On the day the Emperor Alexander, entered Tilsit the whole army was under arms. The Imperial Guard was drawn out in two lines of three deep from the landing-place to the Emperor Napoleon's quarters, and from thence to the quarters of the Emperor of Russia. A salute of 100 guns was fired the moment Alexander stepped ashore on the spot where the Emperor Napoleon was waiting to receive him. The latter carried his attention to his visitor so far as to send from his quarters the furniture for Alexander's bedchamber. Among the articles sent was a camp-bed belonging to the Emperor, which he presented to Alexander, who appeared much pleased with the gift. "This meeting; the first which history records of the same kind and of equal importance, attracted visitors to Tilsit from 100 leagues round. M. de Talleyrand arrived, and after the observance of the usual ceremonies business began to be discussed." (Memoirs of the Duc de Rovigo, tome iii. p. 117). "When," said Napoleon, "I was at Tilsit with the Emperor Alexander and the King of Prussia, I was the most ignorant of the three in military affairs. These two sovereigns, especially the King of Prussia, were completely 'au fait' as to the number of buttons there ought to be in front of a jacket, how many behind, and the manner in which the skirts ought to be cut. Not a tailor in the army knew better than King Frederick how many measures of cloth it took to make a jacket. In fact," continued he laughing, "I was nobody in comparison with them. They continually tormented me about matters belonging to tailors, of which I was entirely ignorant, although, in order not to affront them, I answered just as gravely as if the fate of an army depended upon the cut of a jacket. When I went to see the King of Prussia, instead of a library, I found that he had a large room, like an arsenal, furnished with shelves and pegs; on which were hung fifty or sixty jackets of different patterns. Every day he changed his fashion and put on a different one. He attached more importance to this than was necessary for the salvation of a kingdom." (O'Meara's Napoleon in Exile.)

226 Las Cases mentions that at the time of the treaty of Tilsit Napoleon wrote to the Empress Josephine as follows: "'The Queen of Prussia is really a charming woman. She is fond of coquetting with me; but do not be jealous: I am like oilcloth, along which everything of this

The treaty of peace concluded at Tilsit between France and Russia, on the 7th of July, and ratified two days after, produced no less striking a change in the geographical division of Europe than had been effected the year preceding by the Treaty of Presburg. The treaty contained no stipulation dishonourable to Russia, whose territory was preserved inviolate; but how was Prussia treated? Some historians, for the vain pleasure of flattering by posthumous praises the pretended moderation of Napoleon, have almost reproached him for having suffered some remnants of the monarchy of the great Frederick to survive. There is, nevertheless, a point on which Napoleon has been wrongfully condemned, at least with reference to the campaign of 1807. It has been said that he should at that period have re-established the kingdom of Poland; and certainly there is every reason to regret, for the interests of France and Europe, that it was not re-established. But when a desire, even founded on reason, is not carried into effect, should we conclude that the wished-for object ought to be achieved in defiance of all obstacles? At that time, that is to say, during the campaign of Tilsit, insurmountable obstacles existed.

If, however, by the Treaty of Tilsit, the throne of Poland was not restored to serve as a barrier between old Europe and the Empire of the Czars, Napoleon founded a Kingdom of Westphalia, which he gave to the young 'ensigne de vaisseau' whom he had scolded as a schoolboy, and whom he now made a King, that he might have another crowned prefect under his control. The Kingdom of Westphalia was composed of the States of Hesse-Cassel, of a part of the provinces taken from Prussia by the moderation of the Emperor, and of the States of Paderborn, Fulda, Brunswick, and a part of the Electorate of Hanover. Napoleon, at the same time, though he did not like to do things by halves, to avoid touching the Russian and Austrian provinces of old Poland, planted on the banks of the Vistula the Grand Duchy of Warsaw, which he gave to the King of Saxony, with the intention of increasing or destroying it afterwards as he might find convenient. Thus he allowed the Poles to hope better things for the future, and ensured to himself partisans in the north should the chances of fortune call him thither. Alexander, who was cajoled even more than his father had been by what I may call the political coquetry of Napoleon, consented to all these arrangements, acknowledged 'in globo' all the kings crowned by the Emperor, and accepted some provinces which had belonged to his despoiled ally, the King of Prussia, doubtless by way of consolation for not having been able to get more restored to Prussia. The two Emperors parted the best friends in the world; but the Continental system was still in existence.

---

sort elides without penetrating. It would cost me too dear to play the gallant' "On this subject an anecdote was related in the salon of Josephine. It was said that the Queen of Prussia one day had a beautiful rose in her hand, which the Emperor asked her to give him. The Queen hesitated for a few moments, and then presented it to him, saying, 'Why should I so readily grant what you request, while you remain deaf to all my entreaties?' (She alluded to the fortress of Magdeburg, which she had earnestly solicited)." (Memorial de St. Helene).

CHAPTER XII

1807

The Treaty of Tilsit, as soon as it was known at Altona, spread consternation amongst the emigrants. As to the German Princes, who were awaiting the issue of events either at Altolna or Hamburg, when they learned that a definitive treaty of peace had been signed between France and Russia, and that two days after the Treaty of Tilsit the Prussian monarchy was placed at the mercy of Napoleon, every courier that arrived threw them into indescribable agitation. It depended on the Emperor's will whether they were to be or not to be. The Duke of Mecklenburg- Schwerin had not succeeded in getting himself re-established in his states, by an exceptional decision, like the Duke of Weimar; but at length he obtained the restitution of his territory at the request of the Emperor Alexander, and on the 28th of July he quitted Hamburg to return to his Duchy.

The Danish charge d'affaires communicated to me about the same time an official report from his Government. This report announced that on Monday, the 3d of August, a squadron consisting of twelve ships of the line and twelve frigates, commanded by Admiral Gambier, had passed the Sound. The rest of the squadron was seen in the Categat. At the same time the English troops which were in the island of Rugen had reembarked. We could not then conceive what enterprise this considerable force had been sent upon. But our uncertainty was soon at an end. M. Didelot, the French Ambassador at Copenhagen, arrived at Hamburg, at nine o'clock in the evening of the 12th of August. He had been fortunate enough to pass through the Great Belt, though in sight of the English, without being stopped. I forwarded his report to Paris by an extraordinary courier.

The English had sent 20,000 men and twenty-seven vessels into the Baltic; Lord Cathcart commanded the troops. The coast of Zealand was blockaded by ninety vessels. Mr. Jackson, who had been sent by England to negotiate with Denmark, which she feared would be invaded by the French troops, supported the propositions he was charged to offer to Denmark by a reference to this powerful British force. Mr. Jackson's proposals had for their object nothing less than to induce the King of Denmark to place in the custody of England the whole of his ships and naval stores. They were, it is true, to be kept in deposit, but the condition contained the words, "until the conclusion of a general peace," which rendered the period of their restoration uncertain. They were to be detained until such precautions should be no longer necessary. A menace and its execution followed close upon this demand. After a noble but useless resistance, and a terrific bombardment, Copenhagen surrendered, and the Danish fleet was destroyed. It would be difficult to find in history a more infamous and revolting instance of the abuse of power against weakness.

Sometime after this event a pamphlet entitled "Germania" appeared, which I translated and sent to the Emperor. It was eloquently written, and expressed the indignation which the conduct of England had excited in the author as in every one else.[227]

227 "That expedition," said Napoleon at St. Helena, "showed great energy on the part of your

I have stated what were the principal consequences of the Treaty of Tilsit; it is more than probable that if the bombardment of Copenhagen had preceded the treaty the Emperor would have used Prussia even worse than he did. He might have erased her from the list of nations; but he did not do so, out of regard to the Emperor Alexander. The destruction of Prussia was no new project with Bonaparte. I remember an observation of his to M. Lemercier upon that subject when we first went to reside at Malmaison. M. Lemercier had been reading to the First Consul some poem in which Frederick the Great was spoken of. "You seem to admire him greatly," said Bonaparte to M. Lemercier; "what do you find in him so astonishing? He is not equal to Turenne."—"General," replied M. Lemercier, "it is not merely the warrior that I esteem in Frederick; it is impossible to refrain from admiring a man who was a philosopher even on the throne." To this the First Consul replied, in a half ill-humoured tone, "Certainly, Lemercier; but Frederick's philosophy shall not prevent me from erasing his kingdom from the map of Europe." The kingdom of Frederick the Great was not, however, obliterated from the map, because the Emperor of Russia would not basely abandon a faithful ally who had incurred with him the chances of fortune. Prussia then bitterly had to lament the tergiversations which had prevented her from declaring herself against France during the campaign of Austerlitz.

Napoleon returned to Paris about the end of July after an absence of ten months, the longest he had yet made since he had been at the head of the French Government, whether as Consul or Emperor. The interview at Tilsit, the Emperor Alexander's friendship, which was spoken of everywhere in terms of exaggeration, and the peace established on the Continent, conferred on Napoleon a moral influence in public opinion which he had not possessed since his coronation. Constant in his hatred of deliberative assemblies, which he had often termed collections of babblers, ideologists, and phrasemongers, Napoleon, on his return to Paris, suppressed the Tribunate, which had been an annoyance to him ever since the first day of his elevation. The Emperor, who was 'skillful above all men in speculating on the favourable disposition of opinion, availed himself at this conjuncture of the enthusiasm produced by his interview on the Niemen. He therefore discarded from the fundamental institutions of the government that which still retained the shadow of a popular character. But it was necessary that he should possess a Senate merely to vote men; a mute Legislative Body to vote money; that there should be no opposition in the one and no criticism in the other; no control over him of any description; the power of arbitrarily doing whatever he pleased; an enslaved press;—this was what Napoleon wished, and this he obtained. But the month of March 1814 resolved the question of absolute power!

In the midst of these great affairs, and while Napoleon was dreaming of universal monarchy, I beheld in a less extensive sphere the inevitable consequences of the ambition of a single

---

Ministers: but setting aside the violation of the laws of, nations which you committed—for in fact it was nothing but a robbery—I think that it was; injurious to your interests, as it made the Danish nation irreconcilable enemies to you, and in fact shut you out of the north for three years. When I heard of it I said, I am glad of it, as it will embroil England irrecoverably with the Northern Powers. The Danes being able to join me with sixteen sail of the line was of but little consequence. I had plenty of ships, and only wanted seamen, whom you did not take, and whom I obtained afterwards, while by the expedition your Ministers established their characters as faithless, and as persons with whom no engagements, no laws were binding." (Voice from St. Helena.)

man. Pillage and robbery were carried on in all parts over which my diplomatic jurisdiction extended. Rapine seemed to be legally authorised, and was perpetrated with such fury, and at the same time with such ignorance, that the agents were frequently unacquainted with the value of the articles which they seized. Thus, for example, the Emperor ordered the seizure at Hamburg, Bremen, and Lübeck of all English merchandise, whatever might be its nature or origin. The Prince of Neufchatel (Berthier) wrote to me from the Emperor that I must procure 10,000,000 francs from the Hanse Towns. M. Daru, the Intendant-General, whose business it was to collect this sort of levy, which Napoleon had learned to make in Egypt, wrote to urge me to obtain a prompt and favourable decision. The unfortunate towns which I was thus enjoined to oppress had already suffered sufficiently. I had obtained, by means of negotiation, more than was demanded for the ransom of the English merchandise, which had been seized according to order. Before I received the letters of M. Darn and the Prince of Neufchatel I had obtained from Hamburg 16,000,000 instead of 10,000,000, besides nearly 3,000,000 from Bremen and Lübeck. Thus I furnished the Government with 9,000,000 more than had been required, and yet I had so managed that those enormous sacrifices were not overoppressive to those who made them. I fixed the value of the English merchandise because I knew that the high price at which it sold on the Continent would not only cover the proposed ransom but also leave a considerable profit. Such was the singular effect of the Continental system that when merchandise was confiscated, and when afterwards the permission to sell it freely was given, the price fetched at the sale was so large that the loss was covered, and even great advantage gained.

Peace being concluded with Russia it was necessary to make choice of an Ambassador, not only to maintain the new relations of amity between Napoleon and Alexander, but likewise to urge on the promised intervention of Russia with England,—to bring about reconciliation and peace between the Cabinets of Paris and London. The Emperor confided this mission to Caulaincourt, with respect to whom there existed an unfounded prejudice relating to some circumstances which preceded the death of the Duc d'Enghien. This unfortunate and unjust impression had preceded Caulaincourt to St. Petersburg, and it was feared that he would not experience the reception due to the French Ambassador and to his own personal qualities. I knew at the time, from positive information, that after a short explanation with Alexander that monarch retained no suspicion unfavourable to our Ambassador, for whom he conceived and maintained great esteem and friendship.

Caulaincourt's mission was not, in all respects, easy of fulfilment, for the invincible repugnance and reiterated refusal of England to enter into negotiations with France through the medium of Russia was one of the remarkable circumstances of the period of which I am speaking. I knew positively that England was determined never to allow Napoleon to possess himself of the whole of the Continent,—a project which he indicated too undisguisedly to admit of any doubt respecting it. For two years he had indeed advanced with rapid strides; but England was not discouraged. She was too well aware of the irritation of the sovereigns and the discontent of the people not be certain that when she desired it, her lever of gold would again raise up and arm the Continent against the encroaching power of Napoleon. He, on his part, perceiving that all his attempts were fruitless, and that England would listen to no proposals, devised fresh plans for raising up new enemies against England.

It probably is not forgotten that in 1801 France compelled Portugal to make common cause with her against England. In 1807 the Emperor did again what the First Consul had done. By an inexplicable fatality Junot obtained the command of the troops which were marching against Portugal. I say against Portugal, for that was the fact, though France represented herself as a protector to deliver Portugal from the influence of England. Be that as it may, the choice which the Emperor made of a commander astonished everybody. Was Junot, a compound of vanity and mediocrity, the fit man to be entrusted with the command of an army in a distant country, and under circumstances in which great political and military talents were requisite? For my own part, knowing Junot's incapacity, I must acknowledge that his appointment astonished me. I remember one day, when I was speaking on the subject to Bernadotte, he showed me a letter he had received from Paris, in which it was said that the Emperor had sent Junot to Portugal only for the sake of depriving him of the government of Paris. Junot annoyed Napoleon by his bad conduct, his folly, and his incredible extravagance. He was alike devoid of dignity—either in feeling or conduct. Thus Portugal was twice the place of exile selected by Consular and Imperial caprice: first, when the First Consul wished to get rid of the familiarity of Lannes; and next, when the Emperor grew weary of the misconduct of a favourite.

The invasion of Portugal presented no difficulty. It was an armed promenade and not a war; but how many events were connected with the occupation of that country! The Prince Regent of Portugal, unwilling to act dishonourably to England, to which he was allied by treaties; and unable to oppose the whole power of Napoleon, embarked for Brazil, declaring that all defence was useless. At the same time he recommended his subjects to receive the French troops in a friendly manner, and said that he consigned to Providence the consequences of an invasion which was without a motive. He was answered in the Emperor's name that, Portugal being the ally of England, we were only carrying on hostilities against, the latter country by invading his dominions.

It was in the month of November that the code of French jurisprudence, upon which the most learned legislators had indefatigably laboured, was established as the law of the State, under the title of the Code Napoleon. Doubtless this legislative monument will redound to Napoleon's honour in history; but was it to be supposed that the same laws would be equally applicable throughout so vast an extent as that comprised within the French Empire? Impossible as this was, as soon as the Code Napoleon way promulgated I received orders to establish it in the Hanse Towns.[228]

---

228 This great code of Civil Law was drawn up under Napoleon's orders and personal superintendence. Much had been prepared under the Convention, and the chief merits of it were due to the labours of such men as Tronchet; Partatis, Bigot de Preameneu, Maleville, Cambacérès, etc. But it was debated under and by Napoleon, who took a lively interest in it. It was first called the "Code Civil," but is 1807 was named "Code Napoleon," or eventually "Les Cinq Codes de Napoleon." When completed in 1810 it included five Codes—the Code Civil, decreed March 1803; Code de Procedure Civile, decreed April 1806; Code de Commerce, decreed September 1807; Code d'Instruction Criminelle, decreed November 1808; and the Code Penal, decreed February 1810. It had to be retained by the Bourbons, and its principles have worked and are slowly working their way into the law of every nation. Napoleon was justly proud of this work. The Introduction of the Code into the conquered countries was, as Bourrienne says, made too quickly. Puymaigre, who was employed in the administration of Hamburg after Bourrienne left, says, "I shall always remember the astonishment of the Hamburgers when they were invaded by this cloud of French officials, who, under every form, made researches is their houses, and who came to apply the multiplied demands of the

The long and frequent conversations I had on this subject with the Senators and the most able lawyers of the country soon convinced me of the immense difficulty I should have to encounter, and the danger of suddenly altering habits and customs which had been firmly established by time.

The jury system gave tolerable satisfaction; but the severe punishments assigned to certain offences by the Code were disapproved of. Hence resulted the frequent and serious abuse of men being acquitted whose guilt was evident to the jury, who pronounced them not guilty rather than condemn them to a punishment which was thought too severe. Besides, their leniency had another ground, which was, that the people being ignorant of the new law were not aware of the penalties attached to particular offences. I remember that a man who was accused of stealing a cloak at Hamburg justified himself on the ground that he committed the offence in a fit of intoxication. M. Von Einingen, one of the jury, insisted that the prisoner was not guilty, because, as he said, the Syndic Doormann, when dining with him one day, having drunk more wine than usual, took away his cloak. This defence per Baccho was completely successful. An argument founded on the similarity between the conduct of the Syndic and the accused, could not but triumph, otherwise the little debauch of the former would have been condemned in the person of the latter. This trial, which terminated so whimsically, nevertheless proves that the best and the gravest institutions may become objects of ridicule when suddenly introduced into a country whose habits are not prepared to receive them.

The Romans very wisely reserved in the Capitol a place for the gods of the nations they conquered. They wished to annex provinces and kingdoms to their empire. Napoleon, on the contrary, wished to make his empire encroach upon other states, and to realise the impossible Utopia of ten different nations, all having different customs and languages, united into a single State. Could justice, that safeguard of human rights, be duly administered in the Hanse Towns when those towns were converted into French departments? In these new departments many judges had been appointed who did not understand a word of German, and who had no knowledge of law. The presidents of the tribunals of Lilbeck, Stade, Bremerlehe, and Minden were so utterly ignorant of the German language that it was necessary to explain to them all the pleadings in the council-chamber. Was it not absurd to establish such a judicial system, and above all, to appoint such men in a country

---

fiscal system. Like Proteus, the administration could take any shape. To only speak of my department, which certainly was not the least odious one, for it was opposed to the habits of the Hamburgers and annoyed all the industries, no idea can be formed of the despair of the inhabitants, subjected to perpetual visits, and exposed to be charged with contraventions of the law, of which they knew nothing. "Remembering their former laws, they used to offer to meet a charge of fraud by the proof of their oath, and could not imagine that such a guarantee could be repulsed. When they were independent they paid almost nothing, and such was the national spirit, that in urgent cases when money was wanted the senate taxed every citizen a certain proportion of his income, the tenth or twentieth. A donator presided over the recovery of this tax, which was done in a very strange manner. A box, covered with a carpet, received the offering of every citizen, without any person verifying the sum, and only on the simple moral guarantee of the honesty of the debtor, who himself judged the sum he ought to pay. When the receipt was finished the senate always obtained more than it had calculated on." (Puymaigre, pp, 181.)

so important to France as Hamburg and the Hanse Towns? Add to this the impertinence of some favourites who were sent from Paris to serve official and legal apprenticeships in the conquered provinces, and it may be easily conceived what was the attachment of the people to Napoleon the Great.

CHAPTER XIII

1807-1808

The disorders of Spain, which commenced about the close of the year 1807, in a short time assumed a most complicated aspect. Though far from the theatre of events I obtained an intimate knowledge of all the important facts connected with the extraordinary transactions in the Peninsula. However, as this point of history is one of the most generally, though I cannot say the best, known, I shall omit in my notes and memoranda many things which would be but repetitions to the reading portion of the public. It is a remarkable fact that Bonaparte, who by turns cast his eyes on all the States of Europe, never directed his attention to Spain as long as his greatness was confined to mere projects. Whenever he spoke of his future destiny he alluded to Italy, Germany, the East, and the destruction of the English power; but never to Spain. Consequently, when he heard of the first symptoms of disorder in the Peninsula he paid but little attention to the business, and some time elapsed before he took any part in events which subsequently had so great an influence on his fate.

Godoy reigned in Spain under the name of the imbecile Charles IV. He was an object of execration to all who were not his creatures; and even those whose fate depended upon him viewed him with the most profound contempt. The hatred of a people is almost always the just reward of favourites. What sentiments, therefore, must have been inspired by a man who, to the knowledge of all Spain, owed the favour of the king only to the favours of the queen![229]

Godoy's ascendancy over the royal family was boundless; his power was absolute: the treasures, of America were at his command, and he made the most infamous use of them. In short, he had made the Court of Madrid one of those places to which the indignant muse of Juvenal conducts the mother of Britanicus. There is no doubt that Godoy was one of the principal causes of all the misfortunes which have overwhelmed Spain under so many various forms.

The hatred of the Spaniards against the Prince of the Peace was general. This hatred was shared by the Prince the Asturias[230], who openly declared himself the enemy of Godoy. The latter allied himself with France, from which he hoped to obtain powerful protection against his enemies. This alliance gave rise to great dissatisfaction in Spain, and caused France to be regarded with an unfavourable eye. The Prince of the Asturias was encouraged and supported by the complaints of the Spaniards, who wished to see the overthrow of Godoy's power. Charles IV., on his part, regarded all opposition to the Prince of the Peace as directed against himself, and in November 1807 he accused his son of wishing to dethrone him.

The King of Spain did not confine himself to verbal complaints. He, or rather the Prince of the Peace, acting in his name, arrested the warmest partisans of the Prince of the Asturias.

---

229 Manuel Godoy, originally a private in the guards, became the paramour of Charles IV.'s Queen; then a grandee; and then the supreme ruler of the State.—Editor of 1836 edition.

230 Afterwards Ferdinand VII.

The latter, understanding the sentiments of his father, wrote to Napoleon, soliciting his support. Thus the father and son, at open war, were appealing one against another for the support of him who wished only to get rid of them both, and to put one of his brothers in their place, that he might have one junior more in the college of European kings: but, as I have already mentioned, this new ambition was not premeditated; and if he gave the throne of Spain to his brother Joseph it was only on the refusal of his brother Louis (King of Holland) to accept it.

The Emperor had promised to support Charles IV against his son; and, not wishing to take part in these family quarrels, he had not answered the first letters of the Prince of the Asturias. But finding that the intrigues of Madrid were taking a serious turn, he commenced provisionally by sending troops to Spain. This gave offence to the people, who were averse to the interference of France. In the provinces through which the French troops passed it was asked what was the object: of the invasion. Some attributed it to the Prince of the Peace, others to the Prince of the Asturias; but it excited general indignation, and troubles broke out at Madrid accompanied by all the violence peculiar to the Spanish character.

In these fearful circumstances Godoy proposed that Charles IV. should remove to Seville, where he would be the better enabled to visit the factious with punishment. A proposition from Godoy to his master was, in fact, a command, and Charles IV. accordingly resolved to depart. The people now looked upon Godoy as a traitor. An insurrection broke out, the palace was surrounded, and the Prince of the Peace was on the point of being massacred in an upper apartment, where he had taken refuge.[231] One of the mob had the presence of mind to invoke in his favour the name of the Prince of the Asturias: this saved his life.

Charles IV. did not preserve his crown; he was easily intimidated, and advantage was taken of a moment of alarm to demand that abdication which he had not spirit to refuse. He surrendered up his rights to his son, and thus was overthrown the insolent power of the Prince of the Peace; the favourite was made prisoner, and the Spaniards, who, like all ignorant people, are easily excited, manifested their joy on the occasion with barbarous enthusiasm. Meanwhile the unfortunate King, who had escaped from imaginary rather than real dangers, and who was at first content with having exchanged the right of reigning for the right of living, no sooner found himself in safety than he changed, his mind. He wrote to the Emperor protesting against his abdication, and appealed. to him as the arbiter of his future fate.

During these internal dissensions the French army was continuing its march towards the Pyrenees. Those barriers were speedily crossed, and Murat entered Madrid in the beginning of April 1808. Before I received any despatch from our Government I learned that Murat's presence in Madrid, far from producing a good effect, had only increased the disorder. I

231 French troops had appeared in again some months before, on their way to Portugal, the conquest of which country by Junot was to be aided by Godoy and a Spanish force of 27,000 men, according to a treaty (more disgraceful to the Court of Spain than to Bonaparte) which had been ratified at Fontainebleau on the 27th of October 1807. Charles IV. was little better than an idiot, and Godoy and the French made him believe that Bonaparte world give part, or the whole of Portugal, to Spain. At the time of Junot's march on Lisbon a reserve of 40,000 French troops were assembled at Bayonne— a pretty clear indication, though the factious infatuated Court of Madrid would not see it, that Bonaparte intended to seize the whole of the Peninsula.—Editor of 1838 edition.

obtained this information from a merchant of Lübeck who came to Hamburg on purpose to show me a letter he had received from his correspondent in Madrid. In this letter Spain was said to be a prey which Murat wished to appropriate to himself; and all that afterwards came to my knowledge served only to prove the accuracy of the writer's information. It was perfectly true that Murat wished to conquer Spain for himself, and it is not astonishing that the inhabitants of Madrid should have understood his designs, for he carried his indiscretion so far as openly to express his wish to become King of Spain. The Emperor was informed of this, and gave him to understand, in very significant terms, that the throne of Spain was not destined for him, but that he should not be forgotten in the disposal of other crowns.

However, Napoleon's remonstrances were not sufficient to restrain the imprudence of Murat; and if he did not gain the crown of Spain for himself he powerfully contributed to make Charles IV. lose it. That monarch, whom old habits attached to the Prince of the Peace, solicited the Emperor to liberate his favourite, alleging that he and his family would be content to live in any place of security provided Godoy were with them. The unfortunate Charles seemed to be thoroughly disgusted with greatness.

Both the King and Queen so earnestly implored Godoy's liberation that Murat, whose vanity was flattered by these royal solicitations, took the Prince of the Peace under his protection; but he at the same time declared that, in spite of the abdication of Charles IV., he would acknowledge none but that Prince as King of Spain until he should receive contrary orders from the Emperor. This declaration placed Murat in formal opposition to the Spanish people, who, through their hatred of Godoy, embraced the cause of the heir of the throne; in whose favour Charles IV. had abdicated.

It has been remarked that Napoleon stood in a perplexing situation in this conflict between the King and his son. This is not correct. King Charles, though he afterwards said that his abdication had been forced from him by violence and threats, had nevertheless tendered it. By this act Ferdinand was King, but Charles declared it was done against his will, and he retracted. The Emperor's recognition was wanting, and he, could give or withhold it as he pleased.

In this state of things Napoleon arrived at Bayonne. Thither Ferdinand was also invited to go, under pretence of arranging with the Emperor the differences between his father and himself. It was some time before he could form his determination, but at length his ill-advised friends prevailed on him to set off, and he was caught in the snare. What happened to him, as well as to his father, who repaired to Bayonne with his inseparable friend the Prince of the Peace is well known. Napoleon, who had undertaken to be arbiter between the father and son, thought the best way of settling the difference was to give the disputed throne to his brother Joseph, thus verifying the fable of the "Two Lawyers and the Oyster." The insurrection in Madrid on the 2d of May accelerated the fate of Ferdinand, who was accused of being the author of it; at least this suspicion fell on his friends and adherents.

Charles IV., it was said, would not return to Spain, and solicited an asylum in France. He signed a renunciation of his rights to the crown of Spain, which renunciation was also signed by the Infantas.

Napoleon now issued a decree, appointing "his dearly beloved brother Joseph Napoleon, King of Naples and Sicily, to the crowns of Spain and the Indies." By a subsequent decree, 15th of July, he appointed "his dearly-beloved cousin, Joachim Murat, Grand Duke of Berg, to the throne of Naples and Sicily, which remained vacant by the accession of Joseph Napoleon to the kingdoms of Spain and the Indies." Both these documents are signed Napoleon, and countersigned by the Minister Secretary of State, Maret.

The Prince Royal of Sweden, who was at Hamburg at this time, and the Ministers of all the European power, loudly condemned the conduct of Napoleon with respect to Spain. I cannot say whether or not M. de Talleyrand advised the Emperor not to attempt the overthrow of a branch of the house of Bourbon; his good sense and elevated views might certainly have suggested that advice. But the general opinion was that, had he retained the portfolio of foreign affairs, the Spanish revolution would have terminated with more decorum and good faith than was exhibited in the tragi-comedy acted at Madrid and Bayonne.

After the Treaty of Tilsit and the bonds of friendship which seemed likely to produce a permanent union between the Emperors of France and Russia, the cause of the Bourbons must have been considered irretrievably lost. Indeed, their only hope consisted in the imprudence and folly of him who had usurped their throne, and that hope they cherished. I will here relate what I had the opportunity of learning respecting the conduct of Louis XVIII. after his departure from France; this will naturally bring me to the end of November 1807, at which time I read in the Abeille du Nord published on the 9th of the same month, that the Comte de Lille and the Duc d'Angouleme had set off for England.

The Comte de Provence, as Louis' title then went, left Paris on the 21st of June 1791. He constantly expressed his wish of keeping as near as possible to the frontiers of France. He at first took up his abode at Coblentz, and I knew from good authority that all the emigrants did not regard him with a favourable eye. They could not pardon the wise. principles he had professed at a period when there was yet time to prevent, by reasonable concession, the misfortunes which imprudent irritation brought upon France. When the emigrants, after the campaign of 1792, passed the Rhine, the Comte de Provence resided in the little town of Ham on the Lippe, where he remained until he was persuaded that the people of Toulon had called him to Provence. As he could not, of course, pass through France, Monsieur repaired to the Court of his father-in-law, the King of Sardinia, hoping to embark at Genoa, and from thence to reach the coast of Provence. But the evacuation of Toulon, where the name of Bonaparte was for the first time sounded by the breath of fame, having taken place before he was able to leave Turin, Monsieur remained there four months, at the expiration of which time his father-in-law intimated to him the impossibility of his remaining longer in the Sardinian States. He was afterwards permitted to reside at Verona, where he heard of Louis XVI.'s death. After remaining two years in that city the Senate of Venice forbade his presence in the Venetian States. Thus forced to quit Italy the Comte repaired to the army of Condé.

The cold and timid policy of the Austrian Cabinet afforded no asylum to the Comte de Provence, and he was obliged to pass through Germany; yet, as Louis XVIII. repeated over and over again, ever since the Restoration, "He never intended to shed French blood in Germany for the sake of serving foreign interests." Monsieur had, indeed, too much penetration not to see that his cause was a mere pretext for the powers at war with France. They felt but little for the misfortunes of the Prince, and merely wished to veil their ambition and their hatred of France under the false pretence of zeal for the House of Bourbon.

When the Dauphin died, Louis XVIII. took the title of King of France, and went to Prussia, where he obtained an asylum.[232] But the pretender to the crown of France had not

232 His brother, Charles X., the youngest of the three grandsons of Louis XV. (Louis XVI., Louis XVIII. Charles X.), the Comte d'Artois, afterwards Charles X. emigrated in 1789, and went to Turin and Mantas for 1789 and 1790. In 1791 and 1792 he lived at Coblenta, Worms, Brussels,

yet drained his cup of misfortune. After the 18th Fructidor the Directory required the King of Prussia to send away Louis XVIII., and the Cabinet of Berlin, it must be granted, was not in a situation to oppose the desire of the French Government, whose wishes were commands. In vain Louis XVIII. sought an asylum in the King of Saxony's States. There only remained Russia that durst offer a last refuge to the descendant of Louis XIV. Paul I., who was always in extremes, and who at that time entertained a violent feeling of hatred towards France, earnestly offered Louis XVIII., a residence at Mittau. He treated him with the honours of a sovereign, and loaded him with marks of attention and respect. Three years had scarcely passed when Paul was seized with mad enthusiasm for the man who twelve years later, ravaged his ancient capital, and Louis XVIII. found himself expelled from that Prince's territory with a harshness equal to the kindness with which he had at first been received.

It was during, his three, years' residence at Mittau that Louis XVIII., who was then known by the title of Comte de Lille, wrote to the First Consul those letters which have been referred to in these Memoirs. Prussia, being again solicited, at length consented that Louis XVIII. should reside at Warsaw; but on the accession of Napoleon to the Empire the Prince quitted that residence in order to consult respecting his new situation with the only sovereign who had not deserted him in his misfortune, viz. the King of Sweden. They met at Colmar, and from that city was dated the protest which I have already noticed. Louis XVIII. did not stay long in the States of the King of Sweden. Russia was now on the point of joining her eagles with those of Austria to oppose the new eagles of imperial France. Alexander offered to the Comte de Lille the asylum which Paul had granted to him and afterwards withdrawn. Louis XVIII. accepted the offer, but after the peace of Tilsit, fearing lest Alexander might imitate the second act of his father as well as the first, he plainly saw that he must give up all intention of residing on the Continent; and it was then that I read in the 'Abeille du Nord' the article before alluded to. There is, however, one fact upon which I must insist, because I know it to be true, viz. that it was of his own free will that Louis XVIII. quitted Mittau; and if he was afraid that Alexander would imitate his father's conduct that fear was without foundation. The truth is, that Alexander was ignorant even of the King's intention to go away until he heard from Baron von Driesen, Governor of Mittau, that he had actually departed. Having now stated the truth on this point I have to correct another error, if indeed it be only an error, into which some writers have fallen. It has been falsely alleged that the King left Mittau for the purpose of fomenting fresh troubles in France. The friends of Louis XVIII., who advised him to leave Mittau, had great hopes from the last war. They cherished still greater hopes from the new wars which Bonaparte's ambition could not fail to excite, but they were not so ill-informed respecting the internal condition of France as to expect that disturbances would arise there, or even to believe in the possibility of fomenting them. The pear was not yet ripe for Louis XVIII.

On the 29th of November the contents of a letter which had arrived from London by

---

Vienna, and at Turin. From 1792 to 1812 he lived at Ham on the Lippe at Westphalia at London, and for most of the time at Holyrood, Edinburgh. During this time he visited Russia and Germany, and showed himself on the coast of France. In 1818 he went to Germany, and in 1814 entered France in rear of the allies. In risking his person in the daring schemes of the followers who were giving their lives for the cause of his family he displayed a circumspection which was characterised by them with natural warmth. "Sire, the cowardice of your brother has ruined all;" so Charette is said to have written to Louis XVIII.

way of Sweden were communicated to me. This letter was dated the 3d of November, and contained some particulars respecting the Comte de Lille's arrival in England. That Prince had arrived at Yarmouth on the 31st of October 1807, and it was stated that the King was obliged to wait some time in the port until certain difficulties respecting his landing and the continuance of his journey should be removed. It moreover appeared from this letter that the King of England thought proper to refuse the Comte de Lille permission to go to London or its neighbourhood. The palace of Holyrood in Edinburgh was assigned as his place of residence; and Mr. Ross, secretary to Mr. Canning, conveyed the determination of the King of England to Louis XVIII., at Yarmouth.

The precaution of the English Ministry in not permitting the refugee King to go near London appeared to me remarkable, considering the relative position of the Governments of France and England, and I regarded it as a corroboration of what the Prince Wittgenstein had told me respecting Mr. Canning's inclination for an amicable arrangement. But the moment was approaching when the affairs of Spain were to raise an invincible obstacle to peace, to complicate more than ever the interests of the powers of Europe, and open to Napoleon that vast career of ambition which proved his ruin. He did not allow the hopes of the emigrants to remain chimerical, and the year 1814 witnessed the realization of the prophetic remark made by M. Lemereier, in a conversation with Bonaparte a few days before the foundation of the Empire: "If you get into the bed of the Bourbons, General, you will not lie in it ten year." Napoleon occupied it for nine years and nine months.

Fouché, the grand investigator of the secrets of Europe, did not fail, on the first report of the agitations in Spain, to address to me question on question respecting the Comte de Rechteren, the Spanish Minister at Hamburg, who, however, had left that city, with the permission of his Court, four months after I had entered on my functions. This was going back very far to seek information respecting the affairs of the day. At the very moment when I transmitted a reply to Fouché which was not calculated to please him, because it afforded no ground for suspicion as to the personal conduct of M. de Rechteren, I received from the amiable Josephine a new mark of her remembrance. She sent me the following note:

"M. Milon, who is now in Hamburg, wishes me, my dear Bourrienne, to request that you will use your interest in his favour. I feel the more pleasure in making this request as it affords me an opportunity of renewing the assurance of my regard for you."

Josephine's letter was dated from Fontainebleau, whither the Emperor used to make journeys in imitation of the old Court of France. During these excursions he sometimes partook of the pleasures of the chase, but merely for the sake of reviving an old custom, for in that exercise he found as little amusement as Montaigne did in the game of chess.

At Fontainebleau, as everywhere else, his mind was engaged with the means of augmenting his greatness, but, unfortunately, the exactions he imposed on distant countries were calculated to alienate the affections of the people. Thus, for example, I received an order emanating from him, and transmitted to me by M. Daru, the Intendant-General of the army, that the pay of all the French troops stationed in the Hanse Towns should be defrayed by these towns. I lamented the necessity of making such a communication to the Senates of Bremen, Lübeck, and Hamburg; but my duty compelled me to do so, and I had long been accustomed to fulfil duties even more painful than this. I tried every possible means with the three States, not collectively but separately, to induce them to comply with the measure, in the hope that the assent of one would help me to obtain that of the two others. But, as if they, had been all agreed, I only received evasive expressions of regret.

Knowing as I did, and I may say better than any one else, the hopes and designs of Bonaparte respecting the north of Germany, it was not without pain, nor even without alarm, that I saw him doing everything calculated to convert into enemies the inhabitants of a country which would always have remained quiet had it only been permitted to preserve its neutrality. Among the orders I received were often many which could only have been the result of the profoundest ignorance. For example, I was one day directed to press 3000 seamen in the Hanse Towns. Three thousand seamen out of a population of 200,000! It was as absurd as to think of raising 500,000 sailors in France. This project being impossible, it was of course not executed; but I had some difficulty in persuading the Emperor that a sixth of the number demanded was the utmost the Hanse Towns could supply. Five hundred seamen were accordingly furnished, but to make up that number it was necessary to include many men who were totally unfit for war service.

CHAPTER XIV

1808

In the spring of 1808 a circumstance occurred which gave, me much uneasiness; it was the departure of Bernadotte, Prince of Ponte-Corvo, who received orders to repair to Copenhagen. He left Hamburg on the 8th of March, as he was to reach his destination on the 14th of the same month. The Danish charge d'affaires also received orders to join the Prince, and discharge the functions of King's commissary. It was during his government at Hamburg and his stay in Jutland that Bernadotte unconsciously paved his way to the throne of Sweden. I recollect that he had also his presages and his predestinations. In short, he believed in astrology, and I shall never forget the serious tone in which he one day said to me, "Would you believe, my dear friend, that it was predicted at Paris that I should be a King, but that I must cross the sea to reach my throne?" I could not help smiling with him at this weakness of mind, from which Bonaparte was not far removed. It certainly was not any supernatural influence which elevated Bernadotte to sovereign rank. That elevation was solely due to his excellent character. He had no other talisman than the wisdom of his government, and the promptitude which he always, showed to oppose unjust measures. This it was that united all opinions in his favour.

The bad state of the roads in the north prolonged Bernadotte's journey one day. He set out on the 8th of March; he was expected to arrive at Copenhagen on the 14th, but did not reach there till the 15th. He arrived precisely two hours before the death of Christian, King of Denmark, an event with which he made me acquainted by letter written two days after his arrival.

On the 6th of April following I received a second letter from Bernadotte, in which he desired me to order the Grand Ducal postmaster to keep back all letters addressed to the Spanish troops, who had been placed under his command, and of which the corps of Romana formed part. The postmaster was ordered to keep the letters until he received orders to forward them to their destinations. Bernadotte considered this step indispensable, to prevent the intrigues which he feared might be set on foot in order to shake the fidelity of the Spaniards he commanded. I saw from his despatch that he feared the plotting of Romanillos, who, however, was not a person to cause much apprehension. Romanillos was as commonplace a man as could well be conceived; and his speeches, as well as his writings, were too innocent to create any influence on public opinion.

In addition to the functions with which the Emperor at first invested me, I had to discharge the duties of French Consul-General at Hamburg, and in that character I was obliged to present to the Minister for Foreign Affairs a very singular request, viz. that the judicial notifications, which as Consul-General I had to make known to the people of Hamburg, might be written in a more legible hand. Many of these notifications had been disregarded on account of the impossibility of reading them: With respect to one of them it was declared that it was impossible to discover whether the writing was German, French, or Chinese.

I shall not record all the acts of spoliation committed by second-rate ambitious aspirants who hoped to come in for their share in the division of the Continent: The Emperor's lieutenants regarded Europe as a twelfthcake, but none of them ventured to dispute the best bit with Napoleon. Long would be the litany were I to enregister all the fraud and treachery which they committed, either to augment their fortunes or to win the favour of the chief who wished to have kings for his subjects. The fact is, that all the Princes of Germany displayed the greatest eagerness to range themselves under the protection of Napoleon, by, joining the Confederation of the Rhine. I received from those Princes several letters which served to prove at once the influence of Napoleon in Germany and the facility with which men bend beneath the yoke of a new power. I must say that among the emigrants who remained faithful to their cause there were some who evinced more firmness of character than the foreign Princes. I may mention, for example, M. Hue, the 'valet de chambre' of Louis XVI. I do not intend to deny the high regard I entertained for that faithful servant of the martyred King; but the attentions which I congratulate myself on having shown to an excellent man should not have subjected me to false imputations.

I have read the following statement in a publication:

> "M. Hue retired to Hamburg, where he passed nine, months in perfect obscurity. He afterwards went to Holland, provided with a passport from Bourrienne, who was Napoleon's Minister, though in disgrace, and who, foreseeing what was to happen, sought to ingratiate himself in the favour of the Bourbons."

The above passage contains a falsehood in almost every line. M. Hue wished to reside in Hamburg, but he did not wish to conceal himself. I invited him to visit me, and assured him that he might remain in Hamburg without apprehension, provided he acted prudently. He wished to go to Holland, and I took upon myself to give him a passport. I left M. Hue in the free management of his business, the nature of which I knew very well, and which was very honourable; he was deputed to pay the pensions which Louis XVIII. granted to the emigrants. As for myself, I had tendered my resignation of private secretary to Bonaparte; and even admitting I was in disgrace in that character, I was not so as Minister and Consul-General at Hamburg. My situation, which was of little consequence at the time I was appointed to it, was later on rendered exceedingly important by circumstances. It was, in fact, a sort of watch-tower of the Government, whence all the movements of northern Germany were observed; and during my residence in the Hanse Towns I continually experienced the truth of what Bonaparte said to me at my farewell audience—"Yours is a place independent and apart."

It is absurd to say that the kindness I showed to M. Hue was an attempt to ingratiate myself with the Bourbons. My attentions to him were dictated solely by humanity, unaccompanied by any afterthought. Napoleon had given me his confidence, and by mitigating the verity of his orders I served him better than they who executed them in a way which could not fail to render the French Government odious. If I am accused of extending every possible indulgence to the unfortunate emigrants, I plead guilty; and, far from wishing to defend myself against the charge, I consider it honourable to me. But I defy any one of them to say that I betrayed in their favour the interests with which I was entrusted. They who urged Bonaparte to usurp the crown of France served, though perhaps unconsciously, the cause of the Bourbons. I, on the contrary, used all my endeavours to dissuade him from that measure, which I clearly saw must, in the end, lead to the restoration, though I do not pretend that I was sufficiently clear-sighted to guess that Napoleon's fall was so near at hand. The kindness

I showed to M. Hue and his companions in misfortune was prompted by humanity, and not by mean speculation. As well might it be said that Bernadotte, who, like myself, neglected no opportunity of softening the rigour of the orders he was deputed to execute, was by this means working his way to the throne of Sweden.

Bernadotte had proceeded to Denmark to take the command of the Spanish and French troops who had been removed from the Hanse Towns to occupy that kingdom, which was then threatened by the English. His departure was a great loss to me, for we had always agreed respecting the measures to be adopted, and I felt his absence the more sensibly when I was enabled to make a comparison between him and his successor. It is painful to me to detail the misconduct of those who injured the French name in Germany, but in fulfilment of the task I have undertaken, I am bound to tell the truth.

In April 1808 General Dupas came to take the command of Hamburg, but only under the orders of Bernadotte, who retained the supreme command of the French troops in the Hanse Towns. By the appointment of General Dupas the Emperor cruelly thwarted the wishes and hopes of the inhabitants of Lower Saxony. That General said of the people of Hamburg, "As long as I see those . . . driving in their carriages I can get money from them." It is, however, only just to add, that his dreadful exactions were not made on his own account, but for the benefit of another man to whom he owed his all, and to whom he had in some measure devoted his existence.

I will state some particulars respecting the way in which the generals who commanded the French troops at Hamburg were maintained. The Senate of Hamburg granted to the Marshals thirty friederichs a day for the expenses of their table exclusive of the hotel in which they were lodged by the city. The generals of division had only twenty friederichs. General Dupas wished to be provided for on the same footing as the Marshals. The Senate having, with reason, rejected this demand, Dupas required that he should be daily served with a breakfast and a dinner of thirty covers. This was an inconceivable burden, and Dupas cost the city more than any of his predecessors.

I saw an account of his expenses, which during the twenty-one weeks he remained at Hamburg amounted to 122,000 marks, or about 183,000 francs. None but the most exquisite wines were drunk at the table of Dupas. Even his servants were treated with champagne, and the choicest fruits were brought from the fine hothouses of Berlin. The inhabitants were irritated at this extravagance, and Dupas accordingly experienced the resistance of the Senate.

Among other vexations there was one to which the people could not readily submit. In Hamburg, which had formerly been a fortified town, the custom was preserved of closing the gates at nightfall. On Sundays they were closed three-quarters of an hour later, to avoid interrupting the amusements of the people.

While General Dupas was Governor of Hamburg an event occurred which occasioned considerable irritation in the public mind, and might have been attended by fatal consequences. From some whim or other the General ordered the gates to be closed at seven in the evening, and consequently while it was broad daylight, for it was in the middle of spring; no exception was made in favour of Sunday, and on that day a great number of the inhabitants who had been walking in the outskirts of the city presented themselves at the gate of Altona for admittance. To their surprise they found the gate closed, though it was a greater thoroughfare than any other gate in Hamburg. The number of persons, requiring admittance increased, and a considerable crowd soon collected. After useless entreaties had been addressed to the chief officer of the post the people were determined to send to the Commandant for the keys. The Commandant arrived, accompanied by the General. When they appeared it was supposed they had come for the purpose of opening the gates, and they were accordingly saluted with a general hurrah! which throughout almost all the north is the usual cry for expressing popular satisfaction. General Dupas not understanding the meaning of this hurrah! supposed it to be a signal for sedition, and instead of ordering the gates to be opened he commanded the military to fire upon the peaceful citizens, who only wanted to return to their homes. Several persons were killed, and others more or less seriously wounded. Fortunately, after this first discharge the fury of Dupas was appeased; but still he persisted in keeping the gates closed at night. Next day an order was posted about the city prohibiting the cry of hurrah! under pain of a severe punishment. It was also forbidden that more than three persona should collect together in the streets. Thus it was that certain persons imposed the French yoke upon towns and provinces which were previously happy.

Dupas was as much execrated in the Hanse Towns as Clarke had been in Berlin when he was governor of that capital during the campaign of 1807. Clarke had burdened the people of Berlin with every kind of oppression and exaction. He, as well as many others, manifested a ready obedience in executing the Imperial orders, however tyrannical they might be; and Heaven knows what epithets invariably accompanied the name of Clarke when pronounced by the lips of a Prussian.

Dupas seemed to have taken Clarke as his model. An artillery officer, who was in Hamburg at the time of the disturbance I have just mentioned, told me that it was he who was directed to place two pieces of light-artillery before the gate of Altona. Having executed this order, he went to General Dupas, whom he found in a furious fit of passion, breaking and destroying everything within his reach. In the presence of the officer he broke more than two dozen plates which were on the table before him: these plates, of course, had cost him very little!

On the day after the disturbance which had so fatal a termination I wrote to inform the Prince of Porte-Corvo of what had taken place; and in my letter I solicited the suppression of an extraordinary tribunal which had been created by General Dupas. He returned me an immediate answer, complying with my request. His letter was as follows:

> I have received your letter, my dear Minister: it forcibly conveys the expression of your right feeling, which revolts against oppression, severity, and the abase of power. I entirely concur in your view of the subject, and I am distressed whenever I see such acts of injustice committed. On an examination of the events which took place on the 19th it is impossible to deny that the officer who ordered the gates to be closed so soon was in the wrong; and next, it may be asked, why were not the gates opened instead of the military being ordered to fire on the people? But, on the other hand, did not the people evince decided obstinacy and insubordination? were they not to blame in throwing stones at the guard, forcing the palisades, and even refusing to listen to the voice of the magistrates? It is melancholy that they should have fallen into these excesses, from which, doubtless, they would have refrained had they listened to the civil chiefs, who ought to be their first directors. Finally, my dear Minister, the Senator who distributed money at the gate of Altona to appease the multitude would have done better had he advised them to wait patiently until the gates were opened;

and he might, I think, have gone to the Commandant or the General to solicit that concession. Whenever an irritated mob resorts to violence there is no safety for any one. The protecting power mast then exert its utmost authority to stop mischief. The Senate of ancient Rome, so jealous of its prerogatives, assigned to a Dictator, in times of trouble, the power of life and death, and that magistrate knew no other code than his own will and the axe of his lictors. The ordinary laws did not resume their course until the people returned to submission. The event which took place in Hamburg produced a feeling of agitation of which evil-disposed persons might take advantage to stir up open insurrection. That feeling could only be repressed by a severe tribunal, which, however, is no longer necessary. General Dupas has, accordingly, received orders to dissolve it, and justice will resume her usual course.

J. Bernadotte

Densel,
4th May, 1808.

When Bernadotte returned to Hamburg he sent. Dupas to Lübeck. That city, which was poorer than Hamburg, suffered cruelly from the visitation of such a guest.

Dupas levied all his exactions in kind, and indignantly spurned every offer of accepting money, the very idea of which, he said, shocked his delicacy of feeling. But his demands became so extravagant that the city of Lübeck was utterly unable to satisfy them. Besides his table, which was provided in the same style of profusion as at Hamburg, he required to be furnished with plate, linen, wood, and candles; in short, with the most trivial articles of household consumption.

The Senate deputed to the incorruptible General Dupas M. Nolting, a venerable old man, who mildly represented to him the abuses which were everywhere committed in his name, and entreated that he would vouchsafe to accept twenty Louis a day to defray the expenses of his table alone. At this proposition General Dupes flew into a rage. To offer him money was an insult not to be endured! He furiously drove the terrified Senator out of the house, and at once ordered his 'aide de camp' Barrel to imprison him. M. de Barrel, startled at this extraordinary order, ventured to remonstrate with the General, but in vain; and, though against his heart, he was obliged to obey. The aide de camp accordingly waited upon the Senator Notting, and overcome by that feeling of respect which gray hairs involuntarily inspire in youth, instead of arresting him, he besought the old man not to leave his house until he should prevail on the General to retract his orders. It was not till the following day that M. de Barrel succeeded in getting these orders revoked—that is to say, he obtained M. Notting's release from confinement; for Dupas would not be satisfied until he heard that the Senator had suffered at least the commencement of the punishment to which his capricious fury had doomed him.

In spite of his parade of disinterestedness General Dupas yielded so far as to accept the twenty Louis a day for the expense of his table which M. Notting had offered him on the part of the Senate of Lübeck; but it was not without murmurings, complaints, and menaces that he made this generous concession; and he exclaimed more than once, "These fellows have portioned out my allowance for me." Lübeck was not released from the presence of General

Dupes until the month of March 1809, when he was summoned to command a division in the Emperor's new campaign against Austria. Strange as it may appear, it is nevertheless the fact, that, oppressive as had been his presence at Lübeck, the Hanse Towns soon had reason to regret him.

CHAPTER XV

1808

The year 1808 was fertile in remarkable events. Occupied as I was with my own duties, I yet employed my leisure hours in observing the course of those great acts by which Bonaparte seemed determined to mark every day of his life. At the commencement of 1808 I received one of the first copies of the Code of Commerce, promulgated on the 1st of January by the Emperor's order. This code appeared to me an act of mockery; at least it was extraordinary to publish a code respecting a subject which it was the effect of all the Imperial decrees to destroy. What trade could possibly exist under the Continental system, and the ruinous severity of the customs? The line was already extended widely enough when, by a 'Senatus-consulte', it was still further widened. The Emperor, to whom all the Continent submitted, had recourse to no other formality for the purpose of annexing to the Empire the towns of Kehl, Cassel near Mayence, Wesel, and Flushing, with the territories depending on them.[233]

These conquests, gained by decrees and senatorial decisions, had at least the advantage of being effected without bloodshed. All these things were carefully communicated to me by the Ministers with whom I corresponded, for my situation at Hamburg had acquired such importance that it was necessary I should know everything.

At this period I observed among the news which I received from different places a singular coincidence of dates, worthy of being noted by the authors of ephemrides. On the same day-namely, the 1st of February Paris, Lisbon, and Rome were the scenes of events of different kinds, but, as they all happened on one day, affording a striking example of the rapidity of movement which marked the reign of Bonaparte. At Paris the niece of Josephine, Mademoiselle de Tascher, whom Napoleon had lately exalted to the rank of Princess, was married to the reigning Prince of Ahremberg, while at the same time Junot declared to Portugal that the house of Braganza had ceased to reign, and French troops were, under the command of General Miollis, occupying Rome. This occupation was the commencement of prolonged struggles, during which Pins VII. expiated the condescension he had shown in going to Paris to crown Napoleon.

Looking over my notes, I see it was the day after these three events occurred that Bonaparte gave to his brother-in-law, Prince Borghese, the Governorship-General of the departments beyond the Alps which he had just founded; and of which he made the eighth Grand Dignitary of the Empire. General Menou, whom I had not seen since Egypt, was obliged by this appointment to leave Turin, where he had always remained. Bonaparte, not wishing to permit him to come to Paris, sent Menou to preside over the Junta of Tuscany, of

233 A resolution of the senate, or a "Senatus-consulte" was the means invented by Napoleon for altering the imperial Constitutions, and even the extent of the Empire. By one of these, dated 21st January 1808, the towns of Kehl, Cassel, and Wesel, with Flushing, all already seized, were definitely united to France. The loss of Wesel, which helonged to Murat's Grand Duchy of Berg, was a very sore point with Murat.

which he soon afterwards made another General-Governorship, which he entrusted to the care of his sister Elisa.[234]

My correspondence relative to what passed in the south of France and of Europe presented to me, if I may so express myself, merely an anecdotal interest. Not so the news which came from the north. At Hamburg I was like the sentinel of an advanced post, always on the alert. I frequently informed the Government of what would take place before the event actually happened. I was one of the first to hear of the plans of Russia relative to Sweden. The courier whom I sent to Paris arrived there at the very moment when Russia made the declaration of war. About the end of February the Russian troops entered Swedish Finland, and occupied also the capital of that province, which had at all times been coveted by the Russian Government. It has been said that at the interview at Erfurt Bonaparte consented to the usurpation of that province by Alexander in return for the complaisance of the latter in acknowledging Joseph as King of Spain and the Indies.

The removal of Joseph from the throne of Naples to the throne of Madrid belongs, indeed, to that period respecting which I am now throwing together a few recollections. Murat had succeeded Joseph at Naples, and this accession of the brother-in-law of Napoleon to one of the thrones of the House of Bourbon gave Bonaparte another junior in the college of kings, of which he would have infallibly become the senior if he had gone on as he began.

I will relate a little circumstance which now occurs to me respecting the kings manufactured by Napoleon. I recollect that during the King of Etruria's stay in Paris—the First Consul went with that Prince to the Comedie Francaise, where Voltaire's 'OEdipus' was performed. This piece, I may observe, Bonaparte liked better than anything Voltaire ever wrote. I was in the theatre, but not in the First Consul's box, and I observed, as all present must have done, the eagerness with which the audience applied to Napoleon and the King of Etruria the line in which Philoctetes says—

> "J'ai fait des souverains et n'ai pas voulu l'etre."
> *["I have made sovereigns, but have not wished to be one myself."]*

The application was so marked that it could not fail to become the subject of conversation between the First Consul and me. "You remarked it, Bourrienne?" . . . "Yes, General." . . "The fools! . . . They shall see! They shall see!" We did indeed see. Not content with making kings, Bonaparte, when his brow was encircled by a double crown, after creating princes at length realised the object he had long contemplated, namely, to found a new nobility endowed with hereditary rights. It was at the commencement of March 1808 that he accomplished this project; and I saw in the 'Moniteur' a long list of princes, dukes, counts, barons, and knights of the Empire; there were wanting only viscounts and marquises.

At the same time that Bonaparte was founding a new nobility he determined to raise up

---

234 Prince Camille Philippe Louis Borghese (1755-1832), an Italian, had married, 6th November 1808, Pauline Bonaparte, the sister of Napoleon, and the widow of General Leclerc. He had been made Prince and Duke of Guastalla when that duchy was given to his wife, 30th Marsh 1806. He separated from his wife after a few years. Indeed Pauline was impossible as a wife if half of the stories about her are true. It was she who, finding that a lady was surprised at her having sat naked while a statue of her was being modelled for Canova, believed she had satisfactorily explained matters by saying, "but there was a fire in the room."

the old edifice of the university, but on a new foundation. The education of youth had always been one of his ruling ideas, and I had an opportunity of observing how he was changed by the exercise of sovereign power when I received at Hamburg the statutes of the new elder daughter of the Emperor of the French, and compared them with the ideas which Bonaparte, when General and First Consul, had often expressed to me respecting the education which ought to be given youth. Though the sworn enemy of everything like liberty, Bonaparte had at first conceived a vast system of education, comprising above all the study of history, and those positive sciences, such as geology and astronomy, which give the utmost degree of development to the human mind. The Sovereign, however, shrunk from the first ideas of the man of genius, and his university, confided to the elegant suppleness of M. de Fontaines, was merely a school capable of producing educated subjects but not enlightened men.

Before taking complete possession of Rome, and making it the second city of the Empire, the vaunted moderation of Bonaparte was confined to dismembering from it the legations of Ancona, Urbino, Macerata, and Camerino, which were divided into three departments; and added to the Kingdom of Italy. The patience of the Holy See could no longer hold out against this act of violence, and Cardinal Caprara, who had remained in Paris since the coronation, at last left that capital. Shortly afterwards the Grand Duchies of Parma and Piacenza were united to the French Empire, and annexed to the government of the departments beyond the Alps. These transactions were coincident with the events in Spain and Bayonne before mentioned.

After the snare laid at Bayonne the Emperor entered Paris on the 14th of August, the eve of his birthday. Scarcely had he arrived in the capital when he experienced fresh anxiety in consequence of the conduct of Russia, which, as I have stated, had declared open war with Sweden, and did not conceal the intention of seizing Finland. But Bonaparte, desirous of actively carrying on the war in Spain, felt the necessity of removing his troops from Prussia to the Pyrenees. He then hastened the interview at Erfurt, where the two Emperors of France and Russia had agreed to meet. He hoped that this interview would insure the tranquillity of the Continent, while he should complete the subjection of Spain to the sceptre of Joseph. That Prince had been proclaimed on the 8th of June; and on the 21st of the same month he made his entry into Madrid, but having received, ten days after, information of the disaster at Baylen, he was obliged to leave the Spanish capital.[235]

Bonaparte's wishes must at this time have been limited to the tranquillity of the Continent, for the struggle between him and England was more desperate than ever. England had just sent troops to Portugal under the command of Sir Arthur Wellesley. There was no longer any hope of a reconciliation with Great Britain: The interview at Erfurt having been determined on, the Emperor, who had returned from Bayonne to Paris, again left the capital about the end of September, and arrived at Metz without stopping, except for the purpose of reviewing the regiments which were echeloned on his route, and which were on their march from the Grand Army to Spain.

I had heard some time previously of the interview which was about to take place, and which was so memorable in the life of Napoleon. It excited so much interest in Germany that the roads were covered with the equipages of the Princes who were going to Erfurt to witness the meeting. The French Emperor arrived there before Alexander, and went forward three

235 The important battle of Daylen, where the French, under General Dupont, were beaten by the Spaniards, was fought on the 19th of July 1808.

leagues to meet him. Napoleon was on horseback, Alexander in a carriage. They embraced, it is said, in a manner expressive of the most cordial friendship. This interview was witnessed by most of the sovereign Princes of Germany. However, neither the King of Prussia nor the Emperor of Austria was present. The latter sovereign sent a letter to Napoleon, of which I obtained a copy. It was as follows:

> SIRE, MY BROTHER,—My Ambassador in Paris informs me that your Majesty is about to proceed to Erfurt to meet the Emperor Alexander. I eagerly seize the opportunity of your approach to my frontier to renew those testimonials of friendship and esteem which I have pledged to you; and I send my Lieutenant-General, Baron Vincent, to convey to you the assurance of my unalterable sentiments. If the false accounts that have been circulated respecting the internal institutions which I have established in my monarchy should for a moment have excited your Majesty's doubts as to my intentions, I fatter myself that the explanations given on that subject by Count Metternich to your Minister will have entirely removed them. Baron Vincent is enabled to confirm to your Majesty all that has been said by Count Metternich on the subject, and to add any further explanations, you may wish for. I beg that your Majesty will grant him the same gracious reception he experienced at Paris and at Warsaw. The renewed marks of favour you may bestow on him will be an unequivocal pledge of the reciprocity of your sentiments, and will seal that confidence which will render our satisfaction mutual. Deign to accept the assurance of the unalterable affection and respect with which I am, Sire, my Brother, Your imperial and royal Majesty's faithful brother and friend,
>
> *(Signed)* FRANCIS.
>
> PRESBURG, *8th September 1808.*

This letter appears to be a model of ambiguity, by which it is impossible Napoleon could have been imposed upon. However, as yet he had no suspicion of the hostility of Austria, which speedily became manifest; his grand object then was the Spanish business, and, as I have before observed, one of the secrets of Napoleon's genius was, that he did not apply himself to more than one thing at a time.

At Erfurt Bonaparte attained the principal object he had promised himself by the meeting. Alexander recognized Joseph in his new character of King of Spain and the Indies. It has been said that as the price of this recognition Napoleon consented that Alexander should have Swedish Finland; but for the truth of this I cannot vouch. However, I remember that when, after the interview at Erfurt, Alexander had given-orders to his ambassador to Charles IV. to continue his functions under King Joseph, the Swedish charge d'affaires at Hamburg told me that confidential letters received by him from Erfurt led him to fear that the Emperor Alexander had communicated to Napoleon his designs on Finland, and that Napoleon had given his consent to the occupation. Be this as it may, as soon as the interview was over Napoleon returned to Paris, where he presided with much splendour at the opening of the Legislative Body, and set out in the month of November for Spain.

CHAPTER XVI

1808

Previous to the interview at Erfurt an event took place which created a strong interest in Hamburg and throughout Europe, an event which was planned and executed with inconceivable secrecy. I allude to the defection of the Marquis de la Romans, which I have not hitherto noticed, in order that I might not separate the different facts which came to my knowledge respecting that defection and the circumstances which accompanied it.

The Marquis de la Romans had come to the Hanse Towns at the head of an army corps of 18,000 men, which the Emperor in the preceding campaign claimed in virtue of treaties previously concluded with the Spanish Government. The Spanish troops at first met with a good reception in the Hanse Towns. The difference of language, indeed, occasionally caused discord, but when better acquainted the inhabitants and their visitors became good friends. The Marquis de la Romans was a little swarthy man, of unprepossessing and rather common appearance; but he had a considerable share of talent and information. He had travelled in almost every part of Europe, and as he had been a close observer of all he saw his conversation was exceedingly agreeable and instructive.

During his stay at Hamburg General Romans spent almost every evening at my house, and invariably fell asleep over a game at whist. Madame de Bourrienne was usually his partner, and I recollect he perpetually offered apologies for his involuntary breach of good manners. This, however, did not hinder him from being guilty of the same offence the next evening. I will presently explain the cause of this regular siesta.

On the King of Spain's birthday the Marquis de la Romans gave a magnificent entertainment. The decorations of the ballroom consisted of military emblems. The Marquis did the honours with infinite grace, and paid particular attention to the French generals. He always spoke of the Emperor in very respectful terms, without any appearance of affectation, so that it was impossible to suspect him of harbouring disaffection. He played his part to the last with the utmost address. At Hamburg we had already received intelligence of the fatal result of the battle of the Sierra Morena, and of the capitulation of Dupont, which disgraced him at the very moment when the whole army marked him out as the man most likely next to receive the baton of Marshal of France.

Meanwhile the Marquis de la Romans departed for the Danish island of Funen, in compliance with the order which Marshal Bernadotte had transmitted to him. There, as at Hamburg, the Spaniards were well liked, for their general obliged them to observe the strictest discipline. Great preparations were made in Hamburg on the approach of Saint Napoleon's day, which was then celebrated with much solemnity in every town in which France had representatives. The Prince de Ponte-Corvo was at Travemunde, a small seaport near Lübeck, but that did not prevent him from giving directions for the festival of the 15th of August. The Marquis de la Romana, the better to deceive the Marshal, despatched a courier, requesting permission to visit Hamburg on the day of the fete in order to join his prayers to those of the French, and to receive, on the day of the fete, from the hands of the Prince, the grand order of the Legion of Honour, which he had solicited, and which Napoleon had granted him. Three days after Bernadotte received intelligence of the defection of de la Romana. The Marquis had contrived to assemble a great number of English vessels on the coast, and to escape with all his troops except a depot of 600 men left at Altona. We afterwards heard that he experienced no interruption on his passage, and that he landed with his troops at Corunna. I now knew to what to attribute the drowsiness which always overcame the Marquis de la Romana when he sat down to take a hand at whist. The fact was, he sat up all night making preparations for the escape which he had long meditated, while to lull suspicion he showed himself everywhere during the day, as usual.

On the defection of the Spanish troops I received letters from Government requiring me to augment my vigilance, and to seek out those persons who might be supposed to have been in the confidence of the Marquis de la Romans. I was informed that English agents, dispersed through the Hanse Towns, were endeavouring to foment discord and dissatisfaction among the King of Holland's troops. These manoeuvres were connected with the treason of the Spaniards and the arrival of Danican in Denmark. Insubordination had already broken out, but it was promptly repressed. Two Dutch soldiers were shot for striking their officers, but notwithstanding this severity desertion among the troops increased to an alarming degree. Indefatigable agents in the pay of the English Government laboured incessantly to seduce the soldiers of King Louis (of Holland) from their duty. Some of these agents being denounced to me were taken almost in the act, and positive proof being adduced of their guilt they were condemned to death.

These indispensable examples of severity did not check the manoeuvres of England, though they served to cool the zeal of her agents. I used every endeavour to second the Prince of Ponte-Corvo in tracing out the persons employed by England. It was chiefly from the small island of Heligoland that they found their way to the Continent. This communication was facilitated by the numerous vessels scattered about the small islands which lie along that coast. Five or six pieces of gold defrayed the expense of the passage to or from Heligoland. Thus the Spanish news, which was printed and often fabricated at London, was profusely circulated in the north of Germany. Packets of papers addressed to merchants and well-known persons in the German towns were put into the post-offices of Embden, Kuipphausen, Varel, Oldenburg, Delmenhorst, and Bremen. Generally speaking, this part of the coast was not sufficiently well watched to prevent espionage and smuggling; with regard to smuggling, indeed, no power could have entirely prevented it. The Continental system had made it a necessity, so that a great part of the population depended on it for subsistence.

In the beginning of December 1808 we remarked that the Russian courier who passed through Konigsberg and Berlin, was regularly detained four, five, and even six hours on his way to Hamburg. The trading portion of the population, always suspicious, became alarmed at this chance in the courier's hours, into which they inquired and soon discovered the cause. It was ascertained that two agents had been stationed by the postmaster of the Grand Duchy of Berg at Hamburg, in a village called Eschburg belonging to the province of Lauenburg. There the courier from Berlin was stopped, and his packets and letters opened. As soon as these facts were known in Hamburg there was a general consternation among the trading class-that is to say, the influential population of the city. Important and well-grounded complaints were made. Some letters had been suppressed, enclosures had been taken from one letter and put into another, and several bills of exchange had gone astray. The intelligence soon reached the ears of the Prince of Ponte-Corvo, and was confirmed by the official report of the commissioner for the Imperial and Royal Post-office, who complained of the delay of the courier, of the confusion of the packets, and of want of confidence in the Imperial Post-office. It was impolitic to place such agents in a village where there was not even a post-office, and where the letters were opened in an inn without any supervision. This examination of the letters, sometimes, perhaps, necessary, but often dangerous, and always extremely delicate, created additional alarm, on account of the persons to whom the business was entrusted. If the Emperor wished to be made acquainted with the correspondence of certain persons in the north it would have been natural to entrust the business to his agents and his commissioner at Hamburg, and not to two unknown individuals—another inconvenience attending black cabinets. At my suggestion the Prince of Ponte-Corvo gave orders for putting a stop to the clandestine business at Eschburg. The two agents were taken to Hamburg and their conduct inquired into. They were severely punished. They deserved this, however, less than those who had entrusted them with such an honourable mission; but leaders never make much scruple about abandoning their accomplices in the lower ranks.

But for the pain of witnessing vexations of this sort, which I had not always power to prevent, especially after Bernadotte's removal, my residence at Hamburg would have been delightful. Those who have visited that town know the advantages it possesses from its charming situation on the Elbe, and above all, the delightful country which surrounds it like a garden, and extends to the distance of more than a league along the banks of the Eyder. The manners and customs of the inhabitants bear the stamp of peculiarity; they are fond of pursuing their occupations in the open air. The old men are often seen sitting round tables placed before their doors sipping tea, while the children play before them, and the young people are at their work. These groups have a very picturesque effect, and convey a gratifying idea of the happiness of the people. On seeing the worthy citizens of Hamburg assembled round their doors I could not help thinking of a beautiful remark of Montesquieu. When he went to Florence with a letter of recommendation to the Prime Minister of the Grand Duke of Tuscany he found him sitting at the threshold of his door, inhaling the fresh air and conversing with some friends. "I see," said Montesquieu, "that I am arrived among a happy people, since their Prime Minister can enjoy his leisure moments thus."

A sort of patriarchal simplicity characterises the manners of the inhabitants of Hamburg. They do not visit each other much, and only by invitation; but on such occasions they display great luxury beneath their simple exterior. They are methodical and punctual to an extraordinary degree. Of this I recollect a curious instance. I was very intimate with Baron Woght, a man of talent and information, and exceedingly amiable manners. One day he called to make us a farewell visit as he intended to set out on the following day for Paris. On Madame de Bourrienne expressing a hope that he would not protract his absence beyond six months, the period he had fixed upon, he replied, "Be assured, madame, nothing shall prevent me getting home on the day I have appointed, for I have invited a party of friends to dine with me on the day after my return." The Baron returned at the appointed time, and none of his guests required to be reminded of his invitation at six months' date.

Napoleon so well knew the effect which his presence produced that after a conquest he loved to show himself to the people whose territories he added to the Empire. Duroc, who always accompanied him when he was not engaged on missions, gave me a curious account of Napoleon's journey in 1807 to Venice and the other Italian provinces, which, conformably with the treaty of Presburg, were annexed to the Kingdom of Italy.

In this journey to the Kingdom of Italy Napoleon had several important objects in view.

He was planning great alliances; and he loaded Eugène with favours for the purpose of sounding him and preparing him for his mother's divorce. At the same time he intended to have an interview with his brother Lucien, because, wishing to dispose of the hand of his brother's daughter, he thought of making her marry the Prince of the Asturias (Ferdinand), who before the Spanish war, when the first dissensions between father and son had become manifest, had solicited an alliance with the Emperor in the hope of getting his support. This was shortly after the eldest son of Louis had died in Holland of croup. It has been wrongly believed that Napoleon had an affection for this child beyond that of an uncle for a nephew. I have already said the truth about this.

However this may be, it is certain that Napoleon now seriously contemplated a divorce from Josephine. If there had been no other proof of this I, who from long habit knew how to read Napoleon's thoughts by his acts, found a sufficient one in the decree issued at Milan by which Napoleon adopted Eugène as his son and successor to the crown of Italy, in default of male and legitimate children directly descended from him. Lucien went to Mantua on his brother's invitation, and this was the last interview they had before the Cent Jours. Lucien consented to give his daughter to the Prince of the Asturias, but this marriage did not take place. I learned from Duroc to what a height the enmity of Lucien towards the Beauharnais family, an enmity which I have often had occasion to speak of, had been renewed on this occasion. Lucien could not pardon Josephine for the rebuff of the counsels which he had given her, and which she had rejected with such proper indignation. Lucien had besides another special reason for giving his daughter to the Prince of the Asturias. He particularly wished to prevent that Prince marrying Mademoiselle de Tascher, the niece of Josephine, a marriage for which M. de Beauharnais, then Ambassador of France at Madrid, was working with all his might. Lucien also, with his Republican stolidity, submitted without too much scruple to the idea of having a Bourbon King as son-in-law. It was also during this journey of Napoleon that he annexed Tuscany to the Empire.

Bonaparte returned to Paris on the 1st of January 1808. On his way he stopped for a short time at Chambery, where a young man had been waiting for him several days. This was Madame de Stael's son, who was then not more than seventeen years of age. M. Auguste de Stael lodged at the house of the postmaster of Chambery, and as the Emperor was expected in the course of the night, he gave orders that he should be called up on the arrival of the first courier. The couriers, who had been delayed on the road, did not arrive until six in the morning, and were almost immediately followed by the Emperor himself, so that M, de Stael was awakened by the cries of Vive l'Empereur! He had just time to dress himself hastily, and fly to meet Napoleon, to whom he delivered a letter, which he had prepared beforehand for the purpose of soliciting an audience. Lauriston, the aide de camp on duty, took the letter, it being his business to receive all the letters and petitions which were presented to Napoleon on his way. Before breakfast the Emperor opened the letters which Lauriston had laid on the table; he merely looked at the signatures, and then laid them aside. On opening M. de Stael's letter he said, "Ah! ah! what have we here? a letter from M. de Stael! . . . He wishes to see me: . . . What can he want? . . . Can there be anything in common between me and the refugees of Geneva?"— "Sire," observed Lauriston, "he is a very young man; and, as well as I could judge from the little I saw of him, there is something very prepossessing in his appearance."—"A very young man, say you? . . . Oh, then I will see him. . . . Rustan, tell him to come in." M. de Stael presented himself to Napoleon with modesty, but without any unbecoming timidity. When he had respectfully saluted the Emperor a conversation ensued between them, which

Duroc described to me in nearly the following manner.

As M. de Stael advanced towards the Emperor the latter said, "Whence do you come?"—"From Geneva, Sire."—"Where is your mother?"—"She is either in Vienna or will soon be there."—"At Vienna! . . . Well, that is where she ought to be; and I suppose she is happy. . . . She will now have a good opportunity of learning German."—"Sire, how can you imagine my mother is happy when she is absent from her country and her friends? If I were permitted to lay before your Majesty my mother's confidential letter you would see how unhappy she is in her exile."— "Ah, bah! your mother unhappy, indeed! . . . However, I do not mean to say she is altogether a bad woman. . . . She has talent—perhaps too much; and hers is an unbridled talent. She was educated amidst the chaos of the subverted monarchy and the Revolution; and out of these events she makes an amalgamation of her own! All this might become very dangerous. Her enthusiasm is likely to make proselytes. I must keep watch upon her. She does not like me; and for the interests of those whom she would endanger I must prohibit her coming to Paris."

Young De Stael stated that his object in seeking the interview with the Emperor was to petition for his mother's return to Paris. Napoleon having listened without impatience to the reasons he urged in support of his request, said, "But supposing I were to permit your mother to return to Pairs, six months would not elapse before I should be obliged to send her to the Bicetre or to the Temple. This I should be sorry to do, because the affair would make a noise, and injure me in public opinion. Tell your mother that my determination is formed, that my decision is irrevocable. She shall never set foot in Paris as long as I live."— "Sire, I cannot believe that you would arbitrarily imprison my mother if she gave you no reason for such severity."—"She would give me a dozen! . . . I know her well."—"Sire, permit me to say that I am certain my mother would live in Paris in a way that would afford no ground of reproach; she would live retired, and would see only a very few friends. In spite of your Majesty's refusal I venture to entreat that you will give her a trial, were it only for six weeks or a month. Permit her, Sire, to pass that time in Paris, and I conjure you to come to no final decision beforehand."—"Do you think I am to be deceived by these fair promises? . . . I tell you it cannot be. She would serve as a rallying point for the Faubourg St. Germain. She see nobody, indeed! Could she make that sacrifice? She would visit and receive company. She would be guilty of a thousand follies. She would be saying things which she may consider as very good jokes, but which I should take seriously. My government is no joke: I wish this to be well known by everybody."— "Sire, will your Majesty permit me to repeat that my mother has no wish whatever to mingle in society? She would confine herself to the circle of a few friends, a list of whom she would give to your Majesty. You, Sire, who love France so well, may form some idea of the misery my mother suffers in her banishment. I conjure your Majesty to yield to my entreaties, and let us be included in the number of your faithful subjects."—"You!"—"Yes, Sire; or if your Majesty persist in your refusal, permit a son to inquire what can have raised your displeasure against his mother. Some say that it was my grandfather's last work; but I can assure your Majesty that my mother had nothing to do with that."— "Yes, certainly," added Napoleon, with more ill-humour than he had hitherto manifested. "Yes, certainly, that work is very objectionable. Your grandfather was an ideologist, a fool, an old lunatic. At sixty years of age to think of forming plans to overthrow my constitution! States would be well governed, truly, under such theorists, who judge of men from books and the world from the map."—"Sire, since my grandfather's plans are, in your Majesty's eyes, nothing but vain theories, I cannot conceive why they should so highly excite your displeasure. There is no political economist who has not traced out plans of constitutions."—"Oh! as to political economists, they are mere-visionaries, who are dreaming of plans of finance while they are unfit to fulfil the duties of a schoolmaster in the most insignificant village in the Empire. Your grandfather's work is that of an obstinate old man who died abusing all governments."—"Sire, may I presume to suppose, from the way in which you speak of it, that your Majesty judges from the report of malignant persons, and that you have not yourself read it."

"That is a mistake. I have read it myself from beginning to end."— "Then your Majesty must have seen how my grandfather renders justice to your genius."—"Fine justice, truly! . . . He calls me the indispensable man, but, judging from his arguments, the best thing that could be done would be to cut my throat! Yes, I was indeed indispensable to repair the follies of your grandfather, and the mischief he did to France. It was he who overturned the monarchy and led Louis XVI. to the scaffold."—"Sire, you seem to forget that my grandfather's property was confiscated because he defended the King."—"Defended the King! A fine defence, truly! You might as well say that if I give a man poison and present him with an antidote when he is in the agonies of death I wish to save him! Yet that is the way your grandfather defended Louis XVI . . . . As to the confiscation you speak of, what does that prove? Nothing. Why, the property of Robespierre was confiscated! And let me tell you that Robespierre himself, Marat, and Danton did much less mischief to France than M. Necker. It was he who brought about the Revolution. You, Monsieur de Stael, did not see this; but I did. I witnessed all that passed in those days of terror and public calamity. But as long as I live those days shall never return. Your speculators trace their Utopian schemes upon paper; fools read and believe them. All are babbling about general happiness, and presently the people have not bread to eat; then comes a revolution. Such is usually the fruit of all these fine theories! Your grandfather was the cause of the saturnalia which desolated France. He is responsible for all the blood shed in the Revolution!"

Duroc informed me that the Emperor uttered these last words in a tone of fury which made all present tremble for young De Stael. Fortunately the young man did not lose his self-possession in the conflict, while the agitated expression of his countenance evidently showed what was passing in his mind. He was sufficiently master of himself to reply to the Emperor in a calm though rather faltering voice: "Sire, permit me to hope that posterity will judge of my grandfather more favourably than your Majesty does. During his administration he was ranked by the side of Sully and Colbert; and let me repeat again that I trust posterity will render him justice."—"Posterity will, probably, say little about him."— "I venture to hope the contrary, Sire."

Then, added Duroc, the Emperor turning to us said with a smile, "After all, gentlemen, it is not for me to say too much against the Revolution since I have gained a throne by it." Then again turning to M. de Stael he said, "The reign of anarchy is at au end. I must have subordination. Respect the sovereign authority, since it comes from God. You are young, and well educated, therefore; follow a better course, and avoid those bad principles which endanger the welfare of society."—"Sire, since your Majesty does me the honour to think me well educated, you ought not to condemn the principles of my grandfather and my mother, for it is in those principles that I have been brought up."—"Well, I advise you to keep right in politics, for I will not pardon any offences of the Necker kind. Every one should keep right in politics."

This conversation, Duroc informed me, had continued the whole time of breakfast, and the Emperor rose just as he pronounced these last words: "Every one should keep right in politics." At that moment young De Stael again renewed his solicitations for his mother's recall from exile. Bonaparte then stepped up to him and pinched his ear with that air of familiarity which was customary to him when he was in good humour or wished to appear so.

"You are young," said he; "if you had my age and experience you would judge of things more correctly. I am far from being displeased with your frankness. I like to see a son plead his mother's cause. Your mother has given you a difficult commission, and you have executed it cleverly. I am glad I have had this opportunity of conversing with you. I love to talk with young people when they are unassuming and not too fond of arguing. But in spite of that I will not hold out false hopes to you. Murat has already spoken to me on the subject, and I have told him, as I now tell you, that my will is irrevocable. If your mother were in prison I should not hesitate to liberate her, but nothing shall induce me to recall her from exile."—"But, Sire, is she not as unhappy in being banished from her country and her friends as if she were in prison?"— "Oh! these are your mother's romantic ideas. She is exceedingly unhappy, and much to be pitied, no doubt! . . . With the exception of Paris she has all Europe for her prison."—"But, Sire, her friends are in Paris."—"With her talents she may make friends anywhere. After all, I cannot understand why she should be so anxious to come to Paris. Why should she wish to place herself immediately within the reach of my tyranny? Can she not go to Rome, to Berlin, to Vienna, to Milan, or to London? Yes, let her go to London; that is the place for her. There she may libel me as much as she pleases. In short, she has my full liberty to be anywhere but in Paris. You see, Monsieur de Stael, that is the place of my residence, and there I will have only those who are attached to me. I know from experience that if I were to allow your mother to come to Paris she would spoil everybody about me. She would finish the spoiling of Garat. It was she who ruined the Tribunate. I know she would promise wonders; but she cannot refrain from meddling with politics."—"I can assure your Majesty that my mother does not now concern herself about politics. She devotes herself exclusively to the society of her friends and to literature."—"Ah, there it is! . . . Literature! Do you think I am to be imposed upon by that word? While discoursing on literature, morals, the fine arts, and such matters, it is easy to dabble in politics. Let women mind their knitting. If your mother were in Paris I should hear all sorts of reports about her. Things might, indeed, be falsely attributed to her; but, be that as it may, I will have nothing of the kind going on in the capital in which I reside. All things considered, advise your mother to go to London. That is the best place for her. As for your grandfather, I have not spoken too severely of him. M. Necker knew nothing of the art of government. I have learned something of the matter during the last twenty years."—"All the world, Sire, renders justice to your Majesty's genius, and there is no one but acknowledges that the finances of France are now more prosperous than ever they were before your reign. But permit me to observe that your Majesty must, doubtless, have seen some merit in the financial regulations of my grandfather, since you have adopted some of them in the admirable system you have established."—"That proves nothing; for two or three good ideas do not constitute a good system. Be that as it may, I say again, I will never allow your mother to return to Paris."—"But, Sire, if sacred interests should absolutely require her presence there for a few days would not—"—"How! Sacred interests! What do you mean?"—"Yes, Sire, if you do not allow her to return I shall be obliged to go there, unaided by her advice, in order to recover from your Majesty's Government the payment of a sacred debt."—"Ah! bah! Sacred! Are not all the debts of the State sacred?"—"Doubtless, Sire; but ours is attended with circumstances which give it a peculiar character."—"A peculiar character! Nonsense! Does not every State creditor say the same of his debt? Besides, I know nothing of your claim. It does not concern me, and I will not meddle with it. If you have the law on your side so much the better; but if you want favour I tell you I will not interfere. If I did, I should be rather against you than otherwise."—"Sire, my brother and myself had intended to settle in France, but how can we live in a country where our mother cannot visit us?"—"I do not care for that. I do not advise you to come here. Go to England. The English like wrangling politicians. Go there, for in France, I tell you candidly, that I should be rather against you than for you."

"After this conversation," added Duroc, "the Emperor got into the carriage with me without stopping to look to the other petitions which had been presented to him. He preserved unbroken silence until he got nearly opposite the cascade, on the left of the road, a few leagues from Chambery. He appeared to be absorbed in reflection. At length he said, 'I fear I have been somewhat too harsh with this young man. . . . But no matter, it will prevent others from troubling me. These people calumniate everything I do. They do not understand me, Duroc; their place is not in France. How can Necker's family be for the Bourbons, whose first duty, if ever they returned to France, would be to hang them all.'"

This conversation, related to me by Duroc, interested me so much that I noted it down on paper immediately after my interview.

CHAPTER XVII

1808

When Bonaparte was the chief of the French Republic he had no objection to the existence of a Batavian Republic in the north of France, and he equally tolerated the Cisalpine Republic in the south. But after the coronation all the Republics, which were grouped like satellites round the grand Republic, were converted into kingdoms subject to the Empire, if not avowedly, at least in fact. In this respect there was no difference between the Batavian and Cisalpine Republics. The latter having been metamorphosed into the Kingdom of Italy, it was necessary to find some pretext for transforming the former into the Kingdom of Holland. The government of the Republic of Batavia had been for some time past merely the shadow of a government, but still it preserved, even in its submission to France, those internal forms of freedom which console a nation for the loss of independence. The Emperor kept up such an extensive agency in Holland that he easily got up a deputation soliciting him to choose a king for the Batavian Republic. This submissive deputation came to Paris in 1806 to solicit the Emperor, as a favour, to place Prince Louis on the throne of Holland. The address of the deputation, the answer of Napoleon, and the speech of Louis on being raised to the sovereign dignity, have all been published.

Louis became King of Holland much against his inclination, for he opposed the proposition as much as he dared, alleging as an objection the state of his health, to which certainly the climate of Holland was not favourable; but Bonaparte sternly replied to his remonstrance, "It is better to die a king than live a prince." He was then obliged to accept the crown. He went to Holland accompanied by Hortense, who, however, did mot stay long there. The new King wanted to make himself beloved by his subjects, and as they were an entirely commercial people the best way to win their affections was not to adopt Napoleon's rigid laws against commercial intercourse with England. Hence the first coolness between the two brothers, which ended in the abdication of Louis.

I know not whether Napoleon recollected the motive assigned by Louis for at first refusing the crown of Holland, namely, the climate of the country, or whether he calculated upon greater submission in another of his brothers; but this is certain, that Joseph was not called from the throne of Naples to the throne of Spain until after the refusal of Louis. I have in my possession a copy of a letter written to him by Napoleon on the subject. It is without date of time or place, but its contents prove it to have been written in March or April 1808. It is as follows:—

> Brother:—The King of Spain, Charles IV., has just abdicated. The Spanish people loudly appeal to me. Certain of obtaining no solid peace with England unless I cause a great movement on the Continent, I have determined to place a French King on the throne of Spain. The climate of Holland does not agree with you; besides, Holland cannot rise from her rains. In the whirlwind of events, whether we have peace or not, there is no possibility of her maintaining herself. In this state of things I have

> thought of the throne of Spain for you. Give me your opinions categorically on this measure. If I were to name you King of Spain would you accept the offer? May I count on you? Answer me these two questions. Say, "I have received your letter of such a day, I answer Yes," and then I shall count on your doing what I wish; or say "No" if you decline my proposal. Let no one enter into your confidence, and mention to no one the object of this letter. The thing must be done before we confess having thought about it.
>
> *(Signed)* NAPOLEON.

Before finally seizing Holland Napoleon formed the project of separating Brabant and Zealand from it in exchange for other provinces, the possession of which was doubtful, but Louis successfully resisted this first act of usurpation. Bonaparte was, too intent on the great business in Spain to risk any commotion in the north, where the declaration of Russia against Sweden already sufficiently occupied him. He therefore did not insist upon, and even affected indifference to, the proposed augmentation of the territory of the Empire. This at least may be collected from another letter, dated St. Cloud, 17th August, written upon hearing from M. Alexandre de la Rochefoucauld, his Ambassador in Holland, and from his brother himself, the opposition of Louis to his project.

The letter was as follows:—

> BROTHER—I have received your letter relating to that of the Sieur de la Rochefoucauld. He was only authorised to make the proposals indirectly. Since the exchange does not please you, let us think no more about it. It was useless to make a parade of principles, though I never said that you ought not to consult the nation. The well-informed part of the Dutch people had already acknowledged their indifference to the loss of Brabant, which is connected with France rather than with Holland, and interspersed with expensive fortresses; it might have been advantageously exchanged for the northern provinces. But, once for all, since you do not like this arrangement, let no more be said about it. It was useless even to mention it to me, for the Sieur de la Rochefoucauld was instructed merely to hint the matter.

Though ill-humour here evidently peeps out beneath affected condescension, yet the tone of this letter is singularly moderate,—I may even say kind, in comparison with other letters which Napoleon addressed to Louis. This letter, it is true, was written previously to the interview at Erfurt, when Napoleon, to avoid alarming Russia, made his ambition appear to slumber. But when he got his brother Joseph recognised, and when he had himself struck an important blow in the Peninsula, he began to change his tone to Louis. On the 20th of December he wrote a very remarkable letter, which exhibits the unreserved expression of that tyranny which he wished to exercise over all his family in order to make them the instruments of his despotism. He reproached Louis for not following his system of policy, telling him that he had forgotten he was a Frenchman, and that he wished to become a Dutchman. Among other things he said:

Your Majesty has done more: you took advantage of the moment when I was involved in the affairs of the Continent to renew the relations between Holland and England—to violate the laws of the blockade, which are the only means of effectually destroying the latter power. I expressed my dissatisfaction by forbidding you to come to France, and I have made you feel that even without the assistance of my armies, by merely closing the Rhine, the Weser, the Scheldt, and the Meuse against Holland, I should have placed her in a situation more critical than if I had declared war against her. Your Majesty implored my generosity, appealed to my feelings as brother, and promised to alter your conduct. I thought this warning would be sufficient. I raised my custom-house prohibitions, but your Majesty has returned to your old system.

Your Majesty received all the American ships that presented themselves in the ports of Holland after having been expelled from those of France. I have been obliged a second time to prohibit trade with Holland. In this state of things we may consider ourselves really at war. In my speech to the Legislative Body I manifested my displeasure; for I will not conceal from you that my intention is to unite Holland with France. This will be the most severe blow I can aim against England, and will deliver me from the perpetual insults which the plotters of your Cabinet are constantly directing against me. The mouths of the Rhine and of the Meuse ought, indeed, to belong to me. The principle that the 'Thalweg' (towing-path) of the Rhine is the boundary of France is a fundamental principle.

Your Majesty writes to me on the 17th that you are sure of being able to prevent all trade between Holland and England. I am of opinion that your Majesty promises more than you can fulfil. I shall, however, remove my custom-house prohibitions whenever the existing treaties may be executed. The following are my conditions:—First, The interdiction of all trade and communication with England. Second, The supply of a fleet of fourteen sail-of the line, seven frigates and seven brigs or corvettes, armed and manned. Third, An army of 25,000 men. Fourth, The suppression of the rank of marshals. Fifth, The abolition of all the privileges of nobility which are contrary to the constitution which I have given and guaranteed. Your Majesty may negotiate on these bases with the Duc de Cadore, through the medium of your Minister; but be assured that on the entrance of the first packetboat into Holland I will restore my prohibitions, and that the first Dutch officer who may presume to insult my flag shall be seized, and hanged at the mainyard. Your Majesty will find in me a brother if you prove yourself a Frenchman; but if you forget the sentiments which attach you to our common country you cannot think it extraordinary that I should lose sight of those which nature created between us.

In short, the union of Holland and France will be of all things, most useful to France, to Holland, and the whole Continent, because it will be most injurious to England. This union must be effected willingly or by force. Holland has given me sufficient reason to declare war against her. However, I shall not scruple to consent to an arrangement which will secure to me the limit of the Rhine, and by which Holland will pledge herself to fulfil the conditions stipulated above.[236]

Here the correspondence between the two brothers was suspended for a time; but Louis still continued exposed to new vexations on the part of Napoleon. About the end of 1809 the Emperor summoned all the sovereigns who might be called his vassals to Paris. Among the number was Louis, who, however, did not show himself very willing to quit his States. He called a council of his Ministers, who were of opinion that for the interest of Holland he ought to make this new sacrifice. He did so with resignation. Indeed, every day passed on the throne was a sacrifice made by Louis.

He lived very quietly in Paris, and was closely watched by the police, for it was supposed that as he had come against his will he would not protract his stay so long as Napoleon wished. The system of espionage under which he found himself placed, added to the other circumstances of his situation, inspired him with a degree of energy of which he was not believed to be capable; and amidst the general silence of the servants of the Empire, and even of the Kings and Princes assembled in the capital, he ventured to say, "I have been deceived by promises which were never intended to be kept. Holland is tired of being the sport of France." The Emperor, who was unused to such language as this, was highly incensed at it. Louis had now no alternative but to yield to the incessant exactions of Napoleon or to see Holland united to France. He chose the latter, though not before he had exerted all his feeble power in behalf of the subjects whom Napoleon had consigned to him; but he would not be the accomplice of the man who had resolved to make those subjects the victims of his hatred against England. Who, indeed, could be so blind as not to see that the ruin of the Continent would be the triumph of British commerce?

Louis was, however, permitted to return to his States to contemplate the stagnating effect of the Continental blockade on every branch of trade and industry formerly so active in Holland. Distressed at witnessing evils to which he could apply no remedy, he endeavoured by some prudent remonstrances to avert the utter, ruin with which Holland was threatened. On the 23d of March 1810 he wrote the following letter to Napoleon:—

---

236 Much of the manner in which Napoleon treated occupied countries such as Holland is explained by the spirit of his answer when Beugnot complained to him of the harm done to the Grand Duchy of Berg by the monopoly of tobacco. "It is extraordinary that you should not have discovered the motive that makes me persist in the establishment of the monopoly of tobacco in the Grand Duchy. The question is not about your Grand Duchy but about France. I am very well aware that it is not to your benefit, and that you very possibly lose by it, but what does that signify if it be for the good of France? I tell you, then, that in every country where there is a monopoly of tobacco, but which is contiguous to one where the sale is free, a regular smuggling infiltration must be reckoned on, supplying the consumption for twenty or twenty-five miles into the country subject to the duty. That is what I intend to preserve France from. You must protect yourselves as well as you can from this infiltration. It is enough for me to drive it back more than twenty or twenty-five miles from my frontier." (Beugnot, vol. ii. p. 26).

> If you wish to consolidate the present state of France, to obtain maritime peace, or to attack England with advantage, those objects are not to be obtained by measures like the blockading system, the destruction of a kingdom raised by yourself, or the enfeebling of your allies, and setting at defiance their most sacred rights and the first principles of the law of nations. You should, on the contrary, win their affections for France, and consolidate and reinforce your allies, making them like your brothers, in whom you may place confidence. The destruction of Holland, far from being the means of assailing England, will serve only to increase her strength, by all the industry and wealth which will fly to her for refuge. There are, in reality, only three ways of assailing England, namely, by detaching Ireland, getting possession of the East Indies, or by invasion. These two latter modes, which would be the most effectual, cannot be executed without naval force. But I am astonished that the first should have been so easily relinquished. That is a more secure mode of obtaining peace on good conditions than the system of injuring ourselves for the sake of committing a greater injury upon the enemy.
>
> (*Signed*) LOUIS.

Written remonstrances were no more to Napoleon's taste than verbal ones at a time when, as I was informed by my friends whom fortune chained to his destiny, no one presumed to address a word to him except in answer to his questions. Cambacérès, who alone had retained that privilege in public as his old colleague in the Consulate, lost it after Napoleon's marriage with the daughter of Imperial Austria. His brother's letter highly roused his displeasure. Two months after he received it, being on a journey in the north, he replied from Ostend by a letter which cannot be read without a feeling of pain, since it serves to show how weak are the most sacred ties of blood in comparison with the interests of an insatiable policy. This letter was as follows:

> BROTHER—In the situation in which we are placed it is best to speak candidly. I know your secret sentiments, and all that you can say to the contrary can avail nothing. Holland is certainly in a melancholy situation. I believe you are anxious to extricate her from her difficulties: it is you; and you alone, who can do this. When you conduct yourself in such a way as to induce the people of Holland to believe that you act under my influence, that all your measures and all your sentiments are conformable with mine, then you will be loved, you will be esteemed, and you will acquire the power requisite for re-establishing Holland: when to be my friend, and the friend of France, shall become a title of favour at your court, Holland will be in her natural situation. Since your return from Paris you have done nothing to effect this object. What will be the result of your conduct? Your subjects, bandied about between France and England, will throw themselves into the arms of France, and will demand to be united to her. You know my character, which is to pursue my object unimpeded by any consideration. What, therefore, do you expect me to do? I can dispense with Holland, but Holland cannot dispense with my protection. If, under the dominion of one of my brothers, but looking to me alone for her welfare, she does not

find in her sovereign my image, all confidence in your government is at an end; your sceptre is broken. Love France, love my glory—that is the only way to serve Holland: if you had acted as you ought to have done that country, having becoming a part of my Empire, would have been the more dear to me since I had given her a sovereign whom I almost regarded as my son. In placing you on the throne of Holland I thought I had placed a French citizen there. You have followed a course diametrically opposite to what I expected. I have been forced to prohibit you from coming to France, and to take possession of a part of your territory. In proving yourself a bad Frenchman you are less to the Dutch than a Prince of Orange, to whose family they owe their rank as a nation, and a long succession of prosperity and glory. By your banishment from France the Dutch are convinced that they have lost what they would not have lost under a Schimmelpenninek or a Prince of Orange. Prove yourself a Frenchman, and the brother of the Emperor, and be assured that thereby you will serve the interests of Holland. But you seem to be incorrigible, for you would drive away the few Frenchmen who remain with you. You must be dealt with, not by affectionate advice, but by threats and compulsion. What mean the prayers and mysterious fasts you have ordered? Louis, you will not reign long. Your actions disclose better than your confidential letters the sentiments of your mind. Return to the right course. Be a Frenchman in heart, or your people will banish you, and you will leave Holland an object of ridicule.[237] States must be governed by reason and policy, and not by the weakness produced by acrid and vitiated humours.

(Signed) NAPOLEON.

A few days after this letter was despatched to Louis, Napoleon heard of a paltry affray which had taken place at Amsterdam, and to which Comte de la Rochefoucauld gave a temporary diplomatic importance, being aware that he could not better please his master than by affording him an excuse for being angry. It appeared that the honour of the Count's coachman had been put in jeopardy by the insult of a citizen of Amsterdam, and a quarrel had ensued, which, but for the interference of the guard of the palace, might have terminated seriously since it assumed the character of a party affair between the French and the Dutch. M. de la Rochefoucauld immediately despatched to the Emperor, who was then at Lille, a full report of his coachman's quarrel, in which he expressed himself with as much earnestness as the illustrious author of the "Maxims" evinced when he waged war against kings. The consequence was that Napoleon instantly fulminated the following letter against his brother Louis:

237 It was, on the contrary, became Louis made himself a Dutchman that his people did not banish him, and that he carried away with him the regret of all that portion of his subjects who could appreciate his excellent qualities and possessed good sense enough to perceive that he was not to blame for the evils that weighed upon Holland.—Bourrienne. The conduct of Bonaparte to Murat was almost a counterpart to this. When Murat attempted to consult the interests of Naples he was called a traitor to France.—Editor of 1836 edition.

> BROTHER—At the very moment when you were making the fairest protestations I learn that the servants of my Ambassador have been ill-treated at Amsterdam. I insist that those who were guilty of this outrage be delivered up to me, in order that their punishment may serve as an example to others. The Sieur Serrurier has informed me how you conducted yourself at the diplomatic audiences. I have, consequently, determined that the Dutch Ambassador shall not remain in Paris; and Admiral Yerhuell has received orders to depart within twenty-four hours. I want no more phrases and protestations. It is time I should know whether you intend to ruin Holland by your follies. I do not choose that you should again send a Minister to Austria, or that you should dismiss the French who are in your service. I have recalled my Ambassador as I intend only to have a charge d'affaires in Holland. The Sieur Serrurier, who remains there in that capacity, will communicate my intentions. My Ambassador shall no longer be exposed to your insults. Write to me no more of those set phrases which you have been repeating for the last three years, and the falsehood of which is proved every day. This is the last letter I will ever write to you as long as I live.
>
> (*Signed*) NAPOLEON.

Thus reduced to the cruel alternative of crushing Holland with his own hands, or leaving that task to the Emperor, Louis did not hesitate to lay down his sceptre. Having formed this resolution, he addressed a message to the Legislative Body of the Kingdom of Holland explaining the motives of his abdication. The French troops entered Holland under the command of the Duke of Reggio, and that marshal, who was more a king than the King himself, threatened to occupy Amsterdam. Louis then descended from his throne, and four years after Napoleon was hurled from his.

In his act of abdication Louis declared that he had been driven to that step by the unhappy state of his Kingdom, which he attributed to his brother's unfavourable feelings towards him. He added that he had made every effort and sacrifice to put an end to that painful state of things, and that, finally, he regarded himself as the cause of the continual misunderstanding between the French Empire and Holland. It is curious that Louis thought he could abdicate the crown of Holland in favour of his son, as Napoleon only four years after wished to abdicate his crown in favour of the King of Rome.

Louis bade farewell to the people of Holland in a proclamation, after the publication of which he repaired to the waters at Toeplitz. There he was living in tranquil retirement when he learned that his brother had united Holland to the Empire. He then published a protest, of which I obtained a copy, though its circulation was strictly prohibited by the police. In this protest Louis said:

> The constitution of the state guaranteed by the Emperor, my brother, gave me the right of abdicating in favour of my children. That abdication was made in the form and terms prescribed by the constitution. The Emperor had no right to declare war against Holland, and he has not done so. There is no act, no dissent, no demand of the Dutch nation that can authorise the pretended union. My abdication does not leave the throne vacant. I have abdicated only in favour of my children. As that abdication

left Holland for twelve years under a regency, that is to say, under the direct influence of the Emperor, according to the terms of the constitution, there was no need of that union for executing every measure he might have in view against trade and against England, since his will was supreme in Holland. But I ascended the throne without any other conditions except those imposed upon me by my conscience, my duty, and the interest and welfare of my subjects. I therefore declare before God and the independent sovereigns to whom I address myself— First, That the treaty of the 16th of March 1810, which occasioned the separation of the province of Zealand and Brabant from Holland, was accepted by compulsion, and ratified conditionally by me in Paris, where I was detained against my will; and that, moreover, the treaty was never executed by the Emperor my brother. Instead of 6000 French troops which I was to maintain, according to the terms of the treaty, that number has been more than doubled; instead of occupying only the mouths of the rivers and the coasts, the French custom-horses have encroached into the interior of the country; instead of the interference of France being confined to the measures connected with the blockade of England, Dutch magazines have been seized and Dutch subjects arbitrarily imprisoned; finally, none of the verbal promises have been kept which were made in the Emperor's name by the Duc de Cadore to grant indemnities for the countries ceded by the said treaty and to mitigate its execution, if the King would refer entirely to the Emperor, etc. I declare, in my name, in the name of the nation and my son, the treaty of the 16th of March 1810 to be null and void. Second, I declare that my abdication was forced by the Emperor, my brother, that it was made only as the last extremity, and on this one condition—that I should maintain the rights of Holland and my children. My abdication could only be made in their favour. Third, In my name, in the name of the King my son, who is as yet a minor, and in the name of the Dutch nation, I declare the pretended union of Holland to France, mentioned in the decree of the Emperor, my brother, dated the 9th of July last, to be null, void, illegal, unjust, and arbitrary in the eyes of God and man, and that the nation and the minor King will assert their just rights when circumstances permit them.

(*Signed*) LOUIS.

August 1, 1810.

Thus there seemed to be an end of all intercourse between these two brothers, who were so opposite in character and disposition. But Napoleon, who was enraged that Louis should have presumed to protest, and that in energetic terms, against the union of his Kingdom with the Empire, ordered him to return to France, whither he was summoned in his character of Constable and French Prince. Louis, however, did not think proper to obey this summons, and Napoleon, mindful of his promise of never writing to him again, ordered the following letter to be addressed to him by M. Otto, who had been Ambassador from France to Vienna since the then recent marriage of the Emperor with Maria Louisa—

SIRE:—The Emperor directs me to write to your Majesty as follows:— "It is the duty of every French Prince, and every member of the Imperial family, to reside in France, whence they cannot absent themselves without the permission of the Emperor. Before the union of Holland to the Empire the Emperor permitted the King to reside at Toeplitz, is Bohemia. His health appeared to require the use of the waters, but now the Emperor requires that Prince Louis shall return, at the latest by the 1st of December next, under pain of being considered as disobeying the constitution of the Empire and the head of his family, and being treated accordingly." I fulfil, Sire, word for word the mission with which I have been entrusted, and I send the chief secretary of the embassy to be assured that this letter is rightly delivered. I beg your Majesty to accept the homage of my respect, etc.

(*Signed*) OTTO.[238]

What a letter was this to be addressed by a subject to a prince and a sovereign. When I afterwards saw M. Otto in Paris, and conversed with him on the subject, he assured me how much he had been distressed at the necessity of writing such a letter to the brother of the Emperor. He had employed the expressions dictated by Napoleon in that irritation which he could never command when his will was opposed.[239]

238 The eldest son of Louis, one of the fruits of his unhappy marriage with Hortense Beauharnais, the daughter of Josephine, the wife of his brother Napoleon, was little more than six years of age when his father abdicated the crown of Holland in his favour. In 1830-31 this imprudent young man joined the ill-combined mad insurrection in the States of the Pope. He was present in one or two petty skirmishes, and was, we believe, wounded; but it was a malaria fever caught in the unhealthy Campagna of Rome that carried him to the grave in the twenty-seventh year of his age.—Editor of 1836 edition.— The first child of Louis and of Hortense had died in 1807. The second son, Napoleon Louis (1804-1831) in whose favour he abdicated had been created Grand Duc de Berg et de Cleves by Napoleon in 1809. He married to 1826 Charlotte, the daughter of Joseph Bonaparte, and died in 1831, while engaged in a revolutionary movement in Italy. On his death his younger brother Charles Louis Napoleon, the future Napoleon III., first came forward as an aspirant.

239 With regard to Louis and his conduct in Holland Napoleon thus spoke at St. Helena: "Louis is not devoid of intelligence, and has a good heart, but even with these qualifications a man may commit many errors, and do a great deal of mischief. Louis is naturally inclined to be capricious and fantastical, and the works of Jean Jacques Rousseau have contributed to increase this disposition. Seeking to obtain a reputation for sensibility and beneficence, incapable by himself of enlarged views, and, at most, competent to local details, Louis acted like a prefect rather than a King. "No sooner had he arrived in Holland than, fancying that nothing could be finer than to have it said that he was thenceforth a true Dutchman, he attached himself entirely to the party favourable to the English, promoted smuggling, and than connived with our enemies. It became necessary from that moment watch over him, and even threaten to wage war against him. Louis then seeking a refuge against the weakness of his disposition in the most stubborn obstinacy, and mistaking a public scandal for an act

of glory, fled from his throne, declaiming against me and against my insatiable ambition, my intolerable tyranny, etc. What then remained for me to do? Was I to abandon Holland to our enemies? Ought I to have given it another King? But is that case could I have expected more from him than from my own brother? Did not all the Kings that I created act nearly in the same manner? I therefore united Holland to the Empire, and this act produced a most unfavourable impression in Europe, and contributed not a little to lay the foundation of our misfortunes" (Memorial de Sainte Helene)

CHAPTER XVIII

1809

Bonaparte, the foundations of whose Empire were his sword and his. victories, and who was anxiously looking forward to the time when the sovereigns of Continental Europe should be his juniors, applied for contingents of troops from the States to which I was accredited. The Duchy of Mecklenburg-Schwerin was to furnish a regiment of 1800 men, and the other little States, such as Oldenburg and Mecklenburg-Strelitz, were to furnish regiments of less amount. All Europe was required to rise in arms to second the gigantic projects of the new sovereign. This demand for contingents, and the positive way in which the Emperor insisted upon them, gave rise to an immense correspondence, which, however, was unattended by any result. The notes and orders remained in the portfolios, and the contingents stayed at home.

M. Metternich, whose talent has since been so conspicuously displayed, had been for upwards of a year Ambassador from Austria to Paris. Even then he excelled in the art of guiding men's minds, and of turning to the advantage of his policy his external graces and the favour he acquired in the drawing-room. His father, a clever man, brought up in the old diplomatic school of Thugut and Kaunitz, had early accustomed him to the task of making other Governments believe, by means of agents, what might lead them into error and tend to the advantage of his own Government. His manoeuvres tended to make Austria assume a discontented and haughty tone; and wishing, as she said, to secure her independence, she publicly declared her intention of protecting herself against any enterprise similar to those of which she had so often been the victim. This language, encouraged by the complete evacuation of Germany, and the war in Spain, the unfortunate issue of which was generally foreseen, was used—in time of peace between the two empires, and when France was not threatening war to Austria.[240]

M. Metternich, who had instructions from his Court, gave no satisfactory explanation of those circumstances to Napoleon, who immediately raised a conscription, and brought soldiers from Spain into Germany.

---

240 Metternich arrived in Paris as Ambassador on 4th August 1806, after Austria had been vanquished at Austerlitz. It does not seem probable, either from his views or his correspondence, that he advised the rash attempt of Austria to attack Napoleon by herself; compare Metternich tome 1. p. 69, on the mistake of Prussia in 1805 and 1806; see also tome ii. p. 221, "To provoke a war with France would be madness" (1st July 1808). On the other hand, the tone of his correspondence in 1808 seams calculated to make Austria believe that war was inevitable, and that her forces, "so inferior to those of France before the insurrection in Spain, will at least be equal to them immediately after that event" (tome ii. p. 808). What is curious is that Metternich's conduct towards Napoleon while Ambassador had led even such men as Duke Dalberg to believe that he was really so well disposed towards Napoleon as to serve his cause more than that of Austria.

It was necessary, also, to come to an understanding with Russia, who, being engaged with her war in Finland and Turkey, appeared desirous neither to enter into alliance with Austria nor to afford her support. What, in fact, was the Emperor Alexander's situation with respect to France? He had signed a treaty of peace at Tilsit which he felt had been forced upon him, and he knew that time alone would render it possible for him to take part in a contest which it was evident would again be renewed either with Prussia or Austria.

Every person of common sense must have perceived that Austria, in taking up arms, reckoned, if not on the assistance, at least on the neutrality of Russia. Russia was then engaged with two enemies, the Swedes and the Turks, over whom she hoped to triumph. She therefore rejoiced to see France again engage in a struggle with Austria, and there was no doubt that she would take advantage of any chances favourable to the latter power to join her in opposing the encroachments of France. I never could conceive how, under those circumstances, Napoleon could be so blind as to expect assistance from Russia in his quarrel with Austria. He must, indeed, have been greatly deceived as to the footing on which the two Courts stood with reference to each other—their friendly footing and their mutual agreement to oppose the overgrowing ambition of their common enemy.

The English, who had been compelled to quit Spain, now returned there. They landed in Portugal, which might be almost regarded as their own colony, and marched against Marshal Soult, who left Spain to meet them. Any other man than Soult would perhaps have been embarrassed by the obstacles which he had to surmount. A great deal has been said about his wish to make himself King of Portugal. Bernadotte told me, when he passed through Hamburg, that the matter had been the subject of much conversation at headquarters after the battle of Wagram. Bernadotte placed no faith in the report, and I am pretty sure that Napoleon also disbelieved it. However, this matter is still involved in the obscurity from which it will only be drawn when some person acquainted with the intrigue shall give a full explanation of it.

Since I have, with reference to Soult, touched upon the subject of his supposed ambition, I will mention here what I know of Murat's expectation of succeeding the Emperor. When Romanzow returned from his useless mission of mediation to London the Emperor proceeded to Bayonne. Bernadotte, who had an agent in Paris whom he paid highly, told me one day that he had received a despatch informing him that Murat entertained the idea of one day succeeding the Emperor. Sycophants, expecting to derive advantage from it, encouraged Murat in this chimerical hope. I know not whether Napoleon was acquainted with this circumstance, nor what he said of it, but Bernadotte spoke of it to me as a certain fact. It would, however, have been very wrong to attach great importance to an expression which, perhaps, escaped Murat in a moment of ardour, for his natural temperament sometimes betrayed him into acts of imprudence, the result of which, with a man like Napoleon, was always to be dreaded.

It was in the midst of the operations of the Spanish war, which Napoleon directed in person, that he learned Austria had for the first time raised the landwehr. I obtained some very curious documents respecting the armaments of Austria from the Editor of the Hamburg 'Correspondent'. This paper, the circulation of which amounted to not less than 60,000, paid considerable sums to persons in different parts of Europe who were able and willing to furnish the current news. The Correspondent paid 6000 francs a year to a clerk in the war department at Vienna, and it was this clerk who supplied the intelligence that Austria was preparing for war, and that orders had been issued in all directions to collect and put in motion all the resources of that powerful monarchy. I communicated these particulars to the French Government, and suggested the necessity of increased vigilance and measures of defence. Preceding aggressions, especially that of 1805, were not to be forgotten. Similar information probably reached the French Government from many quarters. Be that as it may, the Emperor consigned the military operations in Spain to his generals, and departed for Paris, where he arrived at the end of January 1809. He had been in Spain only since the beginning of November 1808,' and his presence there had again rendered our banners victorious. But though the insurgent troops were beaten the inhabitants showed themselves more and more unfavourable to Joseph's cause; and it did not appear very probable that he could ever seat himself tranquilly on the throne of Madrid.[241] The Emperor Francis, notwithstanding his counsellors, hesitated about taking the first step; but at length, yielding to the solicitations of England and the secret intrigues of Russia, and, above all, seduced by the subsidies of Great Britain, Austria declared hostilities, not at first against France, but against her allies of the Confederation of the Rhine. On the 9th of April Prince Charles, who was appointed commander-in-chief of the Austrian troops, addressed a note to the commander-in-chief of the French army in Bavaria, apprising him of the declaration of war.

A courier carried the news of this declaration to Strasburg with the utmost expedition, from whence it was transmitted by telegraph to Paris. The Emperor, surprised but not disconcerted by this intelligence, received it at St. Cloud on the 11th of April, and two hours after he was on the road to Germany. The complexity of affairs in which he was then involved seemed to give a new impulse to his activity. When he reached the army neither his troops nor his Guard had been able to come up, and under those circumstances he placed himself at the head of the Bavarian troops, and, as it were, adopted the soldiers of Maximilian. Six days after his departure from Paris the army of Prince Charles, which had passed the Inn, was threatened. The Emperor's headquarters were at Donauwerth, and from thence he addressed to his soldiers one of those energetic and concise proclamations which made them perform so many prodigies, and which was soon circulated in every language by the public journals. This complication of events could not but be fatal to Europe and France, whatever might be its result, but it presented an opportunity favourable to the development of the Emperor's genius. Like his favourite poet Ossian, who loved best to touch his lyre midst the howlings of the tempest, Napoleon required political tempests for the display of his abilities.

During the campaign of 1809, and particularly at its commencement, Napoleon's course was even more rapid than it had been in the campaign of 1805. Every courier who arrived at Hamburg brought us news, or rather prodigies. As soon as the Emperor was informed of the attack made by the Austrians upon Bavaria orders were despatched to all the generals having

241 The successes obtained by Napoleon during his stay of about three months in Spain were certainly very great, and mainly resulted from his own masterly genius and lightning-like rapidity. The Spanish armies, as yet unsupported by British troops, were defeated at Gomenal, Espinosa, Reynosa, Tudela, and at the pass of the Somo sierra Mountains, and at an early hour of the morning of the 4th December Madrid surrendered. On the 20th of December Bonaparte marched with far superior forces against the unfortunate Sir John Moore, who had been sent to advance into Spain both by the wrong route and at a wrong time. On the 29th, from the heights of Benevento, his eyes were delighted by seeing the English in full retreat. But a blow struck him from another quarter, and leaving Soult to follow up Moore he took the road to Paris.

troops under their command to proceed with all speed to the theatre of the war. The Prince of Ponte-Corvo was summoned to join the Grand Army with the Saxon troops under his command and for the time he resigned the government of the Hanse Towns. Colonel Damas succeeded him at Hamburg during that period, but merely as commandant of the fortress; and he never gave rise to any murmur or complaint. Bernadotte was not satisfied with his situation, and indeed the Emperor, who was never much disposed to bring him forward, because he could not forgive him for his opposition on the 18th Brumaire, always appointed him to posts in which but little glory was to be acquired, and placed as few troops as possible under his command.

It required all the promptitude of the Emperor's march upon Vienna to defeat the plots which were brewing against his government, for in the event of his arms being unsuccessful, the blow was ready to be struck. The English force in the north of Germany amounted to about 10,000 men: The Archduke Charles had formed the project of concentrating in the middle of Germany a large body of troops, consisting of the corps of General Am Eude, of General Radizwowitz, and of the English, with whom were to be joined the people who were expected to revolt. The English would have wished the Austrian troops to advance a little farther. The English agent made some representations on this subject to Stadion, the Austrian Minister; but the Archduke preferred making a diversion to committing the safety of the monarchy by departing from his present inactivity and risking the passage of the Danube, in the face of an enemy who never suffered himself to be surprised, and who had calculated every possible event: In concerting his plan the Archduke expected that the Czar would either detach a strong force to assist his allies, or that he would abandon them to their own defence. In the first case the Archduke would have had a great superiority, and in the second, all was prepared in Hesse and in Hanover to rise on the approach of the Austrian and English armies.

At the commencement of July the English advanced upon Cuxhaven with a dozen small ships of war. They landed 400 or 600 sailors and about 50 marines, and planted a standard on one of the outworks. The day after this landing at Cuxhaven the English, who were in Denmark evacuated Copenhagen, after destroying a battery which they had erected there. All the schemes of England were fruitless on the Continent, for with the Emperor's new system of war, which consisted in making a push on the capitals, he soon obtained negotiations for peace. He was master of Vienna before England had even organised the expedition to which I have just alluded. He left Paris on the 11th of April, was at Donauwerth on the 17th, and on the 23d he was master of Ratisbon. In the engagement which preceded his entrance into that town Napoleon received a slight wound in the heel. He nevertheless remained on the field of battle. It was also between Donauwerth and Ratisbon that Davoust, by a bold manoeuvre, gained and merited the title of Prince of Eckmuhl.[242]

At this period fortune was not only bent on favouring Napoleon's arms, but she seemed to take pleasure in realising even his boasting predictions; for the French troops entered Vienna within a month after a proclamation issued by Napoleon at Ratisbon, in which he said he would be master of the Austrian capital in that time.

But while he was thus marching from triumph to triumph the people of Hamburg and the neighbouring countries had a neighbour who did not leave them altogether without

242 The great battle of Eckmuhl, where 100,000 Austrians were driven from all their positions, was fought on the 22d of April.—Editor of 1836 edition.

inquietude. The famous Prussian partisan, Major Schill, after pursuing his system of plunder in Westphalia, came and threw himself into Mecklenburg, whence, I understood, it was his intention to surprise Hamburg. At the head of 600 well-mounted hussars and between 1500 and 2000 infantry badly armed, he took possession of the little fort of Domitz, in Mecklenburg, on the 15th of May, from whence he despatched parties who levied contributions on both banks of the Elbe. Schill inspired terror wherever he went. On the 19th of May a detachment of 30 men belonging to Schill's corps entered Wismar. It was commanded by Count Moleke, who had formerly been in the Prussian service, and who had retired to his estate in Mecklenburg, where the Duke had kindly given him an appointment. Forgetting his duty to his benefactor, he sent to summon the Duke to surrender Stralsund.

Alarmed at the progress of the partisan Schill, the Duke of Mecklenburg and his Court quitted Ludwigsburg, their regular residence, and retired to Doberan, on the seacoast. On quitting Mecklenburg Schill advanced to Bergdorf, four leagues from Hamburg. The alarm then increased in that city. A few of the inhabitants talked of making a compromise with Schill and sending him money to get him away. But the firmness of the majority imposed silence on this timid council. I consulted with the commandant of the town, and we determined to adopt measures of precaution. The custom-house chest, in which there was more than a million of gold, was sent to Holstein under a strong escort. At the same time I sent to Schill a clever spy, who gave him a most alarming account of the means of defence which Hamburg possessed. Schill accordingly gave up his designs on that city, and leaving it on his left, entered Lübeck, which was undefended.

Meanwhile Lieutenant-General Gratien, who had left Berlin by order of the Prince de Neufchatel, with 2500 Dutch and 3000 Swedish troops, actively pursued Schill, and tranquillity was soon restored throughout all the neighbouring country, which had been greatly agitated by his bold enterprise. Schill, after wandering for some days on the shores of the Baltic, was overtaken by General Gratien at Stralsund, whence he was about to embark for Sweden. He made a desperate defence, and was killed after a conflict of two hours. His band was destroyed. Three hundred of his hussars and 200 infantry, who had effected their escape, asked leave to return to Prussia, and they were conducted to the Prussian general commanding a neighbouring town. A war of plunder like that carried on by Schill could not be honourably acknowledged by a power having, any claim to respect. Yet the English Government sent Schill a colonel's commission, and the full uniform of his new rank, with the assurance that all his troops should thenceforth be paid by England.

Schill soon had an imitator of exalted rank. In August 1809 the Duke of Brunswick-OEls sought the dangerous honour of succeeding that famous partisan. At the head of at most 2000 men he for some days disturbed the left bank of the Elbe, and on the 5th entered Bremen. On his approach the French Vice-Consul retired to Osterhulz. One of the Duke's officers presented himself at the hones of the Vice-Consul and demanded 200 Louis. The agent of the Vice-Consul, alarmed at the threat of the place being given up to pillage, capitulated with the officer, and with considerable difficulty got rid of him at the sacrifice of 80 Louis, for which a receipt was presented to him in the name of the Duke. The Duke, who now went by the name of "the new Schill," did not remain long in Bremen.

Wishing to repair with all possible speed to Holland he left Bremen on the evening of the 6th, and proceeded to Dehnenhorst, where his advanced guard had already arrived. The Westphalian troops, commanded by Rewbell, entered Bremen on the 7th, and not finding the Duke of Brunswick, immediately marched in pursuit of him. The Danish troops, who occupied Cuxhaven, received orders to proceed to Bremerlehe, to favour the operations of the Westphalians and the Dutch. Meanwhile the English approached Cuxhaven, where they landed 3000 or 4000 men. The persons in charge of the custom-house establishment, and the few sailors who were in Cuxhaven, fell back upon Hamburg. The Duke of Brunswick, still pursued crossed Germany from the frontiers of Bohemia to Elsfleth, a little port on the left bank of the Weser, where he arrived on the 7th, being one day in advance of his pursuers. He immediately took possession of all the transports at Elsfleth, and embarked for Heligoland.

The landing which the English effected at Cuxhaven while the Danes, who garrisoned that port, were occupied in pursuing the Duke of Brunswick, was attended by no result. After the escape of the Duke the Danes returned to their post which the English immediately evacuated.

CHAPTER XIX

1809

Rapp, who during the campaign of Vienna had resumed his duties as aide de camp, related to me one of those observations of Napoleon which, when his words are compared with the events that followed them, seem to indicate a foresight into his future destiny. When within some days' march of Vienna the Emperor procured a guide to explain to him every village and ruin which he observed on the road. The guide pointed to an eminence on which were a few decayed vestiges of an old fortified castle. "Those," said the guide, "are the ruins of the castle of Diernstein." Napoleon suddenly stopped, and stood for some time silently contemplating the ruins, then turning to Lannes, who was with him, he raid, "See! yonder is the prison of Richard Coeur de Lion. He, like us, went to Syria and Palestine. But, my brave Lannes, the Coeur de Lion was not braver than you. He was more fortunate than I at St. Jean d'Acre. A Duke of Austria sold him to an Emperor of Germany, who imprisoned him in that castle. Those were the days of barbarism. How different from the civilisation of modern times! Europe has seen how I treated the Emperor of Austria, whom I might have made prisoner—and I would treat him so again. I claim no credit for this. In the present age crowned heads must be respected. A conqueror imprisoned!"

A few days after the Emperor was at the gates of Vienna, but on this occasion his access to the Austrian capital was not so easy as it had been rendered in 1805 by the ingenuity and courage of Lannes and Murat. The Archduke Maximilian, who was shut up in the capital, wished to defend it, although the French army already occupied the principal suburbs. In vain were flags of truce sent one after the other to the Archduke. They were not only dismissed unheard, but were even ill-treated, and one of them was almost killed by the populace. The city was then bombarded, and would speedily have been destroyed but that the Emperor, being informed that one of the Archduchesses remained in Vienna on account of ill-health, ordered the firing to cease. By a singular caprice of Napoleon's destiny this Archduchess was no other than Maria Louisa. Vienna at length opened her gates to Napoleon, who for some days took up his residence at Schoenbrunn.

The Emperor was engaged in so many projects at once that they could not all succeed. Thus, while he was triumphant in the Hereditary States his Continental system was experiencing severe checks. The trade with England on the coast of Oldenburg was carped on as uninterruptedly as if in time of peace. English letters and newspapers arrived on the Continent, and those of the Continent found their way into Great Britain, as if France and England had been united by ties of the firmest friendship. In short, things were just in the same state as if the decree for the blockade of the British Isles had not existed. When the custom-house officers succeeded in seizing contraband goods they were again taken from them by main force. On the 2d of July a serious contest took place at Brinskham between the custom-house officers and a party of peasantry, in which the latter remained masters of eighteen wagons laden with English goods: many were wounded on both sides.

If, however, trade with England was carried on freely along a vast extent of coast, it was different in the city of Hamburg, where English goods were introduced only by fraud; and I verily believe that the art of smuggling and the schemes of smugglers were never before carried to such perfection. Above 6000 persons of the lower orders went backwards and forwards, about twenty times a day, from Altona to Hamburg, and they carried on their contraband, trade by many ingenious stratagems, two of which were so curious that they are worth mentioning here.

On the left of the road leading from Hamburg to Altona there was a piece of ground where pits were dug for the purpose of procuring sand used for building and for laying down in the streets. At this time it was proposed to repair the great street of Hamburg leading to the gate of Altona. The smugglers overnight filled the sandpit with brown sugar, and the little carts which usually conveyed the sand into Hamburg were filled with the sugar, care being taken to cover it with a layer of sand about an inch thick. This trick was carried on for a length of time, but no progress was made in repairing the street. I complained greatly of the delay, even before I was aware of its cause, for the street led to a country-house I had near Altona, whither I went daily. The officers of the customs at length perceived that the work did not proceed, and one fine morning the sugar-carts were stopped and seized. Another expedient was then to be devised.

Between Hamburg and Altona there was a little suburb situated on the right bank of the Elbe. This suburb was inhabited, by sailors, labourers of the port, and landowners. The inhabitants were interred in the cemetery of Hamburg. It was observed that funeral processions passed this way more frequently than usual. The customhouse officers, amazed at the sudden mortality of the worthy inhabitants of the little suburb, insisted on searching one of the vehicles, and on opening the hearse it was found to be filled with sugar, coffee, vanilla, indigo, etc. It was necessary to abandon this expedient, but others were soon discovered.

Bonaparte was sensitive, in an extraordinary degree, to all that was said and thought of him, and Heaven knows how many despatches I received from headquarters during the campaign of Vienna directing me not only to watch the vigilant execution of the custom-house laws, but to lay an embargo on a thing which alarmed him more than the introduction of British merchandise, viz. the publication of news. In conformity with these reiterated instructions I directed especial attention to the management of the 'Correspondant'. The importance of this journal, with its 60,000 readers, may easily be perceived. I procured the insertion of everything I thought desirable: all the bulletins, proclamations, acts of the French Government, notes of the 'Moniteur', and the semi-official articles of the French journals: these were all given 'in extenso'. On the other hand, I often suppressed adverse news, which, though well known, would have received additional weight from its insertion in so widely circulated a paper. If by chance there crept in some Austrian bulletin, extracted from the other German papers published in the States of the Confederation of the Rhine, there was always given with it a suitable antidote to destroy, or at least to mitigate, its ill effect. But this was not all. The King of Wurtemberg having reproached the 'Correspondant', in a letter to the Minister for Foreign Affairs, with publishing whatever Austria wished should be made known, and being conducted in a spirit hostile to the good cause, I answered these unjust reproaches by making the Syndic censor prohibit the Hamburg papers from inserting any Austrian order of the day, any Archduke's bulletins, any letter from Prague; in short, anything which should be copied from the other German journals unless those articles had been inserted in the French journals.

My recollections of the year 1809 at Hamburg carry me back to the celebration of Napoleon's fete, which was on the 15th of August, for he had interpolated his patron saint in the Imperial calendar at the date of his birth. The coincidence of this festival with the Assumption gave rise to adulatory rodomontades of the most absurd description. Certainly the Episcopal circulars under the Empire would form a curious collection.[243] Could anything be more revolting than the sycophancy of those Churchmen who declared that "God chose Napoleon for his representative upon earth, and that God created Bonaparte, and then rested; that he was more fortunate than Augustus, more virtuous than Trajan; that he deserved altars and temples to be raised to him!" etc.

Some time after the Festival of St. Napoleon the King of Westphalia made a journey through his States. Of all Napoleon's brothers the King of Westphalia was the one with whom I was least acquainted, and he, it is pretty well known, was the most worthless of the family. His correspondence with me is limited to two letters, one of which he wrote while he commanded the 'Epervier', and another seven years after, dated 6th September 1809. In this latter he said:

> "I shall be in Hannover on the 10th. If you can make it convenient to come there and spend a day with me it will give me great pleasure. I shall then be able to smooth all obstacles to the loan I wish to contract in the Hanse Town. I flatter myself you will do all in your power to forward that object, which at the present crisis is very important to my States. More than ample security is offered, but the money will be of no use to me if I cannot have it at least for two years."

Jerome wanted to contract at Hamburg a loan of 3,000,000 francs. However, the people did not seem to think like his Westphalian Majesty, that the contract presented more than ample security. No one was found willing to draw his purse-strings, and the loan was never raised.

Though I would not, without the Emperor's authority, exert the influence of my situation to further the success of Jerome's negotiation, yet I did my best to assist him. I succeeded in prevailing on the Senate to advance one loan of 100,000 francs to pay a portion of the arrears due to his troops, and a second of 200,000 francs to provide clothing for his army, etc. This scanty supply will cease to be wondered at when it is considered to what a state of desolation the whole of Germany was reduced at the time, as much in the allied States as in those of the enemies of France. I learnt at the time that the King of Bavaria said to an officer of the Emperor's household in whom he had great confidence, "If this continues we shall have to give up, and put the key under the door." These were his very words.

As for Jerome, he returned to Cassel quite disheartened at the unsuccessful issue of his loan. Some days after his return to his capital I received from him a snuffbox with his

243 It will perhaps scarcely be believed that the following words were actually delivered from the pulpit: "God in his mercy has chosen Napoleon to be his representative on earth. The Queen of Heaven has marked, by the most magnificent of presents, the anniversary of the day which witnessed his glorious entrance into her domains. Heavenly Virgin! as a special testimony of your love for the French, and your all-powerful influence with your son, you have connected the first of your solemnities with the birth of the great Napoleon. Heaven ordained that the hero should spring from your sepulchre."—Bourrienne.

portrait set in diamonds, accompanied by a letter of thanks for the service I had rendered him. I never imagined that a token of remembrance from a crowned head could possibly be declined. Napoleon, however, thought otherwise. I had not, it is true, written to acquaint our Government with the King of Westphalia's loan, but in a letter, which I addressed to the Minister for Foreign Affairs on the 22d of September, I mentioned the present Jerome had sent me. Why Napoleon should have been offended at this I know not, but I received orders to return Jerome's present immediately, and these orders were accompanied with bitter reproaches for my having accepted it without the Emperor's authority. I sent back the diamonds, but kept the portrait. Knowing Bonaparte's distrustful disposition, I thought he must have suspected that Jerome had employed threats, or at any rate, that he had used some illegal influence to facilitate the success of his loan. At last, after much correspondence, Napoleon saw clearly that everything was perfectly regular; in a word, that the business had been transacted as between two private persons. As to the 300,000 francs which the Senate had lent to Jerome, the fact is, that but little scruple was made about it, for this simple reason, that it was the means of removing from Hamburg the Westphalian division, whose presence occasioned a much greater expense than the loan.

CHAPTER XX

1809

Napoleon went to inspect all the corps of his army and the field of Wagram, which a short time before had been the scene of one of those great battles in which victory was the more glorious in proportion as it had been valiantly contested.[244]

On that day [the type] of French honour, Macdonald, who, after achieving a succession of prodigies, led the army of Italy into the heart of the Austrian States, was made a marshal on the field of battle. Napoleon said to him, "With us it is for life and for death." The general opinion was that the elevation of Macdonald added less to the marshal's military reputation than it redounded to the honour of the Emperor. Five days after the bombardment of Vienna, namely, on the 17th of May, the Emperor had published a decree, by virtue of which the Papal States were united to the French Empire, and Rome was declared an Imperial City. I will not stop to inquire whether this was good or bad in point of policy, but it was a mean usurpation on the part of Napoleon, for the time was passed when a Julius II. laid down the keys of St. Peter and took up the sword of St. Paul. It was, besides, an injustice, and, considering the Pope's condescension to Napoleon, an act of ingratitude. The decree of union did not deprive the Pope of his residence, but he was only the First Bishop of Christendom, with a revenue of 2,000,000.

Napoleon while at Vienna heard of the affair of Talavera de la Reyna. I was informed, by a letter from headquarters, that he was much affected at the news, and did not conceal his vexation. I verily believe that he was bent on the conquest of Spain, precisely on account of the difficulties he had to surmount. At Talavera commenced the celebrity of a man who, perhaps, would not have been without some glory even if pains had not been taken to build him up a great reputation. That battle commenced the career of Sir Arthur Wellesley, whose after-success, however, has been attended by such important consequences.[245]

Whilst we experienced this check in Spain the English were attempting an expedition to Holland, where they had already made themselves masters of Walcheren. It is true they were obliged to evacuate it shortly after; but as at that time the French and Austrian armies were in a state of inaction, in consequence of the armistice concluded at Znaim, in Moravia, the news unfavourable to Napoleon had the effect of raising the hopes of the Austrian negotiators, who paused in the expectation that fresh defeats would afford them better chances.

---

244 The great battle of Wagram was fought on the 6th of July 1809. The Austrians, who committed a mistake in over-extending their line, lost 20,000 men as prisoners, besides a large number in killed and wounded. There was no day, perhaps, on which Napoleon showed more military genius or more personal courage. He was in the hottest of the fight, and for a long time exposed to showers of grapeshot.— Editor of 1836 edition.

245 The battle of Talavera took place on the 28th of July, twenty-two days after the fatal defeat of the Austrians at Wagram.

It was during these negotiations, the termination of which seemed every day to be farther distant, that Napoleon was exposed to a more real danger than the wound he had received at Ratisbon. Germany was suffering under a degree of distress difficult to be described. Illuminism was making great progress, and had filled some youthful minds with an enthusiasm not less violent than the religious fanaticism to which Henry IV. fell a victim. A young man formed the design of assassinating Napoleon in order to rid Germany of one whom he considered her scourge. Rapp and Berthier were with the Emperor when the assassin was arrested, and in relating what I heard from them I feel assured that I am giving the most faithful account of all the circumstances connected with the event.

"We were at Schoenbrunn," said Rapp, "when the Emperor had just reviewed the troops. I observed a young man at the extremity of one of the columns just as the troops were about to defile. He advanced towards the Emperor, who was then between Berthier and me. The Prince de Neufchatel, thinking he wanted to present a petition, went forward to tell him that I was the person to receive it as I was the aide de camp for the day. The young man replied that he wished to speak with Napoleon himself, and Berthier again told him that he must apply to me. He withdrew a little, still repeating that he wanted to speak with Napoleon. He again advanced and came very near the Emperor; I desired him to fall back, telling him in German to wait till after the parade, when, if he had anything to say, it would be attended to. I surveyed him attentively, for I began to think his conduct suspicious. I observed that he kept his right hand in the breast pocket of his coat; out of which a piece of paper appeared. I know not how it was, but at that moment my eyes met his, and I was struck with his peculiar look and air of fixed determination. Seeing an officer of gendarmerie on the spot, I desired him to seize the young man, but without treating him with any severity, and to convey him to the castle until the parade was ended.

"All this passed in less time than I have taken to tell it, and as every one's attention was fixed on the parade the scene passed unnoticed. I was shortly afterwards told that a large carving-knife had been found on the young man, whose name was Staps. I immediately went to find Duroc, and we proceeded together to the apartment to which Staps had been taken. We found him sitting on a bed, apparently in deep thought, but betraying no symptoms of fear. He had beside him the portrait of a young female, his pocket-book, and purse containing only two pieces of gold. I asked him his name, but he replied that he would tell it to no one but Napoleon. I then asked him what he intended to do with the knife which had been found upon him? But he answered again, 'I shall tell only Napoleon.'—'Did you mean to attempt his life?'—'Yes.'—'Why?'—'I can tell no one but Napoleon.'

"This appeared to me so strange that I thought right to inform the Emperor of it. When I told him what had passed he appeared a little agitated, for you know how he was haunted with the idea of assassination. He desired that the young man should be taken into his cabinet; whither he was accordingly conducted by two gens d'armes. Notwithstanding his criminal intention there was something exceedingly prepossessing in his countenance. I wished that he would deny the attempt; but how was it possible to save a man who was determined to sacrifice himself? The Emperor asked Staps whether he could speak French, and he answered that he could speak it very imperfectly, and as you know (continued Rapp) that next to you I am the best German scholar in Napoleon's Court, I was appointed interpreter on this occasion. The Emperor put the following questions to Staps, which I translated, together with the answers:

"'Where do you come from?'—'From Narremburgh.'—'What is your father?'— 'A

Protestant minister.'—'How old are you?'—'Eighteen.'—'What did you intend to do with your knife?'—'To kill you.'—'You are mad, young man; you are one of the illuminati?'—'I am not mad; I know not what is meant by the illuminati!'—'You are ill, then?'—'I am not; I am very well.'—'Why did you wish to kill me?'—'Because you have ruined my country.'—'Have I done you any harm?'—'Yes, you have harmed me as well as all Germans.'—'By whom were you sent? Who urged you to this crime?'— 'No one; I was urged to it by the sincere conviction that by killing you I should render the greatest service to my country.'—'Is this the first time you have seen me?'—'I saw you at Erfurt, at the time of your interview with the Emperor of Russia.'—'Did you intend to kill me then?'—'No; I thought you would not again wage war against Germany. I was one of your greatest admirers.'—'How long have you been in Vienna?'— 'Ten days.'—'Why did you wait so long before you attempted the execution of your project?'—'I came to Schoenbrunn a week ago with the intention of killing you, but when I arrived the parade was just over; I therefore deferred the execution of my design till today.'—'I tell you, young man, you are either mad or in bad health.'

"The Emperor here ordered Corvisart to be sent for. Staps asked who Corvisart was? I told him that he was a physician. He then said, 'I have no need of him.' Nothing further was said until the arrival of the doctor, and during this interval Steps evinced the utmost indifference. When Corvisart arrived Napoleon directed him to feel the young man's pulse, which he immediately did; and Staps then very coolly said, 'Am I not well, sir?' Corvisart told the Emperor that nothing ailed him. 'I told you so,' said Steps, pronouncing the words with an air of triumph.

"I was really astonished at the coolness and apathy of Staps, and the Emperor seemed for a moment confounded by the young man's behaviour.—After a few moments' pause the Emperor resumed the interrogatory as follows:

"'Your brain is disordered. You will be the ruin of your family. I will grant you your life if you ask pardon for the crime you meditated, and for which you ought to be sorry.'—'I want no pardon. I only regret having failed in my attempt.'—'Indeed! then a crime is nothing to you?'— 'To kill you is no crime: it is a duty.'—'Whose portrait is that which was found on you?'—'It is the portrait of a young lady to whom I am attached.'—'She will doubtless be much distressed at your adventure?'— 'She will only be sorry that I have not succeeded. She abhors you as much as I do.'—'But if I were to pardon you would you be grateful for my mercy?'—'I would nevertheless kill you if I could.'

"I never," continued Rapp, "saw Napoleon look so confounded. The replies of Staps and his immovable resolution perfectly astonished him. He ordered the prisoner to be removed; and when he was gone Napoleon said, 'This is the result of the secret societies which infest Germany. This is the effect of fine principles and the light of reason. They make young men assassins. But what can be done against illuminism? A sect cannot be destroyed by cannon-balls.'

"This event, though pains were taken to keep it secret, became the subject of conversation in the castle of Schoenbrunn. In the evening the Emperor sent for me and said, 'Rapp, the affair of this morning is very extraordinary. I cannot believe that this young man of himself conceived the design of assassinating me. There is something under it. I shall never be persuaded that the intriguers of Berlin and Weimar are strangers to the affair.'—'Sire, allow me to say that your suspicions appear unfounded. Staps has had no accomplice; his placid countenance, and even his fanaticism, are easiest proofs of that.'—'I tell you that he has been instigated by women: furies thirsting for revenge. If I could only obtain proof of it I would have them seized in the midst of their Court.'—'Ah, Sire, it is impossible that either man or woman in the Courts of Berlin or Weimar could have conceived so atrocious a design.'— 'I am not sure of that. Did not those women excite Schill against us while we were at peace with Prussia; but stay a little; we shall see.'— 'Schill's enterprise; Sire, bears no resemblance to this attempt.' You know how the Emperor likes every one to yield to his opinion when he has adopted one which he does not choose to give up; so he said, rather changing his tone of good-humoured familiarity, 'All you say is in vain, Monsieur le General: I am not liked either at Berlin or Weimar.' There is no doubt of that, Sire; but because you are not liked in these two Courts, is it to be inferred that they would assassinate you?'—'I know the fury of those women; but patience. Write to General Lauer: direct him to interrogate Staps. Tell him to bring him to a confession.'

"I wrote conformably with the Emperor's orders, but no confession was obtained from Staps. In his examination by General Lauer he repeated nearly what he had said in the presence of Napoleon. His resignation and firmness never forsook him for a moment; and he persisted in saying that he was the sole author of the attempt, and that no one else was aware of it. Staps' enterprise made a deep impression on the Emperor. On the day when we left Schoenbrunn we happened to be alone, and he said to me, 'I cannot get this unfortunate Staps out of my mind. The more I think on the subject the more I am perplexed. I never can believe that a young man of his age, a German, one who has received a good education, a Protestant too, could have conceived and attempted such a crime. The Italians are said to be a nation of assassins, but no Italian ever attempted my life. This affair is beyond my comprehension. Inquire how Staps died, and let me know.'

"I obtained from General Lauer the information which the Emperor desired. I learned that Staps, whose attempt on the Emperor's life was made on the 23d of October; was executed at seven o'clock in the morning of the 27th, having refused to take any sustenance since the 24th. When any food was brought to him he rejected it, saying, 'I shall be strong enough to walk to the scaffold.' When he was told that peace was concluded he evinced extreme sorrow, and was seized with trembling. On reaching the place of execution he exclaimed loudly, 'Liberty for ever! Germany for ever! Death to the tyrant!'"

Such are the notes which I committed to paper after conversing with Rapp, as we were walking together in the garden of the former hotel of Montmorin, in which Rapp resided. I recollect his showing me the knife taken from Staps, which the Emperor had given him; it was merely a common carving-knife, such as is used in kitchens. To these details may be added a very remarkable circumstance, which I received from another but not less authentic source. I have been assured that the attempt of the German Mutius Scaevola had a marked influence on the concessions which the Emperor made, because he feared that Staps, like him who attempted the life of Porsenna, might have imitators among the illuminati of Germany.

It is well known that after the battle of Wagram conferences were open at Raab. Although peace was almost absolutely necessary for both powers, and the two Emperors appeared to desire it equally, it was not, however, concluded. It is worthy of remark that the delay was occasioned by Bonaparte. Negotiations were therefore suspended, and M. de Champagny had ceased for several days to see the Prince of Lichtenstein when the affair of Staps took place. Immediately after Napoleon's examination of the young fanatic he sent for M. de Champagny: "How are the negotiations going on?" he inquired. The Minister having informed him, the Emperor added, "I wish them to be resumed immediately: I wish for peace; do not hesitate about a few millions more or less in the indemnity demanded from

Austria. Yield on that point. I wish to come to a conclusion: I refer it all to you." The Minister lost no time in writing to the Prince of Lichtenstein: on the same night the two negotiators met at Raab, and the clauses of the treaty which had been suspended were discussed, agreed upon, and signed that very night. Next morning M. de Champagny attended the Emperor's levee with the treaty of peace as it had been agreed on. Napoleon, after hastily examining it, expressed his approbation of every particular, and highly complimented his Minister on the speed with which the treaty had been brought to a conclusion.[246]

246 This definitive treaty of peace, which is sometimes called the Treaty of Vienna, Raab, or Schoenbrunn, contained the following articles: 1. Austria ceded in favour of the Confederation of the Rhine (these fell to Bavaria), Salzburg, Berchtolsgaden, and a part of Upper Austria. 2. To France directly Austria ceded her only seaport, Trieste, and all the countries of Carniola, Friuli, the circle of Vilach, with parts of Croatia end Dalmatia. (By these cessions Austria was excluded from the Adriatic Sea, and cut off from all communication with the navy of Great Britain.) A small lordship, en enclave in the territories of the Grieve League, was also gives up. 3. To the constant ally of Napoleon, to the King of Saxony, in that character Austria ceded some Bohemian enclaves in Saxony end, in his capacity of Grand Duke of Warsaw, she added to his Polish dominions the ancient city of Cracow, and all Western Galicia. 4. Russia, who had entered with but a lukewarm zeal into the war as an ally of France, had a very moderate share of the spoils of Austria. A portion of Eastern Galicia, with a population of 400,000 souls, was allotted to her, but in this allotment the trading town of Brody (almost the only thing worth having) was specially excepted. This last circumstance gave no small degree of disgust to the Emperor Alexander, whose admiration of Napoleon was not destined to have a long duration.—Editor of 1836 edition.

CHAPTER XXI

1809

About this time I had the pleasure of again seeing the son of the reigning Duke of Mecklenburg-Schwerin, whose arrival in the Hanse Towns was speedily followed by that of his sister, Princess Frederica Charlotte of Mecklenburg, married to the Prince Royal of Denmark, Christian Frederick. In November the Princess arrived at Altana from Copenhagen, the reports circulated respecting her having compelled her husband to separate from her. The history of this Princess, who, though perhaps blamable, was nevertheless much pitied, was the general subject of conversation in the north of Germany at the time I was at Hamburg. The King of Denmark, grieved at the publicity of the separation, wrote a letter on the subject to the Duke of Mecklenburg. In this letter, which I had an opportunity of seeing, the King expressed his regret at not having been able to prevent the scandal; for, on his return from a journey to Kiel, the affair had become so notorious that all attempts at reconciliation were vain. In the meantime it was settled that the Princess was to remain at Altona until something should be decided respecting her future condition.

It was Baron Plessen, the Duke of Mecklenburg's Minister of State, who favoured me with a sight of the King of Denmark's letters. M. Plessen told me, likewise, at the time that the Duke had formed the irrevocable determination of not receiving his daughter. A few days after her arrival the Princess visited Madame de Bourrienne. She invited us to her parties, which were very brilliant, and several times did us the honour of being present at ours. But; unfortunately, the extravagance of her conduct, which was very unsuitable to her situation, soon became the subject of general animadversion.

I mentioned at the close of the last chapter how the promptitude of M. de Champagny brought about the conclusion of the treaty known by the name of the Treaty of Schoenbrunn. Under this the ancient edifice of the German Empire was overthrown, and Francis II. of Germany became Francis I., Emperor of Austria. He, however, could not say, like his namesake of France, 'Tout est perdu fors l'honneur'; for honour was somewhat committed, even had nothing else been lost. But the sacrifices Austria was compelled, to make were great. The territories ceded to France were immediately united into a new general government, under the collective denomination of the Illyrian Provinces. Napoleon thus became master of both sides of the Adriatic, by virtue of his twofold title of Emperor of France and King of Italy. Austria, whose external commerce thus received a check, had no longer any direct communication with the sea. The loss of Fiume, Trieste, and the sea-coast appeared so vast a sacrifice that it was impossible to look forward to the duration of a peace so dearly purchased.

The affair of Staps, perhaps, made Napoleon anxious to hurry away from Schoenbrunn, for he set off before he had ratified the preliminaries of the peace, announcing that he would ratify them at Munich. He proceeded in great haste to Nymphenburg, where he was expected on a visit to the Court of Bavaria. He next visited the King of Wurtemberg, whom he pronounced to be the cleverest sovereign in Europe, and at the end of October he arrived at Fontainebleau. From thence he proceeded on horseback to Paris, and he rode so rapidly that only a single chasseur of his escort could keep up with him, and, attended by this one guard, he entered the court of the Tuileries. While Napoleon was at Fontainebleau, before his return to Paris, Josephine for the first time heard the divorce mentioned; the idea had occurred to the Emperor's mind while he was at Schoenbrunn. It was also while at Fontainebleau that Napoleon appointed M. de Montalivet to be Minister of the Interior. The letters which we received from Paris at this period brought intelligence of the brilliant state of the capital during the winter of 1809, and especially of the splendour of the Imperial Court, where the Emperor's levees were attended by the Kings of Saxony, Bavaria, and Wurtemberg, all eager to evince their gratitude to the hero who had raised them to the sovereign rank.

I was the first person in Hamburg who received intelligence of Napoleon's projected marriage with the Archduchess Maria Louisa. The news was brought to me from Vienna by two estafettes. It is impossible to describe the effect produced by the anticipation of this event throughout the north of Germany.[247] From all parts the merchants received orders to buy Austrian stock, in which an extraordinary rise immediately took place. Napoleon's marriage with Maria Louisa was hailed with enthusiastic and general joy. The event was regarded as the guarantee of a long peace, and it was hoped there would be a lasting cessation of the disasters created by the rivalry of France and Austria. The correspondence I received showed that these sentiments were general in the interior of France, and in different countries of Europe; and, in spite of the presentiments I had always had of the return of the Bourbons to France, I now began to think that event problematic, or at least very remote.

About the beginning of the year 1810 commenced the differences between Napoleon and

247 "Napoleon often reflected on the best mode of making this communication to the Empress; still he was reluctant to speak to her. He was apprehensive of the consequences of her susceptibility of feeling; his heart was never proof against the shedding of tears. Ho thought, however, that a favourable opportunity offered for breaking the subject previously to his quitting Fontainebleau. He hinted at it in a few words which he had addressed to the Empress, but he did not explain himself until the arrival of the viceroy, whom he had ordered to join him. He was the first person who spoke openly to his mother and obtained her consent for that bitter sacrifice. He acted on the occasion like a kind son and a man grateful to his benefactor and devoted to his service, by sparing him the necessity of unpleasant explanations towards a partner whose removal was a sacrifice as painful to him as it was affecting: The Emperor, having arranged whatever related to the future condition of the Empress, upon whom he made a liberal settlement, urged the moment of the dissolution of the marriage, no doubt because he felt grieved at the condition of the Empress herself, who dined every day and passed her evenings in the presence of persons who were witnessing her descent from the throne. There existed between him and the Empress Josephine no other bond than a civil act, according to the custom which prevailed at the time of this marriage. Now the law had foreseen the dissolution of such marriage oontracts. A particular day having therefore been fixed upon, the Emperor brought together into his apartments those persons whose ministry was required in this case; amongst others, the Arch-Chancellor and M. Regnault de St. Jean d'Angély. The Emperor then declared in a loud voice his intention of annulling the marriage he had contracted with Josephine, who was present; the Empress also made the same declaration, which was interrupted by her repeated sobs. The Prince Arch-Chancellor having caused the article of the law to be read, he applied it to the cam before him, and declared the marriage to be dissolved." (Memoirs of ad Duc de Rovigo).

his brother Louis, which, as I have already stated, ended in a complete rupture. Napoleon's object was to make himself master of the navigation of the Scheldt which Louis wished should remain free, and hence ensued the union of Holland with the French Empire. Holland was the first province of the Grand Empire which Napoleon took the new Empress to visit. This visit took place almost immediately after the marriage. Napoleon first proceeded to Compiegne, where he remained a week. He next set out for St. Quentin, and inspected the canal. The Empress Maria Louisa then joined him, and they both proceeded to Belgium. At Antwerp the Emperor inspected all the works which he had ordered, and to the execution of which he attached great importance. He returned by way of Ostend, Lille, and Normandy to St. Cloud, where he arrived on the 1st of June 1810. He there learned from my correspondence that the Hanse Towns-refused to advance money for the pay of the French troops. The men were absolutely destitute. I declared that it was urgent to put an end to this state of things. The Hanse towns had been reduced from opulence to misery by taxation and exactions, and were no longer able to provide the funds.

During this year Napoleon, in a fit of madness, issued a decree which I cannot characterise by any other epithet than infernal. I allude to the decree for burning all the English merchandise in France, Holland, the Grand Duchy of Berg, the Hanse Towns; in short, in all places subject to the disastrous dominion of Napoleon. In the interior of France no idea could possibly be formed of the desolation caused by this measure in countries which existed by commerce; and what a spectacle was it to the destitute inhabitants of those countries to witness the destruction of property which, had it been distributed, would have assuaged their misery!

Among the emigrants whom I was ordered to watch was M. de Vergennes, who had always remained at or near Hamburg Since April 1808. I informed the Minister that M. de Vergennes had presented himself to me at this time. I even remember that M. de Vergennes gave me a letter from M. de Rémusat, the First Chamberlain of the Emperor. M. de Rémusat strongly recommended to me his connection, who was called by matters of importance to Hamburg. Residence in this town was, however, too expensive, and he decided to live at Neumuhl, a little village on the Elbe, rather to the west of Altona. There he lived quietly in retirement with an opera dancer named Mademoiselle Ledoux, with whom he had become acquainted in Paris, and whom he had brought with him. He seemed much taken with her. His manner of living did not denote large means.

One duty with which I was entrusted, and to which great importance was attached, was the application and execution of the disastrous Continental system in the north. In my correspondence I did not conceal the dissatisfaction which this ruinous measure excited, and the Emperor's eyes were at length opened on the subject by the following circumstance. In spite of the sincerity with which the Danish Government professed to enforce the Continental system, Holstein contained a great quantity of colonial produce; and, notwithstanding the measures of severity, it was necessary that that merchandise should find a market somewhere. The smugglers often succeeded in introducing it into Germany, and the whole would probably soon have passed the custom-house limits. All things considered, I thought it advisable to make the best of an evil that could not be avoided. I therefore proposed that the colonial produce then in Holstein, and which had been imported before the date of the King's edict for its prohibition, should be allowed to enter Hamburg on the payment of 30, and on some articles 40, per cent. This duty was to be collected at the custom-house, and was to be confined entirely to articles consumed in Germany. The colonial produce in Altona,

Glnckstadt, Husum, and other towns of Holstein, lead been estimated, at about 30,000,000 francs, and the duty would amount to 10,000,000 or 12,000,000. The adoption of the plan I proposed would naturally put a stop to smuggling; for it could not be doubted that the merchants would give 30 or 33 per cent for the right of carrying on a lawful trade rather than give 40 per cent. to the smugglers, with the chance of seizure.

The Emperor immediately adopted my idea, for I transmitted my suggestions to the Minister for Foreign Affairs on the 18th of September, and on the 4th of October a decree was issued conformable to the plan I proposed. Within six weeks after the decree came into operation the custom-house Director received 1300 declarations from persons holding colonial produce in Holstein. It now appeared that the duties would amount to 40,000,000 francs, that is to say, 28,000,000 or 30,000,000 more than my estimate.

Bernadotte had just been nominated Prince Royal of Sweden. This nomination, with all the circumstances connected with it, as well as Bernadotte's residence in Hamburg, before he proceeded to Stockholm, will be particularly noticed in the next chapter. I merely mention the circumstance here to explain some events which took place in the north, and which were, more or less, directly connected with it. For example, in the month of September the course of exchange on St. Petersburg suddenly fell. All the letters which arrived in Hamburg from the capital of Russia and from Riga, attributed the fall to the election of the Prince of Ponte-Corvo as Prince Royal of Sweden. Of thirty letters which I received there was not one but described the consternation which the event had created in St. Petersburg. This consternation, however, might have been excited less by the choice of Sweden than by the fear that that choice was influenced by the French Government.

CHAP XXII

1809-1810

I now come to one of the periods of my life to which I look back with most satisfaction, the time when Bernadotte was with me in Hamburg. I will briefly relate the series of events which led the opposer of the 18th Brumaire to the throne of Sweden.

On the 13th of march 1809 Gustavus Adolphus was arrested, and his uncle, the Duke of Sudermania, provisionally took the reins of Government. A few days afterwards Gustavus published his act of abdication, which in the state of Sweden it was impossible for him to refuse. In May following, the Swedish Diet having been convoked at Stockholm, the Duke of Sudermania was elected King. Christian Augustus, the only son of that monarch, of course became Prince Royal on the accession of his father to the throne. He, however, died suddenly at the end of May 1810, and Count Fersen (the same who at the Court of Marie Antoinette was distinguished by the appellation of 'le beau Fersen'), was massacred by the populace, who suspected, perhaps unjustly, that he had been accessory to the Prince's death.[248] On the 21st of August following Bernadotte was elected Prince Royal of Sweden.

After the death of the Prince Royal the Duke of Sudermania's son, Count Wrede, a Swede, made the first overtures to Bernadotte, and announced to him the intention entertained at Stockholm of offering him the throne of Sweden. Bernadotte was at that time in Paris, and immediately after his first interview with Count Wrede he waited on the Emperor at St. Cloud; Napoleon coolly replied that he could be of no service to him; that events must take their course; that he might accept or refuse the offer as he chose; that he (Bonaparte) would place no obstacles in his way, but that he could give him no advice. It was very evident that the choice of Sweden was not very agreeable to Bonaparte, and though he afterwards disavowed any opposition to it, he made overtures to Stockholm, proposing that the crown of Sweden should be added to that of Denmark.

Bernadotte then went to the waters of Plombieres, and on his return to Paris he sent me a letter announcing his elevation to the rank of Prince Royal of Sweden.

On the 11th of October he arrived in Hamburg, where he stayed only three days. He passed nearly the whole of that time with me, and he communicated to me many curious facts connected with the secret history of the times, and among other things some particulars respecting the battle of Wagram. I was the first to mention to the new Prince Royal of Sweden the reports of the doubtful manner in which the troops under his command behaved. I reminded him of Bonaparte's dissatisfaction at these troops; for there was no doubt of the Emperor being the author of the complaints contained in the bulletins, especially as he had withdrawn the troops from Bernadotte's command. Bernadotte assured me that Napoleon's

248 Count Fereen, alleged to have been one of the favoured lovers of Marie Antoinette, and who was certainly deep in her confidence, had arranged most of the details of the attempted flight to Varennes in 1791, and he himself drove the Royal family their first stage to the gates of Paris.

censure was unjust; during the battle he had complained of the little spirit manifested by the soldiers. "He refused to see me," added Bernadotte, "and I was told, as a reason for his refusal, that he was astonished and displeased to find that, notwithstanding his complaints, of which I must have heard, I had boasted of having gained the battle, and had publicly complimented the Saxons whom I commanded."

Bernadotte then showed me the bulletin he drew up after the battle of Wagram. I remarked that I had never heard of a bulletin being made by any other than the General who was Commander-in-Chief during a battle, and asked how the affair ended. He then handed to me a copy of the Order of the day, which Napoleon said he had sent only to the Marshals commanding the different corps.

Bernadotte's bulletin was printed along with Bonaparte's Order of the Day, a thing quite unparalleled.

Though I was much interested in this account of Bonaparte's conduct after the battle of Wagram; yet I was more curious to hear the particulars of Bernadotte's last communication with the Emperor. The Prince informed me that on his return from Plombieres he attended the levee, when the Emperor asked him, before every one present, whether he had received any recent news from Sweden.

He replied in the affirmative. "What is it?" inquired Napoleon. "Sire, I am informed that your Majesty's charge d'affaires at Stockholm opposes my election. It is also reported to those who choose to believe it that your Majesty gives the preference to the King of Denmark."—"At these words," continued Bernadotte, "the Emperor affected surprise, which you know he can do very artfully. He assured me it was impossible, and then turned the conversation to another subject.

"I know not what to think of his conduct in this affair. I am aware he does not like me;—but the interests of his policy may render him favourable to Sweden. Considering the present greatness and power of France, I conceived it to be my duty to make every personal sacrifice. But I swear to Heaven that I will never commit the honour of Sweden. He, however, expressed himself in the best possible terms in speaking of Charles XIII. and me. He at first started no obstacle to my acceptance of the succession to the throne of Sweden, and he ordered the official announcement of my election to be immediately inserted in the Moniteur'. Ten days elapsed without the Emperor's saying a word to me about my departure. As I was anxious to be off, and all my preparations were made, I determined to go and ask him for the letters patent to relieve me from my oath of fidelity, which I had certainly kept faithfully in spite of all his ill-treatment of me. He at first appeared somewhat surprised at my request, and, after a little hesitation, he said, 'There is a preliminary condition to be fulfilled; a question has been raised by one of the members of the Privy Council.'—'What condition, Sire?'—'You must pledge yourself not to bear arms against me.'—'Does your Majesty suppose that I can bind myself by such an engagement? My election by the Diet of Sweden, which has met with your Majesty's assent, has made me a Swedish subject, and that character is incompatible with the pledge proposed by a member of the Council. I am sure it could never have emanated from your Majesty, and must proceed from the Arch-Chancellor or the Grand Judge, who certainly could not have been aware of the height to which the proposition would raise me.'—'What do you mean?'—'If, Sire, you prevent me accepting a crown unless I pledge myself not to bear arms against you, do you not really place me on a level with you as a General?'

"When I declared positively that my election must make me consider myself a Swedish subject he frowned, and seemed embarrassed. When I had done speaking he said, in a low and faltering voice, 'Well, go. Our destinies will soon be accomplished!' These words were uttered so indistinctly that I was obliged to beg pardon for not having heard what he said, and he repented, 'Go! our destinies will soon be accomplished!' In the subsequent conversations which I had with the Emperor I tried all possible means to remove the unfavourable sentiments he cherished towards me. I revived my recollections of history. I spoke to him of the great men who had excited the admiration of the world, of the difficulties and obstacles which they had to surmount; and, above all, I dwelt upon that solid glory which is founded on the establishment and maintenance of public tranquillity and happiness. The Emperor listened to me attentively, and frequently concurred in my opinion as to the principles of the prosperity and stability of States. One day he took my hand and pressed it affectionately, as if to assure me of his friendship and protection. Though I knew him to be an adept in the art of dissimulation, yet his affected kindness appeared so natural that I thought all his unfavourable feeling towards me was at an end. I spoke to persons by whom our two families were allied, requesting that they would assure the Emperor of the reciprocity of my sentiments, and tell him that I was ready to assist his great plans in any way not hostile to the interests of Sweden.

"Would you believe, my dear friend, that the persons to whom I made these candid protestations laughed at my credulity? They told me that after the conversation in which the Emperor had so cordially pressed my hand. I had scarcely taken leave of him when he was heard to say that I had made a great display of my learning to him, and that he had humoured me like a child. He wished to inspire me with full confidence so as to put me off my guard; and I know for a certainty that he had the design of arresting me.

"But," pursued Bernadotte, "in spite of the feeling of animosity which I know the Emperor has cherished against me since the 18th Brumaire, I do not think, when once I shall be in Sweden, that he will wish to have any differences with the Swedish Government. I must tell you, also he has given me 2,000,000 francs in exchange for my principality of Ponte-Corvo. Half the sum has been already paid, which will be very useful to me in defraying the expenses of my journey and installation. When I was about to step into my carriage to set off, an individual, whom you must excuse me naming, came to bid me farewell, and related to me a little conversation which had just taken place at the Tuileries. Napoleon said to the individual in question, 'Well, does not the Prince regret leaving France?'—'Certainly, Sire.'—'As to me, I should have been very glad if he had not accepted his election. But there is no help for it. . . . He does not like me.'—'Sire, I must take the liberty of saying that your Majesty labours under a mistake. I know the differences which have existed between you and General Bernadotte for the last six years. I know how he opposed the overthrow of the Directory; but I also know that the Prince has long been sincerely attached to you.'—'Well, I dare say you are right. But we have not understood each other. It is now too late. He has his interests and his policy, and I have mine.'"

"Such," added the Prince, "were the Emperor's last observations respecting me two hours before my departure. The individual to whom I have just alluded, spoke truly, my dear Bourrienne. I am indeed sorry to leave France; and I never should have left it but for the injustice of Bonaparte. If ever I ascend the throne of Sweden I shall owe my crown to his ill-treatment of me; for had he not persecuted me by his animosity my condition would have sufficed for a soldier of fortune: but we must follow our fate."

During the three days the Prince spent with me I had many other conversations with him. He wished me to give him my advice as to the course he should pursue with regard to the Continental system. "I advise you," said I, "to reject the system without hesitation. It may be very fine in theory, but it is utterly impossible to carry it into practice, and it will, in the end, give the trade of the world to England. It excites the dissatisfaction of our allies, who, in spite of themselves, will again become our enemies. But no other country, except Russia, is in the situation of Sweden. You want a number of objects of the first necessity, which nature has withheld from you. You can only obtain them by perfect freedom of navigation; and you can only pay for them with those peculiar productions in which Sweden abounds. It would be out of all reason to close your ports against a nation who rules the seas. It is your navy that would be blockaded, not hers. What can France do against you? She may invade you by land. But England and Russia will exert all their efforts to oppose her. By sea it is still more impossible that she should do anything. Then you have nothing to fear but Russia and England, and it will be easy for you to keep up friendly relations with these two powers. Take my advice; sell your iron, timber, leather, and pitch; take in return salt, wines, brandy, and colonial produce. This is the way to make yourself popular in Sweden. If, on the contrary, you follow the Continental system, you will be obliged to adopt laws against smuggling, which will draw upon you the detestation of the people."

Such was the advice which I gave to Bernadotte when he was about to commence his new and brilliant career. In spite of my situation as a French Minister I could not have reconciled it to my conscience to give him any other counsel, for if diplomacy has duties so also has friendship. Bernadotte adopted my advice, and the King of Sweden had no reason to regret having done so.

CHAPTER XXIII

1810

While Bernadotte was preparing to fill the high station to which he had been called by the wishes of the people of Sweden, Napoleon was involved in his misunderstanding with the Pope,[249] and in the affairs of Portugal, which were far from proceeding according to his wishes. Bernadotte had scarcely quitted Hamburg for Sweden when the Duke of Holstein-Augustenburg arrived. The Duke was the brother of the last Prince Royal of Sweden, whom Bernadotte was called to succeed, and he came to escort his sister from Altona to Denmark. His journey had been retarded for some days on account of the presence of the Prince of Ponte-Gorvo in Hamburg: the preference granted to Bernadotte had mortified his ambition, and he was unwilling to come in contact with his fortunate rival. The Duke was favoured, by the Emperor of Russia.

As soon as he arrived in Sweden Bernadotte directed his aide de camp, General Lentil de St. Alphonse, to inform me of his safe passage. Shortly after I received a letter from Bernadotte himself, recommending one of his aides de camp, M. Villatte, who was the bearer of it.

This letter contained the same sentiments of friendship as those I used to receive from General Bernadotte, and formed a contrast with the correspondence of King Jerome, who when he wrote to me assumed the regal character, and prayed that God would have me in his holy keeping. However, the following is the Prince Royal's letter:

> MY DEAR BOURRIENNE—I have directed M. Villatte to see you on his way through Hamburg, and to bear my friendly remembrances to you. Lentil has addressed his letter to you, which I suppose you have already received. Adieu, care for me always, and believe in the inalterable attachment of yours,

---

249 It was about this time that, irritated at what he called the captive Pope's unreasonable obstinacy, Bonaparte conceived, and somewhat openly expressed, his notion of making France a Protestant country, and changing the religion of 30,000,000 of people by an Imperial decree. One or two of the good sayings of the witty, accomplished, and chivalrous Comte Louis de Narbonne have already been given in the course of these volumes. The following is another of them: "I tell you what I will do, Narbonne—I tell you how I will vent my spite on this old fool of a Pope, and the dotards who may succeed him said Napoleon one day at the Tuileries. "I will make a schism as great as that of Luther—I will make France a Protestant country!" "O Sire," replied the Count, "I see difficulties in the way of this project. In the south, in the Vendée, in nearly all the west, the French are bigoted Catholics and even what little religion remains among us in our cities and great towns is of the Roman Church." "Never mind, Narbonne—never mind!—I shall at least carry a large portion of the French people with me—I will make a division!" Sire, replied Narbonne, "I am afraid that there is not enough religion in all France to stand division!"-Editor of 1836 edition.

(*Signed*) CHARLES JOHN.

P.S.—I beg you will present my compliments to madame and all your family. Embrace my little cousin for me.

The little cousin, so called by Bernadotte, was one of my daughters, then a child, whom Bernadotte used to be very fond of while he was at Hamburg.

Departing from the order of date, I will anticipate the future, and relate all I know respecting the real causes of the misunderstanding which arose between Bernadotte and Napoleon. Bonaparte viewed the choice of the Swedes with great displeasure, because he was well aware that Bernadotte had too much integrity and honour to serve him in the north as a political puppet set in motion by means of springs which he might pull at Paris or at his headquarters. His dissatisfaction upon this point occasioned an interesting correspondence, part of which, consisting of letters from Bernadotte to the Emperor, is in my possession. The Emperor had allowed Bernadotte to retain in his service, for a year at least, the French officers who were his aides de camp—but that permission was soon revoked, end the Prince Royal of Sweden wrote to Napoleon a letter of remonstrance.

Napoleon's dissatisfaction with the Prince Royal now changed to decided resentment. He repented having acceded to his departure from France, and he made no secret of his sentiments, for he said before his courtiers, "That he would like to send Bernadotte to Vincennes to finish his study of the Swedish language." Bernadotte was informed of this, but he could not believe that the Emperor had ever entertained such a design. However, a conspiracy was formed in Sweden against Bernadotte, whom a party of foreign brigands were hired to kidnap in the neighbourhood of Raga; but the plot was discovered, and the conspirators were compelled to embark without their prey. The Emperor having at the same time seized upon Swedish Pomerania, the Prince Royal wrote him a second letter in these terms:

From the papers which have just arrived I learn that a division of the army, under the command of the Prince of Eckmuhl, invaded Swedish Pomerania on the night of the 26th of January; that the division continued to advance, entered the capital of the Duchy, and took possession of the island of Rugen. The King expects that your Majesty will explain the reasons which have induced you to act in a manner so contrary to the faith of existing treaties. My old connection with your Majesty warrants me in requesting you to declare your motives without delay, in order that I may give my advice to the King as to the conduct which Sweden ought hereafter to adopt. This gratuitous outrage against Sweden is felt deeply by the nation, and still more, Sire, by me, to whom is entrusted the honour of defending it. Though I have contributed to the triumphs of France, though I have always desired to see her respected and happy; yet I can never think of sacrificing the interests, honour, and independence of the country which has adopted me. Your Majesty, who has so ready a perception of what is just, must admit the propriety of my resolution. Though I am not jealous of the glory and power which surrounds you, I cannot submit to the dishonour of being regarded as a vassal. Your Majesty governs the greatest part of Europe, but your dominion does not extend to the nation which I have been called to govern; my

> ambition is limited to the defence of Sweden. The effect produced upon the people by the invasion of which I complain may lead to consequences which it is impossible to foresee; and although I am not a Coriolanus, and do not command the Volsci, I have a sufficiently good opinion of the Swedes to assure you that they dare undertake anything to avenge insults which they have not provoked, and to preserve rights to which they are as much attached as to their lives.

I was in Paris when the Emperor received Bernadotte's letter on the occupation of Swedish Pomerania. When Bonaparte read it I was informed that he flew into a violent rage, and even exclaimed, "You shall submit to your degradation, or die sword in hand!" But his rage was impotent. The unexpected occupation of Swedish Pomerania obliged the King of Sweden to come to a decided rupture with France, and to seek other allies, for Sweden was not strong enough in herself to maintain neutrality in the midst of the general conflagration of Europe after the disastrous campaign of Moscow. The Prince Royal, therefore, declared to Russia and England that in consequence of the unjust invasion of Pomerania Sweden was at war with France, and he despatched Comte de Lowenhjelm, the King's aide de camp, with a letter explanatory of his views. Napoleon sent many notes to Stockholm, where M. Alquier, his Ambassador, according to his instructions, had maintained a haughty and even insulting tone towards Sweden. Napoleon's overtures, after the manifestations of his anger, and after the attempt to carry off the Prince Royal, which could be attributed only to him, were considered by the Prince Royal merely as a snare. But in the hope of reconciling the duties he owed to both his old and his new country he addressed to the Emperor a moderate letter:

This letter throws great light on the conduct of the Emperor with respect to Bernadotte; for Napoleon was not the man whom any one whatever would have ventured to remind of facts, the accuracy of which was in the least degree questionable. Such then were the relations between Napoleon and the Prince Royal of Sweden. When I shall bring to light some curious secrets, which have hitherto been veiled beneath the mysteries of the Restoration, it will be seen by what means Napoleon, before his fall, again sought to wreak his vengeance upon Bernadotte.

Oh the 4th of December I had the honour to see the Princess Royal of Sweden[250], who arrived that day at Hamburg. She merely passed through the city on her way to Stockholm to join her husband, but she remained but a short time in Sweden,—two months, I believe, at most, not being able to reconcile herself to the ancient Scandinavia. As to the Prince Royal, he soon became inured to the climate, having been for many years employed in the north.

After this my stay at Hamburg was not of long duration. Bonaparte's passion for territorial aggrandisement knew no bounds; and the turn of the Hanse Towns now arrived. By taking possession of these towns and territories he merely accomplished a design formed long previously. I, however, was recalled with many compliments, and under the specious pretext that the Emperor wished to hear my opinions respecting the country in which. I had been residing. At the beginning of December I received a letter from M. de Champagny stating that the Emperor wished to see me in order to consult with me upon different things relating to Hamburg. In this note I was told "that the information I had obtained respecting Hamburg and the north of Germany might be useful to the public interest, which must be

250 Madame Bernadotte, afterwards Queen of Sweden, was a Mademoiselle Clary, and younger sister to the wife of Joseph Bonaparte.

the most gratifying reward of my labours." The reception which awaited me will presently be seen. The conclusion of the letter spoke in very flattering terms of the manner in which I had discharged my duties. I received it on the 8th of December, and next day I set out for Paris. When I arrived at Mayence I was enabled to form a correct idea of the fine compliments which had been paid me, and of the Emperor's anxiety to have my opinion respecting the Hanse Towns. In Mayence I met the courier who was proceeding to announce the union of the Hanse Towns with the French Empire. I confess that, notwithstanding the experience I had acquired of Bonaparte's duplicity, or rather, of the infinite multiplicity of his artifices, he completely took me by surprise on that occasion.

On my arrival in Paris I did not see the Emperor, but the first 'Moniteur' I read contained the formula of a 'Senatus-consulte,' which united the Hanse Towns, Lauenburg, etc., to the French Empire by the right of the strongest. This new and important augmentation of territory could not fail to give uneasiness to Russia. Alexander manifested his dissatisfaction by prohibiting the importation of our agricultural produce and manufactures into Russia. Finally, as the Continental system had destroyed all trade by the ports of the Baltic, Russia showed herself more favourable to the English, and gradually reciprocal complaints of bad faith led to that war whose unfortunate issue was styled by M. Talleyrand "the beginning of the end."

I have now to make the reader acquainted with an extraordinary demand made upon me by the Emperor through the medium of M. de Champagny. In one of my first interviews with that Minister after my return to Paris he thus addressed me: "The Emperor has entrusted me with a commission to you which I am obliged to execute: 'When you see Bourrienne,' said the Emperor, 'tell him I wish him to pay 6,000,000 into your chest to defray the expense of building the new Office for Foreign Affairs.'" I was so astonished at this unfeeling and inconsiderate demand that I was utterly unable to make airy reply. This then was my recompense for having obtained money and supplies during my residence at Hamburg to the extent of nearly 100,000,000, by which his treasury and army had profited in moments of difficulty! M. de Champagny added that the Emperor did not wish to receive me. He asked what answer he should bear to his Majesty. I still remained silent, and the Minister again urged me to give an answer. "Well, then," said I, "tell him he may go to the devil." The Minister naturally wished to obtain some variation from this laconic answer, but I would give no other; and I afterwards learned from Duroc that M. de Champagny was compelled to communicate it to Napoleon. "Well," asked the latter, "have you seen Bourrienne?"—"Yes, Sire."—"Did you tell him I wished him to pay 6,000,000 into your chest?"—"Yes, Sire."—"And what did he say?"—"Sire, I dare not inform your Majesty."—"What did he say? I insist upon knowing."—"Since you insist on my telling you, Sire, M. de Bourrienne said your Majesty might go to the devil."—"Ah! ah! did he really say so?" The Emperor then retired to the recess of a window, where he remained alone for seven or eight minutes, biting his nails; in the fashion of Berthier, and doubtless giving free scope to his projects of vengeance. He then turned to the Minister and spoke to him of quite another subject: Bonaparte had so nursed himself in the idea of making me pay the 6,000,000 that every time he passed the Office for Foreign Affairs he said to those who accompanied hint; "Bourrienne must pay for that after all."[251]

251 This demand of money from Bourrienne is explained in Erreurs (tome ii, p. 228) by the son of Davoust. Bourrienne had been suspected by Napoleon of making large sums at Hamburg by

Though I was not admitted to the honour of sharing the splendour of the Imperial Court; yet I had the satisfaction of finding that; in spite of my disgrace, those of my old friends who were worth anything evinced the same regard for me as heretofore. I often saw Duroc; who snatched some moments from his more serious occupations to come and chat with me respecting all that had occurred since my secession from Bonaparte's cabinet. I shall not attempt to give a verbatim account of my conversations with Duroc, as I have only my memory to guide me; but I believe I shall not depart from the truth in describing them as follows:

On his return from the last Austrian campaign Napoleon; as I have already stated, proceeded to Fontainebleau, where he was joined by Josephine. Then, for the first time, the communication which had always existed between the apartments of the husband and wife was closed. Josephine was fully alive to the fatal prognostics which were to be deduced from this conjugal separation. Duroc informed me that she sent for him, and on entering her chamber, he found her bathed in tears. "I am lost!" she exclaimed in a tone of voice the remembrance of which seemed sensibly to affect Duroc even while relating the circumstance to me: "I am utterly lost! all is over now! You, Duroc, I know, have always been my friend, and so has Rapp. It is not you who have persuaded him to part from me. This is the work of my enemies Savary and Junot! But they are more his enemies than mine. And my poor Eugène I how will he be distressed when he learns I am repudiated by an ungrateful man! Yes Duroc, I may truly call him ungrateful, My God! my God! what will become of us?" . . . Josephine sobbed bitterly while she thus addressed Duroc.

Before I was acquainted with the singular demand which M. de Champagny was instructed to make to me I requested Duroc to inquire of the Emperor his reason for not wishing to see me. The Grand Marshal faithfully executed my commission, but he received only the following answer: "Do you think I have nothing better to do than to give Bourrienne an audience? that would indeed furnish gossip for Paris and Hamburg. He has always sided with the emigrants; he would be talking to me of past times; he was for Josephine! My wife, Duroc, is near her confinement; I shall have a son, I am sure! . . . . Bourrienne is not a man of the day; I have made giant strides since he left France; in short, I do not want to see him. He is a grumbler by nature; and you know, my dear Duroc, I do not like men of that sort."

I had not been above a week in Paris when Duroc related this speech to me. Rapp was not in France at the time, to my great regret. Much against his inclination he had been appointed to some duties connected with the Imperial marriage ceremonies, but shortly after, having given offence to Napoleon by some observation relating to the Faubourg St. Germain, he had received orders to repair to Dantzic, of which place he had already been Governor.

The Emperor's refusal to see me made my situation in Paris extremely delicate; and I was at first in doubt whether I might seek an interview with Josephine. Duroc, however, having assured me that Napoleon would have no objection to it, I wrote requesting permission to wait upon her. I received an answer the same day, and on the morrow I repaired to Malmaison. I was ushered into the tent drawing-room, where I found Josephine and Hortense. When I entered Josephine stretched out her hand to me, saying, "Ah! my friend!" These words she pronounced with deep emotion, and tears prevented her from continuing. She threw

allowing breaches of the Continental system. In one letter to Davoust Napoleon speaks of an "immense fortune," and in another, that Bourrienne is reported to have gained seven or eight millions at Hamburg in giving licences or making arbitrary seizures.

herself on the ottoman on the left of the fireplace, and beckoned me to sit down beside her. Hortense stood by the fireplace, endeavouring to conceal her tears. Josephine took my hand, which she pressed in both her own; and, after a struggle to overcome her feelings, she said, "My dear Bourrienne, I have drained my cup of misery. He has cast me off! forsaken me! He conferred upon me the vain title of Empress only to render my fall the more marked. Ah! we judged him rightly! I knew the destiny that awaited me; for what would he not sacrifice to his ambition!" As she finished these words one of Queen Hortense's ladies entered with a message to her; Hortense stayed a few moments, apparently to recover from the emotion under which she was labouring, and then withdrew, so that I was left alone with Josephine. She seemed to wish for the relief of disclosing her sorrows, which I was curious to hear from her own lips; women have such a striking way of telling their distresses. Josephine confirmed what Duroc had told me respecting the two apartments at Fontainebleau; then, coming to the period when Bonaparte had declared to her the necessity of a separation, she said, "My dear Bourrienne; during all the years you were with us you know I made you the confidant of my thoughts, and kept you acquainted with my sad forebodings. They are now cruelly fulfilled. I acted the part of a good wife to the very last. I have suffered all, and I am resigned! . . . What fortitude did it require latterly to endure my situation, when, though no longer his wife, I was obliged to seem so in the eyes of the world! With what eyes do courtiers look upon a repudiated wife! I was in a state of vague uncertainty worse than death until the fatal day when he at length avowed to me what I had long before read in his looks! On the 30th of November 1809 we were dining together as usual, I had not uttered a word during that sad dinner, and he had broken silence only to ask one of the servants what o'clock it was. As soon as Bonaparte had taken his coffee he dismissed all the attendants, and I remained alone with him. I saw in the expression of his countenance what was passing in his mind, and I knew that my hour was come. He stepped up to me—he was trembling, and I shuddered; he took my hand, pressed it to his heart, and after gazing at me for a few moments in silence he uttered these fatal words: 'Josephine! my dear Josephine! You know how I have loved you! . . . To you, to you alone, I owe the only moments of happiness I have tasted in this world. But, Josephine, my destiny is not to be controlled by my will. My dearest affections must yield to the interests of France.'—'Say no more,' I exclaimed, 'I understand you; I expected this, but the blow is not the less mortal.' I could not say another word," continued Josephine; "I know not what happened after I seemed to lose my reason; I became insensible, and when I recovered I found myself in my chamber. Your friend Corvisart and my poor daughter were with me. Bonaparte came to see me in the evening; and oh! Bourrienne, how can I describe to you what I felt at the sight of him; even the interest he evinced for me seemed an additional cruelty. Alas! I had good reason to fear ever becoming an Empress!"

I knew not what consolation to offer: to Josephine; and knowing as I did the natural lightness of her character, I should have been surprised to find her grief so acute, after the lapse of a year, had I not been aware that there are certain chords which, when struck, do not speedily cease to vibrate in the heart of a woman. I sincerely pitied Josephine, and among all the things I said to assuage her sorrow, the consolation to which she appeared most sensible was the reprobation which public opinion had pronounced on Bonaparte's divorce, and on this subject I said nothing but the truth, for Josephine was generally beloved. I reminded her of a prediction I had made under happier circumstances, viz. on the day that she came to visit us in our little house at Ruel. "My dear friend," said she, "I have not forgotten it, and I have often thought of all you then said. For my part, I knew he was lost from the day he made himself Emperor. Adieu! Bourrienne, come and see me soon again; come often, for we have a great deal to talk about; you know how happy I always am to see you." Such was, to the best of my recollection, what passed at my first interview with Josephine after my return from Hamburg.

CHAPTER XXIV

1811

I had been in Paris about two months when a young man of the name of La Sahla was arrested on the suspicion of having come from Saxony to attempt the life of the Emperor. La Sahla informed the Duc de Rovigo, then Minister of the Police, that he wished to see me, assigning as a reason for this the reputation I had left behind me in Germany. The Emperor, I presume, had no objection to the interview, for I received an invitation to visit the prisoner. I accordingly repaired to the branch office of the Minister of the Police, in the Rue des St. Peres, where I was introduced to a young man between seventeen and eighteen years of age.

My conversation with the young man, whose uncle was, I believe, Minister to the King of Saxony, interested me greatly in his behalf; I determined, if possible, to save La Sahla, and I succeeded. I proceeded immediately to the Duc de Rovigo, and I convinced him that under the circumstances of the case it was important to make it be believed that the young man was insane. I observed that if he were brought before a court he would repeat all that he had stated to me, and probably enter into disclosures which might instigate fresh attempts at assassination. Perhaps an avenger of La Sahla might rise up amongst the students of Leipzig, at which university he had spent his youth. These reasons, together with others, had the success I hoped for. The Emperor afterwards acknowledged the prudent course which had been adopted respecting La Sahla; when speaking at St. Helena of the conspiracies against his life he said, "I carefully concealed all that I could."

In conformity with my advice La Sahla was sent to Vincennes, where he remained until the end of March 1814, He was then removed to the castle of Saumur, from which he was liberated at the beginning of April. I had heard nothing of him for three years, when one day, shortly after the Restoration, whilst sitting at breakfast with my family at my house in the Rue Hauteville, I heard an extraordinary noise in the antechamber, and before I had time to ascertain its cause I found myself in the arms. of a young man, who embraced me with extraordinary ardour. It was La Sahla. He was in a transport of gratitude and joy at his liberation, and at the accomplishment of the events which he had wished to accelerate by assassination. La Sahla returned to Saxony and I saw no more of him, but while I was in Hamburg in 1815, whither I was seat by Louis XVIII., I learned that on the 5th of June a violent explosion was heard in the Chamber of Representatives at Paris, which was at first supposed to be a clap of thunder, but was soon ascertained to have been occasioned by a young Samson having fallen with a packet of detonating powder in his pocket.

On receiving this intelligence I imagined, I know not why, that this young Saxon was La Sahla, and that he had probably intended to blow up Napoleon and even the Legislative Body; but I have since ascertained that I was under a mistake as to his intentions. My knowledge of La Sahla's candour induces me to believe the truth of his declarations to the police; and if there be any inaccuracies in the report of these declarations I do not hesitate to attribute them to the police itself, of which Fouché was the head at the period in question.

It is the latter part of the report which induced me to observe above, that if there were any inaccuracies in the statement they were more likely to proceed from Fouché's police than the false representations of young La Sahla. It is difficult to give credit without proof to such accusations. However, I decide nothing; but I consider it my duty to express doubts of the truth of these charges brought against the two Prussian ministers, of whom the Prince of Wittgenstein, a man of undoubted honour, has always spoken to me in the best of terms.

There is nothing to prove that La Sahla returned to France the second time with the same intentions as before. This project, however, is a mystery to me, and his detonating powder gives rise to many conjectures.

I had scarcely left Hamburg when the Prince of Eckmuhl (Marshal Davoust) was appointed Governor-General of that place on the union of the Hanse Towns with the Empire. From that period I was constantly occupied in contending against the persecutions and denunciations which he racked his imagination to invent. I cannot help attributing to those persecutions the Emperor's coolness towards me on my arrival in Paris. But as Davoust's calumnies were devoid of proof, he resorted to a scheme by which a certain appearance of probability might supply the place of truth. When I arrived in Paris, at the commencement of 1811, I was informed by an excellent friend I had left at Hamburg, M. Bouvier, an emigrant, and one of the hostages of Louis XVI., that in a few days I would receive a letter which would commit me, and likewise M. de Talleyrand and General Rapp. I had never had any connection on matters of business, with either of these individuals, for whom I entertained the most sincere attachment. They, like myself, were not in the good graces of Marshal Davoust, who could not pardon the one for his incontestable superiority of talent, and the other for his blunt honesty. On the receipt of M. Bouvier's letter I carried it to the Duc de Rovigo, whose situation made him perfectly aware of the intrigues which had been carried on against me since I had left Hamburg by one whose ambition aspired to the Viceroyalty of Poland. On that, as on many other similar occasions, the Duc de Rovigo advocated my cause with Napoleon. We agreed that it would be best to await the arrival of the letter which M. Bouvier had announced. Three weeks elapsed, and the letter did not appear. The Duc de Rovigo, therefore, told me that I must have been misinformed. However, I was certain that M. Bouvier would not have sent me the information on slight grounds, and I therefore supposed that the project had only been delayed. I was not wrong in my conjecture, for at length the letter arrived. To what a depth of infamy men can descend! The letter was from a man whom I had known at Hamburg, whom I had obliged, whom I had employed as a spy. His epistle was a miracle of impudence. After relating some extraordinary transactions which he said had taken place between us, and which all bore the stamp of falsehood, he requested me to send him by return of post the sum of 60,000 francs on account of what I had promised him for some business he executed in England by the direction of M. de Talleyrand, General Rapp, and myself. Such miserable wretches are often caught in the snares they spread for others. This was the case in the present instance, for the fellow had committed, the blunder of fixing upon the year 1802 as the period of this pretended business in England, that is to say, two years before my appointment as Minister-Plenipotentiary to the Hanse Towns. This anachronism was not the only one I discovered in the letter.

I took a copy of the letter, and immediately carried the original to the Duc de Rovigo, as had been agreed between us. When I waited on the Minister he was just preparing to go to the Emperor. He took with him the letter which I brought, and also the letter which announced its arrival. As the Duc de Rovigo entered the audience-chamber Napoleon advanced to meet him, and apostrophised him thus: "Well, I have learned fine things of your Bourrienne, whom you are always defending." The fact was, the Emperor had already received a copy of the letter, which had been opened at the Hamburg post-office. The Duc de Rovigo told the Emperor that he had long known what his Majesty had communicated to him. He then entered into a full explanation of the intrigue, of which it was wished to render me the victim, and proved to him the more easily the falsehood of my accusers by reminding him that in 1802 I was not in Hamburg, but was still in his service at home.

It may be supposed that I was too much interested in knowing what had passed at the Tuileries not to return to the Duc de Rovigo the same day. I learned from him the particulars which I have already related. He added that he had observed to the Emperor that there was no connection between Rapp and M. Talleyrand which could warrant the suspicion of their being concerned in the affair in question. "When Napoleon saw the matter in its true light," said Savary, "when I proved to him the palpable existence of the odious machination, he could not find terms to express his indignation. 'What baseness, what horrible villainy!' he exclaimed; and gave me orders to arrest and bring to Paris the infamous writer of the letter; and you may rely upon it his orders shall be promptly obeyed."

Savary, as he had said, instantly despatched orders for the arrest of the writer, whom he directed to be sent to France. On his arrival he was interrogated respecting the letter. He declared that he had written it at the instigation and under the dictation of Marshal Davoust, for doing which he received a small sum of money as a reward. He also confessed that when the letter was put into the post the Prince of Eckmuhl ordered the Director of the Post to open it, take a copy, then seal it again, and send it to its address—that is to say, to me—and the copy to the Emperor. The writer of the letter was banished to Marseilles, or to the Island of Hyeres, but the individual who dictated it continued a Marshal, a Prince, and a Governor-General, and still looked forward to the Viceroyalty of Poland! Such was the discriminating justice of the Empire; and Davoust continued his endeavours to revenge himself by other calumnies for my not having considered him a man of talent. I must do the Duc de Rovigo the justice to say that, though his fidelity to Napoleon was as it always had been, boundless, yet whilst he executed the Emperor's orders he endeavoured to make him acquainted with the truth, as was proved by his conduct in the case I have just mentioned. He was much distressed by the sort of terror which his appointment had excited in the public, and he acknowledged to me that he intended to restore confidence by a more mild system than that of his predecessor. I had observed formerly that Savary did not coincide in the opinion I had always entertained of Fouché, but when once the Duc de Rovigo endeavoured to penetrate the labyrinth of police, counter-police, inspections and hierarchies of espionage, he found they were all bugbears which Fouché had created to alarm the Emperor, as gardeners put up scarecrows among the fruit-trees to frighten away the sparrows. Thus, thanks to the artifices of Fouché, the eagle was frightened as easily as the sparrows, until the period when the Emperor, convinced that Fouché was maintaining a correspondence with England through the agency of Ouvrard, dismissed him.

I saw with pleasure that Savary, the Minister of Police, wished to simplify the working of his administration, and to gradually diminish whatever was annoying in it, but, whatever might be his intentions, he was not always free to act. I acknowledge that when I read his Memoirs I saw with great impatience that in many matters he had voluntarily assumed responsibilities for acts which a word from him might have attributed to their real author. However this may be, what much pleased me in Savary was the wish he showed to learn the real truth in order to tell it to Napoleon. He received from the Emperor more than one severe rebuff. This came from the fact that since the immense aggrandisement of the Empire the ostensible Ministers, instead of rising in credit, had seen their functions diminish by degrees. Thus proposals for appointments to the higher grades of the army came from the cabinet of Berthier, and not from that of the Minister-of-War. Everything which concerned any part of the government of the Interior or of the Exterior, except for the administration of War and perhaps for that of Finance, had its centre in the cabinet of M. Maret, certainly an honest man, but whose facility in saying "All is right," so much helped to make all wrong.

The home trade, manufactures, and particularly several of the Parisian firms were in a state of distress the more hurtful as it contrasted so singularly with the splendour of the Imperial Court since the marriage of Napoleon with Maria Louisa. In this state of affairs a chorus of complaints reached the ears of the Duc de Rovigo every day. I must say that Savary was never kinder to me than since my disgrace; he nourished my hope of getting Napoleon to overcome the prejudices against me with which the spirit of vengeance had inspired him, and I know for certain that Savary returned to the charge more than once to manage this. The Emperor listened without anger, did not blame him for the closeness of our intimacy, and even said to him some obliging but insignificant words about me. This gave time for new machinations against me, and to fill him with fresh doubts when he had almost overcome his former, ideas.

CHAPTER XXV

Since my return to France I had heard much of the intrigues of M. Czernischeff, an aide de camp of the Emperor of Russia, who, under the pretext of being frequently sent to compliment Napoleon on the part of the Emperor Alexander, performed, in fact, the office of a spy. The conduct of Napoleon with regard to M. Czernischeff at that period struck me as singular, especially after the intelligence which before my departure from Hamburg I had transmitted to him respecting the dissatisfaction of Russia and her hostile inclinations. It is therefore clear to me that Bonaparte was well aware of the real object of M. Czernischeffs mission, and that if he appeared to give credit to the increasing professions of his friendship it was only because he still wished, as he formerly did; that Russia might so far commit herself as to afford him a fair pretext for the commencement, of hostilities in the north.

M. Czernischeff first arrived in Paris shortly after the interview at Erfurt, and after that period was almost constantly on the road between Paris and St. Petersburg; it has been computed that in the space of less than four years he travelled more than 10,000 leagues. For a long time his frequent journeyings excited no surmises, but while I was in Paris Savary began to entertain suspicions, the correctness of which it was not difficult to ascertain, so formidable was still the system of espionage, notwithstanding the precaution taken by Fouché to conceal from his successor the names of his most efficient spies. It was known that M. Czernischeff was looking out for a professor of mathematics,—doubtless to disguise the real motives for his stay in Paris by veiling them under the desire of studying the sciences. The confidant of Alexander had applied to a professor connected with a public office; and from that time all the steps of M. Czerniseheff were known to the police. It was discovered that he was less anxious to question his instructor respecting the equations of a degree, or the value of unknown quantities, than to gain all the information he could about the different branches of the administration, and particularly the department of war. It happened that the professor knew some individuals employed in the public offices, who furnished him with intelligence, which he in turn communicated to M. Czernischeff, but not without making a report of it to the police; according to custom, instead of putting an end to this intrigue at once it was suffered fully to develop itself. Napoleon was informed of what was going on, and in this instance gave a new proof of his being an adept in the art of dissimulation, for, instead of testifying any displeasure against M. Czernischeff, he continued to receive him with the same marks of favour which he had shown to him during his former missions to Paris. Being, nevertheless, desirous to get rid of him, without evincing a suspicion that his clandestine proceedings had been discovered, he entrusted him with a friendly letter to his brother of Russia, but Alexander was in such haste to reply to the flattering missive of his brother of France that M. Czernischeff was hurried back to Paris, having scarcely been suffered to enter the gates of St. Petersburg. I believe I am correct in the idea that Napoleon was not really displeased at the intrigues of M. Czernischeff, from the supposition that they afforded an indication of the hostile intentions of Russia towards France; for, whatever he might say on this subject to his confidants, what reliance can we place on the man who formed the camp of Boulogne without the most distant intention of attempting a descent upon England, and who had deceived the whole world respecting that important affair without taking any one into his own confidence?

During the period of my stay in Paris the war with Spain and Portugal occupied much of the public attention; and it proved in the end an enterprise upon which the intuition of Josephine had not deceived her. In general she intermeddled little with political affairs; in the first place, because her doing so would have given offence to Napoleon; and next, because her natural frivolity led her to give a preference to lighter pursuits. But I may safely affirm that she was endowed with an instinct so perfect as seldom to be deceived respecting the good or evil tendency of any measure which Napoleon engaged in; and I remember she told me that when informed of the intention of the Emperor to bestow the throne of Spain on Joseph, she was seized with a feeling of indescribable alarm. It would be difficult to define that instinctive feeling which leads us to foresee the future; but it is a fact that Josephine was endowed with this faculty in a more perfect decree than any other person I have ever known, and to her it was a fatal gift, for she suffered at the same time under the weight of present and of future misfortunes.

I often visited her at Malmaison, as Duroc assured me that the Emperor had no objection to my doing so; yet he must have been fully aware that when Josephine and I were in confidential conversation he would not always be mentioned in terms of unqualified eulogy; and in truth, his first friend and his first wife might well be excused for sometimes commingling their complaints.

Though more than a twelvemonth had elapsed since the divorce grief still preyed on the heart of Josephine. "You cannot conceive, my friend," she often said to me, "all the torments that I have suffered since that fatal day! I cannot imagine how I survived it. You cannot figure to yourself the pain I endure on seeing descriptions of his fetes everywhere. And the first time he came to visit me after his marriage, what a meeting was that! How many tears I shed! The days on which he comes are to me days of misery, for he spares me not. How cruel to speak of his expected heir. Bourrienne, you cannot conceive how heart-rending all this is to me! Better, far better to be exiled a thousand leagues from hence! However," added Josephine, "a few friends still remain faithful in my changed fortune, and that is now the only thing which affords me even temporary consolation." The truth is that she was extremely unhappy, and the most acceptable consolation her friends could offer her was to weep with her. Yet such was still Josephine's passion for dress, that after. having wept for a quarter of an hour she would dry her tears to give audience to milliners and jewellers. The sight of a new hat would call forth all Josephine's feminine love of finery. One day I remember that, taking advantage of the momentary serenity occasioned by an ample display of sparkling gewgaws, I congratulated her upon the happy influence they exercised over her spirits, when she said, "My dear friend, I ought, indeed, to be indifferent to all this; but it is a habit." Josephine might have added that it was also an occupation, for it would be no exaggeration to say that if the time she wasted in tears and at her toilet had been subtracted from her life its duration would have been considerably shortened.

The vast extent of the French Empire now presented a spectacle which resembled rather the dominion of the Romans and the conquests of Charlemagne than the usual form and political changes of modern Europe. In fact, for nearly two centuries, until the period of the Revolution, and particularly until the elevation of Napoleon, no remarkable changes had taken place in the boundaries of European States, if we except the partition of Poland, when two of the co-partitioners committed the error of turning the tide of Russia towards the west! Under Napoleon everything was overturned with astonishing rapidity: customs, manners, laws, were superseded[252] by new customs, new manners, and new laws, imposed by force, and forming a heterogeneous whole, which could not fail to dissolve, as soon as the influence of the power which had created it should cease to operate. Such was the state of Italy that I have been informed by an individual worthy of credit that if the army of Prince Eugène, instead of being victorious, had been beaten on the Piava, a deeply-organised revolution would have broken out in Piedmont, and even in the Kingdom of Italy, where, nevertheless, the majority of the people fully appreciated the excellent qualities of Eugène. I have been also credibly informed that lists were in readiness designating those of the French who were to be put to death, as well as those by whom the severe orders of the Imperial Government had been mitigated, and who were only to be banished. In fact, revolt was as natural to the Italians as submission to the Germans, and as the fury of despair to the Spanish nation. On this subject I may cite an observation contained in one of the works of Alfieri, published fifteen years before the Spanish war. Taking a cursory view of the different European nations he regarded—the Spaniards as the only people possessed of "sufficient energy to struggle against foreign usurpation." Had I still been near the person of Napoleon I would most assuredly have resorted to an innocent artifice, which I had several times employed, and placed the work of Alfieri on his table open at the page I wished him to read. Alfieri's opinion of the Spanish people was in the end fully verified; and I confess I cannot think without shuddering of the torrents of blood which inundated the Peninsula; and for what? To make Joseph Bonaparte a King!

The commencement of 1811 was sufficiently favourable to the French arms in Spain, but towards the beginning of March the aspect of affairs changed. The Duke of Belluno, notwithstanding the valour of his troops, was unsuccessful at Chiclana; and from that day the French army could not make head against the combined forces of England and Portugal. Even Massena, notwithstanding the title of Prince of Eslingen (or Essling), which he had won under the walls of Vienna, was no longer "the favourite child of victory" as he had been at Zurich.

Having mentioned Massena I may observe that he did not favour the change of the French Government on the foundation of the Empire. Massena loved two things, glory and money; but as to what is termed honours, he only valued those which resulted from the command

252 The so-called "French" armies of the time, drawn from all parts of the Empire and from the dependent States, represented the extraordinary fusion attempted by Napoleon. Thus, at the battle of Ocana there were at least troops of the following States, viz. Warsaw, Holland, Baden, Nassau, Hesse-Darmstadt, Frankfort, besides the Spaniards in Joseph's service. A Spanish division went to Denmark, the regiment from Isembourg was sent to Naples, while the Neapolitans crossed to Spain. Even the little Valais had to furnish a battalion. Blacks from San Domingo served in Naples, while sixteen nations, like so many chained dogs, advanced into Russia. Such troops could not have the spirit of a homogeneous army. Already, in 1808, Metternich had written from Paris to his Court, "It is no longer the nation that fights: the present war (Spain) is Napoleon's war; it is not even that of his army." But Napoleon himself was aware of the danger of the Empire from its own extent. In the silence of his cabinet his secretary Meneval sometimes heard him murmur, "L'arc est trop longtemps tendu."

of an army; and his recollections all bound him to the Republic, because the Republic recalled to his mind the most brilliant and glorious events of his military career. He was, besides, among the number of the Marshals who wished to see a limit put to the ambition of Bonaparte; and he had assuredly done enough, since the commencement of the wars of the Republic, to be permitted to enjoy some repose, which his health at that period required. What could he achieve against the English in Portugal? The combined forces of England and Portugal daily augmented, while ours diminished. No efforts were spared by England to gain a superiority in the great struggle in which she was engaged; as her money was lavished profusely, her troops paid well wherever they went, and were abundantly supplied with ammunition and provisions: the French army was compelled, though far from possessing such ample means, to purchase at the same high rate, in order to keep the natives from joining the English party. But even this did not prevent numerous partial insurrections in different places, which rendered all communication with France extremely difficult. Armed bands continually carried off our dispersed soldiers; and the presence of the British troops, supported by the money they spent in the country, excited the inhabitants against us; for it is impossible to suppose that, unsupported by the English, Portugal could have held out a single moment against France. But battles, bad weather, and even want, had so reduced the French force that it was absolutely necessary our troops should repose when their enterprises could lead to no results. In this state of things Massena was recalled, because his health was so materially injured as to render it impossible for him to exert sufficient activity to restore the army to a respectable footing.

Under these circumstances Bonaparte sent Bertrand into Illyria to take the place of Marmont, who was ordered in his turn to relieve Massena and take command of the French army in Portugal Marmont on assuming the command found the troops in a deplorable state. The difficulty of procuring provisions was extreme, and the means he was compelled to employ for that purpose greatly heightened the evil, at the same time insubordination and want of discipline prevailed to such an alarming degree that it would be as difficult as painful to depict the situation of our army at this period, Marmont, by his steady conduct, fortunately succeeded in correcting the disorders which prevailed, and very soon found himself at the head of a well-organised army, amounting to 30,000 infantry, with forty pieces of artillery, but he had only a very small body of cavalry, and those ill-mounted.

Affairs in Spain at the commencement of 1811 exhibited an aspect not very different from those of Portugal. At first we were uniformly successful, but our advantages were so dearly purchased that the ultimate issue of this struggle might easily have been foreseen, because when a people fight for their homes and their liberties the invading army must gradually diminish, while at the same time the armed population, emboldened by success, increases in a still more marked progression. Insurrection was now regarded by the Spaniards as a holy and sacred duty, to which the recent meetings of the Cortes in the Isle of Leon had given, as it were, a legitimate character, since Spain found again, in the remembrance of her ancient privileges, at least the shadow of a Government—a centre around which the defenders of the soil of the Peninsula could rally.[253]

---

253 Lord Wellington gave Massena a beating at Fuentes d'Onore on the 5th of May 1811. It was soon after this battle that Napoleon sent Marmont to succeed Massena. Advancing on the southern frontier of Portugal the skillful Soult contrived to take Badajoz from a wavering Spanish garrison. About this time, however, General Graham, with his British corps, sallied

The Continental system was the cause, if not of the eventual fall, at least of the rapid fall of Napoleon. This cannot be doubted if we consider for a moment the brilliant situation of the Empire in 1811, and the effect simultaneously produced throughout Europe by that system, which undermined the most powerful throne which ever existed. It was the Continental system that Napoleon upheld in Spain, for he had persuaded himself that this system, rigorously enforced, would strike a death blow to the commerce of England; and Duroc besides informed me of a circumstance which is of great weight in this question. Napoleon one day said to him, "I am no longer anxious that Joseph should be King of Spain; and he himself is indifferent about it. I would give the crown to the first comer who would shut his ports against the English."

Murat had come to Paris on the occasion of the Empress' accouchement, and I saw him several times during his stay, for we had always been on the best terms; and I must do him the justice to say that he never assumed the King but to his courtiers, and those who had known him only as a monarch. Eight or ten days after the birth of the King of Rome, as I was one morning walking in the Champs Elysees, I met Murat. He was alone, and dressed in a long blue overcoat. We were exactly opposite the gardens of his sister-in-law, the Princess Borghese. "Well, Bourrienne," said Murat, after we had exchanged the usual courtesies, "well, what are you about now?" I informed him how I had been treated by Napoleon, who, that I might not be in Hamburg when the decree of union arrived there, had recalled me to Paris under a show of confidence. I think I still see the handsome and expressive countenance of Joachim when, having addressed him by the titles of Sire and Your Majesty, he said to me, "Pshaw! Bourrienne, are we not old comrades? The Emperor has treated you unjustly; and to whom has he not been unjust? His displeasure is preferable to his favour, which costs so dear! He says that he made us Kings; but did we not make him an Emperor? To you, my friend, whom I have known long and intimately, I can make my profession of faith. My sword, my blood, my life belong to the Emperor. When he calls me to the field to combat his enemies and the enemies of France I am no longer a King, I resume the rank of a Marshal of the Empire; but let him require no more. At Naples I will be King of Naples, and I will not sacrifice to his false calculations the life, the well-being, and the interests of my subjects. Let him not imagine that he can treat me as he has treated Louis! For I am ready to defend, even against him, if it must be so, the rights of the people over whom he has appointed me to rule. Am I then an advance-guard King?" These last words appeared to me peculiarly appropriate in the mouth of Murat, who had always served in the advance-guard of our armies, and I thought expressed in a very happy manner the similarity of his situation as a king and a soldier.

---

out of Cadiz, and beat the French on the heights of Barrosa, which lie in front of Cadiz, which city the French were then besieging. Encouraged by the successes of our regular armies, the Spanish Guerillas became more and more numerous and daring. By the end of 1811 Joseph Bonaparte found so many thorns in his usurped crown that he implored his brother to put it on some other head. Napoleon would not then listen to his prayer. In the course of 1811 a plan was laid for liberating Ferdinand from his prison in France and placing him at the head of affairs in Spain, but was detected by the emissaries of Bonaparte's police. Ferdinand's sister, the ex-Queen of Etruria, had also planned an escape to England. Her agents were betrayed, tried by a military commission, and shot—the Princess herself was condemned to close confinement in a Roman convent.—Editor of 1836 edition.

I walked with Murat about half an hour. In the course of our conversation he informed me that his greatest cause of complaint against the Emperor was his having first put him forward and then abandoned him. "Before I arrived in Naples," continued he, "it was intimated to me that there was a design of assassinating me. What did I do? I entered that city alone, in full daylight, in an open carriage, for I would rather have been assassinated at once than have lived in the constant fear of being so. I afterwards made a descent on the Isle of Capri, which succeeded. I attempted one against Sicily, and am curtain it would have also been successful had the Emperor fulfilled his promise of sending the Toulon fleet to second my operations; but he issued contrary orders: he enacted Mazarin, and unshed me to play the part of the adventurous Duke of Guise. But I see through his designs. Now that he has a son, on whom he has bestowed the title of King of Rome, he merely wishes the crown of Naples to be considered as a deposit in my hands. He regards Naples as a future annexation to the Kingdom of Rome, to which I foresee it is his design to unite the whole of Italy. But let him not urge me too far, for I will oppose him, and conquer, or perish in the attempt, sword in hand."

I had the discretion not to inform Murat how correctly he had divined the plans of the Emperor and his projects as to Italy, but in regard to the Continental system, which, perhaps, the reader will be inclined to call my great stalking-horse, I spoke of it as I had done to the Prince of Sweden, and I perceived that he was fully disposed to follow my advice, as experience has sufficiently proved. It was in fact the Continental system which separated the interests of Murat from those of the Emperor, and which compelled the new King of Naples to form alliances amongst the Princes at war with France. Different opinions have been entertained on this Subject; mine is, that the Marshal of the Empire was wrong, but the King of Naples right.

The Princes and Dukes of the Empire must pardon me for so often designating them by their Republican names. The Marshals set less value on their titles of nobility than the Dukes and Counts selected from among the civilians. Of all the sons of the Republic Regnault de St. Jean d'Angély was the most gratified at being a Count, whilst, among the fathers of the Revolution no one could regard with greater disdain than Fouché his title of Duke of Otranto; he congratulated himself upon its possession only once, and that was after the fall of the Empire.

I have expressed my dislike of Fouché; and the reason of that feeling was, that I could not endure his system of making the police a government within a government. He had left Paris before my return thither, but I had frequent occasion to speak of that famous personage to Savary, whom, for the reason above assigned, I do not always term Duc de Rovigo. Savary knew better than any one the fallacious measures of Fouché's administration, since he was his successor. Fouché, under pretence of encouraging men of letters, though well aware that the Emperor was hostile to them, intended only to bring them into contempt by making them write verses at command. It was easily seen that Napoleon nourished a profound dislike of literary men, though we must not conclude that he wished the public to be aware of that dislike. Those, besides, who devoted their pens to blazon his glory and his power were sure to be received by him with distinction. On the other hand, as Charlemagne and Louis XIV. owed a portion of the splendour of their reigns to the lustre reflected on them by literature, he wished to appear to patronise authors, provided that they never discussed questions relating to philosophy, the independence of mankind, and civil and political rights. With regard to men of science it was wholly different; those he held in real estimation; but men of letters, properly so called, were considered by him merely as a sprig in his Imperial crown.

The marriage of the Emperor with an Archduchess of Austria had set all the Court poets to work, and in this contest of praise and flattery it must be confessed that the false gods were vanquished by the true God; for, in spite of their fulsome verses, not one of the disciples of Apollo could exceed the extravagance of the Bishops in their pastoral letters. At a time when so many were striving to force themselves into notice there still existed a feeling of esteem in the public mind for men of superior talent who remained independent amidst the general corruption; such was M. Lemercier, such was M. de Chateaubriand. I was in Paris in the spring of 1811, at the period of Chenier's death, when the numerous friends whom Chateaubriand possessed in the second class of the Institute looked to him as the successor of Chenier. This was more than a mere literary question, not only on account of the high literary reputation M. de Chateaubriand already possessed, but of the recollection of his noble conduct at the period of Duc d'Enghien's death, which was yet fresh in the memory of every one; and, besides, no person could be ignorant of the immeasurable difference of opinion between Chenier and M. de Chateaubriand.

M. de Chateaubriand obtained a great majority of votes, and was elected a Member of the Institute. This opened a wide field for conjecture in Paris. Every one was anxious to see how the author of the Genie du Christianisme, the faithful defender of the Bourbons, would bend his eloquence to pronounce the eulogium of a regicide. The time for the admission of the new Member of the Institute arrived, but in his discourse, copies of which were circulated in Paris, he had ventured to allude to the death of Louis XVI., and to raise his voice against the regicides. This did not displease Napoleon; but M. de Chateaubriand also made a profession of faith in favour of liberty, which, he said, found refuge amongst men of letters when banished from the politic body. This was great boldness for the time; for though Bonaparte was secretly gratified at seeing the judges of Louis XVI. scourged by an heroic pen, yet those men held the highest situations under the Government. Cambacérès filled the second place in the Empire, although at a great distance from the first; Merlin de Douai was also in power; and it is known how much liberty was stifled and hidden beneath the dazzling illusion of what is termed glory. A commission was named to examine the discourse of Chateaubriand. MM. Suard, de Segur, de Fontanes, and two or three other members of the same class of the Institute whose names I cannot recollect, were of opinion that the discourse should be read; but it was opposed by the majority.

When Napoleon was informed of what had passed he demanded a sight of the address, which was presented to him by M. Daru. After having perused it he exclaimed; "Had this discourse been delivered I would have shut the gates of the Institute, and thrown M. de Chateaubriand into a dungeon for life." The storm long raged; at length means of conciliation were tried. The Emperor required M. de Chateaubriand to prepare another discourse, which the latter refused to do, in spite of every menace. Madame Gay applied to Madame Regnault de St. Jean d'Angély, who interested her husband in favour of the author of the Genie du Christianisme. M. de Montalivet and Savary also acted on this occasion in the most praiseworthy manner, and succeeded in appeasing the first transports of the Emperor's rage. But the name of Chateaubriand constantly called to mind the circumstances which had occasioned him to give in his resignation; and, besides, Napoleon had another complaint against him. He had published in the 'Merceure' an article on a work of M. Alexandre de Laborde. In that article, which was eagerly read in Paris, and which caused the suppression of the 'Merceure', occurred the famous phrase which has been since so often repeated: "In vain a Nero triumphs: Tacitus is already born in his Empire." This quotation leads me to repeat an observation, which, I believe, I have already made, viz. that it is a manifest misconception to compare Bonaparte to Nero. Napoleon's ambition might blind his vision to political crimes, but in private life no man could evince less disposition to cruelty or bloodshed. A proof that he bore little resemblance to Nero is that his anger against the author of the article in question vented itself in mere words. "What!" exclaimed he, "does Chateaubriand think I am a fool, and that I do not know what he means? If he goes on this way I will have him sabred on the steps of the Tuileries." This language is quite characteristic of Bonaparte, but it was uttered in the first ebullition of his wrath. Napoleon merely threatened, but Nero would have made good his threat; and in such a case there is surely some difference between words and deeds.

The discourse of M. de Chateaubriand revived Napoleon's former enmity against him; he received an order to quit Paris: M. Daru returned to him the manuscript of his discourse, which had been read by Bonaparte, who cancelled some passages with a pencil. We can be sure that the phrase about liberty was not one of those spared by the Imperial pencil. However that may be, written copies were circulated with text altered and abbreviated; and I have even been told that a printed edition appeared, but I have never seen any copies; and as I do not find the discourse in the works of M. de Chateaubriand I have reason to believe that the author has not yet wished to publish it.

Such were the principal circumstances attending the nomination of Chateaubriand to the Institute. I shall not relate some others which occurred on a previous occasion, viz. on the election of an old and worthy visitor at Malmaison, M. Lemercier, and which will serve to show one of those strange inconsistencies so frequent in the character of Napoleon.

After the foundation of the Empire M. Lemercier ceased to present himself at the Tuileries, St. Cloud, or at Malmaison, though he was often seen in the salons of Madame Bonaparte while she yet hoped not to become a Queen. Two places were vacant at once in the second class of the Institute, which still contained a party favourable to liberty. This party, finding it impossible to influence the nomination of both members, contented itself with naming one, it being the mutual condition, in return for favouring the Government candidate, that the Government party should not oppose the choice of the liberals. The liberal party selected M. Lemercier, but as they knew his former connection with Bonaparte had been broken off they wished first to ascertain that he would do nothing to commit their choice. Chenier was empowered to inquire whether M. Lemercier would refuse to accompany them to the Tuileries when they repaired thither in a body, and whether, on his election, he would comply with the usual ceremony of being presented to the Emperor. M. Lemercier replied that he would do nothing contrary to the customs and usages of the body to which he might belong: he was accordingly elected. The Government candidate was M. Esmenard, who was also elected. The two new members were presented to the Emperor on the same day. On this occasion upwards of 400 persons were present in the salon, from one of whom I received these details. When the Emperor saw M. Lemercier, for whom he had long pretended great friendship, he said to him in a kind tone, "Well, Lemercier, you are now installed." Lemercier respectfully bowed to the Emperor; but without uttering a word of reply. Napoleon was mortified at this silence, but without saying anything more to Lemercier he turned to Esmenard, the member who should have been most acceptable to him, and vented upon him the whole weight of his indignation in a manner equally unfeeling and unjust. "Well, Esmenard," said he, "do you still hold your place in the police?" These words were spoken in so loud a tone as to be heard by all present; and it was doubtless this cruel and ambiguous speech which furnished the enemies of Esmenard with arms to attack his reputation as a man of honour, and to give an appearance of disgrace to those functions which he exercised with so much zeal and ability.

When, at the commencement of 1811, I left Paris I had ceased to delude myself respecting the brilliant career which seemed opening before me during the Consulate. I clearly perceived that since Bonaparte, instead of receiving me as I expected, had refused to see me at all, the calumnies of my enemies were triumphant, and that I had nothing to hope for from an absolute ruler, whose past injustice rendered him the more unjust. He now possessed what he had so long and ardently wished for,—a son of his own, an inheritor of his name, his power, and his throne. I must take this opportunity of stating that the malevolent and infamous rumours spread abroad respecting the birth of the King of Rome were wholly without foundation. My friend Corvisart, who did not for a single instant leave Maria Louisa during her long and painful labour, removed from my mind every doubt on the subject. It is as true that the young Prince, for whom the Emperor of Austria stood sponsor at the font, was the son of Napoleon and the Archduchess Maria Louisa as it is false that Bonaparte was the father of the first child of Hortense. The birth of the son of Napoleon was hailed with general enthusiasm. The Emperor was at the height of his power from the period of the birth of his son until the reverse he experienced after the battle of the Moskowa. The Empire, including the States possessed by the Imperial family, contained nearly 57,000,000 of inhabitants; but the period was fast approaching when this power, unparalleled in modern times, was to collapse under its own weight.[254]

254 The little King of Rome, Napoleon Francis Bonaparte, was born on the 20th of March 1811. —Editor of 1836 edition.

CHAPTER XXVI

As I took the most lively interest in all that concerned the Hanse Towns, my first care on returning to Hamburg was to collect information from the most respectable sources concerning the influential members of the new Government. Davoust was at its head. On his arrival he had established in the Duchy of Mecklenburg, in Swedish Pomerania, and in Stralsund, the capital of that province, military posts and custom-houses, and that in a time of profound peace with those countries, and without any previous declaration. The omnipotence of Napoleon, and the terror inspired by the name of Davoust, overcame all obstacles which might have opposed those iniquitous usurpations. The weak were forced to yield to the strong.

At Hamburg a Government Committee was formed, consisting of the Prince of Eekmuhl as President, Comte de Chaban, Councillor of State, who superintended the departments of the Interior and Finance, and of M. Faure, Councillor of State, who was appointed to form and regulate the Courts of Law. I had sometimes met M. de Chaban at Malmaison. He was distantly related to Josephine, and had formerly been an officer in the French Guards. He was compelled to emigrate, having been subjected to every species of persecution during the Revolution.

M. de Chaban was among the first of the emigrants who returned to France after the 18th Brumaire. He was at first made Sub-Prefect of Vendome, but on the union of Tuscany with France Napoleon created him a member of the Junta appointed to regulate the affairs of Tuscany. He next became Prefect of Coblentz and Brussels, was made a Count by Bonaparte, and was afterwards chosen a member of the Government Committee at Hamburg. M. de Chaban was a man of upright principles, and he discharged his various functions in a way that commanded esteem and attachment.[255]

The Hanseatic Towns, united to the Grand Empire professedly for their welfare, soon felt the blessings of the new organisation of a regenerating Government. They were at once presented with; the stamp-duty, registration, the lottery, the droits reunis, the tax on cards, and the 'octroi'. This prodigality of presents caused, as we may be sure, the most lively gratitude; a tax for military quarters and for warlike supplies was imposed, but this did not relieve any one from laving not only officers and soldiers; but even all the chiefs of the administration and their officials billeted on them: The refineries, breweries, and

255 I recollect an anecdote which but too well depicts those disastrous times. The Comte de Chaban, being obliged to cross France during the Reign of Terror, was compelled to assume a disguise. He accordingly provided himself with a smockfrock; a cart and horses, and a load of corn. In this manner he journeyed from place to place till he reached the frontiers. He stopped at Rochambeau, in the Vendomais, where he was recognised by the Marshal de Rochambeau, who to guard against exciting any suspicion among his servants, treated him as if he had really been a carman and said to him, "You may dine in the kitchen."—Bourrienne.

manufactures of all sorts were suppressed. The cash chests of the Admiralty, of the charity houses, of the manufactures, of the savings-banks, of the working classes, the funds of the prisons, the relief meant for the infirm, the chests of the refuges, orphanages; and of the hospitals, were all seized.

More than 200,000 men, Italian, Dutch, and French soldiers came in turn to stay there, but only to be clothed and shod; and then they left newly clothed from head to foot. To leave nothing to be wished for, Davoust, from 1812, established military commissions in all the thirty-second. military division, before he entered upon the Russian campaign. To complete these oppressive measures he established at the same time the High Prevotal Court of the Customs. It was at this time that M. Eudes, the director of the ordinary customs, a strict but just man, said that the rule of the ordinary customs would be regretted, "for till now you have only been on roses . . . " The professed judgments of this court were executed without appeal and without delay. From what I have just said the situation and the misery of the north of Germany, and the consequent discontent, can be judged.

During my stay in Hamburg, which on this occasion was not very long, Napoleon's attention was particularly engaged by the campaign of Portugal, and his discussions with the Pope. At this period the thunderbolts of Rome were not very alarming. Yet precautions were taken to keep secret the excommunication which Pius VII. had pronounced against Napoleon. The event, however, got reported about, and a party in favour of the Pope speedily rose up among the clergy, and more particularly among the fanatics. Napoleon sent to Savona the Archbishops of Nantes, Bourges, Treves, and Tours, to endeavour to bring about a reconciliation with His Holiness. But all their endeavours were unavailing, and after staying a month at Savona they returned to Paris without having done anything. But Napoleon was not discouraged by this first disappointment, and he shortly afterwards sent a second deputation, which experienced the same fate as the first. Cardinal Fesch, Napoleon's uncle, took part with the Pope. For this fact I can vouch, though I cannot for an answer which he is said to have made to the Emperor. I have been informed that when Napoleon was one day speaking to his uncle about the Pope's obstinacy the Cardinal made some observations to him on his (Bonaparte's) conduct to the Holy Father, upon which Napoleon flew into a passion, and said that the Pope and he were two old fools. "As for the Pope," said he, "he is too obstinate to listen to anything. No, I am determined he shall never have Rome again. . . . He will not remain at Savona, and where does he wish I should send him?"—"To Heaven, perhaps," replied the Cardinal.

The truth is, the Emperor was violently irritated against Pius VII. Observing with uneasiness the differences and difficulties to which all these dissensions gave rise, he was anxious to put a stop to them. As the Pope would not listen to any propositions that were made to him, Napoleon convoked a Council, which assembled in Paris, and at which several Italian Bishops were present. The Pope insisted that the temporal and spiritual interests should be discussed together; and, however disposed a certain number of prelates, particularly the Italians, might be to separate these two points of discussion, yet the influence of the Church and well-contrived intrigues gradually gave preponderance to the wishes of the Pope. The Emperor, having discovered that a secret correspondence was carried on by several of the Bishops and Archbishops who had seats in the Council, determined to get rid of some of them, and the Bishops of Ghent, Troyes, Tournay, and Toulouse were arrested and sent to Vincennes. They were superseded by others. He wished to dissolve the Council, which he saw was making no advance towards the object he had in view, and, fearing that it might adopt some act at variance with his supreme wish, every member of the Council was individually required to make a declaration that the proposed changes were conformable to the laws of the Church. It was said at the time that they were unanimous in this individual declaration, though it is certain that in the sittings of the Council opinions were divided. I know not what His Holiness thought of these written opinions compared with the verbal opinions that had been delivered, but certain it is though still a captive at Savona, he refused to adhere to the concessions granted in the secret declarations.

The conflicts which took place in Spain during the year 1811 were unattended by any decisive results. Some brilliant events, indeed, attested the courage of our troops and the skill of our generals. Such were the battle of Albufera and the taking of Tarragona, while Wellington was obliged to raise the siege of Badajoz. These advantages, which were attended only by glory, encouraged Napoleon in the hope of triumphing in the Peninsula, and enabled him to enjoy the brilliant fetes which took place at Paris in celebration of the birth of the King of Rome.

On his return from a tour in Holland at the end of October Napoleon clearly saw that a rupture with Russia was inevitable. In vain he sent Lauriston as Ambassador to St. Petersburg to supersede Caulaincourt, who would no longer remain there: all the diplomatic skill in the world could effect nothing with a powerful Government which had already formed its determination. All the Cabinets in Europe were now unanimous in wishing for the overthrow of Napoleon's power, and the people no less, ardently wished for an order of things less fatal to their trade and industry. In the state to which Europe was reduced no one could counteract the wish of Russia and her allies to go to war with France—Lauriston no more than Caulaincourt.

The war for which Napoleon was now obliged to prepare forced him to neglect Spain, and to leave his interests in that country in a state of real danger. Indeed, his occupation of Spain and his well-known wish to maintain himself there were additional motives for inducing the powers of Europe to enter upon a war which would necessarily divide Napoleon's forces. All at once the troops which were in Italy and the north of Germany moved towards the frontiers of the Russian Empire. From March 1811 the Emperor had all the military forces of Europe at his disposal. It was curious to see this union of nations, distinguished by difference of manners,[256] language, religion, and interests, all ready to fight for one man against a power who had done nothing to offend them. Prussia herself, though she could not pardon the injuries he had inflicted upon her, joined his alliance, but with the intention of breaking it on the first opportunity. When the war with Russia was first spoken of Savary and I had frequent conversations on the subject. I communicated to him all the intelligence I received from abroad respecting that vast enterprise. The Duc de Rovigo shared all my forebodings; and if he and those who thought like him had been listened to, the war would probably have

256 It should be remarked that Napoleon was far from being anxious for the war with Russia. Metternich writing on 26th March 1811, says "Everything seems to indicate that the Emperor Napoleon is at present still far from desiring a war with Russia. But it is not less true that the Emperor Alexander has given himself over, 'nolens volens', to the war party, and that he will bring about war, because the time is approaching when he will no longer be able to resist the reaction of the party in the internal affairs of his Empire, or the temper of his army. The contest between Count Romanzov and the party opposed to that Minister seems on the point of precipitating a war between Russia and France." This, from Metternich, is strong evidence.

been avoided. Through him I learnt who were the individuals who urged the invasion. The eager ambition with which they looked forward to Viceroyalties, Duchies, and endowments blinded them to the possibility of seeing the Cossacks in Paris.

The gigantic enterprise being determined on, vast preparations were made for carrying it into effect. Before his departure Napoleon, who was to take with him all the disposable troops, caused a 'Senatus-consulte' to be issued for levying the National Guards, who were divided into three corps. He also arranged his diplomatic affairs by concluding, in February 1812, a treaty of alliance, offensive and defensive, with Prussia, by virtue of which the two contracting powers mutually guaranteed the integrity of their own possessions, and the European possessions of the Ottoman Porte, because that power was then at war with Russia. A similar treaty was concluded about the beginning of March with Austria, and about the end of the same month Napoleon renewed the capitulation of France and Switzerland. At length, in the month of April, there came to light an evident proof of the success which had attended M. Czernischeff's intrigues in Paris. It was ascertained that a clerk in the War Office, named Michel, had communicated to him the situation of the French forces in Germany. Michel was condemned to death, for the time was gone by when Bonaparte, confident in his genius and good fortune, could communicate his plans to the spy of General Melas.

In March 1812, when I saw that the approaching war would necessarily take Napoleon from France, weary of the persecutions and even threats by which I was every day assailed, I addressed to the Emperor a memorial explaining my conduct and showing the folly and wickedness of my accusers. Among them was a certain Ogier de la Saussaye, who had sent a report to the Emperor, in which the principal charge was, that I had carried off a box containing important papers belonging to the First Consul. The accusation of Ogier de la Saussaye terminated thus: "I add to my report the interrogatories of MM. Westphalen, Osy, Chapeau Rouge, Aukscher, Thierry, and Gumprecht-Mores. The evidence of the latter bears principally on a certain mysterious box, a secret upon which it is impossible to throw any light, but the reality of which we are bound to believe." These are his words. The affair of the mysterious box has been already explained. I have already informed the reader that I put my papers into a box, which I buried lest it should be stolen from me. But for that precaution I should not have been able to lay before the reader the autograph documents in my possession, and which I imagine form the most essential part of these volumes. In my memorial to the Emperor I said, in allusion to the passage above quoted, "This, Sire, is the most atrocious part of Ogier's report.

"Gumprecht being questioned on this point replies that the accuser has probably, as well as himself, seen the circumstance mentioned in an infamous pamphlet which appeared seven or eight years, ago. It was, I think, entitled 'Le Secret du Cabinet des Tuileries,' and was very likely at the time of its appearance denounced by the police. In that libel it is stated, among a thousand other calumnies equally false and absurd, 'that when I left the First Consul I carried away a box full of important papers, that I was in consequence sent to the Temple, where your brother Joseph came to me and offered me my liberation, and a million of francs, if I would restore the papers, which I refused to do,' etc. Ogier, instead of looking for this libel in Hamburg, where I read it, has the impudence to give credit to the charge, the truth of which could have been ascertained immediately: and he adds, 'This secret we are bound to believe.' Your Majesty knows whether I was ever in the Temple, and whether Joseph ever made such an offer to me." I entreated that the Emperor would do me the favour to bring me to trial; for certainly I should have regarded that as a favour rather than to remain as I was, exposed to vague accusations; yet all my solicitations were in vain. My letter to the Emperor remained unanswered; but though Bonaparte could not spare a few moments to reply to an old friend, I learned through Duroc the contempt he cherished for my accusers. Duroc advised me not to be uneasy, and that in all probability the Emperor's prejudices against me would be speedily overcome; and I must say that if they were not overcome it was neither the fault of Duroc nor Savary, who knew how to rightly estimate the miserable intrigues just alluded to.

Napoleon was at length determined to extend the limits of his Empire, or rather to avenge the injuries which Russia had committed against his Continental system. Yet, before he departed for Germany, the resolute refusal of the Pope to submit to any arrangement urgently claimed his consideration. Savona did not appear to him a sufficiently secure residence for such a prisoner. He feared that when all his strength should be removed towards the Niemen the English might carry off the Pope, or that the Italians, excited by the clergy, whose dissatisfaction was general in Italy, would stir up those religious dissensions which are always fatal and difficult to quell. With the view, therefore, of keeping the Pope under his control he removed him to Fontainebleau, and even at one time thought of bringing him to Paris.

The Emperor appointed M. Denon to reside with the Pope at Fontainebleau; and to afford his illustrious prisoner the society of such a man was certainly a delicate mark of attention on the part of Napoleon. When speaking of his residence with Pius VII. M. Denon related to me the following anecdote. "The Pope," said he, "was much attached to me. He always addressed me by the appellation 'my son,' and he loved to converse with me, especially on the subject of the Egyptian expedition. One day he asked me for my work on Egypt, which he said he wished to read; and as you know it is not quite orthodox, and does not perfectly agree with the creation of the world according to Genesis, I at first hesitated; but the Pope insisted, and at length I complied with his wish. The Holy Father assured me that he had been much interested by the perusal of the book. I made some allusion to the delicate points; upon which he said, 'No matter, no matter, my son; all that is exceedingly curious, and I must confess entirely new to me.' I then," continued M. Denon, "told His Holiness why I hesitated to lend him the work, which, I observed, he had excommunicated, together with its author. 'Excommunicated you, my son?' resumed the Pope in a tone of affectionate concern. 'I am very sorry for it, and assure you I was far from being aware of any such thing.'"

When M. Denon related to me this anecdote he told me how greatly he had admired the virtues and resignation of the Holy Father; but he added that it would nevertheless have been easier to make him a martyr than to induce him to yield on any point until he should be restored to the temporal sovereignty of Rome, of which he considered himself the depositary, and which he would not endure the reproach of having willingly sacrificed. After settling the place of the Pope's residence Napoleon set off for Dresden, accompanied by Maria Louisa, who had expressed a wish to see her father.

The Russian enterprise, the most gigantic, perhaps, that the genius of man ever conceived since the conquest of India by Alexander, now absorbed universal attention, and defied the calculations of reason. The Manzanares was forgotten, and nothing was thought of but the Niemen, already so celebrated by the raft of Tilsit. Thither, as towards a common centre, were moving men, horses, provisions, and baggage of every kind, from all parts of Europe. The hopes of our generals and the fears of all prudent men were directed to Russia. The war in Spain, which was becoming more and more unfortunate, excited but a feeble interest;

and our most distinguished officers looked upon it as a disgrace to be sent to the Peninsula. In short, it was easy to foresee that the period was not far distant when the French would be obliged to recross the Pyrenees. Though the truth was concealed from the Emperor on many subjects, yet he was not deceived as to the situation of Spain in the spring of 1812. In February the Duke of Ragusa had frankly informed him that the armies of Spain and Portugal could not, without considerable reinforcements of men and money, hope for any important advantages since Ciudad-Rodrigo and Badajoz had fallen into the hands of the English.

Before he commenced his great operations on the Niemen and the Volga Napoleon made a journey to Dantzic, and Rapp, who was then Governor of that city, informed me of some curious particulars connected with the Imperial visit. The fact is, that if Rapp's advice had been listened to, and had been supported by men higher in rank than himself, Bonaparte would not have braved the chances of the Russian war until those chances turned against him. Speaking to me of the Russians Rapp said, "They will soon be as wise as we are! Every time we go to war with them we teach them how to beat us." I was struck with the originality and truth of this observation, which at the time I heard it was new, though it has been often repeated since.

"On leaving Dresden," said Rapp to me, "Napoleon came to Dantzic. I expected a dressing; for, to tell you the truth, I had treated very cavalierly both his custom-house and its officers, who were raising up as many enemies to France as there were inhabitants in my Government. I had also warned him of all that has since happened in Russia, but I assure you I did not think myself quite so good a prophet. In the beginning of 1812 I thus wrote to him: 'If your Majesty should experience reverses you may depend on it that both Russians and Germans will rise up in a mass to shake off the yoke. There will be a crusade, and all your allies will abandon you. Even the King of Bavaria, on whom you rely so confidently, will join the coalition. I except only the King of Saxony. He, perhaps, might remain faithful to you; but his subjects will force him to make common cause with your enemies. The King of Naples," continued Rapp, "who had the command of the cavalry, had been to Dantzic before the Emperor. He did not seem to take a more favourable view of the approaching campaign than I did. Murat was dissatisfied that the Emperor would not consent to his rejoining him in Dresden; and he said that he would rather be a captain of grenadiers than a King such as he was."

Here I interrupted Rapp to tell him what had fallen from Murat when I met him in the Champs Elysees "Bah!" resumed Rapp, "Murat, brave as he was, was a craven in Napoleon's presence! On the Emperor's arrival in Dantzic the first thing of which he spoke to me was the alliance he had just then concluded with Prussia and Austria. I could not refrain from telling him that we did a great deal of mischief as allies; a fact of which I was assured from the reports daily transmitted to me respecting the conduct of our troops. Bonaparte tossed his bead, as you know he was in the habit of doing when he was displeased. After a moment's silence, dropping the familiar thee and thou, he said, 'Monsieur le General, this is a torrent which must be allowed to run itself out. It will not last long. I must first ascertain whether Alexander decidedly wishes for war.' Then, suddenly changing the subject of conversation, he said, 'Have you not lately observed something extraordinary in Murat? I think he is quite altered. Is he ill?'—'Sire,' replied I, 'Murat is not ill, but he is out of spirits.'—'Out of spirits! but why? Is he not satisfied with being a King?'—'Sire, Murat says he is no King.'—'That is his own fault. Why does he make himself a Neapolitan? Why is he not a Frenchman? When he is in his Kingdom he commits all sorts of follies. He favours the trade of England; that I will not suffer.'

"When," continued Rapp, "he spoke of the favour extended by Murat to the trade between Naples and England I thought my turn would come next; but I was deceived. No more was said on the subject, and when I was about to take my leave the Emperor said to me, as when in his best of humours, 'Rapp, you will sup with me this evening.' I accordingly supped that evening with the Emperor, who had also invited the King of Naples and Berthier. Next day the Emperor visited the fortress, and afterwards returned to the Government Palace, where he received the civil and military authorities. He again invited Murat, Berthier, and me to supper. When we first sat down to table we were all very dull, for the Emperor was silent; and, as you well know, under such circumstances not even Murat himself dared to be the first to speak to him. At length Napoleon, addressing me, inquired how far it was from Cadiz to Dantzic. 'Too far, Sire,' replied I. 'I understand you, Monsieur le General, but in a few months the distance will be still greater.'—'So much the worse, Sire!' Here there was another pause. Neither Murat nor Berthier, on whom the Emperor fixed a scrutinising glance, uttered a word, and Napoleon again broke silence, but without addressing any one of us in particular: 'Gentlemen,' said he in a solemn and rather low tone of voice, 'I see plainly that you are none of you inclined to fight again. The King of Naples does not wish to leave the fine climate of his dominions, Berthier wishes to enjoy the diversion of the chase at his estate of Gros Bois, and Rapp is impatient to be back to his hotel in Paris.' Would you believe it," pursued Rapp, "that neither Murat nor Berthier said a word in reply? and the ball again came to me. I told him frankly that what he said was perfectly true, and the King of Naples and the Prince of Neufchatel complimented me on my spirit, and observed that I was quite right in saying what I did. 'Well,' said I, 'since it was so very right, why did you not follow my example, and why leave me to say all?' You cannot conceive," added Rapp, "how confounded they both were, and especially Murat, though he was very differently situated from Berthier."

The negotiations which Bonaparte opened with Alexander, when he yet wished to seem averse to war, resembled those oratorical paraphrases which do not prevent us from coming to the conclusion we wish. The two Emperors equally desired war; the one with the view of consolidating his power, and the other in the hope of freeing himself from a yoke which threatened to reduce him to a state of vassalage, for it was little short of this to require a power like Russia to close her ports against England for the mere purpose of favouring the interests of France. At that time only two European powers were not tied to Napoleon's fate—Sweden and Turkey. Napoleon was anxious to gain the alliance of these two powers. With respect to Sweden his efforts were vain; and though, in fact, Turkey was then at war with Russia, yet the Grand Seignior was not now, as at the time of Sebastiani's embassy, subject to the influence of France.

The peace, which was soon concluded at Bucharest, between Russia, and Turkey increased Napoleon's embarrassment. The left of the Russian army, secured by the neutrality of Turkey, was reinforced by Bagration's corps from Moldavia: it subsequently occupied the right of the Beresina, and destroyed the last hope of saving the wreck of the French army. It is difficult to conceive how Turkey could have allowed the consideration of injuries she had received from France to induce her to terminate the war with Russia when France was attacking that power with immense forces. The Turks never had a fairer opportunity for taking revenge on Russia, and, unfortunately for Napoleon, they suffered it to escape.

Napoleon was not more successful when he sought the alliance of a Prince whose fortune he had made, and who was allied to his family, but with whom he had never been on terms of good understanding. The Emperor Alexander had a considerable corps of troops in Finland destined to protect that country against the Sweden, Napoleon having consented to that occupation in order to gain the provisional consent of Alexander to the invasion of Spain. What was the course pursued by Napoleon when, being at war with Russia, he wished to detach Sweden from her alliance with Alexander? He intimated to Bernadotte that he had a sure opportunity of retaking Finland, a conquest which would gratify his subjects and win their attachment to him. By this alliance Napoleon wished to force Alexander not to withdraw the troops who were in the north of his Empire, but rather to augment their numbers in order to cover Finland and St. Petersburg. It was thus that Napoleon endeavoured to draw the Prince Royal into his coalition. It was of little consequence to Napoleon whether Bernadotte succeeded or not. The Emperor Alexander would nevertheless have been obliged to increase his force in Finland; that was all that Napoleon wished. In the gigantic struggle upon which France and Russia were about to enter the most trivial alliance was not to be neglected. In January 1812 Davoust invaded Swedish Pomerania without any declaration of war, and without any apparent motive. Was this inconceivable violation of territory likely to dispose the Prince Royal of Sweden to the proposed alliance, even had that alliance not been adverse to the interests of his country? That was impossible; and Bernadotte took the part which was expected of him. He rejected the offers of Napoleon, and prepared for coming events.

The Emperor Alexander wished to withdraw his force from Finland for the purpose of more effectively opposing the immense army which threatened his States. Unwilling to expose Finland to an attack on the part of Sweden, he had an interview on the 28th of August 1812, at Abo, with the Prince-Royal, to come to an arrangement with him for uniting their interests. I know that the Emperor of Russia pledged himself, whatever might happen, to protect Bernadotte against the fate of the new dynasties, to guarantee the possession of his throne, and promised that he should have Norway as a compensation for Finland. He even went so far as to hint that Bernadotte might supersede Napoleon. Bernadotte adopted all the propositions of Alexander, and from that moment Sweden made common cause against Napoleon. The Prince Royal's conduct has been much blamed, but the question resolved itself into one of mere political interest. Could Bernadotte, a Swede by adoption, prefer the alliance of an ambitious sovereign whose vengeance he had to fear, and who had sanctioned the seizure of Finland to that of a powerful monarch, his formidable neighbour, his protector in Sweden, and where hostility might effectually support the hereditary claims of young Gustavus? Sweden, in joining France, would thereby have declared herself the enemy of England. Where, then, would have been her navy, her trade and even her existence?

CHAPTER XXVII

1812

It may now he asked whether Bonaparte, previous to entering upon the last campaign, had resolved on restoring Poland to independence. The fact is that Bonaparte, as Emperor, never entertained any positive wish to reestablish the old Kingdom of Poland, though at a previous period he was strongly inclined to that re-establishment, of which he felt the necessity. He may have said that he would re-establish the Kingdom of Poland, but I beg leave to say that that is no reason for believing that he entertained any such design. He had said, and even sworn, that he would never aggrandise the territory of the Empire! The changeableness of Bonaparte's ideas, plans, and projects renders it difficult to master them; but they may be best understood when it is considered that all Napoleon's plans and conceptions varied with his fortunes. Thus, it is not unlikely that he might at one time have considered the reestablishment of Poland as essential to European policy, and afterwards have regarded it as adverse to the development of his ambition. Who can venture to guess what passed in his mind when dazzled by his glory at Dresden, and whether in one of his dreams he might not have regarded the Empire of the Jagellons as another gem in the Imperial diadem? The truth is that Bonaparte, when General-in-Chief of the army of Egypt and First Consul, had deeply at heart the avenging the dismemberment of Poland, and I have often conversed with him on this most interesting subject, upon which we entirely concurred in opinion. But times and circumstances were changed since we walked together on the terrace of Cairo and mutually deplored the death of young Sulkowski. Had Sulkowski lived Napoleon's favourable intentions with respect to Poland might perhaps have been confirmed. A fact which explains to me the coolness, I may almost say the indifference, of Bonaparte to the resurrection of Poland is that the commencement of the Consulate was the period at which that measure particularly occupied his attention. How often did he converse on the subject with me and other persons who may yet recollect his sentiments! It was the topic on which he most loved to converse, and on which he spoke with feeling and enthusiasm. In the 'Moniteur' of the period here alluded to I could point out more than one article without signature or official character which Napoleon dictated to me, and the insertion of which in that journal, considering the energy of certain expressions, sufficiently proves that they could have emanated from none but Bonaparte. It was usually in the evening that he dictated to me these articles. Then, when the affairs of the day were over, he would launch into the future, and give free scope to his vast projects. Some of these articles were characterised by so little moderation that the First Consul would very often destroy them in the morning, smiling at the violent ebullitions of the preceding night. At other times I took the liberty of not sending them to the 'Moniteur' on the night on which they were dictated, and though he might earnestly wish their insertion I adduced reasons good or bad, to account for the delay. He would then read over the article in question, and approve of my conduct; but he would sometimes add, "It is nevertheless true that with an independent Kingdom of Poland, and 150,000 disposable troops in the east of France, I should always be master of Russia, Prussia, and Austria."—"General," I would reply, "I am entirely of your opinion; but wherefore awaken the suspicions of the interested parties. Leave all to time and circumstances."

The reader may have to learn, and not, perhaps, without some surprise, that in the protocol of the sittings of the Congress of Chatillon Napoleon put forward the spoliation of Poland by the three principal powers allied against him as a claim to a more advantageous peace, and to territorial indemnities for France. In policy he was right, but the report of foreign cannon was already loud enough to drown the best of arguments.

After the ill-timed and useless union of the Hanse Towns to France I returned to Hamburg in the spring of 1811 to convey my family to France. I then had some conversation with Davoust. On one occasion I said to him that if his hopes were realised, and my sad predictions respecting the war with Russia overthrown, I hoped to see the restoration of the Kingdom of Poland. Davoust replied that that event was probable, since he had Napoleon's promise of the Viceroyalty of that Kingdom, and as several of his comrades had been promised starosties. Davoust made no secret of this, and it was generally known throughout Hamburg and the north of Germany.

But notwithstanding what Davoust said respecting. Napoleon's intentions I considered that these promises had been conditional rather than positive.

On Napoleon's arrival in Poland the Diet of Warsaw, assured, as there seemed reason to be, of the Emperor's sentiments, declared the Kingdom free and independent. The different treaties of dismemberment were pronounced to be null; and certainly the Diet had a right so to act, for it calculated upon his support. But the address of the Diet to Napoleon, in which these principles were declared, was ill received. His answer was full of doubt and indecision, the motive of which could not be blamed. To secure the alliance of Austria against Russia he had just guaranteed to his father-in-law the integrity of his dominions. Napoleon therefore declared that he could take no part in any movement or resolution which might disturb Austria in the possession of the Polish provinces forming a part of her Empire. To act otherwise, he said, would be to separate himself from his alliance with Austria, and to throw her into the arms of Russia. But with regard to the Polish-Russian provinces, Napoleon declared he would see what he could do, should Providence favour the good cause. These vague and obscure expressions did not define what he intended to do for the Poles in the event of success crowning his vast enterprises. They excited the distrust of the Poles, and had no other result. On this subject, however, an observation occurs which is of some force as an apology for Napoleon. Poland was successively divided between three powers, Russia, Austria, and Prussia, with each of which Napoleon had been at war, but never with all three at once. He had therefore never been able to take advantage of his victories to re-establish Poland without injuring the interests of neutral powers or of his allies. Hence it may be concluded not only that he never had the positive will which would have triumphed over all obstacles, but also that there never was a possibility of realising those dreams and projects of revenge in which he had indulged on the banks of the Nile, as it were to console the departed spirit of Sulkowski.

Bonaparte's character presents many unaccountable incongruities. Although the most positive man that perhaps ever existed, yet there never was one who more readily yielded to the charm of illusion. In many circumstances the wish and the reality were to him one and the same thing. He never indulged in greater illusions than at the beginning of the campaign of Moscow. Even before the approach of the disasters which accompanied the most fatal retreat recorded in history, all sensible persons concurred in the opinion that the Emperor ought to have passed the winter of 1812-13 in Poland, and have resumed his vast enterprises in the spring. But his natural impatience impelled him forward as it were unconsciously, and he seemed to be under the influence of an invisible demon stronger than even his own strong will. This demon was ambition. He who knew so well the value of time, never sufficiently understood its power, and how much is sometimes gained by delay. Yet Caesar's Commentaries, which were his favourite study, ought to have shown him that Caesar did not conquer Gaul in one campaign. Another illusion by which Napoleon was misled during the campaign of Moscow, and perhaps past experience rendered it very excusable, was the belief that the Emperor Alexander would propose peace when he saw him at the head of his army on the Russian territory. The prolonged stay of Bonaparte at Moscow can indeed be accounted for in no other way than by supposing that he expected the Russian Cabinet would change its opinion and consent to treat for peace. However, whatever might have been the reason, after his long and useless stay in Moscow Napoleon left that city with the design of taking up his winter quarters in Poland; but Fate now frowned upon Napoleon, and in that dreadful retreat the elements seemed leagued with the Russians to destroy the most formidable army ever commanded by one chief. To find a catastrophe in history comparable to that of the Beresina we must go back to the destruction of the legions of Varus.

Notwithstanding the general dismay which prevailed in Paris that capital continued tranquil, when by a singular chance, on the very day on which Napoleon evacuated the burning city of Moscow, Mallet attempted his extraordinary enterprise. This General, who had always professed Republican principles, and was a man of bold decided character, after having been imprisoned for some time, obtained the permission of Government to live in Paris in a hospital house situated near the Barriere de Trove. Of Mallet's, conspiracy it is not necessary to say much after the excellent account given of it in the Memoirs of the Duc de Rovigo. Mallet's plan was to make it be believed that Bonaparte had been killed at Moscow, and that a new Government was established under the authority of the Senate. But what could Mallet do? Absolutely nothing: and had his Government continued three days he would have experienced a more favourable chance than that which he ought reasonably to have expected than asserted that the Emperor was dead, but an estafette from Russia would reveal the truth, resuscitate Napoleon, and overwhelm with confusion Mallet and his proclamation. His enterprise was that of a madman. The French were too weary of troubles to throw themselves into the arms of, Mallet or his associate Lahorie, who had figured so disgracefully on the trial of Moreau., Yet, in spite of the evident impossibility of success, it must be confessed that considerable ingenuity and address marked the commencement of the conspiracy. On the 22d of October Mallet escaped from the hospital house and went to Colonel Soulier, who commanded the tenth cohort of the National Guard, whose barracks were situated exactly behind the hospital house. Mallet was loaded with a parcel of forged orders which he had himself prepared. He introduced himself to Soulier under the name of General La Motte, and said that he came from General Mallet.

Colonel Soulier on hearing of the Emperor's death was affected to tears. He immediately ordered the adjutant to assemble the cohort and obey the orders of General La Motte, to whom he expressed his regret for being himself too ill to leave his bed. It was then two o'clock in the morning, and the forged documents respecting the Emperor's death slid the new form of Government were read to the troops by lamplight. Mallet then hastily set off with 1200 men to La Force, and liberated the Sieurs Gudal and Laholze, who were confined there. Mallet informed them of the Emperor's death and of the change of Government; gave them some orders, in obedience to which the Minister and Prefect of Police were arrested in their hotel. I was then at Courbevoie, and I went to Paris on that very morning to breakfast, as I frequently did, with the Minister of Police. My surprise may be imagined when[257] I learned from the porter that the Duc de Rovigo had been arrested and carried to the prison of La Force. I went into the house and was informed, to my great astonishment, that the ephemeral Minister was being measured for his official suit, an act which so completely denoted the character of the conspirator that it gave me an insight into the business.

Mallet repaired to General Hulin, who had the command of Paris. He informed him that he had been directed by the Minister of Police to arrest him and seal his papers. Hulin asked to see the order, and then entered his cabinet, where Mallet followed him, and just as Hulin was turning round to speak to him he fired a pistol in his face. Hulin fell: the ball entered his cheek, but the wound was not mortal. The most singular circumstance connected with the whole affair is, that the captain whom Mallet had directed to follow him, and who accompanied him to Hulin's, saw nothing extraordinary in all this, and did nothing to stop it. Mallet next proceeded, very composedly, to Adjutant-General Doucet's. It happened that one of the inspectors of the police was there. He recognised General Mallet as being a man under his supervision. He told him that he had no right to quit the hospital house without leave, and ordered him to be arrested. Mallet, seeing that all was over, was in the act of drawing a pistol from his pocket, but being observed was seized and disarmed. Thus terminated this extraordinary conspiracy, for which fourteen lives paid the forfeit; but, with the exception of Mallet, Guidal, and Lahorie, all the others concerned in it were either machines or dupes.

---

257 General Mallet gave out that the Emperor was killed under the walls of Moscow on the 8th of October; he could not take any other day without incurring the risk of being contradicted by the arrival of the regular courier. The Emperor being dead, he concluded that the Senate ought to be invested with the supreme authority, and he therefore resolved to address himself in the name of that body to the nation and the army. In a proclamation to the soldiers he deplored the death of the Emperor; in another, after announcing the abolition of the Imperial system and the Restoration of the Republic, he indicated the manner in which the Government was to be reconstructed, described the branches into which public authority was to be divided, and named the Directors. Attached to the different documents there appeared the signatures of several Senators whose names he recollected but with whom he had ceased to have any intercourse for a great number of years. These signatures were all written by Mallet, and he drew up a decree in the name of the Senate, and signed by the same Senators, appointing himself Governor of Paris, and commander of the troops of the first military division. He also drew up other decrees in the same form which purported to promote to higher ranks all the military officers he intended to make instruments in the execution of his enterprise. He ordered one regiment to close all the barriers of Paris, and allow no person to pass through them. This was done: so that in all the neighbouring towns from which assistance, in case of need, might have been obtained, nothing was known of the transactions in Paris. He sent the other regiments to occupy the Bank, the Treasury, and different Ministerial offices. At the Treasury some resistance was made. The minister of that Department was on the spot, and he employed the guard of his household in maintaining his authority. But in the whole of the two regiments of the Qnard not a single, objection was started to the execution of Mallet's orders (Memoirs of the Duc de Rivogo, tome vi. p. 20.)

This affair produced but little effect in Paris, for the enterprise and its result were make known simultaneously. But it was thought droll enough that the Minister and Prefect of Police should be imprisoned by the men who only the day before were their prisoners. Next day I went to see Savary, who had not yet recovered from the stupefaction caused by his extraordinary adventure. He was aware that his imprisonment; though it lasted only half an hour, was a subject of merriment to the Parisians. The Emperor, as I have already mentioned, left Moscow on the day when Mallet made his bold attempt, that is to say, the 19th of October. He was at Smolensko when he heard the news. Rapp, who had been wounded before the entrance into Moscow, but who was sufficiently recovered to return home, was with Napoleon when the latter received the despatches containing an account of what had happened in Paris. He informed me that Napoleon was much agitated on perusing them, and that he launched into abuse of the inefficiency of the police. Rapp added that he did not confine himself to complaints against the agents of his authority. "Is, then, my power so insecure," said he, "that it may be put in peril by a single individual, and a prisoner? It would appear that my crown is not fixed very firmly on my head if in my own capital the bold stroke of three adventurers can shake it. Rapp, misfortune never comes alone; this is the complement of what is passing here. I cannot be everywhere; but I must go back to Paris; my presence there is indispensable to reanimate public opinion. I must have men and money. Great successes and great victories will repair all. I must set off." Such were the motives which induced the Emperor to leave his army. It is not without indignation that I have heard his precipitate departure attributed to personal cowardice. He was a stranger to such feelings, and was never more happy than on the field of battle. I can readily conceive that he was much alarmed on hearing of Mallet's enterprise. The remarks which he made to Rapp were those which he knew would be made by the public, and he well knew that the affair was calculated to banish those illusions of power and stability with which he endeavoured to surround his government.

On leaving Moscow Napoleon consigned the wrecks of his army to the care of his most distinguished generals to Murat who had so ably commanded the cavalry, but who abandoned the army to return to Naples; and to Ney, the hero, rather than the Prince of the Moskowa, whose name will be immortal in the annals of glory, as his death will be eternal in the annals of party revenge. Amidst the general disorder Eugène, more than any other chief, maintained a sort of discipline among the Italians; and it was remarked that the troops of the south engaged in the fatal campaign of Moscow had endured the rigour of the cold better than those troops who were natives of less genial climates.

Napoleon's return from Moscow was not like his returns from the campaigns of Vienna and Tilsit when he came back crowned with laurels, and bringing peace as the reward of his triumphs. It was remarked that Napoleon's first great disaster followed the first enterprise he undertook after his marriage with Maria Louisa. This tended to confirm the popular belief that the presence of Josephine was favourable to his fortune; and superstitious as he sometimes was, I will not venture to affirm that he himself did not adopt this ides. He now threw off even the semblance of legality in the measures of his government: he assumed arbitrary power, under the impression that the critical circumstances in which he was placed would excuse everything. But, however inexplicable were the means to which the Emperor resorted to procure resources, it is but just to acknowledge that they were the consequence of his system of government, and that he evinced inconceivable activity in repairing his losses so as to place himself in a situation to resist his enemies, and restore the triumph of the French standard. But in spite of all Napoleon's endeavours the disasters of the campaign of Russia were daily more and more sensibly felt. The King of Prussia had played a part which was an acknowledgment of his weakness in joining France, instead of openly declaring himself for the cause of Russia, which was also his. Then took place the defection of General York, who commanded the Prussian contingent to Napoleon's army. The King of Prussia, though no doubt secretly satisfied with the conduct of General York, had him tried and condemned; but shortly after that sovereign commanded in person the troops which had turned against ours. The defection of the Prussians produced a very ill effect, and it was easy to perceive that other defections would follow. Napoleon, foreseeing the fatal chances which this event was likely to draw upon him, assembled a privy council, composed of the Ministers and some of the great officers of his household. MM. de Talleyrand and Cambacérès, and the President of the senate were present. Napoleon asked whether, in the complicated difficulties of our situation, it would be more advisable to negotiate for peace or to prepare for a new war. Cambacérès and Talleyrand gave their opinion in favour of peace, which however, Napoleon would not hear of after a defeat; but the Duc de Feltre, (Clarke) knowing how to touch the susceptible chord in the mind of Bonaparte, said that he would consider the Emperor dishonoured if he consented to the abandonment of the smallest village which had been united to the Empire by a 'Senatus-consulte'. This opinion was adopted, and the war continued. On Napoleon's return to Paris the Pope, who was still at Fontainebleau, determined to accede to an arrangement, and to sign an act which the Emperor conceived would terminate the differences between them. But being influenced by some of the cardinals who had previously incurred the Emperor's displeasure Pius VII. disavowed the new Concordat which he had been weak enough to grant, and the Emperor, who then had more important affairs on his hands, dismissed the Holy Father, and published the act to which he had assented. Bonaparte had no leisure to pay attention to the new difficulties started by Pius VII.; his thoughts were wholly directed to the other side of the Rhine. He was unfortunate, and the powers with whom he was most intimately allied separated from him, as he might have expected, and Austria was not the last to imitate the example set by Prussia. In these difficult circumstances the Emperor, who for some time past had observed the talent and address of the Comte Louis de Narbonne, sent him to Vienna, to supersede M. Otto; but the pacific propositions of M. de Narbonne were not listened to. Austria would not let slip the fair opportunity of taking revenge without endangering herself. Napoleon now saw clearly that since Austria had abandoned him and refused her contingent he should soon have all Europe arrayed against him. But this did not intimidate him.

Some of the Princes of the Confederation of the Rhine still remained faithful to him; and his preparations being completed, he proposed to resume in person the command of the army which had been so miraculously reproduced. But before his departure Napoleon, alarmed at the recollection of Mallet's attempt, and anxious to guard against any similar occurrence during his absence, did not, as on former occasions, consign the reins of the National Government to a Council of Ministers, presided over by the Arch-Chancellor. Napoleon placed my successor with him, M. Meneval, near the Empress Regent as Secretaire des Commandemens (Principal Secretary), and certainly he could not have made a better choice. He made the Empress Maria Louisa Regent, and appointed a Council of Regency to assist her.[258]

258 Meneval, who had held the post of Secretary to Napoleon from the time of Bourrienne's

CHAPTER XXVIII

1813

A considerable time before Napoleon left Paris to join the army, the bulk of which was in Saxony, partial insurrections occurred in many places. The interior of France proper was indeed still in a state of tranquillity, but it was not so in the provinces annexed by force to the extremities of the Empire, especially in the north, and in the unfortunate Hanse Towns, for which, since my residence at Hamburg, I have always felt the greatest interest. The intelligence I received was derived from such unquestionable sources that I can pledge myself for the truth of what I have to state respecting the events which occurred in those provinces at the commencement of 1813; and subsequently I obtained a confirmation of all the facts communicated by my correspondence when I was sent to Hamburg by Louis XVIII. in 1815.

M. Steuve, agent from the Court of Russia, who lived at Altona apparently as a private individual, profited by the irritation produced by the measures adopted at Hamburg. His plans were so well arranged that he was promptly informed of the route of the Grand Army from Moscow, and the approach of the Allied troops. Aided by the knowledge and activity of Sieur Hanft of Hamburg, M. Steuve profited by the discontent of a people so tyrannically governed, and seized the opportunity for producing an explosion. Between eight and nine o'clock on the morning of the 24th of February 1813 an occurrence in which the people were concerned was the signal for a revolt. An individual returning to Hamburg by the Altona gate would not submit to be searched by a fiscal agent, who in consequence maltreated him and wounded him severely. The populace instantly rose, drove away the revenue guard, and set fire to the guard-house. The people also, excited by secret agents, attacked other French posts, where they committed the same excesses. Surprised at this unexpected movement, the French authorities retired to the houses in which they resided. All the respectable inhabitants who were unconnected with the tumult likewise returned to their homes, and no person appeared out of doors.

General Carry St. Cyr had the command of Hamburg after the Prince of Eckmuhl's departure for the Russian campaign.[259] At the first news of the revolt he set about packing up his papers, and Comte de Chaban, M. Konning, the Prefect of Hamburg, and M. Daubignosc, the Director of Police, followed his example. It was not till about four o'clock in the afternoon

disgrace in 1802, had been nearly killed by the hardships of the Russian campaign, and now received an honourable and responsible but less onerous post. He remained with the Empress till 7th May 1815, when, finding that she would not return to her husband, he left her to rejoin his master.

259 General Carry St. Cyr is not to be conFused with the Marshal Gonvion de St. Cyr; he fell into disgrace for his conduct at Hamburg at this time, and was not again employed by Napoleon. Under the Restoration he became Governor of French Guiana.

that a detachment of Danish hussars arrived at Hamburg, and the populace: was then speedily dispersed. All the respectable citizens and men of property assembled the next morning and adopted means for securing internal tranquillity, so that the Danish troops were enabled to return to Altona. Search was then made for the ringleaders of the disturbance. Many persons were arrested, and a military commission, ad hoc; was appointed to try them. The commission, however, condemned only one individual, who, being convicted of being one of the most active voters, was sentenced to be shot, and the sentence was carried into execution.

On the 26th February a similar commotion took place at Lübeck. Attempts were made to attack the French Authorities. The respectable citizens instantly assembled, protected them against outrage, and escorted them in safety to Hamburg, where they arrived on the 27th. The precipitate flight of these persons from Lübeck spread some alarm in Hamburg. The danger was supposed to be greater than it was because the fugitives were accompanied by a formidable body of troops.

But these were not the only attempts to throw off the yoke of French domination, which had become insupportable. All the left bank of the Elbe was immediately in a state of insurrection, and all the official persons took refuge in Hamburg. During these partial insurrections everything was neglected. Indecision, weakness, and cupidity were manifested everywhere. Instead of endeavours to soothe the minds of the people, which had been, long exasperated by intolerable tyranny, recourse was had to rigorous measures. The prisons were crowded with a host of persons declared to be suspected upon the mere representations of the agents of the police. On the 3d of March a special military commission condemned six householders of Hamburg and its neighbourhood to be shot on the glacis for no other offence than having been led, either by chance or curiosity, to a part of the town which was the scene of one of the riots. These executions excited equal horror and indignation, and General Carra St. Cyr was obliged to issue a proclamation for the dissolution of the military commission by whom the men had been sentenced.

The intelligence of the march of the Russian and Prussian troops; who were descending the Elbe, increased the prevailing agitation in Westphalia, Hanover, Mecklenburg, and Pomerania, and all the French troops cantoned between Berlin and Hamburg, including those who occupied the coast of the Baltic, fell back upon Hamburg. General Carra St. Cyr and Baron Konning, the Prefect of Hamburg, used to go every evening to Altona. The latter, worn out by anxiety and his unsettled state of life, lost his reason; and on his way to Hamburg, on the 5th of May, he attempted to cut his throat with a razor. His 'valet de chambre' saved his life by rushing upon him before he had time to execute his design. It was given out that he had broken a blood-vessel, and he was conveyed to Altona, where his wound was cured, and he subsequently recovered from his derangement. M. Konning, who was a native of Holland, was a worthy man, but possessed no decision of character, and but little ability.

At this juncture exaggerated reports were circulated respecting the approach of a Russian corps. A retreat was immediately ordered, and it was executed on the 12th of March. General Carra St. Cyr having no money for the troops, helped himself to 100,000 francs out of the municipal treasury. He left Hamburg at the head of the troops and the enrolled men of the custom-house service. He was escorted by the Burgher Guard, which protected him from the insults of the populace; and the good people of Hamburg never had any visitors of whom they were more happy to be rid.

This sudden retreat excited Napoleon's indignation. He accused General St. Cyr of pusillanimity, in an article inserted in the 'Moniteur', and afterwards copied by his order into all the journals. In fact, had General St. Cyr been better informed, or less easily alarmed, he might have kept Hamburg, and prevented its temporary occupation by the enemy, to dislodge whom it was necessary to besiege the city two months afterwards. St. Cyr had 3000 regular troops, and a considerable body of men in the custom-house service. General Morand could have furnished him with 5000 men from Mecklenburg. He might, therefore, not only have kept possession of Hamburg two months longer, but even to the end of the war, as General Lexnarrois retained possession of Magdeburg. Had not General St. Cyr so hastily evacuated the Elbe he would have been promptly aided by the corps which General Vandamme soon brought from the Wesel, and afterwards by the very, corps with which Marshal Davoust recaptured Hamburg.

The events just described occurred before Napoleon quitted Paris. In the month of August all negotiation was broken off with Austria, though that power, still adhering to her time-serving policy, continued to protest fidelity to the cause of the Emperor Napoleon until the moment when her preparations were completed and her resolution formed. But if there was duplicity at Vienna was there not folly, nay, blindness, in the Cabinet of the Tuileries? Could we reasonably rely upon Austria? She had seen the Russian army pass the Vistula and advance as far as the Saale without offering any remonstrance. At that moment a single movement of her troops, a word of declaration, would have prevented everything. As, therefore, she would not avert the evil when she might have done so with certainty and safety, there must have been singular folly and blindness in the Cabinet who saw this conduct and did not understand it.

I now proceed to mention the further misfortunes which occurred in the north of Germany, and particularly at Hamburg. At fifteen leagues east of Hamburg, but within its territory, is a village named Bergdorf. It was in that village that the Cossacks were first seen. Twelve or fifteen hundred of them arrived there under the command of Colonel Tettenborn. But for the retreat of the French troops, amounting to 3000, exclusive of men in the customhouse service, no attempt would have been made upon Hamburg; but the very name of the Cossacks inspired a degree of terror which must be fresh in the recollection of every one. Alarm spread in Hamburg, which, being destitute of troops and artillery, and surrounded with dilapidated fortifications, could offer no defence. The Senator Bartch and Doctor Know took upon themselves to proceed to Bergdorf to solicit Colonel Tettenborn to take possession of Hamburg, observing that they felt sure of his sentiments of moderation, and that they trusted they would grant protection to a city which had immense commercial relations with Russia. Tettenborn did not place reliance on these propositions because he could not suppose that there had been such a precipitate evacuation; he thought they were merely a snare to entrap him, and refused to accede to them. But a Doctor Von Hess, a Swede, settled in Hamburg some years, and known to Tettenborn as a decided partisan of England and Russia, persuaded the Russian Commander to comply with the wishes of the citizens of Hamburg. However, Tettenborn consented only on the following conditions:—That the old Government should be instantly re-established; that a deputation of Senators in their old costume should invite him to take possession of Hamburg, which he would enter only as a free and Imperial Hanse Town; that if those conditions were not complied with he would regard Hamburg as a French town, and consequently hostile. Notwithstanding the real satisfaction with which the Senators of Hamburg received those propositions they were restrained by the fear of a reverse of fortune. They, however, determined to accept them, thinking that whatever might happen they could screen themselves by alleging that necessity had driven them to the step they took. They therefore declared their compliance with the conditions, and that night and the following day were occupied in assembling the Senate, which had been so long dissolved, and in making the preparations which Tettenborn required.

At four o'clock in the afternoon of the 17th of March a picket of Cossacks, consisting of only forty men, took possession of a town recently flourishing, and containing a population of 124,000, but ruined and reduced to 80,000 inhabitants by the blessing of being united to the French Empire. On the following day, the 18th, Colonel Tettenborn entered Hamburg at the head of 1000 regular and 200 irregular Cossacks. I have described the military situation of Hamburg when it was evacuated on the 12th of March, and Napoleon's displeasure may be easily conceived. Tettenborn was received with all the honours usually bestowed upon a conqueror. Enthusiasm was almost universal. For several nights the people devoted themselves to rejoicing. The Cossacks were gorged with provisions and drink, and were not a little astonished at the handsome reception they experienced.

It was not until the expiration of three or four days that the people began to perceive the small number of the allied troops. Their amount gradually diminished. On the day after the arrival of the Cossacks a detachment was sent to Lübeck, where they were received with the same honours as at Hamburg. Other detachments were sent upon different places, and after four days' occupation there remained in Hamburg only 70 out of the 1200 Cossacks who had entered on the 18th March.

The first thing their commander did was to take possession of the post-office and the treasuries of the different public offices. All the movable effects of the French Government and its agents were seized and sold. The officers evinced a true Cossack disregard of the rights of private property. Counts Huhn, Buasenitz, and Venechtern, who had joined Tettenborn's staff, rendered themselves conspicuous by plundering the property of M. Pyonnier, the Director of the Customs, and M. Gonae, the Postmaster, and not a bottle of wine was left in their cellars. Tettenborn laid hands upon a sum of money, consisting of upwards of 4000 Louis in gold, belonging to M. Gonse, which had been lodged with M. Schwartz, a respectable banker in Hamburg, who filled the office of Prussian Consul. M. Schwartz, with whom this money had been deposited for the sake of security, had also the care of some valuable jewels belonging to Mesdames Carry St. Cyr and Daubignoac; Tettenborn carried off these as well as the money. M. Schwartz remonstrated in his character of Prussian Consul, Prussia being the ally of Russia, but he was considered merely as a banker, and could obtain no redress. Tettenborn, like most of the Cossack chiefs, was nothing but a man for blows and pillage, but the agent of Russia was M. Steuve, whose name I have already mentioned.

Orders were speedily given for a levy of troops, both in infantry and cavalry, to be called Hanseatic volunteers. A man named Hanft, who had formerly been a butcher, raised at his own expense a company of foot and one of lancers, of which he took the command. This undertaking, which cost him 130,000 francs, may afford some idea of the attachment of the people of Hamburg to the French Government! But money, as well as men, was wanting, and a heavy contribution was imposed to defray the expense of enrolling a number of workmen out of employment and idlers, of various kinds. Voluntary donations were solicited, and enthusiasm was so general that even servant-maids gave their rings. The sums thus collected were paid into the chest of Tettenborn's staff, and became a prey to dishonest appropriation. With respect to this money a Sieur Oswald was accused of not having acted with the scrupulous delicacy which Madame de Stael attributes to his namesake in her romance of Corinne.

Between 8000 and 10,000 men were levied in the Hanse Towns and their environs, the population of which had been so greatly reduced within two years. These undisciplined troops, who had been for the most part levied from the lowest classes of society, committed so many outrages that they soon obtained the surname of the Cossacks of the Elbe; and certainly they well deserved it.

Such was the hatred which the French Government had inspired in Hamburg that the occupation of Tettenborn was looked upon as a deliverance. On the colonel's departure the Senate, anxious to give high a testimonial of gratitude, presented him with the freedom of the city, accompanied by 5000 gold fredericks (105,000 francs), with which he was doubtless much more gratified than with the honour of the citizenship.

The restored Senate of Hamburg did not long survive. The people of the Hanse Towns learned, with no small alarm, that the Emperor was making immense preparations to fall upon Germany, where his lieutenants could not fail to take cruel revenge on those who had disavowed his authority. Before he quitted Paris on the 15th of April Napoleon had recalled under the banners of the army 180,000 men, exclusive of the guards of honour, and it was evident that with such a force he might venture on a great game, and probably win it. Yet the month of April passed away without the occurrence of any event important to the Hanse Towns, the inhabitants of which vacillated between hope and fear. Attacks daily took place between parties of Russian and French troops on the territory between Lüneburg and Bremen. In one of these encounters General Morand was mortally wounded, and was conveyed to Lüneburg. His brother having been taken prisoner in the same engagement, Tettenborn, into whose hands he had fallen, gave him leave on parole to visit the General; but he arrived in Lüneburg only in time to see him die.

The French having advanced as far as Haarburg took up their position on the plateau of Schwartzenberg, which commands that little town and the considerable islands situated in that part of the river between Haarburg and Hamburg. Being masters of this elevated point they began to threaten Hamburg and to attack Haarburg. These attacks were directed by Vandamme, of all our generals the most redoubtable in conquered countries. He was a native of Cassel, in Flanders, and had acquired a high reputation for severity. At the very time when he was attacking Hamburg Napoleon said of him at Dresden, "If I were to lose Vandamme I know not what I would give to have him back again; but if I had two such generals I should be obliged to shoot one of them." It must be confessed that one was quite enough.

As soon as he arrived Vandamme sent to inform Tettenborn that if he did not immediately liberate the brother and brother-in-law of Morand, both of whom were his prisoners, he would burn Hamburg. Tettenborn replied that if he resorted to that extremity he would hang them both on the top of St. Michael's Tower, where he might have a view of them. This energetic answer obliged Vandamme to restrain his fury, or at least to direct it to other objects.

Meanwhile the French forces daily augmented at Haarburg. Vandamme, profiting by the negligence of the new Hanseatic troops, who had the defence of the great islands of the Elbe, attacked them one night in the month of May. This happened to be the very night after the battle of Lutzsn, where both sides claimed the victory; and Te Deum was sung in the two hostile camps. The advance of the French turned the balance of opinion in favour of Napoleon, who was in fact really the conqueror on a field of battle celebrated nearly two centuries before by the victory and death of Gustavus Adolphus. The Cossacks of the Elbe could not sustain the shock of the French; Vandamme repulsed the troops who defended Wilhelmsburg, the largest of the two islands, and easily took possession of the smaller one, Fidden, of which the point nearest the right bank of the Elbe is not half a gunshot distant from Hamburg. The 9th of May was a fatal day to the people of Hamburg; for it was then that Davoust, having formed his junction with Vandamme, appeared at the head of a corps of 40,000 men destined to reinforce Napoleon's Grand Army. Hamburg could not hold out against the considerable French force now assembled in its neighbourhood. Tettenborn had, it is true, received a reinforcement of 800 Prussians and 2000, Swedes, but still what resistance could he offer to Davoust's 40,000 men? Tettenborn did not deceive himself as to the weakness of the allies on this point, or the inutility of attempting to defend the city. He yielded to the entreaties of the inhabitants, who represented to him that further resistance must be attended by certain ruin. He accordingly evacuated Hamburg on the 29th of May, taking with him his Hanseatic legions, which had not held out an hour in the islands of the Elbe, and accompanied by the Swedish Doctor Von Hess, whose imprudent advice was the chief cause of all the disasters to which the unfortunate city lied been exposed.

Davoust was at Haarburg, where he received the deputies from Hamburg with an appearance of moderation; and by the conditions stipulated at this conference on the 30th of May a strong detachment of Danish troops occupied Hamburg in the name of the Emperor. The French made their entrance the same evening, and occupied the posts as quietly as if they had been merely changing guard. The inhabitants made not a shadow of resistance. Not a drop of blood was issued; not a threat nor an insult was interchanged. This is the truth; but the truth did not suit Napoleon. It was necessary to getup a pretext for revenge, and accordingly recourse was had to a bulletin, which proclaimed to France and Europe that Hamburg had been taken by main force, with a loss of some hundred men. But for this imaginary resistance, officially announced, how would it have been possible to justify the spoliations and exactions which ensued?

The Dutch General, Hogendorff, became Governor of Hamburg in lieu of Carra St. Cyr, who had been confined at Osnabruck since his precipitate retreat. General Hogendorff had been created one of the Emperor's aides de camp, but he was neither a Rapp, a Lauriston, nor a Duroc. The inhabitants were required to pay all the arrears of taxes due to the different public offices during the seventy days that the French had been absent; and likewise all the allowances that would have been paid to the troops of the garrison had they remained in Hamburg. Payment was also demanded of the arrears for the quartering of troops who were fifty leagues off. However, some of the heads of the government departments, who saw and understood the new situation of the French at Hamburg, did not enforce these unjust and vexatious measures. The duties on registrations were reduced. M. Pyonnier, Director of the Customs, aware of the peculiar difficulty of his situation in a country where the customs were held in abhorrence, observed great caution and moderation in collecting the duties: Personal examination, which is so revolting and indecorous, especially with respect to females, was suppressed. But these modifications did not proceed from the highest quarter; they were due to the good sense of the subordinate agents, who plainly saw that if the Empire was to fall it would not be owing to little infractions in the laws of proscription against coffee and rhubarb.

If the custom-house regulations became less vexatious to the inhabitants of Hamburg it was not the same with the business of the post-office. The old manoeuvres of that department were resumed more actively than ever. Letters were opened without the least reserve, and all the old post-office clerks who were initiated in these scandalous proceedings were recalled. With the exception of the registrations and the customs the inquisitorial system, which had so long oppressed the Hanse Towns, was renewed; and yet the delegates of the French Government were the first to cry out, "The people of Hamburg are traitors to Napoleon: for, in spite of all the blessings he has conferred upon them they do not say with the Latin poet, 'Deus nobis haec otia fecit."

But all that passed was trifling in comparison with what was to come. On the 18th of June was published an Imperial decree, dated the 8th of the same month, by virtue of which were to be reaped the fruits of the official falsehood contained in the bulletin above mentioned. To expiate the crime of rebellion Hamburg was required to pay an extraordinary contribution of 48,000,000 francs, and Lübeck a contribution of 6,000,000. The enormous sum levied on Hamburg was to be paid in the short space of a month, by six equal instalments, either in money, or bills on respectable houses in Paris. In addition to this the new Prefect of Hamburg made a requisition of grain and provisions of every kind, wines, sailcloth, masts, pitch, hemp, iron, copper, steel, in short, everything that could be useful for the supply of the army and navy.

But while these exactions were made on property in Hamburg, at Dresden the liberties of individuals and even lives were attacked. On the 15th of June Napoleon, doubtless blinded by the false reports that were laid before him, gave orders for making out a list of the inhabitants of Hamburg who were absent from the city. He allowed them only a fortnight to return home, an interval too short to enable some of them to come from the places where they had taken refuge. They consequently remained absent beyond the given time. Victims were indispensable but assuredly it was not Bonaparte who conceived the idea of hostages to answer for the men whom prudence kept absent. Of this charge I can clear his memory. The hostages, were, however, taken, and were declared to be also responsible for the payment of the contribution of 48,000,000. In Hamburg they were selected from among the most respectable and wealthy men in the city, some of them far advanced in age. They were conveyed to the old castle of Haarburg on the left bank of the Elbe, and these men, who had been accustomed to all the comforts of life, were deprived even of necessaries, and had only straw to lie on. The hostages from Lübeck were taken to, Hamburg: they were placed between decks on board an old ship in the port: this was a worthy imitation of the prison hulks of England. On the 24th of July there was issued a decree which was published in the Hamburg Correspondent of the 27th. This decree consisted merely of a proscription list, on which were inscribed the names of some of the wealthiest men in the Hanse Towns, Hanover, and Westphalia.

CHAPTER XXIX

1813

On the 2d of May Napoleon won the battle of Lützen. A week after he was at Dresden, not as on his departure for the Russian campaign, like the Sovereign of the West surrounded by his mighty vassals: he was now in the capital of the only one of the monarchs of his creation who remained faithful to the French cause, and whose good faith eventually cost him half his dominions. The Emperor stayed only ten days in Dresden, and then went in pursuit of the Russian army, which he came up with on the 19th, at Bautzen. This battle, which was followed on the two succeeding days by the battles of Wurtchen and Oclikirchen, may be said to have lasted three days—a sufficient proof that it was obstinately disputed. It ended in favour of Napoleon, but he and France paid dearly for it: while General Kirschner and Duroc were talking together the former was killed by a cannon-ball, which mortally wounded the latter in the abdomen. The moment had now arrived for Austria to prove whether or not she. intended entirely to desert the cause of Napoleon.[260] All her amicable demonstrations were

260 There is a running attack in Erreurs (tome, ii. pp, 289-325) on all this part of the Memoirs, but the best account of the negotiations between France, Austria, and the Allies will be found in Metternich, Vol. i. pp. 171-215. Metternich, with good reason, prides himself on the skill with which he gained from Napoleon the exact time, twenty days, necessary for the concentration of the Austrian armies. Whether the negotiations were consistent with good faith on the part of Austria is another matter; but, one thing seems clear—the Austrian marriage ruined Napoleon. He found it impossible to believe that the monarch who had given him his daughter would strike the decisive blow against him. Without this belief there can be no doubt that he would have attacked Austria before she could have collected her forces, and Metternich seems to have dreaded the result. "It was necessary, therefore to prevent Napoleon from carrying out his usual system of leaving an army of observation before the Allied armies, and himself turning to Bohemia to deal a great blow at us, the effect of which it would be impossible to foresee in the present depressed state of the great majority of our men" (Metternich, Vol. i, p. 177). With our knowledge of how Napoleon held his own against the three armies at Dresden we may safely assume that he would have crushed Austria if she had not joined him or disarmed. The conduct of Austria was natural and politic, but it was only successful because Napoleon believed in the good faith of the Emperor Francis, his father-in-law. It is to be noted that Austria only succeeded in getting Alexander to negotiate on the implied condition that the negotiations were not to end in a peace with France. See Metternich, Vol. i. p. 181, where, in answer to the Czar's question as to what would become of their cause if Napoleon accepted the Austrian mediation, he says that if Napoleon declines Austria will join the Allies. If Napoleon accepts, "the negotiations will most certainly show Napoleon to be neither wise nor just, and then the result will be the same. In any case we shall have gained the necessary time to bring our armies into such positions that we need not again fear a separate attack on any one of them, and from which we may ourselves take the offensive."

limited to an offer of her intervention in opening negotiations with Russia. Accordingly, on the 4th of June, an armistice was concluded at Pleiswitz, which was to last till the 8th of July, and was finally prolonged to the 10th of August.

The first overtures after the conclusion of the armistice of Pleiswitz determined the assembling of a Congress at Prague. It was reported at the time that the Allies demanded the restoration of all they had lost since 1805; that is to say, since the campaign of Ulm. In this demand Holland and the Hanse Towns, which had become French provinces, were comprehended. But we should still have retained the Rhine, Belgium, Piedmont, Nice, and Savoy. The battle of Vittoria,[261] which placed the whole of Spain at the disposal of the English, the retreat of Suchet upon the Ebro, the fear of seeing the army of Spin annihilated, were enough to alter the opinions of those counsellors who still recommended war. Notwithstanding Napoleon's opposition and his innate disposition to acquire glory by his victories, probably he would not have been inaccessible to the reiterated representations of sensible men who loved their country, France, therefore, has to reproach his advisers. At this juncture General Moreau arrived; it has been said that he came at the solicitation of Bernadotte. This is neither true nor probable. In the first place, there never was any intimacy between Bernadotte and Moreau; and, in the next, how can it be imagined that Bernadotte wished to see Moreau Emperor! But this question is at once put at rest by the fact, that in the interview at Åbo the Emperor of Russia hinted to Bernadotte the possibility of his succeeding Napoleon. It was generally reported at the time, and I have since learnt that it was true, that the French Princes of the House of Bourbon had made overtures to Moreau through the medium of General Willot, who had been proscribed on the 18th Fructidor; and I have since learned from an authentic source that General Moreau, who was then at Baltimore, refused to support the Bourbon cause. Moreau yielded only to his desire of being revenged on Napoleon; and he found death where he could not find glory.

At the end of July the proceedings of the Congress at Prague were no. further advanced than at the time of its assembling. Far from cheering the French with the prospect of a peace, the Emperor made a journey to Mayence; the Empress went there to see him, and returned to Paris immediately after the Emperor's departure. Napoleon went back to Dresden, and the armistice not being renewed, it died a natural death on the 17th of August, the day appointed for its expiration. A fatal event immediately followed the rupture of the conferences. On the 17th of August Austria, wishing to gain by war as she had before gained by alliances, declared that she would unite her forces with those of the Allies. On the very opening of this disastrous campaign General Jomini went over to the enemy. Jomini belonged to the staff of the unfortunate Marshal Ney, who was beginning to execute with his wonted ability, the orders he had received. There was much surprise at his eagerness to profit by a struggle, begun under such melancholy auspices, to seek a fresh fortune, which promised better than what he had tried under our flag. Public opinion has pronounced judgment on Jomini.[262]

---

261 The news of this decisive battle increased the difficulty of the French plenipotentiaries at Prague, and raised the demands of the Allies. It also shook the confidence of those who remained faithful to us.—Bourrienne.

262 It was on the 11th of August, not the 17th, that Metternich announced to Caulaincourt, Napoleon's plenipotentiary at Prague, that Austria had joined the Allies and declared war with France; At midnight on 10th August Metternich had despatched the passports for the Comte

The first actions were the battle of Dresden, which took place seven days after the rupture of the armistice, and the battle in which Vandamme was defeated, and which rendered the victory of Dresden unavailing. I have already mentioned that Moreau was killed at Dresden. Bavaria was no sooner rid of the French troops than she raised the mask and ranged herself among our enemies.

In October the loss of the battle of Leipsic decided the fate of France. The Saxon army, which had long remained faithful to us, went over to the enemy during the battle. Prince Poniatowski perished at the battle of Leipsic in an attempt to pass the Aster.

I will here mention a fact which occurred before Duroc's departure for the campaign of 1812. I used often to visit him at the Pavilion Marsan, in the Tuileries, where he lodged. One forenoon, when I had been waiting for him a few minutes, he came from the Emperor's apartments, where he had been engaged in the usual business, He was in his court-dress. As soon as he entered he pulled off his coat and hat and laid them aside. "I have just had a conversation with the Emperor about you," said he. "Say nothing to anybody. Have patience, and you will be—" He had, no sooner uttered these words than a footman entered to inform him that the Emperor, wished to see him immediately. "Well," said Duroc, "I must go." No sooner was the servant gone than Duroc stamped violently on the floor, and exclaimed, "That —— never leaves me a moment's rest. If he finds I have five minutes to myself in the course of the morning he is sure to send for me." He then put on his coat and returned to the Emperor, saying, "Another time you shall hear what I have to tell you."

From that time I did not see Duroc until, the month of January 1813. He was constantly absent from Paris, and did not return until the end of 1812. He was much affected at the result of the campaign, but his confidence in Napoleon's genius kept up his spirits. I turned the conversation from this subject and reminded him of his promise to tell me what had passed between the Emperor and himself relative tome. "You shall hear," said he. "The Emperor and I had been playing at billiards, and, between ourselves, he plays very badly. He is nothing at a game which depends on skill. While negligently rolling his balls about he muttered these words: 'Do you ever see Bourrienne now?'—'Yes, Sire, he sometimes dines with me on diplomatic reception-days, and he looks so droll in his old-fashioned court-dress, of Lyons manufacture, that you would laugh if you saw him.'—'What does he say respecting the new regulation for the court-dresses?'—'I confess he says it is very ridiculous; that it will have no other result than to enable the Lyons manufacturers to get rid of their old-fashioned goods; that forced innovations on the customs of a nation are never successful.'—'Oh, that is always the way with Bourrienne; he is never pleased with anything.'— 'Certainly, Sire, he is apt to grumble; but he says what he thinks.'— 'Do you know, Duroc, he served me very well at Hamburg. He raised a good deal of money for me. He is a man who understands business. I will not leave him unemployed. Time must hang heavily on his hands. I will see what I can do for him. He has many enemies.'—'And who has not, Sire?'— 'Many complaints against him were transmitted to me from Hamburg, but the letter which he wrote to me in his justification opened my eyes, and I begin to think that Savary had good motives for defending him. Endeavours are made to dissuade me from employing him, but I shall nevertheless do

---

Louis de Narbonne, Napoleon's Ambassador, and the war manifesto of the Emperor Francis; then he had the beacons lighted which had been prepared from Prague to the Silesian frontier, as a sign of the breech of the negotiations, and the right (i.e. power) of the Allied armies to cross the Silesian frontier (Metternich, vol. i, p. 199).

so at last. I remember that it was he who first informed me of the near approach of the war which we are now engaged in. I forget all that has been said against him for the last two years, and as soon as peace is concluded, and I am at leisure, I will think of him.'"

After relating to me this conversation Duroc said, "you must, of course, feel assured that I said all I think of you, and I will take an opportunity of reminding him of you. But we must we patient. Adieu, my dear friend; we must set off speedily, and Heaven knows when we shall be back again!" I wished him a successful campaign and a speedy return. Alas! I was doomed to see my excellent friend only once again.

Next to the death of Duroc the loss most sincerely regretted during the campaign of 1813 was that of Prince Poniatowski. Joseph Poniatowaki, a nephew of Stanislas Augustus, King of Poland, was born at Warsaw on the 7th of May 1763: At an early age he was remarkable for his patriotic spirit; but his uncle's influence gave him an apparent irresolution, which rendered him suspected by some of the parties in Poland. After his uncle had acceded to the Confederation of Targowitz, Poniatowski left the service accompanied by most of his principal officers. But when, in 1794, the Poles endeavoured to repulse the Russians, he again repaired to the Polish camp and entered the army as a volunteer. His noble conduct obtained for him the esteem of his countrymen. Kosciusko gave him the command of a division, with which he rendered useful services during the two sieges of Warsaw. Immediately after the surrender of that capital Poniatowski went to Vienna. He refused the offers of Catherine and Paul to bear arms in the service of Russia.

Poniatowaki retired to his estate year Warsaw, where he lived like a private gentleman until the creation of the Grand Duchy of Warsaw revived the hopes of the Polish patriots. He then became War Minister. The Archduke Ferdinand having come, in 1809, with Austrian troops to take possession of the Duchy of Warsaw, Poniatowski, who commanded the Polish troops, which were very inferior in numbers to the Austrian force, obliged the latter, rather by dint of skillful maneuvering than by fighting, to evacuate the Grand Duchy. He pursued them into Galicia as far as Cracow.

After this honourable campaign he continued to exercise his functions as Minister until 1812. The war against Russia again summoned him to the head of the Polish army. After taking part in all the events of that war, which was attended by such various chances, Poniatowaki was present at the battle of Leipsic. That battle, which commenced on the 14th of October, the anniversary of the famous battles of Ulm and of Jena, lasted four days, and decided the fate of Europe. Five hundred thousand men fought on a surface of three square leagues.

Retreat having become indispensable, Napoleon took leave at Leipsic of the King of Saxony and his family, whom he had brought with him from Dresden. The Emperor then exclaimed in a loud voice, "Adieu; Saxons," to the people who filled the market-place, where the King of Saxony resided. With some difficulty, and after passing through many turnings and windings, he gained the suburb of Runstadt and left Leipsic by the outer gate of that suburb which leads to the bridge of the Elster, and to Lindenau. The bridge was blown up shortly after he had passed it, and that event utterly prevented the retreat of the part of the army which was on the left bank of the Easter, and which fell into the power of the enemy. Napoleon was at the time accused of having ordered the destruction of the bridge immediately after he had himself passed it in order to secure his own personal retreat, as he was threatened by the active pursuit of the enemy. The English journals were unanimous on this point, and to counteract this opinion, which was very general, an article was inserted in the 'Moniteur'. Before passing the bridge of the Elster Napoleon had directed Poniatowski, in concert with Marshal Macdonald, to cover and protect the retreat, and to defend that part of the suburb of Leipsic which is nearest to the Borne road. For the execution of these orders he had only 2000 Polish infantry. He was in this desperate situation when he saw the French columns in full retreat and the bridge so choked up with their artillery and waggons that there was no possibility of passing it. Then drawing his sword, and turning to the officers who were near him, he said, "Here we must fall with honour!" At the head of a small party of cuirassiers and Polish officers he rushed on the columns of the Allies. In this action he received a ball in his left arm: he had already been wounded on the 14th and 16th. He nevertheless advanced, but he found the suburb filled with Allied troops.[263]

He fought his way through them and received another wound. He then threw himself into the Pleisse, which was the first river he came to. Aided by his officers, he gained the opposite bank, leaving his horse in the river. Though greatly exhausted he mounted another, and gained the Elster, by passing through M. Reichenbach's garden, which was situated on the side of that river. In spite of the steepness of the banks of the Elster at that part, the Prince plunged with his horse into the river: both man and horse were drowned, and the same fate was shared by several officers who followed Poniatawski's example. Marshal Macdonald was, luckily, one of those who escaped. Five days after a fisherman drew the body of the Prince, out of the water. On the 26th of October it was temporarily interred at Leipsic, with all the honours due to the illustrious deceased. A modest stone marks the spot where the body of the Prince was dragged from the river. The Poles expressed a wish to. erect a monument to the memory of their countryman in the garden of M. Reichenbach, but that gentleman declared he would do it at his own expense, which he did. The monument consists of a beautiful sarcophagus, surrounded by weeping willows. The body of the Prince, after bring embalmed, was sent in the following year to Warsaw, and in 1816 it was deposited in the cathedral, among the remains of the Kings and great men of Poland. The celebrated Thorwaldsen was commissioned to execute a monument for his tomb. Prince Poniatowski left no issue but a natural son, born in 1790. The royal race, therefore existed only in a collateral branch of King Stanislas, namely, Prince Stanislas, born in 1754.

263 The Allies were so numerous that they scarcely perceived the losses they sustained. Their masses pressed down upon us in every direction, and it was impossible that victory could fail to be with them. Their success, however, would have been less decisive had it not been for the defection of the Saxons. In the midst of the battle, these troops having moved towards the enemy, as if intending to make an attack, turned suddenly around, and opened a heavy fire of artillery and musketry on the columns by the aids of which they had a few moments before been fighting. I do not know to what page of history such a transaction is recorded. This event immediately produced a great difference in our affairs, which were before in a bad enough train. I ought here mention that before the battle the Emperor dismissed a Bavarian division which still remained with him. He spoke to the officers in terms which will not soon be effaced from their memory. He told them, that, "according to the laws of war, they were his prisoners, since their Government had taken part against him; but that he could not forget the services they had rendered him, and that they were therefore at liberty to return home." These troops left the army, where they were much esteemed, and marched for Bavaria.

CHAPTER XXX

1813

When the war resumed its course after the disaster of Leipsic I am certain that the Allied sovereigns determined to treat with Napoleon only in his own capital, as he, four years before, had refused to treat with the Emperor of Austria except at Vienna. The latter sovereign now completely raised the mask, and declared to the Emperor that he would make common cause with Russia and Prussia against him. In his declaration he made rise of the singular pretext, that the more enemies there were against Napoleon there would be the greater chance of speedily obliging him to accede to conditions which would at length restore the tranquillity of which Europe stood so much in need. This declaration on the part of Austria was an affair of no little importance, for she had now raised an army of 260,000 men. An equal force was enrolled beneath the Russian banners, which were advancing towards the Rhine. Prussia had 200,000 men; the Confederation of the Rhine 150,000: in short, including the Swedes and the Dutch, the English troops in Spain and in the Netherlands, the Danes, who had abandoned us, the Spaniards and Portuguese, whose courage and hopes were revived by our reverses, Napoleon had arrayed against him upwards of a million of armed men. Among them, too, were the Neapolitans, with Murat at their head!

The month of November 1813 was fatal to the fortune of Napoleon. In all parts the French armies were repulsed and driven back upon the Rhine, while-in every direction, the Allied forces advanced towards that river. For a considerable time I had confidently anticipated the fall of the Empire; not because the foreign sovereigns had vowed its destruction, but because I saw the impossibility of Napoleon defending himself against all Europe, and because I knew that, however desperate might be his fortune, nothing would induce him to consent to conditions which he considered disgraceful. At this time every day was marked by a new defection. Even the Bavarians, the natural Allies of France, they whom the Emperor had led to victory at the commencement of the second campaign of Vienna, they whom he had, as it were, adopted on the field of battle, were now against us, and were the bitterest of our enemies.

Even before the battle of Leipsic, the consequences of which were so ruinous to Napoleon, he had felt the necessity of applying to France for a supply of troops; as if France had been inexhaustible. He directed the Empress Regent to make this demand; and accordingly Maria Louisa proceeded to the Senate, for the first time, in great state: but the glories of the Empire were now on the decline. The Empress obtained a levy of 280,000 troops, but they were no sooner enrolled than they were sacrificed. The defection of the Bavarians considerably augmented the difficulties which assailed the wreck of the army that had escaped from Leipsic. The Bavarians had got before us to Hanau, a town four leagues distant from Frankfort; there they established themselves, with the view of cutting off our retreat; but French valour was roused, the little town was speedily carried, and the Bavarians were repulsed with considerable loss. The French army arrived at Mayence; if, indeed, one may give the name of army to a few masses of men destitute, dispirited, and exhausted by fatigue and privation. On the arrival of the troops at Mayence no preparation had been made for receiving them: there were no provisions, or supplies of any kind; and, as the climax of misfortune, infectious epidemics broke out amongst the men. All the accounts I received concurred in assuring me that their situation was dreadful:

However; without counting the wreck which escaped from the disasters of Leipsic, and the ravages of disease; without including the 280,000 men which had been raised by a 'Senatus-consulte, on the application of Maria Louisa, the Emperor still possessed 120,000 good troops; but they were in the rear, scattered along the Elbe, shut up in fortresses such as Dantzic, Hamburg, Torgau, and Spandau. Such was the horror of our situation that if, on the one hand, we could not resolve to abandon them, it was at the same time impossible to aid them. In France a universal cry was raised for peace, at whatever price it could be purchased. In this state of things it may be said that the year 1813 was more fatal to Napoleon than the year 1812. The disasters of Moscow were repaired by his activity and the sacrifices of France; but the disasters of Leipsic were irreparable.

I shall shortly speak of some negotiations in which, if I had chosen, I might have taken a part. After the battle of Leipsic, in which France lost, for the second time, a formidable army, all the powers allied against Napoleon declared at Frankfort, on the 9th of November, that they would never break the bonds which united them; that henceforth it was not merely a Continental peace, but a general peace, that would be demanded; and that any negotiation not having a general peace for its object would be rejected. The Allied powers declared that France was to be confined within her natural limits, the Rhine, the Alps, and the Pyrenees. This was all that was to remain of the vast Empire founded by Napoleon; but still it must be allowed it was a great deal, after the many disasters France had experienced, and when she was menaced with invasion by numerous and victorious armies. But Napoleon could not accede to such proposals, for he was always ready to yield to illusion when the truth was not satisfactory to him.

According to the proposals of the Allies at Frankfort, Germany; Italy, and Spain were to be entirely withdrawn from the dominion of France. England recognised the freedom of trade and navigation, and there appeared no reason to doubt the sincerity of her professed willingness to make great sacrifices to promote the object proposed by the Allies. But to these offers a fatal condition was added, namely, that the Congress should meet in a town, to be declared neutral, on the right bank of the Rhine, where the plenipotentiaries of all the belligerent powers were to assemble; but the course of the war was not to be impeded by these negotiations.[264]

The Duc de Bassano (Maret), who was still Minister for Foreign Affairs, replied, by order of Napoleon, to the overtures wade by the Allies for a general Congress; and stated that the Emperor acceded to them, and wished Mannheim to be chosen as the neutral town. M. Metternich replied in a note, dated Frankfort, the 25th of November, stating that the Allies felt no difficulty in acceding to Napoleon's choice of Mannheim for the meeting of the Congress; but as M. de Bassano's letter contained no mention of the general and summary

---

264 This, system of negotiating and advancing was a realization of Metternich's idea copying Napoleon's own former procedure. "Let us hold always the sword in one head, and the olive branch in the other; always ready to negotiate, but only negotiating whilst advancing. Here is Napoleon's system: may he find enemies who will carry on war . . . as he would carry it on himself." (Metternich vol. ii. p. 346).

bases I have just mentioned, and which had been communicated to M. de St. Aignan at Frankfort, M. Metternich stated that the Allies wished the Emperor Napoleon to declare his determination respecting those bases, in order that insurmountable difficulties might not arrest the negotiations at their very outset. The Duke of Vicenza (Caulaincourt), who had just succeeded the Duc de Bassano, received this letter. Trusting to the declaration of Frankfort he thought he would be justified in treating on those bases; he confidently relied on the consent of Napoleon. But the Allies had now determined not to grant the limits accorded by that declaration. Caulaincourt was therefore obliged to apply for fresh powers, which being granted, he replied, on the 2d of December, that Napoleon accepted the fundamental and summary bases which had been communicated by M. de St. Aignan. To this letter M. Metternich answered that the Emperors of Russia and Austria were gratified to find that the Emperor of France recognised the bases judged necessary by the Allies; that the two sovereigns would communicate without delay the official document to their Allies, and that they were convinced that immediately on receiving their reply the negotiations might be opened without any interruption of the war.

We shall now see the reason why these first negotiations came to no result. In the month of October the Allies overthrew the colossal edifice denominated the French Empire. When led by victory to the banks of the Rhine they declared their wish to abstain from conquest, explained their intentions, and manifested an unalterable resolution to abide by them. This determination of the Allies induced the French Government to evince pacific intentions. Napoleon wished, by an apparent desire for peace, to justify, if I may so express myself, in the eyes of his subjects, the necessity of new sacrifices; which, according to his proclamations, he demanded only to enable him to obtain peace on as honourable conditions as possible. But the truth is, he was resolved not even to listen to the offers made at Frankfort. He always represented the limits of the Rhine as merely a compensation for the dismemberment of Poland and the immense aggrandisement of the English possessions in Asia. But he wanted to gain time, and, if possible, to keep the Allied armies on the right bank of the Rhine.

The immense levies made in France, one after the other, had converted the conscription into a sort of pressgang. Men employed in agriculture and manufactures were dragged from their labours; and the people began to express their dissatisfaction at the measures of Government more loudly than they had hitherto ventured to do; yet all were willing to make another effort, if they could have persuaded themselves that the Emperor would henceforth confine his thoughts to France alone. Napoleon sent Caulaincourt to the headquarters of the Allies; but that was only for the sake of gaining time, and inducing a belief that he was favourably disposed to peace.

The Allies having learned the immense levies of troops which Napoleon was making, and being well acquainted with the state of feeling in France, published the famous manifesto, addressed to the French people, which was profusely circulated, and may be referred to as a warning to subjects who trust to the promises of Governments.

The good faith with which the promises in the manifesto were kept may be judged of from the Treaty of Paris. In the meantime the manifesto did not a little contribute to alienate from Napoleon those who were yet faithful to his cause; for, by believing in the declarations of the Allies, they saw in him the sole obstacle to that peace which France so ardently desired. On this point, too, the Allies were not wrong, and I confess that I did not see without great surprise that the Duc de Rovigo, in that part of his Memoirs where he mentions this manifesto, reproaches those who framed it for representing the Emperor as a madman, who replied to overtures of peace only by conscription levies: After all, I do not intend to maintain that the declaration was entirely sincere; with respect to the future it certainly was not. Switzerland was already tampered with, and attempts were made to induce her to permit the Allied troops to enter France by the bridge of Bale. Things were going on no better in the south of France, where the Anglo-Spanish army threatened our frontiers by the Pyrenees, and already occupied Pampeluna; and at the same time the internal affairs of the country were no less critical than its external position. It was in vain to levy troops; everything essential to an army was wanting. To meet the most pressing demands the Emperor drew out 30,000,000 from the immense treasure which he had accumulated in the cellars and galleries of the Pavillion Marsan, at the Tuileries. These 30,000,000 were speedily swallowed up. Nevertheless it was an act of generosity on the part of Napoleon, and I never could understand on what ground the Legislative Body complained of the outlay, because, as the funds did not proceed from the Budget, there needed no financial law to authorise their application. Besides, why did these rigid legislators, who, while fortune smiled on Bonaparte, dared not utter a word on the subject, demand, previously to the gratuitous gift just mentioned, that the 350,000,000 in the Emperor's privy puree should be transferred to the Imperial treasury and carried to the public accounts? Why did they wink at the accumulation in the Tuileries of the contributions and exactions levied in, conquered countries? The answer is plain: because there would have been danger in opposing it.

Amidst the difficulties which assailed the Emperor he cast his eyes on M. de Talleyrand. But it being required, as a condition of his receiving the portfolio of Foreign Affairs, that he should resign his office of Vice-Grand-Elector, M. de Talleyrand preferred a permanent post to a portfolio, which the caprice of a moment might withdraw. I have been informed that, in a conversation with the Emperor, M. de Talleyrand gave him the extraordinary advice of working upon the ambition of the English family of Wellesley, and to excite in the mind of Wellington, the lustre of whose reputation was now dawning, ambitious projects which would have embarrassed the coalition. Napoleon, however, did not adopt this proposition, the issue of which he thought too uncertain, and above all, too remote, in the urgent circumstances in which it stood. Caulaincourt was then made Minister for Foreign Affairs, in lieu of M. Maret, who was appointed Secretary of State, an office much better suited to him.

Meanwhile the Emperor was wholly intent on the means of repelling the attack which was preparing against him. The critical circumstances in which he was placed seemed to restore the energy which time had in some measure robbed him of. He turned his eyes towards Spain, and resolved to bring the army from that country to oppose the Allies, whose movements indicated their intention of entering France by Switzerland. An event occurred connected with this subject calculated to have a decided influence on the affairs of the moment, namely, the renunciation by Joseph, King of Spain, of all right to the crown, to be followed by the return; as had been agreed on; of Ferdinand to his dominions. Joseph made this sacrifice at the instigation of his brother. The treaty was signed, but an inconceivable delay occurred in its execution, while the torrent, which was advancing upon France, rushed forward so rapidly that the treaty could not be carried into execution. Ferdinand, it is true, re-ascended his throne, but from other causes.

The Emperor was deeply interested in the march of the Allies. It was important to destroy the bridge of Bale, because the Rhine once crossed masses of the enemy would be thrown into France. At this time I had close relations with a foreign diplomat whom I am forbidden by discretion to name. He told me that the enemy was advancing towards the frontier, and that the bridge of Bale would not be destroyed, as it had been so agreed at Berne, where the Allies had gained the day. This astonished me, because I knew, on the other hand, from a person who ought, to have been equally well informed,—that it was hoped the bridge would be blown up. Being much interested in knowing the truth, I sent on my own account, an agent to Bale who on his return told me that the bridge would remain.

On the 19th of December the Legislative Body was convoked. It was on a Wednesday. M. Laine was Vice-President under M. Regnier. A committee was appointed to examine and report on the communications of the Emperor. The report and conclusions of the committee were not satisfactory; it was alleged that they betrayed a revolutionary tendency, of which M. Laine was absurdly accused of having been one of the promoters; but all who knew him must have been convinced of the falsehood of the charge. The Emperor ordered the report to be seized, and then adjourned the Legislative Body. Those who attentively observed the events of the time will recollect the stupor which prevailed in Paris on the intelligence of this seizure and of the adjournment of the Legislative Body. A thousand conjectures were started as to what new occurrences had taken place abroad, but nothing satisfactory was learned.

I considered this a great mistake. Who can doubt that if the Legislative Body had taken the frank and noble step of declaring that France accepted the conditions of Frankfort they would not have been listened to by the Allies? But the words, "You are dishonoured if you cede a single village acquired by a 'Senatus-consulte'," always, resounded in Napoleon's ears: they flattered his secret thoughts, and every pacific proposal was rejected.

The members of the adjourned Legislative Body went as usual to take leave of the Emperor, who received them on a Sunday, and after delivering to them the speech, which is very well known, dismissed the rebels with great ill-humour, refusing to hear any explanation. "I have suppressed your address," he began abruptly: "it was incendiary. I called you round me to do good—you have done ill. Eleven-twelfths of you are well-intentioned, the others, and above all M. Laine, are factious intriguers, devoted to England, to all my enemies, and corresponding through the channel of the advocate Deseze with the Bourbons. Return to your Departments, and feel that my eye will follow you; you have endeavoured to humble me, you may kill me, but you shall not dishonour me. You make remonstrances; is this a time, when the stranger invades our provinces, and 200,000 Cossacks are ready to overflow our country? There may have been petty abuses; I never connived at them. You, M. Raynouard, you said that. Prince Massena robbed a man at Marseilles of his house. You lie! The General took possession of a vacant house, and my Minister shall indemnify the proprietor. Is it thus that you dare affront a Marshal of France who has bled for his country, and grown gray in victory? Why did you not make your complaints in private to me? I would have done you justice. We should wash our dirty linen at home, and not drag it out before the world. You, call yourselves Representatives of the Nation. It is not true; you are only Deputies of the Departments; a small portion of the State, inferior to the Senate, inferior even to the Council of State. The Representatives of the People! I am alone the Representative of the People. Twice have 24,000,000 of French called me to the throne: which of you durst undertake such a burden? It had already overwhelmed (ecrase), your Assemblies, and your Conventions, your Vergniauds and your Guadets, your Jacobins and your Girondins. They are all dead! What, who are you? nothing—all authority is in the Throne; and what is the Throne? this wooden frame covered with velvet?—no, I am the Throne! You have added wrong to reproaches. You have talked of concessions—concessions that even my enemies dared not ask! I suppose if they asked Champaigne you would have had me give them La

Brie besides; but in four months I will conquer peace, or I shall be dead! You advise! how dare you debate of such high matters (de si graves interets)! You have put me in the front of the battle as the cause of war—it is infamous (c'est une atrocité). In all your committees you have excluded the friends of Government— extraordinary commission—committee of finance—committee of the address, all, all my enemies. M. Laine, I repeat it, is a traitor; he is a wicked man, the others are mere intriguers. I do justice to the eleven-twelfths; but the factions I know, and will pursue. Is it, I ask again, is it while the enemy is in France that you should have done this? But nature has gifted me with a determined courage—nothing can overcome me. It cost my pride much too—I made that sacrifice; I—but I am above your miserable declamations—I was in need of consolation, and you would mortify me—but, no, my victories shall crush your clamours! In three months we shall have peace, and you shall repent your folly. I am one of those who triumph or die.

"Go back to your Departments if any one of you dare to print your address I shall publish it in the Moniteur with notes of my own. Go; France stands in more need of me than I do of France. I bear the eleven-twelfths of you in my heart—I shall nominate the Deputies to the two series which are vacant, and I shall reduce the Legislative Body to the discharge of its proper duties. The inhabitants of Alsace and Franche Comte have more spirit than you; they ask me for arms, I send them, and one of my aides de camp will lead them against the enemy."

In after conversations he said of the Legislative Body that "its members never came to Paris but to obtain some favours. They importuned the Ministers from morning till night, and complained if they were not immediately satisfied. When invited to dinner they burn with envy at the splendour they see before them." I heard this from Cambacérès, who was present when the Emperor made these remarks.

CHAPTER XXXI

1813

I am now arrived at the most critical period in Napoleon's career. What reflections must he have made, if he had had leisure to reflect, in comparing the recollections of his rising glory with the sad picture of his falling fortune? What a contrast presents itself when we compare the famous flag of the army of Italy, which the youthful conqueror, Bonaparte, carried to the Directory, with those drooping eagles who had now to defend the aerie whence they had so often taken flight to spread their triumphant wings over Europe! Here we see the difference between liberty and absolute power! Napoleon, the son of liberty, to whom he owed everything, had disowned his mother, and was now about to fall. Those glorious triumphs were now over when the people of Italy consoled themselves for defeat and submitted to the magical power of that liberty which preceded the Republican armies. Now, on the contrary, it was to free themselves from a despotic yoke that the nations of Europe had in their turn taken up arms and were preparing to invade France.

With the violation of the Swiss territory by the Allied armies, after the consent of the Cantons, is connected a fact of great importance in my life, and which, if I had chosen, might have made a great difference in my destiny. On Tuesday, the 28th of December, I dined with my old friend, M. Pierlot, and on leaving home I was in the habit of saying where I might be found in case I should be wanted. At nine o'clock at night an express arrived from the Minister of Police desiring me to come immediately to his office. I confess, considering the circumstances of the times, and knowing the Emperor's prejudices against me, such a request coming at such an hour made me feel some uneasiness, and I expected nothing less then a journey to Vincennes. The Duc de Rovigo, by becoming responsible for me, had as yet warded off the blow, and the supervision to which the Emperor had subjected me—thanks to the good offices of Davoust—consisted in going three times a week to show myself to Savory.

I accordingly, having first borrowed a night-cap, repaired to the hotel of the Minister of Police. I was ushered into a well-lighted room, and when I entered I found Savary waiting for me. He was in full costume, from which I concluded he had just come from the Emperor. Advancing towards me with an air which showed he had no bad news to communicate, he thus addressed me:

"Bourrienne, I have just come from the Emperor, who asked me where you were? I told him you were in Paris, and that I saw you often. 'Well,' continued the Emperor, 'bid him come to me, I want to employ him. It is three years since he has had anything to do. I wish to send him as Minister to Switzerland, but he must set off directly. He must go to the Allies. He understands German well. The King of Prussia expressed by letter satisfaction at his conduct towards the Prussians whom the war forced to retire to Hamburg. He knows Prince Witgenstein, who is the friend of the King of Prussia, and probably is at Lörrach. He will see all the Germans who are there. I confidently rely on him, and believe his journey will have a good result. Caulaincourt will give him his instructions."

Notwithstanding my extreme surprise at this communication I replied without hesitation that I could not accept the mission; that it was offered too late. "It perhaps is hoped;" said I, "that the bridge of Bale will be destroyed, and that Switzerland will preserve her neutrality. But I do not believe any such thing; nay, more, I know positively to the contrary. I can only repeat the offer comes much too late."—"I am very sorry for this resolution," observed Savory, "but Caulaincourt will perhaps persuade you. The Emperor wishes you to go to the Duc de Vicence to-morrow at one o'clock; he will acquaint you with all the particulars, and give you your instructions."—"He may acquaint me with whatever he chooses, but I will not go to Lörrach."—"You know the Emperor better than I do, he wishes you to go, and he will not pardon your refusal."—"He may do as he pleases, but no consideration shall induce me to go to Switzerland."—"You are wrong: but you will reflect on the matter between this and tomorrow morning. Night will bring good counsel, At any rate, do not fail to go to-morrow at one o'clock to Caulaincourt, he expects you, and directions will be given to admit you immediately."

Next morning the first thing I did was to call on M. de Talleyrand. I told him what had taken place, and as he was intimately acquainted with Caulaincourt, I begged him to speak to that Minister in favour of my resolution. M. de Talleyrand approved of my determination not to go to Switzerland, and at one o'clock precisely I proceeded to M. de Caulaincourt's. He told me all he had been instructed to say. From the manner in which he made the communication I concluded that he himself considered the proposed mission a disagreeable one, and unlikely to be attended by any useful result. I observed that he must have heard from Savory that I had already expressed my determination to decline the mission which the Emperor had been pleased to offer me. The Duc de Vicence then, in a very friendly way, detailed the reasons which ought to induce me to accept the offer, and did not disguise from me that by persisting in my determination I ran the risk of raising Napoleon's doubts as to my opinions and future intentions. I replied that, having lived for three years as a private individual, unconnected with public affairs, I should have no influence at the headquarters of the Allies, and that whatever little ability I might be supposed to possess, that would not counterbalance the difficulties of my situation, and the opinion that I was out of favour. I added that I should appear at the headquarters without any decoration, without even that of the Cordon of the Legion of Honour to which the Emperor attached so much importance, and the want of which would almost have the appearance of disgrace; and I said that these trifles, however slightly valued by reasonable men, were not, as he well knew, without their influence on the men with whom I should have to treat. "If that be all," replied Caulaincourt, "the obstacle will speedily be removed. I am authorised by the Emperor to tell you that he will create you a Duke, and give you the Grand Cordon of the Legion of Honour."

After these words I thought I was dreaming, and I was almost inclined to believe that Caulaincourt was jesting with me. However, the offer was serious, and I will not deny that it was tempting; yet I nevertheless persisted in the refusal I had given. At length, after some further conversation, and renewed, but useless, entreaties on the part of M. de Caulaincourt, he arose, which was a signal that our interview was terminated. I acknowledge I remained for a moment in doubt how to act, for I felt we had come to no understanding. M. de' Caulaincourt advanced slowly towards the door of his cabinet: If I went away without knowing his opinion I had done nothing; addressing him, therefore, by his surname, "Caulaincourt;" said I, "you have frequently assured me that you would never forget the services I rendered to you and your family at a time when I possessed some influence. I know you, and therefore speak to you without disguise. I do not now address myself to the Emperor's Minister, but to

Caulaincourt. You are a man of honour, and I can open my heart to you frankly. Consider the embarrassing situation of France, which you know better than I do. I do not ask you for your secrets, but I myself know enough. I will tell you candidly that I am convinced the enemy will pass the Rhine in a few days. The Emperor has been deceived: I should not have time to reach my destination, and I should be laughed at. My correspondents in Germany have made me acquainted with every particular. Now, Caulaincourt, tell me honestly, if you were in my place, and I in yours, and I should make this proposition to you, what determination would you adopt?"

I observed from the expression of Caulaincourt's countenance that my question had made an impression on him, and affectionately pressing my hand he said, "I would do as you do: Enough. I will arrange the business with the Emperor." This reply seemed to remove a weight from my mind, and I left Caulaincourt with feelings of gratitude. I felt fully assured that he would settle the business satisfactorily, and in this conjecture I was not deceived, for I heard no more of the matter.

I must here go forward a year to relate another occurrence in which the Duc de Vicence and I were concerned. When, in March 1815, the King appointed me Prefect of Police, M. de Caulaincourt sent to me a confidential person to inquire whether he ran any risk in remaining in Paris, or whether he had better remove. He had been told that his name was inscribed in a list of individuals whom I had received orders to arrest. Delighted at this proof of confidence, I returned the following answer by the Duc de Vicence's messenger: "Tell M. de Caulaincourt that I do not know where he lives. He need be under no apprehension: I will answer for him."

During the campaign of 1813 the Allies, after driving the French out of Saxony and obliging them to retreat towards the Rhine, besieged Hamburg, where Davoust was shut up with a garrison of 30,000 men, resolutely determined to make it a second Saragossa. From the month of September every day augmented the number of the Allied troops, who were already making rapid progress on the left bank of the Elbe. Davoust endeavoured to fortify Hamburg on so extended a scale that, in the opinion of the most experienced military men, it would have required a garrison of 60,000 men to defend it in a regular and protracted siege. At the commencement of the siege Davoust lost Vandamme, who was killed in a sortie at the head of a numerous corps which was inconsiderately sacrificed.

It is but justice to admit that Davoust displayed great activity in the defence, and began by laying in large supplies.[265] General Bertrand was directed to construct a bridge to form a communication between Hamburg and Haarburg by joining the islands of the Elbe to the Continent along a total distance of about two leagues. This bridge was to be built of wood, and Davoust seized upon all the timber-yards to supply materials for its construction. In the space of eighty-three days the bridge was finished. It was a very magnificent structure, its length being 2529 toises, exclusive of the lines of junction, formed on the two islands.

The inhabitants were dreadfully oppressed, but all the cruel measures and precautions of the French were ineffectual, for the Allies advanced in great force and occupied Westphalia, which movement obliged the Governor of Hamburg to recall to the town the different detachments scattered round Hamburg.

---

265 Vandamme fought under Grouchy in 1815, and died several years afterwards. This killing him at Hamburg is one of the curious mistakes seized on by the Bonapartists to deny the authenticity of these Memoirs.

At Lübeck the departure of the French troops was marked by blood. Before they evacuated the town, an old man, and a butcher named Prahl, were condemned to be shot. The butcher's crime consisted in having said, in speaking of the French, "Der teufel hohle sie" (the devil take them). The old man fortunately escaped his threatened fate, but, notwithstanding the entreaties and tears of the inhabitants, the sentence upon Prahl was carried into execution.

The garrison of Hamburg was composed of French, Italian, and Dutch troops. Their number at first amounted to 30,000, but sickness made great-havoc among them. From sixty to eighty perished daily in the hospitals. When the garrison evacuated Hamburg in May 1814 it was reduced to about 15,000 men. In the month of December provisions began to diminish, and there was no possibility of renewing the supply. The poor were first of all made to leave the town, and afterwards all persons who were not usefully employed. It is no exaggeration to estimate at 50,000 the number of persons who were thus exiled. The colonel commanding the gendarmerie at Hamburg notified to the exiled inhabitants that those who did not leave the town within the prescribed time would receive fifty blows with a cane and afterwards be driven out. But if penance may be commuted with priests so it may with gendarmes. Delinquents contrived to purchase their escape from the bastinado by a sum of money, and French gallantry substituted with respect to females the birch for the cane. I saw an order directing all female servants to be examined as to their health unless they could produce certificates from their masters. On the 25th of December the Government granted twenty-four hours longer to persons who were ordered to quit the town; and two days after this indulgence an ordinance was published declaring that those who should return to the town after once leaving it were to be considered as rebels and accomplices of the enemy, and as such condemned to death by a prevotal court. But this was not enough. At the end of December people, without distinction of sex or age, were dragged from their beds and conveyed out of the town on a cold night, when the thermometer was between sixteen or eighteen degrees; and it was affirmed that several old men perished in this removal. Those who survived were left on the outside of the Altona gates. At Altona they all found refuge and assistance. On Christmas-day 7000 of these unfortunate persons were received in the house of M. Rainville, formerly aide de camp to Dumouriez, and who left France together with that general. His house, which was at Holstein, was usually the scene of brilliant entertainments, but it was converted into the abode of misery, mourning, and death. All possible attention was bestowed on the unfortunate outlaws; but few profited by it, and what is worse, the inhabitants of Altona suffered for their generosity. Many of the unfortunate persons were affected with the epidemic disease which was raging in Hamburg, and which in consequence broke out at Altona.

All means of raising money in Hamburg being exhausted, a seizure was made of the funds of the Bank of that city, which yet contained from seven to eight millions of marks. Were those who ordered this measure not aware that to seize on the funds of some of the citizens of Hamburg was an injury to all foreigners who had funds in the Bank? Such is a brief statement of the vexations and cruelties which long oppressed this unfortunate city. Napoleon accused Hamburg of Anglomania, and by ruining her he thought to ruin England. Hamburg, feeble and bereft of her sources, could only complain, like Jerusalem when besieged by Titus: "Plorans, ploravit in nocte."

CHAPTER XXXII

1813-1814

I want now to proceed to notice the affairs of Italy and the principal events of the Viceroyalty of Eugène. In order to throw together all that I have to say about the Viceroy I must anticipate the order of time.

After the campaign of 1812, when Eugène revisited Italy, he was promptly informed of the more than doubtful dispositions of Austria towards France. He then made preparations for raising an army capable of defending the country which the Emperor had committed to his safeguard. Napoleon was fully aware how much advantage he would derive from the presence on the northern frontiers of Italy of an army sufficiently strong to harass Austria, in case she should draw aside the transparent veil which still covered her policy. Eugène did all that depended on him to meet the Emperor's wishes; but in spite of his efforts the army of Italy was, after all; only an imaginary army to those who could compare the number of men actually enrolled with the numbers stated in the lists. When, in July 1813, the Viceroy was informed of the turn taken by the negotiations at the shadow of a Congress assembled at Prague, he had no longer any doubt of the renewal of hostilities; and foreseeing an attack on Italy he resolved as speedily as possible to approach the frontiers of Austria. He had succeeded in assembling an army composed of French and Italians, and amounting to 45,000 infantry and 5000 cavalry. On the renewal of hostilities the Viceroy's headquarters were at Udine. Down to the month of April 1814 he succeeded in maintaining a formidable attitude, and in defending the entrance of his kingdom by dint of that military talent which was to be expected in a man bred in the great school of Napoleon, and whom the army looked up to as one of its most skillful generals.

During the great and unfortunate events of 1813 all eyes had been fixed on Germany and the Rhine; but the defection of Murat for a time diverted attention to Italy. That event did not so very much surprise me, for I had not forgotten my conversation with the King of Naples in the Champs Elysees, with which I have made the reader acquainted. At first Murat's defection was thought incredible by every one, and it highly excited Bonaparte's indignation. Another defection which occurred about the same period deeply distressed Eugène, for although raised to the rank of a prince, and almost a sovereign, he was still a man, and an excellent man. He was united to the Princess Amelia of Bavaria, who was as amiable and as much beloved as he, and he had the deep mortification to count the subjects of his father-in-law among the enemies whom he would probably have to combat. Fearing lest he should be harassed by the Bavarians on the side of the Tyrol, Eugène commenced his retrograde movement in the autumn of 1813. He at first fell back on the Tagliamento, and successively on the Adige. On reaching that river the army of Italy was considerably diminished, in spite of all Eugène's care of his troops. About the end of November Eugène learned that a Neapolitan corps was advancing upon Upper Italy, part taking the direction of Rome, and part that of Ancona. The object of the King of Naples was to take advantage of the situation of Europe, and he was duped by the promises held out to him as the reward of his treason. Murat seemed to have adopted the artful policy of Austria; for not only had he determined to join the coalition, but he was even maintaining communications with England and Austria, while at the same time he was making protestations of fidelity to his engagements with Napoleon.

When first informed of Murat's treason by the Viceroy the Emperor refused to believe it. "No," he exclaimed to those about him, "it cannot be! Murat, to whom I have given my sister! Murat, to whom I have given a throne! Eugène must be misinformed. It is impossible that Murat has declared himself against me!" It was, however, not only possible but true. Gradually throwing aside the dissimulation beneath which he had concealed his designs, Murat seemed inclined to renew the policy of Italy during the fifteenth and sixteenth centuries, when the art of deceiving was deemed by the Italian Governments the most sublime effort of genius. Without any declaration of war, Murat ordered the Neapolitan General who occupied Rome to assume the supreme command in the Roman States, and to take possession of the country. General Miollis, who commanded the French troops in Rome, could only throw himself, with his handful of men, into the Castle of St. Angelo, the famous mole of Adrian, in which was long preserved the treasury of Sixtus V. The French General soon found himself blockaded by the Neapolitan troops, who also blockaded Civita Vecchia and Ancona.

The treaty concluded between Murat and Austria was definitively signed on the 11th of January 1814. As soon as he was informed of it the Viceroy, certain that he should soon have to engage with the Neapolitans, was obliged to renounce the preservation of the line of the Adige, the Neapolitan army being in the rear of his right wing. He accordingly ordered a retrograde movement to the other side of the Mincio, where his army was cantoned. In this position Prince Eugène, on the 8th of February, had to engage with the Austrians, who had come up with him, and the victory of the Mincio arrested, for some time, the invasion of the Austrian army and its junction with the Neapolitan troops.

It was not until eight days after that Murat officially declared war against the Emperor; and immediately several general and superior officers, and many French troops, who were in his service, abandoned him, and repaired to the headquarters of the Viceroy. Murat made endeavours to detain them; they replied, that as he had declared war against France, no Frenchman who loved his country could remain in his service. "Do you think," returned he, "that my heart is less French than yours? On the contrary, I am much to be pitied. I hear of nothing but the disasters of the Grand Army. I have been obliged to enter into a treaty with the Austrians, and an arrangement with the English, commanded by Lord Bentinck, in order to save my Kingdom from a threatened landing of the English and the Sicilians, which would infallibly have excited an insurrection."

There could not be a more ingenuous confession of the antipathy which Joachim knew the Neapolitans to entertain towards his person and government. His address to the French was ineffectual. It was easy to foresee what would ensue. The Viceroy soon received an official communication from Napoleon's War Minister, accompanied by an Imperial decree, recalling all the French who were in the service of Joachim, and declaring that all who were taken with arms in their hands should be tried by a courtmartial as traitors to their country. Murat commenced by gaining advantages which could not be disputed. His troops almost immediately took possession of Leghorn and the citadel of Ancona, and the French were obliged to evacuate Tuscany.

The defection of Murat overthrew one of Bonaparte's gigantic conceptions. He had planned that Murat and Eugène with their combined forces should march on the rear of the Allies, while he, disputing the soil of France with the invaders, should multiply obstacles to their advance; the King of Naples and the Viceroy of Italy were to march upon Vienna and make Austria tremble in the heart of her capital before the timid million of her Allies, who measured their steps as they approached Paris, should desecrate by their presence the capital of France. When informed of the vast project, which, however, was but the dream of a moment, I immediately recognised that eagle glance, that power of discovering great resources in great calamities, so peculiar to Bonaparte.

Napoleon was yet Emperor of France; but he who had imposed on all Europe treaties of peace no less disastrous than the wars which had preceded them, could not now obtain an armistice; and Caulaincourt, who was sent to treat for one at the camp of the Allies, spent twenty days at Luneville before he could even obtain permission to pass the advanced posts of the invading army. In vain did Caulaincourt entreat Napoleon to sacrifice, or at least resign temporarily, a portion of that glory acquired in so many battles, and which nothing could efface in history. Napoleon replied, "I will sign whatever you wish. To obtain peace I will exact no condition; but I will not dictate my own humiliation." This concession, of course, amounted to a determination not to sign or to grant anything.

In the first fortnight of January 1814 one-third of France was invaded, and it was proposed to form a new Congress, to be held at Chatillon-sur-Seine. The situation of Napoleon grew daily worse and worse. He was advised to seek extraordinary resources in the interior of the Empire, and was reminded of the fourteen armies which rose, as if by enchantment, to defend France at the commencement of the Revolution. Finally, a reconciliation with the Jacobins, a party who had power to call up masses to aid him, was recommended. For a moment he was inclined to adopt this advice. He rode on horseback through the surburbs of St. Antoine and St. Marceau, courted the populace, affectionately replied to their acclamations, and he thought he saw the possibility of turning to account the attachment which the people evinced for him. On his return to the Palace some prudent persons ventured to represent to him that, instead of courting this absurd sort of popularity it would be more advisable to rely on the nobility and the higher classes of society. "Gentlemen," replied he, "you may say what you please, but in the situation in which I stand my only nobility is the rabble of the faubourgs, and I know of no rabble but the nobility whom I have created." This was a strange compliment to all ranks, for it was only saying that they were all rabble together.

At this time the Jacobins were disposed to exert every effort to serve him; but they required to have their own way, and to be allowed freely to excite and foster revolutionary sentiments. The press, which groaned under the most odious and intolerable censorship, was to be wholly resigned to them. I do not state these facts from hearsay. I happened by chance to be present at two conferences in which were set forward projects infected with the odour of the clubs, and these projects were supported with the more assurance because their success was regarded as certain. Though I had not seen Napoleon since my departure for Hamburg, yet I was sufficiently assured of his feeling towards the Jacobins to be convinced that he would have nothing to do with them. I was not wrong. On hearing of the price they set on their services he said, "This is too much; I shall have a chance of deliverance in battle, but I shall have none with these furious blockheads. There can be nothing in common between the demagogic principles of '93 and the monarchy, between clubs of madmen and a regular Ministry, between a Committee of Public Safety and an Emperor, between revolutionary tribunals and established laws. If fall I must, I will not bequeath France to the Revolution from which I have delivered her."

These were golden words, and Napoleon thought of a more noble and truly national mode of parrying the danger which threatened him. He ordered the enrolment of the National Guard of Paris, which was placed under the command of Marshal Moncey. A better choice could not have been made, but the staff of the National Guard was a focus of hidden intrigues, in which the defence of Paris was less thought about than the means of taking advantage of Napoleon's overthrow. I was made a captain in this Guard, and, like the rest of the officers, I was summoned to the Tuileries, on the 23d of January, when the Emperor took leave of the National Guard previously to his departure from Paris to join the army.

Napoleon entered with the Empress. He advanced with a dignified step, leading by the hand his son, who was not yet three years old. It was long since I had seen him. He had grown very corpulent, and I remarked on his pale countenance an expression of melancholy and irritability.

The habitual movement of the muscles of his neck was more decided and more frequent than formerly. I shall not attempt to describe what were my feelings during this ceremony, when I again saw, after a long separation, the friend of my youth, who had become master of Europe, and was now on the point of sinking beneath the efforts of his enemies. There was something melancholy in this solemn and impressive ceremony. I have rarely witnessed such profound silence in so numerous an assembly. At length Napoleon, in a voice as firm and sonorous as when he used to harangue his troops in Italy or in Egypt, but without that air of confidence which then beamed on his countenance, delivered to the assembled officers an address which was published in all the journals of the time. At the commencement of this address he said, "I set out this night to take the command of the army. On quitting the capital I confidently leave behind me my wife and my son, in whom so many hopes are centred." I listened attentively to Napoleon's address, and, though he delivered it firmly, he either felt or feigned emotion. Whether or not the emotion was sincere on his part, it was shared by many present; and for my own part I confess that my feelings were deeply moved when he uttered the words, "I leave you my wife and my son." At that moment my eyes were fixed on the young Prince, and the interest with which he inspired me was equally unconnected with the splendour which surrounded and the misfortunes which threatened him. I beheld in the interesting child not the King of Rome but the son of my old friend. All day long afterwards I could not help feeling depressed while comparing the farewell scene of the morning with the day on which we took possession of the Tuileries. How many centuries seemed the fourteen years which separated the two events.

It may be worth while to remind those who are curious in comparing dates that Napoleon, the successor of Louis XVI., and who had become the nephew of that monarch by his marriage with the niece of Marie Antoinette, took leave of the National Guard of Paris on the anniversary of the fatal 21st of January, after twenty-five years of successive terror, fear, hope, glory, and misfortune.

Meanwhile, a Congress was opened at Chatillon-sur-Seine, at which were assembled the Duke of Vicenza on the part of France, Lords Aderdeen and Cathcart and Sir Charles Stewart as the representatives of England, Count Razumowsky on the part of Russia, Count Stadion for Austria, and Count Humboldt for Prussia. Before the opening of the Congress, the Duke of Vicenza, in conformity with the Emperor's orders, demanded an armistice, which is almost invariably granted during negotiations for peace; but it was now too late: the Allies had long since determined not to listen to any such demand. They therefore answered the Duke of Vicenza's application by requiring that the propositions for peace should be immediately signed. But these were not the propositions of Frankfort. The Allies established as their bases the limits of the old French monarchy. They conceived themselves authorised in so doing by their success and by their situation.

To estimate rightly Napoleon's conduct during the negotiations for peace which took place in the conferences at Chatillon it is necessary to bear in mind the organisation he had received from nature and the ideas with which that organisation had imbued him at an early period of life. If the last negotiations of his expiring reign be examined with due attention and impartiality it will appear evident that the causes of his fall arose out of his character. I cannot range myself among those adulators who have accused the persons about him with having dissuaded him from peace. Did he not say at St. Helena, in speaking of the negotiations at Chatillon, "A thunderbolt alone could have saved us: to treat, to conclude, was to yield foolishly to the enemy." These words forcibly portray Napoleon's character. It must also be borne in mind how much he was captivated by the immortality of the great names which history has bequeathed to our admiration, and which are perpetuated from generation to generation. Napoleon was resolved that his name should re-echo in ages to come, from the palace to the cottage. To live without fame appeared to him an anticipated death. If, however, in this thirst for glory, not for notoriety, he conceived the wish to surpass Alexander and Caesar, he never desired the renown of Erostratus, and I will say again what I have said before, that if he committed actions to be condemned, it was because he considered them as steps which helped him to place himself on the summit of immortality on which he wished to place his name. Witness what he wrote to his brother Jerome, "Better never, to have lived than to live without glory;" witness also what he wrote later to his brother Louis, "It is better to die as a King than to live as a Prince." How often in the days of my intimacy with Bonaparte has he not said to me, "Who knows the names of those kings who have passed from the thrones on which chance or birth seated them? They lived and died unnoticed. The learned, perhaps, may find them mentioned in old archives, and a medal or a coin dug from the earth may reveal to antiquarians the existence of a sovereign of whom they had never before heard. But, on the contrary, when we hear the names of Cyrus, Alexander, Caesar, Mahomet, Charlemagne, Henry IV., and Louis XIV., we are immediately among our intimate acquaintance." I must add, that when Napoleon thus spoke to me in the gardens of Malmaison he only repeated what had often fallen from him in his youth, for his character and his ideas never varied; the change was in the objects to which they were applied.

From his boyhood Napoleon was fond of reading the history of the great men of antiquity; and what he chiefly sought to discover was the means by which those men had become great. He remarked that military glory secures more extended fame than the arts of peace and the noble efforts which contribute to the happiness of mankind. History informs us that great military talent and victory often give the power, which, in its turn, procures the means of gratifying ambition. Napoleon was always persuaded that that power was essential to him, in order to bend men to his will, and to stifle all discussions on his conduct. It was his established principle never to sign a disadvantageous peace. To him a tarnished crown was no longer a crown. He said one day to M. de Caulaincourt, who was pressing him to consent to sacrifices, "Courage may defend a crown, but infamy never." In all the last acts of Napoleon's career I can retrace the impress of his character, as I had often recognised in the great actions of the Emperor the execution of a thought conceived by the General-in-Chief of the Army of Italy.

On the opening of the Congress the Duke of Vicenza, convinced that he could no longer count on the natural limits of France promised at Frankfort by the Allies, demanded new powers. Those limits were doubtless the result of reasonable concessions, and they had been granted even after the battle of Leipsic; but it was now necessary that Napoleon's Minister should show himself ready to make further concessions if he wished to be allowed to negotiate. The Congress was opened on the 5th of February, and on the 7th the Plenipotentiaries of the Allied powers declared themselves categorically. They inserted in the protocol that after the successes which had favoured their armies they insisted on France being restored to her old limits, such as they were during the monarchy before the Revolution; and that she should renounce all direct influence beyond her future limits.

This proposition appeared so extraordinary to M. de Caulaincourt that he requested the sitting might be suspended, since the conditions departed too far from his instructions to enable him to give an immediate answer. The Plenipotentiaries of the Allied powers acceded to his request, and the continuation of the sitting was postponed till eight in the evening. When it was resumed the Duke of Vicenza renewed his promise to make the greatest sacrifices for the attainment of peace. He added that the amount of the sacrifices necessarily depended on the amount of the compensations, and that he could not determine on any concession or compensation without being made acquainted with the whole. He wished to have a general plan of the views of the Allies, and he requested that their Plenipotentiaries would explain themselves decidedly respecting the number and description of the sacrifices and compensations to be demanded. It must be acknowledged that the Duke of Vicenza perfectly fulfilled the views of the Emperor in thus protracting and gaining time by subtle subterfuges, for all that he suggested had already been done.

On the day after this sitting some advantages gained by the Allies, who took Chatillon-sur-Marne and Troves, induced Napoleon to direct Caulaincourt to declare to the Congress that if an armistice were immediately agreed on he was ready to consent to France being restored to her old limits. By securing this armistice Napoleon hoped that happy chances might arise, and that intrigues might be set on foot; but the Allies would not listen to any such proposition.

At the sitting of the 10th of March the Duke of Vicenza inserted in the protocol that the last courier he had received had been arrested and detained a considerable time by several Russian general officers, who had obliged him to deliver up his despatches, which had not been returned to him till thirty-six hours after at Chaumont. Caulaincourt justly complained of this infraction of the law of nations and established usage, which, he said, was the sole cause of the delay in bringing the negotiations to a conclusion. After this complaint he communicated to the Congress the ostensible instructions of Napoleon, in which he authorised his Minister to accede to the demands of the Allies. But in making this communication M. de Caulaincourt took care not to explain the private and secret instructions he had also received. The Allies rejected the armistice because it would have checked their victorious advance; but they consented to sign the definitive peace, which of all things was what the Emperor did not wish.

Napoleon at length determined to make sacrifices, and the Duke of Vicenza submitted new propositions to the Congress. The Allies replied, in the same sitting, that these propositions contained no distinct and explicit declaration on the project presented by them on the 17th of February; that, having on the 28th of the same month, demanded a decisive answer within the term of ten days, they were about to break up the negotiations

Caulaincourt then declared verbally:

1st. That the Emperor Napoleon was ready to renounce all pretension or influence whatever in countries beyond the boundaries of France.

2d. To recognise the independence of Spain, Italy, Switzerland, Germany, and Holland, and that as to England, France would make such concessions as might be deemed necessary in consideration of a reasonable equivalent.

Upon this the sitting was immediately broken up without a reply. It must be remarked that this singular declaration was verbal, and consequently not binding, and that the limits of France were mentioned without being specified. It cannot be doubted that Napoleon meant the limits conceded at Frankfort, to which he was well convinced the Allies would not consent, for circumstances were now changed. Besides, what could be meant by the reasonable equivalent from England? Is it astonishing that this obscurity and vagueness should have banished all confidence on the part of the Plenipotentiaries of the Allied powers? Three days after the sitting of the 10th of March they declared they could not even enter into a discussion of the verbal protocol of the French Minister. They requested that M. de Caulaincourt would declare whether he would accept or reject the project of a treaty presented by the Allied Sovereigns, or offer a counter-project.

The Duke of Vicenza, who was still prohibited, by secret instructions from coming to any conclusion on the proposed basis, inserted in the protocol of the sitting of the 13th of March a very ambiguous note. The Plenipotentiaries of the Allies; in their reply, insisted upon receiving another declaration from the French Plenipotentiary, which should contain an acceptance or refusal of their project of a treaty presented in the conference of the 7th of February, or a counter-project. After much discussion Caulaincourt agreed to draw up a counter-project, which he presented on the 15th, under the following title: "Project of a definitive Treaty between France and the Allies." In this extraordinary project, presented after so much delay, M. de Caulaincourt, to the great astonishment of the Allies, departed in no respect from the declarations of the 10th of March. He replied again to the ultimatum of the Allies, or what he wished to regard as such, by defending a multitude of petty interests, which were of no importance in so great a contest; but in general the conditions seemed rather those of a conqueror dictating to his enemies than of a man overwhelmed by misfortune: As may readily be imagined, they were, for the most part, received with derision by the Allies.

Everything tends to prove that the French Plenipotentiary had received no positive instructions from the 5th of February, and that, after all the delay which Napoleon constantly created, Caulaincourt never had it in his power to answer, categorically, the propositions of the Allies. Napoleon never intended to make peace at Chatillon on the terms proposed. He always hoped that some fortunate event would enable him to obtain more favourable conditions.

On the 18th of March, that is to say, three days after the presentation of this project of a treaty, the Plenipotentiaries of the Allies recorded in the protocol their reasons for rejecting the extraordinary project of the French Minister. For my part, I was convinced, for the reasons I have mentioned, that the Emperor would never agree to sign the conditions proposed in the ultimatum of the Allies, dated the 13th of March, and I remember having expressed that opinion to M. de Talleyrand. I saw him on the 14th, and found him engaged in perusing some intelligence he had just received from the Duke of Vicenza, announcing, as beyond all doubt, the early signature of peace. Caulaincourt had received orders to come to a conclusion. Napoleon, he said, had given him a carte blanche to save the capital, and avoid a battle, by which the last resources of the nation would be endangered. This seemed pretty positive, to be sure; but even this assurance did not, for a moment, alter my opinion. The better to convince me, M. de Talleyrand gave me Caulaincourt's letter to read. After reading it I confidently said, "He will never sign the conditions." M. de Talleyrand could not help thinking me very obstinate in my opinion, for he judged of what the Emperor would do by his situation, while I judged by his character. I told M. de Talleyrand that Caulaincourt might have received written orders to sign; for the sake of showing them to the Plenipotentiaries of the Allies, but that I had no doubt he had been instructed to postpone coming to a conclusion, and to wait for final orders. I added, that I saw no reason to change my opinion, and that I continued to regard the breaking up of the Congress as nearer than appearances seemed to indicate. Accordingly, three days afterwards, the Allies grew tired of the delay and the conferences were broken up. Thus Napoleon sacrificed everything rather than his glory. He fell from a great height, but he never, by his signature, consented to any dismemberment of France.

The Plenipotentiaries of the Allies, convinced that these renewed difficulties and demands had no other object but to gain time, stated that the Allied powers, faithful to their principles, and in conformity with their previous declarations, regarded the negotiations at Chatillon as terminated by the French Government. This rupture of the conferences took place on the 19th of March, six days after the presentation of the ultimatum of the Allied powers. The issue of these long discussions was thus left to be decided by the chances of war, which were not very favourable to the man who boldly contended against armed Europe. The successes of the Allies during the conferences at Chatillon had opened to their view the road to Paris, while Napoleon shrunk from the necessity of signing his own disgrace. In these circumstances was to be found the sole cause of his ruin, and he might have said, "Tout est perdu, fors la gloire." His glory is immortal.[266]

---

266 The conviviality and harmony that reigned between the Ministers made the society and Intercourse at Chatillon most agreeable. The diplomatists dined alternately with each other; M. de Caulaincourt liberally passing for all the Ministers, through the French advanced posts, convoys of all the good cheer in epicurean wises, etc., that Paris could afford; nor was female society wanting to complete the charm and banish ennui from the Chatillon Congress, which I am sure will be long recollected with sensations of pleasure by all the Plenipotentiaries there engaged (Memoirs of Lord Burghersh).

CHAPTER XXXIII

1814

I was always persuaded, and everything I have since seen has confirmed my opinion, that the Allies entering France had no design of restoring the House of Bourbon, or of imposing any Government whatever on the French people. They came to destroy and not to found. That which they wished to destroy from the commencement of their success was Napoleon's supremacy, in order to prevent the future invasions with which they believed Europe would still be constantly threatened. If, indeed, I had entertained any doubt on this subject it would have been banished by the account I heard of General Reynier's conversation with the Emperor Alexander. That General, who was made prisoner at Leipsic, was exchanged, and returned to France. In the beginning of February 1814 he passed through Troves, where the Emperor Alexander then was. Reynier expressed a desire to be allowed to pay his respects to the Emperor, and to thank him for having restored him to liberty. He was received with that affability of manner which was sometimes affected by the Russian monarch.

On his arrival at Paris General Reynier called at the Duc de Rovigo's, where I had dined that day, and where he still was when I arrived. He related in my hearing the conversation to which I have alluded, and stated that it had all the appearance of sincerity on the Emperor's part. Having asked Alexander whether he had any instructions for Napoleon, as the latter, on learning that he had seen his Majesty would not fail to ask him many questions, he replied that he had nothing particular to communicate to him. Alexander added that he was Napoleon's friend, but that he had, personally, much reason—to complain of his conduct; that the Allies would have nothing more to do with him; that they had no intention of forcing any Sovereign upon France; but that they would no longer acknowledge Napoleon as Emperor of the French. "For my part," said Alexander, "I can no longer place any confidence in him. He has deceived me too often." In reply to this Reynier made some remarks dictated by his attachment and fidelity to Bonaparte. He observed that Napoleon was acknowledged as Sovereign of France by every treaty. "But," added Reynier, "if you should persist in forcing him to resign the supreme power, whom will you put in his place?"—"Did you not choose him; why then can you not choose some one else to govern you? I repeat that we do not intend to force any one upon you but we will have no more to do with Napoleon."

Several Generals were then named; and after Reynier had explained the great difficulties which would oppose any such choice, Alexander interrupted him saying, "But, General, there is Bernadotte.' Has he not been voluntarily chosen Prince Royal of Sweden; may he not also be raised to the same rank in France? He is your countryman; surely then you may choose him, since the Swedes took him, though a foreigner." General Reynier, who was a man of firm character, started some objections, which I thought at the time well founded; and Alexander put an end to the conversation by saving, rather in a tone of dissatisfaction, "Well, General, the fate of arms will decide."

The campaign of France forced Napoleon to adopt a kind of operations quite new to him. He had been accustomed to attack; but he was now obliged to stand on his defence, so that, instead of having to execute a previously conceived plan, as when, in the Cabinet of the Tuileries, he traced out to me the field of Marengo, he had now to determine his movements according to those of his numerous enemies. When the Emperor arrived at Chalons-sur-Marne the Prussian army was advancing by the road of Lorraine. He drove it back beyond St. Dizier. Meanwhile the Grand Austro-Russian army passed the Seine and the Yonne at Montereau, and even sent forward a corps which advanced as far as Fontainebleau. Napoleon then made a movement to the right in order to drive back the troops which threatened to march on Paris, and by a curious chance he came up with the troops in the very place where he passed the boyish years in which he cherished what then seemed wild and fabulous dreams of his future fate. What thoughts and recollections must have crowded on his mind when he found himself an Emperor and a King, at the head of a yet powerful army, in the chateau of the Comte de Brienne, to whom he had so often paid his homage! It was at Brienne that he had said to me, thirty-four years before, "I will do these Frenchman all the harm I can." Since then he had certainly changed his mind; but it might be said that fate persisted in forcing the man to realise the design of the boy in spite of himself. No sooner had Napoleon revisited Brienne as a conqueror than he was repulsed and hurried to his fall, which became every moment more certain.

I shall not enter into any details of the campaign of France, because the description of battles forms no part of my plan. Still, I think it indispensable briefly to describe Napoleon's miraculous activity from the time of his leaving Paris to the entrance of the Allies into the capital. Few successful campaigns have enabled our Generals and the French army to reap so much glory as they gained during this great reverse of fortune. For it is possible to triumph without honour, and to fall with glory. The chances of the war were not doubtful, but certainly the numerous hosts of the Allies could never have anticipated so long and brilliant a resistance. The theatre of the military operations soon approached so near to Paris that the general eagerness for news from the army was speedily satisfied, and when any advantage was gained by the Emperor his partisans saw the enemy already repulsed from the French territory. I was not for a moment deceived by these illusions, as I well knew the determination and the resources of the Allied sovereigns. Besides, events were so rapid and various in this war of extermination that the guns of the Invalides announcing a victory were sometimes immediately followed by the distant rolling of artillery, denoting the enemy's near approach to the capital.

The Emperor left Paris on the 25th of January, at which time the Emperors of Russia and Austria and the King of Prussia were assembled at Langres. Napoleon rejoined his Guard at Vitry-le-Francais. On the second day after his departure he drove before him the Prussian army, which he had forced to evacuate St. Dizier. Two days after this the battle of Brienne was fought, and on the 1st of February between 70,000 and 80,000 French and Allied troops stood face to face. On this occasion the commanders on both sides were exposed to personal danger, for Napoleon had a horse killed under him, and a Cossack fell dead by the side of Marshal Blücher. A few days after this battle Napoleon entered Troyes, where he stayed but a short time, and then advanced to Champaubert. At the latter place was fought the battle which hears its name. The Russians were defeated, General Alsufieff was made prisoner, and 2000 men and 30 guns fell into the hands of the French. After this battle the Emperor was under such a delusion as to his situation that while supping with Berthier, Marmont, and his prisoner, General Alsufieff, the Emperor said, "Another such victory as this, gentlemen, and I shall be on the Vistula."

Finding that no one replied, and reading in the countenances of his Marshals that they did not share his hopes, "I see how it is," he added, "every one is growing tired of war; there is no more enthusiasm. The sacred fire is extinct." Then rising from the table, and stepping up to General Drouot, with the marked intention of paying him a compliment which should at the same time convey a censure on the Marshals, "General," said he, patting him on the shoulder, "we only want a hundred men like you, and we should succeed." Drouot replied, with great presence of mind and modesty, "Rather say a hundred thousand, Sire." This anecdote was related to me by the two principal persons who were present on the occasion.

Napoleon soon began to have other subjects of disquietude besides the fate of battles. He was aware that since the beginning of February the Duc d'Angouleme had arrived at St. Jean de Luz, whence he had addressed a proclamation to the French armies in the name of his uncle, Louis XVIII.; and he speedily heard of the Comte d'Artois' arrival at Yesoul, on the 21st of February, which place he did not leave until the 16th of March following.

Meanwhile hostilities were maintained with increased vigor over a vast line of operations. How much useless glory did not our soldiers gain in these conflicts! In spite of prodigies of valour the enemy's masses advanced, and gradually concentrated, so that this war might be compared to the battles of the ravens and the eagle in the Alps. The eagle slays hundreds of his assailants—every blow of his beak is the death of an enemy, but still the vultures return to the charge, and press upon the eagle until they destroy him.

As the month of February drew to its close the Allies were in retreat on several points, but their retreat was not a rout. After experiencing reverses they fell back without disorder, and retired behind the Aube, where they rallied and obtained numerous reinforcements, which daily arrived, and which soon enabled them to resume the offensive.

Still Napoleon continued astonishing Europe, leagued as it was against him. At Craonne, on the 7th of March, he destroyed Blücher's corps in a severe action, but the victory was attended by great loss to the conqueror. Marshal Victor was seriously wounded, as well as Generals Grouchy and La Ferriere.

While Napoleon was resisting the numerous enemies assembled to destroy him it might be said that he was also his own enemy, either from false calculation or from negligence with respect to his illustrious prisoners, who, on his departure from Paris, had not yet been sent to their States. The Pope was then at Fontainebleau, and the Princes of Spain at Valencay. The Pope, however, was the first to be allowed to depart. Surely Bonaparte could never have thought of the service which the Pope might have rendered him at Rome, into which Murat's troops would never have dared to march had his Holiness been present there. With regard to the Spanish Princes Napoleon must have been greatly blinded by confidence in his fortune to have so long believed it possible to retain in France those useless trophies of defeated pretensions. It was, besides, so easy to get rid of the exiles of Valencay by sending them back to the place from whence they had been brought! It was so natural to recall with all speed the troops from the south when our armies in Germany began to be repulsed on the Rhine and even driven into France! With the aid of these veteran troops Napoleon and his genius might have again turned the scale of fortune. But Napoleon reckoned on the nation, and he was wrong, for the nation was tired of him. His cause had ceased to be the cause of France.

The latter days of March were filled up by a series of calamities to Napoleon. On the 23d the rear-guard of the French army suffered considerable loss. To hear of attacks on his rear-guard must indeed have been mortifying to Napoleon, whose advanced guards had been so long accustomed to open the path of victory! Prince Schwartzenberg soon passed the Aube and marched upon Vitry and Chalons. Napoleon, counting on the possibility of defending Paris, threw himself, with the velocity of the eagle, on Schwartzenberg's rear by passing by Doulevant and Bar- sur-Aube. He pushed forward his advanced guards to Chaumont, and there saw the Austrian army make a movement which he took to be a retreat; but it was no such thing. The movement was directed on Paris, while Blücher, who had re-occupied Chalons-sur-Maine, marched to meet Prince Schwartzenberg, and Napoleon, thinking to cut off their retreat, was himself cut off from the possibility of returning to Paris. Everything then depended on the defence of Paris, or, to speak more correctly, it seemed possible, by sacrificing the capital, to prolong for a few days the existence of the phantom of the Empire which was rapidly vanishing. On the 26th was fought the battle of Fere Champenoise, where, valour yielding to numbers, Marshals Marmont and Mortier were obliged to retire upon Sezanne after sustaining considerable loss.

It was on the 26th of March, and I beg the reader to bear this date in mind, that Napoleon suffered a loss which, in the circumstances in which he stood, was irreparable. At the battle of Fere Champenoise the Allies captured a convoy consisting of nearly all the remaining ammunition and stores of the army, a vast quantity of arms, caissons, and equipage of all kinds. The whole became the prey of the Allies, who published a bulletin announcing this important capture. A copy of this order of the day fell into the hands of Marshal Macdonald, who thought that such news ought immediately to be communicated to the Emperor. He therefore repaired himself to the headquarters of Napoleon, who was then preparing to recover Vitre-le-Francais, which was occupied by the Prussians. The Marshal, with the view of dissuading the Emperor from what he considered a vain attempt, presented him with the bulletin.

This was on the morning of the 27th: Napoleon would not believe the news. "No!" said he to the Marshal, "you are deceived, this cannot be true." Then perusing the bulletin with more attention. "Here," said he, "look yourself. This is the 27th, and the bulletin is dated the 29th. You see the thing is impossible. The bulletin is forged!" The Marshal, who had paid more attention to the news than to its date, was astounded. But having afterwards shown the bulletin to Drouot, that General said, "Alas! Marshal, the news is but too true. The error of the date is merely a misprint, the 9 is a 6 inverted!" On what trifles sometimes depend the most important events. An inverted cipher sufficed to flatter Bonaparte's illusion, or at least the illusions which he wished to maintain among his most distinguished lieutenants, and to delay the moment when they should discover that the loss they deplored was too certain. On that very day the Empress left Paris.

CHAPTER XXXIV

1814

The grandees of the Empire and the first subjects of Napoleon were divided into two classes totally distinct from each other. Among these patronised men were many who had been the first patrons of Bonaparte and had favoured his accession to Consular power. This class was composed of his old friends and former companions-in-arms. The others, who may be called the children of the Empire, did not carry back their thoughts to a period which they had not seen. They had never known anything but Napoleon and the Empire, beyond which the sphere of their ideas did not extend, while among Napoleon's old brothers-in-arms it was still remembered that there was once a country, a France, before they had helped to give it a master. To this class of men France was not confined to the narrow circle of the Imperial headquarters, but extended to the Rhine, the Alps, the Pyrenees, and the two oceans.

On the other hand, numbers of ardent and adventurous young men, full of enthusiasm for Bonaparte, had passed from the school to the camp. They were entirely opposed to Napoleon's downfall, because with his power would vanish those dreams of glory and fortune which had captivated their imaginations. These young men, who belonged to the class which I have denominated children of the Empire, were prepared to risk and commit everything to prolong the political life of their Emperor.

The distinction I have drawn between what may be called the men of France and the men of the Empire was not confined to the army, but was equally marked among the high civil functionaries of the State. The old Republicans could not possibly regard Napoleon with the same eyes as those whose elevation dated only from Napoleon; and the members of assemblies anterior to the 18th Brumaire could not entertain the same ideas as those whose notions of national franchises and public rights were derived from their seats as auditors in the Council of State. I know not whether this distinction between the men of two different periods has been before pointed out, but it serves to explain the conduct of many persons of elevated rank during the events of 1814. With regard to myself, convinced as I was of the certainty of Napoleon's fall, I conceived that the first duty of every citizen was claimed by his country; and although I may incur censure, I candidly avow that Napoleon's treatment of me during the last four years of his power was not without some influence on my prompt submission to the Government which succeeded his. I, however, declare that this consideration was not the sole nor the most powerful motive of my conduct. Only those who were in Paris at the period of the capitulation can form an idea of the violence of party feeling which prevailed there both for and against Napoleon, but without the name of the Bourbons ever being pronounced. They were almost unknown to the new generation, forgotten by many of the old, and feared by the conventionalists; at that time they possessed only the frail support of the coteries of the Faubourg St. Germain, and some remains of the emigration. But as it is certain that the emigrants could offer only vain demonstrations and wishes in support of the old family of our Kings, they did little to assist the restoration of the Bourbons. Another thing equally certain is, that they alone, by their follies and absurd pretensions, brought about the return of Bonaparte and the second exile of Louis XVIII. in the following year.

On the 28th of March was convoked an extraordinary Council of Regency, at which Maria Louisa presided. The question discussed was, whether the Empress should remain in Paris or proceed to Blois. Joseph Bonaparte strongly urged her departure, because a letter from the Emperor had directed that in case of Paris being threatened the Empress-Regent and all the Council of Regency should retire to Blois. The Arch-Chancellor and the majority of the Council were of the same opinion, but one of the most influential members of the Council observed to Joseph that the letter referred to had been written under circumstances very different from those then existing, and that it was important the Empress should remain in Paris, where she would, of course, obtain from the Emperor her father and the Allied sovereigns, more advantageous conditions than if she were fifty leagues from Paris. The adoption of this opinion would only have retarded for a few days a change which had become inevitable; nevertheless it might have given rise to great difficulties. It must be admitted that for the interests of Napoleon it was the wisest counsel that could be suggested. However, it was overruled by Joseph's advice.

M. de Talleyrand, as a member of the Council of Regency, also received the order to quit Paris on the 30th of March. At this period I was at his house every day. When I went to him that day I was told he had started. However I went up, and remained some time in his hotel with several of his friends who had met there. We soon saw him return, and for my part I heard with satisfaction that they had not allowed him to pass the barriers. It was said then, and it has been repeated since, that M. de Talleyrand was not a stranger to the gentle violence used towards him. The same day of this visit to M. de Talleyrand I also went to see the Duc de Rovigo (Savary), with the friendly object of getting him to remain, and to profit by his position to prevent disturbances. He refused without hesitating, as he only thought of the Emperor. I found him by his fireside, where there was a large fire, in which he was burning all the papers which might have compromised every one who had served his ministry (Police). I congratulated him sincerely on this loyal occupation: fire alone could purify the mass of filth and denunciations which encumbered the police archives.

On the departure of the Empress many persons expected a popular movement in favour of a change of Government, but the capital remained tranquil. Many of the inhabitants, indeed, thought of defence, not for the sake of preserving Napoleon's government, but merely from that ardour of feeling which belongs to our national character. Strong indignation was excited by the thought of seeing foreigners masters of Paris—a circumstance of which there had been no example since the reign of Charles VII. Meanwhile the critical moment approached. On the 29th of March Marshals Marmont and Mortier fell back to defend the approaches to Paris. During the night the barriers were consigned to the care of the National Guard, and not a foreigner, not even one of their agents, was allowed to enter the capital.

At daybreak on the 30th of March the whole population of Paris was awakened by the report of cannon, and the plain of St. Denis was soon covered with Allied troops, who were debouching upon it from all points. The heroic valour of our troops was unavailing against such a numerical superiority. But the Allies paid dearly for their entrance into the French capital. The National Guard, under the command of Marshal Moncey, and the pupils of the Polytechnic School transformed into artillery men, behaved in a manner worthy of veteran troops. The conduct of Marmont on that day alone would suffice to immortalise him. The corps he commanded was reduced to between 7000 and 8000 infantry and 800 cavalry, with whom, for the space of twelve hours he maintained his ground against an army of 55,000 men, of whom it is said 14,000 were killed, wounded, and taken. Marshal Marmont put himself so forward in the heat of the battle that a dozen of men were killed by the bayonet at his side, and his hat was perforated by a ball. But what was to be done against overwhelming numbers!

In this state of things the Duke of Ragusa made known his situation to Joseph Bonaparte, who authorised him to negotiate.

Joseph's answer is so important in reference to the events which succeeded that I will transcribe it here.

> If the Dukes of Ragusa and Treviso can no longer hold out, they are authorised to negotiate with Prince Schwartzenberg and the Emperor of Russia, who are before them. They will fall back on the Loire.
>
> *(Signed)* JOSEPH
>
> *Montmartre, 30th March 1814, 12 oclock*

It was not until a considerable time after the receipt of this formal authority that Marmont and Mortier ceased to make a vigorous resistance against the Allied army, for the suspension of arms was not agreed upon until four in the afternoon. It was not waited for by Joseph; at a quarter past twelve—that is to say, immediately after he had addressed to Marmont the authority just alluded to Joseph repaired to the Bois de Boulogne to regain the Versailles road, and from thence to proceed to Rambouillet. The precipitate flight of Joseph astonished only those who did not know him. I know for a fact that several officers attached to his staff were much dissatisfied at his alacrity on this occasion.

In these circumstances what was to be done but to save Paris, which there was no possibility of defending two hours longer. Methinks I still see Marmont when, on the evening of the 30th of March, he returned from the field of battle to his hotel in the Rue de Paradis, where I was waiting for him, together with about twenty other persons, among whom were MM. Perregaua and Lafitte. When he entered he was scarcely recognisable: he had a beard of eight days' growth; the greatcoat which covered his uniform was in tatters, and he was blackened with powder from head to foot. We considered what was best to be done, and all insisted on the necessity of signing a capitulation. The Marshal must recollect that the exclamation of every one about him was, "France must be saved." MM. Perregaus and Lafitte delivered their opinions in a very decided way, and it will readily be conceived how great was the influence of two men who were at the head of the financial world. They alleged that the general wish of the Parisians, which nobody had a better opportunity of knowing than themselves, was decidedly averse to a protracted conflict, and that France was tired of the yoke of Bonaparte. This last declaration gave a wider range to the business under consideration. The question was no longer confined to the capitulation of Paris, but a change in the government was thought of, and the name of the Bourbons was pronounced for the first time. I do not recollect which of us it was who, on hearing mention made of the possible recall of the old dynasty, remarked how difficult it would be to bring about a restoration without retrograding to the past. But I think I am perfectly correct in stating that M. Lafitte said, "Gentlemen, we shall have nothing to fear if we have a good constitution which will guarantee the rights of all." The majority of the meeting concurred in this wise opinion, which was not without its influence on Marshal Marmont.

During this painful meeting an unexpected incident occurred. One of the Emperor's aides de camp arrived at Marmont's. Napoleon, being informed of the advance of the Allies on Paris, had marched with the utmost speed from the banks of the Marne on the road of Fontainebleau. In the evening he was in person at Froidmanteau, whence he despatched his envoy to Marshal Marmont. From the language of the aide de camp it was easy to perceive that the state of opinion at the Imperial headquarters was very different from that which prevailed among the population of Paris. The officer expressed indignation at the very idea of capitulating, and he announced with inconceivable confidence the approaching arrival of Napoleon in Paris, which he yet hoped to save from the occupation of the enemy. The officer informed us that Napoleon trusted to the people rising in spite of the capitulation, and that they would unpave the streets to stone the Allies on their entrance. I ventured to dissent from this absurd idea of defence, and I observed that it was madness to suppose that Paris could resist the numerous troops who were ready to enter on the following day; that the suspension of arms had been consented to by the Allies only to afford time for drawing up a more regular capitulation, and that the armistice could not be broken without trampling on all the laws of honour. I added that the thoughts of the people were directed towards a better future; that the French were tired of a despotic Government and of the distress to which continual war had reduced trade and industry; "for," said I, "when a nation is sunk to such a state of misery its hopes can only be directed towards the future; it is natural they should be so directed, even without reflection." Most of the individuals present concurred in my opinion, and the decision of the meeting was unanimous. Marshal Marmont has since said to me, "I have been blamed, my dear Bourrienne: but you were with me on the 30th of March. You were a witness to the wishes expressed by a portion of the principal inhabitants of Paris. I acted as I was urged to do only because I considered the meeting to be composed of men entirely disinterested, and who had nothing to expect from the return of the Bourbons."

Such is a correct statement of the facts which some persons have perverted with the view of enhancing Napoleon's glory. With respect to those versions which differ from mine I have only one comment to offer, which is, that I saw and heard what I describe.

The day after the capitulation of Paris—Marmont went in the evening to see the Emperor at Fontainebleau. He supped with him. Napoleon praised his defence of Paris . . . After supper the Marshal rejoined his corps at Essonne, and six hours after the Emperor arrived there to visit the lines. On leaving Paris Marmont had left Colonels Fabvier and Dent's to direct the execution of the capitulation. These officers joined the Emperor and the Marshal as they were proceeding up the banks of the river at Essonne. They did not disguise the effect which the entrance of the Allies had produced in Paris. At this intelligence the Emperor was deeply mortified, and he returned immediately to Fontainebleau, leaving the Marshal at Essonne.

At daybreak on the 31st of March Paris presented a novel and curious spectacle. No sooner had the French troops evacuated the capital than the principal streets resounded with cries of "Down with Bonaparte!"— "No conscription!"—"No consolidated duties (droits reunis)!" With these cries were mingled that of "The Bourbons for ever!" but this latter cry was not repeated so frequently as the others: in general I remarked that the people gaped and listened with a sort of indifference. As I had taken a very active part in all that had happened during some preceding days I was particularly curious to study what might be called the physiognomy of Paris. This was the second opportunity which had offered itself for such a study, and I now saw the people applaud the fall of the man whom they had received with enthusiasm after the 18th Brumaire. The reason was, that liberty was then hoped for, as it was hoped for in 1814. I went out early in the morning to see the numerous groups of people who had assembled in the streets. I saw women tearing their handkerchiefs and distributing the fragments as the emblems of the revived lily. That same morning I met on the Boulevards, and some hours afterwards on the Place Louis XV., a party of gentlemen who paraded the streets of the capital proclaiming the restoration of the Bourbons and shouting, "Vive le Roi!" and "Vive Louis XVIII!" At their head I recognised MM. Sosthenes de la Rochefoucauld, Comte de Froissard, the Duc de Luxembourg, the Duc de Crussol, Seymour, etc. The cavalcade distributed white cockades in passing along, and was speedily joined by a numerous crowd, who repaired to the Place Vendome. The scene that was acted there is well known, and the enthusiasm of popular joy could scarcely excuse the fury that was directed against the effigy of the man whose misfortunes, whether merited or not, should have protected him from such outrages. These excesses served, perhaps more than is generally supposed, to favour the plans of the leaders of the Royalist party, to whom M. Nesselrode had declared that before he would pledge himself to further their views he must have proofs that they were seconded by the population of Paris.

I was afterwards informed by an eye-witness of what took place on the evening of the 31st of March in one of the principal meetings of the Royalists, which was held in the hotel of the Comte de Morfontaine, who acted as president on the occasion. Amidst a chaos of abortive propositions and contradictory motions M. Sosthenes de la Rochefoucauld proposed that a deputation should be immediately sent to the Emperor Alexander to express to him the wish of the meeting. This motion was immediately approved, and the mover was chosen to head the deputation. On leaving the hotel the deputation met M. de Chateaubriand, who had that very day been, as it were, the precursor of the restoration, by publishing his admirable manifesto, entitled "Bonaparte and the Bourbons." He was invited to join the deputation; but nothing could overcome his diffidence and induce him to speak. On arriving at the hotel in the Rue St. Florentin the deputation was introduced to Count Nesselrode, to whom M. Sosthenes de la Rochefoucauld briefly explained its object; he spoke of the wishes of the meeting and of the manifest desire of Paris and of France. He represented the restoration of the Bourbons as the only means of securing the peace of Europe; and observed, in conclusion, that as the exertions of the day must have been very fatiguing to the Emperor, the deputation would not solicit the favour of being introduced to him, but would confidently rely on the good faith of his Imperial Majesty. "I have just left the Emperor," replied M. Nesselrode, "and can pledge myself for his intentions. Return to the meeting and announce to the French people that in compliance with their wishes his Imperial Majesty will use all his influence to restore the crown to the legitimate monarch: his Majesty Louis XVIII. shall reascend the throne of France." With this gratifying intelligence the deputation returned to the meeting in the Rue d'Anjou.

There is no question that great enthusiasm was displayed on the entrance of the Allies into Paris. It may be praised or blamed, but the fact cannot be denied. I closely watched all that was passing, and I observed the expression of a sentiment which I had long anticipated when, after his alliance with the daughter of the Caesars, the ambition of Bonaparte increased in proportion as it was gratified: I clearly foresaw Napoleon's fall. Whoever watched the course of events during the last four years of the Empire must have observed, as I did, that from the date of Napoleon's marriage with Maria Louisa the form of the French Government became daily more and more tyrannical and oppressive. The intolerable height which this evil had attained is evident from the circumstance that at the end of 1813 the Legislative Body, throwing aside the mute character which it had hitherto maintained, presumed to give a lecture to him who had never before received a lecture from any one. On the 31st of March it was recollected what had been the conduct of Bonaparte on the occasion alluded to, and those of the deputies who remained in Paris related how the gendarmes had opposed their entrance into the hall of the Assembly. All this contributed wonderfully to irritate the public mind against Napoleon. He had become master of France by the sword, and the sword being sheathed, his power was at an end, for no popular institution identified with the nation the new dynasty which he hoped to found. The nation admired but did not love Napoleon, for it is impossible to love what is feared, and he had done nothing to claim the affections of France.

I was present at all the meetings and conferences which were held at M de Talleyrand's hotel, where the Emperor Alexander had taken up his residence. Of all the persons present at these meetings M. de Talleyrand was most disposed to retain Napoleon at the head of the Government, with restrictions on the exercise of his power. In the existing state of things it was only possible to choose one of three courses: first, to make peace with Napoleon, with the adoption of proper securities against him; second, to establish a Regency; and third, to recall the Bourbons.

On the 13th of March I witnessed the entrance of the Allied sovereigns into Paris, and after the procession had passed the new street of the Luxembourg I repaired straight to M. de Talleyrand's hotel, which I reached before the Emperor Alexander, who arrived at a quarter-past one. When his Imperial Majesty entered M. de Talleyrand's drawing-room most of the persons assembled, and particularly the Abbe de Pradt, the Abbe de Montesquieu, and General Dessolles, urgently demanded the restoration of the Bourbons. The Emperor did not come to any immediate decision. Drawing me into the embrasure of a window, which looked upon the street, he made some observations which enabled me to guess what would be his determination. "M. de Bourrienne," said he, "you have been the friend of Napoleon, and so have I. I was his sincere friend; but there is no possibility of remaining at peace with a man of such bad faith." These last words opened my eyes; and when the different propositions which were made came under discussion I saw plainly that Bonaparte, in making himself Emperor, had made up the bed for the Bourbons.

A discussion ensued on the three possible measures which I have above mentioned, and which were proposed by the Emperor Alexander himself. I thought, if I may so express myself, that his Majesty was playing a part, when, pretending to doubt the possibility of recalling the Bourbons, which he wished above all things, he asked M. de Talleyrand what means he proposed to employ for the attainment of that object? Besides the French, there were present at this meeting the Emperor Alexander, the King of Prussia, Prince Schwartzenberg, M. Nesselrode, M. Pozzo-di-Borgo, and Prince Liechtenstein. During the discussion Alexander walked about with some appearance of agitation. "Gentlemen," said, he, addressing us in an elevated tone of voice, "you know that it was not I who commenced the war; you know that Napoleon came to attack me in my dominions. But we are not drawn here by the thirst of conquest or the desire of revenge. You have seen the precautions I have taken to preserve your capital, the wonder of the arts, from the horrors of pillage, to which the chances of war would have consigned it. Neither my Allies nor myself are engaged in a war of reprisals; and I should be inconsolable if any violence were committed on your magnificent city. We are not waging war against France, but against Napoleon, and the enemies of French liberty. William, and you, Prince" (here the Emperor turned towards the King of Prussia and Prince Schwartzenberg, who represented the Emperor of Austria), "you can both bear testimony that the sentiments I express are yours." Both bowed assent to this observation of Alexander, which his Majesty several times repeated in different words. He insisted that France should be perfectly free; and declared that as soon as the wishes of the country were understood, he and his Allies would support them, without seeking to favour any particular government.

The Abbe de Pradt then declared, in a tone of conviction, that we were all Royalists, and that the sentiments of France concurred with ours. The Emperor Alexander, adverting to the different governments which might be suitable to France, spoke of the maintenance of Bonaparte on the throne, the establishment of a Regency, the choice of Bernadotte, and the recall of the Bourbons. M. de Talleyrand next spoke, and I well remember his saying to the Emperor of Russia, "Sire, only one of two things is possible. We must either have Bonaparte or Louis XVIII. Bonaparte, if you can support him; but you cannot, for you are not alone . . . . . . We will not have another soldier in his stead. If we want a soldier, we will keep the one we have; he is the first in the world. After him any other who may be proposed would not have ten men to support him. I say again, Sire, either Bonaparte or Louis XVIII. Anything else is an intrigue." These remarkable words of the Prince de Benevento produced on the mind of Alexander all the effect we could hope for. Thus the question was simplified, being reduced now to only two alternatives; and as it was evident that Alexander would have nothing to do with either Napoleon or his family, it was reduced to the single proposition of the restoration of the Bourbons.

On being pressed by us all, with the exception of M. de Talleyrand, who still wished to leave the question undecided between Bonaparte and Louis XVIII., Alexander at length declared that he would no longer treat with Napoleon. When it was represented to him that that declaration referred only to Napoleon personally, and did not extend to his family, he added, "Nor with any member of his family." Thus as early as the 31st of March the restoration of the Bourbons might be considered as decided.

I cannot omit mentioning the hurry with which Laborie, whom M. de Talleyrand appointed Secretary to the Provisional Government, rushed out of the apartment as soon as he got possession of the Emperor Alexander's declaration. He got it printed with such expedition that in the space of an hour it was posted on all the walls in Paris; and it certainly produced an extraordinary effect. As yet nothing warranted a doubt that Alexander would not abide by his word. The treaty of Paris could not be anticipated; and there was reason to believe that France, with a new Government, would obtain more advantageous conditions than if the Allies had, treated with Napoleon. But this illusion speedily vanished.

On the evening of the 31st of March I returned to M. de Talleyrand's. I again saw the Emperor Alexander, who, stepping up to me, said, "M. de Bourrienne you must take the superintendence of the Post-office department." I could not decline this precise invitation on the part of the Czar; and besides, Lavalette having departed on the preceding day, the business would have been for a time suspended; a circumstance which would have been extremely prejudicial to the restoration which we wished to favour.

I went at once to the hotel in the Rue J. J. Rousseau, where, indeed, I found that not only was there no order to send out the post next day, but that it had been even countermanded.

I went that night to the administrators, who yielded to my requests and, seconded by them, next morning I got all the clerks to be at their post. I reorganised the service, and the post went out on the 1st of April as usual. Such are my remembrances of the 31st of March.

A Provisional Government was established, of which M. de Talleyrand was appointed President. The other members were General Beurnonville, Comte Francois de Jaucourt, the Duc Dalberg, who had married one of Maria Louisa's ladies of honour, and the Abby de Montesquieu. The place of Chancellor of the Legion of Honour was given to the Abbe de Pradt. Thus there were two abbes among the members of the Provisional Government, and by a singular chance they happened to be the same who had officiated at the mass which was performed in the Champ de Mars on the day of the first federation.

Those who were dissatisfied with the events of the 31st of March now saw no hope but in the possibility that the Emperor of Austria would separate from his Allies, or at least not make common cause with them in favour of the re-establishment of the Bourbons. But that monarch had been brought up in the old policy of his family, and was imbued with the traditional principles of his Cabinet. I know for a fact that the sentiments and intentions of the Emperor of Austria perfectly coincided with those of his Allies. Anxious to ascertain the truth on this subject, I ventured, when in conversation with the Emperor Alexander, to hint at the reports I had heard relative to the cause of the Emperor of Austria's absence. I do not recollect the precise words of his Majesty's answer, but it enabled me to infer with certainty that Francis II. was in no way averse to the overthrow of his son-in-law, and that his absence from the scene of the discussions was only occasioned by a feeling of delicacy natural enough in his situation.

Caulaincourt, who was sent by Napoleon to the headquarters of the Emperor Alexander, arrived there on the night of the 30th of March. He, however, did not obtain an interview with the Czar until after his Majesty had received the Municipal Council of Paris, at the head of which was M. de Chabrol. At first Alexander appeared somewhat surprised to see the Municipal Council, which he did not receive exactly in the way that was expected; but this coldness was merely momentary, and he afterwards addressed the Council in a very gracious way, though he dropped no hint of his ulterior intentions.

Alexander, who entertained a personal regard for Caulaincourt, received him kindly in his own character, but not as the envoy of Napoleon. "You have come too late," said the Czar. "It is all over. I can say nothing to you at present. Go to Paris, and I will see you there." These words perfectly enlightened Caulaincourt as to the result of his mission. His next interview with the Emperor Alexander at M. de Talleyrand's did not take place until after the declaration noticed in my last chapter. The conversation they had together remained a secret, for neither Alexander nor the Duke of Vicenza mentioned it; but there was reason to infer, from some words which fell from the Emperor Alexander, that he had received Caulaincourt rather as a private individual than as the ambassador of Napoleon, whose power, indeed, he could not recognise after his declaration. The Provisional Government was not entirely pleased with Caulaincourt's presence in Paris, and a representation was made to the Russian Emperor on the subject. Alexander concurred in the opinion of the Provisional Government, which was expressed through the medium of the Abbe de Pradt. M. de Caulaincourt, therefore, at the wish of the Czar, returned to the Emperor, then at Fontainebleau.

CHAPTER XXXV

1814

On the morning of the 30th of March, while the battle before the walls of Paris was at its height, Bonaparte was still at Troyes. He quitted that town at ten o'clock, accompanied only by Bertrand, Caulaincourt, two aides de camp, and two orderly officers. He was not more than two hours in traveling the first ten leagues, and he and his slender escort performed the journey without changing horses, and without even alighting. They arrived at Sens at one o'clock in the afternoon. Everything was in such confusion that it was impossible to prepare a suitable mode of conveyance for the Emperor. He was therefore obliged to content himself with a wretched cariole, and in this equipage, about four in the morning, he reached Froidmanteau, about four leagues from Paris. It was there that the Emperor received from General Belliard, who arrived at the head of a column of artillery, the first intelligence of the battle of Paris. He heard the news with an air of composure, which was probably affected to avoid discouraging those about him. He walked for about a quarter of an hour on the high road, and it was after that promenade that he sent Caulaincourt to Paris. Napoleon afterwards went to the house of the postmaster, where he ordered his maps to be brought to him, and, according to custom, marked the different positions of the enemy's troops with pine, the heads of which were touched with wax of different colours. After this description of work, which Napoleon did every day, or sometimes several times a day, he repaired to Fontainebleau, where he arrived at six in the morning. He did not order the great apartments of the castle to be opened, but went up to his favourite little apartment, where he shut himself up, and remained alone during the whole of the 31st of March.

In the evening the Emperor sent for the Duke of Ragusa, who had just arrived at Essonne with his troops. The Duke reached Fontainebleau between three and four o'clock on the morning of the 1st of April. Napoleon then received a detailed account of the events of the 30th from Marmont, on whose gallant conduct before Paris he bestowed much praise.

All was gloom and melancholy at Fontainebleau, yet the Emperor still retained his authority, and I have been informed that he deliberated for some time as to whether he should retire behind the Loire, or immediately hazard a bold stroke upon Paris, which would have been much more to his taste than to resign himself to the chances which an uncertain temporising might bring about. This latter thought pleased him; and he was seriously considering his plan of attack when the news of the 31st, and the unsuccessful issue of Caulaincourt's mission, gave him to understand that his situation was more desperate than he had hitherto imagined. Meanwhile the heads of his columns, which the Emperor had left at Troves, arrived on the 1st of April at Fontainebleau, the troops having marched fifty leagues in less than three days, one of the most rapid marches ever performed. On the 2d of April Napoleon communicated the events of Paris to the Generals who were about him, recommending them to conceal the news lest it should dispirit the troops, upon whom he yet relied. That day, during an inspection of the troops, which took place in the court of the Palace, Bonaparte assembled the officers of his Guard, and harangued them as follows:

> Soldiers! the enemy has stolen three marches upon us, and has made himself master of Paris. We must drive him thence. Frenchmen, unworthy of the name, emigrants whom we have pardoned, have mounted the white cockade, and joined the enemy. The wretches shall receive the reward due to this new crime. Let us swear to conquer or die, and to enforce respect to the tri-coloured cockade, which has for twenty years accompanied us on the path of glory and honour.

He also endeavoured to induce the Generals to second his mad designs upon Paris, by making them believe that he had made sincere efforts to conclude peace. He assured them that he had expressed to the Emperor Alexander his willingness to purchase it by sacrifices; that he had consented to resign even the conquests made during the Revolution, and to confine himself within the old limits of France. "Alexander," added Napoleon, "refused; and, not content with that refusal, he has leagued himself with a party of emigrants, whom, perhaps, I was wrong in pardoning for having borne arms against France. Through their perfidious insinuations Alexander has permitted the white cockade to be mounted on the capital. We will maintain ours, and in a few days we will march upon Paris. I rely on you."

When the boundless attachment of the Guards to the Emperor is considered it cannot appear surprising that these last words, uttered in an impressive tone, should have produced a feeling of enthusiasm, almost electrical, in all to whom they were addressed. The old companions of the glory of their chief exclaimed with one voice, "Paris! Paris!" But, fortunately, during the night, the Generals having deliberated with each other saw the frightful abyss into which they were about to precipitate France. They therefore resolved to intimate in discreet terms to the Emperor that they would not expose Paris to destruction, so that on the 3d of April, prudent ideas succeeded the inconsiderate enthusiasm of the preceding day.

The wreck of the army assembled at Fontainebleau, which was the remnant of 1,000,000 of troops levied during fifteen months, consisted only of the corps of the Duke of Reggio (Oudinot), Ney, Macdonald, and General Gerard, which 'altogether did not amount to 25,000 men, and which, joined to the remaining 7000 of the Guard, did not leave the Emperor a disposable force of more than 32,000 men. Nothing but madness or despair could have suggested the thought of subduing, with such scanty resources, the foreign masses which occupied and surrounded Paris.

On the 2d of April the Senate published a 'Senatus-consulte', declaring that Napoleon had forfeited the throne, and abolishing the right of succession, which had been established in favour of his family. Furnished with this set, and without awaiting the concurrence of the Legislative Body, which was given next day, the Provisional Government published an address to the French armies. In this address the troops were informed that they were no longer the soldiers of Napoleon, and that the Senate released them from their oaths. These documents were widely circulated at the time, and inserted in all the public journals.

The address of the Senate was sent round to the Marshals, and was of course first delivered to those who were nearest the capital; of this latter number was Marmont, whose allegiance to the Emperor, as we have already seen, yielded only to the sacred interests of his country. Montessuis was directed by the Provisional Government to convey the address to Marmont, and to use such arguments as were calculated to strengthen those sentiments which had triumphed over his dearest personal affections. I gave Montessuis a letter to Marmont, in which I said:

"My Dear Friend—An old acquaintance of mine will convey to you the remembrances of our friendship. He will, I trust, influence your resolution: a single word will suffice to induce you to sacrifice all for the happiness of your country. To secure that object you, who are so good a Frenchman and so loyal a knight, will not fear either dangers or obstacles. Your friends expect you, long for you, and I trust will soon embrace you."

Montessuis also took one from General Dessolles, whom the Provisional Government had appointed Governor of the National Guard in the room of Marshal Moncey, who had left Paris on the occupation of the Allies. General Dessolles and I did not communicate to each other our correspondence, but when I afterwards saw the letter of Dessolles I could not help remarking the coincidence of our appeal to Marmont's patriotism. Prince Schwartzenberg also wrote to Marmont to induce him to espouse a clause which had now become the cause of France. To the Prince's letter Marmont replied, that he was disposed to concur in the union of the army and the people, which would avert all chance of civil war, and stop the effusion of French blood; and that he was ready with his troops to quit the army of the Emperor Napoleon on the condition that his troops might retire with the honours of war, and that the safety and liberty of the Emperor were guaranteed by the Allies.

After Prince Schwartzenberg acceded to these conditions Marmont was placed in circumstances which obliged him to request that he might be released from his promise.

I happened to learn the manner in which Marshal Macdonald was informed of the taking of Paris. He had been two days without any intelligence from the Emperor, when he received an order in the handwriting of Berthier, couched in the following terms: "The Emperor desires that you halt wherever you may receive this order." After Berthier's signature the following words were added as a postscript: "You, of course, know that the enemy is in possession of Paris." When the Emperor thus announced, with apparent negligence, an event which totally changed the face of affairs, I am convinced his object was to make the Marshal believe that he looked upon, that event as less important than it really was. However, this object was not attained, for I recollect having heard Macdonald say that Berthier's singular postscript, and the tone of indifference in which it was expressed, filled him with mingled surprise and alarm. Marshal Macdonald then commanded the rear-guard of the army which occupied the environs of Montereau. Six hours after the receipt of the order here referred to Macdonald received a second order directing him to put his troops in motion, and he learned the Emperor's intention of marching on Paris with all his remaining force.

On receiving the Emperor's second order Macdonald left his corps at Montereau and repaired in haste to Fontainebleau. When he arrived there the Emperor had already intimated to the Generals commanding divisions in the corps assembled at Fontainebleau his design of marching on Paris. Alarmed at this determination the Generals, most of whom had left in the capital their wives, children, and friends, requested that Macdonald would go with them to wait upon Napoleon and endeavour to dissuade him from his intention. "Gentlemen," said the Marshal, "in the Emperor's present situation such a proceeding may displease him. It must be managed cautiously. Leave it to me, gentlemen, I will go to the chateau."

Marshal Macdonald accordingly went to the Palace of Fontainebleau, where the following conversation ensued between him and the Emperor, and I beg the reader to bear in mind that it was related to me by the Marshal himself. As soon as he entered the apartment in which Napoleon was the latter stepped up to him and said, "Well, how are things going on?"— "Very badly, Sire."—"How? . . . badly! . . . What then are the feelings of your army?"—"My army, Sire, is entirely discouraged . . . appalled by the fate of Paris."—"Will not your troops join me in an advance on Paris?"—"Sire, do not think of such a thing. If I were to give such an order to my troops I should run the risk of being disobeyed."—"But what is to be done? I cannot remain as I am; I have yet resources and partisans. It is said that the Allies will no longer treat with me. Well! no matter. I will march on Paris. I will be revenged on the inconstancy of the Parisians and the baseness of the Senate. Woe to the members of the Government they have patched up for the return of their Bourbons; that is what they are looking forward to. But to-morrow I shall place myself at the head of my Guards, and to-morrow we shall be in the Tuileries."

The Marshal listened in silence, and when at length Napoleon became somewhat calm he observed, "Sire, it appears, then, that you are not aware of what has taken place in Paris—of the establishment of a Provisional Government, and—"—"I know it all: and what then?"—"Sire," added the Marshal, presenting a paper to Napoleon, "here is something which will tell you more than I can." Macdonald then presented to him a letter from General Beurnonville, announcing the forfeiture of the Emperor pronounced by the Senate, and the determination of the Allied powers not to treat with Napoleon, or any member of his family. "Marshal," said the Emperor, before he opened the letter, "may this be read aloud?"—"Certainly, Sire." The letter was then handed to Barre, who read it. An individual who was present on the occasion described to me the impression which the reading of the letter produced on Napoleon. His countenance exhibited that violent contraction of the features which I have often remarked when his mind was disturbed. However, he did not lose his self-command, which indeed never forsook him when policy or vanity required that he should retain it; and when the reading of Beurnonville's letter was ended he affected to persist in his intention of marching on Paris. "Sire," exclaimed Macdonald, "that plan must be renounced. Not a sword would be unsheathed to second you in such an enterprise." After this conversation between the Emperor and Macdonald the question of the abdication began to be seriously thought of. Caulaincourt had already hinted to Napoleon that in case of his abdicating personally there was a possibility of inducing the Allies to agree to a Council of Regency. Napoleon then determined to sign the act of abdication, which he himself drew up in the following terms:—

> The Allied powers having declared that the Emperor Napoleon is the only obstacle to the re-establishment of peace in Europe, the Emperor Napoleon, faithful to his oath, declares that he is ready to descend from the throne, to leave France, and even to lay down his life for the welfare of the country, which is inseparable from the rights of his son, those of the Regency of the Empress, and the maintenance of the laws of the Empire.
>
> Given at *our Palace of Fontainebleau, 2d April 1814.*
>
> (*Signed*) NAPOLEON.

After having written this act the Emperor presented it to the Marshals, saying, "Here, gentlemen! are you satisfied?"

This abdication of Napoleon was certainly very useless, but in case of anything occurring to render it a matter of importance the act might have proved entirely illusory. Its meaning might appear unequivocal to the generality of people, but not to me, who was so well initiated in the cunning to which Napoleon could resort when it suited his purpose. It is necessary to observe that Napoleon does not say that "he descends from the throne," but that "he is ready to descend from the throne." This was a subterfuge, by the aid of which he intended to open new negotiations respecting the form and conditions of the Regency of his son, in case of the Allied sovereigns acceding to that proposition. This would have afforded the means of gaining time.

He had not yet resigned all hope, and therefore he joyfully received a piece of intelligence communicated to him by General Allix. The General informed the Emperor that he had met an Austrian officer who was sent by Francis II. to Prince Schwartzenberg, and who positively assured him that all which had taken place in Paris was contrary to the wish of the Emperor of Austria. That this may have been the opinion of the officer is possible, and even probable. But it is certain from the issue of a mission of the Duc de Cadore (Champagny), of which I shall presently speak, that the officer expressed merely his own personal opinion. However, as soon as General Allix had communicated this good news, as he termed it, to Napoleon, the latter exclaimed to the persons who were about him, "I told you so, gentlemen. Francis II. cannot carry his enmity so far as to dethrone his daughter. Vicenza, go and desire the Marshals to return my act of abdication. I will send a courier to the Emperor of Austria."

Thus Bonaparte in his shipwreck looked round for a saving plank, and tried to nurse himself in illusions. The Duke of Vicenza went to Marshals Ney and Macdonald, whom he found just stepping into a carriage to proceed to Paris. Both positively refused to return the act to Caulaincourt, saying, "We are sure of the concurrence of the Emperor of Austria, and we take everything upon ourselves." The result proved that they were better informed than General Allix.

During the conversation with Marshal Macdonald which has just been described the Emperor was seated. When he came to the resolution of signing the abdication he arose and walked once or twice up and down his cabinet. After he had written and signed the act he said, "Gentlemen, the interests of my son, the interests of the army, and above all, the interests of France, must be defended. I therefore appoint as my commissioners to the Allied powers the Duke of Vicenza, the Prince of the Moskowa, and the Duke of Ragusa. . . . Are you satisfied?" added he, after a pause. "I think these interests are consigned to good hands." All present answered, as with one voice. "Yes, Sire." But no sooner was this answer pronounced than the Emperor threw himself upon a small yellow sofa, which stood near the window, and striking his thigh with his hand with a sort of convulsive motion, he exclaimed, "No, gentlemen: I will have no Regency! With my Guards and Marmont's corps I shall be in Paris to-morrow." Ney and Macdonald vainly endeavoured to undeceive him respecting this impracticable design. He rose with marked ill-humour, and rubbing his head, as he was in the habit of doing when agitated, he said in a loud and authoritative tone, "Retire."

The Marshals withdrew, and Napoleon was left alone with Caulaincourt. He told the latter that what had most displeased him in the proceedings which had just taken place was the reading of Beurnonville's letter. "Sire," observed the Duke of Vicenza, "it was by your order that the letter was read."—"That is true. . . . But why was it not addressed directly to me by Macdonald?"—"Sire, the letter was at first addressed to Marshal Macdonald, but the aide de camp who was the bearer of it had orders to communicate its contents to Marmont on passing through Essonne, because Beurnonville did not precisely know where Macdonald would be found." After this brief explanation the Emperor appeared satisfied, and he said to Caulaincourt, "Vicenza, call back Macdonald."

The Duke of Vicenza hastened after the Marshal, whom he found at the end of the gallery of the Palace, and he brought him back to the Emperor. When Macdonald returned to the cabinet the Emperor's warmth had entirely subsided, and he said to him with great composure, "Well, Duke of Tarantum, do you think that the Regency is the only possible thing?"— "Yes, Sire."—"Then I wish you to go with Ney to the Emperor Alexander, instead of Marmont; it is better that he should remain with his corps, to which his presence is indispensable. You will therefore go with Ney. I rely on you. I hope you have entirely forgotten all that has separated us for so long a time."—"Yes, Sire, I have not thought of it since 1809."—"I am glad of it, Marshal, and I must acknowledge to you that I was in the wrong." While speaking to the Marshal the Emperor manifested unusual emotion. He approached him and pressed his hand in the most affectionate way.

The Emperor's three Commissioners—that is to say, Marshals Macdonald and Ney and the Duke of Vicenza had informed Marmont that they would dine with him as they passed through Essonne, and would acquaint him with all that had happened at Fontainebleau. On their arrival at Essonne the three Imperial Commissioners explained to the Duc of Ragusa the object of their mission, and persuaded him to accompany them to the Emperor Alexander. This obliged the Marshal to inform them how he was situated. The negotiations which Marmont had opened and almost concluded with Prince Schwartzenberg were rendered void by the mission which he had joined, and which it was necessary he should himself explain to the Commander of the Austrian army. The three Marshals and the Duke of Vicenza repaired to Petit Bourg, the headquarters of Prince Schwartzenberg, and there the Prince released Marmont from the promise he had given.

CHAPTER XXXVI

1814

After my nomination as Director-General of the Post office the business of that department proceeded as regularly as before. Having learned that a great many intercepted letters had been thrown aside I sent, on the 4th of April, an advertisement to the 'Moniteur', stating that the letters to and from England or other foreign countries which had been lying at the Post-office for more than three years would be forwarded to their respective addresses. This produced to the Post-office a receipt of nearly 300,000 francs, a fact which may afford an idea of the enormous number of intercepted letters.

On the night after the publication of the advertisement I was awakened by an express from the Provisional Government, by which I was requested to proceed with all possible haste to M. de Talleyrand's hotel. I rose, and I set off immediately, and I got there some minutes before the arrival of the Emperor's Commissioners. I went up to the salon on the first floor, which was one of the suite of apartments occupied by the Emperor Alexander. The Marshals retired to confer with the monarch, and it would be difficult to describe the anxiety—or, I may rather say, consternation—which, during their absence, prevailed among some of the members of the Provisional Government and other persons assembled in the salon where I was.

While the Marshals were with Alexander, I learned that they had previously conversed with M. de Talleyrand, who observed to them, "If you succeed in your designs you will compromise all who have met in this hotel since the 1st of April, and the number is not small. For my part, take no account of me, I am willing to be compromised." I had passed the evening of this day with M. de Talleyrand, who then observed to the Emperor Alexander in my presence, "Will you support Bonaparte? No, you neither can nor will. I have already had the honour to tell your Majesty that we can have no choice but between Bonaparte and Louis XVIII.; anything else would be an intrigue, and no intrigue can have power to support him who may be its object. Bernadotte, Eugène, the Regency, all those propositions result from intrigues. In present circumstances nothing but a new principle is sufficiently strong to establish the new order of things which must be adopted. Louis XVIII. is a principle."

None of the members of the Provisional Government were present at this conference, for no one was willing to appear to influence in any way the determination of the chief of the coalition upon the subject of this important mission. General Dessolles alone, in quality of commander of the National Guard of Paris, was requested to be present. At length the Marshals entered the salon where we were, and their appearance created a sensation which it is impossible to describe; but the expression of dissatisfaction which we thought we remarked in their countenances restored the hopes of those who for some hours had been a prey to apprehensions. Macdonald, with his head elevated, and evidently under the influence of strong irritation, approached Beurnonville, and thus addressed him, in answer to a question which the latter had put to him. "Speak not to me, sir; I have nothing to say to you. You have made me forget a friendship of thirty years!" Then turning to Dupont, "As for you, sir," he continued in the same tone, "your conduct towards the Emperor is not generous. I confess that he has treated you with severity, perhaps he may even have been unjust to you with respect to the affair of Baylen, but how long has it been the practice to avenge a personal wrong at the expense of one's country?"

These remarks were made with such warmth, and in so elevated a tone of voice, that Caulaincourt thought it necessary to interfere, and said, "Do not forget, gentlemen, that this is the residence of the Emperor of Russia." At this moment M. de Talleyrand returned from the interview with the Emperor which he had had after the departure of the Marshals, and approaching the group formed round Macdonald, "Gentlemen," said he, "if you wish to dispute and discuss, step down to my apartments."— "That would be useless," replied Macdonald; "my comrades and I do not acknowledge the Provisional Government." The three Marshals, Ney, Macdonald, and Marmont, then immediately retired with Caulaincourt, and went to Ney's hotel, there to await the answer which the Emperor Alexander had promised to give them after consulting the King of Prussia.

Such was this night-scene; which possessed more dramatic effect than many which are performed on the stage. In it all was real: on its denouement depended the political state of France, and the existence of all those who had already declared themselves in favour of the Bourbons. It is a remarkable fact, and one which affords a striking lesson to men who are tempted to sacrifice themselves for any political cause, that most of those who then demanded the restoration of the Bourbons at the peril of their lives have successively fallen into disgrace.

When the Marshals and Caulaincourt had retired we were all anxious to know what had passed between them and the Emperor of Russia. I learned from Dessolles, who, as I have stated, was present at the conference in his rank of commander of the National Guard of Paris, that the Marshals were unanimous in urging Alexander to accede to a Regency. Macdonald especially supported that proposition with much warmth; and among the observations he made I recollect Dessolles mentioned the following:— "I am not authorised to treat in any way for the fate reserved for the Emperor. We have full powers to treat for the Regency, the army, and France; but the Emperor has positively forbidden us to specify anything personally regarding himself." Alexander merely replied, "That does not astonish me." The Marshals then, resuming the conversation, dwelt much on the respect which was due to the military glory of France. They strongly manifested their disinclination to abandon the family of a man who had so often led them to victory; and lastly, they reminded the Emperor Alexander of his own declaration, in which he proclaimed, in his own name as well as on the part of his Allies, that it was not their intention to impose on France any government whatever.

Dessolles, who had all along declared himself in favour of the Bourbons, in his turn entered into the discussion with as much warmth as the partisans of the Regency. He represented to Alexander how many persons would be compromised for merely having acted or declared their opinions behind the shield of his promises. He repeated what Alexander had already been told, that the Regency would, in fact, be nothing but Bonaparte in disguise. However, Dessolles acknowledged that such was the effect of Marshal Macdonald's powerful and persuasive eloquence that Alexander seemed to waver; and, unwilling to give the Marshals a positive refusal, he had recourse to a subterfuge, by which he would be enabled to execute the design he had irrevocably formed without seeming to take on himself alone the responsibility of a change of government. Dessolles accordingly informed us that Alexander at last gave the following answer to the Marshals: "Gentlemen, I am not alone; in an affair of such importance I must consult the King of Prussia, for I have promised to do nothing without consulting him. In a few hours you shall know my decision." It was this decision which the Marshals went to wait for at Ney's.

Most of the members of the Provisional Government attributed the evasive reply of the Emperor Alexander to the influence of the speech of Dessolles. For my part, while I do justice to the manner in which he declared himself on this important occasion, I do not ascribe to his eloquence the power of fixing Alexander's resolution, for I well know by experience how easy it is to make princes appear to adopt the advice of any one when the counsel given is precisely that which they wish to follow. From the sentiments of Alexander at this time I had not the slightest doubt as to the course he would finally pursue, and I considered what he said about consulting the King of Prussia to be merely a polite excuse, by which he avoided the disagreeable task of giving the Marshals a direct refusal.

I therefore returned home quite satisfied as to the result of the Emperor Alexander's visit to the King of Prussia. I knew, from the persons about the Czar, that he cherished a hatred, which was but too well justified, towards Bonaparte. Frederick William is of too firm a character to have yielded to any of the considerations which might on this subject have been pressed on him as they had been on the Emperor of Russia. But, besides that the King of Prussia had legitimate reasons for disliking Napoleon, policy would at that time have required that he should appear to be his enemy, for to do so was to render himself popular with his subjects. But the King of Prussia did not need to act under the dictates of policy; he followed his own opinion in rejecting the propositions of the Marshals, which he did without hesitation, and with much energy.

While the Marshals had gone to Paris Bonaparte was anxious to ascertain whether his Commissioners had passed the advanced posts of the foreign armies, and in case of resistance he determined to march on Paris, for he could not believe that he had lost every chance. He sent an aide de camp to desire Marmont to come immediately to Fontainebleau: such was Napoleon's impatience that instead of waiting for the return of his aide de camp he sent off a second and then a third officer on the same errand. This rapid succession of envoys from the Emperor alarmed the general who commanded the different divisions of Marmont's corps at Essonne. They feared that the Emperor was aware of the Convention concluded that morning with Prince Schwartzenberg, and that he had sent for Marmont with the view of reprimanding him. The fact was, Napoleon knew nothing of the matter, for Marmont, on departing for Paris with Macdonald and Ney, had left orders that it should be said that he had gone to inspect his lines. Souham; Lebrun des Essarts, and Bordessoulle, who had given their assent to the Convention with Prince Schwartzenberg, deliberated in the absence of Marmont, and, perhaps being ignorant that he was released from his promise, and fearing the vengeance of Napoleon, they determined to march upon Versailles. On arriving there the troops not finding the Marshal at their head thought themselves betrayed, and a spirit of insurrection broke out among them. One of Marmont's aides de camp, whom he had left at Essonne, exerted every endeavour to prevent the departure of his general's corps, but, finding all his efforts unavailing, he hastened to Paris to inform the Marshal of what had happened. 'When Marmont received this news he was breakfasting at Ney's with Macdonald and Caulaincourt: they were waiting for the answer which the Emperor Alexander had promised to send them. The march of his corps on Versailles threw Marmont into despair. He said to the Marshals, "I must be off to join my corps and quell this mutiny;"

and without losing a moment he ordered his carriage and directed the coachman to drive with the utmost speed. He sent forward one of his aides de camp to inform the troops of his approach.

Having arrived within a hundred paces of the place where his troops were assembled he found the generals who were under his orders advancing to meet him. They urged him not to go farther, as the men were in open insurrection. "I will go into the midst of them," said Marmont. "In a moment they shall either kill me or acknowledge me as their chief:" He sent off another aide de camp to range the troops in the order of battle. Then, alighting from the carriage and mounting a horse, he advanced alone, and thus harangued his troops: "How! Is there treason here? Is it possible that you disown me? Am I not your comrade? Have I not been wounded twenty times among you? . . . Have I not shared your fatigues and privations? And am I not ready to do so again?" Here Marmont was interrupted by a general shout of "Vive le Marechal! Vive le Marechal!"

The alarm caused among the members of the Provisional Government by the mission of the Marshals was increased by the news of the mutiny of Marmont's troops. During the whole of the day we were in a state of tormenting anxiety. It was feared that the insurrectionary spirit might spread among other corps of the army, and the cause of France again be endangered. But the courage of Marmont saved everything: It would be impossible to convey any idea of the manner in which he was received by us at Talleyrand's when he related the particulars of what had occurred at Versailles.

On the evening of the day on which Marmont had acted so nobly it was proposed that the army should adopt the white cockade. In reply to this proposition the Marshal said, "Gentlemen, I have made my troops understand the necessity of serving France before all things. They have, consequently, returned to order, and I can now answer for them. But what I cannot answer for is to induce them to abandon the colours which have led them to victory for the last twenty years. Therefore do not count upon me for a thing which I consider to be totally hostile to the interests of France. I will speak to the Emperor Alexander on the subject." Such were Marmont's words. Every one appeared to concur in his opinion, and the discussion terminated. For my own part, I find by my notes that I declared myself strongly in favour of Marmont's proposition.

The Marshal's opinion having been adopted, at least provisionally, an article was prepared for the Moniteur in nearly the following terms:

> The white cockade has been, during the last four days, a badge for the manifestation of public opinion in favour of the overthrow of an oppressive Government: it has been the only means of distinguishing the partisans of the restoration of the old dynasty, to which at length we are to be indebted for repose. But as the late Government is at an end, all colours differing from our national colours are useless: let us, therefore, resume those which have so often led us to victory.

Such was the spirit of the article, though possibly the above copy may differ in a few words. It met with the unqualified approbation of every one present. I was therefore extremely surprised, on looking at the 'Moniteur' next day, to find that the article was not inserted. I knew not what courtly interference prevented the appearance of the article, but I remember that Marmont was very ill pleased at its omission. He complained on the subject to the Emperor Alexander, who promised to write, and in fact did write, to the Provisional

Government to get the article inserted. However, it did not appear, and in a few days we obtained a solution of the enigma, as we might perhaps have done before if we had tried. The Emperor Alexander also promised to write to the Comte d'Artois, and to inform him that the opinion of France was in favour of the preservation of the three colours, but I do not know whether the letter was written, or, if it was, what answer it received.

Marshal Jourdan, who was then at Rouen, received a letter, written without the knowledge of Marmont, informing him that the latter had mounted the white cockade in his corps. Jourdan thought he could not do otherwise than follow Marmont's example, and he announced to the Provisional Government that in consequence of the resolution of the Duke of Ragusa he had just ordered his corps to wear the white cockade. Marmont could now be boldly faced, and when he complained to the Provisional Government of the non-insertion of the article in the Moniteur the reply was, "It cannot now appear. You see Marshal Jourdan has mounted the white cockade: you would not give the army two sets of colours!"

Marmont could make no answer to so positive a fact. It was not till some time after that I learned Jourdan had determined to unfurl the white flag only on the positive assurance that Marmont had already done so. Thus we lost the colours which had been worn by Louis XVI., which Louis XVIII., when a Prince, had adopted, and in which the Comte d'Artois showed himself on his return to the Parisians, for he entered the capital in the uniform of the National Guard. The fraud played off by some members of the Provisional Government was attended by fatal consequences; many evils might have been spared to France had Marmont's advice been adopted.

At the period of the dissolution of the Empire there might be said to be three Governments in France, viz. the Provisional Government in Paris, Napoleon's at Fontainebleau, and the doubtful and ambulatory Regency of "Maria Louisa." Doubtful and ambulatory the Regency might well be called, for there was so little decision as to the course to be adopted by the Empress that it was at first proposed to conduct her to Orleans, then to Tours, and she went finally to Blois.

The uncertainty which prevailed respecting the destiny of Maria Louisa is proved by a document which I have in my possession, and of which there cannot be many copies in existence. It is a circular addressed to the prefects by M. de Montalivet, the Minister of the Interior, who accompanied the Empress. In it a blank is left for the seat of the Government, to which the prefects are desired to send their communications. In the copy I possess the blank is filled up with the word "Blois" in manuscript.

As soon as Maria Louisa was made acquainted with the events that had taken place around Paris she sent for the Duc de Cadore, and gave him a letter addressed to the Emperor of Austria, saying, "Take this to my father, who must be at Dijon. I rely on you for defending the interests of France, those of the Emperor, and above all those of my son." Certainly Maria Louisa's confidence could not be better placed, and those great interests would have been defended by the Duc de Cadore 'si defendi possent.'

After the departure of the Duc de Cadore Maria Louisa published the following proclamation, addressed to the French people:

By the Empress Regent.

A PROCLAMATION

The events of the war have placed the capital in the power of foreigners. The Emperor has marched to defend it at the head of his armies, so often victorious. They are face to face with the enemy before the walls of Paris. From the residence which I have chosen, and from the Ministers of the Emperor, will emanate the only orders which you can acknowledge. Every town in the power of foreigners ceases to be free, and every order which may proceed from them is the language of the enemy, or that which it suits his hostile views to propagate. You will be faithful to your oaths. You will listen to the voice of a Princess who was consigned to your good faith, and whose highest pride consists in being a Frenchwoman, and in being united to the destiny of the sovereign whom you have freely chosen. My son was less sure of your affections in the time of our prosperity; his rights and his person are under your safeguard.

(By order) Montalivet.
(Signed) Maria Louisa

Blois,
3d April 1814.

It is to be inferred that the Regency had within three days adopted the resolution of not quitting Blois, for the above document presents no blanks, nor words filled up in writing. The Empress' proclamation, though a powerful appeal to the feelings of the French people, produced no effect. Maria Louisa's proclamation was dated the 4th of April, on the evening of which day Napoleon signed the conditional abdication, with the fate of which the reader has already been made acquainted. M. de Montalivet transmitted the Empress' proclamation, accompanied by another circular, to the prefects, of whom very few received it.

M. de Champagny, having left Blois with the letter he had received from the Empress, proceeded to the headquarters of the Emperor of Austria, carefully avoiding those roads which were occupied by Cossack troops. He arrived, not without considerable difficulty, at Chanseaux, where Frances II. was expected. When the Emperor arrived the Duc de Cadore was announced, and immediately introduced to his Majesty. The Duke remained some hours with Francis II., without being able to obtain from him anything but fair protestations. The Emperor always took refuge behind the promise he had given to his Allies to approve whatever measures they might adopt. The Duke was not to leave the Emperor's headquarters that evening, and, in the hope that his Majesty might yet reflect on the critical situation of his daughter, he asked permission to take leave next morning. He accordingly presented himself to the Emperor's levee, when he renewed his efforts in support of the claims of Maria Louisa. "I have a great affection for my daughter, and also for my son-in law," said the Emperor. "I bear them both in my heart, and would shed my blood for them"—"Ah, Sire!" exclaimed M. de Champagny, "such a sacrifice is not necessary."—"Yes, Duke, I say again I would shed my blood, I would resign my life for them, but I have given my Allies a promise not to treat without them, and to approve all that they may do. Besides," added the Emperor, "my Minister, M. de Metternich, has gone to their headquarters, and I will ratify whatever he may sign."

When the Duc de Cadore related to me the particulars of his mission, in which zeal could not work an impossibility, I remarked that he regarded as a circumstance fatal to Napoleon the absence of M. de Metternich and the presence of M. Stadion at the headquarters of the Emperor of Austria. Though in all probability nothing could have arrested the course of events, yet it is certain that the personal sentiments of the two Austrian Ministers towards Napoleon were widely different. I am not going too far when I affirm that, policy apart, M. de Metternich was much attached to Napoleon. In support of this assertion I may quote a fact of which I can guarantee the authenticity:

When M. de Metternich was complimented on the occasion of Maria Louisa's marriage he replied, "To have contributed to a measure which has received the approbation of 80,000,000 men is indeed a just subject of congratulation." Such a remark openly made by the intelligent Minister of the Cabinet of Vienna was well calculated to gratify the ears of Napoleon, from whom, however, M. de Metternich in his personal relations did not conceal the truth. I recollect a reply which was made by M. de Metternich at Dresden after a little hesitation. "As to you," said the Emperor, "you will not go to war with me. It is impossible that you can declare yourself against me. That can never be."—"Sire, we are not now quite allies, and some time hence we may become enemies." This hint was the last which Napoleon received from Metternich, and Napoleon must have been blind indeed not to have profited by it. As to M. Stadion, he entertained a profound dislike of the Emperor. That Minister knew and could not forget that his preceding exclusion from the Cabinet of Vienna had been due to the all-powerful influence of Napoleon.

Whether or not the absence of Metternich influenced the resolution of Francis II., it is certain that that monarch yielded nothing to the urgent solicitations of a Minister who conscientiously fulfilled the delicate mission consigned to him. M. de Champagny rejoined the Empress at Orleans, whither she had repaired on leaving Blois. He found Maria Louisa almost deserted, all the Grand Dignitaries of the Empire having successively returned to Paris after sending in their submissions to the Provisional Government.

I had scarcely entered upon the exercise of my functions as Postmaster-General when, on the morning of the 2d of April, I was surprised to see a Prussian general officer enter my cabinet. I immediately recognised him as General Blücher. He had commanded the Prussian army in the battle which took place at the gates of Paris. "Sir," said he, "I consider it one of my first duties on entering Paris to thank you for the attention I received from you in Hamburg. I am sorry that I was not sooner aware of your being in Paris. I assure you that had I been sooner informed of this circumstance the capitulation should have been made without a blow being struck. How much blood might then have been spared!"—"General," said I, "on what do you ground this assurance?"—"If I had known that you were in Paris I would have given you a letter to the King of Prussia. That monarch, who knows the resources and intentions of the Allies, would, I am sure, have authorised you to decide a suspension of arms before the neighbourhood of Paris became the theatre of the war."—"But," resumed I, "in spite of the good intentions of the Allies, it would have been very difficult to prevent resistance. French pride, irritated as it was by reverses, would have opposed insurmountable obstacles to such a measure."—"But, good heavens! you would have seen that resistance could be of no avail against such immense masses."—"You are right, General; but French honour would have been defended to the last."—"I am fully aware of that; but surely you have earned glory enough!"—"Yet our French susceptibility would have made us look upon that glory as tarnished if Paris had been occupied without defence . . . . But under present circumstances I am well pleased that you were satisfied with my conduct in Hamburg, for it induces me to hope that you will observe the same moderation in Paris that I exercised there. The days are past when it could be said, Woe to the conquered."—"You are right; yet," added he, smiling, "you know we are called the northern barbarians."—"Then, General," returned I, "you have a fair opportunity of showing that that designation is a libel."

Some days after Blücher's visit I had the honour of being admitted to a private audience of the King of Prussia. Clarke and Berthier were also received in this audience, which took place at the hotel of Prince Eugène, where the King of Prussia resided in Paris. We waited for some minutes in the salon, and when Frederick William entered from his cabinet I remarked on his countenance an air of embarrassment and austerity which convinced me that he had been studying his part, as great personages are in the habit of doing on similar occasions. The King on entering the salon first noticed Berthier, whom he addressed with much kindness, bestowing praises on the French troops, and complimenting the Marshal on his conduct during the war in Germany. Berthier returned thanks for these well-merited praises, for though he was not remarkable for strength of understanding or energy of mind, yet he was not a bad man, and I have known many proofs of his good conduct in conquered countries.

After saluting Berthier the King of Prussia turned towards Clarke, and his countenance immediately assumed an expression of dissatisfaction. He had evidently not forgotten Clarke's conduct in Berlin. He reminded him that he had rendered the Continental system more odious than it was in itself, and that he had shown no moderation in the execution of his orders. "In short," said his Majesty, "if I have any advice to give you, it is that you never again return to Prussia." The King pronounced these words in so loud and decided a tone that Clarke was perfectly confounded. He uttered some unintelligible observations, which, however, Frederick William did not notice, for suddenly turning towards me he said, with an air of affability, "Ah! M. de Bourrienne, I am glad to see you, and I take this opportunity of repeating what I wrote to you from Gonigsberg. You always extended protection to the Germans, and did all you could to alleviate their condition. I learned with great satisfaction what you did for the Prussians whom the fate of war drove into Hamburg; and I feel pleasure in telling you, in the presence of these two gentlemen, that if all the French agents had acted as you did we should not, probably, be here." I expressed, by a profound bow, how much I was gratified by this complimentary address, and the king, after saluting us, retired.

About the middle of April Bernadotte arrived in Paris. His situation had become equivocal, since circumstances had banished the hopes he might have conceived in his interview with the Emperor Alexander at Åbo. Besides, he had been represented in some official pamphlets as a traitor to France, and among certain worshippers of our injured glory there prevailed a feeling of irritation, and which was unjustly directed towards Bernadotte.

I even remember that Napoleon, before he had fallen from his power, had a sort of national protest made by the police against the Prince Royal of Sweden. This Prince had reserved an hotel in the Rue d'Anjou, and the words, "Down with the traitor! down with the perjurer," were shouted there; but this had no result, as it was only considered an outrage caused by a spirit of petty vengeance.

While Bernadotte was in Paris I saw him every day. He but faintly disguised from me the hope he had entertained of ruling France; and in the numerous conversations to which our respective occupations led I ascertained, though Bernadotte did not formally tell me so, that he once had strong expectations of succeeding Napoleon.

Pressed at last into his final intrenchments he broke through all reserve and confirmed all I knew of the interview of Åbo.

I asked Bernadotte what he thought of the projects which were attributed to Moreau; whether it was true that he had in him a competitor, and whether Moreau had aspired to the dangerous honour of governing France: "Those reports," replied the Prince Royal of Sweden, "are devoid of foundation: at least I can assure you that in the conversations I have had with the Emperor Alexander, that sovereign never said anything which could warrant such a supposition. I know that the Emperor of Russia wished to avail himself of the military talents of Moreau in the great struggle that had commenced, and to enable the exiled general to return to his country, in the hope that, should the war prove fortunate, he would enjoy the honours and privileges due to his past services."

Bernadotte expressed to me astonishment at the recall of the Bourbons, and assured me that he had not expected the French people would so readily have consented to the Restoration. I confess I was surprised that Bernadotte, with the intelligence I knew him to possess, should imagine that the will of subjects has any influence in changes of government!

During his stay in Paris Bernadotte evinced for me the same sentiments of friendship which he had shown me at Hamburg. One day I received from him a letter, dated Paris, with which he transmitted to me one of the crosses of the Polar Star, which the King of Sweden had left at his disposal. Bernadotte was not very well satisfied with his residence in Paris, in spite of the friendship which the Emperor Alexander constantly manifested towards him. After a few days he set out for Sweden, having first taken leave of the Comte d'Artois. I did not see him after his farewell visit to the Count, so that I know not what was the nature of the conversation which passed between the two Princes.

VOLUME IV

1814-1821

CHAPTER I

1814

When Marmont left Paris on the receipt of the intelligence from Essonne, Marshals Macdonald and Ney and the Duke of Vicenza waited upon the Emperor Alexander to learn his resolution before he could have been informed of the movement of Marmont's troops. I myself went during the morning to the hotel of M. de Talleyrand, and it was there I learnt how what we had hoped for had become fact: the matter was completely decided. The Emperor Alexander had walked out at six in the morning to the residence of the King of Prussia in the Rue de Bourbon. The two sovereigns afterwards proceeded together to M. de Talleyrand's, where they were when Napoleon's Commissioners arrived. The Commissioners being introduced to the two sovereigns, the Emperor Alexander, in answer to their proposition, replied that the Regency was impossible, as submissions to the Provisional Government were pouring in from all parts, and that if the army had formed contrary wishes those should have been sooner made known. "Sire," observed Macdonald, "that—was—impossible, as none of the Marshals were in Paris, and besides, who could foresee the turn which affairs have taken? Could we imagine that an unfounded alarm would have removed from Essonne the corps of the Duke of Ragusa, who has this moment left us to bring his troops back to order?" These words produced no change in the determination of the sovereigns, who would hear of nothing but the unconditional abdication of Napoleon. Before the Marshals took leave of the Emperor Alexander they solicited an armistice of forty-eight hours, which time they said was indispensable to negotiate the act of abdication with Napoleon. This request was granted without hesitation, and the Emperor Alexander, showing Macdonald a map of the environs of Paris, courteously presented him with a pencil, saying, "Here, Marshal, mark yourself the limits to be observed by the two armies."—"No, Sire," replied Macdonald, "we are the conquered party, and it is for you to mark the line of demarcation." Alexander determined that the right bank of the Seine should be occupied by the Allied troops, and the left bank by the French; but it was observed that this arrangement would be attended with inconvenience, as it would cut Paris in two, and it was agreed that the line should turn Paris. I have been informed that on a map sent to the Austrian staff to acquaint Prince Schwartzenberg with the limits definitively agreed on, Fontainebleau, the Emperor's headquarters, was by some artful means included within the line. The Austrians acted so implicitly on this direction that Marshal Macdonald was obliged to complain on the subject to Alexander, who removed all obstacles.

When, in discussing the question of the abdication conformably with the instructions he had received, Macdonald observed to the Emperor Alexander that Napoleon wished for nothing for himself, "Assure him," replied Alexander, "that a provision shall be made for him worthy of the rank he has occupied. Tell him that if he wishes to reside in my States he shall be well received, though he brought desolation there. I shall always remember the friendship which united us. He shall have the island of Elba, or something else." After taking leave of the Emperor Alexander, on the 5th of April, Napoleon's Commissioners returned to

Fontainebleau to render an account of their mission. I saw Alexander that same day, and it appeared to me that his mind was relieved of a great weight by the question of the Regency being brought to an end. I was informed that he intended to quit Paris in a few days, and that he had given full powers to M. Pozzo-di-Borgo, whom he appointed his Commissioner to the Provisional Government.

On the same day, the 5th of April, Napoleon inspected his troops in the Palace yard of Fontainebleau. He observed some coolness among his officers, and even among the private soldiers, who had evinced such enthusiasm when he inspected them on the 2d of April. He was so much affected by this change of conduct that he remained but a short time on the parade, and afterwards retired to his apartments.

About one o'clock on the morning of the 6th of April Ney, Macdonald, and Caulaincourt arrived at Fontainebleau to acquaint the Emperor with the issue of their mission, and the sentiments expressed by Alexander when they took leave of him. Marshal Ney was the first to announce to Napoleon that the Allies required his complete and unconditional abdication, unaccompanied by any stipulation, except that of his personal safety, which should be guaranteed. Marshal Macdonald and the Duke of Vicenza then spoke to the same effect, but in more gentle terms than those employed by Ney, who was but little versed in the courtesies of speech. When Marshal Macdonald had finished speaking Napoleon said with some emotion, "Marshal, I am sensible of all that you have done for me, and of the warmth with which you have pleaded the cause of my son. They wish for my complete and unconditional abdication. . . . Very well. I again empower you to act on my behalf. You shall go and defend my interests and those of my family." Then, after a moment's pause, he added, still addressing Macdonald, "Marshal, where shall I go?" Macdonald then informed the Emperor what Alexander had mentioned in the hypothesis of his wishing to reside in Russia. "Sire," added he, "the Emperor of Russia told me that he destined for you the island of Elba, or something else."—"Or something else!" repeated Napoleon hastily, "and what is that something else?"—"Sire, I know not."—"Ah! it is doubtless the island of Corsica, and he refrained from mentioning it to avoid embarrassment! Marshal, I leave all to you."

The Marshals returned to Paris as soon as Napoleon furnished them with new powers; Caulaincourt remained at Fontainebleau. On arriving in Paris Marshal Ney sent in his adhesion to the Provisional Government, so that when Macdonald returned to Fontainebleau to convey to Napoleon the definitive treaty of the Allies, Ney did not accompany him, and the Emperor expressed surprise and dissatisfaction at his absence. Ney, as all his friends concur in admitting, expended his whole energy in battle, and often wanted resolution when out of the field, consequently I was not surprised to find that he joined us before some other of his comrades. As to Macdonald, he was one of those generous spirits who may be most confidently relied on by those who have wronged them. Napoleon experienced the truth of this. Macdonald returned alone to Fontainebleau, and when he entered the Emperor's chamber he found him seated in a small armchair before the fireplace. He was dressed in a morning-gown of white dimity, and he wore his slippers without stockings. His elbows rested on his knees and his head was supported by his hands. He was motionless, and seemed absorbed in profound reflection. Only two persons were in the apartment, the Duke of Bassano; who was at a little distance from the Emperor, and Caulaincourt, who was near the fireplace. So profound was Napoleon's reverie that he did not hear Macdonald enter, and the Duke of Vicenza was obliged to inform him of the Marshal's presence. "Sire," said Caulaincourt, "the Duke of Tarantum has brought for your signature the treaty which is to be ratified to-morrow." The Emperor then, as if roused from a lethargic slumber, turned to Macdonald, and merely said, "Ah, Marshal! so you are here!" Napoleon's countenance was so altered that the Marshal, struck with the change, said, as if it were involuntarily, "Is your Majesty indisposed?"—"Yes," answered Napoleon, "I have passed a very bad night."

The Emperor continued seated for a moment, then rising, he took the treaty, read it without making any observation, signed it, and returned it to the Marshal, saying; "I am not now rich enough to reward these last services."—"Sire, interest never guided my conduct."—"I know that, and I now see how I have been deceived respecting you. I also see the designs of those who prejudiced me against you."—"Sire, I have already told you, since 1809 I am devoted to you in life and death."—"I know it. But since I cannot reward you as I would wish, let a token of remembrance, inconsiderable though it be, assure you that I shall ever bear in mind the services you have rendered me." Then turning to Caulaincourt Napoleon said, "Vicenza, ask for the sabre which was given me by Murad Bey in Egypt, and which I wore at the battle of Mount Thabor." Constant having brought the sabre, the Emperor took it from the hands of Caulaincourt and presented it to the Marshal "Here, my faithful friend," said he, "is a reward which I believe will gratify you." Macdonald on receiving the sabre said, "If ever I have a son, Sire, this will be his most precious inheritance. I will never part with it as long as I live."—"Give me your hand," said the Emperor, "and embrace me." At these words Napoleon and Macdonald affectionately rushed into each other's arms, and parted with tears in their eyes. Such was the last interview between Macdonald and Napoleon. I had the above particulars from the Marshal himself in 1814., a few days after he returned to Paris with the treaty ratified by Napoleon.

After the clauses of the treaty had been guaranteed Napoleon signed, on the 11th of April, at Fontainebleau, his act of abdication, which was in the following terms:—

> "The Allied powers having proclaimed that the Emperor Napoleon is the only obstacle to the re-establishment of peace in Europe, the Emperor Napoleon, faithful to his oath, declares that he renounces for himself and his heirs the thrones of France and Italy, and that there is no personal sacrifice, even that of life, which he is not ready to make for the interests of France."

It was not until after Bonaparte had written and signed the above act that Marshal Macdonald sent to the Provisional Government his recognition, expressed in the following dignified and simple manner:—

> "Being released from my allegiance by the abdication of the Emperor Napoleon, I declare that I conform to the acts of the Senate and the Provisional Government."

It is worthy of remark that Napoleon's act of abdication was published in the 'Moniteur' on the 12th of April, the very day on which the Comte d'Artois made his entry into Paris with the title of Lieutenant-General of the Kingdom conferred on him by Louis XVIII. The 12th of April was also the day on which the Imperial army fought its last battle before Toulouse, when the French troops, commanded by Soult, made Wellington purchase so dearly his entrance into the south of France.[267]

---

267 The battle of Toulouse was fought on the 10th not 12th April — D.W.

Political revolutions are generally stormy, yet, during the great change of 1814 Paris was perfectly tranquil, thanks to the excellent discipline maintained by the commanders of the Allied armies, and thanks also to the services of the National Guard of Paris, who every night patrolled the streets. My duties as Director-General of the Post-office had of course obliged me to resign my captain's epaulette.

When I first obtained my appointment I had been somewhat alarmed to hear that all the roads were covered with foreign troops, especially Cossacks, who even in time of peace are very ready to capture any horses that may fall in their way. On my application to the Emperor Alexander his Majesty immediately issued a ukase, severely prohibiting the seizure of horses or anything belonging to the Post-office department. The ukase was printed by order of the Czar, and filed up at all the post-offices, and it will be seen that after the 20th of March, when I was placed in an embarrassing situation, one of the postmasters on the Lille road expressed to me his gratitude for my conduct while I was in the service.

On the 10th of April a ceremony took place in Paris which has been much spoken of; and which must have had a very imposing effect on those who allow themselves to be dazzled by mere spectacle. Early in the morning some regiments of the Allied troops occupied the north side of the Boulevard, from the site of the old Bastille to the Place Louis XV., in the middle of which an altar of square form was erected. Thither the Allied sovereigns came to witness the celebration of mass according to the rites of the Greek Church. I went to a window of the hotel of the Minister of the Marine to see the ceremony. After I had waited from eight in the morning till near twelve the pageant commenced by the arrival of half a dozen Greek priests, with long beards, and as richly dressed as the high priests who figure in the processions of the opera. About three-quarters of an hour after this first scene the infantry, followed by the cavalry, entered the place, which, in a few moments was entirely covered with military. The Allied sovereigns at length appeared, attended by brilliant staffs. They alighted from their horses and advanced to the altar. What appeared to me most remarkable was the profound silence of the vast multitude during the performance of the mass. The whole spectacle had the effect of a finely-painted panorama. For my own part, I must confess I was heartily tired of the ceremony, and was very glad when it was over. I could not admire the foreign uniforms, which were very inferior to ours. Many of them appeared fanciful, and even grotesque, and nothing can be more unsoldier-like than to see a man laced in stays till his figure resembles a wasp. The ceremony which took place two days after, though less pompous, was much more French. In the retinue which, on the 12th of April, momentarily increased round the Comte d'Artos, there were at least recollections for the old, and hopes for every one.

When, on the departure of the Commissioners whom Napoleon had sent to Alexander to treat for the Regency, it was finally determined that the Allied sovereigns would listen to no proposition from Napoleon and his family, the Provisional Government thought it time to request that Monsieur would, by his presence, give a new impulse to the partisans of the Bourbons. The Abby de Montesquieu wrote to the Prince a letter, which was carried to him by Viscount Sosthenes de la Rochefoucauld, one of the individuals who, in these difficult circumstances, most zealously served the cause of the Bourbons. On the afternoon of the 11th Monsieur arrived at a country-house belonging to Madame Charles de Dames, where he passed the night. The news of his arrival spread through Paris with the rapidity of lightning, and every one wished to solemnise his entrance into the capital. The National Guard formed a double line from the barrier of Bondy to Notre Dame, whither the Prince was first to proceed, in observance of an old custom, which, however, had become very rare in France during the last twenty years.

M. de Talleyrand, accompanied by the members of the Provisional Government, several Marshals and general officers, and the municipal body, headed by the prefect of the Seine, went in procession beyond the barrier to receive Monsieur. M. de Talleyrand, in the name of the Provisional Government, addressed the Prince, who in reply made that observation which has been so often repeated, "Nothing is changed in France: there is only one Frenchman more."[268]

This remark promised much. The Comte Artois next proceeded on horseback to the barrier St. Martin. I mingled in the crowd to see the procession and to observe the sentiments of the spectators. Near me stood an old knight of St. Louis, who had resumed the insignia of the order, and who wept for joy at again seeing one of the Bourbons. The procession soon arrived, preceded by a band playing the air, "Vive Henri Quatre!" I had never before seen Monsieur, and his appearance had a most pleasing effect upon me. His open countenance bore the expression of that confidence which his presence inspired in all who saw him. His staff was very brilliant, considering it was got together without preparation. The Prince wore the uniform of the National Guard, with the insignia of the Order of the Holy Ghost.

I must candidly state that where I saw Monsieur pass, enthusiasm was chiefly confined to his own retinue, and to persons who appeared to belong to a superior class of society. The lower order of people seemed to be animated by curiosity and astonishment rather than any other feeling. I must add that it was not without painful surprise I saw a squadron of Cossacks close the procession; and my surprise was the greater when I learned from General Sacken that the Emperor Alexander had wished that on that day the one Frenchman more should be surrounded only by Frenchmen, and that to prove that the presence of the Bourbons was the signal of reconciliation his Majesty had ordered 20,000 of the Allied troops to quit Paris. I know not to what the presence of the Cossacks is to be attributed, but it was an awkward circumstance at the time, and one which malevolence did not fail to seize upon.

Two days only intervened between Monsieur's entrance into Paris and the arrival of the Emperor of Austria. That monarch was not popular among the Parisians. The line of conduct he had adopted was almost generally condemned, for, even among those who had most ardently wished for the dethronement of his daughter, through their aversion to the Bonaparte family, there were many who blamed the Emperor of Austria's behaviour to Maria Louisa: they would have wished that, for the honour of Francis II., he had unsuccessfully

268 These words were never really uttered by the Comte d'Artois, and we can in this case follow the manufacture of the phrase. The reply actually made to Talleyrand was, "Sir, and gentlemen, I thank you; I am too happy. Let us get on; I am too happy." When the day's work was done, "Let us see," said Talleyrand; "what did Monsieur say? I did not hear much: he seemed much moved, and desirous of hastening on, but if what he did say will not suit you (Beugnot), make an answer for him . . . and I can answer that Monsieur will accept it, and that so thoroughly that by the end of a couple of days he will believe he made it, and he will have made it: you will count for nothing." After repeated attempts, rejected by Talleyrand, Beugnot at last produced, "No more divisions. Peace and France! At last I see her once more, and nothing in her is changed, except that here is one more Frenchman." At last the great critic (Talleyrand) said, "This time I yield; that is really Monsieur's speech, and I will answer for you that he is the man who made it." Monsieur did not disdain to refer to it in his replies, and the prophecy of M. de Talleyrand was completely realised (Beugnot, vol. ii, p. 119)

opposed the downfall of the dynasty, whose alliance he considered as a safeguard in 1809. This was the opinion which the mass of the people instinctively formed, for they judged of the Emperor of Austria in his character of a father and not in his character of a monarch; and as the rights of misfortune are always sacred in France, more interest was felt for Maria Louisa when she was known to be forsaken than when she was in the height of her splendour. Francis II. had not seen his daughter since the day when she left Vienna to unite her destiny with that of the master of half of Europe, and I have already stated how he received the mission with which Maria Louisa entrusted the Duc de Cadore.

I was then too intent on what was passing in Paris and at Fontainebleau to observe with equal interest all the circumstances connected with the fate of Maria Louisa, but I will present to the reader all the information I was able to collect respecting that Princess during the period immediately preceding her departure from France. She constantly assured the persons about her that she could rely on her father. The following words, which were faithfully reported to me, were addressed by her to an officer who was at Blois during the mission of M. de Champagny. "Even though it should be the intention of the Allied sovereigns to dethrone the Emperor Napoleon, my father will not suffer it. When he placed me on the throne of France he repeated to me twenty times his determination to uphold me on it; and my father is an honest man." I also know that the Empress, both at Blois and at Orleans, expressed her regret at not having followed the advice of the members of the Regency, who wished her to stay in Paris.

On leaving Orleans Maria Louisa proceeded to Rambouillet; and it was not one of the least extraordinary circumstances of that eventful period to see the sovereigns of Europe, the dethroned sovereigns of France, and those who had come to resume the sceptre, all crowded together within a circle of fifteen leagues round the capital. There was a Bourbon at the Tuileries, Bonaparte at Fontainebleau, his wife and son at Rambouillet, the repudiated Empress at Malmaison three leagues distant, and the Emperors of Russia and Austria and the King of Prussia in Paris.

When all her hopes had vanished Maria Louisa left Rambouillet to return to Austria with her son. She did not obtain permission to see Napoleon before her departure, though she had frequently expressed a wish to that effect. Napoleon himself was aware of the embarrassment which might have attended such a farewell, or otherwise he would no doubt have made a parting interview with Maria Louisa one of the clauses of the treaty of Paris and Fontainebleau, and of his definitive act of abdication. I was informed at the time that the reason which prevented Maria Louisa's wish from being acceded to was the fear that, by one of those sudden impulses common to women, she might have determined to unite herself to Napoleon's fallen fortune, and accompany him to Elba; and the Emperor of Austria wished to have his daughter back again.

Things had arrived at this point, and there was no possibility of retracting from any of the decisions which had been formed when the Emperor of Austria went to see his daughter at Rambouillet. I recollect it was thought extraordinary at the time that the Emperor Alexander should accompany him on this visit; and, indeed, the sight of the sovereign, who was regarded as the head and arbiter of the coalition, could not be agreeable to the dethroned Empress.[269]

269 Meneval (tome ii. p. 112), then with Maria Louisa as Secretary, who gives some details of her interview with the Emperor Francis on the 16th of April, says nothing about the Czar

The two Emperors set off from Paris shortly after each other. The Emperor of Austria arrived first at Rambouillet, where he was received with respect and affection by his daughter. Maria Louisa was happy to see him, but the many tears she shed were not all tears of joy. After the first effusion of filial affection she complained of the situation to which she was reduced. Her father sympathised with her, but could offer her no consolation, since her misfortunes were irreparable. Alexander was expected to arrive immediately, and the Emperor of Austria therefore informed his daughter that the Russian monarch wished to see her. At first Maria Louisa decidedly refused to receive him, and she persisted for some time in this resolution. She said to her father, "Would he too make me a prisoner before your eyes? If he enters here by force I will retire to my chamber. There, I presume, he will not dare to follow me while you are here." But there was no time to be lost; Francis II. heard the equipage of the Emperor of Russia rolling through the courtyard of Rambouillet, and his entreaties to his daughter became more and more urgent. At length she yielded, and the Emperor of Austria went himself to meet his ally and conduct him to the salon where Maria Louisa remained, in deference to her father. She did not, however, carry her deference so far as to give a favourable reception to him whom she regarded as the author of all her misfortunes. She listened with considerable coldness to the offers and protestations of Alexander, and merely replied that all she wished for was the liberty of returning to her family. A few days after this painful interview Maria Louisa and her son set off for Vienna.[270]

---

having been there; a fact he would have been sure to have remarked upon. It was only on the 19th of April that Alexander visited her, the King of Prussia coming in his turn on the 22d; but Bourrienne is right in saying that Maria Louisa complained bitterly of having to receive Alexander, and considered that she was forced by her father to do so. The poor little King of Rome, then only three years old, had also to be seen by the monarchs. He was not taken with his grandfather, remarking that he was not handsome. Maria Louisa seems, according to Meneval, to have been at this time really anxious to join Napoleon (Meneval, tome ii. p. 94). She left Rambouillet on the 28d of April stopped one day at Grossbois, receiving there her father and Berthier, and taking farewell of several persons who came from Paris for that purpose. On the 25th of April she started for Vienna, and later for Parma, which state she received under the treaty of 1814 and 1815. She yielded to the influence brought to bear on her, became estranged from Napoleon, and eventually married her chamberlain, the Comte de Neipperg, an Austrian general.

270 A few days after this visit Alexander paid his respects to Bonaparte's other wife, Josephine. In this great breaking up of empires and kingdoms the unfortunate Josephine, who had been suffering agonies on account of the husband who had abandoned her, was not forgotten. One of the first things the Emperor of Russia did on arriving at Paris was to despatch a guard for the protection of her beautiful little palace at Malmaison. The Allied sovereigns treated her with delicacy and consideration. "As soon as the Emperor Alexander knew that the Empress Josephine had arrived at Malmaison he hastened to pay her a visit. It is not possible to be more amiable than he was to her. When in the course of conversation he spoke of the occupation of Paris by the Allies, and of the position of the Emperor Napoleon, it was always in perfectly measured language: he never forgot for a single instant that he was speaking before one who had been the wife of his vanquished enemy. On her side the ex-Empress did not conceal the tender sentiments, the lively affection she still entertained for Napoleon. . . . Alexander had

This visit was soon followed by those of the other Allied Princes.

> "The King of Prussia and the Princes, his sons, came rather frequently to pay their court to Josephine; they even dined with her several times at Malmaison; but the Emperor Alexander come much more frequently. The Queen Hortense was always with her mother when she received the sovereigns, and assisted her in doing the honours of the house. The illustrious strangers exceedingly admired Malmaison, which seemed to them a charming residence. They were particularly struck with the fine gardens and conservatories." From this moment, however, Josephine's health rapidly declined, and she did not live to see Napoleon's return from Elba. She often said to her attendant, "I do not know what is the matter with me, but at times I have fits of melancholy enough to kill me." But on the very brink of the grave she retained all her amiability, all her love of dress, and the graces and resources of a drawing-room society. The immediate cause of her death was a bad cold she caught in taking a drive in the park of Malmaison on a damp cold day. She expired on the noon of Sunday, the 26th of May, in the fifty-third year of her age. Her body was embalmed, and on the sixth day after her death deposited in a vault in the church of Ruel, close to Malmaison. The funeral ceremonies were magnificent, but a better tribute to the memory of Josephine was to be found in the tears with which her children, her servants, the neighbouring poor, and all that knew her followed her to the grave. In 1826 a beautiful monument was erected over her remains by Eugène Beauharnais and his sisters with this simple inscription:
>
> TO JOSEPHINE.
> EUGENE. HORTENSE.

---

certainly something elevated and magnanimous in his character, which would not permit him to say a single word capable of insulting misfortune; the Empress had only one prayer to make to him, and that was for her children."

CHAPTER II

1814

I must now direct the attention of the reader to Italy, which was the cradle of Napoleon's glory, and towards which he transported himself in imagination from the Palace of Fontainebleau. Eugène had succeeded in keeping up his means of defence until April, but on the 7th of that month, being positively informed of the overwhelming reverses of France, he found himself constrained to accede to the propositions of the Marshal de Bellegarde to treat for the evacuation of Italy; and on the 10th a convention was concluded, in which it was stipulated that the French troops, under the command of Eugène, should return within the limits of old France. The clauses of this convention were executed on the 19th of April.[271]

Eugène, thinking that the Senate of Milan was favourably disposed towards him, solicited that body to use its influence in obtaining the consent of the Allied powers to his continuance at the head of the Government of Italy; but this proposition was rejected by the Senate. A feeling of irritation pervaded the public mind in Italy, and the army had not proceeded three marches beyond Mantua when an insurrection broke out in Milan. The Finance Minister, Pizna, was assassinated, and his residence demolished, and nothing would have saved the Viceroy from a similar fate had he been in his capital. Amidst this popular excitement, and the eagerness of the Italians to be released from the dominion of the French, the friends of Eugène thought him fortunate in being able to join his father-in-law at Munich almost incognito.[272] Thus, at the expiration of nine years, fell the iron crown which Napoleon had placed on his head saying, "Dieu me l'a donne; gare a qui la touche."

I will now take a glance at the affairs of Germany. Rapp was not in France at the period of the fall of the Empire. He had, with extraordinary courage and skill, defended himself against a year's siege at Dantzic. At length, being reduced to the last extremity, and constrained to surrender, he opened the gates of the city, which presented nothing but heaps of ruins. Rapp had stipulated that the garrison of Dantzic should return to France, and the Duke of Wurtemberg, who commanded the siege, had consented to that condition; but the Emperor of Russia having refused to ratify it, Rapp, having no means of defence, was made prisoner with his troops; and conducted to Kiew, whence he afterwards returned to Paris, where I saw him.

---

271 Lord William Bentinck and Sir Edward Pellew had taken Genoa on the 18th Of April. Murat was in the field with the Austrians against the French.

272 Some time after Eugène visited France and had a long audience of Louis XVIII. He announced himself to that monarch by his father's title of Marquis de Beauharnais. The King immediately saluted him by the title of Monsieur le Marechal, and proposed that he should reside in France with that rank. But this invitation Eugène declined, because as a French Prince under the fallen Government he had commanded the Marshals, and he therefore could not submit to be the last in rank among those illustrious military chiefs. —Bourrienne.

Hamburg still held out, but at the beginning of April intelligence was received there of the extraordinary events which had delivered Europe from her oppressor. Davoust refused to believe this news, which at once annihilated all his hopes of power and greatness. This blindness was persisted in for some time at Hamburg. Several hawkers, who were marked out by the police as having been the circulators of Paris news, were shot. An agent of the Government publicly announced his design of assassinating one of the French Princes, in whose service he was said to have been as a page. He said he would go to his Royal Highness and solicit to be appointed one of his aides de camp, and that, if the application were refused, as it probably would be, the refusal would only confirm him in his purpose.

At length, when the state of things was beyond the possibility of doubt, Davoust assembled the troops, acquainted them with the dethronement of the Emperor, hoisted a flag of truce, and sent his adhesion to the Provisional Government. All then thought of their personal safety, without losing sight of their honestly-acquired wealth. Diamonds and other objects of value and small bulk were hastily collected and packed up. The Governor of Hamburg, Count Hogendorff, who, in spite of some signal instances of opposition, had too often co-operated in severe and vexatious measures, was the first to quit the city. He was, indeed, hurried off by Davoust; because he had mounted the Orange cockade and wished to take his Dutch troops away with him. After consigning the command to General Gerard, Davoust quitted Hamburg, and arrived at Paris on the 18th of June.

I have left Napoleon at Fontainebleau. The period of his departure for Elba was near at hand: it was fixed for the 17th of April.

On that day Maubreuil, a man who has become unfortunately celebrated, presented himself at the Post-office, and asked to speak with me. He showed me some written orders, signed by General Sacken, the Commander of the Russian troops in Palls, and by Baron Brackenhausen, chief of the staff. These orders set forth that Maubreuil was entrusted with an important mission, for the execution of which he was authorised to demand the assistance of the Russian troops; and the commanders of those men were enjoined to place at his disposal as many troops as he might apply for. Maubreuil was also the bearer of similar orders from General Dupont, the War Minister, and from M. Angles, the Provisional Commissary-General of the Police, who directed all the other commissaries to obey the orders they might receive from Maubreuil. On seeing these documents, of the authenticity of which there was no doubt, I immediately ordered the different postmasters to provide Maubreuil promptly with any number of horses he might require.

Some days after I was informed that the object of Maubreuil's mission was to assassinate Napoleon. It may readily be imagined what was my astonishment on hearing this, after I had seen the signature of the Commander of the Russian forces, and knowing as I did the intentions of the Emperor Alexander. The fact is, I did not, and never can, believe that such was the intention of Maubreuil. This man has been accused of having carried off the jewels of the Queen of Westphalia.

Napoleon having consented to proceed to the island of Elba, conformably with the treaty he had ratified on the 13th, requested to be accompanied to the place of embarkation by a Commissioner from each of the Allied powers. Count Schouwaloff was appointed by Russia, Colonel Neil Campbell by England, General Kohler by Austria, and Count Waldbourg-Truchess by Prussia. On the 16th the four Commissioners came for the first time to Fontainebleau, where the Emperor, who was still attended by Generals Drouot and Bertrand, gave to each a private audience on the following day.

Though Napoleon received with coldness the Commissioners whom he had himself solicited, yet that coldness was far from being manifested in an equal degree to all. He who experienced the best reception was Colonel Campbell, apparently because his person exhibited traces of wounds. Napoleon asked him in what battles he had received them, and on what occasions he had been invested with the orders he wore. He next questioned him as to the place of his birth, and Colonel Campbell having answered that he was a Scotchman, Napoleon congratulated him on being the countryman of Ossian, his favourite author, with whose poetry, however, he was only acquainted through the medium of wretched translations. On this first audience Napoleon said to the Colonel, "I have cordially hated the English. I have made war against you by every possible means, but I esteem your nation. I am convinced that there is more generosity in your Government than in any other. I should like to be conveyed from Toulon to Elba by an English frigate."

The Austrian and Russian Commissioners were received coolly, but without any marked indications of displeasure. It was not so with the Prussian Commissioner, to whom he said duly, "Are there any Prussians in my escort?"—"No, Sire."—"Then why do you take the trouble to accompany me?"—"Sire, it is not a trouble, but an honour."—"These are mere words; you have nothing to do here."—"Sire, I could not possibly decline the honourable mission with which the King my master has entrusted me." At these words Napoleon turned his back on Count Truchess.

The Commissioners expected that Napoleon would be ready to set out without delay; but they were deceived. He asked for a sight of the itinerary of his route, and wished to make some alterations in it. The Commissioners were reluctant to oppose his wish, for they had been instructed to treat him with all the respect and etiquette due to a sovereign. They therefore suspended the departure, and, as they could not take upon themselves to acquiesce in the changes wished for by the Emperor, they applied for fresh orders. On the night of the 18th of April they received these orders, authorising them to travel by any road the Emperor might prefer. The departure was then definitively fixed for the 20th.

Accordingly, at ten on the morning of the 20th, the carriages were in readiness, and the Imperial Guard was drawn up in the grand court of the Palace of Fontainebleau, called the Cour du Cheval Blanc. All the population of the town and the neighbouring villages thronged round the Palace. Napoleon sent for General Kohler, the Austrian Commissioner, and said to him, "I have reflected on what I ought to do, and I am determined not to depart. The Allies are not faithful to their engagements with me. I can, therefore, revoke my abdication, which was only conditional. More than a thousand addresses were delivered to me last night: I am conjured to resume the reins of government. I renounced my rights to the crown only to avert the horrors of a civil war, having never had any other object in view than the glory and happiness of France. But, seeing as I now do, the dissatisfaction inspired by the measures of the new Government, I can explain to my Guard the reasons which induced me to revoke my abdication. It is true that the number of troops on which I can count will scarcely exceed 30,000 men, but it will be easy for me to increase their numbers to 130,000. Know, then, that I can also, without injuring my honour, say to my Guard, that having nothing but the repose and happiness of the country at heart, I renounce all my rights, and exhort my troops to follow my example, and yield to the wish of the nation."

I heard these words reported by General Kohler himself, after his return from his mission. He did not disguise the embarrassment which this unexpected address had occasioned; and I recollect having remarked at the time that had Bonaparte, at the commencement of the campaign of Paris, renounced his rights and returned to the rank of citizen, the immense masses of the Allies must have yielded to the efforts of France. General Kohler also stated that Napoleon complained of Maria Louisa not being allowed to accompany him; but at length, yielding to the reasons urged by those about him, he added, "Well, I prefer remaining faithful to my promise; but if I have any new ground of complaint, I will free myself from all my engagements."

At eleven o'clock Comte de Bussy, one of the Emperor's aides de camp, was sent by the Grand Marshal (General Bertrand) to announce that all was ready for departure. "Am I;" said Napoleon, "to regulate my actions by the Grand Marshal's watch? I will go when I please. Perhaps I may not go at all. Leave me!"

All the forms of courtly etiquette which Napoleon loved so much were observed; and when at length he was pleased to leave his cabinet to enter the salon, where the Commissioners were waiting; the doors were thrown open as usual, and "The Emperor" was announced; but no sooner was the word uttered than he turned back again. However, he soon reappeared, rapidly crossed the gallery, and descended the staircase, and at twelve o'clock precisely he stood at the head of his Guard, as if at a review in the court of the Tuileries in the brilliant days of the Consulate and the Empire.

Then took place a really moving scene—Napoleon's farewell to his soldiers. Of this I may abstain from entering into any details, since they are known everywhere, and by everybody, but I may subjoin the Emperor's last address to his old companions-in-arms, because it belongs to history. This address was pronounced in a voice as firm and sonorous as that in which Bonaparte used to harangue his troops in the days of his triumphs. It was as follows:

> "Soldiers of my Old Guard, I bid you farewell. For twenty years I have constantly accompanied you on the road to honour and glory. In these latter times, as in the days of our prosperity, you have invariably been models of courage and fidelity. With men such as you our cause could not be lost, but the war would have been interminable; it would have been civil war, and that would have entailed deeper misfortunes on France. I have sacrificed all my interests to those of the country. I go; but you, my friends, will continue to serve France. Her happiness was my only thought . . . It will still be the object of my wishes. Do not regret my fate: if I have consented to survive, it is to serve your glory. I intend to write the history of the great achievements we have performed together. Adieu, my friends. Would I could press you all to my, heart!"

During the first day cries of "Vive l'Empereur!" resounded along the road, and Napoleon, resorting to his usual dissimulation, censured the disloyalty of the people to their legitimate sovereign, which he did with ill disguised irony. The Guard accompanied him as far as Briars. At that place Napoleon invited Colonel Campbell to breakfast with him. He conversed on the last war in Spain, and spoke in complimentary terms of the English nation and the military talents of Wellington. Yet by that time he must have heard of the battle of Toulouse.

On the night of the 21st Napoleon slept at Nevers, where he was received by the acclamations of the people, who here, as in several other towns, mingled their cries in favour of their late sovereign with imprecations against the Commissioners of the Allies. He left Nevers at six on the morning of the 22d. Napoleon was now no longer escorted by the Guards, who were succeeded by a corps of Cossacks: the cries of "Vive l'Empereur!" accordingly ceased, and he had the mortification to hear in its stead, "Vivent les Allies!" However, I have been informed that at Lyons, through which the Emperor passed on the 23d at eleven at night, the cry of "Vive l'Empereur!" was still echoed among the groups who assembled before the post-office during the change of horses.

Augereau, who was still a Republican, though he accepted the title of Duke of Castiglione from Napoleon, had always been among the discontented. On the downfall of the Emperor he was one of that considerable number of persons who turned Royalists not out of love for the Bourbons but out of hatred to Bonaparte. He held a command in the south when he heard of the forfeiture of Napoleon pronounced by the Senate, and he was one of the first to send his recognition to the Provisional Government. Augereau, who, like all uneducated men, went to extremes in everything, had published under his name a proclamation extravagantly violent and even insulting to the Emperor. Whether Napoleon was aware of this proclamation I cannot pretend to say, but he affected ignorance of the matter if he was informed of it, for on the 24th, having met Augereau at a little distance from Valence, he stopped his carriage and immediately alighted. Augereau did the same, and they cordially embraced in the presence of the Commissioners. It was remarked that in saluting Napoleon took off his hat and Augereau kept on his. "Where are you going?", said the Emperor; "to Court?"—"No, I am going to Lyons."—"You have behaved very badly to me." Augereau, finding that the Emperor addressed him in the second person singular, adopted the same familiarity; so they conversed as they were accustomed to do when they were both generals in Italy. "Of what do you complain?" said he. "Has not your insatiable ambition brought us to this? Have you not sacrificed everything to that ambition, even the happiness of France? I care no more for the Bourbons than for you. All I care for is the country." Upon this Napoleon turned sharply away from the Marshal, lifted his hat to him, and then stepped into his carriage. The Commissioners, and all the persons in Napoleon's suite, were indignant at seeing Augereau stand in the road still covered, with his hands behind his back, and instead of bowing, merely making a contemptuous salutation to Napoleon with his hand. It was at the Tuileries that these haughty Republicans should have shown their airs. To have done so on the road to Elba was a mean insult which recoiled upon themselves.[273]

---

273 The following letter, taken from Captain Bingham's recently published selections from the Correspondence of the first Napoleon, indicates in emphatic language the Emperor's recent dissatisfaction with Marshal Augereau when in command at Lyons during the "death struggle" of 1814:

"TO MARSHAL AUGEREAU.

NOGENT, *21st February, 1814*,

...... What! six hours after having received the first troops coming from Spain you were not in the field! Six hours repose was sufficient. I won the action of Naugis with a brigade of dragoons coming from Spain which, since it had left Bayonne, had not unbridled its horses. The six battalions of the division of Nimes want clothes, equipment, and drilling, say you? What poor reasons you give me there, Augereau! I have destroyed 80,000 enemies with conscripts having nothing but knapsacks! The National Guards, say you, are pitiable; I have 4000 here in round hats, without knapsacks, in wooden shoes, but with good muskets, and I get a great deal out of them. There is no money, you continue; and where do you hope to draw money from! You want waggons; take them wherever you can. You have no magazines; this is too ridiculous. I order you twelve hours after the reception of this letter to take the field. If you

At Valence Napoleon, for the first time, saw French soldiers with the white cockade in their caps. They belonged to Augereau's corps. At Orange the air resounded with tunes of "Vive le Roi!" Here the gaiety, real or feigned, which Napoleon had hitherto evinced, began to forsake him.

Had the Emperor arrived at Avignon three hours later than he did there is no doubt that he would have been massacred.[274] He did not change horses at Avignon, through which he passed at five in the morning, but at St. Andiol, where he arrived at six. The Emperor, who was fatigued with sitting in the carriage, alighted with Colonel Campbell and General Bertrand, and walked with them up the first hill. His valet de chambre, who was also walking a little distance in advance, met one of the mail couriers, who said to him, "Those are the Emperor's carriages coming this way?"—"No, they are the equipages of the Allies."—"I say they are the Emperor's carriages. I am an old soldier. I served in the campaign of Egypt, and I will save the life of my General."—"I tell you again they are not the Emperor's carriages."—"Do not attempt to deceive me; I have just passed through Organ, where the Emperor has been hanged in effigy. The wretches erected a scaffold and hanged a figure dressed in a French uniform covered with blood. Perhaps I may get myself into a scrape by this confidence, but no matter. Do you profit by it." The courier then set off at full gallop. The valet de chambre took General Drouot apart, and told him what he had heard. Drouot communicated the circumstance to General Bertrand, who himself related it to the Emperor in the presence of the Commissioners. The latter, justly indignant, held a sort of council on the highway, and it was determined that the Emperor should go forward without his retinue. The valet de chambre was asked whether he had any clothes in the carriage. He produced a long blue cloak and a round hat. It was proposed to put a white cockade in the hat, but to this Napoleon would not consent. He went forward in the style of a courier, with Amaudru, one of the two outriders who had escorted his carriage, and dashed through Orgon. When the Allied Commissioners arrived there the assembled population were uttering exclamations of "Down with the Corsican! Down with the brigand!" The mayor of Orgon (the same man whom I had seen almost on his knees to General Bonaparte on his return from Egypt) addressed himself to Pelard, the Emperor's valet de chambre, and said, "Do you follow that rascal?"—"No," replied Pelard, "I am attached to the Commisairiers of the Allied powers."—Ah! that is well! I should like to hang the villain with my own hands.

"Ah! if you knew, sir, how the scoundrel has deceived us! It was I who received him on his return from Egypt. We wished to take his horses out and draw his carriage. I should like to avenge myself now for the honours I rendered him at that time."

The crowd augmented, and continued to vociferate with a degree of fury which may be imagined by those who have heard the inhabitants of the south manifest, by cries, their joy or their hatred. Some more violent than the rest wished to force Napoleon's coachman to cry "Vive le Roi!" He courageously refused, though threatened with a stroke of a sabre, when, fortunately; the carriage being ready to start, he whipped the horses and set off at

---

are still Augereau of Castiglione, keep the command, but if your sixty years weigh upon you hand over the command to your senior general. The country is in danger; and can be saved by boldness and alacrity alone . . . . . .

(*Signed*) NAPOLEON

274 The Royalist mob of Avignon massacred Marshal Brune in 1816.

full gallop. The Commissioners would not breakfast at Orgon; they paid for what had been prepared, and took some refreshments away with them. The carriages did not overtake the Emperor until they came to La Calade, where he had arrived a quarter of an hour before with Amaudru.

They found him standing by the fire in the kitchen of the inn talking with the landlady. She had asked him whether the tyrant was soon to pass that way? "Ah! sir," said she, "it is all nonsense to say we have got rid of him. I always, have said, and always will say, that we shall never be sure of being done with him until he be laid at the bottom of a well, covered over with stones. I wish we had him safe in the well in our yard. You see, sir, the Directory sent him to Egypt to get rid of him; but he came back again! And he will come back again, you maybe sure of that, sir; unless—" Here the good woman, having finished skimming her pot, looked up and perceived that all the party were standing uncovered except the individual to whom, she had been speaking. She was confounded, and the embarrassment she experienced at having spoken so ill of the Emperor to the Emperor himself banished all her anger, and she lavished every mark of attention, and respect on Napoleon and his retinue. A messenger was immediately sent to Aix to purchase ribbons for making white cockades. All the carriages were brought into the courtyard of the inn, and the gate was closed; the landlady informed Napoleon that it would not be prudent for him to venture on passing through Aix, where a population of more than 20,000 were waiting to stone him.

Meanwhile dinner was served, and Napoleon sat down to table. He admirably disguised the agitation which he could not fail to experience, and I have been assured, by some of the individuals who were present on that remarkable occasion, that he never made himself more agreeable. His conversation, which was enriched by the resources of his memory and his imagination, charmed every one, and he remarked, with an air of indifference which was perhaps affected, "I believe the new French Government has a design on my life."

The Commissioners, informed of what was going on at Aix, proposed sending to the Mayor an order for closing the gates and adopting measures for securing the public tranquillity. About fifty individuals had assembled round the inn, and one among them offered to carry a letter to the Mayor of Aix. The Commissioners accepted his services, and in their letter informed the Mayor that if the gates of the town were not closed within an hour they would advance with two regiments of uhlans and six pieces of artillery, and would fire upon all who might oppose them. This threat had the desired effect; and the Mayor returned for answer that the gates should be closed, and that he would take upon himself the responsibility of everything which might happen.

The danger which threatened the Emperor at Aix was thus averted; but there was another to be braved. During the seven or eight hours he passed at La Calade a considerable number of people had gathered round the inn, and manifested every disposition to proceed to some excess. Most of them had in their hands five-franc pieces, in order to recognise the Emperor by his likeness on the coin. Napoleon, who had passed two nights without sleep, was in a little room adjoining the kitchen, where he had fallen into a slumber, reclining an the shoulder of his valet de chambre. In a moment of dejection he had said, "I now renounce the political world forever. I shall henceforth feel no interest about anything that may happen. At Porto-Ferrajo I may be happy—more happy than I have ever been! No!—if the crown of Europe were now offered to me I would not accept it. I will devote myself to science. I was right never to esteem mankind! But France and the French people—what ingratitude! I am disgusted with ambition, and I wish to rule no longer!"

When the moment for departure arrived it was proposed that he should put on the greatcoat and fur cap of General Kohler, and that he should go into the carriage of the Austrian Commissioner. The Emperor, thus disguised, left the inn of La Calade, passing between two lines of spectators. On turning the walls of Aix Napoleon had again the mortification to hear the cries of "Down with the tyrant! Down with Nicolas!" and these vociferations resounded at the distance of a quarter of a league from the town.

Bonaparte, dispirited by these manifestations of hatred, said, in a tone of mingled grief and contempt, "These Provencals are the same furious brawlers that they used to be. They committed frightful massacres at the commencement of the Revolution. Eighteen years ago I came to this part of the country with some thousand men to deliver two Royalists who were to be hanged. Their crime was having worn the white cockade. I saved them; but it was not without difficulty that I rescued them from the hands of their assailants; and now, you see, they resume the same excesses against those who refuse to wear the white cockade.". At about a league from Aix the Emperor and his retinue found horses and an escort of gendarmerie to conduct them to the chateau of Luc.

The Princess Pauline was at the country residence of M. Charles, member of the Legislative Body, near the castle of Luc. On hearing of the misfortunes of her brother she determined to accompany him to the isle of Elba, and she proceeded to Fréjus to embark with him. At Fréjus the Emperor rejoined Colonel Campbell, who had quitted the convoy on the road, and had brought into the port the English frigate the 'Undaunted' which was appointed to convey the Emperor to the place of his destination. In spite of the wish he had expressed to Colonel Campbell he manifested considerable reluctance to go on board. However, on the 28th of April he sailed for the island of Elba in the English frigate, in which it could not then be said that Caesar and his fortune were embarked.[275]

In every particular of his conduct he paid great attention to the maintenance of his Imperial dignity. On landing he received the keys of his city of Porto-Ferrajo, and the devoirs of the Governor, prefect, and other dignitaries, and he proceeded immediately under a canopy of State to the parish church, which served as a cathedral. There he heard Te Deum, and it is stated that his countenance was dark and melancholy, and that he even shed tears.

One of Bonaparte's first cares was to select a flag for the Elbese Empire, and after some hesitation he fixed on "Argent, on a bend gules, or three bees," as the armorial ensign of his new dominion. It is strange that neither he nor any of those whom he consulted should have been aware that Elba had an ancient and peculiar ensign, and it is still more remarkable that this ensign should be one singularly adapted to Bonaparte's situation; being no more than "a wheel,—the emblem," says M. Bernaud, "of the vicissitudes of human life, which the Elbese had borrowed from the Egyptian mysteries." This is as curious a coincidence as any we ever recollect to have met; as the medals of Elba with the emblem of the wheel are well known, we cannot but suppose that Bonaparte was aware of the circumstance; yet he is represented as having in vain made several anxious inquiries after the ancient arms of the island.

During the first months of his residence there his life was, in general, one of characteristic

275 It was on the 3d of May 1814 that Bonaparte arrived within sight of Porto-Ferrajo, the capital of his miniature empire; but he did not land till the next morning. At first he paid a short visit incognito, being accompanied by a sergeant's party of marines from the Undaunted. He then returned on board to breakfast, and at about two o'clock made his public entrance, the 'Undaunted' firing a royal salute.

activity and almost garrulous frankness. He gave dinners, went to balls, rode all day about his island, planned fortifications, aqueducts, lazarettos, harbours, and palaces; and the very second day after he landed fitted out an expedition of a dozen soldiers to take possession of a little uninhabited island called Pianosa, which lies a few leagues from Elba; on this occasion he said good-humouredly, "Toute l'Europe dira que j'ai deja fait une conqute" (All Europe will say I have already made a conquest). The cause of the island of Pianosa being left uninhabited was the marauding of the Corsairs from the coast of Barbary, against whom Bonaparte considered himself fully protected by the 4th Article of the Treaty of Fontainebleau.

The greatest wealth of Elba consists in its iron mines, for which the island was celebrated in the days of Virgil. Soon after his arrival Napoleon visited the mines in company with Colonel Campbell, and being informed that they produced annually about 500,000 francs he exclaimed joyfully, "These, then, are my own!" One of his followers, however, reminded him that he had long since disposed of that revenue, having given it to his order of the Legion of Honour, to furnish pensions, etc. "Where was my head when I made that grant?" said he, "but I have made many foolish decrees of that sort!"

Sir Walter Scott, in telling a curious fact, makes a very curious mistake. "To dignify his capital," he says, "having discovered that the ancient name of Porto-Ferrajo was Comopoli (the city of Como), he commanded it to be called Cosmopoli, or the city of all nations." Now the old name of Porto-Ferrajo was in reality not Comopoli, but Cosmopoli, and it obtained that name from the Florentine Cosmo de' Medici, to whose ducal house Elba belonged, as an integral part of Tuscany. The name equally signified the city of Cosmo, or the city of all nations, and the vanity of the Medici had probably been flattered by the double meaning of the appellation. But Bonaparte certainly revived the old name, and did not add a letter to it to dignify his little capital.

The household of Napoleon, though reduced to thirty-five persons, still represented an Imperial Court. The forms and etiquette of the Tuileries and St, Cloud were retained on a diminished scale, but the furniture and internal accommodations of the palace are represented as having been meaner by far than those of an English gentleman of ordinary rank. The Bodyguard of his Imperial Majesty the Emperor of Elba consisted of about 700 infantry and 80 cavalry, and to this handful of troops Napoleon seemed to pay almost as much attention as he had formerly given to his Grande Armee. The men were constantly exercised, particularly in throwing shot and shells, and he soon began to look out for good recruits.

He early announced that he would hold a Court and receive ladies twice a week; the first was on the 7th of May, and a great concourse assembled. Bonaparte at first paid great attention to the women, particularly those who possessed personal attractions, and asked them, in his rapid way, whether they were married? how many children they had, and who their husbands were? To the last question he received one universal answer; it happened that every lady was married to a merchant, but when it came to be further explained that they were merchant butchers and merchant bakers, his Imperial Majesty permitted some expression of his dissatisfaction to escape him and hastily retired. On the 4th of June there was a ball on board the British frigate, in honour of the King's birthday; the whole beauty and fashion of Elba were assembled, and dancing with great glee, when, about midnight, Bonaparte came in his barge, unexpectedly, and masked, to join the festivity. He was very affable, and visited every part of the ship, and all the amusements which had been prepared for the different classes of persons. On his birthday, the 15th of August, he ordered the mayor to give a ball, and for this purpose a temporary building, capable of holding 300 persons, was to be erected, and the whole entertainment, building and all, were to be at the expense of the inhabitants themselves. These were bad auspices, and accordingly the ball completely failed. Madame Mtire, Madame Bertrand, and the two ladies of honour, attended, but not above thirty of the fair islanders, and as the author of the Itineraire remarks, "Le bal fut triste quoique Bonaparte n'y parut pas."

Having in an excursion reached the summit of one of the highest hills on the island, where the sea was visible all round him, he shook his head with affected solemnity, and exclaimed in a bantering tone, "Eh! il faut avouer que mon ile est bien petite."

On this mountain one of the party saw a little church in an almost inaccessible situation, and observed that it was a most inconvenient site for a church, for surely no congregation could attend it. "It is on that account the more convenient to the parson," replied Bonaparte, "who may preach what stuff he pleases without fear of contradiction."

As they descended the hill and met some peasants with their goats who asked for charity, Bonaparte told a story which the present circumstances brought to his recollection, that when he was crossing the Great St. Bernard, previously to the battle of Marengo, he had met a goatherd, and entered into conversation with him. The goatherd, not knowing to whom he was speaking, lamented his own hard lot, and envied the riches of some persons who actually had cows and cornfields. Bonaparte inquired if some fairy were to offer to gratify all his wishes what he would ask? The poor peasant expressed, in his own opinion, some very extravagant desires, such as a dozen of cows and a good farmhouse. Bonaparte afterwards recollected the incident, and astonished the goatherd by the fulfilment of all his wishes.

But all his thoughts and conversations were not as light and pleasant as these. Sometimes he would involve himself in an account of the last campaign, of his own views and hopes, of the defection of his marshals, of the capture of Paris, and finally of his abdication; on these he would talk by the hour with great earnestness and almost fury, exhibiting in very rapid succession traits of eloquence, of military genius, of indignation; of vanity, and of selfishness. With regard to the audience to whom he addressed these tirades he was not very particular.

The chief violence of his rage seemed to be directed against Marshal Marmont whom, as well as Augereau, he sometimes called by names too gross for repetition, and charged roundly with treachery. Marmont, when he could no longer defend Paris by arms, saved it by an honourable capitulation; he preserved his army for the service of his country and when everything else was lost stipulated for the safety of Bonaparte. This last stipulation, however, Bonaparte affected to treat with contempt and indignation.—Editor of 1836 edition.

CHAPTER III

1814

No power is so great as that resulting from the changes produced by time. Wise policy consists in directing that power, but to do so it is requisite to know the wants of the age. For this reason Louis XVIII. appeared, in the eyes of all sensible persons, a monarch expressly formed for the circumstances in which we stood after the fall of Napoleon.

In the winter of 1813-14 some Royalist proclamations had been circulated in Paris, and as they contained the germs of those hopes which the Charter, had it been executed, was calculated to realise, the police opposed their circulation, and I recollect that, in order to multiply the number of copies, my family and I daily devoted some hours to transcribing them. After the definitive declaration of Alexander a very active correspondence ensued between the Provisional Government and Hartwell, and Louis XVIII. was even preparing to embark for Bordeaux when he learned the events of the 31st of March. That news induced the King to alter his determination, and he soon quitted his retirement to proceed to London. Louis XVIII. and the Prince Regent of England exchanged the orders of the Holy Ghost and the Garter, and I believe I may affirm that this was the first occasion on which any but a Catholic Prince was invested with the order of the Holy Ghost.

Louis XVIII. embarked at Dover on board the Royal Sovereign, and landed at Calais on the 24th of April. I need not enter into any description of the enthusiasm which his presence excited; that is generally known through the reports of the journals of the time. It is very certain that all rational persons saw with satisfaction the Princes of the House of Bourbon reascend the throne of their ancestors, enlightened by experience and misfortune, which, as some ancient philosopher observes, are the best counsellors of kings.

I had received a letter addressed to me from London by the Duc de Duras, pointing out the route which Louis XVIII. was to pursue from Calais to Paris: In this he said, "After the zeal, monsieur, you have shown for the service of the King, I do not doubt your activity to prevent his suffering in any way at a moment so happy and interesting for every Frenchman." The King's wishes on this subject were scrupulously fulfilled, and I recollect with pleasure the zeal with which my directions were executed by all the persons in the service of the Postoffice. His Majesty stopped for a short time at Amiens, and then proceeded to Compiegne, where the Ministers and Marshals had previously arrived to present to him their homage and the assurance of their fidelity. Berthier addressed the King in the name of the Marshals, and said, among other things, "that France, groaning for five and twenty years under the weight of the misfortunes that oppressed her, had anxiously looked forward to the happy day which she now saw dawning." Berthier might justly have said for "ten years"; but at all events, even had he spoken the truth, it was ill placed in the mouth of a man whom the Emperor had constantly loaded with favours: The Emperor Alexander also went to Compiegne to meet Louis XVIII., and the two monarchs dined together.

I did not go to Compiegne because the business which I had constantly to execute did not permit me to leave Paris for so long an interval as that journey would have required, but

I was at St. Ouen when Louis XVIII. arrived on the 2d of May. There I had to congratulate myself on being remembered by a man to whom I was fortunate enough to render some service at Hamburg. As the King entered the salon through which he had to pass to go to the dining-room M. Hue recognising me said to his Majesty, "There is M. de Bourrienne." The King then stepping up to me said, "Ah! M. de Bourrienne, I am very glad to see you. I am aware of the services you have rendered me in Hamburg and Paris, and I shall feel much pleasure in testifying my gratitude."

At St. Ouen Louis XVIII. promulgated the declaration which preceded the Charter, and which repeated the sentiments expressed by the King twenty years before, in the Declaration of Colmar. It was also at St, Ouen that project of a Constitution was presented to him by the Senate in which that body, to justify 'in extremis' its title of conservative, stipulated for the preservation of its revenues and endowments.

On the 3d of May Louis XVIII. made his solemn entrance into Paris, the Duchess d'Angouleme being in the carriage with the King. His Majesty proceeded first to Notre Dame. On arriving at the Pont Neuf he saw the model of the statue of Henri IV. replaced, on the pedestal of which appeared the following words: 'Ludovico reduce, Henricus redivivus', which were suggested by M. de Lally-Tollendal, and were greatly preferable to the long and prolix inscription composed for the bronze statue.

The King's entrance into Paris did not excite so much enthusiasm as the entrance of Monsieur. In the places through which I passed on the 3d of May astonishment seemed to be the prevailing feeling among the people. The abatement of public enthusiasm was more perceptible a short time after, when Louis XVIII. restored "the red corps" which Louis XVI. had suppressed long before the Revolution.

It was not a little extraordinary to see the direction of the Government consigned to a man who neither had nor could have any knowledge of France. From the commencement M. de Blacas affected ministerial omnipotence. When I went on the 11th of May to the Tuileries to present, as usual, my portfolio to the King, in virtue of my privilege of transacting business with the sovereign, M. de Blacas wished to take the portfolio from me, which appeared to me the more surprising as, during the seven days I had the honour of coming in contact with Louis XVIII., his Majesty had been pleased to bestow many compliments upon me. I at first refused to give up the portfolio, but M. de Blacas told me the King had ordered him to receive it; I then, of course, yielded the point.

However, it, was not long before I had experience of a courtier's revenge, for two days after this circumstance, that is to say, on the 13th of May, on entering my cabinet at the usual hour, I mechanically took up the 'Moniteur', which I found lying on my desk. On glancing hastily over it what was my astonishment to find that the Comte Ferrand had been appointed Director of the Post-office in my stead. Such was the strange mode in which M. de Blacas made me feel the promised gratitude of the sovereign. Certainly, after my proofs of loyalty, which a year afterwards procured for me the honour of being outlawed in quite a special way, I had reason to complain, and I might have said 'Sic vos non vobis' as justly as Virgil when he alluded to the unmerited favours lavished by Augustus on the Maevii and Bavii of his time.

The measures of Government soon excited complaints in every quarter. The usages of the old system were gradually restored, and ridicule being mingled with more serious considerations, Paris was speedily inundated with caricatures and pamphlets. However, tranquillity prevailed until the month of September, when M. de Talleyrand departed for the Congress of Vienna. Then all was disorder at the Tuileries. Every one feeling himself free from restraint, wished to play the statesman, and Heaven knows how many follies were committed in the absence of the schoolmaster.

Under a feeble Government there is but one step from discontent to insurrection, under an imbecile Government like that of France in 1814, after the departure of M. de Talleyrand, conspiracy has free Scope. During the summer of 1814 were initiated the events which reached their climax on the 20th of March 1815. I almost fancy I am dreaming when I look back on the miraculous incapacity of the persons who were then at the head of our Government. The emigrants, who, as it has been truly said, had neither learned nor forgotten anything, came back with all the absurd pretensions of Coblentz. Their silly vanity reminded one of a character in one of Voltaire's novels who is continually saying, "Un homme comme moi!" These people were so engrossed with their pretended merit that they were blind to everything else. They not only disregarded the wishes and the wants of France; which in overthrowing the Empire hoped to regain liberty, but they disregarded every warning they had received.

I recollect one circumstance which was well calculated to excite suspicion. Prince Eugène proposed going to the waters of Plombieres to join his sister Hortense. The horses, the carriages, and one of the Prince's aides de camp had already arrived at Plombieres, and his residence was prepared; but he did not go. Eugène had, no doubt, received intimation of his sister's intrigues with some of the individuals of the late Court of Napoleon who were then at the waters, and as he had determined to reside quietly at the Court of his father-in-law; without meddling with public affairs, he remained at Munich. This fact, however, passed off unnoticed.

At the end of 1814 unequivocal indications of a great catastrophe were observable. About that time a man, whom I much esteem, and with whom I have always been on terms of friendship, said to me, "You see how things are going on: they are committing fault upon fault. You must be convinced that such a state of things cannot last long. Between ourselves, I am of opinion that all will be over in the month of March; that month will repair the disgrace of last March. We shall then, once for all, be delivered from fanaticism and the emigrants. You see the intolerable spirit of hypocrisy that prevails, and you know that the influence of the priests is, of all things, the most hateful to the nation. We have gone back a long way within the last eight months. I fear you will repent of having taken too active a part in affairs at the commencement of the present year. You see we have gone a very different way from what you expected. However, as I have often told you before, you had good reason to complain; and after all, you acted to the best of your judgment."

I did not attach much importance to this prediction of a change in the month of March. I deplored, as every one did, the inconceivable errors of "Ferrand and Company," and I hoped that the Government would gradually return to those principles which were calculated to conciliate the feelings of the people. A few days after another of my friends called on me. He had exercised important functions, and his name had appeared on a proscription list. He had claims upon the Government, which was by no means favourably disposed towards him. I asked him how things were going on, and he replied, "Very well; no opposition is made to my demands. I have no reason to complain." This reminded me of the man in the 'Lettres Persanes', who admired the excellent order of the finances under Colbert because his pension was promptly paid. I congratulated my friend on the justice which the Government rendered him, as well as on the justice which he rendered to the Government, and I remarked that if the same course were adopted towards every one all parties would speedily be conciliated. "I do not think so," said my friend. "If the Government persist in its present course it cannot possibly stand, and we shall have the Emperor back again."—"That," said I, "would be a very great misfortune; and even if such were the wish of France, it would be opposed by Europe. You who are so devotedly attached to France cannot be indifferent to the danger that would threaten her if the presence of Bonaparte should bring the foreigners back again. Can you endure to think of the dismemberment of our country?"—"That they would never dare to attempt. But you and I can never agree on the question of the Emperor and your Bourbons. We take a totally different view of the matter. You had cause to complain of Bonaparte, but I had only reason to be satisfied with him. But tell me, what would you do if he were to return?"— "Bonaparte return!"—"Yes."—"Upon my word, the best thing I could do would be to set off as speedily as I could, and that is certainly what I should do. I am thoroughly convinced that he would never pardon me for the part I have taken in the Restoration, and I candidly confess that I should not hesitate a moment to save my life by leaving France."—"Well, you are wrong, for I am convinced that if you would range yourself among the number of his friends you might have whatever you wished—titles, honours, riches. Of this I could give you assurance."—"All this, I must tell you, does not tempt me. I love France as dearly, as you do, and I am convinced that she can never be happy under Bonaparte. If he should return I will go and live abroad."

This is only part of a conversation which lasted a considerable time, and, as is often the case after a long discussion, my friend retained his opinion, and I mine. However, this second warning, this hypothesis of the return of Bonaparte, made me reflect, and I soon received another hint which gave additional weight to the preceding ones. An individual with whom I was well acquainted, and whom I knew from his principles and connections to be entirely devoted to the royal cause, communicated to me some extraordinary circumstances which he said alarmed him. Among other things he said, "The day before yesterday I met Charles de Labedoyere, who, you know, is my intimate friend. I remarked that he had an air of agitation and abstraction. I invited him to come and dine with me, but he declined, alleging as an excuse that we should not be alone. He then asked me to go and dine with him yesterday, as he wanted to talk with me. I accepted his invitation, and we conversed a long time on political affair's and the situation of France. You know my sentiments are quite the reverse of his, so we disputed and wrangled, though we are still very good friends. But what alarms me is, that at parting Charles pressed my hand, saying, 'Adieu; to-morrow I set off for Grenoble. In a month you will hear something of Charles de Labedoyere.'"

These three successive communications appeared to me very extraordinary. The two first were made to me by persons interested in the event, and the third by one who dreaded it. They all presented a striking coincidence with the intrigues at Plombieres a few months before. In the month of January I determined to mention the business to M. de Blacas, who then engrossed all credit and all power, and through whose medium alone anything could reach the sovereign. I need scarcely add that my intention was merely to mention to him the facts without naming the individuals from whom I obtained them. After all, however, M. de Blacas did not receive me, and I only had the honour of speaking to his secretary, who, if the fact deserve to be recorded, was an abbe named Fleuriel. This personage, who was an extraordinary specimen of impertinence and self-conceit, would have been an admirable study for a comic poet. He had all the dignity belonging to the great secretary of a great Minister, and, with an air of indifference, he told me that the Count was not there; but M. de Blacas was there, and I knew it.

Devoted as I was to the cause of the Bourbons, I thought it my duty to write that very day to M. de Blacas to request an interview; I received no answer. Two days after I wrote a second letter, in which I informed M. de Blacas that I had something of the greatest importance to communicate to him; this letter remained unnoticed like the first. Unable to account for this strange treatment I again repaired to the Pavilion de Flore, and requested the Abbe Fleuriel to explain to me if he could the cause of his master's silence. "Sir," said he, "I received your two letters, and laid them before the Count; I cannot tell why he has not sent you an answer; but Monsieur le Comte is so much engaged. . . . Monsieur le Comte is so overwhelmed with business that"—"Monsieur le Comte may, perhaps, repent of it. Good morning, sir!"

I thus had personal experience of the truth of what I had often heard respecting M. de Blacas. That favourite, who succeeded Comte d'Avaray, enjoyed the full confidence of the King, and concentrated the sovereign power in his own cabinet. The only means of transmitting any communication to Louis XVIII. was to get it addressed to M. de Blacas by one of his most intimate friends.

Convinced as I was of the danger that threatened France, and unable to break through the blockade which M. de Blacas had formed round the person of the King, I determined to write to M. de Talleyrand at Vienna,' and acquaint him with the communications that had been made to me. M. de Talleyrand corresponded directly with the King, and I doubt not that my information at length reached the ears of his Majesty. But when Louis XVIII. was informed of what was to happen it was too late to avert the danger.

CHAPTER IV

1814-1815

About the middle of summer Napoleon was visited by his mother and his sister the Princess Pauline. Both these ladies had very considerable talents for political intrigue, and then natural faculties in this way had not lain dormant or been injured by want of practice. In Pauline this finesse was partially concealed by a languor and indecision of manner and an occasional assumption of 'niaiserie'; or almost infantine simplicity; but this only threw people the more off their guard, and made her finesse the more sure in its operation. Pauline was handsome too, uncommonly graceful, and had all that power of fascination which has been attributed to the Bonaparte family. She could gain hearts with ease, and those whom her charms enslaved were generally ready to devote themselves absolutely to her brother. She went and came between Naples and Elba, and kept her brother-in-law, Murat, in mind of the fact that the lion was not yet dead nor so much as sleeping, but merely retiring the better to spring forward on his quarry.

Having taken this resolution and chosen his time, Napoleon kept the secret of his expedition until the last moment; and means were found to privately make the requisite preparations. A portion of the soldiers was embarked in a brig called the 'Inconstant' and the remainder in six small craft. It was not till they were all on board that the troops first conceived a suspicion of the Emperor's purpose: 1000 or 1200 men had sailed to regain possession of an Empire containing a population of 30,000,000! He commenced his voyage on Sunday the 26th of February 1815, and the next morning at ten o'clock was not out of sight of the island, to the great annoyance of the few friends he had left behind. At this time Colonel Sir Neil Campbell was absent on a tour to Leghorn, but being informed by the French Consul and by Spanocchi, the Tuscan Governor of the town, that Napoleon was about to sail for the Continent, he hastened back, and gave chase to the little squadron in the Partridge sloop of war, which was cruising in the neighbourhood, but, being delayed by communicating with a French frigate, reached Antibes too late.

There were between 400 and 500 men on board the brig (the 'Inconstant') in which Bonaparte embarked. On the passage they met with a French ship of war, with which they spoke. The Guards were ordered to pull off their caps and lie down on the deck or go below while the captain exchanged some words with the commander of the frigate, whom he afterwards proposed to pursue and capture. Bonaparte rejected the idea as absurd, and asked why he should introduce this new episode into his plan.

As they stood over to the coast of France the Emperor was in the highest spirits. The die was cast, and he seemed to be quite himself again. He sat upon the deck and amused the officers collected round him with a narrative of his campaigns, particularly those of Italy and Egypt. When he had finished he observed the deck to be encumbered with several large chests belonging to him. He asked the maitre d'hotel what they contained. Upon being told they were filled with wine he ordered them to be immediately broken open, saying, "We will divide the booty." The Emperor superintended the distribution himself, and presented bottle by bottle to his comrades, till tired of this occupation he called out to Bertrand, "Grand Marshal, assist me, if you please. Let us help these gentlemen. They will help us some day." It was with this species of bonhomie that he captivated when he chose all around him. The following day he was employed in various arrangements, and among others in dictating to Colonel Raoul the proclamations to be issued on his landing. In one of these, after observing, "we must forget that we have given law to the neighbouring nations," Napoleon stopped. "What have I said?" Colonel Raoul read the passage. "Stop!" said Napoleon. "Omit the word 'neighbouring;' say simply 'to nations.'" It was thus his pride revealed itself; and his ambition seemed to rekindle at the very recollections of his former greatness.

Napoleon landed without any accident on the 1st of March at Cannes, a small seaport in the Gulf of St. Juan, not far from Fréjus, where he had disembarked on his return from Egypt sixteen years before, and where he had embarked the preceding year for Elba. A small party of the Guards who presented themselves before the neighbouring garrison of Antibes were made prisoners by General Corsin, the Governor of the place. Some one hinted that it was not right to proceed till they had released their comrades, but the Emperor observed that this was poorly to estimate the magnitude of the undertaking; before them were 30,000,000 men uniting to be set free! He, however, sent the Commissariat Officer to try what he could do, calling out after him, "Take care you do not get yourself made prisoner too!"

At nightfall the troops bivouacked on the beach. Just before a postillion, in a splendid livery, had been brought to Napoleon. It turned out that this man had formerly been a domestic of the Empress Josephine, and was now in the service of the Prince of Monaco, who himself had been equerry to the Empress. The postillion, after expressing his great astonishment at finding the Emperor there, stated, in answer to the questions that were put to him, that he had just come from Paris; that all along the road, as far as Avignon, he had heard nothing but regret for the Emperor's absence; that his name was constantly echoed from mouth to mouth; and that, when once fairly through Provence, he would find the whole population ready to rally round him. The man added that his laced livery had frequently rendered him the object of odium and insult on the road. This was the testimony of one of the common class of society: it was very gratifying to the Emperor, as it entirely corresponded with his expectations. The Prince of Monaco himself, on being presented to the Emperor, was less explicit. Napoleon refrained from questioning him on political matters. The conversation therefore assumed a more lively character, and turned altogether on the ladies of the former Imperial Court, concerning whom the Emperor was very particular in his inquiries.

As soon as the moon had risen, which was about one or two in the morning of the 2d, the bivouacs were broken up, and Napoleon gave orders for proceeding to Grasse. There he expected to find a road which he had planned during the Empire, but in this he was disappointed, the Bourbons having given up all such expensive works through want of money. Bonaparte was therefore obliged to pass through narrow defiles filled with snow, and left behind him in the hands of the municipality his carriage and two pieces of cannon, which had been brought ashore. This was termed a capture in the bulletins of the day. The municipality of Grasse was strongly in favour of the Royalist cause, but the sudden appearance of the Emperor afforded but little time for hesitation, and they came to tender their submission to him. Having passed through the town he halted on a little height some way beyond it, where he breakfasted. He was soon surrounded by the whole population of the place; and he heard the same sentiments and the same prayers as before he quitted France. A multitude of petitions had already been drawn up, and were presented to him, just as though he had come from Paris and was making a tour through the departments. One complained that his pension had not been paid, another that his cross of the Legion of Honour had been taken from him. Some of the more discontented secretly informed Napoleon that the authorities of the town were very hostile to him, but that the mass of the people were devoted to him, and only waited till his back was turned to rid themselves of the miscreants. He replied, "Be not too hasty. Let them have the mortification of seeing our triumph without having anything to reproach us with." The Emperor advanced with all the rapidity in his power. "Victory," he said, "depended on my speed. To me France was in Grenoble. That place was a hundred miles distant, but I and my companions reached it in five days; and with what weather and what roads! I entered the city just as the Comte d'Artois, warned by the telegraph, was quitting the Tuileries."

Napoleon himself was so perfectly convinced of the state of affairs that he knew his success in no way depended on the force he might bring with him. A 'piquet' of 'gens d'armes', he said, was all that was necessary. Everything turned out as he foresaw. At first he owned he was not without some degree of uncertainty and apprehension. As he advanced, however, the whole population declared themselves enthusiastically in his favour: but he saw no soldiers. It was not till he arrived between Mure and Vizille, within five or six leagues from Grenoble, and on the fifth day after his landing, that he met a battalion. The commanding officer refused to hold even a parley. The Emperor, without hesitation, advanced alone, and 100 grenadiers marched at some distance behind him, with their arms reversed. The sight of Napoleon, his well-known costume, and his gray military greatcoat, had a magical effect on the soldiers, and they stood motionless. Napoleon went straight up to them and baring his breast said, "Let him that has the heart kill his Emperor!" The soldiers threw down their arms, their eyes moistened with tears, and cries of "Vive l'Empereur!" resounded on every side. Napoleon ordered the battalion to wheel round to the right, and all marched on together.

At a short distance from Grenoble Colonel Labedoyere, who had been sent at the head of the 7th regiment to oppose his passage, came to join the Emperor. The impulse thus given in a manner decided the question. Labedoyere's superior officer in vain interfered to restrain his enthusiasm and that of his men. The tri-coloured cockades, which had been concealed in the hollow of a drum, were eagerly distributed by Labedoyere among them, and they threw away the white cockade as a badge of their nation's dishonour. The peasantry of Dauphiny, the cradle of the Revolution, lined the roadside: they were transported and mad with joy. The first battalion, which has just been alluded to, had shown some signs of hesitation, but thousands of the country people crowded round it, and by their shouts of "Vive l'Empereur!" endeavoured to urge the troops to decision, while others who followed in Napoleon's rear encouraged his little troop to advance by assuring them that they would meet with success. Napoleon said he could have taken 2,000,000 of these peasants with him to Paris, but that then he would have been called "the King of the Jaequerie."

Napoleon issued two proclamations on the road. He at first regretted that he had not had them printed before he left Elba; but this could not have been done without some risk of betraying his secret designs. He dictated them on board the vessel, where every man who could write was employed in copying them. These copies soon became very scarce; many of them were illegible; and it was not till he arrived at Gap, on the 5th of March, that he found means to have them printed. They were from that time circulated and read everywhere with the utmost avidity.

The address to the army was considered as being still more masterly and eloquent, and it was certainly well suited to the taste of French soldiers, who, as Bourrienne remarks, are wonderfully pleased with grandiloquence, metaphor, and hyperbole, though they do not always understand what they mean. Even a French author of some distinction praises this address as something sublime. "The proclamation to the army," says he, "is full of energy: it could not fail to make all military imaginations vibrate. That prophetic phrase, 'The eagle, with the national colours, will fly from church steeple to church steeple, till it settles on the towers of Notre Dame,' was happy in the extreme."

These words certainly produced an immense effect on the French soldiery, who everywhere shouted, "Vive l'Empereur!" "Vive le petit Caporal!" "We will die for our old comrade!" with the most genuine enthusiasm.

It was some distance in advance of Grenoble that Labedoyere joined, but he could not make quite sure of the garrison of that city, which was commanded by General Marchand, a man resolved to be faithful to his latest master. The shades of night had fallen when Bonaparte arrived in front of the fortress of Grenoble, where he stood for some minutes in a painful state of suspense and indecision.

It was on the 7th of March, at nightfall, that Bonaparte thus stood before the walls of Grenoble. He found the gates closed, and the commanding officer refused to open them. The garrison assembled on the ramparts shouted "Vive l'Empereur!" and shook hands with Napoleon's followers through the wickets, but they could not be prevailed on to do more. It was necessary to force the gates, and this was done under the mouths of ten pieces of artillery, loaded with grapeshot. In none of his battles did Napoleon ever imagine himself to be in so much danger as at the entrance into Grenoble. The soldiers seemed to turn upon him with furious gestures: for a moment it might be supposed that they were going to tear him to pieces. But these were the suppressed transports of love and joy. The Emperor and his horse were both borne along by the multitude, and he had scarcely time to breathe in the inn where he alighted when an increased tumult was heard without; the inhabitants of Grenoble came to offer him the broken gates of the city, since they could not present him with the keys.

From Grenoble to Paris Napoleon found no further opposition. During the four days of his stay at Lyons, where he had arrived on the 10th, there were continually upwards of 20,000 people assembled before his windows; whose acclamations were unceasing. It would never have been supposed that the Emperor had even for a moment been absent from the country. He issued orders, signed decrees, reviewed the troops, as if nothing had happened. The military corps, the public bodies, and all classes of citizens, eagerly came forward to tender their homage and their services. The Comte d'Artois, who had hastened to Lyons, as the Duc and Duchesse d'Augouleme had done to Bourdeaux, like them in vain attempted to make a stand. The Mounted National Guard (who were known Royalists) deserted him at this crisis, and in his flight only one of them chose to follow him. Bonaparte refused their services when offered to him, and with a chivalrous feeling worthy of being recorded sent the decoration of the Legion of Honour to the single volunteer who had thus shown his fidelity by following the Duke.

As soon as the Emperor quitted Lyons he wrote to Ney, who with his army was at Lons-le-Saulnier, to come and join him. Ney had set off from the Court with a promise to bring Napoleon, "like a wild beast in a cage, to Paris." Scott excuses Ney's heart at the expense of his head, and fancies that the Marshal was rather carried away by circumstances, by vanity, and by fickleness, than actuated by premeditated treachery, and it is quite possible that these protestations were sincerely uttered when Ney left Paris, but, infected by the ardour of his troops, he was unable to resist a contagion so much in harmony with all his antecedents, and to attack not only his leader in many a time of peril, but also the sovereign who had forwarded his career through every grade of the army.

The facts of the case were these:—

On the 11th of March Ney, being at Besancon, learned that Napoleon was at Lyons. To those who doubted whether his troops would fight against their old comrades he said, "They shall fight! I will take a musket from a grenadier and begin the action myself! I will run my sword to the hilt in the body of the first man who hesitates to fire." At the same time he wrote to the Minister of War at Paris that he hoped to see a fortunate close to this mad enterprise.

He then advanced to Lons-le-Saulnier, where, on the night between the 13th and 14th of March, not quite three days after his vehement protestations of fidelity, he received, without hesitation, a letter from Bonaparte, inviting him, by his old appellation of the "Bravest of the Brave," to join his standard. With this invitation Ney complied, and published an order of the day that declared the cause of the Bourbons, which he had sworn to defend, lost for ever.

It is pleaded in extenuation of Ney's defection that both his officers and men were beyond his control, and determined to join their old Master; but in that case he might have given up his command, and retired in the same honourable way that Marshals Macdonald and Marmont and several other generals did. But even among his own officers Ney had an example set him, for many of them, after remonstrating in vain, threw up their commands. One of them broke his sword in two and threw the pieces at Ney's feet, saying, "It is easier for a man of honour to break iron than to break his word."

Napoleon, when at St. Helena, gave a very different reading to these incidents. On this subject he was heard to say, "If I except Labedoyere, who flew to me with enthusiasm and affection, and another individual, who, of his own accord, rendered me important services, nearly all the other generals whom I met on my route evinced hesitation and uncertainty; they yielded only to the impulse about them, if indeed they did not manifest a hostile feeling towards me. This was the case with Ney, with Massena, St. Cyr, Soult, as well as with Macdonald and the Duke of Belluno, so that if the Bourbons had reason to complain of the complete desertion of the soldiers and the people, they had no right to reproach the chiefs of the army with conspiring against them, who had shown themselves mere children in politics, and would be looked upon as neither emigrants nor patriots."

Between Lyons and Fontainebleau Napoleon often travelled several miles ahead of his army with no other escort than a few Polish lancers. His advanced guard now generally consisted of the troops (miscalled Royal) who happened to be before him on the road whither they had been sent to oppose him, and to whom couriers were sent forward to give notice of the Emperor's approach, in order that they might be quite ready to join him with the due military ceremonies. White flags and cockades everywhere disappeared; the tri-colour resumed its pride of place. It was spring, and true to its season the violet had reappeared! The joy of the soldiers and the lower orders was almost frantic, but even among the industrious poor there were not wanting many who regretted this precipitate return to the old order of things—to conscription, war, and bloodshed, while in the superior classes of society there was a pretty general consternation. The vain, volatile soldiery, however, thought of nothing but their Emperor, saw nothing before them but the restoration of all their laurels, the humiliation of England, and the utter defeat of the Russians, Prussians, and Austrians.

On the night between the 19th and 20th of March Napoleon reached Fontainebleau, and again paused, as had formerly been his custom, with short, quick steps through the antiquated but splendid galleries of that old palace. What must have been his feelings on revisiting the chamber in which, the year before, it is said he had attempted suicide!

Louis XVIII., left the Palace of the Tuileries at nearly the same hour that Bonaparte entered that of Fontainebleau.

The most forlorn hope of the Bourbons was now in a considerable army posted between Fontainebleau and Paris. Meanwhile the two armies approached each other at Melun; that of the King was commanded by Marshal Macdonald. On the 20th his troops were drawn up in three lines to receive the invaders, who were said to be advancing from Fontainebleau. There was a long pause of suspense, of a nature which seldom fails to render men more accessible to strong and sudden emotions. The glades of the forest, and the acclivity which leads to it, were in full view of the Royal army, but presented the appearance of a deep solitude. All was silence, except when the regimental bands of music, at the command of the officers, who remained generally faithful, played the airs of "Vive Henri Quatre," "O Richard," "La Belle Gabrielle," and other tunes connected with the cause and family of the Bourbons. The sounds excited no corresponding sentiments among the soldiers.

At length, about noon, a galloping of horse was heard. An open carriage appeared, surrounded by a few hussars, and drawn by four horses. It came on at full speed, and Napoleon, jumping from the vehicle, was in the midst of the ranks which had been formed to oppose him. His escort threw themselves from their horses, mingled with their ancient comrades, and the effect of their exhortations was instantaneous on men whose minds were already half made up to the purpose which they now accomplished. There was a general shout of "Vive Napoleon!" The last army of the Bourbons passed from their side, and no further obstruction existed betwixt Napoleon and the capital, which he was once more—but for a brief space—to inhabit as a sovereign.

Louis, accompanied only by a few household troops, had scarcely turned his back on the capital of his ancestors when Lavalette hastened from a place of concealment and seized on the Post-office in the name of Napoleon. By this measure all the King's proclamations' were intercepted, and the restoration of the Emperor was announced to all the departments. General Excelmans, who had just renewed his oath to Louis, pulled down with his own hands the white flag that was floating over the Tuileries, and hoisted the three-coloured banner.

It was late in the evening of the 20th that Bonaparte entered Paris in an open carriage, which was driven straight to the gilded gates of the Tuileries. He received the acclamations of the military and of the lower classes of the suburbs, but most of the respectable citizens looked on in silent wonderment. It was quite evident then that he was recalled by a party—a party, in truth, numerous and powerful, but not by the unanimous voice of the nation. The enthusiasm of his immediate adherents, however, made up for the silence and lukewarmness of others. They filled and crammed the square of the Carrousel, and the courts and avenues of the Tuileries; they pressed so closely upon him that he was obliged to cry out, "My friends, you stifle me!" and his aides de camp were compelled to carry him in their arms up the grand staircase, and thence into the royal apartments. It was observed, however, that amongst these ardent friends were many men who had been the first to desert him in 1814, and that these individuals were the most enthusiastic in their demonstrations, the loudest in their shouts!

And thus was Napoleon again at the Tuileries, where, even more than at Fontainebleau, his mind was flooded by the deep and painful recollections of the past! A few nights after his return thither he sent for M. Horan, one of the physicians who had attended Josephine during her last illness. "So, Monsieur Horan," said he, "you did not leave the Empress during her malady?"—"No, Sire."

"What was the cause of that malady?"—"Uneasiness of mind . . . grief."—"You believe that?" (and Napoleon laid a strong emphasis on the word believe, looking steadfastly in the doctor's face). He then asked, "Was she long ill? Did she suffer much?"—"She was ill a week, Sire; her Majesty suffered little bodily pain."—"Did she see that she was dying? Did she show courage?"—"A sign her Majesty made when she could no longer express herself leaves me no doubt that she felt her end approaching; she seamed to contemplate it without fear."—"Well!—well!" and then Napoleon much affected drew close to M. Horan, and added, "You say that she was in grief; from what did that arise?"—"From passing events, Sire; from your Majesty's position last year."—"Ah! she used to speak of me then?"—"Very often." Here Napoleon drew his hand across his eyes, which seemed filled with tears. He then went on. "Good woman!—Excellent Josephine! She loved me truly—she—did she not? . . . Ah! She was a Frenchwoman!"—"Yes, Sire, she loved you, and she would have proved it had it not been for dread of displeasing you: she had conceived an idea."—"How? . . . What would she have done?" "She one day said that as Empress of the French she would drive through Paris with eight horses to her coach, and all her household in gala livery, to go and rejoin you at Fontainebleau, and never quit you more."—"She would have done it—she was capable of doing it!"

Napoleon again betrayed deep emotion, on recovering from which he asked the physician the most minute questions about the nature of Josephine's disease, the friends and attendants who were around her at the hour of her death, and the conduct of her two children, Eugène and Hortense.

CHAPTER V

1815

Those who opposed the execution of the treaty concluded with Napoleon at the time of his abdication were guilty of a great error, for they afforded him a fair pretext for leaving the island of Elba. The details of that extraordinary enterprise are known to every one, and I shall not repeat what has been told over and over again. For my own part, as soon as I saw with what rapidity Bonaparte was marching upon Lyons, and the enthusiasm with which he was received by the troops and the people, I prepared to retire to Belgium, there to await the denouement of this new drama.

Every preparation for my departure was completed on the evening of the 13th of March, and I was ready to depart, to avoid the persecutions of which I expected I should be the object, when I received a message from the Tuileries stating that the King desired to see me. I of course lost no time in proceeding to the Palace, and went straight to M. Hue to inquire of him why I had been sent for. He occupied the apartments in which I passed the three most laborious and anxious years of my life. M. Hue, perceiving that I felt a certain degree of uneasiness at being summoned to the Tuileries at that hour of the night, hastened to inform me that the King wished to appoint me Prefect of the Police. He conducted me to the King's chamber, where his Majesty thus addressed me kindly, but in an impressive manner, "M. de Bourrienne, can we rely upon you? I expect much from your zeal and fidelity."—"Your Majesty," replied I, "shall have no reason to complain of my betraying your confidence."—"Well, I re-establish the Prefecture of the Police, and I appoint you Prefect. Do your best, M. de Bourrienne, in the discharge of your duties; I count upon you."

By a singular coincidence, on the very day (the 13th of March) when I received this appointment Napoleon, who was at Lyons, signed the decree which excluded from the amnesty he had granted thirteen individuals, among whose names mine was inscribed. This decree confirmed me in the presentiments I had conceived as soon as I heard of the landing of Bonaparte. On returning home from the Tuileries after receiving my appointment a multitude of ideas crowded on my mind. At the first moment I had been prompted only by the wish to serve the cause of the King, but I was alarmed when I came to examine the extent of the responsibility I had taken upon myself. However, I determined to meet with courage the difficulties that presented themselves, and I must say that I had every reason to be satisfied with the manner in which I was seconded by M. Foudras, the Inspector-General of the Police.

Even now I am filled with astonishment when I think of the Council that was held at the Tuileries on the evening of the 13th of March in M. de Blacas' apartments. The ignorance of the members of that Council respecting our situation, and their confidence in the useless measures they had adopted against Napoleon, exceed all conception.

Will it be believed that those great statesmen, who had the control of the telegraph, the post-office, the police and its agents, money-in short, everything which constitutes power—asked me to give them information respecting the advance of Bonaparte? What could I say to them? I could only repeat the reports which were circulated on the Exchange, and those which I had collected here and there during the last twenty-four hours. I did not conceal that the danger was imminent, and that all their precautions would be of no avail. The question then arose as to what course should be adapted by the King. It was impossible that the monarch could remain at the Capital, and yet, where was he to go? One proposed that he should go to Bordeaux, another to La Vendée, and a third to Normandy, and a fourth member of the Council was of opinion that the King should be conducted to Melun. I conceived that if a battle should take place anywhere it would probably be in the neighbourhood of that town, but the councillor who made this last suggestion assured us that the presence of the King in an open carriage and eight horses would produce a wonderful effect on the minds of the troops. This project was merely ridiculous; the others appeared to be dangerous and impracticable. I declared to the Council that, considering the situation of things, it was necessary to renounce all idea of resistance by force of arms; that no soldier would fire a musket, and that it was madness to attempt to take any other view of things. "Defection," said I, "is inevitable. The soldiers are drinking in their barracks the money which you have been giving them for some days past to purchase their fidelity. They say Louis XVIII., is a very decent sort of man, but 'Vive le petit Caporal!'"

Immediately on the landing of Napoleon the King sent an extraordinary courier to Marmont, who was at Chatillon whither he had gone to take a last leave of his dying mother. I saw him one day after he had had an interview with the King; I think it was on the 6th or 7th of March. After some conversation on the landing of Napoleon, and the means of preventing him from reaching Paris, Marmont said to me, "This is what I dwelt most strongly upon in the interview I have just had with the King. 'Sire,' said I, 'I doubt not Bonaparte's intention of coming to Paris, and the best way to prevent him doing so would be for your Majesty to remain here. It is necessary to secure the Palace of the Tuileries against a surprise, and to prepare it for resisting a siege, in which it would be indispensable to use cannon. You must shut yourself up in your palace, with the individuals of your household and the principal public functionaries, while the Duc d'Angoulome should go to Bordeaux, the Duc de Berri to La Vendée, and Monsieur to, the Franche-Comte; but they must set off in open day, and announce that they are going to collect defenders for your Majesty.[276]

". . . This is what I said to the King this morning, and I added that I would answer for everything if my advice were followed. I am now going to direct my aide de camp, Colonel Fabvier, to draw up the plan of defence." I did not concur in Marmont's opinion. It is certainly probable that had Louis XVIII. remained in his palace the numerous defections which took place before the 20th of March would have been checked and some persons would not have found so ready an excuse for breaking their oaths of allegiance. There can be little doubt, too, but Bonaparte would have reflected well before he attempted the siege of the Tuileries.[277]

276 Monsieur, the brother of the King, the Comte d'Artois later Charles X.

277 Marmont (tome vii. p. 87) gives the full details of his scheme for provisioning and garrisoning the Tuileries which the King was to hold while his family spread themselves throughout the provinces. The idea had nothing strange in it, for the same advice was given by General Mathieu Dumas (Souvenirs, tome iii. p. 564), a man not likely to suggest any rash schemes. Jaucourt, writing to Talleyrand, obviously believed in the wisdom of the King's remaining, as did the Czar; see Talleyrand's Correspondence, vol. ii. pp. 94, 122, 129. Napoleon would

Marmont supported his opinion by observing that the admiration and astonishment excited by the extraordinary enterprise of Napoleon and his rapid march to Paris would be counterbalanced by the interest inspired by a venerable monarch defying his bold rival and courageously defending his throne. While I rendered full justice to the good intentions of the Duke of Ragusa, yet I did not think that his advice could be adopted. I opposed it as I opposed all the propositions that were made in the Council relative to the different places to which the King should retire. I myself suggested Lille as being the nearest, and as presenting the greatest degree of safety, especially in the first instance.

It was after midnight when I left the Council of the Tuileries. The discussion had terminated, and without coming to any precise resolution it was agreed that the different opinions which had been expressed should be submitted to Louis XVIII. in order that his Majesty might adopt that which should appear to him the best. The King adopted my opinion, but it was not acted upon until five days after.

My appointment to the Prefecture of the Police was, as will be seen, a late thought of measure, almost as late indeed as Napoleon's proposition to send me as his Minister Plenipotentiary to Switzerland. In now accepting office I was well convinced of the inutility of any effort that might be made to arrest the progress of the fast approaching and menacing events. Being introduced into the King's cabinet his Majesty asked me what I thought of the situation of affairs. "I think, Sire, that Bonaparte will be here in five or six days."—"What, sir?"—"Yes, Sire."—"But proper measures are taken, the necessary orders given, and the Marshals are faithful to me."—"Sire, I suspect no man's fidelity; but I can assure your Majesty that, as Bonaparte has landed, he will be here within a week. I know him, and your Majesty cannot know him as well as I do; but I can venture to assure your Majesty with the same confidence that he will not be here six months hence. He will be hurried into acts of folly which will ruin him."—"De Bourrienne, I hope the best from events, but if misfortune again compel me to leave France, and your second prediction be fulfilled, you may rely on me." During this short conversation the King appeared perfectly tranquil and resigned.

The next day I again visited the Tuileries, whither I had at those perilous times frequent occasion to repair. On that day I received a list of twenty-five persons whom I was ordered to arrest. I took the liberty to observe that such a proceeding was not only useless but likely to produce a very injurious effect at that critical moment. The reasons I urged had not all the effect I expected. However, some relaxation as to twenty-three of the twenty-five was conceded, but it was insisted that Fouché and Davoust should be arrested without delay. The King repeatedly said, "I wish you to arrest Fouché."—"Sire, I beseech your Majesty to consider the inutility of such a measure."—"I am resolved upon Fouches arrest. But I am sure you will miss him, for Andre could not catch him."

My nocturnal installation as Prefect of the Police took place some time after midnight. I had great repugnance to the arrest of Fouché, but the order having been given, there was no alternative but to obey it. I communicated the order to M. Foudras, who very coolly observed, "Since we are to arrest him you need not be afraid, we shall have him fast tomorrow."

The next day my agents repaired to the Duke of Otranto's hotel, in the Rue d'Artois. On showing their warrant Fouché said, "What does this mean? Your warrant is of no force; it is mere waste-paper. It purports to come from the Prefect of the Police, but there is no such

---

certainly have been placed in a strange difficulty, but a king capable of adopting such a resolution would never have been required to consider it.

Prefect." In my opinion Fouché was right, for my appointment, which took place during the night, had not been legally announced. Be that as it may, on his refusal to surrender, one of my agents applied to the staff of the National Guard, requesting the support, in case of need, of an armed force. General Dessolles repaired to the Tuileries to take the King's orders on the subject. Meanwhile Fouché, who never lost his self-possession, after talking to the police officers who remained with him, pretended to step aside for some indispensable purpose, but the door which he opened led into a dark passage through which he slipped, leaving my unfortunate agents groping about in the obscurity. As for himself, he speedily gained the Rue Taitbout, where he stepped into a coach, and drove off. This is the whole history of the notable arrest of Fouché.

As for Davoust, I felt my hands tied with respect to him. I do not mean to affect generosity, for I acknowledge the enmity I bore him; but I did not wish it to be supposed that I was acting towards him from a spirit of personal vengeance. I therefore merely ordered him to be watched. The other twenty-three were to me in this matter as if they had never existed; and some of them, perhaps, will only learn in reading my Memoirs what dangerous characters they were thought to be.

On the 15th of March, after the conversation which, as I have already related, I had with Louis XVIII, I went to M. de Blacas and repeated to him what I had stated to the King on the certainty of Bonaparte's speedy arrival in Paris. I told him that I found it necessary to devote the short time still in our power to prevent a reaction against the Royalists, and to preserve public tranquillity until the departure of the Royal family, and that I would protect the departure of all persons who had reasons for withdrawing themselves from the scene of the great and perhaps disastrous events that might ensue. "You may readily believe, Count," added I, "that considering the great interests with which I am entrusted, I am not inclined to lose valuable time in arresting the persons of whose names I have received a list. The execution of such a measure would be useless; it would lead to nothing, or rather it would serve to irritate public feeling. My conviction of this fact has banished from me all idea of keeping under restraint for four or five days persons whose influence, whether real or supposed, is nil, since Bonaparte is at Auxerre. Mere supervision appears to me sufficient, and to that I propose confining myself."—"The King," replied M. de Blacas, "relies on you. He knows that though only forty-eight hours have elapsed since you entered upon your functions, you have already rendered greater services than you are perhaps aware of." I then asked M. de Blacas whether he had not received any intimation of Bonaparte's intended departure from the island of Elba by letters or by secret agents. "The only positive information we received," answered the Minister, "was an intercepted letter, dated Elba, 6th February. It was addressed to M. ——, near Grenoble. I will show it you." M. de Blacas opened a drawer of his writing-table and took out the letter, which he gave to me. The writer thanked his correspondent for the information he had transmitted to "the inhabitant of Elba." He was informed that everything was ready for departure, and that the first favourable opportunity would be seized, but that it would be desirable first to receive answers to some questions contained in the letter. These questions related to the regiments which had been sent into the south, and the places of their cantonment. It was inquired whether the choice of the commanders was conformable to what had been agreed on in Paris, and whether Labedoyere was at his post. The letter was rather long and it impressed me by the way in which the plan of a landing on the coast of Provence was discussed. Precise answers were requested on all these points. On returning the letter to M. de Blacas I remarked that the contents of the letter called for the adoption of some decided measures, and I asked him what had been done. He answered, "I immediately sent a copy of the letter to M. d'Andre, that he might give orders for arresting the individual to whom it was addressed."

Having had the opportunity of closely observing the machinery of a vigilant and active Government, I was, I must confess, not a little amazed at the insufficiency of the measures adopted to defeat this well-planned conspiracy. When M. de Blacas informed me of all that had been done, I could not repress an exclamation of surprise. "Well," said he, "and what would you have done?"—"In the first place I would not have lost twenty-four hours, which were an age in such a crisis." I then explained the plan I would have adopted. A quarter of an hour after the receipt of the letter I would have sent trustworthy men to Grenoble, and above all things I would have taken care not to let the matter fall into the hands of the police. Having obtained all information from the correspondent at Grenoble, I would have made him write a letter to his correspondent at Elba to quiet the eagerness of Napoleon, telling him that the movement of troops he spoke of had not been made, that it would take eight days to carry it out, and that it was necessary to the success of the enterprise to delay the embarkation for some days. While Bonaparte was thus delayed I would have sent to the coast of Provence a sufficient body of men devoted to the Royal cause, sending off in another direction the regiments whose chiefs were gained over by Napoleon, as the correspondence should reveal their names. "You are perhaps right, sir," said M. de Blacas, "but what could I do? I am new here. I had not the control of the police, and I trusted to M. d'Andre."—"Well," said I, "Bonaparte will be here on the 20th of March." With these words I parted from M. de Blacas. I remarked a great change in him. He had already lost a vast deal of that hauteur of favouritism which made him so much disliked.

When I entered upon my duties in the Prefecture of Police the evil was already past remedy. The incorrigible emigres required another lesson, and the temporary resurrection of the Empire was inevitable. But, if Bonaparte was recalled, it was not owing to any attachment to him personally; it was not from any fidelity to the recollections of the Empire. It was resolved at any price to get rid of those imbecile councillors, who thought they might treat France like a country conquered by the emigrants. The people determined to free themselves from a Government which seemed resolved to trample on all that was dear to France. In this state of things some looked upon Bonaparte as a liberator, but the greater number regarded him as an instrument. In this last character he was viewed by the old Republicans, and by a new generation, who thought they caught a glimpse of liberty in promises, and Who were blind enough to believe that the idol of France would be restored by Napoleon.

In February 1815, while everything was preparing at Elba for the approaching departure of Napoleon, Murat applied to the Court of Vienna for leave to march through the Austrian Provinces of Upper Italy an army directed on France. It was on the 26th of the same month that Bonaparte escaped from Elba. These two facts were necessarily connected together, for, in spite of Murat's extravagant ideas, he never could have entertained the expectation of obliging the King of France, by the mere force of arms, to acknowledge his continued possession of the throne of Naples. Since the return of Louis XVIII. the Cabinet of the Tuileries had never regarded Murat in any other light than as a usurper, and I know from good authority that the French Plenipotentiaries at the Congress of Vienna were especially instructed to insist that the restoration of the throne of Naples in favour of the Bourbons of the Two Sicilies should be a consequence of the restoration of the throne of France. I also know that the proposition was firmly opposed on the part of Austria, who had always viewed with jealousy the occupation of three thrones of Europe by the single House of Bourbon.

According to information, for the authenticity of which I can vouch, the following were the plans which Napoleon conceived at Elba. Almost immediately after his arrival in France he was to order the Marshals on whom he could best rely to defend to the utmost the entrances to the French territory and the approaches to Paris, by pivoting on the triple line of fortresses which gird the north and east of France. Davoust was 'in petto' singled out for the defence of Paris. He, was to arm the inhabitants of the suburbs, and to have, besides, 20,000 men of the National Guard at his disposal. Napoleon, not being aware of the situation of the Allies, never supposed that they could concentrate their forces and march against him so speedily as they did. He hoped to take them by surprise, and defeat their projects, by making Murat march upon Milan, and by stirring up insurrections in Italy. The Po being once crossed, and Murat approaching the capital of Lombardy, Napoleon with the corps of Suchet, Brune, Grouchy, and Massena, augmented by troops sent, by forced marches, to Lyons, was to cross the Alps and revolutionise Piedmont. There, having recruited his army and joined the Neapolitans in Milan, he was to proclaim the independence of Italy, unite the whole country under a single chief, and then march at the head of 100,000 men on Vienna, by the Julian Alps, across which victory had conducted him in 1797. This was not all: numerous emissaries scattered through Poland and Hungary were to foment discord and raise the cry of liberty and independence, to alarm Russia and Austria. It must be confessed it would have been an extraordinary spectacle to see Napoleon giving liberty to Europe in revenge for not having succeeded in enslaving her.

By means of these bold manoeuvres and vast combinations Napoleon calculated that he would have the advantage of the initiative in military operations. Perhaps his genius was never more fully developed than in this vast conception. According to this plan he was to extend his operations over a line of 500 leagues, from Ostend to Vienna, by the Alps and Italy, to provide himself with immense resources of every kind, to prevent the Emperor of Austria from marching his troops against France, and probably force him to terminate a war from which the hereditary provinces would have exclusively suffered. Such was the bright prospect which presented itself to Napoleon when he stepped on board the vessel which was to convey him from Elba to France. But the mad precipitation of Murat put Europe on the alert, and the brilliant illusion vanished like a dream.

After being assured that all was tranquil, and that the Royal family was secure against every danger, I myself set out at four o'clock on the morning of the 20th of March, taking the road to Lille.—Nothing extraordinary occurred until I arrived at the post-office of Fins, in front of which were drawn up a great number of carriages, which had arrived before mine, and the owners of which, like myself, were impatiently waiting for horses. I soon observed that some one called the postmaster aside in a way which did not appear entirely devoid of mystery, and I acknowledge I felt some degree of alarm. I was in the room in which the travellers were waiting, and my attention was attracted by a large bill fixed against the wall. It was printed in French and Russian, and it proved to be the order of the day which I had been fortunate enough to obtain from the Emperor Alexander to exempt posthorses, etc., from the requisitions of the Allied troops.

I was standing looking at the bill when the postmaster came into the room and advanced towards me. "Sir," said he, "that is an order of the day which saved me from ruin."—"Then surely you would not harm the man by whom it is signed?"—"I know you, sir, I recognised you immediately. I saw you in Paris when you were Director of the Post-office, and you granted a just claim which I had upon you. I have now come to tell you that they are harnessing two horses to your calash, and you may set off at full speed." The worthy man had assigned to my use the only two horses at his disposal; his son performed the office of postilion, and I set off to the no small dissatisfaction of some of the travellers who had arrived before me, and who, perhaps, had as good reasons as I to avoid the presence of Napoleon.

We arrived at Lille at eleven o'clock on the night of the 21st. Here I encountered another vexation, though not of an alarming kind. The gates of the town were closed, and I was obliged to content myself with a miserable night's lodging in the suburb.

I entered Lille on the 22d, and Louis XVIII. arrived on the 23d. His Majesty also found the gates closed, and more than an hour elapsed before an order could be obtained for opening them, for the Duke of Orleans, who commanded the town, was inspecting the troops when his Majesty arrived. The King was perfectly well received at Lille. There indeed appeared some symptoms of defection, but it must be acknowledged that the officers of the old army had been so singularly sacrificed to the promotion of the returned emigrants that it was very natural the former should hail the return of the man who had so often led them to victory. I put up at the Hotel de Grand, certainly without forming any prognostic respecting the future residence of the King. When I saw his Majesty's retinue I went down and stood at the door of the hotel, where as soon as Louis XVIII. perceived me he distinguished me from among all the persons who were awaiting his arrival, and holding out his hand for me to kiss he said, "Follow me, M. de Bourrienne."

On entering the apartments prepared for him the King expressed to me his approval of my conduct since the Restoration, and especially during the short interval in which I had discharged the functions of Prefect of the Police. He did me the honour to invite me to breakfast with him. The conversation naturally turned on the events of the day, of which every one present spoke according to his hopes or fears. Observing that Louis XVIII. concurred in Berthier's discouraging view of affairs, I ventured to repeat what I had already said at the Tuileries, that, judging from the disposition of the sovereigns of Europe and the information which I had received, it appeared very probable that his Majesty would be again seated on his throne in three months. Berthier bit his nails as he did when he wanted to leave the army of Egypt and return to Paris to the object of his adoration. Berthier was not hopeful; he was always one of those men who have the least confidence and the most depression. I could perceive that the King regarded my observation as one of those compliments which he was accustomed to receive, and that he had no great confidence in the fulfilment of my prediction. However, wishing to seem to believe it, he said, what he had more than hinted before, "M. de Bourrienne, as long as I am King you shall be my Prefect of the Police."

It was the decided intention of Louis XVIII. to remain in France as long as he could, but the Napoleonic fever, which spread like an epidemic among the troops, had infected the garrison of Lille. Marshal Mortier, who commanded at Lille, and the Duke of Orleans, expressed to me their well-founded fears, and repeatedly recommended me to urge the King to quit Lille speedily, in order to avoid any fatal occurrence. During the two days I passed with his Majesty I entreated him to yield to the imperious circumstances in which he was placed. At length the King, with deep regret, consented to go, and I left Lille the day before that fixed for his Majesty's departure.

In September 1814 the King had appointed me charge d'affaires from France to Hamburg, but not having received orders to repair to my post I have not hitherto mentioned this nomination. However, when Louis XVIII. was on the point of leaving France he thought that my presence in Hamburg might be useful for the purpose of making him acquainted with all that might interest him in the north of Germany. But it was not there that danger was to be apprehended. There were two points to be watched—the headquarters of Napoleon and the King's Council at Ghent. I, however, lost no time in repairing to a city where I was sure of finding a great many friends. On passing through Brussels I alighted at the Hotel de Bellevue, where the Duc de Berri arrived shortly after me. His Royal Highness then invited me to breakfast with him, and conversed with me very confidentially. I afterwards continued my journey.

CHAPTER VI

1815

At Lille, and again at Hamburg, I received letters from my family, which I had looked for with great impatience. They contained particulars of what had occurred relative to me since Bonaparte's return to Paris. Two hours after my departure Madame de Bourrienne also left Paris, accompanied by her children, and proceeded to an asylum which had been offered her seven leagues from the capital. She left at my house in Paris her sister, two of her brothers, and her friend the Comtesse de Neuilly, who had resided with us since her return from the emigration.

On the very morning of my wife's departure (namely, the 20th of March) a person, with whom I had always been on terms of friendship, and who was entirely devoted to Bonaparte, sent to request that Madame de Bourrienne would call on him, as he wished to speak to her on most important and urgent business. My sister-in-law informed the messenger that my wife had left Paris, but, begging a friend to accompany her, she went herself to the individual, whose name will be probably guessed, though I do not mention it. The person who came with the message to my house put many questions to Madame de Bourrienne's sister respecting my absence, and advised her, above all things, to conjure me not to follow the King, observing that the cause of Louis XVIII. was utterly lost, and that I should do well to retire quietly to Burgundy, as there was no doubt of my obtaining the Emperor's pardon.

Nothing could be more gloomy than Bonaparte's entrance into Paris. He arrived at night in the midst of a thick fog. The streets were almost deserted, and a vague feeling of terror prevailed almost generally in the capital. At nine o'clock on the same evening, the very hour of Bonaparte's arrival at the Tuileries, a lady, a friend, of my family, and whose son served in the Young Guard, called and requested to see Madame de Bourrienne. She refused to enter the house lest she should be seen, and my sister-in-law went down to the garden to speak to her without a light. This lady's brother had been on the preceding night to Fontainebleau to see Bonaparte, and he had directed his sister to desire me to remain in Paris, and to retain my post in the Prefecture of the Police, as I was sure of a full and complete pardon.

On the morning of the 21st General Becton, who has since been the victim of his mad enterprises, called at my house and requested to speak with me and Madame de Bourrienne. He was received by my wife's sister and brothers, and stated that he came from M. de Caulaincourt to renew the assurances of safety which had already been given to me. I was, I confess, very sensible of these proofs of friendship when they came to my knowledge, but I did not for a single moment repent the course I adopted. I could not forget the intrigues of which I had been the object since 1811, nor the continual threats of arrest which, during that year, had not left me a moment's quiet; and since I now revert to that time, I may take the opportunity of explaining how in 1814 I was made acquainted with the real causes of the persecution to which I had been a prey. A person, whose name prudence forbids me mentioning, communicated to me the following letter, the original copy of which is in my possession:

Monsieur Le Duc De Bassano—I send you some very important documents respecting the Sieur Bourrienne, and beg you will make me a confidential report on this affair. Keep these documents for yourself alone. This business demands the utmost secrecy. Everything induces me to believe that Bourrienne has carried a series of intrigues with London. Bring me the report on Thursday. I pray God, etc.

(*Signed*) Napoleon

Paris,
25th December 1811.

I could now clearly perceive what to me had hitherto been enveloped in obscurity; but I was not, as yet, made acquainted with the documents mentioned in Napoleon's epistle. Still, however, the cause of his animosity was an enigma which I was unable to guess, but I obtained its solution some time afterwards.

General Driesen, who was the Governor of Mittau while Louis XVIII. resided in that town, came to Paris in 1814. I had been well acquainted with him in 1810 at Hamburg, where he lived for a considerable time. While at Mittau he conceived a chivalrous and enthusiastic friendship for the King of France. We were at first distrustful of each other, but afterwards the most intimate confidence arose between us. General Driesen looked forward with certainty to the return of the Bourbons to France, and in the course of our frequent conversations on his favourite theme he gradually threw off all reserve, and at length disclosed to me that he was maintaining a correspondence with the King.

He told me that he had sent to Hartwell several drafts of proclamations, with none of which, he said, the King was satisfied. On allowing me the copy of the last of these drafts I frankly told him that I was quite of the King's opinion as to its unfitness. I observed that if the King should one day return to France and act as the general advised he would not keep possession of his throne six months. Driesen then requested me to dictate a draft of a proclamation conformably with my ideas. This I consented to do on one condition, viz. that he would never mention my name in connection with the business, either in writing or conversation. General Driesen promised this, and then I dictated to him a draft which I would now candidly lay before the reader if I had a copy of it. I may add that in the different proclamations of Louis XVIII. I remarked several passages precisely corresponding with the draft I had dictated at Hamburg.

During the four years which intervened between my return to Paris and the downfall of the Empire it several times occurred to me that General Driesen had betrayed my secret, and on his very first visit to me after the Restoration, our conversation happening to turn on Hamburg, I asked him whether he had not disclosed what I wished him to conceal? "Well," said he, "there is no harm in telling the truth now. After you had left Hamburg the King wrote to me inquiring the name of the author of the last draft I had sent him, which was very different from all that had preceded it. I did not answer this question, but the King having repeated it in a second letter, and having demanded an answer, I was compelled to break my promise to you, and I put into the post-office of Gothenberg in Sweden a letter for the King, in which I mentioned your name."

The mystery was now revealed to me. I clearly saw what had excited in Napoleon's mind the suspicion that I was carrying on intrigues with England. I have no doubt as to the way in which the affair came to his knowledge. The King must have disclosed my name to one of those persons whose situations placed them above the suspicion of any betrayal of confidence, and thus the circumstance must have reached the ear of Bonaparte. This is not a mere hypothesis, for I well know how promptly and faithfully Napoleon was informed of all that was said and done at Hartwell.

Having shown General Driesen Napoleon's accusatory letter, he begged that I would entrust him with it for a day or two, saying he would show it to the King at a private audience. His object was to serve me, and to excite Louis XVIII.'s interest in my behalf, by briefly relating to him the whole affair. The general came to me on leaving the Tuileries, and assured me that the King after perusing the letter, had the great kindness to observe that I might think myself very happy in not having been shot. I know not whether Napoleon was afterwards informed of the details of this affair, which certainly had no connection with any intrigues with England, and which, after all, would have been a mere peccadillo in comparison with the conduct I thought it my duty to adopt at the time of the Restoration.

Meanwhile Madame de Bourrienne informed me by an express that seals were to be placed on the effects of all the persons included in the decree of Lyons, and consequently upon mine. As soon as my wife received information of this she quitted her retreat and repaired to Paris to face the storm. On the 29th of March, at nine in the evening, the police agents presented themselves at my house. Madame de Bourrienne remonstrated against the measure and the inconvenient hour that was chosen for its execution; but all was in vain, and there was no alternative but to submit.

But the matter did not end with the first formalities performed by Fouché's alguazils. During the month of May seven persons were appointed to examine, my papers, and among the inquisitorial septemvirate were two men well known and filling high situations. One of these executed his commission, but the other, sensible of the odium attached to it, wrote to say he was unwell, and never came. The number of my inquisitors, 'in domo', was thus reduced to six. They behaved with great rudeness, and executed their mission with a rigour and severity exceedingly painful to my family. They carried their search so far as to rummage the pockets of my old clothes, and even to unrip the linings. All this was done in the hope of finding something that would commit me in the eyes of the new master of France. But I was not to be caught in that way, and before leaving home I had taken such precautions as to set my mind perfectly at ease.

However, those who had declared themselves strongly against Napoleon were not the only persons who had reason to be alarmed at his return. Women even, by a system of inquisition unworthy of the Emperor, but unfortunately quite in unison with his hatred of all liberty, were condemned to exile, and had cause to apprehend further severity. It is for the exclusive admirers of the Chief of the Empire to approve of everything which proceeded from him, even his rigour against a defenceless sex; it is for them to laugh at the misery of a woman, and a writer of genius, condemned without any form of trial to the most severe punishment short of death. For my part, I saw neither justice nor pleasantry in the exile of Madame de Chevreuse for having had the courage (and courage was not common then even among men) to say that she was not made to be the gaoler of the Queen of Spain. On Napoleon's return from. the isle of Elba, Madame de Stael was in a state of weakness, which rendered her unable to bear any sudden and violent emotion. This debilitated state of health had been produced by her flight from Coppet to Russia immediately after the birth of the son who was the fruit of her marriage with M. Rocca. In spite of the danger of a journey in such circumstances she saw greater danger in staying where she was, and she set out on her new exile. That exile was not of long duration, but Madame de Stael never recovered from the effect of the alarm and fatigue it occasioned her.

The name of the authoress of Corinne, naturally calls to mind that of the friend who was most faithful to her in misfortune, and who was not herself screened from the severity of Napoleon by the just and universal admiration of which she was the object. In 1815 Madame Recamier did not leave Paris, to which she had returned in 1814, though her exile was not revoked. I know positively that Hortense assured her of the pleasure she would feel in receiving her, and that Madame Recamier, as an excuse for declining the perilous honour, observed that she had determined never again to appear in the world as long as her friends should be persecuted. The memorial de Sainte Helene, referring to the origin of the ill-will of the Chief of the Empire towards the society of Madame de Stael and Madame Recamier, etc., seems to reproach Madame Recamier, "accustomed," says the Memorial, "to ask for everything and to obtain everything," for having claimed nothing less than the complete reinstatement of her father. Whatever may have been the pretensions of Madame Recamier, Bonaparte, not a little addicted to the custom he complains of in her, could not have, with a good grace, made a crime of her ingratitude if he on his side had not claimed a very different sentiment from gratitude. I was with the First Consul at the time M. Bernard, the father of Madame Reamier, was accused, and I have not forgotten on what conditions the re-establishment would have been granted.

The frequent interviews between Madame Recamier and Madame de Stael were not calculated to bring Napoleon to sentiments and measures of moderation. He became more and more irritated at this friendship between two women formed for each other's society; and, on the occasion of one of Madame Recamier's journeys to Coppet he informed her, through the medium of Fouché, that she was perfectly at liberty to go to Switzerland, but not to return to Paris. "Ah, Monseigneur! a great man may be pardoned for the weakness of loving women, but not for fearing them." This was the only reply of Madame Recamier to Fouché when she set out for Coppet. I may here observe that the personal prejudices of the Emperor would not have been of a persevering and violent character if some of the people who surrounded him had not sought to foment them. I myself fell a victim to this. Napoleon's affection for me would perhaps have got the upper hand if his relenting towards me had not been incessantly combated by my enemies around him.

I had no opportunity of observing the aspect of Paris during that memorable period recorded in history by the name of the Hundred Days, but the letters which I received at the time, together with all that, I afterwards heard, concurred in assuring me that the capital never presented so melancholy a picture as: during those three months. No one felt any confidence in Napoleon's second reign, and it was said, without any sort of reserve, that Fouché, while serving the cause of usurpation, would secretly betray it. The future was viewed with alarm, and the present with dissatisfaction. The sight of the federates who paraded the faubourgs and the boulevards, vociferating, "The Republic for ever!" and "Death to the Royalists!" their sanguinary songs, the revolutionary airs played in our theatres, all tended to produce a fearful torpor in the public mind, and the issue of the impending events was anxiously awaited.

One of the circumstances which, at the commencement of the Hundred Days, most contributed to open the eyes of those who were yet dazzled by the past glory of Napoleon, was the assurance with which he declared that the Empress and his son would be restored to him, though nothing warranted that announcement. It was evident that he could not count on any ally; and in spite of the prodigious activity with which a new army was raised those persons must have been blind indeed who could imagine the possibility of his triumphing over Europe, again armed to oppose him. I deplored the inevitable disasters which Bonaparte's bold enterprise would entail, but I had such certain information respecting the intentions of the Allied powers, and the spirit which animated the Plenipotentiaries at Vienna, that I could not for a moment doubt the issue of the conflict: Thus I was not at all surprised when I received at Hamburg the minutes of the conferences at Vienna in May 1815.

When the first intelligence of Bonaparte's landing was received at Vienna it must be confessed that very little had been done at the Congress, for measures calculated to reconstruct a solid and durable order of things could only be framed and adopted deliberately, and upon mature reflection. Louis XVIII. had instructed his Plenipotentiaries to defend and support the principles of justice and the law of nations, so as to secure the rights of all parties and avert the chances of a new war. The Congress was occupied with these important objects when intelligence was received of Napoleon's departure from Elba and his landing at the Gulf of Juan. The Plenipotentiaries then signed the protocol of the conferences to which I have above alluded.

ANNEX TO THE PRECEDING CHAPTER

The following despatch of Napoleon's to Marshal Davoust (given in Captain Bingham's Translation, vol. iii. p. 121), though not strictly bearing upon the subject of the Duke of Bassano's inquiry (p. 256), may perhaps find a place here, as indicative of the private feeling of the Emperor towards Bourrienne. As the reader will remember, it has already been alluded to earlier in the work:

COMPIEGNE,
3d September 1811.

TO MARSHAL DAVOUST.

I have received your letter concerning the cheating of Bourrienne at Hamburg. It will be important to throw light upon what he has done. Have the Jew, Gumprecht Mares, arrested, seize his papers, and place him in solitary confinement. Have some of the other principal agents of Bourrienne arrested, so as to discover his doings at Hamburg, and the embezzlements he has committed there.

(Signed) NAPOLEON.

CHAPTER VII

1815

Napoleon was scarcely reseated on his throne when he found he could not resume that absolute power he had possessed before his abdication at Fontainebleau. He was obliged to submit to the curb of a representative government, but we may well believe that he only yielded, with a mental reservation that as soon as victory should return to his standards and his army be reorganised he would send the representatives of the people back to their departments, and make himself as absolute as he had ever been. His temporary submission was indeed obligatory.

The Republicans and Constitutionalists who had assisted, or not opposed his return, with Carnot, Fouché, Benjamin Constant, and his own brother Lucien (a lover of constitutional liberty) at their head, would support him only on condition of his reigning as a constitutional sovereign; he therefore proclaimed a constitution under the title of "Acte additionnel aux Constitutions de l'Empire," which greatly resembled the charter granted by Louis XVIII. the year before. An hereditary Chamber of Peers was to be appointed by the Emperor, a Chamber of Representatives chosen by the Electoral Colleges, to be renewed every five years, by which all taxes were to be voted, ministers were to be responsible, judges irremovable, the right of petition was acknowledged, and property was declared inviolable. Lastly, the French nation was made to declare that they would never recall the Bourbons.

Even before reaching Paris, and while resting on his journey from Elba at Lyons, the second city in France, and the ancient capital of the Franks, Napoleon arranged his ministry, and issued sundry decrees, which show how little his mind was prepared for proceeding according to the majority of votes in representative assemblies.

Cambacérès was named Minister of Justice, Fouché Minister of Police (a boon to the Revolutionists), Davoust appointed Minister of War. Decrees upon decrees were issued with a rapidity which showed how laboriously Bonaparte had employed those studious hours at Elba which he was supposed to have dedicated to the composition of his Memoirs. They were couched in the name of "Napoleon, by the grace of God, Emperor of France," and were dated on the 13th of March, although not promulgated until the 21st of that month. The first of these decrees abrogated all changes in the courts of justice and tribunals which had taken place during the absence of Napoleon. The second banished anew all emigrants who had returned to France before 1814 without proper authority, and displaced all officers belonging to the class of emigrants introduced into the army by the King. The third suppressed the Order of St. Louis, the white flag, cockade, and other Royal emblems, and restored the tri-coloured banner and the Imperial symbols of Bonaparte's authority. The same decree abolished the Swiss Guard and the Household troops of the King. The fourth sequestered the effects of the Bourbons. A similar Ordinance sequestered the restored property of emigrant families.

The fifth decree of Lyons suppressed the ancient nobility and feudal titles, and formally confirmed proprietors of national domains in their possessions. (This decree was very acceptable to the majority of Frenchmen). The sixth declared sentence of exile against all emigrants not erased by Napoleon from the list previously to the accession of the Bourbons, to which was added confiscation of their property. The seventh restored the Legion of Honour in every respect as it had existed under the Emperor; uniting to its funds the confiscated revenues of the Bourbon order of St. Louis. The eighth and last decree was the most important of all. Under pretence that emigrants who had borne arms against France had been introduced into the Chamber of Peers, and that the Chamber of Deputies had already sat for the legal time, it dissolved both Chambers, and convoked the Electoral Colleges of the Empire, in order that they might hold, in the ensuing month of May, an extraordinary assembly—the Champ-de-Mai.

This National Convocation, for which Napoleon claimed a precedent in the history of the ancient Franks, was to have two objects: first, to make such alterations and reforms in the Constitution of the Empire as circumstances should render advisable; secondly, to assist at the coronation of the Empress Maria Louisa. Her presence, and that of her son, was spoken of as something that admitted of no doubt, though Bonaparte knew there was little hope of their return from Vienna. These various enactments were well calculated to serve Napoleon's cause. They flattered the army, and at the same time stimulated their resentment against the emigrants, by insinuating that they had been sacrificed by Louis to the interest of his followers. They held out to the Republicans a prospect of confiscation, proscription, and, revolution of government, while, the Imperialists were gratified with a view of ample funds for pensions, offices, and honorary decorations. To proprietors of the national domains security was promised, to the Parisians the grand spectacle of the Champ-de-Mai, and to. France peace and tranquillity, since the arrival of the Empress and her son, confidently asserted to be at hand, was taken as a pledge of the friendship of Austria.

Napoleon at the same time endeavoured to make himself popular with the common people—the mob of the Faubourg St. Antoine and other obscure quarters of Paris. On the first evening of his return, as he walked round the glittering circle met to welcome him, in the State apartments of the Tuileries, he kept repeating, "Gentlemen, it is to the poor and disinterested mass of the people that I owe everything; it is they who have brought me back to the capital. It is the poor subaltern officers and common soldiers that have done all this. I owe everything to the common people and the ranks of the army. Remember that! I owe everything to the army and the people!" Some time after he took occasional rides through the Faubourg St. Antoine, but the demonstrations of the mob gave him little pleasure, and, it was easy to detect a sneer in his addresses to them. He had some slight intercourse with the men of the Revolution—the fierce, blood-thirsty Jacobins—but even now he could not conceal his abhorrence of them, and, be it said to his honour, he had as little to do with them as possible.

When Napoleon, departed for the summer campaign he took care beforehand to leave large sums of money for the 'federes'; in the hands of the devoted Real; under whose management the mob was placed. These sums were to be distributed at appropriate seasons, to make the people cry in the streets of Paris, "Napoleon or death." He also left in the hands of Davoust a written authority for the publication of his bulletins, many clauses of which were written long before the battles were fought that they were to describe. He gave to the same Marshal a plan of his campaign, which he had arranged for the defensive. This was not confided to him without an injunction of the strictest secrecy, but it is said that Davoust communicated the plan to Fouché. Considering Davoust's character this is very unlikely, but if so, it is far from improbable that Fouché communicated the plan to the Allies with whom, and more particularly with Prince Metternich, he is well known to have been corresponding at the time.

Shortly after the Emperor's arrival in Paris Benjamin Constant, a moderate and candid man, was deputed by the constitutional party to ascertain Napoleon's sentiments and intentions. Constant was a lover of constitutional liberty, and an old opponent of Napoleon, whose headlong career of despotism, cut out by the sword, he had vainly endeavoured to check by the eloquence of his pen.

The interview took place at the Tuileries. The Emperor, as was his wont, began the conversation, and kept it nearly all to himself during the rest of the audience. He did not affect to disguise either his past actions or present dispositions.

"The nation," he said, "has had a respite of twelve years from every kind of political agitation, and for one year has enjoyed a respite from war. This double repose has created a craving after activity. It requires, or fancies it requires, a Tribune and popular assemblies. It did not always require them. The people threw themselves at my feet when I took the reins of government. You ought to recollect this, who made a trial of opposition. Where was your support—your strength? Nowhere. I assumed less authority than I was invited to assume. Now all is changed. A feeble government, opposed to the national interests, has given to these interests the habit of standing on the defensive and evading authority. The taste for constitutions, for debates, for harangues, appears to have revived. Nevertheless it is but the minority that wishes all this, be assured. The people, or if you like the phrase better; the multitude, wish only for me. You would say so if you had only seen this multitude pressing eagerly on my steps, rushing down from the tops of the mountains, calling on me, seeking me out, saluting me. On my way from Cannes hither I have not conquered—I have administered. I am not only (as has been pretended) the Emperor of the soldiers; I am that of the peasants of the plebeians of France. Accordingly, in spite of all that has happened, you see the people come back to me. There is sympathy between us. It is not as with the privileged classes. The noblesse have been in my service; they thronged in crowds into my antechambers. There is no place that they have not accepted or solicited. I have had the Montmorencys, the Noailles, the Rohans, the Beauveaus, the Montemarts, in my train. But there never was any cordiality between us. The steed made his curvets—he was well broken in, but I felt him quiver under me. With the people it is another thing. The popular fibre responds to mine. I have risen from the ranks of the people: my voice sets mechanically upon them. Look at those conscripts, the sons of peasants: I never flattered them; I treated them roughly. They did not crowd round me the less; they did not on that account cease to cry, 'Vive l'Empereur!' It is that between them and me there is one and the same nature. They look to me as their support, their safeguard against the nobles. I have but to make a sign, or even to look another way, and the nobles would be massacred in every province. So well have they managed matters in the last ten months! but I do not desire to be the King of a mob. If there are the means to govern by a constitution well and good. I wished for the empire of the world, and to ensure it complete liberty of action was necessary to me. To govern France merely it is possible that a constitution may be better. I wished for the empire of the world, as who would not have done in my place? The world invited me to rule over it. Sovereigns and subjects alike emulously bowed the neck under my sceptre. I have seldom met with opposition in France, but still I have encountered more of it from some obscure and unarmed Frenchmen than from all these Kings so resolute, just now, no longer to have a man of the people for their equal! See then what appears to you possible; let me know your ideas. Public discussion, free elections, responsible ministers, the liberty of the press, I have no objection to all that, the liberty of the press especially; to stifle it is absurd. I am convinced on this point. I am the man of the people: if the people really wish for liberty let them have it. I have acknowledged their sovereignty. It is just that I should lend an ear to their will, nay, even to their caprices. I have never been disposed to oppress them for my pleasure. I conceived great designs; but fate has been against me; I am no longer a conqueror, nor can I be one. I know what is possible and what is not.—I have no further object than to raise up France and bestow on her a government suitable to her. I have no hatred to liberty, I have set it aside when it obstructed my path, but I understand what it means; I was brought up in its school: besides, the work of fifteen years is overturned, and it is not possible to recommence it. It would take twenty years, and the lives of 2,000,000 of men to be sacrificed to it. As for the rest, I desire peace, but I can only obtain it by means of victory. I would not inspire you with false expectations. I permit it to be said that negotiations are going on; there are none. I foresee a hard struggle, a long war. To support it I must be seconded by the nation, but in return I believe they will expect liberty. They shall have it: the circumstances are new. All I desire is to be informed of the truth. I am getting old. A man is no longer at forty-five what he was at thirty. The repose enjoyed by a constitutional king may suit me: it will still more certainly be the best thing, for my son."

From this remarkable address. Benjamin Constant concluded that no change had taken place in Bonaparte's views or feelings in matters of government, but, being convinced that circumstances had changed, he had made up his mind to conform to them. He says, and we cannot doubt it, "that he listened to Napoleon with the deepest interest, that there was a breadth and grandeur of manner as he spoke, and a calm serenity seated on a brow covered with immortal laurels."

Whilst believing the utter incompatibility of Napoleon and constitutional government we cannot in fairness omit mentioning that the causes which repelled him from the altar and sanctuary of freedom were strong: the real lovers of a rational and feasible liberty—the constitutional monarchy men were few—the mad ultra-Liberals, the Jacobins, the refuse of one revolution and the provokers of another, were numerous, active, loud, and in pursuing different ends these two parties, the respectable and the disreputable, the good and the bad, got mixed and confused with one another.

On the 14th of May, when the 'federes' were marshalled in processional order and treated with what was called a solemn festival, as they moved along the boulevards to the Court of the Tuileries, they coupled the name of Napoleon with Jacobin curses and revolutionary songs. The airs and the words that had made Paris tremble to her very centre during the Reign of Terror—the "Marseillaise," the "Carmagnole," the "Jour du depart," the execrable ditty, the burden of which is, "And with the entrails of the last of the priests let us strangle the last of the kings," were all roared out in fearful chorus by a drunken, filthy, and furious mob. Many a day had elapsed since they had dared to sing these blasphemous and antisocial songs in public. Napoleon himself as soon as he had power enough suppressed them, and he was as proud of this feat and his triumph over the dregs of the Jacobins as he was of any of his victories; and in this he was right, in this he proved himself the friend of humanity. As the tumultuous mass approached the triumphal arch and the grand entrance to the Palace he could not conceal his abhorrence. His Guards were drawn up under arms, and numerous pieces of artillery, already loaded were turned out on the Place du Carrousel. He hastily dismissed these dangerous partisans with some praise, some money, and some drink. On coming into close contact with such a mob he did not feel his fibre respond to that of the populace! Like Frankenstein, he loathed and was afraid of the mighty monster he had put together.

But it was not merely the mob that checked the liberalism or constitution of Napoleon, a delicate and doubtful plant in itself, that required the most cautious treatment to make it really take root and grow up in such a soil: Some of his councillors, who called themselves "philosophical statesmen," advised him to lay aside the style of Emperor, and assume that of High President or Lord General of the Republic! Annoyed with such puerilities while the enemy was every day drawing nearer the frontiers he withdrew from the Tuileries to the comparatively small and retired palace of the Elysee, where he escaped these talking-dreamers, and felt himself again a sovereign: Shut up with Benjamin Constant and a few other reasonable politicians, he drew up the sketch of a new constitution, which was neither much better nor much worse than the royal charter of Louis XVIII. We give an epitome of its main features.

The Emperor was to have executive power, and to exercise legislative power in concurrence with the two Chambers. The Chamber of Peers was to be hereditary, and nominated by the Emperor, and its number was unlimited. The Second Chamber was to be elected by the people, and to consist of 629 members; none to be under the age of twenty-five. The President was to be appointed by the members, but approved of by the Emperor. Members were to be paid at the rate settled by the Constituent Assembly, which was to be renewed every five years. The Emperor might prorogue, adjourn, or dissolve the House of Representatives, whose sittings were to be public. The Electoral Colleges were maintained. Land tax and direct taxes were to be voted only for a year, indirect taxes might be imposed for several years. No levy of men for the army nor any exchange of territory was to be made but by a law. Taxes were to be proposed by the Chamber of Representatives. Ministers to be responsible. Judges to be irremovable. Juries to be established. Right of petition, freedom of worship, inviolability of property, were recognised. Liberty of the press was given under legal responsibility, and press offences were to be judged with a jury. No place or part of the territory could be placed in a state of siege except in case of foreign invasion or civil troubles. Finally, the French people declared that in the delegation it thus made of its powers it was not to be taken as giving the right to propose the re-establishment of the Bourbons, or of any Prince of that family on the throne, even in case of the extinction of the imperial dynasty. Any such proposal was formally interdicted to the Chambers or to the citizens, as well as any of the following measures, viz. the re-establishment of the former, feudal nobility, of the feudal and seignorial rights, of tithes, of any privileged and dominant religion, as well as of the power of making any attack on the irrevocability of the sale of the national goods.

Shortly after the return of Napoleon from Elba, believing it to be impossible to make the Emperor of Austria consent to his wife's rejoining him (and Maria Louisa had no inclination to a renewal of conjugal intercourse), Napoleon had not been many days in Paris when he concocted a plan for carrying off from Vienna both his wife and his son: In this project force was no less necessary than stratagem. A number of French of both sexes much devoted to the Emperor, who, had given them rank and fortune, had accompanied Maria Louisa in 1814 from Paris to Blois and thence to Vienna. A correspondence was opened with these persons, who embarked heart and soul in the plot; they forged passports, procured relays, of horses; and altogether arranged matters so well that but for a single individual—one who revealed the whole project a few days previously to that fixed upon for carrying it into effect—there is little room to doubt that the plan would have succeeded, and that the daughter of Austria and the titular King of home would have given such, prestige as their presence could give at the Tuileries and the Champs-de-Mai. No sooner had the Emperor of Austria discovered this plot, which, had it been successful, would have placed him in a very awkward predicament, than he dismissed all the French people about his daughter, compelled her to lay aside the armorial bearings and liveries of Napoleon, and even to relinquish the title of Empress of the French: No force, no art, no police could conceal these things from the people of Paris; who, moreover, and at nearly the same time; were made very uneasy by the failure of Murat's attempt in Italy, which greatly increased the power and political influence of Austria. Murat being disposed of, the Emperor Francis was enabled to concentrate all his forces in Italy, and to hold them in readiness for the re-invasion of France.

"Napoleon," says Lavallette, "had undoubtedly expected that the Empress and his son would be restored to him; he had published his wishes as a certainty, and to prevent it was, in fact, the worst injury the Emperor of Austria could have done, him. His hope was, however, soon destroyed.

"One evening I was summoned to the palace. I found the Emperor in a dimly-lighted closet, warming himself in a corner of the fireplace, and appearing to suffer already from the complaint which never afterwards left him. 'Here is a letter,' he said, 'which the courier from Vienna says is meant for you—read it.' On first casting my eyes on the letter I thought I knew the handwriting, but as it was long I read it slowly, and came at last to the principal object. The writer said that we ought not to reckon upon the Empress, as she did not even attempt to conceal her dislike of the Emperor, and was disposed to approve all the measures that could be taken against him; that her return was not to be thought of, as she herself would raise the greatest obstacles in the way of it; in case it should be proposed; finally, that it was not possible for him to dissemble his indignation that the Empress, wholly enamoured of ——, did not even take pains to hide her ridiculous partiality for him. The handwriting of the letter was disguised, yet not so much but that I was able to discover whose it was. I found; however, in the manner in which the secret was expressed a warmth of zeal and a picturesque style that did not belong to the author of the letter. While reading it, I all of a sudden suspected it was a counterfeit, and intended to mislead the Emperor. I communicated this idea to him, and the danger I perceived in this fraud. As I grew more and more animated I found plausible reasons enough to throw the Emperor himself into some uncertainty. 'How is it possible,' I said, 'that ——— should have been imprudent enough to write such things to me, who am not his friend, and who have had so little connection with him? How can one suppose that the Empress should forget herself, in such circumstances, so far as to manifest aversion to you, and, still more, to cast herself away upon a man who undoubtedly still possesses some power to please, but who is no longer young, whose face is disfigured, and whose person, altogether, has nothing agreeable in it?' 'But,' answered the Emperor, ——- is attached to me; and though he is not your friend, the postscript sufficiently explains the motive of the confidence he places in you.' The following words were, in fact, written at the bottom of the letter: 'I do not think you ought to mention the truth to the Emperor, but make whatever use of it you think proper.' I persisted, however, in maintaining that the letter was a counterfeit; and the Emperor then said to me, 'Go to Caulaincourt. He possesses a great many others in the same handwriting. Let the comparison decide between your opinion and mine.'

"I went to Caulaincourt, who said eagerly to me, 'I am sure the letter is from ——-, and I have not the least doubt of the truth of the particulars it contains. The best thing the Emperor can do is to be comforted; there is no help to be expected from that side.'

"So sad a discovery was very painful to the Emperor, for he was sincerely attached to the Empress, and still hoped again to see his son, whom he loved most tenderly.'

"Fouché had been far from wishing the return of the Emperor. He was long tired of obeying, and had, besides, undertaken another plan, which Napoleon's arrival had broken off. The Emperor, however, put him again at the head of the police, because Savary was worn out in that employment, and a skillful man was wanted there. Fouché accepted the office, but without giving up his plan of deposing the Emperor, to put in his place either his son or a Republic under a President. He had never ceased to correspond with Prince Metternich, and, if he is to be believed, he tried to persuade the Emperor to abdicate in favour of his son. That was also my opinion; but; coming from such a quarter, the advice was not without danger for the person to whom it was given. Besides, that advice having been rejected, it: was the duty of the Minister either to think no more of his plan or to resign his office. Fouché, however, remained in the Cabinet; and continued his correspondence. The Emperor, who placed but little confidence in him; kept a careful eye upon him. One evening the Emperor: had a great deal of company at the Elysee, he told me not to go home, because he wished to speak to me. When everybody was gone the Emperor stopped with Fouché in the apartment next to the one I was in. The door remained half open. They walked up and down together talking very calmly. I was therefore greatly astonished when, after a quarter of, an hour, I heard the Emperor say to him' gravely, 'You are a traitor! Why do you remain Minister of the Police if you wish to betray me? It rests with me to have you hanged, and everybody would rejoice at your death!' I did not hear Fouché's reply, but the conversation lasted above half an hour longer, the parties all the time walking up and down. When Fouché went away he bade me cheerfully, good-night, and said that the Emperor had gone back to his apartments.

"The next day the Emperor spoke to me of the previous night's conversation. 'I suspected,' he said, 'that the wretch was in correspondence with Vienna. I have had a banker's clerk arrested on his return from that city. He has acknowledged that he brought a letter for Fouché from Metternich, and that the answer was to be sent at a fixed time to Bale, where a man was to wait for the bearer on the bridge: I sent for Fouché a few days ago, and kept him three hours long in my garden, hoping that in the course of a friendly conversation he would mention that letter to me, but he said nothing. At last, yesterday evening, I myself opened the subject.' (Here the Emperor repeated to me the words I had heard the night before, 'You are a traitor,' etc.) He acknowledged, in fact, continued the Emperor, 'that he had received such a letter, but that it was not signed and that he had looked upon it as a mystification. He showed it me. Now that letter was evidently an answer, in which the writer again declared that he would listen to nothing more concerning the Emperor, but that, his person excepted, it would be easy to agree to all the rest. I expected that the Emperor would conclude his narrative by expressing his anger against Fouché, but our conversation turned on some other subject, and he talked no more of him.

"Two days afterwards I went to Fouché to solicit the return to Paris of an officer of musqueteers who had been banished far from his family. I found him at breakfast, and sat down next to him. Facing him sat a stranger. 'Do you see this man?' he said to me; pointing with his spoon to the stranger; 'he is an aristocrat, a Bourbonist, a Chouan; it is the Abbe ——-, one of the editors of the Journal des Debats—a sworn enemy to Napoleon, a fanatic partisan of the Bourbons; he is one of our men. I looked, at him. At every fresh epithet of the Minister the Abbe bowed his head down to his plate with a smile of cheerfulness and self-complacency, and with a sort of leer. I never saw a more ignoble countenance. Fouché explained to me, on leaving the breakfast table, in what manner all these valets of literature were men of his, and while I acknowledged to myself that the system might be necessary, I scarcely knew who were really more despicable—the wretches who thus sold themselves to the highest bidder, or the minister who boasted of having bought them, as if their acquisition were a glorious conquest. Judging that the Emperor had spoken to me of the scene I have described above, Fouché said to me, 'The Emperor's temper is soured by the resistance he finds, and he thinks it is my fault. He does not know that I have no power but by public opinion. To morrow I might hang before my door twenty persons obnoxious to public opinion, though I should not be able to imprison for four-and-twenty hours any individual favoured by it. As I am never in a hurry to speak I remained silent, but reflecting on what the Emperor had said concerning Fouché I found the comparison of their two speeches remarkable. The master could have his minister hanged with public applause, and the minister could hang—whom? Perhaps the master himself, and with the same approbation. What a singular situation!—and I believe they were both in the right; so far public opinion, equitable in regard to Fouché, had swerved concerning the Emperor."

The wrath of Napoleon was confined to the Lower House, the Peers, from the nature of their composition, being complacent and passive enough. The vast majority of them were in fact mere shadows gathered round the solid persons of Joseph, Lucien, Louis, and Jerome Bonaparte, and Sieyès, Carnot, and the military men of the Revolution. As a political body Napoleon despised them himself, and yet he wanted the nation to respect them. But respect was impossible, and the volatile Parisians made the Peers a constant object of their witticisms. The punsters of Paris made the following somewhat ingenious play upon words. Lallemand, Labedogure, Drouot, and Ney they called Las Quatre Pairs fides (perfides), which in pronunciation may equally mean the four faithful peers or the four perfidious men. The infamous Vandamme and another were called Pair-siffles, the biased peers, or the biased pair, or (persiffles) men made objects of derision. It was thus the lower orders behaved while the existence of France was at stake.

By this time the thunder-cloud of war had gathered and was ready to burst. Short as the time at his disposal was Napoleon prepared to meet it with his accustomed energy. Firearms formed one of the most important objects of attention. There were sufficient sabres, but muskets were wanting. The Imperial factories could, in ordinary times, furnish monthly 20,000 stands of new arms; by the extraordinary activity and inducements offered this number was doubled. Workmen were also employed in repairing the old muskets. There was displayed at this momentous period the same activity in the capital as in 1793, and better directed, though without the same ultimate success. The clothing of the army was another difficulty, and this was got over by advancing large sums of money to the cloth manufacturers beforehand. The contractors delivered 20,000 cavalry horses before the 1st of June, 10,000 trained horses had been furnished by the dismounted gendarmerie. Twelve thousand artillery horses were also delivered by the 1st of June, in addition to 6000 which the army already had.

The facility with which the Ministers of Finance and of the Treasury provided for all these expenses astonished everybody, as it was necessary to pay for everything in ready money. The system of public works was at the same time resumed throughout France. "It is easy to see," said the workmen, "that 'the great contractor' is returned; all was dead, now everything revives."

"We have just learnt," says a writer who was at Brussels at this time, "that Napoleon had left the capital of France on the 12th; on the 15th the frequent arrival of couriers excited extreme anxiety, and towards evening General Muffing presented himself at the hotel of the Duke of Wellington with despatches from Blücher. We were all aware that the enemy was in movement, and the ignorant could not solve the enigma of the Duke going tranquilly to the ball at the Duke of Richmond's—his coolness was above their comprehension. Had he remained at his own hotel a panic would have probably ensued amongst the inhabitants, which would have embarrassed the intended movement of the British division of the army.

"I returned home late, and we were still talking over our uneasiness when we heard the trumpets sound. Before the sun had risen in full splendour I heard martial music approaching, and soon beheld from my windows the 5th reserve of the British army passing; the Highland brigade were the first in advance, led by their noble thanes, the bagpipes playing their several pibrochs; they were succeeded by the 28th, their bugles' note falling more blithely upon the ear. Each regiment passed in succession with its band playing."

The gallant Duke of Brunswick was at a ball at the assembly-rooms in the Rue Ducale on the night of the 15th of June when the French guns, which he was one of the first to hear, were clearly distinguished at Brussels. "Upon receiving the information that a powerful French force was advancing in the direction of Charleroi. 'Then it is high time for me to be off,' he exclaimed, and immediately quitted, the ball-room."

"At four the whole disposable force under the Duke of Wellington was collected together, but in such haste that many of the officers had no time to change their silk stockings and dancing-shoes; and some, quite overcome by drowsiness, were seen lying asleep about the ramparts, still holding, however, with a firm hand, the reins of their horses, which were grazing by their sides.

"About five o'clock the word march' was heard in all directions, and instantly the whole mass appeared to move simultaneously. I conversed with several of the officers previous to their departure, and not one appeared to have the slightest idea of an approaching engagement.

"The Duke of Wellington and his staff did not quit Brussels till past eleven o'clock, and it was not till some time after they were gone that it was generally known the whole French army, including a strong corps of cavalry, was within a few miles of Quatre Bras."

CHAPTER VIII

THE BATTLES OF LIGNY AND QUATRE BRAS

1815

The moment for striking a decisive blow had now come, and accordingly, early on the morning of the 15th, the whole of the French army was in motion. The 2d corps proceeded to Marchiennes to attack the Prussian outposts at Thuin and Lobes, in order to secure the communication across the Sambre between those places. The 3d corps, covered by General Pajol's cavalry, advanced upon Charleroi, followed by the Imperial Guard and the 6th corps, with the necessary detachments of pontoniers. The remainder of the cavalry, under Grouchy, also advanced upon Charleroi, on the flanks of the 3d and 6th corps. The 4th corps was ordered to march upon the bridge of Chatelet.

On the approach of the French advanced guards an incessant skirmish was maintained during the whole morning with the Prussians, who, after losing many men, were compelled to yield to superior numbers. General Zieten, finding it impossible, from the extent of frontier he had to cover, to check the advance of the French, fell back towards Fleurus by the road to Charleroi, resolutely contesting the advance of the enemy wherever it was possible. In the repeated attacks sustained by him he suffered considerable loss. It was nearly mid-day before a passage through Charleroi was secured by the French army, and General Zieten continued his retreat upon Fleurus, where he took up his position for the night. Upon Zieten's abandoning, in the course of his retreat, the chaussee which leads to Brussels through Quatre Bras, Marshal Ney, who had only just been put in command on the left of the French army, was ordered to advance by this road upon Gosselies, and found at Frasnes part of the Duke of Wellington's army, composed of Nassau troops under the command of Prince Bernard of Saxe-Weimar, who, after some skirmishing, maintained his position. "Notwithstanding all the exertions of the French at a moment when time was of such importance, they had only been able to advance about fifteen English miles during the day, with nearly fifteen hours of daylight."

It was the intention of Napoleon during his operations on this day to effect a separation between the English and Prussian armies, in which he had nearly succeeded. Napoleon's plan for this purpose, and the execution of it by his army, were alike admirable, but it is hardly probable that the Allied generals were taken by surprise, as it was the only likely course which Napoleon could have taken. His line of operation was on the direct road to Brussels, and there were no fortified works to impede his progress, while from the nature of the country his numerous and excellent cavalry could be employed with great effect.

In the French accounts Marshal Ney was much blamed for not occupying Quatre Bras with the whole of his force on the evening of the 16th. "Ney might probably have driven back the Nassau troops at Quatre Bras, and occupied that important position, but hearing a heavy cannonade on his right flank, where General Zieten had taken up his position, he thought it necessary to halt and detach a division in the direction of Fleurus. He was severely censured by Napoleon for not having literally followed his orders and pushed on to Quatre Bras." This accusation forms a curious contrast with that made against Grouchy, upon whom Napoleon threw the blame of the defeat at Waterloo, because he strictly fulfilled his orders, by pressing the Prussians at Wavre, unheeding the cannonade on his left, which might have led him to conjecture that the more important contest between the Emperor and Wellington was at that moment raging.

It was at six o'clock in the evening of the 16th that the Duke of Wellington received the first information of the advance of the French army; but it was not, however, until ten o'clock that positive news reached him that the French army had moved upon the line of the Sambre. This information induced him to push forward reinforcements on Quatre Bras, at which place he himself arrived at an early hour on the 16th, and immediately proceeded to Bry, to devise measures with Marshal Blücher in order to combine their efforts. From the movement of considerable masses of the French in front of the Prussians it was evident that their first grand attack would be directed against them. That this was Napoleon's object on the 16th maybe seen by his orders to Ney and Grouchy to turn the right of the Prussians, and drive the British from their position at Quatre Bras, and then to march down the chaussee upon Bry in order effectually to separate the two armies. Ney was accordingly detached for this purpose with 43,000 men. In the event of the success of Marshal Ney he would have been enabled to detach a portion of his forces for the purpose of making a flank attack upon the Prussians in the rear of St. Amend, whilst Napoleon in person was directing his main efforts against that village the strongest in the Prussian position. Ney's reserve was at Frasnes, disposable either for the purpose of supporting the attack on Quatre Bras or that at St. Amand; and in case of Ney's complete success to turn the Prussian right flank by marching on Bry.

CHAPTER IX

THE BATTLE OF WATERLOO

1815

One of the most important struggles of modern times was now about to commence—a struggle which for many years was to decide the fate of Europe. Napoleon and Wellington at length stood opposite one another. They had never met; the military reputation of each was of the highest kind,[278] the career of both had been marked by signal victory; Napoleon

278 For full details of the Waterloo campaign see Siborne's History of the War in France and Belgium in 1815, giving the English contemporary account; Chesney's Waterloo Lectures, the best English modern account, which has been accepted by the Prussians as pretty nearly representing their view; and Waterloo by Lieutenant-Colonel Prince Edouard de la Tour d'Auvergne (Paris, Plon, 1870), which may be taken as the French modern account. In judging this campaign the reader must guard himself from looking on it as fought by two different armies-the English and the Prussian-whose achievements are to be weighed against one another. Wellington and Blücher were acting in a complete unison rare even when two different corps of the same nation are concerned, but practically unexampled in the case of two armies of different nations. Thus the two forces became one army, divided into two wings, one, the left (or Prussian wing) having been defeated by the main body of the French at Ligny on the 16th of June, the right (or English wing) retreated to hold the position at Waterloo, where the left (or Prussian wing) was to join it, and the united force was to crush the enemy. Thus there is no question as to whether the Prussian army saved the English by their arrival, or whether the English saved the Prussians by their resistance at Waterloo. Each army executed well and gallantly its part in a concerted operation. The English would never have fought at Waterloo if they had not relied on the arrival of the Prussians. Had the Prussians not come up on the afternoon of the 18th of June the English would have been exposed to the same great peril of having alone to deal with the mass of the French army, as the Prussians would have had to face if they had found the English in full retreat. To investigate the relative performances of the two armies is much the same as to decide the respective merits of the two Prussian armies at Sadowa, where one held the Austrians until the other arrived. Also in reading the many interesting personal accounts of the campaign it most be remembered that opinions about the chance of success in a defensive struggle are apt to warp with the observer's position, as indeed General Grant has remarked in answer to criticisms on his army's state at the end of the first day of the battle of Shiloh or Pittsburg Landing. The man placed in the front rank or fighting line sees attack after attack beaten off. He sees only part of his own losses, and most of the wounded disappear, and he also knows something of the enemy's loss by seeing the dead in front of him. Warmed by the contest, he thus believes in success. The man placed in rear or advancing with reinforcements, having nothing of the excitement of

had carried his triumphant legions across the stupendous Alps, over the north of Italy, throughout Prussia, Austria, Russia, and even to the foot of the Pyramids, while Wellington, who had been early distinguished in India, had won immortal renown in the Peninsula, where he had defeated, one after another, the favourite generals of Napoleon. He was now to make trial of his prowess against their Master.

Among the most critical events of modern times the battle of Waterloo stands conspicuous. This sanguinary encounter at last stopped the torrent of the ruthless and predatory ambition of the French, by which so many countries had been desolated. With the peace which immediately succeeded it confidence was restored to Europe.

---

the struggle, sees only the long and increasing column of wounded, stragglers, and perhaps of fliers. He sees his companion fall without being able to answer the fire. He sees nothing of the corresponding loss of the enemy, and he is apt to take a most desponding view of the situation. Thus Englishmen reading the accounts of men who fought at Waterloo are too ready to disbelieve representations of what was taking place in the rear of the army, and to think Thackeray's life-like picture in Vanity Fair of the state of Brussels must be overdrawn. Indeed, in this very battle of Waterloo, Zieten began to retreat when his help was most required, because one of his aides de camp told him that the right wing of the English was in full retreat. "This inexperienced young man," says Muffling, p. 248, "had mistaken the great number of wounded going, or being taken, to the rear to be dressed, for fugitives, and accordingly made a false report." Further, reserves do not say much of their part or, sometimes, no part of the fight, and few people know that at least two English regiments actually present on the field of Waterloo hardly fired a shot till the last advance. The Duke described the army as the worst he ever commanded, and said that if he had had his Peninsular men, the fight would have been over much sooner. But the Duke, sticking to ideas now obsolete, had no picked corps. Each man, trusting in and trusted by his comrades, fought under his own officers and under his own regimental colours. Whatever they did not know, the men knew how to die, and at the end of the day a heap of dead told where each regiment and battery had stood.

CHAPTER X

1815

One of the first public men to see Napoleon after his return from Waterloo was Lavallette. "I flew," says he, "to the Elysee to see the Emperor: he summoned me into his closet, and as soon as he saw me, he came to meet me with a frightful epileptic 'laugh. 'Oh, my God!' he said, raising his eyes to heaven, and walking two or three times up and down the room. This appearance of despair was however very short. He soon recovered his coolness, and asked me what was going forward in the Chamber of Representatives. I could not attempt to hide that party spirit was there carried to a high pitch, and that the majority seemed determined to require his abdication, and to pronounce it themselves if he did not concede willingly. 'How is that?' he said. 'If proper measures are not taken the enemy will be before the gates of Paris in eight days. Alas!' he added, 'have I accustomed them to such great victories that they knew not how to bear one day's misfortune? What will become of poor France? I have done all I could for her!' He then heaved a deep sigh. Somebody asked to speak to him, and I left him, with a direction to come back at a later hour.

"I passed the day in seeking information among all my friends and acquaintances. I found in all of them either the greatest dejection or an extravagant joy, which they disguised by feigned alarm and pity for myself, which I repulsed with great indignation. Nothing favourable was to be expected from the Chamber of Representatives. They all said they wished for liberty, but, between two enemies who appeared ready to destroy it, they preferred the foreigners, the friends of the Bourbons, to Napoleon, who might still have prolonged the struggle, but that he alone would not find means to save them and erect the edifice of liberty. The Chamber of Peers presented a much sadder spectacle. Except the intrepid Thibaudeau, who till, the last moment expressed himself with admirable energy against the Bourbons, almost all the others thought of nothing else but getting out of the dilemma with the least loss they could. Some took no pains to hide their wish of bending again under the Bourbon yoke."

On the evening of Napoleon's return to Paris he sent for Benjamin Constant to come to him at the Elysee about seven o'clock. The Chambers had decreed their permanence, and proposals for abdication had reached the Emperor. He was serious but calm. In reply to some words on the disaster of Waterloo he said, "The question no longer concerns me, but France. They wish me to abdicate. Have they calculated upon the inevitable consequences of this abdication? It is round me, round my name, that the army rallies: to separate me from it is to disband it. If I abdicate to-day, in two days' time you will no longer have an army. These poor fellows do not understand all your subtleties. Is it believed that axioms in metaphysics, declarations of right, harangues from the tribune, will put a stop to the disbanding of an army? To reject me when I landed at Cannes I can conceive possible; to abandon me now is what I do not understand. It is not when the enemy is at twenty-five leagues' distance that any Government can be overturned with impunity. Does any one imagine that the Foreign Powers will be won over by fine words? If they had dethroned me fifteen days ago there would have been some spirit in it; but as it is, I make part of what strangers attack, I make part, then, of what France is bound to defend. In giving me up she gives up herself, she avows her weakness, she acknowledges herself conquered, she courts the insolence of the conqueror. It is not the love of liberty which deposes me, but Waterloo; it is fear, and a fear of which your enemies will take advantage. And then what title has the Chamber to demand my abdication? It goes out of its lawful sphere in doing so; it has no authority. It is my right, it is my duty to dissolve it."

"He then hastily ran over the possible consequences of such a step. Separated from the Chambers, he could only be considered as a military chief: but the army would be for him; that would always join him who can lead it against foreign banners, and to this might be added all that part of the population which is equally powerful and easily, led in such a state of things. As if chance intended to strengthen Napoleon in this train of thought, while he was speaking the avenue of Marigny resounded with the cries of 'Vive l'Empereur!' A crowd of men, chiefly of the poor and labouring class, pressed forward into the avenue, full of wild enthusiasm, and trying to scale the walls to make an offer to Napoleon to rally round and defend him. Bonaparte for some time looked attentively at this group. 'You see it is so,' said he; 'those are not the men whom I have loaded with honours and riches. What do these people owe me? I found them—I left them—poor. The instinct of necessity enlightens them; the voice of the country speaks by their months; and if I choose, if I permit it, in an hour the refractory Chambers will have ceased to exist. But the life of a man is not worth purchasing at such a price: I did not return from the Isle of Elba that Paris should be inundated with blood: He did not like the idea of flight.' 'Why should I not stay here?' he repeated. 'What do you suppose they would do to a man disarmed like me? I will go to Malmaison: I can live there in retirement with some friends, who most certainly will come to see me only for my own sake.'

"He then described with complacency and even with a sort of gaiety this new kind of life. Afterwards, discarding an idea which sounded like mere irony, he went on. 'If they do not like me to remain in France, where am I to go? To England? My abode there would be ridiculous or disquieting. I should be tranquil; no one would believe it. Every fog would be suspected of concealing my landing on the coast. At the first sign of a green coat getting out of a boat one party would fly from France, the other would put France out of the pale of the law. I should compromise everybody, and by dint of the repeated "Behold he comes!" I should feel the temptation to set out. America would be more suitable; I could live there with dignity. But once more, what is there to fear? What sovereign can, without injuring himself, persecute me? To one I have restored half his dominions; how often has the other pressed my hand, calling me a great man! And as to the third, can he find pleasure or honour in humiliation of his son-in-law? Would they wish to proclaim in the face of the world that all they did was through fear? As to the rest, I shall see: I do not wish to employ open force. I came in the hope of combining our last resources: they abandoned me; they do so with the same facility with which they received me back. Well, then, let them efface, if possible, this double stain of weakness and levity! Let them cover it over with some sacrifice, with some glory! Let them do for the country what they will not do for me. I doubt it. To-day, those who deliver up Bonaparte say that it is to save France: to-morrow, by delivering up France, they will prove that it was to save their own heads.'"

The humiliating scenes which rapidly succeeded one another; and which ended in Napoleon's unconditional surrender, may be briefly told. As soon as possible after his arrival at Paris he assembled his counsellors, when he declared himself in favour of still resisting. The question, however, was, whether the Chambers would support him; and Lafayette being treacherously informed, it is said by Fouché, that it was intended to dissolve the Chambers, used his influence to get the chambers to adopt the propositions he laid before them. By these the independence of the nation was asserted to be in danger; the sittings of the Chamber were declared permanent, and all attempts to dissolve it were pronounced treasonable. The propositions were adopted, and being communicated to the Chamber of Peers, that body also declared itself permanent. Whatever might have been the intentions of Bonaparte, it was now manifest that there were no longer any hopes of his being able to make his will the law of the nation; after some vacillation, therefore, on 22d June he published the following declaration:

> TO THE FRENCH PEOPLE
>
> FRENCHMEN!—In commencing war for maintaining the national independence, I relied on the union of all efforts, of all wills, and the concurrence of all the national authorities. I had reason to hope for success, and I braved all the declarations of the powers against me. Circumstances appear to me changed. I offer myself a sacrifice to the hatred of the enemies of France. May they prove sincere in their declarations, and really have directed them only against my power. My political life is terminated, and I proclaim my son under the title of: NAPOLEON II., EMPEROR OF THE FRENCH.
>
> The present Ministers will provisionally form the Council of the Government. The interest which I take in my son induces me to invite the Chambers to form without delay the Regency by a law. Unite all for the public safety, that you may continue an independent nation.
>
> *(Signed)* NAPOLEON.

This declaration was conveyed to both the Chambers, which voted deputations to the late Emperor, accepting this abdication, but in their debates the nomination of his son to the succession was artfully eluded. The Chamber of Representatives voted the nomination of a Commission of five persons, three to be chosen from that Chamber, and two from the Chamber of Peers, for the purpose of provisionally exercising the functions of Government, and also that the Ministers should continue their respective functions under the authority of this Commission. The persons chosen by the Chamber of Representatives were Carnot, Fouché, and Grenier, those nominated by the Peers were the Duke of Vicenza (Caulaincourt) and Baron Quinette. The Commission nominated five persons to the Allied army for the purpose of proposing peace. These proceedings were, however, rendered of little importance by the resolution of the victors to advance to Paris.

Napoleon's behaviour just before and immediately after the crisis is well described by Lavallette. "The next day," he observes, "I returned to the Emperor. He had received the most positive accounts of the state of feeling in the Chamber of Representatives. The reports had, however, been given to him with some little reserve, for he did not seem to me convinced that the resolution was really formed to pronounce his abdication, I was better informed on the matter, and I came to him without having the least doubt in my mind that the only thing he could do was to descend once more from the throne. I communicated to him all the particulars I had just received, and I did not hesitate to advise him to follow the only course worthy of him. He listened to me with a sombre air, and though he was in some measure master of himself, the agitation of his mind and the sense of his position betrayed themselves in his face and in all his motions. 'I know,' said I, 'that your Majesty may still keep the sword drawn, but with whom, and against whom? Defeat has chilled the courage of every one; the army is still in the greatest confusion. Nothing is to be expected from Paris, and the coup d'etat of the 18th Brumaire cannot be renewed.'—'That thought,' he replied, stopping, 'is far from my mind. I will hear nothing more about myself. But poor France!' At that moment Savary and Caulaincourt entered, and having drawn a faithful picture of the exasperation of the Deputies, they persuaded him to assent to abdication. Some words he uttered proved to us that he would have considered death preferable to that step; but still he took it.

"The great act of abdication being performed, he remained calm during the whole day, giving his advice on the position the army should take, and on the manner in which the negotiations with the enemy ought to be conducted. He insisted especially on the necessity of proclaiming his son Emperor, not so much for the advantage of the child as with a view to concentrate all the power of sentiments and affections. Unfortunately, nobody would listen to him. Some men of sense and courage rallied found that proposition in the two Chambers, but fear swayed the majority; and among those who remained free from it many thought that a public declaration of liberty, and the resolution to defend it at any price, would make the enemy and the Bourbons turn back. Strange delusion of weakness and want of experience! It must, however, be respected, for it had its source in love of their country; but, while we excuse it, can it be justified? The population of the metropolis had resumed its usual appearance, which was that of complete indifference, with a resolution to cry 'Long live the King!' provided the King arrived well escorted; for one must not judge of the whole capital by about one-thirtieth part of the inhabitants, who called for arms, and declared themselves warmly against the return of the exiled family.

"On the 23d I returned to the Elysee. The Emperor had been for two hours in his bath. He himself turned the discourse on the retreat he ought to choose, and spoke of the United States. I rejected the idea without reflection, and with a degree of vehemence that surprised him. 'Why not America?' he asked. I answered, 'Because Moreau retired there.' The observation was harsh, and I should never have forgiven myself for having expressed it; if I had not retracted my advice a few days afterwards. He heard it without any apparent ill-humour, but I have no doubt that it must have made an unfavourable impression on his mind. I strongly urged on his choosing England for his asylum.

"The Emperor went to Malmaison. He was accompanied thither by the Duchesse de St. Leu, Bertrand and his family, and the Duc de Bassano. The day that he arrived there he proposed to me to accompany him abroad. Drouot,' he said, 'remains in France. I see the Minister of War wishes him not to be lost to his country. I dare not complain, but it is a great loss for me; I never met with a better head, or a more upright heart. That man was formed to be a prime minister anywhere.' I declined to accompany him at the time, saying, 'My wife is enceinte; I cannot make up my mind to leave her. Allow me some time, and I will join you wherever you may be. I have remained faithful to your Majesty in better times, and you may reckon upon me now. Nevertheless, if my wife did not require all my attention, I should do better to go with you, for I have sad forebodings respecting my fate."

"The Emperor made no answer; but I saw by the expression of his countenance that he had no better augury of my fate than I had. However, the enemy was approaching, and for the last three days he had solicited the Provisional Government to place a frigate at his disposal, with which he might proceed to America. It had been promised him; he was even pressed to set off; but he wanted to be the bearer of the order to the captain to convey him to the United States, and that order did not arrive. We all felt that the delay of a single hour might put his freedom in jeopardy.

"After we had talked the subject over among ourselves, I went to him and strongly pointed out to him how dangerous it might be to prolong his stay. He observed that he could not go without the order. 'Depart, nevertheless,' I replied; your presence on board the ship will still have a great influence over Frenchmen; cut the cables, promise money to the crew, and if the captain resist have him put on shore, and hoist your sails. I have no doubt but Fouché has sold you to the Allies.'— 'I believe it also; but go and make the last effort with the Minister of Marine.' I went off immediately to M. Decres. He was in bed, and listened to me with an indifference that made my blood boil. He said to me, 'I am only a Minister. Go to Fouché; speak to the Government. As for me, I can do nothing. Good-night.' And so saying he covered himself up again in his blankets. I left him; but I could not succeed in speaking either to Fouché or to any of the others. It was two o'clock in the morning when I returned to Malmaison; the Emperor was in bed. I was admitted to his chamber, where I gave him an account of the result of my mission, and renewed my entreaties. He listened to me, but made no answer. He got up, however, and spent a part of the night in walking up and down the room.

"The following day was the last of that sad drama. The Emperor had gone to bed again, and slept a few hours. I entered his cabinet at about twelve o'clock. 'If I had known you were here,' he said, 'I would have had you called in.' He then gave me, on a subject that interested him personally, some instructions which it is needless for me to repeat. Soon after I left him, full of anxiety respecting his fate, my heart oppressed with grief, but still far from suspecting the extent to which both the rigour of fortune and the cruelty of his enemies would be carried."

All the morning of the 29th of June the great road from St. Germain rung with the cries of "Vive l'Empereur!" proceeding from the troops who passed under the walls of Malmaison. About mid-day General Becker, sent by the Provisional Government, arrived. He had been appointed to attend Napoleon. Fouché knew that General Becker had grievances against the Emperor, and thought to find in him willing agent. He was greatly deceived, for the General paid to the Emperor a degree of respect highly to his honour. Time now became pressing. The Emperor, at the moment of departure, sent a message by General Becker himself to the Provisional Government, offering to march as a private citizen at the head of the troops. He promised to repulse Blücher, and afterwards to continue his route. Upon the refusal of the Provisional Government he quitted Malmaison on the 29th.

Napoleon and part of his suite took the road to Rochefort. He slept at Rambouillet on the 29th of June, on the 30th at Tours, on the 1st of July he arrived at Niort, and on the 3d reached Rochefort, on the western coast of France, with the intention of escaping to America; but the whole western seaboard was so vigilantly watched by British men-of-war that, after various plans and devices, he was obliged to abandon the attempt in despair. He was lodged at the house of the prefect, at the balcony of which he occasionally showed himself to acknowledge the acclamations of the people.

During his stay here a French naval officer, commanding a Danish merchant vessel, generously offered to some of Napoleon's adherents to further his escape. He proposed to take Napoleon alone, and undertook to conceal his person so effectually as to defy the most rigid scrutiny, and offered to sail immediately to the United States of America. He required no other compensation than a small sum to indemnify the owners of his ship for the loss this enterprise might occasion them. This was agreed to by Bertrand upon certain stipulations.

On the evening of the 8th of July Napoleon reached Fouras, receiving everywhere testimonies of attachment. He proceeded on board the Saale, one of the two frigates appointed by the Provisional Government to convey him to the United States, and slept on board that night. Very early on the following morning he visited the fortifications of that place, and returned to the frigate for dinner. On the evening of the 9th of July he despatched Count Las Cases and the Duke of Rovigo to the commander of the English squadron, for the purpose of ascertaining whether the passports promised by the Provisional Government to enable him to proceed to America had been received. A negative answer was returned; it was at the same time signified that the Emperor would be attacked by the English squadron if he attempted to sail under a flag of truce, and it was intimated that every neutral vessel would be examined, and probably sent into an English port. Las Cases affirms that Napoleon was recommended to proceed to England by Captain Maitland, who assured him that he would experience no ill-treatment there. The English ship 'Bellerophon' then anchored in the Basque roads, within sight of the French vessels of war. The coast being, as we have stated, entirely blockaded by the English squadron, the Emperor was undecided as to the course he should pursue. Neutral vessels and 'chasse-marees', manned by young naval officers, were proposed, and many other plans were devised.

Napoleon disembarked on the 12th at the Isle of Aix with acclamations ringing on every side. He had quitted the frigates because they refused to sail, owing either to the weakness of character of the commandant, or in consequence of his receiving fresh orders from the Provisional Government. Many persons thought that the enterprise might be undertaken with some probability of success; the wind, however, remained constantly in the wrong quarter.

Las Cases returned to the Bellerophon at four o'clock in the morning of the 14th, to inquire whether any reply had been received to the communication made by Napoleon. Captain Maitland stated that he expected to receive it every moment, and added that, if the Emperor would then embark for England, he was authorized to convey him thither. He added, moreover, that in his own opinion, and many other officers present concurred with him, he had no doubt Napoleon would be treated in England with all-possible attention and respect; that in England neither the King nor Ministers exercised the same arbitrary power as on the Continent; that the English indeed possessed generosity of sentiment and a liberality of opinions superior even to those of the King. Las Cases replied that he would make Napoleon acquainted with Captain Maitland's offer, and added, that he thought the Emperor would not hesitate to proceed to England, so as to be able to continue his voyage to the United States. He described France, south of the Loire, to be in commotion, the hopes of the people resting on Napoleon as long as he was present; the propositions everywhere made to him, and at every moment; his decided resolution not to become the pretext of a civil war; the generosity he had exhibited in abdicating, in order to render the conclusion of a peace more practicable; and his settled determination to banish himself, in order to render that peace more prompt and more lasting.

The messengers returned to their Master, who, after some doubt and hesitation, despatched General Gourgaud with the following well-known letter to the Prince Regent:—

ROCHEFORT,
13th July 1815.

> ROYAL HIGHNESS—A victim to the factions which divide my country, and to the hostility of the greatest Powers of Europe, I have terminated my political career, and come, like Themistocles, to share the hospitality of the British people. I place myself under the protection of their laws, and I claim that from your Royal Highness as the most powerful, the most constant, and the most generous of my enemies.
>
> *(Signed)* NAPOLEON.

About four P.M. Las Cases and Savory returned to the 'Bellerophon', where they had a long conversation with Captain Maitland, in the presence of Captains Sartorius and Gambler, who both declare that Maitland repeatedly warned Napoleon's adherents not to entertain the remotest idea that he was enabled to offer any pledge whatever to their Master beyond the simple assurance that he would convey him in safety to the English coast, there to await the determination of the British Government.

Napoleon had begun to prepare for his embarkation before daylight on the 15th. It was time that he did so, for a messenger charged with orders to arrest him had already arrived at Rochefort from the new Government. The execution of this order was delayed by General Becker for a few hours in order to allow Napoleon sufficient time to escape. At daybreak, he quitted the 'Epervier', and was enthusiastically cheered by the ship's company so long as the boat was within hearing. Soon after six he was received on board the 'Bellerophon' with respectful silence, but without those honours generally paid to persons of high rank. Bonaparte was dressed in the uniform of the 'chasseurs a cheval' of the Imperial Guard, and wore the Grand Cross of the Legion of Honour.

On entering the vessel he took off his hat, and addressing Captain Maitland, said, "I am come to throw myself on the protection of the laws of England." Napoleon's manner was well calculated to make a favourable impression on those with whom he conversed. He requested to be introduced to the officers of the ship, and put various questions to each. He then went round the ship, although he was informed that the men were cleaning and scouring, and remarked upon anything which struck him as differing from what he had seen on French vessels. The clean appearance of the men surprised him. "He then observed," says Captain Maitland, to whose interesting narrative we refer, "'I can see no sufficient reason why your ships should beat the French ones with so much ease. The finest men-of-war in your service are French; a French ship is heavier in every respect than one of yours; she carries more guns, and those guns are of a larger calibre, and she has a great many more men.'" His inquiries, which were minute, proved that he had directed much attention to the French navy.

On the first morning Napoleon took breakfast in the English fashion, but observing that his distinguished prisoner did not eat much, Captain Maitland gave direction that for the future a hot breakfast should be served up after the French manner. 'The Superb', the Admiral's ship, which had been seen in the morning, was now approaching. Immediately on her anchoring Captain Maitland went on board to give an account of all that had happened, and received the Admiral's approbation of what he had done. In the afternoon Admiral Sir Henry Hotham was introduced to Napoleon, and invited by him to dinner. This was arranged, in order to make it more agreeable to him, by Bonaparte's maitre d'hotel. On dinner being announced Napoleon led the way, and seated himself in the centre at one side of the table, desiring Sir Henry Hotham to take the seat on his right, and Madame Bertrand that on his left hand. On this day Captain Maitland took his seat at the end of the table, but on the following day, by Napoleon's request, he placed himself on his right hand, whilst General Bertrand took the top. Two of the ship's officers dined with the Emperor daily, by express invitation. The conversation of Napoleon was animated. He made many inquiries as to the family and connections of Captain Maitland, and in alluding to Lord Lauderdale, who was sent as ambassador to Paris during the administration of Mr. Fox, paid that nobleman some compliments and said of the then Premier, "Had Mr. Fox lived it never would have come to this; but his death put an end to all hopes of peace."

On one occasion he ordered his camp-bed to be displayed for the inspection of the English officers. In two small leather packages were comprised the couch of the once mighty ruler of the Continent. The steel bedstead which, when folded up, was only two feet long, and eighteen inches wide, occupied one case, while the other contained the mattress and curtains. The whole was so contrived as to be ready for use in three minutes.

Napoleon spoke in terms of high praise of the marines on duty in the Bellerophon, and on going through their ranks exclaimed to Bertrand, "How much might be done with a hundred thousand such soldiers as these!" In putting them through their exercise he drew a contrast between the charge of the bayonet as made by the English and the French, and observed that the English method of fixing the bayonet was faulty, as it might easily be twisted off when in close action. In visiting Admiral Hotham's flag-ship, the 'Superb', he manifested the same active curiosity as in former instances, and made the same minute inquiries into everything by which he was surrounded. During breakfast one of Napoleon's suite, Colonel Planat, was much affected, and even wept, on witnessing the humiliation of his Master.

On the return of Bonaparte from the Superb to the 'Bellerophon' the latter ship was got under weigh and made sail for England. When passing within a cable's length of the 'Superb' Napoleon inquired of Captain Maitland if he thought that distance was sufficient for action. The reply of the English officer was characteristic; he told the Emperor that half the distance, or even less, would suit much better. Speaking of Sir Sidney Smith, Bonaparte repeated the anecdote connected with his quarrel at St. Jean d'Acre with that officer, which has already been related in one of the notes earlier in these volumes. Patting Captain Maitland on the shoulder, he observed, that had it not been for the English navy he would have been Emperor of the East, but that wherever he went he was sure to find English ships in the way.

The 'Bellerophon', with Bonaparte on board, sighted the coast of England on Sunday, the 23d of July 1815, and at daybreak on the 24th the vessel approached Dartmouth. No sooner had the ship anchored than an order from Loral Keith was delivered to Captain Maitland, from which the following is an extract:

EXTRACT OF AN ORDER FROM ADMIRAL VISCOUNT KEITH, G. C. B., ADDRESSED TO CAPTAIN MAITLAND, OF H. M. S. "BELLEROPHON," DATED VILLE DE PARIS, HAMOAZE, 23D JULY 1815.

Captain Sartorius, of His Majesty's ship 'Slaney', delivered to me last night, at eleven o'clock, your despatch of the 14th instant, acquainting me that Bonaparte had proposed to embark on board the ship you command, and that you had acceded thereto, with the intention of proceeding to Torbay, there to wait for further orders. I lost no time in forwarding your letter by Captain Sartorius to the Lords Commissioners of the Admiralty, in order that their Lordships might, through him, be acquainted with every circumstance that had occurred on an occasion of so much importance; and you may expect orders from their Lordships for your further guidance. You are to remain in Torbay until you receive such orders; and in the meantime, in addition to the directions already in your possession, you are most positively ordered to prevent every person whatever from coming on board the ship you command, except the officers and men who compose her crew; nor is any person whatever, whether in His Majesty's service or not, who does not belong, to the ship, to be suffered to come on board, either for the purpose of visiting the officers, or on any pretence whatever, without express permission either from the Lords Commissioners of the Admiralty or from me. As I understand from Captain Sartorius that General Gourgaud refused to deliver the letter with which he was charged for the Prince Regent to any person except His Royal Highness, you are to take him out of the 'Slaney' into the ship you command, until you receive directions from the Admiralty on the subject, and order that ship back to Plymouth Sound, when Captain Sartorius returns from London.

It was stated about this time, in some of the English newspapers, that St. Helena would be the place of exile of the ex-Emperor, the bare report of which evidently caused great pain to Napoleon and his suite. General Gourgaud was obliged to return to the 'Bellerophon', not having been suffered to go on shore to deliver the letter from Bonaparte to the Prince Regent with which he had been entrusted. The ship which bore the modern Alexander soon became a natural object of attraction to the whole neighbourhood, and was constantly surrounded by crowds of boats. Napoleon frequently showed himself to the people from shore with a view of gratifying their curiosity. On the 25th of July the number of guard-boats which surrounded the vessel was greatly increased; and the alarm of the captives became greater as the report was strengthened as to the intention of conveying Bonaparte to St. Helena.

In conversation with Captain Maitland, Napoleon, who seemed to be aware that the English fishermen united the occupation of smugglers to their usual trade; stated that many of them had been bribed by him, and had assisted in the escape of French prisoners of war. They had even proposed to deliver Louis XVIII. into his power, but as they would .not answer for the safety of his life, Napoleon refused the offer. Upon the arrival of despatches from London the 'Bellerophon' got under weigh for Plymouth Sound on the 26th of July. This movement tended still further to disconcert the ex-Emperor and his followers. In passing the breakwater Bonaparte could not withhold his admiration of that work, which he considered highly honourable to the public spirit of the nation, and, alluding to his own improvements at Cherbourg, expressed his apprehensions that they would now be suffered to fall into decay.

Captain Maitland was directed by Lord Keith to observe the utmost vigilance to prevent the escape of his prisoners, and with this view no boat was permitted to approach the Bellerophon; the 'Liffey' and 'Eurotas' were ordered to take up an anchorage on each side of the ship, and further precautions were adopted at night.

On the 27th of July Captain Maitland proceeded to Lord Keith, taking with him Bonaparte's original letter to the Prince Regent, which, as General Gourgaud had not been permitted to deliver it personally, Napoleon now desired to be transmitted through the hands of the Admiral. As Lord Keith had now received instructions from his Government as to the manner in which Napoleon was to be treated, he lost no time in paying his respects to the fallen chief.

On the 31st of July the anxiously-expected order of the English Government arrived. In this document, wherein the ex-Emperor was styled "General Bonaparte," it was notified that he was to be exiled to St. Helena, the place of all others most dreaded by him and his devoted adherents. It was, moreover, specified that he might be allowed to take with him three officers, and his surgeon, and twelve servants. To his own selection was conceded the choice of these followers, with the exclusion, however, of Savary and Lallemand, who were on no account to be permitted any further to share his fortunes. This prohibition gave considerable alarm to those individuals, who became excessively anxious as to their future disposal, and declared that to deliver them up to the vengeance of the Bourbons would be a violation of faith and honour.

Napoleon himself complained bitterly on the subject of his destination, and said, "The idea, of it is horrible to me. To be placed for life on an island within the tropics, at an immense distance from any land, cut off from all communication with the world, and everything that I hold dear in it!—c'est pis que la cage de fer de Tamerlan. I would prefer being delivered up to the Bourbons. Among other insults," said he,—"but that is a mere bagatelle, a very secondary consideration—they style me General! They can have no right to call me General; they may as well call me 'Archbishop,' for I was Head of the Church as well as of the Army. If they do not acknowledge me as Emperor they ought as First Counsul; they have sent ambassadors to me as such; and your King, in his letters, styled me 'Brother.' Had they confined me in the Tower of London, or one of the fortresses in England (though not what I had hoped from the generosity of the English people), I should not have so much cause of complaint; but to banish me to an island within the tropics! They might as well have signed my death-warrant at once, for it is impossible a man of my habit of body can live long in such a climate."

Having so expressed himself, he wrote a second letter to the Prince Regent, which was forwarded through Lord Keith. It was the opinion of Generals Montholon and Gourgaud that Bonaparte would sooner kill himself than go to St. Helena. This idea arose from his having been heard emphatically to exclaim, "I will not go to St. Helena!" The generals, indeed, declared that were he to give his own consent to be so exiled they would themselves prevent him. In consequence of this threat Captain Maitland was instructed by Lord Keith to tell those gentlemen that as the English law awarded death to murderers, the crime they meditated would inevitably conduct them to the gallows.

Early on the morning of the 4th of August the 'Bellerophon' was ordered to be ready at a moment's notice for sea. The reason of this was traced to a circumstance which is conspicuous among the many remarkable incidents by which Bonaparte's arrival near the English coast was characterised. A rumour reached Lord Keith that a 'habeas corpus' had been procured with a view of delivering Napoleon from the custody he was then in. This, however, turned out to be a subpoena for Bonaparte as a witness at a trial in the Court of King's Bench; and, indeed, a person attempted to get on board the Bellerophon to serve the document; but he was foiled in his intention; though, had he succeeded, the subpoena would, in the situation wherein the ex-Emperor then stood, have been without avail.

On the 5th Captain Maitland, having been summoned to the flag-ship of Lord Keith, acquainted General Bertrand that he would convey to the Admiral anything which Bonaparte (who had expressed an urgent wish to see his lordship) might desire to say to him. Bertrand requested the captain to delay his departure until a document, then in preparation, should be completed: the "PROTEST OF HIS MAJESTY THE LATE EMPEROR OF THE FRENCH, ETC."

Captain Maitland denied that any snare was laid for Bonaparte, either by himself or by the English Government, and stated that the precautions for preventing the escape of Napoleon from Rochefort were so well ordered that it was impossible to evade them; and that the fugitive was compelled to surrender himself to the English ship.

On the 7th of August Bonaparte, with the suite he had selected, was transferred from the 'Bellerophon' to the 'Northumberland'. Lord Keith's barge was prepared for his conveyance to the latter vessel, and his lordship was present on the occasion. A captain's guard was turned out, and as Napoleon left the 'Bellerophon' the marines presented arms, and the drum was beaten as usual in saluting a general officer. When he arrived on board the Northumberland the squadron got under weigh, and Napoleon sailed for the place of his final exile and grave.'[279]

279 For the continuation of Napoleon's voyage see Chapter XIII.

CHAPTER XI

1815

The fulfilment of my prediction was now at hand, for the result of the Battle of Waterloo enabled Louis XVIII. to return to his dominions. As soon as I heard of the King's departure from Ghent I quitted Hamburg, and travelled with all possible haste in the hope of reaching Paris in time to witness his Majesty's entrance. I arrived at St. Denis on the 7th of July, and, notwithstanding the intrigues that were set on foot, I found an immense number of persons assembled to meet the King. Indeed, the place was so crowded that it was with the greatest difficulty I could procure even a little garret for my lodging.

Having resumed my uniform of a captain of the National Guard, I proceeded immediately to the King's palace. The salon was filled with ladies and gentlemen who had come to congratulate the King on his return. At St. Denis I found my family, who, not being aware that I had left Hamburg, were much surprised to see me.

They informed me that the Parisians were all impatient for the return of the King—a fact of which I could judge by the opposition manifested to the free expression of public feeling. Paris having been declared in a state of blockade, the gates were closed, and no one was permitted to leave the capital, particularly by the Barriere de la Chapelle. It is true that special permission might be obtained, and with tolerable ease, by those who wished to leave the city; but the forms to be observed for obtaining the permission deterred the mass of the people from proceeding to St. Denis, which, indeed, was the sole object of the regulation. As it had been resolved to force Fouché and the tri-coloured cockade upon the King, it was deemed necessary to keep away from his Majesty all who might persuade him to resist the proposed measures. Madame de Bourrienne told me that on her arrival at St. Denis she called upon M. Hue and M. Lefebvre, the King's physician, who both acquainted her with those fatal resolutions. Those gentlemen, however, assured her that the King would resolutely hold out against the tri-coloured cockade, but the nomination of the ill-omened man appeared inevitable.

Fouché Minister of the Police! If, like Don Juan, I had seen a statue move, I could not have been more confounded than when I heard this news. I could not credit it until it was repeated to me by different persons. How; indeed, could I think that at the moment of a reaction the King should have entrusted the most important ministerial department to a man to whose arrest he had a hundred days before attached so much consequence? to a man, moreover, whom Bonaparte had appointed, at Lyons, to fill the same office! This was inconceivable! Thus, in less than twenty-four hours, the same man had been entrusted to execute measures the most opposite, and to serve interests the most contradictory. He was one day the minister of usurpation, and the next the minister of legitimacy! How can I express what I felt when Fouché took the oath of fidelity to Louis XVIII. when I saw the King clasp in his hands the hands of Fouché! I was standing near M. de Chateaubriand, whose feelings must have been similar to mine, to judge from a passage in his admirable work, 'La Monarchie selon la Charte'. "About nine in the evening," he says, "I was in one of the royal antechambers. All at once the door opened, and I saw the President of the Council enter leaning on the arm of the new minister. Oh, Louis-le-Desire! Oh, my unfortunate master! you have proved that there is no sacrifice which your people may not expect from your paternal heart!"

Fouché was resolved to have his restoration as well as M. de Talleyrand, who had had his the year before; he therefore contrived to retard the King's entry into Paris for four days. The prudent members of the Chamber of Peers, who had taken no part in the King's Government in 1814, were the first to declare that it was for the interest of France to hasten his Majesty's entrance into Paris, in order to prevent foreigners from exercising a sort of right of conquest in a city which was a prey to civil dissension and party influence. Blücher informed me that the way in which Fouché contrived to delay the King's return greatly contributed to the pretensions of the foreigners who, he confessed, were very well pleased to see the population of Paris divided in opinion, and to hear the alarming cries raised by the confederates of the Faubourgs when the King was already at St. Denis.

I know for a fact that Louis XVIII. wished to have nothing to do with Fouché, and indignantly refused to appoint him when he was first proposed. But he had so nobly served Bonaparte during the Hundred Days that it was necessary he should be rewarded. Fouché, besides, had gained the support of a powerful party among the emigrants of the Faubourg St. Germain, and he possessed the art of rendering himself indispensable. I have heard many honest men say very seriously that to him was due the tranquillity of Paris. Moreover, Wellington was the person by whose influence in particular Fouché was made one of the counsellors of the King. After all the benefits which foreigners had conferred upon us Fouché was indeed an acceptable present to France and to the King.

I was not ignorant of the Duke of Wellington's influence upon the affairs of the second Restoration, but for a long time I refused to believe that his influence should have outweighed all the serious considerations opposed to such a perfect anomaly as appointing Fouché the Minister of a Bourbon. But I was deceived. France and the King owed to him Fouché's introduction into the Council, and I had to thank him for the impossibility of resuming a situation which I had relinquished for the purpose of following the King into Belgium. Could I be Prefect of Police under a Minister whom a short time before I had received orders to arrest, but who eluded my agents? That was impossible. The King could not offer me the place of Prefect under Fouché, and if he had I could not have accepted it. I was therefore right in not relying on the assurances which had been given me; but I confess that if I had been told to guess the cause why they could not be realised I never should have thought that cause would have been the appointment of Fouché as a Minister of the King of France. At first, therefore, I was of course quite forgotten, as is the custom of courts when a faithful subject refrains from taking part in the intrigues of the moment.

I have already frequently stated my opinion of the pretended talent of Fouché; but admitting his talent to have been as great as was supposed, that would have been an additional reason for not entrusting the general police of the kingdom to him. His principles and conduct were already sufficiently known. No one could be ignorant of the language he held respecting the Bourbons, and in which he indulged as freely after he became the Minister of Louis XVIII. as when he was the Minister of Bonaparte. It was universally known that in his conversation the Bourbons were the perpetual butt for his sarcasms, that he never mentioned them but in terms of disparagement, and that he represented them as unworthy of governing France. Everybody must have been aware that Fouché, in his heart, favoured a Republic, where the part of President might have been assigned to him. Could any one have forgotten the famous postscript he subjoined to a letter he wrote from Lyons to his worthy friend Robespierre: "To celebrate the fete of the Republic suitably, I have ordered 250 persons to be shot?" And to this man, the most furious enemy of the restoration of the monarchy, was consigned the task of consolidating it for the second time! But it would require another Claudian to describe this new Rufinus!

Fouché never regarded a benefit in any other light than as the means of injuring his benefactor. The King, deceived, like many other persons, by the reputation which Fouché's partisans had conjured up for him, was certainly not aware that Fouché had always discharged the functions of Minister in his own interest, and never for the interest of the Government which had the weakness to entrust him with a power always dangerous in his hands. Fouché had opinions, but he belonged to no party, and his political success is explained by the readiness with which he always served the party he knew must triumph, and which he himself overthrew in its turn. He maintained himself in favour from the days of blood and terror until the happy time of the second Restoration only by abandoning and sacrificing those who were attached to him; and it might be said that his ruling passion was the desire of continual change. No man was ever characterised by greater levity or inconstancy of mind. In all things he looked only to himself, and to this egotism he sacrificed both subjects and Governments. Such were the secret causes of the sway exercised by Fouché during the Convention, the Directory, the Empire, the Usurpation, and after the second return of the Bourbons. He helped to found and to destroy every one of those successive Governments. Fouché's character is perfectly unique. I know no other man who, loaded with honours, and almost escaping disgrace, has passed through so many eventful periods, and taken part in so many convulsions and revolutions.

On the 7th of July the King was told that Fouché alone could smooth the way for his entrance into Paris, that he alone could unlock the gates of the capital, and that he alone had power to control public opinion. The reception given to the King on the following day afforded an opportunity of judging of the truth of these assertions. The King's presence was the signal for a feeling of concord, which was manifested in a very decided way. I saw upon the boulevards, and often in company with each other, persons, some of whom had resumed the white cockade, while others still retained the national colours, and harmony was not in the least disturbed by these different badges.

Having returned to private life solely on account of Fouché's presence in the Ministry, I yielded to that consolation which is always left to the discontented. I watched the extravagance and inconsistency that were passing around me, and the new follies which were every day committed; and it must be confessed that a rich and varied picture presented itself to my observation. The King did not bring back M. de Blacas. His Majesty had yielded to prudent advice, and on arriving at Mons sent the unlucky Minister as his ambassador to Naples. Vengeance was talked of, and there were some persons inconsiderate enough to wish that advantage should be taken of the presence of the foreigners in order to make what they termed "an end of the Revolution," as if there were any other means of effecting that object than frankly adopting whatever good the Revolution had produced. The foreigners observed with satisfaction the disposition of these shallow persons, which they thought might be turned to their own advantage. The truth is, that on the second Restoration our pretended allies proved themselves our enemies.

But for them, but for their bad conduct, their insatiable exactions, but for the humiliation that was felt at seeing foreign cannon planted in the streets of Paris, and beneath the very windows of the Palace, the days which followed the 8th of July might have been considered by the Royal Family as the season of a festival. Every day people thronged to the garden of the Tuileries, and expressed their joy by singing and dancing under the King's windows.

This ebullition of feeling might perhaps be thought absurd, but it at least bore evidence of the pleasure caused by the return of the Bourbons.

This manifestation of joy by numbers of persons of both sexes, most of them belonging to the better classes of society, displeased Fouché, and he determined to put a stop to it. Wretches were hired to mingle with the crowd and sprinkle corrosive liquids on the dresses of the females some of them were even instructed to commit acts of indecency, so that all respectable persons were driven from the gardens through the fear of being injured or insulted: As it was wished to create disturbance under the very eyes of the King, and to make him doubt the reality of the sentiments so openly expressed in his favour, the agents of the Police mingled the cry of "Vive l'Empereur!" with that of "Vive le Roi!" and it happened oftener than once that the most respectable persons were arrested and charged by Fouché's infamous agents with having uttered seditious cries. A friend of mine, whose Royalist opinions were well known, and whose father had been massacred during the Revolution, told me that while walking with two ladies he heard some individuals near him crying out "Vive l'Empereur!" This created a great disturbance. The sentinel advanced to the spot, and those very individuals themselves had the audacity to charge my friend with being guilty of uttering the offensive cry. In vain the bystanders asserted the falsehood of the accusation; he was seized and dragged to the guard-house, and after being detained for some hours he was liberated on the application of his friends. By dint of such wretched manoeuvres Fouché triumphed. He contrived to make it be believed that he was the only person capable of preventing the disorders of which he himself was the sole author: He got the Police of the Tuileries under his control. The singing and dancing ceased, and the Palace was the abode of dulness.

While the King was at St. Denis he restored to General Dessoles the command of the National Guard. The General ordered the barriers to be immediately thrown open. On the day of his arrival in Paris the King determined, as a principle, that the throne should be surrounded by a Privy Council, the members of which were to be the princes and persons whom his Majesty might appoint at a future period. The King then named his new Ministry, which was thus composed:

Prince Talleyrand, peer of France, President of the Council of Ministers, and Secretary of State for Foreign Affairs.

Baron Louis, Minister of Finance.

The Duke of Otranto, Minister of the Police.

Baron Pasquier, Minister of Justice, and Keeper of the Seals.

Marshal Gouvion St. Cyr, War Minister.

Comte de Jaucourt, peer of France, Minister of the Marine.

The Duc de Richelieu, peer of France, Minister of the King's Household.

The portfolio of the Minister of the Interior, which was not immediately disposed of, was provisionally entrusted to the Minister of Justice. But what was most gratifying to the public in the composition of this new ministry was that M. de Blacas, who had made himself so odious to everybody, was superseded by M. de Richelieu, whose name revived the memory of a great Minister, and who, by his excellent conduct throughout the whole course of his career, deserves to be distinguished as a model of honour and wisdom.

General satisfaction was expressed on the appointment of Marshal Macdonald to the post of Grand Chancellor of the Legion of Honour in lieu of M. de Pradt. M. de Chabrol resumed the Prefecture of the Seine, which, during the Hundred Days, had been occupied by M. de Bondi, M. de Mole was made Director-General of bridges and causeways. I was superseded in the Prefecture of Police by M. Decazes, and M. Beugnot followed M. Ferrand as Director-General of the Post-office.

I think it was on the 10th of July that I went to St. Cloud to pay a visit of thanks to Blücher. I had been informed that as soon as he learned I had a house at St. Cloud he sent a guard to protect it. This spontaneous mark of attention was well deserving of grateful acknowledgment, especially at a time when there was so much reason to complain of the plunder practised by the Prussians. My visit to Blücher presented to observation a striking instance of the instability of human greatness. I found Blücher residing like a sovereign in the Palace of St. Cloud, where I had lived so long in the intimacy of Napoleon, at a period when he dictated laws to the Kings of Europe before he was a monarch himself.[280]

In that cabinet in which Napoleon and I had passed so many busy hours, and where so many great plans had their birth, I was received by the man who had been my prisoner at Hamburg. The Prussian General immediately reminded me of the circumstance. "Who could have foreseen," said he, "that after being your prisoner I should become the protector of your property? You treated me well at Hamburg, and I have now an opportunity of repaying your kindness. Heaven knows what will be the result of all this! One thing, however, is certain, and that is, that the Allies will now make such conditions as will banish all possibility of danger for a long time to come. The Emperor Alexander does not wish to make the French people expiate too dearly the misfortunes they have caused us. He attributes them to Napoleon, but Napoleon cannot pay the expenses of the war, and they must be paid by some one. It was all very well for once, but we cannot pay the expense of coming back a second time. However," added he, "you will lose none of your territory; that is a point on which I can give you positive assurance. The Emperor Alexander has several times repeated in my presence to the King my master, 'I honour the French nation, and I am determined that it shall preserve its old limits.'"

The above are the very words which Blücher addressed to me. Profiting by the friendly sentiments he expressed towards me I took the opportunity of mentioning the complaints that were everywhere made of the bad discipline of the troops under his command. "What can I do?" said he. "I cannot be present everywhere; but I assure you that in future and at your

280 The English occupied St. Cloud after the Prussians. My large house, in which the children of the Comte d'Artois were inoculated, was respected by them, but they occupied a small home forming part of the estate. The English officer who commanded the troops stationed a guard at the large house. One morning we were informed that the door had been broken open and a valuable looking-glass stolen. We complained to the commanding officer, and on the affair being inquired into it was discovered that the sentinel himself had committed the theft. The man was tried by a court-martial, and condemned to death, a circumstance which, as may naturally be supposed, was very distressing to us. Madame de Bourrienne applied to the commanding officer for the man's pardon, but could only obtain his reprieve. The regiment departed some weeks after, and we could never learn what was the fate of the criminal.—Bourrienne.

recommendation I will severely punish any misconduct that may come to my knowledge."

Such was the result of my visit to Blücher; but, in spite of his promises, his troops continued to commit the most revolting excesses. Thus the Prussian troops have left in the neighbourhood of Paris recollections no less odious than those produced by the conduct of Davoust's corps in Prussia.—Of this an instance now occurs to my memory, which I will relate here. In the spring of 1816, as I was going to Chevreuse, I stopped at the Petit Bicetre to water my horse. I seated myself for a few minutes near the door of the inn, and a large dog belonging to the innkeeper began to bark and growl at me. His master, a respectable-looking old man, exclaimed, "Be quiet, Blücher!"—"How came you to give your dog that name?" said I.—"Ah, sir! it is the name of a villain who did a great deal of mischief here last year. There is my house; they have left scarcely anything but the four walls. They said they came for our good; but let them come back again . . . we will watch them, and spear them like wild boars in the wood." The poor man's house certainly exhibited traces of the most atrocious violence, and he shed tears as he related to me his disasters.

Before the King departed for Ghent he had consented to sign the contract of marriage between one of my daughters and M. Massieu de Clerval, though the latter was at that time only a lieutenant in the navy. The day appointed for the signature of the contract happened to be Sunday, the 19th of March, and it may well be imagined that in the critical circumstances in which we then stood, a matter of so little importance could scarcely be thought about. In July I renewed my request to his Majesty; which gave rise to serious discussions in the Council of Ceremonies. Lest any deviation from the laws of rigid etiquette should commit the fate of the monarchy, it was determined that the marriage contract of a lieutenant in the navy could be signed only at the petty levee. However, his Majesty, recollecting the promise he had given me, decided that the signature should be given at the grand levee. Though all this may appear exceedingly ludicrous, yet I must confess that the triumph over etiquette was very gratifying to me.

A short time after the King appointed me a Councillor of State; a title which I had held under Bonaparte ever since his installation at the Tuileries, though I had never fulfilled the functions of the office. In the month of August; the King having resolved to convoke a new Chamber of Deputies, I was appointed President of the Electoral College of the department of the Yonne. As soon as I was informed of my nomination I waited on M. de Talleyrand for my instructions, but he told me that, in conformity with the King's intentions, I was to receive my orders from the Minister of Police. I observed to M. de Talleyrand that I must decline seeing Fouché, on account of the situation in which we stood with reference to each other. "Go to him, go to him," said M. de Talleyrand, "and be assured Fouché will say to you nothing on the subject."

I felt great repugnance to see Fouché, and consequently I went to him quite against my inclination. I naturally expected a very cold reception. What had passed between us rendered our interview exceedingly delicate. I called on Fouché at nine in the morning, and found him alone, and walking in his garden. He received me as a man might be expected to receive an intimate friend whom he had not seen for a long time. On reflection I was not very much surprised at this, for I was well aware that Fouché could make his hatred yield to calculation. He said not a word about his arrest, and it may well be supposed that I did not seek to turn the conversation on that subject. I asked him whether he had any information to give me respecting the elections of the Yonne. "None at all," said he; "get yourself nominated if you can, only use your endeavours to exclude General Desfouinaux. Anything else is a matter of indifference to me."—"What is your objection to Desfournaux?"—"The Ministry will not have him."

I was about to depart when Fouché; called me back saying, "Why are you in such haste? Cannot you stay a few minutes longer?" He then began to speak of the first return of the Bourbons, and asked me how I could so easily bring myself to act in their favour. He then entered into details respecting the Royal Family which I conceive it to be my duty to pass over in silence: It may be added, however, that the conversation lasted a long time, and to say the least of it, was by no means in favour of "divine right."

I conceived it to be my duty to make the King acquainted with this conversation, and as there was now no Comte de Blacas to keep truth and good advice from his Majesty's ear, I was; on my first solicitation, immediately admitted to, the Royal cabinet. I cautiously suppressed the most startling details, for, had I literally reported what Fouché said, Louis XVIII. could not possibly have given credit to it. The King thanked me for my communication, and I could perceive he was convinced that by longer retaining Fouché in office he would become the victim of the Minister who had been so scandalously forced upon him on the 7th of July. The disgrace of the Duke of Otranto speedily followed, and I had the satisfaction of having contributed to repair one of the evils with which the Duke of Wellington visited France.

Fouché was so evidently a traitor to the cause he feigned to serve, and Bonaparte was so convinced of this,—that during the Hundred Days, when the Ministers of the King at Ghent were enumerated in the presence of Napoleon, some one said, "But where is the Minister of the Police?"

"E-h! Parbleu," said Bonaparte, "that is Fouché?" It was not the same with Carnot, in spite of the indelible stain of his vote: if he had served the King, his Majesty could have depended on him, but nothing could shake the firmness of his principles in favour of liberty. I learned, from a person who had the opportunity of being well informed, that he would not accept the post of Minister of the Interior which was offered to him at the commencement of the Hundred Days until he had a conversation with Bonaparte, to ascertain whether he had changed his principles. Carnot placed faith in the fair promises of Napoleon, who deceived him, as he had deceived others.

Soon after my audience with the King I set off to discharge my duties in the department of the Yonne, and I obtained the honour of being elected to represent my countrymen in the Chamber of Deputies. My colleague was M. Raudot, a man who, in very trying circumstances, had given proofs of courage by boldly manifesting his attachment to the King's Government. The following are the facts which I learned in connection with this episode, and which I circulated as speedily as possible among the electors of whom I had the honour to be President. Bonaparte, on his way from Lyons to Paris, after his landing at the gulf of Juan, stopped at Avalon, and immediately sent for the mayor, M. Raudot. He instantly obeyed the summons. On coming into Napoleon's presence he said, "What do you want, General?" This appellation displeased Napoleon, who nevertheless put several questions to M. Raudot, who was willing to oblige him as a traveller, but not to serve him as an Emperor. Napoleon having given him some orders, this worthy servant of the King replied, "General, I can receive no orders from you, for I acknowledge no sovereign but the King, to whom I have sworn allegiance." Napoleon then directed M. Raudot, in a tone of severity, to withdraw, and I need not add that it was not long before he was dismissed from the mayoralty of Avalon.

The elections of the Yonne being over, I returned to Paris, where I took part in public affairs only as an amateur, while waiting for the opening of the session. I was deeply grieved to see the Government resort to measures of severity to punish faults which it would have been better policy to attribute only to the unfortunate circumstances of the times. No consideration can ever make me cease to regret the memory of Ney, who was the victim of the influence of foreigners. Their object, as Blücher intimated to me at St. Cloud, was to disable France from engaging in war for a long time to come, and they hoped to effect that object by stirring up between the Royal Government and the army of the Loire that spirit of discord which the sacrifice of Ney could not fail to produce. I have no positive proofs of the fact, but in my opinion Ney's life was a pledge of gratitude which Fouché thought he must offer to the foreign influence which had made him Minister.

About this time I learned a fact which will create no surprise, as it affords another proof of the chivalrous disinterestedness of Macdonald's character. When in 1815 several Marshals claimed from the Allied powers their endowments in foreign countries, Madame Moreau, to whom the King had given the honorary title of 'Madame la Marechale', and who was the friend of the Duke of Tarentum, wrote, without Macdonald's knowledge, to M. de Blacas; our ambassador at Naples, begging him to endeavour to preserve for the Marshal the endowment which had been given him in the Kingdom of Naples. As soon as Macdonald was informed of this circumstance he waited upon Madame Moreau, thanked her for her kind intentions, but at the same time informed her that he should disavow all knowledge of her letter, as the request it contained was entirely averse to his principles. The Marshal did, in fact, write the following letter to M. de Blacas:—"I hasten to inform you, sir, that it was not with my consent that Madame Moreau wrote to you, and I beg you will take no step that might expose me to a refusal. The King of Naples owes me no recompense for having beaten his army, revolutionised his kingdom, and forced him to retire to Sicily." Such conduct was well worthy of the man who was the last to forsake Napoleon in, 1814, and the first to rejoin him, and that without the desire of accepting any appointment in 1815. M. de Blacas, who was himself much surprised at Macdonald's letter, communicated it to the King of Naples, whose answer deserves to be recorded. It was as follows:—"If I had not imposed a law upon myself to acknowledge none of the French endowments, the conduct of Marshal Macdonald would have induced me to make an exception in his favour." It is gratifying to see princes such scrupulous observers of the laws they make for themselves!

About the end of August 1815, as I was walking on the Boulevard des Capucines, I had the pleasure of meeting Rapp, whom I had not seen for a long time. He had just come out of the house of Lagrenee, the artist, who was painting his portrait. I was on foot, and Rapp's carriage was waiting, so we both stepped into it, and set off to take a drive in the Bois de Boulogne. We had a great deal to say to each other, for we had not met since the great events of the two Restorations. The reason of this was, that in 1814 I passed a part of the year at Sens, and since the occurrences of March 1815 Rapp himself had been absent from Paris. I found him perfectly resigned to his change of condition, though indulging in a few oaths against the foreigners. Rapp was not one of those, generals who betrayed the King on the 20th of March. He told me that he remained at the head of the division which he commanded at Ecouen, under the orders of the Duc de Berry, and that he did not resign it to the War Minister until after the King's departure. "How did Napoleon receive you?" I inquired. "I waited till he sent for me. You know what sort of fellow I am: I know nothing about politics; not I. I had sworn fidelity to the King. I know my duty, and I would have fought against the Emperor."—"Indeed!"—"Yes, certainly I would, and I told him so myself."—"How! did you venture so far?"—"To be sure. I told him that my resolution was definite. 'Pshaw! . . . replied he angrily. 'I knew well that you were opposed to me. If we had come to an action I should have sought you out on the field of battle. I would have shown you the Medusa's head. Would you have dared to fire on me?'—'Without doubt,' I replied. 'Ah! parbleu this is too much,' he said. 'But your troops would not have obeyed you. They had preserved all their affection for me.'—'What could I do?' resumed I. 'You abdicated, you left France, you recommended us to serve the King—and then you return! Besides; I tell you frankly, I do not augur well of what will happen. We shall have war again. France has had enough of that.' Upon this," continued Rapp, "he assured me that he had other thoughts; that he had no further desire for war; that he wished to govern in peace, and devote himself solely to the happiness of his people. When I hinted opposition on the part of the Foreign Powers, he said that he had made alliances. He then spoke to me of the King, and I said I had been much pleased with him; indeed, the King gave me a very gratifying reception on my return from Kiew, and I see no reason why I should complain, when I am so well used. During the conversation the Emperor much extolled the conduct of the Duke of Orleans. He then gave me some description of his passage from the Isle of Elba and his journey to Paris. He complained of being accused of ambition; and observing that I looked astonished and doubtful—'What?' he continued, 'am I ambitious then?' And patting his belly with both his hands, 'Can a man,' he asked, 'so fat as I am be ambitious?' I could not for my soul help saying, 'Ah! Sire, your Majesty is surely joking.' He pretended, however, to be serious, and after a few moments, noticing my decorations, he began to banter me about the Cross of St. Louis and the Cross of the Lily, which I still wore."

I asked Rapp whether all was true that had been said about the enthusiasm which was manifested along the whole of Napoleon's route from the Gulf of Juan to Paris. "Ma foi!" he replied, "I was not there any more than you, but all those who accompanied him have assured me of the truth of the details which have been published; but I recollect having heard Bertrand say that on one occasion he was fearful for the safety of the Emperor, in case any assassin should have presented himself. At Fossard, where the Emperor stopped to breakfast on his way to Paris, his escort was so fatigued as to be unable to follow, so that he was for some time almost alone on the road, until a squadron which was in garrison at Melun met him and escorted him to Fontainebleau. As to anything else, from all I have heard, the Emperor was exposed to no danger."

We then began to talk of our situation, and the singular chances of our fortune. Rapp told me how, within a few days only, he had ceased to be one of the discontented; for the condition of the generals who had commanded army corps in the campaign of Waterloo was very different in 1815 from what it had been in 1814. "I had determined," he said, "to live a quiet life, to meddle with nothing, and not even to wear my uniform. I had, therefore, since the King's return never presented myself at Court; when, a week ago, while riding on horseback two or three hundred paces from this spot, I saw a group of horsemen on the other side of the avenue, one of whom galloped towards me. I immediately recognised the Duc de Berry, 'How, Monseigneur, is it you?' I exclaimed. 'It is, my dear General; and since you will not come to us, I must come to you. Will you breakfast with me tomorrow morning?'—'Ma foi!" continued Rapp, "what could I do? The tone of kindness in which he gave this invitation quite charmed me. I went, and I was treated so well that I shall go again. But I will ask for nothing: I only want these Prussians and English rascals out of the way!" I complimented Rapp on his conduct, and told him that it was impossible that so loyal and honest a man as he should not, at some time or other, attract the King's notice. I had the happiness to see this prediction accomplished. Since that time I regularly saw Rapp whenever we both happened to be in Paris, which was pretty often.

I have already mentioned that in the month of August the King named me Councillor of State. On the 19th of the following month I was appointed Minister of State and member of the Privy Council. I may close these volumes by relating a circumstance very flattering to me, and connected with the last-mentioned nomination. The King had directed M. de Talleyrand to present to him, in his official character of President of the Council of Ministers, a list of the persons who might be deemed suitable as members of the Privy Council. The King having read the list, said to his Minister, "But, M. de Talleyrand, I do not see here the names of two of our best friends, Bourrienne and Alexis de Noailles."—"Sire, I thought their nomination would seem more flattering in coming directly from your Majesty." The King then added my name to the list, and afterwards that of the Comte Alexis de Noailles, so that both our names are written in Louis XVIII.'s own hand in the original Ordinance.

I have now brought to a conclusion my narrative of the extraordinary events in which I have taken part, either as a spectator or an actor, during the course of a strangely diversified life, of which nothing now remains but recollections.[281]

281 I discharged the functions of Councillor of State until 1818, at which time an Ordinance appeared declaring those functions Incompatible with the title of Minister of State—Bourrienne.

CHAPTER XII

THE CENT JOURS

The extraordinary rapidity of events during the Cent fours, or Hundred Days of Napoleon's reign in 1815, and the startling changes in the parts previously filled by the chief personages, make it difficult to consider it as an historical period; it more resembles a series of sudden theatrical transformations, only broken by the great pause while the nation waited for news from the army.

The first Restoration of the Bourbons had been so unexpected, and was so rapidly carried out, that the Bonapartists, or indeed all France, had hardly realized the situation before Napoleon was again in the Tuileries; and during the Cent Jours both Bonapartists and Royalists were alike rubbing their eyes, asking whether they were awake, and wondering which was the reality and which the dream, the Empire or the Restoration.

It is both difficult and interesting to attempt to follow the history of the chief characters of the period; and the reader must pardon some abrupt transitions from person to person, and from group to group, while the details of some subsequent movements of the Bonaparte family must be thrown in to give a proper idea of the strange revolution in their fortunes. We may divide the characters with which we have to deal into five groups,—the Bonaparte family, the Marshals, the Statesmen of the Empire, the Bourbons, and the Allied Monarchs. One figure and one name will be missing, but if we omit all account of poor, bleeding, mutilated France, it is but leaving her in the oblivion in which she was left at the time by every one except by Napoleon.

The disaster of 1814 had rather dispersed than crushed the Bonaparte family, and they rallied immediately on the return from Elba. The final fall of the Empire was total ruin to them. The provisions of the Treaty of Fontainebleau, which had been meant to ensure a maintenance to them, had not been carried out while Napoleon was still a latent power, and after 1815 the Bourbons were only too happy to find a reason for not paying a debt they had determined never to liquidate; it was well for any of the Bourbons in their days of distress to receive the bounty of the usurper, but there was a peculiar pleasure in refusing to pay the price promised for his immediate abdication.

The flight of the Bonapartes in 1815 was rapid. Metternich writes to Maria Louisa in July 1815: "Madame Mere and Cardinal Fesch left yesterday for Tuscany. We do not know exactly where Joseph is. Lucien is in England under a false name, Jerome in Switzerland, Louis at Rome. Queen Hortense has set out for Switzerland, whither General de Flahault and his mother will follow her. Murat seems to be still at Toulon; this, however, is not certain." Was ever such an account of a dynasty given? These had all been among the great ones of Europe: in a moment they were fugitives, several of them having for the rest of their lives a bitter struggle with poverty. Fortunately for them the Pope, the King of Holland, and the Grand-Duke of Tuscany, were not under heavy obligations to Napoleon, and could thus afford to give to his family the protection denied them by those monarchs who believed themselves bound to redeem their former servility.

When Napoleon landed Maria Louisa was in Austria, and she was eager to assist in taking every precaution to prevent her son, the young King of Rome, being spirited off to join his father, whose fortunes she had sworn to share: She herself was fast falling under the influence of the one-eyed Austrian General, Neipperg, just then left a widower, who was soon to be admitted to share her bed. By 1823 she seemed to have entirely forgotten the different members of the Bonaparte family, speaking of her life in France as "a bad dream." She obtained the Grand-Duchy of Parma, where she reigned till 1847, marrying a third time, it is said, the Count Bombellea, and dying, just too soon to be hunted from her Duchy by the Revolution of 1848.

There is something very touching in most that we know of the poor young King of Rome, from his childish but strangely prescient resistance to his removal from Paris to Blois on the approach of the Allies in 1814, to the message of remembrance sent in after years to the column of the Place Vendome, "his only friend in Paris."

At four years of age Meneval describes him as gentle, but quick in answering, strong, and with excellent health. "Light curly hair in ringlets set off a fresh face, while fine blue eyes lit up his regular features: He was precociously intelligent, and knew more than most children older than himself." When Meneval—the former secretary of his father, giving up his post in Austria with Maria Louisa, as he was about to rejoin Napoleon—took farewell of the Prince in May 1815, the poor little motherless child drew me towards the window, and, giving me a touching look, said in a low tone, "Monsieur Meva, tell him (Napoleon) that I always love him dearly." We say "motherless," because Maria Louisa seems to have yielded up her child at the dictates of policy to be closely guarded as easily as she gave up her husband. "If," wrote Madame de Montesquieu, his governess, "the child had a mother, I would leave him in her hands, and be happy, but she is nothing like a mother, she is more indifferent to his fate than the most utter stranger in her service." His grandfather, the Emperor Francis, to do him justice, seems to have been really kind to the lad, and while, in 1814, 1816, and in 1830, taking care to deprive him of all chance of, his glorious inheritance, still seems to have cared for him personally, and to have been always kind to him. There is no truth in the story that the Austrians neglected his education and connived at the ruin of his faculties. Both his tutor, the Count Maurice Dietrichstein, and Marshal Marmont, who conversed with him in 1831, agree in speaking highly of him as full of promise: Marmont's evidence being especially valuable as showing that the Austrians did not object to the Duke of Reichstadt (as he had been created by his grandfather in 1818), learning all he could of his father's life from one of the Marshals. In 1831 Marmont describes him: "I recognised his father's look in him, and in that he most resembled Napoleon. His eyes, not so large as those of Napoleon, and sunk deeper in their sockets, had the same expression, the same fire, the same energy. His forehead was like that of his father, and so was the lower part of his face and his chin. Then his complexion was that of Napoleon in his youth, with the same pallor and the same colour of the skin, but all the rest of his face recalled his mother and the House of Austria. He was taller than Napoleon by about three inches."

As long as the Duke lived his name was naturally the rallying-point of the Bonapartes, and was mentioned in some of the many conspiracies against the Bourbons. In 1830 Joseph Bonaparte tried to get the sanction of the Austrians to his nephew being put forward as a claimant to the throne of France, vacant by the flight of Charles X., but they held their captive firmly. A very interesting passage is given in the 'Memoirs of Charles Greville', who says that Prince Esterhazy told him a great deal about the Duke of Reichstadt, who, if he had lived, would have probably played a great part in the world. He died of a premature decay, brought on, apparently, by over-exertion and over-excitement; his talents were very conspicuous, he was 'petri d'ambition', worshipped the memory of his father, and for that reason never liked his mother; his thoughts were incessantly turned towards France, and when he heard of the Days of July (overthrow of Charles X.) he said, "Why was I not there to take my chance? He evinced great affection and gratitude to his grandfather, who, while he scrupulously observed all his obligations towards Louis Philippe, could not help feeling a secret pride in the aspiring genius of Napoleon's son. He was well educated, and day and night pored over the history of his father's glorious career. He delighted in military exercises, and not only shone at the head of his regiment, but had already acquired the hereditary art of ingratiating himself with the soldiers." Esterhazy went on to describe how the Duke abandoned everything at a ball when he met there Marshals Marmont and Maison. "He had no eyes or ears but for them; from nine in the evening to five the next morning he devoted himself to these Marshals." There was the true Napoleonic ring in his answer to advice given by Marmont when the Duke said that he would not allow himself to be put forward by the Sovereigns of Europe. "The son of Napoleon should be too great to serve as an instrument; and in events of that nature I wish not to be an advanced guard, but a reserve,—that is, to come as a succour, recalling great memories."

His death in 1832, on the 22d of July, the anniversary of the battle of Salamanca, solved many questions. Metternich visited the Duke on his deathbed: "It was a heartrending sight. I never remember to have seen a more mournful picture of decay." When Francis was told of the death of his grandson he answered, "I look upon the Duke's death as a blessing for him. Whether it be detrimental or otherwise to the public good I do not know. As for myself, I shall ever lament the loss of my grandson."

Josephine was in her grave at Rueil when Napoleon returned. She had died on the 29th of May 1814, at Malmaison, while the Allies were exhibiting themselves in Paris. It seems hard that she should not have lived to enjoy a triumph, however brief, over her Austrian rival. "She, at least," said Napoleon truly, "would never have abandoned me."

Josephine's daughter, Hortense, separated from her husband, Louis Bonaparte, and created Duchess of St Leu by Louis XVIII., was in Paris, much suspected by the Bourbons, but really engaged in a lawsuit with her husband about the custody of her sons. She had to go into hiding when the news of the landing arrived, but her empty house, left unwatched, became very useful for receiving the Bonapartists, who wished for a place of concealment, amongst them, as we shall see, being, of all people, Fouché! Hortense was met by Napoleon with some reproaches for accepting a title from the Bourbons, but she did the honours of the Elysee for him, and it is creditable to both of them that, braving the vile slanders about their intercourse, she was with him to the end; and that one of the last persons to embrace him at Malmaison before he started for the coast was his adopted daughter, the child of his discarded wife. Hortense's presence in Paris was thought to be too dangerous by the Prussian Governor; and she was peremptorily ordered to leave. An appeal to the Emperor Francis received a favourable answer, but Francis always gave way where any act against his son-in-law was in question, and she had to start at the shortest notice on a wandering life to Aix, Baden, and Constance, till the generosity of the small but brave canton of Thurgau enabled her to get a resting-place at the Chateau of Arenenberg.

In 1831 she lost her second son, the eldest then surviving, who died from fever in a revolutionary attempt in which he and his younger brother, the future Napoleon. III., were engaged. She was able to visit France incognito, and even to see Louis Philippe and his Queen; but her presence in the country was soon thought dangerous, and she was urged to leave. In 1836 Hortense's last child, Louis Napoleon, made his attempt at an 'emeule' at Strasburg, and was shipped off to America by the Government. She went to France to plead for him, and then, worn out by grief and anxiety, returned to Arenenberg, which her son, the future Emperor, only succeeded in reaching in time to see her die in October 1837. She was laid with Josephine at Rueil.

Hortense's brother, Prince Eugène, the Viceroy of Italy, was at Vienna when Napoleon returned, and fell under the suspicion of the Allies of having informed the Emperor of the intention of removing him from Elba. He was detained in Bavaria by his father-in-law the King, to whose Court he retired, and who in 1817 created him Duke of Leuchtenberg and Prince of Eichstadt. With the protection of Bavaria he actually succeeded in wringing from the Bourbons some 700,000 francs of the property of his mother. A first attack of apoplexy struck him in 1823, and he died from a second in February 1824 at Munich. His descendants have intermarried into the Royal Families of Portugal, Sweden, Brazil, Russia, 'and Wartemberg; his grandson now (1884) holds the title of Leuchtenberg.

Except Louis, an invalid, all the brothers of the Emperor were around him in the Cent Jours, the supreme effort of their family. Joseph had left Spain after Vittoria, and had remained in an uncomfortable and unrecognised state near Paris until in 1814 he was again employed, and when, rightly or not, he urged the retreat of the Regency from Paris to Blois. He then took refuge at his chateau of Prangins in the canton Vaud in Switzerland, closely watched by the Bourbonists, who dreaded danger from every side except the real point, and who preferred trying to hunt the Bonapartists from place to place, instead of making their life bearable by carrying out the engagements with them.

In 1816, escaping from the arrest with which he was threatened, after having written to urge Murat to action with fatal effect, Joseph joined Napoleon in Paris, and appeared at the Champ de Mai, sitting also in the Chamber of Peers, but, as before, putting forward ridiculous pretensions as to his inherent right to the peerage, and claiming a special seat. In fact, he never could realise how entirely he owed any position to the brother he wished to treat as an equal.

He remained in Paris during the brief campaign, and after Waterloo was concealed in the house of the Swedish Ambassador, where his sister-in-law, the Crown Princess of Sweden, the wife of Bernadotte, was living. Muffling, the Prussian Governor of Paris, wished to arrest him, but as the Governor could not violate the domicile of an Ambassador, he had to apply to the Czar, who arranged for the escape of the ex-King before the Governor could seize him Joseph went to the coast, pretty much following the route of Napoleon. He was arrested once at Saintes, but was allowed to proceed, and he met his brother on the 4th of July, at Rochefort.

It is significant as to the possibility of the escape of Napoleon that Joseph succeeded in getting on the brig Commerce as "M. Bouchard," and, though the ship was thrice searched by the English, he got to New York on the 28th of August, where he was mistaken for Carnot. He was well received, and, taking the title of Comte de Survilliers, he first lived at Lansdowne, Fairmount Park, Philadelphia, where he afterwards always passed part of the year while he was in America. He also bought the property of Point Breeze, at Bordentown, on the Delaware, where he built a house with a fine view of the river. This first house was burnt down, but he erected another, where he lived in some state and in great comfort, displaying his jewels and pictures to his admiring neighbours, and showing kindness to impecunious nephews.

The news of the Revolution of July in 1830, which drove Charles X. from the throne, excited Joseph's hopes for the family of which he considered himself the Regent, and he applied to Metternich to get the Austrian Government to allow or assist in the placing his nephew, the Duke of Reichstadt, on the throne of France. Austria would not even answer.

In July 1832 Joseph crossed to England, where he met Lucien, just arrived from Italy, bringing the news of the death of his nephew. Disappointed, he stayed in England for some time, but returned to America in 1836. In he finally left America, and again came to England, where he had a paralytic stroke, and in 1843 he went to Florence, where he met his wife after a long separation.

Joseph lived long enough to see the two attempts of another nephew, Louis Napoleon, at Strasburg in 1836, and at Boulogne in 1840, which seem to have been undertaken without his knowledge, and to have much surprised him. He died in Florence in 1844; his body was buried first in Santa Croce, Florence, but was removed to the Invalides in 1864. His wife the ex-Queen, had retired in 1815 to Frankfort and to Brussels, where she was well received by the King, William, and where she stayed till 1823, when she went to Florence, dying there in 1845. Her monument is in the Cappella Riccardi, Santa Croce, Florence.

Lucien had retired to Rome in 1804, on the creation of the Empire, and had continued embroiled with his brother, partly from his so-called Republican principles, but chiefly from his adhering to his marriage, his second one, with Madame Jouberthon,—a union which Napoleon steadily refused to acknowledge, offering Lucien anything, a kingdom or the hand of a queen (if we take Lucien's account), if he would only consent to the annulment of the contract.

In August 1810, affecting uneasiness as Napoleon stretched his power over Rome, Lucien embarked for America, but he was captured by the English and taken, first to Malta and then to England, where he passed the years till 1814 in a sort of honourable captivity, first at Ludlow and then at Thorngrove, not far from that town.

In 1814 Lucien was released, when he went to Rome, where he was welcomed by the kindly old Pope, who remembered the benefits conferred by Napoleon on the Church, while he forgot the injuries personal to himself; and the stiff-necked Republican, the one-time "Brutus" Bonaparte, accepted the title of Duke of Musignano and Prince of Canino.

In 1815 Lucien joined his brother, whom he wished to abdicate at the Champ de Mai in favour of the King of Rome, placing his sword only at the disposal of France. This step was seriously debated, but, though it might have placed the Allies in a more difficult position, it would certainly have been disregarded by them, at least unless some great victory had given the dynasty firmer footing. After Waterloo he was in favour of a dissolution of the Chambers, but Napoleon had become hopeless and almost apathetic, while Lucien himself, from his former connection with the 18th and 19th Brumaire, was looked on with great distrust by the Chambers, as indeed he was by his brother. Advantage was taken of his Roman title to taunt him with not being a Frenchman; and all his efforts failed. At the end he fled, and failing to cross to England or to get to Rochefort, he reached Turin on the 12th of July only to find himself arrested. He remained there till the 15th of September, when he was allowed to go to Rome. There he was interned and carefully watched; indeed in 1817 the Pope had to intervene to prevent his removal to the north of Germany, so anxious were the Allies as to the safety of the puppet they had put on the throne of France.

The death of Napoleon in 1821 released Lucien and the Bonaparte family from the constant surveillance exercised over them till then. In 1830 he bought a property, the Croce del Biacco, near Bologna. The flight of the elder branch of the Bourbons from France in 1830 raised his hopes, and, as already said, he went to England in 1832 to meet Joseph and to plan some step for raising Napoleon II. to the throne. The news of the death of his nephew dashed all the hopes of the family, and after staying in England for some time he returned to Italy, dying at Viterbo in 1840, and being buried at Canino, where also his second wife lies. Lucien had a taste for literature, and was the author of several works, which a kindly posterity will allow to die.

Louis Bonaparte had fled from his Kingdom of Holland in 1810, after a short reign of four years, disgusted with being expected to study the interests of the brother to whom he owed his throne, and with being required to treat his wife Hortense with ordinary consideration. He had taken refuge in Austria, putting that Court in great anxiety how to pay him the amount of attention to be expected by the brother of the Emperor, and at the same time the proper coldness Napoleon might wish shown to a royal deserter. Thanks to the suggestions of Metternich, they seem to have been successful in this task. Taking the title of Comte de, St. Len from an estate in France; Louis went first to Toplitz, then to Gratz, and in 1813 he took refuge in Switzerland. In 1814 he went to Rome; and then to Florence, where the Grand-Duke Ferdinand received any of the family who came there with great kindness.

Louis was the least interesting of the family, and it is difficult to excuse his absence from France in 1815. After all, the present of a kingdom is not such an unpardonable offence as to separate brothers for ever, and Napoleon seems to have felt deeply the way in which he was treated by a brother to whom he had acted as a father; still ill-health and the natural selfishness of invalids may account for much. While his son Louis Napoleon was flying about making his attempts on France, Louis remained in the Roman Palace of the French Academy, sunk in anxiety about his religious state. He disclaimed his son's proceedings, but this may have been due to the Pope, who sheltered him. Anyhow, it is strange to mark the difference between the father and his two sons who came of age, and who took to revolution so kindly.

In 1846 Louis was ill at Leghorn when his son escaped from Ham, where he had been imprisoned after his Boulogne attempt. Passports were refused to the son to go from Italy to his father, and Louis died alone on the 25th of July 1846. He was buried at Santa Croce, Florence, but the body was afterwards removed to the village church of St. Leu Taverny, rebuilt by his son Napoleon III.

Jerome, the youngest of the whole family, the "middy," as Napoleon liked to call him, had been placed in the navy, in which profession he passed as having distinguished himself, after leaving his admiral in rather a peculiar manner, by attacking an English convoy, and eventually escaping the English by running into the port of Concarneau, believed to be inaccessible. At that time it was an event for a French man-of-war to reach home.

Jerome had incurred the anger of Napoleon by marrying a beautiful young lady of Baltimore, a Mica Paterson, but, more obedient than Lucien, he submitted to have this marriage annulled by his all-powerful brother, and in reward he received the brand-new Kingdom of Westphalia, and the hand of a daughter of the King of Wartemberg, "the cleverest King in Europe," according to Napoleon. Jerome is said to have ruled rather more as a Heliogabalus than a Solomon, but the new Kingdom had the advantage of starting with good administrators, and with the example of "the Code."

In 1812 Jerome was given the command of the right wing of the Grand Army in its advance against Russia, but he did not fulfil the expectations of his brother, and Davoust took the command instead. Every king feels himself a born general: whatever else they cannot do, war is an art which comes with the crown, and Jerome, unwilling to serve under a mere Marshal, withdrew in disgust. In 1813 he had the good feeling and the good sense to refuse the treacherous offer of the Allies to allow him to retain his kingdom if he joined them against his brother, a snare his sister Caroline fell into at Naples.

On the downfall of Napoleon, Jerome, as the Count of Gratz, went to Switzerland, and then to Gratz and Trieste.

His wife, the ex-Queen Catherine, fell into the hands of Maubreuil, the officer sent on a mysterious mission, believed to be intended for the murder of Napoleon, but which only resulted in the robbery of the Queen's jewels and of some 80,000 francs. The jewels were for the most part recovered, being fished up from the bed of the Seine, but not the cash.

In 1815 Jerome joined his brother, and appeared at the Champ de Mai. A true Bonaparte, his vanity was much hurt, however, by having—he, a real king—to sit on the back seat of the carriage, while his elder brother Lucien; a mere Roman-prince, occupied a seat of honour by the side of Napoleon. In the Waterloo campaign he was given the 6th division, forming part of Reille's corps, General Guilleminot being sent with him to prevent any of the awkwardnesses of 1812. His division was engaged with the Prussians on the 15th of June, and at Quatre Bras he was severely wounded. At Waterloo his division formed the extreme left of the French infantry, opposite Hougomont, and was engaged in the struggle for that post. Whatever his failings may have been, he is acknowledged to have fought gallantly. After the battle he was given the command of the army by his brother, and was told to cover the retreat to Laon, which he reached on the 21st of June, with 18,000 infantry, 3000 cavalry and two batteries which he had rallied. This, be it observed, is a larger force than Ney told the Chambers even Grouchy (none of whose men are included) could have, and Jerome's strength had swollen to 25,000 infantry and 6000 cavalry when he handed over the army to Soult at Laon. Napoleon had intended to leave Jerome with the command of the army, but he eventually took him to Paris.

When Napoleon left the country Jerome was assured by the ambassador of Wurtemberg that he would find a refuge in the dominions of his father-in-law; but when he arrived there he was informed that if he did not wish to be, according to the original intentions of the Allies, handed over to the Prussians, and separated from his wife, he must sign an engagement to remain in Wurtemberg under strict surveillance. He was then imprisoned at Guppingen, and afterwards at Ellwangen, where he was not even allowed to write or receive letters except through the captain of the chateau.

Part of Jerome's troubles came from the conduct of his wife Catherine, who had the idea that, as she had been given in marriage by her father to Jerome, as she had lived for seven years as his wife, and as she had borne a child to him, she was really his wife, and bound to remain with him in his misfortunes! The royal family of Wurtemberg, however, following the illustrious example of that of Austria, looked on her past life as a mere state of concubinage, useful to the family, and to be respected while her husband could retain his kingdom, but which should end the moment there was nothing more to be gained from Napoleon or his brother. It was all proper and decorous to retain the title of King of Wurtemberg, which the former Duke and then Elector had owed to the exile of St. Helena, but King Frederick, and still less his son William, who succeeded him in 1816, could not comprehend Catherine's clinging to her husband when he had lost his kingdom. "I was a Queen; I am still a wife and mother," wrote the Princess to her disgusted father. Another complaint against this extraordinary Princess was that she actually saw Las Cases on his return from St. Helena, and thus obtained news of the exile.

After constant ill treatment Jerome and his wife, as the Count and Countess of Montfort, a rank the King of Wurtemberg afterwards raised to Prince, were allowed to proceed to Hainburg near Vienna, then to Florence, and, later to Trieste, where Jerome was when his sister Elisa died. In 1823 they were permitted to go to Rome, and in 1835 they went to Lausanne, where his true-hearted wife died the same year. Jerome went to Florence, and lived to see the revival of the Empire, and to once more enjoy the rank of a French Prince. He died in 1860 at the chateau of Villegenis in France, and was buried in the Invalides.

The mother of the Emperor, Letitia, in 1814, had retained her title of Imperatrice Mere, and had retired to Rome. She then went to Elba in June, and stayed there with her daughter Pauline until Napoleon had sailed for France. On 2d March 1814 she went from Elba to San Vicenzo near Leghorn, and then to Rome. Her son sent a frigate for her, the 'Melpomene', which was captured by the English 'Rivoli'; another vessel, the 'Dryade', brought her to France, and she joined Napoleon in Paris. We must have a regard for this simple old lady, who was always careful and saving, only half believing in the stability of the Empire; and, like a true mother, always most attentive to the most unfortunate of her children. Her life had been full of startling changes; and it must have been strange for the woman who had been hunted out of Corsica, flying from her house just in time to save her life from the adherents of Paoli, to find herself in grandeur in Paris. She saw her son just before he left, as she thought, for America, and then retired to the Rinuccini—now the Bonaparte-Palace at Rome, where she died in 1836. She had been anxious to join Napoleon at St. Helena, and had refused, as long as Napoleon was alive, to forgive her daughter Caroline, the wife of Murat, for her abandonment of her brother. She was buried at Albano.

Letitia's youngest daughter, the beautiful but frail Pauline, Duchess of Guastalla, married first to General Leclerc, and then to Prince Camille Borgelle, was at Nice when her brother abdicated in 1814. She retired with her mother to Rome, and in October 1814 went to Elba, staying there till Napoleon left, except when she was sent to Naples with a message of forgiveness for Murat. There was a characteristic scene between her and Colonel Campbell when the English Commissioner arrived to find Napoleon gone. Pauline professed ignorance till the last of her brother's intentions, and pressed the Colonel's hand to her heart that he might feel how agitated she was. "She did not appear to be so," says the battered old Colonel, who seems to have been proof against her charms. She then went to Rome, and later to Pisa. Her health was failing, and, unable to join her brother in France, she sent him her only means of assistance, her jewels, which were captured at Waterloo. Her offer to go to St. Helena, repeated several times, was never accepted by Napoleon. She died in 1825 at Florence, from consumption, reconciled to her husband, from whom she had been separated since 1807. She was buried at Sta Maria Maggiore, Rome.

Elisa, the eldest sister of Napoleon, the former Grand Duchess of Tuscany, which Duchy she had ruled well, being a woman of considerable talent, was the first of all to die. In 1814 she had been forced to fly from her Government, and, accompanied by her husband, she had attempted to reach France. Finding herself cut off by the Austrians; she took shelter with Augereau's army, and then returned to Italy. She took the title of Comtesse de Campignana, and retired to Trieste, near which town, at the Chateau of Sant Andrea, under a wearisome surveillance, she expired in 1820, watched by her husband, Felix Baeciocchi, and her sister Caroline. Her monument is in the Bacciocchi Chapel in San Petronio, Bologna.

Caroline, the wife of Murat, was the only one of the family untrue to Napoleon. Very ambitious, and forgetting how completely she owed her Kingdom of Naples to her brother, she had urged Murat in 1814 to separate from Napoleon, and, still worse, to attack Eugène, who held the north of Italy against the Austrians. She relied on the formal treaty with Austria that Murat should retain his Kingdom of Naples, and she may also have trusted to the good offices of her former admirer Metternich. When the Congress of Vienna met, the French Minister, Talleyrand, at once began to press for the removal of Murat. A trifling treaty was not considered an obstacle to the Heaven-sent deliverers of Europe, and Murat, believing his fate sealed, hearing of Napoleon's landing, and urged on by a misleading letter from Joseph Bonaparte, at once marched to attack the Austrians. He was easily routed by the Austrians under Neipperg, the future husband of Maria Louisa. Murat fled to France, and Caroline first took refuge in an English man-of-war, the 'Tremendous', being, promised a free passage to England. She was, however, handed over to the Austrians; who kept her in confinement at Hainburg near Vienna. In October 1815 Murat landed in Calabria in a last wild attempt to recover his throne. He was arrested and immediately shot. After his murder Caroline, taking the title of Countess of Lipona (an anagram of Napoli), was permitted to retire to Trieste with Elisa, Jerome, and his wife. Caroline was almost without means of existence, the Neapolitan Bourbons refusing even to give up the property she had brought there. She married a General Macdonald. When Hortense was buried at Rueil Caroline obtained permission to attend the sad ceremony. In 1838 she went to France to try to obtain a pension, and succeeded in getting one of 100,000 francs. She died from cancer in the stomach in 1839, and was buried in the Campo Santo, Bologna.

Cardinal Fesch, the half-uncle of Napoleon, the Archbishop of Lyons, who had fallen into disgrace with Napoleon for taking the side of the Pope and refusing to accept the see of Paris, to which he was nominated by Napoleon, had retired to Rome in 1814, where he remained till the return of Napoleon, when he went to Paris, and accepted a peerage. After Waterloo he again sought the protection of the Pope, and he remained at Rome till his death in 1839, a few days before Caroline Bonaparte's. He was buried in S. Lorenzo in Lucina, Rome. He had for years been a great collector of pictures, of which he left a large number (1200) to the town of Ajaccio. The Cardinal, buying at the right time when few men had either enough leisure or money to think of pictures, got together a most valuable collection. This was sold in 1843-44 at Rome. Its contents now form some of the greatest treasures in the galleries of Dudley House and of the Marquis of Hertford, now Sir Richard Wallace's. In a large collection there are generally some daubs, but it is an amusing instance of party spirit to find the value of his pictures run down by men who are unwilling to allow any one connected with Napoleon to have even taste in art. He always refused the demands of the Restoration that he should resign his see of Lyons, though under Louis Philippe he offered to do so, and leave his pictures to France, if the Bonaparte family were allowed to enter France: this was refused.

It can hardly be denied that the fate of the Bonapartes was a hard one. Napoleon had been undisputed sovereign of France for fourteen years, Louis had been King of Holland for four years, Jerome was King of Westphalia for six years, Caroline was Queen of Naples for seven years. If Napoleon had forfeited all his rights by leaving Elba after the conditions of his abdication had been broken by the Allies, still there was no reason why the terms stipulated for the other members of the family should not have been carried out, or at least an ordinary income insured to them. With all Napoleon's faults he was always ready to shower wealth on the victims of his policy:—The sovereigns of the Continent had courted and intermarried with the Bonapartes in the fame of that family's grandeur: there was neither generosity nor wisdom in treating them as so many criminals the moment fortune had declared against them. The conduct of the Allies was not influenced simply by the principle of legitimacy, for the King of Saxony only kept his throne by the monarchs falling out over the spoil. If sovereigns were to be respected as of divine appointment, it was not well to make their existence only depend on the fate of war.

Nothing in the history of the Cent Jours is more strange than the small part played in it by the Marshals, the very men who are so identified in our minds with the Emperor, that we might have expected to find that brilliant band playing a most prominent part in his last great struggle, no longer for mere victory, but for very existence. In recording how the Guard came up the fatal hill at Waterloo for their last combat, it would seem but natural to have to give a long roll of the old historic names as leading or at least accompanying them; and the reader is apt to ask, where were the men whose very titles recalled such glorious battle-fields, such achievements, and such rewards showered down by the man who, almost alone at the end of the day, rode forward to invite that death from which it was such cruel kindness to save him?

Only three Marshals were in Belgium in 1815, and even of them one did but count his promotion from that very year, so it is but natural for French writers to dream of what might have been the course of the battle if Murat's plume had waved with the cavalry, if Mortier had been with the Guard, and if Davoust or one of his tried brethren had taken the place of Grouchy. There is, however, little real ground for surprise at this absence of the Marshals. Death, time, and hardships had all done their work amongst that grand array of commanders. Some were old men, veterans of the Revolutionary wars, when first created Marshals in 1804; others, such as Massena, were now but the wreck of themselves; and even before 1812 Napoleon had been struck with the failing energy of some of his original companions: indeed, it might have been better for him if he had in 1813, as he half resolved, cast away his dislike to new faces, and fought his last desperate campaigns with younger men who still had fortunes to win, leaving "Berthier to hunt at Grosbois," and the other Marshals to enjoy their well-deserved rest in their splendid hotels at Paris.

Davoust, Duke of Auerstadt, Prince of Eckmuhl, whose name should be properly spelt Davout, was one of the principal personages at the end of the Cent Jours. Strict and severe, having his corps always in good order, and displaying more character than most of the military men under Napoleon, one is apt to believe that the conqueror at Auerstadt bade fair to be the most prominent of all the Marshals. In 1814 he had returned from defending Hamburg to find himself under a cloud of accusations, and the Bourbons ungenerously and unwisely left him undefended for acts which they must have known were part of his duty as governor of a besieged place. At the time he was attacked as if his first duty was not to hold the place for France, but to organise a system of outdoor relief for the neighbouring population, and to surrender as soon as he had exhausted the money in the Government chest and the provisions in the Government stores. Sore and discontented, practically proscribed, still Davoust would not join in the too hasty enterprise of the brothers Lallemand, who wished him to lead the military rising on the approach of Napoleon; but he was with the Emperor on the day after his arrival in Paris.

Davoust might have expected high command in the army, but, to his annoyance, Napoleon fixed on him as War Minister. For several years the War Minister had been little more than a clerk, and neither had nor was expected to have much influence with the army. Napoleon now wanted a man of tried devotion, and of stern enough character to overawe the capital and the restless spirits in the army. Much against his will Davoust was therefore forced to content himself with the organisation of the forces being hastily raised, but he chafed in his position; and it is characteristic of him that Napoleon was eventually forced to send him the most formal orders before the surly Minister would carry out the Emperor's unlucky intention of giving a command to Bourmont, whom Davoust strongly and rightly suspected of treachery. When Napoleon left the capital Davoust became its governor, and held his post unmoved by the intrigues of the Republicans and the Royalists. When Napoleon returned from the great disaster Davoust gave his voice for the only wise policy,—resistance and the prorogation of the factious Chambers. On the abdication of Napoleon the Provisional Government necessarily gave Davoust the command of the army which was concentrated round Paris.

If Davoust had restricted himself less closely to his duty as a soldier, if he had taken more on himself, with the 100,000 men he soon had under him, he might have saved France from much of her subsequent humiliation, or at least he might have preserved the lives of Ney and of the brave men whom the Bourbons afterwards butchered. Outwitted by Fouché, and unwilling to face the hostility of the Chambers, Davoust at last consented to the capitulation of Paris, though he first gave the Prussian cavalry a sharp lesson. While many of his comrades were engaged in the great struggle for favour or safety, the stern Marshal gave up his Ministry, and, doing the last service in his power to France, stopped all further useless bloodshed by withdrawing the army, no easy task in their then humour, behind the Loire, where he kept what the Royalists called the "Brigands of the Loire" in subjection till relieved by Macdonald. He was the only one of the younger Marshals who had not been tried in Spain, and so far he was fortunate; but, though he was not popular with the army, his character and services seem to point him out as the most fit of all the Marshals for an independent command. Had Napoleon been successful in 1812, Davoust was to have received the Viceroyalty of Poland; and he would probably have left a higher name in history than the other men placed by Napoleon to rule over his outlying kingdoms. In any case it was fortunate for France and for the Allies that a man of his character ruled the army after Napoleon abdicated; there would otherwise have been wild work round Paris, as it was only with the greatest difficulty and by the force of his authority and example that Davoust succeeded in getting the army to withdraw from the capital, and to gradually adopt the white cockade. When superseded by Macdonald he had done a work no other man could have accomplished. He protested against the proscription, but it was too late; his power had departed. In 1819 he was forgiven for his services to France, and was made a peer, but he died in 1823, only fifty-three years old.

Among the Marshals who gave an active support to Napoleon Ney takes the leading part in most eyes; if it were only for his fate, which is too well known for much to be said here concerning it. In 1815 Ney was commanding in Franche-Comte, and was called up to Paris and ordered to go to Besancon to march so as to take Napoleon in flank. He started off, not improbably using the rough brags afterwards attributed to him as most grievous sins, such as that "he would bring back Napoleon in an iron cage." It had been intended to have sent the Duc de Berry, the second son of the Comte d'Artois, with Ney; and it was most unfortunate for the Marshal that this was not done. There can be no possible doubt that Ney spoke and acted in good faith when he left Paris. One point alone seems decisive of this. Ney found under him in command, as General of Division, Bourmont, an officer of well-known Royalist opinions, who had at one time served with the Vendean insurgents, and who afterwards deserted Napoleon just before Waterloo, although he had entreated to be employed in the campaign. Not only did Ney leave Bourmont in command, but, requiring another Divisional General, instead of selecting a Bonapartist, he urged Lecourbe to leave his retirement and join him. Now, though Lecourbe was a distinguished General, specially famed for mountain warfare—witness his services in 1799 among the Alps above Lucerne—he had been long left unemployed by Napoleon on account of his strong Republican opinions and his sympathy with Moreau. These two Generals, Bourmont and Lecourbe, the two arms of Ney as commander, through whom alone he could communicate with the troops, he not only kept with him, but consulted to the last, before he declared for Napoleon. This would have been too dangerous a thing for a tricky politician to have attempted as a blind, but Ney was well known to be only too frank and impulsive. Had the Duc de Berry gone with him, had Ney carried with him such a gage of the intention of the Bourbons to defend their throne, it is probable that he would have behaved like Macdonald; and it is certain that he would have had no better success. The Bonapartists themselves dreaded what they called the wrong-headedness of Ney. It was, however, thought better to keep the Duc de Berry in safety.

Ney found himself put forward singly, as it were, to oppose the man whom all France was joining; he found, as did every officer sent on a similar mission, that the soldiers were simply waiting to meet Napoleon; and while the Princes sought security, while the soldiers plotted against their leaders, came the calls of the Emperor in the old trumpet tone. The eagle was to fly—nay, it was flying from tower to tower, and victory was advancing with a rush. Was Ney to be the one man to shoot down his old leader? could he, as he asked, stop the sea with his hands? On his trial his subordinate, Bourmont, who had by that time shown his devotion to the Bourbons by sacrificing his military honour, and deserting to the Allies, was asked whether Ney could have got the soldiers to act against the Emperor. He could only suggest that if Ney had taken a musket and himself charged, the men would have followed his example. "Still," said Bourmont, "I would not dare to affirm that he (the Marshal) would have won." And who was Ney to charge? We know how Napoleon approached the forces sent to oppose him: he showed himself alone in the front of his own troops. Was Ney to deliberately kill his old commander? was any general ever expected to undergo such a test? and can it be believed that the soldiers who carried off the reluctant Oudinot and chased the flying Macdonald, had such a reverence for the "Rougeot," as they called him, that they would have stood by while he committed this murder? The whole idea is absurd: as Ney himself said at his trial, they would have "pulverized" him. Undoubtedly the honourable course for Ney would have been to have left his corps when he lost control over them; but to urge, as was done afterwards, that he had acted on a preconceived scheme, and that his example had such weight, was only malicious falsehood. The Emperor himself knew well how little he owed to the free will of his Marshal, and he soon had to send him from Paris, as Ney, sore at heart, and discontented with himself and with both sides, uttered his mind with his usual freedom. Ney was first ordered to inspect the frontier from Dunkirk to Bale, and was then allowed to go to his home. He kept so aloof from Napoleon that when he appeared on the Champ de Mai the Emperor affected surprise, saying that he thought Ney had emigrated. At the last moment Marshal Mortier fell ill. Ney had already been sent for. He hurried up, buying Mortier's horses (presumably the ill-fated animals who died under him at Waterloo), and reached the army just in time to be given the command of the left wing.

It has been well remarked that the very qualities which made Ney invaluable for defence or for the service of a rear-guard weighed against him in such a combat as Quatre Bras. Splendid as a corps leader, he had not the commander's eye to embrace the field and surmise the strength of the enemy at a glance. At Bautzen in 1818 his staff had been unable to prevent him from leaving the route which would have brought him on the very rear of the enemy, because seeing the foe, and unable to resist the desire of returning their fire, he turned off to engage immediately. At Quatre Bras, not seeing the force he was engaged with, believing he had the whole English army on his hands from the first, he let himself at the beginning of the day be imposed upon by a mere screen of troops.

We cannot here go into Ney's behaviour at Waterloo except to point out that too little importance is generally given to the fact of the English cavalry having, in a happy moment, fallen on and destroyed the artillery which was being brought up to sweep the English squares at close quarters. At Waterloo, as in so many other combats, the account of Ney's behaviour more resembles that of a Homeric hero than of a modern general. To the ideal commander of to-day, watching the fight at a distance, calmly weighing its course, undisturbed except by distant random shots, it is strange to compare Ney staggering through the gate of Konigsberg all covered with blood; smoke and snow, musket in hand, announcing himself as the rear-guard of France, or appearing, a second Achilles, on the ramparts of Smolensko to encourage the yielding troops on the glacis, or amidst the flying troops at Waterloo, with uncovered head and broken sword, black with powder, on foot, his fifth horse killed under him, knowing that life, honour, and country were lost, still hoping against hope and attempting one more last desperate rally. If he had died—ah! if he had died there—what a glorious tomb might have risen, glorious for France as well as for him, with the simple inscription, "The Bravest of the Brave."

Early on the 19th June a small band of officers retreating from the field found Ney asleep at Marchiennes, "the first repose he had had for four days," and they did not disturb him for orders. "And indeed what order could Marshal Ney have given?" The disaster of the day, the overwhelming horror of the flight of the beaten army, simply crushed Ney morally as well as physically. Rising in the Chambers he denounced all attempt at further resistance. He did not know, he would not believe, that Grouchy was safe, and that the army was fast rallying. Fresh from the field, with all its traces on him, the authority of Ney was too great for the Government. Frightened friends, plotting Royalists, echoed the wild words of Ney brave only against physical dangers. Instead of dying on the battle-field, he had lived to ensure the return of the Bourbons, the fall of Bonaparte, his own death, and the ruin of France.

Before his exception from the amnesty was known Ney left Paris on the 6th of July, and went into the country with but little attempt at concealment, and with formal passports from Fouché. The capitulation of Paris seemed to cover him, and he was so little aware of the thirst of the Royalists for his blood that he let his presence be known by leaving about a splendid sabre presented to him by the Emperor on his marriage, and recognised by mere report by an old soldier as belonging to Ney or Murat; and Ney himself let into the house the party sent to arrest him on the 5th of August, and actually refused the offer of Excelmans, through whose troops he passed, to set him free. No one at the time, except the wretched refugees of Ghent, could have suspected, after the capitulation, that there was any special danger for Ney, and it is very difficult to see on what principle the Bourbons chose their victims or intended victims. Drouot, for example, had never served Louis XVIII., he had never worn the white cockade, he had left France with Napoleon for Elba, and had served the Emperor there. In 1815 he had fought under his own sovereign. After Waterloo he had exerted all his great influence, the greater from his position, to induce the Guard to retire behind the Loire, and to submit to the Bourbons. It was because Davoust so needed him that Drouot remained with the army. Stilt Drouot was selected for death, but the evidence of his position was too strong to enable the Court to condemn him. Cambronne, another selection, had also gone with Napoleon to Elba. Savory, another selection, had, as was eventually acknowledged, only joined Napoleon when he was in full possession of the reins of Government. Bertrand, who was condemned while at St. Helena, was in the same position as Drouot. In fact, if any one were to draw up a list of probable proscriptions and compare it with those of the 24th of July 1815, there would probably be few names common to both except Labedoyere, Mouton Duvernet, etc. The truth is that the Bourbons, and, to do them justice, still more the rancorous band of mediocrities who surrounded them, thirsted for blood. Even they could feel the full ignominy of the flight to Ghent.

While they had been chanting the glories of the Restoration, the devotion of the people, the valour of the Princes, Napoleon had landed, the Restoration had vanished like a bad dream, and the Princes were the first to lead the way to the frontier. To protest that there had been a conspiracy, and that the conspirators must suffer, was the only possible cloak for the shame of the Royalists, who could not see that the only conspiracy was the universal one of the nation against the miserable men who knew not how to govern a high-spirited people.

Ney, arrested on the 5th of August, was first brought before a Military Court on the 9th of November composed of Marshal Jourdan (President), Marshals Massena, Augereau, and Mortier, Lieutenants-General Gazan, Claparede, and Vilatte (members). Moncey had refused to sit, and Massena urged to the Court his own quarrels with Ney in Spain to get rid of the task, but was forced to remain. Defended by both the Berryers, Ney unfortunately denied the jurisdiction of the court-martial over him as a peer. In all probability the Military Court would have acquitted him. Too glad at the moment to be free from the trial of their old comrade, not understanding the danger of the proceeding, the Court, by a majority of five against two, declared themselves non-competent, and on the 21st of November Ney was sent before the Chamber of Peers, which condemned him on the 6th of December.

To beg the life of his brave adversary would have been such an obvious act of generosity on the part of the Duke of Wellington that we maybe pardoned for examining his reasons for not interfering. First, the Duke seems to have laid weight on the fact that if Ney had believed the capitulation had covered him he would not have hidden. Now, even before Ney knew of his exception from the amnesty, to appear in Paris would have been a foolish piece of bravado. Further, the Royalist reaction was in full vigour, and when the Royalist mobs, with the connivance of the authorities, were murdering Marshal Brune and attacking any prominent adherents of Napoleon, it was hardly the time for Ney to travel in full pomp. It cannot be said that, apart from the capitulation, the Duke had no responsibility. Generally a Government executing a prisoner, may, with some force, if rather brutally, urge that the fact of their being able to try and execute him in itself shows their authority to do so. The Bourbons could not even use this argument. If the Allies had evacuated France Louis le Desiree would have ordered his carriage and have been at the frontier before they had reached it. If Frenchmen actually fired the shots which killed Ney, the Allies at least shared the responsibility with the French Government. Lastly, it would seem that the Duke would have asked for the life of Ney if the King, clever at such small artifices, had not purposely affected a temporary coldness to him. Few men would have been so deterred from asking for the life of a dog. The fact is, the Duke of Wellington was a great general, he was a single-hearted and patriotic statesman, he had a thousand virtues, but he was never generous. It cannot be said that he simply shared the feelings of his army, for there was preparation among some of his officers to enable Ney to escape, and Ney had to be guarded by men of good position disguised in the uniform of privates. Ney had written to his wife when he joined Napoleon, thinking of the little vexations the Royalists loved to inflict on the men who had conquered the Continent. "You will no longer weep when you leave the Tuileries." The unfortunate lady wept now as she vainly sought some mercy for her husband. Arrested on the 5th of August, sentenced on the 6th of December, Ney was shot on the 7th of December, and the very manner of his execution shows that, in taking his life there was much more of revenge than of justice.

If Ney were to be shot, it is obvious that it should have been as a high act of justice. If neither the rank nor the services of the criminal were to save him, his death could not be too formal, too solemn, too public. Even an ordinary military execution is always carried out with grave and striking forms: there is a grand parade of the troops, that all may see with their own eyes the last act of the law. After the execution the troops defile past the body, that all may see the criminal actually dead: There was nothing of all this in the execution of Ney. A few chance passers, in the early morning of the 7th of December 1815, saw a small body of troops waiting by the wall of the garden of the Luxemburg. A fiacre drove up, out of which got Marshal Ney in plain clothes, himself surprised by the everyday aspect of the place. Then, when the officer of the firing party (for such the spectators now knew it to be) saw whom it was he was to fire on, he became, it is said, perfectly petrified; and a peer, one of the judges of Ney, the Duke de la Force, took his place. Ney fell at the first volley with six balls in his breast, three in the head and neck, and one in the arm, and in a quarter of an hour the body was removed; "plain Michel Ney" as he had said to the secretary enunciating his title in reading his sentence, "plain Michel Ney, soon to be a little dust."

The Communists caught red-handed in the streets of Paris in 1870 died with hardly less formality than was observed at the death-scene of the Prince of the Moskowa and Duke of Elchingen, and the truth then became plain. The Bourbons could not, dared not, attempt to carry out the sentence of the law with the forms of the law. The Government did not venture to let the troops or the people face the Marshal. The forms of the law could not be carried out, the demands of revenge could be. And if this be thought any exaggeration, the proof of the ill effects of this murder, for its form makes it difficult to call it anything else, is ready to our hands. It was impossible to get the public to believe that Ney had really been killed in this manner, and nearly to this day we have had fresh stories recurring of the real Ney being discovered in America. The deed, however, had really been done. The Marshals now knew that when the Princes fled they themselves must remain to die for the Royal cause; and Louis had at last succeeded in preventing his return to his kingdom amongst the baggage waggons of the Allies from being considered as a mere subject for jeers. One detail of the execution of Ney, however, we are told nothing of: we do not know if his widow, like Madame Labedoyere, had to pay three francs a head to the soldiers of the firing party which shot her husband. Whatever were the faults of the Bourbons, they at least carried out their executions economically.

The statesmen of France, distinguished as they were, certainly did not rise to a level with the situation either in 1814 or in 1815. In 1814, it is true, they were almost stunned by the crash of the Empire, and little as they foresaw the restoration of the Bourbons, still less could they have anticipated the extraordinary follies which were to be perpetrated. In 1815 there was less excuse for their helplessness, and, overawed as they were by the mass of foes which was pouring on them to complete the disaster of Waterloo, still it is disappointing to find that there was no one to seize the helm of power, and, confronting the Allies, to stipulate proper terms for France, and for the brave men who had fought for her. The Steady Davoust was there with his 100,000 men to add weight to their language, and the total helplessness of the older line of the Bourbons had been too evidently displayed to make their return a certainty, so that there is no reason to doubt that a firm-hearted patriot might have saved France from much of the degradation and loss inflicted on her when once the Allies had again got her at their mercy. At-the least the Bourbons might have been deprived of the revenge they sought for in taking some of the best blood of France. Better for Ney and his comrades to have fallen in a last struggle before Paris than to be shot by Frenchmen emboldened by the presence of foreign troops.

Talleyrand, the most prominent figure among the statesmen, was away. His absence at Vienna during the first Restoration was undoubtedly the cause of many of the errors then committed. His ability as displayed under Napoleon has been much exaggerated, for, as the Duke of Wellington said, it was easy enough to be Foreign Minister to a Government in military possession of Europe, but at least he was above the petty trivialities and absurdities of the Bourbon' Court. On the receipt of the news of the landing of Napoleon he really seems to have believed that the enterprise would immediately end in disaster, and he pressed on the outlawing of the man who had overwhelmed him with riches, and who had, at the worst, left him when in disgrace in quiet possession of all his ill-gotten wealth. But, as the power of Napoleon became more and more displayed, as perhaps Talleyrand found that the Austrians were not quite so firm as they wished to be considered, and as he foresaw the possible chances of the Orleans family, he became rather lukewarm in his attention to the King, to whom he had recently been bewailing the hardships of his separation from his loved monarch. He suddenly found that, after a Congress, the first duty of a diplomatist was to look after his liver, and Carlsbad offered an agreeable retreat where he could wait till he might congratulate the winner in the struggle.

Louis deeply resented this conduct of his Foreign Minister, and when Talleyrand at last joined him with all his doubts resolved, the King took the first opportunity of dismissing him, leaving the calm Talleyrand for once stuttering with rage. Louis soon, however, found that he was not the free agent he believed. The Allies did not want to have to again replace their puppet on the throne, and they looked on Talleyrand and Fouché as the two necessary men. Talleyrand was reinstated immediately, and remained for some time at the head of the Ministry. He was, however, not the man for Parliamentary Government, being too careless in business, and trying to gain his ends more by clever tricks than straightforward measures. As for the state into which he let the Government fall, it was happily characterised by M. Beugnot. "Until now," said he, "we have only known three sorts of governments—the Monarchical, the Aristocratic, and the Republican. Now we have invented a new one, which has never been heard of before,—Paternal Anarchy."

In September 1815 the elections to the Chamber were bringing in deputies more Royalist than the King, and Talleyrand sought to gain popularity by throwing over Fouché. To his horror it appeared that, well contented with this step, the deputies next asked when the former Bishop was to be dismissed. Taking advantage of what Talleyrand conceived to be a happy way of eliciting a strong expression of royal support by threatening to resign, the King replaced him by the Duc de Richelieu. It was well to cut jokes at the Duke and say that he was the man in France who knew most of the Crimea (the Duke had been long in the Russian service, with the approval of Napoleon), but Talleyrand was overwhelmed. He received the same office at Court which he had held under Napoleon, Grand Chamberlain, and afterwards remained a sardonic spectator of events, a not unimposing figure attending at the Court ceremonials and at the heavy dinners of the King, and probably lending a helping hand in 1830 to oust Charles X. from the throne. The Monarchy of July sent him as Ambassador to England, where he mixed in local politics, for example, plotting against Lord Palmerston, whose brusque manners he disliked; and in 1838 he ended his strange life with some dignity, having, as one of his eulogists puts it, been faithful to every Government he had served as long as it was possible to save them.

With the darker side of Talleyrand's character we have nothing to do here; it is sufficient for our purposes to say that the part the leading statesman of France took during the Cent Jours was simply nil. In 1814, he had let the reins slip through his hands; 1815 he could only follow the King, who even refused to adopt his advice as to the proper way in which to return to France, and though he once more became Chief Minister, Talleyrand, like Louis XVIII., owed his restoration in 1815 solely to the Allies.

The Comte d'Artois, the brother of the King, and later King himself as Charles X., was sent to Lyons, to which place the Duc d'Orleans followed him, and where the two Princes met Marshal Macdonald. The Marshal did all that man could do to keep the soldiers true to the Bourbons, but he had to advise the Princes to return to Paris, and he himself had to fly for his life when he attempted to stop Napoleon in person. The Duc d'Orleans was then sent to the north to hold Lille, where the King intended to take refuge, and the Comte d'Artois remained with the Court.

The Court was very badly off for money, the King, and Clarke, Duke of Feltre, the War Minister, were the only happy possessors of carriages. They passed their time, as the Abbe Louis once bitterly remarked, in saying foolish things till they had a chance of doing them.

The Comte d'Artois, who, probably wisely, certainly cautiously, had refused to go with De Vitrolles to stir up the south until he had placed the King in safety, had ended by going to Ghent too, while the Duc de Berry was at Alost, close by, with a tiny army composed of the remains of the Maison du Roi, of which the most was made in reports. The Duc d'Orleans, always an object of suspicion to the King, had left France with the Royal party, but had refused to stay in Belgium, as he alleged that it was an enemy's country. He crossed to England where he remained, greatly adding to the anxiety of Louis by refusing to join him.

The end of these Princes is well known. Louis died in 1824, leaving his throne to his brother; but Charles only held it till 1830, when after the rising called "the three glorious days of July," he was civilly escorted from France, and took shelter in England. The Duc Angouleme died without issue. The Duc de Berry was assassinated in 1820, but his widow gave birth to a posthumous son the Duc de Bordeaux, or, to fervid Royalists, Henri V., though better known to us as the Comte de Chambord, who died in 1883 without issue, thus ending the then eldest line of Bourbons, and transmitting his claims to the Orleans family. On the fall of Charles X. the Duc d'Orleans became King of the French, but he was unseated by the Revolution of 1848, and died a refugee in England. As the three Princes of the House of Condé, the Prince de Condé, his son, the Duc de Bourbon, and his: grandson, the Duc d'Enghien, all died without further male issue, that noble line is extinct.

When the news of the escape of Napoleon from Elba reached Vienna on the 7th of March 1815, the three heads of the Allies, the Emperors of Austria and Russia, and the King of Prussia, were still there. Though it was said that the Congress danced but did not advance, still a great deal of work had really been done, and the news of Napoleon's landing created a fresh bond of union between the Allies which stopped all further chances of disunion, and enabled them to practically complete their work by the 9th of June 1815, though the treaties required cobbling for some years afterwards.

France, Austria, and England had snatched the greater part of Saxony from the jaws of Prussia, and Alexander had been forced to leave the King of Saxony to reign over half of his former subjects, without, as he wished, sparing him the pain of such a degradation by taking all from him. Russia had to be contented with a large increase of her Polish dominions, getting most of the Grand-Duchy of Westphalia. Austria had, probably unwisely, withdrawn from her former outlying provinces in Swabia and the Netherlands, which had before the Revolution made her necessarily the guardian of Europe against France, preferring to take her gains in Italy, gains which she has gradually lost in our days; while Prussia, by accepting the Rhine provinces, completely stepped into the former post of Austria. Indeed, from the way in which Prussia was, after 1815, as it were, scattered across Germany, it was evident that her fate must be either to be crushed by France, or else, by annexing the states enclosed in her dominions, to become the predominating power in Germany. It was impossible for her to remain as she was left.

The Allies tightly bound France. They had no desire to have again to march on Paris to restore Louis to the subjects who had such unfortunate objections to being subjected to that desirable monarch. By the second Treaty of Paris, on the 20th of November 1815, France was to be occupied by an Allied force, in military positions on the frontier, not to exceed 150,000 men, to be taken from all the Allied armies, under a commander who was eventually the Duke of Wellington. Originally the occupation was not to exceed five years, but in February 1817 the army was reduced by 30,000 men, one-fifth of each contingent; and by the Treaty of Aix-la-Chapelle of 9th October 1818, France was to-be evacuated by the 30th of November 1818.

The three monarchs were probably not sorry to get the Congress over on any terms. Alexander had had his fill of displaying himself in the salons in his favourite part of an Agamemnon generous towards Troy, and he had worn out his first popularity. He was stung by finding some of his favourite plans boldly opposed by Talleyrand and by Metternich, and, indeed, was anxious to meet the last in open combat. Francis had required all the firmness of what he called his Bohemian head to resist the threats, entreaties, and cajoleries employed to get him to acquiesce in the dethronement of the King of Saxony, and the wiping out of the Saxon nationality by the very alliance which professed to fight only for the rights of nations and of their lawful sovereigns.

All three monarchs had again the satisfaction of entering Paris, but without enjoying the full glories of 1814. "Our friends, the enemies" were not so popular then in France, and the spoliation of the Louvre was not pleasant even to the Royalists. The foreign monarchs soon returned to their own drained and impoverished States.

The Emperor Francis had afterwards a quiet reign to his death in 1835, having only to assist his Minister in snuffing out the occasional flashes of a love of freedom in Germany.

The King of Prussia returned in a triumph well won by his sturdy subjects, and, in the light of his new honours, the Countess Von Voss tells us he was really handsome. He was now at leisure to resume the discussions on uniform, and the work of fastening and unfastening the numerous buttons of his pantaloons, in which he had been so roughly interrupted by Jena. The first institution of the Zollverein, or commercial union with several States, gradually extended, was a measure which did much for the unification of Germany. With his brother sovereigns he revisited Paris at the end of the military occupation in 1818, remaining there longer than the others, "because," said the Parisians, "he had discovered an actor at a small theatre who achieved the feat of making him laugh." He died in 1840. His Queen—heartbroken, it was said—had died in 1810.

Alexander was still brimming over with the best and most benevolent intentions towards every one. The world was to be free, happy, and religious; but he had rather vague ideas as to how his plans were to be carried out. Thus it is characteristic that when his successor desired to have a solemn coronation as King of Poland it was found that Alexander had not foreseen the difficulties which were met with in trying to arrange for the coronation of a Sovereign of the Greek Church as King of a Roman Catholic State. The much-dreaded but very misty Holy Alliance was one of the few fruits of Alexander's visions. His mind is described as passing through a regular series of stages with each influence under which he acted. He ended his life, tired out, disillusioned, "deceived in everything, weighed down with regret;" obliged to crush the very hopes of his people he had encouraged, dying in 1825 at Taganrog, leaving his new Polish Kingdom to be wiped out by-his successors.

The minor sovereigns require little mention. They retained any titles they had received from Napoleon, while they exulted, at being free from his heavy hand and sharp superintendence. Each got a share, small or great, of the spoil except the poor King of Denmark, who, being assured by Alexander on his departure that he carried away all hearts, answered, "Yes, but not any souls."

The reintroduction of much that was bad in the old system (one country even going so far as to re-establish torture), the steady attack on liberty and on all liberal ideas, Wurtemberg being practically the only State which grumbled at the tightening of the reins so dear to Metternich,—all formed a fitting commentary on the proclamations by which the Sovereigns had hounded on their people against the man they represented as the one obstacle to the freedom and peace of Europe. In gloom and disenchantment the nations sat down to lick their wounds: The contempt shown by the monarchs for everything but the right of conquest, the manner in which they treated the lands won from Napoleon as a gigantic "pool" which was to be shared amongst them, so many souls to each; their total failure to fulfil their promises to their subjects of granting liberty,—all these slowly bore their fruits in after years, and their effects are not even yet exhausted. The right of a sovereign to hold his lands was now, by the public law of Europe, to be decided by his strength, The rights of the people were treated as not existing. Truly, as our most gifted poetess has sung—

"The Kings crept out—the peoples sat at home,
And finding the long invocated peace
(A pall embroidered with worn images
Of rights divine) too scant to cover doom
Such as they suffered, nursed the corn that grew
Rankly to bitter bread, on Waterloo."

CHAPTER XIII[282]

1815-1821

The closing scenes in the life of the great Emperor only now remain to be briefly touched upon. In a previous chapter we have narrated the surrender of Napoleon, his voyage to England, and his transference from the Bellerophon to the Northumberland. The latter vessel was in great confusion from the short notice at which she had sailed, and for the two first days the crew was employed in restoring order. The space abaft the mizenmast contained a dining-room about ten feet broad, and extending the whole width of the ship, a saloon, and two cabins. The Emperor occupied the cabin on the left; in which his camp-bedstead had been put up; that on the right was appropriated to the Admiral. It was peremptorily enjoined that the saloon should be in common. The form of the dining-table resembled that of the dining-room. Napoleon sat with his back to the saloon; on his left sat Madame Bertrand, and on his right the Admiral, who, with Madame de Montholon, filled up one side of the table. Next that lady, but at the end of the table, was Captain Ross, who commanded the ship, and at the opposite end M. de Montholon; Madame Bertrand, and the Admiral's secretary. The side of the table facing the Emperor was occupied by the Grand-Marshal, the Colonel of the field Regiment, Las Cases, and Gourgaud. The Admiral invited one or two of the officers to dinner every day, and the band of the 53d, newly-formed, played during dinner-time.

On the 10th of August the Northumberland cleared the Channel, and lost sight of land. The course of the ship was shaped to cross the Bay of Biscay and double Cape Finisterre. The wind was fair, though light, and the heat excessive. Napoleon breakfasted in his own cabin at irregular hours. He sent for one of his attendants every morning to know the distance run, the state of the wind, and other particulars connected with their progress. He read a great deal, dressed towards four o'clock, and then came into the public saloon; here he played at chess with one of the party; at five o'clock the Admiral announced that dinner was on the table. It is well known that Napoleon was scarcely ever more than fifteen minutes at dinner; here the two courses alone took up nearly an hour and a half. This was a serious annoyance to him, though his features and manner always evinced perfect equanimity. Neither the new system of cookery nor the quality of the dishes ever met with his censure. He was waited on by two valets, who stood behind his chair. At first the Admiral was in the habit of offering several dishes to the Emperor, but the acknowledgment of the latter was expressed so coldly that the practice was given up. The Admiral thenceforth only pointed out to the servants what was preferable. Napoleon was generally silent, as if unacquainted with the language, though it was French. If he spoke, it was to ask some technical or scientific question, or to address a few words to those whom the Admiral occasionally asked to dinner.

The Emperor rose immediately after coffee had been handed round, and went on deck, followed by the Grand-Marshal and Las Cases. This disconcerted Admiral Cockburn, who

282 This chapter; by the editor of the 1836 edition, is based upon the 'Memorial', and O'Meara's and Antommarchi's works.

expressed his surprise to his officers; but Madame Bertrand, whose maternal language was English, replied with spirit, "Do not forget, sir, that your guest is a man who has governed a large portion of the world, and that kings once contended for the honour of being admitted to his table."—"Very true," rejoined the Admiral; and from that time he did his utmost to comply with Napoleon's habits. He shortened the time of sitting at table, ordering coffee for Napoleon and those who accompanied him even before the rest of the company had finished their dinner. The Emperor remained walking on deck till dark. On returning to the after-cabin he sat down to play vingt et un with some of his suite, and generally retired in about half an hour. On the morning of the 15th of August all his suite asked permission to be admitted to his presence. He was not aware of the cause of this visit; it was his birthday, which seemed to have altogether escaped his recollection.

On the following day they doubled Cape Finisterre, and up to the 21st, passing off the Straits of Gibraltar, continued their course along the coast of Africa towards Madeira. Napoleon commonly remained in his cabin the whole morning, and from the extreme heat he wore a very slight dress. He could not sleep well, and frequently rose in the night. Reading was his chief occupation. He often sent for Count Las Cases to translate whatever related to St. Helena or the countries by which they were sailing. Napoleon used to start a subject of conversation; or revive that of some preceding day, and when he had taken eight or nine turns the whole length of the deck he would seat himself on the second gun from the gangway on the larboard side. The midshipmen soon observed this habitual predilection, so that the cannon was thenceforth called the Emperor's gun. It was here that Napoleon often conversed for hours together.

On the 22d of August they came within sight of Madeira, and at night arrived off the port. They stopped for a day or two to take in provisions. Napoleon was indisposed. A sudden gale arose and the air was filled with small particles of sand and the suffocating exhalations from the deserts of Africa. On the evening of the 24th they got under weigh again, and progressed smoothly and rapidly. The Emperor added to his amusements a game at piquet. He was but an indifferent chess-player, and there was no very good one on board. He asked, jestingly, "How it was that he frequently beat those who beat better players than himself?" Vingt et un was given up, as they played too high at it; and Napoleon had a great aversion to gaming. One night a negro threw himself overboard to avoid a flogging, which occasioned a great noise and bustle. A young midshipman meeting Las Cases descending into the cabin, and thinking he was going to inform Napoleon, caught hold of his coat and in a tone of great concern exclaimed, "Ah sir, do not alarm the Emperor! Tell him the noise is owing to an accident!" In general the midshipmen behaved with marked respect and attention to Bonaparte, and often by signs or words directed the sailors to avoid incommoding him: He sometimes noticed this conduct, and remarked that youthful hearts were always prone to generous instincts.

On the 1st of September they found themselves in the latitude of the Cape de Verd Islands. Everything now promised a prosperous passage, but the time hung heavily. Las Cases had undertaken to teach his son English, and the Emperor also expressed a wish to learn. He, however, soon grew tired and laid it aside, nor was it resumed until long afterwards. His manners and habits were always the same; he invariably appeared contented, patient, and good-humoured. The Admiral gradually laid aside his reserve, and took an interest in his great captive. He pointed out the danger incurred by coming on deck after dinner, owing to the damp of the evening: the Emperor, would then sometimes take his arm and prolong the conversation, talking sometimes on naval affairs, on the French resources in the south, and on the improvements he had contemplated in the ports and harbours of the Mediterranean, to all which the Admiral listened with deep attention.

Meanwhile Napoleon observed that Las Cases was busily employed, and obtained a sight of his journal, with which he was not displeased. He, however, noticed that some of the military details and anecdotes gave but a meagre idea of the subject of war: This first led to the proposal of his writing his own Memoirs. At length the Emperor came to a determination, and on Saturday, the 9th of September he called his secretary into his cabin and dictated to him some particulars of the siege of Toulon. On approaching the line they fell in with the trade-winds, that blow here constantly from the east. On the 16th there was a considerable fall of rain, to the great joy of the sailors, who were in want of water. The rain began to fall heavily just as the Emperor had got upon deck to take his afternoon walk. But this did not disappoint him of his usual exercise; he merely called for his famous gray greatcoat, which the crew regarded with much interest.

On the 23d of September they passed the line. This was a day of great merriment and disorder among the crew: it was the ceremony which the English sailors call the "christening." No one is spared; and the officers are generally more roughly handled than any one else. The Admiral, who had previously amused himself by giving an alarming description of this ceremony, now very courteously exempted his guests from the inconvenience and ridicule attending it. Napoleon was scrupulously respected through the whole of this Saturnalian festivity. On being informed of the decorum which had been observed with regard to him he ordered a hundred Napoleons to be presented to the grotesque Neptune and his crew; which the Admiral opposed, perhaps from motives of prudence as well as politeness.

Owing to the haste with which they had left England the painting of the ship had been only lately finished, and this circumstance confined Napoleon, whose sense of smell was very acute, to his room for two days. They were now, in the beginning of October, driven into the Gulf of Guinea, where they met a French vessel bound for the Isle of Bourbon. They spoke with the captain, who expressed his surprise and regret when he learnt that Napoleon was on board. The wind was unfavourable, and the ship made little progress. The sailors grumbled at the Admiral, who had gone out of the usual course. At length they approached the termination of their voyage. On the 14th of October the Admiral had informed them that he expected to come within sight of St. Helena that day. They had scarcely risen from table when their ears were saluted with the cry of "land!" This was within a quarter of an hour of the time that had been fixed on. The Emperor went on the forecastle to see the island; but it was still hardly distinguishable. At daybreak next morning they had a tolerably clear view of it.

At length, about seventy days after his departure from England, and a hundred and ten after quitting Paris, Napoleon reached St. Helena. In the harbour were several vessels of the squadron which had separated from them, and which they thought they had left behind. Napoleon, contrary to custom, dressed early and went upon deck: he went forward to the gangway to view the island. He beheld a kind of village surrounded by numerous barren hills towering to the clouds. Every platform, every aperture, the brow of every hill was planted with cannon. The Emperor viewed the prospect through his glass. His countenance underwent no change. He soon left the deck; and sending for Las Cases, proceeded to his day's work. The Admiral, who had gone ashore very early, returned about six much fatigued. He had been walking over various parts of the island, and at length thought he had found a habitation that would suit his captives. The place stood in need of repairs, which might occupy two months. His orders were not to let the French quit the vessel till a house should be prepared to receive them. He, however, undertook, on his own responsibility, to set them on shore the next day.

On the 16th, after dinner, Napoleon, accompanied by the Admiral and the Grand-Marshal, Bertrand, got into a boat to go ashore. As he passed, the officers assembled on the quarter-deck, and the greater part of the crew on the gangways. The Emperor, before he stepped into the boat, sent for the captain of the vessel, and took leave of him, desiring him at the same time to convey his thanks to the officers and crew. These words appeared to produce the liveliest sensation in all by whom they were understood, or to whom they were interpreted. The remainder of his suite landed about eight. They found the Emperor in the apartments which had been assigned to him, a few minutes after he went upstairs to his chamber. He was lodged in a sort of inn in James Town, which consists only, of one short street, or row of houses built in a narrow valley between two rocky hills.

The next day the Emperor, the Grand-Marshal, and the Admiral, riding out to visit Longwood, which had been chosen for the Emperor's residence, on their return saw a small villa, with a pavilion attached to it, about two miles from the town, the residence of Mr. Balcombe; a merchant of the island. This spot pleased Napoleon, and the Admiral was of opinion that it would be better for him to remain here than to return to the town, where the sentinels at his door, with the crowds collected round it, in a manner confined him to his chamber. The pavilion was a sort of summer-house on a pyramidal eminence, about thirty or forty paces from the house, where the family were accustomed to resort in fine weather: this was hired for the temporary abode of the Emperor, and he took possession of it immediately. There was a carriage-road from the town, and the valley was in this part less rugged in its aspect. Las Cases was soon sent for. As he ascended the winding path leading to the pavilion he saw Napoleon standing at the threshold of the door. His body was slightly bent, and his hands behind his back: he wore his usual plain and simple uniform and the well-known hat. The Emperor was alone. He took a fancy to walk a little; but there was no level ground on any side of the pavilion, which was surrounded by huge pieces of rock. Taking the arm of his companion, however, he began to converse in a cheerful strain. When Napoleon was about to retire to rest the servants found that one of the windows was open close to the bed: they barricaded it as well as they could, so as to exclude the air, to the effects of which the Emperor was very susceptible. Las Cases ascended to an upper room. The valets de chambres lay stretched in their cloaks across the threshold of the door. Such was the first night Napoleon passed at the Briars.

An English officer was lodged with them in the house as their guard, and two non-commissioned officers were stationed near the house to watch their movements. Napoleon the next day proceeded with his dictation, which occupied him for several hours, and then took a walk in the garden, where he was met by the two Misses Balcombe, lively girls about fourteen years of age, who presented him with flowers, and overwhelmed him with whimsical questions. Napoleon was amused by their familiarity, to which he had been little accustomed. "We have been to a masked ball," said he, when the young ladies had taken their leave.

The next day a chicken was brought for breakfast, which the Emperor undertook to carve himself, and was surprised at his succeeding so well, it being a long time since he had done so much. The coffee he considered so bad that on tasting it he thought himself poisoned, and sent it away.

The mornings were passed in business; in the evening Napoleon sometimes strolled to the neighbouring villa, where the young ladies made him play at whist. The Campaign of Italy was nearly finished, and Las Cases proposed that the other followers of Napoleon who were lodged in the town should come up every morning to assist in transcribing The Campaign of Egypt, the History of the Consulate, etc. This suggestion pleased the ex-Emperor, so that from that time one or two of his suite came regularly every day to write to his dictation, and stayed to dinner. A tent, sent by the Colonel of the 53d Regiment, was spread out so as to form a prolongation of the pavillion. Their cook took up his abode at the Briars. The table linen was taken from the trunks, the plate was set forth, and the first dinner after these new arrangements was a sort of fete.

One day at dinner Napoleon, casting his eye on one of the dishes of his own campaign-service, on which the-arms of the King had been engraved, "How they have spoiled that!" he exclaimed; and he could not refrain from observing that the King was in great haste to take possession of the Imperial plate, which certainly did not belong to him. Amongst the baggage was also a cabinet in which were a number of medallions, given him by the Pope and other potentates, some letters of Louis XVIII. which he had left behind him on his writing-table in the suddenness of his flight from the Tuileries on the 20th of March, and a number of other letters found in the portfolio of M. De Blacas intended to calumniate Napoleon.

The Emperor never dressed until about four o'clock, he then walked in the garden, which was particularly agreeable to him on account of its solitude—the English soldiers having been removed at Mr. Balcombe's request. A little arbour was covered with canvas; and a chair and table placed in it, and here Napoleon dictated a great part of his Memoirs. In the evening, when he did not go out, he generally contrived to prolong the conversation till eleven or twelve o'clock.

Thus time passed with little variety or interruption. The weather in the winter became delightful. One day, his usual task being done; Napoleon strolled out towards the town, until he came within sight of the road and shipping. On his return he met Mrs. Balcombe and a Mrs. Stuart, who was on her way back from Bombay to England. The Emperor conversed with her on the manners and customs of India, and on the inconveniences of a long voyage at sea, particularly to ladies. He alluded to Scotland, Mrs. Stuart's native country, expatiated on the genius of Ossian, and congratulated his fair interlocutor on the preservation of her clear northern complexion. While the parties were thus engaged some heavily burdened slaves passed near to them. Mrs. Balcombe motioned them to make a detour; but Napoleon interposed, exclaiming, "Respect the burden, madam!" As he said this the Scotch lady, who had been very eagerly scanning the features of Napoleon, whispered to her friend, "Heavens! what a character, and what an expression of countenance! How different to the idea I had formed of him!"

Napoleon shortly after repeated the same walk, and went into the house of Major Hudson. This visit occasioned considerable alarm to the constituted authorities.

The Governor gave a ball, to which the French were invited; and Las Cases about the same time rode over to Longwood to see what advance had been made in the preparations for their reception. His report on his return was not very favourable. They had now been six weeks at the Briars, during which Napoleon had been nearly as much confined as if on board the vessel. His health began to be impaired by it. Las Cases gave it as his opinion that the Emperor did not possess that constitution of iron which was usually ascribed to him;

and that it was the strength of his mind, not of his body, that carried him through the labours of the field and of the cabinet. In speaking on this subject Napoleon himself observed that nature had endowed him with two peculiarities: one was the power of sleeping at any hour or in any place; the other, his being incapable of committing any excess either in eating or drinking: "If," said he, "I go the least beyond my mark my stomach instantly revolts." He was subject to nausea from very slight causes, and to colds from any change of air.

The prisoners removed to Longwood on the 10th of December 1815. Napoleon invited Mr. Balcombe to breakfast with him that morning, and conversed with him in a very cheerful manner. About two Admiral Cockburn was announced; he entered with an air of embarrassment. In consequence of the restraints imposed upon him at the Briars, and the manner in which those of his suite residing in the town had been treated, Bonaparte had discontinued receiving the visits of the Admiral; yet on the present occasion he behaved towards him as though nothing had happened. At length they left the Briars and set out for Longwood. Napoleon rode the horse, a small, sprightly, and tolerably handsome animal, which had been brought for him from the Cape. He wore his uniform of the Chasseurs of the Guard, and his graceful manner and handsome countenance were particularly remarked. The Admiral was very attentive to him. At the entrance of Longwood they found a guard under arms who rendered the prescribed honours to their illustrious captive. His horse, unaccustomed to parades, and frightened by the roll of the drum, refused to pass the gate till spurred on by Napoleon, while a significant look passed among the escort. The Admiral took great pains to point out the minutest details at Longwood. He had himself superintended all the arrangements, among which was a bath-room. Bonaparte was satisfied with everything, and the Admiral seemed highly pleased. He had anticipated petulance and disdain, but Napoleon manifested perfect good-humour.

The entrance to the house was through a room which had been just built to answer the double purpose of an ante-chamber and a dining-room. This apartment led to the drawing-room; beyond this was a third room running in a cross direction and very dark. This was intended to be the depository of the Emperor's maps and books, but it was afterwards converted into the dining-room. The Emperor's chamber opened into this apartment on the right hand side, and was divided into two equal parts, forming a cabinet and sleeping-room; a little external gallery served for a bathing-room: Opposite the Emperor's chamber, at the other extremity of the building, were the apartments of Madame Montholon, her husband, and her son, afterward used as the Emperors library. Detached from this part of the house was a little square room on the ground floor, contiguous to the kitchen, which was assigned to Las Cases. The windows and beds had no curtains. The furniture was mean and scanty. Bertrand and his family resided at a distance of two miles, at a place called Rut's Gate. General Gourgaud slept under a tent, as well as Mr. O'Meara, and the officer commanding the guard. The house was surrounded by a garden. In front, and separated by a tolerably deep ravine, was encamped the 53d Regiment, different parties of which were stationed on the neighbouring heights.

The domestic establishment of the Emperor consisted of eleven persons. To the Grand-Marshal was confided the general superintendence; to M. de Montholon the domestic details; Las Cases was to take care of the furniture and property, and General Gourgaud to have the management of the stables. These arrangements, however, produced discontent among Napoleon's attendants. Las Cases admits that they were no longer the members of one family, each using his best efforts to promote the advantage of all. They were far from practising that which necessity dictated. He says also, "The Admiral has more than once, in the midst of our disputes with him, hastily exclaimed that the Emperor was decidedly the most good-natured, just, and reasonable of the whole set."

On his first arrival he went to visit the barracks occupied by some Chinese living on the island, and a place called Longwood Farm. He complained to Las Cases that they had been idle of late; but by degrees their hours and the employment of them became fixed and regular. The Campaign of Italy being now finished, Napoleon corrected it, and dictated on other subjects. This was their morning's work. They dined between eight and nine, Madame Montholon being seated on Napoleon's right; Las Cases on his left, and Gourgaud, Montholon, and Las Cases' son sitting opposite. The smell of the paint not being yet gone off, they remained not more than ten minutes at table, and the dessert was prepared in the adjoining apartment, where coffee was served up and conversation commenced. Scenes were read from Molière, Racine, and Voltaire; and regret was always expressed at their not having a copy of Corneille. They then played at 'reversis', which had been Bonaparte's favourite game in his youth. The recollection was agreeable to him, and he thought he could amuse himself at it for any length of time, but was soon undeceived. His aim was always to make the 'reversis', that is, to win every trick. Character is displayed in the smallest incidents.

Napoleon read a libel on himself, and contrasted the compliments which had passed between him and the Queen of Prussia with the brutal-behaviour ascribed to him in the English newspapers. On the other hand, two common sailors had at different times, while he was at Longwood and at the Briars, in spite of orders and at all risks, made their way through the sentinels to gain a sight of Napoleon. On seeing the interest they took in him he exclaimed, "This is fanaticism! Yes, imagination rules the world!"

The instructions of the English Ministers with regard to the treatment of Napoleon at St. Helena had been prepared with the view completely to secure his person. An English officer was to be constantly at his table. This order, however, was not carried into effect. An officer was also to accompany Napoleon in all his rides; this order was dispensed with within certain prescribed limits, because Napoleon had refused to ride at all on such conditions. Almost everyday brought with it some new cause of uneasiness and complaint. Sentinels were posted beneath Napoleon's windows and before his doors. This order was, however, doubtless given to prevent his being annoyed by impertinent curiosity. The French were certainly precluded from all free communication with the inhabitants of the island; but this precaution was of unquestionable necessity for the security of the Emperor's person. Las Cases complains that the passwords were perpetually changed, so that they lived in constant perplexity and apprehension of being subjected to some unforeseen insult. "Napoleon," he continues, "addressed a complaint to the Admiral, which obtained for him no redress. In the midst of these complaints the Admiral wished to introduce some ladies (who had arrived in the Doric) to Napoleon; but he declined, not approving this alternation of affronts and civilities." He, however, consented, at the request of their Colonel, to receive the officers of the 53d Regiment. After this officer took his leave, Napoleon prolonged his walk in the garden. He stopped awhile to look at a flower in one of the beds, and asked his companion if it was not a lily. It was indeed a magnificent one. The thought that he had in his mind was obvious. He then spoke of the number of times he had been wounded; and said it had been thought he had never met with these accidents from his having kept them secret as much as possible.'

It was near the end of December. One day, after a walk and a tumble in the mud, Bonaparte returned and found a packet of English newspapers, which the Grand-Marshal translated to him. This occupied him till late, and he forgot his dinner in discussing their contents. After dinner had been served Las Cases wished to continue the translation, but Napoleon would not suffer him to proceed, from consideration for the weak state of his eyes. "We must wait till to-morrow," said he. A few days afterwards the Admiral came in person to visit him, and the interview was an agreeable one. After some animated discussion it was arranged that Napoleon should henceforth ride freely about the island; that the officer should follow him only at a distance; and that visitors should be admitted to him, not with the permission of the Admiral as the Inspector of Longwood, but with that of the Grand-Marshal, who was to do the honours of the establishment. These concessions were, however, soon recalled. On the 30th of this month Piontkowsky, a Pole; who had been left behind, but whose entreaties prevailed upon the English Government, joined Bonaparte. On New-Year's Day all their little party was collected together, and Napoleon, entering into the feelings of the occasion, begged that they might breakfast and pass it together. Every day furnished some new trait of this kind.

On the 14th of April 1816 Sir Hudson Lowe, the new Governor, arrived at St. Helena. This epoch is important, as making the beginning of a continued series of accusations, and counter-accusations, by which the last five years of Napoleon's life were constantly occupied, to the great annoyance of himself and all connected with him, and possibly to the shortening of his own existence.

It would be tedious to detail the progress of this petty war, but, as a subject which has formed so great a portion of the life of Napoleon, it must not be omitted. To avoid anything which may appear like a bias against Napoleon, the details, unless when otherwise mentioned, will be derived from Las Cases, his devoted admirer.

On the first visit of the new Governor; which was the 16th of April, Napoleon refused to admit him, because he himself was ill, and also because the Governor had not asked beforehand for an audience. On the second visit the Governor, was admitted to an audience, and Napoleon seems to have taken a prejudice at first sight, as he remarked to his suite that the Governor was "hideous, and had a most ugly countenance," though he allowed he ought not to judge too hastily. The spirit of the party was shown by a remark made, that the first two days had been days of battle.

The Governor saw Napoleon again on the 30th April, and the interview was stormy. Napoleon argued with the Governor on the conduct of the Allies towards him, said they had no right to dispose of him, who was their equal and sometimes their master. He then declaimed on the eternal disgrace the English had inflicted on themselves by sending him to St. Helena; they wished to kill him by a lingering death: their conduct was worse than that of the Calabrians in shooting Murat. He talked of the cowardliness of suicide, complained of the small extent and horrid climate of St. Helena, and said it would be an act of kindness to deprive him of life at once. Sir H. Lowe said that a house of wood, fitted up with every possible accommodation, was then on its way from England for his use. Napoleon refused it at once, and exclaimed that it was not a house but an executioner and a coffin that he wanted; the house was a mockery, death would be a favour. A few minutes after Napoleon took up some reports of the campaigns of 1814, which lay on the table, and asked Sir H. Lowe if he had written them. Las Cases, after saying that the Governor replied in the affirmative, finishes his account of the interview, but according to O'Meara, Napoleon said they were full of folly and falsehood. The Governor, with a much milder reply than most men would have given, retired, and Napoleon harangued upon the sinister expression of his countenance, abused him in the coarsest manner, and made his servant throw a cup of coffee out of the window because it had stood a moment on a table near the Governor.

It was required that all persons who visited at Longwood or at Hut's Gate should make a report to the Governor, or to Sir Thomas Reade, of the conversations they had held with the French. Several additional sentinels were posted around Longwood House and grounds.

During some extremely wet and foggy weather Napoleon did not go out for several days. Messengers and letters continually succeeded one another from Plantation House. The Governor appeared anxious to see Napoleon, and was evidently distrustful, although the residents at Longwood were assured of his actual presence by the sound of his voice. He had some communications with Count Bertrand on the necessity that one of his officers should see Napoleon daily. He also went to Longwood frequently himself, and finally, after some difficulty, succeeded in obtaining an interview with Napoleon in his bedchamber, which lasted about a quarter of an hour. Some days before he sent for Mr. O'Meara, asked a variety of questions concerning the captive, walked round the house several times and before the windows, measuring and laying down the plan of a new ditch, which he said he would have dug in order to prevent the cattle from trespassing.

On the morning of the 5th of May Napoleon sent for his surgeon O'Meara to come to him. He was introduced into Napoleon's bed-chamber, a description of which is thus given: "It was about fourteen feet by twelve, and ten or eleven feet in height. The walls were lined with brown nankeen, bordered and edged with common green bordering paper, and destitute of skirting. Two small windows without pulleys, one of which was thrown up and fastened by a piece of notched wood, looked towards the camp of the 53d Regiment. There were window-curtains of white long-cloth, a small fire-place, a shabby grate and fire-irons to match, with a paltry mantelpiece of wood, painted white, upon which stood a small marble bust of his son. Above the mantelpiece hung the portrait of Maria Louisa, and four or five of young Napoleon, one of which was embroidered by the hands of his mother. A little more to the right hung also the portrait of the Empress Josephine; and to the left was suspended the alarm chamber-watch of Frederick the Great, obtained by Napoleon at Potsdam; while on the right the Consular watch, engraved with the cipher B, hung, by a chain of the plaited hair of Maria Louisa, from a pin stuck in the nankeen lining. In the right-hand corner was placed the little plain iron camp-bedstead, with green silk curtains, on which its master had reposed on the fields of Marengo and Austerlitz. Between the windows there was a chest of drawers, and a bookcase with green blinds stood on the left of the door leading to the next apartment. Four or five cane-bottomed chairs painted green were standing here and there about the room. Before the back door there was a screen covered with nankeen, and between that and the fireplace an old-fashioned sofa covered with white long-cloth, on which Napoleon reclined, dressed in his white morning-gown, white loose trousers and stockings all in one, a chequered red handkerchief upon his head, and his shirt-collar open without a cravat. His air was melancholy and troubled. Before him stood a little round table, with some books, at the foot of which lay in confusion upon the carpet a heap of those which he had already perused, and at the opposite side of the sofa was suspended Isabey's portrait of the Empress Maria Louisa, holding her son in her arms. In front of the fireplace stood Las Cases with his arms folded over his breast and some papers in one of his hands. Of all the former magnificence of the once mighty Emperor of France nothing remained but a superb wash-hand-stand containing a silver basin and water-jug of the same metal, in the lefthand corner." The object of Napoleon in sending for O'Meara on this occasion was to question him whether in their future intercourse he was to consider him in the light of a spy and a tool of the Governor or as his physician? The doctor gave a decided and satisfactory answer on this point.

"During the short interview that this Governor had with me in my bedchamber, one of the first things he proposed was to send you away," said Napoleon to O'Meara, "and that I should take his own surgeon in your place. This he repeated, and so earnest was he to gain his object that, though I gave him a flat refusal, when he was going out he turned about and again proposed it."

On the 11th a proclamation was issued by the Governor, "forbidding any persons on the island from sending letters to or receiving them from General Bonaparte or his suite, on pain of being immediately arrested and dealt with accordingly." Nothing escaped the vigilance of Sir Hudson Lowe. "The Governor," said Napoleon, "has just sent an invitation to Bertrand for General Bonaparte to come to Plantation House to meet Lady Moira. I told Bertrand to return no answer to it. If he really wanted me to see her he would have put Plantation House within the limits, but to send such an invitation, knowing I must go in charge of a guard if I wished to avail myself of it, was an insult."

Soon after came the Declaration of the Allies and the Acts of Parliament authorising the detention of Napoleon Bonaparte as a prisoner of war and disturber of the peace of Europe. Against the Bill, when brought into the House of Lords, there were two protests, those of Lord Holland and of the Duke of Sussex. These official documents did not tend to soothe the temper or raise the spirits of the French to endure their captivity.

In addition to the misery of his own captivity, Napoleon had to contend with the unmanageable humours of his own followers. As often happens with men in such circumstances, they sometimes disagreed among themselves, and part of their petulance and ill-temper fell upon their Chief. He took these little incidents deeply to heart. On one occasion he said in bitterness, "I know that I am fallen; but to feel this among you! I am aware that man is frequently unreasonable and susceptible of offence. Thus, when I am mistrustful of myself I ask, should I have been treated so at the Tuileries? This is my test."

A great deal of pains has been taken by Napoleon's adherents and others to blacken the character of Sir Hudson Lowe, and to make it appear that his sole object was to harass Napoleon and to make his life miserable. Now, although it may be questioned whether Sir Hudson Lowe was the proper person to be placed in the delicate situation of guard over the fallen Emperor, there is no doubt that quarrels and complaints began long before that officer reached the island; and the character of those complaints will show that at best the prisoners were persons very difficult to satisfy. Their detention at the Briars was one of the first causes of complaint. It was stated that the Emperor was very ill there, that he was confined "in a cage" with no attendance, that his suite was kept from him, and that he was deprived of exercise. A few pages farther in the journal of Las Cases we find the Emperor in good health, and as soon as it was announced that Longwood was ready to receive him, then it was urged that the gaolers wished to compel him to go against his will, that they desired to push their authority to the utmost, that the smell of the paint at Longwood was very disagreeable, etc. Napoleon himself was quite ready to go, and seemed much vexed when Count Bertrand and General Gourgaud arrived from Longwood with the intelligence that the place was as yet uninhabitable. His displeasure, however, was much more seriously excited by the appearance of Count Montholon with the information that all was ready at Longwood within a few minutes after receiving the contrary accounts from Bertrand and Gourgaud. He probably perceived that he was trifled with by his attendants, who endeavoured to make him believe that which suited their own convenience. We may also remark that the systematic opposition which was carried to such a great length against Sir Hudson Lowe had begun during the stay of Admiral Cockburn. His visits were refused; he was accused of caprice, arrogance, and impertinence, and he was nicknamed "the Shark" by Napoleon himself; his own calmness alone probably prevented more violent ebullitions.

The wooden house arrived at last, and the Governor waited on Napoleon to consult with him how and where it should be erected. Las Cases, who heard the dispute in an adjoining room, says that it was long and clamorous.

He gives the details in Napoleon's own words, and we have here the advantage of comparing his statement with the account transmitted by Sir Hudson Lowe to the British Government, dated 17th May 1816. The two accounts vary but little. Napoleon admits that he was thrown quite out of temper, that he received the Governor with his stormy countenance, looked furiously at him, and made no reply to his information of the arrival of the house but by a significant look. He told him that he wanted nothing, nor would receive anything at his hands; that he supposed he was to be put to death by poison or the sword; the poison would be difficult to administer, but he had the means of doing it with the sword. The sanctuary of his abode should not be violated, and the troops should not enter his house but by trampling on his corpse. He then alluded to an invitation sent to him by Sir Hudson Lows to meet Lady Loudon at his house, and said there could not be an act of more refined cruelty than inviting him to his table by the title of "General," to make him an object of ridicule or amusement to his guests. What right had he to call him "General" Bonaparte? He would not be deprived of his dignity by him, nor by any one in the world. He certainly should have condescended to visit Lady Loudon had she been within his limits, as he did not stand upon strict etiquette with a woman, but he should have deemed that he was conferring an honour upon her. He would not consider himself a prisoner of war, but was placed in his present position by the most horrible breach of trust. After a few more words he dismissed the Governor without once more alluding to the house which was the object of the visit. The fate of this unfortunate house may be mentioned here. It was erected after a great many disputes, but was unfortunately surrounded by a sunk fence and ornamental railing. This was immediately connected in Napoleon's mind with the idea of a fortification; it was impossible to remove the impression that the ditch and palisade were intended to secure his person. As soon as the objection was made known, Sir Hudson Lowe ordered the ground to be levelled and the rails taken away. But before this was quite completed Napoleon's health was too much destroyed to permit his removal, and the house was never occupied.

Napoleon seems to have felt that he had been too violent in his conduct. He admitted, when at table with his suite a few days after, that he had behaved very ill, and that in any other situation he should blush for what he had done. "I could have wished, for his sake," he said, "to see him evince a little anger, or pull the door violently after him when he went away." These few words let us into a good deal of Napoleon's character: he liked to intimidate, but his vehement language was received with a calmness and resolute forbearance to which he was quite unaccustomed, and he consequently grew more angry as his anger was less regarded.

The specimens here given of the disputes with Sir Hudson Lowe may probably suffice: a great many more are furnished by Las Cases, O'Meara, and other partisans of Napoleon, and even they always make him the aggressor. Napoleon himself in his cooler moments seemed to admit this; after the most violent quarrel with the Governor, that of the 18th of August 1816, which utterly put an end to anything like decent civility between the parties; he allowed that he had used the Governor very ill, that he repeatedly and purposely offended him, and that Sir Hudson Lowe had not in a single instance shown a want of respect, except perhaps that he retired too abruptly.

Great complaints were made of the scanty way in which the table of the exiles was supplied; and it was again and again alleged by them that they had scarcely anything to eat. The wine, too, was said to be execrable, so bad that in fact it could not be drunk; and, of such stuff as it was, only one bottle a day was allowed to each person—an allowance which Las Cases calls ridiculously small. Thus pressed, but partly for effect, Napoleon resolved to dispose of his plate in monthly proportions; and as he knew that some East India captains had offered as much as a hundred guineas for a single plate, in order to preserve a memorial of him, he determined that what was sold should be broken up, the arms erased, and no trace left which could show that they had ever been his. The only portions left uninjured were the little eagles with which some of the dish-covers were mounted. These last fragments were objects of veneration for the attendants of Napoleon, they were looked upon as relics, with a feeling at once melancholy and religious. When the moment came for breaking up the plate Las Cases bears testimony to the painful emotions and real grief produced among the servants. They could not, without the utmost reluctance, bring themselves to apply the hammer to those objects of their veneration.

The island of St. Helena was regularly visited by East India ships on the return voyage, which touched there to take in water, and to leave gunpowder for the use of the garrison. On such occasions there were always persons anxious to pay a visit to the renowned captive. The regulation of those visits was calculated to protect Napoleon from being annoyed by the idle curiosity of strangers, to which he professed a great aversion. Such persons as wished to wait upon him were, in the first place, obliged to apply to the Governor, by whom their names were forwarded to Count Bertrand. This gentleman, as Grand-Marshal of the household, communicated the wishes of those persons to Napoleon, and in case of a favourable reply fixed the hour for an interview.

Those visitors whom Napoleon admitted were chiefly persons of rank and distinction, travellers from distant countries, or men who had distinguished themselves in the scientific world, and who could communicate interesting information in exchange for the gratification they received. Some of those persons who were admitted to interviews with him have published narratives of their conversation, and all agree in extolling the extreme grace, propriety, and appearance of benevolence manifested by Bonaparte while holding these levees. His questions were always put with great tact, and on some subject with which the person interrogated was well acquainted, so as to induce him to bring forth any new or curious information of which he might be possessed.

Captain Basil Hall, in August 1817, when in command of the Lyra, had an interview with the Emperor, of whom he says: "Bonaparte struck me as differing considerably from the pictures and busts' I had seen of him. His face and figure looked much broader and more square—larger, indeed, in every way than any representation I had met with. His corpulency, at this time universally reported to be excessive, was by no means remarkable. His flesh looked, on the contrary, firm and muscular. There was not the least trace of colour in his cheeks; in fact his skin was more like marble than ordinary flesh. Not the smallest trace of a wrinkle was discernible on his brow, nor an approach to a furrow on any part of his countenance. His health and spirits, judging from appearances, were excellent, though at this period it was generally believed in England that he was fast sinking under a complication of diseases, and that his spirits were entirely gone. His manner of speaking was rather slow than otherwise, and perfectly distinct; he waited with great patience and kindness for my answers to his questions, and a reference to Count Bertrand was necessary only once during the whole conversation. The brilliant and sometimes dazzling expression of his eye could not be overlooked. It was not, however, a permanent lustre, for it was only remarkable when he was excited by some point of particular interest. It is impossible to imagine an expression of more entire mildness, I may almost call it of benignity and kindness, than that which played over his features during the whole interview. If, therefore he were at this time out of health and in low spirits, his power of self-command must have been even more extraordinary than is generally supposed, for his whole deportment, his conversation, and the expression of his countenance indicated a frame in perfect health and a mind at ease."

The manner assumed by Napoleon in the occasional interviews he had with such visitors was so very opposite to that which he constantly maintained towards the authorities in whose custody he was placed, that we can scarcely doubt he was acting a part in one of those situations. It was suggested by Mr. Ellis that he either wished, by means of his continual complaints, to keep alive his interest in England, where he flattered himself there was a party favourable to him, or that his troubled mind found an occupation in the annoyance which he caused to the Governor. Every attempt at conciliation on the part of Sir Hudson Lowe furnished fresh causes for irritation. He sent fowling-pieces to Longwood, and the thanks returned were a reply from Napoleon that it was an insult to send fowling-pieces where there was no game. An invitation to a ball was resented vehemently, and descanted upon by the French party as a great offence. Sir Hudson Lowe at one time sent a variety of clothes and other articles received from England which he imagined might be useful at Longwood. Great offence was taken at this; they were treated, they said, like paupers; the articles, ought to have been left at the Governor's house, and a list sent respectfully to the household, stating that such things were at their command if they wanted them.

An opinion has already been expressed that much of this annoyance was due to the offended pride of Napoleon's attendants, who were at first certainly far more captious than himself. He admitted as much himself on one occasion in a conversation with O'Meara. He said, "Las Cases certainly was greatly irritated against Sir Hudson, and contributed materially towards forming the impressions existing in my mind." He attributed this to the sensitive mind of Las Cases, which he said was peculiarly alive to the ill-treatment Napoleon and himself had been subjected to. Sir Hudson Lowe also felt this, and remarked, like Sir George Cockburn, on more than one occasion, that he always found Napoleon himself more reasonable than the persons about him.

A fertile source of annoyance was the resolution of Napoleon not upon any terms to acknowledge himself a prisoner, and his refusal to submit to such regulations as would render his captivity less burdensome. More than once the attendance of an officer was offered to be discontinued if he would allow himself to be seen once every day, and promise to take no means of escaping. "If he were to give me the whole of the island," said Napoleon, "on condition that I would pledge my word not to attempt an escape, I would not accept it; because it would be equivalent to acknowledging myself a prisoner, although at the same time I would not make the attempt. I am here by force, and not by right. If I had been taken at Waterloo perhaps I might have had no hesitation in accepting it, although even in that case it would be contrary to the law of nations, as now there is no war. If they were to offer me permission to reside in England on similar conditions I would refuse it." The very idea of exhibiting himself to an officer every day, though but for a moment, was repelled with indignation. He even kept loaded pistols to shoot any person who should attempt an intrusion on his privacy. It is stated in a note in O'Meara's journal that "the Emperor was so firmly impressed with the idea that an attempt would be made forcibly to intrude on his privacy, that from a short time after the departure of Sir George Cockburn he always kept four or five pairs of loaded pistols and some swords in his apartment, with which he was determined to despatch the first who entered against his will." It seems this practice was continued to his death.

Napoleon continued to pass the mornings in dictating his Memoirs and the evenings in reading or conversation. He grew fonder of Racine, but his favourite was Corneille. He repeated that, had he lived in his time, he would have made him a prince. He had a distaste to Voltaire, and found considerable fault with his dramas, perhaps justly, as conveying opinions rather than sentiments. He criticised his Mahomet, and said he had made him merely an impostor and a tyrant, without representing him as a great man. This was owing to Voltaire's religious and political antipathies; for those who are free from common prejudices acquire others of their own in their stead, to which they are equally bigoted, and which they bring forward on all occasions. When the evening passed off in conversation without having recourse to books he considered it a point gained.

Some one having asked the Emperor which was the greatest battle that he had fought, he replied it was difficult to answer that question without inquiring what was implied by the greatest battle. "Mine," continued he, "cannot be judged of separately: they formed a portion of extensive plans. They must therefore be estimated by their consequences. The battle of Marengo, which was so long undecided, procured for us the command of all Italy. Ulm annihilated a whole army; Jena laid the whole Prussian monarchy at our feet; Friedland opened the Russian empire to us; and Eckmuhl decided the fate of a war. The battle of the Moskwa was that in which the greatest talent was displayed, and by which we obtained the fewest advantages. Waterloo, where everything failed, would, had victory crowned our efforts, have saved France and given peace to Europe."

Madame Montholon having inquired what troops he considered the best, "Those which are victorious, madam," replied the Emperor. "But," added he, "soldiers are capricious and inconstant, like you ladies. The best troops were the Carthaginians under Hannibal, the Romans under the Scipios, the Macedonians under Alexander, and the Prussians under Frederick." He thought, however, that the French soldiers were of all others those which could most easily be rendered the best, and preserved so. "With my complete guard of 40,000 or 50,000 men I would have undertaken to march through Europe. It is perhaps possible to produce troops as good as those that composed my army of Italy and Austerlitz, but certainly none can ever surpass them."

The anniversary of the battle of Waterloo produced a visible impression on the Emperor. "Incomprehensible day!" said he, dejectedly; "concurrence of unheard-of fatalities! Grouchy, Ney, D'Erlon—was there treachery or was it merely misfortune? Alas! poor France!" Here he covered his eyes with his hands. "And yet," said he, "all that human skill could do was accomplished! All was not lost until the moment when all had succeeded." A short time afterwards, resuming the subject, he exclaimed, "In that extraordinary campaign, thrice, in less than a week, I saw the certain triumph of France slip through my fingers. Had it not been for a traitor I should have annihilated the enemy at the outset of the campaign. I should have destroyed him at Ligny if my left wing had only done its duty. I should have destroyed him again at Waterloo if my right had seconded me. Singular defeat, by which, notwithstanding the most fatal catastrophe, the glory of the conquered has not suffered."

We shall here give Napoleon's own opinion of the battle of Waterloo. "The plan of the battle," said he, "will not in the eyes of the historian reflect any credit on Lord Wellington as a general. In the first place, he ought not to have given battle with the armies divided. They ought to have been united and encamped before the 15th. In the next, the choice of ground was bad; because if he had been beaten he could not have retreated, as there was only one road leading through the forest in his rear. He also committed a fault which might have proved the destruction of all his army, without its ever having commenced the campaign, or being drawn out in battle; he allowed himself to be surprised. On the 15th I was at Charleroi, and had beaten the Prussians without his knowing anything about it. I had gained forty-eight hours of manoeuvres upon him, which was a great object; and if some of my generals had shown that vigour and genius which they had displayed on other occasions, I should have taken his army in cantonments without ever fighting a battle. But they were discouraged, and fancied that they saw an army of 100,000 men everywhere opposed to them. I had not time enough myself to attend to the minutiae of the army. I counted upon surprising and cutting Wellington up in detail. I knew of Bulow's arrival at eleven o'clock, but I did not regard it. I had still eighty chances out of a hundred in my favour. Notwithstanding the great superiority of force against me I was convinced that I should obtain the victory, I had about 70,000 men, of whom 15,000 were cavalry. I had also 260 pieces of cannon; but my troops were so good that I esteemed them sufficient to beat 120,000. Of all those troops, however, I only reckoned the English as being able to cope with my own. The others I thought little of. I believe that of English there were from 35,000 to 40,000. These I esteemed to be as brave and as good as my own troops; the English army was well known latterly on the Continent, and besides, your nation possesses courage and energy. As to the Prussians, Belgians, and others, half the number of my troops, were sufficient to beat them. I only left 34,000 men to take care of the Prussians. The chief causes of the loss of that battle were, first of all, Grouchy's great tardiness and neglect in executing his orders; next, the 'grenadiers a cheval' and the cavalry under General Guyot, which I had in reserve, and which were never to leave me, engaged without orders and without my knowledge; so that after the last charge, when the troops were beaten and the English cavalry advanced, I had not a single corps of cavalry in reserve to resist them, instead of one which I esteemed to be equal to double their own number. In consequence of this the English attacked, succeeded, and all was lost. There was no means of rallying. The youngest general would not have committed the fault of leaving an army entirely without reserve, which, however, occurred here, whether in consequence of treason or not I cannot say. These were the two principal causes of the loss of the battle of Waterloo."

"If Lord Wellington had intrenched himself," continued Napoleon, "I would not have attacked him. As a general, his plan did not show talent. He certainly displayed great courage and obstinacy; but a little must be taken away even from that when you consider that he had no means of retreat, and that had he made the attempt not a man of his army would have escaped. First, to the firmness and bravery of his troops, for the English fought with the greatest courage and obstinacy, he is principally indebted for the victory, and not to his own conduct as a general; and next, to the arrival of Blücher, to whom the victory is more to be attributed than to Wellington, and more credit is due as a general; because he, although beaten the day before, assembled his troops, and brought them into action in the evening. I believe, however," continued Napoleon, "that Wellington is a man of great firmness. The glory of such a victory is a great thing; but in the eye of the historian his military reputation will gain nothing by it."

"I always had a high opinion of your seamen," said Napoleon one day to O'Meara, in a conversation arising out of the expedition to Algiers. "When I was returning from Holland along with the Empress Maria Louisa we stopped to rest at Givet. During the night a violent storm of wind and rain came on, which swelled the Meuse so much that the bridge of boats over it was carried away. I was very anxious to depart, and ordered all the boatmen in the place to be assembled that I might be enabled to cross the river. They said that the waters were so high that it would be impossible to pass before two or three days. I questioned some of them, and soon discovered that they were fresh-water seamen. I then recollected that there were English prisoners in the barracks, and ordered that some of the oldest and best seamen among them should be brought before me to the banks of the river. The waters were very high, and the current rapid and dangerous. I asked them if they could join a number of boats together so that I might pass over. They answered that it was possible, but hazardous. I desired them to set about it instantly. In the course of a few hours they succeeded in effecting what the others had pronounced to be impossible, and I crossed before the evening was over. I ordered those who had worked at it to receive a sum of money each, a suit of clothes, and their liberty. Marchand was with me at the time."

In December 1816 Las Cases was compelled to leave St. Helena. He had written a letter to Lucien Bonaparte, and entrusted it to a mulatto servant to be forwarded to Europe. He was detected; and as he was thus endeavouring to carry on (contrary to the regulations of the island) a clandestine correspondence with Europe, Las Cases and his son were sent off, first to the Cape and then to England, where they were only allowed to land to be sent to Dover and shipped off to Ostend.

Not long after their arrival at St. Helena, Madame Bertrand gave birth to a son, and when Napoleon went to visit her she said, "I have the honour of presenting to your Majesty the first French subject who has entered Longwood without the permission of Lord Bathurst."

It has been generally supposed that Napoleon was a believer in the doctrine of predestination. The following conversation with Las Cases clearly decides that point. "Pray," said he, "am I not thought to be given to a belief in predestination?"—"Yes, Sire; at least by many people."—"Well, well! let them say what they please, one may sometimes be tempted to set a part, and it may occasionally be useful. But what are men? How much easier is it to occupy their attention and to strike their imaginations by absurdities than by rational ideas! But can a man of sound sense listen for one moment to such a doctrine? Either predestination admits the existence of free-will, or it rejects it. If it admits it, what kind of predetermined result can that be which a simple resolution, a step, a word, may alter or modify ad infinitum? If predestination, on the contrary, rejects the existence of free-will it is quite another question; in that case a child need only be thrown into its cradle as soon as it is born, there is no necessity for bestowing the least care upon it, for if it be irrevocably decreed that it is to live, it will grow though no food should be given to it. You see that such a doctrine cannot be maintained; predestination is but a word without meaning. The Turks themselves, the professors of predestination, are not convinced of the doctrine, for in that case medicine would not exist in Turkey, and a man residing in a third floor would not take the trouble of going down stairs, but would immediately throw himself out of the window.

You see to what a string of absurdities that will lead?"

The following traits are characteristic of the man. In the common intercourse of life, and his familiar conversation, Napoleon mutilated the names most familiar to him, even French names; yet this would not have occurred on any public occasion. He has been heard many times during his walks to repeat the celebrated speech of Augustus in Corneille's tragedy, and he has never missed saying, "Take a seat, Sylla," instead of Cinna. He would frequently create names according to his fancy, and when he had once adopted them they remained fixed in his mind, although they were pronounced properly a hundred times a day in his hearing; but he would have been struck if others had used them as he had altered them. It was the same thing with respect to orthography; in general he did not attend to it, yet if the copies which were made contained any faults of spelling he would have complained of it. One day Napoleon said to Las Cases, "Your orthography is not correct, is it?" This question gave occasion to a sarcastic smile from a person who stood near, who thought it was meant to convey a reproach. The Emperor, who saw this, continued, "At least I suppose it is not, for a man occupied with important public business, a minister, for instance, cannot and need not attend to orthography. His ideas must flow faster than his hand can trace them, he has only time to dwell upon essentials; he must put words in letters, and phrases in words, and let the scribes make it out afterwards." Napoleon indeed left a great deal for the copyists to do; he was their torment; his handwriting actually resembled hieroglyphics—he often could not decipher it himself. Las Cases' son was one day reading to him a chapter of The Campaign of Italy; on a sudden he stopped short, unable to make out the writing. "The little blockhead," said Napoleon, "cannot read his own handwriting."—"It is not mine, Sire."—"And whose, then?"—"Your Majesty's."—"How so, you little rogue; do you mean to insult me?" The Emperor took the manuscript, tried a long while to read it, and at last threw it down, saying, "He is right; I cannot tell myself what is written." He has often sent the copyists to Las Cases to read what he had himself been unable to decipher.

We are now approaching the last melancholy epoch of Napoleon's life, when he first felt the ravages of that malady which finally put a period to his existence. Occasional manifestations of its presence had been exhibited for some years, but his usual health always returned after every attack, and its fatal nature was not suspected, although Napoleon himself had several times said that he should die of a scirrhus in the pylorus, the disease which killed his father, and which the physicians of Montpelier declared would be hereditary in his family. About the middle of the year 1818 it was observed that his health grew gradually worse, and it was thought proper by O'Meara to report to the Governor the state in which he was. Even on these occasions Napoleon seized the opportunity for renewing his claim to the title of Emperor. He insisted that the physician should not send any bulletin whatever unless he named him in it by his Imperial designation. O'Meara explained that the instructions of his Government and the orders of Sir Hudson Lowe prohibited him from using the term; but it was in vain. After some difficulty it was agreed upon that the word "patient" should be used instead of the title of General, which caused so much offence, and this substitution got rid of the difficulty.

O'Meara afterwards proposed to call in the assistance of Dr. Baxter, the principal medical officer of the island, but this offer Napoleon refused at once, alleging that, although "it was true he looked like an honest man, he was too much attached to that hangman" (Lows), he also persisted in rejecting the aid of medicine, and determined to take no exercise out-of-doors as long as he should be subjected to the challenge of sentinels. To a representation that his determination might convert a curable to a fatal malady, he replied, "I shall at least have the consolation that my death will be an eternal dishonour to the English nation who sent me to this climate to die under the hands of . . ."

An important incident in Napoleon's monotonous life was the removal of O'Meara, who had attended him as his physician from the time of his arrival on the island. The removal of this gentleman, was occasioned by the suspicion of similar conduct to that which brought about the dismissal of Las Cases twenty months previously, namely, the carrying on secret correspondence with persons out of the island. Napoleon complained bitterly of the loss of his medical attendant, though he had most assuredly very seldom attended to his advice, and repelled as an insult the proffered assistance of Dr. Baxter, insinuating that the Governor wished to have his life in his power. Some time after Dr. Stokes, a naval surgeon, was called in, but withdrawn and eventually tried by court-martial for furnishing information to the French at Longwood. After this Napoleon expressed his determination to admit no more visits from any English physician whatever, and Cardinal Fesch was requested by the British Ministry to select some physician of reputation in Italy who should be sent to St. Helena to attend on Napoleon. The choice fell on Dr. Antommarchi, a young surgeon, who was accordingly sent to St. Helena in company with two Catholic priests, the Abbes Buonavita and Vignale, and two domestics, in compliance with the wish of Napoleon to that effect. The party reached the island on 10th September 1819.

On his first visit the Emperor overwhelmed Antommarchi with questions concerning his mother and family, the Princess Julie (wife of Joseph), and Las Cases, whom Antommarchi had seen in passing through Frankfort, expatiated with satisfaction on the retreat which he had at one time meditated in Corsica, entered into some discussions with the doctor on his profession, and then directed his attention to the details of his disorder. While he examined the symptoms the Emperor continued his remarks. They were sometimes serious, sometimes lively; kindness, indignation, gaiety, were expressed by turns in his words and in his countenance. "Well, doctor!" he exclaimed, "what is your opinion? Am I to trouble much longer the digestion of Kings?"—"You will survive them, Sire."—"Aye, I believe you; they will not be able to subject to the ban of Europe the fame of our victories, it will traverse ages, it will proclaim the conquerors and the conquered, those who were generous and those who were not so; posterity will judge, I do not dread its decision."—"This after-life belongs to you of right. Your name will never be repeated with admiration without recalling those inglorious warriors so basely leagued against a single man. But you are not near your end, you have yet a long career to run."—"No, Doctor! I cannot hold out long under this frightful climate."—"Your excellent constitution is proof against its pernicious effects."—"It once did not yield to the strength of mind with which nature has endowed me, but the transition from a life of action to a complete seclusion has ruined all. I have grown fat, my energy is gone, the bow is unstrung." Antommarchi did not try to combat an opinion but too well-founded, but diverted the conversation to another subject. "I resign myself," said Napoleon, "to your direction. Let medicine give the order, I submit to its decisions. I entrust my health to your care. I owe you the detail of the habits I have acquired, of the affections to which I am subject.

"The hours at which I obey the injunctions of nature are in general extremely irregular. I sleep, I eat according to circumstances or the situation in which I am placed; my sleep is ordinarily sound and tranquil. If pain or any accident interrupt it I jump out of bed, call for a light, walk, set to work, and fix my attention on some subject; sometimes I remain in the dark, change my apartment, lie down in another bed, or stretch myself on the sofa. I rise at two, three, or four in the morning; I call for some one to keep me company, amuse myself with recollections or business, and wait for the return of day. I go out as soon as dawn appears, take a stroll, and when the sun shows itself I reenter and go to bed again, where I remain a longer or shorter time, according as the day promises to turn out. If it is bad, and I feel irritation and uneasiness, I have recourse to the method I have just mentioned. I change my posture, pass from my bed to the sofa, from the sofa to the bed, seek and find a degree of freshness. I do not describe to you my morning costume; it has nothing to do with the sufferings I endure, and besides, I do not wish to deprive you of the pleasure of your surprise when you see it. These ingenious contrivances carry me on to nine or ten o'clock, sometimes later. I then order the breakfast to be brought, which I take from time to time in my bath, but most frequently in the garden. Either Bertrand or Montholon keep me company, often both of them. Physicians have the right of regulating the table; it is proper that I should give you an account of mine. Well, then, a basin of soup, two plates of meat, one of vegetables, a salad when I can take it, compose the whole service; half a bottle of claret; which I dilute with a good deal of water, serves me for drink; I drink a little of it pure towards the end of the repast. Sometimes, when I feel fatigued, I substitute champagne for claret, it is a certain means of giving a fillip to the stomach."

The doctor having expressed his surprise at Napoleon's temperance, he replied, "In my marches with the army of Italy I never failed to put into the bow of my saddle a bottle of wine, some bread, and a cold fowl. This provision sufficed for the wants of the day,—I may even say that I often shared it with others. I thus gained time. I eat fast, masticate little, my meals do not consume my hours. This is not what you will approve the most, but in my present situation what signifies it? I am attacked with a liver complaint, a malady which is general in this horrible climate."

Antommarchi, having gained his confidence, now became companion as well as physician to the Emperor, and sometimes read with him. He eagerly turned over the newspapers when they arrived, and commented freely on their contents. "It is amusing," he would say, "to see the sage measures resorted to by the Allies to make people forget my tyranny!" On one occasion he felt more languid than ordinary, and lighting on the 'Andromache' of Racine; he took up the book, began to read, but soon let it drop from his hands. He had come to the famous passage where the mother describes her being allowed to see her son once a day.

He was moved, covered his face with his hands, and, saying that he was too much affected, desired to be left alone. He grew calmer, fell asleep, and when he awoke, desired Antommarchi to be called again. He was getting ready to shave, and the doctor was curious to witness the operation. He was in his shirt, his head uncovered, with two valets at his side, one holding the glass and a towel, the other the rest of the apparatus. The Emperor spread the soap over one side of his face, put down the brush, wiped his hands and mouth, took a razor dipped in hot water and shaved the right side with singular dexterity. "Is it done, Noverraz?"—"Yes, Sire."—"Well, then, face about. Come, villain, quick, stand still." The light fell on the left side, which, after applying the lather, he shaved in the same manner and with the same dexterity. He drew his hand over his chin. "Raise the glass. Am I quite right?"— "Quite so."—"Not a hair has escaped me: what say you?"—"No, Sire," replied the valet de chambre. "No! I think I perceive one. Lift up the glass, place it in a better light. How, rascal! Flattery? You deceive me at St. Helena? On this rock? You, too, are an accomplice." With this he gave them both a box on the ear, laughed, and joked in the most pleasant manner possible.

An almost incredible instance of the determination of the exiles to make as many enemies as they possibly could was exhibited to Antommarchi on his arrival at Longwood. He states that before he was permitted to enter on his functions as surgeon he was required to take an oath that he would not communicate with the English, and that he would more especially avoid giving them the least information respecting the progress of Napoleon's disorder. He was not allowed to see his illustrious patient until the oath was taken. After exacting such an oath from his physician the attendants of Bonaparte had little right to complain, as they did, that the real state of his disorder was purposely concealed from the world by the English Government. It is more than probable that the constant attempts observed to throw mystery and secrecy around them must have tended to create the suspicion of escape, and to increase the consequent rigour of the regulations maintained by the Governor.

Soon after the arrival of the priests Napoleon determined, we may suppose partly in jest, to elevate one of them to the dignity of bishop, and he chose for a diocese the Jumna. "The last box brought from Europe had been broken open," says Antommarchi; "it contained the vases and church ornaments. "Stop," said Napoleon, "this is the property of St. Peter; have a care who touches it; send for the abbes—but talking of the abbes, do you know that the Cardinal [Fesch] is a poor creature? He sends me missionaries and propagandists, as if I were a penitent, and as if a whole string of their Eminences had not always attended at my chapel. I will do what he ought to have done; I possess the right of investiture, and I shall use it." Abbe Buonavita was just entering the room, "I give you the episcopal mitre."—"Sire!"—"I restore it to you; you shall wear it in spite of the heretics; they will not again take it from you."— "But, Sire!"—"I cannot add to it so rich a benefice as that of Valencia, which Suchet had given you, but at any rate your see shall be secure from the chances of battles. I appoint you Bishop of—let me see—of the Jumna. The vast countries through which that river flows were on the point of entering into alliance with me—all was in readiness, all were going to march. We were about to give the finishing blow to England." The speech concluded with an order to Count Montholon to procure the necessary dress for the abbe in order to strike with awe all the heretics. The upshot of the whole was, that the scarlet and violet coloured clothes necessary to furnish the new bishop with the only valuable portion of his temporalities, his dress, could not be procured in the island, and the abbe remained an abbe in spite of the investiture, and the whole farce was forgotten.

We occasionally see the Exile in better moods, when he listened to the voice of reason, and thought less of the annoyances inseparable from the state to which his ambition, or as he himself always averred, his destiny, had reduced him. He had for a long time debarred himself from all exercise, having, as he expressed it, determined not to expose himself to the insult of being accompanied on his ride by a British officer; or the possibility of being challenged by a sentinel. One day when he complained of his inactive life his medical attendant recommended the exercise of digging the ground; the idea was instantly seized upon by Napoleon with his characteristic ardour. Noverraz, his chasseur, who had been formerly accustomed to rural occupations, was honoured with the title of head gardener, and under his directions Napoleon proceeded to work with great vigour. He sent for Antommarchi to witness his newly acquired dexterity in the use of the spade. "Well, Doctor," said he to him, "are you satisfied with your patient—is he obedient enough? This is better than your pills, Dottoraccio; you shall not physic me any more." At first he soon got fatigued, and complained much of the weakness of his body and delicacy of his hands; but "never mind," said he, "I have always accustomed my body to bend to my will, and I shall bring it to do so now, and inure it to the exercise." He soon grew fond of his new employment, and pressed all the inhabitants of Longwood into the service. Even the ladies had great difficulty to avoid being set to work. He laughed at them, urged them, entreated them, and used all his arts of persuasion, particularly with Madame Bertrand. He assured her that the exercise of gardening was much better than all the doctor's prescriptions—that it was in fact one of his prescriptions. But in this instance his eloquence failed in its effect, and he was obliged, though with much reluctance, to desist from his attempts to make lady gardeners.

But in recompense he had willing labourers on the part of the gentlemen. Antommarchi says, "The Emperor urged us, excited us, and everything around us soon assumed a different aspect. Here was an excavation, there a basin or a road. We made alleys, grottoes, cascades; the appearance of the ground had now some life and diversity. We planted willows, oaks, peach-trees, to give a little shade round the house. Having completed the ornamental part of our labours we turned to the useful. We divided the ground, we manured it, and sowed it with abundance of beans, peas, and every vegetable that grows in the island." In the course of their labours they found that a tank would be of great use to hold water, which might be brought by pipes from a spring at a distance of 3000 feet.

For this laborious attempt it was absolutely necessary to procure additional forces, and a party of Chinese, of whom there are many on the island, was engaged to help them. These people were much amused at Napoleon's working-dress, which was a jacket and large trousers, with an enormous straw hat to shield him from the sun, and sandals. He pitied those poor fellows who suffered from the heat of the sun, and made each of them a present of a large hat like his own. After much exertion the basin was finished, the pipes laid, and the water began to flow into it. Napoleon stocked his pond with gold-fish, which he placed in it with his own hands. He would remain by the pond for hours together, at a time when he was so weak that he could hardly support himself. He would amuse himself by following the motion of the fishes, throwing bread to them, studying their ways, taking an interest in their loves and their quarrels, and endeavouring with anxiety to find out points of resemblance between their motives and those of mankind. He often sent for his attendants to communicate his remarks to them, and directed their observations to any peculiarities he had observed. His favourites at last sickened, they struggled, floated on the water, and died one after another. He was deeply affected by this, and remarked to Antommarchi, "You see very well that there is a fatality attached to me. Everything I love, everything that belongs to me, is immediately struck: heaven and mankind unite to persecute me." From this time he visited them daily in spite of sickness or bad weather, nor did his anxiety diminish until it was discovered that a coppery cement, with which the bottom of the basin was plastered, had poisoned the water. The fish which were not yet dead were then taken out and put into a tub.

Napoleon appears to have taken peculiar interest in observing the instincts of animals, and comparing their practices and propensities with those of men. A rainy day, during which the digging of the tank could not be proceeded with, gave occasion for some observations on the actions of a number of ants, which had made a way into his bedroom, climbed upon a table on which some sugar usually stood, and taken possession of the sugar-basin. He would not allow the industrious little insects to be disturbed in their plans; but he now and then moved the sugar, followed their manoeuvres, and admired the activity and industry they displayed until they found it again; this they had been sometimes even two or three days in effecting, though they always succeeded at last. He then surrounded the basin with water, but the ants still reached it; he finally employed vinegar, and the insects were unable to get through the new obstacle.

But the slight activity of mind that now remained to him was soon to be exchanged for the languor and gloom of sickness, with but few intervals between positive suffering and the most distressing lowness of spirits. Towards the end of the year 1820 he walked with difficulty, and required assistance even to reach a chair in his garden. He became nearly incapable of the slightest action; his legs swelled; the pains in his side and back were increased; he was troubled with nausea, profuse sweats, loss of appetite, and was subject to frequent faintings. "Here I am, Doctor," said he one day, "at my last cast. No more energy and strength left: I bend under the load . . . I am going. I feel that my hour is come."

Some days after, as he lay on his couch, he feelingly expressed to Antommarchi the vast change which had taken place within him. He recalled for a few moments the vivid recollection of past times, and compared his former energy with the weakness which he was then sinking under.

The news of the death of his sister Elisa also affected him deeply. After a struggle with his feelings, which had nearly overpowered him, he rose, supported himself on Antommarchi's arm; and regarding him steadfastly, said, "Well, Doctor! you see Elisa has just shown me the way. Death, which seemed to have forgotten my family, has begun to strike it; my turn cannot be far off. What think you?"—"Your Majesty is in no danger: you are still reserved for some glorious enterprise."— "Ah, Doctor! I have neither strength nor activity nor energy; I am no longer Napoleon. You strive in vain to give me hopes, to recall life ready to expire. Your care can do nothing in spite of fate: it is immovable: there is no appeal from its decisions. The next person of our family who will follow Elisa to the tomb is that great Napoleon who hardly exists, who bends under the yoke, and who still, nevertheless keeps Europe in alarm. Behold, my good friend, how I look on my situation! As for me, all is over: I repeat it to you, my days will soon close on this miserable rock."—"We returned," says Antommarchi, "into his chamber. Napoleon lay down' in bed. 'Close my windows,' he said; leave me to myself; I will send for you by-and-by. What a delightful thing rest is! I would not exchange it for all the thrones in the world! What an alteration! How I am fallen! I, whose activity was boundless, whose mind never slumbered, am now plunged into a lethargic stupor, so that it requires an effort even to raise my eyelids. I sometimes dictated to four or five secretaries, who wrote as fast as words could be uttered, but then I was NAPOLEON—now I am no longer anything. My strength—my faculties forsake me. I do not live—I merely exist.'"

From this period the existence of Napoleon was evidently drawing to a close, his days were counted. Whole hours, and even days, were either passed in gloomy silence or spent in pain, accompanied by distressing coughs, and all the melancholy signs of the approach of death. He made a last effort to ride a few miles round Longwood on the 22d of January 1821, but it exhausted his strength, and from that time his only exercise was in the calash. Even that slight motion soon became too fatiguing.

He now kept his room, and no longer stirred out. His disorder and his weakness increased upon him. He still was able to eat something, but very little, and with a worse appetite than ever. "Ah! doctor," he exclaimed, "how I suffer! Why did the cannon-balls spare me only to die in this deplorable manner? I that was so active, so alert, can now scarcely raise my eyelids!"

His last airing was on the 17th of March. The disease increased, and Antommarchi, who was much alarmed, obtained with some difficulty permission to see an English physician. He held a consultation, on the 26th of March, with Dr. Arnott of the 20th Regiment; but Napoleon still refused to take medicine, and often repeated his favourite saying: "Everything that must happen is written down, our hour is marked, and it is not in our power to take from time a portion which nature refuses us." He continued to grow worse, and at last consented to see Dr. Arnott, whose first visit was on the 1st of April. He was introduced into the chamber of the patient, which was darkened, and into which Napoleon did not suffer any light to be brought, examined his pulse and the other symptoms, and was requested to repeat his visit the next day. Napoleon was now within a month of his death, and although he occasionally spoke with the eloquence and vehemence he had so often exhibited, his mind was evidently giving way. The reported appearance of a comet was taken as a token of his death. He was excited, and exclaimed with emotion, "A comet! that was the precursor of the death of Caesar."

On the 3d of April the symptoms of the disorder had become so alarming that Antommarchi informed Bertrand and Montholon he thought Napoleon's danger imminent, and that Napoleon ought to take steps to put his affairs in order. He was now attacked by fever and by violent thirst, which often interrupted his sleep in the night. On the 14th Napoleon found himself in better spirits, and talked with Dr. Arnott on the merits of Marlborough, whose Campaigns he desired him to present to the 20th Regiment, learning that they did not, possess a copy in their library.

On the 15th of April Napoleon's doors were closed to all but Montholon and Marchand, and it appeared that he had been making his Will. On the 19th he was better, was free from pain, sat up, and ate a little. He was in good spirits, and wished them to read to him. As General Montholon with the others expressed his satisfaction at this improvement he smiled gently, and said, "You deceive yourselves, my friends: I am, it is true, somewhat better, but I feel no less that my end draws near. When I am dead you will have the agreeable consolation of returning to Europe. One will meet his relations, another his friends; and as for me, I shall behold my brave companions-in-arms in the Elysian Fields. Yes," he went on, raising his voice, "Kléber, Desaix, Bessières, Duroc, Ney, Murat, Massena, Berthier, all will come to greet me: they will talk to me of what we have done together. I will recount to them the latest events of my life. On seeing me they will become once more intoxicated with enthusiasm and glory. We will discourse of our wars with the Scipios, Hannibal, Caesar, and Frederick—there will be a satisfaction in that: unless," he added, laughing bitterly, "they should be alarmed below to see so many warriors assembled together!"

He addressed Dr. Arnott, who came in while he was speaking, on the treatment he had received from England said that she had violated every sacred right in making him prisoner, that he should have been much better treated in Russia, Austria, or even Prussia; that he was sent to the horrible rock of St. Helena on purpose to die; that he had been purposely placed on the most uninhabitable spot of that inhospitable island, and kept six years a close prisoner, and that Sir Hudson Lowe was his executioner. He concluded with these words: "You will end like the proud republic of Venice; and I, dying upon this dreary rock, away from those I hold dear, and deprived of everything, bequeath the opprobrium and horror of my death to the reigning family of England."

On the 21st Napoleon gave directions to the priest who was in attendance as to the manner in which he would be placed to lie in state after his death; and finding his religious attendant had never officiated in such a solemnity he gave the most minute instructions for the mode of conducting it. He afterwards declared that he would die, as he was born a Catholic, and desired that mass should be said by his body, and the customary ceremonies should be performed every day until his burial. The expression of his face was earnest and convulsive; he saw Antommarchi watching the contractions which he underwent, when his eye caught some indication that displeased him. "You are above these weaknesses; but what would you have? I am neither philosopher nor physician. I believe in God; I am of the religion of my fathers; every one cannot be an atheist who pleases." Then turning to the priest—"I was born in the Catholic religion. I wish to fulfil the duties which it imposes, and to receive the succour which it administers. You will say mass every day in the adjoining chapel, and you will expose the Holy Sacrament for forty hours. After I am dead you will place your altar at my head in the funeral chamber; you will continue to celebrate mass, and perform all the customary ceremonies; you will not cease till I am laid in the ground." The Abbe (Vignale) withdrew; Napoleon reproved his fellow-countryman for his supposed incredulity. "Can you carry it to this point? Can you disbelieve in God? Everything proclaims His existence; and, besides, the greatest minds have thought so."—"But, Sire, I have never called it in question. I was attending to the progress of the fever: your Majesty fancied you saw in my features an expression which they had not."— "You are a physician, Doctor," he replied laughingly; "these folks," he added, half to himself, "are conversant only with matter; they will believe in nothing beyond."

In the afternoon of the 25th he was better; but being left alone, a sudden fancy possessed him to eat. He called for fruits, wine, tried a biscuit, then swallowed some champagne, seized a bunch of grapes, and burst into a fit of laughter as soon as he saw Antommarchi return. The physician ordered away the dessert, and found fault with the maitre d'hotel; but the mischief was done, the fever returned and became violent. The Emperor was now on his death-bed, but he testified concern for every one. He asked Antommarchi if 500 guineas would satisfy the English physician, and if he himself would like to serve Maria Louisa in quality of a physician? "She is my wife, the first Princess in Europe, and after me you should serve no one else." Antommarchi expressed his acknowledgments. The fever continued unabated, with violent thirst and cold in the feet. On the 27th he determined to remove from the small chamber into the salon. They were preparing to carry him. "No," he said, "not until I am dead; for the present it will be sufficient if you support me."

Between the 27th and 28th the Emperor passed a very bad night; the fever increased, coldness spread over his limbs, his strength was quite gone. He spoke a few words of encouragement to Antommarchi; then in a tone of perfect calmness and composure he delivered to him the following instructions: "After my death, which cannot be far off, I wish you to open my body: I wish also, nay, I require, that you will not suffer any English physician to touch me. If, however, you find it indispensable to have some one to assist you, Dr. Arnott is the only one I am willing you should employ. I am desirous, further, that you should take out my heart, that you put it in spirits of wine, and that you carry it to Parma to my dear Maria Louisa: you will tell her how tenderly I have loved her, that I have never ceased to love her; and you will report to her all that you have witnessed, all that relates to my situation and my death. I recommend you, above all, carefully to examine my stomach, to make an exact detailed report of it, which you will convey to my son. The vomitings which succeed each other without intermission lead me to suppose that the stomach is the one of my organs which is the most deranged, and I am inclined to believe that it is affected with the disease which conducted my father to the grave,—I mean a cancer in the lower stomach. What think you?" His physician hesitating, he continued—"I have not doubted this since I found the sickness become frequent and obstinate. It is nevertheless well worthy of remark that I have always had a stomach of iron, that I have felt no inconvenience from this organ till latterly, and that whereas my father was fond of high-seasoned dishes and spirituous liquors,

I have never been able to make use of them. Be it as it may, I entreat, I charge you to neglect nothing in such an examination, in order that when you see my son you may communicate the result of your observations to him, and point out the most suitable remedies. When I am no more you will repair to Rome; you will find out my mother and my family. You will give them an account of all you have observed relative to my situation, my disorder, and my death on this remote and miserable rock; you will tell them that the great Napoleon expired in the most deplorable state, wanting everything, abandoned to himself and his glory." It was ten in the forenoon; after this the fever abated, and he fell into a sort of doze.

The Emperor passed a very bad night, and could not sleep. He grew light-headed and talked incoherently; still the fever had abated in its violence. Towards morning the hiccough began to torment him, the fever increased, and he became quite delirious. He spoke of his complaint, and called upon Baxter (the Governor's physician) to appear, to come and see the truth of his reports. Then all at once fancying O'Meara present, he imagined a dialogue between them, throwing a weight of odium on the English policy. The fever having subsided, his hearing became distinct; he grew calm, and entered into some further conversation on what was to be done after his death. He felt thirsty, and drank a large quantity of cold water. "If fate should determine that I shall recover, I would raise a monument on the spot where this water gushes out: I would crown the fountain in memory of the comfort which it has afforded me. If I die, and they should not proscribe my remains as they have proscribed my person, I should desire to be buried with my ancestors in the cathedral of Ajaccio, in Corsica. But if I am not allowed to repose where I was born, why, then, let them bury me at the spot where this fine and refreshing water flows." This request was afterwards complied with.

He remained nearly in the same state for some days. On the 1st of May he was delirious nearly all day, and suffered dreadful vomitings. He took two small biscuits and a few drops of red wine. On the 2d he was rather quieter, and the alarming symptoms diminished a little. At 2 P.M., however, he had a paroxysm of fever, and became again delirious. He talked to himself of France, of his dear son, of some of his old companions-in-arms. At times he was evidently in imagination on the field of battle. "Stengel!" he cried; "Desaix! Massena! Ah! victory is declaring itself! run—rush forward—press the charge!—they are ours!"

"I was listening," says Dr. Antommarchi, "and following the progress of that painful agony in the deepest distress, when Napoleon, suddenly collecting his strength, jumped on the floor, and would absolutely go down into the garden to take a walk. I ran to receive him in my arms, but his legs bent under the weight of his body; he fell backwards, and I had the mortification of being unable to prevent his falling. We raised him up and entreated him to get into bed again; but he did not recognise anybody, and began to storm and fall into a violent passion. He was unconscious, and anxiously desired to walk in the garden. In the course of the day, however, he became more collected, and again spoke of his disease, and the precise anatomical examination he wished to be made of his body after death. He had a fancy that this might be useful to his son." "The physicians of Montpelier," he said to Antommarchi, "announced that the scirrhosis in the pylorus would be hereditary in my family; their report is, I believe, in the hands of my brother Louis; ask for it and compare it with your own observations on my case, in order that my son may be saved from this cruel disease. You will see him, Doctor, and you will point out to him what is best to do, and will save him from the cruel sufferings I now experience. This is the last service I ask of you." Later in the day he said, "Doctor, I am very ill—I feel that I am going to die."

The last time Napoleon spoke, except to utter a few short unconnected words, was on the 3d of May. It was in the afternoon, and he had requested his attendants, in case of his losing consciousness, not to allow any English physician to approach him except Dr. Arnott. "I am going to die," said he, "and you to return to Europe; I must give you some advice as to the line of conduct you are to pursue. You have shared my exile, you will be faithful to my memory, and will not do anything that may injure it. I have sanctioned all proper principles, and infused them into my laws and acts; I have not omitted a single one. Unfortunately, however, the circumstances in which I was placed were arduous, and I was obliged to act with severity, and to postpone the execution of my plans. Our reverses occurred; I could not unbend the bow; and France has been deprived of the liberal institutions I intended to give her. She judges me with indulgence; she feels grateful for my intentions; she cherishes my name and my victories. Imitate her example, be faithful to the opinions we have defended, and to the glory we have acquired: any other course can only lead to shame and confusion."

From this moment it does not appear that Napoleon showed any signs of understanding what was going forward around him. His weakness increased every moment, and a harassing hiccough continued until death took place. The day before that event a fearful tempest threatened to destroy everything about Longwood. The plantations were torn up by the roots, and it was particularly remarked that a willow, under which Napoleon usually sat to enjoy the fresh air, had fallen. "It seemed," says Antommarchi, "as if none of the things the Emperor valued were to survive him." On the day of his death Madame Bertrand, who had not left his bedside, sent for her children to take a last farewell of Napoleon. The scene which ensued was affecting: the children ran to the bed, kissed the hands of Napoleon, and covered them with tears. One of the children fainted, and all had to be carried from the spot. "We all," says Antommarchi, "mixed our lamentations with theirs: we all felt the same anguish, the same cruel foreboding of the approach of the fatal instant, which every minute accelerated." The favourite valet, Noverraz, who had been for some time very ill, when he heard of the state in which Napoleon was, caused himself to be carried downstairs, and entered the apartment in tears. He was with great difficulty prevailed upon to leave the room: he was in a delirious state, and he fancied his master was threatened with danger, and was calling upon him for assistance: he said he would not leave him but would fight and die for him. But Napoleon was now insensible to the tears of his servants; he had scarcely spoken for two days; early in the morning he articulated a few broken sentences, among which the only words distinguishable were, "tete d'armee," the last that ever left his lips, and which indicated the tenor of his fancies. The day passed in convulsive movements and low moanings, with occasionally a loud shriek, and the dismal scene closed just before six in the evening. A slight froth covered his lips, and he was no more.

After he had been dead about six hours Antommarchi had the body carefully washed and laid out on another bed. The executors then proceeded to examine two codicils which were directed to be opened immediately after the Emperor's decease. The one related to the gratuities which he intended out of his private purse for the different individuals of his household, and to the alms which he wished to be distributed among the poor of St. Helena; the other contained his last wish that "his ashes should repose on the banks of the Seine, in the midst of the French people whom he had loved so well." The executors notified this request to the Governor, who stated that his orders were that the body was to, remain on the island. On the next day, after taking a plaster cast of the face of Napoleon, Antommarchi proceeded to open the body in the presence of Sir Thomas Reade, some staff officers, and eight medical men.

The Emperor had intended his hair (which was of a chestnut colour) for presents to the different members of his family, and it was cut off and kept for this purpose.

He had grown considerably thinner in person during the last few months. After his death his face and body were pale, but without alteration or anything of a cadaverous appearance. His physiognomy was fine, the eyes fast closed, and you would have said that the Emperor was not dead, but in a profound sleep. His mouth retained its expression of sweetness, though one side was contracted into a bitter smile. Several scars were seen on his body. On opening it it was found that the liver was not affected, but that there was that cancer of the stomach which he had himself suspected, and of which his father and two of his sisters died. This painful examination having been completed, Antommarchi took out the heart and placed it in a silver vase filled with spirits of wine; he then directed the valet de chambre to dress the body as he had been accustomed in the Emperor's lifetime, with the grand cordon of the Legion of Honour across the breast, in the green uniform of a colonel of the Chasseurs of the Guard, decorated with the orders of the Legion of Honour and of the Iron Crown, long boots with little spurs, finally, his three cornered hat. Thus habited, Napoleon was removed in the afternoon of the 6th out of the hall, into which the crowd rushed immediately. The linen which had been employed in the dissection of the body, though stained with blood, was eagerly seized, torn in pieces, and distributed among the bystanders.

Napoleon lay in state in his little bedroom which had been converted into a funeral chamber. It was hung with black cloth brought from the town. This circumstance first apprised the inhabitants of his death. The corpse, which had not been embalmed, and which was of an extraordinary whiteness, was placed on one of the campbeds, surrounded with little white curtains, which served for a sarcophagus. The blue cloak which Napoleon had worn at the battle of Marengo covered it. The feet and the hands were free; the sword on the left side, and a crucifix on the breast. At some distance was the silver vase containing the heart and stomach, which were not allowed to be removed. At the back of the head was an altar, where the priest in his stole and surplice recited the customary prayers. All the individuals of Napoleon's suite, officers and domestics, dressed in mourning, remained standing on the left. Dr. Arnott had been charged to see that no attempt was made to convey away the body.

For some-hours the crowd had besieged the doors; they were admitted, and beheld the inanimate remains of Napoleon in respectful silence. The officers of the 20th and 66th Regiments were admitted first, then the others. The following day (the 7th) the throng was greater. Antommarchi was not allowed to take the heart of Napoleon to Europe with him; he deposited that and the stomach in two vases, filled with alcohol and hermetically sealed, in the corners of the coffin in which the corpse was laid. This was a shell of zinc lined with white satin, in which was a mattress furnished with a pillow. There not being room for the hat to remain on his head, it was placed at his feet, with some eagles, pieces of French money coined during his reign, a plate engraved with his arms, etc. The coffin was closed, carefully soldered up, and then fixed in another case of mahogany, which was enclosed in a third made of lead, which last was fastened in a fourth of mahogany, which was sealed up and fastened with screws. The coffin was exhibited in the same place as the body had been, and was also covered with the cloak that Napoleon had worn at the battle of Marengo. The funeral was ordered for the morrow, 8th May, and the troops were to attend in the morning by break of day.

This took place accordingly: the Governor arrived first, the Rear-Admiral soon after, and shortly all the authorities, civil and military, were assembled at Longwood. The day was fine, the people crowded the roads, music resounded from the heights; never had spectacle so sad and solemn been witnessed in these remote regions. At half-past twelve the grenadiers took hold of the coffin, lifted it with difficulty, and succeeded in removing it into the great walk in the garden, where the hearse awaited them. It was placed in the carriage, covered with a pall of violet-coloured velvet, and with the cloak which the hero wore at Marengo. The Emperor's household were in mourning. The cavalcade was arranged by order of the Governor in the following manner: The Abbe Vignale in his sacerdotal robes, with young Henry Bertrand at his side, bearing an aspersorium; Doctors Arnott and Antommarchi, the persons entrusted with the superintendence of the hearse, drawn by four horses, led by grooms, and escorted by twelve grenadiers without arms, on each side; these last were to carry the coffin on their shoulders as soon as the ruggedness of the road prevented the hearse from advancing; young Napoleon Bertrand, and Marchand, both on foot, and by the side of the hearse; Counts Bertrand and Montholon on horseback close behind the hearse; a part of the household of the Emperor; Countess Bertrand with her daughter Hortense, in a calash drawn by two horses led by hand by her domestics, who walked by the side of the precipice; the Emperor's horse led by his piqueur Archambaud; the officers of marine on horseback and on foot; the officers of the staff on horse-back; the members of the council of the island in like manner; General Coffin and the Marquis Montchenu on horseback; the Rear-Admiral and the Governor on horseback; the inhabitants of the island.

The train set out in this order from Longwood, passed by the barracks, and was met by the garrison, about 2500 in number, drawn up on the left of the road as far as Hut's Gate. Military bands placed at different distances added still more, by the mournful airs which they played, to the striking solemnity of the occasion. When the train had passed the troops followed and accompanied it to the burying-place. The dragoons marched first. Then came the 20th Regiment of infantry, the marines, the 66th, the volunteers of St. Helena, and lastly, the company of Royal Artillery, with fifteen pieces of cannon. Lady Lowe and her daughter were at the roadside at Hut's Gate, in an open carriage drawn by two horses. They were attended by some domestics in mourning, and followed the procession at a distance. The fifteen pieces of artillery were ranged along the road, and the gunners were at their posts ready to fire. Having advanced about a quarter of a mile beyond Hut's Gate the hearse stopped, the troops halted and drew up in line of battle by the roadside. The grenadiers then raised the coffin on their shoulders and bore it thus to the place of interment, by the new route which had been made on purpose on the declivity of the mountain. All the attendants alighted, the ladies descended from their carriages, and the procession followed the corpse without observing any regular order.

Counts Bertrand and Montholon, Marchand and young Napoleon Bertrand, carried the four corners of the pall. The coffin was laid down at the side of the tomb, which was hung with black. Near were seen the cords and pulleys which were to lower it into the earth. The coffin was then uncovered, the Abbe Vignale repeated the usual prayers, and the body was let down into the grave with the feet to the east. The artillery then fired three salutes in succession of fifteen discharges each. The Admiral's vessel had fired during the procession twenty-five minute guns from time to time. A huge stone, which was to have been employed in the building of the new house of the Emperor, was now used to close his grave, and was lowered till it rested on a strong stone wall so as not to touch the coffin. While the grave was closed the crowd seized upon the willows, which the former presence of Napoleon had already rendered objects of veneration. Every one was ambitious to possess a branch or some leaves of these trees which were henceforth to shadow the tomb of this great man, and to preserve them as a precious relic of so memorable a scene. The Governor and Admiral endeavoured to prevent this outrage, but in vain. The Governor, however, surrounded the spot afterwards with a barricade, where he placed a guard to keep off all intruders. The tomb of the Emperor was about a league from Longwood. It was of a quadrangular shape, wider at top than at bottom; the depth about twelve feet. The coffin was placed on two strong pieces of wood, and was detached in its whole circumference.

The companions of Napoleon returned to France, and the island gradually resumed its former quiet state, while the willows weeping over the grave guarded the ashes of the man for whom Europe had been all too small.

Printed in the USA
CPSIA information can be obtained
at www.ICGtesting.com
LVHW021031110823
754842LV00009B/198

9 781528 719384